Java™ Master Reference

Arthur Griffith

IDG
BOOKS
WORLDWIDE

IDG Books Worldwide, Inc.

An International Data Group Company

Foster City, CA ◆ Chicago, IL ◆ Indianapolis, IN ◆ Southlake, TX

Java™ Master Reference

Published by
IDG Books Worldwide, Inc.
An International Data Group Company
919 E. Hillsdale Blvd., Suite 400
Foster City, CA 94404
www.idgbooks.com (IDG Books Worldwide Web site)

Library of Congress Catalog Card No.: 97-74337

ISBN: 0-7645-3084-4

Printed in the United States of America

10 9 8 7 6 5 4 3 2 1

1DD/QS/RS/ZX/FC

Distributed in the United States by IDG Books Worldwide, Inc.

Distributed by Macmillan Canada for Canada; by Transworld Publishers Limited in the United Kingdom; by IDG Norge Books for Norway; by IDG Sweden Books for Sweden; by Woodslane Pty. Ltd. for Australia; by Woodslane Enterprises Ltd. for New Zealand; by Longman Singapore Publishers Ltd. for Singapore, Malaysia, Thailand, and Indonesia; by Simron Pty. Ltd. for South Africa; by Toppan Company Ltd. for Japan; by Distribuidora Cuspide for Argentina; by Livraria Cultura for Brazil; by Ediciencia S.A. for Ecuador; by Addison-Wesley Publishing Company for Korea; by Ediciones ZETA S.C.R. Ltda. for Peru; by WS Computer Publishing Corporation, Inc., for the Philippines; by Unalis Corporation for Taiwan; by Contemporanea de Ediciones for Venezuela; by Computer Book & Magazine Store for Puerto Rico; by Express Computer Distributors for the Caribbean and West Indies. Authorized Sales Agent: Anthony Rudkin Associates for the Middle East and North Africa.

For general information on IDG Books Worldwide's books in the U.S., please call our Consumer Customer Service department at 800-762-2974. For reseller information, including discounts and premium sales, please call our Reseller Customer Service department at 800-434-3422.

For information on where to purchase IDG Books Worldwide's books outside the U.S., please contact our International Sales department at 415-655-3200 or fax 415-655-3295.

For information on foreign language translations, please contact our Foreign & Subsidiary Rights department at 415-655-3021 or fax 415-655-3281.

For sales inquiries and special prices for bulk quantities, please contact our Sales department at 415-655-3200 or write to the address above.

For information on using IDG Books Worldwide's books in the classroom or for ordering examination copies, please contact our Educational Sales department at 800-434-2086 or fax 817-251-8174.

For press review copies, author interviews, or other publicity information, please contact our Public Relations department at 415-655-3000 or fax 415-655-3299.

For authorization to photocopy items for corporate, personal, or educational use, please contact Copyright Clearance Center, 222 Rosewood Drive, Danvers, MA 01923, or fax 508-750-4470.

The IDG Books Worldwide logo is a trademark under exclusive license to IDG Books Worldwide, Inc., from International Data Group, Inc.

ABOUT IDG BOOKS WORLDWIDE

Welcome to the world of IDG Books Worldwide.

IDG Books Worldwide, Inc., is a subsidiary of International Data Group, the world's largest publisher of computer-related information and the leading global provider of information services on information technology. IDG was founded more than 25 years ago and now employs more than 8,500 people worldwide. IDG publishes more than 275 computer publications in over 75 countries (see listing below). More than 60 million people read one or more IDG publications each month.

Launched in 1990, IDG Books Worldwide is today the #1 publisher of best-selling computer books in the United States. We are proud to have received eight awards from the Computer Press Association in recognition of editorial excellence and three from *Computer Currents'* First Annual Readers' Choice Awards. Our best-selling *...For Dummies*® series has more than 30 million copies in print with translations in 30 languages. IDG Books Worldwide, through a joint venture with IDG's Hi-Tech Beijing, became the first U.S. publisher to publish a computer book in the People's Republic of China. In record time, IDG Books Worldwide has become the first choice for millions of readers around the world who want to learn how to better manage their businesses.

Our mission is simple: Every one of our books is designed to bring extra value and skill-building instructions to the reader. Our books are written by experts who understand and care about our readers. The knowledge base of our editorial staff comes from years of experience in publishing, education, and journalism — experience we use to produce books for the '90s. In short, we care about books, so we attract the best people. We devote special attention to details such as audience, interior design, use of icons, and illustrations. And because we use an efficient process of authoring, editing, and desktop publishing our books electronically, we can spend more time ensuring superior content and spend less time on the technicalities of making books.

You can count on our commitment to deliver high-quality books at competitive prices on topics you want to read about. At IDG Books Worldwide, we continue in the IDG tradition of delivering quality for more than 25 years. You'll find no better book on a subject than one from IDG Books Worldwide.

John Kilcullen
CEO
IDG Books Worldwide, Inc.

Steven Berkowitz
President and Publisher
IDG Books Worldwide, Inc.

*Eighth Annual
Computer Press
Awards ➤1992*

*Ninth Annual
Computer Press
Awards ➤1993*

*Tenth Annual
Computer Press
Awards ➤1994*

*Eleventh Annual
Computer Press
Awards ➤1995*

3/24/97

Credits

Acquisitions Editor
Michael Roney

Development Editor
Stefan Grünwedel

Technical Editors
Bruce Woodard
David Williams

Copy Editor
Robert Campbell

Production Coordinator
Susan Parini

Book Designer
Kurt Krames

**Graphics and
Production Specialists**
Ed Penslien
Christopher Pimentel
Trevor Wilson

Illustrators
David Puckett
Pamela Drury Wattenmaker

Proofreader
Jennifer K. Overmyer

About the Author

Arthur Griffith has worked as a computer programmer and consultant specializing in compiler writing for satellite communications, electronic circuit diagnostics, and telephone network analysis for over 20 years. He is the coauthor of IDG Books Worldwide's *Discover Visual Café*.

For Mary

Preface

In a way, I wrote this book for myself. I was trying to write Java code with the help of a pile of books and a few Internet links. The going was slow because I kept having to stop and search here and there for little bits of information—usually for something I already knew but whose details I couldn't remember. It didn't take me long to realize I was doing the same thing I did when I started programming in C, then later in C++. I programmed in C for several years and the problem persisted—a stack of books and no real quick search method. Little questions kept cropping up—such as the exact calling sequence for `fgets()`, the meaning of a value for `errno`, or whether `isgraphic()` applied to the space character. With Java I kept having questions about how to load an image, extract a substring, and open a file. Exactly how does that label thing work with `break`? Would an anonymous class work for this? I could see that working in Java was going to be déjà vu. I wished I had a single alphabetic, cross-referenced source for all the things that were so easy to forget. What I wanted is the very book you now hold in your hands.

What This Book Contains

Java Master Reference presents an alphabetical listing of all pieces and parts that you will need in day-to-day Java programming. I've designed it to be used as a reference for both the language and the API. As the book's name implies, this is a reference book, not a tutorial. I made every attempt to include all of Java's troublesome details—the things that are so easy to forget, the things that were incomplete in tutorials, the things you somehow missed as you learned about this language—as well as Java parts that you have never seen before.

I've also included several helpful appendixes to help you get a handle on the ins and outs of Java and this book. Appendix A, "Table of Methods," lists all method names in alphabetical order, followed by a list of all the classes or interfaces in which they are defined. Once a class or interface is determined, it can be looked up directly by its name in the book. Use this appendix to jog your memory when you remember the name of a method but can't recall the class in which it is defined. Appendix B explains all you need to know about this book's CD-ROM. Appendix C, "Java API Hierarchy Map," contains a diagram of the complete Java API, showing the relative position of every class, along with the interfaces implemented by each.

You will find sample source code throughout the book. I've tried to keep every example as simple as possible—each one is intended to demonstrate only one thing—but every one of them is a stand-alone program.

Some examples are applications, and some are applets. All examples are supplied in both the source and object forms on the book's companion CD-ROM. Source files end with ".java," and object files end with ".class." Here are two examples:

```
AppexampleName.java
AppExampleName.class
```

To run the `AppExampleName` example, you can start it with the Java virtual machine from the command line, like this:

```
java AppExampleName
```

There are also sample applets. An *applet* is designed to be run from commands inside an HTML file being executed by a browser. An applet example is on the CD-ROM in at least three files, such as these:

```
AppletExample.java
AppletExample.class
AppletExample.html
```

If you address the HTML file with a Web browser, the applet will run. A very simple browser (it ignores everything about an HTML file except applet tags) is supplied as part of the Java development kit. It is called `appletviewer`. To run this example, enter this from the command line:

```
appletviewer AppletExample.html
```

The examples were designed to facilitate experimentation. No collection of demo code could possibly contain an example of everything you may want to see or use. Each supplied example can act as a skeleton. It will cover most of what you want to see—but it is also there so you can easily make tests and run experiments. Let's say you want to know whether or not the predecrement operator could be applied to a hexadecimal literal constant inside an expression. The sample code that displays decrement operations is sitting there ready for a quick line to be added to make the test. If you wish, after making the test, you can save the code in its new form to make it a part of your set of examples.

Parts List

The JDK consists of several utility programs and the API. Each utility program is described in the book. Here is a list of them—these are the programs supplied by Sun with JDK 1.1 for both Windows and Solaris. The same set of utilities should be present when the JDK is ported to other systems.

Table 1 Software Utilities Supplied with the Sun JDK

Name	Description
appletviewer	A utility that executes Java applets
jar	A program that compresses files into a single Java Archive (JAR) file
java	A Java Virtual Machine that executes Java programs
javac	The Java language compiler
javadoc	A program that generates documentation from Java source code
javah	A program that reads Java source and creates header files for C code
javakey	A program that generates digital encryption signatures and manages a database of them
javap	The Java disassembler, which reads class files and prints bytecodes
jdb	A Java debugger
native2ascii	A text-conversion utility
rmic	A program that generates the stubs and skeletons needed to implement the Java remote interface
rmiregistry	A program that establishes a server registry for remote interface communications
serialver	A utility that displays the serial VersionUID

Providing Feedback

Every attempt was made to make the contents of this book as complete and accurate as possible, but with a book as large and detailed as this one, there are bound to be errors. I know there must be some because I found a lot of them myself. I corrected the ones I found, and so have my editors but others certainly exist. A Web site is being maintained specifically for this book. It contains updates, as well as entries for all the missing or incorrect information found after the book went to press:

    http://web2.airmail.net/arthur/jref

This Web site also contains links to other useful Java sites as well as information on changes that could affect the way you use the information in this book. Also, if you have some particular question about an entry in the book, and you can't find it on the Web site, let me know:

    arthur98@airmail.net

Finally, let the publisher know what you think of this book. You can register your comments through the IDG Books Worldwide Online Registration Form located at this URL:

    http://my2cents.idgbooks.com

Making Connections

Here is a list of Web sites that contain Java information. This is by no means an exhaustive list. The sites included here are those that seem to be either official or stable and well-maintained.

Sun

Sun Microsystems maintains a Web site that contains all the latest information on Java. This is Java's official home:

```
http://java.sun.com
http://www.javasoft.com
```

Java information sites

Several sites on the Internet carry news and general information on Java:

```
http://www.javaworld.com/
http://www.roaster.com/news/
http://www.javology.com/
```

The Java Lobby

This is the Web page of a group whose stated purpose is to represent the needs and wishes of Java developers to the organizations who have influence over Java's design:

```
http://www.javalobby.org/
```

Unicode

Information on the Unicode Consortium and updates to the unicode standard can be found at:

```
http://www.unicode.org
ftp://unicode.org
```

HTTP

The java.net package has classes that perform Internet communications using the HTTP protocol. This page supplies information about the header fields that can be set and read by the methods of the Java classes:

```
http://www.w3.org/hypertext/WWW/Protocols/
```

URL

This is a good location for information on the structure and content of URLs:

```
http://www.ncsa.uiuc.edu/demoweb/url-primer.html
```

JDBC

This site contains information about the current state of JDBC:

```
http://splash.javasoft.com/jdbc/
```

This site maintains links to various vendors of JDBC drivers. There is also information about Java ODBC drivers at this site:

```
http://splash.javasoft.com/jdbc/jdbc.drivers.html
```

RFC

The RFC (request for comment) system was used to design the Internet. It is a collection of documents online (mostly in plain text, but there is some PostScript here and there) that completely define the protocols of the Internet, including e-mail and the World Wide Web. It also includes information on character sets and compression algorithms. You will find thousands of these documents, indexed and free for the taking, at many Internet locations. Here is one of them:

```
ftp://ds.internic.net/rfc
```

Language codes

Every written language on earth has a lowercase two-letter code assigned to it by ISO-639. Here are some places to find a complete list of these codes:

```
http://sizif.mf.uni-lj.si/linux/cee/std/ISO_639.html
http://www.triacom.com/a.iso639.en.htm
http://www.sil.org/sgml/iso639.html
```

Country codes

Every country has an uppercase two-letter code defined by ISO-3166. Here are some places to find a complete list:

```
http://www.chemie.fu-berlin.de/diverse/doc/ISO_3166.html
http://stiwww.epfl.ch/utile/iso_3166.html
http://www-s.ti.com/ti_me/docs/ctrycode.htm
```

Acknowledgments

I want to thank my wife, Mary, for believing in me and supporting me in writing this book. Without her, I could not have even started this project. The three greatest treasures you can have on earth are freedom, self-confidence, and someone who truly loves you. Anyone who doesn't appreciate them has never been without them.

I want to thank Mike Roney at IDG Books Worldwide for giving me the opportunity to write the book and for keeping things on track as Java and the book evolved. I want to thank Stefan Grünwedel at IDG Books for doing an outstanding job of coordinating all the things that needed to happen to create a book. I also want to thank Margot Maley at Waterside Productions for pointing me in the right direction and helping me keep both oars in the water.

Robert Campbell, the book's copy editor, has the amazing ability to make a few quick edits and convert a collection of disjointed thoughts into a clear and readable sentence. David Wall, author of several computer books, was kind enough to act as an advisor during those periods when I became somewhat bewildered by the writing process.

Bruce Woodard and David Williams did an excellent job of the very difficult task of verifying the technical accuracy and completeness of the book.

Contents

abstract

keyword

This is a modifier used in the declaration of a class, interface, or method. The keyword abstract tells the compiler an actual instance of the item being defined will never occur. Declaring something as abstract defines the item as an incomplete type, for which the details will be supplied later. To specify a class or method is not abstract — sometimes it is referred to as being *concrete*.

abstract method

An abstract method is one that does not have a body defined for it. Some examples of abstract method definitions are:

```
abstract int distance();
abstract void invert(int selection);
```

The declaration of an abstract method has exactly the same format as a normal method declaration, except:

- ◆ It is always preceded by the modifying keyword abstract.
- ◆ It never has a body.

An abstract method can only be defined as part of an abstract class or part of an interface. In fact, defining an abstract method forces the class in which it appears to be abstract, and the class must be declared as such.

A method cannot be both abstract and static. This is so because an abstract method does not have a body, and a static method has its body resident inside the class definition.

abstract interface

The keyword abstract is optional in the definition of an interface. The abstract keyword can be included in the declaration of an interface (the syntax of Java allows it), but it makes no difference—all interfaces are abstract whether or not they are declared as such.

abstract class

An abstract class is declared by using the keyword `abstract` as a modifier in its definition. An abstract class is considered an incomplete class by the compiler — one that cannot be instantiated. Four things can cause a class to become abstract:

- A class that contains one or more abstract methods must be declared as an abstract class.
- If a class extends an abstract class and does not implement methods with bodies for all of the superclass's abstract methods, it must be declared as an abstract class.
- If a class implements an interface but does not supply methods for all the methods defined in the interface, it must be declared as an abstract class.
- A class complete in all respects, but declared using the `abstract` keyword, is an abstract class.

The first three of these examples are actually the same. They all produce a class that contains an abstract method.

While the inclusion of an abstract method effectively does force a class to become abstract, the keyword `abstract` is still required to be used as part of the class definition. This is actually handy as an error-checking mechanism to ensure the programmer creating an abstract class actually intended to do so. Also, it is possible to create an abstract class, for whatever reason, that does not contain an abstract method. The presence of the keyword `abstract` removes all ambiguity.

An abstract class can contain `static` methods. These `static` methods, if they are also declared `public`, can be executed from other classes by preceding the method name with the name of the abstract class. This is reasonable because a static method resides inside the class definition and does not require the instance of an object for execution. One nice side effect of this is an abstract class can have a `main()` enabling it to be executed directly as an application.

A class cannot be declared as both `abstract` and `final`. The two declarations are in conflict because a final class cannot be subclassed, and subclassing is all that can be done with an abstract class.

Abstract class list

A number of abstract classes are in the Java API. Table A-1 lists them.

Table A-1	Names of Java API Abstract Classes		
AWTEvent	FilterWriter	MouseAdapter	RemoteStub
BreakIterator	FocusAdapter	MouseMotionAdapter	ResourceBundle
Calendar	FontMetrics	Number	Signature
ClassLoader	Format	NumberFormat	Signer
Collator	Graphics	ObjectStreamException	SocketImpl
ColorModel	HttpURLConnection	OutputStream	TimeZone
Component	Image	PrintJob	Toolkit
ComponentAdapter	InputEvent	Process	URLConnection
Container	InputStream	Provider	URLStreamHandler
ContainerAdapter	KeyAdapter	RGBImageFilter	WindowAdapter
ContentHandler	KeyPairGenerator	RMISocketFactory	Writer
DatagramSocketImpl	ListResourceBundle	Reader	
DateFormat	MenuComponent	RemoteObject	
FilterReader	MessageDigest	RemoteServer	

Example 1

This example shows the abstract class `AddSub` that contains two methods—one that is abstract and one that is not. The class `AddSubMulDiv` extends `AddSub` and adds a few new methods. Notice `AddSubMulDiv` implements a nonabstract version of the abstract method `subtract()`. It must do this to prevent itself from becoming an abstract class:

```
abstract class AddSub {
    public int add(int x,int y) {
        return(x + y);
    }
    abstract public int subtract(int x,int y);
}

public class AddSubMulDiv extends AddSub {
    public int subtract(int x,int y) {
        return(x-y);
    }
    public int multiply(int x,int y) {
        return(x*y);
    }
    public int divide(int x,int y) {
        return(x/y);
```

```
        }
    }
```

Example 2

This is a modification of the previous example to add another generation. If a class wishes to remain abstract, it need not implement the abstractions of its superclass. Here, the class AddSubMul2 extends the abstract class AddSub2, and it does not implement the abstract method subtract(). This forces AddSubMul2 to be an abstract class. Finally AddSubMulDiv2 extends AddSubMul2 and, to become a concrete class, must implement the subtract() method:

```
abstract class AddSub2 {
    public int add(int x,int y) {
        return(x + y);
    }
    abstract public int subtract(int x,int y);
}

abstract class AddSubMul2 extends AddSub2 {
    public int multiply(int x, int y) {
        return(x*y);
    }
}

public class AddSubMulDiv2 extends AddSub2 {
    public int subtract(int x,int y) {
        return(x-y);
    }
    public int divide(int x,int y) {
        return(x/y);
    }
}
```

 For the inverse of abstract, see **final**. For an alternative to an abstract class, see **interface**. For more on classes, see **class**. For another way of using abstraction, see **inner classes**.

Abstract Windowing Toolkit

 See **awt**.

AbstractMethodError

public class AbstractMethodError

This error is thrown whenever the Virtual Machine detects an attempt to make a call to an abstract method. This can happen if the compiled class files are out of phase with the source files—or if a class file of the correct name and incorrect configuration was loaded from another location.

Inheritance

```
public class java.lang.AbstractMethodError
    extends IncompatibleClassChangeError
            ⇑
    public class java.lang.IncompatibleClassChangeError
        extends LinkageError
                ⇑
        public class java.lang.LinkageError
            extends Error
                    ⇑
            public class java.lang.Error
                extends Throwable
                        ⇑
                public class java.lang.Throwable
                    implements Serializable
                    extends Object
                            ⇑
                        public class java.lang.Object
java.lang.ObjectConstructors
public AbstractMethodError()
public AbstractMethodError(String message)
```

If the `message` string is supplied, it is used as the detailed error message—without it, there will be no detailed message.

access

Access is part of scope. The scope of a name is determined by *where* it is declared, while the access of a name is *how* it is declared. The access qualifiers can be used to modify the scope. Four access qualifiers exist: `public`, `private`, `protected`, and the default access (which has no name, but is sometimes referred to as *package* access).

public

- A public class or interface can be accessed by any code that can access the package in which the class is declared.
- A public class or interface member (variable, method, or constructor) can be accessed by any code that can access the class or interface in which it is declared.
- A public member (variable, method, or constructor) can be accessed directly from a subclass without qualification. If the subclass has overridden the name in the super class, it can still be accessed with an expression of the form `super`.name.
- A public constructor can be accessed from a subclass by the expression `super()`.

private

- A class or interface member (variable, method, or constructor) declared as private can be accessed only from within the compilation unit in which it is declared.

protected

- The protected constructor of a class can be accessed by code in the same package in which the class is declared — or by the code in any subclass of the class in which the protected constructor is declared.
- A protected member (variable, method, or constructor) can be accessed directly from a subclass without qualification. If the subclass has overridden the name in the super class, it can still be accessed with an expression of the form `super`.name.
- A protected constructor can be accessed from a subclass by the expression `super()`.
- A protected variable or method is inherited by any subclass of the class in which it is declared.

The default

If no access modifier is declared, the default is assumed.

- A class that has no access declaration can be accessed only within the package in which it is declared.
- Interface members (methods and variables) default to `public`.

♦ A constructor can be accessed from a subclass by the expression `super()` only if the subclass is in the same package.

♦ A variable or method with default access is inherited only by subclasses that are in the same package as the class in which it is declared.

 Also see **scope**. For access to packages, see **CLASSPATH**.

AccessException

class java.rmi.AccessException

This exception will be thrown by the RMI registry whenever some operation (bind or unbind, for example) is not permitted for the node.

Inheritance

```
public class java.rmi.AccessException
    extends RemoteException
        ⇑
    public class java.rmi.RemoteException
        extends IOException
            ⇑
        public class java.io.IOException
            extends Exception
                ⇑
            public class java.lang.Exception
                extends Throwable
                    ⇑
                public class java.lang.Throwable
                    implements Serializable
                    extends Object
                        ⇑
                    public class java.lang.Object
```

Constructors

```
public AccessException(String message)
public AccessException(Exception detail,String message)
```

The `message` string is used as a detailed message describing this particular exception. This exception can also include another exception to supply more details.

accessor method

The Java beans have standard *accessor* methods. These are the "set" and "get" methods for a property. For example, if a bean property is named "umpa," the accessor methods will have the names `getUmpa()` and `setUmpa()`. This naming convention allows processes wanting to access a bean to create the method names from the name of the property.

 For more information, see **PropertyDescriptor**.

acl

package java.security.acl

Access Control Lists have to do with security. They are collections of system permissions that can be denied or granted. This package is a set of abstractions for managing principals (groups or individuals) and their security access permissions.

 This package supplies only the interfaces and exceptions for the Access Control Lists. The implementation will vary from one system to another. The default implementation is in the sun.security.acl package.

Interfaces

        Acl
        AclEntry
        Group
        Owner
        Permission

Exceptions

        AclNotFoundException
        LastOwnerException
        NotOwnerException

Acl

interface java.security.acl.Acl

This is the interface to a class that contains an ACL (Access Control List). An ACL is a list used to control the granting and removal of access permissions.

Principal

Each member of the list is a principal. A principal can represent an individual or a group. Each principal has a list of permissions associated with it. An individual can simultaneously have a principal entry and be the member of a group that has its own separate principal entry.

Positive or negative

A principal can appear twice in the list—once positive and once negative. The positive entry lists the permissions that will be granted. The negative entry lists the permissions that will be denied.

Conflict

If a positive entry grants the same permission a negative permission denies, it is as if that particular permission were not specified for that principal. The permissions specified for an individual will override that of any group to which the individual may belong. If a user is a member of more than one group, a permission will be considered positive only if it is positive in all the groups, or if it has been specifically set to positive for the user.

Owners

This interface extends the `java.security.acl.Owner` interface. Only owners are allowed to modify the list.

Inheritance

```
public interface java.security.acl.Acl
        extends Owner
            ⇑
    public interface java.security.acl.Owner
```

Methods

addEntry()

```
public abstract boolean addEntry(Principal caller,
        AclEntry aclEntry)
    throws NotOwnerException
```

Associates the `caller` and the `aclEntry` as a single entry in the list. Each `aclEntry` is either positive or negative, and each is associated with one principal. If a match occurs on both the principal and the polarity (positive or negative), no change is made to the list and `false` is returned. If the add succeeds, `true` is returned. If the `caller` is not the owner of the list, a `NotOwnerException` is thrown.

checkPermission()

```
public abstract boolean checkPermission)
```

```
                 Principal principal,Permission permission)
```
Returns `true` only if `principal` has been granted the `permission`. If the `permission` is not specifically granted, it is denied. Conflicts are resolved as previously described.

entries()

```
public abstract Enumeration entries()
```

Returns an enumeration of the `AclEntry`s in the list.

getName()

```
public abstract String getName()
```

Returns the name of this `Acl` object.

getPermissions()

```
public abstract Enumeration getPermissions(Principal principal)
```

Returns an enumerated list of the permissions for `principal`. The complete list of permissions is compiled from the permissions of the principal and any groups to which the principal may belong. Conflicts are resolved as previously described.

removeEntry()

```
public abstract boolean removeEntry(Principal caller,
         AclEntry entry)
    throws NotOwnerException
```

Removes the `entry` from the permissions list of the `principal`. If the `caller` is not an owner of the list, a `NotOwnerException` is thrown.

setName()

```
public abstract void setName(Principal caller,
         String name)
    throws NotOwnerException
```

Assigns a name to this list. The `caller` must be an owner of the list, or a `NotOwnerException` will be thrown.

toString()

```
public abstract String toString()
```

Returns a string representation of the contents of the list.

AclEntry

interface java.security.acl.AclEntry

The purpose of this interface is to specify a set of methods that will be used to associate a list of permissions with a principal. (A principal can be an individual or a group—a group is a collection of principals.) This interface defines methods to maintain and query the list.

Positive or negative

An AclEntry object is in one of two states—it is set to *positive* if the permissions are to be granted and *negative* if they are to be denied. The default is positive. An AclEntry can only be made negative with a call to setNegativePermissions().

Inheritance

```
public interface java.security.acl.AclEntry
    extends Cloneable
          ⇑
    public interface java.lang.Cloneable
```

Methods

addPermission()

```
public abstract boolean addPermission(Permission permission)
```
Adds the permission to the list. A return value of true indicates that the add succeeded. A false return indicates that the permission was already a member of the list.

checkPermission()

```
public abstract boolean checkPermission(Permission permission)
```
If permission is in the list, returns true. If it is not in the list, returns false.

clone()

```
public abstract Object clone()
```

Duplicates this object.

getPrincipal()

```
public abstract Principal getPrincipal()
```

Returns the principal. If none has been set, the return is null.

isNegative()

```
public abstract boolean isNegative()
```

Returns `true` if this is a list of negative permissions. It returns `false` if the list is positive.

permissions()

```
public abstract Enumeration permissions()
```

Returns an enumeration of the permissions.

removePermission()

```
public abstract boolean
          removePermission(Permission permission)
```

Removes the `permission`. The return will be `true` if the permission was removed and `false` if the permission was not in the list.

setNegativePermissions()

```
public abstract void setNegativePermissions()
```

Sets this `AclEntry` to be negative.

setPrincipal()

```
public abstract boolean setPrincipal(Principal user)
```

Specifies the `Principal` for which the list of permissions is to apply.

toString()

```
public abstract String toString()
```

Returns a string representation of this object.

AclNotFoundException

class java.security.acl.AclNotFoundException

This exception is thrown to indicate that there was an attempt to reference a nonexistent `Acl` object.

Inheritance

```
public class java.security.acl.AclNotFoundException
     extends Exception
          ⇑
     public class java.lang.Exception
```

```
extends Throwable
        ⇑
public class java.lang.Throwable
        implements Serializable
        extends Object
                ⇑
        public class java.lang.Object
```

Constructors

AclNotFoundException()

```
public AclNotFoundException()
```

ActionEvent

class java.awt.event.ActionEvent

An *action* is a nonhardware-specific response from the user. That is, an action is, for instance, a button press or selection from a list that could have been made with the keyboard, the mouse, or even some other device. In every case, an ActionEvent is issued from a Java component—not directly from a hardware device.

Modifiers

Certain modifiers can accompany the event. For example, if a button were activated with a mouse click while the control key was held down, the CTRL_MASK modifier should be set in the ActionEvent. The named constants in this class define the possible modifiers.

The id number

Every event has an id number that can supply more information about what type of event it is. These id values range between ACTION_FIRST and ACTION_LAST. The ActionEvent class has only one possible value in the range—the ACTION_PERFORMED value.

Inheritance

```
public class java.awt.event.ActionEvent
    extends AWTEvent
        ⇑
    public class java.awt.event.AWTEvent
        extends EventObject
            ⇑
        public class java.util.EventObject
```

```
implements Serializable
extends Object
        ⇑
public class java.lang.Object
```

Variables and constants

ACTION_FIRST

```
public final static int ACTION_FIRST
```

The lowest possible value of the action event ids.

ACTION_LAST

```
public final static int ACTION_LAST
```

The highest possible value of the action event ids.

ACTION_PERFORMED

```
public final static int ACTION_PERFORMED
```

An action performed event id number.

ALT_MASK

```
public final static int ALT_MASK
```

The alt modifier constant.

CTRL_MASK

```
public final static int CTRL_MASK
```

The control modifier constant.

META_MASK

```
public final static int META_MASK
```

The meta modifier constant.

SHIFT_MASK

```
public final static int SHIFT_MASK
```

The shift modifier constant.

Constructors

```
public ActionEvent(Object source,int id,String command)
public ActionEvent(Object source,int id,String command,
```

```
        int modifiers)
```

This will construct an `ActionEvent` for the specified `source` object. The `id` is always `ACTION_PERFORMED`. The `command` is the string associated with the event — for example, the label on a button or the text of a list member. The optional `modifiers` can be an ORed combination of the mask values defined as constants.

Methods

getActionCommand()

```
public String getActionCommand()
```

Returns the command string that was specified on the constructor.

getModifiers()

```
public int getModifiers()
```

Returns the set of modifier masks that were specified on the constructor.

paramString()

```
public String paramString()
```

Returns debugging information. The return string describes the internal state and values of this object.

Example

This example shows the `ActionEvents` generated from a pair of buttons. The `ActionButtons` class is an `ActionListener`, so it can be added to the list of listeners for the button:

```
import java.awt.*;
import java.awt.event.*;
public class ActionButtons extends Frame
            implements ActionListener {
    Button button;
    public static void main(String[] arg) {
        new ActionButtons();
    }
    ActionButtons() {
        button = new Button("Button Text");
        button.addActionListener(this);
        add("Center",button);
        pack();
        show();
    }
```

```
public void actionPerformed(ActionEvent event) {
    System.out.println(event.getActionCommand());
    System.out.println(event.paramString());
}
}
```

To receive the event, this class implements the `actionPerformed()` method of the `ActionListener` interface. The method is then called with each `ActionEvent` on the button because the button's method `addActionListener()` was called to register the listener. The output from clicking on the button looks like this:

```
Button Text
ACTION_PERFORMED,cmd=Button Text
```

For a list of the AWT events, see the **event** package.

ActionListener

interface java.awt.event.ActionListener

The listener interface for receiving action events.

Implemented by

```
AWTEventMulticaster
```

Inheritance

```
public interface java.awt.event.ActionListener
    extends EventListener
        ⇑
    public interface java.util.EventListener
```

Constructors

Returned by

Objects implementing `ActionListener` are returned from the `AWTEventMulticaster` methods `add()` and `remove()`.

Methods

actionPerformed()

```
public abstract void actionPerformed(ActionEvent event)
```

This is the method that will be invoked whenever an action occurs.

 For an example of using the `ActionListener`, see **ActionEvent**.

adapter class

The term "adapter class" is used in two different ways in Java literature. The first, and probably more correct, definition is a class that implements all the methods of an interface in some sort of default way. This adapter class can then be subclassed for an actual implementation that has to bother to implement only the methods that are important to it. An example of this in the Java API is `java.awt.event.ComponentAdapater`. This type of class can also be called a convenience class.

Another type of class that is also called a convenience class is one that can, under the right circumstances, change its appearance to be that of another class—one that could be entirely different from itself. An example of this would be a class that maintains a collection of objects, with methods to add and delete these objects, and such a class could include a method that returns an `Enumeration` object. The `Enumeration` is an interface, not a class, so the collection object could implement the `Enumeration` interface and return itself as the `Enumeration` object (most likely, it would return a clone of itself). The returned object would have all the methods of the Enumeration interface implemented and would behave exactly as if it were a special Enumeration object that just happened to contain the same group of items as the original container.

 Also see **convenience**.

Adjustable

interface java.awt.Adjustable

This interface is implemented by classes that have an integer value that can be adjusted between a pair of upper and lower bounds. Think of a scrollbar (which uses this interface) and its various value settings. It has both upper and lower bounds, and the current value is the position of the slider. The size of the slider represents the visible amount.

The increments

The value of an `Adjustable` object can be modified in three ways. First, it can simply be set to a value in the range. Second, it can be moved up or down by the unit increment amount—the smallest amount the slider can be adjusted. The unit amount is normally one, but cases arise in which it is greater than one. An example of this is in the display of text, in which each unit is the scrolled height of the font. Third, the block amount can be set to a convenient value (usually a multiple of the unit value) for making large jump movements. An example of this would be displaying an entire page of text with each jump.

Implemented by

```
Scrollbar
```

Inheritance

```
public interface java.awt.Adjustable
```

Variables and constants

HORIZONTAL

```
public final static int HORIZONTAL
```

A constant used to specify horizontal orientation.

VERTICAL

```
public final static int VERTICAL
```

A constant used to specify vertical orientation.

Constructors

Returned by

Objects implementing this interface are returned by
`AdjustmentEvent.getAdjustable()`, `ScrollPane.getHAdjustable()`, and
`ScrollPane.getVAdjustable()`.

Methods

addAdjustmentListener()

```
public abstract void addAdjustmentListener(
        AdjustmentListener listener)
```

Adds a listener that will be notified when the adjustable values change.

getBlockIncrement()

```
public abstract int getBlockIncrement()
```

Returns the block value increment for the adjustable object.

getMaximum()

```
public abstract int getMaximum()
```

Returns the maximum allowable value of the adjustable object.

getMinimum()

```
public abstract int getMinimum()
```

Returns the minimum allowable value of the adjustable object.

getOrientation()

```
public abstract int getOrientation()
```

Returns the current orientation of the object — it is either VERTICAL or HORIZONTAL.

getUnitIncrement()

```
public abstract int getUnitIncrement()
```

Returns the unit value increment for the adjustable object.

getValue()

```
public abstract int getValue()
```

Returns the current value of the adjustable object.

getVisibleAmount()

```
public abstract int getVisibleAmount()
```

Returns the length of the proportional indicator.

removeAdjustmentListener()

```
public abstract void removeAdjustmentListener(
        AdjustmentListener listener)
```

Removes a listener that had been added by addAdjustmentListener().

setBlockIncrement()

```
public abstract void setBlockIncrement(int b)
```

Sets the block value increment.

setMaximum()

```
public abstract void setMaximum(int value)
```

Sets the maximum value.

setMinimum()

```
public abstract void setMinimum(int value)
```

Sets the minimum value.

setUnitIncrement()

```
public abstract void setUnitIncrement(int value)
```

Sets the unit increment value.

setValue()

```
public abstract void setValue(int value)
```

Sets the current value. The value must be within the range specified by the minimum and maximum.

setVisibleAmount()

```
public abstract void setVisibleAmount(int value)
```

Sets the length of the proportional indicator of the adjustable object.

 For an example, see **Scrollbar**.

AdjustmentEvent

class java.awt.event.AdjustmentEvent

This event is issued to notify listeners that an adjustment has occurred. This event is delivered to a registered AdjustmentListener. This is used in the ScrollPane to notify listeners of a change.

The ID number

Events have an ID number that can supply more information about the initiation of the event. The range of the ID value is between ADJUSTMENT_FIRST and ADJUSTMENT_LAST. For the AdjustmentEvent, there is only one value in the range—the ADJUSTMENT_VALUE_CHANGED value.

Inheritance

```
public class java.awt.event.AdjustmentEvent
    extends AWTEvent
            ⇑
    public class java.awt.AWTEvent
        extends EventObject
```

```
                    ⇑
    public class java.util.EventObject
            implements Serializable
            extends Object
                    ⇑
        public class java.lang.Object
```

Variables and constants

ADJUSTMENT_FIRST

```
    public final static int ADJUSTMENT_FIRST
```

The lowest value of the `AdjustmentEvent` id numbers.

ADJUSTMENT_LAST

```
    public final static int ADJUSTMENT_LAST
```

The highest value of the `AdjustmentEvent` id numbers.

ADJUSTMENT_VALUE_CHANGED

```
    public final static int ADJUSTMENT_VALUE_CHANGED
```

The only valid id value for the `AdjustmentEvent` id.

BLOCK_DECREMENT

```
    public final static int BLOCK_DECREMENT
```

Identifies the event as a block decrement adjustment type.

BLOCK_INCREMENT

```
    public final static int BLOCK_INCREMENT
```

Identifies the event as a block increment adjustment type.

TRACK

```
    public final static int TRACK
```

Identifies the event as an absolute tracking adjustment type.

UNIT_DECREMENT

```
    public final static int UNIT_DECREMENT
```

Identifies the event as a unit decrement adjustment type.

UNIT_INCREMENT

```
    public final static int UNIT_INCREMENT
```

Identifies the event as a unit increment adjustment type.

Constructors

AdjustmentEvent()

```
public AdjustmentEvent(Adjustable source,int id,
                int type,int value)
```

The construction of an AdjustmentEvent requires that an event source object be specified, as well as the id (which is always ADJUSTMENT_VALUE_CHANGED), the type of adjustment that is being made, and the numeric value of the adjustment. The type is one of UNIT_DECREMENT, UNIT_INCREMENT, BLOCK_DECREMENT, BLOCK_INCREMENT, or TRACK. The value specifies the amount of the adjustment.

Methods

getAdjustable()

```
public Adjustable getAdjustable()
```

Returns the Adjustable object that originated the event.

getAdjustmentType()

```
public int getAdjustmentType()
```

Returns the type of the adjustment.

getValue()

```
public int getValue()
```

Returns the value of the adjustment.

paramString()

```
public String paramString()
```

Returns debugging information. The return string describes the internal state and values of this object.

For an example, see **ScrollPane**. For the listener interface, see **AdjustmentListener**.

a
b
c

AdjustmentListener

interface java.awt.event.AdjustmentListener

This must be implemented for a listener to be able to receive an
`AdjustmentEvent`.

Implemented by

`AWTEventMulticaster`

Inheritance

```
public interface java.awt.event.AdjustmentListener
extends EventListener
        ⇑
    public interface java.util.EventListener
```

Constructors

Returned by

Objects implementing this interface are returned from the `AWTEventMulticaster`
methods `add()` and `remove()`.

Methods

adjustmentValueChanged()

```
public abstract void
        adjustmentValueChanged(AdjustmentEvent event)
```

This method will be called for all the `AdjustmentEvent` occurrences for which the object
is registered.

 For a description of the event, see **AdjustmentEvent**.

Adler32

class java.util.zip.Adler32

This class can be used to compute an Adler 32 checksum. This type of checksum is almost, but not quite, as reliable as a CRC 32, but it has the advantage
of being much faster to calculate.

Inheritance

```
public class java.util.zip.Adler32
    implements Checksum
    extends Object
        ⇑
    public class java.lang.Object
```

Constructors

```
public Adler32()
```

Methods

getValue()

```
public long getValue()
```

Returns the internal checksum value.

reset()

```
public void reset()
```

Resets the internal checksum to its initial value.

update()

```
public void update(byte array[],int offset,int length)
public void update(byte array[])
public void update(int value)
```

Updates the checksum calculation to include the supplied bytes. A single byte can be specified as the value. A block of bytes can be specified as array, and the checksum will be updated for length bytes beginning at offset. If offset and length are not specified, the entire array is used. This method can be called repeatedly to have new data included in the calculation.

 For another method of calculating a checksum, see **CRC32**.

AlreadyBoundException

class java.rmi.AlreadyBoundException

This exception is thrown by the RMI registry whenever an attempt is made to bind a name that has already been bound.

Inheritance

```
public class java.rmi.AlreadyBoundException
extends Exception
          ⇑
    public class java.lang.Exception
        extends Throwable
              ⇑
        public class java.lang.Throwable
            implements Serializable
            extends Object
                ⇑
            public class java.lang.Object
```

Constructors

```
public AlreadyBoundException()
public AlreadyBoundException(String message)
```

If the `message` string is supplied, it is used as a detailed message describing this particular exception.

 For an interface that has a method to throw this exception, see **Registry**.

ampersand

&   &=

These operators can be used for either bitwise ANDing (on integer types) or logical ANDing (on `boolean` types). Which action is performed depends on which data types they operate on.

Bitwise operation

If the expression on one side is an integer, the other side must also be an integer. If the integers are not the same size, one of them will be widened and a bitwise ANDing operation will take place on the two. Integer widening involves sign extension on the left, and the resulting 1s or 0s will be used in the ANDing operation.

Boolean operation

If the expression on one side is a `boolean`, the other side must also be a `boolean`. Both `boolean` expressions will be evaluated, and if they are both true, the result of the expression is `true`—otherwise the result is `false`. The example demonstrates that both sides of the expression are always evaluated.

Example

This example evaluates two `boolean` AND expressions. One with both sides `true`—one with both sides `false`. Each expression actually evaluated causes a line to print. The logical AND operator with a single ampersand will always evaluate the expressions to each side of it even when the evaluation of only one of them is necessary to determine the result. This example includes samples of a logical AND between two `false` values and two `true` values:

```
public class LogicalAnd {
    public static void main(String[] arg) {
        boolean state;
        state = alwaysTrue(1) & alwaysTrue(2);
        state = alwaysFalse(3) & alwaysFalse(4);
        state &= alwaysTrue(5);
    }
    static boolean alwaysTrue(int value) {
        System.out.println("True for " + value);
        return(true);
    }
    static boolean alwaysFalse(int value) {
        System.out.println("False for " + value);
        return(false);
    }
}
```

In the first case it is necessary to evaluate both sides to determine that the two expressions both result in `true`. In the second case, where both are `false`, it is really only necessary to evaluate one expression—but as you can see from the output, both are evaluated.

```
True for 1
True for 2
False for 3
False for 4
True for 5
```

This is always the case, with the single-ampersand form. The double-ampersand works differently—it will evaluate only one of its terms if that is all that is needed.

For the double ampersand logical operator, see **ampersand ampersand**. For the logical and arithmetic OR, see **bar** and **bar bar**. For more on integer widening, see **conversion**.

ampersand ampersand

&&

This operator can be used to perform the logical AND operation between two
`boolean` expressions.

The Boolean operation

The operation begins by evaluating the expression on the left side. If that is found to be
`false`, the expression on the right is not evaluated. This is demonstrated in the example.

Example

This example evaluates two `boolean` AND expressions. One with both sides
`true`—one with both sides `false`. Each expression actually evaluated causes a
line to print:

```
public class LogicalAnd2 {
    public static void main(String[] arg) {
        boolean state;
        state = alwaysTrue(1) && alwaysTrue(2);
        state = alwaysFalse(3) && alwaysFalse(4);
    }
    static boolean alwaysTrue(int value) {
        System.out.println("True for " + value);
        return(true);
    }
    static boolean alwaysFalse(int value) {
        System.out.println("False for " + value);
        return(false);
    }
}
```

Here is the output from the example:

```
True for 1
True for 2
False for 3
```

The call to `alwaysFalse(4)` was not made, because the evaluation of
`alwaysFalse(3)` was sufficient to produce the result. The single ampersand
operator works differently.

 For another logical AND operator, see **ampersand**. There are also logical and
arithmetic OR operators; see **bar** and **bar bar**.

AND

 To perform operations on an array of `boolean` values, see **BitSet**. For bitwise operations on primitive data types, including the `boolean` type, see **ampersand**. For logical expression evaluation, see **ampersand ampersand**.

anonymous class

 For a description with an example, see **inner classes**.

API

Application Program Interface

For Java, the complete set of classes supplied with the JDK is the API (Application Program Interface). They are grouped into packages.

 For a list of the packages making up the API, see **java**.

applet

There are two kinds of programs that can be written in Java—one is an application and the other is an applet. An *applet* is a program that is intended to be named in an HTML document that is loaded into a Web browser to be executed. The Java Virtual Machine is built in—it's part of the Web browser—so the browser has complete control of the running of the applet. This includes things like interapplet messaging and security. The Web browser can be configured to any level of applet security including reading and writing files, accessing system configuration parameters, and so on.

A Static Applet

This is a description of a very simple applet, how to compile it, and how to run it. All it does is display a string as shown in Figure A-1:

```
import java.awt.*;
import java.applet.*;

public class StaticApplet extends Applet {
```

```
private String displayString = "Static Applet";
private Font font;
private Rectangle rectangle;
private int stringY;
private int stringX;

public void init() {
    rectangle = new Rectangle();
    font = new Font("Courier",Font.BOLD,35);
    setBackground(Color.lightGray);
}

public void paint(Graphics g) {
    if(!rectangle.equals(getBounds())) {
        rectangle = getBounds();
        FontMetrics fm = g.getFontMetrics(font);
        stringX = rectangle.width;
        stringX -= fm.stringWidth(displayString);
        stringX /= 2;
        stringY = rectangle.height;
        stringY -= fm.getAscent() + fm.getDescent();
        stringY /= 2;
        stringY += fm.getAscent();
    }
    g.setColor(Color.lightGray);
    g.fillRect(0,0,getSize().width,getSize().height);
    g.setColor(Color.red);
    g.setFont(font);
    g.drawString(displayString,stringX,stringY);
    g.dispose();
    }
}
```

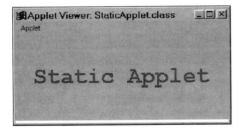

Figure A-1 StaticApplet displays a character string.

It extends Applet

All applets have `Applet` as their superclass. The `Applet` superclass has certain methods defined that are called by the browser. This simple example overloads two of them — `init()` and `paint()`.

The `init()` method

This method is the first one called by the browser in any applet. It can be used to set up initial values and do any other preliminary setup work that must come first. In this example, the font and background colors are defined. The font will be used later. The `setBackground()` method is called to provide a default for use by the browser in clearing space for the applet window. A rectangular object is created here for convenience — just so one will exist later on.

The `paint()` method

This method is called by the browser to paint the entire applet window. The first thing we do is check whether or not the rectangle we have is the same size as the applet, so we compare our rectangle to the current `getBounds()` of the applet and — if the two don't match — we calculate the coordinate values needed to put the string in the center of the display. Doing this rectangle comparison each time we display the applet causes the applet to automatically resize whenever something changes.

The last line of code in the `paint()` method is a call to the `dispose()` method of the `Graphics` object. This will cause the `Graphics` object to release any system-level resources it is holding. This is necessary if the paint method is going to be called often to make sure the resources are not exhausted.

Compiling the applet

To compile the applet, enter the command

```
javac StaticApplet.java
```

This will produce a file named StaticApplet.class. It is this file that is used to run the applet.

Running the applet

The display of an applet is the responsibility of a browser of some sort, and a very simple browser is supplied with the JDK — the appletviewer. Like all browsers, the appletviewer reads HTML files and follows the instructions it finds there. Here is the HTML (in a file named StaticApplet.html) to run StaticApplet:

```
<html>
<head>
<title> A simple static applet </title>
</head>
<body>
```

```
<center>
<applet code="StaticApplet.class"
        width=330 height=130></applet>
</center>

</body>

</html>
```

To run the applet, enter this command:

```
appletviewer StaticApplet.html
```

An applet with a component

This applet demonstrates how to include a component in an applet. The component in the example is a simple button. Each time the button is pressed, it changes its color and its label. You will notice that no paint() method appears. It was unnecessary since we have nothing to paint—a layout manager comes with the applet to manage the location and display of components. Figure A-2 shows what the displayed window looks like.

```
import java.awt.*;
import java.awt.event.*;
import java.applet.*;

public class ButtonApplet extends Applet
        implements ActionListener {
    private Button button;
    private int index;
    private String[] colorName = {
        "White","Yellow","Green","Pink"
    }
    private Color[] color = {
        Color.white,Color.yellow,Color.green,Color.pink
    }

    public void init() {
        setBackground(Color.lightGray);
        index = 0;
        button = new Button(colorName[index]);
        button.setBackground(color[index]);
        button.addActionListener(this);
        add(button);
    }
```

```
public void actionPerformed(ActionEvent event) {
    if(++index >= colorName.length)
        index = 0;
    button.setBackground(color[index]);
    button.setLabel(colorName[index]);
}
}
```

Figure A-2   The display of the ButtonApplet.

ButtonApplet **implements** ActionListener

For a class to have the ability to receive events from a component, it must be a registered listener of that component. The ActionListener requires the implementation of one method—the actionPerformed() method.

The init() **method**

When the browser calls this method—to initialize the applet—a button is constructed. It is assigned an initial label and color from the arrays. The addActionListener() method of the component is called to register this applet as a listener for events that will be coming from it. The add() method of the applet is called to add the component to the applet. It will be the responsibility of the layout manager to position the button on the display.

The actionPerformed() **method**

With each button event—the mouse button being pressed is an event—this method will be called, because it was registered in init(). The applet need not query the contents of the ActionEvent to find out which component generated it because we have only one component. We just set the background color and the button label to the next ones in the arrays.

An animation applet

Several ways exist to configure an animation applet. All of them require that the applet launch a separate thread. This particular form has been used successfully as a basis for dozens of applets. In this example, we bounce a colored circle around the window like a ball around a billiard table. A screen shot of it is shown in Figure A-3.

```java
import java.awt.*;
import java.applet.*;

public class AnimationApplet extends Applet
        implements Runnable {
    private static final int MARGIN = 30;
    private static final int DOT_DIAMETER = 8;
    private static final int PAUSE = 3;
    private static final Color DOT_COLOR = Color.red;
    private static final int ADVANCE = 3;

    private static final byte UP = 1;
    private static final byte DOWN = 2;
    private static final byte LEFT = 1;
    private static final byte RIGHT = 2;

    private Image image;
    private Font font;
    private byte vertical;
    private byte horizontal;
    private int x_dot;
    private int y_dot;
    private Thread looper;
    private Rectangle rectangle;
    private int y_string;
    private int x_string;

    public void init() {
        vertical = DOWN;
        horizontal = RIGHT;
        x_dot = MARGIN;
        y_dot = MARGIN;
        rectangle = new Rectangle();
        setBackground(Color.lightGray);
    }
    public void start() {
        if(looper == null) {
            looper = new Thread(this);
            looper.start();
        }
    }
    public void stop() {
```

```
                    if(looper != null) {
                        looper.stop();
                        looper = null;
                    }
            }
            public void run() {
                try {
                    while(true) {
                        repaint();
                        Thread.sleep(PAUSE);
                    }
                } finally {
                    return;
                }
            }
            public void update(Graphics g) {
                if(looper.isAlive()) {
                    if(!rectangle.equals(getBounds()) ||
                            (image == null)) {
                        rectangle = getBounds();
                        image = createImage(rectangle.width,
                                rectangle.height);
                    }
                    nextFrame();
                    paint(image.getGraphics());
                    g.drawImage(image,0,0,null);
                }
            }
            public void paint(Graphics g) {
                g.setColor(Color.lightGray);
                g.fillRect(0,0,getSize().width,getSize().height);
                g.setColor(DOT_COLOR);
                g.fillOval(x_dot,y_dot,DOT_DIAMETER,DOT_DIAMETER);
            }
            private void nextFrame() {
                for(int i=0; i<ADVANCE; i++) {
                    if(horizontal == RIGHT) {
                        int edge = rectangle.width -
                                MARGIN - DOT_DIAMETER;
                        if((x_dot += 3) > edge) {
                            x_dot = edge;
                            horizontal = LEFT;
                        }
                    } else {
```

```
                    if((x_dot -= 3) < MARGIN) {
                        x_dot = MARGIN;
                        horizontal = RIGHT;
                    }
                }
                if(vertical == DOWN) {
                    int bottom = rectangle.height -
                            MARGIN - DOT_DIAMETER;
                    if((y_dot += 3) > bottom) {
                        y_dot = bottom;
                        vertical = UP;
                    }
                } else {
                    if((y_dot -= 3) < MARGIN) {
                        y_dot = MARGIN;
                        vertical = DOWN;
                    }
                }
            }
        }
    }
}
```

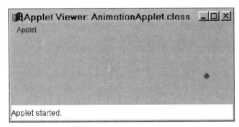

Figure A-3   The moving dot.

It implements Runnable

To be able to do animation, an applet needs to run continuously. To run continuously—and leave the browser free to do other things— it has to crank up a separate thread in which to run. Any class implementing the Runnable interface can be executed as a separate thread.

The init() method

This is the first method called by the browser. It is used to perform the one-time initialization required for the applet.

The start() method

This method is called each time the applet is to begin execution. A new Thread object is created using this as its runnable target—this being the object that has implemented the run() method of the Runnable interface. As soon as the thread is created, its start() method is called to get it running. Once the thread is running, it will call the run() method of the applet.

This can be a bit confusing because there are two start() methods—one in the applet and one in the thread. The one in the applet calls the one in the thread, and then the one in the thread calls run() in the applet.

The start() method of the applet could be called several times during the life of the applet, so it is necessary to make sure that the applet is not already running before creating a new thread. This is done by checking whether or not looper is null.

The stop() method

This method is called each time the applet is to cease execution. This could be a temporary stop—there could be another call to start() following this, so nothing should be destroyed. We just want to shut down the thread, which we do by calling its stop() method. The reference to the thread, looper, is set to null so start() will know a new thread will need to be created to restart the applet. The start() and stop() methods of the applet can be called again and again as the applet is suspended and restarted when, say, the browser is hidden behind another window or the applet is scrolled off the display.

The run() method

This is the method that is required by the Runnable interface. When a thread is started, this method is called. The thread will continue to run until this method returns, so this becomes the main loop of the applet—all the animation is controlled from here. It simply goes into an infinite loop alternately calling repaint() and Thread.sleep(). The repaint() method causes the system to schedule a call to update() and then returns.

While this loop is going on, if the browser makes a call to the applet's stop() method, the thread is halted. This causes the Thread.sleep() method to throw an exception in run(). This exception breaks the try block causing run() to return—the applet has been stopped. A call to start() is all that is needed to bring it back to life.

The update() method

This method is called after one or more calls to repaint(). In our example, the only call to repaint() is in the loop of the run() method, but it could have been called from anywhere. Several calls to repaint() before update() is called will cause only one call to update(). A default version of update() just makes a call to paint().

It is possible that this method gets called at a point where the thread is not active. We are dealing with asynchronous threads here, and there are some race conditions. For that reason, we have to make sure that the thread is running by calling looper.isAlive().

If the applet has been resized (or if we have just gotten our first size—remember we created a zero-sized rectangle at the beginning), we save a copy of the current rectangle and create an `Image` object of the size of the rectangle. This image is to be used as a work area. Doing all the painting to the work area and then displaying it all at once eliminates flicker.

We call the `nextFrame()` method to set up the values to be used in drawing the next frame of our moving picture. The `paint()` method is called to draw the entire new picture frame on the RAM image. Finally, the `drawImage()` method is the `Graphics` object used to paint the RAM form of the picture on the actual display.

The `paint()` method

This method paints the entire frame using the graphics object supplied to it. This method cannot assume that any parts of the picture have been already drawn—the entire window could have just popped up from an icon. In this example, we simply fill the entire rectangle with the background color and then draw a colored dot in the location specified by `x_dot` and `y_dot`.

The `nextFrame()` method

This is the only method in the applet that is not an overloading of an `Applet` class method or implementation of a `Runnable` interface method. It is here as a convenience to do the calculations to move the display values from one picture frame to the next. It moves the dot by `ADVANCE` pixels in both the horizontal and vertical directions, changing directions when an edge is hit.

applet

package java.applet

This package contains the class and the interfaces on which all Java applets are based.

Interfaces

```
AppletContext
AppletStub
AudioClip
```

Classes

```
Applet
```

Applet

class java.applet.Applet

This is the superclass of all applets. An applet is a program intended to be executed inside the context of a Web browser (or some other applet viewer) by having its name and location included in an HTML document.

As you can see by its inheritance, the `Applet` class brings a lot of things with it. It is a panel container that can be used to display graphics. The applet has almost complete control over what it displays; however, for most browsers, the actual size of its displayable area is not under control of the applet—the size is determined by the browser, which normally uses the dimension values embedded in the HTML document.

Inheritance

```
public class java.applet.Applet
    extends Panel
        ⇑
    public class java.awt.Panel
        extends Container
            ⇑
        public class java.awt.Container
            extends Component
                ⇑
            public class java.awt.Component
                implements ImageObserver
                implements MenuContainer
                implements Serializable
                extends Object
                    ⇑
                public class java.lang.Object
```

Constructors

```
public Applet()
```

Returned by

An `Applet` object is returned by `AppletContext.getApplet()`.

Methods

destroy()

```
public void destroy()
```

This method is called by the browser whenever the applet is to be destroyed. If some resources are being held by the applet, they should be released in this method. Most applets will have no need to override this method. The method `stop()` is always called before `destroy()`.

getAppletContex()

```
public AppletContext getAppletContext()
```

Returns an `AppletContext` object for this applet.

getAppletInfo()

```
public String getAppletInfo()
```

Returns a string that describes the applet. A default string is provided, but any applet can override this method to return a descriptive string of its own—commonly author and copyright information.

getAudioClip()

```
public AudioClip getAudioClip(URL url)

public AudioClip getAudioClip(URL url,String name)
```

Loads the audio clip specified by `url`. If the `name` is present as the second argument, the `url` is used to locate the directory and the name is used as the name of the file itself. A `null` return indicates it cannot be found. The format understood by Java is the `.au` file format.

getCodeBase()

```
public URL getCodeBase()
```

Retrieves the URL of the applet class file (which may or may not be the URL of the HTML document).

getDocumentBase()

```
public URL getDocumentBase()
```

Retrieves the URL of the HTML document (which may or may not be the URL of the applet class file).

getImage()

```
public Image getImage(URL url)
public Image getImage(URL url,String name)
```

Schedules the retrieval of an image file. If the `name` is present as the second argument, the `url` is used to locate the directory and the name is used as the name of the file itself. If the name is not supplied, the `url` must contain the filename. A `null` return indicates it cannot be found. You can get the URL of the applet or the HTML document with `getCodeBase()` and `getDocumentBase()`. The formats understood by Java are .jpeg and .gif.

getLocale()

```
public Locale getLocale()
```

If a special `Locale` has been set for the applet, it is returned — otherwise, the default is returned by making a call to `Locale.getDefault()`.

getParameter()

```
public String getParameter(String name)
```

Get a parameter string from an HTML document.

getParameterInfo()

```
public String[][] getParameterInfo()
```

Returns a two-dimensional array of strings that describes the parameters understood by this applet. The value of the first subscript is the same as the number of parameters; the second is 3, because there are always three strings used to describe a parameter—the first is its name, the second is its type, and the third is a description of it. The default method returns `null`.

init()

```
public void init()
```

Your applet should override this method to do any one-time initializations. A Web browser — or other applet viewer — will call this method when it first loads the applet.

isActive()

```
public boolean isActive()
```

The return value of this method is `false` until immediately prior to the call to `start()`, when it becomes `true`. It will remain `true` until just before the call to `stop()`, when it is set back to `false`.

play()

```
public void play(URL url)
public void play(URL url,String name)
```

Loads and plays an audio clip once. The name of the clip file is specified by its URL, or by the URL of the directory in which it is kept and the name of the file. No errors are reported — if the file cannot be found or won't play after it loads, no action is taken.

a

b

c

resize()

```
public void resize(Dimension d)
public void resize(int width,int height)
```

Makes a request for the applet to be resized. For an applet to be actually resized depends on actions taken by the applet viewer, so the request may be entirely ignored. The size is in pixels.

setStub()

```
public final void setStub(AppletStub stub)
```

This method will be called automatically to assign the AppletStub used by some of the other methods to retrieve information from the environment.

showStatus()

```
public void showStatus(String message)
```

Displays a string on the status bar of the Web browser. This is normally a small window that displays a single line of text somewhere below the main viewing window—there may not be one.

start()

```
public void start()
```

Your applet should override this method to include any code that should be executed each time the applet begins execution. Each call to start() will be matched by a call to stop() to halt the applet. The start() and stop() methods may be called several times during the life of an applet.

stop()

```
public void stop()
```

Your applet should override this method to include any code that should be executed each time the applet ceases execution. There will have been a call to start() prior to this call. The start() and stop() methods may be called several times during the life of an applet. This method is always called before destroy() is called.

Example

This code snippet demonstrates the format of data required to implement the getParameterInfo() method. Each set of three strings defines a single parameter with its name, its type, and some descriptive text.

```
static String[][] parmInfo = {
    {"maximum", "50-100", "The maximum setting" },
    {"minimum", "1-30",   "The minimum setting" },
    {"filename","url",     "The url of the file" },
};
```

```
public String[][] getParameterInfo() {
    return(parmInfo);
}
```

 For examples of applets, see **applet**. For more capabilities of an applet, see **AppletContext**. For an example of an applet reading parameters from HTML, see **HTML**. For an example of loading and displaying an image, see **Image**. For the ability to run an applet with the full set of capabilities normally limited to applications, see **JAR** and **javakey**.

AppletContext

interface java.applet.AppletContext

This interface defines methods that are available to all applets. Applets are executed by an interpreter of HTML—a Web browser or the applet viewer. These methods can be used to get information from the interpreter. The methods in an `AppletContext` can be used to discover all sorts of information, including the names of other applets that are currently running.

Inheritance

```
public interface java.applet.AppletContext
```

Constructors

Returned by

An object implementing this interface is returned from `Applet.getAppletContext()` and `AppletStub.getAppletContext()`.

Methods

getApplet()

```
public abstract Applet getApplet(String name)
```

Returns a reference to the named applet. If the named applet is not found, it returns `null`.

getApplets()

```
public abstract Enumeration getApplets()
```

Returns an enumeration of all applets, including the one making the call. If an applet exists but is not accessible, it will not be included.

getAudioClip()

```
public abstract AudioClip getAudioClip(URL url)
```

Loads the audio clip specified by `url`. This method will block until it is loaded.

getImage()

```
public abstract Image getImage(URL url)
```

Retrieves an image specified by `url`. The method does not actually get the image—it schedules the retrieval of the image and returns immediately. For an example, see `MediaTracker`.

showDocument()

```
public abstract void showDocument(URL url)
public abstract void showDocument(URL url,String target)
```

Displays the document specified by `url`. The `target` specifies where the document should be displayed and can take on the values found in Table A-2. The browser, or other software being used to display the applet, may simply ignore this method call. See Example 1.

Table A-2 Target Options for `showDocument()`

Target	Where It Is to Be Displayed
"_self"	Displays the document in the current frame.
"_parent"	Displays it in the parent frame.
"_top"	Displays it in the topmost frame.
"_blank"	Displays it in a new unnamed top-level window.
name	Using any string value other than the four just listed will cause the display to be in a top-level window of the specified name.

showStatus()

```
public abstract void showStatus(String status)
```

Displays `status` on the status line of the browser. This is the line of text usually found at the bottom of the browser window. The browser may simply ignore this call.

Example

This is an applet that has a pull-down list of some Web sites and a button that will link to the one currently selected. The factory method getAppletContext() is used to get the context of this applet. It is then simply a matter of creating a URL object and calling showDocument():

```java
import java.awt.*;
import java.awt.event.*;
import java.applet.*;
import java.net.*;

public class ShowDocumentApplet extends Applet {
    private String[] linkName = {
                "http://www.idgbooks.com",
                "http://www.javasoft.com",
                "http://java.sun.com"
    };
    private Choice choice;
    private Button button;
    private URL actualURL;
    private AppletContext context;

    public void init() {
        setBackground(Color.lightGray);
        context = getAppletContext();
        choice = new Choice();
        for(int i=0; i<linkName.length; i++)
            choice.addItem(linkName[i]);
        add(choice);
        button = new Button("Go");
        add(button);
        getActualURL(linkName[0]);
    }

    public boolean action(Event event,Object object) {
        if(event.target == choice) {
            getActualURL(object.toString());
            return(true);
        } else if(event.target == button) {
            context.showDocument(actualURL);
            return(true);
        }
        return(false);
    }
```

```
private void getActualURL(String urlString) {
    try {
        actualURL = new URL(urlString);
    } catch(Exception e) {
        e.printStackTrace();
    }
}
}
```

This example uses the older Java 1.0 event model. It was written this way because an Internet connection is required for the applet to run, and by using the older event model, the example will work for any Java-enabled Web browser.

 See **Applet**.

AppletStub

interface java.applet.AppletStub

This is the set of methods to be called by a browser or applet viewer to interface with an applet. This interface is not normally used by applet programmers—the same set of methods are available in the `Applet` class.

Inheritance

```
public interface java.applet.AppletStub
```

Methods

appletResize()

```
public abstract void appletResize(int width,int height)
```

This method is called to make a request to resize the applet. The request may be ignored.

getAppletContext()

```
public abstract AppletContext getAppletContext()
```

Returns an `AppletContext` for this applet.

getCodeBase()

```
public abstract URL getCodeBase()
```

Returns the `URL` of the class file of the applet.

getDocumentBase()

```
public abstract URL getDocumentBase()
```

Gets the URL of the HTML file executing the applet.

getParameter()

```
public abstract String getParameter(String name)
```

Given the name of a parameter, returns its value.

isActive()

```
public abstract boolean isActive()
```

Returns true if the applet is currently active.

 For programmer access to these methods, see **Applet**.

appletviewer

program

This is a utility that you can use to run applets outside of a Web browser. It uses the same input as a Web browser—an HTML file—but it discards everything except any applet tags that it finds.

Multiple applets

The applet viewer is capable of running several applets at once. A separate window will pop up for each applet tag found in an HTML file. Also, the applet viewer can accept several HTML files on the command line and will execute the applets found in all of them.

Syntax

The syntax of the command line:

```
appletviewer [options] url [url ...]
```

Options

-debug

This will cause the applet to be executed by jdb, the applet debugger.

-J<java option>

This will pass *java option* through to the interpreter (java or jdb) that runs the applet. The java option string cannot contain spaces—to specify multiple options, use multiple -J flags.

No space appears between -J and the option string. For example, to have the Java interpreter print out a list of the available options:

```
appletviewer -J-help SoundOnLoad.html
```

 For debugging applets, see **jdb**. For options that can be passed to the Java interpreter, see **java**.

application

Two kinds of programs can be written in Java. One is an applet and the other is an application. An applet is executed by a browser whenever it is found in an HTML document. An application is executed by a stand-alone Java interpreter.

Any nonabstract class can be made into an application by adding a main() method. This means that the same class can be both an application and an applet. This is a simple application that prints a line of text:

```
public class OneLiner {
    public void static main(String[] arg) {
        System.out.println("This will print");
    }
}
```

When the Java interpreter is instructed to execute the OneLiner class like this—

```
java OneLiner
```

—it loads the class —from a file named OneLiner.class—and calls the method main(). If any arguments appear on the command line like this—

```
java OneLiner -j -m
```

—they are passed to main() in the String arg[] array. The first argument is arg[0], the second is arg[1], and so on. The main() method can then load and execute all the classes it needs.

For a simple application, when main() returns, the application will cease execution. On the other hand, if main() has created an object that is still doing work, it will be left running. An example of this is a pop-up dialog waiting for user response. The Java interpreter will continue to execute as the window is waiting for user response.

 For more information on starting applications from the command line, see **java**.

AreaAveragingScaleFilter

class java.awt.image.AreaAveragingScaleFilter

This is an image filter that will accept an image and produce a copy of it scaled to a different size.

Scaling by averaging

An image is reduced in size by a simple area averaging algorithm that produces a smoother result than the more familiar nearest neighbor algorithm. To reduce the size of an image, each new pixel is created as an average of the pixel values that the new single pixel is to represent. To increase the size, the algorithm works in a way analogous to increasing the image by an even multiple in both directions and then using the averaging algorithm to bring it back to the requested size.

Top down left right

For the smoothing to work properly, the input image must be delivered in top-down left-right order. That is, each row of pixels, starting with the top one, is sent in left-to-right order. If the data arrives in any other order, a simple pixel replication algorithm will be applied, and then the `requestTopDownLeftRight()` method will be used to refilter the pixels using the better algorithm. This can cause the image data to be transmitted twice, but only if the source of the image, the ImageProducer, was capable of sending it in top-down, left-right order but did not do so the first time.

 Normally, you will not need to create this object directly. The method `Image.getScaledInstance()` will create an object of the class and return the scaled image. If you need to perform your own image filtering, however, see **ImageFilter** for examples.

Inheritance

```
public class java.awt.image.AreaAveragingScaleFilter
     extends ReplicateScaleFilter
          ⇑
     public class java.awt.image.ReplicateScaleFilter
          extends ImageFilter
               ⇑
          public class java.awt.image.ImageFilter
               implements ImageConsumer
               implements Cloneable
               extends Object
                    ⇑
               public class java.lang.Object
```

Constructors

```
public AreaAveragingScaleFilter(int width,int height)
```

The constructor specifies the desired height and width of the output image.

Methods

setHints()

```
public void setHints(int hintFlags)
```

This method is called to supply information about how the image will be delivered. The information passed in as hintFlags will determine which algorithm is used. For the possible values of hintFlags, see **ImageConsumer**.

setPixels()

```
public void setPixels(int x,int y,int w,int h,
        ColorModel model,byte pixels[],
        int off,int scansize)
public void setPixels(int x,int y,int w,int h,
        ColorModel model,int pixels[],
        int off,int scansize)
```

 These are the methods that do the actual filtering. For an explanation of the arguments and an example, see **ImageFilter**.

Example

This example loads an image into RAM and, with each click of the mouse, displays a copy of it in its original size and another copy that has been scaled:

```
import java.awt.*;
import java.applet.*;
import java.net.*;
import java.awt.image.*;
import java.util.*;

public class ScaleFilterApplet extends Applet {
    private static final int startScale = 10;
    private static final int incrementScale = 10;
    private static final int endScale = 200;
    private int scale = startScale;
    private Image image;
    private Image scaleImage;
```

```
public void init() {
    setBackground(Color.lightGray);
    URL url = getCodeBase();
    image = getImage(url,"bluemarble.gif");
    MediaTracker mt = new MediaTracker(this);
    mt.addImage(image,1);
    try {
        mt.waitForAll();
    } catch(Exception e) {
        e.printStackTrace();
    }
    repaint();
}

public void paint(Graphics g) {
    g.setColor(Color.lightGray);
    g.fillRect(0,0,getSize().width,getSize().height);
    g.drawImage(image,0,0,this);
    if(scaleImage != null) {
        g.drawImage(scaleImage,0,
                    image.getHeight(this),this);
    }
    g.dispose();
}

public boolean mouseDown(Event event,int x,int y) {
    AreaAveragingScaleFilter sf =
            new AreaAveragingScaleFilter(scale,scale);
    ImageProducer ip = image.getSource();
    ImageProducer is = new FilteredImageSource(ip,sf);
    scaleImage = getToolkit().createImage(is);
    repaint();
    if((scale += incrementScale) > endScale)
        scale = startScale;
    return(true);
}
}
```

The applet uses the value of scale to determine the size of the new image. It starts by reducing the size of the image and then changes the scaling (by increasing the value of scale) as the mouse is clicked. After just a couple of mouse clicks, it looks like Figure A-4. After a few mouse clicks, it begins to expand instead of contract, as shown in Figure A-5.

Figure A-4   The image being reduced from its original size.

Figure A-5   The image being expanded from its original size.

 This example demonstrates something else about a filter. If you run the program, you will notice that each time you change the scaling, the new image slowly draws in the display. That is because scaling an image is very similar to loading an image—the action is scheduled and the method returns immediately. Whenever the incomplete image is drawn on the applet window, another call to `paint()` is scheduled. This continues until the whole thing is displayed. To prevent this from happening, you can use a `MediaTracker` to prevent display until the image is loaded—just as this applet behaves as the original image is loaded in `init()`.

 For more examples of image processing, see **CropImageFilter, Image, ImageFilter,** and **RGBImageFilter**. For another example of scaling an image, see **Image**. For the scaling of an image within a component, see **Component.prepareImage()**.

argument

 See **method**.

ArithmeticException

class java.lang.ArithmeticException

This exception is thrown to report any of several arithmetic conditions. A divide-by-zero exception is one example.

Inheritance

```
public class java.lang.ArithmeticException
    extends RuntimeException
        ⇑
    public class java.lang.RuntimeException
        extends Exception
            ⇑
        public class java.lang.Exception
            extends Throwable
                ⇑
            public class java.lang.Throwable
                implements Serializable
                extends Object
                    ⇑
                public class java.lang.Object
```

Constructors

```
public ArithmeticException()
public ArithmeticException(String message)
```

If the `message` string is supplied, it is used as a detailed message describing this particular exception.

array

Arrays are objects. Just like all other objects, they are created by new, accessed by references, and automatically garbage-collected when no more references to them remain.

Two steps to create an array

The creation of an array is a two-step process. First, the reference is declared, and then the array is created. For example, a reference to an array of 15 `double` values is created by simply declaring it:

```
double[] dvalue;
```

At this point, dvalue is a null pointer to an array of unknown size. The keyword new is used to create the actual array:

```
dvalue = new double[15];
```

We now have the array. Each member of it can be accessed by the subscript notation dvalue[0] through dvalue[14].

Combining the two steps into one

Optionally, the two steps just described can be combined into one and the reference and the array can both be created in a single statement this way:

```
double[] dvalue = new double[15];
```

An array with initial values

A set of values can be used both to initialize the array and to determine its size, like this:

```
double[] dvalue = { 1.0, 2.0, 3.0, 4.0 };
```

This creates the array reference dvalue and initializes it with an array of four double values.

Multidimensional arrays

This is the declaration of a reference to a two-dimensional array:

```
int[][] ivalue;
```

To declare an actual array, do this:

```
ivalue = new int[5][10];
```

Or here's another way to do the same thing:

```
ivalue = new int[5][];
for(int i=0; i<5; i++)
        ivalue[i] = new int[10];
```

The subarrays of multidimensional arrays do not have to be the same size. In this example, there is no requirement for all the int arrays to have 10 elements.

The size of an array

Each array has a built-in constant, named length, that contains a count of the number of elements in the array. For example, this will print the number 35:

```
char[] cvalue = new char[35];
System.out.println("Array length: " + cvalue.length);
```

Conversions

Objects can be converted by being cast to one of their interfaces or superclasses. An array object cannot be converted to any object type other than Object or String. An array cannot be converted to any interface except Cloneable, which is implemented by all arrays. An array of one type cannot be converted to an array of another type if there is no conversion between the types of the members of the arrays.

The array Class

Like all other objects in Java, each array has a Class object. Also like all other objects in Java, each array has the Object class as its superclass. As in the case of all the subclasses of Object, all the methods of Object are available. One of these is the getClass() method that returns an object of the class Class — the class of the array. To find out things like the name of the class of an array, use the methods of the Class object.

Example

This example demonstrates how the Class object of an array can be obtained and how information can be gotten from it. The names of the classes are in a special format containing characters that are not normally part of valid Java names. This example prints the class names for some arrays:

```
public class ArrayClasses {
    public static void main(String[] arg) {
        byte[] barr = new byte[10];
        System.out.println("byte[10] --- \"" +
            barr.getClass().getName() + "\"");
        short[] sharr = new short[10];
        System.out.println("short[10] --- \"" +
            sharr.getClass().getName() + "\"");
        char[] charr = new char[10];
        System.out.println("char[10] --- \"" +
            charr.getClass().getName() + "\"");
        int[] iarr = new int[10];
        System.out.println("int[10] --- \"" +
            iarr.getClass().getName() + "\"");
        long[] larr = new long[10];
        System.out.println("long[10] --- \"" +
            larr.getClass().getName() + "\"");
        float[] farr = new float[10];
        System.out.println("float[10] --- \"" +
            farr.getClass().getName() + "\"");
        double[] darr = new double[10];
        System.out.println("double[10] --- \"" +
            darr.getClass().getName() + "\"");
```

```
        ArrayClasses[] rcarr = new ArrayClasses[10];
        System.out.println("reference[10] --- \"" +
            rcarr.getClass().getName() + "\"");
    }
}
```

The output looks like this:

```
byte[10] --- "[B"
short[10] --- "[S"
char[10] --- "[C"
int[10] --- "[I"
long[10] --- "[J"
float[10] --- "[F"
double[10] --- "[D"
reference[10] --- "[LArrayClasses;"
```

As you can see, the names of array classes of the primitive data types have a left bracket and a type-identifying letter. The last line shows the name of the `Class` object for the `ArrayClasses` class.

 To perform a fast array copy, see **System.arraycopy()**. For some special operations on arrays, see **Array**.

Array

class java.lang.reflect.Array

This class is a collection of static methods to dynamically create and manipulate Java arrays. These are very low-level operations that will seldom be required in an application.

Conversions

Several `get()` methods convert the members of an array from one type to another. This conversion must always be widening — a narrowing conversion is not allowed and will always throw an exception.

Inheritance

```
public final class java.lang.reflect.Array
    extends Object
            ⇑
    public class java.lang.Object
```

Methods

get()

```
public static Object get(Object array,int index)
        throws IllegalArgumentException
        throws ArrayIndexOutOfBoundsException
```

Returns a member of array. If array is made up of primitive types, an appropriate wrapper class will be created. For example, an Integer object will be created if array is an array of ints. If array is null, a NullPointerException will be thrown. If array is not an array, an IllegalArgumentException will be thrown. If the index is out of bounds, an ArrayIndexOutOfBoundsException will be thrown.

getBoolean()

```
public static boolean getBoolean(Object array,int index)
        throws IllegalArgumentException
        throws ArrayIndexOutOfBoundsException
```

Returns a member of array as a boolean value. If array is null, a NullPointerException will be thrown. If array is not an array, or if the member cannot be converted to a boolean value, an IllegalArgumentException will be thrown. If the index is out of bounds, an ArrayIndexOutOfBoundsException will be thrown.

getByte()

```
public static byte getByte(Object array,int index)
        throws IllegalArgumentException
        throws ArrayIndexOutOfBoundsException
```

Returns a member of array as a byte value. If array is null, a NullPointerException will be thrown. If array is not an array, or if the member cannot be converted to a byte value, an IllegalArgumentException will be thrown. If the index is out of bounds, an ArrayIndexOutOfBoundsException will be thrown.

getChar()

```
public static char getChar(Object array,int index)
        throws IllegalArgumentException
        throws ArrayIndexOutOfBoundsException
```

Returns a member of array as a char value. If array is null, a NullPointerException will be thrown. If array is not an array, or if the member cannot be converted to a char value, an IllegalArgumentException will be thrown. If the index is out of bounds, an ArrayIndexOutOfBoundsException will be thrown.

getDouble()

```
public static double getDouble(Object array,int index)
        throws IllegalArgumentException
```

```
throws ArrayIndexOutOfBoundsException
```

Returns a member of array as a double value. If array is null, a NullPointerException will be thrown. If array is not an array, or if the member cannot be converted to a double value, an IllegalArgumentException will be thrown. If the index is out of bounds, an ArrayIndexOutOfBoundsException will be thrown.

getFloat()

```
public static float getFloat(Object array,int index)
    throws IllegalArgumentException
    throws ArrayIndexOutOfBoundsException
```

Returns a member of array as a float value. If array is null, a NullPointerException will be thrown. If array is not an array, or if the member cannot be converted to a float value, an IllegalArgumentException will be thrown. If the index is out of bounds, an ArrayIndexOutOfBoundsException will be thrown.

getInt()

```
public static int getInt(Object array,int index)
    throws IllegalArgumentException
    throws ArrayIndexOutOfBoundsException
```

Returns a member of array as an int value. If array is null, a NullPointerException will be thrown. If array is not an array, or if the member cannot be converted to an int value, an IllegalArgumentException will be thrown. If the index is out of bounds, an ArrayIndexOutOfBoundsException will be thrown.

getLength()

```
public static int getLength(Object array)
    throws IllegalArgumentException
```

Returns the number of members of array. If array is not an array, the IllegalArgumentException will be thrown.

getLong()

```
public static long getLong(Object array,int index)
    throws IllegalArgumentException
    throws ArrayIndexOutOfBoundsException
```

Returns a member of array as a long value. If array is null, a NullPointerException will be thrown. If array is not an array, or if the member cannot be converted to a long value, an IllegalArgumentException will be thrown. If the index is out of bounds, an ArrayIndexOutOfBoundsException will be thrown.

getShort()

```
public static short getShort(Object array,int index)
```

```
throws IllegalArgumentException
throws ArrayIndexOutOfBoundsException
```

Returns a member of `array` as a `short` value. If `array` is `null`, a `NullPointerException` will be thrown. If `array` is not an array, or if the member cannot be converted to a `short` value, an `IllegalArgumentException` will be thrown. If the `index` is out of bounds, an `ArrayIndexOutOfBoundsException` will be thrown.

newInstance()

```
public static Object newInstance(Class componentType,
         int length)
    throws NegativeArraySizeException
```

Creates an array of the `componentType` and `length`. The result is identical to the expression

```
new componentType[length];
```

If `componentType` is `null`, a `NullPointerException` is thrown. If `length` is negative, a `NegativeArraySizeException` is thrown.

newInstance()

```
public static Object newInstance(Class componentType,
         int dimensions[])
    throws IllegalArgumentException
    throws NegativeArraySizeException
```

Creates a multidimensional array of the `componentType` with the specified `dimensions`. It is the same as

```
new componentType[dimensions[0]][dimensions[1]]...
```

If any of the `dimensions` values is zero, or if the requested number of dimensions is greater than 255, an `IllegalArgumentException` is thrown. If any of the requested `dimensions` is less than zero, a `NegativeArraySizeException` is thrown.

set()

```
public static void set(Object array,int index,
         Object value)
    throws IllegalArgumentException
    throws ArrayIndexOutOfBoundsException
```

Sets the member of the `array` at the `index` to the `value`. If `array` is a primitive type, the `value` is automatically unwrapped. If `array` is `null`, or if `array` is a primitive type and `value` is `null`, a `NullPointerException` is thrown. If `array` is not an array, or if the `value` cannot be converted to the type of `array`, an `IllegalArgumentException` is thrown. If the `index` does not address a member of `array`, an `ArrayIndexOutOfBoundsException` is thrown.

setBoolean()

```
public static void setBoolean(Object array,
        int index,boolean value)
    throws IllegalArgumentException
    ArrayIndexOutOfBoundsException
```

Sets the member of the array at index to the value. If array is null, a NullPointerException is thrown. If array is not an array, or if value cannot be converted to the type of a member of array, an IllegalArgumentException is thrown. If index does not address a member of array, an ArrayIndexOutOfBoundsException is thrown.

setByte()

```
public static void setByte(Object array,
        int index,byte value)
    throws IllegalArgumentException
    ArrayIndexOutOfBoundsException
```

Sets the member of the array at index to the value. If array is null, a NullPointerException is thrown. If array is not an array, or if value cannot be converted to the type of a member of array, an IllegalArgumentException is thrown. If index does not address a member of array, an ArrayIndexOutOfBoundsException is thrown.

setChar()

```
public static void setChar(Object array,
        int index,char value)
    throws IllegalArgumentException
    ArrayIndexOutOfBoundsException
```

Sets the member of the array at index to the value. If array is null, a NullPointerException is thrown. If array is not an array, or if value cannot be converted to the type of a member of array, an IllegalArgumentException is thrown. If index does not address a member of array, an ArrayIndexOutOfBoundsException is thrown.

setDouble()

```
public static void setDouble(Object array,
        int index,double value)
    throws IllegalArgumentException
    ArrayIndexOutOfBoundsException
```

Sets the member of the array at index to the value. If array is null, a NullPointerException is thrown. If array is not an array, or if value cannot be converted to the type of a member of array, an IllegalArgumentException is thrown. If index does not address a member of array, an ArrayIndexOutOfBoundsException is thrown.

setFloat()

```
public static void setFloat(Object array,
        int index,float value)
    throws IllegalArgumentException
    ArrayIndexOutOfBoundsException
```

Sets the member of the array at index to the value. If array is null, a NullPointerException is thrown. If array is not an array, or if value cannot be converted to the type of a member of array, an IllegalArgumentException is thrown. If index does not address a member of array, an ArrayIndexOutOfBoundsException is thrown.

setInt()

```
public static void setInt(Object array,
        int index,int value)
    throws IllegalArgumentException
    ArrayIndexOutOfBoundsException
```

Sets the member of the array at index to the value. If array is null, a NullPointerException is thrown. If array is not an array, or if value cannot be converted to the type of a member of array, an IllegalArgumentException is thrown. If index does not address a member of array, an ArrayIndexOutOfBoundsException is thrown.

setLong()

```
public static void setLong(Object array,
        int index,long value)
    throws IllegalArgumentException
    ArrayIndexOutOfBoundsException
```

Sets the member of the array at index to the value. If array is null, a NullPointerException is thrown. If array is not an array, or if value cannot be converted to the type of a member of array, an IllegalArgumentException is thrown. If index does not address a member of array, an ArrayIndexOutOfBoundsException is thrown.

setShort()

```
public static void setShort(Object array,
        int index,short value)
    throws IllegalArgumentException
    ArrayIndexOutOfBoundsException
```

Sets the member of the `array` at `index` to the `value`. If `array` is `null`, a `NullPointerException` is thrown. If `array` is not an array, or if `value` cannot be converted to the type of a member of `array`, an `IllegalArgumentException` is thrown. If `index` does not address a member of `array`, an `ArrayIndexOutOfBoundsException` is thrown.

 To perform a fast array copy, see **System.arraycopy()**.

ArrayIndexOutOfBoundsException

class java.lang.ArrayIndexOutOfBoundsException

This exception is thrown when an invalid index (too large or too small) has been used. The smallest valid index value is zero; the largest is one less than the size of the array.

Inheritance

```
public class java.lang.ArrayIndexOutOfBoundsException
    extends IndexOutOfBoundsException
        ⇑
    public class java.lang.IndexOutOfBoundsException
    extends RuntimeException
            ⇑
        public class java.lang.RuntimeException
            extends Exception
                ⇑
            public class java.lang.Exception
                extends Throwable
                    ⇑
                public class java.lang.Throwable
                    implements Serializable
                    extends Object
                        ⇑
                    public class java.lang.Object
```

Constructors

```
public ArrayIndexOutOfBoundsException()
public ArrayIndexOutOfBoundsException(int index)
public ArrayIndexOutOfBoundsException(String message)
```

The exception can be constructed by specifying the offending `index` value or the string form of a detailed `message`.

ArrayStoreException

class java.lang.ArrayStoreException

This exception is thrown whenever an attempt is made to store an inappropriate type of object into an array.

Inheritance

```
public class java.lang.ArrayStoreException
      extends RuntimeException
          ⇑
      public class java.lang.RuntimeException
          extends Exception
              ⇑
          public class java.lang.Exception
              extends Throwable
                  ⇑
              public class java.lang.Throwable
                  implements Serializable
                  extends Object
                      ⇑
                  public class java.lang.Object
```

Constructors

```
public ArrayStoreException()
public ArrayStoreException(String message)
```

If the message string is supplied, it is used as a detailed message describing this particular exception.

ASCII

The ASCII (American Standard Code for Information Interchange) character set of the ANSI (American National Standards Institute) is the set of Latin characters and control codes that are represented by numeric values 0 through 127 (in hex, that's 0x00 through 0x7F). Any ASCII character value will fit into seven bits. It is the predominant character set of modern computing.

The ASCII character set

Table A-3 is a list of the ASCII characters with their octal, decimal, and hexadecimal values. The hexadecimal characters are shown in their Java 16-bit

Unicode format. The nondisplayable characters each have acronyms of two or three letters. Some of these characters have special escape sequences, and some have more than one name.

Table A-3 The ASCII Character Set

Octal	Decimal	Unicode	Name	Description
000	0	\u0000	NUL	Ctrl-@
001	1	\u0001	SOH	Ctrl-A, start of header
002	2	\u0002	STX	Ctrl-B, start of text
003	3	\u0003	ETX	Ctrl-C, end of text
004	4	\u0004	EOT	Ctrl-D, end of tape
005	5	\u0005	ENQ	Ctrl-E, inquire
006	6	\u0006	ACK	Ctrl-G, acknowledge
007	7	\u0007	BEL	Ctrl-G, bell
010	8	\u0008	BS	Ctrl-H, backspace, \b
011	9	\u0009	HT	Ctrl-I, horizontal tab, \t
012	10	\u000a	LF	Ctrl-J, linefeed, newline, \n
013	11	\u000b	VT	Ctrl-K, vertical tab
014	12	\u000c	FF	Ctrl-L, form feed, new page, \f
015	13	\u000d	CR	Ctrl-M, carriage return, \r
016	14	\u000e	SO	Ctrl-N, Shift out
017	15	\u000f	SI	Ctrl-O, Shift in
020	16	\u0010	DLE	Ctrl-P, data link escape
021	17	\u0011	DC1	Ctrl-Q, device control 1, XON
022	18	\u0012	DC2	Ctrl-R, device control 2
023	19	\u0013	DC3	Ctrl-S, device control 3, XOFF
024	20	\u0014	DC4	Ctrl-T, device control 4
025	21	\u0015	NAK	Ctrl-U, negative acknowledgement
026	22	\u0016	SYN	Ctrl-V, synchronous idle
027	23	\u0017	ETB	Ctrl-W, end transmission block
030	24	\u0018	CAN	Ctrl-X, cancel
031	25	\u0019	EM	Ctrl-Y, end of medium
032	26	\u001a	SUB	Ctrl-Z, substitute
033	27	\u001b	ESC	Ctrl-[, Escape
034	28	\u001c	FS	Ctrl-\, file separator
035	29	\u001d	GS	Ctrl-], group separator
036	30	\u001e	RS	Ctrl-^, record separator
037	31	\u001f	US	Ctrl-_, unit separator
040	32	\u0020		Space

continued

Table A-3 *continued*

Octal	Decimal	Unicode	Name	Description
041	33	\u0021	!	Exclamation mark
042	34	\u0022	"	Double quote, \ "
043	35	\u0023	#	Hash, octothorp, pound sign
044	36	\u0024	$	Dollar
045	37	\u0025	%	Percent
046	38	\u0026	&	Ampersand
047	39	\u0027	'	Single quote, quote, \ '
050	40	\u0028	(	Open parenthesis, left parenthesis
051	41	\u0029	)	Close parenthesis, right parenthesis
052	42	\u002a	*	Asterisk, star
053	43	\u002b	+	Plus
054	44	\u002c	,	Comma
055	45	\u002d	-	Minus
056	46	\u002e	.	Period, dot, full stop
057	47	\u002f	/	Slash, stroke
060	48	\u0030	0	Zero
061	49	\u0031	1	One
062	50	\u0032	2	Two
063	51	\u0033	3	Three
064	52	\u0034	4	Four
065	53	\u0035	5	Five
066	54	\u0036	6	Six
067	55	\u0037	7	Seven
070	56	\u0038	8	Eight
071	57	\u0039	9	Nine
072	58	\u003a	:	Colon
073	59	\u003b	;	Semicolon
074	60	\u003c	<	Less than
075	61	\u003d	=	Equals
076	62	\u003e	>	Greater than
077	63	\u003f	?	Question mark
0100	64	\u0040	@	At sign
0101	65	\u0041	A	
0102	66	\u0042	B	
0103	67	\u0043	C	
0104	68	\u0044	D	
0105	69	\u0045	E	
0106	70	\u0046	F	

Octal	Decimal	Unicode	Name	Description
0107	71	\u0047	G	
0110	72	\u0048	H	
0111	73	\u0049	I	
0112	74	\u004a	J	
0113	75	\u004b	K	
0114	76	\u004c	L	
0115	77	\u004d	M	
0116	78	\u004e	N	
0117	79	\u004f	O	
0120	80	\u0050	P	
0121	81	\u0051	Q	
0122	82	\u0052	R	
0123	83	\u0053	S	
0124	84	\u0054	T	
0125	85	\u0055	U	
0126	86	\u0056	V	
0127	87	\u0057	W	
0130	88	\u0058	X	
0131	89	\u0059	Y	
0132	90	\u005a	Z	
0133	91	\u005b	[	Open bracket, open square bracket, left bracket
0134	92	\u005c	\	Backslash, \\
0135	93	\u005d	]	Close bracket, close square bracket, right bracket
0136	94	\u005e	^	Caret
0137	95	\u005f	_	Underscore
0140	96	\u0060	`	Backquote, grave accent
0141	97	\u0061	a	
0142	98	\u0062	b	
0143	99	\u0063	c	
0144	100	\u0064	d	
0145	101	\u0065	e	
0146	102	\u0066	f	
0147	103	\u0067	g	
0150	104	\u0068	h	
0151	105	\u0069	i	
0152	106	\u006a	j	
0153	107	\u006b	k	
0154	108	\u006c	l	
0155	109	\u006d	m	

continued

Table A-3 *continued*

Octal	Decimal	Unicode	Name	Description
0156	110	\u006e	n	
0157	111	\u006f	o	
0160	112	\u0070	p	
0161	113	\u0071	q	
0162	114	\u0072	r	
0163	115	\u0073	s	
0164	116	\u0074	t	
0165	117	\u0075	u	
0166	118	\u0076	v	
0167	119	\u0077	w	
0170	120	\u0078	x	
0171	121	\u0079	y	
0172	122	\u007a	z	
0173	123	\u007b	{	Open curly bracket, left brace, open brace
0174	124	\u007c	|	Bar, vertical bar
0175	125	\u007d	}	Close curly bracket, right brace, close brace
0176	126	\u007e	~	Tilde
0177	127	\u007f	DEL	Delete

For the position of ASCII in the scheme of the larger character sets, see **Unicode**. For the construction of nonprintable characters, see **escapes**. For information on the character stream input to the Java compiler, see **lexical structure**.

at sign

@

The at sign is used inside comments that are to be processed into documentation by javadoc.

See **javadoc**.

AudioClip

interface java.applet.AudioClip

This is a high-level abstraction of audio. You can get an object that implements this interface with a call to `Applet.getAudioClip()`.

Inheritance

```
public interface java.applet.AudioClip
```

Constructors

Returned by

An object implementing this interface is returned from `Applet.getAudioClip()` and `AppletContext.getAudioClip()`.

Methods

loop()

```
public abstract void loop()
```

Plays the audio clip in a continuous loop. It plays until `stop()` is called.

play()

```
public abstract void play()
```

Plays the audio clip once all the way through. If the method is called while the clip is playing, it will restart from the beginning. If this method is called for more than one audio clip, the two will play simultaneously.

stop()

```
public abstract void stop()
```

If the audio clip is currently playing, it will stop.

Example

This applet loads a sound file and plays it. It plays it once when the applet loads, and again in response to a mouse button.

```
import java.awt.*;
import java.awt.event.*;
import java.applet.*;
import java.net.*;
```

```
public class SoundOnLoad extends Applet {
    private String soundFileName = "crash.au";
    private AudioClip audioClip;

    public void init() {
        setBackground(Color.lightGray);
        URL url = getCodeBase();
        audioClip = getAudioClip(url,soundFileName);
        audioClip.play();
        enableEvents(AWTEvent.MOUSE_EVENT_MASK);
    }

    public void paint(Graphics g) {
        g.setColor(Color.lightGray);
        g.fillRect(0,0,getSize().width,getSize().height);
        g.setColor(Color.black);
        g.drawString("Hear that?",30,30);
        g.dispose();
    }

    public void processMouseEvent(MouseEvent event) {
        if(event.getID() == MouseEvent.MOUSE_RELEASED)
            audioClip.play();
    }
}
```

The init() method calls getCodeBase() to get the URL of the directory holding the applet. Using this URL and the name of the audio file, a call is made to the factory method getAudioClip() to load the audio clip into RAM. The getAudioClip() method blocks until the file is loaded (or an error occurs), so we can play the audio immediately. The audio is played again every time a mouse button is pressed and released.

 To retrieve an audio clip over the Net, see **Applet** and **AppletContext**.

awt

package java.awt

This is the graphical user interface, or GUI, package. It has classes that can be used to construct labels, buttons, menus, and the like. It also has classes that handle image and audio processing. The letters AWT stand for Abstract Windowing Toolkit.

Packages

```
java.awt.datatransfer
java.awt.event
java.awt.image
java.awt.peer
```

Interfaces

```
Adjustable
ItemSelectable
LayoutManager
LayoutManager2
MenuContainer
PrintGraphics
Shape
```

Classes

```
AWTEvent
AWTEventMulticaster
BorderLayout
Button
Canvas
CardLayout
Checkbox
CheckboxGroup
CheckboxMenuItem
Choice
Color
Component
Container
Cursor
Dialog
Dimension
Event
EventQueue
FileDialog
FlowLayout
Font
FontMetrics
Frame
Graphics
GridBagConstraints
GridBagLayout
```

a
b
c

GridLayout
Image
Insets
Label
List
MediaTracker
Menu
MenuBar
MenuComponent
MenuItem
MenuShortcut
Panel
Point
Polygon
PopupMenu
PrintJob
Rectangle
ScrollPane
Scrollbar
SystemColor
TextArea
TextComponent
TextField
Toolkit
Window

Exceptions

AWTException
IllegalComponentStateException

Errors

AWTError

AWTError

class java.awt.AWTError

This is thrown for any of the AWT errors.

Inheritance

```
public class java.awt.AWTError
    extends Error
        ⇑
    public class java.lang.Error
        extends Throwable
            ⇑
        public class java.lang.Throwable
            implements Serializable
            extends Object
                ⇑
            public class java.lang.Object
```

Constructors

```
public AWTError(String message)
```

The `message` string is used as a detailed message describing this particular error.

AWTEvent

class java.awt.AWTEvent

This is the superclass of all AWT events.

Either listen or enable

No events are delivered by default—a program must request that they be sent. This can be done in two different ways. First, a call can be made to `enableEvents()` of a component with a mask specifying which events are to be delivered. Second, a call can be made to `addListener()` to specify a listener that is to receive events.

Enabling the events

To receive events, a call to `enableEvents()` is made with a mask that specifies which events are to be received. The masks are defined as constants in this class. This is necessary only for subclasses of `Component` wishing to register for events that would not normally be delivered. For example, a `Button` component would not normally receive focus events, but a subclass may need them.

Listening for the events

Any class the implements the `EventListener` interface can be registered to receive the events from any component. Normally, this is done by implementing a subinterface of `EventListener`. For example, a class that implements `ActionListener` will be sent the action events of any component to which it is registered. For an example of this, see `ActionEvent`.

consumed

Some events will be sent down to the peer (the system-level component) for processing, and others will be processed at the Java API/application level. Once an event reaches the stage, at any of these levels, that no more processing is necessary, it is flagged as having been *consumed*. If an event has been consumed already, it is not sent to the peer. If it has not been consumed, it will be sent to the peer for consumption.

 This class supercedes the `java.awt.Event` class—using this class is the preferred way to field events. At any rate, it is recommended that you do not mix `AWTEvent` and `Event` in the same program—the results can be so confusing that your program may not run. Do not mix event models.

Extended by

```
ActionEvent
ComponentEvent
ItemEvent
TextEvent
AdjustmentEvent
```

Inheritance

```
public class java.awt.AWTEvent
    extends EventObject
           ⇑
    public class java.util.EventObject
        implements Serializable
        extends Object
               ⇑
        public class java.lang.Object
```

Variables and constants

ACTION_EVENT_MASK

```
public final static long ACTION_EVENT_MASK
```

The mask for selecting action events.

ADJUSTMENT_EVENT_MASK

```
public final static long ADJUSTMENT_EVENT_MASK
```

The mask for selecting adjustment events.

COMPONENT_EVENT_MASK

```
public final static long COMPONENT_EVENT_MASK
```

The mask for selecting component events.

consumed

```
protected boolean consumed
```

Indicates whether or not this event has been consumed.

CONTAINER_EVENT_MASK

```
public final static long CONTAINER_EVENT_MASK
```

The mask for selecting container events.

FOCUS_EVENT_MASK

```
public final static long FOCUS_EVENT_MASK
```

The mask for selecting focus events.

id

```
protected int id
```

This value is set by the subclass as an identification of the event type.

ITEM_EVENT_MASK

```
public final static long ITEM_EVENT_MASK
```

The mask for selecting item events.

KEY_EVENT_MASK

```
public final static long KEY_EVENT_MASK
```

The mask for selecting key events.

MOUSE_EVENT_MASK

```
public final static long MOUSE_EVENT_MASK
```

The mask for selecting mouse events.

MOUSE_MOTION_EVENT_MASK

```
public final static long MOUSE_MOTION_EVENT_MASK
```

The mask for selecting mouse motion events.

RESERVED_ID_MAX

```
public static final int RESERVED_ID_MAX
```

The maximum value that will be used internally for AWT event id numbers. A program defining its own event id numbers should use values greater than this.

TEXT_EVENT_MASK

```
public final static long TEXT_EVENT_MASK
```

The mask for selecting text events.

WINDOW_EVENT_MASK

```
public final static long WINDOW_EVENT_MASK
```

The mask for selecting window events.

Constructors

```
public AWTEvent(Event event)
public AWTEvent(Object source,int id)
```

An AWTEvent can be constructed from an Event object of the 1.0 form. One can also be constructed by specifying its source and assigning it an id number to indicate its type.

Returned by

Objects of this class are returned from the EventQueue methods getNextEvent() and peekEvent().

Methods

consume()

```
protected void consume()
```

Flags this event as having been consumed by setting consumed to true.

getId()

```
public int getId()
```

This returns the id number that specifies the event type.

isConsumed()

```
protected boolean isConsumed()
```

Returns true if this event has been consumed and false if it has not.

paramString()

```
public String paramString()
```

Returns debugging information. The return string describes the internal state and values of this object.

toString()

```
public String toString()
```

Returns a string representation of the event.

For the various event classes derived from AWTEvent, see the package **java.awt.event**. The mask values defined here are used as argument values in a call to **Component.enableEvents()**. The class that queues AWTEvents is **EventQueue**.

AWTEventMulticaster

class java.awt.AWTEventMulticaster

This class is capable of maintaining a list of event listeners and has the ability to dispatch events to all the listeners on the list.

This class is used internally in the Component class to distribute events. You would only need this class if for some reason you wished to manage the distribution of events yourself. It could be useful in writing your own components, or for writing some sort of component simulation.

How the chaining works

Each object of this class can be thought of as a node in a binary tree. Each node contains references to a pair of EventListeners as a and b. This class is an EventListener itself, because this class implements all the EventListener interfaces. Each time an object of this class is asked to add a new member, it does so by placing a reference to it in either a or b— whichever is null. If neither a nor b is null, a new AWTEventMulticaster object is created to hold both the new one being added along with either a or b (it doesn't matter which). The newly created AWTEventMulticaster is then used to replace either a or b— whichever was used for the new object. This way, a binary tree is formed that holds them all. The returned value is, then, the root of a binary tree containing all the EventListeners.

Inheritance

```
public class java.awt.AWTEventMulticaster
    implements ActionListener
    implements AdjustmentListener
```

```
        implements ComponentListener
        implements ContainerListener
        implements FocusListener
        implements ItemListener
        implements KeyListener
        implements MouseListener
        implements MouseMotionListener
        implements TextListener
        implements WindowListener
        extends Object
              ⇑
        public class java.lang.Object
```

Variables and constants

a
```
protected EventListener a
```

b
```
protected EventListener b
```

Constructors
```
protected AWTEventMulticaster(EventListener arga,
        EventListener argb)
```

The constructor accepts two EventListener objects, which it stores in the root of its internal tree. Either arga or argb can be null.

Methods

actionPerformed()
```
public void actionPerformed(ActionEvent event)
```
Handles the event by invoking the actionPerformed() methods on a and b.

add()
```
public static ActionListener add(
        ActionListener arga,ActionListener argb)

public static AdjustmentListener add(
        AdjustmentListener arga,AdjustmentListener argb)

public static ComponentListener add(
```

```
                ComponentListener arga,ComponentListener argb)
public static ContainerListener add(
                ContainerListener arga,ContainerListener argb)
public static FocusListener add(
                FocusListener arga,FocusListener argb)
public static ItemListener add(
                ItemListener arga,ItemListener argb)
public static KeyListener add(
                KeyListener arga,KeyListener argb)
public static MouseListener add(
                MouseListener arga,MouseListener argb)
public static MouseMotionListener add(
                MouseMotionListener arga,MouseMotionListener argb)
public static TextListener add(
                TextListener arga,TextListener argb)
public static WindowListener add(
                WindowListener arga,WindowListener argb)
```

Links `arga` and `argb` and returns the resulting multicast listener.

addInternal()

```
protected static EventListener addInternal(
                EventListener arga,EventListener argb)
```

This will return an `EventListener` constructed from `arga` and `argb`. If `argb` is `null`, it will return `arga`—if `arga` is `null`, it will return `argb`. If neither is `null`, it creates an `AWTEventMulticaster` object and returns it.

adjustmentValueChanged()

```
public void adjustmentValueChanged(AdjustmentEvent e)
```

Calls the `adjustmentValueChanged()` methods in a and b.

componentAdded()

```
public void componentAdded(ContainerEvent e)
```

Calls the `componentAdded()` methods in a and b.

componentHidden()

```
public void componentHidden(ComponentEvent e)
```

Calls the `componentHidden()` methods in a and b.

componentMoved()

```
public void componentMoved(ComponentEvent e)
```

Calls the `componentMoved()` methods in a and b.

componentRemoved()

```
public void componentRemoved(ContainerEvent e)
```

Calls the `componentRemoved()` methods in a and b.

componentResized()

```
public void componentResized(ComponentEvent e)
```

Calls the `componentResized()` methods in a and b.

componentShown()

```
public void componentShown(ComponentEvent e)
```

Calls the `componentShown()` methods in a and b.

focusGained()

```
public void focusGained(FocusEvent e)
```

Calls the `focusGained()` methods in a and b.

focusLost()

```
public void focusLost(FocusEvent e)
```

Calls the `focusLost()` methods in a and b.

itemStateChanged()

```
public void itemStateChanged(ItemEvent e)
```

Calls the `itemStateChanged()` methods in a and b.

keyPressed()

```
public void keyPressed(KeyEvent e)
```

Calls the `keyPressed()` methods in a and b.

keyReleased()

```
public void keyReleased(KeyEvent e)
```

Calls the `keyReleased()` methods in a and b.

keyTyped()

```
public void keyTyped(KeyEvent e)
```

Calls the `keyTyped()` methods in a and b.

mouseClicked()

```
public void mouseClicked(MouseEvent e)
```

Calls the `mouseClicked()` methods in a and b.

mouseDragged()

```
public void mouseDragged(MouseEvent e)
```

Calls the `mouseDragged()` methods in a and b.

mouseEntered()

```
public void mouseEntered(MouseEvent e)
```

Calls the `mouseEntered()` methods in a and b.

mouseExited()

```
public void mouseExited(MouseEvent e)
```

Calls the `mouseExited()` methods in a and b.

mouseMoved()

```
public void mouseMoved(MouseEvent e)
```

Calls the `mouseMoved()` methods in a and b.

mousePressed()

```
public void mousePressed(MouseEvent e)
```

Calls the `mousePressed()` methods in a and b.

mouseReleased()

```
public void mouseReleased(MouseEvent e)
```

Calls the `mouseReleased()` methods in a and b.

remove()

```
public static ActionListener remove(
        ActionListener removedFrom,
        ActionListener toBeRemoved)

public static AdjustmentListener remove(
```

```
                         AdjustmentListener removedFrom,
                         AdjustmentListener toBeRemoved)

        public static ComponentListener remove(
                         ComponentListener removedFrom,
                         ComponentListener toBeRemoved)

        public static ContainerListener remove(
                         ContainerListener removedFrom,
                         ContainerListener toBeRemoved)

        public static EventListener remove(
                         EventListener removedFrom,
                         EventListener toBeRemoved)

        public static FocusListener remove(
                         FocusListener removedFrom,
                         FocusListener toBeRemoved)

        public static ItemListener remove(
                         ItemListener removedFrom,
                         ItemListener toBeRemoved)

        public static KeyListener remove(
                         KeyListener removedFrom,
                         KeyListener toBeRemoved)

        public static MouseListener remove(
                         MouseListener removedFrom,
                         MouseListener toBeRemoved)

        public static MouseMotionListener remove(
                         MouseMotionListener removedFrom,
                         MouseMotionListener toBeRemoved)

        public static TextListener remove(
                         TextListener removedFrom,
                         TextListener toBeRemoved)

        public static WindowListener remove(
                         WindowListener removedFrom,
                         WindowListener toBeRemoved)
```

This method will search, starting with a and b of the removedFrom chain of links, attempting to find toBeRemoved. If it is found, it is removed from the chain. The resulting object is returned.

removeInternal()

```
        protected static EventListener removeInternal(
                         EventListener removedFrom,
```

```
EventListener toBeRemoved)
```

This method will search the removedFrom chain of links (both a and b) attempting to find toBeRemoved. If it is found, it is removed from the chain. If either argument is null, the return is null.

textValueChanged()

```
public void textValueChanged(TextEvent e)
```

Calls the textValueChanged() methods in a and b.

windowActivated()

```
public void windowActivated(WindowEvent e)
```

Calls the windowActivated() methods in a and b.

windowClosed ()

```
public void windowClosed(WindowEvent e)
```

Calls the windowClosed() methods in a and b.

windowClosing()

```
public void windowClosing(WindowEvent e)
```

Calls the windowClosing() methods in a and b.

windowDeactivated()

```
public void windowDeactivated(WindowEvent e)
```

Calls the windowDeactivated() methods in a and b.

windowDeiconified()

```
public void windowDeiconified(WindowEvent e)
```

Calls the windowDeiconified() methods in a and b.

windowIconified()

```
public void windowIconified(WindowEvent e)
```

Calls the windowIconified() methods in a and b.

windowOpened()

```
public void windowOpened(WindowEvent e)
```

Calls the windowOpened() methods in a and b.

For a higher-level interface to this class, see **Component**.

AWTException

class java.awt.AWTException

This is thrown to indicate that an Abstract Window Toolkit exception has occurred.

Inheritance

```
public class java.awt.AWTException
    extends Exception
        ⇑
    public class java.lang.Exception
        extends Throwable
            ⇑
        public class java.lang.Throwable
            implements Serializable
            extends Object
                ⇑
            public class java.lang.Object
```

Constructors

AWTException()

```
public AWTException(String message)
```

It is constructed with a message giving details of the cause of the exception.

B

backslash

\

 For how this is used to create escape sequences for special characters in strings, see **escapes**.

bar

| |=

These operators can be used for either bitwise ORing (on integer types) or logical ORing (on Boolean types). Which action they perform is determined by the data types they are operating on.

The bitwise operation

If the expression on one side is an integer, the other side must also be an integer. If the integers are not the same size, one of them will be widened and a bitwise ORing operation will take place between the two.

The Boolean operation

If the expression on one side is a `boolean`, the other side must also be a `boolean`. Both Boolean expressions will be evaluated and if either is `true`, the result of the expression is `true`—otherwise the result is `false`. Both sides of the expression are always evaluated.

Example

This example evaluates three Boolean OR expressions. One has both sides true, one, both sides false, and one, a true and a false. The operator |= uses its left operand as one of its argument values and also as the recipient of the result. Each expression that is actually evaluated causes a line to print. The logical OR operator with a single bar will always evaluate the expressions on each side even when the evaluation of only one of them is necessary to determine the result:

```
public class LogicalOr {
    public static void main(String[] arg) {
        boolean state;
        state = alwaysTrue(1) | alwaysTrue(2);
        state = alwaysFalse(3) | alwaysFalse(4);
        state |= alwaysTrue(5);
    }
    static boolean alwaysTrue(int value) {
        System.out.println("True for " + value);
        return(true);
    }
    static boolean alwaysFalse(int value) {
        System.out.println("False for " + value);
        return(false);
    }
}
```

In the first case, it is only necessary to evaluate one side to determine that the result will be true. In the second case, where both terms are false, it is necessary to evaluate both expressions. As you can see from the output, however, both terms are always evaluated in either case:

```
True for 1
True for 2
False for 3
False for 4
True for 5
```

This is always the case with the single-bar form. The double-bar form works differently.

 For the double-bar logical operator, see **bar bar**. For the AND operations, see **ampersand** and **ampersand ampersand**.

bar bar

||

This operator can be used to perform the logical OR operation between two Boolean expressions.

The Boolean operation

The operation begins by evaluating the expression on the left side. If that is found to be true, the expression on the right is not evaluated. This is demonstrated in the example.

Example

This example evaluates two Boolean OR expressions, one with both sides true, and one with both sides false. Each expression that is actually evaluated causes a line to print:

```
public class LogicalOr2 {
    public static void main(String[] arg) {
        boolean state;
        state = alwaysTrue(1) || alwaysTrue(2);
        state = alwaysFalse(3) || alwaysFalse(4);
    }
    static boolean alwaysTrue(int value) {
        System.out.println("True for " + value);
        return(true);
    }
    static boolean alwaysFalse(int value) {
        System.out.println("False for " + value);
        return(false);
    }
}
```

Here is the output from the example:

```
True for 1
False for 3
False for 4
```

The call to alwaysTrue(2) was not made because the evaluation of alwaysTrue(1) was sufficient to produce the result. On the other hand, the call to alwaysFalse(3) did not determine the outcome, so it was necessary to make the call to alwaysFalse(4). The single bar operator works differently.

 For another logical OR operator, see **bar**. For the AND operations, see **ampersand** and **ampersand ampersand**.

base class

 See **superclass**.

BeanDescriptor

class java.beans.BeanDescriptor

A `BeanDescriptor` contains class information about a bean. Methods are available to return the `Class` object of either the bean or the bean's customizer.

Inheritance

```
public class java.beans.BeanDescriptor
    extends FeatureDescriptor
        ⇑
    public class java.beans.FeatureDescriptor
        extends Object
            ⇑
        public class java.lang.Object
```

Constructors

```
public BeanDescriptor(Class beanClass)
public BeanDescriptor(Class beanClass, Class customizerClass)
```

The `beanClass` is the `Class` object of the Java class implementing the bean. The `customizerClass` is the `Class` object of the Java class implementing the bean's customizer.

Returned by

You can find `getBeanDescriptor()` methods in `BeanInfo` and `SimpleBeanInfo`.

Methods

getBeanClass()

```
public Class getBeanClass()
```

This returns the `Class` object of the bean.

getCustomizerClass()

```
public Class getCustomizerClass()
```

This returns the `Class` object of the bean's customizer. If the bean does not have a customizer, this will be `null`.

BeanInfo

interface java.beans.BeanInfo

This interface is implemented by a class being designed to supply specific information about a Java bean's methods, events, and other properties. A class implementing this interface will be used during automatic analysis of the bean.

Options exist

The amount of information available will vary. It could be quite minimal. Any information not supplied here could be available by automatic analysis using low-level reflection of the methods of the bean.

A simpler approach

If you want to supply a minimal subset, it may be simpler to use the `SimpleBeanInfo` class. It implements this interface with a complete set of dummy methods. You have only to override the dummies for the methods that you need to implement.

Implemented by

```
SimpleBeanInfo
```

Inheritance

```
public interface java.beans.BeanInfo
```

Variables and constants

ICON_COLOR_16x16

```
public final static int ICON_COLOR_16x16
```

Constant to indicate a 16×16 color icon to the method `getIcon()`.

ICON_COLOR_32x32

```
public final static int ICON_COLOR_32x32
```

Constant to indicate a 32×32 color icon to the method `getIcon()`.

ICON_MONO_16x16

```
public final static int ICON_MONO_16x16
```

Constant to indicate a 16×16 monochrome icon to the method `getIcon()`.

ICON_MONO_32x32

```
public final static int ICON_MONO_32x32
```

Constant to indicate a 32×32 monochrome icon to the method getIcon().

Constructors

Returned by

The Introspector class has a getBeanInfo() method to return an object that implements BeanInfo.

Methods

getAdditionalBeanInfo()

```
public abstract BeanInfo[] getAdditionalBeanInfo()
```

Returns an array of other BeanInfo objects to provide additional information about the bean. The array is possibly null. If conflicts arise between the information in this bean and a member of the array, the information in this bean takes precedence. Later elements in the array (those with larger indexes) take precedence over earlier ones.

getBeanDescriptor()

```
public abstract BeanDescriptor getBeanDescriptor()
```

Returns a BeanDescriptor object for the bean. The return value may be null, indicating that the information should be obtained by automatic analysis.

getDefaultEventIndex()

```
public abstract int getDefaultEventIndex()
```

Returns an index to the default event. A bean may have a particular event that occurs more often than the others during human interaction. This method will return the index to it in the array of events returned by getEventSetDescriptors(). If there is no such default event, −1 is returned.

getDefaultPropertyIndex()

```
public abstract int getDefaultPropertyIndex()
```

Returns an index to the default property. A bean may have some property that a user most often chooses for update when customizing the bean. This method returns the index to it in the array returned by getPropertyDescriptors(). If there is no such default property, −1 is returned.

getEventSetDescriptors()

```
public abstract EventSetDescriptor[] getEventSetDescriptors()
```

Returns an array containing the kinds of events that can be issued from this bean. A null return indicates that the information should be obtained by automatic analysis.

getIcon()

```
public abstract Image getIcon(int iconKind)
```

Returns a displayable image that can be used to represent the bean. If there is no image for the bean, a null is returned. The value of iconKind determines the type of image to be returned—whether it is 16×16 or 32×32, and whether or not it is color. The possible values of iconKind are defined as constants in this class.

getMethodDescriptors()

```
public abstract MethodDescriptor[] getMethodDescriptors()
```

Returns an array containing descriptions of the externally accessible methods of the bean. If the information should be obtained by automatic analysis, a null is returned.

getPropertyDescriptors()

```
public abstract PropertyDescriptor[] getPropertyDescriptors()
```

This returns an array of property descriptions describing the editable properties of this bean. A null return indicates that the information should be obtained by automatic analysis.

It is possible that a member of the array is an IndexedPropertyDescriptor object—a subclass of PropertyDescriptor. This requires that you use instanceof to distinguish one from the other.

 For a base class having fewer implementation requirements for what has to be implemented, see **SimpleBeanInfo**. For more information, see **Introspector**.

beans

package java.beans

This package supplies a model for the construction of component software. Its purpose is to enable the development of software components that can be used by programmers inside their applications. A bean has a standard interface that can be used by an IDE to manipulate the bean, giving the programmer information and control of the bean for insertion into an application. A bean also has a standard form for its API that can be deciphered at runtime. This allows the programmer's code to determine the capabilities of a bean and interface with it unambiguously. A bean also has the Java characteristic of being entirely portable. Although a bean is most commonly thought of as being some sort of GUI component, it is also possible to have a bean that has no human interface.

Interfaces

```
BeanInfo
Customizer
PropertyChangeListener
PropertyEditor
VetoableChangeListener
Visibility
```

Classes

```
BeanDescriptor
Beans
EventSetDescriptor
FeatureDescriptor
IndexedPropertyDescriptor
Introspector
MethodDescriptor
ParameterDescriptor
PropertyChangeEvent
PropertyChangeSupport
PropertyDescriptor
PropertyEditorManager
PropertyEditorSupport
SimpleBeanInfo
VetoableChangeSupport
```

Exceptions

```
IntrospectionException
PropertyVetoException
```

Beans

class java.beans.Beans

This class is a collection of general-purpose beans control methods.

The name of a bean

When specifying the name of a bean, note that the name is a qualified string of dot-separated names—the same naming convention as for package names. To convert the bean name to the name of a serialized object for loading, append the suffix ".ser." For example, if the bean name is "all.beans.fred," a search will be made for "all/beans/fred.ser."

When the bean is an applet

If the bean being instantiated is an applet (that is, if it has `Applet` as its superclass), some special initialization must be done. The bean will be supplied with an `AppletStub` and an `AppletContext`. If it is instantiated from a serialized object, there is nothing else to do (since it will have been initialized before being serialized). If, however, it is instantiated from a class, the `init()` method will be called.

Once the applet is loaded, you must install it in a visible AWT container and then call the `start()` method. An applet loaded in this way will not have access to parameters normally supplied in the HTML, so an applet to be used in this way should have methods that can be called to set the values.

Inheritance

```
public class java.beans.Beans
      extends Object
          ⇑
      public class java.lang.Object
```

Constructors

```
public Beans()
```

Methods

getInstanceOf()

```
public static Object getInstanceOf(Object bean,
        Class targetType)
```

Returns an object that represents a certain view of the `bean`. The `targetType` specifies the type of view being requested. The returned object may be the bean itself, or it may be an entirely different object constructed to represent the view. If the requested view is not available, the bean itself is always returned.

This method is provided as a hook in Java beans version 1.0 to allow for more flexibility to be added to future versions of a bean.

instantiate()

```
public static Object instantiate(ClassLoader loader,
        String beanName)
    throws IOException
    throws ClassNotFoundException
```

Institutes a bean and returns a reference to it. The `loader` controls the security and search methods to be used for loading the bean named `beanName`. If `loader` is null, the system

`ClassLoader` is used. The `ClassNotFoundException` is thrown if the class of a loaded bean cannot be determined.

 An attempt is made to use the name to load a serialized object, and then the name is used to load a class. These are the only two forms available in Java beans 1.0, but more loading mechanisms may be added to later versions.

isDesignTime()

```
public static boolean isDesignTime()
```

Returns `true` if execution is taking place inside an IDE or some other application construction environment.

isGuiAvailable()

```
public static boolean isGuiAvailable()
```

Returns `true` if the current environment is a GUI—that is, if a mouse, a keyboard, and a graphical display are available.

isInstanceOf()

```
public static boolean isInstanceOf(Object bean,
        Class targetType)
```

Returns `true` if `bean` can be viewed as the specified `targetType`. This method can be called to determine whether a call to `getInstanceOf()` would succeed for the specified `targetType`. A return value of `true` indicates that a call to the `getInstanceOf()` could successfully return an object of the specified `targetType`.

setDesignTime()

```
public static void setDesignTime(boolean setting)
    throws SecurityException
```

Sets the flag indicating whether or not execution is taking place inside an IDE or some other application construction environment.

setGuiAvailable()

```
public static void setGuiAvailable(boolean setting)
    throws SecurityException
```

Sets the flag indicating if the current environment is a GUI—that is, if a mouse, a keyboard, and a graphical display are available.

BindException

class java.net.BindException

This exception is thrown to indicate a failed attempt to bind a socket to a local address and port. Most likely, this happened because the port was already in use or the local address could not be assigned.

Inheritance

```
public class java.net.BindException
    extends SocketException
        ⇑
    public class java.net.SocketException
        extends IOException
            ⇑
        public class java.io.IOException
            extends Exception
                ⇑
            public class java.lang.Exception
                extends Throwable
                    ⇑
                public class java.lang.Throwable
                    implements Serializable
                    extends Object
                        ⇑
                    public class java.lang.Object
```

Constructors

```
public BindException()
public BindException(String message)
```

If the message string is supplied, it is used as a detailed message describing this particular exception.

big endian

In any of the integer types (byte, char, short, int, or long), the leftmost bit is the most significant bit. The "big end" comes first as you read from left to right. Java imposes this as the standard format for its integer data even on hardware that has a different format. The opposite of "big endian" is "little endian."

BigDecimal

class java.math.BigDecimal

This is an immutable arbitrary precision signed decimal number. It has a non-negative *scale* value. The scale specifies the number of the digits to the right of the decimal point. The BigDecimal class provides methods to perform arithmetic, as well as scaling, format conversion, and comparison.

Scaling

The value represented is determined by the string of digits it contains and by the scale used to position the decimal point. For example, if the string of digits is "345678" and value of the scale is 4, the actual value is 34.5678 because four of the digits go on the right of decimal.

Trailing zeroes are significant. They are necessary as placeholders for the scale.

Rounding modes

Rounding is a matter of determining the action to be taken on a digit after the one to its right has been discarded. Should it be incremented, decremented, or left as it is?

Eight modes can be set to control the type of rounding that will take place during the arithmetic operations. They are all described in this entry with the constant values that designate them. These modes are used to control all operations — including scaling.

Inheritance

```
public class java.math.BigDecimal
      extends Number
         ⇑
      public class java.lang.Number
            implements Serializable
            extends Object
               ⇑
            public class java.lang.Object
```

Variables and constants

ROUND_CEILING

```
public final static int ROUND_CEILING
```

Round toward the more positive value. If the value is positive, increment the last digit. If the value is negative, decrement the last digit.

ROUND_DOWN

```
public final static int ROUND_DOWN
```

Never increment a digit during rounding, which means never increase the magnitude of a number. Always round toward zero.

ROUND_FLOOR

```
public final static int ROUND_FLOOR
```

Round to the more negative value. If the value is positive, decrement the last digit. If the value is negative, increment the last digit.

ROUND_HALF_DOWN

```
public final static int ROUND_HALF_DOWN
```

Increment the last digit if the discarded digit was greater than 5 — otherwise, leave the new last digit as it is. This will almost balance the rounding, but rounding down has a 5 to 4 statistical edge.

ROUND_HALF_EVEN

```
public final static int ROUND_HALF_EVEN
```

Increment the last digit if the discarded digit is equal to 5. If it is greater than five, only increment the last digit if it is even. This will balance the rounding assuming that half the digits are even and half are odd.

ROUND_HALF_UP

```
public final static int ROUND_HALF_UP
```

Increment the last digit if the discarded digit was greater than or equal to 5 — otherwise, leave the new last digit as it is. This will almost balance the rounding, but rounding up has a 5 to 4 statistical edge.

ROUND_UNNECESSARY

```
public final static int ROUND_UNNECESSARY
```

This mode will not round. Using this mode implies that rounding will not be necessary, and if it turns out that it is, an ArithmeticException will be thrown.

ROUND_UP

```
public final static int ROUND_UP
```

If the discarded digit is nonzero, always increment the remaining digit. This method will never decrease the magnitude of a number. It always rounds away from zero.

Constructors

```
public BigDecimal(String svalue)
    throws NumberFormatException
```

```
public BigDecimal(double dvalue)
    throws NumberFormatException

public BigDecimal(BigInteger bivalue)

public BigDecimal(BigInteger bivalue,int scale)
    throws NumberFormatException
```

The svalue is a string of decimal digits that may be preceded by a minus sign and may contain a decimal point. The scale will be determined by the number of digits to the right of the decimal point (if there are none, the scale is 0). Any spurious characters — white space or whatever — will result in a NumberFormatException. Whether or not a character is a valid digit, and the value of the digit, is determined by Character.digit().

The dvalue is a double that will determine the value and the scale of the BigDecimal. The scale is the smallest power of 10 that, when multiplied by dvalue, will result in only zeroes to the right of the decimal point. If dvalue equals –infinity, +infinity, or NaN, a NumberFormatException will be thrown.

Using bivalue will create a BigDecimal from the BigInteger value. If the scale is not specified, it will default to zero. The scale value will shift the decimal point into the number. For example, if the integer value is 12345, a scale of 2 will result in a BigDecimal value of 123.45. A negative value for scale will result in a NumberFormatException being thrown.

Returned by

Because a BigDecimal is immutable, all methods in this class that perform operations return a new object. There are also getBigDecimal() methods in CallableStatement and ResultSet.

Methods

abs()

```
public BigDecimal abs()
```

Returns a BigDecimal that is the same as the current object, except that a negative number will be changed to positive.

add()

```
public BigDecimal add(BigDecimal value)
```

Returns a BigDecimal that is the sum of the value of the current object and value. The scale of the result will be the larger of the two.

compareTo()

```
public int compareTo(BigDecimal value)
```

If the value of this `BigDecimal` is less than `value`, return −1. If it is greater, return 1. If they are the same, return 0. The size of the scale is not considered. For example, 123.400 is equal to 123.4.

divide()

```
public BigDecimal divide(BigDecimal value,int scale,
        int roundingMode)
    throws ArithmeticException
    throws IllegalArgumentException

public BigDecimal divide(BigDecimal value,int roundingMode)
    throws ArithmeticException
    throws IllegalArgumentException
```

Divides this `BigDecimal` by `value` and returns a new `BigDecimal`. The `scale` specifies the scale of the result. If `scale` is not specified, the scale of this object is used. If rounding must be done, use the specified `roundingMode`. An `ArithmeticError` is thrown on an attempt to divide by zero. An `IllegalArgumentException` occurs if `roundingMode` is not valid.

doubleValue()

```
public double doubleValue()
```

Returns the value as a `double`. This could cause narrowing because not only can a `BigDecimal` hold more digits than a double, but it can also contain numbers of greater magnitude. If the magnitude is too large to fit in a `double`, the return value will be positive or negative infinity.

equals()

```
public boolean equals(Object object)
```

Returns `true` if `object` is a `BigDecimal` containing the same numeric value and scale as the current object.

floatValue()

```
public float floatValue()
```

Returns the value as a `float`. This could cause narrowing because not only can a `BigDecimal` hold more digits than a `float`, but it can also contain numbers of greater magnitude. If the magnitude is too large to fit in a `float`, the return value will be positive or negative infinity.

hashCode()

```
public int hashCode()
```

Returns the hashcode value for this object. `BigDecimal` objects with the same value but different scales will have different hashcodes.

intValue()

```
public int intValue()
```

Returns the value as an int. Narrowing could take place—in particular, any fractional portion will be truncated.

longValue()

```
public long longValue()
```

Returns the value as a long. Narrowing could take place—in particular, any fractional portion will be truncated.

max()

```
public BigDecimal max(BigDecimal value)
```

Returns either this BigDecimal or value—whichever is larger as determined by a call to compareTo(). If they are equal, either one could be returned.

min()

```
public BigDecimal min(BigDecimal value)
```

Returns either this BigDecimal or value—whichever is smaller as determined by a call to compareTo(). If they are equal, either one could be returned.

movePointLeft()

```
public BigDecimal movePointLeft(int shift)
```

Returns a BigDecimal that has had shift added to its scale value. If shift is negative, it is converted to positive and a call is made to movePointRight().

movePointRight()

```
public BigDecimal movePointRight(int shift)
```

Returns a BigDecimal that has had shift subtracted from its scale value. If shift is greater than the current scale value, the new scale is simply set to zero and the numeric value is sized appropriately. If shift is negative, it is converted to positive and a call is made to movePointLeft().

multiply()

```
public BigDecimal multiply(BigDecimal value)
```

Returns a BigDecimal that is the product of this and the value, and that has a scale that is the sum of the scales of the two.

negate()

```
public BigDecimal negate()
```

Returns a `Big Decimal` that has the same scale as this one and has a value of the oppostie sign.

scale()

```
public int scale()
```

Returns the scale value.

setScale()

```
public BigDecimal setScale(int scale,int roundingMode)
    throws ArithmeticException
    throws IllegalArgumentException
```

```
public BigDecimal setScale(int scale)
    throws ArithmeticException
    throws IllegalArgumentException
```

Returns a `BigDecimal` that has a scale specified by the `scale` argument and has its value multiplied or divided by the appropriate power of 10 to maintain the magnitude of the original value. If the specified `scale` is smaller than the scale of this object, then the number must be divided and precision could be lost. During division, rounding could be applied. The default rounding Mode is `ROUND_UNNECESSARY`.

An `ArithmeticException` is thrown if `scale` is negative or the `roundingMode` is `ROUND_UNNECESSARY` and rounding would have been required. An `IllegalArgumentException` is thrown if `roundingMode` is invalid.

signum()

```
public int signum()
```

Returns −1 if this number is negative, +1 if it is positive, and 0 if it is zero.

subtract()

```
public BigDecimal subtract(BigDecimal value)
```

Returns a `BigDecimal` with `value` subtracted from the value of this `BigDecimal`; the scale is set to whichever is the larger of the two.

toBigInteger()

```
public BigInteger toBigInteger()
```

Returns a `BigInteger` object that has the value of the nonfractional portion of this `BigDecimal`. The fractional portion is truncated.

toString()

```
public String toString()
```

Returns a string representation of this number. The method `Character.forDigit()` is used to convert the values to a base-10 string. A minus sign and decimal point are inserted.

valueOf()

```
public static BigDecimal valueOf(long value,int scale)
    throws NumberFormatException
```

```
public static BigDecimal valueOf(long value)
```

Converts the value to a `BigDecimal` and then sets the `scale` as specified. If `scale` is not specified, 0 is assumed. For example, a long `value` of 45678 and a `scale` of 2 will result in a `BigDecimal` value of 456.78. A `NumberFormatException` will be thrown for a negative value of the scale.

 Also see **BigInteger**.

BigInteger

class java.math.BigInteger

This class contains an immutable arbitrary-precision integer. It has methods to perform unary and binary operations on these integers.

Two's complement

The bitwise operations work as if the internal value were a two's complement value. That is, they work just like the Java language operators on the primitive integer types. Also, a family of methods is included to perform the sort of actions that the `Math` class performs on primitive integral types.

The leading bits and the sign

With an unlimited number of leading bits, an unsigned shift, it isn't necessary. In fact, no single-bit operation can reverse the sign of a number. You can think of a `BigInteger` as always having some leading bits no matter how many you are working with.

The degree of certainty of primes

This class includes ways to work with large prime numbers. Large prime numbers can take a long time to calculate, so some shortcuts can be used (for many practical purposes, a number that appears to be prime can be just as useful as a number that is actually prime). The *degree of certainty* is a positive number that is less than one. The smaller the value, the less the certainty that the number is actually prime. The larger the degree of certainty, however, the longer the calculation takes. The certainty value used as an argument to the constructor, and some of the methods, is used to calculate the degree this way:

degree = 1 - (1 / 2^x)

—where x is the certainty argument value. That is, if you pass the method a 1, the degree will be 0.5. If you pass a 2, the degree will be 0.75, and so on. The larger the certainty value you specify, the closer the degree is to 1.0, and the more certain you can be that the number is actually prime.

Inheritance

```
public class java.math.BigInteger
    extends Number
        ⇑
    public class java.lang.Number
        implements Serializable
        extends Object
            ⇑
        public class java.lang.Object
```

Constructors

```
public BigInteger(byte barray[])
    throws NumberFormatException

public BigInteger(int signum,byte magnitude[])
    throws NumberFormatException

public BigInteger(String svalue,int radix)
    throws NumberFormatException

public BigInteger(String svalue)
    throws NumberFormatException

public BigInteger(int bitCount,Random random)
    throws IllegalArgumentException

public BigInteger(int bitCount,int certainty,
        Random random)
```

The byte array barray contains the binary form of a number—an extended two's complement value with a leading sign bit. It is in big-endian form. The most significant byte is barray[0], and the most significant bit of each byte is in position 0. A NumberFormatException is thrown on a zero-length barray.

The combination of signum and magnitude is the byte-magnitude form of a constructor. The signum argument specifies the sign; that is, −1 for a negative number, +1 for a positive number, and 0 for zero. The unsigned binary value of the number is contained in the byte array `magnitude`. A `NumberFormatException` will be thrown if the `signum` value is invalid, or if `signum` is 0 and `magnitude` is nonzero. A zero-length `magnitude` array is permissible with a zero `signum`.

The string `svalue` is a string of characters, of the specified radix, that represents the number. If the radix is not specified, the default radix of 10 is used. The characters are converted to digits by `Character.digit()`. A `NumberFormatException` is thrown if there are any characters, including white space, other than those that are valid for the radix. The valid digits are in the range `Character.MIN_RADIX` through `Character.MAX_RADIX`.

The form that accepts `bitCount` and `random` returns a `BigInteger` that contains a random number value that can be contained in `bitCount` bits. The returned value is always a positive number. The value of `certainty` will specify the degree of certainty that the returned value will be a prime number—the larger the number, the greater the certainty that the number is prime. Also, the larger the number, the longer the time the constructor takes to verify the primeness of the number. An `IllegalArgumentException` occurs if `bitCount` is not greater than one.

Returned by

Because a `BigInteger` is immutable, all methods in this class that perform operations return a new object. Several methods are included in `DSAPublicKey` that return a `BigInteger`.

Methods

abs()

```
public BigInteger abs()
```

Returns a `BigInteger` that contains a positive number with the same value contained in the current object.

add()

```
public BigInteger add(BigInteger value)
    throws ArithmeticException
```

Returns a `BigInteger` that is the sum of this one and `value`.

and()

```
public BigInteger and(BigInteger value)
```

Returns a `BigInteger` that is the result of a bitwise (`this` & `value`). The return value will be negative only if both values are negative.

andNot()

```
public BigInteger andNot(BigInteger value)
```

Returns a `BigInteger` that is the result of a bitwise (`this` & (~`value`)). The return value is negative only if `this` is negative and `value` is positive.

bitCount()

```
public int bitCount()
```

Returns a count of the number of bits that are different from the sign bit.

bitLength()

```
public int bitLength()
```

Returns a count of the minimum number of bits required to represent the absolute value of this `BigInteger` in the two's complement form.

clearBit()

```
public BigInteger clearBit(int bitNumber)
    throws ArithmeticException
```

Returns a `BigInteger` that is the result of a single bit being cleared in the current value. It calculates a bitwise (`this` & ~(1<< `bitNumber`)).

compareTo()

```
public int compareTo(BigInteger value)
```

Returns −1 if this number is less than `value`, +1 if it is greater than, and 0 if the two are equal.

divide()

```
public BigInteger divide(BigInteger value)
    throws ArithmeticException
```

Returns a `BigInteger` that is the quotient of dividing this number by `value`. An `ArithmeticException` is thrown if value is zero.

divideAndRemainder()

```
public BigInteger[] divideAndRemainder(BigInteger value)
    throws ArithmeticException
```

Returns an array of two `BigIntegers` that contain the quotient and remainder of the division of this number by the `value`. `BigInteger[0]` holds the quotient, and `BigInteger[1]` holds the remainder. An `ArithmeticException` is thrown if value is zero.

doubleValue()

```
public double doubleValue()
```

Returns the value as a `double`. This could cause narrowing because it is possible for a `BigInteger` to hold more digits than a `double`.

equals()

```
public boolean equals(Object object)
```

Returns `true` if `object` is a `BigInteger` that contains the same value as this one.

flipBit()

```
public BigInteger flipBit(int bitNumber)
    throws ArithmeticException
```

Returns a `BigInteger` that is the same as this one except the bit designated by bitNumber has been toggled. It calculates a bitwise (`this ^ (1<<bitNumber)`).

floatValue()

```
public float floatValue()
```

Returns the value as a `float`. This could cause narrowing because it is possible for a `BigInteger` to hold more digits than a `float`.

gcd()

```
public BigInteger gcd(BigInteger value)
```

Returns a `BigInteger` that has the value of the greatest common divisor of the absolute value of this `BigInteger` and the absolute value of `value`. If either number is zero, the other number is returned.

getLowestSetBit()

```
public int getLowestSetBit()
```

Returns a count of the number zero bits to the right of the rightmost one bit. If there is no one bit in the number, return −1.

hashCode()

```
public int hashCode()
```

Returns a hashcode value for this object.

intValue()

```
public int intValue()
```

Returns the number as an `int`. This narrowing could cause loss of magnitude.

isProbablePrime()

```
public boolean isProbablePrime(int certainty)
```

Returns `true` if this number can be verified as being prime to the specified level of certainty.

longValue()

```
public long longValue()
```

Returns the number as a `long`. This narrowing could cause loss of magnitude.

max()

```
public BigInteger max(BigInteger value)
```

Returns a `BigInteger` that is the larger of this number and `value`. If they are equal, either one may be returned.

min()

```
public BigInteger min(BigInteger value)
```

Returns a `BigInteger` that is the smaller of this number and `value`. If they are equal, either one may be returned.

mod()

```
public BigInteger mod(BigInteger value)
```

Returns a `BigInteger` that is this number modulo `value`. It calculates a bitwise (`this & value`). An `ArithmeticException` is thrown if `value` is not greater than zero.

modInverse()

```
public BigInteger modInverse(BigInteger value)
    throws ArithmeticException
```

Returns the multiplicative inverse of this number modulo `value`. An `ArithmeticException` is thrown if `value` is not a positive number, or if there is no multiplicative inverse. (There is no multiplicative inverse if this number and `value` are not mutually prime—that is, if the greatest common divisor of the two numbers is not 1).

modPow()

```
public BigInteger modPow(BigInteger exp,BigInteger value)
```

Returns a `BigInteger` that is this value raised to the power of `exp` and then modulo `value`. The exponent can be positive or negative. An `ArithmeticException` is thrown if `value` is not greater than zero.

multiply()

```
public BigInteger multiply(BigInteger value)
```

Returns a `BigInteger` that is the product of this number and `value`.

negate()

```
public BigInteger negate()
```

Returns a `BigInteger` that has the same value but opposite sign of this number.

not()

```
public BigInteger not()
```

Returns a `BigInteger` that is a one's complement of this number. It performs a bitwise (`~this`). The sign of the returned `BigInteger` will be the opposite of this one.

or()

```
public BigInteger or(BigInteger val)
```

Returns a `BigInteger` that is the result of a bitwise OR operation (`this | value`). The return value will be negative if and only if either of the values are negative.

pow()

```
public BigInteger pow(int exponent)
    throws ArithmeticException
```

Returns a `BigInteger` that has the value of this one raised to the power of the exponent. An `ArithmeticException` is thrown if the exponent is less than zero (because the result would not be an integer value).

remainder()

```
public BigInteger remainder(BigInteger value)
    throws ArithmeticException
```

Returns a `BigInteger` that is this number modulo `value`. The method performs the operation (`this % value`). An `ArithmeticException` is thrown if the value is equal to zero.

setBit()

```
public BigInteger setBit(int bitNumber)
    throws ArithmeticException
```

Returns a `BigInteger` that has the value of this number with the bit at `bitNumber` set to 1. The returned number is the result of a bitwise OR operation (`this | (1<<bitNumber)`).

shiftLeft()

```
public BigInteger shiftLeft(int shift)
```

Returns a `BigInteger` that is the result of this number being shifted left by `shift` bits.

shiftRight()

```
public BigInteger shiftRight(int shift)
```

Returns a `BigInteger` that is the result of performing a sign-extended shift to the right by `shift` bits.

signum()

```
public int signum()
```

Returns −1 if this number is negative, +1 if it is positive, and 0 if it is zero.

subtract()

```
public BigInteger subtract(BigInteger value)
```

Returns a `BigNumber` that is the result of subtracting `value` from this number.

testBit()

```
public boolean testBit(int bitNumber)
        throws ArithmeticException
```

Returns `true` if the `bitNumber` bit of this number is set. An `ArithmeticException` is thrown if `bitNumber` is negative.

toByteArray()

```
public byte[] toByteArray()
```

The returned byte array contains the binary form of this number—an extended two's complement value with a leading sign bit. It is in big-endian form. The most significant byte is on the left, byte[0], and the most significant bit of each byte is also on the left.

toString()

```
public String toString()
public String toString(int radix)
```

This method returns a string representation of the number in the specified radix. If the value of `radix` is outside the range `Character.MIN_RADIX` and `Character.MAX_RADIX`, or if the radix is not specified, it defaults to 10. A leading minus sign is included for a negative number. The values are converted to digits by calling `Character.forDigit()`.

valueOf()

```
public static BigInteger valueOf(long value)
```

Returns a `BigInteger` containing the value of the `long`.

xor()

```
public BigInteger xor(BigInteger value)
```

Returns a `BigInteger` that is the result of a bitwise exclusive-or of this number and `value`. The return value will be negative if one, but not both, of the values are negative.

 Also see **BigDecimal.**

bit operations

 For a class that manipulates bit arrays, see **BitSet**. For the bitwise operators of the Java language, see **ampersand, bar, caret, shift left,** and **shift right**.

BitSet

class java.util.Bitset

This is an array of `boolean` values. Each member of the array is uniquely identified by its index value. The lowest index value is 0. The size of the array will automatically grow as needed. The default value of any member of the array is `false`. The class is defined as final — it cannot be subclassed.

The skip-fill

While there is no specified upper limit to the index value, it is probably not a good idea to use an unnecessarily large number. The setting to `true` of one of the Boolean values causes the Java interpreter to allocate a space for all Booleans with smaller index values. For example, if you were to set the Boolean value with the index of 9832, Java would allocate space enough to hold at least 9832 Boolean values. That may not be what you intended.

Both bit and Boolean

The terms *bit* and *Boolean* get a little mixed up here. Although the word "bit" appears in the name of the class and the methods that return the value of one of these "bits" actually return a `boolean` data type, in places in Java, a distinct difference occurs between the two. A byte is composed of eight bits, not `boolean`s — and a bit can be either 1 or 0, not `true` or `false`. But for the purposes of this class, they can be considered to be exactly the same.

Inheritance

```
public final class java.util.BitSet
        implements Cloneable
        implements Serializable
        extends Object
                ⇑
        public class java.lang.Object
```

Constructors

BitSet()

```
public BitSet()
```

```
public BitSet(int bitCount)
```

Both constructors create a `BitSet` object with all bits set to `false`. The value `bitCount` will determine the number of bits that are initially allocated. If `bitCount` is not specified, the initial size of the array is implementation-dependent. Not knowing the actual array size should be of no consequence, because all members of the array are initialized to `false`, and nonexistent bits are reported as being `false`. See Example 1.

Methods

and()

```
public void and(BitSet set)
```

This array of bits is logically ANDed with the bits in `set`, and the result is placed in this object. If one array is longer than the other, the resulting bits beyond the end of the array are `false` in the result. See Example 3.

clear()

```
public void clear(int index)
```

The bit at the `index` is set to `false`.

clone()

```
public Object clone()
```

Makes an exact copy of this `BitSet` object.

equals()

```
public boolean equals(Object object)
```

Returns `true` if `object` is a `BitSet` object and it has the same set of `true` bits as this object—the size of the internal array does not matter. See Example 2.

get()

```
public boolean get(int index)
```

Returns the bit at index. See Example 1.

hashCode()

```
public int hashCode()
```

Returns the hashcode. See Example 2.

or()

```
public void or(BitSet set)
```

This method performs a logical OR of the bits in this BitSet with the bits in set and leaves the result in this BitSet. See Example 3.

set()

```
public void set(int index)
```

This will set the bit at index to true. See Examples 2 and 3.

size()

```
public int size()
```

This method returns a count of the number of bits currently allocated for the object. The number could be greater than that required to hold all the bits that are currently set. The allocation normally proceeds in chunks (the current implementation increases the array 64 bits at a time). See Examples 1 and 2.

toString()

```
public String toString()
```

This method will convert this object to a string. The string includes the index values of all the bits that are set to true. See Example 3.

xor()

```
public void xor(BitSet set)
```

This method performs a logical XOR (exclusive or) of the bits in this BitSet with the bits in set and leaves the result in this BitSet. See Example 3.

Example 1

This example will display the default size for your compiler and will also demonstrate that a value beyond the range of the current size will simply be assumed to be false:

```
import java.util.BitSet;

public class BitSetSize {
    public static void main(String arg[]) {
        BitSet bitset = new BitSet();
        System.out.println("size: " + bitset.size());
        System.out.println("bit 100: " + bitset.get(100));
        System.out.println("size: " + bitset.size());
    }
}
```

Here is a typical listing of the output from this example. In this example, the initial array size was 64. Notice that the get() method returns the default value of false for the undefined member. Also, testing the nonexistent bit did not change the size of the bit array:

```
size: 64
bit 100: false
size: 64
```

Example 2

This example demonstrates the operation of the equals() and hashCode() methods. In the example, two BitSet objects, bs1 and bs2, are created. One has its size specified as 300; the other takes the default size, which is nominally 64.

```
public class BitSetEqual {
    static public void main(String arg[]) {
        BitSet bs1 = new BitSet();
        BitSet bs2 = new BitSet(300);
        System.out.println("bs1 hashcode: " +
                bs1.hashCode());
        System.out.println("bs2 hashcode: " +
                bs2.hashCode());
        bs1.set(10);
        bs1.set(15);
        System.out.println(bs1.equals(bs2));
        System.out.println("bs1 hashcode: " +
                bs1.hashCode());
        System.out.println("bs2 hashcode: " +
                bs2.hashCode());
        bs2.set(10);
        bs2.set(15);
        System.out.println(bs1.equals(bs2));
        System.out.println("bs1 hashcode: " +
```

```
                              bs1.hashCode());
              System.out.println("bs2 hashcode: " +
                              bs2.hashCode());
          }
      }
```

Setting bits will cause the hashcode to change. Having the same group of bits set (that is, such that the two objects contain the same value) causes their hashcodes to be the same. Here is an example of the output from this example:

```
bs1 hashcode: 1234
bs2 hashcode: 1234
false
bs1 hashcode: 32978
bs2 hashcode: 1234
true
bs1 hashcode: 32978
bs2 hashcode: 32978
```

This shows that it is the pattern of true bits that determine equality—either with the equals() or hashCode() methods. The internal length of the array has no effect on either method.

Example 3

This example demonstrates the actions that are taken by the methods and(), or(), and xor(). Each is tested twice—once applying a short array to a long one, and once, a long array to a short one:

```
import java.util.*;
public class BitSetLogical {
    static BitSet bLong;
    static BitSet bShort;
    public static void main(String[] arg) {
        newBitSets();
        showBitSets("When they are newly created");
        newBitSets();
        bLong.and(bShort);
        showBitSets("Anding the short into the long");
        newBitSets();
        bShort.and(bLong);
        showBitSets("Anding the long into the short");
        newBitSets();
        bLong.or(bShort);
        showBitSets("Oring the short into the long");
        newBitSets();
```

```
        bShort.or(bLong);
        showBitSets("Oring the long into the short");
        newBitSets();
        bLong.xor(bShort);
        showBitSets("Xoring the short into the long");
        newBitSets();
        bShort.xor(bLong);
        showBitSets("Xoring the long into the short");
    }

    public static void newBitSets() {
        bLong = new BitSet(128);
        bShort = new BitSet();
        bLong.set(1);
        bShort.set(2);
        bLong.set(3);
        bShort.set(3);
        bLong.set(100);
        bShort.set(50);
    }

    public static void showBitSets(String arg) {
        System.out.println("--- " + arg);
        System.out.println(" long: " + bLong +
            "(array size=" + bLong.size() + ")");
        System.out.println("short: " + bShort +
            "(array size=" + bShort.size() + ")");
    }
}
```

The internal lengths of the arrays have no effect on the outcome of the operation. If the shorter array needs to be lengthened to include a newly created true bit to satisfy the operation, then it is extended. Here is the output of this example:

```
--- When they are newly created
 long: {1, 3, 100}(array size=128)
short: {2, 3, 50}(array size=64)
--- Anding the short into the long
 long: {3}(array size=128)
short: {2, 3, 50}(array size=64)
--- Anding the long into the short
 long: {1, 3, 100}(array size=128)
short: {3}(array size=64)
--- Oring the short into the long
```

```
long: {1, 2, 3, 50, 100}(array size=128)
short: {2, 3, 50}(array size=64)
--- Oring the long into the short
 long: {1, 3, 100}(array size=128)
short: {1, 2, 3, 50, 100}(array size=128)
--- Xoring the short into the long
 long: {1, 2, 50, 100}(array size=128)
short: {2, 3, 50}(array size=64)
--- Xoring the long into the short
 long: {1, 3, 100}(array size=128)
short: {1, 2, 50, 100}(array size=128)
```

As you can see, the size of the shorter array was extended only as needed to hold a true bit.

block

A *block* is a group of executable statements that act as a single unit. The statements all execute from top to bottom as a unit. A block normally begins with a left brace ({) and ends with a right brace (}). For example:

```
{
    int i = 12;
    System.out.println("i=" + i);
}
```

Because the two statements are enclosed in a block, they will execute as a unit. The scope of the variable i is limited to the block—it will cease to exist when the flow of execution leaves the block.

A one-line block

A special case exists in which a block can be defined without the braces, but it can only consist of a single statement. In this example—

```
if(a < b)
    System.out.println("a is less than b");
```

—the line that does the printing makes up the entire block and will only be executed if the Boolean expression is true.

Nested blocks

Because a block is a collection of one or more statements that acts like a single statement, a block can be used as a single statement within another block.

A body block

The most common blocks are the bodies of methods. All the executable statements of a method are enclosed in a pair of braces. The body of a class or an interface is also a block enclosed in braces.

boolean

The `boolean` type is one of the primitive data types in the Java language. Conceptually, at least, it is a single bit. A `boolean` variable can take on one of two values designated by the constant values `true` and `false`.

Literals

There are two `boolean` literals—`true` and `false`. These two words are of the data type `boolean`. The keywords `true` and `false` are the only `boolean` literals. It is not possible to use 1 or 0—or any other value—and have it assume the characteristics of a `boolean` value.

Operators

Table B-1 lists the operators that are valid on `boolean` data types.

Table B-1	Valid Boolean Operators
Operator(s)	**Description**
`= =` `!=`	The relational operators
`!`	The logical-complement operator
`&` `^` `|`	The logical operators
`&&` `||` `?:`	The conditional operators
`+`	With one `boolean` and one `String` operand, this causes the `boolean` to be converted to a `String` object containing either "true" or "false."

Control flow

The operands of `if`, `while`, `do`, and `for` *must* be `boolean` expressions. The first operand of the trinary operator `?` `:` also must be a `boolean` expression.

Conversion to and from an integer

No built-in relationship exists between a boolean type and any other primitive data type. To convert between a boolean and another type requires specific code—it cannot be done with casting. This line of code will convert an int to a boolean, where a zero int value is considered false and a nonzero int value is considered true (as in C and C++):

```
boolean bvalue = (ivalue == 0) ? false : true;
```

This will convert a boolean value true to an int value of 1, and a boolean value false to a 0.

```
int ivalue = bvalue ? 1 : 0;
```

 For more on true and false, see **literals**.

Boolean

class java.lang.Boolean

This is a wrapper class for the primitive type boolean.

immutable

A Boolean object is created with a setting of either true or false and cannot be changed.

Inheritance

```
public final class java.lang.Boolean
        implements Serializable
        extends Object
                ⇑
        public class java.lang.Object
```

Variables and constants

FALSE

```
public final static Boolean FALSE
```

A constant Boolean object that is set to false.

TRUE

```
public final static Boolean TRUE
```

A constant Boolean object that is set to true.

TYPE

```
public final static Class TYPE
```

The Class object representing the primitive type boolean.

Constructors

```
public Boolean(boolean value)
public Boolean(String stringValue)
```

A Boolean type, when created, must be set to true or false. The value can be any expression that results in a boolean type. The stringValue can be some form of "true" or "True" or "TRUE" (case doesn't matter) to be true. Any other string is assumed to be false.

Methods

booleanValue()

```
public boolean booleanValue()
```

Returns the internal boolean primitive value of true or false.

equals()

```
public boolean equals(Object object)
```

Returns true if object is a Boolean object and has the same value setting as this Boolean object. This is, if they are both true, return true — or if they are both false, return true.

getBoolean()

```
public static boolean getBoolean(String name)
```

Returns the boolean value of a system property. For example, if there is a system property named "java.home.localdisk" that has the string value "true", the following method call will return true.

```
boolean bn = Boolean.getBoolean("java.home.localdisk");
```

The method will return false either if the the property does not exist or if it does exist and its value is not a "true" string.

hashCode()

```
public int hashCode()
```

Returns the hashcode value of this object.

toString()

```
public String toString()
```

Returns a string representation of the object. The return value is either "true" or "false" according to the object's value.

valueOf()

```
public static Boolean valueOf(String string)
```

Converts `string` into a `Boolean` object. If `string` is "true" (not case sensitive), the value of the returned `Boolean` is `true`; otherwise, it is `false`.

 The wrappers of the other primitive types are **Byte, Character, Integer, Short, Long, Float,** and **Double.**

BorderLayout

class java.awt.BorderLayout

This is a layout manager that is able to manage the positioning of a maximum of five components. It is capable of placing one against each of the four edges of its rectangle, and one other in the center.

Placement by compass points and center

The components are laid out as if the container were a map. North is at the top, and West is on the left. To specify the placement, the names of the four points of the compass are used:

```
"North"
"South"
"East"
"West"
```

The component in the center can be placed with the string

```
"Center"
```

If the String is not one of these—or if no string is specified—the default is "Center." The constants declared in this class can be used in lieu of the literal strings.

Fitting

The components are made to fit this way. The "North" and "South" components are sized horizontally to fit the window and allowed to use their preferred sizes vertically. Next, the "East" and "West" components are sized to fit vertically in the space available and allowed to use their preferred sizes horizontally. The "Center" component is made to fit whatever space is left over.

Inheritance

```
public class java.awt.BorderLayout
    implements LayoutManager2
    implements Serializable
    extends Object
        ⇑
    public class java.lang.Object
```

Variables and constants

CENTER

```
public final static String CENTER
```

The value to indicate that the component is to be in the center.

EAST

```
public final static String EAST
```

The value to indicate that the component is to be placed to the East.

NORTH

```
public final static String NORTH
```

The value to indicate that the component is to be placed to the North.

SOUTH

```
public final static String SOUTH
```

The value to indicate that the component is to be placed to the South.

WEST

```
public final static String WEST
```

The value to indicate that the component is to be placed to the West.

Constructors

BorderLayout()

```
public BorderLayout()
public BorderLayout(int horizontalGap,int verticalGap)
```

The size of the gaps between components can be specified—if not, they default to zero. The gaps specify the number of pixels that will appear between adjacent components.

Methods

addLayoutComponent()

```
public void addLayoutComponent(Component component,
        Object constraint)
```

```
public void addLayoutComponent(String name,
        Component comp)*** deprecated ****
```

The component is added to the layout manager according to the constraint. If the constraint is not a String naming one of the four compass points, "Center" is assumed. Note that the second form, the one with the String name argument, has been deprecated— only the first form should be used.

getHgap()

```
public int getHgap()
```

Returns the value of the horizontal gap.

getLayoutAlignmentX()

```
public float getLayoutAlignmentX(Container parent)
```

Returns the relative horizontal position in the parent window. With the origin at the left, the leftmost value is 0.0 and the rightmost is 1.0.

getLayoutAlignmentY()

```
public float getLayoutAlignmentY(Container parent)
```

Returns the relative vertical position in the parent window. With the origin at the top, the top value is 0.0 and the bottom value is 1.0.

getVgap()

```
public int getVgap()
```

Returns the value of the vertical gap.

invalidateLayout()

```
public void invalidateLayout(Container target)
```

Commands the layout manager to discard any positioning information it may have and recalculate it all.

layoutContainer()

```
public void layoutContainer(Container target)
```

Performs the action of laying out the components in the target container. Takes into account the size constraints of the target, the gap sizes, and the size requirements of the various components.

maximumLayoutSize()

```
public Dimension maximumLayoutSize(Container target)
```

Uses the values from the various components, and the gap information, to arrive at the maximum size that could be filled with the layout.

minimumLayoutSize()

```
public Dimension minimumLayoutSize(Container target)
```

Uses the values from the various components, and the gap information, to arrive at the minimum size that could be used to contain all the components.

preferredLayoutSize()

```
public Dimension preferredLayoutSize(Container target)
```

Uses the values from the various components, and the gap information, to arrive at the preferred layout size.

removeLayoutComponent()

```
public void removeLayoutComponent(Component component)
```

Removes the component from the layout.

setHgap()

```
public void setHgap(int hgap)
```

Sets the value of the horizontal gap.

setVgap()

```
public void setVgap(int vgap)
```

Sets the value of the vertical gap.

toString()

```
public String toString()
```

Returns the String representation of the BorderLayout object.

Example 1

This example places five buttons in an applet window using the BorderLayout manager:

```
import java.awt.*;
import java.applet.*;
```

```
public class BorderLayout1 extends Applet {
    public void init() {
        setLayout(new BorderLayout());
        add("North",new Button("North"));
        add("South",new Button("South"));
        add("East",new Button("East"));
        add("West",new Button("West"));
        add("Center",new Button("Center"));
    }
}
```

The layout manager is created and assigned to the applet by a call to `setLayout()`. The buttons are added using the `add()` method of the container. The applet window displays as shown in Figure B-1.

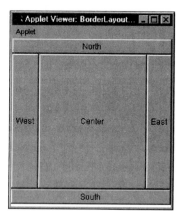

Figure B-1 Five buttons in a BorderLayout manager.

The placement follows this procedure:

1. The North and South items are configured by using their preferred sizes vertically and setting their horizontal sizes to fit the available space.

2. The East and West items are configured by using their preferred sizes horizontally and stretching them vertically to fit the available space.

3. The Center item is resized both vertically and horizontally to fill the available space.

 A combination of the String constants in BorderLayout and the overloading of the `add()` methods of Container makes it possible to add a component in any one of four different ways. All of the following statements are equivalent:

```
add("North",new Button("North"));
```

```
add(BorderLayout.NORTH,new Button("North"));
add(new Button("North"),"North");
add(new Button("North"),BorderLayout.NORTH);
```

None of these are deprecated and they all work equally well, but it is possible to argue that the last one is more correct because it is more consistent with other changes made in moving from 1.0 to 1.1.

Example 2

This example is the same as Example 1, except that a couple of buttons are missing:

```
import java.awt.*;
import java.applet.*;

public class BorderLayout2 extends Applet {
    public void init() {
        setLayout(new BorderLayout());
        add("North",new Button("North"));
        add("East",new Button("East"));
        add("Center",new Button("Center"));
    }
}
```

Nothing is placed at either the South or West positions. Figure B-2 shows that the BorderLayout manager follows the rules of placement. The North member is stretched to fill the horizontal width, the East member is stretched vertically to fill completely to the bottom of the window, and the one in the Center will fill whatever is left over.

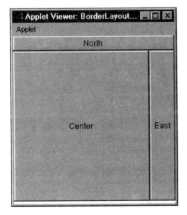

Figure B-2   It isn't necessary to supply a component for all positions.

Example 3

This is the same as Example 1, except that spaces have been inserted between the components:

```
import java.awt.*;
import java.applet.*;

public class BorderLayout3 extends Applet {
    public void init() {
        setLayout(new BorderLayout(5,10));
        add("North",new Button("North"));
        add("South",new Button("South"));
        add("East",new Button("East"));
        add("West",new Button("West"));
        add("Center",new Button("Center"));
    }
}
```

Figure B-3 shows the resulting applet window with a horizontal spacing of 5 pixels and a vertical spacing of 10 pixels.

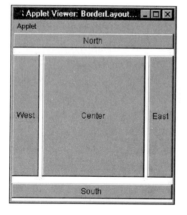

Figure B-3 The spacing between components is determined by constant settings.

Example 4

This example shows how to use BorderLayout managers in an application (by using a Frame as the container), and how one BorderLayout can be nested inside another (by using Panel as the component in one and the container of another):

```
import java.awt.*;
public class BorderLayoutApp extends Frame {
    public static void main(String[] arg) {
```

```
        BorderLayoutApp bla = new BorderLayoutApp();
        bla.show();
    }
    BorderLayoutApp() {
        setLayout(new BorderLayout());
        add("North",new Button("North"));
        add("South",new Button("South"));
        add("East",new Button("East"));
        add("West",new Button("West"));
        Panel p = new Panel();
        p.setLayout(new BorderLayout());
        p.add("North",new Button("N"));
        p.add("South",new Button("S"));
        p.add("East",new Button("E"));
        p.add("West",new Button("W"));
        p.add("Center",new Button("C"));
        add("Center",p);
        setSize(300,300);
        pack();
        show();
    }
}
```

Once the layout manager is defined, components can be added just as they were in the applet examples just given. A `Panel` is created, given its own `BorderLayout` manager and a set of buttons, and added as the "Center" component. The result is shown in Figure B-4.

Figure B-4   A `Panel` is used to nest one layout manager inside another.

braces

{}

Braces (sometimes called "squiggly braces" or "curly braces") are used to create code blocks.

See **block**.

brackets

[]

Brackets (sometimes called "square brackets") are used in the declaration and access of arrays.

See **array**.

break

keyword

The break statement is used to interrupt the flow of execution inside a `for`, `do`, `while`, or `switch-case` block and exit it. It can optionally have a label used to perform a multilevel break out of nested blocks.

For examples of break statements, see **for**, **do**, **while**, and **switch**. Another keyword that performs a somewhat similar function is **continue**. To exit an entire method, see **return**. To see how to handle an error condition, which could possibly entail exiting one or more methods, see **throw**.

BreakIterator

class java.text.BreakIterator

This is a lexical scanner. This class contains methods for extracting tokens by locating boundaries and delimiters in text. A `BreakIterator` contains an internal cursor that can be moved through the text and return information about boundaries used to break up the text.

A `BreakIterator` is intended for natural language text. It was not designed for use on a programming language.

Reading the input

The `BreakIterator` uses a `CharacterIterator` for its input. This means that it can use as input any object that implements the `CharacterIterator` interface. A `StringCharacterIterator` is used to scan input from `String` objects.

Factory methods for different types of iterators

A BreakIterator can be acquired from the factory methods of this class. There are different kinds of iterators—there are those that work with words, lines, sentences, or characters. They can be combined to break down text into its component parts.

Line boundary

Line boundary analysis determines where a text string can be broken when line-wrapping. It is aware of punctuation and word hyphenation.

Sentence

This iterator is able to locate trailing punctuation marks that are used to terminate sentences. It can handle things like quotation marks, parentheses, and periods used as decimal points in numbers.

Word

This iterator is able to locate individual words or other tokens in the text. It can differentiate between the punctuation marks that appear inside words and those that separate words. It will extract characters that are not part of a word (delimiting symbols and punctuation marks) by placing a word break on each side of them.

Inheritance

```
public abstract class java.text.BreakIterator
      implements Cloneable
      implements Serializable
      extends Object
            ⇑
      public class java.lang.Object
```

Variables and constants

DONE

```
public final static int DONE
```

Indicates end of text (for both forward and backward scanning).

Constructors

```
protected BreakIterator()
```

The object created from the default constructor is stateless—it has no defined behavior.

Factory

This class contains factory methods `getCharacterInstance()`, `getLineInstance()`, `getSentenceInstance()`, and `getWordInstance()`. Each of these produces a different kind of `BreakIterator`.

Methods

clone()

```
public Object clone()
```

Returns a duplicate of this object.

current()

```
public abstract int current()
```

Returns the index of the current cursor position. It will be the one last found by a call to `next()`, `previous()`, `first()`, or `last()`.

first()

```
public abstract int first()
```

Sets the current position to the first boundary in the text and returns its index.

following()

```
public abstract int following(int offset)
```

Returns the first boundary found by starting at `offset` and moving forward. If there is a boundary at `offset`, it is skipped. If no boundary is found, the method returns DONE. If `offset` is invalid, an `IllegalArgumentException` will be thrown.

getAvailableLocales()

```
public static synchronized Locale[] getAvailableLocales()
```

Returns the set of `Locale`s for which `TextBoundaries` are installed.

getCharacterInstance()

```
public static BreakIterator getCharacterInstance()

public static BreakIterator
      getCharacterInstance(Locale locale)
```

Creates and returns a `BreakIterator` for character breaks. A *character break* is a boundary made up of combined character sequences. If `locale` is not specified, or if it is one that cannot be used, the default is used.

getLineInstance()

```
public static BreakIterator getLineInstance()

public static BreakIterator getLineInstance(Locale locale)
```

Creates and returns a BreakIterator for line breaks. A *line break* is a place in the text where a logical line break *could* occur. If locale is not specified, or if it is one that cannot be used, the default is used.

getSentenceInstance()

```
public static BreakIterator getSentenceInstance()

public static BreakIterator getSentenceInstance(Locale locale)
```

Creates and returns a BreakIterator for sentence breaks. If locale is not specified, or if it is one that cannot be used, the default is used.

getText()

```
public abstract CharacterIterator getText()
```

Returns a CharacterIterator object for the text being scanned.

getWordInstance()

```
public static BreakIterator getWordInstance()

public static BreakIterator getWordInstance(Locale locale)
```

Creates and returns a BreakIterator for word breaks. If locale is not specified, or if it is one that cannot be used, the default is used.

last()

```
public abstract int last()
```

Sets the current position to the last boundary in the text and returns its index.

next()

```
public abstract int next()
public abstract int next(int count)
```

Moves the current position forward count number of boundaries in the text and returns the index. The default count is 1. A negative count will move toward the beginning of the text. A zero does nothing. If the beginning or end of the text is hit, DONE is returned.

previous()

```
public abstract int previous()
```

Moves the current position one boundary prior to the current one. If the beginning of the text is hit, DONE is returned.

setText()

```
public void setText(String newText)
public abstract void setText(CharacterIterator newText)
```

This defines a new string to be scanned. The current scanning position is set to first().

Example

This example uses a word iterator to divide the words and punctuation in a sentence and insert a vertical bar at the position of each break:

```
import java.text.*;
public class WordText {
    static String input =
            "\"This,\" he said, \"is a sentence.\"";
    public static void main(String args[]) {
        System.out.println(input);
        BreakIterator bi = BreakIterator.getWordInstance();
        bi.setText(input);
        int index1 = bi.first();
        int index2 = bi.next();
        String output = "|";
        while(index2 != BreakIterator.DONE) {
            output += input.substring(index1,index2);
            output += "|";
            index1 = index2;
            index2 = bi.next();
        }
        System.out.println(output);
    }
}
```

The output of the example consists of before and after versions of the string, like this:

```
"This," he said, "is a sentence."
|"|This|,|"| |he| |said|,| |"|is| |a| |sentence|.|"|
```

 For iteration through the characters of a String, see **StringCharacterIterator**. Also see **CharacterIterator**.

BufferedInputStream

class java.io.BufferedInputStream

This class will read data from an input stream and perform internal buffering.
It reads data in larger blocks than your program requires. This prevents a
physical read each time your program requests a small amount of data.

Inheritance

```
public class java.io.BufferedInputStream
    extends FilterInputStream
        ⇑
    public class java.io.FilterInputStream
        extends InputStream
            ⇑
        public class java.io.InputStream
            extends Object
                ⇑
            public class java.lang.Object
```

Variables and constants

buf

```
protected byte buf[]
```

The internal array that holds the buffered data.

count

```
protected int count
```

The number of bytes currently held in buf.

marklimit

```
protected int marklimit
```

The current maximum value set by mark() that determines the number of already-read
bytes that must be retained in case there is a call to reset().

markpos

```
protected int markpos
```

The index into buf of the current position set by mark().

pos

```
protected int pos
```

The index to the current input byte in buf.

Constructors

```
public BufferedInputStream(InputStream input)
public BufferedInputStream(InputStream in,int size)
```

A BufferedInputStream is constructed using input. The size argument specifies the size of the buffer. If the size is not specified, a default value is assumed.

Methods

available()

```
public abstract int available()
    throws IOException
```

Returns the number of bytes immediately available—the number that can be read without blocking.

close()

```
public void close()
    throws IOException
```

This will terminate the input stream. This must be called to release any system-level resources associated with the stream.

mark()

```
public synchronized void mark(int readlimit)
```

This will mark the current position in the input stream; a subsequent call to reset() will restore the input to this position. The value of readlimit specifies the number of bytes that can be read before the mark is discarded. For mark() to work, the return value from markSupported() must be true.

markSupported()

```
public boolean markSupported()
```

This method returns true if the mark() and reset() methods can be used to mark the current position of the input stream.

read()

```
public abstract int read()
```

```
        throws IOException
    public int read(byte barray[],int offset,int length)
        throws IOException
```

If no argument is supplied, this will read one `byte` of data and return it as an `int`. If `barray` is supplied, the input data is placed in the array and the number of bytes read is returned. If `offset` and `length` are specified, the input data will appear beginning at `barray[offset]` for a maximum of `length` bytes. This method will block as long as there is unread data available. A return value of −1 indicates a normal end to the input stream.

reset()

```
    public synchronized void reset()
        throws IOException
```

This will reposition the input stream to the location of the last call to `mark()`. The exception is thrown if there is no active mark. A mark will be removed (causing this method to throw an exception) if more bytes have been read than the number specified on the call to `mark()`.

skip()

```
    public long skip(long count)
        throws IOException
```

Calling this method makes a request to have the input stream skip over `count` number of input bytes. The return value is the actual number of bytes skipped.

Example

A `BufferedInputStream` can be inserted in front of any input stream. This example reads its own source file and echoes it to standard output:

```java
import java.io.*;
public class BinStream {
    public static void main(String[] arg) {
        FileInputStream fis;
        BufferedInputStream bis;
        try {
            fis = new FileInputStream("BinStream.java");
            bis = new BufferedInputStream(fis);
            while(true) {
                int character = bis.read();
                if(character < 0)
                    break;
                System.out.print((char)character);
```

```
                    }
                } catch(IOException e) {
                    e.printStackTrace();
                }
            }
        }
```

For buffering input from a reader, see **BufferedReader**. For buffering output to a stream, see **BufferedOutputStream**.

BufferedOutputStream

class java.io.BufferedOutputStream

This class will write data to an output stream. The data is buffered to reduce the actual number of physical writes by placing the data in an output buffer and writing it only when the buffer is full, the output is closed, or the buffer is flushed.

The last data written by an application could be held in a buffer that is not flushed until the finalizer is called. Finalizers are not called immediately, and they are not always called on program exit. Your application could exit and discard unwritten data in the buffer. It is important that either close() or flush() be called when you are through writing.

Inheritance

```
public class java.io.BufferedOutputStream
    extends FilterOutputStream
        ⇑
    public class java.io.FilterOutputStream
        extends OutputStream
            ⇑
        public class java.io.OutputStream
            extends Object
                ⇑
            public class java.lang.Object
```

Variables and constants

buf

```
protected byte buf[]
```

The storage location of buffered output data.

count

```
protected int count
```

The number of bytes being held in buf.

Constructors

```
public BufferedOutputStream(OutputStream out)
public BufferedOutputStream(OutputStream out,int size)
```

A BufferedOutputStream is constructed using out. The size parameter will determine the size of the output buffer—if it is not specified, a default size is used.

Methods

flush()

```
public void flush()
    throws IOException
```

This will flush the stream by forcing a write of any buffered output bytes.

write()

```
public void write(byte barray[],int offset,int length)
    throws IOException

public abstract void write(int bvalue)
    throws IOException
```

This method will write one or more bytes to the output. If bvalue is specified, it is written as a single byte. For barray, writing will begin at offset and continue for length bytes.

Example

A BufferedOutputStream can be inserted in front of any output stream. This example reads its own source code and, using a BufferedOutputStream to a file, makes a duplicate copy of it. Notice that close() is called to flush the buffer once the output has been written:

```
import java.io.*;
public class BoutStream {
    public static void main(String[] arg) {
        FileInputStream fis;
        FileOutputStream fos;
        BufferedOutputStream bos;
        try {
```

```
                    fis = new FileInputStream("BoutStream.java");
                    fos = new FileOutputStream("duplicate");
                    bos = new BufferedOutputStream(fos);
                    while(true) {
                            int character = fis.read();
                            if(character < 0)
                                    break;
                            bos.write(character);
                    }
                    bos.close();
            } catch(IOException e) {
                    e.printStackTrace();
            }
        }
    }
```

 For buffering output to a writer, see **BufferedWriter**. For buffering input from a stream, see **BufferedInputStream**.

BufferedReader

class java.io.BufferedReader

This class can be used to execute a buffered read from an input character stream. A block of bytes is read from the input stream, held in a buffer, and converted to characters as needed by the reader.

Efficiency

This class is designed for efficiency. The conversion from bytes to characters is done locally in the buffering instead of possibly being done during the physical read. It is possible, for some types of input streams, that expensive accesses are executed for each byte being read.

Extended by

```
    LineNumberReader
```

Inheritance

```
    public class java.io.BufferedReader
        extends Reader
            ⇑
        public class java.io.Reader
```

```
           extends Object
                 ⇑
           public class java.lang.Object
```

Constructors

```
           public BufferedReader(Reader input)
           public BufferedReader(Reader input,int bufferSize)
```

This will create a BufferedReader that uses input for data. If the bufferSize is not specified, the default value will be used.

Methods

close()

```
           public abstract void close()
              throws IOException
```

Closes the stream. Any attempt to access the file after this method has been called will cause an IOException to be thrown.

mark()

```
           public synchronized void mark(int readlimit)
```

This will mark the current position in the input stream; a subsequent call to reset() will restore the input to this position. The value of readlimit specifies the number of characters that can be read before the mark is discarded. For mark() to work, the return value from markSupported() must be true.

markSupported()

```
           public boolean markSupported()
```

This method returns true if the mark() and reset() methods can be used to alter the flow of the input stream.

read()

```
           public int read()
              throws IOException
```

```
           public int read(char carray[],int offset,int length)
              throws IOException
```

If no argument is specified, this will read one character and return it as an int. If carray is specified, the input data is placed in the array and the number of characters read is returned. Also, if carray is specified, the input data will appear beginning at carray[offset] for a maximum of length characters. This method will block as long as there is unread data available. A return value of −1 indicates a normal end to the input stream.

readLine()

```
public String readLine()
    throws IOException
```

Reads a line of text from the input stream. There are three forms of line terminator: a line feed character, a carriage return, or a carriage return immediately followed by a line feed. The returned string does not include the line termination.

ready()

```
public boolean ready()
    throws IOException
```

This method returns `true` if there is data that can be read without blocking and `false` otherwise.

reset()

```
public synchronized void reset()
    throws IOException
```

This will reposition the input stream to the location of the last call to `mark()`. The exception is thrown if there is no active mark. A mark will be removed (causing this method to throw an exception) if more bytes have been read than the number specified on the most recent call to `mark()`.

skip()

```
public long skip(long count)
    throws IOException
```

Calling this method makes a request to have the input stream skip over `count` number of input characters. The return value is the actual number of characters skipped.

Example

This example uses a `BufferedReader` to read its own source file and then echo it to standard output:

```java
import java.io.*;
public class BinReader {
    public static void main(String[] arg) {
        FileReader fr;
        BufferedReader br;
        try {
            fr = new FileReader("BinReader.java");
            br = new BufferedReader(fr);
            while(true) {
                int character = br.read();
```

```
                    if(character < 0)
                         break;
                    System.out.print((char)character);
               }
          } catch(IOException e) {
               e.printStackTrace();
          }
     }
}
```

 For buffering input from a stream, see **BufferedInputStream**. For buffering output to a writer, see **BufferedWriter**.

BufferedWriter

class java.io.BufferedWriter

This class supplies buffered writing of text for single characters, character arrays, or character strings. It uses an internal buffer to increase the efficiency of writing—the buffer size has a reasonable default, but its size can be specified.

The newline

This class writes text for the local system. This is why there is a `newLine()` method that should be used instead of the '\n' character.

 The last pieces of data written could be held in a buffer that is not to be flushed until the finalizer is called. Finalizers are not called immediately, and they are not always called on program exit. Your application could exit and discard unwritten data in the buffer. It is important that either `close()` or `flush()` be called when you are through writing.

Inheritance

```
public class java.io.BufferedWriter
     extends Writer
          ⇑
     public class java.io.Writer
          extends Object
               ⇑
          public class java.lang.Object
```

Constructors

```
public BufferedWriter(Writer out)
public BufferedWriter(Writer out,int size)
```

If size is not specified, the object will be created with a buffer of the default size.

Methods

close()

```
public abstract void close()
    throws IOException
```

This method will first call flush() and then close the output stream. Further calls to write() or flush() will not work. It is not an error to call close() more than once.

flush()

```
public abstract void flush()
    throws IOException
```

Any pending output is written. If there are any pending output characters anywhere in the output stream, they will be sent immediately to their final destination at the end of the stream chain.

newLine()

```
public void newLine()
    throws IOException
```

This will write a line separator to the stream. The output is determined by the contents of the system property line.separator (which may or may not be '\n').

write()

```
public abstract void write(char carray[], int offset,int length)
    throws IOException
```

```
public void write(int character)
    throws IOException
```

```
public void write(String string,
        int stroffset,int strlength)
    throws IOException
```

Writes an array of characters, a string of characters, or a single character to the stream. The lowest-order 16 bits of character are written to the stream as a single Unicode character (the high-order 16 bits are ignored). For an array, the writing will begin at carray[offset] and continue for length characters. If string is specified, the character beginning at stroffset and continuing for strlength characters will be written.

Example

A `BufferedWriter` can be inserted in front of any writer. This example reads its own source code and, using a `BufferedWriter`, makes a duplicate of it. Notice that `close()` is called to flush the buffer once the output has been written:

```
import java.io.*;
public class BoutWriter {
    public static void main(String[] arg) {
        FileReader fr;
        FileWriter fw;
        BufferedWriter bw;
        try {
            fr = new FileReader("BoutStream.java");
            fw = new FileWriter("duplicate");
            bw = new BufferedWriter(fw);
            while(true) {
                int character = fr.read();
                if(character < 0)
                    break;
                bw.write(character);
            }
            bw.close();
        } catch(IOException e) {
            e.printStackTrace();
        }
    }
}
```

 For buffering output to a stream, see **BufferedOutputStream**. For buffering input from a reader, see **BufferedReader**.

Button

class java.awt.Button

This is a graphical pushbutton with a textual label.

Inheritance

```
public class java.awt.Button
    extends Component
        ⇑
    public abstract class java.awt.Component
```

```
implements ImageObserver
implements MenuContainer
implements Serializable
extends Object
          ⇑
public class java.lang.Object
```

Constructors

```
public Button()
public Button(String label)
```

If no label is specified, the button will be blank.

Methods

addActionListener()

```
public void addActionListener(ActionListener listener)
```

Adds a listener to receive events from this button.

addNotify()

```
public void addNotify()
```

Creates the underlying system-dependent peer for this object. This method is not normally called by the application. It is called by the container.

getActionCommand()

```
public String getActionCommand()
```

This will return the command name of the button. By default, this is the label string, but could have been set to any value with the setActionCommand().

getLabel()

```
public String getLabel()
```

Returns the button label. See Example 1.

paramString()

```
protected String paramString()
```

Returns debugging information. The return string describes the internal state and values of this object.

processActionEvent()

```
protected void processActionEvent(ActionEvent event)
```

This method will be called so that the button events can be processed. It will be called only if a call has been made to `enableEvents()` or to `addActionListener()`.

processEvent()

```
protected void processEvent(AWTEvent event)
```

If the `event` is an `ActionEvent`, it is dispatched to all the listeners with a call to `processActionEvent()`—otherwise, this method calls `super.processEvent()`.

removeActionListener()

```
public void removeActionListener(ActionListener listener)
```

Removes a previously added action listener from the button.

setActionCommand()

```
public void setActionCommand(String command)
```

This sets the action command of the button. By default, it is the same as the button label.

setLabel()

```
public synchronized void setLabel(String label)
```

Sets the label string of the button.

Example 1

This is a simple applet that contains one button. Whenever this applet is executed by the applet viewer, it will print "Button pushed" each time the button is activated with the mouse:

```
import java.awt.*;
import java.awt.event.*;
import java.applet.*;
public class SimpleButton extends Applet
        implements ActionListener {
    public void init() {
        Button button = new Button("Push Me");
        add(button);
        button.addActionListener(this);
    }
    public void actionPerformed(ActionEvent event) {
        System.out.println("Button pushed");
    }
}
```

The applet implements the `ActionListener` interface so that it will be capable of receiving events. The button is created, and the `add()` method is used to attach it to the applet. The button's `addActionListener()` method is called to add the applet to the list of listeners of events from the button. Because this applet is a registered listener of button actions, the method `actionPerformed()` will be called for every button event. Figure B-5 shows what the applet looks like.

Figure B-5   A simple applet with a single button.

Example 2

If there is more than one button , we need to be able to determine which one was pressed. This applet has three buttons:

```
import java.awt.*;
import java.awt.event.*;
import java.applet.*;
public class ThreeButtons extends Applet
        implements ActionListener {
    public void init() {
        Button button;
        button = new Button("First");
        button.setActionCommand("1");
        button.addActionListener(this);
        add(button);
        button = new Button("Second");
        button.addActionListener(this);
        add(button);
        button = new Button("Third");
        button.addActionListener(this);
        add(button);
    }
    public void actionPerformed(ActionEvent event) {
        System.out.println("Command: " +
                event.getActionCommand());
    }
}
```

Its display window is shown in Figure B-6.

Figure B-6   An applet with three buttons.

Each button is created with a label, has its `addActionListener()` method called to add the applet to its list of listeners, and is attached to the applet with the `add()` method. The `actionPerformed()` method is called for each button event and prints out the action command string. Clicking the mouse on each of the buttons, in turn, generates this text:

```
Command: 1
Command: Second
Command: Third
```

The button labeled "First" had its command string changed with a call to `setActionCommand()`. The other two buttons use their labels as the string.

The other components are **Canvas**, **Checkbox**, **Choice**, **Label**, **List**, **Scrollbar**, **TextArea**, and **TextField**. The menu components are **Menu**, **MenuBar**, **MenuItem**, and **CheckboxMenuItem**.

byte

primitive data type

The Java byte data type is an eight-bit signed integer. It can hold values ranging from –127 to 128.

literals

Literals can be declared in decimal, octal, or hexadecimal. Any of these can be declared negative by being preceded with a minus sign.

The compiler checks the validity of the range of literal constants in the context in which they are being used. For example, one of these literal values will work while the other will be out of range:

```
byte b;
b = 20;
b = 200;   // Error
```

The value 20 is within the range held by a byte—the value 200 is not.

Base-10 literal

A number beginning with any digit other than 0 and containing nothing other than the digits 0 through 9 is a base-10 literal. Here are some examples:

```
82    -6    100
```

The largest positive value is 127, and the largest negative value is –128.

Hexadecimal literal

A hexadecimal (base-16) integer begins with 0x or 0X. It can contain the digits 0 through 9 and the letters A through F. The letters A through F (which represent the decimal values 10 through 15) can be either upper- or lowercase. A valid byte value can hold only two hexadecimal digits, since each digit defines four bits. Some examples of hexadecimal literals include:

```
0x022    0XB    0x9a    0X7F
```

Hexadecimal values greater than 0x7F are positive values that have no representation as a byte—the values from 0x80 through 0xFF will fit into a byte but represent negative values. The Java compiler will generate an error for this statement:

```
byte b = 0xFF;    // Error
```

The insertion of the value can be forced by using a cast, like this:

```
byte b = (byte)0xFF;
```

The values of a byte range from –128 to +127. The range of byte hexadecimal literals is from –0x7F to +0x7F—which does not include –128 (internally represented as 0x80). To write this value in hex, it is necessary to cast it this way:

```
byte b = (byte)0x80;
```

Octal literal

An octal (base-8) literal always has a 0 as its leftmost digit and contains only the digits 0 through 7. One octal digit represents, at most, three bits. These are examples of octal literals:

```
05    052    0177
```

Octal values greater than 0177 are positive values that have no representation as a byte—the values from 0200 through 0377 will fit into a byte but represent negative values. The Java compiler will generate an error for this statement:

```
byte b = 0377;    // Error
```

The insertion of the value can be forced by using a cast, like this:

```
byte b = (byte)0x377;
```

The range of values of a byte are from −128 to +127. The range of byte
octal literals is from −0177 to +0177 — which does not include −128 (internally represented as 0377). To write this value in octal, it is necessary to cast it
this way:

```
byte b = (byte)0377;
```

Example

This is a simple program that demonstrates the value-setting rules just
described:

```
public class ByteLiteral {
    static public void main(String arg[]) {
        byte b;
        b = 20;
        System.out.println("Assigning 20: " + b);
        b = -128;
        System.out.println("Assigning -128: " + b);
        b = 127;
        System.out.println("Assigning 127: " + b);
        b = 0x7F;
        System.out.println("Assigning 0x7F: " + b);
        b = -0x7F;
        System.out.println("Assigning -0x7F: " + b);
        b = (byte)0x80;
        System.out.println("Assigning (byte)0x80: " + b);
        b = (byte)0xFF;
        System.out.println("Assigning (byte)0xFF: " + b);
        b = 077;
        System.out.println("Assigning 077: " + b);
        b = 0100;
        System.out.println("Assigning 0100: " + b);
        b = 0177;
        System.out.println("Assigning 0177: " + b);
        b = -0177;
        System.out.println("Assigning -0177: " + b);
        /* These statements all cause out-of-range errors.
        b = 200;
        b = -0xFF;
```

```
                              b = 0xFF;
                              b = 0377;
                              */
                         }
                    }
```

 For other integer types, see **char**, **int**, **short**, and **long**.

Byte

class java.lang.Byte

This is a Java class wrapper for the primitive type `byte`.

Inheritance

```
public final class java.lang.Byte
      extends Number
           ⇑
      public class java.lang.Number
            implements Serializable
            extends Object
                 ⇑
            public class java.lang.Object
```

Variables and constants

MAX_VALUE

```
public final static byte MAX_VALUE
```

The maximum value that can be held in a byte. It is 127.

MIN_VALUE

```
public final static byte MIN_VALUE
```

The minimum value that can be held in a byte. It is −128.

TYPE

```
public final static Class TYPE
```

The Class object that represents the byte primitive type.

Constructors

```
public Byte(byte value)
public Byte(String string)
```

A `Byte` object can be constructed from either a byte value or the string representation of a byte value. If the `string` is not a valid byte value, a `NumberFormatException` will be thrown. The string must be a base-10 number —neither hex nor octal are valid.

Returned by

The methods `decode()` and `valueOf()` belonging to this class will create `Byte` objects.

Methods

byteValue()

```
public byte byteValue()
```

Returns the value of the `byte`.

decode()

```
public static Byte decode(String string)
    throws NumberFormatException
```

Converts `string` to a `Byte`. The string can be in the form of a base-10, hexadecimal, or octal constant. If the format of the number is not valid, a `NumberFormatException` is thrown.

doubleValue()

```
public double doubleValue()
```

Returns the value of the `byte` as a `double`.

equals()

```
public boolean equals(Object object)
```

Returns `true` if `object` is a `Byte` object and holds the same value as this `Byte`.

floatValue()

```
public float floatValue()
```

Returns the value of the `byte` as a `float`.

hashCode()

```
public int hashCode()
```

Returns the hashcode value for this object.

intValue()

```
public int intValue()
```

Returns the value of the `byte` as an `int`.

longValue()

```
public long longValue()
```

Returns the `byte` value as a `long`.

parseByte()

```
public static byte parseByte(String string)
    throws NumberFormatException

public static byte parseByte(String string,int radix)
    throws NumberFormatException
```

Converts `string` to a `byte`. The string must be all base-10 digits unless another radix is specified. If a radix greater than 10 is specified, the digits greater than 10 are A, B, C, and so on. If the format of the number is not valid, a `NumberFormatException` is thrown.

shortValue()

```
public short shortValue()
```

Returns the value as a `short`.

toString()

```
public String toString()
public static String toString(byte value)
```

Returns a `String` representation of the `value`. If the value is not specified, the internal value of the `Byte` object is used.

valueOf()

```
public static Byte valueOf(String string)
    throws NumberFormatException

public static Byte valueOf(String string,int radix)
    throws NumberFormatException
```

Converts the `string` to a `Byte` object. Unless specified otherwise, a radix of 10 is assumed. If the number cannot be parsed and evaluated to a number that fits into a `byte`, a `NumberFormatException` will be thrown.

 The wrappers of the other primitive types are **Boolean, Character, Integer, Short, Long, Float,** and **Double.**

ByteArrayInputStream

class java.io.ByteArrayInputStream

This class allows you read a RAM-resident byte array as an input stream.

Inheritance

```
public class java.io.ByteArrayInputStream
extends InputStream
            ⇑
    public class java.io.InputStream
            extends Object
                ⇑
        public class java.lang.Object
```

Variables and constants

buf

```
protected byte buf[]
```

A reference to the input data supplied by the constructor.

count

```
protected int count
```

The number of bytes currently held in buf.

pos

```
protected int pos
```

Index into buf of the next character to be read.

Constructors

ByteArrayInputStream()

```
public ByteArrayInputStream(byte barray[])
public ByteArrayInputStream(byte barray[],
        int offset,int length)
```

A ByteArrayInputStream is constructed using barray as its input source. If offset and length are specified, it will limit the input to the bytes beginning at barray[offset] and continuing for length characters. If offset and length are not specified, the entire array is used. The supplied array is not copied—the streamed data is read byte by byte from the array you supply.

Methods

available()

```
public synchronized int available()
```

This returns the number of bytes yet to be read from the array.

read()

```
public synchronized int read()
public synchronized int read(byte outArray[],
            int offset,int length)
```

Data can be read one byte at a time (and returned as an int value), or it can be read into an array. In either case, −1 is returned to indicate the end of the input. If outArray is specified, the data from the input array is placed into outArray beginning at the index offset and continuing for length bytes. When reading into outArray, the return value is the number of actual bytes read (which could be less than the number requested by length).

reset()

```
public synchronized void reset()
```

Resets the input stream back to its beginning.

skip()

```
public synchronized long skip(long count)
```

This will move the index of the next input byte forward by count bytes. The return value is the number of bytes actually skipped.

Example

This example uses the ByteArrayOutputStream to construct an array of bytes containing the 26 uppercase letters of the Latin alphabet. It then uses a ByteArrayInputStream to read the members of the array and print them to standard output:

```
import java.io.*;
public class ByteInOut {
    public static void main(String[] arg) {
        int character = 'A';
        ByteArrayOutputStream bout;
        bout = new ByteArrayOutputStream();
        for(int i=0; i<26; i++)
            bout.write(character++);
        byte[] abc = bout.toByteArray();
        ByteArrayInputStream bin;
        bin = new ByteArrayInputStream(abc);
```

```
            character = bin.read();
            while(character > 0) {
                System.out.print((char)character);
                character = bin.read();
            }
            System.out.println();
        }
    }
```

The character variable is initialized to 'A' and is incremented with each write. The `write()` method uses only the lower eight bits of its argument and places the value in its internal array. The method `toByteArray()` is used to get a reference to the array of bytes. The array of bytes is then used as the input data to a `ByteArrayInputStream`. Each byte is read and, after being cast to a `char` type, is printed to standard output. The output is simply:

```
ABCDEFGHIJKLMNOPQRSTUVWXYZ
```

Also see **ByteArrayOutputStream**.

ByteArrayOutputStream

class java.io.ByteArrayOutputStream

This class is an output stream that writes to a byte array in RAM. The array is automatically expanded as data is written to it.

Inheritance

```
public class java.io.ByteArrayOutputStream
    extends OutputStream
        ⇑
    public class java.io.OutputStream
        extends Object
            ⇑
        public class java.lang.Object
```

Variables and constants

buf

```
protected byte buf[]
```

As data is written to the stream, it is stored here.

count

```
protected int count
```

The number of bytes currently held in `buf`.

Constructors

```
public ByteArrayOutputStream()
public ByteArrayOutputStream(int size)
```

The `ByteArrayOutputStream` can optionally be constructed with a specified initial size of the internal array. If the size is not specified, a default will be assumed. The only consideration here is efficiency, because the internal array will automatically expand as needed.

Methods

reset()

```
public synchronized void reset()
```

Resets the count of the number of bytes of the internal buffer to zero. This way, you can start reusing the array without doing a reallocation.

size()

```
public int size()
```

This method returns the allocated size of the internal buffer.

toByteArray()

```
public synchronized byte[] toByteArray()
```

This method makes a copy of the internal buffer and returns it.

toString()

```
public String toString()
public String toString(String encoding)
     throws UnsupportedEncodingException
public String toString(int hibyte)   deprecated
```

This method will convert the byte values in the internal buffer to a string using the local default character encoding. If the encoding is specified, the named encoding is used instead of the local default encoding method.

The form that requires the `hibyte` to be specified is deprecated. It does the conversion by setting the high-order eight bits of the resulting characters to the `hibyte` value and using the raw byte values as the low-order eight bits.

write()

```
public synchronized void write(byte barray[],
        int offset,int length)
public synchronized void write(int bytevalue)
```

The bytes in barray from barray[offset] for a count of length are written to the output. If bytevalue is supplied, the lower eight bits are used as a single byte value for writing.

writeTo()

```
public synchronized void writeTo(OutputStream outstream)
    throws IOException
```

This will write the entire contents of the internal buffer to outstream.

 For an example, see **ByteArrayInputStream**.

bytecode

 For a description of the Virtual Machine and how it interprets bytecodes, see **Virtual Machine**.

Calendar

class java.util.Calendar

This is an abstract class designed to be used as the superclass of classes handling calendar arithmetic and the conversion dates from one format to another. An object of this class will contain a date setting that is capable of being accurate to the millisecond level.

Insufficient information

One of the primary jobs of this class is the conversion of date information. Circumstances can arise in which an insufficient amount of information is supplied from the input format to fill all the requirements of the output format. For example, the string "May 4, 1994" does not specify a time, so a default must be selected. The default date/time values are based on January 1, 1960, at 00:00:00 and any unspecified portion (day, month, or whatever) will draw from this default—our example would become May 4, 1994, at 00:00:00.

Contradictory information

It is possible to supply a date that has incorrect or contradictory information. For example, the date, "Friday, January 23, 1997", is in error because January 23 is actually a Thursday. To solve this, a set of precedences is used to allow the class to discard contradictory information. Certain combinations of data will take precedence and will be used to decide what parts of the input are to be discarded. What follows is a list of the precedence combinations. The process that reads the date string starts pattern matching at the top of the list, and if it finds a string that has a matching combination, it will ignore contradictory information that matches combinations further down the list. For example, if the input data contains both the month and the day of month, it will match the first entry in the table. If the input also contains a day-of-week value, it will be ignored because that value isn't defined until later in the table. Here are the precedence combinations:

- month + day-of-month
- month + week-of-month + day-of-week
- month + day-of-week-of-month + day-of-week
- day-of-year
- day-of-week + week-of-year

- hour-of-day
- ampm + hour-of-ampm

 For an example of how this list of formats is used, see **GregorianCalendar**.

Specifying time

An ambiguity can arise when one is specifying a time. The time "24:00:00" will become "00:00:00" and will trip the date over to the following day.

A.M. and P.M.

An ambiguity has always existed as to exactly where A.M. leaves off and P.M. begins. With this class, 12:00 A.M. is midnight, and 12:00 P.M. is noon.

Fields

These fields are used as a sort of "parametric overloading." A group of field value constants are used as arguments to some of the methods. The purpose of these is to specify which part of the date and time is to be operated on.

For example, the first argument to the `add()` method will be taken as a field-definition argument. It will be something like `Calendar.MINUTE` or `Calendar.HOUR`. This argument specifies which part of the date is to receive the addition.

Numeric value ranges

Many of the methods require numeric values for items that normally have names. This class defines constants so that you can use names for input, but the output values are numeric. A numeric value for a year is the full four-digit number. Months are numbered from 0 for January through 11 for December. Days of the month are numbered normally, 1 through 31. Hours of the day are numbered 0 through 23. Minutes are numbered 0 through 59. Seconds are numbered 0 through 59. The days of the week are numbered from 1 for Sunday through 7 for Saturday.

Input leniency

As date strings are scanned as input for conversion into numeric dates, the class will operate in one of two modes. When the leniency setting is `false`, every attempt is made to parse the date but a failure will throw an exception. If leniency is `true`, the parse will do the best it can, but it will ignore any errors or unknown characters in the input string. For example, the date February 31 would throw an exception without leniency—with leniency it would result in some day in March. In both cases, defaults are assumed for unspecified values.

Extended by

```
GregorianCalendar
```

Inheritance

```
public abstract class java.util.Calendar
     implements Serializable
     implements Cloneable
     extends Object
          ⇑
          public class java.lang.Object
```

Variables and constants

Most of these constants are self-explanatory. Many of them are used in the subclass GregorianCalendar.

AM

```
public final static int AM
```

This is a constant to be used with a 12-hour clock.

AM_PM

```
public final static byte AM_PM
```

This constant is used by other classes to specify a 12-hour clock form when converting time data to a string.

APRIL

```
public final static int APRIL
```

A month constant.

areFieldsSet

```
protected boolean areFieldsSet
```

The flag value indicating whether the time fields are set in the calendar.

AUGUST

```
public final static int AUGUST
```

A month constant.

DATE

```
public final static byte DATE
```

This is used in time fields as the name for the day of the month.

DAY_OF_MONTH

```
public final static byte DAY_OF_MONTH
```

This is used in time fields as the number of the day of the month.

DAY_OF_WEEK

```
public final static byte DAY_OF_WEEK
```

This is used in time fields as the day of the week.

DAY_OF_WEEK_IN_MONTH

```
public final static byte DAY_OF_WEEK_IN_MONTH
```

This is used in time fields as the day of the week in the month.

DAY_OF_YEAR

```
public final static byte DAY_OF_YEAR
```

This is used in time fields as the day of the year.

DECEMBER

```
public final static int DECEMBER
```

A month constant.

DST_OFFSET

```
public final static byte DST_OFFSET
```

This is used in time fields as the daylight standard time offset.

ERA

```
public final static byte ERA
```

This is used in time fields — its meaning is calendar specific.

FEBRUARY

```
public final static int FEBRUARY
```

A month constant.

FIELD_COUNT

```
public final static byte FIELD_COUNT
```

This is used in time fields. It is used for the creation of the time field array.

fields

```
protected int fields[]
```

This is used internally to hold the binary form of the date and time values.

FRIDAY

```
public final static int FRIDAY
```

A day constant.

HOUR

```
public final static byte HOUR
```

This is used in the time fields to specify the hour for a 12-hour clock.

HOUR_OF_DAY

```
public final static byte HOUR_OF_DAY
```

This is used in the time fields to specify the hour for a 24-hour clock.

isSet

```
protected boolean isSet[]
```

The flags to indicate whether or not a specific time field is set.

isTimeSet

```
protected boolean isTimeSet
```

The flag that indicates if the current time is set for the calendar.

JANUARY

```
public final static int JANUARY
```

A month constant.

JULY

```
public final static int JULY
```

A month constant.

JUNE

```
public final static int JUNE
```

A month constant.

MARCH

```
public final static int MARCH
```

A month constant.MAY

```
public final static int MAY
```

A month constant.

MILLISECOND

```
public final static byte MILLISECOND
```

This is used in the time fields to specify milliseconds.

MINUTE

```
public final static byte MINUTE
```

This is used in the time fields to specify minutes.

MONDAY

```
public final static int MONDAY
```

A day constant.

MONTH

```
public final static byte MONTH
```

This is used in the time fields to specify months.

NOVEMBER

```
public final static int NOVEMBER
```

A month constant.

OCTOBER

```
public final static int OCTOBER
```

A month constant.

PM

```
public final static int PM
```

This is a constant to be used with a 12-hour clock.

SATURDAY

```
public final static int SATURDAY
```

A day constant.

SECOND

```
public final static byte SECOND
```

This is used in the time fields to specify seconds.

SEPTEMBER

```
public final static int SEPTEMBER
```

A month constant.

SUNDAY

```
public final static int SUNDAY
```

A day constant.

THURSDAY

```
public final static int THURSDAY
```

A day constant.

time

```
protected long time
```

The binary form of the current date and time. It is a count of the number of milliseconds since midnight, January 1, 1960.

TUESDAY

```
public final static int TUESDAY
```

A day constant.

UNDECIMBER

```
public final static int UNDECIMBER
```

This is an artificial name that represents the thirteenth month of a lunar calendar.

WEDNESDAY

```
public final static int WEDNESDAY
```

A day constant.

WEEK_OF_MONTH

```
public final static byte WEEK_OF_MONTH
```

This is used in time fields to represent the week number of the month.

WEEK_OF_YEAR

```
public final static byte WEEK_OF_YEAR
```

This is used in time fields to represent the week number of the year.

YEAR

```
public final static byte YEAR
```

This is used in time fields to represent the year.

ZONE_OFFSET

```
public final static byte ZONE_OFFSET
```

This is used in time fields to represent the time zone offset from universal time.

Constructors

```
protected Calendar()
protected Calendar(TimeZone zone,Locale locale)
```

This is an abstract class, but there is an option beyond the default constructor. If zone and locale are not specified on a call to super(), they will default to TimeZone.getDefault() and the current locale.

Returned by

A Calendar object can be returned from a call to either Calendar.getInstance() or DateFormat.getCalendar().

Methods

add()

```
public abstract void add(byte field,int amount)
          throws IllegalArgumentException
```

Adds an incremental value to the time. If the amount is negative, it will subtract. The field determines the meaning of the amount. For example, if field is DAY, the amount is a number of days.

after()

```
public abstract boolean after(Object when)
```

Returns true if when is after the time of this object. The comparison is made by converting the two to universal time. The when argument is a Calendar object.

before()

```
public abstract boolean before(Object when)
```

Returns `true` if `when` is before the time of this object. The comparison is made by converting the two to universal time. The `when` argument is a `Calendar` object.

clear()

```
public final void clear()
```

```
public final void clear(byte field)
          throws IllegalArgumentException
```

Resets the specified `field` to its initial values. If no `field` is specified, it resets them all.

clone()

```
public Object clone()
```

Duplicates this object.

complete()

```
protected void complete()
          throws IllegalArgumentException
```

If any fields have not been set, this will fill them in with the default.

computeFields()

```
protected abstract void computeFields()
```

Sets the internal universal time to that of the internal fields and then reinitializes the field settings. This method is supplied so that a subclass can synchronize its internal field data with any new universal time value it receives. It is the inverse of `computeTime()`.

computeTime()

```
protected abstract void computeTime()
```

Sets the internal field value settings to the internal universal time. This method is supplied so that a subclass can synchronize its internal universal time with any new field values that it receives. It is the inverse of `computeFields()`.

equals()

```
public abstract boolean equals(Object when)
```

Returns `true` if `when` is a `Calendar` object of the same type as this one, and they are both set to the same universal time.

get()

```
public final int get(byte field)
            throws IllegalArgumentException
```

Returns the value for the specified field. This method can cause the time values to be calculated, which will not happen with `internalGet()`.

getAvailableLocales()

```
public static synchronized Locale[] getAvailableLocales()
```

Returns the list of locales for which `Calendars` are installed.

getFirstDayOfWeek()

```
public int getFirstDayOfWeek()
```

Returns the number of the day that is locally considered to be the first in the week—the one
that appears in the leftmost column of a wall calendar. In the U.S., it is Sunday.

getGreatestMinimum()

```
public abstract int getGreatestMinimum(byte field)
```

For the specified field, the method will return the largest possible minimum value. For the
Gregorian calendar, this is always the same as `getMinimum()`.

getInstance()

```
public static synchronized Calendar getInstance()
public static synchronized CalendargetInstance(Locale locale)
public static synchronized CalendargetInstance(TimeZone zone)
public static synchronized Calendar
            getInstance(TimeZone zone,Locale locale)
```

Returns a `Calendar` based on the specified time zone and locale. If the `zone` or `locale`
is not specified, the current defaults will be used.

getLeastMaximum()

```
public abstract int getLeastMaximum(byte field)
```

Returns the smallest possible maximum value of the field. For example, for the Gregorian
calendar, the field Calendar.DAY_OF_MONTH will return a value of 28.

getMaximum()

```
public abstract int getMaximum(byte field)
```

Returns the largest possible value of the `field`. An example for the Gregorian calendar
would be the field value `Calendar.DAYOFMONTH` returning 31.

getMinimalDaysInFirstWeek()

```
public int getMinimalDaysInFirstWeek()
```

Returns the minimum number of days that can be included in the first week of the year. A Gregorian calendar can begin with the last day of a week, so the return value would be 1. There are calendars that require the year to begin on the first day of the week—the return value would then be 7.

getMinimum()

```
public abstract int getMinimum(byte field)
```

This method returns the minimum possible value for the field type. For example, the Gregorian calendar would return 1 for Calendar.DAYOFMONTH.

getTime()

```
public final Date getTime()
```

Returns a Date object that contains the date and time of this object.

getTimeInMillis()

```
protected long getTimeInMillis()
```

Returns the internal setting of this Calendar as a count of the number of milliseconds since midnight, January 1, 1960.

getTimeZone()

```
public TimeZone getTimeZone()
```

Returns the TimeZone object of this Calendar.

internalGet()

```
protected final int internalGet(int field)
            throws IllegalArgumentException
```

This will return the numeric value of the specified field. This method will not cause the time values to be calculated, as is done with get().

isLenient()

```
public boolean isLenient()
```

Returns true if the date and time interpretations are to be lenient.

isSet()

```
public final boolean isSet(int field)
         throws IllegalArgumentException
```

This method returns `true` if the specified field has some value set for it, or `false` if it has been left to the default.

roll()

```
public abstract void roll(byte field,boolean up)
         throws IllegalArgumentException
```

To *roll* a date or time is to move it forward or backward (that is, up or down) one from its current position. For example, rolling the time 10:53 P.M. up by one hour would make it 11:53 P.M. Of course, rolling one field can force another to follow. If we roll our example one more time, it will move from 11:53 P.M. to 12:53 A.M. of the next day—the day will have rolled, which could cause the month and even the year to roll also.

Hours are rolled by using a 24-hour clock—that is, the values range from 0 through 23. Months vary in length, which can cause a roll to skip a month. For example, if the date of January 31 is rolled up by one month, the resulting date will be March 3. This is the result of rolling forward according to the number of days in January.

set()

```
public final void set(byte field,int value)
         throws IllegalArgumentException

public final void set(int year,int month,int date)

public final void set(int year,int month,int date,
         int hour,int minute)

public final void set(int year,int month,int date,
         int hour,int minute,int second)
```

This family of `set()` method forms can be used to set the various fields. Any individual field can be addressed in the first form of the `set()` method by naming the `field` and its `value`. The other three forms of `set()` can be used to set specific fields.

setFirstDayOfWeek()

```
public void setFirstDayOfWeek(byte value)
```

This sets which day is to be considered the first day of the week. In the U.S., it is Sunday.

setLenient()

```
public void setLenient(boolean setting)
```

Specifies the level of leniency to be used in analyzing textual data input. If the setting is true, the analysis will be lenient and indecipherable portions will be ignored — if the setting is false, analysis will be strict and an exception will be thrown in the event of an error.

setMinimalDaysInFirstWeek()

```
public void setMinimalDaysInFirstWeek(byte value)
```

This method sets the minimum number of days that can be in the first week of the year.

setTime()

```
public final void setTime(Date date)
```

This method will set the internal time to match that of date.

setTimeInMillis()

```
protected void setTimeInMillis(long millis)
```

This method will set the current time from the long value.

setTimeZone()

```
public void setTimeZone(TimeZone value)
```

Sets the TimeZone for this Calendar.

 For examples of some of the method calls, see **GregorianCalendar**. For other date and time classes, see **Date**.

CallableStatement

interface java.sql.CallableStatement

A CallableStatement object is a wrapper around an SQL stored procedure. It has methods to create the stored procedure and to execute it. It is a standard interface that defines a standard way of calling stored procedures for all databases.

Know your SQL types

Several methods are available for setting IN parameter values. The methods all have names in the form of setSomething() (the set methods are defined in the superinterface PreparedStatement). Care must be taken that the data types match the SQL types. For example, if the IN parameter has the SQL type INTEGER, then setInt() should be used. The "get" methods of this interface can be used to retrieve the value after the statement has been executed.

The OUT parameter, the one returned by getObject(), must have its type defined in a call to registerOutParameter() before the procedure can be executed—the types of the IN parameters are determined at the time they are set.

The parameterIndex

Once a stored procedure is defined, it can be controlled by using its parameters. The parameters can be used for input, output, or both. The methods used to access parameter values all use a parameterIndex value to specify which parameter is being addressed. The first parameter is index number one, not zero. The "set" methods are defined in the superinterface; the "get" methods are defined in this interface.

The exception

Every method of this interface is capable of throwing an SQLException. This means it will be necessary to call the methods of this class inside a try-catch block.

Inheritance

```
public interface java.sql.CallableStatement
        extends PreparedStatement
```

Constructors

Returned by

A class implementing this interface is returned from a call to Connection.prepareCall().

Methods

getBigDecimal()

```
public abstract BigDecimal getBigDecimal⇑
            int parameterIndex,int scale⇑
        throws SQLException
```

Returns the value of a NUMERIC parameter as a BigDecimal object. The scale value is the number of digits to the right of the decimal point. A null will be returned if the value of the parameter is SQL NULL.

getBoolean()

```
public abstract boolean getBoolean(int parameterIndex)
        throws SQLException
```

Returns the value of an SQL BIT parameter as a boolean. If the value is SQL NULL, the returned value is false.

getByte()

```
public abstract byte getByte(int parameterIndex)
    throws SQLException
```

Returns the value of an SQL TINYINT parameter as a byte. If the value is SQL NULL, the returned value is zero.

getBytes()

```
public abstract byte[] getBytes(int parameterIndex)
    throws SQLException
```

Returns the value of an SQL BINARY or VARBINARY parameter as a byte array. If the value is SQL NULL, a null is returned.

getDate()

```
public abstract Date getDate(int parameterIndex)
    throws SQLException
```

Returns the value of an SQL DATE parameter as a Date. If the value is SQL NULL, a null is returned.

getDouble()

```
public abstract double getDouble(int parameterIndex)
    throws SQLException
```

Returns the value of an SQL DOUBLE parameter as a double. If the value is SQL NULL, the return value is zero.

getFloat()

```
public abstract float getFloat(int parameterIndex)
    throws SQLException
```

Returns the value of an SQL FLOAT parameter as a float. If the value is SQL NULL, the return value is zero.

getInt()

```
public abstract int getInt(int parameterIndex)
    throws SQLException
```

Returns the value of an SQL INTEGER as an int. If the value is SQL NULL, the return value is zero.

getLong()

```
public abstract long getLong(int parameterIndex)
    throws SQLException
```

Returns the value of an SQL BIGINT parameter as a `long`. If the value is SQL NULL, the return value is zero.

getObject()

```
public abstract Object getObject(int parameterIndex
    throws SQLException
```

Returns the value of a parameter as a Java object. The type of object will correspond to the SQL type that was registered for this parameter in a call to `registerOutParameter()`.

 This method can be used to read database-specific types by having the parameter type defined as `java.sql.Types.OTHER`. This will allow the driver to create an object according to the database type.

getShort()

```
public abstract short getShort(int parameterIndex)
    throws SQLException
```

Returns the value of an SQL SMALLINT parameter as a `short`. If the value is SQL NULL, the return value is zero.

getString()

```
public abstract String getString(int parameterIndex)
    throws SQLException
```

Returns the value of an SQL CHAR, VARCHAR, or LONGVARCHAR parameter as a `String`. If the value is SQL NULL, a `null` is returned.

getTime()

```
public abstract Time getTime(int parameterIndex)
    throws SQLException
```

Returns the value of an SQL TIME parameter as a `Time` object. If the value is SQL NULL, a `null` is returned.

getTimestamp()

```
public abstract Timestamp getTimestamp(int parameterIndex)
    throws SQLException
```

Returns the value of an SQL TIMESTAMP parameter as a `Timestamp` object. If the value is SQL NULL, a `null` is returned.

registerOutParameter()

```
public abstract void registerOutParameter(
        int parameterIndex,int sqlType)
```

```
        throws SQLException

public abstract void registerOutParameter⇑
            int parameterIndex,int sqlType,int scale)
        throws SQLException
```

Registers the type of the specified output parameter. Its type will be determined by sqlType as one of the types defined in the Types class. This must be done before executing a stored procedure. For sqlType settings of NUMERIC or DECIMAL, it is necessary to specify the scale to define decimal point positioning.

wasNull()

```
public abstract boolean wasNull()
        throws SQLException
```

This method will return true if the last parameter read had the value SQL NULL.

 For information on the SQL database types, see **Types**. The other classes involved with executing SQL commands are **Statement** and **PreparedStatement**.

Canvas

class java.awt.Canvas

This is the simplest of all displayable components. It is an inactive rectangle filled with the background color. It can be used by the graphics methods for drawing directly to the display. It can be subclassed to construct components — for example, it can be used to create a button that contains a graphic instead of text.

Inheritance

```
public class java.awt.Canvas
    extends Component
        ⇑
    public abstract class java.awt.Component
        implements ImageObserver
        implements MenuContainer
        implements Serializable
        extends Object
            ⇑
        public class java.lang.Object
```

Constructors

```
public Canvas()
```

Methods

addNotify()

```
public void addNotify()
```

Creates the underlying system-dependent peer for this object. This method is not normally called by the application. It is called by the container.

paint()

```
public void paint(Graphics g)
```

This method, normally overridden, simply fills the rectangle with the background color.

Example

This example shows how to construct a Canvas object and have it displayed. The main() method of the CanvasDrawing class creates a Frame to hold the Canvas, and then it creates a SimpleCanvas to place in the Frame. The Canvas must be sized because it defaults to zero size.

```
import java.awt.*;
public class CanvasDrawing {
    public static void main(String[] arg) {
        Frame f = new Frame("Canvas");
        SimpleCanvas sc = new SimpleCanvas();
        sc.setSize(150,100);
        f.add(sc);
        f.pack();
        f.show();
    }
}
class SimpleCanvas extends Canvas {
    public void paint(Graphics g) {
        g.setColor(Color.lightGray);
        g.fillOval(0,0,getSize().width,getSize().height);
        g.setColor(Color.black);
        g.drawLine(0,0,getSize().width,getSize().height);
        g.drawLine(0,getSize().height,getSize().width,0);
    }
}
```

The SimpleCanvas class overloads the paint() method from its superclass to do the drawing. The paint() method is called each time the Canvas needs to be displayed. In this example, we use the Graphics object to set the colors and do some drawing that fits the size of the Canvas. The displayed window is shown in Figure C-1.

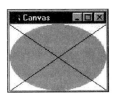

Figure C-1   A simple Canvas drawing.

CardLayout

class java.awt.CardLayout

This is a layout manager that will display only one component member at a time. You can think of it as a stack of cards where only one card is visible at any one time. Methods are available that can be used to change which card is visible.

A circular list

Displayable items are added to the layout manager in the order in which they are to appear with calls to next() and previous(). The list is circular. Calling the next() method while the last item added is being displayed will cause the first item to be displayed. Also, calling previous() while the first item is being displayed will cause the last item to be displayed.

Inheritance

```
public class java.awt.CardLayout
    implements LayoutManager2
    implements Serializable
    extends Object
        ⇑
    public class java.lang.Object
```

Constructors

```
public CardLayout()
public CardLayout(int horizontalGap,int verticalGap)
```

The values of horizontalGap and verticalGap specify the number of pixels left as a border between the displayed component and the edge of the window. If the gap values are not specified, they default to zero.

Methods

addLayoutComponent()

```
public void addLayoutComponent(Component comp,
        Object constraint)
```

```
public void addLayoutComponent(String name,
        Component component)  *** deprecated ***
```

This method will add a new component to the layout manager. The constraint is an iden-tifying tag that can be used by the show() method to cause the component to be displayed. The constraint must be a String object, or an IllegalArgumentException will be thrown. The second form—with the name argument—has been deprecated.

first()

```
public void first(Container parent)
```

Displays the first component.

getHgap()

```
public int getHgap()
```

Returns the value of the horizontal gap.

getLayoutAlignmentX()

```
public float getLayoutAlignmentX(Container parent)
```

Returns the horizontal alignment value. This value indicates how this component would pre-fer to be aligned with its neighbors. The far left is 0.0, and the far right is 1.0. This method always returns 0.5 to indicate the center.

getLayoutAlignmentY()

```
public float getLayoutAlignmentY(Container parent)
```

Returns the vertical alignment value. This value indicates how this component would prefer to be aligned with its neighbors. The top is 0.0, and the bottom is 1.0. This method always returns 0.5 to indicate the center.

getVgap()

```
public int getVgap()
```

Returns the value of the vertical gap.

invalidateLayout()

```
public void invalidateLayout(Container target)
```

Invalidates the layout. All positioning information acquired from the components will need to be reacquired, and the layout will need to be redone.

last()

```
public void last(Container parent)
```

Displays the last component.

layoutContainer()

```
public void layoutContainer(Container parent)
```

Recalculates the layout of the components.

maximumLayoutSize()

```
public Dimension maximumLayoutSize(Container parent)
```

Returns the maximum size that could be taken up by laying out the contained components in the parent container.

minimumLayoutSize()

```
public Dimension minimumLayoutSize(Container parent)
```

Returns the minimum size that could be used to lay out the contained components in the parent container.

next()

```
public void next(Container parent)
```

Displays the next component.

preferredLayoutSize()

```
public Dimension preferredLayoutSize(Container parent)
```

Returns the preferred size that would be used to lay out the contained components in the parent container.

previous()

```
public void previous(Container parent)
```

Displays the previous component.

removeLayoutComponent()

```
public void removeLayoutComponent(Component component)
```

Removes the specified component from the layout.

setHgap()

```
public void setHgap(int hgap)
```

Sets the size of the horizontal gap.

setVgap()

```
public void setVgap(int vgap)
```

Sets the size of the vertical gap.

show()

```
public void show(Container parent,String name)
```

Displays the named component. The name is the one assigned to the component in the call to addLayoutComponent().toString().

```
public String toString()
```

Returns a string description of the layout values.

Example

This example creates a group of Canvas objects and displays them in a panel using the CardLayout manager. Four buttons can be used to move the display from one to the other:

```
import java.awt.*;
import java.awt.event.*;
public class CardCanvases extends Frame
        implements ActionListener {
    CardLayout cardLayout = new CardLayout();
    Panel cardPanel = new Panel();
    Panel buttonPanel = new Panel();
    public static void main(String[] arg) {
        CardCanvases cc = new CardCanvases();
        cc.show();
    }
    CardCanvases() {
        Button button;
        cardPanel.setLayout(cardLayout);
        cardPanel.add("A",
        new CardCanvas("The first card",Color.pink));
        cardPanel.add("B",
        new CardCanvas("The second card",Color.yellow));
```

```
            cardPanel.add("C",
            new CardCanvas("The third card",Color.red));
            cardPanel.add("D",
            new CardCanvas("The fourth card",Color.green));
            buttonPanel.setLayout(new GridLayout(1,4));
            button = new Button("First");
            button.addActionListener(this);
            buttonPanel.add(button);
            button = new Button("<<");
            button.addActionListener(this);
            buttonPanel.add(button);
            button = new Button(">");
            button.addActionListener(this);
            buttonPanel.add(button);
            button = new Button("Last");
            button.addActionListener(this);
            buttonPanel.add(button);
            add("North",buttonPanel);
            add("Center",cardPanel);
            pack();
        }
    public void actionPerformed(ActionEvent event) {
        String command = event.getActionCommand();
        if(command.equals("First"))
            cardLayout.first(cardPanel);
        else if(command.equals("Last"))
            cardLayout.last(cardPanel);
        else if(command.equals("<<"))
            cardLayout.previous(cardPanel);
        else if(command.equals(">"))
            cardLayout.next(cardPanel);
    }
}
class CardCanvas extends Canvas {
    String name;
    Color color;
    CardCanvas(String name,Color color) {
        this.name = name;
        this.color = color;
        setSize(150,100);
    }
    public void paint(Graphics g) {
        g.setColor(color);
        g.fillOval(0,0,getSize().width,getSize().height);
```

```
                    g.setColor(Color.black);
                    g.drawString(name,0,50);
              }
        }
```

The window displayed by `CardCanvas`es is shown in Figure C-2. Using the `add()` method of the container, the `CardLayout` manager is given a collection of `CardCanvas` objects to be displayed. Each `CardCanvas` object will display a different string and a different color oval. A set of buttons — one for each of the positional controls — appears in a separate `Panel` at the top of the window. Each button is associated with a positional method and can be used to flip the displayed card from one to another.

Figure C-2   The CardLayout manager.

caret

^   ^=

The caret character is used in Java to perform the bitwise exclusive-OR operation. The operation can be used on any of the integer types. The operation sets bit values in its result according to the bit settings of its two operands. If two corresponding bits are alike (either both 1 or both 0), the resulting bit is 0 — if they are different, the resulting bit is 1.

There are two forms of the operator:

```
a = b ^ c;
```

For this form, the bit patterns of b and c are exclusive-ORed and the result is placed in a.

```
a ^= b;
```

In this form, the bit patterns of a and b are exclusive-ORed and the result is used to overwrite the value in a.

Example

This example performs an exclusive-OR with the values in b and c and puts
the result in a:

```
public class Caret {
    public static void main(String[] arg) {
        int b = 0x07E5F0FA;
        int c = 0x0E74FF05;
        int a = b ^ c;
        showBits("b=",b);
        showBits("c=",c);
        showBits("a=",a);
    }
    private static void showBits(String tag,int value) {
        String bstring = Integer.toBinaryString(value);
        while(bstring.length() < 32)
            bstring = "0" + bstring;
        System.out.println(tag + bstring);
    }
}
```

The values are all printed as a stream of bits (zero-padded on the left so
that they will line up vertically) displaying the fact that each resulting bit (in
the last line) is determined by whether or not the bits directly above it are different or the same. The output looks like this:

```
b=00000111111001011111000011111010
c=00001110011101001111111100000101
a=00001001100100010000111111111111
```

 For the other bit-wise operators, see **ampersand** and **bar**. Java also uses the
term "caret" to refer to the text-editing cursor in **TextArea**, **TextComponent**,
and **TextField**.

case

 See **Switch**.

casting

Casting is used to force an explicit conversion of data from one type to another. Casting has rules, and there is no way to force an invalid conversion. For instance, it is not possible to cast a reference to an `int`.

Ambiguity and validation

Depending on what type is being cast to what other type, the actual conversion can take place either at run time or at execution time. If the compiler can unambiguously determine exactly what sort of conversion is to take place, the compiler will generate the code to do the conversion and the run-time system has no decisions to make—it just runs the generated code. If it is possible that the conversion would be valid at run time, but the compiler cannot make the determination for certain, the compiler will generate code that causes the Virtual Machine to make the conversion at run time—but to also test and make sure the conversion is valid. If there is no way that the conversion could be valid, the compiler generates an error.

The syntax of a cast

To specify a cast, it is only necessary to prepend the item to be cast with the desired type in parentheses. For example, to force the conversion of an `int` to a `float`, do this:

```
int ivalue;
float fvalue;
fvalue = (float)ivalue;
```

Of course, in this example, the cast is unnecessary because the compiler would have automatically made the conversion. Times will arise, however, when you will need to use casting to tell Java what you want done. Here is an example of a conversion where casting is required:

```
byte bvalue;
int ivalue;
bvalue = (byte)ivalue;
```

Loss of data is possible when you are converting the `byte` to the `int`, so you will need to insert the cast to tell the compiler that you know what is being done.

Casting primitives

Here is an example of using casting to cause calculations to occur the way that you would like them to:

```
int a = 100;
int b = 200;
float result;
result = a / b;
```

In this example, the result will be zero. That is because the division will be done with the `int` values before the result is converted to a `float`. Using casting will change the way the calculation is done, and it will change the result.

```
result = (float)a / (float)b;
```

This will cause the values `a` and `b` to both be converted before the division takes place; the value of the result will be 0.5.

For conversion rules among the primitives, see **conversion** and **method**. For casting objects (instances of classes and interfaces), see **reference**.

catch

keyword

For examples and an explanation of exception handling using `catch`, see **try**.

Certificate

interface java.security.Certificate

This interface defines methods to be used in managing an identity certificate.

An identity certificate

An identity certificate is used to validate the ownership of a public key. It is a guarantee by one principal that a public key is the correct one for another principal. There is no need for the certificates to be of the same type—for example, a principal could use a PGP certification to validate an X.509 certificate. The different types of certification can share this same interface.

Another level of validation

Before an object with this interface can confidently be used to validate certificates, the object itself will be need to be validated. There is no inherent way of doing this—it is the responsibility of the party implementing this interface to provide a method of validating the object.

Inheritance

```
public interface java.security.Certificate
```

Constructors

Returned by

An array of `Certificate` objects is returned from `Identity.certificates()`.

Methods

decode()

```
public abstract void decode(InputStream stream)
    throws KeyException
    throws IOException
```

Decodes the certificate read from the input `stream`. The incoming certificate is expected to have the format returned by `getFormat()` and produced by `encode()`. A `KeyException` is thrown if the incoming certificate is malformed. An `IOException` will be thrown if there is an error reading from the `stream`.

encode()

```
public abstract void encode(OutputStream stream)
    throws KeyException
    throws IOException
```

The certificate is encoded and written to the `stream` in such a form that it could be read by `decode()`. A `KeyException` will be thrown if the certificate has not been initialized or has data missing. An `IOException` is thrown if there is an error writing to the `stream`.

getFormat()

```
public abstract String getFormat()
```

Returns the name of the coding format used by `encode()` and `decode()`. For example, it could be "PGP" or "X.509."

getGuarantor()

```
public abstract Principal getGuarantor()
```

Returns the `Principal` that certifies that this public key is the one belonging to the `Principal` that is returned from a call to `getPrincipal()`. For certain types of keys, the returned `Principal` here will be some sort of certifying authority being used to guarantee the key.

getPrincipal()

```
public abstract Principal getPrincipal()
```

Returns the `Principal` that is being certified as being the owner of the key.

getPublicKey()

```
public abstract PublicKey getPublicKey()
```

Returns the `PublicKey` that is having its ownership certified.

toString()

```
public abstract String toString(boolean detailed)
```

Returns a string that represents the contents of the `Certificate`. If `detailed` is true, the string will contained detailed information.

 Also see **Key**, **PublicKey**, **PrivateKey**, **KeyPair**, and **KeyPairGenerator**. For a listing of the algorithm names, see **security**.

char

primitive data type

The `char` primitive data type is a 16-bit unsigned integer. It is the only unsigned data type in Java. The `char` data type was designed to hold a Unicode character value.

 Although a `char` is an integer and can be used to hold numeric values and perform arithmetic, there is almost no need to ever do so. Every value that can be held in a `char` can also be held in an `int`. In fact, no matter what kind of value you put into a `char`, Java will always treat it as a Unicode character. The only way that the value inside a `char` variable can be printed is by first converting the value to another form—such as an `int`—since any of the Java formatting and printing functions will convert the `char` value into its Unicode character equivalent. Of course, there are times when you will need to do character arithmetic, and the `char` data type is perfect for that.

Table C-1 lists all the ways in which the maximum and minimum values for a `char` can be declared.

Table C-1	Different Forms of Declaring Maximum and Minimum Values	
Type	**Maximum**	**Minimum**
Unicode	\uFFFF	\u0000
Decimal	32767	-0
Octal	0177777	0
Hexadecimal	0xFFFF	0x0000
Predefined	Character.MAX_VALUE	Character.MIN_VALUE

The letter J

This program demonstrates several ways to initialize a char to an uppercase J:

```
public class CharLiteral {
    static public void main(String arg[]) {
        char c;
        c = 74;
        System.out.println("Assigning 74: " + c);
        c = 'J';
        System.out.println("Assigning 'J': " + c);
        c = 0x4A;
        System.out.println("Assigning 0x4A: " + c);
        c = 0112;
        System.out.println("Assigning 0112: " + c);
        c = '\112';
        System.out.println("Assigning '\\112': " + c);
        c = '\u004A';
        System.out.println("Assigning '\\u004A': " + c);
        c = 32767;
        System.out.println("Assigning 32767: " + c);
        c = 0x8000;
        System.out.println("Assigning 0x8000: " + c);
        c = 0xFFFF;
        System.out.println("Assigning 0xFFFF: " + c);
        c = 0177777;
        System.out.println("Assigning 0177777: " + c);
    }
}
```

As you can see, several ways exist to initialize a char variable, but no matter how you do it, the contents will always be interpreted by Java to be a displayable character. This is the output from the program:

```
Assigning 74: J
Assigning 'J': J
Assigning 0x4A: J
Assigning 0112: J
Assigning '\112': J
Assigning '\u004A': J
Assigning 32767: ?
Assigning 0x8000: ?
Assigning 0xFFFF: ?
Assigning 0177777: ?
```

Some values did not display at all (they were converted to '?' characters in the output). That is because Java interpreted them as Unicode characters but did not have any displayable graphics to use for those specific values.

Character literal

A character literal is surrounded by single quotes. Inside the quotes is either a single character or an escape sequence. The single character form is the simplest—here are some examples:

```
'J'    '$'    'r'
```

 It is possible to use escape sequences inside quotes of a character literal to specify any character—regardless of whether the character can or cannot be typed in and displayed. The escape character used for this is a backslash. A special set is defined of single-character escape sequences. See **escapes**.

Decimal literal

A number beginning with any digit other than 0, and containing only the digits 0 through 9, is a decimal (base-10) literal. Some examples of decimal char literals:

```
82    12910    852
```

Hexadecimal literal

A hexadecimal (base-16) integer begins with 0x or 0X. It can contain the digits 0 through 9 and the letters A through F. The letters A through F (which represent the decimal values 10 through 15) can be either upper- or lowercase. Some examples of hexadecimal char literals are:

```
0x022    0X71B9    0x99a    0X2a
```

Octal literal

An octal (base-8) literal begins with a 0 and contains only the digits 0 through 7. One octal digit represents, at most, three bits. These are examples of octal literals:

```
05    052    017777
```

 For a general discussion on character-constant escape sequences, see **escapes**. For a wrapper class that defines special char operations, see **Character**. For information on character values and their meanings, see **Unicode**. For other integer types, see **byte**, **short**, **int**, and **long**.

Character

class java.lang.Character

The is the Java wrapper class of the `char` data type and can be used for general character manipulations.

Inheritance

```
public final class java.lang.Character
      implements Serializable
      extends Object
           ⇑
      public class java.lang.Object
```

Variables and constants

COMBINING_SPACING_MARK

```
public final static byte COMBINING_SPACING_MARK
```

A character type.

CONNECTOR_PUNCTUATION

```
public final static byte CONNECTOR_PUNCTUATION
```

A character type.

CONTROL

```
public final static byte CONTROL
```

A character type.

CURRENCY_SYMBOL

```
public final static byte CURRENCY_SYMBOL
```

A character type.

DASH_PUNCTUATION

```
public final static byte DASH_PUNCTUATION
```

A character type.

DECIMAL_DIGIT_NUMBER

```
public final static byte DECIMAL_DIGIT_NUMBER
```

A character type.

ENCLOSING_MARK

```
public final static byte ENCLOSING_MARK
```

A character type.

END_PUNCTUATION

```
public final static byte END_PUNCTUATION
```

A character type.

FORMAT

```
public final static byte FORMAT
```

A character type.

LETTER_NUMBER

```
public final static byte LETTER_NUMBER
```

A character type.

LINE_SEPARATOR

```
public final static byte LINE_SEPARATOR
```

A character type.

LOWERCASE_LETTER

```
public final static byte LOWERCASE_LETTER
```

A character type.

MATH_SYMBOL

```
public final static byte MATH_SYMBOL
```

A character type.

MAX_RADIX

```
public final static int MAX_RADIX
```

The maximum radix available for conversion to and from Strings. The maximum value is 36.

MAX_VALUE

```
public final static char MAX_VALUE
```

The maximum value that can be contained in a char type. The maximum value is '\uFFFF'.

MIN_RADIX

```
public final static int MIN_RADIX
```

The minimum radix available for conversion to and from Strings. The minimum value of a radix is 2.

MIN_VALUE

```
public final static char MIN_VALUE
```

The minimum value that can be contained in a `char` type. The minimum value is '\u0000'.

MODIFIER_LETTER

```
public final static byte MODIFIER_LETTER
```

A character type.

MODIFIER_SYMBOL

```
public final static byte MODIFIER_SYMBOL
```

A character type.

NON_SPACING_MARK

```
public final static byte NON_SPACING_MARK
```

A character type.

OTHER_LETTER

```
public final static byte OTHER_LETTER
```

A character type.

OTHER_NUMBER

```
public final static byte OTHER_NUMBER
```

A character type.

OTHER_PUNCTUATION

```
public final static byte OTHER_PUNCTUATION
```

A character type.

OTHER_SYMBOL

```
public final static byte OTHER_SYMBOL
```

A character type.

PARAGRAPH_SEPARATOR

```
public final static byte PARAGRAPH_SEPARATOR
```

A character type.

PRIVATE_USE

```
public final static byte PRIVATE_USE
```

A character type.

SPACE_SEPARATOR

```
public final static byte SPACE_SEPARATOR
```

A character type.

START_PUNCTUATION

```
public final static byte START_PUNCTUATION
```

A character type.

SURROGATE

```
public final static byte SURROGATE
```

A character type.

TITLECASE_LETTER

```
public final static byte TITLECASE_LETTER
```

A character type.

TYPE

```
public final static Class TYPE
```

The Class object representing the primitive type char.

UNASSIGNED

```
public final static byte UNASSIGNED
```

A character type.

UPPERCASE_LETTER

```
public final static byte UPPERCASE_LETTER
```

A character type.

Constructors

```
public Character(char value)
```

A `Character` object is constructed that contains the specified `value`.

Methods

charValue()

```
public char charValue()
```

Returns the `char` value of this object.

digit()

```
public static int digit(char character,int radix)
```

Returns the numeric value of the `character`. The `character` must be a digit in the range of the specified `radix`, or −1 is returned.

The `radix` value must be between `MIN_RADIX` and `MAX_RADIX`. To be a digit, the `character` must be a Unicode decimal digit or a letter of the Latin alphabet (A is ten, B is eleven, and so on). Uppercase and lowercase letters are treated the same. The value of each `character` must fall within the range limitations set by `radix`.

equals()

```
public boolean equals(Object object)
```

Returns `true` if the argument `object` is the same as this. They are considered the same if they both are `Character` objects and contain the same value.

forDigit()

```
public static char forDigit(int digit,int radix)
```

Given the value of a digit, and the radix for the digit, returns the Unicode character for that digit. If the digit-radix combination is not valid, the return value is zero.

getNumericValue()

```
public static int getNumericValue(char character)
```

Returns the numeric value assigned to the `character` whenever it is used as a digit in a numeric character string. The `character` can be one used for any base up to `MAX_RADIX`. The radix need not be specified, because every character has its unique value no matter what the radix—for example, the character 'A' will always return the value 10, and the character 'j' will return 19.

If the `character` has no assigned numeric value, −1 is returned. If the character is one with a special fractional value (that cannot be represented as an `int`), −2 is returned.

getType()

```
public static int getType(char character)
```

Returns the type of the `character`. It will be one of the constants defined in the `Character` class.

hashCode()

```
public int hashCode()
```

Returns the hashcode for this `Character` object.

isDefined()

```
public static boolean isDefined(char character)
```

Returns `true` if `character` is a valid Unicode character; otherwise, returns `false`.

isDigit()

```
public static boolean isDigit(char character)
```

Returns `true` if the `character` is a Unicode digit and `false` if it is not. The basic Latin digits (the ASCII digits) have the Unicode values \u0030 through \u0039. A Unicode character is considered to be a digit if its Unicode category is "Nd." For a list of the Unicode digit characters, see **Unicode**.

isIdentifierIgnorable()

```
public static boolean
    isIdentifierIgnorable(char character)
```

Returns `true` if the character should be ignored in a Java identifier or in a Unicode identifier. Table C-2 lists the characters that will cause this method to return `true`.

Table C-2   Ignorable Characters

Range	Description
\u0000 – \u0008	ISO control characters
\u000E – \u001B	ISO control characters
\u007F – \u009F	ISO control characters
\u200C – \u200F	Join controls
\u200A – \u200E	Bidirectional controls
\u206A – \u206F	Format controls
\uFEFF	Zero-width no-break space

isISOControl()

```
public static boolean isISOControl(char character)
```

Returns true if the character is an ISO control character. The return value will be true for any value from \u0000 through \u001F or from \u007F through \u009F.

isJavaIdentifierPart()

```
public static booleanisJavaIdentifierPart(char character)
```

Returns true if the character is one that can be included in a Java identifier (but not necessarily be the leading character of the identifier). To qualify, it must be one of these:

- A letter
- A currency symbol (such as the dollar symbol)
- A connecting punctuation character (such as the underscore)
- A digit
- A numeric letter (such as a Roman numeral character)
- A combining mark
- A nonspacing mark
- An ignorable control character

isJavaIdentifierStart()

```
public static boolean
    isJavaIdentifierStart(char character)
```

Returns true if the character is one that can be used as the leading character in a Java identifier. To qualify, it must be one of these:

- A letter
- A currency symbol (such as the dollar symbol)
- A connecting punctuation character (such as the underscore)

isJavaLetter()   deprecated

```
public static boolean isJavaLetter(char character)
```

Returns true if the character is a Java letter, a currency symbol, or the underscore character. This method is deprecated as of version 1.1. Use isJavaIdentifierStart().

isJavaLetterOrDigit()   deprecated

```
public static boolean isJavaLetterOrDigit(char character)
```

Returns true if the character is a valid Java letter (as defined by isJavaLetter()) or a digit. This method is deprecated as of version 1.1. Use isJavaIdentifierPart().

isLetter()

```
public static boolean isLetter(char character)
```

Returns `true` if the character is a letter.

A character is considered to be a letter if it is the Unicode category "Lu," "Ll," "Lt," "Lm," or "Lo."

isLetterOrDigit()

```
public static boolean isLetterOrDigit(char character)
```

Returns `true` if the `character` is a letter or a digit. A character is a letter or a digit if either `isLetter()` or `isDigit()` returns `true`. In other words, a Unicode character is considered to be a letter or a digit if it is the category "Lu," "Ll," "Lt," "Lm," "Lo," or "Nd."

isLowerCase()

```
public static boolean isLowerCase(char character)
```

Returns `true` if the `character` is lowercase.

A character is considered to be lowercase if its Unicode category is "Ll."

isSpace()   deprecated

```
public static boolean isSpace(char character)
```

Returns `true` if the character is an ISO-LATIN-1 whitespace character. This method is deprecated as of version 1.1. This method handles only ISO-LATIN-1 space characters—use `isWhitespace()`.

isSpaceChar()

```
public static boolean isSpaceChar(char character)
```

Returns `true` if the `character` is a Unicode space character.

A character is considered to be a space character if its Unicode category is "Zs," "Zl," or "Zp."

isTitleCase()

```
public static boolean isTitleCase(char character)
```

Returns `true` if the `character` is a titlecase character.

A character is considered to be a titlecase character if its Unicode category is "Lt."

isUnicodeIdentifierPart()

```
public static booleanisUnicodeIdentifierPart(char character)
```

Returns `true` if this character is valid as part of a Unicode identifier. To qualify, it must be one of the following:

- A letter
- A connecting punctuation character (such as underscore)
- A digit
- A numeric letter (such as a Roman numeral character)
- A combining mark
- A nonspacing mark
- An ignorable control character

isUnicodeIdentifierStart()

```
public static booleanisUnicodeIdentifierStart(char character)
```

Returns `true` if the `character` is one that could be used as the first character in a Unicode identifier—which can happen only if it is a Unicode letter.

isUpperCase()

```
public static boolean isUpperCase(char character)
```

Returns `true` if the `character` is uppercase.
A character is considered to be a titlecase character if its Unicode category is "Lu." This includes the Unicode values \u0042 through \u005A (the ASCII characters A through Z).

isWhitespace()

```
public static boolean isWhitespace(char character)
```

Returns `true` if the `character` is a whitespace character in the Java language. To be a whitespace character, it can be any one of the following:

- A character in the Unicode category "Zs" (space separator) but not in the range \u00A0 or \uFEFF (a break space)
- A unicode line separator (category "Zl")
- A unicode paragraph separator (category "Zp")
- A horizontal tab (\u0009)
- A line feed (\u000A)
- A vertical tab (\u000B)
- A form feed (\u000C)
- A carriage return (\u000D)
- A file separator (\u001C)
- A group separator (\u001D)
- A record separator (\u001E)
- A unit separator (\u001F)

toLowerCase()

```
public static char toLowerCase(char character)
```

The `character` is converted to its lowercase equivalent If there is no lowercase form of the character, it is returned unchanged.

Particular Unicode characters in the range \u2000 through \u2FFF will be mapped to lowercase (Roman numeral digits, for example) although the characters themselves will not return `true` from `isUpperCase()`.

toString()

```
public String toString()
```

Returns a `String` representation of the character.

toTitleCase()

```
public static char toTitleCase(char character)
```

The `character` is converted to its titlecase equivalent. If the character has no title case, it is returned unchanged.

toUpperCase()

```
public static char toUpperCase(char character)
```

The `character` is converted to its uppercase equivalent. If the character has no upper case, it is returned unchanged.

 For more on the primitive data type, see **char**. For more on the Unicode character set, see **Unicode**. The wrappers of the other primitive types are **Boolean, Byte, Integer, Short, Long, Float,** and **Double**.

CharacterIterator

Interface java.text.CharacterIterator

This interface defines a standard set of methods that can be used to move back and forth over text. A class implementing this interface will need to create the methods required to read and return the character values. There is no writing to the text—only reading from it.

Beginning and ending

The implementing class will maintain an internal index that is manipulated by the various methods. This index acts like a cursor that tracks a current position in the text. The method `first()` sets the index to the first character of the text. The method `last()` will set the index to the last character in the text.

Implemented by

```
StringCharacterIterator
```

Inheritance

```
public interface java.text.CharacterIterator
    extends Cloneable
        ⇑
public interface java.lang.Cloneable
```

Variables and constants

DONE

```
public final static char DONE
```

This is the constant value returned when an iterator has come to the end of the text by moving either forward or backward. Its value is '\uFFFF', which, according to Unicode, is an invalid value that should never occur.

Constructors

Returned by

An object that implements this interface can be returned from a call to `BreakIterator.getText()`.

Methods

clone()

```
public abstract Object clone()
```

Returns a duplicate of the object implementing this interface.

current()

```
public abstract char current()
```

Returns the character at the current position — or returns DONE if the current position is beyond the end of the text.

first()

```
public abstract char first()
```

Sets the current index to the first character and returns the character.

getBeginIndex()

```
public abstract int getBeginIndex()
```

Returns the starting index of the text.

getEndIndex()

```
public abstract int getEndIndex()
```

Returns the index of the first character beyond the end of the text.

getIndex()

```
public abstract int getIndex()
```

Returns the current index.

last()

```
public abstract char last()
```

Sets the index to the last character in the text—that is, sets the index to endIndex() −1.

next()

```
public abstract char next()
```

The index is incremented, and the character at the new index position is returned. If the index, after being incremented, is beyond the end of the text, the current index is set to one past the end of text and the value DONE is returned.

previous()

```
public abstract char previous()
```

The index is decremented, and the character at the new index position is returned. If the new index value is before the beginning of the text, the index is set to the first character and the value DONE is returned.

setIndex()

```
public abstract char setIndex(int position)
```

The index is set to the specified position, and the character at the new index is returned. If the requested position is outside the valid range, an IllegalArgumentException is thrown.

 For an example of class implementing this interface, see **BreakIterator**. For iteration through the characters in a String, see **StringCharacterIterator**.

CharArrayReader

class java.io.CharArrayReader

This class is an input stream wrapper around a character array.

Inheritance

```
public class java.io.CharArrayReader
    extends Reader
      ⇑
    public class java.io.Reader
       extends Object
         ⇑
       public class java.lang.Object
```

Variables and constants

buf

```
protected char buf[]
```

The internal array from which char values are read.

count

```
protected int count
```

The number of characters in buf.

markedPos

```
protected int markedPos
```

The index to the currently marked position in buf.

pos

```
protected int pos
```

The index of the next character to be read from buf.

Constructors

CharArrayReader()

```
public CharArrayReader(char carray[])

public CharArrayReader(char carray[],int offset,int length)
```

This will create a `CharArrayReader` that will use `carray` as its input. If `offset` and `length` are supplied, the input will begin at `carray[offset]` and continue for `length` characters. The `carray` data is not copied—the characters are read directly from the array that you supply.

Methods

close()

```
public void close()
```

Closes the stream.

mark()

```
public void mark(int readlimit)
    throws IOException
```

This will mark the current position in the stream such that a subsequent call to `reset()` will cause the internal read cursor to return to this location. The `readlimit` is the maximum number of input characters that can be read before the marked position is lost.

markSupported()

```
public boolean markSupported()
```

This method always returns `true` to indicate that the `CharArrayReader` supports `mark()` and `reset()`.

read()

```
public int read()
    throws IOException
```

```
public int read(char barray[],int offset,int length)
    throws IOException
```

If no argument is specified, a single character is read and returned as an `int`. If `barray` is specified, `length` characters are read and placed into the array beginning at `barray[offset]`. A return of −1 indicates no characters were read. If characters are read into the array, the actual number of characters read is returned.

ready()

```
public boolean ready()
    throws IOException
```

This method returns `true` if a call to `read()` would return at least one character.

reset()

```
public void reset()
```

```
        throws IOException
```

This will move the input marker to the position of the most recent call to `mark()`. If no call has been made to `mark()`, the input is returned to the beginning.

skip()

```
    public long skip(long count)
        throws IOException
```

This will cause the input cursor to skip over `count` characters. The return value is the actual number of characters skipped.

 To read characters from a `String` object, see **StringReader**. To write to an array of characters, see **CharArrayWriter**.

CharArrayWriter

class java.io.CharArrayWriter

This class is an output stream that writes to an internal RAM-resident array. The size of the array expands automatically as data is written to it.

Inheritance

```
    public class java.io.CharArrayWriter
        extends Writer
            ⇑
        public class java.io.Writer
            extends Object
                ⇑
            public class java.lang.Object
```

Variables and constants

buf

```
    protected char buf[]
```

The internal array to store data written to the stream.

count

```
    protected int count
```

The number of characters that have been written to `buf`.

Constructors

CharArrayWriter()

```
public CharArrayWriter()

public CharArrayWriter(int initialSize)
```

If no initialSize is supplied, the internal array will be of the default size. The default size in Java 1.1 is 32.

Methods

close()

```
public void close()
```

This method closes the stream so that it can no longer accept data, but the internal data remains intact and accessible.

flush()

```
public void flush()
```

Flushes the stream.

reset()

```
public void reset()
```

Sets the number of characters to zero and restarts writing at the beginning. The internally allocated array remains intact—there is no reallocation of RAM.

size()

```
public int size()
```

Returns the count of the number of characters that can be held in the internal array without requiring a new RAM allocation.

toCharArray()

```
public char[] toCharArray()
```

Creates and returns an array that holds the data that has been written into the internal buffer.

toString()

```
public String toString()
```

Creates and returns a String object from the array of characters that have been written to the internal buffer.

write()

```
public void write(char carray[],int offset,int length)

public void write(int character)

public void write(String string,int offset,int length)
```

These methods are used to write characters to this stream. If `carray` or `string` is specified, the characters beginning at the index `offset` are written for a count of `length` characters. If `character` is specified, its lower 16 bits are written as a `char` value. All characters written are appended to the end of the current data.

writeTo()

```
public void writeTo(Writer outstream)
    throws IOException
```

This method writes all the characters that it is holding in its internal buffer to `outstream`.

 To write characters to a `String` object, see **StringWriter**. To read from an array of characters, see **CharArrayReader**.

CharConversionException

class java.io.CharConversionException

This is the base class for the character conversion exceptions.

Inheritance

```
public class java.io.CharConversionException
    extends IOException
        ⇑
    public class java.io.IOException
        extends Exception
            ⇑
        public class java.lang.Exception
            extends Throwable
                ⇑
            public class java.lang.Throwable
                implements Serializable
                extends Object
                    ⇑
                public class java.lang.Object
```

Constructors

```
public CharConversionException()
public CharConversionException(String message)
```

If the message string is supplied, it is used as a detailed message describing this particular exception.

Checkbox

class java.awt.Checkbox

A Checkbox is a graphical object that has a Boolean state. The state can be changed by the user. It is normally used to enable the user to select or deselect some option within an application.

Inheritance

```
public class java.awt.Checkbox
      implements ItemSelectable
      extends Component
            ⇑
      public class java.awt.Component
            implements ImageObserver
            implements MenuContainer
            implements Serializable
            extends Object
                  ⇑
            public class java.lang.Object
```

Constructors

```
public Checkbox()
public Checkbox(String label)
public Checkbox(String label,boolean state)
public Checkbox(String label,boolean state,
        CheckboxGroup group)
public Checkbox(String label,CheckboxGroup group,
        boolean state)
```

The constructor of a checkbox can have the identifying label specified, along with whether its initial state is true or false. The name of a CheckBoxGroup can be specified; doing so will enable this checkbox to interact with other checkboxes (to make things work like radio-button groups). The default is a checkbox without a label that is in the `false` state and is not a member of a `CheckBoxGroup`.

Returned by

Objects of this class are returned from `CheckboxGroup.getCurrent()` and `CheckboxGroup.getSelectedCheckbox()`.

Methods

addItemListener()

```
public void addItemListener(ItemListener listener)
```

This will add an `ItemListener`. The job of the `ItemListener` is to receive events from the `Checkbox`. There can be more than one `ItemListener` for a single `Checkbox`.

addNotify()

```
public void addNotify()
```

Creates the underlying system-dependent peer for this object. This method is not normally called by the application. It is called by the container.

getCheckboxGroup()

```
public CheckboxGroup getCheckboxGroup()
```

Returns the `CheckBoxGroup`. If this `Checkbox` is not in a group, `null` is returned.

getLabel()

```
public String getLabel()
```

Returns the `String` that is the label of this `Checkbox`. If this `Checkbox` has no label, `null` is returned.

getSelectedObjects()

```
public Object[] getSelectedObjects()
```

Returns `null` if the `Checkbox` is not selected. If it is selected, an array of size one will be returned that contains the `Checkbox` label.

getState()

```
public boolean getState()
```

Returns the current state of this `Checkbox` — either `true` or `false`. See Example 2.

paramString()

```
protected String paramString()
```

Returns debugging information. The return string describes the internal state and values of this object.

processEvent()

```
protected void processEvent(AWTEvent e)
```

Processes events on this Checkbox. If the event is an ItemEvent, it invokes the processItemEvent() method; otherwise, it calls processEvent() of the superclass.

processItemEvent()

```
protected void processItemEvent(ItemEvent event)
```

This method is called whenever an event occurs on this Checkbox. The Checkbox dispatches the event to its ItemListener objects.

This method will be called by the system only if an ItemListener has been added by a call to addItemListener() or a call has been made to enableEvents().

removeItemListener()

```
public void removeItemListener(ItemListener listener)
```

Removes listener from the list of objects that receives events from this checkbox.

setCheckboxGroup()

```
public void setCheckboxGroup(CheckboxGroup group)
```

This will set the CheckboxGroup for this Checkbox.

setLabel()

```
public synchronized void setLabel(String label)
```

This method sets the label for the Checkbox.

setState()

```
public void setState(boolean state)
```

This method sets the state of the Checkbox to either true or false.

Example 1

This example creates and displays a simple Checkbox:

```
import java.awt.*;
import java.awt.event.*;
public class SimpleCheckbox extends Frame
        implements ItemListener {
    Checkbox checkbox;
    public static void main(String[] arg) {
```

```
            SimpleCheckbox sc = new SimpleCheckbox();
        }
        SimpleCheckbox() {
            super("SimpleCheckbox");
            checkbox = new Checkbox("The label string");
            checkbox.addItemListener(this);
            add("Center",checkbox);
            pack();
            show();
        }
        public void itemStateChanged(ItemEvent event) {
            System.out.println("State: " + checkbox.getState());
        }
    }
```

The Checkbox is constructed with a label and lets the initial state default to false. The initial window—the false setting—looks like Figure C-3.

Figure C-3   A *Checkbox* with a false setting.

One click with the mouse will change it to true, and it will look like Figure C-4.

Figure C-4   A *Checkbox* with a true setting.

The SimpleCheckbox class implements ItemListener, so a call to addItemListener() can be made to register itself with the Checkbox. This means the method itemStateChanged() is called each time the state changes between true and false. Each mouse click modifies the state, and three consecutive clicks will print this output:

```
State: true
State: false
State: true
```

Example 2

A number of Checkboxes can be grouped together in such a way that the user can select from any combination of things—that is, the boxes can be all true, all false, or any combination of true and false.

```java
import java.awt.*;
public class CheckboxSelection extends Frame {
    Checkbox[] box;
    public static void main(String[] arg) {
        new CheckboxSelection();
    }
    CheckboxSelection() {
        setLayout(new GridLayout(4,1));
        box = new Checkbox[4];
        box[0] = new Checkbox("Bell");
        box[1] = new Checkbox("Book");
        box[2] = new Checkbox("Candle");
        box[3] = new Checkbox("Bus ticket");
        for(int i=0; i<4; i++)
            add(box[i]);
        pack();
        show();
    }
}
```

Here we construct and display four checkboxes. In this sort of configuration, the checkboxes aren't even aware of each other's existence. They can all be switched on and off independently as shown in Figure C-5.

Figure C-5 An unrelated collection of checkboxes.

Example 3

This example is very much like the previous example, except that the checkboxes are included in groups:

```java
import java.awt.*;
public class CheckboxExclusive extends Frame {
    Checkbox[] box;
```

```
CheckboxGroup group;
public static void main(String[] arg) {
    new CheckboxExclusive();
}
CheckboxExclusive() {
    group = new CheckboxGroup();
    setLayout(new GridLayout(4,1));
    box = new Checkbox[4];
    box[0] = new Checkbox("Bell");
    box[1] = new Checkbox("Book");
    box[2] = new Checkbox("Candle");
    box[3] = new Checkbox("Bus ticket");
    for(int i=0; i<4; i++) {
        box[i].setCheckboxGroup(group);
        add(box[i]);
    }
    pack();
    show();
}
}
```

Each `Checkbox` is added to the `CheckboxGroup` named `group`. They now become aware of each other's existence, and their behavior changes. Along with a slight change in appearance, they are distinguished by the fact that it is only possible for one of them to be set to true—every time one of them is set to true, all the others are set to false. The window is shown in Figure C-6.

Figure C-6 A group of *Checkboxes* in a *CheckboxGroup*.

To group checkboxes into a collection of mutually exclusive selectors, see **CheckBoxGroup**. The other components are **Canvas, Button, Choice, Label, List, Scrollbar, ScrollPane, TextArea,** and **TextField**. The menu components are **Menu, MenuBar, MenuItem,** and **CheckboxMenuItem**.

CheckboxGroup

class java.awt.CheckboxGroup

This class will establish a relationship with two or more Checkbox components to make them mutually exclusive — make them into a set of radio buttons. Using the mouse to select any Checkbox in the group will cause the others to become unselected.

Inheritance

```
public class java.awt.CheckboxGroup
    implements Serializable
    extends Object
        ⇑
    public class java.lang.Object
```

Constructors

```
public CheckboxGroup()
```

Returned by

A CheckBoxGroup object is returned from the method getCheckBoxGroup().

Methods

getCurrent()   **deprecated**

```
public Checkbox getCurrent()
```

Returns the Checkbox that is currently selected. This method is deprecated — use getSelectedCheckbox() instead.

getSelectedCheckbox()

```
public Checkbox getSelectedCheckbox()
```

Returns the Checkbox that is currently selected.

setCurrent()   **deprecated**

```
public synchronized void setCurrent(Checkbox checkbox)
```

Causes the Checkbox to be the one currently selected. This method is deprecated — use setSelectedCheckbox() instead.

setSelectedCheckbox()

```
public synchronized voidsetSelectedCheckbox(Checkbox checkbox)
```

Causes the Checkbox to be the one currently selected. If the Checkbox is not a member of this group, no action is taken and there is no error.

toString()

```
public String toString()
```

Returns a string that contains the values and settings of the CheckBoxGroup.

 For an example, see **Checkbox**.

CheckboxMenuItem

class java.awt.CheckboxMenuItem

This is a checkbox that appears as a choice on a menu.

On and off

A CheckboxMenuItem has two states. The mouse can be used to toggle from one state to another, and the current state is displayed in some form as being either selected or unselected. These states can also be thought of as on or off, depending on the sort of thing being selected. Within the program, the values are true for on and false for off.

Inheritance

```
public class java.awt.CheckboxMenuItem
    implements ItemSelectable
    extends MenuItem
        ⇑
    public class java.awt.MenuItem
        extends MenuComponent
            ⇑
        public abstract class java.awt.MenuComponent
            implements Serializable
            extends Object
                ⇑
            public class java.lang.Object
```

Constructors

```
public CheckboxMenuItem()
public CheckboxMenuItem(String label)
public CheckboxMenuItem(String label,boolean state)
```

By default, state is set to false—the *off* state. If no label is specified, the CheckboxMenuItem will be blank.

Returned by

A CheckboxMenuItem is returned from a call to Toolkit.createCheckboxMenuItem().

Methods

addItemListener()

```
public void addItemListener(ItemListener listener)
```

Adds the listener to the list of ItemListeners that will receive events from the checkbox.

addNotify()

```
public void addNotify()
```

Creates the underlying system-dependent peer for this object. This method is not normally called by the application. It is called by the container.

getSelectedObjects()

```
public synchronized Object[] getSelectedObjects()
```

If the CheckboxMenuItem is currently true—the *on* state—returns a single-member array with one member—the CheckboxMenuItem. If it is *off*, returns null.

getState()

```
public boolean getState()
```

Returns true if the checkbox is *on* and false if it is *off*.

paramString()

```
public String paramString()
```

Returns debugging information. The return string describes the internal state and values of this object.

processEvent()

```
protected void processEvent(AWTEvent event)
```

If the event is an ItemEvent, processes the event. All other event types are passed to the superclass method processEvent().

processItemEvent()

```
protected void processItemEvent(ItemEvent event)
```

This method is called whenever an event occurs on this Checkbox. The Checkbox dispatches the event to its ItemListener objects.

This method will be called by the system only if an ItemListener has been added with a call to addItemListener() or a call has been made to enableEvents().

removeItemListener()

```
public void removeItemListener(ItemListener listener)
```

Removes the listener from the list of those that will receive ItemEvents from this object.

setState()

```
public synchronized void setState(boolean setting)
```

If setting is true, the CheckboxMenuItem will be set to *on*. If setting is false, it will be set to *off*.

Example

Here is a simple menu example with some CheckboxMenuItems on it. The menu is constructed normally, and the CheckboxMenuItem objects are added in the same way regular menu String entries are normally added:

```
import java.awt.*;
import java.awt.event.*;
public class MenuChecking extends Frame
        implements ItemListener {
    public static void main(String[] arg) {
        MenuChecking mc = new MenuChecking();
    }
    MenuChecking() {
        super("MenuChecking");
        MenuBar menubar = new MenuBar();
        Menu menu = new Menu("Mode");
        menubar.add(menu);
        menu.add("Open");
        menu.add("Close");
        CheckboxMenuItem checkBox;
        checkBox = new CheckboxMenuItem("Save locally");
        checkBox.addItemListener(this);
```

```
            menu.add(checkBox);
            checkBox = new CheckboxMenuItem("Save inverted");
            checkBox.addItemListener(this);
            menu.add(checkBox);
            checkBox = new CheckboxMenuItem("Save stamps");
            checkBox.addItemListener(this);
            menu.add(checkBox);
            menu.add("Save");
            setMenuBar(menubar);
            setSize(50,50);
            show();
        }
    public void itemStateChanged(ItemEvent event) {
            System.out.print(event.getItem());
            switch(event.getStateChange()) {
            case ItemEvent.DESELECTED:
                System.out.println(" DESELECTED");
                break;
            case ItemEvent.SELECTED:
                System.out.println(" SELECTED");
                break;
            }
        }
    }
```

For the program to receive notification of the checkboxes being turned on and off, it is necessary to implement the ItemListener interface, supply an itemStateChanged() method, and register itself as a listener by calling addItemListener() for each CheckBoxMenuItem. The itemStateChanged() method will be called each time the user selects one of the checkboxes. It is necessary to determine which of them was toggled, and whether it was toggled on or off. The current state of a CheckboxMenuItem is indicated on the display of the menu. After a few toggles, the window looks like the one shown in Figure C-7.

Figure C-7 A *CheckboxMenuItem* example.

The output prints one line with toggle and looks like this:

```
Save locally SELECTED
Save inverted SELECTED
Save stamps SELECTED
Save inverted DESELECTED
```

 The other parts that go into a menu are **Menu, MenuBar, MenuContainer, MenuItem,** and **MenuShortcut**.

CheckedInputStream

class java.util.zip.CheckedInputStream

This is an input stream that calculates a checksum of the data being read.

Inheritance

```
public class java.util.zip.CheckedInputStream
    extends FilterInputStream
        ⇑
    public class java.io.FileInputStream
        extends InputStream
            ⇑
        public class java.io.InputStream
            extends Object
                ⇑
            public class java.lang.Object
```

Constructors

```
public CheckedInputStream(InputStream instream,
    Checksum checksum)
```

Creates CheckedInputStream, **which will read** instream **and use** checksum to do the calculations. The two Checksum **classes included with Java are** CRC32 **and** Adler32.

Methods

getChecksum()

```
public Checksum getChecksum()
```

Returns the Checksum object that was assigned to this stream on the constructor. A calculated checksum value, one that can be used to validate the data, can be extracted from the Checksum object.

read()

```
public int read()
        throws IOException

public int read(byte barray[],int offset,int length)
        throws IOException
```

If no argument is supplied, this will read one byte of data and return it as an int. If barray is supplied, the input data is placed in the array and the number of bytes actually read is returned. The input data will appear beginning at barray[offset] for a maximum of length bytes. This method will block until data has been read or the end of the input stream has been reached. A return value of −1 indicates a normal end to the input stream.

skip()

```
public long skip(long count)
        throws IOException
```

This method makes a request to have the input stream skip over count number of input bytes. The return value is the actual number of bytes skipped.

For a Checksum class that can be used by this class, see **CRC32** and **Adler32**. Also see **CheckedOutputStream**.

CheckedOutputStream

class java.util.zip.CheckedOutputStream

This is an output stream that calculates a checksum on the data being written.

Inheritance

```
public class java.util.zip.CheckedOutputStream
    extends FilterOutputStream
        ⇑
    public class java.io.FilterOutputStream
        extends OutputStream
            ⇑
        public class java.io.OutputStream
            extends Object
                ⇑
```

```
public class java.lang.Object
```

Constructors

```
public CheckedOutputStream(OutputStream outstream,
        Checksum checksum)
```

Creates CheckedOutputStream, which will write outstream and use checksum to do the calculations. The twoChecksum classes included with Java are CRC32 and Adler32.

Methods

getChecksum()

```
public Checksum getChecksum()
```

Returns the Checksum object that was assigned to this stream on the constructor. The computed checksum value can be retrieved from the Checksum object.

write()

```
public void write(int value)
    throws IOException
```

```
public void write(byte barray[],int offset,int length)
    throws IOException
```

This method will write one or more bytes to the output. If value is specified, its lower eight bits are written as a single byte. If barray is specified, the writing will begin at barray[offset] and continue for length bytes. The method blocks until the writing is complete.

 For Checksum class that can be used by this class, see **CRC32** and **Adler32**. Also see **CheckedInputStream**.

Checksum

interface java.util.zip.Checksum

This is the interface to be implemented by a class that is capable of calculating a checksum of some sort over a block of data.

Implemented by

```
Adler32
CRC32
```

Inheritance

```
public interface Checksum
```

Constructors

Returned by

Objects implementing this interface can be returned from the `getChecksum()` methods of `CheckedInputStream` and `CheckedOutputStream`.

Methods

getValue()

```
public long getValue()
```

Returns the internal checksum.

reset()

```
public void reset()
```

Resets the internal checksum to its initial value.

update()

```
public void update(byte array[],int offset,int length)
```

```
public void update(int value)
```

This will update the checksum calculation to include the supplied bytes. A single byte can be specified as the `value`. A block of bytes can be specified as `array`, and the checksum will be updated for `length` bytes beginning at `offset`.

 A `Checksum` can be calculated while reading or writing data through **CheckedInputStream** and **CheckedOutputStream**.

Choice

class java.awt.Choice

A `Choice` is a component that displays a list of items for selection with the mouse. Unless activated by the mouse, the list displays a single line of text containing the currently selected item.

The items and their indexes

A `Choice` maintains an internal list of items. Each item is a `String` object that is displayed for the user to make a selection. Inside the program, the members of the list can be located by name—by doing a string comparison—or by an index number. The index of the first member of the list is 0.

The current selection

One item in the list is always currently selected (unless the list is empty). The currently selected member of the list is the one displayed when the `Choice` is not popped up. When the list is popped up, the currently selected item is the one that is highlighted. Methods are available to specify the current selection, and to inquire which one is selected.

Inheritance

```
public class java.awt.Choice
      implements ItemSelectable
      extends Component
            ⇑
      public abstract class java.awt.Component
            implements ImageObserver
            implements MenuContainer
            implements Serializable
            extends Object
                  ⇑
            public class java.lang.Object
```

Constructors

```
public Choice()
```

Methods

add()

```
public synchronized void add(String item)
```

Identical to `addItem()`.

addItem()

```
public synchronized void addItem(String item)
```

Adds an `item` to the end of the list. A `NullPointerException` will be thrown if `item` is `null`.

addItemListener()

```
public void addItemListener(ItemListener listener)
```

Adds listener to the list of those that will receive ItemEvents from this object.

addNotify()

```
public void addNotify()
```

Creates the underlying system-dependent peer for this object. This method is not normally called by the application. It is called by the container.

countItems()   deprecated

```
public int countItems()
```

Returns the total number of items listed in the Choice. This method is deprecated — use getItemCount() instead.

getItem()

```
public String getItem(int index)
```

Returns the item at the specified index. The index values begin with zero.

getItemCount()

```
public int getItemCount()
```

Returns the total number of items in the Choice.

getSelectedIndex()

```
public int getSelectedIndex()
```

Returns the index value of the currently selected item. If the list is empty, return −1.

getSelectedItem()

```
public synchronized String getSelectedItem()
```

Returns the currently selected item. If there is no selected item, or the list is empty, a null is returned.

getSelectedObjects()

```
public synchronized Object[] getSelectedObjects()
```

Returns an array that has only one member — the String of the currently selected item. If there are no items in the Choice, null is returned.

insert()

```
public synchronized void insert(String item,int index)
```

Inserts the item at the index. The item and this index, and all the ones with larger indexes, are moved up one position to make room. An `IllegalArgumentException` is thrown if the index is out of bounds.

paramString()

```
protected String paramString()
```

Returns debugging information. The return string describes the internal state and values of this object.

processEvent()

```
protected void processEvent(AWTEvent event)
```

Processes the `event`. If `event` is an `ItemEvent`, a call will be made to `processItemEvent()`. If it is not an `ItemEvent`, a call will be made to `processEvent()` of the superclass.

processItemEvent()

```
protected void processItemEvent(ItemEvent event)
```

This method is called whenever an event occurs on this `Choice`. The `Choice` dispatches the event to its `ItemListener` objects.

This method will be called by the system only if an `ItemListener` has been added with a call to `addItemListener()` or a call has been made to `enableEvents()`.

remove()

```
public synchronized void remove(String item)

public synchronized void remove(int index)
```

Removes the named or indexed item from the list. An `IllegalArgumentException` is thrown if `item` is not in the list or `index` is out of range.

removeAll()

```
public synchronized void removeAll()
```

Removes all items from the list.

removeItemListener()

```
public void removeItemListener(ItemListener listener)
```

Removes `listener` from the list of `ItemListener`s that will be notified whenever `ItemEvent` occurs on this object.

select()

```
public synchronized void select(int index)
```

```
public synchronized void select(String item)
```

Causes the item, or the one at the index, to be the one currently selected. An IllegalArgumentException is thrown if the item is not found or index is out of bounds.

Example

You can choose either of two approaches to reading the selection from a Choice. By implementing the ItemListener interface, you arrange that the program will be notified each time a selection is made—this means that the choices can be read as they are made. It is also possible, depending on the requirements of your application, to wait until later and simply read the final choice made by the user. This example uses both options:

```
import java.awt.*;
import java.awt.event.*;
public class Choosing extends Frame
        implements ActionListener, ItemListener {
    Choice choice;
    Button report;
    public static void main(String[] arg) {
        new Choosing();
    }
    Choosing() {
        choice = new Choice();
        choice.addItemListener(this);
        choice.addItem("First choice");
        choice.addItem("Second choice");
        choice.addItem("Third choice");
        choice.addItem("Fourth choice");
        add("North",choice);
        report = new Button("Report");
        report.addActionListener(this);
        add("South",report);
        pack();
        show();
    }
    public void itemStateChanged(ItemEvent event) {
        System.out.println("Chosen: " +
                choice.getSelectedItem());
    }
    public void actionPerformed(ActionEvent event) {
        System.out.println("Reported: " +
                choice.getSelectedItem());
```

```
        }
    }
```

The method itemStateChanged() will be called whenever a choice is made. A button has been added that causes a call to actionPerformed() whenever it is pressed. In both cases, it is simply a matter of querying the Choice with a call to getSelectedItem() to discover the current selection.

A Choice has two appearances. Figure C-8 shows the Choice without its list showing—it just shows the current selection. Figure C-9 shows the Choice after the button on the right has been selected—it lists all the items for the user to make a selection. If the list is too long to be displayed all at once, a scroll bar will automatically be added.

Figure C-8   A *Choice* showing the current selection.

Figure C-9   A *Choice* showing the list of selectable items.

The other components are **Canvas, Button, Choice, Label, List, Scrollbar, ScrollPane, TextArea,** and **TextField.** The menu components are **Menu, MenuBar, MenuItem,** and **CheckboxMenuItem.**

ChoiceFormat

class java.text.ChoiceFormat

This class provides a mapping between an array of numbers and an array of strings.

Descriptive examples

A ChoiceFormat can be used to map the number 1 to the string "first," 2 to "second," and so on. It can be used to format messages so that the language matches the count. A message could be constructed that says, "There X in the basket." A ChoiceFormat could be used to format X according to a numeric value. If the number is 0, X would be changed to the string "are no snakes." If the number is 1, X would be "is one snake," and if it is greater than 1, X would be "are snakes."

Graphic example

One simple example would be the days of the week. The numbers and strings would be set up in a pair of arrays like this:

```
double[] dayNum = {0,1,2,3,4,5,6};
String[] dayName = {"Sun","Mon","Tue","Wed","Thu","Fri","Sat"};
```

The number 0 maps to "Sun," 1 to "Mon," and so on.

Missing numbers

The numbers are declared in the array as doubles because there can be gaps. A simple mapping will convert any value you supply to a value that is a member of the array (that is why the array is referred to as a set of limits). Whenever a number does not exactly match one in the list, the next smaller number is chosen. A number less than the first one in the list will cause the first one to be chosen. For example, take this mapping:

```
double[] dayNum = {1,4,5};
String[] dayName = {"Mon","Thu","Fri"};
```

The numbers 2 or 3 (as well as 2.54 or 3.6, for that matter) would map to the next lower number, 1, and result in the string "Mon." Any number is valid. A number less than 1 will cause 1 to be chosen. A number greater than 5 will cause 5 to be chosen.

Inheritance

```
public class java.text.ChoiceFormat
    extends NumberFormat
        ⇑
    public class java.text.NumberFormat
        implements Cloneable
        extends Format
            ⇑
        public class java.text.Format
            implements Serializable
            implements Cloneable
            extends Object
                ⇑
            public class java.lang.Object
```

Constructors

```
public ChoiceFormat(double limits[],String formats[])
public ChoiceFormat(String pattern)
```

The limits array is the set of numbers, and formats is the array of strings —these two arrays have a one-to-one correspondence as described previously. The format of pattern is described in MessageFormat.

Methods

applyPattern()

```
public void applyPattern(String newPattern)
```

For a description of the form of newPattern, see MessageFormat.

clone()

```
public Object clone()
```

Returns a duplicate of this object.

equals()

```
public boolean equals(Object object)
```

Returns true if object is a ChoiceFormat with its two arrays identical to this one.

format()

```
public StringBuffer format(long number,
        StringBuffer appendTo,FieldPosition position)

public StringBuffer format(double number,
        StringBuffer appendTo,FieldPosition position)
```

Formats number into a string. The generated string will be appended on the end of the one in appendTo. The appendTo object is then used as the return value. The position is updated with the location of the resulting string in the returned StringBuffer.

 If the number is specified as a long, you should be aware that it will be converted to a double internally with possible loss of precision.

getFormats()

```
public Object[] getFormats()
```

Returns the array of formats.

getLimits()

```
public double[] getLimits()
```

Returns the array of numeric values associated with the formats.

hashCode()

```
public int hashCode()
```

Returns the hashcode value of this object.

nextDouble()

```
public final static double nextDouble(double value)

public static double nextDouble(double value,boolean increment)
```

Increments or decrements the value by the smallest possible amount and returns the result. The smallest possible amount is the value that will change the base number by one. This will affect the exponent only if there is underflow or overflow. If increment is false, value will be decremented. If increment is true, value will be incremented. The default is true. The only exception to returning a valid value is if value is the IEEE NaN value, then NaN is returned.

parse()

```
public Number parse(String text,ParsePosition position)
```

Reads the text string and converts it to a numeric value. If the value is within the range that can be contained in a long, a Long wrapper is returned. If the number cannot be represented as a long, a Double wrapper will be returned. The position will determine the starting position in text, and position will be updated to point to the character just beyond the last one read.

previousDouble()

```
public final static double previousDouble(double value)
```

This is the same as calling nextDouble(value,false).

setChoices()

```
public void setChoices(double limits[],String formats[])
```

Sets both arrays. This replaces those that were supplied to the constructor.

toPattern()

```
public String toPattern()
```

Returns the internal pattern string. For the format of patterns strings, see MessageFormat.

Example

This example will, when given a number, print a description of the magnitude of the number. It does some estimating:

```java
import java.text.*;
public class Estimator {
    static double[] limits = {0,1,2,6,7,12,13};
    static String[] format = {
        "are no apples",
        "is one apple",
        "are fewer than six apples",
        "are a half dozen apples",
        "are less than a dozen apples",
        "are a dozen apples",
        "are more than a dozen apples"
    };
    public static void main(String[] arg) {
        ChoiceFormat form =
                new ChoiceFormat(limits,format);
        for(int i=0; i< 15; i++)
            System.out.println(i + ": There " +
                form.format(i) + " in the tree.");
    }
}
```

Calling the format() method will return the String that corresponds with the value. As you can see, the list of numbers defined as limits has some gaps in it. Any number passed to form.format() that addresses one of the gaps will default to the next larger number. For this example, any number from 7 through 11 will be translated as "less than a dozen." Any number from 13 up will be "more than a dozen." The output of the program looks like this:

```
0: There are no apples in the tree.
1: There is one apple in the tree.
2: There are fewer than six apples in the tree.
3: There are fewer than six apples in the tree.
4: There are fewer than six apples in the tree.
5: There are fewer than six apples in the tree.
6: There are a half dozen apples in the tree.
7: There are less than a dozen apples in the tree.
8: There are less than a dozen apples in the tree.
9: There are less than a dozen apples in the tree.
10: There are less than a dozen apples in the tree.
11: There are less than a dozen apples in the tree.
12: There are a dozen apples in the tree.
```

```
13: There are more than a dozen apples in the tree.
14: There are more than a dozen apples in the tree.
```

 For an example using patterns, see **MessageFormat**.

class

keyword

A *class* is a plan—a sort of blueprint—from which an object can be constructed. If an object can be considered a cookie, then its class is a cookie cutter. When writing a Java program, you are writing a collection of classes, and when you write a class, you are simply designing the cookie cutter.

The contents of a class

The term *member* has special meaning for a Java class. A class contains both members and nonmembers. The members of a class are:

- ◆ Variables
- ◆ Constants
- ◆ Methods
- ◆ Static methods
- ◆ Static variables
- ◆ Static constants

The nonmembers of a class are:

- ◆ Static initializers
- ◆ Constructors

Members can be inherited by subclasses—nonmembers cannot. Further, only members that are declared as `protected` or `public` can be inherited.

The variables and constants are collectively called *fields*. Any field can have an initializer—in fact, the constants are required to have initializers. When you group the fields together as one type of thing, the list of the contents of a class assumes the new form that follows.

The members of a class then are:

- ◆ Fields
- ◆ Methods

The nonmembers of a class are:

- ◆ Static initializers
- ◆ Constructors

Java allows a field and a method to have the same name because the syntax that refers to them will not allow for any ambiguities (a reference to the name of a method is always followed by a pair of parentheses). Two fields cannot have the same names. Two methods can have the same names, as long as their signature lists of argument types differ.

There are three ways a member can be included in a class:

- ◆ It can be declared directly in the class.
- ◆ It can be inherited from any of its superinterfaces.
- ◆ It can be inherited from its superclass. Its superclass could have, in turn, inherited it from its superclass or one of its superinterfaces.

Variables

A *variable* is a named type declaration. A variable can optionally have an initializing expression. Each time an instance is created from the class, a new copy of the variable will be created. See **variable**.

Constants

A *constant* is declared the same way that a variable is except (1) it has the modifier final and (2) it must have an initializer. See **constant**.

Static variables

A *static variable* is also called a *class variable*. A static variable will only have one incarnation — there will never be more than one copy of it. It is static in the sense that it always exists, regardless of whether any instances of the class in which it is defined exist. Two separate objects making references to the same static variable name — whether in their own class or another — will be referring to the same variable and will be working with the same value. See **static**.

Static constants

A *static constant* declaration is the same as a static variable declaration except (1) it has the modifier final and (2) it must have an initializer. A static constant is also declared with the modifier static, which tells Java that there need be only one copy of it. See **constant**.

Methods

Methods are the containers of the executable code. They have a name, an optional list of parameters, an optional return value, and a block of zero or more executable statements. See **method**.

Constructors

A *constructor* is a special sort of method. It has the same name as the class in which it is defined. It has no declared return type, but it returns a reference to the object being constructed. It is called only once, when an object is being instantiated from the class. A constructor has an optional list of parameters and a block of zero or more executable statements. See **constructor**.

Initializers

An *initializer* is any expression that is used to assign an initial value to a field. See **variable**.

Static initializers

A *static initializer* is the initializer expression for a static variable. A nonstatic initializer is one that executes each time a class is instantiated into an object. A static initializer initializes the class variables, so it only executes once.

Inner classes

It is possible to define one class inside another. See **inner classes**.

Class hierarchy

The *class hierarchy* is the relationship derived from the structure of one class inheriting from another. One class inherits from another with the keyword extend. For example, this is how the class Bicycle would inherit from (or extend) the class Vehicle:

```
class Bicycle extends Vehicle {
    . . .
}
```

One class is the parent class of all other classes — it is the class named java.lang.Object. If a class is declared without an extends clause, the class Object is assumed. All classes are extended from Object at the root of their inheritance tree.

In the family tree of classes, every class has a single parent. This single-parent structure is known as *single inheritance*. The immediate parent of any class is known as its *superclass*. A class has only one superclass. The child class of a superclass is called a *subclass*. A superclass can have any number of subclasses.

A class can implement one or more *interfaces*. An interface is a special sort of abstract class that can hold only constant values and method declarations. A class may implement an interface by supplying method bodies for all the method definitions—the interface then becomes a *superinterface* of the class. A class may have several superinterfaces.

If there is an implementation of an interface anywhere in the family tree of a class, the class inherits it along with the implementation of the methods for it.

Class modifiers

Public

A class can be declared as `public`. This allows access to the class from outside its package. Here is an example of the syntax used to make a class publicly accessible:

```
public class CookieJar {
    . . .
}
```

Abstract

If a class is declared as being *abstract,* it cannot be instantiated—it is considered to be incomplete. It can be used only as the superclass of another class. Any class that contains at least one abstract method must be declared abstract because it cannot be instantiated without the method body. The abstract method could be inherited from a superclass or from a superinterface. Here is the syntax used to declare a class abstract:

```
abstract class FloorPlan {
    . . .
}
```

A class cannot be both `abstract` and `final`. A class that implements an interface but does not supply all the method definitions of the interface is an abstract class and must be declared as such.

Final

A class that is declared as *final* can be instantiated, but it cannot be used as a superclass. Here is an example of the declaration of a final class:

```
final class Molecule {
    . . .
}
```

A class cannot be both `final` and `abstract`.

Default

If no modifier is specified for a class, it will assume the default accessibility. It will be accessible from inside any class in its same package. For example:

```
package mypackage;
class Rombus {
    ...
}
```

The class Rombus is declared as being inside a package named mypackage. Any other classes declared inside mypackage will be able to access Rombus.

Constructors

Every class has at least one constructor. A *constructor* is a special sort of method that has the same name as the class in which it is defined. Several constructors can be defined for one class by overloading. If you do not supply a constructor, Java will supply one for you. The one supplied by Java does nothing—it allows all the fields to assume their default values.

A simple class

Here is the declaration of a very simple class:

```
package furniture;

class ElectricLamp {
    int wattage;
}
```

Here are the things we know about it from the declaration:

- It is in the package known as furniture.
- It has the default scope (since neither public nor private were declared) of being accessible throughout the package.
- Its name is ElectricLamp.
- It contains the field wattage that will assume the initial value of zero (the Java default value for an int). This field assumes the default accessibility, which means it is available only to this class and any subclasses in this same package.
- The class has java.lang.Object as its superclass. This is always the case when there is no extends clause.

A class with an interface

This is another version of the ElectricLamp class—this time with an interface that allows the lamp to be turned on and off:

```
package furniture;

interface LampSwitch {
    void switchOn();
    void switchOff();
}

class ElectricLamp implements interface LampSwitch {
    boolean lampTurnedOn;
    int wattage;
    void switchOn() {
        lampTurnedOn = true;
    }
    void switchOff() {
        lampTurnedOn = false;
    }
}
```

Here is what we know about this version:

◆ The interface LampSwitch is in the package furniture.

◆ The interface LampSwitch contains the prototypes of two methods —switchOn() and switchOff().

◆ The class ElectricLamp implements the interface LampSwitch— which means method bodies need to be supplied in the class for the methods specified in the interface.

◆ The class ElectricLamp contains the fields lampTurnedOn and wattage. These are available only to this class and its subclasses.

A class with multiple interfaces

One class can implement several interfaces. Only one interface statement may appear, but it can have any number of interface names separated by commas. Here is an example:

```
import java.awt.*;
class ViolaBox implements Adjustable, Shape {
    ...
}
```

- The `import` statement makes the interfaces of the java.awt package available without their having to be fully qualified.
- The class `ViolaBox` implements two interfaces from the Java API: `java.awt.Adjustable` and `java.awt.Shape`.

A subclass

This is the declaration of a subclass of the `ElectricLamp` class of the previous example:

```
package furniture;

class TableLamp extends ElectricLamp {
    int height = 34;
}
```

- This class is in the package `furniture`.
- The class has `furniture.ElectricLamp` as its superclass.
- It contains the field `height`, which has an initial value of 34.
- It contains the fields `wattage` and `lampTurnedOn`, inherited from its superclass.
- It contains the methods `switchOn()` and `switchOff()`, inherited from its superclass.

The subclass of a subclass

There is no limit to the level of subclassing. Here is an extension of the `TableLamp` class from the previous example:

```
class ShadedTableLamp extends TableLamp {
    int shadeHeight;
    int shadeDiameter;
    int getShadeHeight() {
        return(shadeHeight);
    }
    void setShadeHeight(int setting) {
        shadeHeight = setting;
    }
}
```

- This class inherits all the methods and data from the `TableLamp` class.
- This class contains the values `shadeHeight` and `shadeDiameter`.

- ◆ It has the method setShadeHeight(), which can be used to set the value of shadeHeight.
- ◆ It has the method getShadeHeight(), which can be used to return the shadeHeight value to the caller.

A simple class with a constructor

A *constructor* is a special sort of method that is executed once—when a class is instantiated. A constructor is easy to spot—it always has the same name as its containing class. Here is a version of the TableLamp class with a constructor:

```
class TableLamp {
    int height;
    TableLamp() {
        height = 34;
    }
}
```

- ◆ The only field in this class is height.
- ◆ The class has one constructor (which sets the height to 34). Since it has no arguments, that method becomes the default constructor.

A class with multiple constructors

A class can have several constructors. They are differentiated by being over-loaded—that is, they have a different list of argument types:

```
class TableLamp {
    int wattage;
    int height;
    TableLamp() {
        wattage = 100;
        height = 34;

    }
    TableLamp(int w) {
        wattage = w;
        height = 34;
    }
    TableLamp(int w,int h) {
        wattage = w;
        height = h;
    }
}
```

- This class has three constructors—all of which initialize the fields `wattage` and `height`.
- The first constructor is the default constructor; it has no arguments and will set the wattage to 100 and the height to 34.
- The second constructor sets the wattage to the parameter value and sets the height to 34.
- The third constructor retrieves both `height` and `wattage` from the parameter values.

There are three ways to instantiate this class—any one of the following will work:

```
TableLamp t = new TableLamp();
TableLamp t = new TableLamp(26);
TableLamp t = new TableLamp(26,150);
```

All of these will have the same result (creating a `TableLamp` object) with the only difference among them being the `height` value and `wattage` value settings.

A simple class with methods

This is a simple class to demonstrate how methods interface with the fields and version of `TableLamp` that has methods for changing the wattage:

```
class TableLamp {
    int wattage;
    void setWattage(int w) {
        wattage = w;
    }
    int getWattage() {
        return(wattage);
    }
```

- This class contains the single variable `wattage`, which will always have an initial value of zero (since it is not being set by a constructor).
- The method `setWattage()` has the ability to set the value of `wattage`.
- The method `getWattage()` has the ability to return the current value of `wattage` to the caller.

Nonpublic classes

You should be aware of something when defining more than one class in a single file: Each class—public, private, or otherwise—will be put into its own `.class` file when it is compiled. And that `.class` file will have the same name as the class itself. Therefore, if you have two private classes of the same name, you will have an error—the last one compiled will simply overwrite the other. The basic rule: Each class within a package must have a unique name. This applies to the unnamed package also.

For defining one class inside another, see **inner classes**. For the run-time form of a class, see **object**. For information on field and method accessibility, see **access** and **scope**. For the specifics of designing and implementing an interface, see **interface**. For more about class constructors, see **constructor**. For examples of abstract classes and methods, see **abstract**. For examples of final classes and methods, see **final**. For information on inheritance, see **extends** and **implements**.

Class

class java.lang.Class

A `Class` object is an object that contains a complete description of some class. A `Class` object can be acquired for every Java object—including arrays and primitive types. Methods are found in `Class` to access the full path name of an object, the list of fields, the list of constructors, and even the list of interfaces that it implements. There is a unique `Class` object for every Java class.

The Java Virtual Machine creates a `Class` object for every class it loads; it uses the information in them to manipulate the objects and perform operations on them. Having this information available on classes makes possible the most complete run-time identification system imaginable. Not only is it quick and easy to find out what class an object was instantiated from, it is also possible to find out almost everything about the class. The kinds of things done with the methods here are the kinds of things the compiler and the interpreter would both need to do—this is a sort of peek inside the Java mechanism.

Inheritance

```
public final class java.lang.Class
    implements Serializable
    extends Object
        ⇑
    public class java.lang.Object
```

Constructors

This class has no public constructors, but there are several ways to get a `Class` object.

Acquire the `Class` from an object

A call to the method `getClass()` will return a `Class` object. This method is declared in `Object` and is inherited by every class in Java. The method is final and cannot be overridden.

Acquire the Class from an object name

The `Class` object contains the method `forName()`, which can be used to retrieve a `Class` object. The method is described later under this heading.

Acquire the Class for a primitive type

Each of the primitive types has a wrapper, and each of the wrappers has a constant called `TYPE` that is the `Class` object of the primitive. The `getClass()` method also works for these wrappers, but they return the `Class` object of the wrapper, not of the primitive. There are nine wrapper classes: `Boolean`, `Byte`, `Character`, `Short`, `Integer`, `Long`, `Float`, `Double`, and `Void`.

Acquire a `Class` From a Special Method

Class objects can be returned from the following methods:

```
BeanDescriptor.getBeanClass()
BeanDescriptor.getCustomizerClass()
Class.forName()
Class.getComponentType()
Class.getDeclaringClass()
Class.getSuperclass()
ClassLoader.defineClass()
ClassLoader.findLoadedClass()
ClassLoader.findSystemClass()
ClassLoader.loadClass()
Constructor.getDeclaringClass()
DataFlavor.getRepresentationClass()
EventSetDescriptor.getListenerType()
Field.getDeclaringClass()
Field.getType()
IndexedPropertyDescriptor.getIndexedPropertyType()
LoaderHandler.loadClass()
Member.getDeclaringClass()
Method.getDeclaringClass()method.getReturnType()
Object.getClass()
```

```
ObjectInputStream.resolveClass()
ObjectStreamClass.forClass()
PropertyDescriptor.getPropertyEditorClass()
PropertyDescriptor.getPropertyType()
RMIClassLoader.loadClass()
SecurityManager.currentLoadedClass()
```

Acquire an Array of Classes

An array of Class objects can be returned from the following methods:

```
Class.getClasses()
Class.getDeclaredClasses()
Class.getInterfaces()
Constructor.getExceptionTypes()
Constructor.getParameterTypes()
Method.getExceptionTypes()
Method.getParameterTypes()
SecurityManager.getClassContext()
```

Methods

Some of the methods—such as getMethods() and getDeclaredMethods()—
are paired and do very much the same thing. The only difference is that the
one without the word "Declared" in its middle will get items only that are
public, and the one with "Declared" will get all items, whether public or not.

forName()

```
public static Class forName(String className)
    throws ClassNotFoundException
```

This method can be used to get the Class object for a named class. The class does not
have to have been previously loaded.

The className is the fully qualified name of a class for which a Class object is
desired. If the named class is found, its Class object is returned. If the className is not
found, the ClassNotFoundException is thrown.

getClasses()

```
public Class[] getClasses()
```

Returns an array of public classes and interfaces that are represented by this Class object.
If there are none, a zero-length array is returned.

getClassLoader()

```
public ClassLoader getClassLoader()
```

Returns the class loader that loaded the class. Returns `null` if the class was not loaded by a class loader.

getComponentType()

```
public Class getComponentType()
```

Returns the `Class` object of the component of an array. If the class is not an array, returns `null`. See Example 1.

getConstructor()

```
public Constructor getConstructor(Class parameterTypes[])
    throws NoSuchMethodException
    throws SecurityException
```

Finds the matching public constructor and returns a `Constructor` object for it. The array `parameterTypes` describes the argument list — it is an array of `Class` objects specifying the argument types that are to be expected (in array order).

If no match is found, a `NoSuchMethodException` is thrown. If the matching constructor is not available (it could be private), a `SecurityException` is thrown.

getConstructors()

```
public Constructor[] getConstructors()
    throws SecurityException
```

Returns an array of `Constructor` objects — one for each public constructor of the class. If there are no public constructors, a `SecurityException` is thrown. See Example 2.

getDeclaredClasses()

```
public Class[] getDeclaredClasses()
    throws SecurityException
```

Returns an array of classes and interfaces that are members of the class. If there are none, a zero-length array is returned. All of them, regardless of their declared access, are returned. If access is denied, a `SecurityException` is thrown.

getDeclaredConstructor()

```
public Constructor
        getDeclaredConstructor(Class parameterTypes[])
    throws NoSuchMethodException
    throws SecurityException
```

Finds the matching constructor (whether or not it is public) and returns a `Constructor` object for it. The array `parameterTypes` describes the argument list — it is an array of `Class` objects specifying the argument types that are to be expected (in array order).

If no match is found, a `NoSuchMethodException` is thrown. If the matching constructor is not available, a `SecurityException` is thrown.

getDeclaredConstructors()

```
public Constructor[] getDeclaredConstructors()
    throws SecurityException
```

Returns an array of Constructor objects—one for each constructor, public or not, of the class. If the information is denied, a SecurityException is thrown.

getDeclaredField()

```
public Field getDeclaredField(String name)
    throws NoSuchFieldException
    throws SecurityException
```

Returns the Field object for the field specified by its name. If access is denied, a SecurityException is thrown. If there is no field of the specified name, a NoSuchFieldException is thrown.

getDeclaredFields()

```
public Field[] getDeclaredFields()
    throws SecurityException
```

Returns an array of Field objects—one for each field declared in the interface or class represented by the Class object. A Field object is returned for all fields, regardless of access. If there are no fields declared in the object, a zero-length array is returned. If the information is denied, a SecurityException is thrown. See Example 3.

getDeclaredMethod()

```
public Method getDeclaredMethod(String name,
        Class parameterTypes[])
    throws NoSuchMethodException
    throws SecurityException
```

Returns a Method object that represents the specified method. A method is defined by its name and the list of parameter types. The parameters are specified by the array of parameterTypes—in array order.

If no method is found to match the criteria, a NoSuchMethodException is thrown. If access to the method is denied, a SecurityException is thrown.

getDeclaredMethods()

```
public Method[] getDeclaredMethods()
    throws SecurityException
```

Returns an array of all the methods declared in a class. The return value is an array of Method objects—each of which represents one method of the class. If there are no methods, a zero-length array is returned. If access is denied, a SecurityException is thrown.

getDeclaringClass()

```
public Class getDeclaringClass()
```

If this class is an inner class, returns the Class object representing the outer class. This method has not been implemented in 1.1 and always returns null.

getField()

```
public Field getField(String name)
    throws NoSuchFieldException
    throws SecurityException
```

Returns a Field object that represents the one named by name. The field must be publicly accessible, or a SecurityException will be thrown. If there is no field of the specified name, a NoSuchFieldException is thrown.

getFields()

```
public Field[] getFields()
    throws SecurityException
```

Returns an array of Field objects that represents all the publicly accessible fields of the class. The publicly available fields of all the superclasses and superinterfaces — all the inherited public fields — will also be included in the array. If there are no publicly accessible fields, a zero-length array is returned. If access is denied, a SecurityException will be thrown.

getInterfaces()

```
public Class[] getInterfaces()
```

Returns an array of Class objects that represent all the interfaces implement by the represented class. If there are none, returns a zero-length array. If this Class object represents an interface, the return is an array representing its superinterfaces.

getMethod()

```
public Method getMethod(String name,Class parameterTypes[])
    throws NoSuchMethodException
    throws SecurityException
```

Returns a Method object that represents the specified method. The method sought must have public access. A method is defined by its name and the list of parameter types. The parameters are specified by the array of parameterTypes — in array order.

If no method is found to match the criteria, a NoSuchMethodException is thrown. If access to the method is denied, a SecurityException is thrown.

getMethods()

```
public Method[] getMethods()
    throws SecurityException
```

Returns an array of all the public methods declared in a class. The return value is an array of `Method` objects—each of which represents one method of the class. If there are no methods, a zero-length array is returned. If access is denied, a `SecurityException` is thrown.

getModifiers()

```
public int getModifiers()
```

This method returns the Java language modifiers for the class (`public`, `private`, `protected`, `final`, and `interface`) encoded into an `int`. The `int` can be decoded by using methods of the `Modifier` class.

getName()

```
public String getName()
```

Returns the fully qualified name of the object represented by the `Class`.

getResourceAsStream()

```
public InputStream getResourceAsStream(String name)
```

Finds the named resource and opens a stream from which it can be read. If there is no resource by the specified `name`, a `null` is returned. The rules for performing the search are determined by the `ClassLoader` of the class. The resource can be a file or any other entity capable of being read through a stream.

If the `name` begins with '/', it is assumed to be an absolute path. If it is not an absolute path name, the full path will be constructed by appending `name` onto the end of the path name of the class.

getSigners()

```
public Object[] getSigners()
```

Returns an array of the signers of the class. The signers, if any, will have been set in the class with a call to `ClassLoader.setSigners()`.

getSuperclass()

```
public Class getSuperclass()
```

Returns the `Class` reference of the superclass. If the class is `Object`, or if this is a `Class` representation of an interface, the return value is `null`. See Example 4.

isArray()

```
public boolean isArray()
```

Returns `true` if this class represents an array.

isAssignableFrom()

```
public boolean isAssignableFrom(Class otherClass)
```

A return of `true` indicates that an object represented by `otherClass` can be assigned directly to a reference to an object of the type represented by this `Class`. This method compares the object represented by `otherClass` to the object represented by this `Class` and returns `true` if `otherClass` is

- ◆ The same class
- ◆ A superclass
- ◆ The same interface
- ◆ A superinterface
- ◆ A primitive type that can be widened to this type

isInstance()

```
public boolean isInstance(Object object)
```

This is the run-time equivalent of `instanceof`. The method will return `true` if `object` can be cast to the type represented by this `Class` without raising a `ClassCastException`. Returns `true` if

- ◆ The object is an instance of the class represented by this `Class`.
- ◆ The object is an instance of any subclass of the class represented by this `Class`.
- ◆ This `Class` represents an interface that is implemented by `object`.
- ◆ This `Class` represents an array and the `object` is an array that can be assigned to it without narrowing.

isInterface()

```
public boolean isInterface()
```

Returns `true` if this `Class` object represents an interface.

isPrimitive()

```
public boolean isPrimitive()
```

Returns `true` if this `Class` represents one of the Java primitive types.

newInstance()

```
public Object newInstance()
      throws InstantiationException
      throws IllegalAccessException
```

Returns a new instance of the class represented by this `Class`. If it is not possible to instantiate an object (it could be an abstract class or a primitive type), an `InstantiationException` is thrown. An `IllegalAccessException` is thrown if the class or an initializer is not accessible.

toString()

```
public String toString()
```

This method returns a descriptive name of the class or interface being represented. The string begins with the word "class" or "interface" and is followed by its fully qualified name. If the Class represents a primitive type, the string is the name of the primitive type.

Example 1

This example demonstrates the way to get the Class object of an array and how the Class object can be used to determine the type of the elements of the array:

```
public class ArrayComponent {
    public static void main(String[] arg) {
        long[] arr = new long[5];
        Class c = arr.getClass();
        Class cc = c.getComponentType();
        System.out.println(cc);
    }
}
```

The toString() method of the Class class prints the simple name of the class. In this example, the output is

```
long
```

Example 2

Here is an example of a Class object being used to list the names of the constructors of an Integer. The method getConstructors() is used to retrieve the array and then each member of the array is printed:

```
import java.lang.reflect.*;

public class ClassConstructorList {
    public static void main(String[] arg) {
        Integer in = new Integer(22);
        Class c = in.getClass();
        Constructor[] con = c.getConstructors();
        System.out.println("The class has " +
            con.length + " constructors.");
        for(int i=0; i<con.length; i++)
            System.out.println(con[i]);
    }
}
```

The output from this example looks like this:

```
The class has 2 constructors.
public java.lang.Integer(int)
public java.lang.Integer(java.lang.String)
            throws java.lang.NumberFormatException
```

Example 3

Here is an example of using `getDeclaredFields()` to get a list of all the fields that have been declared inside a class:

```
import java.lang.reflect.*;

public class ClassFieldList {
    public static void main(String[] arg) {
        Integer in = new Integer(23);
        Class c = in.getClass();
        Field arr[] = c.getDeclaredFields();
        for(int i=0; i<arr.length; i++)
            System.out.println(arr[i]);
    }
}
```

The output from this class looks like this:

```
public static final int java.lang.Integer.MIN_VALUE
public static final int java.lang.Integer.MAX_VALUE
public static final java.lang.Classjava.lang.Integer.TYPE
private int java.lang.Integer.value
private static final longjava.lang.Integer.serialVersionUID
```

Example 4

By repeatedly finding the superclasses of each class, you can determine the entire hierarchy of an object:

```
import java.util.*;
public class ClassHierarchy {
    public static void main(String[] arg) {
        Properties p = new Properties();
        Class c = p.getClass();
        while(c != null) {
            System.out.println(c);
            c = c.getSuperclass();
```

```
            }
          }
        }
```

The output of the program looks like this:

```
class java.util.Properties
class java.util.Hashtable
class java.util.Dictionary
class java.lang.Object
```

ClassCastException

class java.lang.ClassCastException

This exception is thrown whenever an invalid class cast occurs.

Inheritance

```
public class java.lang.ClassCastException
    extends RuntimeException
        ⇑
    public class java.lang.RuntimeException
        extends Exception
            ⇑
        public class java.lang.Exception
            extends Throwable
                ⇑
            public class java.lang.Throwable
                implements Serializable
                extends Object
                    ⇑
                public class java.lang.Object
```

Constructors

```
public ClassCastException()
public ClassCastException(String message)
```

If the message string is supplied, it is used as the detailed error message—without it, there will be no detailed message.

ClassCircularityError

class java.lang.ClassCircularityError

This exception is thrown whenever a nonresolvable circularity has been detected during the initialization of a class — that is, when some sort of inter-dependency exists between two or more classes such that each requires the other to be resolved first.

Inheritance

```
public class java.lang.ClassCircularityError
    extends LinkageError
        ⇑
    public class java.lang.LinkageError
        extends Error
            ⇑
        public class java.lang.Error
            extends Throwable
                ⇑
            public class java.lang.Throwable
                implements Serializable
                extends Object
                    ⇑
                public class java.lang.Object
```

Constructors

```
public ClassCircularityError()
public ClassCircularityError(String message)
```

If the message string is supplied, it is used as the detailed message.

classes.zip

This is part of the standard JDK (Java Development Kit) distributed by Sun. This file contains the class files (the executable bytecode files) of the Java API. It should not be unzipped—the Java Virtual Machine is capable of extracting the objects directly from the file during execution. The location of this file must be included in the CLASSPATH so that the Virtual Machine can find the API.

 For a description of ways to address the classes.zip file, see **CLASSPATH**, **java**, and **appletviewer**.

ClassFormatError

class java.lang.ClassFormatError

Thrown to indicate the occurrence of an invalid file format.

Inheritance

```
public class java.lang.ClassFormatError
    extends LinkageError
        ⇑
    public class java.lang.LinkageError
        extends Error
            ⇑
        public class java.lang.Error
        extends Throwable
                ⇑
            public class java.lang.Throwable
                implements Serializable
                extends Object
                    ⇑
                public class java.lang.Object
```

Constructors

```
public ClassFormatError()
public ClassFormatError(String message)
```

If the message string is supplied, it is used as the detailed message.

ClassLoader

class java.lang.ClassLoader

This is an abstract class that is used to define the methods and procedures used by the Virtual Machine to load classes from .class files.

What the ClassLoader **is not**

Classes are normally loaded from a class file—or a zip file, or a JAR file—on disk. The disk location is determined by the class name used in the program and the java.class.path property (which is set by the browser, the environment variable CLASSPATH, or the classpath option of the interpreter). This mechanism is somewhat platform-dependent and does not involve a ClassLoader.

What ClassLoader **is**

Classes may be loaded from locations other than the disk — such as over the network — by using ClassLoader. Classes can be stored in different forms also. A ClassLoader can be used to receive classes from, say, a stream of bytes over a serial link. The ClassLoader instructs the system to convert the byte stream into the instance of a class. Once a class is loaded, ClassLoader will try to resolve references to methods and variables by loading other classes — the ones containing the references — from the same source.

Inheritance

```
public abstract class java.lang.ClassLoader
      extends Object
         ⇑
      public class java.lang.Object
```

Constructors

```
protected ClassLoader()
```

Returned by

ClassLoader objects can be returned from calls to Class.getClassLoader() and SecurityManager.currentClassLoader().

Methods

defineClass()

```
protected final Class defineClass(byte indata[],
        int offset,int length)     ** deprecated **
    throws ClassFormatError

protected final Class defineClass(String name,
        byte indata[],int offset,int length)
    throws ClassFormatError
```

Converts indata into an instance of a Class object for a class — one that represents the loaded class. The resulting Class cannot be used until its references are resolved (which could entail further ClassLoader actions). A ClassFormatError is thrown if indata cannot be deciphered.

The parameter name is the name of the class. If the name is unknown, use null. Package name qualifications in the name string should use '.' instead of '/' to describe the path. The offset is the starting position of the class data in the indata array — the length is the number of bytes of class data in indata. See Example 1.

The form of defineClass() without the name parameter has been deprecated as of version 1.1.

findLoadedClass()

```
protected final Class findLoadedClass(String name)
```

Returns the Class representation of a previously loaded class. If the named class is not found, null is returned.

findSystemClass()

```
protected final Class findSystemClass(String name)
        throws ClassNotFoundException
        throws NoClassDefFoundError
```

Returns the Class object of the named system class. A system class is one that is loaded from the local file system without using a ClassLoader. The actual loading process is system-dependent.

getResource()

```
public URL getResource(String name)
```

Locates the named resource and returns its URL. A call to URL.getContent() could return an Image, AudioClip, or an InputStream. The resource can be anything that can be represented by a URL.

getResourceAsStream()

```
public InputStream getResourceAsStream(String name)
```

Finds the named resource and opens a stream from which it can be read. If there is no resource found by the specified name, a null is returned. The rules for performing the search are determined by the ClassLoader.

getSystemResource()

```
public URL getSystemResource(String name)
```

Locates the named system resource and returns its URL. A call to URL.getContent() could return an Image, an AudioClip, or an InputStream. The search for the resource will be in the places specified by CLASSPATH. A system resource is one that resides on the local computer.

getSystemResourceAsStream()

```
public final static InputStream
            getSystemResourceAsStream(String name)
```

Finds the named system resource and opens a stream from which it can be read. If there is no resource by the specified name, a null is returned. The rules for performing the search are determined by the ClassLoader. The search for the resource will be in the places specified by CLASSPATH. A system resource is one that resides on the local computer.

loadClass()

```
public Class loadClass(String name)
    throws ClassNotFoundException

protected abstract Class loadClass(String name,boolean resolve)
    throws ClassNotFoundException
```

Returns the Class representation for the named class. The ClassNotFoundException is thrown if the class definition is not found. Setting resolve to true will cause the Class to be resolved through a call to resolveClass() before the method returns. Note that one of the methods—the one with the resolve parameter—is abstract, which means it must be defined by the subclass.

 This method can cause the same Class to be loaded a number of times—once for each time it is called. To prevent this from happening, it will be necessary to keep a list of preloaded Classes in a table.

resolveClass()

```
protected final void resolveClass(Class resClass)
```

This will resolve the references made by resClass. This resolution must occur before the class referenced by resClass can be used. The resolving is done by calls to loadClass(). The process of resolving a class could cause other classes to be loaded, which, in turn, will be resolved.

setSigners()

```
protected final void setSigners(Class cl,Object signers[])
```

This will assign the array of signers of a class. This is called by signature-aware software after the class itself is designed. The signer array can be retrieved by a call to Class.getSigners().

Example 1

This example is really a collection of code snippets to give you an idea of how a ClassLoader object could be defined and used. This is how some implementation of a ClassLoader would look. For this example, we will be loading classes over a numbered serial port:

```
public class SerialLoader extends ClassLoader {
    int ttyNumber;
    byte bArray[];
    Hashtable table = new Hashtable();
    public SerialLoader(int ttyNumber) {
        this.ttyNumber = ttyNumber;
    }
```

```
public Class loadClass(String name,
                boolean resolve)
            throws ClassNotFoundException {
    Class newClass = table.get(name);
    if(newClass != null)
        return(newClass);
    // Insert code to load bArray from the port.
    newClass = defineClass(name,bArray,0,bArray.length);
    // If resolve is true, resolve reference here.
    table.put(name,newClass);
    return(newClass);
}
```

The class loader first looks to see whether the class is already in the table and, if it is, simply returns the table entry. If the class is not in the table, it must be loaded. The byte-array form of the class is loaded through the port. Once loaded, a class is defined from the data, and the class is then resolved—if need be—by loading the necessary resolving classes. Finally, the finished class is put into the table and returned to the caller.

All that is left to do is to create an instance of the class, like this:

```
SerialLoader sl = new SerialLoader(4);
Object whopper = sl.loadClass("Whopper").newInstance();
```

It is important that any classes loaded through the SerialLoader be resolved by also using the SerialLoader. This is because, quite often, the references to classes will be resolved as the other classes are loaded from the same location—in this case, through the same serial port.

Example 2

This example shows how to access a system resource. The exact string form is system-dependent—in this case, running under Windows 95, the CLASS-PATH was set to include C:\TMP, and an audio file, Fred.au, was placed in that directory. The method getSystemResource() looked through the directories listed in CLASSPATH until it found the file. It then returned a URL for the file:

```
import java.net.*;
public class SystemResource {
    public static void main(String[] arg) {
        URL url = ClassLoader.getSystemResource("fred.au");
        System.out.println(url.toExternalForm());
        try {
            System.out.println(url.getContent());
```

```
        } catch(Exception e) {
            System.out.println(e);
        }
    }
}
```

In the example, we print the external form and the content type of the URL. The output looks like this:

```
systemresource:/FILEc:\tmp/+/fred.au
class sun.applet.AppletAudioClip[null]
```

 For loading classes from a remote system, see **RMIClassLoader**.

ClassNotFoundException

class java.lang.ClassNotFoundException

This exception is thrown if an attempt was made to load a class that does not exist or cannot be found.

Inheritance

```
public class java.lang.ClassNotFoundException
    extends Exception
        ⇑
    public class java.lang.Exception
        extends Throwable
            ⇑
        public class java.lang.Throwable
            implements Serializable
            extends Object
                ⇑
            public class java.lang.Object
```

Constructors

```
public ClassNotFoundException()
public ClassNotFoundException(String message)
```

If the message string is supplied, it is used as the detailed message.

CLASSPATH

environment variable

During compilation (and again during execution), Java needs to resolve the meanings of references to names not found inside a class. The CLASSPATH environment variable is designed to aid in directing the search. It should be noted that use of CLASSPATH is part of the Sun JDK and that there are other Java software development systems that have their own methods of resolving file and directory names.

Some systems (UNIX and Windows, for example) have a hierarchical file system for which environment variables can be set. When this is the case, the environment variable CLASSPATH can be set to the list of directories into which Java will search for packages.

For example, say that CLASSPATH is set to

```
/pkgs/hummer;/sun/java
```

If the Java compiler were to encounter the statement

```
int i = gobat.fred.Skimpy();
```

then the compiler would look for the directory named gobat in /pkgs/hummer, and if it failed, it would look again in /sun/java. Once the directory was located, the compiler would look inside it for something called fred and go on from there. In this example, it would expect a file named fred.class to contain a method named Skimpy().

A zip file

A collection of files in a directory is only one form of storage for class files — they can also be kept in a zip file or a JAR file. One example of this is the Java API that is kept in the classes.zip file somewhere on the CLASSPATH. The file is included in the path the same way that a directory would be, for example:

```
/pkgs/hummer/java/classes.zip
```

This requires the full path /pkgs/hummer/java/classes.zip be included in CLASSPATH, and Java will look inside the zip file just as if it were a directory.

 Also see **java**, the interpreter, and its classpath option.

Clipboard

class java.awt.datatransfer.Clipboard

This class implements the underlying mechanism that can be used to implement GUI interface cut-and-paste and copy-and-paste operations.

Inheritance

```
public class java.awt.datatransfer.Clipboard
    extends Object
        ⇑
    public class java.lang.Object
```

Variables and constants

contents

```
protected Transferable contents
```

The object that has been cut or copied from one location and is to be pasted into another.

owner

```
protected ClipboardOwner owner
```

The class that provided the Transferable object.

Constructors

```
public Clipboard(String name)
```

A Clipboard object is assigned a name that can be used as identification.

Returned by

The system clipboard can be acquired by a call to Toolkit.getSystemClipboard().

Methods

getContents()

```
public synchronized TransferablegetContents(Object requester)
```

Returns the Transferable object that is already on the clipboard. If there is no Transferable object, null is returned. The requester is the object requesting the data.

getName()

```
public String getName()
```

Returns the name of this clipboard.

setContents()

```
public synchronized void setContents(
        Transferable contents,ClipboardOwner owner)
```

Puts contents onto the clipboard and assigns ownership of it to owner. If there is already a registered owner, it is notified that it is no longer the owner of the contents of the clipboard.

Example

This is a simple example of posting an object to the system clipboard from one class and retrieving it in another. In a windowing environment, this could be used to implement a drag-and-drop operation with the mouse, but for this example, we just post a line of text to a clipboard and read it back:

```java
import java.awt.*;
import java.awt.datatransfer.*;
import java.io.*;

public class PostAndRetrieve {
    public static void main(String[] arg) {
        Poster poster = new Poster();
        poster.post("This is the posted string.");
        Retriever retriever = new Retriever();
        String string = retriever.retrieve();
        System.out.println(string);
        System.exit(0);
    }
}

class Poster implements ClipboardOwner {
    public void post(String string) {
        Toolkit tk = Toolkit.getDefaultToolkit();
        Clipboard board = tk.getSystemClipboard();
        System.out.println("Poster (the board): " +
                board.getName());
        StringSelection ss = new StringSelection(string);
        System.out.println("Poster (Transferable): " + ss);
        board.setContents(ss,this);
    }
    public void lostOwnership(Clipboard board,
            Transferable tran) {
        System.out.println("Poster lost ownership:");
        System.out.println("  Clipboard: " + board);
        System.out.println("  Transferable: " + tran);
    }
}
```

```
class Retriever implements ClipboardOwner {
    public String retrieve() {
        Toolkit tk = Toolkit.getDefaultToolkit();
        Clipboard board = tk.getSystemClipboard();
        System.out.println("Retriever (the board): " +
                board.getName());
        Transferable tran = board.getContents(this);
        System.out.println("Retriever (tran): " + tran);
        DataFlavor[] flavor = tran.getTransferDataFlavors();
        for(int i=0; i<flavor.length; i++) {
            System.out.println("Retriever (flavor): " +
                    flavor[i].getHumanPresentableName());
        }
        String string = "Fail";
        try {
            string = (String)tran.getTransferData(
                    DataFlavor.stringFlavor);
        } catch(UnsupportedFlavorException e) {
            System.out.println(e);
        } catch(IOException e) {
            System.out.println(e);
        }
        // Post it back just to force change of ownership.
        board.setContents(tran,this);
        return(string);
    }
    public void lostOwnership(Clipboard b,Transferable t) {
    }
}
```

The main() method creates a Poster object and uses it to put a string on the clipboard; it then creates a Retriever object to read it back.

The Poster first gets a copy of the system Clipboard from the default Toolkit. A StringSelection object is created to hold the Unicode string to be posted. The StringSelection class implements the Transferable interface, enabling it to be posted to a Clipboard. The call to setContents() of the Clipboard posts the data. The first argument is the transferable object, and the second is the owner of the data being transferred. In this example, the owner is Poster, which implements the ClipboardOwner interface. The Clipboard owner interface requires the implementation of the method lostOwnerShip() that will be called whenever the data is no longer on the clipboard.

The Retriever class also gets a copy of the system Clipboard and calls getContents() to retrieve the data that was stored there. There is no way of knowing what the retrieved data is, so a call is made to `getTransferDataFlavors()` to get a list of all the forms in which the data could possibly be retrieved. In our example, we know what the data is, so we just ignore the array of flavors (other than to print the list) and retrieve the data as a `String` object by calling `getTransferData()` and specifying the `DataFlavor.stringFlavor` (which is the specification of a Java `String`). It is necessary to retrieve the data inside a try block because there are a couple of exceptions that can be thrown—one if the flavor is unknown to the stored `Transferable` object and the other if the data is no longer there to be retrieved.

As one final step in `Retrieve`—before returning to `main()` with the `String`—calls the `setContents()` method of the `Clipboard` to post the data back to it. This is not necessary for retrieving data—it is used in this example to demonstrate that loss of ownership will cause the `lostOwnerShip()` method of the original owner to be called. It is not necessary to actually do anything when ownership is lost—it is simply a notification. In fact, the `lostOwnership()` method does nothing but print to standard output. Here is the output from this example:

```
Poster (the board): System
Poster (Transferable):
java.awt.datatransfer.StringSelection@1cc92e
Retriever (the board): System
Retriever (tran): java.awt.datatransfer.StringSelection@1cc95e
Retriever (flavor): Unicode String
Retriever (flavor): Plain Text
Poster lost ownership:
   Clipboard: sun.awt.windows.WClipboard@1cc91b
   Transferable: java.awt.datatransfer.StringSelection@1cc92e
This is the posted string.
```

As you can see, two possible flavors of data could have been retrieved from the `Transferable`. One was the Unicode `String` object (the one we used), and the other was a plain text string of characters. You can also see that the output from the `Poster` class was printed when it lost ownership of the `Clipboard` as the `Retriever` assumed ownership by posting a new `Transferable`.

 Data that resides on a clipboard implements the **Transferable** interface. The owner of clipboard data implements the **ClipboardOwner** interface. The data characteristics are identified by having a **DataFlavor**.

ClipboardOwner

interface java.awt.datatransfer.ClipboardOwner

This is the interface for a class that can write information to a `Clipboard`. An object assumes ownership of a `Clipboard` by posting data to it.

Implemented by

```
StringSelection
```

Inheritance

```
public interface java.awt.datatransfer.ClipboardOwner
```

Methods

lostOwnership()

```
public abstract void lostOwnership(
        Clipboard clipboard,Transferable contents)
```

This method is called to notify the object that it has lost ownership of the clipboard and its contents. This will happen whenever another object takes ownership of the `Clipboard` by posting data to it.

 An object implementing this interface can communicate with a **Clipboard**. Data that resides on a clipboard implements the **Transferable** interface. The data characteristics are identified by having a **DataFlavor**.

Cloneable

interface java.lang.Cloneable

This interface has no members—however, this interface must be implemented for a call to the `clone()` method to succeed. The `clone()` method, inherited from the `Object` class, will throw a `CloneableNotImplemented` exception when called, unless the class implements this interface.

Implemented by

```
BitSet
BreakIterator
Calendar
Collator
Date
DateFormatSymbols
DecimalFormatSymbols
DateFormat
Format
GridBagConstraints
```

```
Hashtable
Insets
ImageFilter
Locale
NumberFormat
TimeZone
Vector
```

Extended by

```
AclEntry
CharacterIterator
```

Inheritance

```
public interface java.lang.Cloneable
```

 For examples of using the clone() method, see **Object**.

CloneNotSupportedException

class java.lang.CloneNotSupportedException

This exception is thrown whenever the method clone() is called but the class has not implemented the Cloneable interface.

Extended by

```
ServerCloneException
```

Inheritance

```
public class java.lang.CloneNotSupportedException
    extends Exception
        ⇑
    public class java.lang.Exception
        extends Throwable
            ⇑
        public class java.lang.Throwable
            implements Serializable
            extends Object
```

⇑
```
public class java.lang.Object
```

Constructors
```
public CloneNotSupportedException()
public CloneNotSupportedException(String message)
```

If the `message` string is supplied, it is used as the detailed message.

 For the interface, see **Cloneable**. For the `clone()` method, see **Object**.

coercion

 For Java's ability to force data conversion from one type to another, see **expressions**.

collation

The action of comparing two characters, or strings of characters, to one other to determine which should come before the other is known as *collation*. Because we are dealing with the Unicode character set—which includes all the major alphabets of the world—the process is a bit more complicated than the simple ordering of the ASCII character set.

The strength of comparison

Three things can happen in comparing character A to character B: A can be less than B, A can be greater than B, or A and B can be identical. Some languages include a concept known as the *strength* of the comparison—this has to do with a degree of the difference between two characters. The strengths of the differences (in descending order of magnitude) are primary, secondary, tertiary, and identical.

The letters e and f have primary differences. The letters e and e are identical. The Czech letters e and ě have only secondary differences, and e and E have only tertiary differences.

Multi-character comparisons

Circumstances arise in which the comparison of a string involves more than a one-for-one comparison of the characters. For example, in Spanish, while the string "ca" would break down to a c and then an *a*, the string "cha" would break down to "ch" and *a*. In German, the string "äb" breaks down to *a*, then *e*, and then *b*.

A caseless compare

The special capabilities of the Java collation classes and their configurable character strengths can be handy even when working just with the ASCII character set. The characters *e* and *E* could be given identical primary differences with one or the other having a greater secondary difference (depending on whether you wanted upper- or lowercase to come first). This would give you the option of comparing strings with or without considering case.

The key in three parts

The collation value of any one character is determined by the magnitude of its key. The key for a character is composed of three parts—the 16-bit primary, the 8-bit secondary, and the 8-bit tertiary order.

A key value for a character can be acquired by calling the appropriate method. When returned separately, the primary value is returned as an `int`, while the secondary and tertiary values are each returned as a `short`. It is done this way to eliminate problems with signed/unsigned values.

The key as an int

Whenever the entire key value is formatted as an `int`, it is packed this way: The first 16 bits hold the primary value, the next 8 bits hold the secondary value, and the last 8 bits hold the tertiary value.

 For classes that implement these principles, see **CollationElementIterator**, **CollationKey**, **RuleBasedCollator**, and **Collator**.

CollationElementIterator

class java.text.CollationElementIterator

This is an iterator that will walk through a string character by character and return the collation keys for each character. It can be used to collate Unicode strings following the rules defined by the characteristics of a specific language. The ordering priority of a character is known as its *key*. The keys of the characters can be used to make the comparisons.

Inheritance

```
public final class java.text.CollationElementIterator
      extends Object
         ⇑
      public class java.lang.Object
```

Variables and constants

NULLORDER

```
public final static int NULLORDER
```

This value indicates that the end of the string has been reached.

Constructors

```
CollationElementIterator(String sourceText,
            RuleBasedCollator order)
```

The sourceText is the string to be used to generate the set of key values. The order is the collator that will be used to determine the key value of any one specific character.

Returned by

A CollationElementIterator is returned from a call to RuleBaseCollator.getCollationElementIterator().

Methods

next()

```
public int next()
```

Returns the 32-bit ordering key value of the next character in the string. After the return, the internal cursor will have been moved to the next character. If there are no more characters, it returns NULLORDER.

primaryOrder()

```
public final static int primaryOrder(int order)
```

Extracts and returns the primary value of the key order.

reset()

```
public void reset()
```

This method will return the internal cursor to the first character in the string. After this call, a call to next() will return the key value of the first character in the string.

secondaryOrder()

```
public final static short secondaryOrder(int order)
```

Extracts and returns the secondary value of the key order.

tertiaryOrder()

```
public final static short tertiaryOrder(int order)
```

Extracts and returns the tertiary value of the key `order`.

 For a description of the meanings of the keys, see **collation**. The other classes dealing with collation are **CollationKey**, **Collator**, and **RuleBasedCollator**.

CollationKey

class java.text.CollationKey

A `CollationKey` represents a single string and can be compared to another `CollationKey` object to determine the proper ordering of the two strings.

It's a matter of speed

It is simpler to use the `Collator.compare()` method to make string comparisons, but if you are going to be making a lot of comparisons (as could be the case in a sorting algorithm), it could be faster to perform the comparisons using the `CollationKey` object for each string. You will have to weigh the cost of the overhead of creating a `CollationKey` for each string against the cost of each comparison for the number of comparisons you will be making.

The comparison is done with the bits

A `CollationKey` is generated for an entire string. The key itself is a string of bits that can be compared very quickly. The comparison method only looks as far into the string of bits as it must to find a mismatch that determines the ordering.

Inheritance

```
public final class java.text.CollationKey
    extends Object
            ⇑
    public class java.lang.Object
```

Constructors

Returned by

Objects of this class are acquired by the `getCollationKey()` methods of `Collator` and `RuleBasedCollator`. Important: Only `CollationKey` objects from the same `Collator` can be compared with one another.

Methods

compareTo()

```
public int compareTo(CollationKey target)
```

Returns the results of a comparison of the key values of this CollationKey and the target. A negative value means this key is less than the target, a positive value indicates greater-than, and zero means they are equal.

equals()

```
public boolean equals(Object target)
```

Compares the key value of this Collation key to the key value of the target and returns true if they are equal.

getSourceString()

```
public String getSourceString()
```

Returns the string that this key represents.

hashCode()

```
public int hashCode()
```

Returns the hash value that is calculated from the key value. Two CollationKey objects representing the same string will have the same hashcode values.

toByteArray()

```
public byte[] toByteArray()
```

Returns the internal key—the string of bits used for comparison—in an array of bytes. The most significant bytes are first.

Example

This is a simple example of a sort to demonstrate the mechanics of using a CollationKey:

```
import java.text.*;
public class CollationKeyMechanics {
    public static void main(String[] arg) {
        Collator collator = Collator.getInstance();
        CollationKey[] key = new CollationKey[4];
        key[0] = collator.getCollationKey("lions");
        key[1] = collator.getCollationKey("tigers");
        key[2] = collator.getCollationKey("bears");
        key[3] = collator.getCollationKey("oh my");
        sort(key);
```

```
        for(int i=0; i<key.length; i++)
            System.out.println(key[i].getSourceString());
    }
    private static void sort(CollationKey[] key) {
        int i = 1;
        while(i<key.length) {
            if(key[i-1].compareTo(key[i]) > 0) {
                CollationKey hold = key[i];
                key[i] = key[i-1];
                key[i-1] = hold;
                i = 1;
            } else {
                i++;
            }
        }
    }
}
```

An array of keys is acquired from a Collator by calling getCollationKey() with the strings to be collated. These keys encapsulate both the string and the collation rules. A sort() routine is used (in this case, a very simple sort routine) to put the keys in collation order. The output of the example looks like this:

```
bears
lions
oh my
tigers
```

 For a description of the meanings of the keys, see **collation**. The other classes dealing with collation are **CollationElementIterator**, **Collator**, and **RuleBasedCollator**.

Collator

class java.text.Collator

An object of this class is capable of performing locale-specific comparisons of Unicode character strings. This abstract class is used to construct classes capable of using specific collation rules for making string comparisons in the local language.

A matter of efficiency

Once a `Collator` object exists, there are two different ways to use it to compare strings. The `compare()` method of this class can be called to directly compare strings, or a `CollationKey` object can be constructed for each string to be compared. The `CollationKey` method requires that a new object be created for each string, but the comparisons are much quicker. If the same string will be used in a comparison several times (as in a sort procedure), the `CollationKey` could be faster.

One important note: `CollationKeys` from different `Collator` objects cannot be compared to one another.

Extended by

```
RuleBasedCollator
```

Inheritance

```
public abstract class java.text.Collator
    implements Cloneable
    implements Serializable
    extends Object
        ⇑
    public class java.lang.Object
```

Variables and constants

CANONICAL_DECOMPOSITION

```
public final static int CANONICAL_DECOMPOSITION
```

The default decomposition mode setting. Any character defined by Unicode 2.0 to be a variant will be appropriately decomposed for collation.

FULL_DECOMPOSITION

```
public final static int FULL_DECOMPOSITION
```

An optional decomposition mode setting. This is the most complete and, as a result, the slowest of the decomposition settings. With this setting, both Unicode canonical variants and Unicode compatibility variants will be decomposed for collation. This means that accented characters and characters that have special formats will be collated with their nominal forms. For example, the half-width and full-width ASCII and Katakana characters are collated together.

IDENTICAL

```
public final static int IDENTICAL
```

A comparison strength setting. This means that all differences are considered—primary, secondary, and tertiary—to determine the comparison results.

NO_DECOMPOSITION

```
public final static int NO_DECOMPOSITION
```

A decomposition mode setting. This means that accented characters are not decomposed for collation. This is the fastest of the collation modes but could produce incorrect results for languages that use accents.

PRIMARY

```
public final static int PRIMARY
```

A comparison strength setting. This will cause comparisons to be made on the primary key values of the characters being compared. For example, this could cause *a* and *ä* to be considered to be identical.

SECONDARY

```
public final static int SECONDARY
```

A comparison strength setting. This will cause the primary and secondary key values to be taken into account for the comparison, but any tertiary values are ignored. For example, this could cause *a* and *ä* to be considered not the same.

TERTIARY

```
public final static int TERTIARY
```

A comparison strength setting. This will cause all the shadings of differences to be taken into account when comparing two characters. For example, this could cause *a* and *A* to be considered different because they differ in case.

Constructors

```
protected Collator()
```

The default constructor is protected so that it will be accessible from the derived classes only.

Returned by

The default Collator for the locale can be acquired by calling getInstance().

Methods

clone()

```
public Object clone()
```

Creates a duplicate of this object.

compare()

```
public abstract int compare(String source,String target)
```

Uses the comparison rules of this `Collator` and compares the source string to the target string. Returns the value resulting from the comparison as negative if `source` is less than `target`, positive if `source` is greater, and zero if the two strings are equal.

equals()

```
public boolean equals(String source,String target)

public boolean equals(Object object)
```

The form that requires two `String` objects is a convenience function that returns `true` if the `source` and `target` strings are equal. The other form will return `true` if `object` is a `Collator` that is equal to this one.

getAvailableLocales()

```
public static synchronized Locale[] getAvailableLocales()
```

Returns all the `Locale` objects for which there is a `Collator` installed.

getCollationKey()

```
public abstract CollationKeygetCollationKey(String source)
```

Constructs and returns a `CollationKey` object for the `source` string. For an example, see `CollationKey`.

getDecomposition()

```
public synchronized int getDecomposition()
```

Returns the decomposition mode of this `Collator`. The returned value is `NO_DECOMPO-SITION`, `CANONICAL_DECOMPOSITION`, or `FULL_DECOMPOSITION`.

getInstance()

```
public static synchronized CollatorgetInstance(Locale locale)
public static synchronized Collator getInstance()
```

Returns the `Collator` instance for the locale. If no `locale` is specified, the current default is assumed.

getStrength()

```
public synchronized int getStrength()
```

Returns the value of the strength used for comparisons by this Collator. The returned value is PRIMARY, SECONDARY, TERTIARY, or IDENTICAL.

hashCode()

```
public synchronized abstract int hashCode()
```

Returns the hashcode value for this object.

setDecomposition()

```
public synchronized void setDecomposition(int mode)
```

Sets the decomposition mode to NO_DECOMPOSITION, CANONICAL_DECOMPOSITION, or FULL_DECOMPOSITION. An IllegalArgumentException is thrown if mode is not one of these values.

setStrength()

```
public synchronized void setStrength(int strength)
```

Sets the strength to either PRIMARY, SECONDARY, TERTIARY, or IDENTICAL. An IllegalArgumentException is thrown if mode is not one of these values.

Example

This example shows how to use the collator of the default locale to make string comparisons:

```
import java.text.*;
public class CollatorCompare {
    static Collator collator;
    public static void main(String[] arg) {
        collator = Collator.getInstance();
        showCompare("apples","oranges");
        showCompare("oranges","apples");
        showCompare("apples","apples");
        showCompare("Apples","apples");
        showCompare("apples","Apples");
    }
    private static void showCompare(String s1,String s2) {
        System.out.println("Compare " + s1 + " to " + s2 +
            " = " + collator.compare(s1,s2));
    }
}
```

The default Collator is acquired by calling getInstance(). The results of the comparison are –1, 0, and 1. The output from this example looks like this:

```
Compare apples to oranges = -1
```

```
Compare oranges to apples = 1
Compare apples to apples = 0
Compare Apples to apples = 1
Compare apples to Apples = -1
```

 There is one generalized subclass of `Collator` as a part of the Java API. See **RuleBasedCollator**.

Color

class java.awt.Color

This class encapsulates RGB colors.

RGB

The color values are made up of three components — red, green, and blue. Each one of these can be assigned a value from 0 through 255. A value of 0 means none of that color is included, and a value of 255 means the maximum amount of that color is included. If all three colors are at their maximum values — that is, (255,255,255) — the color is white. The lowest value for all three (0,0,0) is black. Figure C-10 shows the format used by Java to store the three 8-bit color components in standard big-endian format as a 32-bit `long`.

Figure C-10 The format of RGB stored as a `long`.

The predefined colors

A number of `Color` objects are statically defined as constants in this class. There is nothing magic about this set of colors — they are made up of a fairly standard set of RGB values that have been found to show up quite well on various systems. This makes them quite portable. The actual color displayed will vary from one system to another. It depends on the software that converts RGB to the local system's format, the characteristics of the phosphors in the display, the brightness and contrast settings, and even the ambient light in the room.

An HSB color

An alternative method of defining a color is the HSB method—that is, hue, saturation, and brightness. Each of the three values are floating-point numbers that range from 0.0 to 1.0. A brightness value of 0.0 is black, and a brightness of 1.0 is white.

Extended by

```
SystemColor
```

Inheritance

```
public class java.awt.Color
    implements Serializable
    extends Object
        ⇑
    public class java.lang.Object
```

Variables and constants

black

```
public final static Color black
```

The color black: (0,0,0).

blue

```
public final static Color blue
```

The color blue: (0,0,255).

cyan

```
public final static Color cyan
```

The color cyan: (0,255,255).

darkGray

```
public final static Color darkGray
```

The color dark gray: (64,64,64)

gray

```
public final static Color gray
```

The color gray: (128,128,128)

green

```
public final static Color green
```

The color green: (0,255,0)

lightGray

```
public final static Color lightGray
```

The color light gray: (192,192,192)

magenta

```
public final static Color magenta
```

The color magenta: (255,0,255)

orange

```
public final static Color orange
```

The color orange: (255,200,0)

pink

```
public final static Color pink
```

The color pink: (255,175,175)

red

```
public final static Color red
```

The color red: (255,0,0)

white

```
public final static Color white
```

The color white: (255,255,255)

yellow

```
public final static Color yellow
```

The color yellow: (255,255,0)

Constructors

```
public Color(int R,int G,int B)
public Color(float R,float G,float B)
public Color(int RGB)
```

Three ways exist to specify the same thing. A `Color` is created by specifying the values of the red, green, and blue components. Each of the `int` values R, G, and B can range from a minimum color intensity of zero to a maximum of 255. Each `float` value can range from a minimum color intensity of 0.0 to a maximum of 1.0. If all three colors are included as a single `int` value, that value is expected to be in the `RGB` format described previously.

Returned by

Aside from the `Color` constants described earlier, some methods in this class return `Color` objects; they are `brighter()`, `darker()`, `decode()`, `getColor()`, and `getHSBColor()`. `Color` objects are also returned from `Graphics.getColor()`, `Component.getBackground()`, and `Component.getForeground()`.

Methods

brighter()

```
public Color brighter()
```

Returns a brighter version of this color. Not all colors will return a brighter version (black and white, for example), and even if a brighter version is returned, it may not display differently from the original on any given system.

darker()

```
public Color darker()
```

Returns a darker version of this color. Not all colors will return a darker version (black, for example), and even if a darker version is returned, it may not display differently from the original on any given system.

decode()

```
public static Color decode(String colorValue)
    throws NumberFormatException
```

Returns a `Color` for the color named as `colorValue`. A call is made to `Integer.decode()` to convert `colorValue` to an `int`, and then the three eight-bit values are extracted from it. The `int` is expected to be in the same format that can be supplied as an `RGB` argument to a `Color` constructor.

equals()

```
public boolean equals(Object object)
```

Returns `true` if object is a `Color` object that represents the same color value as this one.

getBlue()

```
public int getBlue()
```

Returns the blue component of the color as a value from 0 to 255.

getColor()

```
public static Color getColor(String colorName)

public static Color getColor(String colorValue,
        Color defaultColor)

public static Color getColor(String colorName,
        int defaultColor)
```

Returns the `Color` defined by the system property `colorName`. If no property is defined for `colorName`, but either `defaultColor` or `defaultColorValue` has been specified, the default is returned. If no property is defined and no default was supplied, a `null` is returned.

A call is made to `Integer.getValue()` to convert `colorName` from a system property to an `int`, and then the three eight-bit values are extracted from the `int`. The `int` is expected to be the same format that can be supplied as an `RGB` argument to a `Color` constructor.

getGreen()

```
public int getGreen()
```

Returns the green component of the color as a value from 0 to 255.

getHSBColor()

```
public static Color getHSBColor(float h,float s,float b)
```

Returns a `Color` object constructed from the HSB values.

getRed()

```
public int getRed()
```

Returns the red component of the color as a value from 0 to 255.

getRGB()

```
public int getRGB()
```

Returns the 32-bit form of the RGB color.

hashCode()

```
public int hashCode()
```

Returns the hashcode value for this object.

HSBtoRGB()

```
public static int HSBtoRGB(float hue,float saturation,
```

```
            float brightness)
```

Given the three HSB values of a color; returns the 32-bit RGB value for it.

RGBtoHSB()

```
public static float[] RGBtoHSB(int r,int g,int b,
           float hsbvals[])
```

Converts the RGB values in an array of HSB values. Puts the values into the hsbvals array. Returns the hsbvals array.

toString()

```
public String toString()
```

Returns the string representation of the color values.

 For an example of using a Color object to do drawing, see **Graphics**. For some system-dependent considerations, see the two **ColorModels**: **DirectColorModel** and **IndexColorModel**.

ColorModel

class java.awt.image.ColorModel

This is an abstract class that the defines methods for converting color data into the default format and extracting information from the result.

The default color model

Java has a default way to represent colors: it is called the RGB model. It is a 32-bit value that has a special meaning assigned to each byte of a standard big-endian long, as shown in Figure C-11.

The leftmost byte is the *alpha* value. This is a measure of the transparency of the color. An alpha value of 0 means the color is completely transparent. A value of 255 means the color is completely opaque.

The other three bytes are the intensity of the primary colors red, green, and blue. A value of 0 means that the primary color has zero inclusion, and a value of 255 means that it has maximum inclusion.

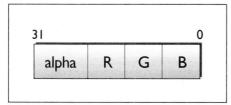

Figure C-11   The format of RGB with an alpha component.

Extended by

```
DirectColorModel
IndexColorModel
```

Inheritance

```
public abstract class java.awt.image.ColorModel
    extends Object
        ⇑
    public class java.lang.Object
```

Returned by

The method `getRGBdefault()` will return a `ColorModel` object that works with the default color model. There are `getColorModel()` methods in `Component`, `ComponentPeer`, `PixelGrabber`, and `Toolkit`.

Variables and constants

pixel_bits

```
protected int pixel_bits
```

This holds a count of the number of bits per pixel required to define a color.

Constructors

```
public ColorModel(int pixelBits)
```

A `ColorModel` is constructed by specifying the number of bits per pixel, which is stored in `pixel_bits`.

Methods

finalize()

```
public void finalize()
```

Called by the garbage collector before memory of the object is reclaimed.

getAlpha()

```
public abstract int getAlpha(int pixel)
```

Returns the alpha component of the color. The values range from 0, which is transparent, to 255, which is opaque.

getBlue()

```
public abstract int getBlue(int pixelColor)
```

Returns the blue component of `pixelColor`. The return value ranges from 0, which is no blue, to 255, which is maximum blue.

getGreen()

```
public abstract int getGreen(int pixelColor)
```

Returns the green component of `pixelColor`. The return value ranges from 0, which is no green, to 255, which is maximum green.

getPixelSize()

```
public int getPixelSize()
```

Returns the number of bits per pixel.

getRed()

```
public abstract int getRed(int pixelColor)
```

Returns the red component of `pixelColor`. The return value ranges from 0, which is no red, to 255, which is maximum red.

getRGB()

```
public int getRGB(int pixelColor)
```

Converts the `pixelColor` to the default RGB color model form.

getRGBdefault()

```
public static ColorModel getRGBdefault()
```

Returns a `ColorModel` object capable of performing operations using pixels colors of the default format.

The two color model classes derived from this one are **DirectColorModel** and **IndexColorModel**.

colon

:

Making labels

A colon is used as part of the definition of a label when tagging a `for`, `do`, or `while` loop. For example:

```
looptop: for(int i=0; i<10; i++) ...
```

defines `looptop` as a label tagged to the beginning of the `for` loop.

Making cases

A colon is used as part of the definition of a `case` or `default` statement in a `switch`/`case` block. It looks like this:

```
switch(value) {
case 1:
    ...
case 2:
    ...
default:
    ...
}
```

Making conditionals

A colon, in combination with a question mark, can be used in the creation of a simplified if-then-else statement. For example, this statement will set the value of x to the larger of either a or b:

```
x = a > b ? a : b;
```

 For examples using colons to define a label used by `break` and `continue`, see **for**, **do**, or **while**. For examples of using colons in switch/case statements, see **switch**. For more on the construction of conditionals, see **question mark**.

comma

,

A comma has two uses in Java.

A comma can be used to separate expressions in the first and third parts of a for statement. For example:

```
for(i=0, j=10, k=0; i<10; i++, j--, k += 2) ...
```

The first section is for initialization, and the comma allows for the initialization of more than one variable. The third section is the expression executed at the bottom of the loop, and the comma allows for more than one to be executed. Unlike C, Java does not allow the comma to be used on the conditional in the center.

The second purpose of the comma is to separate a list of values when initializing an array. For example:

```
int[] fred = {1,2,3,4};
```

comment

/* /** // */

Java offers three forms of comments. There is the traditional form that was inherited from other languages (such as in C and C++), the documentation form (very much like the traditional form), and the end-of-line form (as found in C++).

Traditional form

The traditional form of a comment (sometimes called a slash-asterisk comment) begins with a slash-asterisk pair.

```
/* This is the traditional form. */
```

Because Java is a free-form language, a comment of this form can be continued for several lines by using one pair of delimiters. It is not uncommon to construct a comment block using a form similar to this:

```
/*
 *     This is an example of a comment block
 *     that continues for a few lines. The compiler
 *     skips everything until the comment closes.
 */
```

A traditional comment can be placed anywhere a single white space character can be placed. These statements are all identical:

```
toast = bread + heat;
toast = bread + heat /* No butter */;
toast /* Medium brown */ = bread + heat;
```

However, it is not valid to split a token with a comment, like this:

```
toast = br/*Bad*/ead + heat;  *** error ***
```

Documentation form

The documentation form is really the same as the traditional form—it's just that an added asterisk at the beginning marks it as containing information that can be used for special processing as documentation.

```
/** This is the documentation form. */
```

A comment of this form is created to be extracted for documentation. The standard tool to do this is *javadoc*.

The four-character sequence /**/ will be taken to be an empty documentation comment. The second asterisk serves the double purpose of tagging it and ending it.

End-of-line form

In a way, this form is simpler than the other two. This form begins with a double slash and continues to the end of the line. It looks like this:

```
// Everything to the end of the line is a comment.
```

Slash-slash, slash-asterisk, or asterisk-slash characters can appear to the right of the initial slash-slash, but they will be ignored. This form can begin anywhere on the line—anything to the left of the slash-slash is not part of the comment. For example:

```
compare = apples & oranges; // An odd comparison
```

Comments do not nest

The slash-asterisk style comments do not nest. You cannot use a comment to surround another comment. This is not valid:

```
/* Begin outer /* inner */ end outer */
```

The slash-asterisk pair immediately before `inner` will be ignored, and the asterisk-slash will terminate the comment—the compiler will become confused when it comes to `end outer`. Care must be taken not to accidentally terminate a comment like this:

```
/* An embedded asterisk slash (*/) ends a comment. */
```

You can nest a slash-slash style comment within a slash-asterisk style comment. This is valid:

```
/* This is the beginning of the comment.
   This is inside. // And this is inside.
   This will end the comment. */
```

 Failure to close a comment can cause a mysterious error message to occur at some point far away from the actual error. The compiler will treat everything as a comment until it finds a */ pair to close it, and that could be dozens of lines past the missing close.

 For how the compiler goes about processing comments, see **lexical structure**. For writing documentation comments and converting them to documents, see **javadoc**.

comparison

```
< > <= >= == !=
```

The Java primitive data types `byte`, `char`, `short`, `int`, `long`, `float`, and `double` can be compared using the six basic comparison operators:

`<`	less than
`>`	greater than
`<=`	less than or equal to
`>=`	greater than or equal to
`==`	equal
`!=`	not equal

A comparison operator always produces a `boolean` data type as the result. This result can be assigned directly to a `boolean` data type, as in

```
boolean result = a > b;
```

Or, more commonly, it can be used as the `boolean` expression in a conditional as in

```
if(a > b) ...
```

Widening for comparison

Primitives of different types can be compared because of the built-in widening rules of Java. If necessary, one operand will be widened to the type of the other before the actual comparison is performed.

Object comparison

It is not possible to use the built-in operators to execute comparisons on objects. Many objects have methods for doing comparisons.

compilation unit

A Java compilation unit is a text file—a Java program source code file—that has three parts. All the parts are optional, but a compilation unit without at least one class or interface definition is pointless.

1. A package declaration will specify the name of the package that will contain all the types defined in this file. If no package name is specified, the types defined in the file will be in the unnamed package.
2. One or more import statements may be used that will allow statements in this file to access public names from other packages.
3. The unit must contain the definition of one or more classes and interfaces.

Name of the compilation unit

The name of a compilation unit file normally ends with `.java`. (It is possible to have a system where a different file-naming convention would be necessary.) Also, a compilation unit can only define one public name, and that name must be the same as the filename. For example, the class

```
public class RunAbout {
    ...
}
```

must be in a source file named

```
RunAbout.java
```

Example

Here is an example of a compilation unit that contains all three parts:

```
package jpack;
```

```
import java.util.*;

public class CompilationUnit {
    public static void main(String arg[]) {
        Hashtable ht = new Hashtable();
        System.out.println(ht.toString());
    }
}
```

This compilation unit is to be part of a package named jpack (the package name also corresponds to the name of the directory in which it resides). The import statement adds all the types of the package java.util to the local namespace. The third part is the definition of the type CompilationUnit. Of course, since CompilationUnit is a public class, the name of the file must be CompilationUnit.java.

 Compilation units are grouped into packages—see **package**. To address names in other packages, see **import**.

compiler

 See **javac**.

Compiler

class java.lang.Compiler

These are a set of methods that can be used to communicate with a compiler that is capable of converting Java bytecodes directly into system-dependent machine code. No compiler is supplied as part of the standard JDK, but there are several third-party suppliers of JIT (Just In Time) compilers for applets, and there are native-mode compilers that can be used to convert applications into local executables.

The identifying property

The property java.compiler.exists should name the compiler library that can be used in a call to System.loadLibrary(), which can, in turn, be used to activate the compiler.

Inheritance

```
public final class Compiler
```

```
extends Object
     ⇑
public class java.lang.Object
```

Constructors

This class has no public constructors—all the methods are static.

Methods

command()

```
public static Object command(Object argument)
```

The argument object is passed to the compiler. Exactly what the argument is, and what will be done with it, is compiler-dependent. This method returns null if there is no compiler, or if the compiler has been disabled.

compileClass()

```
public static boolean compileClass(Class description)
```

A description of the class—in the form of a Class object—to be compiled is passed to the compiler. The class should be compiled into machine code. This method returns false if there is no compiler, or if the compiler has been disabled.

compileClasses()

```
public static boolean compileClasses(String names)
```

The argument names holds a list of the names of one or more classes to be compiled. The exact format of names is compiler-dependent. A return value of true indicates a successful compile. This method returns false if there is no compiler, or if the compiler has been disabled.

disable()

```
public static void disable()
```

Disables the compiler.

enable()

```
public static void Enable()
```

Enables the compiler.

Component

class java.awt.Component

This is an abstract class that is the superclass of all the windowing and displayable classes.

GUI

The graphical user interface of Java is defined by this class. Every mouse-clickable and keyboard-enterable object displayed in a window is a subclass of this class. A component is either a single element on the window (such as a button or a menu selection) or a group of elements (such as a collection of radio buttons or a pull-down list). Components can be nested inside one another.

The deprecation

You will find many deprecated methods in this class. This happened because of the change in the event model when Java moved from version 1.0 to version 1.1. This class is very involved with fielding and processing events, and the method of doing this was changed radically between versions 1.0 and 1.1. The deprecated methods should not be used in new software but are still supported for existing software. Use one or the other—the two event models should not be mixed in one program.

Extended by

```
Button
Canvas
Checkbox
Choice
Container
Label
List
Scrollbar
TextComponent
```

Inheritance

```
public abstract class java.awt.Component
    implements ImageObserver
    implements MenuContainer
    implements Serializable
    extends Object
        ⇑
    public class java.lang.Object
```

Variables and constants

BOTTOM_ALIGNMENT

```
public final static float BOTTOM_ALIGNMENT
```

This specifies alignment at the bottom of the component. It is for convenience in checking the return value from `getAlignmentY()`.

CENTER_ALIGNMENT

```
public final static float CENTER_ALIGNMENT
```

This specifies alignment in the center of the component. It is for convenience in checking the return value from `getAlignmentY()` and `getAlignmentX()`.

LEFT_ALIGNMENT()

```
public final static float LEFT_ALIGNMENT
```

This specifies alignment on the left of the component. It is for convenience in checking the return value from `getAlignmentX()`.

RIGHT_ALIGNMENT

```
public final static float RIGHT_ALIGNMENT
```

This specifies alignment on the right of the component. It is for convenience in checking the return value from `getAlignmentX()`.

TOP_ALIGNMENT

```
public final static float TOP_ALIGNMENT
```

This specifies alignment at the top of the component. It is for convenience in checking the return value from `getAlignmentY()`.

Constructors

```
protected Component()
```

Returned by

Objects of this class are returned from calls to

```
Component.getComponentAt()
Component.locate()
ComponentEvent.getComponent()
Container.add()
Container.getComponent()
Container.getComponentAt()
Container.locate()
```

```
ContainerEvent.getChild()
PropertyEditor.getCustomEditor()
PropertyEditorSupport.getCustomEditor()
Window.getFocusOwner()
```

An array of components is returned from `Container.getComponents()`.

Methods

action()   **deprecated**

```
public boolean action(Event event,Object what)
```

This method is called whenever an action is performed on the component. The `event` is accompanied by `what`, an object that can contain further details about the action.

add()

```
public synchronized void add(PopupMenu popup)
```

Adds the specified `popup` to the component. This is a menu that can be popped up instead of pulled down from a menu bar.

addComponentListener()

```
public synchronized void
        addComponentListener(ComponentListener listen)
```

Adds `listen` as a component listener.

addFocusListener()

```
public synchronized void
        addFocusListener(FocusListener listen)
```

Adds a listener that will detect loss and gain of focus.

addKeyListener()

```
public synchronized void
        addKeyListener(KeyListener listen)
```

Adds a listener that will receive keyboard events.

addMouseListener()

```
public synchronized void
        addMouseListener(MouseListener listen)
```

Adds a listener to the mouse events.

addMouseMotionListener()

```
public synchronized void
        addMouseMotionListener(MouseMotionListener listen)
```

Adds a listener that will be sent the mouse motion events.

addNotify()

```
public void addNotify()
```

Creates the underlying system-dependent peer for this object. This method is not normally called by the application. It is called by the container.

bounds()   deprecated

```
public Rectangle bounds()
```

This method is deprecated—use getBounds().

checkImage()

```
public int checkImage(Image image,ImageObserver observer)

public int checkImage(Image image,int width,
        int height,ImageObserver observer)
```

The return value is the logical OR of the set of ImageObserver flags describing the status of an image being loaded and/or being prepared for display. If width and height are specified, the method checks on the preparation of a version of the image that is being scaled to that size. The observer argument specifies the ImageObserver that is to have its imageUpdate() method called as the preparation proceeds. This method does not initiate the preparation of an image—it only checks the status.

contains()

```
public boolean contains(int x,int y)

public boolean contains(Point p)
```

Returns true if the point lies within the component. The coordinates are relative to the component itself.

createImage()

```
public Image createImage(ImageProducer producer)

public Image createImage(int width,int height)
```

These methods will create an image from the producer or create an empty image of the specified width and height.

deliverEvent()   **deprecated**

```
public void deliverEvent(Event event)
```

This method is deprecated—use dispatchEvent(AWTEvent e).

disable()   **deprecated**

```
public void disable()
```

This method is deprecated—use setEnabled().

disableEvents()

```
protected final void disableEvents(long eventMask)
```

This will disable the events specified by the eventMask. The values are defined in AWTEvent.

dispatchEvent()

```
public final void dispatchEvent(AWTEvent event)
```

The event is either processed by this Component or it is dispatched to an appropriate sub-component.

doLayout()

```
public void doLayout()
```

This requests that the component be laid out. Normally, this only has meaning when the component is being used as a container of some sort. This method is called requesting that its contained components are to be configured by the layout manager.

enable()   **deprecated**

```
public void enable()

public void enable(boolean b)
```

This method is deprecated—use setEnabled().

enableEvents()

```
protected final void enableEvents(long eventMask)
```

This will cause the events specified by eventMask to become enabled—that is, the events will be delivered to this component. There is no need to call this method if an event listener has been registered—the events of that type will have already been enabled. This is only necessary for subclasses that wish to receive the events even if there is no registered listener. The eventMask values are defined in AWTEvent.

getAlignmentX()

```
public float getAlignmentX()
```

Returns the horizontal alignment value—a floating-point number from 0.0 to 1.0, with 0.0 being the far left and 1.0 being the far right. Some constant values are defined as part of this class as convenience values for this method.

getAlignmentY()

```
public float getAlignmentY()
```

Returns the vertical alignment value—a floating-point number from 0.0 to 1.0, with 0.0 being the top and 1.0 being the bottom. Some constant values are defined as part of this class as convenience values for this method.

getBackground()

```
public Color getBackground()
```

Returns the background color. If no background color has been specified, the color of its parent is returned.

getBounds()

```
public Rectangle getBounds()
```

Returns a Rectangle that contains the bounds of this component.

getColorModel()

```
public ColorModel getColorModel()
```

Returns the ColorModel used to display the component.

getComponentAt()

```
public Component getComponentAt(int x,int y)

public Component getComponentAt(Point p)
```

This has meaning for container components—it returns the contained component that is at the specified location.

getCursor()

```
public Cursor getCursor()
```

Returns the Cursor object set for this component.

getFont()

```
public Font getFont()
```

Returns the Font for this component. If it does not have one, the Font of its parent is returned.

getFontMetrics()

```
public FontMetrics getFontMetrics(Font font)
```

Returns a FontMetrics object that can be used to determine information about the font.

getForeground()

```
public Color getForeground()
```

Returns the foreground color used in this component. If there is none, the foreground color of its parent is returned.

getGraphics()

```
public Graphics getGraphics()
```

Returns the Graphics object that can be used for drawing to the component. If the component is not currently being displayed, a null will be returned.

 Whenever you are finished using the Graphics object returned from this method, it is a good idea to call its dispose() method so that any system resources it holds will be freed. This will eventually be done automatically, but it could happen that you need the resource again before garbage collection.

getLocale()

```
public Locale getLocale()
    throws IllegalComponentStateException
```

This will return the Locale object for this component. If none has been specified, the Locale of its parent will be returned. If the Locale cannot be determined from a parent (for instance, if the component has not been added to a hierarchy), the exception is thrown.

getLocation()

```
public Point getLocation()
```

Returns the location of this component in the parent's window.

getLocationOnScreen()

```
public Point getLocationOnScreen()
```

Returns the screen location of this component.

getMaximumSize()

```
public Dimension getMaximumSize()
```

Returns the maximum size of this component.

getMinimumSize()

```
public Dimension getMinimumSize()
```

Returns the minimum size of this component.

getName()

```
public String getName()
```

Gets the name of the component.

getParent()

```
public Container getParent()
```

Gets the parent of the component.

getPeer()   **deprecated**

```
public ComponentPeer getPeer()
```

Returns the peer of this component.

getPreferredSize()

```
public Dimension getPreferredSize()
```

Returns the preferred size of this component.

getSize()

```
public Dimension getSize()
```

Returns the current size of this component.

getToolkit()

```
public Toolkit getToolkit()
```

Returns the component's Toolkit. The Toolkit for a component can be changed by adding the component to a Frame container. The Toolkit could be changed again by moving the component to another Frame.

getTreeLock()

```
public final Object getTreeLock()
```

Returns the locking object for AWT component-tree and layout operations. This method will always return the same Object. It is one that can be used to synchronize actions on the component. By locking the object returned from this method, you will have effectively locked the locking object of this component and all of its subcomponents.

gotFocus()   **deprecated**

```
public boolean gotFocus(Event event,Object what)
```

Returns true if the component has received the input focus. This method has been replaced by processFocusEvent(FocusEvent event).

handleEvent()   **deprecated**

```
public boolean handleEvent(Event event)
```

This method handles events and returns true if the event has been handled and false if the event should be passed onto the parent of this component. This method is deprecated —use processEvent().

hide()   **deprecated**

```
public void hide()
```

This method is deprecated—use setVisible().

imageUpdate()

```
public boolean imageUpdate(Image image,int flags,
             int x,int y,int width,int height)
```

This method is implemented to fulfill the requirements of implementing the ImageObserver interface. If a call has been made to any methods of the image request-ing a status update, and if the information was not available, this method is called whenever the information becomes available. This will repaint the component if the image has changed. A return value of true indicates that the image has completely loaded (or has completely failed to load), and false indicates loading is still in progress.

inside()   **deprecated**

```
public boolean inside(int x,int y)
```

This method is deprecated—use contains().

invalidate()

```
public void invalidate()
```

This will invalidate this component, and all those above it in the component hierarchy, by marking them as needing a layout.

isEnabled()

```
public boolean isEnabled()
```

Returns true if the component is enabled. All components are initially enabled.

isFocusTraversable()

```
public boolean isFocusTraversable()
```

Returns `true` if this component can be traversed by using the Tab (or Shift+Tab) key.

isShowing()

```
public boolean isShowing()
```

Returns `true` if the component is visible and showing—this will be `false` if its window is hidden or iconified.

isValid()

```
public boolean isValid()
```

Returns `true` if the component is valid. This is for containers. A container is valid if it has a current and correct layout of all its contained components.

isVisible()

```
public boolean isVisible()
```

Returns `true` if this component will be displayed if its container is unobscured. This does not indicate whether it is actually showing.

keyDown()   deprecated

```
public boolean keyDown(Event event,int key)
```

This is called with the keystroke value whenever a key is pressed. Replaced by `processKeyEvent()`.

keyUp()   deprecated

```
public boolean keyUp(Event event,int key)
```

This is called with the keystroke value whenever a key is released. Replaced by `processKeyEvent()`.

layout()   deprecated

```
public void layout()
```

Replaced by `doLayout()`.

list()

```
public void list()
public void list(PrintStream out)
public void list(PrintStream out,int indent)
public void list(PrintWriter out)
public void list(PrintWriter out,int indent)
```

Prints a listing of the contents of this component. If `out` is not specified, the listing goes to `System.out`. An indention can be specified to make nested listings more readable.

locate()   **deprecated**

    public Component locate(int x,int y)

This method is deprecated—use getComponentAt().

location()   **deprecated**

    public Point location()

This method is deprecated—use getLocation().

lostFocus()   **deprecated**

    public boolean lostFocus(Event event,Object what)

This method is called when the component loses the keyboard/mouse focus. Replaced by processFocusEvent().

minimumSize()   **deprecated**

    public Dimension minimumSize()

This method is deprecated—use getMinimumSize().

mouseDown()   **deprecated**

    public boolean mouseDown(Event event,int x,int y)

This method is called whenever a mouse button is pressed. This method is deprecated—use processMouseEvent().

mouseDrag()   **deprecated**

    public boolean mouseDrag(Event event,int x,int y)

This method is called at each position the mouse occupies while being moved with a button held down. This method is deprecated—use processMouseMotionEvent().

mouseEnter()   **deprecated**

    public boolean mouseEnter(Event event,int x,int y)

This method is called whenever the mouse pointer enters the component window. This method is deprecated—use processMouseEvent().

mouseExit()   **deprecated**

    public boolean mouseExit(Event event,int x,int y)

This method is called whenever the mouse pointer leaves the component window. This method is deprecated—use processMouseEvent().

mouseMove()   **deprecated**

    public boolean mouseMove(Event evt,int x,int y)

This method is called whenever the mouse pointer arrives at a new location in the component window. This method is deprecated—use `processMouseMotionEvent()`.

mouseUp()   **deprecated**
```
public boolean mouseUp(Event evt,int x,int y)
```
This method is called each time the mouse button is released. This method is deprecated—use `processMouseEvent()`.

move()   **deprecated**
```
public void move(int x,int y)
```
This method is deprecated—use `setLocation()`.

nextFocus()   **deprecated**
```
public void nextFocus()
```
This method is deprecated—use `transferFocus()`.

paint()
```
public void paint(Graphics g)
```
This method will paint the component using the supplied `Graphics` object. Under normal circumstances, this method should not be called directly. Calls to it should be scheduled by calling `repaint()`.

paintAll()
```
public void paintAll(Graphics g)
```
This method will paint the component and all its subcomponents using the supplied `Graphics` object.

paramString()
```
protected String paramString()
```
Returns debugging information. The return string describes the internal state and values of this object.

preferredSize()   **deprecated**
```
public Dimension preferredSize()
```
This method is deprecated—use `getPreferredSize()`.

prepareImage()
```
public boolean prepareImage(Image image,ImageObserver observer)
```

```
public boolean prepareImage(Image image,
            int width,int height,ImageObserver observer)
```

This method starts a separate thread and returns immediately. The separate thread loads the image data and prepares it for screen representation. The return value of true indicates that the image is fully prepared (probably from a previous call to this method). If the height and width are specified, a newly scaled version of the image is prepared. A return of false indicates that a thread has been spawned to do the work. The observer is given the task of tracking the loading process.

print()

```
public void print(Graphics g)
```

This method can be overloaded if there is something special to be done to print the component. The default version simply calls paint().

printAll()

```
public void printAll(Graphics g)
```

This method will print the component and all its subcomponents.

processComponentEvent()

```
protected voidprocessComponentEvent(ComponentEvent event)
```

This method will dispatch any received ComponentEvent to the all registered ComponentListeners. This method will not be called unless there is at least one ComponentListener registered by a call to addComponentListener() or component events are enabled by a call to enableEvents().

processEvent()

```
protected void processEvent(AWTEvent event)
```

This is the method that is called with all events. By default, this method distributes incoming events to the various other event-processing methods of the component—such as processComponentEvent() and processMouseEvent().

processFocusEvent()

```
protected void processFocusEvent(FocusEvent event)
```

This method will dispatch any received FocusEvent to all registered FocusListeners. This method will not be called unless there is at least one FocusListener registered by a call to addFocusListener() or focus events are enabled by a call to enableEvents().

processKeyEvent()

```
protected void processKeyEvent(KeyEvent event)
```

This method will dispatch any received `KeyEvent` to all registered `KeyListeners`. This method will not be called unless there is at least one `KeyListener` registered by a call to `addKeyListener()` or keyboard events are enabled by a call to `enableEvents()`.

processMouseEvent()

```
protected void processMouseEvent(MouseEvent event)
```

This method will dispatch any received `MouseEvent` — except those having to do with mouse movement — to all registered `MouseListeners`. This method will not be called unless there is at least one `MouseListener` registered by a call to `addMouseListener()` or mouse events are enabled by a call to `enableEvents()`. This method receives all `MouseEvents` except `MOUSE_MOVE` and `MOUSE_DRAG`.

processMouseMotionEvent()

```
protected void processMouseMotionEvent(MouseEvent event)
```

This method will dispatch any received `MouseEvent` to all registered `MouseMotionListeners`. This method will not be called unless there is at least one `MouseMotionListener` registered by a call to `addMouseMotionListener()` or mouse motion events are enabled by a call to `enableEvents()`. This method will receive only the `MOUSE_MOVE` and `MOUSE_DRAG` `MouseEvents`.

remove()

```
public synchronized void remove(MenuComponent popup)
```

Removes the specified `popup` menu from the component.

removeComponentListener()

```
public synchronized void
        removeComponentListener(ComponentListener listen)
```

This removes the `ComponentListener` — it will no longer receive component events.

removeFocusListener()

```
public synchronized void
        removeFocusListener(FocusListener listen)
```

This removes the `FocusListener` — it will no longer receive focus events.

removeKeyListener()

```
public synchronized voidremoveKeyListener(KeyListener listen)
```

This removes the `KeyListener` — it will no longer receive keyboard events.

removeMouseListener()

```
public synchronized void
        removeMouseListener(MouseListener listen)
```

This removes the `MouseListener` — it will no longer receive mouse button or mouse enter/leave events.

removeMouseMotionListener()

```
public synchronized void removeMouseMotionListener(
        MouseMotionListener listen)
```

This removes the `MouseMotionListener` — it will no longer receive mouse move or mouse drag events.

removeNotify()

```
public void removeNotify()
```

This method is called by the container as this component is removed from it. It is a signal to the component that it should clean up by destroying its peer.

repaint()

```
public void repaint()
public void repaint(int x,int y,int width,int height)
public void repaint(long tm)
public void repaint(long tm,int x,int y,
        int width,int height)
```

This method will schedule a call to `update()`. Since this is an asynchronous operation, there can be several calls to this method before a call is made to `repaint()`, but this will result in only a single call to `repaint()`. The dimensions specify the region of the component that is to be redrawn. If no dimensions are supplied, the entire component is redrawn. The `tm` value adds the requirement that the call to update must occur within `tm` milliseconds.

requestFocus()

```
public void requestFocus()
```

A call to this method is a request for the input focus. This request may be denied. For one thing, the component must be visible on the screen for this to work.

reshape()   **deprecated**

```
public void reshape(int x,int y,int width,int height)
```

This method is deprecated — use `setBounds()`.

resize()   **deprecated**

```
public void resize(Dimension d)
public void resize(int width,int height)
```

This method is deprecated—use `setSize()`.

setBackground()

```
public void setBackground(Color c)
```

Sets the background color.

setBounds()

```
public void setBounds(int x,int y,int width,int height)
```

```
public void setBounds(Rectangle rect)
```

This will resize and reposition the component in the specified bounding box.

setCursor()

```
public synchronized void setCursor(Cursor cursor)
```

Sets the `cursor` for this component.

setEnabled()

```
public void setEnabled(boolean setting)
```

If setting is `true`, this method will enable the component—if it is `false`, it will disable it. Unless a component is enabled, it will not respond to keyboard or mouse events. By default, components are enabled.

setFont()

```
public synchronized void setFont(Font font)
```

Sets the font of the component.

setForeground()

```
public void setForeground(Color c)
```

Sets the component foreground color.

setLocale()

```
public void setLocale(Locale locale)
```

Sets the locale of this component.

setLocation()

```
public void setLocation(int x,int y)

public void setLocation(Point p)
```

This will move the upper-left corner of the component to the specified location in the parent's window.

setName()

```
public void setName(String name)
```

This method sets the name of the component.

setSize()

```
public void setSize(Dimension d)

public void setSize(int width,int height)
```

This method will change the size of the component.

setVisible()

```
public void setVisible(boolean setting)
```

If the setting is false, the component will be hidden. If it is true, the component will be visible. Even though a component is not being hidden, it still may not appear on the screen. It could be obscured by another window or iconized.

show()   **deprecated**

```
public void show()

public void show(boolean setting)
```

This method is deprecated—use setVisible().

size()   **deprecated**

```
public Dimension size()
```

This method is deprecated—use getSize().

toString()

```
public String toString()
```

Returns a String representation of this component.

transferFocus()

```
public void transferFocus()
```

Transfers the focus away from this component to the next one.

update()

```
public void update(Graphics g)
```

This will be called because there has been one or more calls to repaint(). It can be assumed that the background of the component has not been cleared — this call is made to modify the previously painted display.

validate()

```
public void validate()
```

This method is intended for containers to ensure that the component has a valid layout. If the component is currently invalid, its layout manager is called on to correct the layout and, thus, validate the component.

 For more on events see **ActionEvent, AWTEvent, ComponentEvent, ItemEvent, TextEvent,** and **AdjustmentEvent.** For the more on distributing events, see **AWTEventMulticaster.**

ComponentAdapter

class java.awt.event.ComponentAdapter

This abstract class is a convenience for implementing a ComponentListener. This class defines a complete set of empty methods for the ComponentListener interface. If you want to create a ComponentListener but only implement one or two of the methods, you can subclass from this class and skip the step of writing stubs for all the other methods.

Inheritance

```
public abstract class java.awt.event.ComponentAdapter
    implements ComponentListener
    extends Object
        ⇑
    public class java.lang.Object
```

Constructors

```
public ComponentAdapter()
```

Methods

componentHidden()

```
public void componentHidden(ComponentEvent e)
```

componentMoved()

```
public void componentMoved(ComponentEvent e)
```

componentResized()

```
public void componentResized(ComponentEvent e)
```

componentShown()

```
public void componentShown(ComponentEvent e)
```

ComponentEvent

class java.awt.event.ComponentEvent

This is the superclass of all component-level events.

Nothing to be done

These events are available to an application only for the sake of notification. The AWT automatically handles the events of this class.

Extended by

```
ContainerEvent
FocusEvent
InputEvent
PaintEvent
WindowEvent
```

Inheritance

```
public class java.awt.event.ComponentEvent
    extends AWTEvent
        ⇑
    public class java.awt.AWTEvent
        extends EventObject
            ⇑
```

```
public class java.util.EventObject
        implements Serializable
        extends Object
           ⇑
        public class java.lang.Object
```

Variables and constants

COMPONENT_FIRST

```
public final static int COMPONENT_FIRST
```

This is the lowest possible value of a component event id number.

COMPONENT_HIDDEN

```
public final static int COMPONENT_HIDDEN
```

The id of the component-hidden event.

COMPONENT_LAST

```
public final static int COMPONENT_LAST
```

This is the largest possible value of a component event id number.

COMPONENT_MOVED

```
public final static int COMPONENT_MOVED
```

The id of the component-moved event.

COMPONENT_RESIZED

```
public final static int COMPONENT_RESIZED
```

The id of the component-resized event.

COMPONENT_SHOWN

```
public final static int COMPONENT_SHOWN
```

The id of the component-shown event.

Constructors

```
public ComponentEvent(Component source,int id)
```

A `ComponentEvent` is contracted using the `Component` that is the `source` of the event and the `id` number specifying the type of component event.

Methods

getComponent()

```
public Component getComponent()
```

Returns the component that caused the event.

paramString()

```
public String paramString()
```

Returns debugging information. The return string describes the internal state and values of this object.

 These events can be monitored by a **ComponentListener**.

ComponentListener

interface java.awt.event.ComponentListener

The interface used to implement listener of ComponentEvents.

Nothing to be done

These events are available to an application only for the sake of notification. The AWT automatically handles the events of this class, so there is no action that needs to be taken by an application.

Implemented by

```
AWTEventMulticaster
ComponentAdapter
```

Inheritance

```
public interface java.awt.event.ComponentListener
    extends EventListener
            ⇑
    public interface java.util.EventListener
```

Constructors

Returned by

Objects that implement this interface are returned from AWTEventMulticaster.add() and AWTEventMulticaster.remove().

Methods

componentHidden()

```
public abstract void componentHidden(ComponentEvent e)
```

This method is called whenever a component has become hidden.

componentMoved()

```
public abstract void componentMoved(ComponentEvent e)
```

This method is called whenever a component has been moved.

componentResized()

```
public abstract void componentResized(ComponentEvent e)
```

This method is called whenever a component has been resized.

componentShown()

```
public abstract void componentShown(ComponentEvent e)
```

This method is called whenever a component becomes visible.

 For a description of the event received by a ComponentListener, see **ComponentEvent**.

ConnectException

class java.net.ConnectException

This exception is thrown when an error occurs during an attempt to make a socket connection with a remote host. Commonly, this will occur if the remote port number is not valid. This can also happen if no processes are actively monitoring the port on the remote system.

 Another class by the name ConnectException occurs in the java.rmi package.

Inheritance

```
public class java.net.ConnectException
    extends SocketException
        ⇑
    public class java.net.SocketException
        extends IOException
            ⇑
        public class java.io.IOException
```

```
                      extends Exception
                          ⇑
            public class java.lang.Exception
                      extends Throwable
                              ⇑
                public class java.lang.Throwable
                          implements Serializable
                          extends Object
                                  ⇑
                    public class java.lang.Object
```

Constructors

```
    public ConnectException()
    public ConnectException(String message)
```

If the message string is supplied, it is used as a detailed message describing this particular exception.

ConnectException

class java.rmi.ConnectException

This exception is thrown in the case of a connection error while attempting a remote method invocation.

 Another class by the name ConnectException occurs in the java.net package.

Inheritance

```
    public class java.rmi.ConnectException
        extends RemoteException
            ⇑
        public class java.rmi.RemoteException
            extends IOException
                ⇑
            public class java.io.IOException
                extends Exception
                    ⇑
                public class java.lang.Exception
                    extends Throwable
                        ⇑
                    public class java.lang.Throwable
                        implements Serializable
```

```
                    extends Object
                         ⇑
                    public class java.lang.Object
```

Constructors

```
        public ConnectException(String message)
        public ConnectException(String message,Exception e)
```

A remote exception is created with a detailed `message` describing the exception, and it optionally can include a copy of the original exception that caused this one to be thrown.

ConnectIOException

class java.rmi.ConnectIOException

This exception is thrown to indicate that an `IOException` has occurred during a remote method invocation.

Inheritance

```
        public class java.rmi.ConnectIOException
             extends RemoteException
                  ⇑
             public class java.rmi.RemoteException
                  extends IOException
                       ⇑
                  public class java.io.IOException
                       extends Exception
                            ⇑
                       public class java.lang.Exception
                            extends Throwable
                                 ⇑
                            public class java.lang.Throwable
                                 implements Serializable
                                 extends Object
                                      ⇑
                                 public class java.lang.Object
```

Constructors

```
        public ConnectIOException(String message)
```

```
public ConnectIOException(String message,Exception e)
```

A remote exception is created with a detailed message describing the exception, and it optionally can include a copy of the original exception that caused this one to be thrown.

Connection

interface java.sql.Connection

A Connection object represents a single session with a database. A session consists of issuing SQL statements and retrieving the results of their execution.

What is available

The methods of this interface can provide information about the tables of the database, the SQL grammar that is supported, and stored procedures.

Commit

The default for a connection is to execute a commit on every SQL statement. This can be disabled, resulting in the requirement that an explicit commit statement be issued at some point—or no commit will ever be issued.

When autocommit is enabled, the actual commit will occur whenever an SQL statement completes, or when the execution of another SQL statement begins—whichever is first. For statements returning a ResultSet, the statement is considered complete when the ResultSet has been either retrieved or closed. In the cases where multiple ResultSets are returned, the commit will occur when the last of them has been retrieved.

The exception

Every method in this interface is capable of throwing an SQLException in the case of a database error, so it will be necessary for the call to any of these methods to be placed inside a try-catch block or inside a method that also throws SQLException.

A couple of terms

A *dirty read* is the result of a transaction that proceeds regardless of the status of other transactions and could result in data being read that has not been committed. A *nonrepeatable read* is one that successfully performed a rollback but got different data on reading again. A *phantom read* is one in which conflicting data is read from two different records because of an update occurring on one while the process was reading from the other.

Inheritance

```
public interface java.sql.Connection
```

Variables and constants

TRANSACTION_NONE

```
public final static int TRANSACTION_NONE
```

Indicates that transactions are not supported.

TRANSACTION_READ_COMMITTED

```
public final static int TRANSACTION_READ_COMMITTED
```

Indicates that dirty reads are prevented, but nonrepeatable reads and phantom reads may occur.

TRANSACTION_READ_UNCOMMITTED

```
public final static int TRANSACTION_READ_UNCOMMITTED
```

Indicates that dirty reads, nonrepeatable reads, and phantom reads can occur.

TRANSACTION_REPEATABLE_READ

```
public final static int TRANSACTION_REPEATABLE_READ
```

Indicates that dirty reads and nonrepeatable reads are prevented, but phantom reads can occur.

TRANSACTION_SERIALIZABLE

```
public final static int TRANSACTION_SERIALIZABLE
```

Indicates that dirty reads, nonrepeatable reads, and phantom reads are prevented.

Constructors

Returned by

Objects that implement this interface are returned from calls to `Driver.connect()` and `DriverManager.getConnection()`.

Methods

clearWarnings()

```
public abstract void clearWarnings()
    throws SQLException
```

This will clear any internally held warnings. After this, a call to `getWarnings()` will return `null` until a new warning is reported for the connection.

close()

```
public abstract void close()
```

```
throws SQLException
```

This will drop the connection to the database. It is not absolutely necessary to call this method, because the connection will be severed during garbage collection—but it may be advisable to release the system resources sooner rather than later.

commit()

```
public abstract void commit()
    throws SQLException
```

This will commit any changes and release any locks made since the last commit or rollback. A call to this method should not be made unless the automatic commits have been disabled with a call to setAutoCommit().

createStatement()

```
public abstract Statement createStatement()
    throws SQLException
```

Returns a Statement object that can be used to both execute SQL statements and retrieve the results from their execution.

getAutoCommit()

```
public abstract boolean getAutoCommit()
    throws SQLException
```

Returns true if autocommit is on and false if it is off.

getCatalog()

```
public abstract String getCatalog()
    throws SQLException
```

Returns the current catalog name.

getMetaData()

```
public abstract DatabaseMetaData getMetaData()
    throws SQLException
```

Returns a DatabaseMetaData object that can be used to query detailed information about the database and its capabilities.

getTransactionIsolation()

```
public abstract int getTransactionIsolation()
    throws SQLException
```

Returns the transaction mode. The return value is one of the constants defined in this class.

getWarnings()

```
public abstract SQLWarning getWarnings()
    throws SQLException
```

Returns the linked-list of warnings that have been issued on the connections. The oldest one is returned with any newer ones chained to it.

isClosed()

```
public abstract boolean isClosed()
    throws SQLException
```

Returns `true` if the `Connection` has been closed.

isReadOnly()

```
public abstract boolean isReadOnly()
    throws SQLException
```

Returns `true` if the `Connection` is operating in read-only mode.

nativeSQL()

```
public abstract String nativeSQL(String sql)
    throws SQLException
```

The SQL statement supplied as the `sql` argument is translated by the database driver to a database-specific SQL statement and returned. The `sql` argument may contain one or more '?' parameter placeholders. The returned form is the one the driver would have actually sent to the database.

prepareCall()

```
public abstract CallableStatement prepareCall(String sql)
    throws SQLException
```

Creates a stored procedure using the `sql` statement passed in as an argument. The stored procedure is returned in the form of a `CallableStatement` that supplies methods for setting up the IN and OUT parameters, as well as methods to execute the procedure.

 The actual activity involved will vary from one database to the next. Some drivers will send the call statement to the database for immediate execution, whereas others will wait for the execution of the `CallableStatement`. The only effect `prepareCall()` has at this level is that it could alter the source of certain `SQLExceptions`.

prepareStatement()

```
public abstract PreparedStatementprepareStatement(String sql)
    throws SQLException
```

Creates a precompiled SQL statement by using the `sql` command passed in as an argument. The statement may or may not include IN parameters. The precompiled statement is returned as a `PreparedStatement` object, which can be used to execute the statement, with or without modifications, any number of times.

 The actual activity involved will vary from one database to the next. If the driver supports precompilation, the statement may be sent directly to the database for immediate compilation, while other statements will wait for the execution of the `PreparedStatement`. The only effect `prepareStatement()` has at this level is that it could alter the source of certain `SQLExceptions`.

rollback()

```
public abstract void rollback()
    throws SQLException
```

Either drops all changes made since the last commit or rolls back and releases any database locks. A call to this method only makes sense when autocommit has been disabled.

setAutoCommit()

```
public abstract void setAutoCommit(boolean setting)
    throws SQLException
```

Turns autocommit on or off. If `setting` is `true`, autocommit is turned on and a commit will be issued automatically following the execution of every SQL statement. If the `setting` is `false`, autocommit is turned off and a commit will be issued only upon a call to `commit()`.

setCatalog()

```
public abstract void setCatalog(String catalog)
    throws SQLException
```

A catalog name can be specified for the `Connection`. If the driver does not support catalogs, this call is ignored.

setReadOnly()

```
public abstract void setReadOnly(boolean setting)
    throws SQLException
```

Specify whether or not access to the database will be read-only. If `setting` is `true`, the driver will operate read-only. The driver can use this information to operate more efficiently. This method cannot be called while a transaction is in progress.

setTransactionIsolation()

```
public abstract void setTransactionIsolation(int level)
    throws SQLException
```

Change the transaction level. The value of level must be one of the transaction level values defined in this class. This method cannot be called while a transaction is in progress. A call should be made to `DatabaseMetaData.supportsTransactionIsolationLevel()` to determine whether a valid request is being made.

 For more about communication with a database, see **ResultSet** and **DatabaseMetaData**. For driver-level operations, see **Driver** and **DriverManager**. For information on forming SQL statements, see **Statement** and **PreparedStatement**.

const

keyword

This keyword is reserved by the Java language and it may be used in the future, but it serves no purpose now.

 A keyword in Java that is something like `const` in C++ is **final.**

constant

 Constants are created in the same way as variables, with the addition of the **final** modifier.

constructor

A *constructor* is very much like a method, but with a few fundamental differences. The name of a constructor is always the same as the name of the class. A constructor has no declared return type — its return type automatically becomes a reference to the object that the constructor has just initialized. It is as if any return statements in the constructor were automatically translated to `return(this)`. The first thing a constructor does is call `super()` — if you don't code a call to `super()` as the first thing your constructor does, a call is inserted automatically.

A constructor can be declared as `public`, `private`, or `protected`. A `public` constructor is the normal case. A `private` constructor can only be called from within the class. A `protected` constructor can only be called from within the class or one of its subclasses. A constructor cannot be declared `static` because it references an object — the `this` keyword can be used inside a constructor.

Overloading constructors

Constructors can be overloaded, the same as any other methods. This fact allows an object to be constructed in various ways. Many of the classes of the Java API have overloaded constructors—some good examples are File and String. By using different combinations of arguments on the constructors, one may construct the same kind of object in different ways.

The default constructor

If no constructor is declared for a class, one is automatically generated. It is a simple constructor that has no arguments and simply allows all the members of the class to assume their default values. A default constructor will always call the default constructor of its superclass. If you supply a constructor with no arguments, it will become the default constructor. If you supply one or more constructors with arguments but don't supply a default constructor, no default constructor will exist and arguments must be supplied every time you instantiate the class.

Constructors are not inherited

The public methods of a class are inherited and can be called externally by using a dot reference. This is not true of constructors. The constructor of a superclass can be called only by using the keyword super. For example, if the superclass has a constructor that requires an int value as its argument, that constructor can be called like this:

```
super(44);
```

To call a constructor

It is okay to call a constructor from another constructor within the object. The call is made by using the keyword this. Take this simple example:

```
public class Wa {
    private int value;
    Wa(int argument) {
        value = argument;
    }
    Wa() {
        this(15);
    }
}
```

The constructor without an argument invokes the one with an argument by using `this`. Having one constructor call another is a convenient way to set up default values.

 Remember that every constructor has embedded in it a call to `super()`—the constructor of its parent class. Whenever a constructor is called, constructors of all the parent classes back to the `Object` class are called. This may not be what you want.

 To retrieve information about constructors from objects, see **Class**. For some examples of constructor usage, see **class**.

Constructor

class java.lang.reflect.Constructor

This class will provide information about a particular constructor. That is, it *reflects* the constructor.

Widening and narrowing

`Constructor` permits widening conversions to occur when matching the actual parameters to the formal parameters. An `IllegalArgumentException` is thrown if a narrowing conversion would occur. That is, if you specify an argument type of `int` but the actual argument type is `double`, there will be a match because an `int` can be widened to a `double`. If, however, you specify an `int` but the actual argument is a `short`, the exception will be thrown.

Inheritance

```
public final class java.lang.reflect.Constructor
    implements Member
    extends Object
        ⇑
    public class java.lang.Object
```

Constructors

Returned by

Objects of this class are returned from these methods of the `Class` class: `getConstructor()`, `getConstructors()`, `getDeclaredConstructor()`, and `getDeclaredConstructors()`.

Methods

equals()

```
public boolean equals(Object object)
```

Returns `true` if object is a `Constructor` that reflects the same constructor of the same class as this one.

getDeclaringClass()

```
public Class getDeclaringClass()
```

Returns the `Class` object for the class that holds the constructor reflected by this object.

getExceptionTypes()

```
public Class[] getExceptionTypes()
```

Returns an array of `Class` objects reflecting all the checked exceptions thrown by the constructor. If there are none, an array of length zero is returned.

getModifiers()

```
public int getModifiers()
```

Returns the Java language modifiers for the reflected constructor. To decode the modifiers, see `Modifier`.

getName()

```
public String getName()
```

Returns the name of the reflected constructor—which is always the same name as the constructor's class.

getParameterTypes()

```
public Class[] getParameterTypes()
```

This will return an ordered array of `Class` objects that represent the argument types of the reflected constructor. If there are no arguments, a zero-length array is returned.

hashCode()

```
public int hashCode()
```

Returns the hashcode of this object—which is the same hashcode as the underlying reflected constructor's class name.

newInstance()

```
public Object newInstance(Object initargs[])
     throws InstantiationException
     throws IllegalAccessException
```

```
throws IllegalArgumentException
throws InvocationTargetException
```

Creates and returns a new instance of the class. This is done by using the constructor being reflected by this object.

The arguments from the array `initargs` are passed to the constructor. If an argument is a primitive, the `initargs` array should contain a wrapper of the appropriate type—the wrapper will automatically be converted to the correct type. Widening conversions will be performed as necessary.

An `InstantiationException` is thrown if the class is abstract. An `InstantiationException` is thrown if language access control is enforced and the constructor is inaccessible. An `IllegalArgumentException` is thrown if the supplied arguments do not match (or cannot be widened to) those required by the constructor.

Exceptions beyond those listed here could be thrown from the constructor itself. They will always be rethrown to the caller of `newInstance()`.

toString()

```
public String toString()
```

Returns a string that describes the reflected constructor's access modifiers, the fully qualified class name, and a list of the parameter types for the constructor. It looks very much like the source code declaration of the constructor. For a constructor, the only possible modifiers are `public`, `private`, and `protected`.

Example

This example demonstrates how to get the list of `Constructor` objects from a `Class`:

```java
import java.util.*;
import java.lang.reflect.*;
public class DateConstructor {
    public static void main(String[] arg) {
        Date date = new Date();
        Class dateClass = date.getClass();
        System.out.println(dateClass);
        try {
            Constructor[] cons =
                    dateClass.getConstructors();
            for(int i=0; i<cons.length; i++)
                System.out.println(cons[i]);
        } catch(Exception e) {
            System.out.println(e);
        }
    }
}
```

The method getClass() is called to get the Class object. An array of Constructor objects is returned by calling getConstructors(), and the description of each is printed. The output looks like this:

```
public java.util.Date()
public java.util.Date(long)
public java.util.Date(int,int,int)
public java.util.Date(int,int,int,int,int)
public java.util.Date(int,int,int,int,int,int)
public java.util.Date(java.lang.String)
```

 To create Constructor objects, see **Class**.

Container

class java.awt.Container

This abstract class can be extended to create a container. A container is a class that is capable of containing a group of components (displayable objects) and displaying them on the screen. It can also use a layout manager to arrange the components for display.

The list of components

The container maintains an internal list of its components. Components may be added to and deleted from the list individually. This is an ordered list. The ordering will affect things like the position of the component in its parent window, which component will appear over the top of another, and which component will receive the focus next in a tab sequence. Unless specified otherwise, each newly added component goes to the end of the list. Because the components are normally displayed starting from the beginning of the list, the last one is displayed last in the list and will, thus, be on top of the stack of displayed components.

Layout manager

The Container itself does not assume the responsibility of sizing and positioning the components—this is done by a layout manager. There are several layout managers, and each one has a different set of rules for positioning components.

Extended by

```
Panel
ScrollPane
Window
```

Inheritance

```
public abstract class java.awt.Container
    extends Component
        ⇑
    public class java.awt.Component
        implements ImageObserver
        implements MenuContainer
        implements Serializable
        extends Object
            ⇑
        public class java.lang.Object
```

Constructors

```
protected Container()
```

Returned by

Container objects are returned from Component.getParent(),
ContainerEvent.getContainer(), and Toolkit.getNativeContainer().

Methods

add()

```
public Component add(Component component)
public Component add(Component component,int index)
public void add(Component component,Object constraint)
public void add(Component component,Object constraint,
        int index)
public Component add(String name,Component component)
        *** deprecated ***
```

This method will add the component to the container. If the index is specified, the component will be inserted at that position in the list. If the index is not specified or is −1, the component will be added to the end of the list. If the index is not valid (too large or less than −1), an InvalidArgumentException is thrown. Any constraint specified will need to be compatible with the layout manager being used—for example, it would need to be String for the BorderLayout manager. If no constraint is supplied, a null is used.

 The last form listed, the one with the String name argument, has been deprecated. This was done to allow for a more generalized form—a form that allows the constraint to be something other than a String object.

addContainerListener()

```
public void addContainerListener(
        ContainerListener listener)
```

Adds a listener to the list of those that will receive `ContainerEvents`.

addImpl()

```
protected void addImpl(Component component,
        Object constraint,int index)
```

This method is used by the add() set of methods and has the same set of arguments. You can override this method to monitor every add, but if you do, it will be necessary to include a call to `super.addImpl()` so that the components will actually be added.

addNotify()

```
public void addNotify()
```

Creates the underlying system-dependent peer for this object. This method is not normally called by the application. It is called by the container.

countComponents()   **deprecated**

```
public int countComponents()
```

This method is deprecated—use `getComponentCount()`.

deliverEvent()   **deprecated**

```
public void deliverEvent(Event event)
```

This method is deprecated—use `dispatchEvent()`.

doLayout()

```
public void doLayout()
```

This method should not be called by an application—use `validate()` instead. This will cause the container to invoke the layout manager to size and position the components.

getAlignmentX()

```
public float getAlignmentX()
```

Returns the relative alignment along the horizontal axis, where 0.0 is at the far left and 1.0 is on the far right.

getAlignmentY()

```
public float getAlignmentY()
```

Returns the relative alignment along the horizontal axis, where 0.0 is at the top and 1.0 is on the bottom.

getComponent()

```
public Component getComponent(int index)
```

This method will return the component at the specified index. If the index is not valid, an ArrayIndexOutOfBoundsException is thrown.

getComponentAt()

```
public Component getComponentAt(int x,int y)
```

```
public Component getComponentAt(Point p)
```

This returns the component located at the specified position. If there is more than one component at the position, the topmost one is returned. If the specified point is outside the bounds of the container, null is returned. If the point is inside the container, but there is no child component at that location, the container itself is returned.

getComponentCount()

```
public int getComponentCount()
```

Returns the number of components in the container.

getComponents()

```
public Component[] getComponents()
```

Returns an array that contains all the component references.

getInsets()

```
public Insets getInsets()
```

The Insets indicates the size of the borders around the container. For example, a Frame will always have a border at its top the height of its title bar.

getLayout()

```
public LayoutManager getLayout()
```

Returns the layout manager.

getMaximumSize()

```
public Dimension getMaximumSize()
```

Returns the maximum display size of this container and its components.

getMinimumSize()

```
public Dimension getMinimumSize()
```

Returns the minimum display size of this container and its components.

getPreferredSize()

```
public Dimension getPreferredSize()
```

Returns the preferred size of this container and its components.

insets()   **deprecated**

```
public Insets insets()
```

This method is deprecated—use getInsets().

invalidate()

```
public void invalidate()
```

This method will immediately invalidate the container and all parents above it. After this call, any attempt to display the container and its components will cause all the positions and sizes to be calculated.

isAncestorOf()

```
public boolean isAncestorOf(Component component)
```

This method returns true if the component is contained in this container or in any container in the hierarchy below it.

layout()   **deprecated**

```
public void layout()
```

This method is deprecated—use doLayout().

list()

```
public void list(PrintStream out,int indent)

public void list(PrintWriter out,int indent)
```

Prints a hierarchical listing of the component members of this container. The entire listing will be indented by the amount of indent.

locate()   **deprecated**

```
public Component locate(int x,int y)
```

This method is deprecated—use getComponentAt().

minimumSize()   **deprecated**

```
public Dimension minimumSize()
```

This method is deprecated—use getMinimumSize().

paint()

```
public void paint(Graphics g)
```

This method will paint the container and all the components that it contains. If a child component is completely obscured or, otherwise, not included in the current clip region, its `paint()` method will not be called.

If this method is overridden, it should be called via `super.paint()` so that the lightweight components are drawn.

paintComponents()

```
public void paintComponents(Graphics g)
```

Paints only the components of this container.

paramString()

```
protected String paramString()
```

Returns debugging information. The return string describes the internal state and values of this object.

preferredSize()   **deprecated**

```
public Dimension preferredSize()
```

This method is deprecated—use `getPreferredSize()`.

print()

```
public void print(Graphics g)
```

This method will print the container and all the components that it contains.
If this method is overridden, it should be called via `super.print()` so that the lightweight components are drawn.

printComponents()

```
public void printComponents(Graphics g)
```

Prints only the components of the container.

processContainerEvent()

```
protected void
        processContainerEvent(ContainerEvent event)
```

This method will dispatch the event to any registered `ContainerListeners`. This method will be called only if there has been a call to either `addContainerListener()` or `enableEvents()`.

processEvent()

```
protected void processEvent(AWTEvent event)
```

If the event is a `ContainerEvent`, this method calls `processContainerEvent()`. If event is not a `ContainerEvent`, this method calls `super.processEvent()`.

remove()

```
public void remove(Component component)

public void remove(int index)
```

Removes a component from the container. The component can be specified either by a reference or by its index in the internal list.

removeAll()

```
public void removeAll()
```

Removes all the components from this container.

removeContainerListener()

```
public void removeContainerListener(ContainerListener listener)
```

This will remove the specified listener from the list of ContainerListeners.

removeNotify()

```
public void removeNotify()
```

This is a request that the container remove its peer. This method should not be called by the application—it is called by the component superclass.

setLayout()

```
public void setLayout(LayoutManager manager)
```

Sets the layout manager for the container.

validate()

```
public void validate()
```

Validates this container by performing component sizing and placement.

validateTree()

```
protected void validateTree()
```

Recursively descends the component tree and validates the layout for any components marked as invalid.

 For specific Container objects, see **Window**, **Panel**, and **ScrollPane**. For positioning the components within a Container, see **LayoutManager**. Also see **ContainerEvent** and **ContainerListener**.

ContainerAdapter

class java.awt.event.ContainerAdapter

This abstract class is a convenience for implementing a `ContainerListener`. This class implements a complete set of empty methods for the `ContainerListener` interface. If you want to create a `ContainerListener` that has just one method, you can subclass from this class and skip the step of writing stubs for the other method.

Inheritance

```
public abstract class java.awt.event.ContainerAdapter
      implements ContainerListener
      extends Object
         ⇑
      public class java.lang.Object
```

Constructors

```
public ContainerAdapter()
```

Methods

componentAdded()

```
public void componentAdded(ContainerEvent e)
```

componentRemoved()

```
public void componentRemoved(ContainerEvent e)
```

ContainerEvent

class java.awt.event.ContainerEvent

This is the class for all container-level events.

Nothing to be done

These events are available to an application only for the sake of notification. The AWT automatically handles the events of this class.

Inheritance

```
public class java.awt.event.ContainerEvent
    extends ComponentEvent
        ⇑
    public class java.awt.event.ComponentEvent
        extends AWTEvent
            ⇑
        public class java.awt.AWTEvent
            extends EventObject
                ⇑
            public class java.util.EventObject
                implements Serializable
                extends Object
                    ⇑
                public class java.lang.Object
```

Variables and constants

COMPONENT_ADDED

```
public final static int COMPONENT_ADDED
```

The id of the component-added event.

COMPONENT_REMOVED

```
public final static int COMPONENT_REMOVED
```

The id of the component-removed event.

CONTAINER_FIRST

```
public final static int CONTAINER_FIRST
```

This is the smallest possible value of a container event id number.

CONTAINER_LAST

```
public final static int CONTAINER_LAST
```

This is the largest possible value of a container event id number.

Constructors

```
public ContainerEvent(Component source,int id,Component child)
```

The construction of a ContainerEvent requires the container that is the source of the event, the event id number, and the child component within the container that caused the event.

Methods

getChild()

```
public Component getChild()
```

Returns the child component of the container that caused the event to be issued.

getContainer()

```
public Container getContainer()
```

Returns the container originating the event.

paramString()

```
public String paramString()
```

Returns debugging information. The return string describes the internal state and values of this object.

 For a class that will process events of this type, see **ContainerListener**.

ContainerListener

interface java.awt.event.ContainerListener

This is the interface for classes that wish to receive container events.

Nothing to be done

These events are available to an application only for the sake of notification. The AWT automatically handles the events of this class.

Implemented by

```
AWTEventMulticaster
ContainerAdapter
```

Inheritance

```
public interface ContainerListener
    extends EventListener
        ⇑
    public interface java.util.EventListener
```

Constructors

Returned by

Classes that implement this interface are returned from calls to `AWTEventMulticaster.add()` and `AWTEventMulticaster.remove()`.

Methods

componentAdded()

```
public abstract void componentAdded(ContainerEvent e)
```

This method is called whenever a component is added to the container.

componentRemoved()

```
public abstract void componentRemoved(ContainerEvent e)
```

This method is called whenever a component has been removed from the container.

 An abstract class that can aid in writing an object with this interface is **ContainerAdapter**.

ContentHandler

class java.net.ContentHandler

This is the abstract class that is the superclass of all classes that create objects by reading the description of the object from the input stream of a `URLConnection`.

Works inside URLConnection

The method of this class is normally not called directly by an application. Normally, a call is made to `getContent()` of `URLConnection`. First, `URLConnection` reads a MIME string from the socket. Next, it makes a call to `ContentHandlerFactory`, passing it the MIME string. Then `ContentHandlerFactory` returns an instance of `ContentHandler`. Finally, `URLConnection` calls the `getContent()` method of `ContentHandler` to create the object.

Inheritance

```
public abstract class java.net.ContentHandler
    extends Object
         ⇑
    public class java.lang.Object
```

Constructors

```
public ContentHandler()
```

Returned by

An object of this class is returned from
ContentHandlerFactory.createContentHandler().

Methods

getContent()

```
public abstract Object getContent(URLConnection urlc)
    throws IOException
```

Reads the incoming stream from the urlc and creates an object from it. The urlc must be positioned at the beginning of the stream representing the object. An IOException is thrown if there is an error during the read.

 For more about how objects of this class are used, see **URLConnectionHandler** and **ContentHandlerFactory**.

ContentHandlerFactory

interface java.net.ContentHandlerFactory

This is the interface for a factory object that produces ContentHandler objects. A ContentHandlerFactory will map MIME-type descriptions to a ContentHandler.

Used by the reader of data

An object of this class is used by a URLStreamHandler to retrieve the appropriate ContentHandler to translate an incoming stream of data into an Object. The selection of the translator is made based on the MIME type of the incoming stream compared to the MIME type understood by a ContentHandler.

Inheritance

```
public interface ContentHandlerFactory
```

Methods

createContentHandler()

```
public abstract ContentHandler
            createContentHandler(String MIMEtype)
```

Returns a `ContentHandler` capable of creating an object from the `MIMEtype` of the incoming `URLStreamHandler` data.

 For more about how objects of this class are used, see **URLConnection** and **ContentHandler**.

continue

keyword

The `continue` statement is used to interrupt the flow of execution inside a `for`, `do`, or `while` loop and cause the next iteration to begin immediately. It can optionally refer to a label that will cause execution to break out of an inner loop and restart the iteration of an outer loop.

 For examples of `continue`, see **for**, **do**, and **while**. To break out of a loop without continuing the iteration, see **break**, **return**, and **throw**.

convenience

A convenience method

A convenience method is one that allows the programmer to code a common sequence of steps in a simpler way. That is, the method does not add any real functionality—everything it does can be done some other way—but it can be convenient and/or logical to have a simple convenience method do the chore. A convenience method commonly implements a call to two or three methods to perform multiple tasks as if they were one. Sometimes, a convenience method will do the same job as another method, but it simply requires different arguments.

A convenience class

A convenience class is sometimes called an adapter class. Whenever a class implements an interface, it is required that the class implement every method defined in the interface. A convenience class is one that implements an interface by implementing all the methods to perform some default action, or do nothing at all. This way, another class can extend the convenience class and have the advantage of only being required to actually implement the methods required for it to do its job.

Java includes many convenience methods—for an example, see **Integer.getInteger()**. An example of a convenience class is **ContainerAdapter**. Also see **adapter**.

conversion

Every object has a class, and every primitive has a type. There are rules concerning the conversion from one type to another and from one object to another. The rules described here are the ones that apply during variable assignment and expression evaluation. They also apply to arguments being passed to method calls, except for some minor differences having to do with constants.

Widening and narrowing of primitives

A conversion of data from one primitive to another that does not cause loss of magnitude is called *widening*. A conversion of data from one primitive to another that could cause loss of magnitude is called *narrowing*.

For example, converting a byte value to an int is widening because every possible value that can be contained in a byte can also be contained in an int. On the other hand, converting a long to an int is narrowing because of the possible loss of data. Table C-3 contains a list of the widening and narrowing for each of the primitives.

Table C-3   The Widening and Narrowing of Primitives

Type	Narrows To	Widens To
byte	char	short, int, long, float, double
char	byte, short	int, long, float, double
short	byte, char	int, long, float, double
int	byte, short, char	long, float, double
long	byte, short, char, int	float, double
float	byte, short, char, int, long	double
double	byte, short, char, int, long, float	

A char is larger than a byte (16 bits compared to 8), but a byte can contain both positive and negative values. Each of these can hold numbers that the other can't, so it is narrowing to convert between them in either direction.

Widening

Converting from a `long` or an `int` to a `float` is widening because the range of values of a `float` includes all the values of a `long` or an `int`. There will be no change in the magnitude of the value. However, there could be some loss of precision because a `long` uses 64 bits to represent its value, an `int` uses 32, and a `float` only uses 23. The program `Widening.java` shows the sort of thing that can happen with loss of precision:

```
public class Widening {
    public static void main(String[] arg) {
        float fval;
        long lval = 0x7AAAAAAAAAAAAAAAL;
        fval = lval;
        long newlval = (long)fval;
        System.out.println("   from long=" + lval);
        System.out.println("    to float=" + fval);
        System.out.println("back to long=" + newlval);
        int ival = 0x7AAAAAAA;
        fval = ival;
        int newival = (int)fval;
        System.out.println("   from int=" + ival);
        System.out.println("    to float=" + fval);
        System.out.println("back to int=" + newival);
    }
}
```

Here is the output:

```
   from long=8839064868652493482
    to float=8.8390647E18
back to long=8839064685400555520
   from int=2058005162
    to float=2.05800512E9
back to int=2058005120
```

The larger the number, the more pronounced the loss of precision. This example uses very large numbers, and by comparing the before and after values, you can see that least significant digits were altered because of the truncation.

Narrowing

Narrowing can cause loss of data. The high-order bits of the larger primitive data type are simply trimmed off, leaving only the bits that the smaller primitive is able to hold. Since the integers are all represented in two's complement notation, narrowing an integer could reverse the sign of the result—a positive value could become negative, or a negative value could become positive. Narrowing a floating-point type to an integer could result in zero (if the floating-point value is less than one), or it could result in the maximum value representable by the integer type (if the floating-point number is larger than the maximum value of the integer type).

 The Java compiler allows widening without comment—just assign one value to another and it is done. Narrowing is a different matter. Because narrowing could cause loss of magnitude, it will be necessary to cast the wider type to the narrower type or the compiler will complain. This has the double advantage of helping you prevent accidental loss of data, and of documenting the conversion by pointing out where possible loss of data could occur.

Narrowing never causes a run-time exception. Since the programmer knew of the possibility of the loss of data, the Java runtime system ignores any overflow, underflow, or truncation.

Rounding

Even when there is no loss of magnitude, a conversion from a real number to an integer will normally cause loss of data. Anything to the right of the decimal point is truncated whenever this sort of casting forces the conversion:

```
public class Truncation {
    public static void main(String[] arg) {
        double from;
        int to;
        from = 1.3;
        for(int i=0; i<5; i++) {
            to = (int)from;
            System.out.println("Double " + from +
                    " becomes int " + to);
            from += 0.2;
        }
    }
}
```

Here is the output:

```
Double 1.3 becomes int 1
Double 1.5 becomes int 1
Double 1.7 becomes int 1
Double 1.9 becomes int 1
Double 2.1 becomes int 2
```

If rounding is desired, adding 0.5 to the value being narrowed will achieve the desired result. Here is a modification of the previous example:

```
public class Rounding {
    public static void main(String[] arg) {
```

```
                    double from;
                    int to;

                    from = 1.3;
                    for(int i=0; i<5; i++) {
                        to = (int)(from + 0.5);
                        System.out.println("Double " + from +
                                " becomes int " + to);
                        from += 0.2;
                    }
                }
            }
```

Here is the output:

```
Double 1.3 becomes int 1
Double 1.5 becomes int 2
Double 1.7 becomes int 2
Double 1.9 becomes int 2
Double 2.1 becomes int 2
```

For conversion of references, see **reference**. For passing constants to methods, see **method**. To force conversions, see **casting**.

core classes

Certain class definitions are very much a part of the language — these are referred to as the *core classes*. The core classes are the public classes in the `java.*` package, and they are all included in this book. This is the minimum set of classes available on all Java platforms. If an application, or an applet, has all its classes based on the core classes, it is considered to be 100 percent Java and will run on any Java platform.

Some classes seem to be a little more "core" than others. Some have a special relationship with the compiler or the Virtual Machine. `Object`, for example, is the base class of all classes — and a `String` object is generated by the compiler whenever a quoted string is found in the source.

CRC32

class java.util.zip.CRC32

This class can be used to calculate a 32-bit CRC (cyclical redundancy check) checksum. A CRC is a bit more reliable than an `Adler32` checksum, but it takes longer to calculate.

Inheritance

```
public class java.util.zip.CRC32
    implements Checksum
    extends Object
        ⇑
    public class java.lang.Object
```

Constructors

```
public CRC32()
```

Methods

getValue()

```
public long getValue()
```

Returns the calculated checksum.

reset()

```
public void reset()
```

Resets the internal checksum to its initial value.

update()

```
public void update(int value)
public void update(byte array[])
public void update(byte array[],int offset,int length)
```

This will update the checksum calculation to include the supplied bytes. This method can be called repeatedly until the checksum has been calculated for all the data. A single byte can be specified as the value. A block of bytes can be specified as array, and the checksum will be updated for length bytes beginning at array[offset]. If the length and offset are not specified, the entire array is used.

 For another method of calculating a checksum, see **Adler32**.

CropImageFilter

class java.awt.image.CropImageFilter

This is an image filter that will produce a new image by extracting a rectangular region from an existing image. A CropImageFilter accepts input produced from a `FilteredImageSource` object to produce a cropped version of the original image.

Inheritance

```
public class java.awt.image.CropImageFilter
    extends ImageFilter
        ⇑
    public class java.awt.image.ImageFilter
        implements ImageConsumer
        implements Cloneable
        extends Object
            ⇑
        public class java.lang.Object
```

Constructors

```
public CropImageFilter(int x,int y,int width,int height)
```

The area of the input image that will become the new cropped image has its upper-left-hand corner at x and y and has the specified width and height.

Methods

setDimensions()

```
public void setDimensions(int width,int height)
```

This will change the width and height values from those specified on the constructor.

setPixels()

```
public void setPixels(int x,int y,int w,int h,
        ColorModel model,byte pixels[],
        int off,int scansize)
```

```
public void setPixels(int x,int y,int w,int h,
        ColorModel model,int pixels[],
        int off,int scansize)
```

This does the actual filtering of the data supplied in the pixels array. This method is called with the entire image, but only the pixels within the cropped region are passed through to the output. For a description of the arguments, see ImageFilter.

setProperties()

```
public void setProperties(Hashtable props)
```

This method is called by the image producer to pass along a set of properties that describes the source and processing of the image. The `CropImageFilter` adds a property that is a `Rectangle` object (specifying the cropped area) with a `String` key of "croprect." The properties are then passed onto the next image consumer.

Example

This example uses `CropImageFilter` to create a new image from a small square extracted from a larger image and display it on top of the existing image:

```
import java.awt.*;
import java.applet.*;
import java.net.*;
import java.awt.image.*;
import java.util.*;

public class CropImageFilterApplet extends Applet {
    private Image image;
    private Image cropImage;

    public void init() {
        setBackground(Color.lightGray);
        URL url = getCodeBase();
        image = getImage(url,"halebopp.jpg");
        MediaTracker mt = new MediaTracker(this);
        mt.addImage(image,1);
        try {
            mt.waitForAll();
        } catch(Exception e) {
            e.printStackTrace();
        }
        CropImageFilter cf =
                new CropImageFilter(350,10,100,100);
        ImageProducer ip = image.getSource();
        FilteredImageSource is =
                new FilteredImageSource(ip,cf);
        cropImage = getToolkit().createImage(is);
        repaint();
    }

    public void paint(Graphics g) {
        g.drawImage(image,0,0,this);
        g.drawImage(cropImage,20,200,this);
        g.dispose();
    }
}
```

The entire image is first loaded from disk into image. A CropImageFilter is created with dimensions that will enclose a 100×100 square toward the upper-right of the image (the full input image is 515×362). An image is created by calling createImage() using the CropImageFilter as the image source. The paint() method simply draws the smaller image on top of the larger one, such that it shows up as an insert in the lower left. Figure C-12 shows the final result.

Figure C-12   The CropImageFilter is used to extract an image subset.

Cursor

class java.awt.Cursor

An instance of this class contains a bitmap that can be used as the graphic for the mouse cursor.

The cursors are predefined

Because of the portability issue, the cursors are all predefined. Different systems have different ways of producing displaying cursors—some use simple bitmaps that can be modified and others have a predefined set of cursors that cannot be changed. Java uses a predefined set of cursors (Java 1.1 includes a total of 14 different cursors). This results in a standard set of Cursor type names that can be implemented to work on any system.

The cursor definition values

A cursor is defined as an integer that is an index into the array of predefined cursors. The default cursor has an index value of zero.

Inheritance

```
public class java.awt.Cursor
    implements Serializable
    extends Object
        ⇑
    public class java.lang.Object
```

Variables and constants

CROSSHAIR_CURSOR

```
public final static int CROSSHAIR_CURSOR
```

A cursor composed of one vertical and one horizontal line to indicate a point at its center.

DEFAULT_CURSOR

```
public final static int DEFAULT_CURSOR
```

This is the cursor that is used whenever no specific cursor is set.

E_RESIZE_CURSOR

```
public final static int E_RESIZE_CURSOR
```

The East resize cursor. Normally an arrow pointing left to indicate window expansion or contraction on its left side.

HAND_CURSOR

```
public final static int HAND_CURSOR
```

The hand cursor. This often is made to look like a human hand pointing with the forefinger.

MOVE_CURSOR

```
public final static int MOVE_CURSOR
```

The move cursor. This is usually something like a crosshair or a four-way arrow to indicate that the item under the cursor is being moved.

N_RESIZE_CURSOR

```
public final static int N_RESIZE_CURSOR
```

The North resize cursor. Normally an arrow pointing up to indicate window expansion or contraction on its upper edge.

NE_RESIZE_CURSOR

```
public final static int NE_RESIZE_CURSOR
```

The Northeast resize cursor. Normally an arrow pointing up and to the right to indicate window expansion or contraction on its upper and right edges.

NW_RESIZE_CURSOR

```
public final static int NW_RESIZE_CURSOR
```

The Northwest resize cursor. Normally an arrow pointing up and to the left to indicate window expansion or contraction on its upper and left edges.

predefined

```
protected static Cursor predefined[]
```

The array of predefined Cursor objects.

S_RESIZE_CURSOR

```
public final static int S_RESIZE_CURSOR
```

The South resize cursor. Normally an arrow pointing down to indicate window expansion or contraction on its lower edge.

SE_RESIZE_CURSOR

```
public final static int SE_RESIZE_CURSOR
```

The Southeast resize cursor. Normally an arrow pointing down and to the right to indicate window expansion or contraction on its lower and right edges.

SW_RESIZE_CURSOR

```
public final static int SW_RESIZE_CURSOR
```

The Southwest resize cursor. Normally an arrow pointing down and to the left to indicate window expansion or contraction on its lower and left edges.

TEXT_CURSOR

```
public final static int TEXT_CURSOR
```

The text cursor. A special cursor used to indicate the current position in text—often some sort of vertical bar.

W_RESIZE_CURSOR

```
public final static int W_RESIZE_CURSOR
```

The West resize cursor. Normally an arrow pointing left to indicate window expansion or contraction on its left edge.

WAIT_CURSOR

```
public final static int WAIT_CURSOR
```

The wait cursor. A cursor that indicates the user should wait until some action has completed — usually a clock face or an hourglass.

Constructors

```
public Cursor(int type)
```

The `type` value must be one of those defined in this class; otherwise, an `IllegalArgumentException` is thrown.

Returned by

Methods of this class that produce `Cursor` objects are `getDefaultCursor()` and `getPredefinedCursor()`. A `Cursor` object can also be acquired from `Component.getCursor()`.

Methods

getDefaultCursor()

```
public static Cursor getDefaultCursor()
```

Returns the default `Cursor`.

getPredefinedCursor()

```
public static Cursor getPredefinedCursor(int type)
```

Returns a `Cursor` that is defined by one of the constant values listed previously.

getType()

```
public int getType()
```

Returns the type value of this `Cursor`.

 There are `setCursor()` methods in **Component** and **Frame**. The cursor constant values defined here are also defined in **Frame**.

Customizer

interface java.beans.Customizer

This interface should be implemented by an object that controls the interactive customization of a bean. It is used to notify the bean's parent object — the one responsible for display of the bean being customized — each time the bean needs to be redisplayed because of some modification that has been made to it.

Other Customizer characteristics

A customizer should inherit from `Component` so that it will be capable of being included as a component in `Container`. A customizer should have a default constructor that requires no arguments. The only information it will need to perform its job is the bean to be customized and the listeners to be notified when the bean has been changed — these are both supplied by the methods of this interface.

Inheritance

```
public interface java.beans.Customizer
```

Methods

addPropertyChangeListener()

```
public abstract void addPropertyChangeListener(
        PropertyChangeListener listener)
```

Adds a `listener` to the list of objects that will receive a `PropertyChangeEvent`. The customizer will call the `propertyChange()` method of the `listener` whenever it changes the bean in such a way that its display may need to be updated.

removePropertyChangeListener()

```
public abstract void removePropertyChangeListener(
        PropertyChangeListener listener)
```

Removes the `listener` from the list of those that will receive a `PropertyChangeEvent`.

setObject()

```
public abstract void setObject(Object bean)
```

Specifies the `bean` to be customized. This method should only be called once — and this call should be made before the `Customizer` has been added to a parent AWT container.

 For a description of the event, see **PropertyChangeEvent**. Also see **BeanDescriptor**.

D

daemon

For a description of daemon threads, see **thread**.

DatabaseMetaData

interface java.sql.DatabaseMetaData

The purpose of this interface is to provide information about a database. It has a number of methods, each of which returns one specific piece of information about the database. This "data about data" type of information is called *metadata*.

This interface definition is quite unique. It is really much more than just a convenience interface—it is a contract that can be agreed upon between an application and a database. The contract is defined in the Java API, it can be implemented by a database, and it can be complied with by an application. By implementing this interface, a database agrees to return certain information about itself to a Java application. In turn, a Java application can use the methods of this interface to query the database to determine its capabilities and characteristics. If a database supplies the information, and if an application uses it properly, the application will be able to successfully use the database without having to program specifically for it. Using this interface, a database will be portable across all of Java, and an application will be portable across several databases.

Because of the contractual nature of this interface, the documentation here was brought over virtually intact from the original API documentation. Some minor additions have been made here and there for clarification.

The types of information

Some of the information returned by methods defined in this interface is simple identification. For example, it is possible to determine the name and version number of the database.

Some of the information has to do with the presence or absence of a capability. For example, the database can be queried as to whether or not it supports nested outer joins; a simple `true` or `false` will be returned.

Some of the information has to do with procedures that must be followed by the application. For example, some databases will automatically close all cursors whenever the data is committed, and others will leave the cursors open. It is important for the application to know which will happen so that it will know whether it must close the cursors on completion, or, on the other hand, whether it will need to reopen the cursors to continue processing.

The ResultSets objects contain rows and columns

Some of the methods return a `ResultSet` object. The information is in the form of a table in a row/column format, and you can use the methods of the `ResultSet` class to extract it. In the descriptions, as in SQL, the columns are numbered, with the leftmost column being number one. For the methods of this interface that return a `ResultSet`, the descriptions include a numbered list of the columns. For those in which the order could matter, the ordering is also specified.

Exceptions for no metadata

If a method is called requesting data that are not available from this particular database, or if the called method is not supported by this database, an `SQLException` will be thrown. It is also possible to have an empty `ResultSet` returned if data are unavailable.

The string patterns

Some of the methods require that you supply a string pattern that will be used to qualify the query. Two characters have a special meaning in a pattern:

```
'%'   Match a substring of zero or more characters.
'_'   Match any single character.
```

To include one of these characters in a pattern as the character itself—not as a pattern generator—precede it with the escape character returned from `getSearchStringEscape()`.

SQL92

This interface definition is based on international SQL standard ISO/IEC 9075:1992 of July 1992. This standard is commonly known as either SQL92 or ANSI92. The standard defines the SQL database language used to define data structures, specify data integrity, invoke operations on SQL data, and create procedures embedded in the database. It is designed to provide portability between SQL implementations and interconnections between databases.

Inheritance

```
public interface java.sql.DatabaseMetaData
```

Variables and constants

There are some standard column names in some of the tables enclosed in the ResultSet object returned from the methods. These standard columns will contain standard values defined here as constants. For example, a column named `NULLABLE` will contain either the contant `columnNullable` or the constant `columnNoNulls`. The constants are listed here along with the name of the column in which they will appear.

bestRowNotPseudo

```
public final static int bestRowNotPseudo
```

BEST ROW PSEUDO_COLUMN—is not a pseudocolumn.

bestRowPseudo

```
public final static int bestRowPseudo
```

BEST ROW PSEUDO_COLUMN—is a pseudocolumn.

bestRowSession

```
public final static int bestRowSession
```

BEST ROW SCOPE—valid for the remainder of the current session.

bestRowTemporary

```
public final static int bestRowTemporary
```

BEST ROW SCOPE—is very temporary, while using row.

bestRowTransaction

```
public final static int bestRowTransaction
```

BEST ROW SCOPE—valid for the remainder of the current transaction.

bestRowUnknown

```
public final static int bestRowUnknown
```

BEST ROW PSEUDO_COLUMN—may or may not be a pseudocolumn.

columnNoNulls

```
public final static int columnNoNulls
```

COLUMN NULLABLE—may not allow NULL values.

columnNullable

```
public final static int columnNullable
```

COLUMN NULLABLE—definitely allows NULL values.

columnNullableUnknown

```
public final static int columnNullableUnknown
```

COLUMN NULLABLE—nullability unknown.

importedKeyCascade

```
public final static int importedKeyCascade
```

IMPORT KEY UPDATE_RULE and DELETE_RULE—to update, change the imported key to agree with the primary key update. To delete, delete rows that import a deleted key.

importedKeyInitiallyDeferred

```
public final static int importedKeyInitiallyDeferred
```

IMPORT KEY DEFERRABILITY—see SQL92 for the definition.

importedKeyInitiallyImmediate

```
public final static int importedKeyInitiallyImmediate
```

IMPORT KEY DEFERRABILITY—see SQL92 for the definition.

importedKeyNoAction

```
public final static int importedKeyNoAction
```

IMPORT KEY UPDATE_RULE and DELETE_RULE—do not allow update or deletion of the primary key if it has been imported.

importedKeyNotDeferrable

```
public final static int importedKeyNotDeferrable
```

IMPORT KEY DEFERRABILITY—see SQL92 for definition.

importedKeyRestrict

```
public final static int importedKeyRestrict
```

IMPORT KEY UPDATE_RULE and DELETE_RULE—do not allow update or deletion of the primary key if it has been imported.

importedKeySetDefault

```
public final static int importedKeySetDefault
```

IMPORT KEY UPDATE_RULE and DELETE_RULE—change the imported key to default values if its primary key has been updated or deleted.

importedKeySetNull

```
public final static int importedKeySetNull
```

IMPORT KEY UPDATE_RULE and DELETE_RULE—change the imported key to NULL if its primary key has been updated or deleted.

procedureColumnIn

```
public final static int procedureColumnIn
```

COLUMN_TYPE—IN parameter.

procedureColumnInOut

```
public final static int procedureColumnInOut
```

COLUMN_TYPE—INOUT parameter.

procedureColumnOut

```
public final static int procedureColumnOut
```

COLUMN_TYPE—OUT parameter.

procedureColumnResult

```
public final static int procedureColumnResult
```

COLUMN_TYPE—result column in ResultSet.

procedureColumnReturn

```
public final static int procedureColumnReturn
```

COLUMN_TYPE—procedure return value.

procedureColumnUnknown

```
public final static int procedureColumnUnknown
```

COLUMN_TYPE—the purpose of the column is unknown.

procedureNoNulls

```
public final static int procedureNoNulls
```

TYPE NULLABLE—does not allow NULL values.

procedureNoResult

```
public final static int procedureNoResult
```

PROCEDURE_TYPE—does not return a result.

procedureNullable

```
public final static int procedureNullable
```

TYPE NULLABLE—allows NULL values.

procedureNullableUnknown

```
public final static int procedureNullableUnknown
```

TYPE NULLABLE—nullability unknown.

procedureResultUnknown

```
public final static int procedureResultUnknown
```

PROCEDURE_TYPE—may return a result.

procedureReturnsResult

```
public final static int procedureReturnsResult
```

PROCEDURE_TYPE—returns a result.

tableIndexClustered

```
public final static short tableIndexClustered
```

INDEX INFO TYPE—identifies a clustered index.

tableIndexHashed

```
public final static short tableIndexHashed
```

INDEX INFO TYPE—identifies a hashed index.

tableIndexOther

```
public final static short tableIndexOther
```

INDEX INFO TYPE—identifies some other form of index.

tableIndexStatistic

```
public final static short tableIndexStatistic
```

INDEX INFO TYPE—identifies table statistics that are returned in conjunction with a table's index descriptions.

typeNoNulls

```
public final static int typeNoNulls
```

TYPE NULLABLE—does not allow NULL values.

typeNullable

```
public final static int typeNullable
```

TYPE NULLABLE—allows NULL values.

typeNullableUnknown

```
public final static int typeNullableUnknown
```

TYPE NULLABLE—nullability unknown.

typePredBasic

```
public final static int typePredBasic
```

TYPE INFO SEARCHABLE—supported except for WHERE ... LIKE.

typePredChar

```
public final static int typePredChar
```

TYPE INFO SEARCHABLE—only supported with WHERE ... LIKE.

typePredNone

```
public final static int typePredNone
```

TYPE INFO SEARCHABLE—search is not supported.

typeSearchable

```
public final static int typeSearchable
```

TYPE INFO SEARCHABLE—supported for all WHERE.

versionColumnNotPseudo

```
public final static int versionColumnNotPseudo
```

VERSION COLUMNS PSEUDO_COLUMN—is not a pseudocolumn.

versionColumnPseudo

```
public final static int versionColumnPseudo
```

VERSION COLUMNS PSEUDO_COLUMN—is a pseudocolumn.

versionColumnUnknown

```
public final static int versionColumnUnknown
```

VERSION COLUMNS PSEUDO_COLUMN—may or may not be a pseudocolumn.

Constructors

Returned by

An object implementing this interface is returned from `Connection.getMetaData()`.

Methods

allProceduresAreCallable()

```
public abstract boolean allProceduresAreCallable()
    throws SQLException
```

Returns `true` if all the procedures returned by `getProcedures()` can be called by the current user.

allTablesAreSelectable()

```
public abstract boolean allTablesAreSelectable()
    throws SQLException
```

Returns `true` if all the tables returned by `getTable()` can be SELECTed by the current user.

dataDefinitionCausesTransactionCommit()

```
public abstract boolean dataDefinitionCausesTransactionCommit()
    throws SQLException
```

Returns `true` if a data definition statement within a transaction will force the transaction to commit.

dataDefinitionIgnoredInTransactions()

```
public abstract boolean
        dataDefinitionIgnoredInTransactions()
    throws SQLException
```

Returns `true` if a data definition statement within a transaction will be ignored.

doesMaxRowSizeIncludeBlobs()

```
public abstract boolean doesMaxRowSizeIncludeBlobs()
    throws SQLException
```

Returns `true` if `getMaxRowSize()` includes LONGVARCHAR and LONGVARBINARY blobs.

getBestRowIdentifier()

```
public abstract ResultSet
        getBestRowIdentifier(String catalog,String schema,
```

```
       String table,int scope,boolean nullable)
   throws SQLException
```

Returns a description of a table's optimal set of columns that uniquely identifies a row. They are ordered by SCOPE. The `catalog` argument is a catalog name. A `catalog` string of "" will retrieve those columns without a catalog. A `null catalog` will cause the catalog criteria not to be used. A `schema` pattern of "" will retrieve those without a schema. A table name can be specified with `table`. The `scope` can be any of the values described here for SCOPE. If `nullable` is `false`, columns that are nullable will not be included.

The return value is a list of column descriptions. Each member of the set has the following columns:

1   SCOPE `short`. This is the actual scope of the result. If it is `bestRowTemporary`, it is very temporary. If it is `bestRowTransaction`, it is valid for remainder of current transaction. If it is `bestRowSession`, it is valid for remainder of the current session.
2   COLUMN_NAME `String`. The column name
3   DATA_TYPE `short`. The SQL data type from `java.sql.Types`
4   TYPE_NAME `String`. The data source–dependent type name
5   COLUMN_SIZE `int`. The precision
6   BUFFER_LENGTH `int`. Not used
7   DECIMAL_DIGITS `short`. The scale
8   PSEUDO_COLUMN `short`. Indicates whether this is this a pseudocolumn like an Oracle ROWID. If its value is `bestRowUnknown`, it may or may not be pseudo column. If it is `bestRowNotPseudo`, it is not a pseudocolumn. If it is `bestRowPseudo`, it is a pseudocolumn.

getCatalogs()

```
   public abstract ResultSet getCatalogs()
       throws SQLException
```

The return value is a list of catalog names available in this database. Each member of the set has the following column:

1   TABLE_CAT `String`. The catalog name

getCatalogSeparator()

```
   public abstract String getCatalogSeparator()
       throws SQLException
```

Returns the string that is used for a separator between the catalog and the table name.

getCatalogTerm()

```
   public abstract String getCatalogTerm()
       throws SQLException
```

Returns the database vendor's preferred term for "catalog."

getColumnPrivileges()

```
public abstract ResultSet getColumnPrivileges(
        String catalog,String schema,String table,
        String columnNamePattern)
    throws SQLException
```

Gets a description of the access rights for the columns of a specific table. Only privileges matching the column name criteria are returned. The `catalog` argument is a catalog name. A `catalog` string of "" will retrieve those columns without a catalog. A `null` `catalog` will cause the catalog criteria not to be used. A `schema` pattern of "" will retrieve those columns without a schema. A table name can be specified with `table`. The `columnNamePattern` specifies a pattern match required for the name of the column. The descriptions are ordered by COLUMN_NAME and PRIVILEGE. Each privilege description has the following columns:

1   TABLE_CAT `String`. The table catalog, which could be null
2   TABLE_SCHEM `String`. The table schema, which could be null
3   TABLE_NAME `String`. The name of the table
4   COLUMN_NAME `String`. The name of the column
5   GRANTOR `String`. The grantor of access, which may be null
6   GRANTEE `String`. The grantee of access
7   PRIVILEGE `String`. The name of the access privilege. It could be "SELECT", "INSERT", "UPDATE", "REFERENCES", etc.
8   IS_GRANTABLE `String`. This is "YES" if the grantee is permitted to grant permission to others. It is "NO" if it is not permitted. It is `null` if unknown.

getColumns()

```
public abstract ResultSet getColumns(String catalog,
        String schemaPattern,String tableNamePattern,
        String columnNamePattern)
    throws SQLException
```

Returns a descriptor of the table columns available in a catalog. The `catalog` argument is a catalog name. A `catalog` string of "" will retrieve those columns without a catalog. A `schemaPattern` of "" will retrieve those without a schema. The `tableNamePattern` specifies a pattern-match required for the name of the table. The `columnNamePattern` specifies a pattern match required for the name of the column.

The descriptions are ordered by TABLE_SCHEM, TABLE_NAME, and ORDINAL_POSITION. Each description returned has the following columns:

1   TABLE_CAT `String`. The name of the table catalog, which could be `null`
2   TABLE_SCHEM `String`. The name of the table schema, which could be `null`
3   TABLE_NAME `String`. The name of the table
4   COLUMN_NAME `String`. The name of the column
5   DATA_TYPE `short`. The SQL type from java.sql.Types
6   TYPE_NAME `String`. The data source–dependent type name

7   COLUMN_SIZE `int`. The size of the column. For `char` or `date` types, this is the maximum number of characters. For numeric or decimal types, this is the precision.
8   BUFFER_LENGTH. Not used
9   DECIMAL_DIGITS `int`. The number of fractional digits
10   NUM_PREC_RADIX `int`. The radix of a numeric type (typically either 10 or 2)
11   NULLABLE `int`. Specifies whether NULL is allowed. If the value is `columnNoNulls`, NULL values may or may not be allowed. If the value is `columnNullable`, NULL values are allowed. If it is `columnNullableUnknown`, it is not known whether they are allowed.
12   REMARKS `String`. This is a comment describing column, which could be NULL.
13   COLUMN_DEF `String`. This is the default value of the column, which could be NULL.
14   SQL_DATA_TYPE `int`. Not used
15   SQL_DATETIME_SUB `int`. Not used
16   CHAR_OCTET_LENGTH `int`. For character types, this is the maximum allowable number of bytes.
17   ORDINAL_POSITION `int`. This is the index of columns in the table. The index of the first column is 1.
18   IS_NULLABLE String. A value of "NO" means column does not allow NULL values. A value of "YES" means the column might allow NULL values. Any other value indicates it is unknown.

getCrossReference()

```
public abstract ResultSet getCrossReference(
        String primaryCatalog,String primarySchema,
        String primaryTable,String foreignCatalog,
        String foreignSchema,String foreignTable)
    throws SQLException
```

Returns a description of the foreign key columns that are in the foreign key table and that reference the primary key columns of the primary key table. Effectively, this is a description of how one table imports the keys of another table. Normally, this is a single foreign key/primary key pair.

A `catalog` string of "" will retrieve those columns without a catalog. A `null catalog` means that the catalog is not included in the selection criteria. A `primarySchema` pattern of "" will retrieve those columns without a schema. The `primaryTable` is the name of the table that exports the key. A `foreignCatalog` of "" will retrieve those columns without a foreign catalog. A `null foreignCatalog` means that the foreign catalog is not included in the selection criteria. A `foreignSchema` of "" will retrieve those columns without a foreign schema. The `foreignTable` is the table name that imports the key.

The return values are ordered by FKTABLE_CAT, FKTABLE_SCHEM, FKTABLE_NAME, and KEY_SEQ. Each foreign key column description has the following columns:

1   PKTABLE_CAT `String`. The name of the primary key table catalog, which may be `null`

2   PKTABLE_SCHEM `String`. The name of the primary key table schema, which may be `null`

3   PKTABLE_NAME `String`. The name of the primary key table

4   PKCOLUMN_NAME `String`. The name of the primary key column

5   FKTABLE_CAT `String`. The name of the foreign key table catalog being exported, which may be `null`

6   FKTABLE_SCHEM `String`. The name of the foreign key table schema being exported, which may be `null`

7   FKTABLE_NAME `String`. The name of the foreign key table being exported

8   FKCOLUMN_NAME `String`. The name of the foreign key column being exported

9   KEY_SEQ `short`. The sequence number within the foreign key

10 UPDATE_RULE `short`. Specifies what happens to the foreign key when the primary is updated. If it is `importedNoAction` or `importedKeyRestrict`, it does not allow update of the primary key if it has been imported. If it is `importedKeyCascade`, a change is made to the imported key to make it agree with the primary key update. If it is `importedKeySetNull`, the imported key is set to NULL if its primary key has been updated. If it is `importedKeySetDefault`, the imported key will be set to its default values if its primary key has been updated.

11 DELETE_RULE `short`. Specifies what happens to the foreign key when its primary is deleted. If the value is `importedKeyNoAction` or `importedKeyRestrict`, the deletion of the primary key is not allowed if it has been imported. If it is `importedKeyCascade`, the rows that import a deleted key are deleted. If it is `importedKeySetNull`, the imported key is set to NULL if its primary key has been deleted. If it is `importedKeySetDefault`, the imported key is set to default if its primary key has been deleted.

12 FK_NAME `String`. The foreign key name, which may be null

13 PK_NAME `String`. The primary key name, which may be null

14 DEFERRABILITY `short`. Determines whether the evaluation of foreign key constraints be deferred until commit time. The possible values are `importedKeyInitiallyDeferred`, `importedKeyInitiallyImmediate`, and `importedKeyNotDeferrable`. See SQL92 for the definition of these terms.

getDatabaseProductName()

```
public abstract String getDatabaseProductName()
    throws SQLException
```

Returns the name of the database.

getDatabaseProductVersion()

```
public abstract String getDatabaseProductVersion()
    throws SQLException
```

Returns the version of the database.

getDefaultTransactionIsolation()

```
public abstract int getDefaultTransactionIsolation()
    throws SQLException
```

Returns the default transaction isolation level of the database. The possible values are defined in java.sql.Connection.

getDriverMajorVersion()

```
public abstract int getDriverMajorVersion()
```

Returns the major version number of the JDBC driver.

getDriverMinorVersion()

```
public abstract int getDriverMinorVersion()
```

Returns the minor version number of the JDBC driver.

getDriverName()

```
public abstract String getDriverName()
    throws SQLException
```

Returns the name of the JDBC driver.

getDriverVersion()

```
public abstract String getDriverVersion()
    throws SQLException
```

Returns the version of the JDBC driver.

getExportedKeys()

```
public abstract ResultSet getExportedKeys(String catalog,
        String schema,String table)
    throws SQLException
```

Returns the descriptions of the foreign key columns that reference the primary key columns of a table — that is, the foreign keys exported by a table. They are ordered by FKTABLE_CAT, FKTABLE_SCHEM, FKTABLE_NAME, and KEY_SEQ.

A catalog name of "" will retrieve those columns without a catalog. A null catalog means that the catalog name will not be included in the selection criteria. A schema pattern of "" will retrieve those columns without a schema. The table is the name of a table.

Each foreign key column description has the following columns:

1   PKTABLE_CAT String. The name of the primary key table catalog, which may be null

2   PKTABLE_SCHEM String. The name of the primary key table schema, which may be null

3   PKTABLE_NAME String. The name of the primary key table
4   PKCOLUMN_NAME String . The name of the primary key column
5   FKTABLE_CAT String. The name of the foreign key table catalog, which may be null
6   FKTABLE_SCHEM String. The name of the foreign key table schema, which may be null
7   FKTABLE_NAME String. The name of the foreign key table
8   FKCOLUMN_NAME String. The name of the foreign key column
9   KEY_SEQ short. The sequence number within the foreign key
10   UPDATE_RULE short. An indication of what happens to the foreign key when the primary key is updated. If the value is importedNoAction or importedKeyRestrict, the update of the primary is not allowed if it has been imported. If it is importedKeyCascade, the imported key is changed to agree with the primary key update. If it is importedKeySetNull, the imported key is changed to NULL if its primary key has been updated. If it is importedKeySetDefault, the imported key is changed to its default values whenever its primary key is updated.
11   DELETE_RULE short. Specifies what happens to the foreign key when its primary is deleted. If the value is importedKeyNoAction or importedKeyRestrict, dele-tion of the primary is not allowed if it has been imported. If it is importedKeyCascade, the rows that import a deleted key are deleted. If it is importedKeySetNull, the imported key is set to NULL if its primary key has been deleted. If it is importedKeySetDefault, the imported key is set to its default if its primary key has been deleted.
12   FK_NAME String. The foreign key name, which may be null
13   PK_NAME String. The primary key name, which may be null
14   DEFERRABILITY short. Indicates whether the evaluation of foreign key constraints may be deferred until commit time. The possible values are importedKeyInitiallyDeferred, importedKeyInitiallyImmediate, and importedKeyNotDeferrable. See SQL92 for the definitions.

getExtraNameCharacters()

```
public abstract String getExtraNameCharacters()
    throws SQLException
```

Returns a string that contains characters allowed in names other than the normal ones. The normal set of characters includes a–z, A–Z, 0–9, and the underscore character.

getIdentifierQuoteString()

```
public abstract String getIdentifierQuoteString()
    throws SQLException
```

Returns the string used to quote SQL identifiers. A string composed of a single space is returned if identifier quoting is not supported. A JDBC-compliant driver will return a string containing a single double-quote character.

getImportedKeys()

```
public abstract ResultSet getImportedKeys(String catalog,
        String schema,String table)
    throws SQLException
```

Returns a description of the primary key columns that are referenced by a table's foreign key columns — that is, the primary keys imported by a table.

A `catalog` name of "" will retrieve those columns without a catalog. A `null catalog` means the catalog will not be included in the criteria. The `schema` is a name pattern. A `schema` pattern of "" will retrieve those columns without a schema. The `table` is the name of the table.

They are ordered by PKTABLE_CAT, PKTABLE_SCHEM, PKTABLE_NAME, and KEY_SEQ. Each primary key column description has the following columns:

1   PKTABLE_CAT `String`. The primary key table catalog being imported, which could be `null`
2   PKTABLE_SCHEM `String`. The primary key table schema being imported, which may be `null`
3   PKTABLE_NAME `String`. The primary key table name being imported
4   PKCOLUMN_NAME `String`. The primary key column name being imported
5   FKTABLE_CAT `String`. The foreign key table catalog, which may be `null`
6   FKTABLE_SCHEM `String`. The foreign key table schema, which may be `null`
7   FKTABLE_NAME `String`. The name of the foreign key table
8   FKCOLUMN_NAME `String`. The name of the foreign key column
9   KEY_SEQ `short`. The sequence number within the foreign key
10   UPDATE_RULE `short`. Specifies what happens to the foreign key when the primary key is updated. If it is `importedNoAction` or `importedKeyRestrict`, an update of the primary key is not allowed if it has been imported. If it is `importedKeyCascade`, the imported key is changed to agree with the primary key. If it is `importedKeySetNull`, the imported key is changed to NULL if its primary key has been updated. If it is `importedKeySetDefault`, the imported key is changed to its default values if its primary key has been updated.
11   DELETE_RULE `short`. Specifies what happens to the foreign key when the primary key is deleted. If the value is `importedKeyNoAction` or `importedKeyRestriction`, deletion of the primary key is not allowed if it has been imported. If it is `importedKeyCascade`, rows that import a deleted key are deleted. If it is `importedKeySetNull`, the imported key is set to NULL if its primary key has been deleted. If it is `importedKeySetDefault`, the imported key is set to its default if its primary key has been deleted.
12   FK_NAME `String`. The name of the foreign key, which may be `null`
13   PK_NAME `String` . The name of the primary key, which may be `null`
14   DEFERRABILITY `short`. Specifies whether the evaluation of a foreign key constraints can be deferred until commit time. Its value will be `importedKeyInitiallyDeferred`, `importedKeyInitiallyImmediate`, or `importedKeyNotDeferrable`. See SQL92 for the definitions.

getIndexInfo()

```
public abstract ResultSet getIndexInfo(String catalog,
        String schema,String table,
        boolean unique,boolean approximate)
    throws SQLException
```

Returns a description of the table indexes and statistics.

A catalog name of "" will retrieve those indexes without a catalog. A null catalog name will drop the catalog form the selection criteria. A schema pattern of "" will retrieve those indexes without a schema. The table is the table name. If unique is true, only indexes with unique values will be included. If approximate is true, the return value could include approximate or out-of-date values.

The returned data are ordered by NON_UNIQUE, TYPE, INDEX_NAME, and ORDINAL_POSITION. Each index column description has the following columns:

1 TABLE_CAT String. The name of the table catalog, which may be null
2 TABLE_SCHEM String. The name of the table schema, which may be null
3 TABLE_NAME String. The table name
4 NON_UNIQUE boolean. Set to true if index values may be nonunique. Set to false when TYPE is tableIndexStatistic
5 INDEX_QUALIFIER String. The name of the index catalog, which will be NULL when TYPE is tableIndexStatistic
6 INDEX_NAME String. The index name. It is null when TYPE is tableIndexStatistic.
7 TYPE short. Specifies the index type. If the value is tableIndexStatistic, this identifies table statistics that are returned in conjunction with a table's index descriptions. If it is tableIndexClustered, this is a clustered index. If it is tableIndexHashed, this is a hashed index. If it is tableIndexOther, this is some other style of index.
8 ORDINAL_POSITION short. The column sequence number within the index. It is zero when TYPE is tableIndexStatistic.
9 COLUMN_NAME String. This is the name of the column. It is null when TYPE is tableIndexStatistic.
10 ASC_OR_DESC String. This designates the column sort order. It is "A" for ascending and "D" for descending. It will be null if sort sequence is not supported or when the TYPE is tableIndexStatistic.
11 CARDINALITY int. If the TYPE is tableIndexStatistic, then this is the number of rows in the table; otherwise, it is the number of unique values in the index.
12 PAGES int. If the TYPE is tableIndexStatistic, then this is the number of pages used for the table; otherwise, it is the number of pages used for the current index.
13 FILTER_CONDITION String. The filter condition, which may be null

getMaxBinaryLiteralLength()

```
public abstract int getMaxBinaryLiteralLength()
```

```
throws SQLException
```

Returns the maximum number of hexadecimal characters that can be included in an inline binary literal.

getMaxCatalogNameLength()

```
public abstract int getMaxCatalogNameLength()
    throws SQLException
```

Returns the maximum length of a catalog name.

getMaxCharLiteralLength()

```
public abstract int getMaxCharLiteralLength()
    throws SQLException
```

Returns the maximum length of a character literal.

getMaxColumnNameLength()

```
public abstract int getMaxColumnNameLength()
    throws SQLException
```

Returns the maximum length of a column name.

getMaxColumnsInGroupBy()

```
public abstract int getMaxColumnsInGroupBy()
    throws SQLException
```

Returns the maximum number of columns allowed in a "GROUP BY" clause.

getMaxColumnsInIndex()

```
public abstract int getMaxColumnsInIndex()
    throws SQLException
```

Returns the maximum number of columns allowed in an index.

getMaxColumnsInOrderBy()

```
public abstract int getMaxColumnsInOrderBy()
    throws SQLException
```

Returns the maximum number of columns allowed in an "ORDER BY" clause.

getMaxColumnsInSelect()

```
public abstract int getMaxColumnsInSelect()
    throws SQLException
```

Returns the maximum number of columns allowed in a "SELECT" list.

getMaxColumnsInTable()

```
public abstract int getMaxColumnsInTable()
    throws SQLException
```

Returns the maximum number of columns allowed in a table.

getMaxConnections()

```
public abstract int getMaxConnections()
    throws SQLException
```

Returns the maximum number of connections that can be simultaneously active.

getMaxCursorNameLength()

```
public abstract int getMaxCursorNameLength()
    throws SQLException
```

Returns the maximum length of the name of a cursor.

getMaxIndexLength()

```
public abstract int getMaxIndexLength()
    throws SQLException
```

Returns the maximum number of bytes that can be included in an index.

getMaxProcedureNameLength()

```
public abstract int getMaxProcedureNameLength()
    throws SQLException
```

Returns the maximum length allowed for a procedure name.

getMaxRowSize()

```
public abstract int getMaxRowSize()
    throws SQLException
```

Returns the maximum length allowed for a single row.

getMaxSchemaNameLength()

```
public abstract int getMaxSchemaNameLength()
    throws SQLException
```

Returns the maximum length allowed for a schema name.

getMaxStatementLength()

```
public abstract int getMaxStatementLength()
    throws SQLException
```

Returns the maximum length allowed for an SQL statement.

getMaxStatements()

```
public abstract int getMaxStatements()
    throws SQLException
```

Returns the maximum number of active statements that can be opened to the database.

getMaxTableNameLength()

```
public abstract int getMaxTableNameLength()
    throws SQLException
```

Returns the maximum length allowed for a table name.

getMaxTablesInSelect()

```
public abstract int getMaxTablesInSelect()
    throws SQLException
```

Returns the maximum number of tables allowed in a SELECT statement.

getMaxUserNameLength()

```
public abstract int getMaxUserNameLength()
    throws SQLException
```

Returns the maximum length allowed for a user name.

getNumericFunctions()

```
public abstract String getNumericFunctions()
    throws SQLException
```

Returns a comma-separated list of math functions.

getPrimaryKeys()

```
public abstract ResultSet getPrimaryKeys(String catalog,
        String schema,String table)
    throws SQLException
```

Returns a description of the primary keys of a table.

A `catalog` name of "" will retrieve those keys without a catalog. A `null catalog` will leave the catalog name out of the search criteria. A `schema` pattern of "" will retrieve those keys without a schema. The `table` argument is the name of the table.

They are ordered by COLUMN_NAME. Each primary key column description has the following columns:

1　TABLE_CAT `String`. The name of the table catalog, which may be `null`
2　TABLE_SCHEM `String` The name of the table schema, which may be `null`
3　TABLE_NAME `String`. The name of the table
4　COLUMN_NAME `String`. The column name

5   KEY_SEQ `short`. The sequence number within the primary key
6   PK_NAME `String`. The name of the primary key, which may be `null`

getProcedureColumns()

```
public abstract ResultSet getProcedureColumns(
        String catalog,String schemaPattern,
        String procedureNamePattern,
        String columnNamePattern)
    throws SQLException
```

Returns a description of a catalog's stored procedure parameters and the result columns. Only descriptions matching the schema, procedure, and parameter name criteria are returned. A `catalog` name of "" will retrieve those columns without a catalog. A `null` `catalog` means that the catalog will not be used in the search criteria. A `schemaPattern` of "" will retrieve those columns without a schema. The `procedureNamePattern` is a pattern used to select the procedure name. The `columnNamePattern` is a pattern used to select the column name.

The returned data are ordered by PROCEDURE_SCHEMA and PROCEDURE_NAME. Within this, the return value, if any, is first. Next are the parameter descriptions in call order. The column descriptions follow in column number order. Each row in the `ResultSet` is a parameter description or column description with the following fields:

1   PROCEDURE_CAT `String`. The name of the procedure catalog, which may be `null`
2   PROCEDURE_SCHEM `String`. The name of the procedure schema, which may be `null`
3   PROCEDURE_NAME `String`. The name of the procedure
4   COLUMN_NAME `String`. The column/parameter name
5   COLUMN_TYPE `Short`. The kind of column/parameter. If the value is `procedureColumnUnknown`, it is unknown. If it is `procedureColumnIn`, it is an IN parameter. It is `procedureColumnInOut`, it is an INOUT parameter. If it is `procedureColumnOut`, it is an OUT parameter. If it is `procedureColumnReturn`, it is a return-value procedure. If it is `procedureColumnResult`, it is a result column in `ResultSet`.
6   DATA_TYPE `short`. The SQL type from `java.sql.Types`
7   TYPE_NAME `String`. The SQL type name
8   PRECISION `int`. The precision
9   LENGTH `int`. The length of the data in bytes
10 SCALE `short`. The scale
11 RADIX `short`. The radix
12 NULLABLE `short`. Specifies whether or not the column can be NULL. If the value is `procedureNoNulls`, NULL values are not allowed. If it is `procedureNullable`, NULL values are allowed. If it is `procedureNullableUnknown`, it is not known whether or not the column allows NULL.

13   REMARKS `String`. A description of the parameter/column. This may be NULL. Also, additional columns beyond REMARKS can be defined by the database.

getProcedures()

```
public abstract ResultSet getProcedures(String catalog,
        String schemaPattern,String procedureNamePattern)
throws SQLException
```

Returns a description of the stored procedures available in a catalog.

Only procedure descriptions matching the schema and procedure name criteria are returned. A catalog name of "" will retrieve those stored procedures without a `catalog`. A `null catalog` will leave the catalog out of the selection criteria. A `schemaPattern` of "" will retrieve those stored procedures without a schema. The `procedureNamePattern` is a pattern used to select the procedure name.

The returned data are ordered by PROCEDURE_SCHEM, and then by PROCEDURE_NAME. Each procedure description has the following columns:

1   PROCEDURE_CAT `String`. The name of the procedure catalog, which may be `null`
2   PROCEDURE_SCHEM `String`. The name of the procedure schema, which may be `null`
3   PROCEDURE_NAME `String`. The procedure name
4   Reserved for future use
5   Reserved for future use
6   Reserved for future use
7   REMARKS `String`. An explanatory comment
8   PROCEDURE_TYPE `short`. An indicator of the kind of procedure: If the value is `procedureResultUnknown`, the procedure may return a result. If it is `procedureNoResult`, the procedure does not return a result. If it is `procedureReturnsResult`, the procedure returns a result.

getProcedureTerm()

```
public abstract String getProcedureTerm()
    throws SQLException
```

Returns the database vendor's preferred term for "procedure."

getSchemas()

```
public abstract ResultSet getSchemas()
    throws SQLException
```

Returns the names of the schemas that are available in this database. The results are ordered by schema name. The schema column is:

1   TABLE_SCHEM String. The name of the schema

getSchemaTerm()

```
public abstract String getSchemaTerm()
    throws SQLException
```

Returns the database vendor's preferred term for "schema."

getSearchStringEscape()

```
public abstract String getSearchStringEscape()
    throws SQLException
```

This is the escape character that can be used in the pattern strings. Placing the contents of this string in front of a '%' character or an underscore will cause it to lose its pattern-building powers and become a regular character in the stream.

getSQLKeywords()

```
public abstract String getSQLKeywords()
    throws SQLException
```

Returns a comma-separated list of all the SQL keywords that are not defined in SQL92.

getStringFunctions()

```
public abstract String getStringFunctions()
    throws SQLException
```

Returns a comma-separated list of string function names.

getSystemFunctions()

```
public abstract String getSystemFunctions()
    throws SQLException
```

Returns a comma-separated list of system functions.

getTablePrivileges()

```
public abstract ResultSet getTablePrivileges(
        String catalog,String schemaPattern,
        String tableNamePattern)
    throws SQLException
```

Returns a description of the access right for each table in a catalog.

 A table-level privilege applies to one or more columns in the table. It cannot be assumed that it applies to all the columns.

Only privileges matching the schema and table name criteria are returned. A catalog name of "" will retrieve those tables without a catalog. A null catalog will exclude the catalog from the selection criteria. A schemaPattern of "" will retrieve those tables without a schema. The tableNamePattern is a pattern to select the table name.

The returned data are ordered by TABLE_SCHEM, TABLE_NAME, and PRIVILEGE. Each privilege description has the following columns:

1   TABLE_CAT `String`. The name of the table catalog, which may be `null`
2   TABLE_SCHEM `String`. The name of the table schema, which may be `null`
3   TABLE_NAME `String`. The table name
4   GRANTOR. `String`. The grantor of access, which may be `null`
5   GRANTEE `String`. The grantee of access
6   PRIVILEGE `String`. The name of the access (SELECT, INSERT, UPDATE, REFER-ENCES, . . .)
7   IS_GRANTABLE `String`. The string is "YES" if the grantee is permitted to grant per-missions to others. It is "NO" if not and `null` if unknown.

getTables()

```
public abstract ResultSet getTables(String catalog,
        String schemaPattern,String tableNamePattern,
        String types[])
    throws SQLException
```

Returns a description of the tables available in a catalog. Some databases will not return information for all tables.

Only table descriptions matching the catalog, the schema, the table name, and the type criteria are returned. A `catalog` name of "" will retrieve those tables without a catalog. A `null catalog` will exclude the catalog from the selection criteria. A `schemaPattern` of "" will retrieve those tables without a schema. The `tableNamePattern` is a pattern to select the table name. The `types` array is a list of types to be returned. A `null types` argument will return all types.

The returned data are ordered by TABLE_TYPE, TABLE_SCHEM, and TABLE_NAME. Each table description has the following columns:

1   TABLE_CAT `String`. The name of the table catalog, which may be `null`
2   TABLE_SCHEM `String`. The name of the table schema, which may be `null`
3   TABLE_NAME `String`. The name of the table
4   TABLE_TYPE `String`. A string defining the table type. Typical types are:
    "TABLE"
    "VIEW"
    "SYSTEM TABLE"
    "GLOBAL TEMPORARY"
    "LOCAL TEMPORARY"
    "ALIAS"
    "SYNONYM"
5   REMARKS `String`. A description of the table

getTableTypes()

```
public abstract ResultSet getTableTypes()
```

```
throws SQLException
```

Returns the types of tables that are available in this database as a `ResultSet` with a single column. The table type is this:

1 TABLE_TYPE String. The name of a table type. Typical types are:
   "TABLE"
   "VIEW"
   "SYSTEM TABLE"
   "GLOBAL TEMPORARY"
   "LOCAL TEMPORARY"
   "ALIAS"
   "SYNONYM"

getTimeDateFunctions()

```
public abstract String getTimeDateFunctions()
    throws SQLException
```

Returns a comma-separated list of date and time functions.

getTypeInfo()

```
public abstract ResultSet getTypeInfo()
    throws SQLException
```

Returns a description of all the standard SQL types supported by this database. The list is ordered by DATA_TYPE and then by how closely the data type maps to the corresponding JDBC SQL type. Each type description has the following columns:

1   TYPE_NAME String. The name of the type
2   DATA_TYPE short. The SQL data type as defined in `java.sql.Types`
3   PRECISION int. The maximum precision
4   LITERAL_PREFIX String. The prefix used to quote a literal, which may be null
5   LITERAL_SUFFIX String. The suffix used to quote a literal, which may be null
6   CREATE_PARAMS String. The parameters used in creating the type, which may be null
7   NULLABLE short. Specifies whether or not you can use NULL for this type. If the value is typeNoNulls, the type cannot be set to NULL. If it is typeNullable, the type allows NULL values. If it is typeNullableUnknown, it is unknown.
8   CASE_SENSITIVE boolean. This is true if the SQL type is case-sensitive.
9   SEARCHABLE short. Specifies whether or not WHERE can be used based on this type. If the value is typePredNone, it cannot be used. If it is typePredChar, all that is supported is WHERE/LIKE. If it is typePredBasic, it is supported except for WHERE/LIKE. If it is typeSearchable, there is support for all WHERE.
10 UNSIGNED_ATTRIBUTE boolean. Set to true if the SQL type is unsigned
11 FIXED_PREC_SCALE boolean. Set to true if the SQL type can be used as a money value

12   AUTO_INCREMENT boolean. Set to true if the SQL type be used for an auto-increment value.
13   LOCAL_TYPE_NAME String. A localized version of the type name, which could be null
14   MINIMUM_SCALE short. The minimum scale supported
15   MAXIMUM_SCALE short. The maximum scale supported
16   SQL_DATA_TYPE int. Unused
17   SQL_DATETIME_SUB int. Unused
18   NUM_PREC_RADIX int. The radix value—usually 2 or 10

getURL()

```
public abstract String getURL()
     throws SQLException
```

Returns the URL for this database.

getUserName()

```
public abstract String getUserName()
     throws SQLException
```

Returns the user name, as known to the database.

getVersionColumns()

```
public abstract ResultSet getVersionColumns(
         String catalog,String schema,String table)
     throws SQLException
```

Returns a description of a table's columns that are automatically updated when any value in a row is updated. A catalog name of "" will retrieve those columns without a catalog. A null catalog will exclude the catalog from the selection criteria. A schema of "" will retrieve those columns without a schema. The table argument is the name of the table. Each column description has the following columns:

1   SCOPE short. Not used
2   COLUMN_NAME String. The name of the column
3   DATA_TYPE short. The SQL data type as defined in java.sql.Types
4   TYPE_NAME String. The data-source dependent type name
5   COLUMN_SIZE int. The precision
6   BUFFER_LENGTH int. The length of column value in bytes
7   DECIMAL_DIGITS short. The scale
8   PSEUDO_COLUMN short. Indicates whether or not this is a pseudocolumn (like an Oracle ROWID). If the value is versionColumnUnknown, it may or may not be pseudocolumn. If it is versionColumnNotPseudo, it is not a pseudocolumn. If it is versionColumnPseudo, it is a pseudocolumn.

isCatalogAtStart()

```
public abstract boolean isCatalogAtStart()
    throws SQLException
```

Returns `true` if a catalog appears at the beginning of a qualified table name and returns `false` if it appears at the end.

isReadOnly()

```
public abstract boolean isReadOnly() throws SQLException
```

Returns `true` if the database is in the read-only mode.

nullPlusNonNullIsNull()

```
public abstract boolean nullPlusNonNullIsNull()
    throws SQLException
```

Returns `true` if a concatenation of a non-NULL value with a NULL value will result in a NULL value. A JDBC-compliant driver will always return `true`.

nullsAreSortedAtEnd()

```
public abstract boolean nullsAreSortedAtEnd()
    throws SQLException
```

Returns true if NULL values are sorted at the end of the sorting order regardless of whether the sorting order is ascending or descending.

nullsAreSortedAtStart()

```
public abstract boolean nullsAreSortedAtStart()
    throws SQLException
```

Returns `true` if NULL values are sorted at the start of the sorting order regardless of whether the sort is ascending or descending.

nullsAreSortedHigh()

```
public abstract boolean nullsAreSortedHigh()
    throws SQLException
```

Returns true if NULL values are sorted as being higher than any other value.

nullsAreSortedLow()

```
public abstract boolean nullsAreSortedLow()
    throws SQLException
```

Returns `true` if NULL values are sorted as being lower than any other value.

storesLowerCaseIdentifiers()

```
public abstract boolean storesLowerCaseIdentifiers()
    throws SQLException
```

Returns true if the database treats mixed-case unquoted SQL identifiers as case-insensitive and stores them in lowercase.

storesLowerCaseQuotedIdentifiers()

```
public abstract boolean
        storesLowerCaseQuotedIdentifiers()
    throws SQLException
```

Returns true if the database treats mixed-case quoted SQL identifiers as case-insensitive and stores them as lowercase.

storesMixedCaseIdentifiers()

```
public abstract boolean storesMixedCaseIdentifiers()
    throws SQLException
```

Returns true if the database treats mixed-case unquoted SQL identifiers as case-insensitive but stores them as mixed-case strings.

storesMixedCaseQuotedIdentifiers()

```
public abstract boolean storesMixedCaseQuotedIdentifiers()
    throws SQLException
```

Returns true if the database treats mixed-case quoted SQL identifiers as case-insensitive but stores them as mixed-case strings.

storesUpperCaseIdentifiers()

```
public abstract boolean storesUpperCaseIdentifiers()
    throws SQLException
```

Returns true if the database treats mixed-case unquoted SQL identifiers as case insensitive and stores them in upper-case.

storesUpperCaseQuotedIdentifiers()

```
public abstract boolean storesUpperCaseQuotedIdentifiers()
    throws SQLException
```

Returns true if the database treats mixed-case quoted SQL identifiers as case-insensitive and stores them in uppercase.

supportsAlterTableWithAddColumn()

```
public abstract boolean supportsAlterTableWithAddColumn()
    throws SQLException
```

Returns true if "ALTER TABLE" with an add column is supported.

supportsAlterTableWithDropColumn()

```
public abstract boolean supportsAlterTableWithDropColumn()
    throws SQLException
```

Returns true if "ALTER TABLE" with a drop column is supported.

supportsANSI92EntryLevelSQL()

```
public abstract boolean supportsANSI92EntryLevelSQL()
    throws SQLException
```

Returns true if ANSI92 entry-level SQL grammar is supported. All JDBC-compliant drivers must return true.

supportsANSI92FullSQL()

```
public abstract boolean supportsANSI92FullSQL()
    throws SQLException
```

Returns true if the full ANSI92 SQL grammar is supported.

supportsANSI92IntermediateSQL()

```
public abstract boolean supportsANSI92IntermediateSQL()
    throws SQLException
```

Returns true if the ANSI92 intermediate SQL grammar is supported.

supportsCatalogsInDataManipulation()

```
public abstract boolean supportsCatalogsInDataManipulation()
    throws SQLException
```

Returns true if a catalog name can be used in a data manipulation statement.

supportsCatalogsInIndexDefinitions()

```
public abstract boolean supportsCatalogsInIndexDefinitions()
    throws SQLException
```

Returns true if a catalog name can be used in an index definition statement.

supportsCatalogsInPrivilegeDefinitions()

```
public abstract boolean supportsCatalogsInPrivilegeDefinitions()
    throws SQLException
```

Returns `true` if a catalog name can be used in a privilege definition statement.

supportsCatalogsInProcedureCalls()

```
public abstract boolean supportsCatalogsInProcedureCalls()
    throws SQLException
```

Returns `true` if a catalog name can be used in a procedure call statement.

supportsCatalogsInTableDefinitions()

```
public abstract boolean supportsCatalogsInTableDefinitions()
    throws SQLException
```

Returns `true` if a catalog name can be used in a table definition statement.

supportsColumnAliasing()

```
public abstract boolean supportsColumnAliasing()
    throws SQLException
```

Returns `true` if column aliasing is supported, meaning the SQL "AS" clause can be used to provide names for computed columns or to provide alias names for columns. A JDBC-compliant driver will always return `true`.

supportsConvert()

```
public abstract boolean supportsConvert()
    throws SQLException
```

Returns `true` if the CONVERT function between SQL types is supported.

supportsConvert()

```
public abstract boolean supportsConvert(int fromType,
        int toType)
    throws SQLException
```

Returns `true` if an SQL CONVERT statement can convert data from the `fromType` to the `toType`.

supportsCoreSQLGrammar()

```
public abstract boolean supportsCoreSQLGrammar()
    throws SQLException
```

Returns `true` if the ODBC Core SQL grammar is supported.

supportsCorrelatedSubqueries()

```
public abstract boolean supportsCorrelatedSubqueries()
    throws SQLException
```

Returns `true` if correlated subqueries are supported. A JDBC-compliant driver always returns `true`.

supportsDataDefinitionAndDataManipulationTransactions()

```
public abstract boolean
    supportsDataDefinitionAndDataManipulationTransactions()
    throws SQLException
```

Returns `true` if both data definition and data manipulation statements within a transaction are supported.

supportsDataManipulationTransactionsOnly()

```
public abstract boolean
        supportsDataManipulationTransactionsOnly()
    throws SQLException
```

Returns `true` if data manipulation statements within a transaction are supported.

supportsDifferentTableCorrelationNames()

```
public abstract boolean
        supportsDifferentTableCorrelationNames()
    throws SQLException
```

Returns `true` if table correlation names are supported and are restricted to being different from the names of the tables.

supportsExpressionsInOrderBy()

```
public abstract boolean supportsExpressionsInOrderBy()
    throws SQLException
```

Returns `true` if expressions in "ORDER BY" lists are supported.

supportsExtendedSQLGrammar()

```
public abstract boolean supportsExtendedSQLGrammar()
    throws SQLException
```

Returns `true` if the ODBC Extended SQL grammar is supported.

supportsFullOuterJoins()

```
public abstract boolean supportsFullOuterJoins()
    throws SQLException
```

Returns `true` if full nested outer joins are supported.

supportsGroupBy()

```
public abstract boolean supportsGroupBy()
    throws SQLException
```

Returns true if some form of a "GROUP BY" clause is supported.

supportsGroupByBeyondSelect()

```
public abstract boolean supportsGroupByBeyondSelect()
    throws SQLException
```

Returns true if a "GROUP BY" clause can add columns not in the SELECT provided that it specifies all the columns in the SELECT.

supportsGroupByUnrelated()

```
public abstract boolean supportsGroupByUnrelated()
    throws SQLException
```

Returns true if a "GROUP BY" clause can use columns not in the SELECT.

supportsIntegrityEnhancementFacility()

```
public abstract boolean supportsIntegrityEnhancementFacility()
    throws SQLException
```

Returns true if the SQL Integrity Enhancement Facility is supported.

supportsLikeEscapeClause()

```
public abstract boolean supportsLikeEscapeClause()
    throws SQLException
```

Returns true if the escape character in "LIKE" clauses is supported. A JDBC-compliant driver always returns true.

supportsLimitedOuterJoins()

```
public abstract boolean supportsLimitedOuterJoins()
    throws SQLException
```

Returns true if there is at least limited support for outer joins. This will always be true if supportFullOuterJoins() is true.

supportsMinimumSQLGrammar()

```
public abstract boolean supportsMinimumSQLGrammar()
    throws SQLException
```

Returns true if the ODBC Minimum SQL grammar is supported. All JDBC-compliant drivers must return true.

supportsMixedCaseIdentifiers()

```
public abstract boolean supportsMixedCaseIdentifiers()
    throws SQLException
```

Returns true if the database treats mixed-case unquoted SQL identifiers as case-sensitive and, as a result, stores them in mixed case. A JDBC-compliant driver will always return false.

supportsMixedCaseQuotedIdentifiers()

```
public abstract boolean supportsMixedCaseQuotedIdentifiers()
    throws SQLException
```

Returns true if the database treats mixed-case quoted SQL identifiers as case-sensitive and, as a result, stores them in mixed case. A JDBC-compliant driver will always return true.

supportsMultipleResultSets()

```
public abstract boolean supportsMultipleResultSets()
    throws SQLException
```

Returns true if multiple ResultSets being returned from a single execution is supported.

supportsMultipleTransactions()

```
public abstract boolean supportsMultipleTransactions()
    throws SQLException
```

Returns true if multiple transactions (on different connections) can be open simultaneously.

supportsNonNullableColumns()

```
public abstract boolean supportsNonNullableColumns()
    throws SQLException
```

Returns true if columns can be defined as nonnullable. A JDBC-compliant driver always returns true.

supportsOpenCursorsAcrossCommit()

```
public abstract boolean supportsOpenCursorsAcrossCommit()
    throws SQLException
```

Returns true if cursors remain open across commits. A return of false indicates that they may not remain open.

supportsOpenCursorsAcrossRollback()

```
public abstract boolean supportsOpenCursorsAcrossRollback()
    throws SQLException
```

Returns true if cursors remain open across rollbacks. A return of false indicates that they may not remain open.

supportsOpenStatementsAcrossCommit()

```
public abstract boolean supportsOpenStatementsAcrossCommit()
    throws SQLException
```

Returns true if statements remain open across commits.

supportsOpenStatementsAcrossRollback()

```
public abstract boolean supportsOpenStatementsAcrossRollback()
    throws SQLException
```

Returns true if statements remain open across rollbacks.

supportsOrderByUnrelated()

```
public abstract boolean supportsOrderByUnrelated()
    throws SQLException
```

Returns true if an "ORDER BY" clause can use columns not in the SELECT.

supportsOuterJoins()

```
public abstract boolean supportsOuterJoins()
    throws SQLException
```

Returns true if some form of outer join is supported.

supportsPositionedDelete()

```
public abstract boolean supportsPositionedDelete()
    throws SQLException
```

Returns true if a positioned DELETE is supported.

supportsPositionedUpdate()

```
public abstract boolean supportsPositionedUpdate()
    throws SQLException
```

Returns true if a positioned UPDATE is supported.

supportsSchemasInDataManipulation()

```
public abstract boolean supportsSchemasInDataManipulation()
    throws SQLException
```

Returns true if a schema name can be used in a data manipulation statement.

supportsSchemasInIndexDefinitions()

```
public abstract boolean supportsSchemasInIndexDefinitions()
    throws SQLException
```

Returns true if a schema name may be used in an index definition statement.

supportsSchemasInPrivilegeDefinitions()

```
public abstract boolean supportsSchemasInPrivilegeDefinitions()
    throws SQLException
```

Returns true if a schema name may be used in a privilege definition statement.

supportsSchemasInProcedureCalls()

```
public abstract boolean supportsSchemasInProcedureCalls()
    throws SQLException
```

Returns true if a schema name may be used in a procedure call statement.

supportsSchemasInTableDefinitions()

```
public abstract boolean supportsSchemasInTableDefinitions()
    throws SQLException
```

Returns true if a schema name may be used in a table definition statement.

supportsSelectForUpdate()

```
public abstract boolean supportsSelectForUpdate()
    throws SQLException
```

Returns true if SELECT for UPDATE is supported.

supportsStoredProcedures()

```
public abstract boolean supportsStoredProcedures()
    throws SQLException
```

Returns true if stored procedure calls using the stored procedure escape syntax are supported.

supportsSubqueriesInComparisons()

```
public abstract boolean supportsSubqueriesInComparisons()
    throws SQLException
```

Returns true if subqueries in comparison expressions are supported. A JDBC-compliant driver always returns true.

supportsSubqueriesInExists()

```
public abstract boolean supportsSubqueriesInExists()
```

```
            throws SQLException
```

Returns `true` if subqueries in "exists" expressions are supported. A JDBC-compliant driver always returns `true`.

supportsSubqueriesInIns()

```
    public abstract boolean supportsSubqueriesInIns()
            throws SQLException
```

Returns `true` if subqueries in "in" statements are supported. A JDBC-compliant driver always returns `true`.

supportsSubqueriesInQuantifieds()

```
    public abstract boolean supportsSubqueriesInQuantifieds()
            throws SQLException
```

Returns `true` if subqueries in quantified expressions are supported. A JDBC-compliant driver always returns `true`.

supportsTableCorrelationNames()

```
    public abstract boolean supportsTableCorrelationNames()
            throws SQLException
```

Returns `true` if table correlation names are supported. A JDBC-compliant driver always returns `true`.

supportsTransactionIsolationLevel()

```
    public abstract boolean
            supportsTransactionIsolationLevel(int level)
            throws SQLException
```

Returns `true` if the database supports the specified transaction isolation level. The level values are defined in `java.sql.Connection`.

supportsTransactions()

```
    public abstract boolean supportsTransactions()
            throws SQLException
```

Returns `true` if transactions are supported. If not, a commit will be a noop and the isolation level is TRANSACTION_NONE.

supportsUnion()

```
    public abstract boolean supportsUnion()
            throws SQLException
```

Returns `true` if SQL UNION is supported.

supportsUnionAll()

```
public abstract boolean supportsUnionAll()
    throws SQLException
```

Returns `true` if SQL UNION ALL is supported.

usesLocalFilePerTable()

```
public abstract boolean usesLocalFilePerTable()
    throws SQLException
```

Returns `true` if the database uses a separate file for each table.

usesLocalFiles()

```
public abstract boolean usesLocalFiles()
    throws SQLException
```

Returns `true` if the database stores tables in a local file.

 For making connections to a database, see **Driver** and **DriverManager**. For information on database compliance, see **JDBC**.

DataFlavor

class java.awt.datatransfer.DataFlavor

A `DataFlavor` object is the representation of a data format. It represents the format as it would appear on a clipboard, attached to an e-mail message, in a drag-and-drop operation, or as a file on disk.

Data can be stored on the clipboard in one flavor and retrieved in another. The original data flavor is set by the poster of the data. For this to work, there must be a conversion method to convert the data from one flavor to another.

Inheritance

```
public class java.awt.datatransfer.DataFlavor
    extends Object
            ⇑
    public class java.lang.Object
```

Variables and constants

plainTextFlavor

```
public static DataFlavor plainTextFlavor
```

A predefined `DataFlavor` representing Unicode text. The representation class is `InputStream`, and its MIME type is "text/plain; charset=unicode."

stringFlavor

```
public static DataFlavor stringFlavor
```

A predefined `DataFlavor` representing a Java Unicode string. The representation class is `java.lang.String`, and its MIME type is "application/x-java-serialized-object."

Constructors

```
public DataFlavor(Class representationClass,
        String humanPresentableName)

public DataFlavor(String mimeType,
        String humanPresentableName)
```

Specifying `representationClass` will construct a `DataFlavor` that represents a Java class. Transmitted data will be in the form of a serialized class. Its MIME type will default to "application/x-java-serialized-object."

If `mimeType` is used to specify the MIME type, the representation class will default to `InputStream`.

The `humanPresentableName` is a description used to identify this flavor.

Returned by

Arrays of `DataFlavor` objects are returned from the `getTransferDataFlavors()` methods in `StringSelection` and `Transferable`.

Methods

equals()

```
public boolean equals(DataFlavor dataFlavor)
```

Returns true if `dataFlavor` is the same as this `DataFlavor`.

getHumanPresentableName()

```
public String getHumanPresentableName()
```

Returns the description of the flavor, as it was supplied to the constructor.

getMimeType()

```
public String getMimeType()
```

Returns the MIME encoding type.

getRepresentationClass()

```
public Class getRepresentationClass()
```

Returns the Class object that would normally be returned by an object of the type represented by this DataFlavor.

isMimeTypeEqual()

```
public boolean isMimeTypeEqual(String mimeType)

public final boolean
         isMimeTypeEqual(DataFlavor dataFlavor)
```

Returns true if the MIME type of this flavor and the one specified as either mineType or dataFlavor are *functionally* the same. That is, one may have some option specified that the other does not—but if the one that is specified is the same as the default, the two are functionally the same and this method will return true.

normalizeMimeType()

```
protected String normalizeMimeType(String mimeType)
```

This will convert the mimeType string to a normalized MIME form.

This method is called to normalize all MIME strings, which allows for some flexibility in the definition of a normalized form. For example, it could be that the normalized form would include all the possible options with their default values inserted. The initial release of Java 1.1 simply returns the input string with no modifications.

normalizeMimeTypeParameter()

```
protected String normalizeMimeTypeParameter(
         String parameterName,String parameterValue)
```

This is called to normalize every MIME parameter. This is to allow DataFlavor subclasses to overload the method to handle special parameters. The default method returns the string

```
parameterName + "=" + parameterValue
```

setHumanPresentableName()

```
public void setHumanPresentableName(String
humanPresentableName)
```

Changes the description from the one supplied on the constructor to humanPresentableName.

For an example of transferring data from one program to another, see **Clipboard**. For converting data from one flavor to another, see **Transferable**.

DataFormatException

class java.util.zip.DataFormatException

This exception is thrown to indicate that an error in data formatting has occurred.

Inheritance

```
public class java.util.zip.DataFormatException
    extends Exception
        ⇑
    public class java.lang.Exception
        extends Throwable
            ⇑
        public class java.lang.Throwable
            implements Serializable
            extends Object
                ⇑
            public class java.lang.Object
```

Constructors

```
public DataFormatException()
public DataFormatException(String message)
```

If the message string is supplied, it is used as a detailed message describing this particular exception.

datagram

A *datagram* is the basic message unit used to transmit data over an internet. It is part of the TCP/IP protocol definition.

The Internet datagram

A datagram is used by the Internet to transmit data packages without the requirement of establishing a connection. The packet contains the address of the recipient and, optionally, routing information. A collection of datagrams may be used to compose a single message. Because the Internet may route the datagrams differently, they could arrive in a different order than that in which they were transmitted.

The complete address

An Internet address has two parts: The IP number is a 32-bit number that uniquely identifies a computer. The port number uniquely identifies some application running on the computer.

The port number

To transmit a datagram, it is necessary to know the remote port number as well as the remote IP address. Certain port numbers are standard (such as for FTP and HTTP) and are referred to as *well-known* ports. Others are dynamically assigned. Whenever a datagram is sent, the sender's full address (IP and port) is included so that the receiver can respond. Port numbers are unsigned 16-bit values.

DatagramPacket

class java.net.DatagramPacket

This is a wrapper class for an Internet datagram.

Inheritance

```
public final class java.net.DatagramPacket
    extends Object
        ⇑
    public class java.lang.Object
```

Constructors

```
public DatagramPacket(byte ibuf[],int ilength)
public DatagramPacket(byte ibuf[],int ilength,
        InetAddress iaddr,int iport)
```

If `iaddr` and `iport` are specified, the `DatagramPacket` may be used to transmit a message—otherwise, it can only be used to receive a message. The `ibuf` array holds the body of the message. The `ilength` argument is the number of bytes of message that are in `ibuf` for sending a message, or the number of bytes that should be read when receiving a message.

Methods

getAddress()

```
public synchronized InetAddress getAddress()
```

Returns the IP address. This will be the Internet address of the remote host—the one which is to receive this datagram, or from which the datagram has been received.

getData()

```
public synchronized byte[] getData()
```

Returns the data. This will be either the data to be sent or the data that has been received.

getLength()

```
public synchronized int getLength()
```

Returns the length of the data. This is the size of the data to be sent or the data that has been received.

getPort()

```
public synchronized int getPort()
```

Returns the port number of the remote host.

setAddress()

```
public synchronized void setAddress(InetAddress iaddr)
```

Specifies the IP address of the remote host.

setData()

```
public synchronized void setData(byte ibuf[])
```

The data in `ibuf` will be stored in the message block of this object.

setLength()

```
public synchronized void setLength(int ilength)
```

Specifies the number of bytes of data being held in this object.

setPort()

```
public synchronized void setPort(int iport)
```

Specifies the port number of the remote host.

 For sending and receiving datagrams, see **DatagramSocket**. For a description of a datagram, see **datagram**.

DatagramSocket

class java.net.DatagramSocket

This class represents a UDP socket and may be used to send and receive datagrams over an internet.

A socket

A *socket* is one end of a connectionless communications link. It is connectionless in the sense that it does not establish and one-to-one link with another socket — it can be addressed by and communicate with any number of other sockets. A socket is uniquely identified by the IP address of the host on which it resides and its port number on that host. When a socket is created, it must be assigned an available port number — this is called *binding* the socket to its port.

Socket timeout

This is the number of milliseconds the `receive()` method will block while waiting to receive a datagram. When the time expires, an exception is thrown.

Extended by

```
MulticastSocket
```

Inheritance

```
public class java.net.DatagramSocket
    extends Object
        ⇑
    public class java.lang.Object
```

Constructors

```
public DatagramSocket()
    throws SocketException

public DatagramSocket(int port)
    throws SocketException

public DatagramSocket(int port,InetAddress localAddress)
    throws SocketException
```

If the port is not specified, the constructor will bind the socket to the first available port number. The localAddress must be a valid IP address for this host (it is possible for a host to have more than one). A SocketException is thrown if the socket could not be opened or if it could not bind to the specified port.

Methods

close()

```
public void close()
```

Closes the socket.

getLocalAddress()

```
public InetAddress getLocalAddress()
```

Returns the IP address of the local host. This will be the address to which this socket is bound.

getLocalPort()

```
public int getLocalPort()
```

Returns the port number of this socket. This will be the port number to which this socket is bound.

getSoTimeout()

```
public synchronized int getSoTimeout()
    throws SocketException
```

Returns the setting of the socket timeout. If the timeout is infinite, a zero is returned.

receive()

```
public synchronized void receive(DatagramPacket packet)
    throws IOException
```

Receives a datagram from this socket and inserts the data and the sender's address (IP and port number) into `packet`. This method will block until a either a datagram is received or the socket timeout occurs. The `DatagramPacket` is defined with a fixed block size for the data, and if the actual data block is too large, it will be truncated. An `IOException` is thrown if an error occurs or if there is a timeout.

send()

```
public void send(DatagramPacket packet)
    throws IOException
```

Sends a datagram packet. The packet should have been initialized with the data as well as the IP address and port number of the intended recipient. An `IOException` is thrown if an error occurs.

setSoTimeout()

```
public synchronized void setSoTimeout(int timeout)
    throws SocketException
```

Sets the socket timeout. The value of `timeout` is the number of milliseconds a call to `receive()` will block and wait for the arrival of a datagram. A timeout of zero will cause `receive()` to have no timeout—it will block forever.

For a description of a datagram, see **datagram**. This is a UDP socket—for a TCP socket, see **ServerSocket** and **Socket**.

DatagramSocketImpl

class java.net.DatagramSocketImpl

This is an abstract class for implementing a UDP multicast datagram and socket.

Multicast

Multicasting allows datagrams to be sent to several locations at once. Because of the special handling involved, a special group of addresses is set aside for multicasting. A 23-bit IP multicast address can be identified because its leading (leftmost) four bits are always 1110.

Extended by

```
PlainDatagramSocketImpl
```

Inheritance

```
public abstract class java.net.DatagramSocketImpl
    implements SocketOptions
    extends Object
        ⇑
    public class java.lang.Object
```

Variables and constants

fd

```
protected FileDescriptor fd
```

The file descriptor of the socket.

localPort

```
protected int localPort
```

The port number on the local host.

Constructors

```
public DatagramSocketImpl()
```

Methods

bind()

```
protected abstract void bind(int lport,InetAddress laddr)
    throws SocketException
```

Binds the socket to a local port and IP address.

close()

```
protected abstract void close()
```

Closes the socket.

create()

```
protected abstract void create()
    throws SocketException
```

Creates a datagram socket.

getFileDescriptor()

```
protected FileDescriptor getFileDescriptor()
```

Returns the file descriptor of the socket.

getLocalPort()

```
protected int getLocalPort()
```

Returns the local port number of the socket.

getTTL()

```
protected abstract byte getTTL()
    throws IOException
```

Returns the time-to-live option. This is the count of the maximum number of hops that can be taken by this datagram before the Internet will destroy it.

join()

```
protected abstract void join(InetAddress inetaddr)
    throws IOException
```

Joins the group that has the multicast address specified by `inetaddr`.

leave()

```
protected abstract void leave(InetAddress inetaddr)
    throws IOException
```

Leaves the group that has the multicast address specified by `inetaddr`.

peek()

```
protected abstract int peek(InetAddress inetaddr)
        throws IOException
```

Returns the IP address of the last packet received.

receive()

```
protected abstract void receive(DatagramPacket packet)
        throws IOException
```

Receives a datagram packet and stores the information from it in `packet`.

send()

```
protected abstract void send(DatagramPacket packet)
        throws IOException
```

Sends the datagram `packet`. The packet contains the data and the information about the intended recipient.

setTTL()

```
protected abstract void setTTL(byte ttl)
        throws IOException
```

Sets the time-to-live option to the `ttl` value. This is the count of the maximum number of hops that can be taken by this datagram before the Internet will destroy it.

 For a description of a datagram, see **datagram**. This is a UDP socket—for a TCP socket, see **ServerSocket** and **Socket**.

DataInput

interface java.io.DataInput

This is the interface definition for classes that have the ability to read input in a standard format for the Java primitive types.

Implemented by

```
DataInputStream
RandomAccessFile
```

Extended by

```
ObjectInput
```

Inheritance

```
public interface java.io.DataInput
```

Methods

readBoolean()

```
public abstract boolean readBoolean()
    throws IOException
```

Reads a boolean value. An EOFException is thrown on an unexpected end-of-file.

readByte()

```
public abstract byte readByte()
    throws IOException
```

Reads a byte value. An EOFException is thrown on an unexpected end-of-file.

readChar()

```
public abstract char readChar()
    throws IOException
```

Reads a char value. An EOFException is thrown on an unexpected end-of-file.

readDouble()

```
public abstract double readDouble()
    throws IOException
```

Reads a double value. An EOFException is thrown on an unexpected end-of-file.

readFloat()

```
public abstract float readFloat()
    throws IOException
```

Reads a float value. An EOFException is thrown on an unexpected end-of-file.

readFully()

```
public abstract void readFully(byte barray[])
    throws IOException

public abstract void readFully(byte barray[],
        int offset,int length)
    throws IOException
```

Reads an array of bytes into barray. The data will be placed into barray beginning at offset and continuing for length bytes. If offset and length are not specified, all of `barray` will be filled. This is a blocking read—it will not return until there is enough data to fill `barray`. An `EOFException` is thrown on an unexpected end-of-file.

readInt()

```
public abstract int readInt()
    throws IOException
```

Reads an `int` value. An `EOFException` is thrown on an unexpected end-of-file.

readLine()

```
public abstract String readLine() throws IOException
```

Reads a `String`. An `EOFException` is thrown on an unexpected end-of-file.

readLong()

```
public abstract long readLong()
    throws IOException
```

Reads a `long` value. An `EOFException` is thrown on an unexpected end-of-file.

readShort()

```
public abstract short readShort()
    throws IOException
```

Reads a `short` value. An `EOFException` is thrown on an unexpected end-of-file.

readUnsignedByte()

```
public abstract int readUnsignedByte()
    throws IOException
```

Reads an eight-bit byte as an unsigned value and returns it as an `int` in the range 0 to 255. An `EOFException` is thrown on an unexpected end-of-file.

readUnsignedShort()

```
public abstract int readUnsignedShort()
    throws IOException
```

Reads a 16-bit short as an unsigned value and returns it as an `int` in the range 0 to 65,535. An `EOFException` is thrown on an unexpected end-of-file.

readUTF()

```
public abstract String readUTF()
    throws IOException
```

Reads a string of UTF-formatted Unicode characters and converts them all to their 16-bit Unicode form. An `EOFException` is thrown on an unexpected end-of-file.

skipBytes()

```
public abstract int skipBytes(int count)
    throws IOException
```

Requests the input stream to skip past `count` number of bytes. An `EOFException` is thrown on an unexpected end-of-file.

 For an example, see **DataInputStream**. For the inverse of this interface, see **DataOutput**.

DataInputStream

class java.io.DataInputStream

This class can be used to read Java primitive data types in a system-independent manner.

Inheritance

```
public class java.io.DataInputStream
    implements DataInput
    extends FilterInputStream
        ⇑
    public class java.io.FilterInputStream
        extends OutputStream
            ⇑
        public class java.io.InputStream
            extends Object
                ⇑
            public class java.lang.Object
```

Constructors

DataInputStream()

```
public DataInputStream(InputStream input)
```

This creates a `DataInputStream` that uses `input` for its data.

Methods

read()

```
public final int read(byte barray[])
    throws IOException
```

```
public final int read(byte barray[], int offset,int length)
    throws IOException
```

Reads an array of bytes. The input data is placed in `barray`, and the number of bytes read is returned. If `offset` and `length` are specified, the input data will appear beginning at `barray[offset]` for a maximum of `length` bytes. The default `offset` is 0, and the default `length` is the size of `barray`. This method will block as long as there is unread data available. A return value of −1 indicates a normal end to the input stream.

readBoolean()

```
public final boolean readBoolean()
    throws IOException
```

Reads a `boolean` value. An `EOFException` is thrown on an unexpected end-of-file.

readByte()

```
public final byte readByte()
    throws IOException
```

Reads a `byte` value. An `EOFException` is thrown on an unexpected end-of-file.

readChar()

```
public final char readChar()
    throws IOException
```

Reads a `char` value. An `EOFException` is thrown on an unexpected end-of-file.

readDouble()

```
public final double readDouble()
    throws IOException
```

Reads a `double` value. An `EOFException` is thrown on an unexpected end-of-file.

readFloat()

```
public final float readFloat()
    throws IOException
```

Reads a `float` value. An `EOFException` is thrown on an unexpected end-of-file.

readFully()

```
public final void readFully(byte barray[])
    throws IOException
```

```
public final void readFully(byte barray[], int offset,int
length)
    throws IOException
```

Reads an array of bytes into `barray`. The data will be placed into `barray` beginning at `offset` and continuing for `length` bytes. If `offset` and `length` are not specified, all of `barray` will be filled. This is a blocking read—it will not return until there is enough data to fill `barray`. An `EOFException` is thrown on an unexpected end-of-file.

readInt()

```
public final int readInt()
    throws IOException
```

Reads an `int` value. An `EOFException` is thrown on an unexpected end-of-file.

readLine()   deprecated

```
public final String readLine()
    throws IOException
```

Reads a `String` that is terminated with a line feed, carriage return, a line feed and carriage return pair, or an end-of-file. This method has been deprecated because it does not properly convert bytes to characters—the preferred method is `BufferedReader.readLine()`.

readLong()

```
public final long readLong()
    throws IOException
```

Reads a `long` value. An `EOFException` is thrown on an unexpected end-of-file.

readShort()

```
public final short readShort()
    throws IOException
```

Reads a `short` value. An `EOFException` is thrown on an unexpected end-of-file.

readUnsignedByte()

```
public final int readUnsignedByte()
    throws IOException
```

Reads an eight-bit `byte` as an unsigned value and returns it as an `int` in the range 0 to 255. An `EOFException` is thrown on an unexpected end-of-file.

readUnsignedShort()

```
public final int readUnsignedShort()
    throws IOException
```

Reads a 16-bit `short` as an unsigned value and returns it as an `int` in the range 0 to 65,535. An `EOFException` is thrown on an unexpected end-of-file.

readUTF()

```
public static final String readUTF()
    throws IOException

public final static String readUTF(DataInput input)
    throws IOException
```

Reads a string of UTF-formatted Unicode characters and converts them all to their 16-bit Unicode form. The default input stream is this — if input is specified, it will be used as the source for reading. An EOFException is thrown on an unexpected end-of-file.

skipBytes()

```
public final int skipBytes(int count)
    throws IOException
```

Requests that the input stream skip count number of bytes of the input stream. An EOFException is thrown on an unexpected end-of-file.

Example

This example uses a disk file to demonstrate DataOutputStream and DataInputStream. Once the DataOutputStream is constructed, data is written to it using some of the type-specific methods of the class. After the data is written, the output is closed and a DataInputStream is opened using the same file for its input. In a reverse of the writing, the same data types are read in the same order in which they had been written:

```
import java.io.*;
public class DataOutInStream {
    public static void main(String[] arg) {
        try {
            FileOutputStream fout = new
                FileOutputStream("datafile.dat");
            DataOutputStream dout = new
                DataOutputStream(fout);
            writeStuff(dout);
            dout.close();
        } catch(IOException e) {
            System.out.println(e);
        }
        try {
            FileInputStream fin = new
                FileInputStream("datafile.dat");
            DataInputStream din = new
                DataInputStream(fin);
            readStuff(din);
```

```
            din.close();
        } catch(IOException e) {
            System.out.println(e);
        }
    }

    static void writeStuff(DataOutputStream dout)
            throws IOException {
        dout.writeUTF("ABC\u4444");
        dout.writeBoolean(true);
        dout.writeChar('x');
        dout.writeInt(9988);
        dout.writeDouble(99.88);
    }

    static void readStuff(DataInputStream din)
            throws IOException {
        String svalue = din.readUTF();
        System.out.println(svalue);
        boolean bvalue = din.readBoolean();
        System.out.println(bvalue);
        char cvalue = din.readChar();
        System.out.println(cvalue);
        int ivalue = din.readInt();
        System.out.println(ivalue);
        double dvalue = din.readDouble();
        System.out.println(dvalue);
    }
}
```

Each item read from the file is printed to standard out, which looks like this:

```
ABC?
true
x
9988
99.88
```

This output verifies that the values written to the file are the same ones that are read back in. Notice that the unprintable character was translated to '?'. This is a hex dump of the file showing the disk-resident form of the data, and a description of its parts.

```
00 06 41 42 43 E4 91 84 01 00 78 00 00 27 04 40
58 F8 51 EB 85 1E B8
```

00 06 41 42 43 E4 91 84

This is the string in UTF format. The first two bytes are a count of the number of bytes the string consumes in the file. The values 41, 42, and 43 are the ASCII characters 'A', 'B', and 'C'. The three-byte sequence "E4 91 84" is the UTF encoding of '\u4444'.

01

A Boolean value is encoded as a single byte. It is 00 for `false` and 01 for `true`.

00 78

The single character 'x' was written to the file in its full 16-bit Unicode format.

00 00 27 04

The binary form of the `int` value 9988.

40 58 F8 51 EB 85 1E B8

The binary form of the `double` value 99.88.

 For the inverse of this class, see **DataOutputStream**.

DataOutput

interface java.io.DataOutput

An interface defining the methods to be used to write the primitive data types to a stream in a system-independent format.

Implemented by

```
DataOutputStream
RandomAccessFile
```

Extended by

```
ObjectOutput
```

Inheritance

```
public interface java.io.DataOutput
```

Methods

write()

```
public abstract void write(byte barray[])
    throws IOException
```

```
public abstract void write(byte barray[],
        int offset,int length)
    throws IOException
```

```
public abstract void write(int bvalue)
    throws IOException
```

This method will write one or more bytes to the stream. If bvalue is specified, the least-significant eight bits of it are written as a byte. If barray is specified, an array of bytes is written. If offset and length are specified, the bytes written will begin with barray[offset] and continue for length bytes. If offset and length are not specified, the entire array is written.

writeBoolean()

```
public abstract void writeBoolean(boolean value)
    throws IOException
```

Writes a boolean value.

writeByte()

```
public abstract void writeByte(int value)
    throws IOException
```

Writes the least significant eight bits of value to the stream as a byte value.

writeBytes()

```
public abstract void writeBytes(String string)
    throws IOException
```

Writes the characters of string as a series of byte values.

writeChar()

```
public abstract void writeChar(int value)
    throws IOException
```

Writes the low-order 16 bits of the int as a char.

writeChars()

```
public abstract void writeChars(String string)
    throws IOException
```

Writes the contents of the `string` as a sequence of `char` values.

writeDouble()

```
public abstract void writeDouble(double value)
    throws IOException
```

Writes the `double` value.

writeFloat()

```
public abstract void writeFloat(float value)
    throws IOException
```

Writes the `float` value.

writeInt()

```
public abstract void writeInt(int value)
    throws IOException
```

Writes the `int` value.

writeLong()

```
public abstract void writeLong(long value)
    throws IOException
```

Writes the `long` value.

writeShort()

```
public abstract void writeShort(int value)
    throws IOException
```

Writes the least significant 16 bits of the `int` as a `short`.

writeUTF()

```
public abstract void writeUTF(String string)
    throws IOException
```

Writes the `string` in UTF format.

For an example, see **DataInputStream**. For the inverse of this interface, see **DataInput**.

DataOutputStream

class java.io.DataOutputStream

This class is capable of writing the primitive data types to a stream in a platform-independent format.

Inheritance

```
public class java.io.DataOutputStream
    implements DataOutput
    extends FilterOutputStream
        ⇑
    public class java.io.FilterOutputStream
        extends OutputStream
            ⇑
        public class java.io.OutputStream
            extends Object
                ⇑
            public class java.lang.Object
```

Variables and constants

written

```
protected int written
```

A running count of the number of bytes written.

Constructors

```
public DataOutputStream(OutputStream outstream)
```

A DataOutputStream is constructed to use outstream.

Methods

flush()

```
public void flush()
    throws IOException
```

Writes any buffered bytes to the stream.

size()

```
public final int size()
```

Returns a count of the number of bytes that have been written.

write()

```
public void write(byte barray[],
        int offset,int length)
    throws IOException

public void write(int bvalue)
    throws IOException
```

Writes one or more bytes to the stream. If bvalue is specified, the least significant eight bits of it are written as a byte. If barray is specified, the bytes written will begin with barray[offset] and continue for length bytes. The method will block until the data is written.

writeBoolean()

```
public void writeBoolean(boolean value)
    throws IOException
```

Writes a boolean value.

writeByte()

```
public void writeByte(int value)
    throws IOException
```

Writes the least significant eight bits of value as a byte value.

writeBytes()

```
public void writeBytes(String string)
    throws IOException
```

Writes characters of string as a series of byte values. The high-order byte of each character is discarded.

writeChar()

```
public void writeChar(int value)
    throws IOException
```

Writes the low-order 16 bits of the int as a char.

writeChars()

```
public void writeChars(String string)
    throws IOException
```

Writes the contents of the string as a sequence of char values.

writeDouble()

```
public void writeDouble(double value)
    throws IOException
```

Writes the double value.

writeFloat()

```
public void writeFloat(float value)
    throws IOException
```

Writes the float value.

writeInt()

```
public void writeInt(int value)
    throws IOException
```

Writes the int value.

writeLong()

```
public void writeLong(long value)
    throws IOException
```

Writes the long value.

writeShort()

```
public void writeShort(int value)
    throws IOException
```

Writes the least significant 16 bits of the int as a short.

writeUTF()

```
public void writeUTF(String string)
    throws IOException
```

Writes the string in UTF format.

 For an example, see **DataInputStream**.

datatransfer

package java.awt.datatransfer

This package contains classes to aid in the development of interprocess data transfer using facilities such as drag-and-drop and e-mail attachments.

Interfaces

ClipboardOwner
Transferable

Classes

Clipboard
DataFlavor
StringSelection

Exceptions

UnsupportedFlavorException

DataTruncation

class java.sql.DataTruncation

If data is unexpectedly truncated on reading from a JDBC database, a warning is issued by having a DataTruncation object attached to the exception thrown by the object that was the cause of the truncation. If the data is truncated on writing, a DataTruncation object is thrown as an exception.

Inheritance

```
public class java.sql.DataTruncation
    extends SQLWarning
        ⇑
    public class java.sql.SQLWarning
        extends SQLException
            ⇑
        public class java.sql.SQLException
            extends Exception
                ⇑
            public class java.lang.Exception
                extends Throwable
                    ⇑
                public class java.lang.Throwable
                    implements Serializable
                    extends Object
                        ⇑
                    public class java.lang.Object
```

Constructors

```
public DataTruncation(int index,boolean parameter,
        boolean read,int dataSize,int transferSize)
```

The index value indicates which parameter or column. The value of parameter is true to indicate that it was a parameter that was truncated. The value of read is true if the truncation occurred on a read operation and false if it occurred on a write operation. The dataSize is the original size of the data, and the transferSize is the size after truncation.

The constructor will set the SQLState to "01004," which is the code for data truncation. The vendorCode will be set to the SQLException default.

Methods

getDataSize()

```
public int getDataSize()
```

Returns a count of the number of bytes that should have been transferred. The value could be approximate in the case of data conversion. The value is −1 if the true count is not known.

getIndex()

```
public int getIndex()
```

Returns the index to the parameter or column that was truncated. It can be −1 to indicate that the value is unknown. If the value is unknown, the return value of getParameter() should be ignored.

getParameter()

```
public boolean getParameter()
```

Returns true if it was a parameter that was truncated. A false return indicates that it was a column.

getRead()

```
public boolean getRead()
```

Returns true if the truncation occurred on a read operation. Returns false if it was a write that was truncated.

getTransferSize()

```
public int getTransferSize()
```

Returns a count of the number of bytes that were successfully transferred. This value could be −1 to indicate that the number is unknown.

See **SQLWarning** and **SQLException** (the superclasses of this class) for more details.

date

The Java internal representation of the date and time is a signed 64-bit count of the number of milliseconds from midnight, January 1, 1970. Negative values go backward in time—positive values go forward.

How far this can take us

By using a 64-bit value as a count of milliseconds, Java is capable of tracking dates and times for over a quarter of a million years into the past or the future.

The names of time

The standard basis of time in Java is UT (Universal Time). This also is known as UTC (Coordinated Universal Time) and GMT (Greenwich Mean Time). The date January 1, 1970, at 00:00:00 is known as the epoch. A period of 1,000 years is called a millennium. The periods of time on each side of year zero, known as B.C. and A.D., are called eras.

Internal standard

The internal time value is the same on all systems—that is, two computers in different time zones will both maintain the same value internally. The 64-bit value is based on UT, but the software interpreting the time will translate it differently to enable the display to be in the local time zone. This makes it possible for networked systems to transmit time stamps without the complication of translating from one time system to another.

An approximation

There is a sort of built-in error. The Java clock gets its value from the clock of the host computer. The fact is that the host clock is seldom maintained at anywhere near the accuracy of one millisecond (many of them don't even have one-millisecond granularity). Even if it were, there is also the occasional (about once a year) adjustment of one second to allow for discrepancies in the rotation of the Earth.

For a wrapper of a date value, see **Date**. For other time and date classes, see **Calendar.** For a method to acquire the current time, see **System.currentTimeMillis()**.

Date

class java.util.Date

The Java date is a 64-bit counter of the number of milliseconds since January 1, 1970. The Date class is a wrapper for the Java date.

Extended by

```
java.sql.Date
Time
Timestamp
```

Inheritance

```
public class java.util.Date
    implements Serializable
    implements Cloneable
    extends Object
            ⇑
    public class java.lang.Object
```

Constructors

```
public Date()
public Date(long date)
```

The default Date contains the date and time of the moment of its construction. A date value is the standard Java binary form—a count of milliseconds since January 1, 1970.

 The following constructors that accept integer values for year, month, day, hour, minute, and second have all been deprecated. Also, the form that accepts string has been deprecated.

```
public Date(int year,int month,int day)      deprecated
public Date(int year,int month,int day,int hour,
        int minute)      deprecated
public Date(int year,int month,int day,int hour,
        int minute,int second)      deprecated
public Date(String string)      deprecated
```

If a year is specified, it must be a year after 1900. A month is a value from 0 to 11. The day is a value from 1 to 31. A day number that is too large will cause a rollover—that is, September 31 will be interpreted as October 1. The hour value ranges from 0 to 23. The minute and second values ranges from 0 to 59. The string must be one that is acceptable to parse().

Returned by

Objects of the Date class are returned from Calendar.getTime(), CallableStatement.getDate(), Date.valueOf(), DateFormat.parse(), GregorianCalendar.getGregorianChange(), ResultSet.getDate(), and SimpleDateFormat.parse().

Methods

after()

```
public boolean after(Date when)
```

Returns true if this Date is after the one specified as when.

before()

```
public boolean before(Date when)
```

Returns true if this Date is before the one specified as when.

equals()

```
public boolean equals(Object obj)
```

Returnss true if obj is a Date with the same time as this one.

getDate()   deprecated

```
public int getDate()
```

Returns the day of the month—a number in the range 1 to 31.

getDay()   deprecated

```
public int getDay()
```

Returns the day of the week—a number in the range 0 to 6, with 0 as Sunday.

getHours()   deprecated

```
public int getHours()
```

Returns the hour of the day—a number in the range 0 to 23.

getMinutes()   deprecated

```
public int getMinutes()
```

Returns the minute—a number in the range 0 to 59.

getMonth() deprecated

```
public int getMonth()
```

Returns the month—a number in the range 0 to 11, with 0 as January.

getSeconds() deprecated

```
public int getSeconds()
```

Returns the seconds—a number in the range 0 to 59.

getTime()

```
public long getTime()
```

Returns the internal form of the date—the 64-bit count of the number of milliseconds since January 1, 1970.

getTimezoneOffset() deprecated

```
public int getTimezoneOffset()
```

Returns the offset from UT for the current locale. The returned value is in minutes. The returned value will vary with daylight savings time.

getYear() deprecated

```
public int getYear()
```

Returns the internal two-digit year number after adding 1900 to it.

hashCode()

```
public int hashCode()
```

This method computes and returns the hashcode value. Two Date objects that contain the same time value will return the same hashcode.

parse() deprecated

```
public static long parse(String string)
```

If the string is in a recognizable date format, its binary form will be returned. One recognizable form would be "Sat, 12 Aug 1995 13:30:00 GMT." This method understands time zone abbreviations, and it also understands time zone offsets, such as "Sat, 12 Aug 1995 13:30:00 GMT+0430" where the zone is four hours and thirty minutes west of Greenwich. If no time zone is specified, the local time zone is taken as the default.

setDate() deprecated

```
public void setDate(int date)
```

Sets the internal date (day of the month) to the specified value.

setHours()   **deprecated**

```
public void setHours(int hours)
```

Sets the hours value.

setMinutes()   **deprecated**

```
public void setMinutes(int minutes)
```

Sets the minutes value.

setMonth()   **deprecated**

```
public void setMonth(int month)
```

Sets the month value.

setSeconds()   **deprecated**

```
public void setSeconds(int seconds)
```

Sets the seconds value.

setTime()

```
public void setTime(long time)
```

Sets the internal time to the specified system time.

setYear()   **deprecated**

```
public void setYear(int year)
```

Sets the year value.

toGMTString()   **deprecated**

```
public String toGMTString()
```

Returns a string form of the internal date in the GMT format.

toLocaleString()   **deprecated**

```
public String toLocaleString()
```

Returns a string form of the internal date—it uses the local time zone for its formatting.

toString()

```
public String toString()
```

Returns a string form of the internal date. The string is localized—it looks like this: "Mon Jan 27 10:48:19 1997."

UTC() **deprecated**

```
public static long UTC(int year,int month,int date,
        int hrs,int min,int sec)
```

Uses the values passed to it to create a standard Java 64-bit binary date.

 For other time and date classes, see **Calendar**. To simply get the raw binary form of the time, see **System.currentTimeMillis()**. For a description of the Java internal format, see **date**. For database operations, there is also a **java.sql.Date** class.

Date

class java.sql.Date

This is a thin wrapper around `java.util.Date` to enable a JDBC to identify this as an SQL DATE value. To do this, this class extends `java.util.Date` by adding some formatting and parsing methods.

 In the initial release of Java 1.1, the methods `getHours()`, `getMinutes()`, `getSeconds()`, `setHours()`, `setMinutes()`, and `setSeconds()` of this class do nothing other than throw an `IllegalArgumentException`.

Inheritance

```
public class java.sql.Date
    extends Date
        ⇑
    public class java.util.Date
        implements Serializable
        implements Cloneable
        extends Object
            ⇑
        public class java.lang.Object
```

Constructors

```
public Date(int year,int month,int day)
public Date(long date)
```

The `year` is specified as the actual year minus 1900—that is, the year 2005 is represented as 105. The `month` is a number from 0 to 11. The `day` is the day of the month—a number from 1 to 31. The `date` is the standard Java system date—a count of the number of milliseconds since midnight, January 1, 1970.

Methods

getHours()

```
public int getHours()
```

Returns the hour.

getMinutes()

```
public int getMinutes()
```

Returns the number of minutes past the hour represented by this date.

getSeconds()

```
public int getSeconds()
```

Returns the number of seconds past the minute represented by this date.

setHours()

```
public void setHours(int i)
```

Sets the hour of this date to the specified value.

setMinutes()

```
public void setMinutes(int i)
```

Sets the minutes of this date to the specified value.

setSeconds()

```
public void setSeconds(int i)
```

Sets the seconds of this date to the specified value.

setTime()

```
public void setTime(long date)
```

Sets a Date using a milliseconds time value.

toString()

```
public String toString()
```

Returns a string in JDBC date-escape format. This is the *yyyy-mm-dd* format, where *yyyy* is four digits and both *mm* and *dd* are two digits (with leading zeroes if necessary).

valueOf()

```
public static Date valueOf(String string)
```

Converts string from a JDBC date-escape format to a Date object. The string must be in the format *yyyy-mm-dd*.

For more date operations, see **java.util.Date**. For a description of the Java internal date format, see **date**.

DateFormat

class java.text.DateFormat

This abstract class is the base class of locale-based date and time string formatting classes. There are methods for converting milliseconds to strings and converting strings to milliseconds. Ideally, it should be possible to maintain all date values internally as millisecond values or Date objects, and the string appearance to the user should automatically adjust itself to his locale.

Formatting styles

Within a locale, some standard formatting styles exist. A date can be formatted FULL, LONG, MEDIUM, or SHORT. The exact meaning of each of these will vary from one implementation to another. The SHORT form is completely numeric, for example, "3/1/97" or "14:10." The MEDIUM form adds a little text to the short form, for example, "Mar 1, 1997" or "2:10pm." The LONG form spells it all out, for example, "March 1, 1997" or "2:10:18pm." The FULL form includes all the information, for example "Saturday, March 1, 1997, AD" or "2:10:18pm CST."

An efficiency consideration

If you are going to be formatting a lot of date strings, it would be best to create a single DateFormat object and reuse it. There is a bit more expense in creating a new DateFormat object than in storing and reusing one.

Cast it for more control

Try casting the DateFormat you get from getDateInstance() to a SimpleDateFormat object. This will work if you have one in the extended form SimpleDateFormat.

Extended by

```
SimpleDateFormat
```

Inheritance

```
public abstract class java.text.DateFormat
    implements Cloneable
    extends Format
        ⇑
    public class java.text.Format
```

```
implements Serializable
implements Cloneable
extends Object
       ⇑
public class java.lang.Object
```

Variables and constants

AM_PM_FIELD

```
public final static int AM_PM_FIELD
```

Used in the FieldPosition object as an argument passed to methods of this class.

calendar

```
protected Calendar calendar
```

The calendar used internally by the DateFormat object. Subclasses should initialize this to the calendar from the locale used by the DateFormat object.

DATE_FIELD

```
public final static int DATE_FIELD
```

Used in the FieldPosition object as an argument passed to methods of this class.

DAY_OF_WEEK_FIELD

```
public final static int DAY_OF_WEEK_FIELD
```

Used in the FieldPosition object as an argument passed to methods of this class.

DAY_OF_WEEK_IN_MONTH_FIELD

```
public final static int DAY_OF_WEEK_IN_MONTH_FIELD
```

Used in the FieldPosition object as an argument passed to methods of this class.

DAY_OF_YEAR_FIELD

```
public final static int DAY_OF_YEAR_FIELD
```

Used in the FieldPosition object as an argument passed to methods of this class.

DEFAULT

```
public final static int DEFAULT
```

This constant can be used as an argument to methods that require a style argument to specify that the default style be used.

ERA_FIELD

```
public final static int ERA_FIELD
```

Used in the `FieldPosition` object as an argument passed to methods of this class.

FULL

```
public final static int FULL
```

This is a value used as a style argument to specify that the `FULL` style be used.

HOUR0_FIELD

```
public final static int HOUR0_FIELD
```

Used in the `FieldPosition` object as an argument passed to methods of this class to specify using a zero–base hour system in a 12-hour clock. That is, a quarter-hour past midnight will be formatted as "00:15am" instead of "12:15am."

HOUR1_FIELD

```
public final static int HOUR1_FIELD
```

Used in the `FieldPosition` object as an argument passed to methods of this class to specify using a one–base hour system in a 12-hour clock. That is, a quarter-hour past midnight will be formatted as "12:15am" instead of "00:15am."

HOUR_OF_DAY0_FIELD

```
public final static int HOUR_OF_DAY0_FIELD
```

Used in the `FieldPosition` object as an argument passed to methods of this class to specify using a zero–base hour system in a 24-hour clock. That is, a quarter-hour past midnight will be formatted as "00:15am" instead of "24:15am."

HOUR_OF_DAY1_FIELD

```
public final static int HOUR_OF_DAY1_FIELD
```

Used in the `FieldPosition` object as an argument passed to methods of this class to specify using a one–base hour system in a 24-hour clock. That is, a quarter-hour past midnight will be formatted as "24:15am" instead of "00:15am."

LONG

```
public final static int LONG
```

This is a value used as a style argument to specify that the `LONG` style be used.

MEDIUM

```
public final static int MEDIUM
```

This is a value used as a style argument to specify that the MEDIUM style be used.

MILLISECOND_FIELD

```
public final static int MILLISECOND_FIELD
```

Used in the FieldPosition object as an argument passed to methods of this class.

MINUTE_FIELD

```
public final static int MINUTE_FIELD
```

Used in the FieldPosition object as an argument passed to methods of this class.

MONTH_FIELD

```
public final static int MONTH_FIELD
```

Used in the FieldPosition object as an argument passed to methods of this class.

numberFormat

```
protected NumberFormat numberFormat
```

This is the number formatter that is used by DateFormat to format the numeric portions of the string form of the dates and times it produces. Subclasses should initialize this with the NumberFormat object from the locale that is being used.

SECOND_FIELD

```
public final static int SECOND_FIELD
```

Used in the FieldPosition object as an argument passed to methods of this class.

SHORT

```
public final static int SHORT
```

This is a value used as a style argument to specify that the SHORT style be used.

TIMEZONE_FIELD

```
public final static int TIMEZONE_FIELD
```

Used in the FieldPosition object as an argument passed to methods of this class.

WEEK_OF_MONTH_FIELD

```
public final static int WEEK_OF_MONTH_FIELD
```

Used in the FieldPosition object as an argument passed to methods of this class.

WEEK_OF_YEAR_FIELD

```
public final static int WEEK_OF_YEAR_FIELD
```

Used in the `FieldPosition` object as an argument passed to methods of this class.

YEAR_FIELD

```
public final static int YEAR_FIELD
```

Used in the `FieldPosition` object as an argument passed to methods of this class.

Constructors

```
protected DateFormat()
```

Returned by

`DateFormat` objects are returned from calls to `getDateInstance()`, `getDateTimeInstance()`, `getInstance()`, and `getTimeInstance()`.

Methods

clone()

```
public Object clone()
```

Creates a duplicate of this object.

equals()

```
public boolean equals(Object object)
```

Returns `true` if `object` is a `DateFormat` and is identical to this one.

format()

```
public final StringBuffer format(Object object,
        StringBuffer appendTo,FieldPosition position)

public abstract StringBuffer format(Date date,
        StringBuffer appendTo,FieldPosition position)

public final String format(Date date)
```

Uses the `date` to produce a character string. If something other than a date object is used, it must be some kind of time object. An example would be a `Number` object (normally a `Long`) that contains a number of milliseconds. The argument `appendTo` will be returned with the newly created string appended to it.

When the method returns, position will have been updated to contain some field position information. For example, if the constant used to create the position was `DateFormat.YEAR_FIELD`, and the output string was `"Mar 1, 1997"`, `position.getBeginIndex()` would return 7 and `position.getEndIndex()` would return 10.

getAvailableLocales()

```
public static Locale[] getAvailableLocales()
```

Returns an array that contains all the locales for which DateFormats are installed.

getCalendar()

```
public Calendar getCalendar()
```

Returns the Calendar being used by this DateFormat.

getDateInstance()

```
public final static DateFormat getDateInstance()

public final static DateFormat getDateInstance(int style)

public final static DateFormat getDateInstance(int style,
        Locale locale)
```

Returns an instance of a DateFormat object that will format date strings without any of the time data. If the style is specified, a DateFormat with the specified style will be returned. The possible styles are FULL, MEDIUM, SHORT, and LONG. The default is SHORT. If no locale is specified, the default locale will be used.

getDateTimeInstance()

```
public final static DateFormat getDateTimeInstance()

public final static DateFormat getDateTimeInstance(
        int dateStyle,int timeStyle)

public final static DateFormat getDateTimeInstance(
        int dateStyle,int timeStyle,Locale locale)
```

Returns an instance of a DateFormat object that will format both date and time into one string. The styles of the date and time formatting can be specified separately. The possible styles are FULL, MEDIUM, SHORT, and LONG. The default is SHORT. If no locale is specified, the default locale will be used.

getInstance()

```
public final static DateFormat getInstance()
```

This is the same as the call to getDateTimeInstance() with no arguments.

getNumberInstance()

```
public NumberFormat getNumberInstance()
```

Returns the number formatter used by this DateFormat object to format the numeric portions.

getTimeInstance()

```
public final static DateFormat getTimeInstance()

public final static DateFormat getTimeInstance(int style)

public final static DateFormat getTimeInstance(int style,
        Locale locale)
```

Returns an instance of a DateFormat object that will format time strings without any date information. If the style is specified, a DateFormat with the specified style will be returned. The possible styles are FULL, MEDIUM, SHORT, and LONG. The default is SHORT. If no locale is specified, the default locale will be used.

getTimeZone()

```
public TimeZone getTimeZone()
```

Returns the TimeZone object from the Calendar object that is being used by this DateFormat.

hashCode()

```
public int hashCode()
```

Returns the hashcode of this object.

isLenient()

```
public boolean isLenient()
```

Returns true if the scanning of input time/date strings is to be lenient.

parse()

```
public Date parse(String text)
    throws ParseException

public abstract Date parse(String text, ParsePosition
position)
```

Reads the text and converts the string into a Date object. The input string is normally read from the beginning—unless position specifies another location. On output, the position will reflect where the parse halted—success or failure. If the conversion is not possible and position was not specified, a ParseException is thrown. If it fails with a position specified, a null is returned.

By default, the translation is lenient—that is, if the string is in an unexpected format (one not generated by a DateFormat object) but one that can still be translated into a Date, no exception is thrown.

parseObject()

```
public Object parseObject(String source, ParsePosition
position)
```

This is the same as a call to parse(source,position).

setCalendar()

```
public void setCalendar(Calendar calendar)
```

Specifies the Calendar to be used by this DateFormat. When this object was initialized, the Calendar of the initial locale was used.

setLenient()

```
public void setLenient(boolean setting)
```

This will set the leniency of input string scanning to setting. See parse().

setNumberFormat()

```
public void setNumberFormat(NumberFormat numberFormat)
```

The will set the NumberFormat object used to format the numeric portions of the produced strings of dates and times.

setTimeZone()

```
public void setTimeZone(TimeZone zone)
```

This will change the time zone to the one specified as zone.

Example 1

This example creates a Date object and prints examples of different formatting forms:

```
import java.util.*;
import java.text.*;
public class DateAndTimeFormatting {
    public static void main(String[] arg) {
        Date date = new Date();
        DateFormat df;
        df = DateFormat.getDateInstance(DateFormat.SHORT);
        System.out.println("SHORT: " + df.format(date));
        df =
DateFormat.getDateInstance(DateFormat.MEDIUM);
        System.out.println("MEDIUM: " + df.format(date));
        df = DateFormat.getDateInstance(DateFormat.FULL);
        System.out.println("FULL: " + df.format(date));
```

```
        df = DateFormat.getDateInstance(DateFormat.LONG);
        System.out.println("LONG: " + df.format(date));
        df = DateFormat.getTimeInstance(DateFormat.SHORT);
        System.out.println("SHORT: " + df.format(date));
        df =
DateFormat.getTimeInstance(DateFormat.MEDIUM);
        System.out.println("MEDIUM: " + df.format(date));
        df = DateFormat.getTimeInstance(DateFormat.FULL);
        System.out.println("FULL: " + df.format(date));
        df = DateFormat.getTimeInstance(DateFormat.LONG);
        System.out.println("LONG: " + df.format(date));
        df = DateFormat.getDateTimeInstance(
                DateFormat.SHORT,DateFormat.SHORT);
        System.out.println("SHORT: " + df.format(date));
        df = DateFormat.getDateTimeInstance(
                DateFormat.MEDIUM,DateFormat.MEDIUM);
        System.out.println("MEDIUM: " + df.format(date));
        df = DateFormat.getDateTimeInstance(
                DateFormat.FULL,DateFormat.FULL);
        System.out.println("FULL: " + df.format(date));
        df = DateFormat.getDateTimeInstance(
                DateFormat.LONG,DateFormat.LONG);
        System.out.println("LONG: " + df.format(date));
    }
}
```

There are three types of DateFormat objects: one that will format time values, one that will format date values, and one that will format both. Furthermore, each of these has four ways of formatting its output: SHORT, MEDIUM, FULL, and LONG. This program prints an example line of each of the twelve possibilities.

The output looks like this:

```
SHORT: 3/19/97
MEDIUM: 19-Mar-97
FULL: Wednesday, March 19, 1997
LONG: March 19, 1997
SHORT: 5:17 PM
MEDIUM: 5:17:03 PM
FULL: 5:17:03 o'clock PM PST
LONG: 5:17:03 PM PST
SHORT: 3/19/97 5:17 PM
MEDIUM: 19-Mar-97 5:17:03 PM
FULL: Wednesday, March 19, 1997 5:17:03 o'clock PM PST
LONG: March 19, 1997 5:17:03 PM PST
```

Example 2

This example uses the same Date object and formats the output for two different time zones:

```
import java.util.*;
import java.text.*;
public class ZoneFormat {
    public static void main(String[] arg) {
        Date date = new Date();
        DateFormat df = DateFormat.getTimeInstance(
                DateFormat.FULL);
        System.out.println("Default: " + df.format(date));
        TimeZone tz = TimeZone.getTimeZone("EST");
        df.setTimeZone(tz);
        System.out.println("Changed: " + df.format(date));
    }
}
```

The output looks like this:

```
Default: 5:40:57 o'clock AM PST
Changed: 8:40:57 o'clock AM EST
```

 Associated classes are **SimpleDateFormat**, **Calendar**, **GregorianCalendar**, and **TimeZone**.

DateFormatSymbols

class java.text.DateFormatSymbols

This class holds date and time formatting data such as the names of the months, the days of the week, and the names of the times zones. The DateFormat and SimpleDateFormat classes use these symbols.

Direct extraction is not encouraged

This class was specifically designed for use by DateFormat objects. Rather than extract the information directly from this class, it is considered more appropriate to acquire a DateFormat object or extend it to a class that will do what you need to have done. Once you have this object, pass it the data from which you wish to build a string and let it do the work. Accessing this class directly will circumvent the built-in localization of the Java API.

Direct modification is encouraged

A `DateFormatSymbols` object is clonable. You can make a copy modify the date and time formatting data within the one you are using. In this way, the `DateFormat` object you are using to construct date strings will use whatever symbolic data you would like. Also, you can subclass this class to add an entirely new set of symbols to be used by your `DateFormat` class.

Inheritance

```
public class java.text.DateFormatSymbols
    implements Serializable
    implements Cloneable
    extends Object
         ⇑
    public class java.lang.Object
```

Constructors

```
public DateFormatSymbols()
public DateFormatSymbols(Locale locale)
```

If no `locale` is specified, the default is used. The constructor gets whatever data it needs from the resources defined in the locale. If it is unable to get the required resources from the locale, a `MissingResourceException` is thrown.

Returned by

A `DateFormatSymbols` object is returned from a call to `SimpleDateFormat.getDateFormatSymbols()`.

Methods

clone()

```
public Object clone()
```

Makes a duplicate of this object.

equals()

```
public boolean equals(Object object)
```

Returns `true` if `object` is a `DateFormatSymbols` that is based on the same locale as this one.

getAmPmStrings()

```
public String[] getAmPmStrings()
```

Returns the A.M. and P.M. strings; for example, "AM" and "PM" are possible strings.

getEras()

```
public String[] getEras()
```

Returns the era strings, for example, "AD" and "BC."

getLocalPatternChars()

```
public String getLocalPatternChars()
```

Returns the set of localized time-pattern characters.

getMonths()

```
public String[] getMonths()
```

Returns an array of the month strings, for example, "January" and "February."

getShortMonths()

```
public String[] getShortMonths()
```

Returns an array of the short versions of the month strings, for example, "Jan" and "Feb."

getShortWeekdays()

```
public String[] getShortWeekdays()
```

Returns an array of the short versions of the names of the days of the week, for example, "Mon" and "Tue."

getWeekdays()

```
public String[] getWeekdays()
```

Returns an array of the names of the days of the week, for example, "Monday" and "Tuesday."

getZoneStrings()

```
public String[][] getZoneStrings()
```

Returns the time zone strings.

hashCode()

```
public int hashCode()
```

Returns a hashcode for this object.

setAmPmStrings()

```
public void setAmPmStrings(String newAmpms[])
```

Sets the A.M. and P.M. strings, for example, "AM" and "PM."

setEras()
```
public void setEras(String newEras[])
```
Returns the era strings, for example, "AD" and "BC."

setLocalPatternChars()
```
public void setLocalPatternChars(String patternChars)
```
Sets the string of local time pattern characters.

setMonths()
```
public void setMonths(String newMonths[])
```
Sets the array of the month strings, for example, "January" and "February."

setShortMonths()
```
public void setShortMonths(String newShortMonths[])
```
Sets the array of the short versions of the month strings, for example, "Jan" and "Feb."

setShortWeekdays()
```
public void setShortWeekdays(String newShortWeekdays[])
```
Sets the array of the short versions of the names of the days of the week, for example, "Mon" and "Tue."

setWeekdays()
```
public void setWeekdays(String newWeekdays[])
```
Sets the array of the names of the days of the week, for example, "Monday" and "Tuesday."

setZoneStrings()
```
public void setZoneStrings(String newZoneStrings[][])
```
Sets the time zone strings.

Example

This program prints the strings that are available from this object:

```
import java.text.*;
public class ShowFormatSymbols {
    public static void main(String[] arg) {
        DateFormatSymbols sym = new DateFormatSymbols();
        showString("AmPm",sym.getAmPmStrings());
```

```
        showString("LocalPattern",
                    sym.getLocalPatternChars());
        showString("Months",sym.getMonths());
        showString("ShortMonths",sym.getShortMonths());
        showString("Weekdays",sym.getWeekdays());

        showString("ShortWeekdays",sym.getShortWeekdays());
        showString("Zone",sym.getZoneStrings());
    }

    private static void showString(String tag,String s) {
        System.out.println(tag + ": \"" + s + "\"");
    }
    private static void showString(String tag,String[] s) {
        System.out.print(tag + ":");
        for(int i=0; i<s.length; i++)
            System.out.print(" \"" + s[i] + "\"");
        System.out.println();
    }
    private static void showString(String tag,
                    String[][] s) {
        for(int i=0; i<s.length; i++) {
            System.out.print(tag + "[" + i + "]:");
            for(int j=0; j<s[i].length; j++) {
                System.out.print(" \"" + s[i][j] + "\"");
            }
            System.out.println();
        }
    }
}
```

The output looks like this:

```
AmPm: "AM" "PM"
LocalPattern: "GyMdkHmsSEDFwWahKz"
Months: "January" "February" "March" "April" "May"
            "June" "July" "August" "September" "October"
            "November" "December" ""
ShortMonths: "Jan" "Feb" "Mar" "Apr" "May" "Jun" "Jul"
            "Aug" "Sep" "Oct" "Nov" "Dec" ""
Weekdays: "" "Sunday" "Monday" "Tuesday" "Wednesday"
            "Thursday" "Friday" "Saturday"
ShortWeekdays: "" "Sun" "Mon" "Tue" "Wed" "Thu"
            "Fri" "Sat"
Zone[0]: "PST" "Pacific Standard Time" "PST"
            "Pacific Daylight Time" "PDT" "San Francisco"
```

```
Zone[1]: "MST" "Mountain Standard Time" "MST"
                "Mountain Daylight Time" "MDT" "Denver"
Zone[2]: "CST" "Central Standard Time" "CST"
                "Central Daylight Time" "CDT" "Chicago"
Zone[3]: "EST" "Eastern Standard Time" "EST"
                "Eastern Daylight Time" "EDT" "New York"
```

As you can see, the string arrays for the months begin with January at index 0. The arrays for the weekdays begin with Sunday at index 1. There are four time zones, and each one has several names.

 For more formatting, date formatting, and a definition of the pattern characters, see **SimpleDateFormat**.

debugging

 For the standard Java debugging utility, see **jdb**.

DecimalFormat

class java.text.DecimalFormat

This class is used to format decimal numbers into strings. It uses standard patterns to lay out the character strings. The patterns control both the placement of the digits and the placement of the punctuation that goes with them. The characters used for digits can be localized for Western, Arabic, or Indic languages.

The pattern

To format the numbers, a pattern is used. It's sort of a cookie-cutter. The pattern is composed of characters defined in a `DecimalFormatSymbols` object (there is a `DecimalFormatSymbols` object inside every `DecimalFormat` object).

Prefixes, suffixes, and separators

Some number formats have external prefixes and suffixes (such as minus and plus signs). Some number formats require internal separators (such as commas and decimal points). Care must be taken that the same character is not used both internally and externally — it causes confusion on input of the character form for conversion back to binary.

Some special cases

- A float or double NaN will be formatted as a single character — normally \uFFFD.

- A float or double infinity (either positive or negative) is formatted as a single character, normally \u221E, along with any specified positive/negative prefix/suffix character.

- If a negative number is formatted but there is no specific placement of a negation symbol in the pattern, a leading minus-sign character will be added.

The pattern of a pattern

Patterns are made up of strings of special characters that act as a series of commands directing the details of formatting a number. Each pattern string has either one or two patterns separated by the special pattern separation character. The first pattern is used for positive numbers, and the second, for negative numbers. If the second pattern is not included (it is optional), the positive-number pattern will be used and a minus sign will be added to the front of it.

The characters of a pattern

Each character in a pattern is a formatting command. Table D-1 shows the characters and what they mean. Some variations may be made to the values displayed in the table; see **DecimalFormatSymbols**.

Table D-1 Symbols Used to Compose Formatting Patterns

Character	Meaning
0	A digit will be placed in this position. If there is no value for the position, it will print a zero. For example, this can be used to guarantee such things as the placement of digits in a monetary value format such as "$0.00."
#	A digit will be placed in this position unless the digit is a leading or trailing zero. For example, leading zeroes could be suppressed with a format like "###0."
.	A period specifies the location of the decimal point. If the decimal point character is different for a locale, it will be replaced during formatting.
,	A comma is a placeholder for a grouping separator. For example, separation of the thousands from the hundreds could be done in a format like "###,##0."
;	This is the character used to separate the positive number format from the negative number format in the pattern string, for example, "###0.0;-###0.0."
−	This symbol is used for the negative prefix format, for example, "###;-###."
%	This is an instruction to divide the number by 100 and display it as a percentage.
'	Single quotes are used to insert characters into the string that would otherwise have a special meaning. For example, to prepend a three-digit number with a hashmark, do this: "'#'##0."
X	Any character that is not given a special meaning (by being included in this list) will be included literally into the output string, For example "##0.00CR."

Grouping

Only one grouping separator needs to be specified in the format string. For example, the format "######,###" is the same as "###,###,###." When the formatting is being done, a count is made of the number of digits that appear between the last grouping character and the end of the format string. This count is then used for all grouping. All but the last grouping character is ignored, for example, the format "#,#,#,###" is the same as "###,###."

Inheritance

```
public class java.text.DecimalFormat
    extends NumberFormat
        ⇑
    public class java.text.NumberFormat
        implements Cloneable
        extends Format
            ⇑
        public class java.text.Format
            implements Serializable
            implements Cloneable
            extends Object
                ⇑
            public class java.lang.Object
```

Constructors

```
public DecimalFormat()
public DecimalFormat(String pattern)
public DecimalFormat(String pattern,
        DecimalFormatSymbols symbols)
```

The default constructor creates a DecimalFormat with a set of patterns and symbols for the default locale. If the pattern is specified, it will be used in place of the default. If symbols is specified, it will be used in place of the default set of symbols determined by the locale. An IllegalArgumentException will be thrown if the pattern is invalid.

These constructors can be used if you wish to ignore the built-in internationalization and create your own highly customized formatting. You could do this to create some kind of localized number formatting. It is more normal to get an object of this class from an object factory.

Returned by

To obtain an object of this class for a specific locale, call the method `NumberFormat.getNumberInstance()`. Once obtained, it can be modified for any special requirements you might have. The other methods that return number formatting objects are `NumberFormat.getInstance()`, `NumberFormat.getCurrencyInstance()`, and `NumberFormat.getPercentInstance()`.

Methods

applyLocalizedPattern()

```
public void applyLocalizedPattern(String pattern)
```

Replaces the formatting pattern string of this `DecimalFormat` with the localized `pattern`. A `ParseException` is thrown if the `pattern` is not valid.

applyPattern()

```
public void applyPattern(String pattern)
```

Replaces the formatting pattern string of this `DecimalFormat` with the `pattern`. A `ParseException` is thrown if the `pattern` is not valid.

clone()

```
public Object clone()
```

Returns a duplicate of this object.

equals()

```
public boolean equals(Object object)
```

Returns `true` if the `object` is a `DecimalFormat` with the same pattern as this one.

format()

```
public StringBuffer format(double number,
        StringBuffer result,FieldPosition position)

public StringBuffer format(long number,
        StringBuffer result,FieldPosition position)
```

Uses `number` to produce a formatted character string as the returned `StringBuffer`. The argument `result` will be returned with the newly created string appended to it. The `position` is set by the caller to indicate a portion of the number, and on return, it contains the location of that portion in the `result` string.

getDecimalFormatSymbols()

```
public DecimalFormatSymbols getDecimalFormatSymbols()
```

Returns the `DecimalFormatSymbols` object being used to format the strings.

getGroupingSize()

```
public int getGroupingSize()
```

Returns the number of digits that will be grouped for large numbers. For example, if the output format looks like 654,345,821, the return value is 3.

getMultiplier()

```
public int getMultiplier()
```

Returns the multiplier used to calculate the percent or permill values. For a percent, the suffix should be '%' and multiplier, 100. For permill, the suffix should be '?' and the multiplier, 1,000.

getNegativePrefix()

```
public String getNegativePrefix()
```

Returns the negative prefix string. This is the string that will be placed on the front of every negative value formatted.

getNegativeSuffix()

```
public String getNegativeSuffix()
```

Returns the negative suffix string. This is the string that will be placed on the end of every negative value formatted.

getPositivePrefix()

```
public String getPositivePrefix()
```

Returns the positive prefix string. This is the string that will be placed on the front of every positive value formatted.

getPositiveSuffix()

```
public String getPositiveSuffix()
```

Returns the positive suffix string. This is the string that will be placed on the end of every positive value formatted.

hashCode()

```
public int hashCode()
```

Returns the hashcode for this object.

isDecimalSeparatorAlwaysShown()

```
public boolean isDecimalSeparatorAlwaysShown()
```

Returns `true` if the decimal separator character is included when there is no fractional part to the number.

parse()

```
public Number parse(String text,ParsePosition status)
```

Scans the `text` beginning at the location specified by `status` and converts the input string to a `Number`. If the scanned value has no fractional part and its value fits within the range of a `long`, a `Long` is returned—otherwise, a `Double` is returned. On return, the `status` will have been updated to point to the character in the `text` after the last one is used for input. A `ParseException` is thrown if the input `text` is not valid.

setDecimalFormatSymbols()

```
public void setDecimalFormatSymbols(
        DecimalFormatSymbols symbols)
```

This method can be used to specify a new `DecimalFormatSymbols` object to be used for formatting.

 A call to this method should be made with care. If you must make changes to the formatting string, it would be better to call `getDecimalFormatSymbols()` and make changes to the one already there. That way, anything you don't change will still be valid for the locale.

setDecimalSeparatorAlwaysShown()

```
public void setDecimalSeparatorAlwaysShown(boolean setting)
```

If `setting` is `false`, the decimal separator will only be shown when there is a fractional part to a number. If `setting` is `true`, the decimal separator will always be shown.

setGroupingSize()

```
public void setGroupingSize(int newValue)
```

This method will specify the number of digits that are placed in groups for larger numbers. For example, a `newValue` of 3 would cause a six-digit number to print as 123,456, inserting a separator every three digits.

setMultiplier()

```
public void setMultiplier(int newValue)
```

Sets the value of the multiplier to be used in calculating percentages and permills. It is normal to make the percent suffix a "%" with a multiplier of 100 and the permill suffix a "?" with a multiplier of 1,000.

setNegativePrefix()

```
public void setNegativePrefix(String newValue)
```

Specifies the string to be affixed to the front of every negative number formatted.

setNegativeSuffix()

```
public void setNegativeSuffix(String newValue)
```

Specifies the string to be appended to the end of every negative number formatted.

setPositivePrefix()

```
public void setPositivePrefix(String newValue)
```

Specifies the string to be affixed to the front of every positive number formatted.

setPositiveSuffix()

```
public void setPositiveSuffix(String newValue)
```

Specifies the string to be appended to the end of every positive number formatted.

toLocalizedPattern()

```
public String toLocalizedPattern()
```

Returns a new localized pattern string. It is created by using the initial pattern string and applying the various settings and changes that have been made to it.

toPattern()

```
public String toPattern()
```

Returns a new localized pattern string. It is created by using the initial pattern string and applying the various settings and changes that have been made to it.

Example

This example demonstrates the use of the two format strings — one for the positive value and one for the negative:

```
import java.text.*;
import java.util.*;
public class TwoFormatStrings {
    public static void main(String[] arg) {
        DecimalFormat numForm =
            new DecimalFormat("$#,##0.00;$#,##0.00CR");
        System.out.println("Positive: " +
            numForm.format(345.678));
        System.out.println("Negative: " +
```

```
                                numForm.format(-345.678));
            }
    }
```

The output looks like this:

```
Positive: $345.67
Negative: $345.67CR
```

The negative and positive strings differ only by the addition of the "CR" at the end of the negative number. The leading zeroes were suppressed because their positions were defined with '#' instead of '0'. A separator character — the comma — was suppressed because the digits surrounding it were suppressed. The last digit was also truncated — any digits left over after the format had been satisfied were simply discarded.

 For more examples, see **NumberFormat**. For more on the formatting of numeric values, see **Format**, **NumberFormat**, and **ChoiceFormat**.

DecimalFormatSymbols

class java.text.DecimalFormatSymbols

This class represents the set of symbols used to format numbers. These symbols are used to define the actual characters used by a DecimalFormat object when constructing the displayable string of a numeric value. When a DecimalFormat object is instantiated, it creates its own internal DecimalFormatSymbols object from the locale data. If you need to alter these symbols, get access to the object by calling DecimalFormat.getDecimalFormatSymbols().

Inheritance

```
public final class java.text.DecimalFormatSymbols
    implements Cloneable
    implements Serializable
    extends Object
          ⇑
    public class java.lang.Object
```

Constructors

```
public DecimalFormatSymbols()
public DecimalFormatSymbols(Locale locale)
```

This creates an object based on the specified locale. If no locale is specified, the default is used.

Returned by

A `DecimalFormatSymbols` object is returned from
`DecimalFormat.getDecimalFormatSymbols()`.

Methods

equals()

```
public boolean equals(Object object)
```

Returns `true` if `object` is a `DecimalFormatSymbols` object with the same set of symbols as this one.

getDecimalSeparator()

```
public char getDecimalSeparator()
```

Returns the character used for the decimal point.

getDigit()

```
public char getDigit()
```

Returns the character used to represent a digit in a pattern.

getGroupingSeparator()

```
public char getGroupingSeparator()
```

Returns the character used to group digits in large numbers. For example, a comma is used as the separator in 34,567.

getInfinity()

```
public String getInfinity()
```

Returns the character used to represent infinity.

getMinusSign()

```
public char getMinusSign()
```

Returns the character to be used as the minus sign.

getNaN()

```
public String getNaN()
```

Returns the character used to represent NaN.

getPatternSeparator()

```
public char getPatternSeparator()
```

Returns the character used as the pattern separator—the character that marks the end of one pattern and the beginning of another in the same string.

getPercent()

```
public char getPercent()
```

Returns the character used for the percent sign.

getPerMill()

```
public char getPerMill()
```

Returns the character used for the permill sign.

getZeroDigit()

```
public char getZeroDigit()
```

Returns the digit used to represent zero.

hashCode()

```
public int hashCode()
```

Returns the hashcode value of this object.

setDecimalSeparator()

```
public void setDecimalSeparator(char decimalSeparator)
```

Sets the character to be used as the decimal point.

setDigit()

```
public void setDigit(char digit)
```

Sets the character used in a pattern to represent a digit.

setGroupingSeparator()

```
public void setGroupingSeparator(char groupingSeparator)
```

Sets the character to be used to group digits in large numbers. For example, a comma is used as a separator in 34,567.

setInfinity()

```
public void setInfinity(String infinity)
```

Sets the character to be used to represent infinity.

setMinusSign()

```
public void setMinusSign(char minusSign)
```

Sets the character to be used as the minus sign.

setNaN()

```
public void setNaN(String NaN)
```

Sets the character to be used to represent a NaN value.

setPatternSeparator()

```
public void setPatternSeparator(char patternSeparator)
```

Sets the character to be used as the pattern separator — the character that marks the end of one pattern and the beginning of another in the same string.

setPercent()

```
public void setPercent(char percent)
```

Sets the character to be used as the percent sign.

setPerMill()

```
public void setPerMill(char perMill)
```

Sets the character to be used for the permill sign. (A permill value is based on a thousand, just as a percent value is based on a hundred.)

setZeroDigit()

```
public void setZeroDigit(char zeroDigit)
```

Sets the character to be used as the zero digit.

 The class that uses an object of this class is **NumberFormat**.

decrement

—

This is an operator in the Java language. It is a unary operator that will reduce the value of an integer primitive type by one. It can be used in two ways: as a postdecrement or as a predecrement. A postdecrement will reduce the value *after* it has been used in an expression, and a predecrement will reduce the value *before* it has been used. A predecrement operator looks like this:

```
--x
```

and a postdecrement operator looks like this:

```
x--
```

 For examples of the decrement operator, and a description of the increment operator, see **increment**.

default

keyword

In a switch/case statement, the default case is the one that will be chosen whenever the value does not match any of the other cases.

 For examples of its use, see **switch**.

Deflater

class java.util.zip.Deflater

This class provides general-purpose decompression using the ZLIB compression library.

Inheritance

```
public class java.util.zip.Deflater
    extends Object
        ⇑
    public class java.lang.Object
```

Variables and constants

BEST_COMPRESSION

```
public final static int BEST_COMPRESSION
```

Compression level setting for the best compression.

BEST_SPEED

```
public final static int BEST_SPEED
```

Compression level setting for the fastest compression.

DEFAULT_COMPRESSION

```
public final static int DEFAULT_COMPRESSION
```

The default setting of the compression level.

DEFAULT_STRATEGY

```
public final static int DEFAULT_STRATEGY
```

The default setting of the strategy.

DEFLATED

```
public final static int DEFLATED
```

Used to specify that compression uses the deflate algorithm.

FILTERED

```
public final static int FILTERED
```

Specifies a compression strategy that is best used on data consisting mostly of small values of a somewhat random distribution. This will do more Huffman coding and less string matching.

HUFFMAN_ONLY

```
public final static int HUFFMAN_ONLY
```

Specifies the compression strategy to be only Huffman coding.

NO_COMPRESSION

```
public final static int NO_COMPRESSION
```

This is used to set the compression level not to do any actual compression.

Constructors

```
public Deflater()
public Deflater(int level)
public Deflater(int level,boolean nowrap)
```

Creates a Deflater that will operate at the specified level. The compression level is one of the values listed previously, or it is a value from 0 to 9 (which could be one of the constants defined in this class). If no level is specified, the default will be used. If nowrap is true, the header and checksum fields will not be used—this is to support the compression format used by GZIP and PKZIP.

Methods

deflate()

```
public synchronized int deflate(byte barray[],
          int offset,int length)

public int deflate(byte barray[])
```

This is the return of the deflated data. The array is filled with a maximum of length bytes of compressed data beginning at barray[offset]. If length and offset are not supplied, the entire array is used. The return value is the actual number of compressed bytes placed in the array. A return value of zero indicates that needsInput() should be called to determine if more data is available.

end()

```
public synchronized void end()
```

This will discard any unprocessed input and free the internal data.

finalize()

```
protected void finalize()
```

Frees the compressor when garbage is collected.

finish()

```
public synchronized void finish()
```

This will indicate that the object now has all the data to be compressed and the processing will stop with the data currently in the input buffer.

finished()

```
public synchronized boolean finished()
```

Returns true if the end of the compressed data output stream has been reached.

getAdler()

```
public synchronized int getAdler()
```

Returns the Adler-32 checksum of the uncompressed data.

getTotalIn()

```
public synchronized int getTotalIn()
```

Returns the number of bytes that have been input so far.

getTotalOut()

```
public synchronized int getTotalOut()
```

Returns the number of bytes that have been output so far.

needsInput()

```
public boolean needsInput()
```

Returns `true` if the input buffer is empty and `setInput()` should be called to provide more data.

reset()

```
public synchronized void reset()
```

Resets the internals to allow a new set of input data to be processed. The compression level and strategy remain unchanged.

setDictionary()

```
public void setDictionary(byte barray[])

public synchronized void setDictionary(byte barray[],
        int offset,int length)
```

This will specify the optional dictionary to be used for compression. The dictionary is either the entire `barray` or `length` bytes of it beginning at `barray[offset]`. The same dictionary must be used to decompress the data. If a dictionary is specified, it is not included in the compressed data, so the program that will be doing the decompression must have access to the dictionary.

setInput()

```
public void setInput(byte barray[])

public synchronized void setInput(byte barray[],
        int offset,int length)
```

Supplies input data for compression. This should be called each time `needsInput()` returns `true`. If `offset` and `length` are specified, `length` bytes will be used beginning at `barray[offset]`. If `offset` and `length` are not specified, the entire array is used.

setLevel()

```
public synchronized void setLevel(int Level)
```

Sets the compression level to the specified `level`. An `IllegalArgumentException` is thrown for an invalid `level` value.

setStrategy()

```
public synchronized void setStrategy(int strategy)
```

Sets the compression strategy to the specified strategy. This must be one of the strategy constant values defined in this class. An IllegalArgumentException is thrown for an invalid strategy value.

Example

This example uses its own source code as input to the deflater and outputs a deflated version of itself to disk in a file named "DeflateMyself.zip":

```java
import java.util.zip.*;
import java.io.*;
public class DeflateMyself {
    public static void main(String[] arg) {
        int tocount;
        int fromcount;
        byte[] toblock = new byte[10];
        byte[] fromblock = new byte[10];
        Deflater def = new Deflater();
        try {
            FileInputStream fi = new FileInputStream(
                    "DeflateMyself.java");
            FileOutputStream fo = new FileOutputStream(
                    "DeflateMyself.zip");
            tocount = fi.read(toblock);
            while(tocount > 0) {
                while(!def.needsInput()) {
                    fromcount = def.deflate(fromblock);
                    fo.write(fromblock,0,fromcount);
                }
                def.setInput(toblock,0,tocount);
                tocount = fi.read(toblock);
            }
            def.finish();
            fromcount = def.deflate(fromblock);
            while(fromcount > 0) {
                fo.write(fromblock,0,fromcount);
                fromcount = def.deflate(fromblock);
            }
            System.out.println("Total bytes in: "
                    + def.getTotalIn());
            System.out.println("Total bytes out: "
                    + def.getTotalOut());
            System.out.println("The Adler-32 checksum: "
                    + def.getAdler());
            fi.close();
```

```
            fo.close();
        } catch(Exception e) {
            System.out.println(e);
        }
    }
}
```

The input is read in ten-byte blocks and passed to the deflater. Before any data is written to the deflater, a call is made to `needsInput()` to make sure that the deflater has room for it. As long as there is no room for input, it is necessary to read some output by calling `deflate()` to read compressed data. This loop continues until all the data has been written to the deflater. A call is made to `finish()` to inform the deflater that no more data will be coming. After that, calls are made to `deflate()` until all the data is returned. On completion, we print the number of bytes in and out, along with the value of the checksum, like this:

```
Total bytes in: 1149
Total bytes out: 434
The Adler-32 checksum: 924997327
```

 For information about the compression algorithm, see **ZLIB**. For the inverse of this class, see **Inflater**. To perform deflation directly to a file, see **DeflaterOutputStream**.

DeflaterOutputStream

class java.util.zip.DeflaterOutputStream

This is an output stream that will compress data. It can be used to write directly to a file, or any other output stream.

Extended by

```
GZIPOutputStream
ZipOutputStream
```

Inheritance

```
public class java.util.zip.DeflaterOutputStream
    extends FilterOutputStream
        ⇑
    public class java.io.FilterOutputStream
```

```
extends OutputStream
            ⇑
public class java.io.OutputStream
      extends Object
            ⇑
      public class java.lang.Object
```

Variables and constants

buf

```
protected byte buf[]
```

The output buffer used to hold the compressed output data.

def

```
protected Deflater def
```

The data compression object.

Constructors

```
public DeflaterOutputStream(OutputStream out)
public DeflaterOutputStream(OutputStream out,
        Deflater def)
public DeflaterOutputStream(OutputStream out,
        Deflater def,int size)
```

The DeflaterOutputStream will write to the stream out using the deflater def. If def is not specified, the default deflater will be used. If the size is specified, it defines the size of the output buffer.

Methods

close()

```
public void close()
    throws IOException
```

Writes the remaining compressed data from the output buffer to the stream and closes the stream. An IOException is thrown on an error writing to the stream.

deflate()

```
protected void deflate()
    throws IOException
```

Writes the next block of compressed data to the output stream. An IOException is thrown on an error writing to the stream.

finish()

```
public void finish()
    throws IOException
```

Flushes the compressed data in the internal buffer to the output stream without closing the stream. This method can be useful when multiple filters are connected in series on the same stream. An IOException is thrown on an error writing to the stream.

write()

```
public void write(int byteValue)
    throws IOException

public void write(byte barray[],int offset,int length)
    throws IOException
```

Compresses data and writes it to the output stream. This method will block until the data has been written. Either a single byteValue or length bytes beginning at barray[offset] are written. An IOException is thrown on an error writing to the stream.

Example

This example reads its own source file for data and writes a compressed version of it to "StreamDeflateMyself.zip":

```
import java.util.zip.*;
import java.io.*;
public class StreamDeflateMyself {
    public static void main(String[] arg) {
        int count;
        byte[] block = new byte[10];
        try {
            FileInputStream fi = new FileInputStream(
                    "StreamDeflateMyself.java");
            FileOutputStream fo = new FileOutputStream(
                    "StreamDeflateMyself.zip");
            DeflaterOutputStream def =
                    new DeflaterOutputStream(fo);
            count = fi.read(block);
            while(count > 0) {
                def.write(block,0,count);
                count = fi.read(block);
            }
            def.close();
```

```
                                        fi.close();
                            } catch(Exception e) {
                                System.out.println(e);
                            }
                    }
            }
```

   The output stream is opened and used to construct a
DeflaterOutputStream object. The data is read from the disk and written
directly to the output stream. Once all the data has been written, the stream is
closed, which flushes the balance of the output to disk. This example reads a
file of 622 bytes and compresses it into an output file of 297 bytes.

 The class used to perform deflation is **Deflater**. The inverse of this class is
InflaterInputStream.

deprecated

   There are certain methods and classes that are described as being deprecated.
   These are methods that existed in version 1.0 of the Java API but should not
   be used in version 1.1. They are still present and fully functional (and will be
   for the foreseeable future), but they will eventually be omitted. They should
   not be used. In most cases, they have been replaced by methods that are more
   complete, better named, or more accurate.

 For tracking deprecated items, see **javadoc**.

dgc

package java.rmi.dgc

   This package deals with the distributed garbage collection portion of the
   remote method invocation.

   Interfaces

   DGC

   Classes

   Lease
   VMID

 See **rmi**.

DGC

interface java.rmi.dgc.DGC

This is the interface to the server side of distributed garbage collection.

Leasing objects

In a distributed system, there are both remote and local references to objects. Whenever a remote virtual machine is referencing a local object, it is said to have a *lease* on the object. Either the lease can be canceled by the remote machine, or it can expire after a certain period of time (every lease has an expiration time).

Dirty

A call to `dirty()` is used to add a new remote virtual machine to the list of those that are holding references to this object through RMI. This establishes a lease for a specified period of time. The lease can be renewed by making subsequent calls to `dirty()`. If all leases for an object expire, the object will be made available for garbage collection.

Clean

A call to `clean()` is used to remove a remote virtual machine from the list of those that are holding references to this object through RMI. This immediately causes the lease to expire.

Sequence numbers

The server and the client can get out of synchronization with one another because of the order of the packets delivered over the communications link. This is why the calls to these two methods have sequence numbers. A call to `dirty()` specifies a starting sequence number that is used as a rolling ID that is incremented to sequence later calls to prevent out-of-sequence messages from causing problems. A subsequent call to `dirty()` or `clean()` with a smaller sequence number than that of the last call to either method will be ignored.

Inheritance

```
public interface DGC
    extends Remote
        ⇑
    public interface java.rmi.Remote
```

Methods

clean()

```
public abstract void clean(ObjID ids[],long sequenceNum,
        VMID vmid,boolean strong)
    throws RemoteException
```

Removes vmid from the reference list of every object listed in the ids array. The sequenceNum is the same value that was specified on the call to dirty() and is used for synchronization. If strong is true, then this call is being made because of a failed call to dirty(). Whenever there is a failed call to dirty(), a "strong" call to clean() must be made so that the sequence number will be remembered.

dirty()

```
public abstract Lease dirty(ObjID ids[],long sequenceNum,
        Lease lease)
    throws RemoteException
```

Adds a lease for all of the remote objects referenced in the ids array. The lease argument contains the VMID and the lease period. The value of sequenceNum is used to synchronize this call with later calls to clean() — it should be increased with each call. Because of security restrictions, some clients cannot create a VMID, so a null VMID is acceptable and the garbage collection will assign a VMID to the client.

The returned Lease contains the VMID (which could have been generated) and the period of the lease (which could be shorter than the requested period). The returned VMID is the one that must be used on the call to clean().

This call can be made any number of times to renew a lease — but the call must be made before the lease expires.

 For more information, see **RMI**.

Dialog

class java.awt.Dialog

This is a window that is capable of managing components that are able to accept mouse and keyboard input from the user.

Layout manger

The default layout manager is the BorderLayout.

Events

The events that can be generated by a Dialog are WindowOpened, WindowClosing, WindowClosed, WindowActivated, and WindowDeactivated.

Extended by

```
FileDialog
```

Inheritance

```
public class java.awt.Dialog
    extends Window
        ⇑
    public class java.awt.Window
        extends Container
            ⇑
        public abstract class java.awt.Container
            extends Component
                ⇑
            public class java.awt.Component
                implements ImageObserver
                implements MenuContainer
                implements Serializable
                extends Object
                    ⇑
                public class java.lang.Object
```

Constructors

```
public Dialog(Frame parent)
public Dialog(Frame parent,boolean modal)
public Dialog(Frame parent,String title)
public Dialog(Frame parent,String title,boolean modal)
```

The dialog box requires a `Frame` as its `parent`. If no `title` is specified, the window will have a blank title. If `modal` is `true`, the `Dialog` will grab the mouse and keyboard input while blocking input to other windows.

Methods

addNotify()

```
public void addNotify()
```

Creates the underlying system-dependent peer for this object. This method is not normally called by the application. It is called by the container.

getTitle()

```
public String getTitle()
```

Returns the text of the dialog box title.

isModal()

```
public boolean isModal()
```

Returns `true` if this is a modal dialog box.

isResizable()

```
public boolean isResizable()
```

Returns `true` if the user has the ability to resize the dialog box.

paramString()

```
protected String paramString()
```

Returns debugging information. The return string describes the internal state and values of this object.

setModal()

```
public void setModal(boolean setting)
```

Specifies whether or not this is a modal dialog box. A `setting` of `true` makes the dialog box modal, and `false` makes it nonmodal.

setResizable()

```
public synchronized void setResizable(boolean setting)
```

Specifies whether or not this dialog box is resizable by the user. A `setting` of `true` makes it resizable, and `false` makes it nonresizable.

setTitle()

```
public synchronized void setTitle(String title)
```

Sets the title of the dialog box.

show()

```
public void show()
```

Displays the dialog box. This makes it visible, if necessary, and brings it to the front of the stacking order. If the dialog box is modal, this call will block until the dialog box is taken down with a call to `hide()` or `dispose()`.

It is valid to call this method from a thread that is dispatching the events because the Toolkit will ensure that another dispatching thread runs while this one is blocked.

Example 1

This is a simple modal `Dialog` that contains one button:

```java
import java.awt.*;
import java.awt.event.*;

public class Quit extends Frame {
    public static void main(String[] arg) {
        new Quit();
    }
    Quit() {
        QuitDialog qd = new QuitDialog(this);
    }
}

class QuitDialog extends Dialog
                implements ActionListener {
    QuitDialog(Frame frame) {
        super(frame,"Quit!",true);
        Button quitButton = new Button("quit");
        quitButton.addActionListener(this);
        add(quitButton,BorderLayout.CENTER);
        pack();
        setVisible(true);
    }

    public void actionPerformed(ActionEvent event) {
        setVisible(false);
        System.exit(0);
    }
}
```

Figure D-1 shows the dialog box being displayed.

Figure D-1   A simple dialog box with a single button.

Extend and implement

The dialog box, being a pop-up window, is a separate class named `QuitDialog`. The class extends `Dialog` (thus, becoming a `Dialog`). It also implements ActionListener so that it will be able to listen to information sent from any components it may contain—in this case a single button.

Calling super

The constructor of the superclass is called explicitly to provide a title for the title bar at the top, and to specify that we want this to be a modal dialog box. If super is not called, the title line will be blank and the dialog will be nonmodal.

Adding a button

A button is created and added as the "Center" component (see BorderLayout). To be able to listen to the button, it is necessary for the Dialog to register itself as a listener. This is done with the call to addActionListener(). This means that the method actionPerformed() will be called whenever the button is pressed. In this example, this will only happen once because the actionPerformed() simply exits.

Pack and show

The method pack() will position all the components and resize the dialog window to fit the packing. Once all this is done, a call to show() causes the dialog box to display itself and wait for mouse input.

Example 2

In this example, we change to a FlowLayout manager and let it position several buttons:

```java
import java.awt.*;
import java.awt.event.*;

public class ButtonButton extends Frame {
    public static void main(String[] arg) {
        new ButtonButton();
    }
    ButtonButton() {
        ButtonButtonDialog qd = new
ButtonButtonDialog(this);
    }
}


class ButtonButtonDialog extends Dialog
            implements ActionListener {
    Button[] button;
    ButtonButtonDialog(Frame frame) {
        super(frame,"Quit!",true);
        setLayout(new FlowLayout());
        button = new Button[5];
        for(int i=0; i<5; i++) {
            button[i] = new Button("Button " + i);
```

```
            button[i].addActionListener(this);
            add(button[i]);
        }
        Button quitButton = new Button("quit");
        quitButton.addActionListener(this);
        add(quitButton);
        pack();
        setVisible(true);
    }

    public void actionPerformed(ActionEvent event) {
        if(event.getActionCommand().equals("quit")) {
            setVisible(false);
            System.exit(1);
        }
        System.out.println(event.getActionCommand());
    }
}
```

In this example, we replace the default layout manager with a FlowLayout manager so that we can add components freely and the layout manager will place them for us. A group of buttons are added to the dialog. Five of them have the labels "Button 0" through "Button 4," and the sixth button is labeled "quit." The method addActionListener() is called for each button, so the method actionPerformed() will be called for all of them.

For all but the Quit button, we simply print the command (which, in this case, is also the button label). The text of the command is used to tell which button has been pressed; if the Quit button is pressed, the program will exit. Figure D-2 shows what the dialog box looks like.

Figure D-2 A dialog box with several buttons.

Example 3

This example adds more than buttons to the dialog box. We change the layout manager to a GridLayout so that we can place all the components in a column and then add the components in the order we would like for them to appear:

```
import java.awt.*;
import java.awt.event.*;

public class Grouping extends Frame {
```

```
        public static void main(String[] arg) {
            new Grouping();
        }
        Grouping() {
            GroupingDialog qd = new GroupingDialog(this);
        }
}

class GroupingDialog extends Dialog
              implements ActionListener, ItemListener {
    Button quitButton;
    Label choiceLabel;
    Choice choice;
    Label listLabel;
    List list;
    GroupingDialog(Frame frame) {
        super(frame,"Group",true);
        setLayout(new GridLayout(5,1,10,5));
        choiceLabel = new Label("The choices...");
        add(choiceLabel);
        choice = new Choice();
        choice.addItem("First choice");
        choice.addItem("Second choice");
        choice.addItem("Third choice");
        choice.addItemListener(this);
        add(choice);
        listLabel = new Label("The list...");
        add(listLabel);
        list = new List(2,false);
        list.addItem("First item");
        list.addItem("Second item");
        list.addItem("Third item");
        list.addItem("Fourth item");
        list.addItemListener(this);
        add(list);
        quitButton = new Button("quit");
        quitButton.addActionListener(this);
        add(quitButton);
        pack();
        setVisible(true);
    }

    public void actionPerformed(ActionEvent event) {
        if(event.getActionCommand().equals("quit")) {
```

```
                    setVisible(false);
                    System.exit(1);
            }
            System.out.println(event.paramString());
        }

        public void itemStateChanged(ItemEvent event) {
            System.out.println(event.paramString());
        }
    }
```

We want to receive information from the `Choice` and the `List`, so we need to implement the `ItemListener` interface by adding the method `itemStateChanged()`. We register with the `Choice` and the `List` as an `ItemListener`, which will cause the `itemStateChanged()` method to be called every time a new selection is made. In this example, the text from the selection is printed to standard out. Figure D-3 shows what the window looks like.

Figure D-3   A dialog box with several components.

 The parent of a `Dialog` is always a **Frame**. The standard AWT `Components` that can be added to a dialog are **Canvas, Button, Panel, Checkbox, Choice, Label, List, Scrollbar, Scrollpane, TextArea,** and **TextField.** The available layout managers are **BorderLayout, CardLayout, FlowLayout, GridBagLayout,** and **GridLayout.**

Dictionary

class java.util.Dictionary

This is an abstract class. It defines a collection of methods that can be used to maintain a set of key/value pairs. Both the key and the value are Java objects.

Extended by

```
Hashtable
```

Inheritance

```
public class Dictionary
    extends Object
        ⇑
    public class java.lang.Object
```

Constructors

```
public Dictionary()
```

Methods

elements()

```
public abstract Enumeration elements()
```

Returns an Enumeration object that contains references to all the objects in the Dictionary.

get()

```
public abstract Object get(Object key)
```

This method uses the key to retrieve an object. The key must be an exact match of the one used to store the object. If the key is not found in the table, null is returned.

isEmpty()

```
public abstract boolean isEmpty()
```

Returns true if the Dictionary is empty.

keys()

```
public abstract Enumeration keys()
```

Returns an Enumeration object that contains references to all the keys in the Dictionary.

put()

```
public abstract Object put(Object key,Object value)
```

This will add a new key and its associated value to the Dictionary. If the key is already in the table, the value is assumed to be a new object to be associated with the key and the value is inserted into the table, replacing the one already there. If the key is new to the table, null is returned. If the key is already in the table, its previously associated value is returned. If either the key or the value is null, a NullPointerException will be thrown.

remove()

```
public abstract Object remove(Object key)
```

Removes the key and its associated value object from the table. The returned object is the key itself if it was found and deleted. The return is null if the key was not found.

size()

```
public abstract int size()
```

Returns a count of the number of entries in the Dictionary.

 See the **Hashtable** class, which extends Dictionary. For more about the hashcode, see **hashcode** and **Object**.

DigestException

class java.security.DigestException

This is the generic MessageDigest exception.

Inheritance

```
public class java.security.DigestException
    extends Exception
        ⇑
    public class java.lang.Exception
        extends Throwable
            ⇑
        public class java.lang.Throwable
            implements Serializable
            extends Object
                ⇑
            public class java.lang.Object
```

Constructors

```
public DigestException()
public DigestException(String message)
```

If the `message` string is supplied, it is used as a detailed message describing this particular exception.

 See **MessageDigest**.

DigestInputStream

class java.security.DigestInputStream

This class can be used to attach a `MessageDigest` object to an input stream. The `read()` methods will return streamed data to the caller and also pass the data to the `MessageDigest`. In effect, this is an input stream with a `MessageDigest` monitoring the stream enabling you to read the data and generate a hashcode value at the same time. Once all the data is read, a call to the `digest()` method of the `MessageDigest` object can be made to return the encoded value.

On and off

It is possible to turn the `MessageDigest` input on and off while data is being processed so that only the desired parts of the data will be included in the calculation of the digested value. When it is off, the data can be read normally, but nothing is passed to the `MessageDigest`. The default is to have it on.

You only get one

A `MessageDigest` can only perform the final calculations once. If you need to get intermediate results, you can clone the object at any point you wish and have the clone calculate a value. In this way, the original will be untouched and will continue to accept input data. Alternatively, you could connect more than one `DigestInputStream` in a series and turn each one of them on and off as desired.

Inheritance

```
public class java.security.DigestInputStream
    extends FilterInputStream
        ⇑
    public class java.io.FilterInputStream
        extends InputStream
            ⇑
        public class java.io.InputStream
            extends Object
                ⇑
            public class java.lang.Object
```

Variables and constants

digest

```
protected MessageDigest digest
```

The MessageDigest used by this stream.

Constructors

```
public DigestInputStream(InputStream stream,
        MessageDigest digest)
```

A new DigestInputStream object is constructed by associating the stream with the digest.

Methods

getMessageDigest()

```
public MessageDigest getMessageDigest()
```

Returns the MessageDigest object.

on()

```
public void on(boolean setting)
```

If setting is true, subsequent data read from the stream will also be passed to the MessageDigest. If setting is false, data can be read but will not be passed to the MessageDigest. The default is on.

read()

```
public int read()
    throws IOException
```

```
public int read(byte barray[],int offset,int length)
    throws IOException
```

Reads a byte, or an array of bytes, from the stream and passes the data to the MessageDigest. If a single byte is read, it is returned as an int. If barray is specified, input data is placed into it beginning at barray[offset] and continuing for length bytes. For barray, the actual number of bytes read is returned. The return value is −1 to indicate end-of-file. This method blocks until data has been read. An IOException is thrown if an error occurs on the stream.

setMessageDigest()

```
public void setMessageDigest(MessageDigest digest)
```

This will associate the digest, replacing the one specified on the constructor.

toString()

```
public String toString()
```

Returns a string representation of the input stream and the message digest.

Example

This example generates a message digest value on its own source file by attaching a MessageDigest to an input stream and then reading the file:

```
import java.security.*;
import java.io.*;
public class DigestInputFile {
    public static void main(String[] arg) {
        int count;
        byte[] block = new byte[10];
        try {
            FileInputStream fis = new FileInputStream(
                    "DigestInputFile.java");
            MessageDigest md =
                        MessageDigest.getInstance("MD5");
            DigestInputStream dis =
                        new DigestInputStream(fis,md);
            count = dis.read(block);
            while(count > 0)
                count = dis.read(block);
            dis.close();
            byte[] hash = md.digest();
            for(int i=0; i<hash.length; i++)
                System.out.print(hexByte(hash[i]));
            System.out.println();
        } catch(Exception e) {
            System.out.println(e);
        }
    }
    private static String hexByte(byte b) {
        String hex =
            Integer.toHexString((int)b & 0x000000FF);
        if(hex.length() < 2)
            return("0" + hex);
        return(hex);
    }
}
```

Once the input stream has been opened, it can be used to create a `DigestInputStream`. To do this, we use a `MessageDigest` that uses the MD5 algorithm for generating the encoded value. It is then a simple matter to read the entire file (throwing away the input data), which causes the value to be calculated. The value is returned as a byte array with a call to `digest()`. The code is printed as a string of 16 hexadecimal digits. Here is the output:

```
f246c95c0a3300de6627b36280a343eb
```

For a description of the message digest encryption, see **MessageDigest**. For an output stream of this type, see **DigestOutputStream**.

DigestOutputStream

class java.security.DigestOutputStream

This class can be used to attach a `MessageDigest` object to an output stream. The `write()` methods will send the data to the stream and also pass the data to the `MessageDigest`. In effect, this is an output stream with a `MessageDigest` monitoring the stream enabling you to write the data and generate the hashcode value at the same time. Once all the data has been written, a call to the `digest()` method of the `MessageDigest` object can be made to generate the encoded value.

On and off

It is possible to turn the `MessageDigest` input on and off so that only the desired parts of the data will be included in the calculation of the digested value. When it is off, the data can be written normally, but nothing is passed to the `MessageDigest`. The default is on.

You only get one

A `MessageDigest` can only perform the final calculations once. If you need to get intermediate results, you could clone the `MessageDigest` object at any point and have the clone calculate a value. In this way, the original will be untouched and will continue to accept input data. Alternatively, you could connect more than one `DigestOutputStream` in a series, turning each `MessageDigest` on and off as desired.

Inheritance

```
public class java.security.DigestOutputStream
    extends FilterOutputStream
        ⇑
    public class java.io.FileOutputStream
        extends OutputStream
```

⇑
```
public class java.io.OutputStream
          extends Object
```
⇑
```
public class java.lang.Object
```

Variables and constants

digest
```
protected MessageDigest digest
```
The MessageDigest used by this stream.

Constructors
```
public DigestOutputStream(OutputStream stream,
          MessageDigest digest)
```
A new DigestOutputStream object is constructed by associating the stream with the digest.

Methods

getMessageDigest()
```
public MessageDigest getMessageDigest()
```
Returns the MessageDigest object.

on()
```
public void on(boolean setting)
```
If the setting is true, subsequent data written to the stream will also be passed to the MessageDigest. If setting is false, data can be written but will not be passed to the MessageDigest. The default is on.

setMessageDigest()
```
public void setMessageDigest(MessageDigest digest)
```
This will associate the digest. This will replace the one specified on the constructor.

toString()
```
public String toString()
```
Returns a string representation of the output stream and the message digest.

write()

```
public void write(int byte)
    throws IOException

public void write(byte barray[],int offset,int length)
    throws IOException
```

Writes a byte, or an array of bytes, to the stream and passes the data to the MessageDigest. If barray is specified, output data is written from it beginning at barray[offset] and continuing for length bytes. This method blocks until data has been written. An IOException is thrown if an error occurs on the stream.

Example

This example generates a message digest value by copying its own source code to another file while attaching a MessageDigest to the output stream:

```
import java.security.*;
import java.io.*;
public class DigestOutputFile {
    public static void main(String[] arg) {
        int count;
        byte[] block = new byte[10];
        try {
            FileInputStream fis = new FileInputStream(
                    "DigestOutputFile.java");
            FileOutputStream fos = new FileOutputStream(
                    "DigestOutputFile.clone");
            MessageDigest md =
                    MessageDigest.getInstance("MD5");
            DigestOutputStream dos =
                    new DigestOutputStream(fos,md);
            count = fis.read(block);
            while(count > 0) {
                dos.write(block,0,count);
                count = fis.read(block);
            }
            fis.close();
            dos.close();
            byte[] hash = md.digest();
            for(int i=0; i<hash.length; i++)
                System.out.print(hexByte(hash[i]));
            System.out.println();
        } catch(Exception e) {
            System.out.println(e);
```

```
            }
        }
        private static String hexByte(byte b) {
            String hex =
                Integer.toHexString((int)b & 0x000000FF);
            if(hex.length() < 2)
                return("0" + hex);
            return(hex);
        }
    }
```

The input and output streams are both opened, and a `DigestOutputStream` object is created by using a `MessageDigest` object and the output stream. The data is read from the input stream and written to the output stream—this causes the output stream to automatically calculate the value. Once the two streams are closed, the `digest()` method is called to return the array of bytes that is the message digest. These bytes are printed out as a string of hexadecimal digits that looks like this:

```
1deae2a375b3ae55b9198f162430f2c9
```

 For a description of the message digest encryption, see **MessageDigest**. For an input stream of this type, see **DigestInputStream**.

Dimension

class java.awt.Dimension

This is a wrapper for a height and width dimension-value pair. It is the size of a rectangle.

Inheritance

```
public class java.awt.Dimension
    implements Serializable
    extends Object
        ⇑
    public class java.lang.Object
```

Variables and constants

height

```
public int height
```

The variable that holds the height.

width

```
public int width
```

The variable that holds the width.

Constructors

```
public Dimension()
public Dimension(Dimension dimension)
public Dimension(int width,int height)
```

If no size is specified, width and height default to zero. A Dimension object can be constructed as the copy of another Dimension object, or by having the width and height specified.

Returned by

A Dimension object can be cloned with a call to getSize(). This is a utility object that is used throughout the Java API—it is returned from more that 50 methods.

Methods

equals()

```
public boolean equals(Object object)
```

Returns true if object is Dimension object with the same width and height as this one.

getSize()

```
public Dimension getSize()
```

Returns a new Dimension object with the same width and height as this one.

setSize()

```
public void setSize(Dimension dimension)
```

```
public void setSize(int width,int height)
```

Sets the width and height of this object to those in dimension or in width and height.

toString()

```
public String toString()
```

Returns a string representation of the width and height.

For a similar class that includes the position as well as the size, see **Rectangle**. For similar wrappers, see **Inset, Point, Polygon,** and **Shape**.

DirectColorModel

class java.awt.image.DirectColorModel

This is a `ColorModel` class that performs operations on pixel colors. For this model, the pixel values hold the actual color information (as opposed to systems that use table indexing for the color values). This color model is quite similar to the X11 TrueColor model.

Color bits

The color information is held directly in the pixel data. This is normally achieved by assigning a certain group of bits to each of the primary colors of red, blue, and green. An alpha value is also included that defines the degree of transparency. An alpha value of 0 is completely transparent, and 255 is completely opaque.

Some assumptions are made

Some assumptions are made by the underlying graphics code, and these assumptions are reflected in the methods of this class. The methods are all defined as being final—you can subclass this class, but you cannot modify the behavior of any of its methods.

Inheritance

```
public class java.awt.image.DirectColorModel
    extends ColorModel
        ⇑
    public abstract class java.awt.image.ColorModel
        extends Object
            ⇑
        public class java.lang.Object
```

Constructors

```
public DirectColorModel(int pixelBits,
        int redMask,int greenMask,int blueMask)

public DirectColorModel(int pixelBits,
        int redMask,int greenMask,int blueMask,
        int alphaMask)
```

The value of `pixelBits` defines the number of bits in each pixel. The masks each specify the number and position of the bits that will be assumed by each of the color components and by the alpha component. If `alphaMask` is not specified, a completely opaque color (and alpha value of 255) will be assumed.

The masks must combine to use the exact number of bits specified in `pixelBits`. Each mask must define a set of contiguous bits, and the masks must fit together without overlap. For example, a 16-bit color system could assign four bits to each color and use a four-bit alpha mask in this way:

```
redMask:   0x000F
blueMask   0x00F0
greenMask  0x0F00
alphaMask  0xF000
```

Returned by

A `ColorModel` object correct for the current system (which may or may not be a `DirectColorModel` object) can be returned with a call to `getColorModel()` in `Component`, `ComponentPeer`, `PixelGrabber`, and `Toolkit`.

Methods

getAlpha()

```
public final int getAlpha(int pixel)
```

Returns the alpha value, which is a number from 0 to 255.

getAlphaMask()

```
public final int getAlphaMask()
```

Returns the alpha mask as specified on the constructor. It will be 255 if none was specified in the constructor.

getBlue()

```
public final int getBlue(int pixel)
```

Returns the value of the blue component of this pixel color as a value from 0 to 255.

getBlueMask()

```
public final int getBlueMask()
```

Returns the value of the mask as supplied to the constructor.

getGreen()

```
public final int getGreen(int pixel)
```

Returns the value of the green component of this pixel color as a value from 0 to 255.

getGreenMask()

```
public final int getGreenMask()
```

Returns the value of the mask as supplied to the constructor.

getRed()

```
public final int getRed(int pixel)
```

Returns the value of the red component of this pixel color as a value from 0 to 255.

getRedMask()

```
public final int getRedMask()
```

Returns the value of the mask as supplied to the constructor.

getRGB()

```
public final int getRGB(int pixel)
```

Converts the pixel value into the RGB color model.
Returns the color of the pixel in the default RGB color model.

 For a description of the Java default RGB model, and examples of working with the default model, see **ColorModel**. The other color model class of the Java API is **IndexColorModel**.

divide

/ /=

The operators / and /= are the Java arithmetic division operators. These operators are only valid for the Java primitive data types. Mixed-mode arithmetic is supported—the narrower type is widened before the operation is performed.

The / operator performs division but does not modify the operands. The /= operator performs division and places the results in the left operand. These two statements are equivalent:

```
a = a / b;
a /= b;
```

Integer division

Integer division will perform truncation. The remainder is discarded. Division by zero will throw an ArithmeticException.

Floating point division

Floating-point division will never throw an exception. The results, however, could be positive or negative infinity, or NaN.

 For an operation that performs integer division and returns the remainder, see **remainder**. For information on real numbers, see **floating-point numbers**.

do

keyword

The keyword do, combined with the keyword while, performs an iteration where the test is made at the bottom of the loop. Because the test is at the bottom, the loop is guaranteed to execute at least once.

The do block

A loop is written with do at the top and while at the bottom like this:

```
do {
    body of the loop
} while(boolean expression);
```

The body of the loop will execute before the boolean expression is tested. If the boolean expression results in true, the body will be executed again. This continues until the boolean expression is false.

The break statement

A break statement will cause the do/while block to be exited immediately. This loop will print the values 0 and 1 and then exit the loop:

```
int i = 0;
do {
    if(i == 2)
        break;
    System.out.println(i);
} while(i++ < 5);
```

It is also possible to use a label on the break statement by labeling the loop itself, in this way:

```
int i = 0;
doLabel: do {
    if(i == 2)
```

```
        break doLabel;
    System.out.println(i);
} while(i++ < 5);
```

The advantage of using a label is the ability to break from nested loops of do, for, and while. This break statement will break both loops because it breaks out to the label:

```
int i = 0;
doLabel: do {
    int j = 0;
    do {
        if(j == 2)
            break doLabel;
        System.out.println(j);
    } while(j++ < 5);
} while(i++ < 5);
```

The *continue* statement

A continue statement will cause the do/while block to jump to the bottom and test for the next iteration. This loop will print the values 0, 1, 3, 4 and 5. The value 2 is skipped by the continue statement:

```
int i = 0;
do {
    if(i == 2)
        continue;
    System.out.println(i);
} while(i++ < 5);
```

It is also possible to use a label on the continue statement by labeling the loop itself, in this way:

```
int i = 0;
doLabel: do {
    if(i == 2)
        continue doLabel;
    System.out.println(i);
} while(i++ < 5);
```

The advantage of using a label is the ability to continue the iteration of an outer loop in the case of nested do, for, and while loops. This continue statement will go to the test at the bottom of the outer do loop:

```
int i = 0;
doLabel: do {
```

```
                int j = 0;
                do {
                     if(j == 2)
                          continue doLabel;
                     System.out.println(j);
                } while(j++ < 5);
          } while(i++ < 5);
```

 The other iteration keywords are **for** and **while**. There is conditional execution with **if** and **switch**.

documentation

 For a utility to generate documentation from Java source code, see **javadoc**.

double

primitive data type

The Java double data type is implemented according to the 64-bit double-precision IEEE 754-1985 standard.

Internal format

The 64 bits of the double have one bit allocated for the sign bit, an 11-bit exponent, and a 52-bit mantissa. A base-2 radix is assumed. The 64 bits of a double are allocated as shown in Figure D-4.

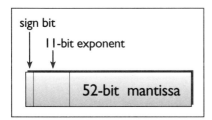

Figure D-4 The internal format of the double primitive data type.

The sign bit is set to 1 to indicate a negative number, and 0 for positive.

The mantissa is a 52-bit number that has a value range from 0 to 72,057,594,037,927,935. With the exception of the special case of zero, there is always at least one bit in the mantissa that is set to 1. The mantissa is normalized by shifting the first nonzero bit completely to the left (adjusting the exponent appropriately). Since all normalized numbers are represented with their leading bit being 1, there is no need to actually include it. The mantissa is shifted left once more, moving the leading bit to the "invisible bit" position—it is assumed.

The exponent is an unsigned 11-bit value that can range in value from 0 to 2047. To be able to represent both positive and negative exponents, the value is offset by 1023. That is, to determine the actual value of the exponent, subtract 1023 from the 11-bit value.

Here is how to calculate the value of a `double` by looking at its bits. Prefix the mantissa with a 1 and the binary point (it's base-2, not -10), and then raise 2 to the power of the adjusted exponent. If M is the mantissa and E is the exponent, it takes this form:

$$1.M \times 2^{(E - 1023)}$$

This sample program uses the `Double` and `Long` wrapper classes to display double values in hexadecimal format:

```
public class HexDouble {
    public static void main(String arg[]) {
        HexDouble hd = new HexDouble();
        System.out.println(
            " 3.0: " + hd.toHexString(3.0));
        System.out.println(
            " 2.0: " + hd.toHexString(2.0));
        System.out.println(
            " 1.0: " + hd.toHexString(1.0));
        System.out.println(
                " 0.5: " + hd.toHexString(0.5));
    }
    final private String toHexString(double value) {
        long lvalue = Double.doubleToLongBits(value);
        return(Long.toHexString(lvalue));
    }
}
```

The output looks like this:

```
3.0: 4008000000000000
2.0: 4000000000000000
1.0: 3ff0000000000000
0.5: 3fe0000000000000
```

You will notice the suppression of any leading 1's. The number 3 requires two leading 1 bits, so its second bit shows up—the other values have only a single 1 bit, and it is always in the "invisible" position. The exponent value for 1.0 in the code as 1023 (3ff in hex), so according to the formula just given, it is actually zero. The exponent for 0.5 is 1022 (3fe in hex), so it is actually –1.

Special values

The largest magnitude value for a `double`—positive or negative—is 1.79769313486231570e+308. The smallest magnitude value—positive or negative—is 4.94065645841246544e–324. These values are defined as positive numbers as the static constants `Double.MAX_VALUE` and `Double.MIN_VALUE`. Table D-2 lists the special values as defined by IEEE standard 754-1985.

Table D-2 Formats of IEEE 754 Double-Precision Floating Special Values

Type	Sign Bit	Exponent	Value
Signaling NaN	u	2047 (max)	0uuuuu...u *(see note)*
Quiet NaN	u	2047 (max)	1uuuuu...u *(see note)*
Negative infinity	1	2047 (max)	000000...0
Positive infinity	0	2047 (max)	000000...0
Negative zero	1	0	000000...0
Positive zero	0	0	000000...0

Note: The letter 'u' is used to mark the place of a bit that may be either 0 or 1. For signaling NaN, at least one of the 'u' bits must be 1. The value of NaN (not a number) results from undefined operations, such as dividing zero by zero. There is an NaN constant predefined as `Double.NaN`.

Too large and too small

If a nonzero literal is rounded to fit into a `double` and is found to result in zero, a compile-time error is generated. If the rounding of a small literal results in any nonzero value, the conversion is made and no compile-time error results.

Positive infinity results from *overflow* (a number becoming larger than that maximum value), and negative infinity results from *underflow* (a number becoming too small to be represented). The values of positive and negative infinity are special representations that are outside the range of the normal numbers. Java allows the value of positive infinity to be derived from expressions such as 1.0/0.0—or you can use the predefined constant `Double.POSITIVE_INFINITY`. Similarly, negative infinity can be entered as –1.0/0.0 or by using the constant `Double.NEGATIVE_INFINITY`.

For single-precision real numbers, see **float**. For the format of real literals, see **real numbers**. For a wrapper class that contains the special `double` constants and performs some special functions, see **Double**.

Double

class java.lang.Double

This is a wrapper class of the primitive type `double`.

Inheritance

```
public final class java.lang.Double
    extends Number
        ⇑
    public class Number
        implements Serializable
        extends Object
            ⇑
        public class java.lang.Object
```

Variables and constants

MAX_VALUE

```
public final static double MAX_VALUE
```

The largest magnitude value that can be held in a `double`. The value of this constant is positive, but the value of the largest magnitude number is the same whether positive or negative. It is 1.79769313486231570e+308d.

MIN_VALUE

```
public final static double MIN_VALUE
```

The smallest magnitude value (other than zero) that can be held in a `double`. The value of this constant is positive, but the values of the smallest magnitude number is the same whether positive or negative. It is 4.94065645841246544e–324d.

NaN

```
public final static double NaN
```

This is an IEEE Not-a-Number value. It cannot be successfully compared to anything—even itself.

NEGATIVE_INFINITY

```
public final static double NEGATIVE_INFINITY
```

This is a special value that will compare as less than any value other than itself.

POSITIVE_INFINITY

```
public final static double POSITIVE_INFINITY
```

This is a special value that will compare as greater than any value other than itself.

TYPE

```
public final static Class TYPE
```

This is the `Class` object that represents the `double` primitive type.

Constructors

```
public Double(double value)
public Double(String string)
        throws NumberFormatException
```

A value of some kind must be supplied to a constructor. If the `string` is specified, a wrapper will be created for it unless the format of the string is not valid — in which case, a `NumberFormatException` will be thrown. The string format must be in a base-10 form with optional signs and exponentiation — it does not accept the hexadecimal or octal format.

Returned by

A `Double` object is returned by the method `valueOf()`.

Methods

byteValue()

```
public byte byteValue()
```

The `double` value is cast to a `byte` and returned.

doubleToLongBits()

```
public static long doubleToLongBits(double value)
```

A `double` and a `long` are both 64-bit primitives. This method takes the bit pattern of the `double` and returns it — unaltered — as a `long`.

doubleValue()

```
public double doubleValue()
```

Returns the internal `double` value.

equals()

```
public boolean equals(Object object)
```

If `object` is a `Double` object, and if it contains the same value as this one, a `true` is returned—otherwise, `false` is returned. If both of them are NaN values, they are considered by this method to be equal (contrary to the IEEE specification, which specifies that NaN values are never equal).

floatValue()

```
public float floatValue()
```

The `double` value is cast to a `float` and returned.

hashCode()

```
public int hashCode()
```

A hashcode for this object is returned. Two distinct `Double` objects that contain identical value will return identical hashcodes.

intValue()

```
public int intValue()
```

The `double` is cast to an `int` and returned.

isInfinite()

```
public boolean isInfinite()

public static boolean isInfinite(double value)
```

Returns `true` if the `value` is no smaller than `POSITIVE_INFINITY`. If no `value` is supplied, the test is made against the internal value of this object.

isNaN()

```
public boolean isNaN()

public static boolean isNaN(double value)
```

Returns `true` if the `value` is NaN. If no `value` is supplied, the test is made against the internal value of this object.

longBitsToDouble()

```
public static double longBitsToDouble(long bits)
```

A `double` and a `long` are both 64-bit primitives. This method takes the bit pattern found in the `long` and returns it—unaltered—as a `double`.

longValue()

```
public long longValue()
```

The internal value is cast to a `long` and returned.

shortValue()

```
public short shortValue()
```

The internal value is cast to a `short` and returned.

toString()

```
public String toString()

public static String toString(double value)
```

Returns the `String` form of the double. If no `value` is supplied, the internal value of the object is used.

valueOf()

```
public static Double valueOf(String string)
        throws NumberFormatException
```

The method converts the `string` into a `Double` object. If the number is not in a recognizable base-10 format, a `NumberFormatException` is thrown.

 The wrappers of the other primitive types are **Boolean**, **Byte**, **Character**, **Short**, **Long**, **Float**, and **Integer**.

double quote

"

The double-quote character is used as the front and back delimiter of literal strings.

 For examples of using literal strings to create `String` objects, see **string literals**.

Driver

interface java.sql.Driver

This interface should be implemented by each SQL driver.

The driver and the manager

When making a connection, the `DriverManager` will load as many drivers as it can find. It will make a connection request to each one using the URL it was supplied. Because several drivers will be loaded at one time, efficiency requires that a driver be as small as possible.

When a driver loads, it should register itself with the `DriverManager`. This will allow a user to load a driver with a call to `Class.forName()`.

Inheritance

```
public interface java.sql.Driver
```

Constructors

Returned by

A `Driver` object is returned from a call to `DriverManager.getDriver()`.

Methods

acceptsURL()

```
public abstract boolean acceptsURL(String url)
    throws SQLException
```

This method is called by the `DriverManager` to request a connection. A return value of `true` indicates the driver has determined that it could be possible to open a connection. A `true` return is not a confirmation of a connection—but it is a confirmation that the driver can read and understand all the protocol of the `url`. An `SQLException` is thrown in the event of a database access error.

connect()

```
public abstract Connection connect(String url, Properties info)
    throws SQLException
```

This method is called to try to make a connection to the database specified by the `url`. A `null` return indicates that this is not the correct driver type for the given `url`. An `SQLException` should be thrown only if the driver is the right one to make the connection to the `url` but the driver is unable to make the connection. If a `Connection` object is returned, a connection has been made.

The `info` argument can be used to pass values as connection arguments. Normally, this is at least a "user" property and a "password" property.

getMajorVersion()

```
public abstract int getMajorVersion()
```

Returns the major version number of the driver.

getMinorVersion()

```
public abstract int getMinorVersion()
```

Returns the minor version number of the driver.

getPropertyInfo()

```
public abstract DriverPropertyInfo[] getPropertyInfo(
        String url,Properties info)
    throws SQLException
```

Returns properties that can be used by a GUI tool to construct the necessary set of prompts needed to acquire the information to make a connection. The `url` is that of the database. The `info` argument contains a set of known properties needed to connect to the database. An `SQLException` is thrown on a database error.

Calling this method could be an iterative process. If this method returns a set of prompts (one or more), these prompts are then presented to the user for answers. The answers are then added to the `info` object, and this method is called again. This process continues until there are no further questions to be answered—that is, no more prompts return from the method call.

jdbcCompliant()

```
public abstract boolean jdbcCompliant()
```

Returns `true` if the driver is JDBC-compliant. A driver will return only `true` if it passes the JDBC compliance tests.

 For loading drivers and connecting to the database, see **DriverManager** and **Connection**. For information on database compliance, see **JDBC**.

DriverManager

class java.sql.DriverManager

This class will manage one or more JDBC drivers.

Loading the drivers

During initialization, the `DriverManager` will attempt to load all the driver classes it finds referenced in the "jdbc.drivers" system property. This will allow an application—by making modifications to its own set of system properties—to control which database driver, or drivers, will be used.

A program can load a JDBC driver at any time by making a call to `Class.forName()` with the name of the class file of the driver.

Making a database connection

When the `DriverManager` attempts to make a connection, it tries all the drivers that have been loaded. The interface to the drivers is such that if a driver is not the correct one for a particular database, no action will be taken.

Inheritance

```
public class java.sql.DriverManager
    extends Object
        ⇑
    public class java.lang.Object
```

Constructors

This class has no constructors—it is a collection of static methods.

Methods

deregisterDriver()

```
public static void deregisterDriver(Driver driver)
    throws SQLException
```

Removes `driver` from the `DriverManager` list. Applets can only remove drivers that they loaded with their own class loader. An `SQLException` is thrown if there is a database access violation.

getConnection()

```
public static synchronized Connection getConnection(
        String url,Properties info)
    throws SQLException
```

```
public static synchronized Connection getConnection(
        String url,String user,String password)
    throws SQLException
```

```
public static synchronized Connection
        getConnection(String url)
    throws SQLException
```

Attempts to establish a connection. The `url` is that of the database. The `info` is other information that is needed for the connection, usually including "user" and "password." The `user` and `password` can be passed individually as strings if no other arguments are required. An `SQLException` is thrown if there is a database error.

getDriver()

```
public static Driver getDriver(String url)
    throws SQLException
```

Passes this url to the drivers and returns the driver that claims to understand it. This is the normal method used to select the correct driver when making a connection.

getDrivers()

```
public static Enumeration getDrivers()
```

Returns an enumeration of all the currently loaded drivers.

getLoginTimeout()

```
public static int getLoginTimeout()
```

Returns the maximum number of seconds that all the drivers can wait when attempting to log on to a database.

getLogStream()

```
public static PrintStream getLogStream()
```

Returns the logging and tracing PrintStream that is used by the DriverManager and all the drivers. If it is disabled, the return is null.

println()

```
public static void println(String message)
```

Prints a message to the current log stream.

registerDriver()

```
public static synchronized void registerDriver(Driver driver)
    throws SQLException
```

This method is called by a newly loaded driver to register itself with the DriverManager. This should be done by every driver when it loads.

setLoginTimeout()

```
public static void setLoginTimeout(int seconds)
```

This specifies the maximum number of seconds that the drivers can wait when attempting to log on to a database.

setLogStream()

```
public static void setLogStream(PrintStream output)
```

This will specify the `output` stream as the one to be used for logging by the `DriverManager` and all the drivers.

 For more information about JDBC access, see **Driver** and **Connection**.

DriverPropertyInfo

class java.sql.DriverPropertyInfo

This class is not normally required for an application. It is of interest only to those who need to interface closely with a JDBC database driver to ascertain the information required by the driver to make a connection and to log on. An object of this class holds a description of one of these pieces of information—the complete piece of information will normally require an array of `DriverPropertyInfo` objects.

Inheritance

```
public class java.sql.DriverPropertyInfo
        extends Object
            ⇑
    public class java.lang.Object
```

Variables and constants

choices

```
public String choices[]
```

If the value of the property can be selected from a list of options, these are the options. If it is not selectable in this way, this will be `null`.

description

```
public String description
```

This is a description of the property. It could be `null`.

name

```
public String name
```

The name of the property.

required

```
public boolean required
```

This will be `true` if a value for this property is required by the driver.

value

```
public String value
```

This is the current value of the property. If the property value has not been specified, this will be `null`.

Constructors

```
public DriverPropertyInfo(String name,String value)
```

The constructor supplies the `name` and the `value`. The other fields default to their initial values.

Returned by

An array of `DriverPropertyInfo` objects can be acquired in a call to `Driver.getPropertyInfo()`.

 For more information about JDBC drivers, see **Driver**.

DSA

The DSA (Digital Security Algorithm) is based on the DSS (Digital Signature Standard) of the NIST (National Institute of Standards and Technology). The NIST was formerly the National Bureau of Standards.

A signature

A *digital signature* is information that is generated by using an encryption key and the body of a message. The signature is then included with the message to verify its authenticity. To check the authenticity of a message, the receiver of the message uses the public key of the signer to verify the combination of message and signature.

Building a signature

A hash value is generated for the entire body of the message. The hash value is then encrypted with the private key, and the resulting encryption is appended to the message. The receiver, using the same algorithm, recalculates the hash value from the data and compares it to the hash value he or she decrypts using the original sender's public key. It they match, the message has not been altered.

Level of security

The level of security is considered to be very strong. The estimate is that a 1,024-bit key would take 1.4E16 mips-years to crack.

The Java interfaces that define a set of DSA operations are **DSAKey**, **DSAKeyPairGenerator**, **DSAParams**, **DSAPrivateKey**, **DSAPublicKey**, and **KeyPairGenerator**.

DSAKey

interface java.security.interfaces.DSAKey

This is the interface to a DSA key.

Extended by

```
DSAPrivateKey
DSAPublicKey
```

Inheritance

```
public interface java.security.interfaces.DSAKey
```

Methods

getParams()

```
public abstract DSAParams getParams()
```

Returns the DSA-specific key parameters. These are always public values.

 For a description of DSA, see **DSA**. Also see **Key** and **Signature**.

DSAKeyPairGenerator

interface java.security.interfaces.DSAKeyPairGenerator

This is the interface to an object that is capable of generating the pair of DSA keys—one public and one private.

 This interface defines a DSA algorithm–specific initialization that can be used to override the defaults. It is not necessary to use this initialization method.

Initialize

The initialize method may be called any number of times. If the initialize method is not called, the size of the generated keys is 1,024 bits using precomputed p, q, and g parameters and with `SecureRandom` as the bit source.

Inheritance

```
public interface java.security.interfaces.DSAKeyPairGenerator
```

Methods

initialize()

```
public abstract void initialize(DSAParams params,
        SecureRandom random)
    throws InvalidParameterException
```

```
public abstract void initialize(int modlen,
        boolean genParams,SecureRandom random)
    throws InvalidParameterException
```

If `params` is specified, initializes the key pair generator using the p, q, and g values from `params` along with the DSA family parameters.

If `params` is not specified, a key of `modlen` length is generated without parameters. The value of `modlen` must be an even multiple of 8 from 512 to 1,024. If `genParms` is `true`, new values will be computed for p, q, and g. If `genParams` is `false`, the precomputed values for the specified value of `modlen` will be used — and if there are no precomputed values for the specified `modlen` value, an exception will the thrown. It is guaranteed that there will always be values for lengths of 512 and 1,024.

The `random` object is used to generate the bits for the key. An `InvalidParameterException` is thrown on a `null` or otherwise invalid parameter.

Example

This example shows how this interface can be used to generate a pair of DSA keys:

```
import java.security.*;
import java.security.interfaces.*;
public class GenerateDSA {
    public static void main(String[] arg) {
        KeyPairGenerator kpg = null;
        try {
            kpg = KeyPairGenerator.getInstance("DSA");
        } catch(NoSuchAlgorithmException e) {
            System.out.println(e);
```

```
                    System.exit(1);
                }
                SecureRandom random = new SecureRandom();
                DSAKeyPairGenerator dsakpg =
                    (DSAKeyPairGenerator)kpg;
                dsakpg.initialize(512,true,random);
                KeyPair kp = kpg.generateKeyPair();
            }
        }
```

The getInstance() method of KeyPairGenerator is called to create a generator of a DSA key. The KeyPairGenerator is then cast to a DSAKeyPairGenerator, and the initialize() method is called. Once this is done, the actual KeyPair is generated with a call to generateKeyPair().

 For a description of DSA, see **DSA**. Also see **Key** and **KeyPairGenerator**.

DSAParams

interface java.security.interfaces.DSAParams

Certain specific values are used in the calculation of a DSA key. In the definition of the encryption method, these are named q, p, and g—also called the *subprime*, the *prime*, and the *base*. This is an interface to a class that will produce this set of parameters.

Inheritance

```
        public interface java.security.interfaces.DSAParams
```

Constructors

Returned by

An object implementing this interface is returned from DSAKey.getParams().

Methods

getG()

```
        public abstract BigInteger getG()
```

Returns the base, g.

getP()

```
public abstract BigInteger getP()
```

Returns the prime, p.

getQ()

```
public abstract BigInteger getQ()
```

Returns the subprime, q.

 For a description of DSA, see **DSA**. Also see **Key** and **KeyPairGenerator**.

DSAPrivateKey

interface java.security.interfaces.DSAPrivateKey

This is the interface providing access to a DSA private key.

Inheritance

```
public interface java.security.interfaces.DSAPrivateKey
    extends DSAKey
    extends PrivateKey
```

Methods

getX()

```
public abstract BigInteger getX()
```

Returns the value of the private key.

 For a description of DSA, see **DSA**. Also see **DSAKey** and **DSAPublicKey**.

DSAPublicKey

interface java.security.interfaces.DSAPublicKey

This is the interface providing access to a DSA public key.

Inheritance

```
public interface java.security.interfaces.DSAPublicKey
```

```
extends DSAKey
extends PublicKey
```

Methods

getY()

```
public abstract BigInteger getY()
```

Returns the value of the public key.

 For a description of DSA, see **DSA**. Also see **DSAKey** and **DSAPrivateKey**.

else

 See **if**.

EmptyStackException

class java.util.EmptyStackException

An attempt was made to access data while the stack was empty. This exception is thrown by the `Stack` class.

Inheritance

```
public class java.util.EmptyStackException
    extends RuntimeException
        ⇑
    public class java.lang.RuntimeException
        extends Exception
            ⇑
        public class java.lang.Exception
            extends Throwable
                ⇑
            public class java.lang.Throwable
                implements Serializable
                extends Object
                    ⇑
                public class java.lang.Object
```

Constructors

```
public EmptyStackException()
```

 See the class **Stack**.

Enumeration

interface java.util.Enumeration

This is an interface used to set up an iteration through a list of objects. Once an enumeration object has been constructed, its methods can be used to retrieve the objects in the list one at a time.

The Implementation Will Vary

This interface has methods that all enable its contents to be accessed as members of a linear list. The actual operation could be quite different—moving from one member to the next could cause a traversal from one node to another in a binary tree, bump the index value of an array, or even read a keyed value from a file.

Implemented by

```
StringTokenizer
```

Inheritance

```
public interface java.util.Enumeration
```

Constructors

Returned by

Several classes supply Enumeration objects to list their contents. They are:

```
Acl.entries()
Acl.getPermissions()
AclEntry.permissions()
AppletContext.getApplets()
Dictionary.elements()
Dictionary.keys()
DriverManager.getDrivers()
FeatureDescriptor.attributeNames()
Group.members()
Hashtable.elements()
Hashtable.keys()
IdentityScope.identities()
ListResourceBundle.getKeys()
MenuBar.shortcuts()
Properties.propertyNames()
PropertyResourceBundle.getKeys()
ResourceBundle.getKeys()
```

```
Vector.elements()
ZipFile.entries()
```

Methods

hasMoreElements()

```
public abstract boolean hasMoreElements()
```

Returns true if a call to nextElement() would return an object. If a call to nextElement() would throw a NoSuchElementException, this method returns false.

nextElement()

```
public abstract Object nextElement()
```

Returns the next object in the list of enumerated objects and shifts the internal index to the next object in the list. If the list has been exhausted, this method will throw a NoSuchElementException.

Example 1

You will find that most container classes—classes that have the ability to contain groups of objects—have methods that return Enumeration objects that can be used to access all the objects held in the container. This example demonstrates how one of these—the one for the Vector class—can be used to access all the members of the container:

```
import java.util.*;

public class EnumVector {
    public static void main(String[] arg) {
        Vector v = new Vector();
        v.addElement("This is the first string added.");
        v.addElement("This is the second string.");
        v.addElement("The third string looks like this.");
        Enumeration enum = v.elements();
        while(enum.hasMoreElements()) {
            String string = (String)enum.nextElement();
            System.out.println(string);
        }
    }
}
```

This example constructs a Vector object and adds three Strings to it. The Vector class has the method elements(), which returns an Enumeration object containing a list of the items in the vector—in this case, it is the three strings. When constructed, an `Enumeration` object has its internal index set to the first object in the list. Each call to `nextElement()` returns a reference to the object and moves the internal index to the next one. The method `hasMoreElements()` will continue to return `true` until the index has moved past the last element.

You will notice that it is necessary to cast the object returned from `nextElement()` to an object of an appropriate type. This is necessary since an `Enumeration` operates at the object level—it is capable of enumerating objects of completely different types in the same list. The output looks like this:

```
This is the first string added.
This is the second string.
The third string looks like this.
```

Example 2

This is an example of a container supplying an `Enumeration` object. The container is a simple array of strings. The `Enumeration` is written in the form of an inner class named `EnumList`:

```
import java.util.*;
public class EnumerateMyself {
    private String string[] = {
        "The first string",
        "The second string",
        "The third string",
        "The cheerleaders"
    };
    public static void main(String[] arg) {
        EnumerateMyself em = new EnumerateMyself();
        Enumeration enum = em.getEnumeration();
        while(enum.hasMoreElements()) {
            String str = (String)enum.nextElement();
            System.out.println(str);
        }
    }
    public Enumeration getEnumeration() {
        return(new EnumList());
    }
    class EnumList implements Enumeration {
        private int index;
        EnumList() {
            index = 0;
        }
```

```
public boolean hasMoreElements() {
    return(index < string.length);
}
public Object nextElement() {
    if(index < string.length)
        return(string[index++]);
    else
        throw new NoSuchElementExcption();
}
}
}
```

The inner class `EnumList` has full access to the variables of its enclosing class, so it is able to return the strings when requested to do so. It also has the private variable `index`, which it uses to track its current position. Because `index` is private, any number of these enumeration objects can be instantiated and each one will maintain its own position in the array of strings.

 Because this example enumerates a static array of strings, the data can be modified underneath the enumerator without any problems. If, however, it is possible for items to be added and deleted from a list, it may be necessary to make `hasMoreElements()` a little smarter. It could, for example, be designed to grab a copy of the next item in the list and have `nextElement()` return the copy. Without this, it is possible that an item could be deleted between the calls to `hasMoreElements()` and `nextElement()`.

Also, if it is possible that the list could be reordered, it may be advisable for the `Enumeration` class to make its own copy of the entire list of objects. This way, the `Enumeration` would be a safe "snapshot" of the list at one point in time.

EOFException

class java.io.EOFException

This is thrown to signal that an end-of-file condition has been hit during input.

Inheritance

```
public class java.io.EOFException
    extends IOException
        ⇑
    public class java.io.IOException
        extends Exception
            ⇑
```

```
public class java.lang.Exception
    extends Throwable
         ⇑
    public class java.lang.Throwable
        implements Serializable
        extends Object
             ⇑
        public class java.lang.Object
```

Constructors

```
public EOFException()
public EOFException(String message)
```

If the message string is supplied, it is used as a detailed message describing this particular exception.

equal

=

The equal sign—more correctly called the assignment operator—is used as a command for Java to evaluate the expression to its right and place the result in the location named to its left. It will work only with the primitive types and references—array members must be assigned individually.

Combined forms of assignment

The assignment operator has other forms, in which it is combined with other binary operators. For example, a multiplication whereby the product of a and b is assigned to a can be written as

```
a = a * b;
```

or as

```
a *= b;
```

The other forms of this type of operation are:

+=	Addition
-=	Subtraction
*=	Multiplication
/=	Division
%=	Remainder
|=	Bitwise OR

&= Bitwise AND

<<= Shift left

>>= Signed shift right

>>>=Unsigned shift right

Combined forms for comparison

The equal-sign character is also used to create some of the comparison operators. None of these actually perform assignment operations. Each one evaluates the expressions to its left and right and, after performing a comparison of the results, result in a `boolean` value of `true` or `false`. The comparison operators are:

< Less than

> Greater than

<= Less than or equal to

>= Greater than or equal to

== Equal to

!= Not equal to

It is possible for data to be converted from one form to another while being moved across an equal-sign; see **conversion** and **casting**.

Error

class java.lang.Error

The `Error` class is the parent of the family of throwable classes that are intended to be caught by the system.

System-level errors

Members of this class are system-level errors that are thrown only by the virtual machine. It is possible for you to write code to catch errors—but be sure you know what you are doing because you could wind up preempting some action that should be taken by the system. Because of this fact, if you are going to catch one of these errors, it is a good idea to rethrow it after it has been caught.

Methods don't need to be declared

You never need to specify an `Error` in the `throws` clause of a method. They are defined as being *unchecked* because the compiler does not check to make sure they are handled.

Extended by

AWTError

```
LinkageError
ThreadDeath
VirtualMachineError
```

Inheritance

```
public class java.lang.Error
    extends Throwable
        ⇑
    public class java.lang.Throwable
        implements Serializable
        extends Object
            ⇑
        public class java.lang.Object
```

Constructors

```
public Error()
public Error(String message)
```

If the `message` string is supplied, it is used as the detailed message.

 For a general description of error handling, see **exception**.

escapes

An escape is a special character that, when used in a sequence of characters, alters the meaning of the character (or characters) to its right.

The backslash escape

In Java, the escape character is the backslash (\). Certain characters, when used in conjunction with the backslash, will take on a special meaning. The compiler will report an error whenever it encounters a backslash followed by any character other than *b, t, n, f, r, u, ", ', \,* or the digits *0* through *7*.

The octal escape

It is possible to use character escapes to specify numeric values. The octal escape takes the form

`'\ddd'`

where `ddd` is from one to three octal digits in the range \000 through \377. The resulting values are the base-10 numbers from 0 to 255.

The octal character escapes were included in Java to provide C and C++ com-patibility. Since the octal escapes can cover only a small range of `char` values (admittedly, an important range), it is probably best to use the Unicode escapes for consistent numeric representation of characters.

The special predefined escapes

A few specific characters can be generated by using special two-character codes. These are listed in Table E-1. They are simply a convenient shorthand form of the longer Unicode escapes.

Table E-1 Character Escape Sequences

Escape	Unicode	Name	Description
\b	\u0008	BS	Backspace
\t	\u0009	HT	Horizontal tab
\n	\u000a	LF	Line feed
\f	\u000c	FF	Form feed
\r	\u000d	CR	Carriage return
\"	\u0022	"	Double quote
\'	\u0027	'	Single quote
\\	\u005c	\	Backslash

The Unicode escapes

Whenever the Java compiler is reading source to be compiled, it translates all characters directly into Unicode 16-bit characters. At the same time, it translates the special Unicode escape sequences directly into Unicode. These escape sequences are designed to allow any Java program to be expressed in ASCII with Unicode characters inserted into it as escape sequences. A Unicode escape sequence consists of a backslash (\), the lower case letter *u*, and four hexadecimal digits, like this:

> \u*XXXX*

The hex digits can be in upper- or lowercase. There must be exactly four hex digits, or a compiler error will result.

   This Unicode escape format is not just for input. Whenever there is output and the proper Unicode printable character is not available, its six-character escape sequence should be used (this is not universally true, but it is often done this way).

Unicode escapes everywhere

A Unicode escape sequence can be used anywhere in the source code that a character can be used — the source is translated into Unicode by the Java compiler before it takes any other action. The example that follows prints eight copies of exactly the same string. Part of the source code itself is written using the Unicode escape values for the characters.

The value of tilde (~) is \u007E, and the value of a single quote (') is \u0027. These Unicode escapes can be used anywhere the characters can be used—notice that \u0022 (the double-quote character) is used to create a quoted string, and that a pair of parentheses are written as \u0029 and \u0029. The letters inside names can be inserted as escapes; note, for instance, that \u0065 is used to generate the letter e both inside the string and in the name "System" used by the compiler to reference a class:

```
public class UnicodeEscape {
    static public void main(String arg[]) {
        System.out.println
            ("The '~' is a tilde");
        System.out.println
            ("The '\u007e' is a tilde");
        System.out.println
            ("The \u0027~\u0027 is a tilde");
        System.out.println
            (\u0022The '~' is a tilde\u0022);
        System.out.println
            \u0028"The '~' is a tilde"\u0029;
        System\u002eout\u002eprintln
            ("The '~' is a tilde");
        Syst\u0065m.out.println
            ("Th\u0065 '~' is a tild\u0065");
        System.out.println
            ("The\u0020\u0027~\u0027\u0020is a tilde");
    }
}
```

The output from this program is this same line printed eight times:

```
The '~' is a tilde
```

Beware the end of the line

You should not use \u000A (line feed) or \u000D (carriage return) escape sequences inside a string. You should use \n and \r instead. This is because Java translates the Unicode characters before breaking the input line into tokens (as you can see from the preceding examples). These characters, if inserted into a string, would cause an end-of-line condition to occur in the middle of a string and would generate a very mysterious-looking compilation error.

The escape of quotes

A character literal is any character between a pair of single quotes. A character literal is also called a character constant. These are character constants:

```
'A'   'J'   '*'   '"'
```

A character constant containing a single quote looks like this:

```
'\''
```

The backslash is needed to insert a single-quote character between two single-quote characters.

In a similar fashion, it is necessary to escape the presence of a double quote inside a quoted string, like this:

```
"The \" character must be escaped."
```

If the interior double quote were not preceded with a backslash, it would terminate the string.

Escape escape

Because the backslash character is used as the escape character, it will also need to be escaped to be included as a character. A character constant of a single backslash looks like this:

```
'\\'
```

This also works for double quotes in a string, like this:

```
"The \\ character must be escaped."
```

Paired backslashes generate a single backslash—but the backslash resulting from such a pairing will *not* participate in generating escape sequences. Here is an example of what happens when the compiler processes a series of backslashes:

```
public class EscapeEscape {
    public static void main(String arg[]) {
        System.out.println("1: \u0058");
        System.out.println("2: \\u0058");
        System.out.println("3: \\\u0058");
        System.out.println("4: \\\\u0058");
    }
}
```

Each pair of backslashes generates a single backslash, and the generated backslashes are not used to build escape sequences. With an odd number of backslashes, one is left over to do the escaping. The Unicode escape \u0058 is the ASCII character X, so the output looks like this:

```
1: X
2: \u0058
3: \X
4: \\u0058
```

A \uu is just a \u

A Unicode escape can contain several u characters. The compiler combines them all into one. Here is an example:

```
public class DoubleU {
    public static void main(String arg[]) {
        System.out.println("1: \u0058");
        System.out.println("2: \uu0058");
        System.out.println("3: \uuu0058");
        System.out.println("4: \uuuu0058");
    }
}
```

Here is the output:

```
1: X
2: X
3: X
4: X
```

This characteristic makes it very handy for transforming text between ASCII and Unicode, as described next.

Transformation between ASCII and Unicode

Unicode is a 16-bit character set living in an 8-bit world. ASCII (which only takes up 7 bits) is the predominantly used character set, and the Internet has been designed to accommodate it. At times, a Unicode file must be represented in ASCII. This can be done by adding and deleting the u's in the Unicode escape sequences.

Let's say this string is written using 16-bit Unicode characters:

```
"The escape \u03a3 is the Greek letter @sigma."
```

A correct conversion from Unicode to ASCII would add a u to any existing escape sequences and convert any non-ASCII characters to escape sequences with a single u. Passing this string through a converter would result in this ASCII string:

```
"The escape \uu03a3 is the Greek letter \u03a3."
```

It could then be converted back to its original form by simply reversing the process—any escape sequences with a single u would be converted to the actual Unicode character. The others would simply have a u removed.

For more information on character sets, see **Unicode** and **ASCII**. For more on constructing strings, see **string literal**. For information on how the Java compiler reads source code, see **lexical structure**. For non–escape character constants, see **char**.

event

package java.awt.event

This package contains the set of event handlers and listeners that are derived from `AWTEvent`.

Interfaces

```
ActionListener
AdjustmentListener
ComponentListener
ContainerListener
FocusListener
ItemListener
KeyListener
MouseListener
MouseMotionListener
TextListener
WindowListener
```

Classes

```
ActionEvent
AdjustmentEvent
ComponentAdapter
ComponentEvent
ContainerAdapter
ContainerEvent
FocusAdapter
FocusEvent
InputEvent
ItemEvent
KeyAdapter
KeyEvent
MouseAdapter
MouseEvent
MouseMotionAdapter
PaintEvent
TextEvent
WindowAdapter
WindowEvent
```

Event

class java.awt.Event

This is a platform-independent class used as a packet for delivering events from the GUI to the application or applet. Subclasses of this class encapsulate mouse, keyboard, and other special events.

 The AWTEvent class should be used instead of this class. There is an old model and a new model of event handling. The new model was introduced in Java version 1.1. This class is the old model event. It is continuing to be supported so that existing software can be maintained—the two event models should not be mixed in the same program. For the new model, see AWTEvent.

The event types

Each event carries an id number that indicates its type. From its type, it can be deduced which of its other fields contain valid data. For example, keyboard events will contain values indicating which key was pressed.

Inheritance

```
public class java.awt.Event
    implements Serializable
    extends Object
        ⇑
    public class java.lang.Object
```

Variables and constants

ACTION_EVENT

```
public static final int ACTION_EVENT
```

The ID of an action event.

ALT_MASK

```
public static final int ALT_MASK
```

An indicator of a keyboard Alt key.

arg

```
public Object arg
```

An object that will contain different object types depending on the type of event.

BACK_SPACE

```
public static final int BACK_SPACE
```

The Backspace key.

CAPS_LOCK

```
public static final int CAPS_LOCK
```

The Caps Lock key.

clickCount

```
public int clickCount
```

This is a count of a number of mouse clicks when the id is MOUSE_DOWN. It will be 1 for a normal click, 2 for a double-click, and so on.

CTRL_MASK

```
public static final int CTRL_MASK
```

Indicates that the Ctrl key was being held down.

DELETE

```
public static final int DELETE
```

The Delete key.

DOWN

```
public static final int DOWN
```

The down-arrow key.

END

```
public static final int END
```

The End key.

ENTER

```
public static final int ENTER
```

The Enter key.

ESCAPE

```
public static final int ESCAPE
```

The Escape key.

evt

```
public Event evt
```

This is the next event. It can be used to link events together in a sequence.

F1

```
public static final int F1
```

The function key F1.

F2

```
public static final int F2
```

The function key F2.

F3

```
public static final int F3
```

The function key F3.

F4

```
public static final int F4
```

The function key F4.

F5

```
public static final int F5
```

The function key F5.

F6

```
public static final int F6
```

The function key F6.

F7

```
public static final int F7
```

The function key F7.

F8

```
public static final int F8
```

The function key F8.

F9

```
public static final int F9
```

The function key F9.

F10

```
public static final int F10
```

The function key F10.

F11

```
public static final int F11
```

The function key F11.

F12

```
public static final int F12
```

The function key F12.

GOT_FOCUS

```
public static final int GOT_FOCUS
```

An event id indicating that a component has gotten the keyboard/mouse focus.

HOME

```
public static final int HOME
```

The Home key.

id

```
public int id
```

The value indicating the type of event.

INSERT

```
public static final int INSERT
```

The Insert key.

key

```
public int key
```

The variable holding the key code identifying the pressed key.

KEY_ACTION

```
public static final int KEY_ACTION
```

An id number identifying the event as a key action.

KEY_ACTION_RELEASE

```
public static final int KEY_ACTION_RELEASE
```

An id number indicating that a key has been released.

KEY_PRESS

```
public static final int KEY_PRESS
```

An id number indicating that a key has been pressed.

KEY_RELEASE

```
public static final int KEY_RELEASE
```

An id number indicating a key release.

LEFT

```
public static final int LEFT
```

The left-arrow key.

LIST_DESELECT

```
public static final int LIST_DESELECT
```

An event id indicating that a list member has been deselected.

LIST_SELECT

```
public static final int LIST_SELECT
```

An event id indicating that a list member has been selected.

LOAD_FILE

```
public static final int LOAD_FILE
```

The id number of a file-loading event.

LOST_FOCUS

```
public static final int LOST_FOCUS
```

An id indicating that a component has lost the mouse/keyboard focus.

META_MASK

```
public static final int META_MASK
```

An indicator that a metakey was being held down.

modifiers

```
public int modifiers
```

The variable that holds the modifier mask values for keyboard and mouse events.

MOUSE_DOWN

```
public static final int MOUSE_DOWN
```

The id of a mouse-button-press event.

MOUSE_DRAG

```
public static final int MOUSE_DRAG
```

An event id reporting that the mouse has been moved while a button was being held down.

MOUSE_ENTER

```
public static final int MOUSE_ENTER
```

An event id indicating that the mouse pointer has entered the area of a component.

MOUSE_EXIT

```
public static final int MOUSE_EXIT
```

An event id indicating that the mouse pointer has moved out of the area of a component.

MOUSE_MOVE

```
public static final int MOUSE_MOVE
```

An event id indicating that the mouse was moved without a button being held down.

MOUSE_UP

```
public static final int MOUSE_UP
```

An event id indicating that a mouse button has been released.

NUM_LOCK

```
public static final int NUM_LOCK
```

The Num Lock key.

PAUSE

```
public static final int PAUSE
```

The Pause key.

PGDN

```
public static final int PGDN
```

The Page Down key.

PGUP

```
public static final int PGUP
```

The Page Up key.

PRINT_SCREEN

```
public static final int PRINT_SCREEN
```

The Print Screen key.

RIGHT

```
public static final int RIGHT
```

The right-arrow key.

SAVE_FILE

```
public static final int SAVE_FILE
```

The id of a file-saving event.

SCROLL_ABSOLUTE

```
public static final int SCROLL_ABSOLUTE
```

The id of an absolute-scroll event.

SCROLL_BEGIN

```
public static final int SCROLL_BEGIN
```

The id number of a scroll-begin event.

SCROLL_END

```
public static final int SCROLL_END
```

The id number of a scroll-end event.

SCROLL_LINE_DOWN

```
public static final int SCROLL_LINE_DOWN
```

The id of an event indicating a scroll down of one line.

SCROLL_LINE_UP

```
public static final int SCROLL_LINE_UP
```

The id of an event indicating a scroll up of one line.

SCROLL_LOCK

```
public static final int SCROLL_LOCK
```

The Scroll Lock key.

SCROLL_PAGE_DOWN

```
public static final int SCROLL_PAGE_DOWN
```

The id of an event indicating a scroll down of one page.

SCROLL_PAGE_UP

```
public static final int SCROLL_PAGE_UP
```

The id of an event indicating a scroll up of one page.

SHIFT_MASK

```
public static final int SHIFT_MASK
```

The mask indicating that the Shift key was held down.

TAB

```
public static final int TAB
```

The Tab key.

target

```
public Object target
```

The component that caused the event to be issued.

UP

```
public static final int UP
```

The up-arrow key.

when

```
public long when
```

The time stamp of the Event. It is a count of the number of milliseconds since January 1, 1970.

WINDOW_DEICONIFY

```
public static final int WINDOW_DEICONIFY
```

The id number of an event indicating that the window was deiconified.

WINDOW_DESTROY

```
public static final int WINDOW_DESTROY
```

The id number of an event indicating that the window has been destroyed.

WINDOW_EXPOSE

```
public static final int WINDOW_EXPOSE
```

The id number of an event indicating that the window has been exposed.

WINDOW_ICONIFY

```
public static final int WINDOW_ICONIFY
```

The id number of an event indicating that the window has been iconified.

WINDOW_MOVED

```
public static final int WINDOW_MOVED
```

The id number of an event indicating that the window has been moved.

x

```
public int x
```

The x coordinate of the event. This will indicate the mouse position.

y

```
public int y
```

The y coordinate of the event. This will indicate the mouse position.

Constructors

```
public Event(Object target,long when,int id,int x,
             int y,int key,int modifiers,Object arg)
public Event(Object target,long when,int id,int x,
```

```
                          int y,int key,int modifiers)
    public Event(Object target,int id,Object arg)
```

The constructor is overloaded because not all values are required for all events. Using a constructor that doesn't specify some value allows that value to default to zero or `null`.

The `target` component is the one that is reporting the event. The value of `when` is set to the time of the event origination. The `x` and `y` values are the pixel coordinates of the location of the event on the face of the component. The `key` is the identifying value used for keyboard events. The `modifiers` can be any combination of the mask values (defined as constants in this class) to indicate keys that were being held down. The `arg` value can be any other object necessary to supply other data required for certain other event types.

Methods

controlDown()

```
    public boolean controlDown()
```

Returns `true` if the Ctrl key was held down when the event was issued.

metaDown()

```
    public boolean metaDown()
```

Returns `true` if the meta key was held down when the event was issued.

paramString()

```
    protected String paramString()
```

Creates the underlying system-dependent peer for this object. This method is not normally called by the application. It is called by the container.

shiftDown()

```
    public boolean shiftDown()
```

Returns `true` if the Shift key was held down when the event was issued.

toString()

```
    public String toString()
```

Returns a string representation of the values of the `Event`.

translate()

```
    public void translate(int dx,int dy)
```

This method translates the internal x and y coordinates of the event by simply adding dx and dy to them. This can be used for translation of the coordinates of the Event to another location, or for mapping the coordinates into a larger containing window.

 For the newer version of event handling, see **AWTEvent**.

EventListener

interface java.util.EventListener

The interface has no methods. It is a tag interface that must be implemented by every event listener. An event listener is an object that is capable of receiving AWTEvents. This is the superinterface of the event listener interfaces in the java.awt.event package.

Extended by

```
ActionListener
ComponentListener
ContainerListener
FocusListener
ItemListener
TextListener
AdjustmentListener
KeyListener
MouseListener
MouseMotionListener
PropertyChangeListener
WindowListener
VetoableChangeListener
```

Inheritance

```
public interface java.util.EventListener
```

Constructors

Returned by

Items that implement this interface are returned from the methods addInternal(), remove(), and removeInternal() in AWTEventMulticaster.

EventObject

class java.util.EventObject

This is the superclass of `AWTEvent`. It could be considered a wrapper class for a reference to the object that is the source of an event.

Extended by

```
AWTEvent
PropertyChangeEvent
```

Inheritance

```
public class java.util.EventObject
    implements Serializable
    extends Object
        ⇑
    public class java.lang.Object
```

Variables and constants

source

```
protected transient Object source
```

This is the object that is the source of the event.

Constructors

```
public EventObject(Object source)
```

The `source` reference supplied on the constructor is held in the object and is returned with a call to `getSource()`.

Methods

getSource()

```
public Object getSource()
```

This method returns the source object that was supplied to the constructor.

toString()

```
public String toString()
```

Returns the string representation of this object.

For the subclasses of EventObject, see the **AWTEvent** class and the **java.awt.event** package.

EventQueue

class java.awt.EventQueue

This class maintains a first-in first-out list of AWTEvent objects.

Inheritance

```
public class java.awt.EventQueue
    extends Object
        ⇑
    public class java.lang.Object
```

Constructors

```
public EventQueue()
```

Returned by

An EventQueue object is returned from a call to either getSystemEventQueue() or getSystemEventQueueImpl() of Toolkit.

Methods

getNextEvent()

```
public synchronized AWTEvent getNextEvent()
    throws InterruptedException
```

Returns the oldest AWTEvent in the queue *and* removes it from the queue. This is a blocking call—if there is no event currently in the queue, this method will not return until one has been posted there by some other thread. An InterruptedException is thrown if there is an interruption by another thread.

peekEvent()

```
public synchronized AWTEvent peekEvent()

public synchronized AWTEvent peekEvent(int id)
```

Returns an AWTEvent in the queue without removing it from the queue. If the id is specified, the oldest event with that id number is returned. If the id is not specified, the oldest event in the queue is returned. This is not a blocking call—if there are no events in the queue (or matching the `id`), a `null` will be returned.

postEvent()

```
public synchronized void postEvent(AWTEvent theEvent)
```

Adds `theEvent` to the queue as the newest event.

EventSetDescriptor

class java.beans.EventSetDescriptor

This class provides access to the descriptions of the set of events that can be issued from a bean.

The naming convention

A naming pattern is assumed. The event *set name* is the name used to construct the name of the event, and to construct the name of its associated classes and methods. The set name normally begins with a lowercase letter. For example, an event set name of "fred" will deliver "FredEvent" events to an object implementing the "FredListener" interface that has been registered by a call to "addFredListener()." The event delivery will be made by calling the method of the "FredListener" object with an argument of a "FredEvent" object. The "FredListener" object can be removed from the list of listeners with a call to "removeFredListener()." Looking at the arguments on the constructors, you can see where it is possible to default to this naming convention or override it with a set of names of your own.

Inheritance

```
public class java.beans.EventSetDescriptor
    extends FeatureDescriptor
        ⇑
    public class java.beans.FeatureDescriptor
        extends Object
            ⇑
        public class java.lang.Object
```

Constructors

```
public EventSetDescriptor(Class sourceClass,
        String eventSetName,
        Class listenerType,
        String listenerMethodName)
    throws IntrospectionException
```

```
public EventSetDescriptor(Class sourceClass,
        String eventSetName,
        Class listenerType,
        String listenerMethodNames[],
        String addListenerMethodName,
        String removeListenerMethodName)
    throws IntrospectionException

public EventSetDescriptor(String eventSetName,
        Class listenerType,
        Method listenerMethods[],
        Method addListenerMethod,
        Method removeListenerMethod)
    throws IntrospectionException

public EventSetDescriptor(String eventSetName,
        Class listenerType,
        MethodDescriptor listenerMethodDescriptors[],
        Method addListenerMethod,
        Method removeListenerMethod)
    throws IntrospectionException
```

sourceClass is the class that will issue the event. eventSetName (normally beginning with a lowercase letter) is the name of the event. listenerType is the Class object of the listener of the event. listenerMethodName is the name of the method that will be called whenever the event is being issued. listenerMethodNames[] is an array of names of the methods that will be called whenever the event is being issued. addListenerMethodName and removeListenerMethodName are the names of the methods used to register and deregister listeners.

Instead of Strings, Method objects can be used to specify listenerMethods as well as addListenerMethod and RemoveListenerMethod. Also, an array of MethodDescriptor objects can be used to specify the listener methods.

An IntrospectionException will be thrown for any exception that occurs during introspection.

Returned by

A array of EventSetDescriptor objects can be returned from calls to BeanInfo.getEventSetDescriptors() and SimpleBeanInfo.getEventSetDescriptors().

Methods

getAddListenerMethod()

```
public Method getAddListenerMethod()
```

Returns the method used to register an event listener.

getListenerMethodDescriptors()

```
public MethodDescriptor[] getListenerMethodDescriptors()
```

Returns the array of listener methods that will be called to deliver the events.

getListenerMethods()

```
public Method[] getListenerMethods()
```

Returns the array of listener methods that will be called to deliver the events.

getListenerType()

```
public Class getListenerType()
```

Returns the Class object of the interface of the listener.

getRemoveListenerMethod()

```
public Method getRemoveListenerMethod()
```

Returns the method used to deregister event listeners.

isInDefaultEventSet()

```
public boolean isInDefaultEventSet()
```

Returns true if this event set is marked as being in the default set.

isUnicast()

```
public boolean isUnicast()
```

Returns true if this event is *unicast*—that is, if is sent to a single recipient instead of a list of several registrants. A unicast event is a special case.

setInDefaultEventSet()

```
public void setInDefaultEventSet(boolean setting)
```

If setting is true, this event set will be marked as being in the default set. If false, it is marked as not being in the default set. The default is true.

setUnicast()

```
public void setUnicast(boolean setting)
```

If setting is true, this event will be marked as being unicast. The default is false.

exception

The exception is the Java facility for handling error conditions.

What is an exception?

An *exception* exists in the form of an object — the same as any other object in Java. Exceptions are divided into two main groups — those that are subclasses of java.lang.Exception and those that are subclasses of java.lang.Error. They can generally be identified by their names — the names in one group always end with "Exception" (as in NoSuchMethodException), and the names in the other group always end in "Error" (as in NoSuchFieldError).

Throwing exceptions

All exceptions have one characteristic in common — they all implement Throwable, which means that any one of them can be used as an argument on the throw Java keyword. An Exception object can be thrown by any method, and if it is thrown, it must be caught somewhere.

Catching errors and exceptions

Except under the most unique of circumstances, Error exceptions should not be caught by the program. They can be caught — but you need to be sure you know what you are doing. At the very least, if you do decide to catch an Error, it would be best to rethrow it. The system may need to catch it to handle some special situations.

Checked and unchecked

Certain exceptions are not checked by the compiler. If an unchecked exception is thrown by a method, the method is not required to specify the fact in a throws clause. The class RunTimeException and all its subclasses are the unchecked exceptions — all others are checked.

Example 1

This is a very simple example of catching a thrown exception:

```
import java.io.*;
public class SimpleException {
    public static void main(String[] arg) {
        try {
            FileReader fw = new FileReader("missing.file");
        } catch(Exception e) {
            System.out.println(e);
        }
    }
}
```

The constructor of the `FileReader` throws an exception when it attempts to open the file. The example uses `catch` to catch the exception. The string form of the exception is then printed; it looks like this:

```
java.io.FileNotFoundException: missing.file
```

The code of the previous example was designed to catch any exception thrown—it catches an `Exception` object, the superclass of all exceptions. It could have been designed to catch the specific exception, like this:

```
import java.io.*;
public class SimpleException2 {
    public static void main(String[] arg) {
        try {
            FileReader fw = new FileReader("missing.file");
        } catch(FileNotFoundException e) {
            System.out.println(e);
        }
    }
}
```

Because the `FileNotFoundException` is the only one thrown by `FileReader`, the behavior of this program is the same as that of the previous one. If a circumstance arises in which a method could throw any one of several exceptions, each one could have its own `catch`, like this:

```
try {
    ...
} catch(OneKindOfException e) {
    ...
} catch(AnotherKindOfException e) {
    ...
```

This way, you can handle each exception in a different way.

Example 2

It isn't necessary to immediately catch a thrown exception. You can simply pass it on up to the method that called you. If it is a checked exception, you will find it necessary to use a `throws` expression so that the compiler will know that you are doing it:

```
import java.io.*;
public class ContinueException {
    public static void main(String[] arg) {
        try {
            openFile();
        } catch(FileNotFoundException e) {
```

```
                    System.out.println(e);
                }
            }
            public static void openFile()
                        throws FileNotFoundException {
                FileReader fw = new FileReader("missing.file");
            }
        }
```

This can be a convenient thing to do if, for example, you are opening and closing a lot of files in different places but would like to handle the exceptions in one place.

Example 3

A number of exception-clause lines of code can appear within a single `try` block. Execution of statements will continue in the `try` block until an exception is encountered, whereupon the rest of the statements will be skipped. That is, whenever an exception occurs, the `try` block exits immediately—the next thing executed will be the `catch` block:

```
import java.io.*;
public class MultiException {
    public static void main(String[] arg) {
        try {
            System.out.println("Enetered the try block.");
            FileWriter fw = new FileWriter("fred");
            System.out.println("The output file is open.");
            FileReader fr = new FileReader("missing.file");
            System.out.println("This line will not
print.");
        } catch(Exception e) {
            System.out.println(e);
        }
    }
}
```

The output looks like this:

```
Entered the try block.
The output file is open.
java.io.FileNotFoundException: missing.file
```

Each statement of the `try` block was executed until an exception was thrown, which caused execution to jump immediately to the `catch` block.

Example 4

Any code included in the finally clause of a try/catch block will be executed
every time the block is executed. This is true whether or not an exception is
thrown. It is true even if a return statement is executed. Once the block has
been entered, there is no way to escape without executing the finally clause:

```
import java.io.*;
public class FinallyException {
    public static void main(String[] arg) {
        try {
            FileReader fw = new FileReader("missing.file");
        } catch(Exception e) {
            System.out.println(e);
            return;
        } finally {
            System.out.println("This will always print");
        }
    }
}
```

This example will always print the line from the finally block, even when
the exception occurs and the return statement is executed.

Example 5

Exceptions are normal Java objects that implement the Throwable interface.
This example extends Exception (which implements Throwable) to create a
NumberTooLargeException:

```
public class SizeChecker {
    int hourNumber;
    public static void main(String[] arg) {
        SizeChecker se = new SizeChecker();
        try {
            se.setHourNumber(13);
        } catch(Exception e) {
            System.out.println(e);
        }
    }
    public void setHourNumber(int number)
            throws NumberTooLargeException {
        if(number > 12)
            throw new NumberTooLargeException(number);
        hourNumber = number;
    }
```

```
      }

      class NumberTooLargeException extends Exception {
          NumberTooLargeException(int number) {
              super("number=" + number);
          }
      }
```

The method setHourNumber() is declared as a method that will throw the NumberTooLargeException for any number greater than 12. The exception is defined with a constructor that takes the number as an argument and uses it to build a string. The call to super() will invoke the Exception constructor with the string. This is the output from the program:

```
NumberTooLargeException: number=13
```

As you can see, the Exception class appends the message string onto the end of the name of the exception to generate the output string.

The NumberTooLargeException is a normal Java class and could have included any number of variables and methods—you can make your exceptions as informative as you need them to be.

 The keywords involved in exception handling are **try, catch, finally, throw,** and **throws**. An exception object is one that is subclassed from **Exception**. The Exception class implements **Throwable**.

Exception

class java.lang.Exception

This is the superclass of all the exception classes that are used in throw, throws, and catch clauses.

Extended by

```
AclNotFoundException
AlreadyBoundException
AWTException
ClassNotFoundException
CloneNotSupportedException
DataFormatException
DigestException
IllegalAccessException
InstantiationException
InterruptedException
```

```
IntrospectionException
InvocationTargetException
IOException
KeyException
LastOwnerException
NoSuchAlgorithmException
NoSuchFieldException
NoSuchMethodException
NoSuchProviderException
NotBoundException
NotOwnerException
ParseException
PropertyVetoException
RuntimeException
ServerNotActiveException
SignatureException
SQLException
TooManyListenersException
UnsupportedFlavorException
```

Inheritance

```
public class java.lang.Exception
    extends Throwable
              ⇑
    public class java.lang.Throwable
          implements Serializable
          extends Object
                    ⇑
          public class java.lang.Object
```

Constructors

```
public Exception()
public Exception(String message)
```

If the `message` string is supplied, it is used as the detailed message.

 For examples of throwing, catching, and creating new exceptions, see **exception**.

ExceptionInInitializerError

class java.lang.ExceptionInInitializerError

This error is thrown whenever an unexpected exception occurs during the execution of a static initializer.

Inheritance

```
public class java.lang.ExceptionInInitializerError
    extends LinkageError
        ⇑
    public class java.lang.LinkageError
        extends Error
            ⇑
        public class java.lang.Error
            extends Throwable
                ⇑
            public class java.lang.Throwable
                implements Serializable
                extends Object
                    ⇑
                public class java.lang.Object
```

Constructors

```
public ExceptionInInitializerError()
public ExceptionInInitializerError(String message)
public ExceptionInInitializerError(Throwable thrown)
```

If the message string is supplied, it is used as a detailed message describing this particular exception. If thrown is supplied, it will be retained and made available through the getException() method—it can be included because this exception is always a rethrow from a previously caught exception.

Methods

getException()

```
public Throwable getException()
```

This returns the original exception that caused this one to be thrown. The original exception is the Throwable that was supplied as an argument to the constructor.

exclusive-or

 For the exclusive-or operator, see **caret**.

ExportException

class java.rmi.server.ExportException

This exception will be thrown to indicate a failed attempt was made by the server to export a remote stub.

Extended by

```
SocketSecurityException
```

Inheritance

```
public class java.rmi.server.ExportException
    extends RemoteException
        ⇑
    public class java.rmi.RemoteException
        extends IOException
            ⇑
        public class java.io.IOException
            extends Exception
                ⇑
            public class java.lang.Exception
                extends Throwable
                    ⇑
                public class java.lang.Throwable
                    implements Serializable
                    extends Object
                        ⇑
                    public class java.lang.Object
```

Constructors

```
public ExportException(String message)

public ExportException(String message,
        Exception exception)
```

If the `message` string is supplied, it is used as a detailed message describing this particular exception. If the `exception` is included, it is the one originally thrown that caused this one to be thrown.

expression

The Java language has a number of unary operators and binary operators—it even has one ternary operator.

The type of an expression

Every expression has a type. This type is a result of the combination of the types of the literals, variables, and methods used in the expression and the operators that are used on them. It is possible to mix types in an expression and have Java make type conversions (by widening or narrowing the expression members). The result will be a single type.

Operator precedence

The order in which operations are performed is determined by the precedence and associativity of the individual operators. For operators of different precedences, the one with the smaller precedence number is executed first (for example, multiplication is always performed before addition). Because two adjacent operators can have the same precedence, a tie breaker is needed. That's where associativity comes in—either the one on the left or the one on the right is chosen to go first. For example, take the expression

```
a * b / c
```

where the multiply and divide operators have the same value of 3. But they also have left-to-right (LtoR) associativity. This means that they are evaluated from left to right, so the multiplication will be performed first.

By using a pair of parentheses, you can force the order of evaluation to be something other than the normal Java default. In the preceding example, we could force the division to be performed first by enclosing it like this:

```
a * ( b / c )
```

The precedence and associativity of the Java operators are shown in Table E-2.

Table E-2   Java Operator Precedence and Associativity

Operator(s)	Precedence	Associativity	Description
( ) [ ] .	1	LtoR	The primary expression operators
++ @-	2	RtoL	Unary post- and preincrement
+ -	2	RtoL	Unary plus and minus
~	2	RtoL	One's complement
!	2	RtoL	Boolean complement
( )	2	RtoL	Casting of types
* / %	3	LtoR	Multiplication, division, and modulo
+	4	LtoR	Addition and string concatenation
-	4	LtoR	Subtraction
<< >> >>>	5	LtoR	Shift left, shift right, shift right without sign extension
< > <= >=	6	LtoR	Less than, greater than, less than or equal, greater than or equal
instanceof	6	LtoR	Type comparison
== !=	7	LtoR	Equal, not equal
&	8	LtoR	Boolean AND and bitwise AND
^	9	LtoR	Boolean XOR and bitwise XOR
|	10	LtoR	Boolean OR and bitwise OR
&&	11	LtoR	Conditional AND
||	12	LtoR	Conditional OR
? :	13	RtoL	Conditional ternary operator
= *= /= %= += -= <<= >>= >>>= &= ^= ~=	14	RtoL	Assignment operators

Operation exceptions

The integer operations have no built-in detection for overflow—whenever addition or subtraction results in a value that will not fit, the integer simply wraps around. The only integer operations that can throw exceptions are / and % (division and remainder), which will both throw an `ArithmeticException` if the right-hand operand is zero.

The floating-point operations do not produce exceptions. If there is overflow, the result is either positive or negative infinity. Any operation that has an undefined or indeterminate result will produce NaN.

Binary operator coercion rules

It is possible to perform binary operations between two different data types. A set of rules is used to convert the operands into compatible types before the operations are performed. This automatic conversion by the various operators is known as *coercion*. The coercion rules are fairly well-defined. Here is what happens:

1. If the operator is += and the left-hand operand is a String object, the right operand is converted to a String object and the right is concatenated to the left.

   Otherwise...

2. If the operator is + and either of the operands is a String, the other is converted to a String and the two are concatenated together.

   Otherwise...

3. If either operand is a double, the other operand is — if necessary — widened to a double and the result of the operation is of type double.

   Otherwise...

4. If either operand is a float, the other operand is — if necessary — widened to a float and the result of the operation is of type float.

   Otherwise...

5. If both operations are integral types, and if the operator is a shift, the shift is executed and the result is the integral type that was shifted.

   Otherwise...

6. If either operand is a long, the other operand is — if necessary — widened to a long, the operation is carried out using 64-bit precision, and the result is of type long.

   Otherwise...

7. Both operands — if necessary — are widened to ints, the operation is carried out using 32-bit precision, and the result of the operation is an int.

 For more on conversion of one type to another, see **conversion**.

extends

The extends keyword is used in Java for one class to inherit from another.

Superclass, subclass, and Object

Whenever one class extends another, the class being extended is called the *superclass* and the class doing the extending is called the *subclass*. A subclass can have only one superclass —this is called single inheritance. If no superclass is specified for a class, the default super- class of Object is used—therefore, in Java, every class except Object has a superclass.

Overriding

A method defined as having the same name and list of argument types as one in the super- class will override the one in the superclass. The only way to call the one in the superclass is to use the keyword super. For example, if the overridden method is called getMaximum(), a call to the one in the superclass will take the form super.getMaximum().

Abstract extending

If a class extends an abstract class and does not implement method bodies of all the abstract methods of its superclass, it will necessarily be an abstract class itself. That is, an abstract method, whether declared locally or inherited, will cause a class to be abstract.

Inheritance of things public and protected

The public and protected members of the superclass are inherited by the subclass. Things can be declared to be more accessible but not less accessible. That is, a protected method can be overridden to become public, but a public method cannot be overridden to become protected or private.

Constructor calling

Every constructor in a subclass will call a constructor of its superclass. This is done by using the keyword super. If a constructor is written that does not have a specific call to super() as its first line of code, the call will be automatically inserted by the compiler. It is only nec- essary to specifically insert a call to super() if you wish to call some constructor other than the default constructor.

Hiding fields

If a field in the subclass has the same name as one in the superclass, the one in the super- class is hidden. The one in the superclass is still there, and it is the one still being addressed by methods of the superclass, but it can only be referenced in the subclass by specifically using the keyword super.

Extension prevention

If a class is defined as final, it cannot be extended. If a method is defined as final, it can- not be overridden.

Interface Extensions

A class can extend another class, but a class cannot extend an interface. An interface can extend another interface, but an interface cannot extend a class. For an example of an interface extending another interface, see KeyListener. An interface can extend more than one interface— to do this, they are all included on a single extends statement and separated by commas.

 See also **class**. For a variation on extends, see **implements**. For more on communications with the superclass, see **super**.

Externalizable

interface java.io.Externalizable

This interface defines the methods that are used for writing the contents of an object to a stream and for reading a stream of previously externalized data into an object.

Storage format

The data members of an object are input and output using the methods in DataOutput and DataInput. These methods are capable of reading and writing the primitive types. The methods ObjectOutput.writeObject() and ObjectInput.readObject() are used to read and write objects, arrays, and strings. When implementing this interface, note that the method readExternal() must read the data in the same order that writeExternal() writes it.

Extended by

RemoteRef

Inheritance

```
public interface java.io.Externalizable
    extends Serializable
        ⇑
    public interface java.io.Serializable
```

Methods

readExternal()

```
public abstract void readExternal(ObjectInput input)
    throws IOException
    throws ClassNotFoundException
```

This method is used to restore the contents of the object from input. If there is no class for the object being restored, the ClassNotFoundException is thrown.

writeExternal()

```
public abstract void writeExternal(ObjectOutput output)
    throws IOException
```

This method will write the contents of the object to output.

 For examples of serialization, see **Serializable**.

factory

Some methods exist only to create and return objects of a certain type. Some of these can be termed object *factories*. Factory methods are ones that supply objects that can't be created any other way, that are very inconvenient to create in some other way, or that are being held inside another object. This is more of a concept than it is a feature of the Java language or its API.

A simple factory

A true factory method will construct an object for the sole purpose of having it returned to the caller. Examples of this are found in String and BigInteger. Each of these classes has several methods that construct objects from the supplied arguments and/or from internal values. For example, performing a concatenation on a String or performing addition on a BigInteger both require methods that produce new objects.

Access to Internal Objects

Cases arise in which an object has another object inside it, and it is possible to get a reference to the internal object via a method call. An example of this would be the getGraphics() method of an off-screen Image object. It may be possible to draw to the Image, but one must use its Graphics object to do it.

System objects

Certain objects exist at the system level and can be acquired only through calls to methods — an application simply cannot construct one. An example of this is the SecurityManager. There is never more than one SecurityManager on a system, and once it has been created and installed, it cannot be replaced. The only way to get a reference to the SecurityManager is to call System.getSecurityManager().

Containers

It could be argued that a container is not really a factory because the objects returned from it had to be created and inserted into it first. Once a container has a collection of objects, however, its access methods act very much like those of a factory.

The factory interface

Some interfaces do nothing more than define methods to be used as factories. An example of this is the URLStreamHandlerFactory interface, which defines a method that can be called to create a stream that is based on a particular protocol. In a way, this is the purest form of a factory because it will generate the constructor arguments necessary to create a proper stream.

false

keyword

This is the constant boolean value. It is part of the Java language.

FeatureDescriptor

class java.beans.FeatureDescriptor

This is the base class of the family of bean descriptor classes. It contains methods to access information common to all bean descriptors. This class also is a way for descriptive strings, and other objects, to be attached as part of the description of the feature. A descriptor is a class that contains information about one particular feature of a bean.

Extended by

```
BeanDescriptor
EventSetDescriptor
MethodDescriptor
ParameterDescriptor
PropertyDescriptor
```

Inheritance

```
public class java.beans.FeatureDescriptor
    extends Object
        ⇑
    public class java.lang.Object
```

Constructors

```
public FeatureDescriptor()
```

Methods

attributeNames()

```
public Enumeration attributeNames()
```

Returns an enumeration of the locale-independent names of the attributes that have been registered with setValue().

getDisplayName()

```
public String getDisplayName()
```

Returns a localized display name. Unless set to another string with a call to setDisplayName(), this method will return the same string as getName() would.

getName()

```
public String getName()
```

Returns the simple name of the object.

getShortDescription()

```
public String getShortDescription()
```

Returns a short description of the object. This method is normally overridden in a subclass. If it is not overriden, its default is to return the same value as getName() would.

getValue()

```
public Object getValue(String attribute)
```

Returns the object associated with the locale-independent attribute. If no attribute is found matching the argument, a null is returned.

isExpert()

```
public boolean isExpert()
```

Returns true if the feature is intended for expert users only.

isHidden()

```
public boolean isHidden()
```

Returns true if the feature is intended for automated access—to be used by software tools only—not by typical Java applications.

setDisplayName()

```
public void setDisplayName(String name)
```

Specifies the string to be returned by getDisplayName().

setExpert()

```
public void setExpert(boolean setting)
```

Determines the value to be returned by getExpert(). A setting of true indicates that this feature is for expert users only.

setHidden()

```
public void setHidden(boolean setting)
```

Determines the value to be returned by getHidden(). A setting of true indicates that this feature should only be accessed by bean manipulation tools and not made available to users.

setName()

```
public void setName(String name)
```

Specifies the string that will be returned by getName().

setShortDescription()

```
public void setShortDescription(String text)
```

Specifies the string that is to provide a short description of the feature. The descriptive text should be less that 40 characters.

setValue()

```
public void setValue(String attribute,Object value)
```

Associates the attribute and the value.

field

A variable or a constant (which is declared inside a class) is known as a *field*. See **variable**.

Field

class java.lang.reflect.Field

An object of this class provides information about—and access to—a single field within a class or an interface. That is, it *reflects* the field. The field can be the static field of a class or a dynamically allocated field of an object.

Inheritance

```
public final class java.lang.reflect.Field
    implements Member
    extends Object
        ⇑
    public class java.lang.Object
```

Constructors

Returned by

Members of this class are returned from the methods `Class.getFields()`, `Class.getField()`, `Class.getDeclaredFields()`, and `Class.getDeclaredField()`.

Methods

equals()

```
public boolean equals(Object object)
```

Returns `true` if `object` is a `Field` object that reflects the same field that this object does.

get()

```
public Object get(Object object)
    throws IllegalArgumentException
    throws IllegalAccessException
```

Returns the value of the reflected field from the specified `object`. If the value of the field is a primitive type, it will be converted to a wrapper object of the appropriate class. If the reflected field is static, the object argument is ignored and may be `null`. A `NullPointerException` is thrown for a nonstatic field and a null `object`. An `IllegalArgumentException` is thrown if `object` is not of the correct class. An `IllegalAccessException` will be thrown if access is denied.

getBoolean()

```
public boolean getBoolean(Object object)
    throws IllegalArgumentException
    throws IllegalAccessException
```

Gets the value of the reflected field as a `boolean`. An `IllegalAccessException` will be thrown if access is denied. An `IllegalArgumentException` is thrown if the field cannot be widened to `boolean`.

getByte()

```
public byte getByte(Object object)
```

```
        throws IllegalArgumentException
        throws IllegalAccessException
```

Gets the value of the reflected field as a byte. An IllegalAccessException is if access is denied. An IllegalArgumentException is thrown if the field cannot be widened to byte.

getChar()

```
public char getChar(Object object)
        throws IllegalArgumentException
        throws IllegalAccessException
```

Gets the value of the reflected field as a char. An IllegalAccessException will be thrown if access is denied. An IllegalArgumentException is thrown if the field cannot be widened to char.

getDeclaringClass()

```
public Class getDeclaringClass()
```

Returns the Class object that represents the class or interface that declares the field reflected by this Field object.

getDouble()

```
public double getDouble(Object object)
        throws IllegalArgumentException
        IllegalAccessException
```

Gets the value of the reflected field as a double. An IllegalAccessException is if access is denied. An IllegalArgumentException is thrown if the field cannot be widened to double.

getFloat()

```
public float getFloat(Object object)
        throws IllegalArgumentException
        throws IllegalAccessException
```

Gets the value of the reflected field as a float. An IllegalAccessException is if access is denied. An IllegalArgumentException is thrown if the field cannot be widened to float.

getInt()

```
public int getInt(Object object)
        throws IllegalArgumentException
        throws IllegalAccessException
```

Gets the value of the reflected field as an `int`. An `IllegalAccessException` is if access is denied. An `IllegalArgumentException` is thrown if the field cannot be widened to `int`.

getLong()

```
public long getLong(Object object)
    throws IllegalArgumentException
    throws IllegalAccessException
```

Gets the value of the reflected field as a `long`. An `IllegalAccessException` is if access is denied. An `IllegalArgumentException` is thrown if the field cannot be widened to `long`.

getModifiers()

```
public int getModifiers()
```

Returns the source-code modifiers that were used to declare the field. They are returned as an `int` in a format that can be decoded by the `Modifiers` class.

getName()

```
public String getName()
```

Returns the declared name of the reflected field.

getShort()

```
public short getShort(Object object)
    throws IllegalArgumentException
    IllegalAccessException
```

Gets the value of the reflected field as a `short`. An `IllegalAccessException` is if access is denied. An `IllegalArgumentException` is thrown if the field cannot be widened to `short`.

getType()

```
public Class getType()
```

Returns a `Class` object that represents the data type declared for the reflected field.

hashCode()

```
public int hashCode()
```

Returns a hashcode for this object. It is produced as a combination of the hashcodes of the reflected field name and the name of its declaring class.

set()

```
public void set(Object object,Object value)
    throws IllegalArgumentException
    throws IllegalAccessException
```

Places the value into the reflected field of object. If the field is a primitive type, the supplied value is expected to be a wrapper that can be unwrapped and widened to fit the field. If the reflected field is static, the object argument can be null (it is ignored). A NullPointerException will be thrown if the object is null and the field is not static. If the object is not of the correct class, or if the value is something that cannot be widened to the appropriate type, an IllegalArgumentException will be thrown. An IllegalAccessException will be thrown if access is denied or the reflected field is final.

setBoolean()

```
public void setBoolean(Object object,boolean setting)
    throws IllegalArgumentException
    throws IllegalAccessException
```

Sets the value of the reflected field to the specified setting. If the reflecting field is inaccessible, an IllegalAccessException is thrown. If the object is of the wrong class, or if setting cannot be widened to the field type, an IllegalArgumentException is thrown.

setByte()

```
public void setByte(Object object,byte value)
    throws IllegalArgumentException
    throws IllegalAccessException
```

Sets the value of the reflected field to value. If the reflecting field is inaccessible, an IllegalAccessException is thrown. If the object is of the wrong class, or if the value cannot be widened to the field type, an IllegalArgumentException is thrown.

setChar()

```
public void setChar(Object object,char value)
    throws IllegalArgumentException
    throws IllegalAccessException
```

Sets the value of the reflected field to value. If the reflecting field is inaccessible, an IllegalAccessException is thrown. If the object is of the wrong class, or if the value cannot be widened to the field type, an IllegalArgumentException is thrown.

setDouble()

```
public void setDouble(Object object,double value)
    throws IllegalArgumentException
    throws IllegalAccessException
```

Sets the value of the reflected field to value. If the reflecting field is inaccessible, an IllegalAccessException is thrown. If the object is of the wrong class, or if the value cannot be widened to the field type, an IllegalArgumentException is thrown.

setFloat()

```
public void setFloat(Object object,float value)
    throws IllegalArgumentException
    throws IllegalAccessException
```

Sets the value of the reflected field to value. If the reflecting field is inaccessible, an IllegalAccessException is thrown. If the object is of the wrong class, or if the value cannot be widened to the field type, an IllegalArgumentException is thrown.

setInt()

```
public void setInt(Object object,int value)
    throws IllegalArgumentException
    IllegalAccessException
```

Sets the value of the reflected field to value. If the reflecting field is inaccessible, an IllegalAccessException is thrown. If the object is of the wrong class, or if the value cannot be widened to the field type, an IllegalArgumentException is thrown.

setLong()

```
public void setLong(Object object,long value)
    throws IllegalArgumentException
    throws IllegalAccessException
```

Sets the value of the reflected field to value. If the reflecting field is inaccessible, an IllegalAccessException is thrown. If the object is of the wrong class, or if the value cannot be widened to the field type, an IllegalArgumentException is thrown.

setShort()

```
public void setShort(Object object,short value)
    throws IllegalArgumentException
    throws IllegalAccessException
```

Sets the value of the reflected field to value. If the reflecting field is inaccessible, an IllegalAccessException is thrown. If the object is of the wrong class, or if the value cannot be widened to the field type, an IllegalArgumentException is thrown.

toString()

```
public String toString()
```

Returns the string describing the reflected field. The string includes the field's declared modifiers, the data type, the fully qualified name of the class, and the name of the field.

Example

This example class extracts its own Field definitions, and lists the fields and their values to standard output:

```
import java.lang.reflect.*;
public class ShowFields {
    private int intValue = 22;
    public double doubleValue = 55.44;
    long longValue = 99;
    public static void main(String[] arg) {
        ShowFields sf = new ShowFields();
        Class thisClass = sf.getClass();
        Field[] fields = thisClass.getDeclaredFields();
        for(int i=0; i<fields.length; i++) {
            System.out.println(fields[i]);
            try {
                double value = fields[i].getDouble(sf);
                System.out.println(" value: " + value);
            } catch(IllegalAccessException e) {
                System.out.println
                    (" value not available");
            }
        }
    }
}
```

The output from the example looks like this:

```
private int ShowFields.intValue
  value: 22.0
public double ShowFields.doubleValue
  value: 55.44
long ShowFields.longValue
  value: 99.0
```

FieldPosition

class java.text.FieldPosition

Objects of this class are used as in/out arguments to subclasses of Format to track and control the character field positions of objects inputted for formatting. A FieldPosition object is passed to the format() method of Format to specify a particular field and becomes updated with the location of the next character in the output string.

Inheritance

```
public class java.text.FieldPosition
```

```
extends Object
        ⇑
public class java.lang.Object
```

Constructors

```
public FieldPosition(int position)
```

A FieldPosition object is constructed with a constant value used to identify a specific field within an object.

Methods

getBeginIndex()

```
public int getBeginIndex()
```

Returns the index of the first character in the produced output stream.

getEndIndex()

```
public int getEndIndex()
```

Returns the index of the first character past the end of the produced output string.

getField()

```
public int getField()
```

Returns the field-identifying number that was supplied to the constructor.

For an example, see **NumberFormat**.

File

class java.io.File

An object of this class represents a single disk file or directory. It contains the name of the file along with other information (such as type and accessibility). The file does not need to actually exist, and so this object can be instantiated before the file is created. This class is designed to be used as a convenient abstraction in referencing a file. It encapsulates all the host-dependent file-naming conventions.

The filename

The name of the file can be relative or absolute. If it is absolute, the entire path from the root of the directory system is included as part of its name. If it is relative, the file (or the directory tree in which the file resides) is in the current default directory.

The filename uses the naming conventions of the host platform. For example, a Windows path name may start with a drive letter and contain backslashes, and a UNIX path name could start with a slash and may contain slashes.

The separators

Constants occur in this class that contain the system-dependent path and file separators. The separator (sometimes called the file separator) is the character used in a path name to separate the individual directory names and the filename. The path separator is the character used in a list of path names to separate them. These differ from system to system. They are supplied as both `char` and `String` constants for convenience.

Inheritance

```
public class java.io.File
    implements Serializable
    extends Object
        ⇑
    public class java.lang.Object
```

Variables and constants

pathSeparator

```
public final static String pathSeparator
```

The system-dependent path separator string.

pathSeparatorChar

```
public final static char pathSeparatorChar
```

The system-dependent path separator character.

separator

```
public final static String separator
```

The system-dependent file separator string.

separatorChar

```
public final static char separatorChar
```

The system-dependent file separator character.

Constructors

```
public File(String pathname)
public File(File directory,String name)
public File(String path,String name)
```

The `pathname` is used to construct the object—a `null` path name will cause a `NullPointerException` to be thrown. If the directory is supplied, the path name from it has the `name` appended to it to construct a new path name for the new `File` object. A `File` object can be constructed from two strings— the first one is assumed to be the path, and the second one, the name.

The full path name to the file is constructed by combining the strings `path` and `name` by inserting a single file separator between them. This means that if the path name is already terminated with a file separator, the resulting string will have a pair of them back to back. Normally, this doesn't matter to the system, but it can be prevented by trimming the directory name with code like this:

```
if(path.endsWith(File.separator)) {
    path = path.substring(0,path.length() - sep.length());
}
```

Methods

canRead()

```
public boolean canRead()
```

Returns `true` if the file exists and is readable.

canWrite()

```
public boolean canWrite()
```

Returns `true` if the file exists and can be written to.

delete()

```
public boolean delete()
```

Deletes the file and returns `true` if the delete succeeded.

equals()

```
public boolean equals(Object object)
```

Returns `true` if `object` is a `File` object representing the same file as this one.

exists()

```
public boolean exists()
```

Returns `true` if the file exists.

getAbsolutePath()

```
public String getAbsolutePath()
```

Returns the absolute path name of the file.

getCanonicalPath()

```
public String getCanonicalPath()
        throws IOException
```

Gets the official, canonical path of the File.

getName()

```
public String getName()
```

Returns the name of the file without any path information.

getParent()

```
public String getParent()
```

Gets the name of the parent directory.

getPath()

```
public String getPath()
```

Gets the path of the file.

hashCode()

```
public int hashCode()
```

Computes the hashcode for this object.

isAbsolute()

```
public boolean isAbsolute()
```

Returns `true` if the filename is described by an absolute path name.

isDirectory()

```
public boolean isDirectory()
```

Returns `true` if the file exists and is a directory.

isFile()

```
public boolean isFile()
```

Returns `true` if the file exists and is a normal file—that is, it is not a directory.

lastModified()

```
public long lastModified()
```

Returns the last-modified date of the file. This is not an absolute time and should only be used for comparison with other modification dates.

length()

```
public long length()
```

Returns the length of the file.

list()

```
public String[] list()

public String[] list(FilenameFilter filter)
```

Returns the names of the files in a directory. The directory names "." and ".." are not included. If a filter is specified, only the names that pass the filtering are included in the list.

mkdir()

```
public boolean mkdir()
```

Creates a directory. It will return true if the creation succeeds and false on failure—if the directory already exists, it is considered a failure.

mkdirs()

```
public boolean mkdirs()
```

Creates all the directories necessary on the path required to create the directory at the deepest level. It returns true if the deepest-level directory was created, false otherwise. If the directory already exists, that is considered a failure and false is returned.

renameTo()

```
public boolean renameTo(File destination)
```

Renames the file to the name of the destination. A return of true indicates that the rename succeeded.

toString()

```
public String toString()
```

Returns the file path.

Example 1

This program will print the file separator and path separator characters for your system:

```
import java.io.*;
public class FilePathSeparators {
    public static void main(String[] arg) {
        System.out.println(
            "path separator: " + File.pathSeparator);
        System.out.println(
            "file separator: " + File.separator);
    }
}
```

On a Windows system, the output looks like this:

```
path separator: ;
file separator: \
```

On a UNIX system, the output looks like this:

```
path separator: :
file separator: /
```

Example 2

This example prints out some of the information it can find out about its own source file:

```
import java.io.*;
public class FileDescription {
    public static void main(String[] arg) {
        File file = new File("FileDescription.java");
        System.out.println("name: " + file.getName());
        System.out.println("path: " + file.getPath());
        System.out.println("absolute path: " +
                file.getAbsolutePath());
        try {
            System.out.println("canonical path: " +
                    file.getCanonicalPath());
        } catch(Exception e) {
            System.out.println("no canonical path");
        }
        System.out.println("length: " + file.length());
    }
}
```

The output looks like this:

```
name: FileDescription.java
path: FileDescription.java
```

```
absolute path: C:\jr.cd\f\FileDescription.java
canonical path: C:\jr.cd\f\FileDescription.java
length: 533
```

 For examples of using File objects to open input and output streams, see **FileInputStream**.

files

A file-naming convention followed by Java is shown in Table F-1.

Table F-1   Java File-Naming Convention

Extension	Contains
.class	A bytecode file output from the Java compiler
.DSA	A file generated by javakey as the "associated security" file used for JAR security
.jar	A Java JAR file containing compressed classes and resources
.java	A file containing the source code for Java classes
.SF	A file generated by javakey as a Signature File used in a JAR file for security
.zip	A compressed collection of .class files readable by the Java Virtual Machine

A group of special-purpose property files appear in the lib directory of the JDK that contain the word properties. The file awt.properties deals with settings for the mouse and keyboard. Font property files, such as font.properties.ja, are included for several locales. There is also a java.security file.

FileDescriptor

class java.io.FileDescriptor

This is the handle of an open device, such as a file or socket.

Standard in, standard out, and standard error

Three static file descriptors are opened whenever a Java program begins execution. These are named System.in, System.out, and System.err and are the functional equivalents of stdin, stdout, and stderr of C.

Stream access

It is unusual to access the `FileDescriptor` directly. Normally, one of the stream classes is used as an interface to a file descriptor.

Inheritance

```
public final class java.io.FileDescriptor
      extends Object
          ⇑
      public class java.lang.Object
```

Returned by

Objects of this class are returned from `DatagramSocketImpl.getFileDescriptor`, `FileInputStream.getFD`, `FileOutputStream.getFD`, `RandomAccessFile.getFD`, and `SocketImpl.getFileDescriptor`.

Variables and constants

err

```
public final static FileDescriptor err
```

The file descriptor of standard error.

in

```
public final static FileDescriptor in
```

The file descriptor of standard in.

out

```
public final static FileDescriptor out
```

The file descriptor of standard out.

Constructors

```
public FileDescriptor()
```

Methods

sync()

```
public void sync()
      throws SyncFailedException
```

This will synchronize the data held in RAM with the device. For example, if the `FileDescriptor` is for a disk file that has been opened for writing, this method will not return until all data held in RAM has been flushed to the physical disk. This method is the one used by the `flush()` and `close()` methods in the stream classes to guarantee that the data has reached its destination.

The `SyncFailedException` is thrown if it is not possible to synchronize the data in RAM with data in the device.

valid()

```
public boolean valid()
```

Returns `true` if this is a valid `FileDescriptor`.

FileDialog

class java.awt.FileDialog

This is a component class that displays a dialog box from which a filename and directory can be selected. You can expect it to have a different appearance on different operating systems because of basic differences in the file systems —but the functions it performs are the same. It deals with two separate items: the directory name and the filename. You can set both of these to specific values before displaying the window, or you can let them default to the current directory. The dialog box is modal—that is, it blocks users from accessing other windows as long as it is being displayed.

Controlling which files are listed

The default is for the window to list every file found in a directory, but it is possible to impose restrictions on which files are listed. This is done by creating a class that implements the `FilenameFilter` interface. The `FilenameFilter` interface specifies the method `accept()`, which will be called once for each file to be listed. If the `accept()` method returns `true`, the file (or directory) will be included in the list; if the return is `false`, the file will not be included.

Inheritance

```
public class java.awt.FileDialog
    extends Dialog
        ⇑
    public class java.awt.Dialog
        extends Window
            ⇑
        public class java.awt.Window
```

```
extends Container
        ⇑
public abstract class java.awt.Container
        extends Component
                ⇑
        public class java.awt.Component
                implements ImageObserver
                implements MenuContainer
                implements Serializable
                extends Object
                        ⇑
                public class java.lang.Object
```

Variables and constants

LOAD

```
public static final int LOAD
```

The constant used to indicate that the FileDialog is to be used to locate an existing file.

SAVE

```
public static final int SAVE
```

The constant used to indicate that the chosen filename is to be a writeable file that may or may not already exist.

Constructors

```
public FileDialog(Frame parent)
public FileDialog(Frame parent,String title)
public FileDialog(Frame parent,String title,int mode)
```

A FileDialog requires a Frame for its parent. The title will appear at the top of the dialog window—if not specified, it will be blank. The mode is either FileDialog.SAVE or FileDialog.LOAD—it will default to FileDialog.LOAD.

Methods

addNotify()

```
public void addNotify()
```

Creates the underlying system-dependent peer for this object. This method is not normally called by the application. It is called by the container.

getDirectory()

```
public String getDirectory()
```

Returns the selected directory.

getFile()

```
public String getFile()
```

Returns the selected file.

getFilenameFilter()

```
public FilenameFilter getFilenameFilter()
```

Returns the `FilenameFilter` being used by this dialog.

getMode()

```
public int getMode()
```

Returns the mode that was set by the constructor. It will be either `FileDialog.LOAD` or `FileDialog.SAVE`.

paramString()

```
protected String paramString()
```

Returns debugging information. The return string describes the internal state and values of this object.

setDirectory()

```
public synchronized void setDirectory(String dir)
```

Specifies the directory containing the files to be displayed. This method should be called before the dialog is displayed.

setFile()

```
public synchronized void setFile(String file)
```

Specifies the file to be used as the current selection. This method should be called before the dialog is displayed.

setFilenameFilter()

```
public synchronized void setFilenameFilter(
            FilenameFilter filter)
```

Specifies the filter to be used on the file and directory names.

setMode()

```
public void setMode(int mode)
```

Sets the mode to either FileDialog.LOAD or FileDialog.SAVE. This should be done before the dialog is displayed.

Example

This example creates a FileDialog object configured to select a filename for loading (that is, it must be an existing file) and sets its starting directory as the one entered in the main window (as shown in Figure F-1):

```
import java.awt.*;
import java.io.*;
import java.awt.event.*;
public class LoadingFiles extends Frame
        implements ActionListener {
    private TextField directoryText;
    private TextField fileText;
    public static void main(String[] arg) {
        new LoadingFiles();
    }
    LoadingFiles() {
        GridBagLayout gbl  = new GridBagLayout();
        GridBagConstraints gbc = new GridBagConstraints();
        Panel panel = new Panel();
        panel.setLayout(gbl);
        Label label = new Label("Directory: ");
        label.setAlignment(Label.RIGHT);
        panel.add(label);
        gbc.gridx = 0;
        gbc.gridy = 0;
        gbl.setConstraints(label,gbc);
        directoryText = new TextField(30);
        panel.add(directoryText);
        gbc.gridx = 1;
        gbc.gridy = 0;
        gbl.setConstraints(directoryText,gbc);
        label = new Label("File: ");
        label.setAlignment(Label.RIGHT);
        panel.add(label);
        gbc.gridx = 0;
        gbc.gridy = 1;
        gbl.setConstraints(label,gbc);
        fileText = new TextField(30);
```

```
        panel.add(fileText);
        gbc.gridx = 1;
        gbc.gridy = 1;
        gbl.setConstraints(fileText,gbc);
        add("Center",panel);
        Panel buttonPanel = new Panel();
        Button load = new Button("Load");
        load.addActionListener(this);
        buttonPanel.add("West",load);
        Button quit = new Button("Quit");
        quit.addActionListener(this);
        buttonPanel.add("East",quit);
        add("South",buttonPanel);
        pack();
        show();
    }
    public void actionPerformed(ActionEvent event) {
        if(event.getActionCommand().equals("Load")) {
            FileDialog fd = new FileDialog(this,
                    "Loading",FileDialog.LOAD);
            String dirName = directoryText.getText();
            if(dirName.length() > 0)
                fd.setDirectory(dirName);
            String fileName = fileText.getText();
            if(fileName.length() > 0)
                fd.setDirectory(dirName);
            fd.show();
            directoryText.setText(fd.getDirectory());
            fileName = fd.getFile();
            if(fileName != null)
                fileText.setText(fileName);
            else
                fileText.setText("");
        } else if(event.getActionCommand().equals("Quit"))
            {System.exit(0);
        }
    }
}
```

Figure F-1 The main window of *LoadingFiles.*

    The `show()` method is called to display the dialog, and—because the `FileDialog` is modal and takes control of the mouse and keyboard—the method does not return until the user has either made a file selection (as shown in Figure F-2) or canceled the operation. After the return from `show()`, the name of the directory is retrieved (so it can be used later as the next starting point) and the name of the file is returned. If the returned filename is `null`, no file was selected.

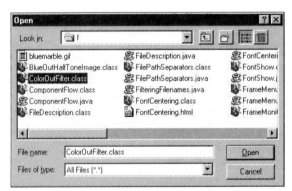

Figure F-2 The file selection window of *LoadingFiles.*

 For details and an example of restricting the listed files to specific file types, see **FilenameFilter**.

FileInputStream

class java.io.FileInputStream

    A class designed to act as a stream for reading from a file.

Extended by

`SocketInputStream`

Inheritance

```
public class java.io.FileInputStream
    extends InputStream
      ⇑
public class java.io.InputStream
    extends Object
      ⇑
    public class java.lang.Object
```

Constructors

```
public FileInputStream(String filename)
    throws FileNotFoundException

public FileInputStream(File file)
    throws FileNotFoundException

public FileInputStream(FileDescriptor descriptor)
```

A `FileInputStream` can be constructed by using the name of an existing readable file (as either a string or a `File` object), or it can be constructed using an existing file descriptor.

Methods

available()

```
public int available()
    throws IOException
```

Returns the number of bytes immediately available—the number that can be read without blocking.

close()

```
public void close()
    throws IOException
```

Terminates the input stream. This must be called to release any system-level resources associated with the stream.

finalize()

```
protected void finalize()
    throws IOException
```

Closes the stream. It is called during garbage collection.

getFD()

```
public final FileDescriptor getFD()
     throws IOException
```

Returns the FileDescriptor object being written to by this stream.

read()

```
public abstract int read()
     throws IOException

public int read(byte barray[])
     throws IOException

public int read(byte barray[],int offset,int length)
     throws IOException
```

If no argument is supplied, this will read one byte of data and return it as an int. If barray is supplied, the input data is placed in the array and the number of bytes read is returned. If offset and length are specified, the input data will appear beginning at barray[offset] for a maximum of length bytes. The default offset is 0, and the default length is the size of barray. This method will block as long as there is unread data available. A return value of −1 indicates a normal end to the input stream.

skip()

```
public long skip(long count)
     throws IOException
```

Calling this method makes a request to have the input stream skip over count number of input bytes. The return value is the actual number of bytes skipped.

Example

This example uses a FileInputStream and a FileOutputStream to copy one file to another. It gets the names of the input and output files from the command line:

```
import java.io.*;
public class FileCopy {
    public static void main(String[] arg) {
        if(arg.length != 2) {
            System.out.println("Usage: FileCopy from to");
            System.exit(1);
        }
        new FileCopy(arg[0],arg[1]);
    }
    FileCopy(String fromName,String toName) {
```

```
        try {
            FileInputStream from=openInputStream(fromName);
            FileOutputStream to=openOutputStream(toName);
            byte[] array = new byte[100];
            int count;
            while((count = from.read(array)) > 0)
                to.write(array,0,count);
            from.close();
            to.close();
        } catch(IOException e) {
            System.err.println(e);
        }
    }
    private FileInputStream openInputStream(String name)
            throws IOException {
        File file = new File(name);
        if(!file.isFile())
            throw new IOException(name +
                " is not a file.");
        if(!file.canRead())
            throw new IOException(name +
                " is not readable.");
        return(new FileInputStream(file));
    }
    private FileOutputStream openOutputStream(String name)
            throws IOException {
        File file = new File(name);
        if(file.isDirectory())
            throw new IOException(name +
                " is a directory.");
        return(new FileOutputStream(file));
    }
}
```

FilenameFilter

interface java.io.FilenameFilter

This interface is implemented by a class that wishes to determine whether certain files and/or directories are to be included in a list.

The qualifying method

When used with the `FileDialog`, the `accept()` method is called once for each file. Both the directory and the filename are supplied to the method, because the `FileDialog` allows the user to move from one directory to another and whether a file should be accepted could depend on which directory it is in.

Inheritance

```
public interface java.io.FilenameFilter
```

Constructor

Returned by

A class implementing this interface is returned from `FileDialog.getFilenameFilter()`.

Methods

accept()

```
public abstract boolean accept(File directory,String fileName)
```

The `directory` is the name of the directory containing the file `fileName`. This method returns `true` if the named file is to be included and `false` if not.

Example

This is an example of using the `FilenameFilter` with a `FileDialog` to limit the files being displayed to those that have the extension `.Java`:

 As of JDK 1.1.3, the implementation of this interface by `FileDialog` did not work properly. The `accept()` method is never actually called. This example should work once the bug is fixed.

```
import java.awt.*;
import java.io.*;
import java.awt.event.*;
public class FilteringFilenames extends Frame
        implements ActionListener, FilenameFilter {
    public static void main(String[] arg) {
        new FilteringFilenames();
    }
    FilteringFilenames() {
        Button load = new Button("filter");
        load.addActionListener(this);
```

```
        add("Center",load);
        pack();
        show();
    }
    public void actionPerformed(ActionEvent event) {
        FileDialog fd = new
            FileDialog(this,"Filtering",FileDialog.LOAD);
        fd.setFilenameFilter(this);
        fd.show();
    }
    public boolean accept(File directory,String name) {
        if(name.endsWith(".java"))
            return(true);
        return(false);
    }
}
```

 For filenames in a selection window, see **FileDialog**.

FileNameMap

interface java.net.FileNameMap

This interface defines a single method that, when given the name of a file, will return the MIME-type description of the file.

Inheritance

```
    public interface java.net.FileNameMap
```

Methods

getContentTypeFor()

```
    public abstract String getContentTypeFor(String fileName)
```

Returns a string that is the MIME description for the type of the named file.

FileNotFoundException

class java.io.FileNotFoundException

This exception is thrown to indicate that a requested file was not found.

Inheritance

```
public class java.io.FileNotFoundException
    extends IOException
        ⇑
    public class java.io.IOException
        extends Exception
            ⇑
        public class java.lang.Exception
            extends Throwable
                ⇑
            public class java.lang.Throwable
                implements Serializable
                extends Object
                    ⇑
                public class java.lang.Object
```

Constructors

```
public IOException()
public IOException(String message)
```

If the message string is supplied, it is used as a detailed message describing this particular exception.

FileOutputStream

class java.io.FileOutputStream

A class designed to act as a stream for writing to a file.

Extended by

```
SocketOutputStream
```

Inheritance

```
public class java.io.FileOutputStream
    extends OutputStream
        ⇑
    public class java.io.OutputStream
        extends Object
            ⇑
        public class java.lang.Object
```

Constructors

FileOutputStream()

```
public FileOutputStream(String filename)
    throws IOException
```

```
public FileOutputStream(String filename,boolean append)
    throws IOException
```

```
public FileOutputStream(File file)
    throws IOException
```

```
public FileOutputStream(FileDescriptor descriptor)
```

The constructor requires the name of the file. The filename is the system-dependent form of the name—for more portability, use either the File or FileDescriptor form of the constructor.

Methods

close()

```
public void close()
    throws IOException
```

Closes the output stream. It must be called to release any resources associated with the stream.

finalize()

```
protected void finalize()
    throws IOException
```

This is the method that is called when the garbage is collected. If the file has not already been closed, it will be closed by this method.

getFD()

```
public final FileDescriptor getFD()
    throws IOException
```

Returns the FileDescriptor object being read by this stream.

read()

```
public abstract int read()
    throws IOException

public int read(byte barray[])
    throws IOException

public int read(byte barray[],int offset,int length)
    throws IOException
```

If no argument is supplied, this will read one byte of data and return it as an int. If barray is supplied, the input data is placed in the array and the number of bytes read is
returned. If offset and length are specified, the input data will appear beginning at
barray[offset] for a maximum of length bytes. The default offset is 0, and the
default length is the size of barray. This method will block as long as there is unread data
available. A return value of −1 indicates a normal end to the input stream.

For an example, see **FileInputStream**.

FileReader

class java.io.FileReader

This is a convenience class (it defines no methods itself) for reading characters
from files. It provides constructors that can be used to create an
InputStreamReader without the requirement of instantiating an input stream
first.

The set of defaults

This class uses its own set of defaults for character encoding and buffer sizes. If you need
more control than this class offers, use an InputStreamReader.

Inheritance

```
public class java.io.FileReader
    extends InputStreamReader
           ⇑
    public class java.io.InputStreamReader
        extends Reader
               ⇑
        public class java.io.Reader
            extends Object
```

```
        ⇑
public class java.lang.Object
```

Constructors

```
public FileReader(String filename)
    throws FileNotFoundException

public FileReader(File file)
    throws FileNotFoundException

public FileReader(FileDescriptor descriptor)
```

A `FileReader` may be constructed based on a filename (in a host-dependent format), a `File` object, or the `descriptor` of a file that is already open.

 For an example, see **FileWriter**. Also see **FileInputStream**.

FileWriter

class java.io.FileWriter

This is a convenience class for writing to character files. It provides no output methods itself—it just provides constructors that can be used to create an `InputStreamReader` without the requirement of instantiating an input stream first.

The set of defaults

This class uses its own set of defaults for character encoding and buffer sizes. If you need more control than this class offers, use an `OutputStreamWriter`.

Inheritance

```
public class java.io.FileWriter
    extends OutputStreamWriter
        ⇑
    public class java.io.OutputStreamWriter
        extends Writer
            ⇑
        public class java.io.Writer
            extends Object
                ⇑
            public class java.lang.Object
```

Constructors

FileWriter()

```
public FileWriter(String fileName)
    throws IOException

public FileWriter(File file)
    throws IOException

public FileWriter(String fileName,boolean append)
    throws IOException

public FileWriter(FileDescriptor fd)
```

If fileName is specified, it is in the system-dependent format.

Example

This example copies its own source file into another file using FileReader and FileWriter objects. The methods read() and write() are inherited from the superclasses OutputStreamWriter and InputStreamReader:

```java
import java.io.*;
public class Duplicator {
    public static void main(String[] arg) {
        FileWriter writer;
        FileReader reader;
        try {
            reader = new FileReader("Duplicator.java");
            writer = new FileWriter("duplicate");
            int character = reader.read();
            while(character >= 0) {
                writer.write(character);
                character = reader.read();
            }
            reader.close();
            writer.close();
        } catch(IOException e) {
            System.err.println(e);
        }
    }
}
```

 Also see **FileOutputStream**.

FilteredImageSource

class java.awt.image.FilteredImageSource

This class combines an `ImageProducer` with an `ImageFilter` to create a new `ImageProducer`. The output image of the new `ImageProducer` is the output of the original `ImageProducer` after being passed through the `ImageFilter`.

Inheritance

```
public class java.awt.image.FilteredImageSource
    implements ImageProducer
    extends Object
          ⇑
    public class java.lang.Object
```

Constructors

```
public FilteredImageSource(ImageProducer producer,
        ImageFilter filter)
```

A new `ImageProducer` (in the form of a `FilteredImageSource` object) is created by piping the output of `producer` through `filter`.

Methods

addConsumer()

```
public synchronized void addConsumer(ImageConsumer consumer)
```

Adds `consumer` to the list of `ImageConsumer` objects to receive the output of the image filtering.

isConsumer()

```
public synchronized boolean isConsumer(ImageConsumer consumer)
```

Returns `true` if `consumer` is on the list to receive image data from the filter.

removeConsumer()

```
public synchronized void
        removeConsumer(ImageConsumer consumer)
```

Removes the `consumer` from the list of those to receive data from the filtering.

requestTopDownLeftRightResend()

```
public void requestTopDownLeftRightResend(
        ImageConsumer consumer)
```

This is a request from `consumer` that the data it received be delivered again—this time in top-down left-right order. This request is simply passed on to the `ImageFilter`.

startProduction()

```
public void startProduction(ImageConsumer consumer)
```

This will add `consumer` to the list of `ImageConsumer`s to receive output data and immediately start delivery of the data to the `ImageConsumer` interface.

Example

This example displays the same image three different ways, as shown in Figure F-3. The leftmost image is unaltered. The center image is displayed with the red removed. The image on the right has the green removed, and it has been shifted to a halftone image:

```java
import java.awt.*;
import java.awt.image.*;
public class MarbleFilter extends Frame {
    public static void main(String[] arg) {
        new MarbleFilter();
    }
    MarbleFilter() {
        Image marbleImage;
        try {
            marbleImage =
                getToolkit().getImage("bluemarble.gif");
            MediaTracker mt = new MediaTracker(this);
            mt.addImage(marbleImage,1);
            mt.waitForAll();
            add("West",new UnfilteredImage(marbleImage));
            add("Center",new RedOutImage(marbleImage));
            add("East",
                new BlueOutHalfToneImage(marbleImage));
        } catch(Exception e) {
            e.printStackTrace();
        }
        pack();
        show();
    }
}
```

```
class UnfilteredImage extends Canvas {
    Image image;
    UnfilteredImage(Image image) {
        this.image = image;

        setSize(image.getWidth(this),image.getHeight(this));
    }
    public void paint(Graphics g) {
        g.drawImage(image,0,0,this);
    }
}

class RedOutImage extends Canvas {
    Image image;
    RedOutImage(Image image) {
        ImageProducer ip1 = image.getSource();
        ColorOutFilter cof = new
        ColorOutFilter(0x00FF0000);
        ImageProducer ip2 =
            new FilteredImageSource(ip1,cof);
        this.image = getToolkit().createImage(ip2);

        setSize(image.getWidth(this),image.getHeight(this));
    }
    public void paint(Graphics g) {
        g.drawImage(image,0,0,this);
    }
}
class BlueOutHalfToneImage extends Canvas {
    Image image;
    BlueOutHalfToneImage(Image image) {
        ImageProducer ip1 = image.getSource();
        ColorOutFilter cof = new
        ColorOutFilter(0x0000FF00);
        ImageProducer ip2 =
            new FilteredImageSource(ip1,cof);
        HalfToneFilter htf = new HalfToneFilter();
        ImageProducer ip3 =
            new FilteredImageSource(ip2,htf);

        this.image = getToolkit().createImage(ip3);

        setSize(image.getWidth(this),image.getHeight(this));
    }
    public void paint(Graphics g) {
```

```
                    g.drawImage(image,0,0,this);
         }
    }
    class ColorOutFilter extends RGBImageFilter {
         int mask;
         ColorOutFilter(int mask) {
              this.mask = ~mask;
              canFilterIndexColorModel = true;
         }
         public int filterRGB(int x,int y,int rgb) {
              return(rgb & mask);
         }
    }
    class HalfToneFilter extends RGBImageFilter {
         HalfToneFilter() {
              canFilterIndexColorModel = true;
         }
         public int filterRGB(int x,int y,int rgb) {
              int rgbOut = rgb & 0xFF000000;
              rgbOut |= ((rgb & 0x00FF0000) > 1) & 0x00FF0000;
              rgbOut |= ((rgb & 0x0000FF00) > 1) & 0x0000FF00;
              rgbOut |= ((rgb & 0x000000FF) > 1) & 0x000000FF;
              return(rgbOut);
         }
    }
```

Figure F-3   Image filtering

The UnfilteredImage class is a simple extension of Canvas and is used to display an unmodified image. The image is supplied on the constructor; the constructor just sets its size and waits for the paint() method to be called to actually display the image.

The RedOutImage class accepts an Image as an argument to its constructor and filters the red out of the image before storing it locally. To do this, it first gets the ImageProducer of the original image. It then instantiates a ColorOutFilter object with the mask set to specify the red portion of the RGB color format. These two, ip1 and cof, are combined by instantiating a FilteredImageSource—this creates the new ImageProducer ip2. The createImage() method of the Toolkit is called to cause the actual filtering to take place. The resulting Image object is stored locally to be displayed by the paint() method.

The BlueOutHalfToneImage class has the same structure as the RedOutImage object, but it adds one more filter. The ColorOutFilter is used again (this time it removes the blue component of the RGB). The resulting ImageProducer is used as the input to another filter—the HalfToneFilter— through the instantiation of a second FilteredImageSource object. The output Image produced from this second filter is stored for later display.

The ColorOutFilter and HalfToneFilter classes are examples of extensions of the RGBImageFilter class. The ColorOutFilter has a bitmap mask that is used to zero out parts of the RGB values passed to it. The HalfToneFilter separately halves each of the three color components of the RGB.

 Other classes that deal with image filtering are **ImageFilter**, **RGBImageFilter**, **CropImageFilter**, and **ReplicateScaleFilter**.

FilterInputStream

class java.io.FilterInputStream

This class represents a filtered input byte stream. The purpose of this class is to act as the superclass in the creation of a standard set of filtering classes that can be chained sequentially in a single input stream.

Extended by

```
BufferedInputStream
CheckedInputStream
DataInputStream
DigestInputStream
InflaterInputStream
LineNumberInputStream
PushbackInputStream
```

Inheritance

```
public class java.io.FilterInputStream
    extends InputStream
        ⇑
    public class java.io.InputStream
        extends Object
            ⇑
```

```
public class java.lang.Object
```

Variables and constants

in

```
protected InputStream in
```

The actual input stream.

Constructors

FilterInputStream()

```
protected FilterInputStream(InputStream inputStream)
```

Creates a FilterInputStream object that uses inputStream.

Methods

available()

```
public abstract int available()
    throws IOException
```

Returns the number of bytes immediately available — the number that can be read without blocking.

close()

```
public void close()
    throws IOException
```

Terminates the input stream. This must be called to release any system-level resources associated with the stream.

mark()

```
public synchronized void mark(int readlimit)
```

Marks the current position in the input stream. A subsequent call to reset() will restore the input to this position. The value of readlimit specifies the number of bytes that can be read before the mark is automatically discarded. For this to work, the return value from markSupported() must be true.

markSupported()

```
public boolean markSupported()
```

Returns true if the mark() and reset() methods can be used to alter the flow of the input stream.

read()

```
public abstract int read()
    throws IOException

public int read(byte barray[])
    throws IOException

public int read(byte barray[],int offset,int length)
    throws IOException
```

If no argument is supplied, this will read one `byte` of data and return it as an `int`. If `barray` is supplied, the input data is placed in the array and the number of bytes read is returned. If `offset` and `length` are specified, the input data will appear beginning at `barray[offset]` for a maximum of `length` bytes. The default `offset` is 0, and the default `length` is the size of `barray`. This method will block as long as unread data is available. A return value of −1 indicates a normal end to the input stream.

reset()

```
public synchronized void reset()
    throws IOException
```

This will reposition the input stream to the location of the last call to `mark()`. An `IOException` is thrown if there is no active mark. A mark will be removed (causing this method to throw an exception) if more bytes have been read than the number specified on the call to `mark()`.

skip()

```
public long skip(long count)
    throws IOException
```

Calling this method makes a request to have the input stream skip over `count` number of input bytes. The return value is the actual number of bytes skipped.

FilterOutputStream

class java.io.FilterOutputStream

This class represents a filtered output byte stream. The purpose of this class is to act as the superclass in the creation of a standard set of filtering classes that can be chained in a series on a single output stream.

Extended by

```
BufferedOutputStream
CheckedOutputStream
```

```
DataOutputStream
DeflaterOutputStream
DigestOutputStream
PrintStream
```

Inheritance

```
public class java.io.FilterOutputStream
    extends OutputStream
        ⇑
    public class java.io.OutputStream
        extends Object
            ⇑
        public class java.lang.Object
```

Variables and constants

out

```
protected OutputStream out
```

The actual output stream.

Constructors

```
public FilterOutputStream(OutputStream out)
```

Constructs a FilterOutputStream based on out.

Methods

close()

```
public void close()
    throws IOException
```

Closes the output stream. It must be called to release any resources associated with the stream.

flush()

```
public void flush()
    throws IOException
```

Flushes the stream by forcing a write of any buffered output bytes.

write()

```
public void write(byte barray[])
```

```
        throws IOException
public void write(byte barray[],int offset,int length)
        throws IOException

public abstract void write(int bvalue)
        throws IOException
```

Writes one or more bytes to the output. If `bvalue` is specified, it is written as a single byte. The writing of `barray` will begin at `barray[offset]` and continue for `length` bytes. The default value for `offset` is 0, and the default `length` is the entire length of the array. The method blocks until the writing is complete.

FilterReader

class java.io.FilterReader

Abstract class for reading filtered character streams.

Extended by

```
PushbackReader
```

Inheritance

```
public abstract class java.io.FilterReader
    extends Reader
        ⇑
    public class java.io.Reader
        extends Object
            ⇑
        public class java.lang.Object
```

Variables and constants

in

```
protected Reader in
```

This is the actual input stream. It is `null` if the stream has been closed.

Constructors

```
protected FilterReader(Reader input)
```

This will create a `FilterReader` using input for its data.

Methods

close()

```
public void close()
        throws IOException
```

Closes the stream. Any attempt to access the file after this method has been called will cause an IOException to be thrown.

mark()

```
public void mark(int readlimit)
        throws IOException
```

Marks the current position in the input stream. A subsequent call to reset() will restore the input to this position. The value of readlimit specifies the number of characters that can be read before the mark is discarded. For this to work, the return value from markSupported() must be true.

markSupported()

```
public boolean markSupported()
```

Returns true if the mark() and reset() methods can be used to alter the flow of the input stream.

read()

```
public int read()
        throws IOException

public int read(char carray[],int offset,int length)
        throws IOException
```

If no argument is supplied, this will read one character and return it as an int. If carray is supplied, the input data is placed in the array and the number of characters read is returned. The input data will appear beginning at carray[offset] for a maximum of length characters. This method will block as long as there is unread data available. A return value of −1 indicates a normal end to the input stream.

ready()

```
public boolean ready()
        throws IOException
```

Returns true if there is data that can be read without blocking and false otherwise.

reset()

```
public synchronized void reset()
        throws IOException
```

This method will reposition the input stream to the location of the last call to `mark()`. An `IOException` is thrown if there is no active mark. A mark will be removed (causing this method to throw an exception) if more bytes have been read than the number specified on the call to `mark()`.

skip()

```
public long skip(long count)
    throws IOException
```

Calling this method makes a request to have the input stream skip over `count` number of input characters. The return value is the actual number of characters skipped.

FilterWriter

class java.io.FilterWriter

An abstract class for writing filtered character streams.

Inheritance

```
public abstract class java.io.FilterWriter
    extends Writer
        ⇑
public class java.io.Writer
    extends Object
        ⇑
        public class java.lang.Object
```

Variables and constants

out

```
protected Writer out
```

The actual stream to which the writing is done.

Constructors

```
protected FilterWriter(Writer output)
```

Constructs a FilterWriter using the output stream.

Methods

close()

```
public void close()
    throws IOException
```

This method will first call flush() and then close the output stream. Further calls to write() or flush() will not work. No error results from calling close() more than once.

flush()

```
public void flush()
    throws IOException
```

Writes any pending output. If there are any pending output characters anywhere in the output stream, they will be sent immediately to their final destination at the end of the stream chain.

write()

```
public void write(char carray[],
        int offset,int length)
    throws IOException
```

```
public void write(int character)
    throws IOException
```

```
public void write(String string,
        int stroffset,int strlength)
    throws IOException
```

Writes an array of characters, a string of characters, or a single character to the stream. For an array, the writing will begin at carray[offset] and continue for length characters. If string is specified, the character beginning at offset stroffset and continuing for strlength characters will be written.

final

keyword

This is used as a modifier in the definition of a class, method, or variable and has a slightly different meaning in each case. The basic idea is that nothing further can be done to modify or extend anything that is declared as final.

final class

A final class cannot be subclassed. This simply means that using its name on the extends statement of any other class will generate a compiler error.

Declaring a class as `final` will allow the compiler to generate more efficient code. Because the compiler knows that the class will never be subclassed, all of the methods in the class are implicitly final and can be called directly or generated as inline code.

 A class cannot be declared to be both `abstract` and `final`. The two declarations are in conflict since a `final` class cannot be subclassed, and subclassing is the only thing that can be done with an `abstract` class.

final method

You can effectively declare a method as final in either of two ways: by using the `final` keyword as a modifier, or by declaring it inside a final class.

A final method cannot be overridden. That is, if the class in which the final method resides is subclassed, there is no way to override the final method.

Using `final` to declare a method will enable the compiler to generate more efficient code. Since the compiler knows that the method can never be overridden, the compiler can do two things: It can generate the body of the method inline, or it can have the method be called directly without the indirection of the table that enables overriding.

final variable

A variable that is declared as final is a constant. Its contents can never be modified. This means that the declaration of a `final` variable must include an initial value or there will be a compiler error. A final declaration gives the compiler the opportunity to generate more efficient code when the value is referenced. One way it can do this is to place the constant value directly inline.

 For examples of using `final` to construct named constants, see **constant.** For the optimization that can be caused by declaring final methods, see **inline.**

finalize

 See **garbage collection.**

finally

keyword

This keyword can optionally appear as a part of the `try` clause. If it is present, it will be the last part of the clause to execute. It will execute following execution of the body of the `try` statement and the body of any of the `catch` statements.

The `finally` clause will execute whether or not an exception is thrown.

For a more information and examples, see **exception**.

float

primitive data type

The Java `float` data type is implemented as the 32-bit single precision IEEE 754-1985 standard.

Internal format

The 32 bits of a `float` have 1 bit allocated for the sign bit, an 8-bit exponent, and a 23-bit mantissa. A base-2 radix is assumed. The 32 bits of a float are allocated as shown in Figure F-4.

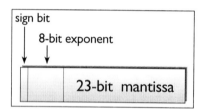

Figure F-4   The internal format of the `float` primitive data type.

The sign bit is set to 1 to indicate a negative number and 0 for a positive number.

The mantissa is a 23-bit number that has a value range from 0 to 8,388,607. With the exception of the special case of zero, at least one bit in the mantissa will always have the value of 1. The mantissa is normalized by shifting the leftmost nonzero bit completely to the left (adjusting the exponent appropriately). Since all normalized numbers are represented with their leading bit being 1, there is no need to actually include it. The mantissa is shifted left once more, moving the leading bit to the "invisible bit" position — it is assumed.

The exponent is an unsigned 8-bit value that can range in value from 0 to 255. To be able to represent both positive and negative exponents, the value is offset by 127. That is, to determine the actual value of the exponent, subtract 127 from the actual 8-bit value.

Here is how to calculate the value of a float by looking at its bits. Prepend the mantissa with a 1 and the binary point (it's base-2, not base-10), and then raise 2 to the power of the adjusted exponent. If M is the mantissa and E is the exponent, it takes this form:

```
1.M * 2^(E - 127)
```

This sample program uses the Float and Int wrapper classes to display float values in hexadecimal format:

```
public class HexFloat {
    public static void main(String arg[]) {
        HexFloat hf = new HexFloat();
        System.out.println(
            " 3.0: " + hf.toHexString(3.0f));
        System.out.println(
            " 2.0: " + hf.toHexString(2.0f));
        System.out.println(
            " 1.0: " + hf.toHexString(1.0f));
        System.out.println(
            " 0.5: " + hf.toHexString(0.5f));
    }
    final private String toHexString(float value) {
        int ivalue = Float.floatToIntBits(value);
        return(Integer.toHexString(ivalue));
    }
}
```

The output looks like this:

```
3.0: 40400000
2.0: 40000000
1.0: 3f800000
0.5: 3f000000
```

You will notice the suppression of any leading ones. The number 3 requires two leading ones, so it has a one-bit present — the other values require only a single one-bit, and it is always in the "invisible" position. The exponent value for 1.0 is 127, so, according to the formula above, it becomes 0 during calculation. The exponent for 0.5 is 126, so it will be –1 during calculation.

Special values

The largest magnitude value for a float — positive or negative — is 3.40282347e+38f. The smallest magnitude value — positive or negative — is 1.40239846e – 45f. These values are defined as positive numbers as the static constants Float.MAX_VALUE and Float.MIN_VALUE. Table F-2 lists the special values as defined by IEEE standard 754-1985.

Table F-2 Formats of IEEE 754 Double-Precision Floating Special Values

Type	Sign bit	Exponent	Value
signalling NaN	u	255 (*max*)	0uuuuu--u (*see note*)
quiet NaN	u	255 (*max*)	1uuuuu--u (*see note*)
negative infinity	1	255 (*max*)	000000--0
positive infinity	0	255 (*max*)	000000--0
negative zero	1	0	000000--0
positive zero	0	0	000000--0

Note: The letter *u* is used in the place of a bit that may be either 0 or 1. For signaling NaN, at least one of the *u* bits must be 1. The value of NaN (not a number) results from undefined operations, such as dividing 0 by 0. There is an NaN constant predefined as `Float.NaN`.

Too large and too small

If a nonzero literal value is rounded to fit into a float and is found to result in 0, a compile-time error is generated. If, however, the rounding of a small literal results in a nonzero value, the conversion is made and no compile-time error results.

Positive infinity results from overflow (a number becoming larger than that maximum value), and negative infinity results from underflow (a number becoming too small to be represented). The values of positive and negative infinity are special representations that are outside the range of the normal numbers. Java allows the value of positive infinity to be derived from expressions such as 1.0f/0.0f—or you can use the predefined constant `Float.POSITIVE_INFINITY`. Similarly, negative infinity can be entered as –1.0f/0.0f or by using the constant `Float.NEGATIVE_INFINITY`.

 For double-precision real numbers, see **double**. For the format of real literals, see **real numbers**. For a wrapper that implements some special operations, see **Float**.

Float

class java.lang.Float

This is a wrapper class for the primitive data type `float`.

Inheritance

```
public final class java.lang.Float
    extends Number
            ⇑
public class java.lang.Number
        implements Serializable
        extends Object
                ⇑
            public class java.lang.Object
```

Constants

MAX_VALUE

```
public final static float MAX_VALUE
```

The largest magnitude value that can be contained in a float. The value is 3.40282346638528860e+38.

MIN_VALUE

```
public final static float MIN_VALUE
```

The smallest magnitude value (other than 0) that can be contained in a float. The value is 1.40129846432481707e -45.

NaN

```
public final static float NaN
```

This is an IEEE not-a-number value. It cannot be successfully compared to anything — even itself.

NEGATIVE_INFINITY

```
public final static float NEGATIVE_INFINITY
```

This is a special value that will compare as less than any value other than itself.

POSITIVE_INFINITY

```
public final static float POSITIVE_INFINITY
```

This is a special value that will compare as greater than any value other than itself.

TYPE

```
public final static Class TYPE
```

This is the Class object that represents the float primitive type.

Constructors

```
public Float(double dvalue)
public Float(float fvalue)
public Float(String string)
          throws NumberFormatException
```

A value of some kind must be supplied to a constructor. If fvalue is specified, the result will be a wrapper that contains it. If dvalue is supplied, it will be cast to a float (with possible loss of precision) and the resulting value will be contained in the wrapper. If the string is specified, it will be converted to a float and there will be a wrapper for it unless the format of the string is not valid—in which case, a NumberFormatException will be thrown. The string format must be in a base-10 form with optional signs and exponentiation—it does not accept the hexadecimal or octal format.

Returned by

An object of this class is returned from the method valueOf().

Methods

byteValue()

```
public byte byteValue()
```

The internal float value is cast to a byte and returned.

doubleValue()

```
public double doubleValue()
```

The internal float value is returned as a double.

equals()

```
public boolean equals(Object obj)
```

If object is a Float object, and if the two contain the same value, a true is returned—otherwise, the method returns false. If both of them are NaN values, they are considered to be equal (contrary to the IEEE specification, which specifies that NaN values are never equal).

floatToIntBits()

```
public static int floatToIntBits(float value)
```

A float and an int are both 32-bit primitives. This method takes the bit pattern of the float and returns it—unaltered—as an int.

floatValue()

```
public float floatValue()
```

Returns the float value.

hashCode()

```
public int hashCode()
```

A hashcode for this object is returned. Two different Float objects that contain identical values will return identical hashcodes.

intBitsToFloat()

```
public static float intBitsToFloat(int bits)
```

Both a float and an int are 32-bit primitives. This method takes the bit pattern found in the int and returns it—unaltered—as a float.

intValue()

```
public int intValue()
```

The float is cast to an int and returned.

isInfinite()

```
public boolean isInfinite()
```

```
public static boolean isInfinite(float value)
```

Returns true if the value is no smaller than POSITIVE_INFINITY. If no value is supplied, the test is made against the internal value of this object.

isNaN()

```
public boolean isNaN()
```

```
public static boolean isNaN(float value)
```

Returns true if the value is an IEEE NaN (not a number). If no value is supplied, the test is made against the internal value of this object.

longValue()

```
public long longValue()
```

The internal value is cast to a long and returned.

shortValue()

```
public short shortValue()
```

The internal value is cast to a short and returned.

toString()

```
public String toString()

public static String toString(float f)
```

Returns the String form of the float. If no value is supplied, the internal value of the object is used.

valueOf()

```
public static Float valueOf(String string)
              throws NumberFormatException
```

The method converts the string into a Float object. If the number is not in a recognizable base-10 format, a NumberFormatException is thrown.

 The wrappers of the other primitive types are **Boolean, Byte, Character, Short, Long, Integer,** and **Double.** For a description of wrappers, see **wrapper.** For a discussion of the float data type, see **floating point numbers.**

floating-point numbers

Java uses the IEEE 754-1985 standard for floating-point numbers (also called real numbers). It uses the single-precision 32-bit format for float and the double-precision 64-bit format for its double type.

Literals

All real number literals are specified in base-10 digits. Table F-3 lists the characters used in forming floating-point literals. Except for the plus sign, the minus sign, and the digits, the presence of any one of the characters in the table will cause the Java compiler to assume the number is a floating-point value and convert it to either a float or a double.

Table F-3 Characters Used in Forming Literals of Real Numbers

Characters	Meaning
0–9	Base-10 digits
.	Decimal point; this can appear anywhere inside the base, not the exponent.
e or E	Exponent; this is necessary whenever an exponent is part of the literal.
f or F	Suffix indicating float
d or D	Suffix indicating double
+ or –	A plus or minus sign can be used for the base and the exponent.

The format of a floating-point literal looks like this:

`sAAA.BBBxmCCCi`

where

s	The sign of the value—this is either a plus sign or a minus sign. If neither is present, a plus sign is the default.
AAA	This is the "whole number" part of the base.
.	The decimal point. This is optional but must be present to signify the presence of a fractional portion of the base.
BBB	The fractional part of the base.
x	The exponentiation indicator is either an e or an E. It is necessary to indicate the presence of an exponent.
m	The sign of the exponent—this is either a plus sign or a minus sign. If neither is present, a plus sign is the default.
CCC	The numeric value of the exponent.
i	Either an f or F to specify float, or a d or D to specify double. The default is double.

The formal definition of the format makes it look more difficult than it really is. Here are some examples of `float` and `double` literals. All of these examples are of type `double`, except the ones that end with f or F:

```
1.0    0.1    .942    8e5    9f    32D
-44e-1 88e10  34.     .004F  -.9   +44.44E44d
```

 For 32-bit real numbers, see **float**. For 64-bit real numbers, see **double**. For real number wrappers, see **Float** and **Double**.

FlowLayout

class java.awt.FlowLayout

This layout manager places as many components as possible into the containing window. It starts in the upper-left corner placing them side by side until there is no more room across the window. It then goes down one line, returns to the left, and repeats the process— just as characters are displayed on a screen, wrapping from line to line. Any components that are left over after the window area is filled are simply not included.

Inheritance

```
public class java.awt.FlowLayout
      implements LayoutManager
      implements Serializable
      extends Object
              ⇑
      public class java.lang.Object
```

Variables and constants

CENTER

```
public static final int CENTER
```

The value used to specify that each row of components be centered.

LEFT

```
public static final int LEFT
```

The value used to specify that each row of components be left-justified.

RIGHT

```
public static final int RIGHT
```

The value used to specify that each row of components be right-justified.

Constructors

```
public FlowLayout()
public FlowLayout(int align)
public FlowLayout(int align,int hgap,int vgap)
```

The `align` value is used to position each horizontal row — the default is CENTER. The values `hgap` and `vgap` are the numbers of horizontal and vertical pixels that will be inserted for spacing between the components — the default for both of them is 5.

Methods

addLayoutComponent()

```
public void addLayoutComponent(String name,Component comp)
```

This method does nothing. For other layout managers, it will add a component to the layout.

getAlignment()

```
public int getAlignment()
```

Returns the alignment value—it is LEFT, RIGHT, or CENTER.

getHgap()

```
public int getHgap()
```

Returns the value of the horizontal gap between components.

getVgap()

```
public int getVgap()
```

Returns the value of the vertical gap between components.

layoutContainer()

```
public void layoutContainer(Container target)
```

This will cause the FlowLayout manager to do all the necessary sizing and positioning of the individual components and lay them out in the container window. The target is the container holding the components.

minimumLayoutSize()

```
public Dimension minimumLayoutSize(Container target)
```

Returns the minimum-sized window that can be used to lay out the components. The target is the container holding the components.

preferredLayoutSize()

```
public Dimension preferredLayoutSize(Container target)
```

Returns the size of the window to lay out the components with their preferred sizes and spacing. The target is the container holding the components.

removeLayoutComponent()

```
public void removeLayoutComponent(Component comp)
```

This method does nothing. For other layout managers, it can be used to remove a component.

setAlignment()

```
public void setAlignment(int align)
```

Sets the alignment of the horizontal rows of components to RIGHT, CENTER, or LEFT.

setHgap()

```
public void setHgap(int hgap)
```

Sets the number of pixels to be used in spacing the components horizontally.

setVgap()

```
public void setVgap(int vgap)
```

Sets the number of pixels to be used in spacing the components vertically.

toString()

```
public String toString()
```

Returns a string representation of the values of this object.

Example

This example adds several components to a Frame that is using a FlowLayout manager:

```
import java.awt.*;
import java.awt.event.*;
public class ComponentFlow extends Frame
        implements ActionListener {
    public static void main(String[] arg) {
        new ComponentFlow();
    }
    ComponentFlow() {
        setLayout(new FlowLayout());
        for(int i=0; i<3; i++)
            add(new Button("Button" + i));
        Choice choice = new Choice();
        choice.addItem("First item");
        choice.addItem("Second item");
        add(choice);
        add(new Label("I'm a Label"));
        Button quit = new Button("Quit");
        quit.addActionListener(this);
        add(quit);
        pack();
        show();
    }
    public void actionPerformed(ActionEvent event) {
        if(event.getActionCommand().equals("Quit")) {
            System.exit(0);
```

```
            }
        }
    }
```

Each component is added to the Frame in the order in which it is to be placed by the FlowLayout manager. Resizing the window will cause the layout manager to relocate the components to make them fit. Figures F-5 through F-7 show some different ways that the window redisplays itself after being resized.

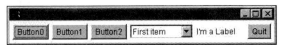

Figure F-5   The default layout of *ComponentFlow*.

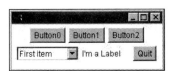

Figure F-6   The *ComponentFlow* window resized.

Figure F-7   The *ComponentFlow* window resized again.

   The other layout managers are **BorderLayout, CardLayout, GridLayout**, and **GridBagLayout**.

FocusAdapter

class java.awt.event.FocusAdapter

This is an adapter class that implements both the methods of the FocusListener interface as empty methods. Its purpose is to allow subclassing in a way only the desired methods of FocusListener need be overridden.

Inheritance

```
public abstract class FocusAdapter
     implements FocusListener
     extends Object
          ⇑
     public class java.lang.Object
```

Constructors

```
public FocusAdapter()
```

Methods

focusGained()

```
public void focusGained(FocusEvent e)
```

focusLost()

```
public void focusLost(FocusEvent e)
```

FocusEvent

class java.awt.event.FocusEvent

This event is issued whenever a component gains or loses focus.

Permanent and Temporary focus

There are two types of focus transferal. Whenever focus is lost indirectly (such as when a component's container is iconized or a modal dialog box grabs the focus), this is said to be a temporary focus change. It is temporary in the sense that some action could cause the focus to automatically default back to where it was. Whenever focus moves directly from one component to another (such as within a tab group, or a mouse selection), this is referred to as permanent. It is permanent in the sense that no action could be taken to cause the focus to "default" back to its previous location.

Inheritance

```
public class FocusEvent
     extends ComponentEvent
          ⇑
```

```
public class java.awt.event.ComponentEvent
    extends AWTEvent
         ⇑
    public class AWTEvent
        extends EventObject
             ⇑
        public class java.util.EventObject
            implements Serializable
            extends Object
                 ⇑
            public class java.lang.Object
```

Variables and constants

FOCUS_FIRST

```
public static final int FOCUS_FIRST
```

The smallest possible value of a focus event ID number.

FOCUS_GAINED

```
public static final int FOCUS_GAINED
```

The ID number of the event indicating focus has been gained.

FOCUS_LAST

```
public static final int FOCUS_LAST
```

The largest possible value of a focus event ID number.

FOCUS_LOST

```
public static final int FOCUS_LOST
```

The ID number of the event indicating that the focus has been lost.

Constructors

```
public FocusEvent(Component source,int id)
public FocusEvent(Component source,int id,boolean temporary)
```

A FocusEvent is constructed for the source component gaining or losing focus and the id number indicating gained or lost focus. If temporary is true or is not specified, this is a temporary focus change—otherwise, it is permanent.

Methods

isTemporary()

```
public boolean isTemporary()
```

Returns `true` if this is a temporary focus change.

paramString()

```
public String paramString()
```

Returns debugging information. The return string describes the internal state and values of this object.

 `FocusEvents` are retrieved by a **FocusListener**. A `FocusListener` can be implemented by extending **FocusAdapter**.

FocusListener

interface java.awt.event.FocusListener

This is the interface defining the methods used to receive the focus events of a component.

Implemented by

```
AWTEventMulticaster
FocusAdapter
```

Inheritance

```
public interface FocusListener
    extends EventListener
        ⇑
    public interface java.util.EventListener
```

Constructors

Returned by

Objects that implement this interface are returned from `AWTEventMulticaster.add()` and `AWTEventMulticastor.remove()`.

Methods

focusGained()

```
public abstract void focusGained(FocusEvent e)
```

This method is called whenever a component gains the focus.

focusLost()

```
public abstract void focusLost(FocusEvent e)
```

This method is called whenever a component loses the focus.

 A `FocusListener` can be implemented by extending **FocusAdapter**.

font

 The Java classes to define and manipulate fonts are **Font** and **FontMetrics**. To find a list of the font names, see **Toolkit**.

Font

class java.awt.Font

This class contains the definition of a displayable font.

Inheritance

```
public class java.awt.Font
    implements Serializable
    extends Object
        ⇑
    public class java.lang.Object
```

Variables and constants

BOLD

```
public static final int BOLD
```

A flag used to specify that the font be displayed as bold.

ITALIC

```
public static final int ITALIC
```

A flag used to specify that the font be displayed as italic.

name

```
protected String name
```

The name of the font.

PLAIN

```
public static final int PLAIN
```

A flag used to specify that the font be displayed as plain (neither bold nor italic).

size

```
protected int size
```

The point size of the font.

style

```
protected int style
```

This is the style of the font. It contains the flags that indicate whether the font is bold, italic, bold italic, or plain.

Constructors

```
public Font(String name,int style,int size)
```

This will create a font of the specified name. This size is the point size of the font. The style is one of these:

```
BOLD
ITALIC
BOLD | ITALIC
PLAIN
```

Returned by

Objects of this class are returned from the getFont() and decode() methods of this class. There are also getFont() methods in Component, FontMetrics, Graphics, MenuComponent, and MenuContainer.

Methods

decode()

```
public static Font decode(String fontName)
```

Returns the font specified by fontName.

equals()

```
public boolean equals(Object object)
```

Returns `true` if `object` is a `Font` object for a font with the same name, style, and point size as this one.

getFamily()

```
public String getFamily()
```

Returns a platform-specific name for this font. The name returned here could vary from one system to another, but the `getName()` method will always return the same name for the same font.

getFont()

```
public static Font getFont(String propName)
```

```
public static Font getFont(String propName,Font defaultFont)
```

If there is a property with the key `propName`, and if the name is a valid font name for this system, returns a `Font` object for it. If `propName` is not a valid name, returns `defaultFont`. If `propName` is not valid and `defaultFont` is not specified, a `null` is returned.

getName()

```
public String getName()
```

Returns the name of the font. This is the portable Java name—the method `getFamily()` will return the system-dependent name, which could be different.

getPeer()

```
public FontPeer getPeer()
```

Returns the peer object for this `Font`.

getSize()

```
public int getSize()
```

Returns the point size of the font.

getStyle()

```
public int getStyle()
```

Returns the style of the font. It is some combination of the flags defined as constants in this class.

hashCode()

```
public int hashCode()
```

Returns a hashcode for this font.

isBold()

```
public boolean isBold()
```

Returns true if this is a bold font.

isItalic()

```
public boolean isItalic()
```

Returns true if this is an italic font.

isPlain()

```
public boolean isPlain()
```

Returns true if this font is neither bold nor italic.

toString()

```
public String toString()
```

Returns a string representation of this object.

Example

This program is capable of showing all the fonts on the system in either bold, italic, or both—and in point sizes ranging from 6 to 72:

```
import java.awt.*;
import java.awt.event.*;
public class FontShow extends Frame
        implements ActionListener, ItemListener {
    private Canvas canvas;
    private Choice fontChoice;
    private Choice pointChoice;
    private Checkbox bold;
    private Checkbox italic;

    private int smallestPoint = 6;
    private int largestPoint = 72;
    private int canvasWidth = 300;
    private int canvasHeight = 100;

    private String fontName;
```

```
    private int fontStyle;
    private int pointSize;

    public static void main(String[] arg) {
        new FontShow();
    }
    FontShow() {
        canvas = new Canvas();
        canvas.setSize(canvasWidth,canvasHeight);
        add("Center",canvas);
        Panel p = new Panel();
        createFontChoice();
        p.add(fontChoice);
        createPointChoice();
        p.add(pointChoice);
        bold = new Checkbox("Bold");
        bold.addItemListener(this);
        p.add(bold);
        italic = new Checkbox("Italic");
        italic.addItemListener(this);
        p.add(italic);
        Button quit = new Button("Quit");
        quit.addActionListener(this);
        p.add(quit);
        add("South",p);
        pack();
        showString();
        show();
    }
    private void createFontChoice() {
        fontChoice = new Choice();
        fontChoice.addItemListener(this);
        String[] fontList;
        fontList =
            Toolkit.getDefaultToolkit().getFontList();
        for(int i=0; i<fontList.length; i++)
            fontChoice.addItem(fontList[i]);
        fontName = fontList[0];
    }
    private void createPointChoice() {
        pointChoice = new Choice();
        pointChoice.addItemListener(this);
        for(int i=smallestPoint; i<=largestPoint; i++)
            pointChoice.addItem(i + " pt");
```

```
                pointChoice.select("20 pt");
                pointSize = 20;
        }
        private void showString() {
                Font font = new
                Font(fontName,fontStyle,pointSize);
                Graphics gc = canvas.getGraphics();
                canvas.paint(gc);
                gc.setFont(font);
                gc.setColor(Color.black);
                gc.drawString(fontName,5,canvasHeight / 2);
        }
        public void itemStateChanged(ItemEvent event) {
                fontName = fontChoice.getSelectedItem();
                if(bold.getState() && italic.getState())
                        fontStyle = Font.BOLD | Font.ITALIC;
                else if(bold.getState())
                        fontStyle = Font.BOLD;
                else if(italic.getState())
                        fontStyle = Font.ITALIC;
                else
                        fontStyle = Font.PLAIN;
                pointSize = pointChoice.getSelectedIndex();
                pointSize += smallestPoint;
                showString();
        }
        public void actionPerformed(ActionEvent event) {
                System.exit(0);
        }
    }
}
```

The FontShow constructor builds FontShowCanvas, which will be used to display strings in various fonts. It also constructs a row of controls across the bottom of the window.

The method createFontChoice() creates a choice box that lists the names of all the fonts on the system. It gets the list of names from the system by calling the Toolkit method getFontList(). The method createPointChoice() simply sets up a selectable list of point sizes—the values 6 and 72 were chosen arbitrarily; the actual values can be beyond this range. There are checkboxes to select, or to deselect, bold and italic. Each time the user makes a selection from any of these, the itemStateChanged() method is called—it just reads all of them and calls showString() to display the string with the new settings.

The `FontShowCanvas.setValues()` method creates a new `Font` object from the settings and displays the name of the chosen font using the `Font` object created from the settings. Figure F-8 is a typical display.

Figure F-8 The *FontShow* window displaying a font.

 For a list of the font names on the local system, see **Toolkit.getFontList()**. To determine size and other font characteristics, see **FontMetrics**.

FontMetrics

class java.awt.FontMetrics

This class can be used to determine the sizes and extents of a particular font. Figure F-9 shows how measurements are made on characters of a font.

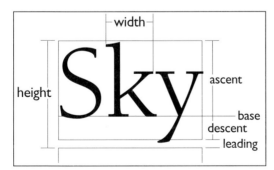

Figure F-9 Font measurements made by *FontMetrics*.

Pixels and Points

Characters, and character fonts, traditionally have their sizes defined in terms of points. A point is $\frac{1}{72}$ of an inch. This class, however, does not deal in points—it deals in pixels. The height, width, ascent, and so on are all given in pixels because that is the most useful measure for graphical purposes.

Advance

The *advance* is the total width of a string of characters. It is called the advance because it is the distance that a pixel-based cursor would move in displaying the string.

Ascent

The *ascent* is the distance measured from the baseline to the top of the characters of the font. The ascent of some characters could actually be slightly more than this. Fonts exist that have characters that go a bit above the ascent, but you can generally assume the ascent to be the top of the tallest character—the part that goes above the ascent is usually nonessential and decorative.

Descent

The *descent* is the distance measured from the baseline to the bottom of the characters of the font. The descent of some characters will be slightly more than this. Some fonts have characters that actually go a bit below the descent, but you can generally assume the descent to be the bottom of the lowest-reaching character—the part that goes below the descent is usually nonessential and decorative.

Height

The *height* of a line of text is the sum of the ascent, the descent, and the leading—effectively, it is the distance from the baseline of one line to the baseline of the next one. This is normally used as vertical spacing, but it offers no guarantee that characters will not overlap, because some fonts go beyond their ascent and descent values.

Leading

The *leading* is the vertical spacing. It is the space that would normally be left between the descent of a line of text and the ascent of the line below it.

Width

The *width* is the number of horizontal pixels consumed by a character. This width includes the spacing, if any, between the characters. In a variable-pitch font, different characters will have different widths, so simply multiplying the width of one character by the number of characters in a string will not result in the width of the string.

A note about subclassing this class

Some methods of this class perform mutual recursion. Care must be taken to prevent an infinite recursion situation when you are overriding the methods. To prevent this, a subclass should always override these methods: `getAscent()`, `getDescent()`, `getLeading()`, `getMaxAdvance()`, `charWidth()`, and `charsWidth()`.

Inheritance

```
public abstract class java.awt.FontMetrics
    implements Serializable
    extends Object
        ⇑
    public class java.lang.Object
```

Variables and constants

font

```
protected Font font
```

The `Font` object being used to extract metric information.

Constructors

```
protected FontMetrics(Font font)
```

A `FontMetrics` object is created for a specific font.

Returned by

`FontMetrics` objects are returned from calls to the `getFontMetrics()` methods in `Component`, `Graphics`, and `Toolkit`.

Methods

bytesWidth()

```
public int bytesWidth(byte data[],int offset,int length)
```

Returns the total advance (width) it would take to display `data` as a string of characters. The measurement begins with `data[offset]` and continues for `length` bytes.

charsWidth()

```
public int charsWidth(char data[],int offset,int length)
```

Returns the total advance (width) it would take to display `data` as a string of characters. The measurement begins with `data[offset]` and continues for `length` characters.

charWidth()

```
public int charWidth(int character)

public int charWidth(char character)
```

Returns the advance (width) it would take to display the single character.

getAscent()

```
public int getAscent()
```

Returns the ascent for this font.

getDescent()

```
public int getDescent()
```

Returns the descent for this font.

getFont()

```
public Font getFont()
```

Returns the Font object that was supplied on the constructor.

getHeight()

```
public int getHeight()
```

Returns the height of the font.

getLeading()

```
public int getLeading()
```

Returns the leading of the font.

getMaxAdvance()

```
public int getMaxAdvance()
```

Returns the advance (the width) of the widest character in this font. A return of −1 indicates the advance is not known.

getMaxAscent()

```
public int getMaxAscent()
```

Returns the maximum ascent value for this font. This may or may not be larger than the return from getAscent(), but it is guaranteed that no character will extend beyond this height.

getMaxDecent()   **deprecated**

```
public int getMaxDecent()
```

This method is deprecated because of the misspelling—use getMaxDescent().

getMaxDescent()

```
public int getMaxDescent()
```

Returns the minimum descent value for this font. This may or may not be larger than the return from getDescent(), but it is guaranteed that no character will extend beyond this height.

getWidths()

```
public int[] getWidths()
```

Returns the actual advance (width) of each of the first 256 characters of the font.

stringWidth()

```
public int stringWidth(String string)
```

Returns the sum of the widths of the characters in string. This will be the actual advance required to display the string.

toString()

```
public String toString()
```

Returns a string representation of this object.

Example

This example applet uses FontMetrics to display a string in the center of a window:

```
import java.awt.*;
import java.applet.*;

public class FontCentering extends Applet {
    private static final String outputString =
        "This will center";
    private static final String fontName = "Courier";
    private static final int fontStyle = Font.BOLD;
    private static final int fontSize = 35;
    private static final Color fontColor = Color.black;

    private Font font;
    private int stringY;
```

```
private int stringX;

public void init() {
    font = new Font(fontName,fontStyle,fontSize);
}
public void paint(Graphics g) {
    calculate(g);
    g.setColor(Color.lightGray);
    g.fillRect(0,0,getSize().width,getSize().height);
    g.setColor(fontColor);
    g.setFont(font);
    g.drawString(outputString,stringX,stringY);
    g.dispose();
}
private void calculate(Graphics g) {
    Rectangle rectangle = getBounds();
    FontMetrics fm = g.getFontMetrics(font);
    stringX = rectangle.width;
    stringX -= fm.stringWidth(outputString);
    stringX /= 2;
    stringY = rectangle.height;
    stringY -= fm.getAscent() + fm.getDescent();
    stringY /= 2;
    stringY += fm.getAscent();
}
}
```

The `paint` method retrieves a `Rectangle` that is the size of the displayed window and uses it to calculate the `stringX` and `stringY` locations. The horizontal position is determined by taking half the distance remaining after subtracting the width of the string from the width of the window—this value is the number of pixels left on each end of the string and is, therefore, the proper value of `stringX`. The value of `stringY` is determined from the same sort of calculation in the vertical direction. The height of the string is taken to be the sum of the ascent and the descent. This is used to calculate the vertical location of the top of the string, and then the ascent is added back to it to locate the baseline. Figure F-10 shows the result.

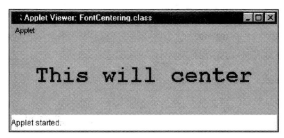

Figure F-10 The display from the *FontCentering* applet.

 To display a font, see **Graphics**.

for

keyword

The keyword for is used to create an iterative loop. The iterative test is made at the top of the loop, making it possible that the body of a for loop is never executed.

Basic syntax of the for

The for statement has three sections. The first is used for initialization, the second, for testing for completion, and the third, for adjusting values for the next iteration. The three sections are enclosed in parentheses and separated with semicolons. A simple for statement would look like this:

```
for(ival = 0; ival < 10; ival++) { ...
```

In this example, the initialization sets the variable ival to zero. The completion test is made by checking whether ival is less than 10. The value adjustment is the increment of ival.

Commas are allowed

Commas may be used to perform more than one initialization, like this:

```
for(ival = 0, jval = 0;...;...) { ...
```

It is also valid to use commas in the third part of the statement to perform more than one variable adjustment, like this:

```
for(...;...;ival++, jval--) { ...
```

Commas may not be used in the test section—it must consist of a single expression that results in a boolean data type.

Special scoping rule

A special case involves variable scoping in the for statement. Normally, a block will begin whenever a left brace ({) is encountered and will end with its companion right brace (}). A for statement works the same way, except that the region inside the parentheses is also included in the scope. For example:

```
for(int k=0; k<20; k++) {
    System.out.println("k=" + k);
}

System.out.println("Final: k=" + k);
```

The println() statement inside the loop will print all the values of k, as you would expect. However, the println() statement outside the loop will generate a compile error, since the scope of k ends with the closing brace of the loop.

Unlabeled break and continue

There are two ways to abruptly abandon a for loop. The break statement will exit the loop immediately and continue with the next line of code below it. The continue statement will drop immediately to the bottom of the loop to perform an update of the variables and then on to the top of the loop to perform the test again.

Labeled break and continue

Circumstances arise in which you must break out of nested loops (or other nested blocks). This can be done with a labeled break or continue. Here is an example:

```
outer: for(int i=0; i<10;i++) {
    for(int j=0; j<20; j++) {
        . . .
        if(mm[i][j] == -1)
            break outer;
    }
}
```

The code in this nested loop finds that it needs to break both the inner and outer for loops. If it were to execute a normal break, the outer loop would continue with its next iteration. The label outer in the break statement tells Java that the outer loop should be broken as well.

The same sort of labeling works with the continue statement, as shown in this example:

```
outer: for(int i=0; i<10;i++) {
    for(int j=0; j<20; j++) {
        . . .
        if(mm[i][j] == -1)
            continue outer;
    }
}
```

Because of the labeling, this example actually breaks out of the inner loop and continues the outer loop with its next iteration.

 For more on scoping, see **scope**.

forward reference

Generally speaking, Java resolves forward references. There is just one case where a forward reference will cause a compile error. Constants and variables must be declared before they are used in a block of code—this is true for both class-level and method-level variables. This is the only forward reference restriction in the language. Classes and interfaces can be declared in any order inside a file, and methods can be declared in any order inside a class.

 If you think of data declarations as executable statements designed to bring data items into existence in the order in which they are declared, this all makes sense. Methods, on the other hand, are created by the compiler and sit in the class waiting to be called—there is no real order required for them to come into existence at runtime.

Format

class java.text.Format

This is an abstract class that is used as a basis for classes that are to format data based on locale information—things like dates and numbers.

Subclassing

As a minimum, subclasses must implement two methods. The format() method is used to convert an object to a string, and parseObject() converts that string back into an object.

Most subclasses implement getInstance(), which returns a Format object appropriate for the locale. Some subclasses will also implement methods for returning specialized Format objects (such as the getDateTimeInstance() method of the DateFormat class and the getPercentInstance() of the NumberFormat class).

If the subclass is to allow the creation of objects for specific locales, it will be necessary to implement getAvailableLocales() to return an array of available locales.

Extended by

```
DateFormat
MessageFormat
NumberFormat
```

Inheritance

```
public abstract class java.text.Format
    implements Serializable
    implements Cloneable
    extends Object
        ⇑
    public class java.lang.Object
```

Constructors

```
public Format()
```

Returned by

An array of Format objects is returned from MessageFormat.getFormats().

Methods

clone()

```
public Object clone()
```

Creates a new object of the same class as this.

format()

```
public final String format(Object object)
```

```
public abstract StringBuffer format(Object object,
        StringBuffer appendTo,FieldPosition position)
```

Uses the data contained in the object to produce a character string. Subclasses should override the StringBuffer version to format a particular object. The argument appendTo will be returned with the newly created string appended to it.

An IllegalArgumentException is thrown if no formatting is defined for the object type specified. If formatting is defined for the object type but there is something malformed about the object, the character '\uFFFD' will be inserted (this is the Unicode replacement character).

parseObject()

```
public abstract Object parseObject(String source,
        ParsePosition position)
```

```
public Object parseObject(String source)
    throws ParseException
```

Reads the `source` string and converts the data into an object. The `position` is passed in containing the index into the `source` for the first character to be read. On return, `position` is set to next character after the last one used by this method. If an error occurs, `position` is unchanged. Leading white space is skipped, but on return, `position` will be set to the beginning of any trailing white space.

A subclass that overloads the form without a `ParsePosition` argument should throw a `ParseException` to indicate that no text was found in the source string. The return value can also be `null` to indicate an error.

It is possible to override this method to return several different types of objects. The type of the returned object can simply be determined by whatever is encountered in the input `source` string. In this case, it is the responsibility of the caller to sort them out.

For an example of a subclass that formats dates, see **DateFormat**. For a subclass that formats messages, see **MessageFormat**. For a subclass that formats numbers, see **NumberFormat**. Also see **ParsePosition** and **FieldPosition**.

Frame

class java.awt.Frame

A top-level window. It has a title bar and a border—and the capability of containing a menu. It was designed to be the main window of an application.

Layout manager

The default layout manager is `BorderLayout`.

Events

The events generated by a `Frame` are `WindowOpened`, `WindowClosing`, `WindowClosed`, `WindowIconified`, `WindowDeiconified`, `WindowActivated`, and `WindowDeactivated`.

Cursors

A set of cursor constants is defined for `Frame`s—the same set that is defined in the `Cursor` class. The methods to define cursors in the `Frame` class have been deprecated because cursor setting is now done at the `Component` level. Even though these are not officially deprecated, it would probably be best to use the constants in `Cursor`.

Inheritance

```
public class java.awt.Frame
```

```
          implements MenuContainer
          extends Window
               ⇑
          public class java.awt.Window
               extends Container
                    ⇑
               public abstract class java.awt.Container
                    extends Component
                         ⇑
                    public abstract class java.awt.Component
                         implements ImageObserver
                         implements MenuContainer
                         implements Serializable
                         extends Object
                              ⇑
                         public class java.lang.Object
```

Variables and constants

CROSSHAIR_CURSOR

```
public static final int CROSSHAIR_CURSOR
```

The crosshair cursor.

DEFAULT_CURSOR

```
public static final int DEFAULT_CURSOR
```

The default cursor.

E_RESIZE_CURSOR

```
public static final int E_RESIZE_CURSOR
```

The east resize cursor.

HAND_CURSOR

```
public static final int HAND_CURSOR
```

The hand cursor.

MOVE_CURSOR

```
public static final int MOVE_CURSOR
```

The move cursor.

N_RESIZE_CURSOR

```
public static final int N_RESIZE_CURSOR
```

The north resize cursor.

NE_RESIZE_CURSOR

```
public static final int NE_RESIZE_CURSOR
```

The northeast resize cursor.

NW_RESIZE_CURSOR

```
public static final int NW_RESIZE_CURSOR
```

The northwest resize cursor.

S_RESIZE_CURSOR

```
public static final int S_RESIZE_CURSOR
```

The south resize cursor.

SE_RESIZE_CURSOR

```
public static final int SE_RESIZE_CURSOR
```

The southeast resize cursor.

SW_RESIZE_CURSOR

```
public static final int SW_RESIZE_CURSOR
```

The southwest resize cursor.

TEXT_CURSOR

```
public static final int TEXT_CURSOR
```

The text cursor.

W_RESIZE_CURSOR

```
public static final int W_RESIZE_CURSOR
```

The west resize cursor.

WAIT_CURSOR

```
public static final int WAIT_CURSOR
```

The wait cursor.

e
f
g

Constructors

```
public Frame()
public Frame(String title)
```

A newly constructed Frame is initially not visible. If a title is supplied to the constructor, it will be displayed by the Frame at the top of the window.

Methods

addNotify()

```
public void addNotify()
```

Creates the underlying system-dependent peer for this object. This method is not normally called by the application. It is called by the container.

dispose()

```
public synchronized void dispose()
```

Disposes of the Frame and releases all its resources. This will also dispose of all components owned by the Frame.

getCursorType()   **deprecated**

```
public int getCursorType()
```

Returns the current cursor. This method is deprecated—use Component.getCursor().

getIconImage()

```
public Image getIconImage()
```

Returns the Image object being used as the icon for this Frame.

getMenuBar()

```
public MenuBar getMenuBar()
```

Returns the MenuBar of this Frame.

getTitle()

```
public String getTitle()
```

Returns the Frame title string.

isResizable()

```
public boolean isResizable()
```

Returns true if the Frame can be resized.

paramString()

```
protected String paramString()
```

Returns debugging information. The return string describes the internal state and values of this object.

remove()

```
public synchronized void remove(MenuComponent m)
```

Removes the MenuComponent from this Frame.

setCursor()

```
public synchronized void setCursor(int cursorType)
```

Sets the current cursor. This method is deprecated — use Component.setCursor().

setIconImage()

```
public synchronized void setIconImage(Image image)
```

Specifies the image to be used as an icon for this Frame.

setMenuBar()

```
public synchronized void setMenuBar(MenuBar mb)
```

Specifies the MenuBar to be used by this Frame.

setResizable()

```
public synchronized void setResizable(boolean setting)
```

Sets the resizable flag. A setting of true indicates that the Frame can be resized — a setting of false indicates that its size must remain constant.

setTitle()

```
public synchronized void setTitle(String title)
```

Specifies the title string to be used on the bar at the top of the Frame.

Example 1

Here is a simple Frame with a menu that can be used to select the cursors:

```
import java.awt.*;
import java.awt.event.*;
public class FrameMenu extends Frame
        implements ActionListener {
    String[] cursorName = {
```

```
                "Crosshair", "Default", "Hand",
                "Text", "Wait"
        };
        public static void main(String[] arg) {
            new FrameMenu();
        }
        FrameMenu() {
            super("Frame Menu");
            MenuItem menuItem;
            MenuBar menubar = new MenuBar();
            Menu fileMenu = new Menu("File");
            menuItem = new MenuItem("Exit");
            menuItem.addActionListener(this);
            fileMenu.add(menuItem);
            menubar.add(fileMenu);
            Menu cursorMenu = new Menu("Cursor");
            for(int i=0; i<cursorName.length; i++) {
                menuItem = new MenuItem(cursorName[i]);
                menuItem.addActionListener(this);
                cursorMenu.add(menuItem);
            }
            menubar.add(cursorMenu);
            setMenuBar(menubar);
            Canvas canvas = new Canvas();
            canvas.setSize(250,250);
            add("Center",canvas);
            pack();
            show();
        }
        public void actionPerformed(ActionEvent event) {
            if(event.getActionCommand().equals("Exit"))
                System.exit(0);
            else
    if(event.getActionCommand().equals("Crosshair"))
                setCursor(new Cursor(Cursor.CROSSHAIR_CURSOR));
            else if(event.getActionCommand().equals("Default"))
                setCursor(new Cursor(Cursor.DEFAULT_CURSOR));
            else if(event.getActionCommand().equals("Hand"))
                setCursor(new Cursor(Cursor.HAND_CURSOR));
            else if(event.getActionCommand().equals("Move"))
                setCursor(new Cursor(Cursor.MOVE_CURSOR));
            else if(event.getActionCommand().equals("Text"))
                setCursor(new Cursor(Cursor.TEXT_CURSOR));
            else if(event.getActionCommand().equals("Wait"))
```

```
        setCursor(new Cursor(Cursor.WAIT_CURSOR));
    }
}
```

As shown in Figure F-11, this example is intended to display the mechanics of constructing a `Frame` with a menu; the `actionPerformed()` method is used to respond to the user's menu requests. Selecting an entry from the Cursor menu will change the displayed cursor of the `Frame`, and the `Exit` menu selection will shut down the program.

Figure F-11 *FrameMenu* with its menu showing.

Example 2

A `Frame` normally displays the system menu and/or buttons, and there is usually an Exit button somewhere that needs to be honored. The actual appearance of the display, and which capabilities exist, will vary from one operating system to another. This example shows a way of receiving the event issued when the user requests that the window be closed:

```
import java.awt.*;
import java.awt.event.*;
public class FrameSystemKill extends Frame {
    public static void main(String[] arg) {
        new FrameSystemKill();
    }
    FrameSystemKill() {
        enableEvents(AWTEvent.WINDOW_EVENT_MASK);
        add("Center",new Button("Do Nothing"));
        pack();
        show();
    }
    public void processWindowEvent(WindowEvent event) {
        if(event.getID() == WindowEvent.WINDOW_CLOSING)
            System.exit(0);
    }
}
```

The method `enableEvents()` is called with the `WINDOW_EVENT_MASK` to request that `WindowEvent` events be delivered to this object. This means that the method `processWindowEvent()` will be called with every event from the window. The event `WINDOW_CLOSING` is sent whenever the user has requested for the window to be closed—this is an opportunity for the program to do whatever cleanup needs to be done before shutting down. If the method returns, the window will not close, so it is necessary to shut it down in the call to `processWindowEvent()`. Its window is shown as Figure F-12.

Figure F-12 *FrameSystemKill* can be closed from the system menu.

Example 3

Several window events can be issued from a `Frame`. The `WindowListener` interface defines a method for each one of these. If you need two or three of them, you can avoid implementing all the methods by using an inner class that extends the `WindowAdapter` class:

```java
import java.awt.*;
import java.awt.event.*;
public class FrameMonitor extends Frame {
    private Monitor monitor;
    public static void main(String[] arg) {
        new FrameMonitor();
    }
    FrameMonitor() {
        monitor = new Monitor();
        addWindowListener(monitor);
        add("Center",new Button("Do Nothing"));
        pack();
        show();
    }
    class Monitor extends WindowAdapter {
        public void windowClosing(WindowEvent event) {
            System.exit(0);
        }
        public void windowIconified(WindowEvent event) {
            System.out.println("Iconified");
        }
        public void windowDeiconified(WindowEvent event) {
            System.out.println("Deiconified");
        }
```

```
        }
    }
```

The `WindowAdapter` class is an implementation of the `WindowListener` interface that has stubs for all the required methods. The inner class `Monitor` extends `WindowAdapater` and overrides three of its methods. The class reports to standard out every time the main window is iconified or deiconified. It also has a method that performs a shutdown from the system menu.

An alternative way of doing this is to have the main class—the one that extends the `Frame` object—implement the `WindowListener` interface, but that does require that all the methods be implemented.

 For more information on cursors and cursor definitions, see **Component** and **Cursor**. The classes used to construct menus are **Menu, MenuBar, MenuComponent, MenuContainer, MenuItem,** and **MenuShortcut.**

garbage collection

Whenever an object is no longer in use, its RAM, along with any other resources it may be holding, is eligible to be recycled by the system to be made available again. This action is automatic on the part of Java and occurs normally with no intervention required on the part of the application.

How does the system know?

Whenever an object is instantiated, a reference (its address) is returned to the creator. This address is stored in a *reference* variable of the correct type. Once this reference variable is destroyed or has its value changed, the application no longer has a way to locate the object. The system monitors this condition and gathers up all "orphaned" objects and prepares them to be recycled (or garbage-collected).

Self referencing

An object will not be garbage-collected as long as one of its methods is in execution even if there are no external references to the object. The executing method itself is enough to keep the object in existence because every nonstatic method has a `this` reference to itself. Even if the method doesn't make use of it, it is still there. Once all the methods have returned (that is, once no threads are still executing anywhere in the object), the object will be garbage-collected. This is completely safe because if no object has a reference to it, none of its methods can ever be called again.

The finalizer

The last step taken by Java garbage collection before the memory from the object is recycled to the system is to *finalize* the object. This is done by calling the `finalize()` method of the object. Every object has a `finalize()` method—it is inherited from `Object`.

It is conceivable that an object could override the `finalize()` method and insert code that would cause the object to become referenced again. This means it would no longer be eligible for garbage collection. If this happens, the object is removed from the list of inactive objects and resumes its status as a referenced object. If it comes around for garbage collection again, however, the garbage collection routine will consider it already finalized and the `finalize()` method will not be called again—the object will simply be recycled.

When does garbage collection occur?

The point at which an object is actually recycled depends on several factors. Mainly, it is determined by how much RAM is available at the time a new object needs to be created. If not enough space exists to allocate RAM to some new object, Java will perform garbage collection until enough space becomes available. Just when and how (or even whether) this occurs will vary from one system to the next. For all practical purposes, an application should not depend on garbage collection ever being performed on any particular object, because, if there is sufficient RAM, nothing may be garbage-collected until after the program has completed execution. In fact, if the Virtual Machine is halted at the conclusion of the program, it could be that no garbage collection ever occurs.

The collection of classes

Some versions of the Java Virtual Machine also garbage-collect class definitions that have been loaded but never used or that have been used but are no longer in use. Sun added this feature to its Virtual Machine in version 1.1 of the JDK.

goto

This is a language reserved word. It has not been implemented, and its usage is not defined, but it is held as a reserved word in case it is needed in the future.

 To exit from inside a `for`, `do`, `while`, or `switch`, see **break.** To jump to the bottom of a `for`, `do`, or `while` loop, see **continue.** To exit from the body of a method, see **return.** To conditionally branch or return due to an error condition, see **exception.**

graph

 For a description of the graph of an object, see **Serializable.**

Graphics

class java.awt.Graphics

This is the abstract base class for all objects that allow an application to render graphical images. The drawing can be on a component or on an off-screen drawable object, such as an `Image` object.

Encapsulated

A Graphics object contains all the information it needs to do the drawing. Here is a list of the information it maintains internally:

- The object to receive the drawing. This is either a Component or an off-screen image.
- A coordinate translation setting that controls the position of the drawing and clipping
- A current clipping rectangle
- A Color object that will be used for all drawing
- A Font object that will be used to draw all text
- The current pixel operation mode — either paint or exclusive-OR
- The Color object for exclusive-OR drawing

It's all pixels

The drawing sizes and positions are measured in pixels.

The region x, y, width, and height

A number the methods of this class operate on rectangular regions of the drawable object. These rectangles are specified by the x-y coordinates of their upper-left corners along with the width and height of the rectangular region.

Down and to the right

Pixels are addressed by x-y coordinates. The coordinates are actually not those of the pixel, but of the juncture to its upper left. That is, the coordinate points lie between the pixels, not on them. You can think of the drawing pen as locating a pixel by hanging it down and to the right of the coordinate point. For most operations, this subtle difference doesn't matter — but some consequences come to light in connection with the slightly different actions performed with outline and filling.

Drawing and filling a rectangle

Figure G-1 shows the results of drawing a rectangle with a width of 8 and a height of 6. Eight pixels are drawn across, and six pixels down. On the other hand, Figure G-2 shows the results of filling a rectangle with a width of 8 and a height of 6. This figure has only seven pixels (width minus one) across and five down (height minus one). The filling occurred to all pixels inside the rectangle, and the boundaries of the rectangles lie *between* the pixels, not on them. For example, if you were to draw a red rectangle and then fill a blue rectangle — both at the same location with the same dimensions — a solid blue rectangle would appear with a single line of red pixels on the right and bottom.

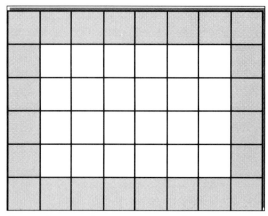

Figure G-1   A drawn rectangle of width 8 and height 6

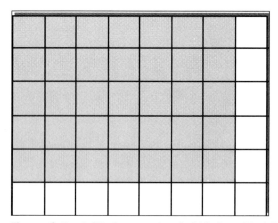

Figure G-2   A filled rectangle of width 8 and height 6.

Positioning text

A line of text is positioned by a single *x-y* coordinate point. The string will be drawn with its left end at the *x* coordinate position. The *y* coordinate specifies the baseline of the text. The size of the text is controlled by the Font.

Coordinates and translation

All drawing is done on an *x-y* coordinate system in which *x* increases to the right and *y* increases downward. The point (0,0) is, by default, at the upper-left corner of the window. The origin point, normally (0,0), can be moved, or *translated*, by making a call to translate().

Clipping

The default clipping region is the entire area of the drawable object. Once a clipping rectangle is set in a Graphics object, the only pixels that will be drawn are the ones within the rectangle. It is possible to use clipping to protect previously drawn areas. A more common practice is to use clipping for efficiency. If only a small portion of the entire picture needs to be redrawn, the Graphics object can be clipped to the area that needs to be drawn and the methods can be called to draw the whole area, but only the clipping region will actually be drawn.

Inheritance

```
public abstract class java.awt.Graphics
    extends Object
        ⇑
    public class java.lang.Object
```

Constructors

```
protected Graphics()
```

Returned by

There are no public constructors. Objects of this class can be acquired by calling Component.getGraphics(), Graphics.create(), Image.getGraphics(), and PrintJob.getGraphics().

Methods

clearRect()

```
public abstract void clearRect(int x,int y,
        int width,int height)
```

Clears the rectangular region by filling it with the background color.

clipRect()

```
public abstract void clipRect(int x,int y,
        int width,int height)
```

Sets the clipping rectangle. Only one clipping area is defined at any one time, and it is always rectangular. The default clipping rectangle is the entire drawing area of the drawable object.

This method can only reduce the area of a clip — never expand it. Figure G-3 shows the results of specifying a clipping region on a Graphic object that already has one. The resulting clip will be the intersection of the two rectangles. If the rectangles don't overlap, the entire area will be clipped and nothing will be drawn.

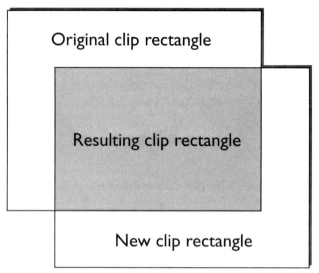

Figure G-3 The result of clipping a *Graphic* that already has a clip rectangle.

copyArea()

```
public abstract void copyArea(int x,int y,
        int width,int height,int dx,int dy)
```

Copies a rectangular area of pixels from one location to another. The rectangle with its upper-left corner at (x,y) will be copied to the rectangle with its upper-left corner at (x+dx,y+dy). The values dx and dy can be negative to copy up or to the left.

If the sending and receiving areas of the copy overlap, copyArea() executes as if the rectangle were copied to another location first and then copied back. If a portion of the source rectangle is outside the bounds of the drawing area, that area will be redrawn by calling the paint() method.

create()

```
public abstract Graphics create()
```

```
public Graphics create(int x,int y,int width,int height)
```

This method returns a new Graphics object that is a copy of this one. If x and y are specified, the new Graphics object will have that location in the drawable as its origin. The width and height will specify the size of a clipping area that will be a rectangle in the upper-left corner of its drawing area.

dispose()

```
public abstract void dispose()
```

Releases any resources that may be being held by the Graphics object. This is not absolutely necessary because the normal Java garbage collection will release the resources.

 In practice, it is best to call this method whenever you are finished with a Graphics object because some systems can run out of resources and cause problems. This appears to be the case for Windows 95. It is particularly true if a lot of Graphics objects could be created in a short period of time—as is the case with animation.

Graphics objects passed to your applet or application from the system will be automatically disposed of by Java. Calling dispose() on these objects does no harm, but it is not strictly necessary to do so for any Graphics objects other than the ones you create.

draw3DRect()

```
public void draw3DRect(int x,int y,
        int width,int height,boolean raised)
```

Draws a rectangle with a 3-D appearance. This method is used to draw the beveled-edge borders around Buttons and other components. The value of raised is set to true to cause the border to have a raised appearance, and false for it to appear to be inset.

drawArc()

```
public abstract void drawArc(int x,int y,
        int width,int height,int startAngle,int arcAngle)
```

Draws a portion of an ellipse or circle. The figure is bounded by the rectangle with its upper-left corner at (x,y) and of the specified height and width. The arc is drawn beginning at the angle specified as startAngle and will continue as specified by the angle arcAngle. Both startAngle and arcAngle are specified in degrees, with 0 degrees being on the right and 90 degrees at the top, as in the Cartesian coordinate system. A positive value for arcAngle rotates counterclockwise, and a negative value rotates clockwise.

drawBytes()

```
public void drawBytes(byte data[],int offset,int length,
        int x,int y)
```

Interprets the bytes from data[offset] for length bytes as characters and draws the resulting character string.

drawChars()

```
public void drawChars(char data[],int offset,int length,
        int x,int y)
```

Draws the characters from data[offset] for length characters as a string.

drawImage()

```
public abstract boolean drawImage(Image image,
        int x,int y,ImageObserver observer)
```

```
public abstract boolean drawImage(Image image,
        int x,int y,int width,int height,
        ImageObserver observer)
```

```
public abstract boolean drawImage(Image image,
        int x,int y,Color background,
        ImageObserver observer)
```

```
public abstract boolean drawImage(Image image,
        int x,int y,int width,int height,
        Color background,ImageObserver observer)
```

```
public abstract boolean drawImage(Image image,
        int dx1,int dy1,int dx2,int dy2,
        int sx1,int sy1,int sx2,int sy2,
        ImageObserver observer)
```

```
public abstract boolean drawImage(Image image,
        int dx1,int dy1,int dx2,int dy2,
        int sx1,int sy1,int sx2,int sy2,
        Color background,ImageObserver observer)
```

Draws the image with its upper-left-hand corner at (x,y). If height and width are specified, the image will be scaled to that size—if not, the image will not be scaled and will have the size defined in the image file itself. If the background is specified, it is the color that will show up in the transparent portions of the image (this form has the same effect as filling the background with the color and then drawing the image on top of it).

If you need more control over the mapping from the image to the drawing, you can use the methods with the source/destination rectangle definitions. The rectangle defined by the points (sx1,sy1) and (sx2,sy2) will be the portion of the source image to be displayed. The points (dx1,dy1) and (dx2,dy2) define the destination rectangle in which the image is to be displayed. If necessary, the extracted image from the source will be automatically scaled to fit the destination rectangle.

All or portions of the image may not be ready to be drawn. This method will draw any parts that are ready and return immediately—it will not wait for the image to finish being prepared (loaded from a file, scaled, or whatever). A return of false will indicate that the drawing of the image was not completed, and that the ImageObserver will be notified as image preparation proceeds.

drawLine()

```
public abstract void drawLine(int x1,int y1,int x2,int y2)
```

Draws a line from (x1,y1) to (x2,y2).

drawOval()
```
public abstract void drawOval(int x,int y,
        int width,int height)
```
Draws an ellipse or circle. The figure is bounded by the rectangle with its upper-left corner at (x,y) and of the specified height and width.

drawPolygon()
```
public abstract void drawPolygon(int xPoints[],
        int yPoints[],int count)
```
```
public void drawPolygon(Polygon p)
```
Draws the outline of a polygon defined by arrays of the *x* and *y* coordinate points. The *x-y* coordinates of each vertex of the polygon are specified either by the values stored in xPoints and yPoints (where lines will be drawn to join count points) or by a Polygon object. Unlike in drawPolyline(), if the beginning and ending points in the array are not the same, they will be joined by one more segment added to the drawing.

drawPolyline()
```
public abstract void drawPolyline(int xPoints[],
        int yPoints[],int nPoints)
```
Draws the outline of a polygon defined by arrays of the *x* and *y* coordinates of its vertices. The *x-y* coordinates of each vertex of the polygon are specified by the values stored in xPoints and yPoints. The value of nPoints is the number of points in the arrays. Unlike in drawPolygon(), the ending point is not automatically joined to the beginning point.

drawRect()
```
public void drawRect(int x,int y,int width,int height)
```
The outline of a rectangle of the specified height and width is drawn with its upper-left corner at (x,y).

drawRoundRect()
```
public abstract void drawRoundRect(int x,int y,
        int width,int height,int arcWidth,int arcHeight)
```
Draws the outline of a rectangle with rounded corners. The edges of the rectangle will be the region with its upper-left corner at (x,y) and the specified width and height. The arcWidth is the number of pixels away from each corner, along the *x*-axis, that the curvature begins. The arcHeight is the number of pixels away from each corner, along the *y*-axis, that the curvature begins.

drawString()

```
public abstract void drawString(String str,int x,int y)
```

Draws a string of characters in the current font and color at the (x,y) location. The string will have its left end at x and its baseline at y. Its extent and height will be determined by the current Font object of the Graphics object.

For more details and examples, see Font and FontMetrics.

fill3DRect()

```
public void fill3DRect(int x,int y,
        int width,int height,boolean raised)
```

Fills a rectangle with the current color and has it appear as either raised or inset. If raised is true, the rectangle will have a darker border on the bottom and right, and a lighter border on top and left. If raised is false, it will appear to be inset by having a border that is darker on the top and left, and lighter on the bottom and right.

fillArc()

```
public abstract void fillArc(int x,int y,
        int width,int height,int startAngle,int arcAngle)
```

Draws a filled portion of an ellipse or circle. The figure is bounded by the rectangle with its upper-left corner at (x,y) and of the specified height and width. The arc is filled beginning at the angle specified as startAngle and will continue as specified by the angle arcAngle.

Both startAngle and arcAngle are specified in degrees, with 0 degrees being on the right and 90 degrees at the top, as in the Cartesian coordinate system. A positive value for arcAngle rotates counterclockwise, and a negative value rotates clockwise.

fillOval()

```
public abstract void fillOval(int x,int y,
        int width,int height)
```

Draws a filled portion of an ellipse or circle. The figure is bounded by the rectangle with its upper-left corner at (x,y) and of the specified height and width.

fillPolygon()

```
public abstract void fillPolygon(int xPoints[],
        int yPoints[],int count)
```

```
public void fillPolygon(Polygon p)
```

Draws a filled portion of a polygon defined by arrays of the x and y coordinate points. The x-y coordinates of each vertex of the polygon are specified either by the values stored in xPoints and yPoints (where lines will be drawn to join count points) or by a Polygon object. If the beginning and ending points in the array are not the same, they will be joined by one more segment being added.

fillRect()

```
public abstract void fillRect(int x,int y,
        int width,int height)
```

A rectangle with its upper-left corner at (x,y) and of the specified height and width is filled with the current color.

fillRoundRect()

```
public abstract void fillRoundRect(int x,int y,
        int width,int height,int arcWidth,int arcHeight)
```

Draws a filled portion of a rectangle with rounded corners. The edges of the rectangle will be the region with its upper-left corner at (x,y) and the specified width and height. The arcWidth is the number of pixels away from each corner, along the x-axis, that the curving begins. The arcHeight is the number of pixels away from each corner, along the y-axis, that the curving begins.

finalize()

```
public void finalize()
```

This method will dispose of any system resources being held by the Graphics object. This method is used by Java garbage collection when reclaiming the object.

getClip()

```
public abstract Shape getClip()
```

Returns a Shape object that defines the current clipping region.

getClipBounds()

```
public abstract Rectangle getClipBounds()
```

Returns a Rectangle that encloses the current clipping area.

getClipRect()   deprecated

```
public Rectangle getClipRect()
```

Returns a Rectangle that encloses the current clipping area. This method is deprecated— use getClipBounds().

getColor()

```
public abstract Color getColor()
```

Returns the current Color.

getFont()

```
public abstract Font getFont()
```

Returns the current Font.

getFontMetrics()

```
public FontMetrics getFontMetrics()

public abstract FontMetrics getFontMetrics(Font font)
```

Returns a FontMetrics object for the font. If font is not specified, the current Font of the Graphics object is used.

setClip()

```
public abstract void setClip(int x,int y,
        int width,int height)

public abstract void setClip(Shape clipregion)
```

This will set the current clipping region. The region will be set to the rectangle of the specified height and width with its upper-left corner at (x,y), or to the shape specified by clipregion. The only Shape objects supported are ones returned by getClip() and Rectangle.

setColor()

```
public abstract void setColor(Color c)
```

Sets the current color. A Graphics only has one color setting at a time used for all drawing.

setFont()

```
public abstract void setFont(Font font)
```

Sets the current Font.

setPaintMode()

```
public abstract void setPaintMode()
```

Sets the logical pixel-writing operation to the overwrite mode. This is the default mode. All pixels written to the drawable object will simply replace the pixel value already there.

setXORMode()

```
public abstract void setXORMode(Color color)
```

Sets the logical pixel-writing operation to the exclusive-OR mode. The written pixels will all be written in an exclusive-OR operation with the existing pixel. Either one of two actions takes place for the painting of each pixel. One, if the argument color is the same as the pixel color, no painting takes place. Two, if the argument color is not the same as the pixel color, a new pixel bit pattern results from an exclusive-OR performed on the two existing ones. In any case, painting the same figure twice will restore the original pixel values. For more information, see **exclusive-OR**.

toString()

```
public String toString()
```

Returns a string representing the `Graphics` object.

translate()

```
public abstract void translate(int x,int y)
```

Translates the origin to the point (x,y) of the current coordinate system. All future drawing will be done relative to the new origin. The default origin is (0,0).

For example, if you wish to have the origin leave a margin of 10 pixels on the top and left, call `translate(10,10)` and any drawing at (0,0) will automatically be translated to (10,10). It is still possible to draw in the margin by using negative drawing coordinates.

Negative numbers can be used to move the origin up or to the left. For example, if the origin has been translated to the point `(10,30)`, to return the origin to back to the default, use the translation values `(-10,-30)`.

Example 1

This an applet that uses `drawImage()` to display a graphic file and then calls `copyArea()` to perform an overlapped copy of pixels:

```java
import java.awt.*;
import java.applet.*;
import java.awt.image.*;
import java.util.*;
import java.net.*;

public class OverlapCopy extends Applet {
    private Image marble;
    public void init() {
        URL url = getCodeBase();
        marble = getImage(url,"bluemarble.gif");
        MediaTracker mt = new MediaTracker(this);
        mt.addImage(marble,1);
        try {
            mt.waitForAll();
        } catch(Exception e) {
            e.printStackTrace();
        }
    }
```

```
public void paint(Graphics g) {
    g.drawImage(marble,0,0,this);
    g.copyArea(0,0,72,72,28,28);
    g.dispose();
}
}
```

The output of the program is shown in Figure G-4.

Figure G-4 The display of a graphic file with a pixel copy.

Example 2

This example calls create() to get a second Graphics object that is clipped to a rectangle within the original:

```
import java.awt.*;
import java.applet.*;
import java.awt.image.*;
import java.util.*;
import java.net.*;

public class OverlapTranslate extends Applet {
    private Image marble;
    public void init() {
        URL url = getCodeBase();
        marble = getImage(url,"bluemarble.gif");
        MediaTracker mt = new MediaTracker(this);
        mt.addImage(marble,1);
        try {
            mt.waitForAll();
        } catch(Exception e) {
            e.printStackTrace();
        }
    }

    public void paint(Graphics g) {
        g.drawImage(marble,0,0,this);
```

```
        Graphics gc = g.create(28,28,50,50);
        gc.drawImage(marble,0,0,this);
        g.dispose();
    }
}
```

The second `Graphics` object was used to draw the marble image at its origin, but it was instantiated with its origin offset from the first. Also, it does not draw the entire image because it was instantiated with a clip region smaller than the drawing area of the component. Figure G-5 shows the output of the program.

Figure G-5   Drawing an image with a relocated and clipped Graphics object.

Example 3

Drawing a three-dimensional rectangle can cause its contents to appear to be raised or lowered. This example draws one that appears raised and another that appears lowered.

```
import java.awt.*;
import java.applet.*;
import java.awt.image.*;
import java.util.*;
import java.net.*;

public class RaisedMarble extends Applet {
    private Image marble;
    public void init() {
        URL url = getCodeBase();
        marble = getImage(url,"bluemarble.gif");
        MediaTracker mt = new MediaTracker(this);
        mt.addImage(marble,1);
        try {
            mt.waitForAll();
        } catch(Exception e) {
            e.printStackTrace();
        }
        setBackground(Color.black);
```

```
        }

    public void paint(Graphics g) {
        int thickness = 3;
        int x = 10;
        int y = 10;
        g.drawImage(marble,x,y,this);
        g.setColor(Color.lightGray);
        int w = marble.getWidth(this);
        int h = marble.getHeight(this);
        for(int i=0; i<thickness; i++)
            g.draw3DRect(--x,--y,w+(2*i),h+(2*i),false);
        x = 92;
        y = 10;
        g.drawImage(marble,x,y,this);
        g.setColor(Color.lightGray);
        w = marble.getWidth(this);
        h = marble.getHeight(this);
        for(int i=0; i<thickness; i++)
            g.draw3DRect(--x,--y,w+(2*i),h+(2*i),true);
    }
}
```

The method `draw3DRect()` uses the current color to create a frame. As shown in figure G-6, the resulting frame is made darker on the top and left to appear inset, and is made lighter on the top and left to appear raised. The current `Graphics` object color is used by `draw3DRect()` for both by calling `Color.darker()` for the shaded portion and `Color.lighter()` for the lighted portion.

The thickness of the border drawn by `draw3DRect()` is only one pixel. To make a thicker border, it is necessary to draw more than one of them. This is done by setting the thickness variable and looping while changing the position of the upper-left corner and the dimension of the rectangle. The output is shown in Figure G-6.

Figure G-6 An example of one raised and one inset frame.

Example 4

This applet will display a raised or inset rectangle. The rectangle will change with the pressing of a mouse button. This is very much like the action of the `Button` component:

```
import java.awt.*;
import java.awt.event.*;
import java.applet.*;

public class RaisedRect extends Applet {
    boolean raised;
    public void init() {
        setBackground(Color.lightGray);
        raised = true;
        enableEvents(AWTEvent.MOUSE_EVENT_MASK);
    }
    public void paint(Graphics g) {
        g.setColor(Color.lightGray);
        Rectangle rectangle = getBounds();
        g.fill3DRect(5,5,
            rectangle.width-10,rectangle.height-10,raised);
    }
    public void processMouseEvent(MouseEvent event) {
        if(event.getID() == MouseEvent.MOUSE_PRESSED)
            raised = false;
        else if(event.getID() ==
        MouseEvent.MOUSE_RELEASED)
            raised = true;
        repaint();
    }
}
```

The `boolean` value `raised` determines whether the rectangle appears raised or inset. Whenever the mouse button is pressed, `raised` is set to `false` so that the rectangle is redrawn as inset. Releasing the mouse button will cause the rectangle to be redrawn as raised again. Figure G-7 shows the raised rectangle, and Figure G-8 shows the inset rectangle.

Figure G-7   A raised rectangle.

Figure G-8   An inset rectangle.

Example 5

This is an example of arc drawing and filling:

```
import java.awt.*;
import java.applet.*;

public class DrawFillArc extends Applet {
    public void init() {
        setBackground(Color.lightGray);
    }
    public void paint(Graphics g) {
        g.setColor(Color.blue);
        Rectangle rectangle = getBounds();
        g.drawArc(0,0,
            rectangle.width,rectangle.height/2,
            45,270);
        g.fillArc(0,rectangle.height/2,
            rectangle.width,rectangle.height/2,
            45,270);
    }
}
```

This applet uses `drawArc()` to inscribe an arc in its rectangle beginning at 45 degrees and continuing for 270 degrees. Then it does the same thing right below it with `fillArc()`. Figure G-9 shows the displayed window of the applet.

Figure G-9   A drawn arc and a filled arc.

Example 6

This example displays the same image three different ways. It scales it smaller, leaves the scaling unmodified, and scales it larger:

```java
import java.awt.*;
import java.applet.*;
import java.awt.image.*;
import java.util.*;
import java.net.*;

public class ScaledMarble extends Applet {
    private Image marble;
    public void init() {
        URL url = getCodeBase();
        marble = getImage(url,"bluemarble.gif");
        MediaTracker mt = new MediaTracker(this);
        mt.addImage(marble,1);
        try {
            mt.waitForAll();
        } catch(Exception e) {
            e.printStackTrace();
        }
        setBackground(Color.black);
    }

    public void paint(Graphics g) {
        g.drawImage(marble,0,0,36,36,this);
        g.drawImage(marble,36,0,this);
        g.drawImage(marble,108,0,144,144,this);
    }
}
```

As shown in Figure G-10, the three drawings are displayed side by side. The default scaling is 72 by 72.

Figure G-10 Images can be scaled larger and smaller.

Example 7

This applet draws the outline of an oval in the top half of its window and a filled oval in the bottom half:

```
import java.awt.*;
import java.applet.*;

public class DrawFillOval extends Applet {
    public void init() {
        setBackground(Color.lightGray);
    }
    public void paint(Graphics g) {
        g.setColor(Color.blue);
        Rectangle rectangle = getBounds();
        g.drawOval(0,0,
            rectangle.width,rectangle.height/2);
        g.fillOval(0,rectangle.height/2,
            rectangle.width,rectangle.height/2);
    }
}
```

To do the drawing, the applet uses the methods drawOval() and fillOval(). The display it produces is shown in Figure G-11.

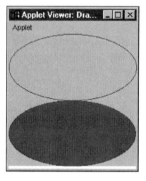

Figure G-11 An example of a drawn oval and a filled oval.

Example 8

This applet draws a polygon from a set of coordinate points and then—by shifting the vertical component of the coordinate to the bottom half of the window—performs a fill on the same polygon:

```
import java.awt.*;
import java.applet.*;
```

```
public class DrawFillPolygon extends Applet {
    int[] x = {5,40,80,160,120,190 };
    int[] y = {5,90,10, 15, 80, 50 };
    public void init() {
        setBackground(Color.lightGray);
    }
    public void paint(Graphics g) {
        g.setColor(Color.red);
        Rectangle rectangle = getBounds();
        g.drawPolygon(x,y,6);
        int[] y2 = new int[6];
        for(int i=0; i<6; i++)
            y2[i] += y[i] + (rectangle.height / 2);
        g.fillPolygon(x,y2,6);
    }
}
```

The beginning and ending points do not need to match because a final joining line will always be assumed and drawn by `drawPolygon()` and `fillPolygon()`. As shown in Figure G-12, the `fillPolygon()` method continues to fill the portion between the lines even after the lines have crossed one another.

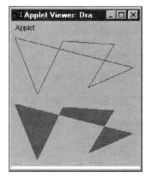

Figure G-12   The drawing and filling of a polygon.

Example 9

This applet demonstrates the drawing and filling of a rectangle:

```
import java.awt.*;
import java.applet.*;

public class DrawFillRect extends Applet {
    public void init() {
        setBackground(Color.lightGray);
```

```
      }
      public void paint(Graphics g) {
          g.setColor(Color.black);
          Rectangle rectangle = getBounds();
          g.drawRect(5,5,
              rectangle.width-10,(rectangle.height/2)-10);
          g.fillRect(5,(rectangle.height/2) + 5,
              rectangle.width-10,(rectangle.height/2)-10);
      }
  }
```

As shown in Figure G-13, a rectangle is drawn in the upper half of the window, and a rectangle is filled in the lower half.

Figure G-13   A drawn rectangle and a filled rectangle.

Example 10

This applet draws a rounded rectangle in the top half of its window and a filled rounded rectangle in the bottom:

```
import java.awt.*;
import java.applet.*;

public class DrawFillRoundRect extends Applet {
    public void init() {
        setBackground(Color.lightGray);
    }
    public void paint(Graphics g) {
        g.setColor(Color.black);
        Rectangle rectangle = getBounds();
        g.drawRoundRect(5,5,
            rectangle.width-10,(rectangle.height/2)-10,
            35,35);
        g.fillRoundRect(5,(rectangle.height/2) + 5,
```

```
             rectangle.width-10,(rectangle.height/2)-10,
             35,35);
    }
}
```

The window it produces is shown in Figure G-14.

Figure G-14   A rounded rectangle and a
filled rounded rectangle.

 For examples of drawing character strings, see **Font** and **FontMetrics**. Also
see **PrintJob** and **PrintGraphics**.

GregorianCalendar

class java.util.GregorianCalendar

This is an implementation of the Gregorian calendar—the calendar used by
most of the world.

Fields

Several of the methods have *field* parameters. These are constant values that instruct the
method as to which part of the date field the method call is to address. Most of the constant
values used as the field specifications are defined in the Calendar class—BC and AD are
defined in this class.

Numeric value ranges

Many of the methods require numeric values for items that may normally have names. A
numeric value for a year is the full four-digit number. Months are numbered from 0 for
January through 11 for December. Days of the month are numbered normally, 1 through 31.
Hours of the day are numbered 0 through 23. Minutes are numbered 0 through 59. Seconds
are numbered 0 through 59. The days of the week are numbered from 1 for Sunday through
7 for Saturday. The days of the year are numbered with January 1 being day 1.

Era

The Gregorian calendar has two eras—AD and BC.

1582

When it was discovered that the Julian calendar did not exactly match the real world—there was a drift of just over eleven minutes a year—the concept of leap year was introduced and some days were skipped to correct the error that had accumulated. In 1582, the day October 5 was declared to be October 15, thus eliminating 10 days from the calendar and adjusting for the leap years that should have been. This class takes this adjustment into consideration when calculating dates.

The exact date of the shift was not worldwide—in some countries, the shift occurred on other dates. For this reason, this class has added the capabilities to change the date of the adjustment to something other than the default.

Inheritance

```
public class java.util.GregorianCalendar
    extends Calendar
              ⇑
    public class java.util.Calendar
          implements Serializable
          implements Cloneable
          extends Object
                ⇑
              public class java.lang.Object
```

Variables and constants

AD

```
public final static byte AD
```

The field value that indicates the era beginning at Gregorian year 0.

BC

```
public final static byte BC
```

The field value that indicates the era prior to the Gregorian year 0.

Constructors

```
public GregorianCalendar()

public GregorianCalendar(int year,int monthNumber,
        int dayOfMonth)
```

```
public GregorianCalendar(int year,int monthNumber,
        int dayOfMonth,int hour,int minute)
```

```
public GregorianCalendar(int year,int monthNumber,
        int dayOfMonth,int hour,int minute,int second)
```

```
public GregorianCalendar(Locale locale)
```

```
public GregorianCalendar(TimeZone zone)
```

```
public GregorianCalendar(TimeZone zone,Locale locale)
```

A GregorianCalendar is always constructed with a time zone and a locale, and these cannot be changed once the object exists. If none is supplied, the default values (system time zone and locale) are assumed. The default date and time settings are January 1, 1960, 00:00:00.

Methods

add()

```
public void add(byte field,int amount)
        throws IllegalArgumentException
```

Adds the specified amount to the portion of the date specified by the field. For example, if the field is Calendar.HOUR, the amount will be added to the hour component of the date. To execute a subtraction, use a negative amount.

after()

```
public boolean after(Object when)
```

Returns true if when is after the time of this object. The comparison is made by converting the two to Universal time. The object when must be a GregorianCalendar.

before()

```
public abstract boolean before(Object when)
```

Returns true if when is before the time of this object. The comparison is made by converting the two to Universal time. The object when must be a GregorianCalendar.

clone()

```
public Object clone()
```

Duplicates this object.

computeFields()

```
protected void computeFields()
```

Uses the various field settings—if any have been made—to calculate a new universal time internally. This guarantees the `long` time value is synchronized with the values of all the field settings.

computeTime()

```
protected void computeTime()
```

Uses the internal long value that holds the universal time to calculate and set all the various field settings. This guarantees that the field values are all synchronized with the `long` value.

equals()

```
public boolean equals(Object object)
```

Returns true if `object` is a `GregorianCalendar` with identical time settings to this one.

getGreatestMinimum()

```
public int getGreatestMinimum(byte field)
```

For `GregorianCalendar`, this is the same as `getMinimum()`.

getGregorianChange()

```
public final Date getGregorianChange()
```

Returns the date of the change from Julian dates to Gregorian dates.

getLeastMaximum()

```
public int getLeastMaximum(byte field)
```

Returns the smallest possible maximum value for the specified field. For example, if the argument is `Calendar.DAYOFMONTH`, the return value will be 28.

getMaximum()

```
public int getMaximum(byte field)
```

Returns the largest possible value for the specified `field`. For example, if `field` is `Calendar.DAYOFMONTH`, the return value will be 31.

getMinimum()

```
public int getMinimum(byte field)
```

Returns the smallest possible value for the specified field.

hashCode()

```
public synchronized int hashCode()
```

Two `GregorianCalendar` objects containing the same time will return the same hash-code value.

isLeapYear()

```
public boolean isLeapYear(int year)
```

Returns true if year is a leap year.

roll()

```
public void roll(byte field,boolean up)
            throws IllegalArgumentException
```

Adjusts the internal date by incrementing or decrementing the field value. For example, it can be used to move the clock to the next hour or to the previous month. For more information, see Calendar.

setGregorianChange()

```
public void setGregorianChange(Date date)
```

Sets the date at which the Julian calendar was switched to the Gregorian calendar.

Example 1

This example creates a GregorianCalendar and rolls certain fields forward and backward:

```
import java.util.*;

public class GregoryRoll {
    static public void main(String[] argv) {
        GregorianCalendar g = new GregorianCalendar(
            1998,Calendar.NOVEMBER,30,23,56,45);
        System.out.println(g.getTime());
        System.out.println(" ** roll up 3 years ** ");
        for(int i=0; i<3; i++) {
            g.roll(Calendar.YEAR,true);
            System.out.println(g.getTime());
        }
        System.out.println(" ** roll down 2 years ** ");
        for(int i=0; i<2; i++) {
            g.roll(Calendar.YEAR,false);
            System.out.println(g.getTime());
        }
        System.out.println(" ** roll up 6 months ** ");
        for(int i=0; i<6; i++) {
            g.roll(Calendar.MONTH,true);
            System.out.println(g.getTime());
        }
```

```
System.out.println(" ** roll up 6 minutes ** ");
for(int i=0; i<6; i++) {
    g.roll(Calendar.MINUTE,true);
    System.out.println(g.getTime());
}
        }
    }
}
```

The rolling works for only one field — changing the value in one field does not change the values in the others.

Here is the output:

```
Mon Nov 30 23:56:45 CST 1998
 ** roll up 3 years **
Tue Nov 30 23:56:45 CST 1999
Thu Nov 30 23:56:45 CST 2000
Fri Nov 30 23:56:45 CST 2001
 ** roll down 2 years **
Thu Nov 30 23:56:45 CST 2000
Tue Nov 30 23:56:45 CST 1999
 ** roll up 6 months **
Thu Dec 30 23:56:45 CST 1999
Sat Jan 30 23:56:45 CST 1999
Tue Mar 02 23:56:45 CST 1999
Tue Mar 30 23:56:45 CST 1999
Fri Apr 30 23:56:45 CDT 1999
Sun May 30 23:56:45 CDT 1999
 ** roll up 6 minutes **
Sun May 30 23:57:45 CDT 1999
Sun May 30 23:58:45 CDT 1999
Sun May 30 23:59:45 CDT 1999
Sun May 30 23:00:45 CDT 1999
Sun May 30 23:01:45 CDT 1999
Sun May 30 23:02:45 CDT 1999
```

This example rolls the years forward and back across the millennium boundary successfully, but the months and minutes don't fare so well. Rolling from December to January does not cause the year to roll over, and rolling one month forward from January 30 causes the result to be March 2. Also, rolling the minutes forward past midnight does not cause an advance to the next day. This may or may not be what you would like — see Example 2.

Example 2

This example creates a GregorianCalendar object and uses the add() method to adjust it forward and backward in time:

```
import java.util.*;

public class GregoryAdd {
    static public void main(String[] argv) {
        GregorianCalendar g = new GregorianCalendar(
            1998,Calendar.NOVEMBER,30,23,56,45);
        System.out.println(g.getTime());
        System.out.println(" ** add 3 years ** ");
        for(int i=0; i<3; i++) {
            g.add(Calendar.YEAR,1);
            System.out.println(g.getTime());
        }
        System.out.println(" ** subtract 2 years ** ");
        for(int i=0; i<2; i++) {
            g.add(Calendar.YEAR,-1);
            System.out.println(g.getTime());
        }
        System.out.println(" ** add 6 months ** ");
        for(int i=0; i<6; i++) {
            g.add(Calendar.MONTH,1);
            System.out.println(g.getTime());
        }
        System.out.println(" ** add 6 minutes ** ");
        for(int i=0; i<6; i++) {
            g.add(Calendar.MINUTE,1);
            System.out.println(g.getTime());
        }
    }
}
```

The add() method successfully modifies the individual field values in much the same way that the roll() method does in Example 1. The year values move successfully across the millennium boundary, but adjusting the month or minute values doesn't cause the other values around them to be altered.

Here is the output:

```
Mon Nov 30 23:56:45 CST 1998
 ** add 3 years **
Tue Nov 30 23:56:45 CST 1999
Thu Nov 30 23:56:45 CST 2000
Fri Nov 30 23:56:45 CST 2001
 ** subtract 2 years **
Thu Nov 30 23:56:45 CST 2000
Tue Nov 30 23:56:45 CST 1999
```

```
     ** add 6 months **
Thu Dec 30 23:56:45 CST 1999
Sun Jan 30 23:56:45 CST 2000
Wed Mar 01 23:56:45 CST 2000
Thu Mar 30 23:56:45 CST 2000
Sun Apr 30 23:56:45 CDT 2000
Tue May 30 23:56:45 CDT 2000
     ** add 6 minutes **
Tue May 30 23:57:45 CDT 2000
Tue May 30 23:58:45 CDT 2000
Tue May 30 23:59:45 CDT 2000
Wed May 31 00:00:45 CDT 2000
Wed May 31 00:01:45 CDT 2000
Wed May 31 00:02:45 CDT 2000
```

Rolling from December to January does not cause the year to roll over, and rolling one month forward from January 30 causes the result to be March 1. Also, rolling the minutes forward past midnight does not cause an advance to the next day. This may or may not be what you would like—see Example 3.

Example 3

This example shows how the GregorianCalendar class can be extended and the protected methods can be used to cause the adjustment to one field to be reflected in the other fields:

```
import java.util.*;

public class GregoryExtend {
    static public void main(String[] argv) {
        new GregoryExtend();
    }
    GregoryExtend() {
        Cal g = new Cal(1998,Calendar.NOVEMBER,30,23,56,45);
        System.out.println(g.getTime());
        System.out.println(" ** add 3 years ** ");
        for(int i=0; i<3; i++) {
            g.add(Calendar.YEAR,1);
            System.out.println(g.getTime());
        }
        System.out.println(" ** subtract 2 years ** ");
        for(int i=0; i<2; i++) {
            g.add(Calendar.YEAR,-1);
            System.out.println(g.getTime());
        }
```

```
                System.out.println(" ** add 6 months ** ");
                for(int i=0; i<6; i++) {
                    g.add(Calendar.MONTH,1);
                    System.out.println(g.getTime());
                }
                System.out.println(" ** add 6 minutes ** ");
                for(int i=0; i<6; i++) {
                    g.add(Calendar.MINUTE,1);
                    System.out.println(g.getTime());
                }
        }
        class Cal extends GregorianCalendar {
            Cal(int year,int month,int dayOfMonth,
                    int hour,int minute,int second) {
                super(year,month,dayOfMonth,hour,minute, second);
            }
            public void add(byte field,int amount) {
                super.add(field,amount);
                computeFields();
            }
        }
    }
}
```

The inner class `Cal` extends `GregorianCalendar`. To simplify the example, only one of the constructors was overridden. The purpose of extending the class is just to override the `add()` method to execute a call to `computeFields()` following the call to `super.add()`. Calling `super.add()` modifies one of the date fields, and then the `computeFields()` method recalculates the internal date/time value from the fields. The computation takes into consideration all the necessary range and bounds checking on the individual fields and resolves any conflicting field information. The calculated value is then used to derive new values for each of the fields.

Here is the output:

```
Mon Nov 30 23:56:45 CST 1998
 ** add 3 years **
Tue Nov 30 23:56:45 CST 1999
Thu Nov 30 23:56:45 CST 2000
Fri Nov 30 23:56:45 CST 2001
 ** subtract 2 years **
Thu Nov 30 23:56:45 CST 2000
Tue Nov 30 23:56:45 CST 1999
 ** add 6 months **
Thu Dec 30 23:56:45 CST 1999
Sun Jan 30 23:56:45 CST 2000
```

```
Wed Mar 01 23:56:45 CST 2000
Thu Mar 30 23:56:45 CST 2000
Sun Apr 30 23:56:45 CDT 2000
Tue May 30 23:56:45 CDT 2000
 ** add 6 minutes **
Tue May 30 23:57:45 CDT 2000
Tue May 30 23:58:45 CDT 2000
Tue May 30 23:59:45 CDT 2000
Wed May 31 00:00:45 CDT 2000
Wed May 31 00:01:45 CDT 2000
Wed May 31 00:02:45 CDT 2000
```

The recalculation of the fields resolves some of the issues of the two previous examples—but not all of them. In this version, adding enough minutes to cause the time to move past midnight will trip both the hour and the day of the month to the next day. There is still a situation that arises when moving to the next month—if the day of the month does not exist (as in the case of an attempt to go from January 30 to February 30), the GregorianCalendar just moves into the month following (in this example, it moved to March 1).

 For other date and time classes, see **Date** and **Calendar**. To simply get the raw binary form of the current time, see **System.currentTimeMillis().**

GridBagConstraints

class java.awt.GridBagConstraints

An object of this class is used as an argument when adding a component to a GridBagLayout manager to specify the constraints the manager should use in laying out the component. It is simply a wrapper of the complete set of constraint variables used by GridBagLayout to size and position a component.

There are no set and get methods

An object of this class is simply a container for a set of public variables. The variables are addressed directly instead of indirectly through methods, which is the normal way. When a GridBagConstraints object is created, the constructor initializes it with a set of default values; it is up to the program to change, one by one, any variables that need to have different values. Because it often happens that a program needs to have several of these objects with similar, but not identical, settings, the clone() method has been implemented so that a new one can be easily created and modified.

Inheritance

```
public class java.awt.GridBagConstraints
    implements Cloneable
    implements Serializable
    extends Object
        ⇑
    public class java.lang.Object
```

Variables and constants

anchor

```
public int anchor
```

Specifies the placement of the component inside its allocated display area when its display area is larger than it is able to fill. The valid values are CENTER, NORTHWEST, NORTH, NORTHEAST, EAST, SOUTHEAST, SOUTH, SOUTHWEST, and WEST.

BOTH

```
public static final int BOTH
```

Stretches the component both horizontally and vertically.

CENTER

```
public static final int CENTER
```

Centers the component.

EAST

```
public static final int EAST
```

Places the component to the east — that is, to the right.

fill

```
public int fill
```

Specifies what action to take when a component is not large enough to fill the area assigned to it. The default value is NONE, which indicates that no action is taken—the component will not be resized. If the value is HORIZONTAL, the component will be stretched horizontally to fit, but not vertically. If the value is VERTICAL, the component will be stretched vertically to fit, but not horizontally. If the value is BOTH, it will be stretched to fit vertically and horizontally.

gridheight

```
public int gridheight
```

Specifies the height, in cells, of the component. The default is 1. The value REMAINDER is used when the component is to be the last one in its column and should use all the remaining cells. The value RELATIVE is used to indicate that the component will be the next to last one in its column.

gridwidth

```
public int gridwidth
```

Specifies the width, in cells, of this component. The default is 1. The value REMAINDER is used when the component is to be the last one in its row and should use all the remaining cells. The value RELATIVE is used to indicate that the component will be the next to last one in its row.

gridx

```
public int gridx
```

Specifies the horizontal positioning. This is the column of cells into which the left side of this component will be placed. The leftmost column is 0. The default value is RELATIVE, which means it will be placed in the next column after the component that was last added to the container's layout manager.

gridy

```
public int gridy
```

Specifies the vertical positioning. This is the row of cells into which the top of this component will be placed. The top row is 0. The default value is RELATIVE, which means it will be placed in a position following the component that was last added to the component's layout manager.

HORIZONTAL

```
public static final int HORIZONTAL
```

Stretches the component horizontally, but not vertically, to fit.

insets

```
public Insets insets
```

This is the external padding value. The default is 0. It will add the specified number of pixels to the outside of the component on all four sides. That is, the component will be fit into its rectangular space and be inset from its neighbors by the specified amount.

ipadx

```
public int ipadx
```

The internal padding value is used to expand the horizontal minimum size of the component. The horizontal minimum-size value of the component is increased by twice the value of `ipadx` (one pixel in each direction).

ipady

```
public int ipady
```

The internal padding value is used to expand the vertical minimum size of the component. The vertical minimum-size value of the component is increased by twice the value of `ipady` (one pixel in each direction).

NONE

```
public static final int NONE
```

Does not resize the component.

NORTH

```
public static final int NORTH
```

Places the component to the north — that is, to the top.

NORTHEAST

```
public static final int NORTHEAST
```

Places the component to the northeast — that is, to the upper right.

NORTHWEST

```
public static final int NORTHWEST
```

Places the component to the northwest — that is, to the upper left.

RELATIVE

```
public static final int RELATIVE
```

Indicates that the component will be the next to last one in its row.

REMAINDER

```
public static final int REMAINDER
```

Indicates that component is to be the last one in its column and should use all the remaining cells.

SOUTH

```
public static final int SOUTH
```

Places the component to the south — that is, to the bottom.

SOUTHEAST

```
public static final int SOUTHEAST
```

Places the component to the southeast — that is, to the lower right.

SOUTHWEST

```
public static final int SOUTHWEST
```

Places the component to the southwest, that is, to the lower left.

VERTICAL

```
public static final int VERTICAL
```

Stretches the component vertically, but not horizontally, to fit.

weightx

```
public double weightx
```

This value specifies how the component size will be increased or decreased horizontally to fit the window. If the value is 0 (the default), the component will not be resized when the window is resized. A value of 1 or more will force resizing. The larger the value, the larger the percentage of the leftover area will be assigned to this component.

weighty

```
public double weighty
```

This value specifies how the component size will be increased or decreased vertically to fit the window. If the value is 0 (the default), the component will not be resized when the window is resized. A value of 1 or more will force resizing. The larger the value, the larger the percentage of the leftover area will be assigned to this component.

WEST

```
public static final int WEST
```

Places the component to the west — that is, to the left.

Constructors

```
public GridBagConstraints()
```

Returned by

A GridBagConstraints object is returned from the getConstraints() and lookupConstraints() methods of GridBagLayout.

Methods

clone()

```
public Object clone()
```

Duplicates this object.

 For examples and more information, see **GridBagLayout**.

GridBagLayout

class java.awt.GridBagLayout

This is a layout manager that is capable of aligning components of different sizes.

A rectangle of cells

The GridBagLayout manager uses a rectangular grid of cells. A single component may occupy one or more of these cells. The widths and heights of the cells are not necessarily uniform. Each cell is addressed by its (,y) coordinates as shown in Figure G-15.

(0,0)	(1,0)	(2,0)
(0,1)	(1,1)	(2,1)
(0,2)	(1,2)	(2,2)
(0,3)	(1,3)	(2,3)

Figure G-15   The cell coordinates of the GridBag.

The constraints

Each component is associated with an instance of a GridBagConstraints object. The constraint values in the GridBagConstraints object supply the information necessary for the layout manager to position and size the component. The component itself supplies information about its maximum, minimum, and preferred sizes. The container also has maximum, minimum, and preferred sizes.

The weights of components

The GridBagLayout keeps row and column weight values that are used to distribute the space left over after all the components have been placed. This weighted distribution happens as the final step of the initial layout, and happens again following each container resize.

Each component has a pair of weight values—a vertical weight and a horizontal weight —assigned to it through its GridBagConstraints values. By summing the weight values of the components, both across and down, the layout manager is able to assign a weight value to each row and column. The weight value of an individual component is then used to determine what percentage of the leftover space it should get. For example, if the sum of the weights for a row is 10, and if one component has a weight of 2, it will get 20 percent of any free space added.

If there are no weights in a row or column—if all the component weights are set to zero in the GridBagConstraints for each component—the new space is added to each side of the grouping of the components in a row, or above and below those in a column. In effect, the row or column will be centered with the new space added as a margin between it and the outer edges of the container window.

Only components with weights are resized whenever the window is resized.

Inheritance

```
public class java.awt.GridBagLayout
    implements LayoutManager2
    implements Serializable
    extends Object
        ⇑
    public class java.lang.Object
```

Variables and constants

columnWeights

```
public double columnWeights[]
```

The total weight of each column.

columnWidths

```
public int columnWidths[]
```

The width of each column.

comptable

```
protected Hashtable comptable
```

A table to contain the cached information about component positioning that has been calculated by the GridBagLayout manager.

defaultConstraints

```
protected GridBagConstraints defaultConstraints
```

This is a GridBagConstraints object that contains the default values.

layoutInfo

```
protected GridBagLayoutInfo layoutInfo
```

This object is used internally to hold the constraint information for each component.

MAXGRIDSIZE

```
protected static final int MAXGRIDSIZE
```

The maximum number of cells in a GridBagLayout.

MINSIZE

```
protected static final int MINSIZE
```

A constant to indicate that the layout should use the minimum size of a component.

PREFERREDSIZE

```
protected static final int PREFERREDSIZE
```

A constant to indicate that the layout should use the preferred size of a component.

rowHeights

```
public int rowHeights[]
```

The minimum height of each row of cells.

rowWeights

```
public double rowWeights[]
```

The weight values of each row.

Constructors

```
public GridBagLayout()
```

Methods

addLayoutComponent()

```
public void addLayoutComponent(String name,Component comp)

public void addLayoutComponent(Component comp,
    Object constraints)
```

Adds a component to the layout. If a `name` is specified, it is the name of the component. The `constraints` will be assigned to this component—if no `constraints` are specified, the default set of constraints will be used.

AdjustForGravity()

```
protected void AdjustForGravity(
          GridBagConstraints constraints,Rectangle rect)
```

This method will—using the information from `constraints` and `rect`—calculate the position and extent of the components and put the bounds of the resulting rectangle into `rect`.

ArrangeGrid()

```
protected void ArrangeGrid(Container parent)
```

Performs the actual work of positioning components inside the `parent` rectangle.

getConstraints()

```
public GridBagConstraints getConstraints(Component component)
```

Returns the constraints assigned to the `component`. A copy is returned so that modifying the returned values will not modify the restraints for the `component`.

getLayoutAlignmentX()

```
public float getLayoutAlignmentX(Container parent)
```

Returns the preferred horizontal position of this layout manager in its parent window. The returned value is relative, with the left side being 0.0 and the right, 1.0.

getLayoutAlignmentY()

```
public float getLayoutAlignmentY(Container parent)
```

Returns the preferred vertical position of this layout manager in its parent window. The returned value is relative, with the top being 0.0 and the bottom, 1.0.

getLayoutDimensions()

```
public int[][] getLayoutDimensions()
```

The returned pair of arrays contains the column widths and row heights of the layout. The value at [0][c] is the width of column c, and the value at [1][r] is the height of row r.

GetLayoutInfo()

```
protected GridBagLayoutInfo GetLayoutInfo(
          Container parent,int sizeflag)
```

Returns a `GridBagLayoutInfo` object that contains the constraint information being used for the various components. This method is intended for debugging.

getLayoutOrigin()

```
public Point getLayoutOrigin()
```

When the components are laid out, space may be left as a margin between them and the edge of the parent window. This method returns the `Point` that is the upper-left corner of the rectangle containing the laid-out components—which may or may not be the upper-left corner of the parent window.

getLayoutWeights()

```
public double[][] getLayoutWeights()
```

The returned pair of arrays contains the sums of the weights in each column and row in the layout. The value at [0][c] is the weight of column c, and the value at [1][r] is the weight of row r.

GetMinSize()

```
protected Dimension GetMinSize(Container parent,
        GridBagLayoutInfo info)
```

Returns the minimum size that will be consumed by the layout.

invalidateLayout()

```
public void invalidateLayout(Container target)
```

Invalidates the layout. If the layout manager has stored any information about the layout, it will be discarded and must be acquired again before the components can be laid out.

layoutContainer()

```
public void layoutContainer(Container parent)
```

Lays out the components, using their constraints, within the `parent` container.

location()

```
public Point location(int x,int y)
```

The return `Point` value contains the coordinates of the cell that contains the pixel point (x,y).

lookupConstraints()

```
protected GridBagConstraints lookupConstraints(
        Component component)
```

Returns the constraints of the `component`.

maximumLayoutSize()

```
public Dimension maximumLayoutSize(Container target)
```

Returns the maximum size of the layout within the specified target container.

minimumLayoutSize()

```
public Dimension minimumLayoutSize(Container parent)
```

Returns the minimum size of the layout within the specified target container.

preferredLayoutSize()

```
public Dimension preferredLayoutSize(Container parent)
```

Returns the preferred size of the layout within the specified target container.

removeLayoutComponent()

```
public void removeLayoutComponent(Component component)
```

This method does nothing—it is defined to satisfy the requirements of the LayoutManager2 interface.

setConstraints()

```
public void setConstraints(Component component,
          GridBagConstraints constraints)
```

Specifies the set of constraints to be used for the component.

toString()

```
public String toString()
```

Returns a string representation of this object and its values.

Example 1

 Each example of the GridBagLayout is a complete program. Each one is designed to demonstrate some specific characteristic of the constraints. To do this, we have presented them in a specific sequence. The first example is the simplest, and each one, in turn, adds a single constraint to the one before it. It is possible to look at the window displayed by any example and—by comparing it to the window of the example before it—see how the addition of one particular constraint affects the display. To get a better idea of how the constraints work, you may want to run the example programs and change the sizes of the windows with the mouse to see how the component positions are managed.

The first example creates a few buttons and places them in a `Frame` container. The (x,y) grid positions are specified, but all the other constraint settings are allowed to default:

```java
import java.awt.*;

public class GridBagSimple extends Frame {
    GridBagLayout gridbag;
    GridBagConstraints con;
    public static void main(String[] arg) {
        new GridBagSimple();
    }
    public GridBagSimple() {
        setBackground(Color.lightGray);
        gridbag = new GridBagLayout();
        con = new GridBagConstraints();
        setLayout(gridbag);
        newButton(0,0);
        newButton(1,0);
        newButton(2,0);
        newButton(3,0);
        newButton(0,1);
        newButton(0,2);
        setSize(200,200);
        show();
    }
    private void newButton(int x,int y) {
        Button b = new Button("("+x+","+y+")");
        con.gridx = x;
        con.gridy = y;
        add(b);
        gridbag.setConstraints(b,con);
    }
}
```

The output is shown in Figure G-16. Each button is placed in its appropriate grid position according to the (x,y) coordinates stored in `gridx` and `gridy`. Because there are no weights on the buttons, they are not resized to fit the window.

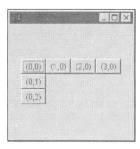

Figure G-16 Some buttons on a GridBagLayout
using the default constraints.

Example 2

This example is a minor modification of Example 1. In this example, each of
the buttons has been assigned a weight of 1, both vertically and horizontally:

```
import java.awt.*;

public class GridBagWeighted extends Frame {
    GridBagLayout gridbag;
    GridBagConstraints con;
    public static void main(String[] arg) {
        new GridBagWeighted();
    }
    public GridBagWeighted() {
        setBackground(Color.lightGray);
        gridbag = new GridBagLayout();
        con = new GridBagConstraints();
        setLayout(gridbag);
        newButton(0,0);
        newButton(1,0);
        newButton(2,0);
        newButton(3,0);
        newButton(0,1);
        newButton(0,2);
        setSize(200,200);
        show();
    }
    private void newButton(int x,int y) {
        Button b = new Button("("+x+","+y+")");
        con.gridx = x;
        con.gridy = y;
        con.weightx = 1;
        con.weighty = 1;
        add(b);
        gridbag.setConstraints(b,con);
```

      }

   }

    Because the buttons are assigned a weight value, the vacant space that was left around the perimeter in the previous examples is now included in each of the grid locations, as shown in Figure G-17. Each button is placed in a grid rectangle large enough to contain it, and there is no resizing, because the constraint value fill was allowed to default to NONE.

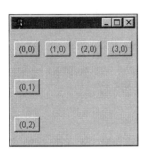

Figure G-17   Buttons with weights are awarded more area.

Example 3

    This example is the same as the previous one except that each Button has its fill constraint set to BOTH:

```
import java.awt.*;

public class GridBagFill extends Frame {
    GridBagLayout gridbag;
    GridBagConstraints con;
    public static void main(String[] arg) {
        new GridBagFill();
    }
    public GridBagFill() {
        setBackground(Color.lightGray);
        gridbag = new GridBagLayout();
        con = new GridBagConstraints();
        setLayout(gridbag);
        newButton(0,0);
        newButton(1,0);
        newButton(2,0);
        newButton(3,0);
        newButton(0,1);
        newButton(0,2);
        setSize(200,200);
        show();
```

```
        }
    private void newButton(int x,int y) {
        Button b = new Button("("+x+","+y+")");
        con.gridx = x;
        con.gridy = y;
        con.weightx = 1;
        con.weighty = 1;
        con.fill = GridBagConstraints.BOTH;
        add(b);
        gridbag.setConstraints(b,con);
    }
}
```

The Buttons all expand both vertically and horizontally to fill their cells in the grid as shown in Figure G-18. Because the weights are all the same magnitude, the buttons are all the same size.

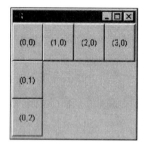

Figure G-18   Each button expands to fill its cell.

Example 4

This example modifies the previous example by assigning different weights to the buttons:

```
import java.awt.*;

public class GridBagVariableWeight extends Frame {
    GridBagLayout gridbag;
    GridBagConstraints con;
    public static void main(String[] arg) {
        new GridBagVariableWeight();
    }
    public GridBagVariableWeight() {
        setBackground(Color.lightGray);
        gridbag = new GridBagLayout();
        con = new GridBagConstraints();
        setLayout(gridbag);
```

```
            newButton(0,0,1,1);
            newButton(1,0,1,1);
            newButton(2,0,3,1);
            newButton(3,0,1,1);
            newButton(0,1,1,3);
            newButton(0,2,1,5);
            setSize(200,200);
            show();
        }
    private void newButton(int x,int y,int wx,int wy) {
            Button b = new Button("("+x+","+y+")");
            con.gridx = x;
            con.gridy = y;
            con.weightx = wx;
            con.weighty = wy;
            con.fill = GridBagConstraints.BOTH;
            add(b);
            gridbag.setConstraints(b,con);
        }
    }
```

The `GridBagLayout` manager begins by determining the preferred size of each of the components and uses that as a starting value for each cell size. If there is space left over, as in this case, it is doled out according to the weight of the components. The buttons in the left column are assigned vertical weight values of 1, 3, and 5, giving a total weight value for the column of 8. This means that the extra space will be allocated with the first button getting $\frac{1}{8}$, the second getting $\frac{3}{8}$, and the bottom button getting $\frac{5}{8}$ of the vertical space available. This is shown in Figure G-19.

In the horizontal row at the top, all the buttons have a weight of 1, except the button at (2,0), which has a weight of 3, giving a total for the row of 6. As you can see from Figure G-19, even though the button at (2,0) will get 50 percent of the space left over, there is not enough of it to make much of a difference. However, as shown in Figure G-20, when the window is widened, the button (2,0) gets a larger portion of the newly available space than the others do.

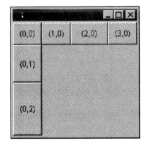

Figure G-19 Available space is allocated according to weights.

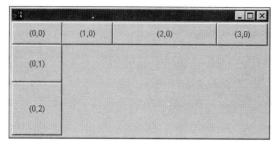

Figure G-20   As the window widens, those with
larger weight values get more space.

Example 5

This is a modification of the previous example to add width and height settings to each of the buttons:

```
import java.awt.*;

public class GridBagVariableSize extends Frame {
    GridBagLayout gridbag;
    GridBagConstraints con;
    public static void main(String[] arg) {
        new GridBagVariableSize();
    }
    public GridBagVariableSize() {
        setBackground(Color.lightGray);
        gridbag = new GridBagLayout();
        con = new GridBagConstraints();
        setLayout(gridbag);
        newButton(0,0,1,1,1,1);
        newButton(1,0,1,1,1,1);
        newButton(2,0,3,1,1,2);
        newButton(3,0,1,1,1,3);
        newButton(0,1,1,3,2,1);
        newButton(0,2,1,5,3,1);
        setSize(200,200);
        show();
    }
    private void newButton(int x,int y,int wx,int wy,
            int sx,int sy) {
        Button b = new Button("("+x+","+y+")");
        con.gridx = x;
```

```
        con.gridy = y;
        con.weightx = wx;
        con.weighty = wy;
        con.fill = GridBagConstraints.BOTH;
        con.gridwidth = sx;
        con.gridheight = sy;
        add(b);
        gridbag.setConstraints(b,con);
    }
}
```

The `gridwidth` and `gridheight` constraints default to 1—this is the number of cells that a component will consume. In this example, we set some of the buttons to cover 2 or 3 cells across, and some to cover 2 or 3 cells down. This causes the buttons to expand and fill the gaps to cover the entire window as shown in Figure G-21.

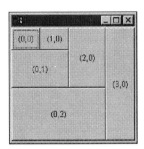

Figure G-21 Components can be designated as covering more than one cell.

With the configurations as defined, the window can now be resized, and the `GridBagLayout` manager will make every effort—following the rules of the constraints—to keep the ratios of the buttons in the requested proportions. Figures G-22 and G-23 show the results of using the mouse to expand the window horizontally and vertically.

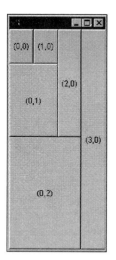

Figure G-22 The constraints maintain vertical size ratios.

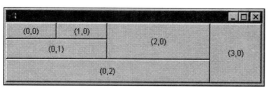

Figure G-23 The constraints maintain horizontal size ratios.

 The other layout managers are **FlowLayout**, **GridLayout**, **BorderLayout**, and **CardLayout**.

GridLayout

class java.awt.GridLayout

This is a layout manager that will position components on the displayable area of a container by laying them out on a uniform grid of rows and columns.

Inheritance

```
public class java.awt.GridLayout
    implements LayoutManager
    implements Serializable
    extends Object
```

⇑
```
public class java.lang.Object
```

Constructors
```
public GridLayout()
public GridLayout(int rows,int columns)
public GridLayout(int rows,int columns,int hgap,int vgap)
```

A rectangular grid is defined as having a specific number of `rows` and `columns`. The horizontal and vertical spacing between components can be set with `hgap` and `vgap`. The default `GridLayout` has one row and will place the components in it from left to right. If either the `row` or `column` value is less than one, an `IllegalArgumentException` is thrown.

Methods
addLayoutComponent()
```
public void addLayoutComponent(String name,
        Component component)
```

This method does nothing. It is here to satisfy the requirements of the `LayoutManager` interface.

getColumns()
```
public int getColumns()
```

Returns the number of columns.

getHgap()
```
public int getHgap()
```

Returns the value of the horizontal gap.

getRows()
```
public int getRows()
```

Returns the number of rows.

getVgap()
```
public int getVgap()
```

Returns the value of the vertical gap.

layoutContainer()

```
public void layoutContainer(Container parent)
```

Lays out the components in the parent window.

minimumLayoutSize()

```
public Dimension minimumLayoutSize(Container parent)
```

Returns the minimum size that it would take to lay out the components in the parent window.

preferredLayoutSize()

```
public Dimension preferredLayoutSize(Container parent)
```

Returns the preferred size for laying out the components in the parent window.

removeLayoutComponent()

```
public void removeLayoutComponent(Component comp)
```

This method does nothing. It exists to satisfy the requirements of the LayoutManager interface.

setColumns()

```
public void setColumns(int cols)
```

Specifies the number of columns.

setHgap()

```
public void setHgap(int hgap)
```

Specifies the horizontal gap between components.

setRows()

```
public void setRows(int rows)
```

Specifies the number of rows.

setVgap()

```
public void setVgap(int vgap)
```

Specifies the vertical gap between components.

toString()

```
public String toString()
```

Returns a string representation of this object and its values.

Example

This example creates a GridLayout manager with two rows and three columns:

```
import java.awt.*;
import java.awt.event.*;
public class ComponentGrid extends Frame
        implements ActionListener {
    public static void main(String[] arg) {
        new ComponentGrid();
    }
    ComponentGrid() {
        setLayout(new GridLayout(2,3));
        for(int i=0; i<3; i++)
            add(new Button("Button" + i));
        Choice choice = new Choice();
        choice.addItem("First item");
        choice.addItem("Second item");
        add(choice);
        add(new Label("I'm a Label"));
        Button quit = new Button("Quit");
        quit.addActionListener(this);
        add(quit);
        setSize(250,250);
        pack();
        show();
    }
    public void actionPerformed(ActionEvent event) {
        if(event.getActionCommand().equals("Quit")) {
            System.exit(0);
        }
    }
}
```

The layout manager divides the available space into equal-sized cells and places one component in each. The components are all resized to fit their cell. Figure G-24 shows the window as it first appears. Figures G-25 and G-26 demonstrate how the components are resized to fit the window as its dimensions change.

Figure G-24 A group of components controlled by the GridLayout manager.

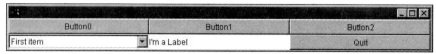

Figure G-25   Narrowing the window will narrow the components.

Figure G-26   Widening the window will widen the components.

 The other layout managers are **FlowLayout**, **GridBagLayout**, **BorderLayout**, and **CardLayout**.

Group

interface java.security.acl.Group

This interface is implemented by an object that maintains an internal collection of `Principal` objects.

The `Group` is also a `Principal`

This interface extends the `Principal` interface. This enables it to contain other `Group` objects as well as `Principal` objects. The result of this is that a `Group` object can contain an entire hierarchy of `Principal`s by having them contained in other `Group` objects. The class that implements the methods of this interface is expected to implement them in such a way that the search and remove operations are recursive and will traverse the entire hierarchy.

Inheritance

```
public interface java.security.acl.Group
    extends Principal
        ⇑
    public interface java.security.Principal
```

Methods

addMember()

```
public abstract boolean addMember(Principal user)
```

Adds this `Principal` to the group. Returns `true` if the add succeeds and `false` if the user is already a member.

isMember()

```
public abstract boolean isMember(Principal user)
```

Returns `true` if the `Principal` is a member of this group. The search is recursive. If the user belongs to a `Group` that is a member of this `Group`, it will be found.

members()

```
public abstract Enumeration members()
```

Returns an `Enumeration` object containing all the members of the group.

removeMember()

```
public abstract boolean removeMember(Principal user)
```

Removes the `Principal` from this `Group`. Returns `true` to indicate that the `user` was found and removed and `false` to indicate that the `user` was not a member of the group.

 See **Principal**.

GZIP

 See **ZLIB**.

GZIPInputStream

class java.util.zip.GZIPInputStream

This is an input stream designed to read and uncompress data that has been compressed in the GZIP format.

Inheritance

```
public class java.util.zip.GZIPInputStream
    extends InflaterInputStream
            ⇑
    public class java.util.zip.InflaterInputStream
        extends FilterInputStream
                ⇑
        public class java.io.FilterInputStream
            extends InputStream
                    ⇑
            public class java.io.InputStream
                extends Object
                        ⇑
                public class java.lang.Object
```

Variables and constants

crc

```
protected CRC32 crc
```

The 32-bit CRC of the uncompressed data.

eos

```
protected boolean eos
```

This is set to `true` to indicate that the end of the input stream has been reached.

GZIP_MAGIC

```
public static final int GZIP_MAGIC
```

This is the magic number that is embedded in the file header for identification of the file type.

Constructors

```
public GZIPInputStream(InputStream instream)
```

```
        throws IOException

public GZIPInputStream(InputStream instream,int size)
        throws IOException
```

A `GZIPInputStream` uses `instream` to read the compressed data. The `size` of the internal working buffer can be specified by `size` or allowed to default.

Methods

close()

```
public void close()
        throws IOException
```

Closes the input stream.

read()

```
public int read(byte barray[],int offset,int length)
        throws IOException
```

Compressed data from the input stream is uncompressed and placed into the array at `barray[offset]` for `length` bytes. The return value is the number of bytes actually placed in `barray`. This method will block until either data is available or the end of the input stream has been reached. The value −1 is returned to indicate the end of the input stream.

Example

This example reads its own source file and compresses it into a GZIP file. It then reads the GZIP file, uncompresses it, and writes it out in its original uncompressed form:

```
import java.io.*;
import java.util.zip.*;
public class FileGZIP {
    public static void main(String[] arg) {
        FileGZIP fg = new FileGZIP();
        fg.compress("FileGZIP.java","FileGZIP.gzip");
        fg.uncompress("FileGZIP.gzip","FileGZIP.ungzip");
    }
    public void compress(String infile,String outfile) {
        int length;
        byte[] barray = new byte[10];
        FileInputStream instream;
        FileOutputStream outstream;
        GZIPOutputStream gzipstream;
        try {
```

```
                    instream = new FileInputStream(infile);
                    outstream = new FileOutputStream(outfile);
                    gzipstream = new GZIPOutputStream(outstream);
                    while((length = instream.read(barray,
                                   0,barray.length)) > 0)
                        gzipstream.write(barray,0,length);
                    instream.close();
                    gzipstream.close();
                } catch(Exception e) {
                    e.printStackTrace();
                }
            }
        public void uncompress(String infile,String outfile) {
            int length;
            byte[] barray = new byte[10];
            FileInputStream instream;
            GZIPInputStream gzipstream;
            FileOutputStream outstream;
            try {
                    instream = new FileInputStream(infile);
                    gzipstream = new GZIPInputStream(instream);
                    outstream = new FileOutputStream(outfile);
                    while((length = gzipstream.read(barray,
                                   0,barray.length)) > 0)
                        outstream.write(barray,0,length);
                    gzipstream.close();
                    outstream.close();
                } catch(Exception e) {
                    e.printStackTrace();
                }
            }
        }
    }
```

As you can see from the example, once the GZIPInputStream or GZIPOutputStream has been opened, it can be used for reading and writing just like any other stream. It is important that the output file be closed to flush the output buffer because it is possible for the program to cease execution without performing the garbage collection that would normally flush the data.

 The companion class to this one is **GZIPOutputStream**. For other compression streaming classes, see **ZipInputStream**, **ZipOutputStream**, **DeflaterInputStream**, and **DeflaterOutputStream**. Also see **ZLIB**.

GZIPOutputStream

class java.util.zip.GZIPOutputStream

This class will compress data in the GZIP format and write the compressed data to a stream.

Inheritance

```
public class java.util.zip.GZIPOutputStream
    extends DeflaterOutputStream
        ⇑
    public class java.util.zip.DeflaterOutputStream
        extends FilterOutputStream
            ⇑
        public class java.io.FilterOutputStream
            extends OutputStream
                ⇑
            public class java.io.OutputStream
                extends Object
                    ⇑
                public class java.lang.Object
```

Variables and constants

crc

```
protected CRC32 crc
```

The 32-bit CRC of the uncompressed data.

Constructors

```
public GZIPOutputStream(OutputStream outstream)
    throws IOException

public GZIPOutputStream(OutputStream outstream,int size)
    throws IOException
```

The creation of a GZIPOutputStream requires an OutputStream to receive the compressed data. The size of its internal working buffer may be specified, or it may be allowed to default.

682 · GZIPOutputStream

Methods

close()

```
public void close()
    throws IOException
```

Writes any data remaining in the internal buffers, writes the trailing information, and then closes the underlying stream.

finish()

```
public void finish()
    throws IOException
```

Writes any data remaining in the internal buffers and writes the trailing information that ends the block of compressed data, but does not close the underlying stream. The next write() will be the start of a new block of data. This is convenient when multiple blocks of compressed data are to be written to the same stream.

write()

```
public synchronized void write(byte barray[],
        int offset,int length)
    throws IOException
```

Writes length bytes from barray beginning at barray[offset]. This method will block until all the data in the array have been compressed and written.

 For an example, see **GZIPInputStream**. For other compression streaming classes, see **ZipInputStream**, **ZipOutputStream**, **DeflaterInputStream**, and **DeflaterOutputStream**. Also see **ZLIB**.

hashcode

Every class in Java has a hashCode() method that returns a 32-bit hashcode value. The Object class has a hashCode() method that some classes override and some do not.

These values are not guaranteed to be entirely unique—nor can you use the hashcode to determine whether objects are identical. For example, the returned hashcodes from two Object objects will return different hashcode values even though the two are identical in every other way. On the other hand, two Byte objects that contain the same values will always return identical hashcodes.

About all you can be sure of is that two objects that return different hashcodes are not the same object. Generally speaking, the hashcode values can be used to differentiate objects kept in a table because objects with the same hashcodes are interchangeable.

Hashtable

class java.util.Hashtable

A Hashtable object maps keys to values. The key can be any object. For an object to be stored and retrieved, it must implement both the hashCode() and equals() methods—and because these methods are a part of the Object class (inherited by all the others), any Java object can be included in a Hashtable.

The load factor

The load factor of a hash table determines when the rehash() method will be called to increase capacity. The load factor is a number between 0.0 and 1.0. For example, a load factor of 0.75 will cause an increase in capacity when the current table is 75 percent full. A large load factor speeds the process of adding new entries by grabbing more RAM each time, but it will cause the location of any one entry to take a bit longer. A small load factor will save space by grabbing less RAM each time, but it will take more time to add entries.

The capacity rule of thumb

The capacity of a hash table will expand automatically as it is needed. If a hash table needs a large number of entries, it is best to create it with a large initial capacity to reduce the rehashing necessary whenever the capacity has to be expanded.

Extended by

```
Properties
```

Inheritance

```
public class java.util.Hashtable
    implements Cloneable
    implements Serializable
    extends Dictionary
        ⇑
    public class java.util.Dictionary
        extends Object
            ⇑
        public class java.lang.Object
```

Constructors

```
public Hashtable()
public Hashtable(int initialCapacity)
public Hashtable(int initialCapacity,float loadFactor)
```

If the `initialCapacity` is specified, space will be allocated immediately to hold that number of entries. If no `initialCapacity` is specified, a default will be assumed. The `initialCapacity` has no effect on the number of entries the `Hashtable` can hold—it will grow on demand to accept as many entries as the system permits. The `loadFactor` will set the load factor to trigger expanding the capacity.

An `IllegalArgumentError` will be thrown if either the specified `loadFactor` or `initialCapacity` is not greater than zero.

Methods

clear()

```
public synchronized void clear()
```

Removes all entries from the `Hashtable`.

clone()

```
public synchronized Object clone()
```

This is a shallow-copy clone—the keys and the values are not cloned. A new table is constructed with new references to the same objects. This can be an expensive operation if the table is very large.

contains()

```
public synchronized boolean contains(Object value)
```

Looks through the entries in the table to try to find the value. It returns true if it is found and false if not. If you have a choice, it would be better to use containsKey() because of efficiency. If value is null, a NullPointerException is thrown.

containsKey()

```
public synchronized boolean containsKey(Object key)
```

Returns true if key is found in the table.

elements()

```
public synchronized Enumeration elements()
```

Returns an Enumeration object that contains all the values currently stored in the table.

get()

```
public synchronized Object get(Object key)
```

Returns the value object associated with key. If it is not in the table, the method returns null.

isEmpty()

```
public boolean isEmpty()
```

Returns true if the table is empty.

keys()

```
public synchronized Enumeration keys()
```

Returns an Enumeration object that contains all the keys currently stored in the table.

rehash()

```
protected void rehash()
```

Rehashes the entire table into a new table of larger size. This method is called automatically whenever the table fills to the threshold setting.

remove()

```
public synchronized Object remove(Object key)
```

Removes key and its associated value from the table. If key is not found, no action is taken. The return value is the key, or null if the key was not found.

size()

```
public int size()
```

Returns the number of key/value pairs that are in the table.

toString()

```
public synchronized String toString()
```

This will convert the contents of the table to a String. The more entries in the table, the longer the String.

Example

This example not only shows the basics of using a hash table but also demonstrates that any kind of object can be used for either the key or the value:

```
import java.awt.*;
import java.util.*;
public class HashInAndOut {
    public static void main(String[] arg) {
        HashInAndOut hino = new HashInAndOut();
        hino.string2color();
        hino.color2string();
    }
    public void string2color() {
        Hashtable ht = new Hashtable();
        ht.put("red",Color.red);
        ht.put("blue",Color.blue);
        ht.put("green",Color.green);

        Color color = (Color)ht.get("blue");
        if(color != null)
            System.out.println(color);
    }
    public void color2string() {
        Hashtable ht = new Hashtable();
        ht.put(Color.red,"red");
        ht.put(Color.blue,"blue");
        ht.put(Color.green,"green");
```

```
        String colorName = (String)ht.get(Color.blue);
        if(colorName != null)
            System.out.println(colorName);
    }
}
```

The method `string2color()` creates a `Hashtable` and inserts three `Color` objects into it—each one keyed by a string. A string is then used to return the `Color` object. The result is that names are assigned to the colors.

The method `color2string()` creates a `Hashtable` and inserts the color names into it—each one keyed by a `Color` object. A `Color` object is then used to return the string. The result is the ability to determine the name of a `Color`.

 For other classes that act as containers of objects, see **Vector** and **Stack**.

hexadecimal

A hexadecimal number is a base-16 number. The characters 0 through 9 assume their usual values, and the characters A through F (upper- or lower-case) assume the values 10 through 15.

 For a description of hexadecimal literals, see **char**, **byte, short, int**, and **long**. To convert an integer to a base-16 `String`, see `toHexString()` in **Integer** and **Long**.

host

A host is any computer that is connected to an internet and, thus, has an IP address. It can be used to refer to a client, a server, a gateway, or a router.

HTML

Here is an HTML file that can be used to execute an applet:

```
<html>
<head>
<title> PageTitle </title>
</head>
<body>

<applet code="AppletName.class"
```

```
                    width=200
                    height=100>
      </applet>

      </body>

      </html>
```

This HTML code will run the applet in the file `AppletName.class` in a window 200 pixels wide by 100 pixels high. There are several parameters that can be specified, but as a minimum, `code`, `width`, and `height` must be given.

Inside the <applet>tag

The <applet> can contain a number of parameter settings. Aside from the required `code`, `width`, and `height`, there are some optional tags. Here is a description of them all:

archive

This is the name of the JAR file that holds the applet. The JAR can also hold other classes, resource files (image, audio, data, and so on), and other applets. The browser will load the entire archive file. When a file is needed, the files contained in the loaded JAR file will be searched before the `codebase` directory.

codebase

This is a URL that will specify the directory where the applet is to be found. This is the name of a directory and can be absolute or relative. If this is not specified, the directory holding the HTML document will be used.

code

This is the name of the applet. The file named here is the one that contains the compiled form of the applet. This can be a directory path, but it must be a relative path because this name is tacked onto the end of the `<codebase>` or onto the URL of the current directory.

width

This is the width, in pixels, of the applet window.

height

This is the height, in pixels, of the applet window.

alt

This is an alternate line of text that will be displayed by browsers that understand the applet tag but do not support applets.

name

This will assign a name to the instance of the applet. Applets running in the same browser can locate each other by name and communicate.

align

This will align the applet window on the page. This should support the same set of alignment settings as the <img> tag. Values include `top`, `middle`, and `bottom`.

vspace

This can be used to specify the number of pixels that the browser should leave at the top and bottom of the applet window.

hspace

This can be used to specify the number of pixels that the browser should leave on the left and right sides of the applet window.

Between <applet> and </applet>

It is possible to specify parameters in the HTML and have the applet read them. Any number of parameters can be specified—each has its own name and value. This HTML file executes an applet and sets up one parameter for it:

```
<html>
<head>
<title> ShowParmString </title>
</head>
<body>
<applet code="ShowParmString.class"
    width=330
    height=130>
<param name="OUTSTRING" value="Show Me!">
</applet>
</body>
</html>
```

This applet will read the parameter OUTSTRING with a call to `getParameter()` and display the string in the center of its window:

```
import java.awt.*;
import java.applet.*;

public class ShowParmString extends Applet {
    private static final String fontName = "Courier";
    private static final int fontStyle = Font.BOLD;
    private static final int fontSize = 35;
```

```
private String outString;
private Font font;
private Rectangle rectangle;
private int stringY;
private int stringX;

public void init() {
    font = new Font(fontName,fontStyle,fontSize);
    setBackground(Color.lightGray);
    if((outString = getParameter("OUTSTRING")) == null)
        outString = "Not Specified";
}

public void paint(Graphics g) {
    calculate(g);
    g.setColor(Color.black);
    g.setFont(font);
    g.drawString(outString,stringX,stringY);
    g.dispose();
}

private void calculate(Graphics g) {
    rectangle = getBounds();
    FontMetrics fm = g.getFontMetrics(font);
    stringX = rectangle.width;
    stringX -= fm.stringWidth(outString);
    stringX /= 2;
    stringY = rectangle.height;
    stringY -= fm.getAscent() + fm.getDescent();
    stringY /= 2;
    stringY += fm.getAscent();
}
}
```

The display from the applet is shown in Figure H-1.

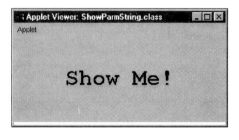

Figure H-1 Output showing a string passed in as a parameter.

The Archive tag

The class file of the applet can be compressed into a JAR file. The same JAR file can also contain other classes and resources (image and sound files) needed by the applet. Here is a version of the previous example that will load the applet from a JAR file:

```
<html>
<head>
<title> ShowParmString </title>
</head>
<body>
<applet code="ShowParmString.class"
  archive="showstuff.jar"
     width=330
     height=130>
<param name="OUTSTRING" value="Show Me!">
</applet>
</body>
</html>
```

The only difference between this example and the previous one is the addition of the `archive` flag. The file showstuff.jar can contain more than one applet, so it is still necessary to specify the name of the applet itself with the `code` tag. It is possible to specify several JAR files by separating them with commas, like this:

```
archive="ripple.jar, pictures.jar, sounds.jar"
```

 For more information on running applets, see **applet**. For the creation of JAR files, see **JAR**.

HttpURLConnection

class java.net.HttpURLConnection

This class encapsulates data and methods for communicating with a Web server. This is an abstract subclass of `URLConnection` adding features specific to HTTP.

Inheritance

```
public abstract class HttpURLConnection
     extends URLConnection
        ⇑
```

```
public abstract class java.net.URLConnection
        extends Object
          ⇑
    public class java.lang.Object
```

Variables and constants

The constants defined here that begin with HTTP_ are the standard error and status codes of the HTTP protocol. These values are sent from the server in a header field that contains the number and its descriptive string. Normally, they look something like this:

```
HTTP/1.0 200 OK
HTTP/1.0 404 Not Found
```

These examples specify the version number to be 1.0. The first has a status of 200, which means "OK," and the other has a status of 404, meaning "Not Found."

HTTP_ACCEPTED

```
public static final int HTTP_ACCEPTED = 202;
```

The request has been accepted for processing.

HTTP_BAD_GATEWAY

```
public static final int HTTP_BAD_GATEWAY = 502;
```

The server—while acting as a gateway or a proxy—received bad information from a server upstream.

HTTP_BAD_METHOD

```
public static final int HTTP_BAD_METHOD = 405;
```

The requested method is not allowed for the resource that was addressed.

HTTP_BAD_REQUEST

```
public static final int HTTP_BAD_REQUEST = 400;
```

The request was not understood by the proxy.

HTTP_CLIENT_TIMEOUT

```
public static final int HTTP_CLIENT_TIMEOUT = 408;
```

The client did not produce a response in the amount of time alloted to it by the server.

HTTP_CONFLICT

```
public static final int HTTP_CONFLICT = 409;
```

The server was not able to fulfill the request because of a conflict with the current state of the resource. A message of this type will have information the client can use to resolve the conflict.

HTTP_CREATED

```
public static final int HTTP_CREATED = 201;
```

According to the request, a new resource has been created.

HTTP_ENTITY_TOO_LARGE

```
public static final int HTTP_ENTITY_TOO_LARGE = 413;
```

The requested entity is too large.

HTTP_FORBIDDEN

```
public static final int HTTP_FORBIDDEN = 403;
```

The server is refusing the request.

HTTP_GATEWAY_TIMEOUT

```
public static final int HTTP_GATEWAY_TIMEOUT = 504;
```

The server—while acting as a gateway or proxy—did not receive a timely response from a server upstream.

HTTP_GONE

```
public static final int HTTP_GONE = 410;
```

The requested resource is no longer to be found at the server.

HTTP_INTERNAL_ERROR

```
public static final int HTTP_INTERNAL_ERROR = 501;
```

The client has made a request that requires a capability not implemented by the server.

HTTP_LENGTH_REQUIRED

```
public static final int HTTP_LENGTH_REQUIRED = 411;
```

The server refuses to honor a request that does not specify the length of the content.

HTTP_MOVED_PERM

```
public static final int HTTP_MOVED_PERM = 301;
```

The requested resource has been permanently moved to a different URL.

HTTP_MOVED_TEMP

```
public static final int HTTP_MOVED_TEMP = 302;
```

The requested resource has been temporarily moved to a different URL.

HTTP_MULT_CHOICE

```
public static final int HTTP_MULT_CHOICE = 300;
```

The request was not specific enough and the server is returning a list of multiple choices that the client can use to make a new request.

HTTP_NO_CONTENT

```
public static final int HTTP_NO_CONTENT = 204;
```

The server has fulfilled the request but there is no information to send back.

HTTP_NOT_ACCEPTABLE

```
public static final int HTTP_NOT_ACCEPTABLE = 406;
```

The requested resource is not capable of generating a response in a form acceptable to the client.

HTTP_NOT_AUTHORITATIVE

```
public static final int HTTP_NOT_AUTHORITATIVE = 203;
```

The information returned in the header is not directly from an authoritative source and could be out of date.

HTTP_NOT_FOUND

```
public static final int HTTP_NOT_FOUND = 404;
```

The server cannot find anything that matches the requested resource.

HTTP_NOT_MODIFIED

```
public static final int HTTP_NOT_MODIFIED = 304;
```

The conditional GET request was not executed because the resource has not been modified.

HTTP_OK

```
public static final int HTTP_OK = 200;
```

Request fulfilled.

HTTP_PARTIAL

```
public static final int HTTP_PARTIAL = 206;
```

The server has fulfilled a partial GET for the requested resources.

HTTP_PAYMENT_REQUIRED

```
public static final int HTTP_PAYMENT_REQUIRED = 402;
```

This code reserved for future use.

HTTP_PRECON_FAILED

```
public static final int HTTP_PRECON_FAILED = 412;
```

A precondition—imposed by the client as part of the request—failed at the server causing the server not to fulfill the request.

HTTP_PROXY_AUTH

```
public static final int HTTP_PROXY_AUTH = 407;
```

The client must first authenticate itself to the proxy before any requests will be honored.

HTTP_REQ_TOO_LONG

```
public static final int HTTP_REQ_TOO_LONG = 414;
```

The server did not fulfill the request because the URL was too long.

HTTP_RESET

```
public static final int HTTP_RESET = 205;
```

The server has fulfilled the request but the user should reset the document view. This normally has to do with data in forms.

HTTP_SEE_OTHER

```
public static final int HTTP_SEE_OTHER = 303;
```

The requested resource is to be found at another URL.

HTTP_SERVER_ERROR

```
public static final int HTTP_SERVER_ERROR = 500;
```

An unexpected error condition has arisen on the server causing the request not to be fulfilled.

HTTP_UNAUTHORIZED

```
public static final int HTTP_UNAUTHORIZED = 401;
```

This request was denied because of lack of authentication.

HTTP_UNAVAILABLE

```
public static final int HTTP_UNAVAILABLE = 503;
```

The request cannot be fulfilled because of temporary overloading or maintenance.

HTTP_UNSUPPORTED_TYPE

```
public static final int HTTP_UNSUPPORTED_TYPE = 415;
```

The request is in a format that is not supported by the server.

HTTP_USE_PROXY

```
public static final int HTTP_USE_PROXY = 305;
```

The requested resource must be accessed through the proxy.

HTTP_VERSION

```
public static final int HTTP_VERSION = 505;
```

The server does not support this version of HTTP.

method

```
protected String method
```

responseCode

```
protected int responseCode
```

responseMessage

```
protected String responseMessage
```

Constructors

```
protected HttpURLConnection(URL url)
```

An `HttpURLConnection` is constructed for a specific `url`.

Methods

disconnect()

```
public abstract void disconnect()
```

Closes the connection to the Web server.

getFollowRedirects()

```
public static boolean getFollowRedirects()
```

getRequestMethod()

```
public String getRequestMethod()
```

Returns the name of the request method.

getResponseCode()

```
public int getResponseCode()
    throws IOException
```

Returns the HTTP code sent by the server. The returned code will be one of the HTTP_ constants defined in this class. A −1 is returned if no code is available.

getResponseMessage()

```
public String getResponseMessage()
    throws IOException
```

Returns the HTTP response message sent by the server. This is the text associated with the response code. For example, it will be "OK" for a 202 code and "Not Found" for a 404.

setFollowRedirects()

```
public static void setFollowRedirects(boolean setting)
```

Setting this to `true` will cause HTTP redirects to be followed automatically. The default is `false`. It cannot be changed in an applet.

setRequestMethod()

```
public void setRequestMethod(String method)
    throws ProtocolException
```

Sets the `method` command for the URL request. The `method` is one of these:

```
"DELETE"
"GET"
"HEAD"
"OPTIONS"
"POST"
"PUT"
"TRACE"
```

The default is "GET". A `ProtocolException` is thrown if `method` is invalid.

usingProxy()

```
public abstract boolean usingProxy()
```

This will return `true` if the connection has been made through a proxy.

identifiers

An identifier is a sequence of characters beginning with a letter and containing letters and digits. The letters and digits are not limited to ASCII—Java has the entire Unicode set of characters to draw from. Letters and digits from the ASCII character set can be intermixed freely with those of any other alphabet, or numeric set, found in Unicode. There is no limit to the number of characters in an identifier.

The Java letters include the ASCII uppercase A–Z and lowercase a–z. The Java digits include the ASCII 0–9. For purposes of constructing Java identifiers, the ASCII dollar sign and underscore are also considered to be Java letters. It is recommended that the dollar sign be used only to access legacy code or for identifiers in automatically generated code. Here are some sample identifiers:

```
Sp    jump2    MAX_SETTING    maximumSetting
```

Any valid Java letter or number can be included in an identifier—all you need is a text editor that will let you put them in. Here are some identifiers using non-ASCII characters:

```
@sigma@pi    jum@pi
```

If, however, you must insert the special characters but only have an ASCII editor, the same two identifiers can be created by using escapes, like this:

```
\u03A3\u03D6    jum\u03D6
```

Also see **names**. For identifiers used as labels, see **break** and **continue**. For information on other Java tokens, see **lexical structure**. For some special identifiers, see **keywords**. For information on Java letters and digits, see **letters**, **digits**, **Unicode**, and **ASCII**. For ASCII insertion of Unicode characters, see **escapes**. There are methods to distinguish letters and digits from other Unicode characters in the **Character** class.

699

Identity

class java.security.Identity

This class is used to represent real-world objects, including people, smart cards, companies, or other things that can have identities authenticated by using a public key.

The name and the key

All identities have both a name and a public key. The name is immutable. Both the name and the key are unique within their scope of existence. An identity may have a set of one or more certificates to verify its authenticity.

Certification

A certificate is used to validate an identity. It is a guarantee by one principal that a public key is the correct one for another principal. Before a certificate can confidently be used to validate an identity, the certificate itself will need to be validated. There is no inherent way of doing this—it is the responsibility of the party providing the certificate to provide a method of validating it.

Subclassing

The identity class can be subclassed to add extensions such as postal addresses, e-mail addresses, telephone numbers, images of people, and logos.

Extended by

```
IdentityScope
Signer
```

Inheritance

```
public abstract class java.security.Identity
    implements Principal
    implements Serializable
    extends Object
        ⇑
    public class java.lang.Object
```

Constructors

```
protected Identity()

public Identity(String name)
```

```
public Identity(String name,IdentityScope scope)
    throws KeyManagementException
```

The name is the name of the entity being identified, and scope is the scope of the identity. If the scope is not specified, an Identity is constructed without scope. The default constructor is supplied only for streaming. The KeyManagementException is thrown if there is already an Identity with this name in the scope.

Returned by

An object of this class is returned from IdentityScope.getIdentity().

Methods

addCertificate()

```
public void addCertificate(Certificate certificate)
    throws KeyManagementException
```

Adds a certificate to the identity. If the Identity has a public key, the public key in certificate must match it. If the Identity does not have a public key, it will have its public key set to the one in certificate.

certificates()

```
public Certificate[] certificates()
```

Returns an array containing all the certificates of this Identity.

equals()

```
public final boolean equals(Object object)
```

If the object is an Identity containing the same name and scope as this one, returns true — otherwise, a call is made to identityEquals() to make the determination.

getInfo()

```
public String getInfo()
```

Returns a descriptive string of general information about the identity.

getName()

```
public final String getName()
```

Returns the name of the identity.

getPublicKey()

```
public PublicKey getPublicKey()
```

Returns the public key of the identity.

getScope()

```
public final IdentityScope getScope()
```

Returns the scope of the identity.

hashCode()

```
public int hashCode()
```

Returns the hashcode value for this Identity.

identityEquals()

```
protected boolean identityEquals(Identity identity)
```

This method should be overloaded by subclasses to return true if the specified identity is the same as this one. The default method returns true only if the names and public keys are both identical.

removeCertificate()

```
public void removeCertificate(Certificate certificate)
        throws KeyManagementException
```

Removes the certificate from this identity. A KeyManagementException is thrown if the certificate is not found.

setInfo()

```
public void setInfo(String info)
```

This will specify the general information string for the identity.

setPublicKey()

```
public void setPublicKey(PublicKey key)
        throws KeyManagementException
```

Specifies the public key for this identity. The existing key and all the certificates will be removed. The KeyManagementException will be thrown if another Identity in the same scope has the same key.

toString()

```
public String toString()
```

```
public String toString(boolean detailed)
```

Returns a string that includes the name and scope of this identity. If detailed is true, more information will be provided.

Also see **IdentityScope**, **Signer**, and **Principal**.

IdentityScope

class java.security.IdentityScope

This class represents a scope for identities and is a container of the identities within the scope. Every `Identity` object has a unique name within its scope.

An `IdentityScope` **is also an** `Identity`

Because an `IdentityScope` is an `Identity`—complete with a name, an optional public key, and a collection of certificates—it can be included inside another `IdentityScope`. Different kinds of `Identity` objects exist, and all of them—including signers— can be contained in an `IdentityScope`. Different `IdentityScopes` may apply different sets of rules for operations on different kinds of identities.

Unique key

Each `Identity` in the `IdentityScope` is unique. No two `Identity` objects can contain the same key value and—since each identity is accessed by name—no two identities can have the same name.

Inheritance

```
public abstract class java.security.IdentityScope
    extends Identity
        ⇑
    public abstract class java.security.Identity
        implements Principal
        implements Serializable
        extends Object
            ⇑
        public class java.lang.Object
```

Constructors

```
protected IdentityScope()

public IdentityScope(String name)

public IdentityScope(String name,IdentityScope scope)
    throws KeyManagementException
```

The `name` is the name of the new `IdentityScope`, and `scope` is the encompassing scope into which this one is to fit. If the `scope` is not specified, an `IdentityScope` is constructed without scope. The default constructor is supplied only for streaming. The `KeyManagementException` is thrown if an `Identity` with this name already exists in the `scope`.

Returned by

An object of this class is returned from `Identity.getScope()` and `IdentityScope.getSystemScope()`.

Methods

addIdentity()

```
public abstract void addIdentity(Identity identity)
    throws KeyManagementException
```

Adds a new `Identity` to the scope. The `KeyManagementException` will the thrown if a duplicate name exists, a duplicate key exists, or the `Identity` is otherwise invalid.

getIdentity()

```
public abstract Identity getIdentity(String name)
```

Returns the `Identity` with the specified name. If none exists by the name, return `null`.

getIdentity()

```
public Identity getIdentity(Principal principal)
```

Returns the `Identity` that has the same name as the `principal`. Return `null` if there is no match.

getIdentity()

```
public abstract Identity getIdentity(PublicKey key)
```

Returns the `Identity` that contains the specified public key. Return `null` if there is no match.

getSystemScope()

```
public static IdentityScope getSystemScope()
```

Returns the `IdentityScope` of the system.

identities()

```
public abstract Enumeration identities()
```

Returns an `Enumeration` of all the `Identity` objects in this `IdentityScope`.

removeIdentity()

```
public abstract void removeIdentity(Identity identity)
    throws KeyManagementException
```

Removes the `identity` from this `IdentityScope`. The `KeyManagementException` is thrown if the `identity` is not in this scope.

setSystemScope()

```
protected static void setSystemScope(IdentityScope scope)
```

Sets the `IdentityScope` of the system.

size()

```
public abstract int size()
```

Returns a count of the number of `Identity` objects in this `IdentityScope`.

toString()

```
public String toString()
```

Returns a string describing this object. The description includes the name, the scope name, and a count of the number of `Identity` objects.

For more information on objects contained in a scope, see **Identity**. Also see **Signer**, **Principal**, and **Key**.

IEEE 754

Java uses the floating-point format defined by the IEEE Standard for Binary Floating-Point Arithmetic, ANSI/IEEE Standard 754-1985 (IEEE, New York). Java uses the 32-bit form for the `float` primitive type and the 64-bit form for the `double` primitive type.

For details of each, see **float** and **double**.

if
---

keyword

The keyword `if` is used to evaluate a Boolean expression and, depending on the results of the evaluation, either executes, or skips, over a block of code.

The conditional expression in an `if` statement must result in a `boolean`. Unlike similar expressions in C and C++, this is not a test for zero or nonzero —it is a test for `true` or `false`. In Java, no conversion is made between a `boolean` type and any other type.

The simple if statement

In its simplest form, the if statement has a Boolean expression in parentheses and a single statement to execute, like this:

```
if(a < b)
    j = 45;
```

If more than one statement is to be executed, they will need to be grouped with braces, like this:

```
if(a < b) {
    j = 45;
    k = 52;
}
```

The else statement

By using an else statement, you can set up an if statement that will execute one block or the other, like this:

```
if(a < b)
    j = 192;
else
    j = -6
```

If multiple statements are to be executed by the if statement, they will need to be grouped into a block, like this:

```
if(a < b) {
    j = 44;
    k = 56;
} else {
    j = 22;
    k = 0;
}
```

The if-else statement

The if-else statement is really nothing syntactically special—it is simply a consequence of the way the syntax is designed for if and else. If you need to execute one of several statements (or one of several blocks of statements), they can be included in a string of if-else statements, like this:

```
if(a > b) {
    j = 44;
} else if(a == c) {
```

```
        j = 10;
   } else if(a == 0) {
        j = 90;
   } else {
        j = -1;
   }
```

In this string of statements, if a is greater than b, j will be set to 44 and the rest of the statement will be skipped. If a is not greater than b but does equal c, j is set to 10 and the rest of the statement will be skipped. If neither of the first two blocks is executed, and if a is 0, j will be set to 90. Finally, if none of the other blocks executed, j will be set to –1.

Labeling an if block

A label can be placed on an if statement to make it the target of a break statement of a for, do, while, or switch statement inside the block of the if statement. Consider this example:

```
int k = 4;
kiff: if(k == 4) {
    for(int i=0; i<10; i++) {
        for(j=0; j<10; j++) {
            if(j == k)
                break kiff;
        }
    }
    x = 55;
}
k = 22;
```

In this example, the value of x will never be set to 55. Inside the inner loop, when j is equal to k, the break statement will break out of the loop to the level labeled kiff. This label tags the entire if block as the level of the break, so execution will continue by setting k to 22.

 For other ways to do conditional execution, see **switch** and **question mark**. The iteration keywords are **do**, **for**, and **while**.

IllegalAccessError

class java.lang.IllegalAccessError

This is thrown when there is an attempt to access some member of a class and the access is denied. This can happen when a program has been compiled referencing one version of a class and then is executed with another version. That is, something that was accessible during the compilation has become inaccessible during execution.

All the classes need to be compiled again because something is out of phase. Recompiling all the classes will either fix the problem or generate a compiler error where the access has been denied.

Inheritance

```
public class java.lang.IllegalAccessError
    extends IncompatibleClassChangeError
            ⇑
    public class java.lang.IncompatibleClassChangeError
        extends LinkageError
                ⇑
        public class java.lang.LinkageError
            extends Error
                    ⇑
            public class java.lang.Error
                extends Throwable
                        ⇑
                public class java.lang.Throwable
                    implements Serializable
                    extends Object
                            ⇑
                    public class java.lang.Object
```

Constructors

```
public LinkageError()
public LinkageError(String message)
```

If the message string is supplied, it is used as a detailed message describing this particular exception.

IllegalAccessException

class java.lang.IllegalAccessException

Java has the capability of loading classes by name at runtime. This exception is thrown whenever a class has been successfully loaded but an attempt has been made to access an inaccessible member of the class.

Inheritance

```
public class java.lang.IllegalAccessException
    extends Exception
            ⇑
    public class java.lang.Exception
        extends Throwable
                ⇑
        public class java.lang.Throwable
            implements Serializable
            extends Object
                    ⇑
            public class java.lang.Object
```

Constructors

```
public IllegalAccessException()
public IllegalAccessException(String message)
```

If the message string is supplied, it is used as a detailed message describing this particular exception.

IllegalArgumentException

class java.lang.IllegalArgumentException

This is thrown to indicate that the value of an argument that has been passed to a method is not valid. The data type of the argument is correct—it is the value that is in error. An example would be an attempt to pass a negative number to a square-root method.

Extended by

```
IllegalThreadStateException
InvalidParameterException
NumberFormatException
```

Inheritance

```
public class java.lang.IllegalArgumentException
    extends RuntimeException
            ⇑
    public class java.lang.RuntimeException
```

```
extends Exception
       ⇑
public class java.lang.Exception
    extends Throwable
           ⇑
    public class java.lang.Throwable
        implements Serializable
        extends Object
               ⇑
            public class java.lang.Object
```

Constructors

```
public RuntimeException()
public RuntimeException(String message)
```

If the message string is supplied, it is used as a detailed message describing this particular exception.

IllegalComponentStateException

class java.awt.IllegalComponentStateException

This exception is thrown to indicate that an AWT component is not in the correct state for the requested operation.

Inheritance

```
public class java.awt.IllegalComponentStateException
    extends IllegalStateException
       ⇑
    public class java.lang.IllegalStateException
        extends RuntimeException
           ⇑
        public class java.lang.RuntimeException
            extends Exception
               ⇑
            public class java.lang.Exception
                extends Throwable
                   ⇑
                public class java.lang.Throwable
                    implements Serializable
                    extends Object
```

```
              ⇑
    public class java.lang.Object
```

Constructors

```
    public IllegalComponentStateException()
    public IllegalComponentStateException(String message)
```

If the `message` string is supplied, it is used as a detailed message describing this particular exception.

IllegalMonitorStateException

class java.lang.IllegalMonitorStateException

This exception it thrown to signal that a monitor operation has been attempted when the monitor is in an invalid state.

Inheritance

```
    public class java.lang.IllegalMonitorStateException
        extends RuntimeException
                    ⇑
        public class java.lang.RuntimeException
            extends Exception
                    ⇑
            public class java.lang.Exception
                extends Throwable
                    ⇑
                public class java.lang.Throwable
                    implements Serializable
                    extends Object
                        ⇑
                        public class java.lang.Object
```

Constructors

```
    public IllegalMonitorStateException()
    public IllegalMonitorStateException(String message)
```

If the `message` string is supplied, it is used as a detailed message describing this particular exception.

For information on monitoring, see **synchronize**. Also see the wait() and notify() methods of **Object**.

IllegalStateException

class java.lang.IllegalStateException

This exception indicates that a method has been invoked at a time when the object was not in a state to handle it. For example, the StreamTokenizer will throw this exception if an attempt is made to read data before the file has been opened.

Extended by

IllegalComponentStateException

Inheritance

```
public class java.lang.IllegalStateException
    extends RuntimeException
        ⇑
    public class java.lang.RuntimeException
        extends Exception
            ⇑
        public class java.lang.Exception
            extends Throwable
                ⇑
            public class java.lang.Throwable
                implements Serializable
                extends Object
                    ⇑
                public class java.lang.Object
```

Constructors

```
public IllegalStateException()
public IllegalStateException(String message)
```

If the message string is supplied, it is used as a detailed message describing this particular exception.

IllegalThreadStateException

class java.lang.IllegalThreadStateException

This is an exception indicating that a thread is not in the proper state for the requested operation. For example, an attempt to start a thread that has already been started will cause this exception to be thrown.

Inheritance

```
public class java.lang.IllegalThreadStateException
     extends IllegalArgumentException
              ⇑
     public class java.lang.IllegalArgumentException
          extends RuntimeException
                   ⇑
          public class java.lang.RuntimeException
               extends Exception
                        ⇑
               public class java.lang.Exception
                    extends Throwable
                             ⇑
                    public class java.lang.Throwable
                         implements Serializable
                         extends Object
                                  ⇑
                         public class java.lang.Object
```

Constructors

```
public IllegalArgumentException()
public IllegalArgumentException(String message)
```

If the `message` string is supplied, it is used as a detailed message describing this particular exception.

image

package java.awt.image

This package contains classes and interfaces that have to do with the modification, scaling, filtering, and general manipulation of graphical images.

Interfaces

```
ImageConsumer
ImageObserver
ImageProducer
```

Classes

```
AreaAveragingScaleFilter
ColorModel
CropImageFilter
DirectColorModel
FilteredImageSource
ImageFilter
IndexColorModel
MemoryImageSource
PixelGrabber
ReplicateScaleFilter
RGBImageFilter
```

 For a Java graphical image object, see **Image**. For drawing an image on the display, see **Graphics**.

Image

class java.awt.Image

This is an abstract class used as the superclass of the platform-dependent implementation of the RAM-resident form of an image. An image is a rectangular area containing pixel values suitable for being painted onto a displayable, printable, or RAM-resident graphic object. This class also includes methods that can take image data and modify it, creating a new `Image` object the reflects the modification.

Inheritance

```
public abstract class java.awt.Image
    extends Object
        ⇑
    public class java.lang.Object
```

Variables and constants

SCALE_AREA_AVERAGING

```
public static final int SCALE_AREA_AVERAGING
```

This is used to request that the `AreaAveragingScaleFilter` should be used to scale the image. The request can be ignored and another algorithm—one that is more efficient for a particular platform—used instead.

SCALE_DEFAULT

```
public static final int SCALE_DEFAULT
```

This is used to request that the default image scaling algorithm be used.

SCALE_FAST

```
public static final int SCALE_FAST
```

This is used to request that the most efficient scaling algorithm be used to scale the image. The selected scaling method could sacrifice quality for speed.

SCALE_REPLICATE

```
public static final int SCALE_REPLICATE
```

This is used to request that the `ReplicateScaleFilter` image scaling algorithm should be used to scale the image. The request can be ignored and another algorithm—one that is more efficient for a particular platform—used instead.

SCALE_SMOOTH

```
public static final int SCALE_SMOOTH
```

This is used to request that a smoothing image scaling algorithm should be used to scale the image. This selection may cause speed to be sacrificed for the sake of smoothing.

UndefinedProperty

```
public static final Object UndefinedProperty
```

This object should be returned when a request is made for a property that is unknown or invalid for this particular image.

Constructors

```
public Image()
```

Returned by

An `Image` object is returned from calls to any of these methods:

```
Applet.getImage()
AppletContext.getImage()
BeanInfo.getIcon()
Component.createImage()
ComponentPeer.createImage()
Frame.getIconImage()
Image.getScaledInstance()
SimpleBeanInfo.getIcon()
SimpleBeanInfo.loadImage()
Toolkit.createImage()
Toolkit.getImage()
```

Methods

flush()

```
public abstract void flush()
```

Frees any resources being held by this Image. The Image is still usable after this call, but if some sort of caching of pixels or precalculation of values had been executed, that will have been discarded by the call to flush() and will have to be recreated or refetched before the Image will become usable again.

getGraphics()

```
public abstract Graphics getGraphics()
```

Returns a Graphics object that can be used to draw to this Image. This is used for off-screen rendering into a RAM-resident Image.

getHeight()

```
public abstract int getHeight(ImageObserver observer)
```

Returns the height of the image. If the height is not known (as is sometime the case while the image is being loaded), the return value is −1.

getProperty()

```
public abstract Object getProperty(String name,
        ImageObserver observer)
```

Returns the named property. Which actual properties are available depends on the format of an image. If a property is not defined, the return value will be an UndefinedProperty object. A null return value indicates that the property values are not yet known but the ImageObserver will be notified when they are.

The property name "comment" should respond with information about the image — such things as the name of the image, its source, and its creator.

getScaledInstance()

```
public Image getScaledInstance(int width,int height,int hints)
```

Returns a new Image that is a scaled version of this one. The new image will be of the specified width and height. Either the width or the height can be specified as a negative number to be replaced by the appropriate value to maintain the aspect ratio of the image. The value of hints should be one of the constants defined in this class to indicate the desired scaling algorithm.

getSource()

```
public abstract ImageProducer getSource()
```

Returns the object that was the source of the internal image—the one that produced the pixel values. This method is used for image filtering, conversion, and scaling to acquire the input stream of pixels.

getWidth()

```
public abstract int getWidth(ImageObserver observer)
```

Returns the width of the image. It the width is not known (as is sometime the case while the image is being loaded), the return value is −1.

Example

This example loads an image file from the disk and allows the user to expand and shrink the image:

```java
import java.awt.*;
import java.awt.event.*;
import java.awt.image.*;
import java.net.*;
import java.util.*;

public class ImageScaling extends Frame
        implements ActionListener {
    private Panel mainPanel;
    private Panel buttonPanel;
    private BlueMarble blueMarble;
    private Button largerButton;
    private Button smallerButton;
    private Button quitButton;

    public static void main(String arg[]) {
        ImageScaling is = new ImageScaling();
    }
```

```
ImageScaling() {
    super("ImageScaling");
    mainPanel = new Panel();
    mainPanel.setLayout(new BorderLayout());
    blueMarble = new BlueMarble();
    mainPanel.add("North",blueMarble);
    buttonPanel = new Panel();
    smallerButton = new Button("Smaller");
    smallerButton.addActionListener(this);
    buttonPanel.add(smallerButton);
    largerButton = new Button("Larger");
    largerButton.addActionListener(this);
    buttonPanel.add(largerButton);
    quitButton = new Button("Quit");
    quitButton.addActionListener(this);
    buttonPanel.add(quitButton);
    mainPanel.add("South",buttonPanel);
    add(mainPanel);
    pack();
    show();
}

public void actionPerformed(ActionEvent event) {
    if(event.getActionCommand().equals("Larger"))
        makeLarger();
    else if(event.getActionCommand().equals("Smaller"))
        makeSmaller();
    else if(event.getActionCommand().equals("Quit"))
        System.exit(0);
}

private void makeLarger() {
    blueMarble.makeLarger();
}

private void makeSmaller() {
    blueMarble.makeSmaller();
}
}

class BlueMarble extends Canvas {
    private Image stillImage;
    private Image zoomImage;
```

```java
    private int stillHeight;
    private int stillWidth;
    private int zoomHeight;
    private int zoomWidth;
    BlueMarble() {
        setBackground(Color.black);
        loadImageFromFile();
        setSize(150,150);
    }
    private void loadImageFromFile() {
        stillImage =
            getToolkit().getImage("bluemarble.gif");
        waitForImage(stillImage);
        stillHeight = stillImage.getHeight(this);
        stillWidth = stillImage.getWidth(this);
        zoomWidth = stillWidth;
        zoomHeight = zoomWidth;
        zoomImage = stillImage;
    }
    private void waitForImage(Image image) {
        MediaTracker mt = new MediaTracker(this);
        mt.addImage(image,1);
        try {
            mt.waitForAll();
        } catch(Exception e) {
            e.printStackTrace();
            System.exit(0);
        }
    }
    public void paint(Graphics g) {
        g.drawImage(stillImage,0,0,this);
        g.drawImage(zoomImage,0,stillHeight + 2,this);
    }
    public void makeSmaller() {
        zoomImage = stillImage.getScaledInstance(
            --zoomWidth,--zoomHeight,
            Image.SCALE_AREA_AVERAGING);
        waitForImage(zoomImage);
        repaint();
    }
    public void makeLarger() {
        zoomImage = stillImage.getScaledInstance(
            ++zoomWidth,++zoomHeight,
            Image.SCALE_AREA_AVERAGING);
```

```
            waitForImage(zoomImage);
            repaint();
        }
    }
```

The class `BlueMarble` extends `Canvas` and handles all the image work. It starts off by loading the unscaled image into `stillImage` by using the `getImage()` method in the `Toolkit`. The `waitForImage()` method is called— it blocks until the image is fully loaded. A copy is made of the image and its dimensions. The `paint()` method displays the two copies of the image—one above the other.

Each time a button is pressed to make the image smaller or larger, a new `zoomImage` is created with a new set of width and height values. The `waitForImage()` method is called each time (if you run the program, you will probably notice the pause here) a new `zoomImage` is created by scaling the original to a new width and height. Figure I-1 shows the result of pressing the Smaller button a few times, and Figure I-2 shows the result of pressing Larger a few times.

Figure I-1   The display after the image has been reduced a few times.

Figure I-2   The display after the image has been enlarged a few times.

For information on displaying an image, see **Graphics**. For information on loading an image from a file, see the `getImage()` method of **Toolkit**, **Applet**, and **AppletContext**. To monitor image loading, see **MediaTracker**. For image manipulation, see **ImageConsumer**, **ImageProducer**, **ImageObserver**, and **ImageFilter**. For information on image scaling, see **ReplicateScaleFilter** and **AreaAveragingScaleFilter**.

ImageConsumer

interface java.awt.image.ImageConsumer

This interface is implemented by classes wishing to receive image pixel data from an `ImageProducer`.

How they connect

When an `ImageConsumer` is registered with an `ImageProducer`, the `ImageProducer` will deliver all the data to the `ImageConsumer`. This is done using the methods of the two interfaces. A single class can be both an `ImageConsumer` and an `ImageProducer` to act as an image filter.

Hints

Some flag constants defined in the class are meant to be used by an `ImageProducer` as hints about how pixels should be delivered to the `ImageConsumer`. These values, used as arguments to the `setHints()` method, are called "hints" because they may be ignored. Their purpose is to allow the image consumer to implement some optimizations. The hint values are one-bit flags that can be used in combinations.

The color model

It is possible to specify a color model to be used by the `ImageConsumer`, but it should not be assumed that the `ImageProducer` will always use this model. Each set of pixels delivered via `setPixels()` has its own accompanying `ColorModel`. It is conceivable that a multiframe image could be delivered using more than one color model—the color model could be altered only for the frames that have been modified by a filter somewhere upstream.

Implemented by

```
ImageFilter
PixelGrabber
```

Inheritance

```
public interface java.awt.image.ImageConsumer
```

Variables and constants

COMPLETESCANLINES

```
public static final int COMPLETESCANLINES
```

This is a hint specifying that the pixels be delivered in groups of one or more complete scan lines.

IMAGEABORTED

```
public static final int IMAGEABORTED
```

This status indicates that the production of the image has been aborted.

IMAGEERROR

```
public static final int IMAGEERROR
```

This status indicates that the production of the image encountered an error.

RANDOMPIXELORDER

```
public static final int RANDOMPIXELORDER
```

This hint is used to state that the pixels may be delivered in any order that suits the producer. The ImageConsumer cannot perform any optimizations that assume the pixels will be received in any particular order. RANDOMPIXELORDER should be the assumption in the absence of any other information.

SINGLEFRAME

```
public static final int SINGLEFRAME
```

This hint is used to indicate a single static image—no animation or changes of any kind. The pixels will be defined in calls to the setPixels() method, and then the imageComplete() method will be called with the STATICIMAGEDONE flag. At this point, no further image data will be delivered.

SINGLEFRAMEDONE

```
public static final int SINGLEFRAMEDONE
```

This status indicates that a complete frame has been delivered but there are more frames to come.

SINGLEPASS

```
public static final int SINGLEPASS
```

This hint indicates that the pixels will be delivered in a single pass—each pixel is going to appear only once in each call to setPixels(). (Some image types, such as JPEG, will send the pixels in multiple passes, with each pass being more detailed than the previous.)

STATICIMAGEDONE

```
public static final int STATICIMAGEDONE
```

This status signals that the image is complete. There are no more pixels to be delivered.

TOPDOWNLEFTRIGHT

```
public static final int TOPDOWNLEFTRIGHT
```

This hint states that the pixels will be delivered in top-down left-right order. Knowing this can allow the processing of the pixels to be optimized as a stream instead of being buffered and processed all at once.

Methods

imageComplete()

```
public abstract void imageComplete(int status)
```

This method is called by the ImageProducer to indicate a completion status, when, for instance, no more pixels will be delivered or one frame of a multiframe image is complete. It could also indicate an error. The value of status is one or more of the status constants defined in this interface. Unless the ImageConsumer is interested in receiving more data from the ImageProducer, it should remove itself as a registered consumer.

setColorModel()

```
public abstract void setColorModel(ColorModel model)
```

Specifies the color model to be used. Exactly what this means is up to the ImageConsumer —this does not guarantee that the incoming pixels will be delivered using this model.

setDimensions()

```
public abstract void setDimensions(int width,int height)
```

The ImageProducer reports the size of the image that is to be sent to the ImageConsumer by calling this method.

setHints()

```
public abstract void setHints(int hintflags)
```

This method is called by the ImageProducer with information about how the pixels are going to be delivered. These hints—a combination of one or more of the hint flag values defined above—can be used by the ImageConsumer to optimize its processing. The ImageConsumer can expect that this method will be called before any calls to setPixels() to deliver pixels—if it is called after pixels have been delivered, the results are undefined.

setPixels()

```
public abstract void setPixels(int x,int y,
        int width,int height,
        ColorModel model,byte pixels[],
        int offset,int scansize)

public abstract void setPixels(int x,int y,
        int width,int height,
        ColorModel model,int pixels[],
        int offset,int scansize)
```

This method is called by the ImageProducer to deliver pixels to the ImageConsumer. The entire image can be delivered in one method call, or it can take several calls.

The values of x and y specify the upper-left corner of the section of the image being delivered. The width and height values specify the count of the number of pixels being delivered in each dimension. If the entire image is being delivered, the values of x and y will both be zero, and the width and height will be the size of the entire image.

The ColorModel is that of the pixels being delivered.

The pixels array contains the actual pixel values. Depending on the color model, each pixel is stored as either 32 bits or 8 bits. Because the format of the pixel data matches the ColorModel argument, this argument should be used for any processing of the pixel data. The implementation of this interface normally requires that the two versions of this method (one for 8-bit data and one for 32-bit data) be identical except for the difference in the sizes of the individual pixels.

The offset is an index to the first pixel in the array. The scansize is the width of each horizontal row of pixels in the delivered rectangle. These two values are used to address the individual pixels. The address of an individual pixel is

```
pixels[px + (py * scansize) + offset]
```

where px and py are the *x* and *y* coordinates of the pixel.

setProperties()

```
public abstract void setProperties(Hashtable props)
```

Sets the list of properties associated with this image.

Example

This example implements an ImageConsumer that prints the information about the image to System.out.

The getImage() method of the default Toolkit is used to create an Image object from a disk file. The ImageProducer of the Image has an instance of the ImageLister registered with it as being an ImageConsumer—this is done with a call to startProduction() that causes the ImageProducer to call the appropriate methods of the ImageConsumer:

```java
import java.util.*;
import java.awt.*;
import java.awt.image.*;
public class ImageLister implements ImageConsumer {
    public static void  main(String[] arg) {
        Toolkit tk = Toolkit.getDefaultToolkit();
        Image image = tk.getImage("bluemarble.gif");
        ImageProducer ip = image.getSource();
        ImageLister lister = new ImageLister();
        ip.startProduction(lister);
    }
    public void imageComplete(int status) {
        boolean exit = true;
        String outstring = "imageComplete(";
        switch(status) {
        case IMAGEABORTED:
            outstring += "IMAGEABORTED";
            break;
        case IMAGEERROR:
            outstring += "IMAGEERROR";
            break;
        case SINGLEFRAMEDONE:
            outstring += "SINGLEFRAMEDONE";
            exit = false;
            break;
        case STATICIMAGEDONE:
            outstring += "STATICIMAGEDONE";
            break;
        default:
            outstring += status;
            break;
        }
        System.out.println(outstring + ")");
        if(exit)
            System.exit(0);
    }
    public void setColorModel(ColorModel model) {
        System.out.println("setColorModel(" + model + ")");
    }
    public void setDimensions(int width,int height) {
        System.out.println("setDimension(" +
            width + "," + height + ")");
    }
    public void setHints(int hints) {
```

```
                String outstring = "";
                if((hints & COMPLETESCANLINES) != 0)
                    outstring += "COMPLETESCANLINES ";
                if((hints & RANDOMPIXELORDER) != 0)
                    outstring += "RANDOMPIXELORDER ";
                if((hints & SINGLEFRAME) != 0)
                    outstring += "SINGLEFRAME ";
                if((hints & STATICIMAGEDONE) != 0)
                    outstring += "STATICIMAGEDONE ";
                if((hints & TOPDOWNLEFTRIGHT) != 0)
                    outstring += "TOPDOWNLEFTRIGHT ";
                System.out.println(outstring);
        }
        public void setPixels(int x,int y,int width,int height,
                ColorModel model,byte pixels[],
                int offset,int scansize) {
            System.out.println("setPixels(byte pixels)");
            System.out.println("    x=" + x + " y=" + y +
                " width=" + width + " height=" + height);
            System.out.println("   ColorModel: " + model);
            System.out.println("    offset=" + offset +
                " scansize=" + scansize);
        }
        public void setPixels(int x,int y,int width,int height,
                ColorModel model,int pixels[],
                int offset,int scansize) {
            System.out.println("setPixels(int pixels)");
            System.out.println("    x=" + x + " y=" + y +
                " width=" + width + " height=" + height);
            System.out.println("   ColorModel: " + model);
            System.out.println("    offset=" + offset +
                " scansize=" + scansize);
        }
        public void setProperties(Hashtable props) {
            System.out.println("setProperties(" + props + ")");
        }
    }
```

Each method of the ImageConsumer interface is implemented with a method that prints out the data passed to it. This gives us a look at the order in which things happen and the sort of things that are passed to the ImageConsumer. Different image sources will have different results, but the process will be the same. Here is the output from this example:

```
setDimension(72,72)
```

```
setProperties({})
setColorModel(java.awt.image.IndexColorModel@1cc949)
COMPLETESCANLINES SINGLEFRAME STATICIMAGEDONE TOPDOWNLEFTRIGHT
setPixels(byte pixels)
    x=0 y=0 width=72 height=1
    ColorModel: java.awt.image.IndexColorModel@1cc949
    offset=0 scansize=0
setPixels(byte pixels)
    x=0 y=1 width=72 height=1
    ColorModel: java.awt.image.IndexColorModel@1cc949
    offset=0 scansize=0
setPixels(byte pixels)
    x=0 y=2 width=72 height=1
    ColorModel: java.awt.image.IndexColorModel@1cc949
    offset=0 scansize=0

    ... lines deleted ...

setPixels(byte pixels)
    x=0 y=70 width=72 height=1
    ColorModel: java.awt.image.IndexColorModel@1cc949
    offset=0 scansize=0
setPixels(byte pixels)
    x=0 y=71 width=72 height=1
    ColorModel: java.awt.image.IndexColorModel@1cc949
    offset=0 scansize=0
imageComplete(STATICIMAGEDONE)
```

 The interface for the class that invokes this one is **ImageProducer**. For more image processing, see **FilteredImageSource**, **ImageFilter**, **ImageObserver**, **PixelGrabber**, and **RGBImageFilter**.

ImageFilter

class java.awt.image.ImageFilter

This class is a generic filter that will receive an image from an `ImageProducer` and pass it onto an image `ImageConsumer`.

This the base

This is a base class that has no effect on the image being passed through it. To construct a filter that will modify the image, it will be necessary to subclass `ImageFilter`.

Filtering action

This class is designed to receive the output from an ImageProducer object and pass the filtered image to a ImageConsumer. Specifically, it expects the data in the form generated from a FilteredImageSource object.

Extended by

```
CropImageFilter
ReplicateScaleFilter
RGBImageFilter
```

Inheritance

```
public class java.awt.image.ImageFilter
    implements ImageConsumer
    implements Cloneable
    extends Object
        ⇑
    public class java.lang.Object
```

Variables and constants

consumer

```
protected ImageConsumer consumer
```

This class, an ImageProducer, passes the filtered image to this ImageConsumer.

Constructors

ImageFilter()

```
public ImageFilter()
```

The filter is constructed without the consumer being initialized.

Returned by

An ImageFilter object is returned from getFilterInstance().

Methods

clone()

```
public Object clone()
```

Creates a clone of this object.

getFilterInstance()

```
public ImageFilter getFilterInstance(ImageConsumer consumer)
```

This does two things. It defines the consumer of the image to be filtered and returns a clone of this object. Note that this method must be called because it is the only way to specify the consumer.

imageComplete()

```
public void imageComplete(int status)
```

This method is called by the ImageProducer to indicate a completion status, such as that no more pixels will be delivered, or that one frame of a multiframe image is complete. It could also imply an error. The value of status is one or more of the status constants defined in this class. Unless the ImageFilter is interested in receiving more data from the ImageProducer, it should remove itself as a registered consumer.

resendTopDownLeftRight()

```
public void resendTopDownLeftRight(ImageProducer producer)
```

This method is called to request that the image previously processed be processed again — but this time in top-down left-right order. This method can do three things:

1. It can request that the producer send the data again in the requested top-down left-right order. If the producer is capable of doing this, this object simply filters the image again and passes it onto the consumer.

2. It could hold the entire image in RAM and convert it to top-down left-right order.

3. If neither this object nor the producer has the ability to generate the image in the requested order, this method simply returns, and no further action is taken.

setColorModel()

```
public void setColorModel(ColorModel model)
```

Specifies the color model to be used.

setDimensions()

```
public void setDimensions(int width,int height)
```

The size of the image that is to be sent is reported to the ImageFilter by calling this method.

setHints()

```
public void setHints(int hints)
```

This method is called by the `ImageProducer` with information about how the pixels are going to be delivered. These hints—a combination of one or more of the hint flag values defined in the `ImageConsumer` interface—can be used by the `ImageFilter` to optimize its processing. The `ImageFilter` can expect that this method will be called before any calls to `setPixels()` to deliver pixels—if it is called after pixels have been delivered, the results are undefined.

setPixels()

```
public void setPixels(int x,int y,
          int width,int height,
          ColorModel model,byte pixels[],
          int off,int scansize)

public void setPixels(int x,int y,
          int width,int height,
          ColorModel model,int pixels[],
          int off,int scansize)
```

This method is called by the `ImageProducer` to deliver pixels to the `ImageFilter`. The entire image can be delivered in one call, or it can take several calls.

The values of x and y specify the upper-left corner of the section of the image being delivered. The `width` and `height` values specify the count of the number of pixels being delivered in each dimension. If the entire image is being delivered, the values of x and y will both be zero, and the `width` and `height` will be the size of the entire image.

The `ColorModel` is that of the pixels being delivered.

The `pixels` array contains the actual pixel values. Depending on the color model, each pixel is stored in either 32 bits or 8 bits. Because the format of the pixel data matches the `ColorModel` argument, this argument should be used for any processing of the pixel data. The implementation of this interface normally requires that the two versions of this method (one for 8-bit data and one for 32-bit data) be identical except for the difference in the sizes of the individual pixels.

The `offset` is an index to the first pixel in the array. The `scansize` is the width of each horizontal row of pixels in the delivered rectangle. These two values are used to address the individual pixels. The address of an individual pixel is

```
pixels[px + (py * scansize) + offset]
```

where px and py are the *x* and *y* coordinates of the pixel.

setProperties()

```
public void setProperties(Hashtable props)
```

This method is called by the image producer as it passes along the properties associated with the image. This class then appends its `toString()` value to the property keyed to "filters" in the table and then passes the properties onto the next image consumer.

Example

This example loads an image from a file and displays two versions of it—one unaltered and the other passed through a filter that rotates it 90 degrees:

```
import java.awt.*;
import java.awt.image.*;
public class RollMarble extends Frame {
    public static void main(String[] arg) {
        new RollMarble();
    }
    RollMarble() {
        add("Center",new TwoMarble());
        setSize(72,200);
        show();
    }
}
class TwoMarble extends Canvas {
    Image upright;
    Image tilted;
    TwoMarble() {
        setBackground(Color.black);
        upright = getToolkit().getImage("bluemarble.gif");
        MediaTracker mt = new MediaTracker(this);
        mt.addImage(upright,1);
        try {
            mt.waitForAll();
        } catch(Exception e) {
            e.printStackTrace();
            System.exit(0);
        }
        ImageProducer ip = upright.getSource();
        TiltFilter tf = new TiltFilter();
        FilteredImageSource fip =
                new FilteredImageSource(ip,tf);
        tilted = getToolkit().createImage(fip);
    }
    public void paint(Graphics g) {
        g.drawImage(upright,0,0,this);
        g.drawImage(tilted,0,
                upright.getHeight(this)+2,this);
    }
}
class TiltFilter extends ImageFilter {
    int width;
```

```
        int height;
        public void setDimensions(int width,int height) {
            this.width = width;
            this.height = height;
            super.setDimensions(width,height);
        }
        public void setHints(int hint) {
            hint |= ImageConsumer.TOPDOWNLEFTRIGHT;
            super.setHints(hint);
        }
        public void setPixels(int x,int y,int width,int height,
                ColorModel model,byte pixels[],
                int offset,int scansize) {
            byte pnew[] = new byte[width * height];
            for(int px=0; px<width; px++) {
                for(int py=0; py<height; py++) {
                    int oldIndex =
                        px + (py*scansize) + offset;
                    int newIndex =
                        py + (px*scansize) + offset;
                    pnew[newIndex] = pixels[oldIndex];
                }
            }
            super.setPixels(x,y,height,width,
                    model,pnew,offset,scansize);
        }
        public void setPixels(int x,int y,int width,int height,
                ColorModel model,int pixels[],
                int offset,int scansize) {
            int pnew[] = new int[width * height];
            for(int px=0; px<width; px++) {
                for(int py=0; py<height; py++) {
                    int oldIndex =
                        px + (py*scansize) + offset;
                    int newIndex =
                        py + (px*scansize) + offset;
                    pnew[newIndex] = pixels[oldIndex];
                }
            }
            super.setPixels(x,y,height,width,
                    model,pnew,offset,scansize);
        }
    }
```

The TwoMarble class prepares both images in its constructor. The unaltered image is loaded from disk and stored in upright. The upright image is then passed through the filter to create the tilted image. This is done by creating a new FilteredImageSource object using the upright image and the TiltFilter on the constructor—this causes images to be created by being passed through the filter. The actual image creation occurs on the call to createImage(). The result is shown in Figure I-3.

Figure I-3 An image rotated by 90 degrees.

The class TiltFilter is an extension of ImageFilter. ImageFilter implements all the methods in such a way that if no methods are overridden, a subclass will simply be a null filter—the image will pass through unchanged. You will notice that for each method overridden in TiltFilter there is a call to the superclass version of the same method. This is necessary because we are working with a filter—all data coming in must be passed on whether or not it is altered. The setDimensions() method is used to grab a copy of the dimensions of the image, and the values are passed on. The setHints() method is used to make certain that a request exists to send the pixel data in top-down left-right order, and the flags are then passed on. The image is modified in setPixels() by reading an input pixel at (x,y) and writing an output pixel to (y,x), thus rotating the image 90 degrees.

ImageObserver

interface java.awt.image.ImageObserver

This interface is implemented by any class that wants to be able to receive status update information on an Image while it is being constructed.

All components have it

This interface is implemented by Component, which means that the information is available to all the Java graphical components.

Getting and using the information

An `Image` notifies an `ImageObserver` of a change in the status of the `Image` by calling the callback method `imageUpdate()` with new information. The `ImageObserver` can use the information supplied from the loading image to know when it is possible to draw a partially complete image.

Implemented by

`Component`

Inheritance

`public interface java.awt.image.ImageObserver`

Variables and constants

ABORT

`public static final int ABORT`

This flag bit indicates that an `Image` being observed was aborted before it was completed. The image production has stopped, and there will be no more information. If a no `ERROR` flag accompanied the `ABORT` flag, an attempt can be made to restart image production.

ALLBITS

`public static final int ALLBITS`

This flag indicates that all the bits of image are now complete. A static image that was previously drawn is now complete and can be drawn again in its final form.

ERROR

`public static final int ERROR`

This flag indicates that an image that was being tracked has encountered an error. No further information will be available, and any attempt to draw the image will fail. This flag can be accompanied by the `ABORT` flag to indicate the cause of the failure.

FRAMEBITS

`public static final int FRAMEBITS`

This flag is used whenever a frame of a multiframe image that has been previously drawn is ready to be drawn again. The frame may not be entirely complete yet, but it is more complete than it was when it was previously drawn.

HEIGHT

```
public static final int HEIGHT
```

This flag indicates that the height of the image is available as the height argument to the imageUpdate() callback method.

PROPERTIES

```
public static final int PROPERTIES
```

This flag indicates that the properties of the image are now available.

SOMEBITS

```
public static final int SOMEBITS
```

This flag indicates that more pixels are available to be drawn. The rectangle defining the available pixels is itself defined by the x, y, width, and height arguments passed to the imageUpdate() callback method.

WIDTH

```
public static final int WIDTH
```

This flag indicates that the width of the image is available as the width argument to the imageUpdate() callback method.

Methods

imageUpdate()

```
public abstract boolean imageUpdate(Image image,
          int infoflags,int x,int y,int width,int height)
```

This method is called whenever a change in state occurs in the image. The image argument is the one being observed. The infoflags setting is one or more of the flag values defined as constants in this interface—these flags specify the reason for this method call.

The values of x, y, width, and height will vary a bit in meaning with the purpose of the method call. For example, if the flag SOMEBITS is set, the rectangle specified will be the area of the new pixels. If the flag is ALLBITS or FRAMEBITS, the values should be ignored. If the HEIGHT or WIDTH flags are set, the height and width values are those of the full-sized image.

This method should continue to return true as long as further updates are needed—once false has been returned, the method should not be called again.

If you implement this method, you will need to take the necessary actions to make sure that the image is drawn properly. The default version of this method in Component calls repaint().

Example

This is an example of observing an Image being loaded from disk:

```
import java.awt.*;
import java.applet.*;
import java.net.*;
public class LoadTrack extends Applet {
    Image image;
    public void init() {
        URL url = getCodeBase();
        image = getImage(url,"bluemarble.gif");
    }
    public void paint(Graphics g) {
        g.drawImage(image,0,0,this);
    }
    public boolean imageUpdate(Image image,int flags,
            int x,int y,int width,int height) {
        String outstring = "";
        if((flags & ABORT) != 0)
            outstring += "ABORT ";
        if((flags & ALLBITS) != 0)
            outstring += "ALLBITS ";
        if((flags & ERROR) != 0)
            outstring += "ERROR ";
        if((flags & FRAMEBITS) != 0)
            outstring += "FRAMEBITS ";
        if((flags & HEIGHT) != 0)
            outstring += "HEIGHT ";
        if((flags & PROPERTIES) != 0)
            outstring += "PROPERTIES ";
        if((flags & SOMEBITS) != 0)
            outstring += "SOMEBITS ";
        if((flags & WIDTH) != 0)
            outstring += "WIDTH ";
        System.out.println(outstring);
        System.out.println("    x=" + x + " y=" + y +
            " width=" + width + " height=" + height);
        return(super.imageUpdate(image,flags,
            x,y,width,height));
    }
}
```

There is no need to explicitly implement the interface, because it is implemented in Component. In fact, a full implementation of the imageUpdate() method in the Component class contains all the code necessary to track the loading of the `Image` and issue calls to `repaint()` whenever there is new data for the image — this is the implementation of the incremental mode of displaying images. This example implements the `imageUpdate()` method only to print the values being passed in; it then calls the superclass version of the method to handle the actual display. The output from this program looks like this: HEIGHT WIDTH

```
    x=0 y=0 width=72 height=72
PROPERTIES
    x=0 y=0 width=0 height=0
SOMEBITS
    x=0 y=0 width=72 height=1
SOMEBITS
    x=0 y=1 width=72 height=1
SOMEBITS
    x=0 y=2 width=72 height=1
SOMEBITS
    x=0 y=3 width=72 height=1

    ... <lines deleted> ...

SOMEBITS
    x=0 y=68 width=72 height=1
SOMEBITS
    x=0 y=69 width=72 height=1
SOMEBITS
    x=0 y=70 width=72 height=1
SOMEBITS
    x=0 y=71 width=72 height=1
ALLBITS
    x=0 y=0 width=72 height=72
```

The first two calls to `imageUpdate()` supply the `height` and `width` of the image and the fact that the property information associated with the `Image` is available. This is followed by a method call for each horizontal row of pixels until all 72 have been delivered. The final entry is the notification that all bits have been delivered.

 For a more application-level way of tracking images, see **MediaTracker**.

ImageProducer

interface java.awt.image.ImageProducer

This interface is implemented by classes that have the ability to produce pixel-level image data.

There is one in every `Image`

An `ImageProducer` is included inside every `Image` object. It is used to reconstruct the image whenever it is needed by an `ImageConsumer`. For example, if a scaled copy of the image is requested, the `ImageProducer` will do the scaling and generate a new set of pixels.

Top-down left-right

The method `requestTopDownLeftRightResend()` can be called by a recipient of the data produced here to request that the data be sent again in top-down left-right order. The `ImageProducer` can ignore the request, or it can honor it. Circumstances may arise in which an ImageConsumer will be able to process a higher-quality image if the data arrives in this order.

Implemented by

```
FilteredImageSource
MemoryImageSource
```

Inheritance

```
public interface java.awt.image.ImageProducer
```

Constructors

Returned by

An object implementing this interface can be returned from `Image.getSource()`.

Methods

addConsumer()

```
public abstract void addConsumer(ImageConsumer consumer)
```

Adds `consumer` to the list of objects that are to receive output when the image is being produced. The `ImageProducer` may start delivering image data immediately, but it is not required to do so—it could wait until there is a call to the `startProduction()` method.

isConsumer()

```
public abstract boolean isConsumer(
        ImageConsumer consumer)
```

Returns `true` if `consumer` is registered with this `ImageProducer` to receive image data.

removeConsumer()

```
public abstract void removeConsumer(
        ImageConsumer consumer)
```

Removes `consumer` from the list of objects registered to receive image data. No error ensues if `consumer` is not registered.

requestTopDownLeftRightResend()

```
public abstract void requestTopDownLeftRightResend(
        ImageConsumer consumer)
```

This method can be used by a `consumer` to request that the data be sent again, and this time in top-down left-right order. This request can be honored or ignored.

If the request is going to be honored, the calls to the `ImageConsumer` methods should take this form:

```
consumer.setHints(TOPDOWNLEFTRIGHT,...);
for( ... )
        consumer.setPixels(...);
consumer.imageComplete();
```

This sequence will tell the `consumer` that data in the requested format is coming, send the data, and then signal the `consumer` that the image is complete.

startProduction()

```
public abstract void startProduction(ImageConsumer consumer)
```

Adds the `consumer` to the list of `ImageConsumer`s to receive a copy of the output data, and immediately starts producing image data. No error arises if the `consumer` is already registered.

 For a class to produce images in RAM, see **MemoryImageSource**. Also see **ImageConsumer**.

immutable

Something that is immutable cannot be changed. In Java, when a class is referred to as being *immutable,* it means the contents of the objects of the class cannot be changed. For example, the `String` object is immutable. When a

`String` object is created, it is created containing a string of characters that cannot be changed. To get a `String` object with a different set of characters, it is necessary to create a new object.

implements

keyword

The `implements` keyword is used in the definition of a class to declare names of the interfaces being implemented by methods of the class.

 For examples of implementing an interface, see **interface**.

import

keyword

The `import` statement may appear in a compilation unit to tell Java where to locate external type names that are to be found in other packages. The `import` statement can include the name of a specific class (for example, `java.awt.image.ColorModel`), or it can use a wildcard notation to make available all the classes in a package (for example, `java.awt.image.*`).

 The `import` statement is not an "include" statement like the one in C—there is no preprocessor in Java. The `import` statement simply tells the compiler where it should look to resolve references to names that are not found locally. The `import` statement is more like the "extern" of assembly language than the "include" of C. If you can imagine an extern statement that allows directory paths and wildcard names, you have the idea.

It is just a matter of convenience

Strictly speaking, `import` statements are not necessary—any program that can be written with them can also be written without them. They simply create a sort of shorthand for resolving external references—they just tell Java where to look. The same thing could be achieved by using fully qualified names in all references.

The default imports

A compilation unit never has to `import` anything in its own package. Every Java compilation unit in a package has access to every defined class or interface in that same package—there is an implicit `import` statement for it.

There is another implicit `import` statement. The `java.lang` package is automatically imported. While the packages `java.io` and `java.util` must always be available for importation, they are not automatically imported. Although it isn't necessary, it is not an error to name the current package or the `java.lang` package in an `import` statement.

There is no hiding

Package names do not hide other package names—more `import` statements just give the compiler more places to look. Because names are never hidden, there is never a need to import something from the same package in which a compilation unit is found—all public names are implicitly imported inside the same package.

Importation of a single type

This is the simplest and most direct form of an import statement—it imports one specific type from a package. Here are some examples:

```
import java.awt.Rectangle;
import java.applet.AudioClip;
import java.util.Vector;
```

In each of these a specific class is imported. A reference to any one of the names will be resolved directly. For example, the statement

```
Rectangle rec = new Rectangle();
```

can be written instead of

```
java.awt.Rectangle rec = new java.awt.Rectangle();
```

In the presence of the `import` statement, the two statements are identical.

Importation of a package

All the names and types in an entire package can be imported in a single statement by using wildcard notation. All the classes in `java.util` can be imported with the single statement

```
import java.util.*;
```

The Java compiler will look in the package to find any names that are otherwise undefined. Since the `java.util` package contains, among other things, the class definition of `Stack`, this statement could be used to create a `Stack` object:

```
Stack st = new Stack();
```

The compiler will check to make sure that the package named in the `import` statement is accessible.

It is not valid to split a path name to a package—the code reference must be either a simple name or a fully qualified name. For example, the class `Inflater` is in the package `java.util.zip`. There are two ways to reference the name. Without an import statement, this is valid:

```
java.util.zip.Inflater inf =
            new java.util.zip.Inflater();
```

The same result can be achieved with an import statement in this way:

```
import java.util.zip.*;
...
Inflater inf = new Inflater();
```

This is not valid:

```
import java.util.*;
...
zip.Inflater inf = new zip.Inflater(); //Error
```

 To put classes and interfaces into packages, see **package**. For the position of the import statement in a source file, see **compilation unit**. For a list of the classes that are automatically imported, see **java.lang**.

IncompatibleClassChangeError

class java.lang.IncompatibleClassChangeError

This error is thrown when a class has been modified in such a way that it no longer interfaces correctly with another class. This can happen when a class is modified and recompiled, but another class—one that interfaces with it—has not been recompiled. A quick solution is to recompile all the classes—either the error will clear up or the compiler will report the problem.

Extended by

```
AbstractMethodError
IllegalAccessError
InstantiationError
NoSuchFieldError
NoSuchMethodError
```

Inheritance

```
public class java.lang.IncompatibleClassChangeError
    extends LinkageError
            ⇑
    public class java.lang.LinkageError
        extends Error
                ⇑
        public class java.lang.Error
            extends Throwable
```

$$\Uparrow$$
```
public class java.lang.Throwable
       implements Serializable
       extends Object
```
$$\Uparrow$$
```
            public class java.lang.Object
```

Constructors

```
public IncompatibleClassChangeError()
public IncompatibleClassChangeError(String message)
```

If the `message` string is supplied, it is used as a detailed message describing this particular exception.

increment

++

This is an operator in the Java language. It is a unary operator that will increase the value of a primitive type by one. It can be used in two ways—as a postincrement or as a preincrement. A postincrement will reduce the value *after* it has been used in an expression, and a preincrement will reduce the value *before* it has been used. A preincrement operator looks like this:

```
++x
```

and a postincrement operator looks like this:

```
x++
```

There is a companion operator, the decrement operator, that will reduce the value by one. A predecrement operator looks like this:

```
--x
```

and a postdecrement operator looks like this:

```
x--
```

Example

This example demonstrates the effects of the increment and decrement operators being applied to an `int` and a `double`. In each case, the value of the primitive type is adjusted by exactly 1:

```
public class IncrDecr {
```

```
public static void main(String[] arg) {
    int a;
    int b;
    double x;
    double y;

    System.out.println
        ("Before     Operation    After");
    a = 5;
    System.out.print("int a=" + a);
    System.out.print("          b = a++;");
    b = a++;
    System.out.println("    b=" + b + " a=" + a);
    a = 5;
    System.out.print("int a=" + a);
    System.out.print("          b = ++a;");
    b = ++a;
    System.out.println("    b=" + b + " a=" + a);
    a = 5;
    System.out.print("int a=" + a);
    System.out.print("          b = a--;");
    b = a--;
    System.out.println("    b=" + b + " a=" + a);
    a = 5;
    System.out.print("int a=" + a);
    System.out.print("          b = --a;");
    b = --a;
    System.out.println("    b=" + b + " a=" + a);

    x = 5.5;
    System.out.print("double x=" + x);
    System.out.print("    y = x++;");
    y = x++;
    System.out.println("    y=" + y + " x=" + x);
    x = 5.5;
    System.out.print("double x=" + x);
    System.out.print("    y = ++x;");
    y = ++x;
    System.out.println("    y=" + y + " x=" + x);
    x = 5.5;
    System.out.print("double x=" + x);
    System.out.print("    y = x--;");
    y = x--;
    System.out.println("    y=" + y + " x=" + x);
```

```
            x = 5.5;
            System.out.print("double x=" + x);
            System.out.print("    y = --x;");
            y = --x;
            System.out.println("      y=" + y + " x=" + x);
        }
    }
```

Pre- and postincrement and pre- and postdecrement operations are shown for integer and real data types. This is a total of eight operations. The output looks like this:

```
Before           Operation    After
int a=5          b = a++;     b=5 a=6
int a=5          b = ++a;     b=6 a=6
int a=5          b = a--;     b=5 a=4
int a=5          b = --a;     b=4 a=4
double x=5.5     y = x++;     y=5.5 x=6.5
double x=5.5     y = ++x;     y=6.5 x=6.5
double x=5.5     y = x--;     y=5.5 x=4.5
double x=5.5     y = --x;     y=4.5 x=4.5
```

IndexColorModel

class java.awt.image.IndexColorModel

The `IndexColorModel` is a map of color values (the indexes) into an array of actual pixel values (the palette). This means that the actual color values begin with 0 and continue to a maximum of the number of colors that can be held in the palette.

A color model

A color model defines the format of the contents of color pixel information in RAM. A `ColorModel` object defines the methods for extracting and inserting alpha, red, green, and blue color components of the pixels.

Transparency — the alpha value

There is an optional transparency value that can be set. This is known as the *alpha* value of the pixel. When painted onto an image, pixels of the transparent color are not painted, or are partially painted, thus allowing the background to "show through." The alpha values range from 0 for completely transparent to 255 for completely opaque.

Internal assumptions

Many of the methods of this class are `final` because there are some assumptions made about the layout, and the implementation and operation of the class reflect the assumptions.

Inheritance

```
public class java.awt.image.IndexColorModel
    extends ColorModel
        ⇑
    public abstract class java.awt.image.ColorModel
        extends Object

        public class java.lang.Object
```

Constructors

```
public IndexColorModel(int bits,int size,
    byte red[],byte green[],byte blue[])

public IndexColorModel(int bits,int size,
    byte red[],byte green[],byte blue[],int trans)

public IndexColorModel(int bits,int size,
    byte red[],byte green[],byte blue[],byte alpha[])

public IndexColorModel(int bits,int size,
    byte colorMap[],int start,boolean hasalpha)

public IndexColorModel(int bits,int size,
    byte colorMap[],int start,
    boolean hasalpha,int trans)
```

An `IndexColorModel` is constructed by specifying the number of bits in each pixel. The size is the size of the arrays that make up the palette.

The arrays `red`, `green`, and `blue` hold the pixel values for each of the three colors for each value of the index — these three arrays are the palette. If an `alpha` array is specified, it holds the transparency value for each pixel (255 being completely opaque, and 0 being completely transparent).

If a `trans` value is specified, it is the index into the palette where the value of a completely transparent pixel can be found. If no `trans` value is specified and no `alpha` values are specified, no color is transparent. If no `alpha` values are specified, all colors — except the one designated as being transparent by `trans` — have an alpha value of 255.

If the `colorMap` is specified, the red, green, and blue (and the optional alpha) arrays are constructed from the values packed into the `colorMap`. The `colorMap` must have enough values to fill arrays of the specified `size`. The value of `start` is the index of the first value in `colorMap`. If `hasalpha` is true, the alpha values are also included in the `colorMap`.

Returned by

An object of this class is returned from calls to `RGBImageFilter.filterIndexColorModel()`.

Methods

getAlpha()

```
public final int getAlpha(int pixel)
```

Returns the alpha transparency value for the specified `pixel`. The return value will be in the range of 0 to 255.

getAlphas()

```
public final void getAlphas(byte alpha[])
```

Copies the array of alpha values into the `alpha` array.

getBlue()

```
public final int getBlue(int pixel)
```

Returns the blue color component for the specified pixel. It will be a value from 0 to 255.

getBlues()

```
public final void getBlues(byte blue[])
```

Copies the array of blue pixel values into the `blue` array.

getGreen()

```
public final int getGreen(int pixel)
```

Returns the green color component for the specified pixel. It will be a value from 0 to 255.

getGreens()

```
public final void getGreens(byte green[])
```

Copies the array of green pixel values into the `green` array.

getMapSize()

```
public final int getMapSize()
```

Returns the size of the red, green, and blue color arrays.

getRed()

```
public final int getRed(int pixel)
```

Returns the red color component for the specified pixel. It will be a value from 0 to 255.

getReds()

```
public final void getReds(byte red[])
```

Copies the array of red pixel values into the `red` array.

getRGB()

```
public final int getRGB(int pixel)
```

Returns the color of the specified `pixel` packed in the default RGB color model.

getTransparentPixel()

```
public final int getTransparentPixel()
```

Returns the index of the transparent pixel. If there is no transparent pixel, the method returns −1.

For a description of the standard color model, see **RGB**. Also see **ColorModel** and **DirectColorModel**.

IndexedPropertyDescriptor

class java.beans.IndexedPropertyDescriptor

An object of this class is the description of a property that acts like an array—one that uses an index as a method argument for reading and writing specific members. Along with the indexed property, there may also be nonindexed methods that read and write entire arrays of the same type as that of the indexed read and write.

Accessor methods

The accessor methods follow a naming convention that enables a process to derive the names of the methods from the name of the property. For example, if the name of a property is `umpaMaximum`, the accessor methods would be `getUmpaMaximum()` and `setUmpaMaximum()`. The name of a property begins with a lowercase letter—to derive the accessor methods, switch it to uppercase and prepend "set" or "get."

The same method-naming convention is used for accessing indexed items in the array and accessing individual members of the array. The names are simply overloaded to have index or array arguments.

Constrained and vetoable

A constrained property, also called a *vetoable* property, is one that has limits imposed on changes that can be made to it. Whenever the "set" method of a vetoable property is called, one or more objects implementing the `VetoableChangeListener` interface may be notified via a `PropertyChangeEvent`. Any one of these is capable of throwing a `PropertyVetoException` to prevent the change from occurring.

Bound

A bound property is one that can cause `PropertyChangeEvent` to be distributed to a list of registered `PropertyChangeListener` objects. This is very similar to a constrained property, except that there is no veto power.

Inheritance

```
public class java.beans.IndexedPropertyDescriptor
    extends PropertyDescriptor
        ⇑
    public class java.beans.PropertyDescriptor
        extends FeatureDescriptor
            ⇑
        public class java.beans.FeatureDescriptor
            extends Object
                ⇑
            public class java.lang.Object
```

Constructors

```
public IndexedPropertyDescriptor(String propertyName,
        Class beanClass)
    throws IntrospectionException

public IndexedPropertyDescriptor(String propertyName,
        Class beanClass,
        String getterName,String setterName,
        String indexedGetterName,String indexedSetterName)
    throws IntrospectionException

public IndexedPropertyDescriptor(String propertyName,
        Method getter,Method setter,
        Method indexedGetter,Method indexedSetter)
    throws IntrospectionException
```

An `IndexedPropertyDescriptor` is constructed from the `propertyName`, which is the name of the property within a bean, and the `beanClass`, which is the `Class` object for the bean that contains the property.

Instead of allowing the accessor method names to be generated — as described above — it is possible to specify the names of the methods. The `getterName` and the `setterName` methods are used to read and write the property as an array. If `getterName` is `null`, the property is write-only. If `setterName` is `null`, the property is read-only. The `indexedGetterName` and `indexedSetterName` methods are used to read and write individual elements of the array.

The accessor names can also be specified as the `Method` objects `getter`, `setter`, `indexedGetter`, and `indexedSetter`.

An `IntrospectionException` is thrown if there is an error during introspection.

Methods

getIndexedPropertyType()

```
public Class getIndexedPropertyType()
```

Returns the `Class` object of an individual member of the array of the indexed property type. If the property is an array of primitive Java types, the appropriate wrapper `Class` object will be returned.

getIndexedReadMethod()

```
public Method getIndexedReadMethod()
```

Returns the `Method` object of the "get" accessor method used to read a single indexed member. If the property is write-only, this will return `null`.

getIndexedWriteMethod()

```
public Method getIndexedWriteMethod()
```

Returns the `Method` object of the "set" accessor method used to write a single indexed member. If the property is read-only, this will return `null`.

 For the editing of properties, see **PropertyEditor** and **PropertyEditorManager**. For more on constrained properties, see **VetoableChangeListener** and **VetoableChangeSupport**. For more on bound properties, see **PropertyChangeListener** and **PropertyChangeSupport**.

IndexOutOfBoundsException

class java.lang.IndexOutOfBoundsException

The subscript of an array is either less than zero or greater than the size of the array.

Extended by

```
ArrayIndexOutOfBoundsException
StringIndexOutOfBoundsException
```

Inheritance

```
public class java.lang.IndexOutOfBoundsException
extends RuntimeException
            ⇑
    public class java.lang.RuntimeException
        extends Exception
            ⇑
        public class java.lang.Exception
            extends Throwable
                ⇑
            public class java.lang.Throwable
                implements Serializable
                extends Object
                    ⇑
                public class java.lang.Object
```

constructors

```
public IndexOutOfBoundsException()
public IndexOutOfBoundsException(String message)
```

If the message string is supplied, it is used as a detailed message describing this particular exception.

InetAddress

class java.net.InetAddress

This class represents an Internet Protocol (IP) address.

Inheritance

```
public final class java.net.InetAddress
    implements Serializable
    extends Object
        ⇑
    public class java.lang.Object
```

Constructors

Returned by

An object of this class is returned from getByName(), getLocalHost(), and getAllByName(). InetAddress objects are also returned from DatagramPacket.getAddress(), DatagramSocket.getLocalAddress(), MulticastSocket.getInterface(), ServerSocket.getInetAddress(), Socket.getInetAddress(), Socket.getLocalAddress(), and SocketImpl.getInetAddress(). An array of InetAdress objects is returned from getAllByName().

Methods

equals()

```
public boolean equals(Object object)
```

Returns true if object is an InetAddress object representing the same address as this one.

getAddress()

```
public byte[] getAddress()
```

Returns the binary form of the IP address represented by this object. The array holds the 32-bit address in network order—the same big-endian order as 32-bit integers in Java.

getAllByName()

```
public static InetAddress[] getAllByName(String host)
    throws UnknownHostException
```

Returns the IP list of addresses of the named host. The host string can be null to represent the local host. The name can be a machine name (such as "java.sun.com") or a string representing the address value (such as "206.26.48.100"). An UnknownHostException is thrown if the host is unknown.

getByName()

```
public static InetAddress getByName(String host)
    throws UnknownHostException
```

Returns the IP address of the named `host`. The `host` string can be `null` to represent the local host. The name can be a machine name (such as "java.sun.com") or a string representing the address value (such as "206.26.48.100"). An `UnknownHostException` is thrown if the host is unknown.

getHostAddress()

```
public String getHostAddress()
```

Returns the IP address as a string in the form of four base-10 numbers separated by periods (such as "206.26.48.100").

getHostName()

```
public String getHostName()
```

Returns the name of the host of the represented address. A null host name indicates that the address is one of those of the local machine.

getLocalHost()

```
public static InetAddress getLocalHost()
    throws UnknownHostException
```

Returns an `InetAddress` object representing the IP address of the local host. An `UnknownHostException` is thrown if no address for the local host could be found.

hashCode()

```
public int hashCode()
```

Returns the hashcode value for this IP address.

isMulticastAddress()

```
public boolean isMulticastAddress()
```

Returns `true` if this IP address is a multicast address. A *multicast* address, also called a class D address, is one that can be used to send a single message to multiple recipients. The first four bits of a multicast address are always 1110.

toString()

```
public String toString()
```

Returns a string form of the IP address.

Inflater

class java.util.zip.Inflater

This class was designed to provide general-purpose decompression for use with the ZLIB and GZIP formats.

Inheritance

```
public class java.util.zip.Inflater
    extends Object
        ⇑
    public class java.lang.Object
```

Constructors

```
public Inflater()
public Inflater(boolean nowrap)
```

If nowrap is true, the ZLIB header and checksum fields will not be used. Setting nowrap to true will support GZIP-compatible compression.

Methods

end()

```
public native synchronized void end()
```

Frees the internal data. This will discard any unprocessed input.

finalize()

```
protected void finalize()
```

This is called by the garbage collector to free the decompressor.

finished()

```
public synchronized boolean finished()
```

Returns true if the end of the input compressed data stream has been reached.

getAdler()

```
public native synchronized int getAdler()
```

Returns the Adler-32 value that has been calculated for the decompressed data.

getRemaining()

```
public synchronized int getRemaining()
```

Returns a count of the number of bytes remaining in the input buffer. This can be used to find out how much is left after decompression has finished.

getTotalIn()

```
public native synchronized int getTotalIn()
```

Returns the count of the number of bytes that have been input so far.

getTotalOut()

```
public native synchronized int getTotalOut()
```

Returns the count of the number of bytes that have been output so far.

inflate()

```
public native synchronized int inflate(byte barray[],
        int offset,int length)
    throws DataFormatException
```

```
public int inflate(byte b[])
    throws DataFormatException
```

Processes input data and places the decompressed results in barray. If offset and length are specified, the results will be a maximum of length bytes beginning at barray[offset]. The return value is actual number of bytes placed in the array. A return value of 0 means needsInput() or needsDictionary() should be called to see if more input is needed or if a preset dictionary is required. A DataFormatException is thrown if the incoming data are not valid.

needsDictionary()

```
public synchronized boolean needsDictionary()
```

Returns true if a preset dictionary is needed for decompression.

needsInput()

```
public synchronized boolean needsInput()
```

Returns true if there is no input data available to be decompressed.

reset()

```
public native synchronized void reset()
```

Resets the inflator to its initial state. After this call, a new set of input data can be processed.

setDictionary()

```
public void setDictionary(byte barray[])

public native synchronized void setDictionary(
        byte barray[],int offset,int length)
```

Sets the byte array of the preset dictionary. If length and offset are specified, there are length dictionary bytes starting at barray[offset]. If length and offset are not specified, the entire array is used. When inflate() returns 0 and needsDictionary() returns true, a present dictionary is required. The method getAdler() can be used to get the Adler-32 value of the needed dictionary.

setInput()

```
public void setInput(byte barray[])

public synchronized void setInput(byte barray[],
        int offset,int length)
```

Supplies compressed input data for decompression. This method should be called whenever needsInput() returns true and there is still data to be decompressed. If length and offset are specified, there are length dictionary bytes starting at barray[offset]. If length and offset are not specified, the entire array is used.

 For an example of data compression, see **Deflater**. To inflate data from a disk file, see **InflaterInputStream**.

InflaterInputStream

class java.util.zip.InflaterInputStream

This is a stream filter that will decompress data in the "deflate" compression format. It also serves as a base class for other decompression stream classes such as GZIPInputStream.

Extended by

```
GZIPInputStream
ZipInputStream
```

Inheritance

```
public class java.util.zip.InflaterInputStream
    extends FilterInputStream
        ⇑
```

```
public class java.io.FilterInputStream
      extends InputStream
            ⇑
      public class java.io.InputStream
            extends Object
               ⇑
         public class java.lang.Object
```

Variables and constants

buf

```
protected byte buf[]
```

The input buffer used for decompression.

inf

```
protected Inflater inf
```

The decompressor used by this stream.

len

```
protected int len
```

The size of the input buffer.

Constructors

```
public InflaterInputStream(InputStream instream)
```

```
public InflaterInputStream(InputStream insream,
      Inflater inflater)
```

```
public InflaterInputStream(InputStream instream,
      Inflater inflater,int size)
```

An InflaterInputStream is constructed by specifying the instream that will supply the data, the inflater that will be used to decompress the data, and the size of the internal buffer that will be used for the decompression work. If the buffer size is not specified, a default value will be assumed. If the inflater is not specified, an Inflater object will be instantiated.

Methods

fill()

```
protected void fill()
      throws IOException
```

Reads from the input stream and fills the input buffer with data to be decompressed.

read()

```
public int read()
    throws IOException

public int read(byte barray[],int offset,int length)
    throws IOException
```

If `barray` is specified, decompressed data is placed into it at `barray[offset]` for `length` bytes. The return value is the number of bytes actually placed in `barray`. If `barray` is not specified, this method will read a single byte of decompressed data and return it as an `int`. This method will block until either data is available or the end of the input stream has been reached. The value −1 is returned to indicate the end of the input stream. A `ZipException` will be thrown if a ZIP format error occurs.

skip()

```
public long skip(long count)
    throws IOException
```

Discards `count` bytes of decompressed data.

For an example, see **DeflaterOutputStream**. The other classes that work with the "deflate" compression format are **Inflater** and **Deflater**. For input streams in other compression formats, see **GZIPInputStream** and the **ZipInputStream**.

inheritance

See **extends** and **implements**.

initializer

For initialization expressions, see **variables**. For the special case of the static initializer, see **class**.

inline

 See **final**.

inner classes

It is possible to define one class inside another. It is even possible to define a class inside a method. It is also possible to define a class that has no name by creating a class definition and an instance of the class in a single statement.

Example 1

This example detects the mouse pointer entering its window. This could have been done by having the class extend the MouseListener interface, but that would require that all the methods of the interface be implemented. The MouseAdapter class has already implemented all these methods as stubs, so it just needs to be extended, and the extended class only needs to implement the mouseEntered() method. The Mousing class can't extend the MouseAdapter class because it has already extended the Frame class, so it was necessary to implement this with another class:

```
import java.awt.*;
import java.awt.event.*;
public class Mousing extends Frame {
    public static void main(String[] arg) {
        new Mousing();
    }
    Mousing() {
        addMouseListener(new MousingEntrance());
        setSize(100,100);
        show();
    }
    class MousingEntrance extends MouseAdapter {
        public void mouseEntered(MouseEvent event) {
            System.out.println(event.getPoint());
        }
    }
}
```

The MousingEntrance class is defined inside the Mousing class and has its own superclass. The compiler creates a separate class file for each inner class but appends the name of the outer class onto the front of it. This way, no name conflict arises even if two classes have inner classes of the same names. The files output from compilation of this example are

```
Mousing$MousingEntrance.class
Mousing.class
```

Example 2

This example is very similar to the previous one with the exception that the inner class is defined inside a method:

```
import java.awt.*;
import java.awt.event.*;
public class Mousing2 extends Frame {
    public static void main(String[] arg) {
        new Mousing2();
    }
    Mousing2() {
        class MousingEntrance extends MouseAdapter {
            public void mouseEntered(MouseEvent event) {
                System.out.println(event.getPoint());
            }
        }
        addMouseListener(new MousingEntrance());
        setSize(100,100);
        show();
    }
}
```

The `MousingEntrance` class is defined inside the constructor of the `Mousing2` class. The compiler still outputs a separate class file for the inner class, but it appends a number and the name of the outer class onto the front of it. This way, no name conflict arises even if two methods have inner classes of the same names. The files output from compilation of this example are

```
Mousing2$1$MousingEntrance.class
Mousing2.class
```

Notice that the number guaranteeing uniqueness is inserted in the middle of the generated name surrounded by '$' characters.

Example 3

Here is a third way to do the same sort of thing. This example demonstrates the use of an anonymous class. The example actually has an inner class defined within another inner class, and the innermost one is anonymous:

```
import java.awt.*;
import java.awt.event.*;
public class InnerMonitor extends Frame {
    public static void main(String[] arg) {
        new InnerMonitor();
    }
    public InnerMonitor() {
        addWindowListener(new WindowAdapter() {
                public void windowClosing(
                        WindowEvent event) {
                    System.exit(0);
                }
            }
        );
        setSize(50,50);
        show();
    }
}
```

An inner class named `InnerMonitor` is given the chore of monitoring for the event signifying the window closing. It sets up the monitoring by making a call to `addWindowListener()`. The window listener object itself is an unnamed subclass of the `WindowAdapter` class. The Java `new` command is used to create an instance of the `WindowAdapter` that overrides the method that is called with the window closing event. This new class is defined and instantiated at the same point in the code — it is never given a name but, instead, has its reference passed as an argument to the `addWindowListener()` method. The class is anonymous because it never has a named class definition.

 For an example of using an inner class to supply an `Enumeration`, see
Enumeration.

InputEvent

class java.awt.event.InputEvent

The is the superclass for the device-level events of the mouse and the keyboard.

Extended by
```
KeyEvent
MouseEvent
```

Inheritance

```
public abstract class java.awt.event.InputEvent
    extends ComponentEvent
        ⇑
    public class java.awt.event.ComponentEvent
        extends AWTEvent
            ⇑
        public class java.awt.AWTEvent
            extends EventObject
                ⇑
            public class java.util.EventObject
                implements Serializable
                extends Object
                    ⇑
                public class java.lang.Object
```

Variables and constants

ALT_MASK

```
public static final int ALT_MASK
```

The constant value used to indicate the Alt key being held down.

BUTTON1_MASK

```
public static final int BUTTON1_MASK
```

The mask value used to indicate mouse button one.

BUTTON2_MASK

```
public static final int BUTTON2_MASK
```

The mask value used to indicate mouse button two.

BUTTON3_MASK

```
public static final int BUTTON3_MASK
```

The mask value used to indicate mouse button three.

CTRL_MASK

```
public static final int CTRL_MASK
```

The mask value used to indicate the Ctrl key being held down.

META_MASK

```
public static final int META_MASK
```

The mask value used to indicate the meta key being held down.

SHIFT_MASK

```
public static final int SHIFT_MASK
```

The mask value used to indicate the Shift key being held down.

Constructors

```
InputEvent(Component source,int id,long when,int modifiers)
```

There are no public constructors. This constructor requires the `source` component that is the source of the event, the `id` of the event type, the time of the origination of the event, and the mask values of the `modifier` keys that were held down when the event occurred.

Methods

consume()

```
public void consume()
```

This will consume the event so that it will not be processed further.

getModifiers()

```
public int getModifiers()
```

Returns the modifier masks that were set when the event was constructed.

getWhen()

```
public long getWhen()
```

Returns the time stamp that indicates when the event occurred.

isAltDown()

```
public boolean isAltDown()
```

Returns `true` if the Alt key was held down when this event occurred.

isConsumed()

```
public boolean isConsumed()
```

Returns `true` if this event has been consumed.

isControlDown()

```
public boolean isControlDown()
```

Returns true if the Ctrl key was held down when this event occurred.

isMetaDown()

```
public boolean isMetaDown()
```

Returns true if the meta key was held down when this event occurred.

isShiftDown()

```
public boolean isShiftDown()
```

Returns true if the Shift key was held down when this event occurred.

InputStream

class java.io.InputStream

All input streams are based on this abstract class, which represents a stream of bytes.

Mark and reset

Methods are included that can be used to mark a spot in the input stream and then rewind to it later—these are mark() and reset(). These were not intended to be used to reposition a file over great distances. The idea is to supply the ability to perform a quick look ahead of a few bytes and then return. There is only one mark—they do not nest into mark-reset pairs.

Extended by

```
ByteArrayInputStream
FileInputStream
FilterInputStream
ObjectInputStream
PipedInputStream
SequenceInputStream
StringBufferInputStream
```

Inheritance

```
public abstract class java.io.InputStream
    extends Object
```

⇑
```
public class java.lang.Object
```

Constructors
```
public InputStream()
```

Returned by

An object of this class is returned from any of these methods:

```
Class.getResourceAsStream()
ClassLoader.getResourceAsStream()
ClassLoader.getSystemResourceAsStream()
Process.getErrorStream()
Process.getInputStream()
ResultSet.getAsciiStream()
ResultSet.getBinaryStream()
ResultSet.getUnicodeStream()
Runtime.getLocalizedInputStream()
Socket.getInputStream()
SocketImpl.getInputStream()
URL.openStream()
URLConnection.getInputStream()
ZipFile.getInputStream()
```

Methods

available()
```
public abstract int available()
    throws IOException
```

Returns the number of bytes immediately available—the number that can be read without blocking.

close()
```
public void close()
    throws IOException
```

Terminates the input stream. This must be called to release any system-level resources associated with the stream.

mark()
```
public synchronized void mark(int readlimit)
```

Marks the current position in the input stream; a subsequent call to `reset()` will restore the input to this position. The value of `readlimit` specifies the number of bytes that can be read before the mark is discarded. For this to work, the return value from `markSupported()` must be `true`.

markSupported()

```
public boolean markSupported()
```

Returns `true` if the `mark()` and `reset()` methods can be used to alter the flow of the input stream.

read()

```
public abstract int read()
    throws IOException

public int read(byte barray[])
    throws IOException

public int read(byte barray[],int offset,int length)
    throws IOException
```

If no argument is supplied, this will read one `byte` of data and return it as an `int`. If `barray` is supplied, the input data is placed in the array and the number of bytes read is returned. If `offset` and `length` are specified, the input data will appear beginning at `barray[offset]` for a maximum of `length` bytes. The default `offset` is 0, and the default `length` is the size of `barray`. This method will block as long as there is unread data available. A return value of −1 indicates a normal end to the input stream.

reset()

```
public synchronized void reset()
    throws IOException
```

This will reposition the input stream to the location of the last call to `mark()`. The exception is thrown if there is no active mark. A mark will be removed (causing this method to throw an exception) if more bytes have been read than the number specified on the call to `mark()`.

skip()

```
public long skip(long count)
    throws IOException
```

Calling this method makes a request to have the input stream skip over `count` number of input bytes. The return value is the actual number of bytes skipped.

InputStreamReader

class java.io.InputStreamReader

This class reads from a `byte` stream and converts the incoming data into a character stream.

Encoding

The encoding used to do the conversion from bytes to characters can be either the default encoding or a specified encoding. The encoding is determined by the constructor. For this class to return a character, it may be necessary for it to read more than one byte from the input stream—this depends on the encoding.

Extended by

```
FileReader
```

Inheritance

```
public class java.io.InputStreamReader

    extends Reader
        ⇑
    public class java.io.Reader
        extends Object
            ⇑
        public class java.lang.Object
```

Constructors

InputStreamReader()

```
public InputStreamReader(InputStream input)
```

```
public InputStreamReader(InputStream input,String encoding)
    throws UnsupportedEncodingException
```

The stream `input` is used to read `bytes`. If `encoding` is specified, it is used instead of the system default character encoding. The `UnsupportedEncodingException` is thrown if the named `encoding` scheme is unknown.

Methods

close()

```
public void close()
```

```
     throws IOException
```

Closes the stream. Any attempt to access the file after this method has been called will cause an `IOException` to be thrown.

getEncoding()

```
public String getEncoding()
```

Returns the name of the character encoding scheme. If the stream has been closed, a `null` may be returned.

read()

```
public int read()
     throws IOException

public int read(char carray[],int offset,int length)
     throws IOException
```

If no argument is supplied, this will read one character and return it as an `int`. If `carray` is supplied, the input data is placed in the array and the number of characters read is returned. The input data will appear beginning at `carray[offset]` for a maximum of `length` characters. This method will block as long as unread data is available. A return value of −1 indicates a normal end to the input stream.

ready()

```
public boolean ready()
     throws IOException
```

This method returns `true` if there is data that can be read without blocking and `false` otherwise.

Insets

class java.awt.Insets

Objects of this class are used as configuration settings within containers specifying the number of pixels to leave as margins around components as they are laid out.

Inheritance

```
public class java.awt.Insets
     implements Cloneable
     implements Serializable
     extends Object
```

⇑
```
public class java.lang.Object
```

Variables and constants

bottom
```
public int bottom
```
The pixel inset from the bottom.

left
```
public int left
```
The pixel inset from the left.

right
```
public int right
```
The pixel inset from the right.

top
```
public int top
```
The pixel inset from the top.

Constructors

```
public Insets(int top,int left,int bottom,int right)
```

An Insets object is created by specifying values for all four of the inset variables.

Returned by

Objects of this class are returned from the Container methods getInsets() and insets().

Methods

clone()
```
public Object clone()
```
Makes a duplicate of this object.

equals()
```
public boolean equals(Object object)
```

Returns `true` if object is an `Inset` object containing the same values as this one.

toString()

```
public String toString()
```

Returns a string that contains the inset values.

 For information on how objects of this class are used, see **Container**. For similar wrappers, see **Dimension**, **Point**, **Polygon**, **Rectangle**, and **Shape**.

instance and instantiation

A class is a plan—set of blueprint instructions—for the creation of an object. The `new` keyword creates an object from the class. This object is known as an *instance* of the class, and the process of creating the object is called *instantiation*.

instanceof

keyword

This is an operator in the Java language that results in a `boolean` value. It will result in `true` if the object to its left is an instance of the class or interface to its right. If the left side is `null`, it always returns `false`.

Example

This example creates an object and then tests it against several classes:

```
import java.awt.*;
import java.awt.image.*;
public class InstanceOfTest extends Frame {
    public static void main(String[] arg) {
        Object obj = (Object)(new InstanceOfTest());
        if(obj instanceof InstanceOfTest)
            System.out.println("is InstanceOfTest");
        else
            System.out.println("is not InstanceOfTest");
        if(obj instanceof Frame)
            System.out.println("is Frame");
        else
            System.out.println("is not Frame");
        if(obj instanceof Panel)
            System.out.println("is Panel");
```

```
            else
                System.out.println("is not Panel");
            if(obj instanceof Container)
                System.out.println("is Container");
            else
                System.out.println("is not Container");
            if(obj instanceof MenuContainer)
                System.out.println("is MenuContainer");
            else
                System.out.println("is not MenuContainer");
            if(obj instanceof Button)
                System.out.println("is Button");
            else
                System.out.println("is not Button");
            if(obj instanceof ImageObserver)
                System.out.println("is ImageObserver");
            else
                System.out.println("is not ImageObserver");
        }
    }
```

This is the output:

```
is InstanceOfTest
is Frame
is not Panel
is Container
is MenuContainer
is not Button
is ImageObserver
```

The object is an `InstanceOfTest` that extends `Frame`, so it is both of those. It is neither a `Panel` nor a `Button`, because neither the `Panel` class nor the `Button` class is to be found anywhere in the lineage of a `Frame`. However, it is a `Container`, since `Container` is a superclass of `Frame`, a couple of generations up the tree. It is a `MenuContainer` because the `Frame` class implements the `MenuContainer` interface. It is an `ImageObserver` because one of its superclasses, the `Component` class, implements the `ImageObserver` interface.

InstantiationError

class java.lang.InstantiationError

An attempt was made to instantiate an abstract class or an interface.

Inheritance

```
public class java.lang.InstantiationError
    extends IncompatibleClassChangeError
        ⇑
    public class java.lang.IncompatibleClassChangeError
        extends LinkageError
            ⇑
        public class java.lang.LinkageError
            extends Error
                ⇑
            public class java.lang.Error
                extends Throwable
                    ⇑
                public class java.lang.Throwable
                    implements Serializable
                    extends Object
                        ⇑
                    public class java.lang.Object
```

Constructors

```
public InstantiationError()
public InstantiationError(String message)
```

If the `message` string is supplied, it is used as a detailed message describing this particular exception.

InstantiationException

class java.lang.InstantiationException

Signals that an attempt has been made to instantiate an abstract class or an interface.

Inheritance

```
public class java.lang.InstantiationException
    extends Exception
        ⇑
    public class java.lang.Exception
        extends Throwable
            ⇑
        public class java.lang.Throwable
```

```
implements Serializable
extends Object
       ⇑
public class java.lang.Object
```

Constructors

```
public InstantiationException()
public InstantiationException(String message)
```

If the `message` string is supplied, it is used as a detailed message describing this particular exception.

int

primitive data type

An `int` is a 32-bit signed integer.

The largest magnitude negative value of an `int` is –2,147,483,648. The largest positive value of an `int` is 2,147,483,647.

Table I-1 lists all the ways in which the maximum and minimum values for an `int` can be declared.

Table I-1   Different Forms of Declaring Maximum and Minimum Values

Type	Maximum	Minimum	Minus One
Decimal	2147483647	-2147483648	-1
Octal	017777777777	020000000000	03777777777
Hexadecimal	0x7fffffff	0x80000000	0xffffffff
Predefined	Integer.MAX_VALUE	Integer.MIN_VALUE	

Literals

Integer literals can be declared in decimal, octal, or hexadecimal. Any of these can be declared negative by being preceded with a minus sign.

Base-10 literal

A number beginning with any digit other than 0, and not containing anything other than the digits 0 through 9, is a base-10 int literal. Some examples of base-10 literals:

```
82    6326    852
```

Hexadecimal literal

A hexadecimal (base-16) integer begins with 0x or 0X. It can contain the digits 0 through 9 and the letters A through F. The letters A through F (which represent the numeric values 10 through 15) can be either upper- or lowercase. Some examples of hexadecimal literals:

```
0x022    0XA1B9    0x99a    0X2a
```

Octal literal

An octal (base-8) integer begins with a 0 and contains only the digits 0 through 7. These are examples of octal literals:

```
05    027    06124531
```

For a class to perform special int operations, see **Integer**. For other integer types, see **byte**, **char**, **short**, and **long**.

Integer

class java.lang.Integer

This is a wrapper class for the primitive data type int. It is a constant—the value contained in an Integer is set by its constructor and cannot be changed.

Inheritance

```
public final class java.lang.Integer
    extends Number
        ⇑
    public abstract class java.lang.Number
        extends Object
            ⇑
        public class java.lang.Object
```

Variables and constants
MAX_VALUE

```
public final static int MAX_VALUE
```

The largest magnitude negative value that can be contained in an int. It can be represented as 2147483647 or 0x7FFFFFFF.

MIN_VALUE

```
public final static int MIN_VALUE
```

The largest magnitude negative value that can be contained in an int. It can be represented as −2147483648 or 0x80000000.

TYPE

```
public final static java.lang.Class TYPE
```

A Class object representing the primitive type int.

Constructors

```
public Integer(int value)

public Integer(String string)
    throws NumberFormatException
```

An Integer object can be constructed directly from an int value or from a String object. The String must be the base-10 character form of an integer value, or a NumberFormatException is thrown.

Returned by

An Integer object is returned from the decode(), getInteger(), and valueOf() methods.

Methods

byteValue()

```
public byte byteValue()
```

The value of the int is returned as a byte. There is possible loss of data. Overrides byteValue() in Number.

decode()

```
public static Integer decode(String nm)
    throws NumberFormatException
```

Converts a String into an Integer object. The standard Java numeric literal forms of decimal, hexadecimal, and octal numbers are recognized.

doubleValue()

```
public double doubleValue()
```

The value of the int is returned as a double.

equals()

```
public boolean equals(Object obj)
```

Returns true if obj is an Integer object with the same value as this one. Overrides equals() in Object.

floatValue()

```
public float floatValue()
```

The value of the int is returned as a float. The magnitude will stay the same, but it is possible to lose a few digits of accuracy. Overrides floatValue() in Number.

getInteger()

```
public static Integer getInteger(String nm)

public static Integer getInteger(String nm,int val)

public static Integer getInteger(String nm,
    Integer valobj)
```

These are convenience methods. They call System.getProperty() with nm as the key. If a property is found, its value is interpreted as a character string form of an int and is passed to Integer.decode() for translation to an Integer.

If the property is not found—or if the property doesn't have a valid integer string value—the default value is returned. If you don't supply a default with either val or valobj, the default will be an Integer with the value 0.

hashCode()

```
public int hashCode()
```

Returns a hashcode for this object. Overrides hashCode() in Object.

intValue()

```
public int intValue()
```

Returns the int value. Overrides intValue() in Number.

longValue()

```
public long longValue()
```

Returns the value as a long. Overrides longValue() in Number.

parseInt()

```
public static int parseInt(String istr)
    throws NumberFormatException
```

```
public static int parseInt(String istr,int radix)
    throws NumberFormatException
```

The characters in istr are converted to an int value. The base is specified by radix—if radix is not specified, base 10 is assumed. The exception is thrown if any character other than those that are valid for the base is found. For bases larger than 10, the letters of the alphabet are used. For example, base 16 includes the letters A through F, base 17 includes G, and so on.

shortValue()

```
public short shortValue()
```

Returns the int value as a short. There is possible loss of data from narrowing. Overrides shortValue() in Number.

toBinaryString()

```
public static String toBinaryString(int ivalue)
```

Returns a string of 32 1s and 0s representing the bits of ivalue.

toHexString()

```
public static String toHexString(int ivalue)
```

Returns the unsigned hexadecimal representation of ivalue. It generates lowercase letters with no leading '0x' sequence and no leading zeroes. Negative numbers are represented with leading 'f' characters (as necessary).

toOctalString()

```
public static String toOctalString(int ivalue)
```

Returns the unsigned octal representation of ivalue. It does not include any leading zeroes. Negative numbers are represented with leading 3s and 7s (as necessary).

toString()

```
public String toString()

public static String toString(int ivalue)

public static String toString(int ivalue,int radix)
```

Returns a String object representing the value of the int. If ivalue is not specified, the internal value of the object is used. If no radix is supplied, a radix of 10 is assumed. Negative numbers, no matter what the radix, are preceded with a minus sign. The form without arguments overrides toString() in Object.

valueOf()

```
public static Integer valueOf(String istr)
    throws NumberFormatException

public static Integer valueOf(String istr,int radix)
    throws NumberFormatException
```

These are convenience methods. They call the method parseInt()—with the appropriate radix—to get an int value. The value is then used to construct and return a new Integer object.

 The wrappers of the other primitive types are **Boolean, Byte, Character, Short, Long, Float,** and **Double.**

interface

An *interface* is the named definition of a collection of methods and/or constants. None of these methods have bodies; therefore, they are all abstract. In one sense, an interface is an abstract class that contains only abstract methods. Because it is totally abstract, the rules of inheritance are not as limiting as those of a class—a class can implement several interfaces but extend only one other class.

An interface is implemented

Before it can be used, an interface must be implemented by a class—that is, a class must assume the responsibility of implementing bodies for all the abstract methods defined in the interface. If the class does not implement all the methods of the interface, the class is abstract. Whenever a class implements an interface, it inherits any of the constant values defined in the interface.

The abstract keyword

An `interface` may or may not have the keyword `abstract` in its definition. It doesn't matter—an interface is always abstract.

Variables in an interface

Any variable names defined in an interface must be both `static` and `final`—that is, they are constants. The initial value must also be defined in the interface.

Extending an interface

One interface can extend another interface in the same way that one class can extend another class. It is done using the `extends` keyword, just as in classes.

An inherited interface becomes part of the class lineage

Whenever a class implements an interface, it is known as a *superinterface* of that class. Subclasses inherit the implementation interfaces. A subclass can override the superclass implementation of any or all of the interface methods. A class that implements an interface but does not supply all the method definitions of the interface is an abstract class.

Multiple interface ambiguity

It is possible for a class to implement two (or more) interfaces with a method of the same name, but the methods' signatures must result in an unambiguous reference. That is, if the methods have different argument types, they will be different methods, and each one must be implemented separately. If they have the same argument signatures, they also must have the same return type.

Multiple implementation

It is possible for more than one class in a hierarchy of classes to implement the same interface. That is, the same interface can be implemented by a class and its superclass—this will result in any methods implemented in the superclass being overridden. Java will consider it to be implemented only once, and it may be referred to without ambiguity.

Example 1

Here is an example of a simple interface definition being implemented by a couple of classes:

```
interface AreaResizable {
    public double getArea();
    public void setArea(double area);
}
```

```
class Square implements AreaResizable {
    double width = 100;
    public double getArea() {
        return(width * width);
    }
    public void setArea(double area) {
        width = Math.sqrt(area);
    }
}

class Circle implements AreaResizable {
    double radius = 20.0;
    public double getArea() {
        return(Math.PI * radius * radius);
    }
    public void setArea(double area) {
        radius = Math.sqrt(area / Math.PI);
    }
}
```

This example defines a simple interface that allows an area value to be set and to be read back. Two classes implement the interface—one for a circle and the other for a square. Each method has its own internal equations for dealing with the values, but the external calls to the methods are guaranteed to be the same because they both adhere to the same interface definition.

Example 2

Here is an example of an implementation of two interfaces that have the same method:

```
interface Umpa {
    public int fifteen();
}
interface Oola {
    public int fifteen();
}
public class InterfaceCollision
        implements Umpa, Oola {
    public static void main(String[] arg) {
        InterfaceCollision ic = new InterfaceCollision();
        System.out.println(ic.fifteen());
    }
    public int fifteen() {
```

```
        return(15);
    }
}
```

In this example, both interfaces define the method named fifteen(), and the class implements them both. There is no problem, because the implementation of the method fifteen() in the class satisfies both interface definitions. If, however, the two interfaces had been declared this way:

```
interface Umpa {
    public int fifteen();
}
interface Oola {
    public double fifteen();
}
```

the class would have had no way to implement a method to satisfy them both.

Example 3

This example demonstrates how one interface can extend another:

```
interface Guz {
    public int fifteen();
}
interface Wiz extends Guz {
    public int forty();
}
public class InterfaceExtension
        implements Guz {
    public static void main(String[] arg) {
        InterfaceExtension ie = new InterfaceExtension();
        System.out.println(ie.fifteen());
        System.out.println(ie.forty());
    }
    public int fifteen() {
        return(15);
    }
    public int forty() {
        return(40);
    }
}
```

By extending Guz, the Wiz interface includes the method fifteen(). Because the class implements Guz, it is obliged to provide methods for both fifteen() and forty().

For some simple interface examples, see **class**. For an example of using an interface for polymorphism, see **reference**.

interfaces

package java.security.interfaces

This is a collection of interfaces used in the construction and maintenance of encryption key values.

Interfaces

```
DSAKey
DSAKeyPairGenerator
DSAParams
DSAPrivateKey
DSAPublicKey
```

InternalError

class java.lang.InternalError

Some sort of internal error has occurred in the Java Virtual Machine. Something is fundamentally wrong—but not necessarily with the Virtual Machine. There could have been an encounter with an unknown bytecode or some other condition that should not have occurred.

Inheritance

```
public class java.lang.InternalError
    extends VirtualMachineError
        ⇑
    public class java.lang.VirtualMachineError
        extends Error
            ⇑
        public class java.lang.Error
            extends Throwable
                ⇑
            public class java.lang.Throwable
                implements Serializable
                extends Object
```

⇑
```
public class java.lang.Object
```

Constructors

```
public InternalError()
public InternalError(String message)
```

If the message string is supplied, it is used as a detailed message describing this particular exception.

InterruptedException

class java.lang.InterruptedException

This exception is thrown as notification that this thread has been interrupted.

Inheritance

```
public class java.lang.InterruptedException
extends Exception
        ⇑
    public class java.lang.Exception
        extends Throwable
            ⇑
        public class java.lang.Throwable
            implements Serializable
            extends Object
                ⇑
            public class java.lang.Object
```

Constructors

```
public InterruptedException()
public InterruptedException(String message)
```

If the message string is supplied, it is used as a detailed message describing this particular exception.

InterruptedIOException

class java.io.InterruptedIOException

Signals that an I/O operation has been interrupted.

Inheritance

```
public class java.io.InterruptedIOException
    extends IOException
        ⇑
    public class java.io.IOException
        extends Exception
            ⇑
        public class java.lang.Exception
            extends Throwable
                ⇑
            public class java.lang.Throwable
                implements Serializable
                extends Object
                    ⇑
                public class java.lang.Object
```

Variables and constants

bytesTransferred

```
public int bytesTransferred
```

This is the number of bytes that had been successfully transferred prior to the interruption.

Constructors

```
public InterruptedIOException()
public InterruptedIOException(String message)
```

If the message string is supplied, it is used as a detailed message describing this particular exception.

IntrospectionException

class java.beans.IntrospectionException

This exception is thrown whenever an error occurs during introspection.

Inheritance

```
public class java.beans.IntrospectionException
    extends Exception
        ⇑
    public class java.lang.Exception
        extends Throwable
            ⇑
        public class java.lang.Throwable
            implements Serializable
            extends Object
                ⇑
            public class java.lang.Object
```

Constructors

```
public IntrospectionException(String message)
```

The `message` string is used as a detailed message describing this particular exception.

Introspector

class java.beans.Introspector

This class can be used to inspect a Java bean to discover its properties, events, and methods. This class has the capability of analyzing the bean's class—and all of its superclasses—to find information. The information is then used to construct a `BeanInfo` object containing the information.

Finding the BeanInfo file

A naming convention is used to create the name of a `BeanInfo` class for a bean—it is the name of the described bean with "BeanInfo" appended to it. For example, if the class name is "Umpa," its `BeanInfo` class will be named "UmpaBeanInfo." The `UmpaBeanInfo` class is first assumed to be in the same package as `Umpa`. If the complete package name is `COM.skunk.works`, we would have started looking for `COM.skunk.works.UmpaBeanInfo`.

If it is not found in the same package, all the packages of the same hierarchy are searched. Next the search will continue by using the search path to each of the package names supplied to the introspector in a call to `getBeanInfoSearchPath()`. For example, if the supplied search paths are `anime.slug` and `anime.slug.general`, then a search will be made for `anime.slug.UmpaBeanInfo` and `anime.slug.general.UmpaBeanInfo`.

As the superclass hierarchy tree is climbed, if a correctly named `BeanInfo` class is located, the information found there is added to any information obtained from analyzing any of the subclasses. The information in the `BeanInfo` object is considered to be definitive, and the search goes no further.

Each time the hierarchy tree is climbed and a `BeanInfo` class is not found, low-level reflection is used to determine as much information as possible about the methods of the class. Standard design patterns are applied (method names that begin with "get" and "set" and so on) to discover information about the bean.

Inheritance

```
public class Introspector
    extends Object
        ⇑
    public class java.lang.Object
```

Constructors

This class has no constructors—all the pubic methods are static.

Methods

decapitalize()

```
public static String decapitalize(String name)
```

Converts a string from one form to another by changing the pattern of capital letters. The leading character of the name is converted from upper- to lowercase. The only exception to this is that if there is a second letter in the `name` and it is also uppercase, the leading letter will not be modified.

getBeanInfo()

```
public static BeanInfo getBeanInfo(Class beanClass)
    throws IntrospectionException
```

```
public static BeanInfo getBeanInfo(Class beanClass,
        Class stopClass)
    throws IntrospectionException
```

Performs introspection on `beanClass` and returns its findings in the form of a `BeanInfo` object. Introspection will proceed up the hierarchy through all the superclasses, but it will not include (nor go past) the `stopClass`.

getBeanInfoSearchPath()

```
public static String[] getBeanInfoSearchPath()
```

Returns the array of package names that will be searched for any `BeanInfo` classes during introspection. The default search path is `sun.beans.infos`.

setBeanInfoSearchPath()

```
public static void setBeanInfoSearchPath(String path[])
```

Changes the array of package names that will be searched to find any BeanInfo classes during introspection.

InvalidClassException

class java.io.InvalidClassException

This exception is thrown when one of the following difficulties arises in the serialization of a class:

- ◆ The serial number of the object does not match the serial number found in the stream.
- ◆ The class contains a data type for which no serialization has been defined.
- ◆ The class does not implement both readObject() and writeObject().
- ◆ The class is not public.
- ◆ The class does not have an accessible default constructor.

Inheritance

```
public class java.io.InvalidClassException
    extends ObjectStreamException
        ⇑
    public class java.io.ObjectStreamException
        extends IOException
            ⇑
        public class java.io.IOException
            extends Exception
                ⇑
            public class java.lang.Exception
                extends Throwable
                    ⇑
                public class java.lang.Throwable
                    implements Serializable
                    extends Object
                        ⇑
                    public class java.lang.Object
```

Variables and constants

classname

```
public String classname
```

The name of the class causing the exception to be thrown.

Constructors

```
public InvalidClassException()

public InvalidClassException(String message, String className)
```

The message string is supplied as a detailed message describing this particular exception. It is optional to specify the name of the class causing the exception to be thrown.

Methods

getMessage()

```
public String getMessage()
```

Returns the message string that was supplied on the constructor.

InvalidKeyException

class java.security.InvalidKeyException

This exception is thrown to report an invalid Key. It could be an invalid encoding, an incorrect key length, or simply that the Key has not been initialized.

Inheritance

```
public class java.security.InvalidKeyException
    extends KeyException
        ⇑
    public class java.security.KeyException
        extends Exception
            ⇑
        public class java.lang.Exception
            extends Throwable
                ⇑
            public class java.lang.Throwable
                implements Serializable
                extends Object
```

```
             ⇑
    public class java.lang.Object
```

Constructors

```
    public InvalidKeyException()
    public InvalidKeyException(String message)
```

If the `message` string is supplied, it is used as a detailed message describing this particular exception.

InvalidObjectException

class java.io.InvalidObjectException

This is the exception thrown by a class that is specifically not allowing itself to be serialized.

Inheritance

```
    public class java.io.InvalidObjectException
        extends ObjectStreamException
            ⇑
        public class java.io.ObjectStreamException
            extends IOException
                ⇑
            public class java.io.IOException
                extends Exception
                    ⇑
                public class java.lang.Exception
                    extends Throwable
                        ⇑
                    public class java.lang.Throwable
                        implements Serializable
                        extends Object
                            ⇑
                        public class java.lang.Object
```

Constructors

```
    public InvalidObjectException(String message)
```

If the `message` string is supplied, it is used as a detailed message describing this particular exception—it is normally the name of the class throwing the exception.

InvalidParameterException

class java.security.InvalidParameterException

This exception is thrown to report that an invalid parameter has been passed to a method.

Inheritance

```
public class java.security.InvalidParameterException
    extends IllegalArgumentException
        ⇑
    public class java.lang.IllegalArgumentException
        extends RuntimeException
            ⇑
        public class java.lang.RuntimeException
            extends Exception
                ⇑
            public class java.lang.Exception
                extends Throwable
                    ⇑
                public class java.lang.Throwable
                    implements Serializable
                    extends Object
                        ⇑
                    public class java.lang.Object
```

Constructors

```
public InvalidParameterException()
public InvalidParameterException(String message)
```

If the `message` string is supplied, it is used as a detailed message describing this particular exception.

InvocationTargetException

class java.lang.reflect.InvocationTargetException

This is a checked exception that can be used to wrap an otherwise unchecked exception.

Inheritance

```
public class java.lang.reflect.InvocationTargetException
    extends Exception
        ⇑
    public class java.lang.Exception
        extends Throwable
            ⇑
        public class java.lang.Throwable
            implements Serializable
            extends Object
                ⇑
            public class java.lang.Object
```

Constructors

```
protected InvocationTargetException()

public InvocationTargetException(Throwable target)

public InvocationTargetException(Throwable target,
        String message)
```

The exception can be constructed to contain another exception and a descriptive message supplying more details.

Methods

getTargetException()

```
public Throwable getTargetException()
```

Returns the target exception that was supplied to the constructor.

invoke

To call a method is to *invoke* a method. The two terms, "call" and "invoke," mean almost the same thing. To "invoke" a method, however, more commonly refers to calling a method that has overridden another method, or one that uses the RMI facility to call a method that uses the RMI facility to call a further method remotely.

io

package java.io

This package contains the interfaces and classes that handle Java input and output.

Interfaces

```
DataInput
DataOutput
Externalizable
FilenameFilter
ObjectInput
ObjectInputValidation
ObjectOutput
Serializable
```

Classes

```
BufferedInputStream
BufferedOutputStream
BufferedReader
BufferedWriter
ByteArrayInputStream
ByteArrayOutputStream
CharArrayReader
CharArrayWriter
DataInputStream
DataOutputStream
File
FileDescriptor
FileInputStream
FileOutputStream
FileReader
FileWriter
FilterInputStream
FilterOutputStream
FilterReader
FilterWriter
InputStream
```

InputStreamReader
LineNumberInputStream
LineNumberReader
ObjectInputStream
ObjectOutputStream
ObjectStreamClass
OutputStream
OutputStreamWriter
PipedInputStream
PipedOutputStream
PipedReader
PipedWriter
PrintStream
PrintWriter
PushbackInputStream
PushbackReader
RandomAccessFile
Reader
SequenceInputStream
StreamTokenizer
StringBufferInputStream
StringReader
StringWriter
Writer

Exceptions

CharConversionException
EOFException
FileNotFoundException
IOException
InterruptedIOException
InvalidClassException
InvalidObjectException
NotActiveException
NotSerializableException
ObjectStreamException
OptionalDataException
StreamCorruptedException
SyncFailedException
UTFDataFormatException
UnsupportedEncodingException
WriteAbortedException

IOException

class java.io.IOException

This is thrown to indicate that some sort of I/O exception has occurred.

Extended by

```
CharConversionException
EOFException
FileNotFoundException
InterruptedIOException
MalformedURLException
ObjectStreamException
ProtocolException
RemoteException
SocketException
SyncFailedException
UnknownHostException
UnknownServiceException
UnsupportedEncodingException
UTFDataFormatException
ZipException
```

Inheritance

```
public class java.io.IOException
    extends Exception
        ⇑
    public class java.lang.Exception
        extends Throwable
            ⇑
        public class java.lang.Throwable
            implements Serializable
            extends Object
                ⇑
            public class java.lang.Object
```

Constructors

```
public Exception()
public Exception(String message)
```

If the `message` string is supplied, it is used as a detailed message describing this particular exception.

ItemEvent

class java.awt.event.ItemEvent

This is the event issued by components that have selectable items to indicate that a change in the selection has occurred.

Inheritance

```
public class java.awt.event.ItemEvent
    extends AWTEvent
        ⇑
    public class java.awt.AWTEvent
        extends EventObject
            ⇑
        public class java.util.EventObject
            implements Serializable
            extends Object
                ⇑
            public class java.lang.Object
```

Variables and constants

DESELECTED

```
public static final int DESELECTED
```

This value is used to indicate the state change of the item that became deselected.

ITEM_FIRST

```
public static final int ITEM_FIRST
```

This is the smallest possible numeric value of a type of ItemEvent.

ITEM_LAST

```
public static final int ITEM_LAST
```

This is the largest possible numeric value of a type of ItemEvent.

ITEM_STATE_CHANGED

```
public static final int ITEM_STATE_CHANGED
```

This event type indicates that there has been a state change.

SELECTED

```
public static final int SELECTED
```

This value is used to indicate the state change of the item that became selected.

Constructors

```
public ItemEvent(ItemSelectable source,int id,
          Object item,int stateChange)
```

The source is the ItemSelectable object issuing the event. The id value is the type of ItemEvent (this is always ITEM_STATE_CHANGED). The item is the one that had its state changed. The value of stateChange is either SELECTED or DESELECTED.

Methods

getItem()

```
public Object getItem()
```

Returns an object that indicates which item was selected. For example, the List component sends this as an Integer object containing the index of the selected (or deselected) item.

getItemSelectable()

```
public ItemSelectable getItemSelectable()
```

Returns the ItemSelectable object that issued the event.

getStateChange()

```
public int getStateChange()
```

Returns the state indicator—this is either SELECTED or DESELECTED.

paramString()

```
public String paramString()
```

Returns debugging information. The return string describes the internal state and values of this object.

For an example, see **ItemListener**. This event is issued from classes that implement **ItemSelectable**, such as **List**, **Checkbox**, **Choice**, and **CheckboxMenuItem**.

ItemListener

interface java.awt.event.ItemListener

This interface is implemented by classes that want to receive `ItemEvents`.

Implemented by

```
AWTEventMulticaster
```

Inheritance

```
public interface java.awt.event.ItemListener
    extends EventListener
        public interface java.util.EventListener
```

Constructors

Returned by

Objects implementing this interface are returned from the `add()` and `remove()` methods of `AWTEventMulticaster`.

Methods

itemStateChanged()

```
public abstract void itemStateChanged(ItemEvent event)
```

This method is called with the `ItemEvent` to report the change of state of some item in the selectable component.

Example

This example constructs and displays a `List`. The `ItemListener` interface is implemented to respond to selections by the mouse. The `itemStateChanged()` method displays, in a TextField, the `paramString()` from the `ItemEvent` object:

```
import java.awt.*;
import java.awt.event.*;
public class ListItems extends Frame
                implements ItemListener {
    List list;
    TextField textField;
    public static void main(String[] arg) {
        ListItems ml = new ListItems();
```

```
        }
        public ListItems() {
            setBackground(Color.lightGray);
            list = new List(4);
            list.addItemListener(this);
            list.addItem("First Item");
            list.addItem("Second Item");
            list.addItem("Third Item");
            list.addItem("Fourth Item");
            add("Center",list);
            textField = new TextField(60);
            add("South",textField);
            pack();
            show();
        }
        public void itemStateChanged(ItemEvent event) {
            textField.setText(event.paramString());
        }
    }
```

Figure I-4 shows what the screen looks like after a selection has been made.

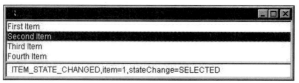

Figure I-4   The parameter string describing the
ItemEvent of a selection.

 Also see **ItemEvent** and **ItemSelectable**.

ItemSelectable

interface java.awt.ItemSelectable

This interface is implemented by displayable components that allow the user to make selections.

Implemented by

```
Checkbox
CheckboxMenuItem
Choice
List
```

Inheritance

```
public interface java.awt.ItemSelectable
```

Constructors

Returned by

An object implementing this interface is returned from
`ItemEvent.getItemSelectable()`.

Methods

addItemListener()

```
public abstract void addItemListener(ItemListener listener)
```

Adds the `listener` to the list of those that will receive an `ItemEvent` whenever the selection changes.

getSelectedObjects()

```
public abstract Object[] getSelectedObjects()
```

Returns the list of currently selected items. Returns `null` if no items are selected.

removeItemListener()

```
public abstract void removeItemListener(
        ItemListener listener)
```

Removes the `listener` to the list of those that will receive an `ItemEvent` whenever the selection changes.

 Also see **ItemEvent** and **ItemListener**.

JAR

Java ARchive

JAR (Java ARchive) is based on the ZIP file format and is used to combine several Java files into one. It was designed to combine class files, images, sounds, and other applet resources into a single file. This allows all the separate files required for an applet to be transmitted over the Internet as a single compressed file.

The thing that differentiates a JAR file from a regular ZIP file is that it is possible to have individual files in a JAR digitally signed for authentication. A JAR file contains a special directory named META-INF. This directory contains a manifest file, a collection of signature instruction files, and signature files.

The manifest file is just what its name implies — it is a list of the signed contents of the JAR file. The JAR may contain files without signatures, and it may also contain files that have multiple signatures, a feature that allows the recipient to use whichever signature it wants (normally, each signature uses a different algorithm and the recipient can select the signature that goes with the algorithm that it has implemented locally).

JAR files are created and examined by using **jar**. JAR files can be opened by a browser using the archive flag of **HTML.** For the capability of running applets without their normal security limitations, see **javakey**.

jar

utility

This is a utility program for creation and manipulation of JAR files.

If you are familiar with the syntax of the UNIX tar utility, you already know the most of the `jar` syntax.

Synopsis

```
jar [options] [manifest] [destination] input-files
```

options

c

Create a new JAR file from the list of `input-files`. It will either be written to standard output or to the file named by the `f` option.

t

List the contents of the JAR file to standard output.

x <filename>

Extract the file from the archive. If no filename is specified, all files are extracted.

f

This indicates that the name of the destination JAR file is present. If this is a `t` or `x` operation, it will be the name of an existing JAR file. If this is a `c` operation, it will be the name of the JAR file to be created. If `f` is not specified, a `t` or `x` operation will read from the standard input and a `c` operation will write to the standard output.

m<filename>

Used in conjunction with the `c` option to read the manifest data from a specific file.

M

Used in conjunction with the `c` option to suppress the creation of manifest data.

0

Only store the files. Do not use ZIP compression.

v

Write a verbose description of all activities to the standard error output.

manifest

Every JAR file has a manifest file entry. To specify the name of a manifest file, it is necessary to specify it with the `m` option. A manifest file named META-INF/MANIFEST.INF will be automatically generated if you don't specify one.

The manifest file contains a list of the files in the archive that have verification signatures. The content of the manifest file is of the format defined in RFC822—the basis of e-mail and HTTP. Here is an example showing the format of a manifest file:

```
Manifest-Version: 1.0
```

```
Name: common/class1.class
Digest-Algorithms: MD5
MD5-Digest: (base64 representation of MD5 digest)

Name: common/class2.class
Digest-Algorithms: MD5, SHA
MD5-Digest: (base64 representation of MD5 digest)
SHA-Digest: (base64 representation of SHA digest)
```

destination

This is the name of a JAR file to be used for either input or output. To include the destination filename, it will be necessary to specify the f option.

input-files

These are the files to be inserted into the new JAR file. If any of these names is a directory, the directory is processed recursively.

Example 1

This command will create a JAR file from the class files in the current directory:

```
jar cf myjarfile *.class
```

The name of the JAR file is myjarfile. A manifest file will be created and included as the first file in the JAR.

Example 2

This command will create a JAR file from all the class files in the current directory:

```
jar cmf myManifestFile myJarFile *.class
```

The manifest included in the JAR will be the file named myManifestFile. The name of the JAR file will be myJarFile.

Example 3

This example will list the names of the files in the JAR file:

```
jar xf myJarFile
```

All the filenames in the JAR file myJarFile will be listed to the standard output.

 Jar files can be opened by a browser using the archive flag of **HTML.** For the capability of adding signatures and running applets without their normal security limitations, see **javakey**.

java

utility

This is the command-line executable form of the Java Virtual Machine supplied as a part of the standard Sun Java Development Kit. It can be used to run any Java application.

The name of the class file on the command line can contain periods—just like the `import` statement in the source code of a Java class—that it will use as path names to locate classes inside packages.

Synopsis

```
java [options] classname <arguments>
java_g [options] classname <arguments>
javaw [options] classname <arguments>
javaw_g [options] classname <arguments>
```

The forms ending with _g are for debugging. These are nonoptimized versions designed to be used with interactive debuggers, such as `jdb`.

The forms named javaw and javaw_g are only for Win32. They are the same as the java and java_g forms except that they suppress the appearance of the console window. All four use the same set of options.

classname

This file contains the bytecodes to be executed. It is normally created as the output of a Java compiler, such as javac. These files all end with the file extension .class. The interpreter will load the class and call a method in the class that is declared this way:

```
static public void main(String[] args)
```

The class file must be in a directory included in the list of directories defined by the CLASSPATH environment variable. If it is in a package—that is, in a directory underneath a CLASSPATH directory—it must be fully qualified by including its package in the name, for example:

```
java mypackage.utility.hexdump
```

The values of the CLASSPATH variable can be overridden on the command line by using the `-classpath` option.

arguments

The arguments are passed to the application and will appear in the `args` array of the `main()` method.

options
-classpath <path>

Specify the complete path name to be used in place of the environment variable CLASS-PATH. The directory names are separated by colons or semicolons (colons are used for UNIX and Mac; semicolons are used for Win32). Specifying the class path this way removes the default path to the Java system classes, so they will have to be included also.

-cs or -checksource

The compiler will check the modification time of each class file against the modification time of its source file. If the source file is newer than the class file, it will be recompiled.

-D<property>=<value>

Assign the value to the property name. If the property is already defined, this will replace it. Any number of -D options can appear on one command line.

-debug

Allow the jdb debugger to attach itself to the running program. This option will cause a password to be displayed. This password must be used to start the debugging session.

-help

Print a message describing the arguments and options.

-ms <size>

Specify the amount of memory initially assigned to the allocation pool. The default is 1 megabyte. The minimum is 1000 bytes. By default, the size value is specified in bytes, but you can specify it in megabytes with an m or kilobytes with a k (as in 16m or 1024k). The minimum size is 1000 bytes.

-mx <size>

Specify the size of the memory allocation pool used to create objects and by the garbage collection routines. The default size is 16 megabytes. The size value is specified in bytes, but you can specify it in megabytes with an m or kilobytes with a k (as in 16m or 1024k). The minimum size is 1000 bytes.

-noasyncgc

Turn off asynchronous garbage collection. No garbage collection will take place unless it is either explicitly requested by a call to gc( ) or the program runs out of memory. Without this option, garbage collection will run continuously in a separate thread.

-noclassgc

Disable garbage collection of classes.

-noverify

Turn bytecode verification off.

-oss \<size\>

Set the maximum stack size that can be used by Java code in any one thread. Every thread will be assigned a Java-code stack of this size. By default, the size value is specified in bytes, but you can specify it in megabytes with an m or kilobytes with a k (as in 16m or 1024k). The minimum size is 1000 bytes.

-prof

Enable Java profiling, with the output going into a file named java.prof.

-prof: \<file\>

Enable Java profiling with the output going into the named file.

-ss \<size\>

Set the maximum stack size that can be used by native code in any one thread. Every thread will be assigned a native code stack of this size. By default, the size value is specified in bytes, but you can specify the value in megabytes with an m or in kilobytes with a k (as in 16m or 1024k). The minimum size is 1000 bytes.

-t

Print a trace of each instruction executed. This is valid only for java_g or javaw_g.

-tm

Print a trace of each method call. This is valid only for java_g or javaw_g.

-v or -verbose

Print a message as each item of a class file is loaded.

-version

Print the version information.

-verbosegc

The garbage collector will print a message whenever it frees memory.

-verify

Run the bytecode verifier on all code no matter how it is loaded.

-verifyremote

Run the bytecode verifier on all code that is loaded via a class loader. This is the default setting.

For debugging while executing, see **jdb**. For more information on command line arguments, see **application**. To run a Java applet, see **appletviewer**. For more information about the inner workings of the Java run time, see **Virtual Machine**.

java

package

The name of the default package is java. This is the package that holds all the API classes.

Three system-level classes must be present for the compiler and interpreter to operate properly: `java.util`, `java.lang`, and `java.io`. These three are so tightly woven into the fabric of Java that they can be considered to be a part of the language.

The API

A part of the Java language supplied with the compiler and the other utilities is the API. The API is supplied in the form of the default package, which contains a large number of precompiled classes. This is a brief description of all the packages.

package java.applet

This package includes only one class—`java.applet.Applet`. This is the superclass of all applets. The package also contains some interfaces that can be used by applets.

package java.awt

This is the *Abstract Windowing Toolkit*. It contains classes and interfaces that can be used to control the display of windows and respond to user input.

package java.awt.datatransfer

These classes implement cut and paste and can be used to implement drag-and-drop operations. Data, along with its type information, can be transferred from one application to another.

package java.awt.event

These are the Java events (mouse, keyboard, and so on) and the interfaces of the event listeners.

package java.awt.image

These are classes to manipulate and display graphical images.

package java.awt.peer

This is the set of low-level classes used to communicate between the Java AWT and the underlying operating system. The peer classes specify the method calls that must be implemented by a system for it to interface with Java.

package java.beans

These are the Java classes and interfaces used for introspection and property descriptions necessary for the beans operation.

package java.io

This package covers input and output.

package java.lang

This contains some of the core classes and interfaces. It includes wrappers for the primitive types, multithreading, security, access to Java internals, and access to underlying system.

package java.lang.reflect

This is an API providing capabilities for internal inspection and manipulation of Java objects. It has low-level methods that can be used to modify elements of arrays, construct new classes, and access fields within objects.

package java.math

These are classes that handle extended-precision numbers.

package java.net

This has classes dealing with Internet sockets and communications protocols.

package java.rmi

This is the RMI (Remote Access Invocation) package. This is the set of communication facilities that enable the construction of distributed Java applications.

package java.rmi.dgc

This package deals with the distributed garbage collection portion of the remote method invocation.

package java.rmi.registry

This covers access to the registry that exists on every host using remote method invocation.

package java.rmi.server

This includes the classes and interfaces on the server side of remote method invocation.

package java.security

This is a collection of general security classes and interfaces, including classes for identification, validation, key encryption, and decryption.

package java.security.acl

These are Access Control Lists, a set of abstractions for managing principals and their access permissions.

package java.security.interfaces

This is a standard set of interfaces that can be used to implement various techniques and levels of security.

package java.sql

This is a set of classes that defines the methods for querying and updating relational databases.

package java.text

This package contains several classes that can be used to format various kinds of data into strings. It also parses strings and does special collations for sorting.

package java.util

This contains a set of utility classes that can be used for a variety of things from data and calendar arithmetic, linked lists, stacks, and system properties to bit manipulation and multilingual resources. There are several classes for date and time manipulation.

package java.util.zip

This is the data compression and decompression package.

Java

 For Java Beans, see **Beans**. For Java digits, see **digit**. For Java letters, see **letter**. For the Java Virtual Machine, see **Virtual Machine**.

Java Chip

There are three Java-language hardware chips. They all implement the Java bytecodes in CPU form for faster execution.

picoJava

This is the smallest of the three. It is designed for cellular phones and peripheral devices such as printers.

microJava

This chip is a step up in size from picoJava. It adds I/O, memory, communications, and control functions. This chip is intended for kiosks and telecommunications equipment.

UltraJava

This is the largest and most powerful of the chips. It uses advanced graphics circuits and features. It is designed for use in 3-D graphics and other multimedia compute-intensive applications.

javac

utility

The Java compiler. It is used to compile Java source files into bytecodes.

Synopsis

```
javac [options] source-files
javac_g [options] source-files
```

The javac_g version is a nonoptimizing compiler suitable for use with jdb or other debuggers.

options
-classpath <path>

This is the list of directories that javac will use to locate the any class files that may be needed to resolve references. This replaces the path specified by the CLASSPATH environment variable. On UNIX and Mac, the directory names are separated by colons; on Win32, they are separated by semicolons. Specifying this option completely replaces the data from CLASSPATH, so it will be necessary to include the system classes in the path.

-d <directory>

Specify the root directory of the class file hierarchy to be output from the compilation. For example, specifying /usr/classes would cause the compiler to place all class files in that directory—and if a class were defined as being in a package named fred, it would be put into the directory /usr/classes/fred. If this option is not specified, the current directory is assumed. Although it is normal for the output directory to be one of those defined by CLASSPATH, it is not a requirement.

-depend

In its normal operation, the compiler will load class files to resolve references. This flag tells the compiler to compare the modification times of those loaded class files to those of their source files, and to compile the ones that have had their source files updated. Without this flag, the compiler will recompile only class files that are missing or are specified on the command line.

-g

Debugging information will be created by the compiler. This information includes line numbers and local variable names. This information is used by jdb and other debugging tools. Without this flag, only line numbers are generated (unless -O is turned on to suppress them).

-J <option>

This is an option that will be passed through to the Java interpreter that is running the compiler. No spaces may be embedded in the argument — multiple arguments are specified by preceding each with its own -J. This could be handy for setting, for example, the amount of memory available for the compilation.

-nowarn

Turns off warnings.

-O

The compiler will optimize the code. Static and final methods will be compiled into inline code. Because code is generated inline, class files may actually be larger than they would be otherwise.

-verbose

Messages will be printed that describe which source files are being compiled and which class files are being loaded.

source-files

A Java source file is a text file that ends with the file extension .java. Several source-files may be included on the command line of the compiler.

Several classes may be defined in one source file, but only one of them can be declared public. The filename must be the same as the public class name. For example, if the name of a public class is PublicClassName, it must be in a file named PublicClassName.java. The output of the compiler will be put in the file named PublicClassName.class. If there is more than one class in the file, their bytecodes will each be placed in separate files using the name of the class and ending with .class.

To resolve references to external names, the compiler will search the CLASSPATH for files with the appropriate names. When the compiler makes a search, it looks for both the source file and the class file. If a source file is found and there is no class file for it, the source file will be compiled.

Environment

Property java.pipe

Setting the property `java.pipe.output` to `true` will cause the compiler to write output messages to `System.out`. Setting it to `false` (or not having it set) will cause the compiler to write its output messages to `System.err`.

CLASSPATH

This environment variable is used to supply the compiler with a list of directories that hold the class files that will be used to resolved references. It is a list of directory names separated by colons on UNIX and Apple, and by semicolons on Win32.

Dynamic resolution

The Java compiler will load, or even create, the class files it needs to resolve references to names. It is able to accept circular references — that is, compilation unit A can refer to something in compilation unit B while there is also a reference in compilation unit B to something in A. If the compiler encounters a reference to a class that does not exist, but there is a source file for it, it will create the class file from the source file.

Compile errors

There is an error condition that can be quite hard to find. Say a reference occurs in a.java to some method in b.java and, when compiling a.java, you get a report that is no such method exists in b.java. When you look at the code, you can see the method. This could be caused by an unterminated comment (a /* without an */) somewhere earlier in b.java. The compilation skipped past the method until it found another */ pair to terminate the comment — it compiled without an error, but the method is not in the class file.

javadoc

utility

This program will read all the Java source files in a directory, recursively descending the directory tree, and create a set of documents in HTML format that describe the classes. To do this, it extracts the text from specially formatted comments. The text of these comments may contain tags that supply specific information for the documentation. It is even possible to include preformatted HTML in the comments and have it translated directly into the documentation.

Synopsis

```
javadoc [options] [package | source.java]*
```

Documentation is generated from the hierarchical tree starting from a single package or from a list of one or more Java source files.

The output

The generated output is more than one HTML file.

One for each source

One html file is produced for each Java source file input to javadoc.

tree.html

This file contains documentation of the class hierarchy of all the packages involved.

AllNames.html

This file contains an index of the members of the packages. It is a list of all the fields and all the methods along with their signatures.

The input

Specially formatted comments are used to generated descriptions. Any comment that begins with /** and ends with */ will be picked up as part of the documentation. For a documentation comment to be used, it must come immediately before a class, interface, field, constructor, or method definition.

The discarded parts

The leading /** and trailing */ are discarded. The comment is free-form and can be several lines long. All spaces or tabs at the beginning of a line are discarded. If an asterisk is found as the first nonwhitespace character on a line, it is also discarded. For example, the comment block

```
/**
 * This will document.
 */
```

will result in the documentation line being "This will document."

The HTML parts

HTML formatting tags may be included in the body of the comment; they will be passed through. For example, the comment block

```
/**
 * This <i>will</i> be documented.
 */
```

will result in the HTML documentation being "This <i>will</i> be documented." The italic tags will be left in place.

Don't use any heading tags such as <h3> and </h3> because they will conflict with the headings in the generated HTML. Most tags are not harmful, but be careful. You may want to examine some javadoc output to see if your tag will work. The tags <pre> and </pre> are used quite often to prevent the browser from reformatting example code.

Sentence structure

The body of the comment is a collection of sentences and tags. The first sentence should be general and descriptive because it will be extracted and used in the summary at the top of the HTML. The first sentence ends with the first period that is followed by white space. The entire comment block—lead sentence and all—will be used in the actual description.

Tags

As the paragraphs are being parsed for the documentation, javadoc recognizes certain tags and uses them in special ways. All tags being with an at-sign. None of the tags are required, and you can have as many of them as you wish.

A tag must begin at the beginning of a line. It can be preceded by white space but no other characters. If tag names need to be repeated, keep tags with the same names together so that javadoc can gather them into a single list. There are three categories of tags: the class/interface tags, field tags, and constructor/method tags.

Some of the tags contain data that is to be processed by javadoc, such as a class name or filename. Other tags are not processed in any way by javadoc and can be entered as free-form text.

Class/interface tags
@author <name>

The author's name is entered as free-form text. There can be multiple author tags for a single class or interface.

@deprecated <description>

The class, method, or interface is deprecated and may disappear in a future release. This is normally followed by a @see tag pointing to its replacement.

@see <name>

This will cause the insertion of an HTML link to the named class or interface. There can be any number of these tags in one comment block. The object of the link can be specified as simply a class or interface name, a class or interface name with an HTML-type tag for one of its members, or the normal HTML link format addressing any URL. Here are some examples:

```
@see java.lang.String
@see String
```

The # character can be used to separate the name of the class from a class member:

```
@see String#equals
@see Character#MAX_RADIX
```

In the case of overloaded methods, the signature list of arguments can be specified. Spaces are important — if a method has more than one argument, a single space must appear between each argument and the next.

```
@see java.lang.Object#wait(int)
@see java.io.File#File(java.io.File, java.lang.String)
```

The tag can be used to create a link with any URL on the Internet. It takes the form of a standard HTML link:

```
@see <a href="spec.html">Java Spec</a>
```

@since <text>

The text is free-form. This is used to indicate when the particular feature was introduced to the system. For example, this tag is used on new classes that were added to the JDK since version 1.1.

@version <version>

The version can be entered as free-form text. There can be only one version tag for each class or interface.

Field tags
@deprecated <description>

The field is deprecated and may disappear in a future release. This is normally followed by a @see tag pointing to the new field (or access method), if there is one.

@see <name>

This takes the same form as the @see tag for classes and interfaces.

Constructor and method tags
@deprecated <description>

The method is deprecated and may disappear in a future release. This is normally followed by a @see tag pointing to the correct method.

@param <parameter-name> <description>

This requests that the parameter be added to the "Parameters" section in the generated HTML. The description can continue to the next line.

@return <description>

This will add a "Returns" section to the HTML and include the description of the return value.

@see <name>

This tag takes the same form as the @see tag for classes and interfaces.

@exception <fully-qualified-class-name> <description>

This tag can be used to include the name and the description of exceptions thrown by the method. There will be a link to the exception.

options
-author

Include the @author tag information. If this flag is not specified, no author information will be included in the output.

-classpath <path>

This is the list of directories that javac will use to locate any .class files or .java files that may be needed to resolve references. On UNIX and the Mac, the directory names are separated by colons; on Win32, they are separated by semicolons. Specifying this option completely replaces the data from CLASSPATH, so it will be necessary to include the system class in the path.

If you use both options, it may be necessary to have -classpath come before -sourcepath on the command line.

-d <directory>

This gives the name of the directory used by javadoc to store the generated HTML files. The directory can be relative or absolute.

-docencoding <name>

The name is the output HTML file encoding scheme.

-encoding <name>

The name is a source file encoding name, such as EUCJIS\SJIS. If none is specified, the default name for the platform default converter will be used.

-J <flag>

This is an option that will be passed through to the Java interpreter that is running javadoc. No spaces are permitted in the argument. Multiple arguments are specified by beginning each with its own -J. This could be handy for setting, for example, the amount of memory available for generating the documentation.

-nodeprecated

Do not create the deprecation notification found on the @deprecated tag.

-noindex

Do not create the package index. If this flag is not specified, a package index will be created.

-notree

Do not create the class/interface hierarchy. If this flag is not specified, the class/interface hierarchy will be created.

-public

Include only public classes and members.

-protected

Include only protected and public classes and members. This is the default.

-package

Include only package, protected, and public classes and members.

-private

Include all classes and members—private, package, protected, and public.

-sourcepath <path>

This is the path that will be used to find the source files (it has no effect on the search path for class files). The default source path is the current directory.

If you are generating the documentation for a subpackage, you will want to be able to include references to the package in the documentation. For example, if the package being documented is

```
d:\mypackage\subpackage\*.java
```

then you would want to set up the source path like this:

```
-sourcepath d:\mypackage
```

so that references to the appropriate superclass could be included.

If you are generating the documentation for only one class, the situation is quite different. For example, if you are getting the documentation for this single class:

```
d:\mypackage\subpackage\HyperText.java
```

then you will need to set the source path to the directory containing the class, like this:

```
-sourcepath d:\mypackage\subpackage
```

-verbose

This flag will cause javadoc to report on the source files as they are loaded, the generation of the output documents, and the sorting process, along with information about the time all these processes take.

-version

Include the @version tag information. If this flag is not specified, they will not be included.

Environment

CLASSPATH

This environment variable is used to supply javadoc with a list of directories that holds the files that it will use to resolve references. It is a list of directory names separated by colons on UNIX and Apple, and by semicolons on Win32.

Example 1

This is an example of a documentation comment block for a class. This one uses the <pre> and </pre> tags to insert some preformatted text:

```
/**
This class is an n-space rotation of a tesseract. Its
default operation is in the fourth dimension.
<pre>
    Tspin spin = new Tspin();
    spin.show();
</pre>
@author Bertha D. Blues
@version Pre-release 4.2
@see java.awt.Frame
@see spinpackage.blue.FourSpin
@see <a href="http://www.intersticial.com">Slices</a>
*/
public class Tspin extends Frame {
    ...
}
```

Example 2

This is an example showing the format of a documentation comment for a method:

```
/** Returns an approximation of the position of the
 * hypercube in n-space. This can be only an
 * an approximation because the tesseract could be
 * trans-dimensional during the test.
 * @param dimLimit The upper limit of the
 *     trans-dimensional reach.
 * @return The n-space position. The minimum value
 *     is 3 and any value beyond 12 should be
 *     considered hypothetical.
 * @exception SpaceOutOfRangeException If the cube is
 *     currently beyond reach.
```

```
    */
public int getDimension(int dimLimit) {
    ...
}
```

javah

utility

This program will read Java class files and generate C source header files that can be used to create native C code that will link to Java classes.

 The process of linking to native code in Java 1.0 required the use of the output from javah. The Java Native Interface introduced with Java 1.1 does not require the header files or stub files from javah. As a convenience, however, the -jni option of javah can still be used to generate native method prototypes for your header file.

The header file

The generated C header file contains a struct definition with a layout that parallels that of the Java class. There is a field in the struct for each instance variable in the class. The names of the header file and the struct are derived from the class name and, if the class is a member of a package, the package name.

Synopsis

```
javah [options] classname. ...
javah_g [options] classname. ...
```

The javah_g form is a nonoptimized version for use with debuggers such as jdb.

options
-classpath <path>

This is the list of directories that javah will use to locate the class files. This replaces the path specified by the CLASSPATH environment variable. On UNIX and Mac, the directory names are separated by colons; on Win32, they are separated by semicolons.

-d <directory>

Specify the name of the directory where the header file or files will be written. The default is the current directory.

-help

Print the help message describing the options.

-jni

Create an output file containing the prototypes needed for JNI-style native methods.

-o <outputfile>

This will cause the output from all the `classname`s on the command line to have their header-file output concatenated into a single file.

-stubs

Generate empty C function stubs from the information in the Java class file.

-td <directory>

The name of the working directory that javah will use to store temporary files. If this is not specified, a default will be used.

The UNIX default is `/tmp`. On Win32, the environment variables TEMP and TMP will be checked for the default—if neither of these is defined, a directory named C:\TMP will be created.

-trace

Insert tracing information into the stubs file.

-v

This is the verbose mode. Messages will be printed about the files being generated.

-version

Print the javah version.

classname

More than one `classname` may be included on the command line. Unless the flag options specify otherwise, one header file will be generated for each `classname`. The header files, having their names and contents derived from the Java classes, will, by default, be created in the current directory.

Environment

CLASSPATH

This environment variable is used to supply javah with a list of directories that holds the source files that will be used to resolve references. It is a list of directory names separated by colons on UNIX and Apple, and by semicolons on Win32.

For an example of how the `-jni` type header files are used, see **JNI.**

javakey

utility

This is a utility program that will manage a database of entities and keys. The entities (individuals, companies, and so on) are kept in the database along with their private keys, public keys, signatures, and certificates.

The primary purpose of javakey is to generate digital signatures for archive files. A signature verifies that a file came from a specified entity—the signer. The signature is generated using the entity's private and public keys, along with one or more authentication certificates. The authentication certificates are needed to verify that the keys actually belong to the entity.

Entities

An *entity*, also called an *identity*, is a real-world person, company, or organization of some sort that has a public key. An entity may also have one or more certificates. Entities are identified in the javakey database by a user name. Some entities are tagged as being trusted entities—ones that are trusted to sign certificates vouching for other entities.

Certificate

A *certificate* is a digitally signed statement from one entity that verifies the authenticity of the ownership of a key by another entity. The theory is that if you can trust the first entity, you can safely ascribe the correct ownership to the second entity. The javakey utility can handle X.509 certificates.

Signer

A *signer* is an entity that has private key in addition to its public key.

Private key

A *private key* is used for signing a certificate (or other document). The associated public key can be used to verify the signature.

Public key

A *public key* is used to verify the identity of the signer of a certificate (or other document).

Out of the sandbox

The applet viewer allows the applets from a downloaded JAR file that are signed by a trusted entity to have the same full execution rights as local applications. These applets are not restricted to the sandbox.

For this to work, the javakey database must hold a copy of a certificate for the public key of the entity signing the JAR.

The database file

The default name of the database file is `identitydb.obj`. Also by default, it will be in the directory with the JDK installation. The location of the file can be changed by setting the property `identity.database` to the desired property name. The `identity.database` property definition is found in the file java.home\lib\security\java.security. The file should be kept in a secure location because it could contain private keys.

Encryption algorithm

The javakey utility defaults to using DSA (digital signature algorithm). Another algorithm—such as RSA—can be used if it is a standard key generation algorithm and there is a statically installed implementation of the key generator.

Synopsis

```
javakey [options]
```

options

Only one option at a time may be specified on a javakey command. The options may be specified with or without the leading minus sign.

-c identityName {true | false}

Create a new entity in the database with the name `identityName`. If `true`, it will be a trusted entity. If `false` or unspecified, the entity will not trusted.

-dc certfile

Display information about the certificate in the file `certfile`.

-ec identityName certNumber certOutputFile

Export the certificate with the serial number `certNumber` of the named entity to the file `certOutputFile`.

-ek identityName publicFile {privateFile}

Export the public key for the entity to the `publicFile`, and optionally export the private key to the `privateFile`. They keys are written in X.509 format.

-g identityName algorithm keysize {publicFile} {privateFile}

The same as `-gk`.

-gc directivefile

Generate a certificate according to the information in the file. See the example that follows.

-gk identityName algorithm keysize {publicFile} {privateFile}

Using the specified `algorithm` and `keysize`, generate a public key and a private key for the entity specified by `identityName`. The `keysize` is the number of bits. If `publicFile` is specified, the public key will be written to it—also, if `privateFile` is specified, the private key will be written to it.

Note that no facility is provided to specify algorithm-specific key generation parameters such as the p, q, and g parameters of DSA.

-gs directiveFile jarFile

Sign the JAR file according to the information provided in the `directiveFile`. See the example that follows.

-ic identityName certsrcfile

Import the public key certificate in the file `certsrcfile` and associate it with the named entity. If the entity already has a public key, javakey will report an error if the new key is not the same as the existing one.

-ii identityName

This will cause javakey to prompt for information to be added to that of the entity identified by `identityName`. You can enter as many lines of information as you would like. Input is terminated by Ctrl+D on UNIX and Ctrl+Z on Win32.

-ik identityName keysrcfile

Import the public key in the file `keysrcfile` and associate it with the named entity. The key must be in X.509 format.

-ikp identityName publicFile privateFile

Import the public key and the private key, form the two files, and associate them with the entity. The keys must be in X.509 format.

-l

List the user names of all entities in the database.

-ld

List the user names and detailed information about all the entities in the database.

-li identityName

List detailed information about the named entity.

-r identityName

Remove the named entity from the database.

-t identityName {true|false}

Change the trust of the entity `identityName`. If `true`, the entity will become trusted. If `false` or unspecified, the entity will be become untrusted.

Example 1

This command will add `fred` as a trusted signer:

```
javakey -cs fred true
```

The default is not to be trusted. The following two entities are added as untrusted:

```
javakey -cs blackie false
```

```
javakey -cs slickWillie
```

A DSA pair of keys—one public and one private—can be generated for the trusted signer in this way:

```
javakey -gk fred DSA 512
```

Example 2

Quite a bit of information is required to create a certificate, so it can all be entered into a file that javakey will read. This is an example of creating a certificate from a directive file:

```
javakey -gc fredCertification
```

This will create a certificate using the information in the file named `fredCertification`. Here is an example of what `fredCertificate` could look like:

```
#
issuer.name=fred
#
issuer.cert=1
#
subject.name=mlaunay
subject.real.name=Kat Williams
subject.org.unit=Research
subject.org=XYZ Camera Company
subject.country=USA
#
start.date=12 Oct 1997
end.date=31 Dec 1998
serial.number=1234
#
```

```
signature.algorithm=MD5/RSA
#
out.file=cert.cer
```

The following is a description of the meaning of each of the fields. They are all required unless stated otherwise.

issuer.name

This is the name of the entity that will be issuing the certificate.

issuer.cert

This specifies which of the issuer's certificates is to be used to validate the new certificate. It is the number assigned to the certificate by javakey. This field is not required for a self-signed certificate—that is, when the issuer and the subject are the same.

subject.name

This is the entity that is being authenticated by the issuer of the certificate.

subject.real.name

The real-world name of the subject.

subject.org.unit

The subect's organizational unit.

subject.org

The subject's organization.

subject.country

The subject's country.

start.date

This is the starting date of the validity certificate, in a form that can be read by the Java `Date` class (including the time is optional).

end.date

This is the ending date of the validity certificate, in a form that can be read by the Java `Date` class (including the time is optional).

serial.number

This number must be unique for a given issuer. It is used as the ID number of the certificate.

signature.algorithm

This will name the algorithm to be used to create the signature on the certificate. It only needs to be specified to choose some algorithm other than DSA (Digital Signature Algorithm). A non-DSA algorithm can be used if there is a statically installed provider that supplies an implementation for it.

out.file

This is the name of the file that will receive the output.

Example 3

A signature is added to a JAR file after first being generated for an entity in the javakey database. The entity must be in the database, have an associated key pair, and have at least one certificate. Adding the signature is done using the -gs command with a directives file. Here is an example of a directives file:

```
signer=fred
cert=1234
chain=0
signature.file=FREDSIG
out.file=final.jar
```

signer

The name of the signer.

cert

This is the certificate serial number that was assigned when the certificate was associated with the signer. The available certificate numbers can be determined with the ld or li command.

chain

The chain depth of the linked certificates. This is currently not supported.

signature.file

This name, which must be eight characters or less, will be used as the basis to construct the names of the output files. The signature file will be the name with the extension .SF appended to it. The signature block file will be the name with the extension .DSA appended to it.

out.file

This is optional—it is the name of the JAR file.

Once the directive file has been created, it can be used to add the signature to the JAR file this way:

```
javakey -gs directivefile jarfile
```

If the out.file property was specified in the directives, it will be the name of the signed JAR file. If it was not specified, the output file will have the same name as the input file, except that the extension will be .sig.

The generated .SF and .DSA files will both be added to the JAR file in the META-INF directory. Thus, using the names from the preceding example, the output JAR file will be final.jar and will contain the files META-INF/FRED-SIG.SF and META-INF/FREDSIG.DSA. If files by these names already existed in the JAR file, they will be overwritten.

 For more on Java security, see the package **security**.

javap

utility

This is the Java class file disassembler. It will read a class file and print its internal information in human-readable form.

The actual output is controlled by the command line flags. If no options flags are specified, it will simply print a list of the public fields and methods.

Synopsis

```
javap [options] class ...
```

class

One or more class filenames can be included on the command line. The class filenames are specified without their .class extensions.

options
-l

Print the local variable tables. The local variable names are only available if the -g option was used on javac. There will be no line numbers if the -O option was used on javac.

-b

Ensure backward compatibility with earlier versions of javap.

-public

Print only public classes and members.

-protected

Print both public and protected classes and members.

-package

Print package, protected, and public classes and members. This is the default.

-private

Print all classes and members.

-J <flag>

Pass this flag to the Java Virtual Machine executing javap.

-s

Print the internal type signatures for each member.

-c

Print the bytecode instructions that make up the executable bodies of the methods.

-classpath <path>

This is the list of directories that javap will use to locate the class files. This replaces the path specified by the CLASSPATH environment variable. On UNIX and Mac, the directory names are separated by colons; on Win32, they are separated by semicolons.

-verbose

Print information such as the stack size, the number of local variables, and the arguments for methods.

-verify

Run the verifier. The output will be a succeed or fail message.

-version

Print the javap version string.

Environment

CLASSPATH

This environment variable is used to supply javap with a list of directories that holds the class files that will be used to resolved references. It is a list of directory names separated by colons on UNIX and Apple, and by semicolons on Win32.

jdb

utility

This is the Java debugger.

The Java debugger is a command line debugger (very much like the UNIX debugger dbx). It provides the ability to control the execution of a Java program and inspect its values and status. It can operate with a local or remote Java interpreter.

There are two ways to start the interpreter. The more common method is to have the debugger start the interpreter along with the Java program to be debugged. It is also possible to have jdb attach itself to an already-running program.

The jdb debugger requires that debugging information be included in the class file by the compiler. Before debugging, the class files should be compiled by using the -g flag. The debugger will run without it, but certain information will not be available.

Synopsis

```
jdb [options]
```

options

When starting jdb, any command line arguments, other than those listed here, are passed onto the Java interpreter that will be running the program (for example, -classpath). Two command line arguments are used when attaching jdb to a running process:

-host <hostname>

The name of the host on which the program is running.

For this to be done locally, a loopback address must exist in the hosts file. On Win32, it will be necessary to create a file in the WINDOWS directory named hosts (you can copy or rename the one named hosts.sam). Make sure it includes the line:

```
127.0.0.1   localhost
```

This is the special loopback IP address and is used for a computer to address itself.

-password <password>

This is the password that was printed by the remote Java interpreter when it was started with the -debug option. This is a security measure—any interpreter that does not print a password will not allow a debugger to take control of a program that it may be running.

Starting jdb
Starting with no arguments

The debugger can be started with no arguments. It will come up and prompt for a command. Simply enter

```
jdb
```

The debugger will initialize itself and prompt for input. At this point, you can use the `load` command to name the class file to be debugged.

Starting with a class file

If you name a class file on the command line when starting jdb, it will load it when it starts. Enter

```
jdb ClassName.class
```

The debugger will load the file ClassName.class. Once the file is loaded, the program will prompt you for input. You are ready to start your debugging session.

Attaching jdb to a running program

Circumstances arise in which it could be convenient to attach the debugger to a program after it has already started. This can be done, but it takes a little preplanning. The `-debug` flag must be used to start the program running. This is for security reasons because jdb can be used to take control of a running program on a remote system.

When you start a program you wish to debug using the `java -debug` option, it will print a password that can be used by jdb to start the debugging session. The line containing the password will look something like this:

```
Agent password=4k43ug
```

The program will then go into execution—it will not wait for jdb to attach itself. To attach jdb, use the name of the host and the password, like this:

```
jdb -host rimshot -password 4k43ug
```

Commands
?

List the available commands. This is the same as help.

!!

Repeat the previous command.

catch <class ID>

Break for the exception specified by its class ID. If no exception is specified, the debugger will list the exceptions to be caught.

classes

List all the currently loaded classes.

clear <class ID>:<line>

Clear a breakpoint.

cont

Continue execution from the current breakpoint.

down [n frames]

Move down in a thread's stack frame. The default is one frame.

dump <ID> [ID(s)]

Print all the information about variables, methods, superclasses, and implemented interfaces of the specified objects. The objects are specified by their hexadecimal object ID numbers, or by name. If the class has already been loaded, its simple name can be used (that is, `Button` can be used for `java.awt.Button`). Detailed information can be extracted by using expressions such as `0xABCD1234.barray[3]`.

exit

Exit the debugger. This is the same as quit.

gc

Perform garbage collection to free RAM held by unused objects.

help

List the available commands. This is the same as `?`.

ignore <class ID>

Ignore the specified exception.

list [line number | method]

Print the source code at the line number or method. If neither are specified, the line number of the current stack frame is used.

load <classname>

Load the named class into the debugger.

locals

Print the local variables in the current stack frame.

memory

Report memory usage.

methods \<class ID\>

List the methods of the class.

print \<ID\> [ID(s)]

Call the `toString()` method of the object and display the returned `String`. The classes to print can be specified by the hexadecimal object ID number or by name. If the class has already been loaded, its simple name can be used (that is, `Button` can be used for `java.awt.Button`).

quit

Exit the debugger. This is the same as exit.

resume [thread ID(s)]

Resume the specified threads. If no threads are specified, all suspended threads will be resumed.

run \<class\> [args]

Execute the named class by calling its `main()` method with the args. The named class must be already loaded.

step

Execute one line of code.

stop at \<class ID\>:\<line\>

Set a break point at a line. The class and the source-code line number are used to set the break-point. For example, `ClassName:37` would set the breakpoint at line number 37 of `ClassName`.

stop in \<class ID\>.\<method\>

Set a breakpoint in a method.

suspend [thread ID(s)]

Suspend the specified threads. If no threads are specified, they will all be suspended.

thread \<thread ID\>

During a debugging session, most commands are addressed to the default thread. This command specifies the default thread.

threadgroup \<name\>

Set the current thread group.

threadgroups

List the thread groups.

threads [threadgroup]

List all the currently running threads. The listed threads are organized by thread group. A thread is identified by its object ID. Those in the default thread group are identified by an ID the form t@<index>. For example, t@3 would be the third thread in the default group.

up [n frames]

Move up in a thread's stack frame. If no number is specified, the default is one frame.

use [source file path]

If the source file path is not specified, this command will print the path being used to locate the source files. If the path has been specified, the command will change the path.

where [thread ID] | all

Dump the thread stack. If there are no arguments, it will dump the current thread. Using all as the argument will cause it to dump all threads in the current threadgroup. One or more thread ids can be specified, and those will be dumped. A thread ID takes the form t@<index>—for example, t@3.

Exceptions

In the Java interpreter, without the debugger, an uncaught exception will print a stack trace and halt execution. In jdb, an uncaught exception is treated as a nonrecoverable breakpoint, and execution will simply halt where the exception is thrown. At this point, the local variables can be examined to determine the cause of the exception.

It is also possible to catch certain exceptions by using the catch command of jdb. Having an exception caught by jdb is is like hitting a breakpoint. Those set by the catch command can be unset with the ignore command.

Environment

CLASSPATH

This environment variable is used to supply javap with a list of directories that hold the class files that will be used to resolved references. It is a list of directory names separated by colons on UNIX and Apple, and by semicolons on Win32.

JDBC

Java DataBase Connectivity

The JDBC (Java DataBase Connectivity) is a standard SQL interface between a particular database and Java. The interface is designed to handle the not-so-standard facets of SQL that appear in the various database implementations. There is also an ODBC bridge that can be used to implement the JDBC in terms of the C language ODBC API.

The database meta data

For an application to intelligently work with the variations that come about in SQL, the application will need to have some way of finding out just what those variations are. To do this, Java has implemented the idea of a database driver. Not only will the driver accept SQL command and pass them to the database for execution, it will also answer questions about its characteristics.

One of the things that a driver will do is report whether or not it is JDBC compliant. If it is, then not only will it answer other questions about database operations, but it will also obey certain commands in predictable ways.

JDBC Compliance

A database that is JDBC compliant is one that fully supports the JDBC API and all of the SQL 92 entry level standard specification. The Java driver for the database will return true or false on a query about this compliance.

The compliance is not intended to prohibit other database interfaces. This standard interface was designed with the idea of lightweight databases in mind.

 For more information, see the classes of the **sql** package; in particular, see the class **DatabaseMetaData**.

JDK

Java Development Kit

The JDK is the collection of classes and programs supplied from Sun to be used for Java software development. It contains all the fundamental items needed for Java software development and execution. It contains all the classes and programs described in this book. Table J-1 contains a list of the programs and utilities that come with the JDK.

Table J-1 Software Utilities Supplied with the JDK

Name	Description
applet viewer	A utility that will execute Java applets
jar	A program to compress files into a single Java Archive (JAR) file
java	A Java Virtual Machine used to execute Java programs
javac	The Java language compiler
javadoc	A program to generate documentation from Java source code
javah	A program to read Java source and create header files for C code
javakey	A program to generate digital encryption signatures and manage a database of them
javap	The Java disassembler, which reads class files and prints bytecodes
jdb	A Java debugger
native2ascii	A text conversion utility
rmic	A program that generates the stubs and skeletons needed to implement the Java remote interface
rmiregistry	A program that establishes a server registry for remote interface communications
serialver	A utility to display the serial VersionUID

 For a functional subset of the JDK, see **JRE**.

JNI

Java Native Interface

There is a facility that allows Java to interface with native code written for a local machine. A machine-specific executable is known as *native* code.

Exactly how this is done will necessarily vary from one operating system to another. It is also dependent on which compiler and which language is being used. The example supplied here is for the C language on Win32 and on Solaris. The process for linking with native code should be very similar on other systems and for other languages.

 This is a strictly nonportable part of Java. The exact procedure will vary greatly from one system to another, one language to another, one compiler to another, and even from one version of Java to another. When it becomes necessary for you to do this—and there are circumstances in which it may become necessary—it would be a good idea to get the latest information available. Even armed with the most recent information, you will probably have to experiment before you can get it to work the way you would like. The latest information can always be found at the Sun Java site http://www.javasoft.com.

Step 1: Write code to load the library.

The native executable must be loaded from a shared library:

```
public class Limerick {
    public native void printLimerick();
    static {
        System.loadLibrary("lim");
    }
}
```

The `Limerick` class contains the definition of a `native` function named `printLimerick()`. They keyword `native` tells the compiler not to generate code to call a Java method, but that code should be generated to call a native function.

The static initializer, which will execute once when the class is loaded, loads the library named `lim`. The library holds the function `printLimerick()`. The library name will differ from one system to another. On Win32, it will be called `LIM.DLL`, and on a Solaris system, and most other UNIX systems, it will be `liblim.so`.

Step 2: Write a call to the native function.

A program needs to be written that will call the native function. This is a simple demonstration program that calls the function:

```
public class LimerickDemo {
    public static void main(String[] args) {
        Limerick lim = new Limerick();
        lim.printLimerick();
    }
}
```

There is no difference between the syntax of a call to a native function and to a Java method. This small program creates a `Limerick` object and calls the method `printLimerick()`. When the `Limerick` object is created, its class is loaded, causing the shared library—the one containing the native function—to be loaded by the static initializer of the `Limerick` class. This means that the library will have been loaded by the time the call to `printLimerick()` is made.

Step 3: Compile the Java code.

The two Java classes from the previous steps need to be compiled. The native library is not required for this because it is loaded at run time, not compile time.

Step 4: Create a header file for the C code.

Run javah to create the Limerick.h file. The command to do this is

```
javah -jni Limerick
```

Javah reads the file Limerick.java and creates prototypes for all the `native` methods it finds there. In this example, there is a prototype for the C function `printLimerick()`.

The name of the function will almost certainly be changed. It could have the string "java_" added to the front of it. It could also have the name of the defining class added to it. You will need to examine the file to determine the exact function name, and you will need to implement your function with that name.

Here is the header file generated by the Win32 version of javah:

```
/* DO NOT EDIT THIS FILE - it is machine generated */
#include <jni.h>
/* Header for class Limerick */
#ifndef _Included_Limerick
#define _Included_Limerick
#ifdef __cplusplus
extern "C" {
#endif
/*
 * Class:     Limerick
 * Method:    printLimerick
 * Signature: ()V
 */
JNIEXPORT void JNICALL Java_Limerick_printLimerick
  (JNIEnv *, jobject);

#ifdef __cplusplus
}
#endif
#endif
```

Two things are immediately apparent. The name of the function has been changed, and the function itself has two arguments (even though the original definition had none).

Step 5: Write the native method in C.

Here is an implementation of the printLimerick() function as it was defined in the generated header. This is an example stored in the file LimerickImp.c:

```
#include "Limerick.h"
#include <stdio.h>

JNIEXPORT void JNICALL Java_Limerick_printLimerick
  (JNIEnv *env, jobject obj)
{
    printf("There was a young man from St Bees\n");
    printf("who was stung on the arm by a wasp.\n");
    printf("When asked does it hurt,\n");
    printf("he said \"It sure does,\n");
    printf("I'm just glad that it wasn't a hornet.\"\n");
}
```

Step 6: Create the Shared Library.

Compile the native language code into an object file and place it in a shared library. Exactly how you do this depends on your operating system and compiler. For Solaris, a command line would look like this:

```
cc -G -I/usr/local/java/include \
        -I/usr/local/java/include/solaris \
        LimerickImp.c -o liblim.so
```

A command to build the shared library on Win32 could look like this:

```
cl -Ic:\java\include -Ic:\java\include\win32
-LD LimerickImp.c -Felim.dll
```

Step 7: Run the example.

The example is run the same as any other Java application. The command

```
Java LimerickDemo
```

will print the five lines

```
There was a young man from St Bees
who was stung on the arm by a wasp.
When asked does it hurt,
he said "It sure does,
I'm just glad that it wasn't a hornet."
```

 For details on generating the header files, see **javah**.

JRE

Java Runtime Environment

The JRE is a subset of the JDK. It contains all the software necessary to execute Java programs, but it has none of the software development utilities. It is the smallest subset of the JDK that will run Java programs.

JVM

Java Virtual Machine

 See **Virtual Machine**.

Key

interface java.security.Key

This interface defines a set of methods for wrappers of security keys.

The algorithm

Every key has an algorithm associated with it. Example algorithms are DSA and RSA. The algorithm is used in conjunction with the actual key value for encryption/decryption.

The Encoded Form

For a key to be transmitted from one location to another, it needs to have an encoded form —a form other than the binary representation used internally by the algorithm. The form must be standard so that it can be converted back to its binary form by the recipient.

Extended by

```
PrivateKey
PublicKey
```

Inheritance

```
public interface java.security.Key
    extends Serializable
        ⇑
    public interface java.io.Serializable
```

Methods

getAlgorithm()

```
public abstract String getAlgorithm()
```

Returns the name of the algorithm. For example, this could be "DSA" or "RSA." If the algorithm is not known, this will return null.

getEncoded()

```
public abstract byte[] getEncoded()
```

Returns the encoded form of the key—the form that is used to transmit the key from one location to another. If the key does not have an encoded form, returns `null`.

getFormat()

```
public abstract String getFormat()
```

Returns the name of the format in which the key is encoded. If the key does not have a format, returns `null`.

 Also see **PublicKey**, **PrivateKey**, **KeyPair**, and **KeyPairGenerator**. For a listing of the algorithm names, see **security**.

KeyAdapter

class java.awt.event.KeyAdapter

This is an adapter class that implements the methods of the `KeyListener` interface as stubs that do nothing. Its purpose is to allow convenient subclassing that will require that only the desired method of `KeyListener` need be overridden.

Inheritance

```
public abstract class java.awt.event.KeyAdapter
    implements KeyListener
    extends Object
        ⇑
    public class java.lang.Object
```

Constructors

```
public KeyAdapter()
```

Methods

keyPressed()

```
public void keyPressed(KeyEvent e)
```

keyReleased()

```
public void keyReleased(KeyEvent e)
```

keyTyped()

```
public void keyTyped(KeyEvent e)
```

Example

This example uses a `KeyAdapter` to listen only for the keys when they are released, but ignores them when they are pressed:

```java
import java.awt.*;
import java.awt.event.*;
import java.applet.*;

public class Keystrokes extends Frame {
    private String outstring;
    private Font font;

    public static void main(String[] arg) {
        Keystrokes ks = new Keystrokes();
    }
    public Keystrokes() {
        font = new Font("Courier",Font.BOLD,35);
        setBackground(Color.lightGray);
        outstring = "?";
        CaptureKeystrokes capture = new
        CaptureKeystrokes();
        addKeyListener(capture);
        setSize(250,80);
        show();
    }

    public void paint(Graphics g) {
        g.setColor(Color.lightGray);
        g.fillRect(0,0,getSize().width,getSize().height);
        g.setColor(Color.black);
        g.setFont(font);
        g.drawString(outstring,10,50);
        g.dispose();
    }

    class CaptureKeystrokes extends KeyAdapter {
```

```
            public void keyReleased(KeyEvent event) {
                int code = event.getKeyCode();
                outstring = KeyEvent.getKeyText(code);
                repaint();
            }
        }
    }
}
```

The class `CaptureKeystrokes` is an inner class that is a `KeyAdapter`. The only method of the `KeyListener` interface it actually implements is `keyReleased()`. The `getKeyText()` method is used to get a full description of the most recent key pressed. The description is displayed as shown in Figure K-1.

Figure K-1   A description of each key is displayed as it is released.

 For more on keyboard event handling, see **KeyEvent** and **KeyListener**.

keyboard

 For reading keystrokes from the keyboard, see **KeyAdapter**, **KeyEvent**, and **KeyListener**.

KeyEvent

class java.awt.event.KeyEvent

This event is received to report an individual keystroke.

Virtual key codes

A number of constants are defined here that have the form VK_*XXX*. The VK stands for "virtual key." These are the constant values associated with specific keys on the keyboard. They are termed "virtual" keys because some specific key may not be present on the keyboard, but an alternative way may exist to generate an event that simulates the keystroke. For example, the Ctrl+H combination could be mapped to a VK_BACK_SPACE. Also, for debugging or simulation, a KeyEvent could originate from some source other than a physical keyboard.

Some known values

The virtual key values that represent visible characters use the same values as the Unicode character set. For example, the key values VK_0 through VK_9 have the values \u0030 through \u0039. The values VK_A through VK_Z have the values \u0041 through \u005A (the uppercase Latin alphabet).

The values are subject to change

Except for the values that are defined as being members of the Unicode character set, the actual virtual key values have no particular meaning. To detect a particular key, it is always best to use the VK names because the values could be changed in a later release.

There can be missing keys

Key values are defined that do not exist on some keyboards. Java does not attempt to artificially generate these keys—the presence of a constant that defines a key does not mean that it will be produceable by all keyboards.

The form of the event

Pressing a key on the keyboard will always cause a KeyEvent to be issued with an ID value of KEY_PRESSED. The key code will be one of the VK_*XXX* values that designate which key was pressed. For example, if the Shift key is pressed, a KEY_PRESSED event will be generated with a VK_SHIFT key code. If the Shift key is not released and the A key is pressed, another KEY_PRESSED event will be generated with VK_A as the key code—also the SHIFT_MASK will have been set for the letter *A* and isShiftDown() will return true (see the superclass InputEvent).

Inheritance

```
public class java.awt.event.KeyEvent
    extends InputEvent
        ⇑
    public abstract class java.awt.event.InputEvent
        extends ComponentEvent
            ⇑
        public class java.awt.event.ComponentEvent
            extends AWTEvent
                ⇑
            public class java.awt.AWTEvent
                extends EventObject
                    ⇑
                public class java.util.EventObject
                    implements Serializable
                    extends Object
                        ⇑
                    public class java.lang.Object
```

Variables and constants

CHAR_UNDEFINED

```
public static final char CHAR_UNDEFINED
```

This is the value included with KEY_PRESSED and KEY_RELEASED events that do not map to a valid Unicode character.

KEY_FIRST

```
public static final int KEY_FIRST
```

The is the smallest possible value of the key event ID numbers.

KEY_LAST

```
public static final int KEY_LAST
```

This is the largest possible value of the key event ID numbers.

KEY_PRESSED

```
public static final int KEY_PRESSED
```

The key-pressed event ID number.

KEY_RELEASED

```
public static final int KEY_RELEASED
```

The key-released event ID number.

KEY_TYPED

```
public static final int KEY_TYPED
```

The key-typed event ID number. This event is generated by a combination of a keypress followed by a key release.

VK_0

```
public static final int VK_0
```

The 0 key on the main keyboard.

VK_1

```
public static final int VK_1
```

The 1 key on the main keyboard.

VK_2

```
public static final int VK_2
```

The 2 key on the main keyboard.

VK_3

```
public static final int VK_3
```

The 3 key on the main keyboard.

VK_4

```
public static final int VK_4
```

The 4 key on the main keyboard.

VK_5

```
public static final int VK_5
```

The 5 key on the main keyboard.

VK_6

```
public static final int VK_6
```

The 6 key on the main keyboard.

VK_7

```
public static final int VK_7
```

The 7 key on the main keyboard.

VK_8

```
public static final int VK_8
```

The 8 key on the main keyboard.

VK_9

```
public static final int VK_9
```

The 9 key on the main keyboard.

VK_A

```
public static final int VK_A
```

The A key.

VK_ACCEPT

```
public static final int VK_ACCEPT
```

The Accept key.

VK_ADD

```
public static final int VK_ADD
```

The Add (+) key.

VK_ALT

```
public static final int VK_ALT
```

The Alt key.

VK_B

```
public static final int VK_B
```

The B key.

VK_BACK_QUOTE

```
public static final int VK_BACK_QUOTE
```

The back quote (`) key.

VK_BACK_SLASH

```
public static final int VK_BACK_SLASH
```

The backslash (\) key.

VK_BACK_SPACE

```
public static final int VK_BACK_SPACE
```

The Backspace key.

VK_C

```
public static final int VK_C
```

The C key.

VK_CANCEL

```
public static final int VK_CANCEL
```

The Cancel key.

VK_CAPS_LOCK

```
public static final int VK_CAPS_LOCK
```

The Caps Lock key.

VK_CLEAR

```
public static final int VK_CLEAR
```

The Clear key.

VK_CLOSE_BRACKET

```
public static final int VK_CLOSE_BRACKET
```

The close bracket (]) key.

VK_COMMA

```
public static final int VK_COMMA
```

The comma key.

VK_CONTROL

```
public static final int VK_CONTROL
```

The Ctrl key.

VK_CONVERT

```
public static final int VK_CONVERT
```

The Convert key.

VK_D

```
public static final int VK_D
```

The D key.

VK_DECIMAL

```
public static final int VK_DECIMAL
```

The Decimal (.) key.

VK_DELETE

```
public static final int VK_DELETE
```

The Delete key.

VK_DIVIDE

```
public static final int VK_DIVIDE
```

The divide (/) key.

VK_DOWN

```
public static final int VK_DOWN
```

The Down Arrow key.

VK_E

```
public static final int VK_E
```

The E key.

VK_END

```
public static final int VK_END
```

The End key.

VK_ENTER

```
public static final int VK_ENTER
```

The Enter key.

VK_EQUALS

```
public static final int VK_EQUALS
```

The equals (=) key.

VK_ESCAPE

```
public static final int VK_ESCAPE
```

The Escape key.

VK_F

```
public static final int VK_F
```

The F key.

VK_F1

```
public static final int VK_F1
```

The F1 key.

VK_F2

```
public static final int VK_F2
```

The F2 key.

VK_F3

```
public static final int VK_F3
```

The F3 key.

VK_F4

```
public static final int VK_F4
```

The F4 key.

VK_F5

```
public static final int VK_F5
```

The F5 key.

VK_F6

```
public static final int VK_F6
```

The F6 key.

VK_F7

```
public static final int VK_F7
```

The F7 key.

VK_F8

```
public static final int VK_F8
```

The F8 key.

VK_F9

```
public static final int VK_F9
```

The F9 key.

VK_F10

```
public static final int VK_F10
```

The F10 key.

VK_F11

```
public static final int VK_F11
```

The F11 key.

VK_F12

```
public static final int VK_F12
```

The F12 key.

VK_FINAL

```
public static final int VK_FINAL
```

The Final key. This constant is specifically for the Asian keyboard.

VK_G

```
public static final int VK_G
```

The G key.

VK_H

```
public static final int VK_H
```

The H key.

VK_HELP

```
public static final int VK_HELP
```

The Help key.

VK_HOME

```
public static final int VK_HOME
```

The Home key.

VK_I

```
public static final int VK_I
```

The I key.

VK_INSERT

```
public static final int VK_INSERT
```

The Insert key.

VK_J

```
public static final int VK_J
```

The J key.

VK_K

    public static final int VK_K

The K key.

VK_KANA

    public static final int VK_KANA

The Kana key.

VK_KANJI

    public static final int VK_KANJI

The Kanji key.

VK_L

    public static final int VK_L

The L key.

VK_LEFT

    public static final int VK_LEFT

The Left Arrow key.

VK_M

    public static final int VK_M

The M key.

VK_META

    public static final int VK_META

The Meta key.

VK_MODECHANGE

    public static final int VK_MODECHANGE

The Mode Change key.

VK_MULTIPLY

    public static final int VK_MULTIPLY

The Multiply (×) key.

VK_N

```
public static final int VK_N
```

The N key.

VK_NONCONVERT

```
public static final int VK_NONCONVERT
```

The Nonconvert key.

VK_NUM_LOCK

```
public static final int VK_NUM_LOCK
```

The Num Lock key.

VK_NUMPAD0

```
public static final int VK_NUMPAD0
```

The 0 key on the numerical keypad.

VK_NUMPAD1

```
public static final int VK_NUMPAD1
```

The 1 key on the numerical keypad.

VK_NUMPAD2

```
public static final int VK_NUMPAD2
```

The 2 key on the numerical keypad.

VK_NUMPAD3

```
public static final int VK_NUMPAD3
```

The 3 key on the numerical keypad.

VK_NUMPAD4

```
public static final int VK_NUMPAD4
```

The 4 key on the numerical keypad.

VK_NUMPAD5

```
public static final int VK_NUMPAD5
```

The 5 key on the numerical keypad.

VK_NUMPAD6

```
public static final int VK_NUMPAD6
```

The 6 key on the numerical keypad.

VK_NUMPAD7

```
public static final int VK_NUMPAD7
```

The 7 key on the numerical keypad.

VK_NUMPAD8

```
public static final int VK_NUMPAD8
```

The 8 key on the numerical keypad.

VK_NUMPAD9

```
public static final int VK_NUMPAD9
```

The 9 key on the numerical keypad.

VK_O

```
public static final int VK_O
```

The O key.

VK_OPEN_BRACKET

```
public static final int VK_OPEN_BRACKET
```

The open bracket ([) key.

VK_P

```
public static final int VK_P
```

The P key.

VK_PAGE_DOWN

```
public static final int VK_PAGE_DOWN
```

The Page Down key.

VK_PAGE_UP

```
public static final int VK_PAGE_UP
```

The Page Up key.

VK_PAUSE

```
public static final int VK_PAUSE
```

The Pause key.

VK_PERIOD

```
public static final int VK_PERIOD
```

The period (.) key.

VK_PRINTSCREEN

```
public static final int VK_PRINTSCREEN
```

The Print Screen key.

VK_Q

```
public static final int VK_Q
```

The Q key.

VK_QUOTE

```
public static final int VK_QUOTE
```

The quote (') key.

VK_R

```
public static final int VK_R
```

The R key.

VK_RIGHT

```
public static final int VK_RIGHT
```

The Right Arrow key.

VK_S

```
public static final int VK_S
```

The S key.

VK_SCROLL_LOCK

```
public static final int VK_SCROLL_LOCK
```

The Scroll Lock key.

VK_SEMICOLON

```
public static final int VK_SEMICOLON
```

The semicolon (;) key.

VK_SEPARATER

```
public static final int VK_SEPARATER
```

The Separater key.

VK_SHIFT

```
public static final int VK_SHIFT
```

The Shift key.

VK_SLASH

```
public static final int VK_SLASH
```

The forward slash (/) key.

VK_SPACE

```
public static final int VK_SPACE
```

The Spacebar.

VK_SUBTRACT

```
public static final int VK_SUBTRACT
```

The minus (–) key.

VK_T

```
public static final int VK_T
```

The T key.

VK_TAB

```
public static final int VK_TAB
```

The Tab key.

VK_U

```
public static final int VK_U
```

The U key.

VK_UNDEFINED

```
public static final int VK_UNDEFINED
```

An undefined key.

VK_UP

```
public static final int VK_UP
```

The Up Arrow key.

VK_V

```
public static final int VK_V
```

The V key.

VK_W

```
public static final int VK_W
```

The W key.

VK_X

```
public static final int VK_X
```

The X key.

VK_Y

```
public static final int VK_Y
```

The Y key.

VK_Z

```
public static final int VK_Z
```

The Z key.

Constructors

```
public KeyEvent(Component source,int id,long when,
        int modifiers,int keyCode,char keyChar)

public KeyEvent(Component source,int id,long when,
        int modifiers,int keyCode)
```

The construction of a KeyEvent requires the component that is the source of the event, the id indicating the type of the event, and a time stamp specifying when the event occurred. The modifiers are the mask values defined in InputEvent. The keyCode is one of the VK_XXX values, and the keyChar is the displayable form of the character (if it has one).

Methods

getKeyChar()

```
public char getKeyChar()
```

Returns the key character value specified on the constructor. If none was specified, the return value is CHAR_UNDEFINED.

getKeyCode()

```
public int getKeyCode()
```

Returns the key code value. For KEY_TYPED events, this will always be VK_UNDEFINED.

getKeyModifiersText()

```
public static String getKeyModifiersText(int modifiers)
```

Returns a string describing the modifiers. For example, this could be "Shift" or "Ctrl+Shift." The descriptive strings are found in the awt.properties file.

getKeyText()

```
public static String getKeyText(int keyCode)
```

Returns a string description of the key code. For example, it could be "PAGE DOWN," "F10," or "X." The strings are the ones set in the awt.properties file.

isActionKey()

```
public boolean isActionKey()
```

Returns true if this is an action key. The action keys are the function keys, up arrow, left arrow, home, and the like.

paramString()

```
public String paramString()
```

Returns debugging information. The return string describes the internal state and values of this object.

setKeyChar()

```
public void setKeyChar(char keyChar)
```

Sets the character for this key.

setKeyCode()

```
public void setKeyCode(int keyCode)
```

Sets the code value for the key.

setModifiers()

```
public void setModifiers(int modifiers)
```

Specifies the set of modifier mask values.

 For the definition of the key modifiers, see **InputEvent**. For more information on keyboard events, see **KeyAdapter** and **KeyListener**.

KeyException

class java.security.KeyException

This is the basic security key exception.

Extended by

```
InvalidKeyException
KeyManagementException
```

Inheritance

```
public class java.security.KeyException
    extends Exception
        ⇑
    public class java.lang.Exception
        extends Throwable
            ⇑
        public class java.lang.Throwable
            implements Serializable
            extends Object
                ⇑
            public class java.lang.Object
```

Constructors

```
public KeyException()
public KeyException(String message)
```

If the message string is supplied, it is used as a detailed message describing this particular exception.

KeyListener

interface java.awt.event.KeyListener

This is the interface for a class that will receive keyboard events.

Implemented by

```
AWTEventMulticaster
KeyAdapter
```

Inheritance

```
public interface KeyListener
    extends EventListener
        ⇑
    public interface java.util.EventListener
```

Constructor

Returned by

Methods that return objects implementing this class are `AWTEventMulticaster.add()` and `AWTEventMulticaster.remove()`.

Methods

keyPressed()

```
public abstract void keyPressed(KeyEvent e)
```

This method is called whenever a key is pressed.

keyReleased()

```
public abstract void keyReleased(KeyEvent e)
```

This method is called whenever a key is released.

keyTyped()

```
public abstract void keyTyped(KeyEvent e)
```

The method is called whenever a key has been typed—that is, when it has been pressed and then released.

Example 1

This example uses an inner class to implement the KeyListener interface:

```java
import java.awt.*;
import java.awt.event.*;
import java.applet.*;

public class Keyboard extends Frame {
    private String outstring;
    private Font font;

    public static void main(String[] arg) {
        Keyboard kb = new Keyboard();
    }
    public Keyboard() {
        font = new Font("Courier",Font.BOLD,25);
        setBackground(Color.lightGray);
        outstring = "?";
        CaptureKeystrokes capture = new
        CaptureKeystrokes();
        addKeyListener(capture);
        setSize(450,80);
        show();
    }

    public void paint(Graphics g) {
        g.setColor(Color.lightGray);
        g.fillRect(0,0,getSize().width,getSize().height);
        g.setColor(Color.black);
        g.setFont(font);
        g.drawString(outstring,10,50);
        g.dispose();
    }

    class CaptureKeystrokes implements KeyListener {
        public void keyReleased(KeyEvent event) {
            int code = event.getKeyCode();
            outstring = "RELEASE: " +
                    KeyEvent.getKeyText(code);
            System.out.println(outstring);
            repaint();
        }
        public void keyPressed(KeyEvent event) {
            int code = event.getKeyCode();
```

```
                outstring = "PRESSED: " +
                        KeyEvent.getKeyText(code);
                System.out.println(outstring);
                repaint();
            }
            public void keyTyped(KeyEvent event) {
                int code = event.getKeyCode();
                outstring = "TYPED: " +
                        KeyEvent.getKeyText(code);
                System.out.println(outstring);
                repaint();
            }
        }
    }
```

An instance of the `CaptureKeystrokes` class is created and added to the `Frame` as a listener with a call to `addKeyListener()`. Using an inner class in this way has the advantage that the private variable `outstring` of the `Keyboard` class is available, and `repaint()` can be called directly. The result is that the last event received is shown in the window of the application. To make the sequence of events more clear, they are also printed to System.out. Figure K-2 shows its window display.

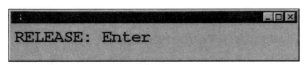

Figure K-2   The display immediately after the enter key has been released.

Here is some typical output written to `System.out`:

```
PRESSED: Shift
PRESSED: H
TYPED: Unknown keyCode: 0x0
RELEASE: H
RELEASE: Shift
PRESSED: I
TYPED: Unknown keyCode: 0x0
RELEASE: I
PRESSED: Enter
TYPED: Unknown keyCode: 0x0
RELEASE: Enter
```

This is the output resulting from typing "Hi" and pressing the Enter key. You can see that the Shift key was pressed before the H was pressed and released afterward. The fact that the Shift key was being held down could have been determined with a call to `isShiftDown()`—or a call to `getModifiers()` could have been made and the mask bits tested for the Shift key. (These are in the superclass `InputEvent`.)

Example 2

This is a variation of the previous example. This one is designed to demonstrate reading strings of characters and responding to the action keys:

```java
import java.awt.*;
import java.awt.event.*;
import java.applet.*;

public class Keystring extends Frame {
    private String outstring;
    private Font font;

    public static void main(String[] arg) {
        Keystring ks = new Keystring();
    }
    public Keystring() {
        font = new Font("Courier",Font.BOLD,25);
        setBackground(Color.lightGray);
        outstring = "";
        CaptureKeystrokes capture = new
        CaptureKeystrokes();
        addKeyListener(capture);
        setSize(450,80);
        show();
    }

    public void paint(Graphics g) {
        g.setColor(Color.lightGray);
        g.fillRect(0,0,getSize().width,getSize().height);
        g.setColor(Color.black);
        g.setFont(font);
        g.drawString(outstring,10,50);
        g.dispose();
    }

    class CaptureKeystrokes implements KeyListener {
        public void keyReleased(KeyEvent event) {
```

```java
            char keyChar = event.getKeyChar();
            if(event.isActionKey()) {
                int code = event.getKeyCode();
                System.out.println("Action: " +
                        KeyEvent.getKeyText(code));
            } else if(keyChar == KeyEvent.VK_ENTER) {
                System.out.println(outstring);
                outstring = "";
            } else if(keyChar != KeyEvent.CHAR_UNDEFINED)
{

                outstring += keyChar;
            }
            repaint();
        }
        public void keyPressed(KeyEvent event) { }
        public void keyTyped(KeyEvent event) { }
    }
}
```

The inner class CaptureKeyStrokes implements only the keyReleased()
method of the KeyListener interface. If the incoming key is an action key, its
description is printed to System.out. If it is the Enter key, any characters that
have been gathered into outstring are printed to System.out and outstring
is cleared so that we can start over. Any event that represents a defined character (one that is printable) will have its character added to outstring. The
current collection of characters in outstring is displayed in the window as
shown in Figure K-3.

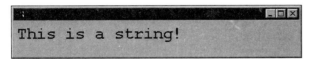

Figure K-3   The string display is updated as characters
are added to it.

For another way to implement a KeyListener, see **KeyAdapter**. For more
methods to determine the input, see the superclass **InputEvent**.

KeyManagementException

class java.security.KeyManagementException

This exception is thrown to indicate a problem in the management of security keys.

Inheritance

```
public class java.security.KeyManagementException
    extends KeyException
        ⇑
    public class java.security.KeyException
        extends Exception
            ⇑
        public class java.lang.Exception
            extends Throwable
                ⇑
            public class java.lang.Throwable
                implements Serializable
                extends Object
                    ⇑
                public class java.lang.Object
```

Constructors

```
public KeyManagementException()
public KeyManagementException(String message)
```

If the message string is supplied, it is used as a detailed message describing this particular exception.

KeyPair

class java.security.KeyPair

This is a simple wrapper to hold a pair of security keys—one private key and one public key. There is no security in this class, so whenever it contains the keys, it should be closely held as a private key.

Inheritance

```
public final class java.security.KeyPair
```

```
extends Object
      ⇑
public class java.lang.Object
```

Constructors

```
public KeyPair(PublicKey publicKey,PrivateKey privateKey)
```

A `KeyPair` object is constructed with the key values it is to hold.

Returned by

An object of this class is returned from `KeyPairGenerator.generateKeyPair()`.

Methods

getPrivate()

```
public PrivateKey getPrivate()
```

Returns the private key.

getPublic()

```
public PublicKey getPublic()
```

Returns the public key.

KeyPairGenerator

class java.security.KeyPairGenerator

This is the superclass of classes that generates a pair of encryption keys—one public key and one private key.

Generalized key generation

A couple of things are common to the generation of key pairs for all algorithms. They all are based on some sort of randomness, and they all have a strength setting of some sort.

But there are differences also. The generalization of an algorithm for generating pairs of keys is not straightforward because different kinds of keys require different information for their creation. A pair of DSA keys can use the values p, q, and g, and RSA does not.

To solve this, more than one way is provided to generate a key pair with this class. The only difference occurs when the object is initialized—after that, everything is the same. This initialization is done by calling the method `initialize()` with the values you want to use.

Inheritance

```
public abstract class java.security.KeyPairGenerator
    extends Object
        ⇑
    public class java.lang.Object
```

Constructors

```
protected KeyPairGenerator(String algorithm)
```

The algorithm is the name of the one to be used to construct the key pair.

Returned by

The normal way to acquire an object of this class is to call getInstance() with an argument that specifies the algorithm.

Methods

generateKeyPair()

```
public abstract KeyPair generateKeyPair()
```

Generates a KeyPair. The generation will use the built-in defaults for the algorithm unless initialize() has been called to change them.

getAlgorithm()

```
public String getAlgorithm()
```

Returns the name of the algorithm used to generate the keys.

getInstance()

```
public static KeyPairGenerator getInstance(String algorithm)
    throws NoSuchAlgorithmException
```

```
public static KeyPairGenerator getInstance(
        String algorithm,String provider)
    throws NoSuchAlgorithmException
    throws NoSuchProviderException
```

Returns a KeyPairGenerator object that implements the named algorithm. Certain algorithms require a provider for the actual key generation. A NoSuchAlgorithmException will be thrown if the specified algorithm name is unknown or is not available on this platform. A NoSuchProviderException will be thrown if the provider is unknown or unavailable.

initialize()

```
public void initialize(int strength)

public abstract void initialize(int strength,
        SecureRandom random)
```

This will initialize the `strength` and `random` settings to something other than the default. The `strength` is an algorithm-specific metric—such as a modulus length or a number of bits.

 For the encryption algorithm names, see **security**. For another class that generates key pairs, see **DSAKeyPairGenerator**.

keywords

This is a list of the keyword and the reserved words of Java.

Reserved words

A keyword is a part of the Java language and cannot be used for any other purpose. A reserved word is one that may become a part of the Java language in the future, so it cannot be used for anything else. The words `const` and `goto` are reserved by Java but have no implementations.

Table K-1   Java Keywords and Reserved Words

Identifier	Description
abstract	An abstract class cannot be instantiated—it can only be extended by a subclass.
boolean	A primitive data type that can only take on the values of true or false.
break	A control flow command used to exit from inside a for, while, do, or switch block.
byte	A primitive data type. It is a signed eight-bit integer.
case	A control flow command that is used as the receiving location of the branch generated by a switch command.
catch	An exception-handling command used following a try as the receiving location of the branch generated by a throw command.
char	A primitive data type. It is an unsigned 16-bit integer intended to be used to contain a single Unicode character.
class	The keyword used in the declaration of a class.
const	Unused. Java reserves this word for possible future use.
continue	A control flow command used to immediately jump to the next iteration of a for, while, or do block.
default	A control flow command that is used as a receiving location of the branch generated by a switch command.
do	A control flow command used to construct a loop that always executes at least once.
double	A primitive data type. It is a 64-bit real number.

continued

Table K-1	*continued*
Identifier	**Description**
else	A control flow command that defines a block that is to be executed as an alternative to an if block.
extends	Used as part of a class declaration to specify the name of the superclass of the class being declared.
false	A constant boolean value.
final	Used in declarations. If this keyword is applied to a variable, it makes it a constant. If it is applied to a class, the class cannot be as a superclass to derive other classes. If it is used to define a method, the method cannot be overridden.
finally	An exception-handling command that defines a block of code to be executed following a try/catch sequence.
float	A primitive data type. It is a 32-bit real number.
for	A control flow command that defines a loop with counters and tests for exiting the loop.
goto	Unused. Java reserves this word for possible future use.
if	A control flow statement that evaluates a Boolean expression to determine whether to execute a block of code.
implements	Used in a class declaration to name an interface that is being locally implemented.
import	Used at the top of source modules to qualify the path of external searches for names.
instanceof	A boolean operator that tests for an object being of a certain class.
int	A primitive data type. It is a signed 32-bit integer.
interface	The keyword used in the definition of a named collection of constants, variables, and abstract method signatures.
long	A primitive data type. It is a 64-bit signed integer.
native	When used as part of a method declaration, it means that the method itself is defined elsewhere and is machine-native executable code.
new	Used to allocate memory and execute constructor methods during object construction.
null	The value contained in a reference when it does not address an object.
package	When used at the beginning of a class definition file, it places the definition of any class or interface into the named package.
private	Used as part of a declaration to limit the scope to the single class.
protected	Used as part of a declaration to limit the scope to the single class and its derived classes.
public	Used as part of a declaration to remove scope limitations and make the name global.
return	A flow control statement used to exit from a method.
short	A primitive data type. It is a 16-bit signed integer.
static	Used in a declaration to cause the declared item to exist in the class instead of in each generated object.
super	Used to address data and methods in the parent class.
switch	A flow control statement that is used in conjunction with case and break statements to select a single block of code for execution.

Identifier	Description
synchronized	Used as a modifier to mark a block of code as being uninterruptable during multithreaded execution.
this	Used to address data and methods in the current object. It is always the name of the current object.
throw	Used in exception handling. This statement will throw an exception that must be caught by a catch command.
throws	Used in a class declaration to specify that this class throws, but does not catch, a specific exception.
transient	Unused. Java reserves this word for possible future use.
true	A constant boolean value.
try	Used in exception handling to execute code that contains one or more throw statements.
void	Defines methods that do not return values.
volatile	When used to declare a variable, it is a warning to the compiler that the value may change unexpectedly from some external source.
while	A flow control statement used to define an iteration that is to continue as long as a boolean expression is true.

Label

class java.awt.Label

This is a component used to display a single line of noneditable text.

Inheritance

```
public class java.awt.Label
    extends Component
        ⇑
    public abstract class java.awt.Component
        implements ImageObserver
        implements MenuContainer
        implements Serializable
        extends Object
            ⇑
        public class java.lang.Object
```

Variables and constants

CENTER

```
public static final int CENTER
```

The constant used to specify that the text be centered.

LEFT

```
public static final int LEFT
```

The constant used to specify that the text be left-justified.

RIGHT

```
public static final int RIGHT
```

The constant used to specify that the text be right-justified.

Constructors

```
public Label()
public Label(String text)
public Label(String text,int alignment)
```

A Label can be constructed with or without a string of text to display. The alignment value is either RIGHT, LEFT, or CENTER—the default is LEFT.

Methods

addNotify()

```
public void addNotify()
```

Creates the underlying system-dependent peer for this object. This method is not normally called by the application. It is called by the container.

getAlignment()

```
public int getAlignment()
```

Returns the alignment setting of this Label.

getText()

```
public String getText()
```

Returns the text of the label.

paramString()

```
protected String paramString()
```

Returns debugging information. The return string describes the internal state and values of this object.

setAlignment()

```
public synchronized void setAlignment(int alignment)
```

Sets the alignment of the displayed text to RIGHT, LEFT, or CENTER. If alignment is not one of these values, an IllegalArgumentException will be thrown.

setText()

```
public synchronized void setText(String text)
```

Sets the text of the Label.

Example

This example demonstrates how to set the font, text, and text position of a label.

```java
import java.awt.*;
import java.awt.event.*;
public class ModLabel extends Frame
                implements ActionListener {
    Label label;
    TextField textField;
    public static void main(String[] arg) {
        ModLabel ml = new ModLabel();
    }
    public ModLabel() {
        setBackground(Color.lightGray);
        label = new Label("I'm here");
        Font font = new Font("Courier",Font.BOLD,25);
        label.setFont(font);
        add("Center",label);

        Panel p = new Panel();
        Button b = new Button("Left");
        b.addActionListener(this);
        p.add(b);
        b = new Button("Center");
        b.addActionListener(this);
        p.add(b);
        b = new Button("Right");
        b.addActionListener(this);
        p.add(b);
        b = new Button("Quit");
        b.addActionListener(this);
        p.add(b);
        add("South",p);

        p = new Panel();
        textField = new TextField(40);
        p.add(textField);
        b = new Button("Set");
        b.addActionListener(this);
        p.add(b);
        add("North",p);

        setSize(450,150);
```

```
        show();
    }
    public void actionPerformed(ActionEvent event) {
        if(event.getActionCommand().equals("Quit"))
            System.exit(0);
        else if(event.getActionCommand().equals("Left"))
            label.setAlignment(Label.LEFT);
        else if(event.getActionCommand().equals("Center"))
            label.setAlignment(Label.CENTER);
        else if(event.getActionCommand().equals("Right"))
            label.setAlignment(Label.RIGHT);
        else if(event.getActionCommand().equals("Set"))
            label.setText(textField.getText());
    }
}
```

The Label is placed in the center of the window. Figure L-1 shows the window as it first appears, with the text of the label on the left.

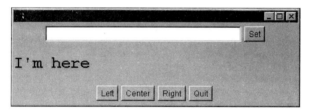

Figure L-1   The display as it first appears.

Three buttons appear across the bottom of the window that can be used to set the position of the text. There is a TextField at the top of the window that can be used to change the text string. Figure L-2 shows the window after the "Right" button has been pressed to move the text to the right side of the Label.

Figure L-2   The display after the text has been moved to the right of the label.

The other noncontainer components are **Button**, **List**, **Checkbox**, **Canvas**, **Scrollbar**, **Choice**, **TextArea**, and **TextField**.

lang

package java.lang

This is the package that contains the group of classes that are a part of the fundamental core of Java. Some of these classes are very closely tied to the definition of the language itself. The `Object` and `String` classes, for example, are known to the Java compiler. Exactly which classes are a part of the fundamental definition of Java has not been precisely defined, but every member of this package is a contender for membership.

Packages

```
java.lang.reflect
```

Interfaces

```
Cloneable
Runnable
```

Classes

```
Bignum
Boolean
Byte
Character
Class
ClassLoader
Compiler
Double
Float
Integer
Long
Math
Number
Object
Process
Runtime
SecurityManager
Short
String
```

StringBuffer
System
Thread
ThreadGroup
Throwable
Void

Exceptions

ArithmeticException
ArrayIndexOutOfBoundsException
ArrayStoreException
ClassCastException
ClassNotFoundException
CloneNotSupportedException
Exception
IllegalAccessException
IllegalArgumentException
IllegalMonitorStateException
IllegalStateException
IllegalThreadStateException
IndexOutOfBoundsException
InstantiationException
InterruptedException
NegativeArraySizeException
NoSuchFieldException
NoSuchMethodException
NullPointerException
NumberFormatException
RuntimeException
SecurityException
StringIndexOutOfBoundsException

Errors

AbstractMethodError
ClassCircularityError
ClassFormatError
Error
ExceptionInInitializerError
IllegalAccessError
IncompatibleClassChangeError
InstantiationError
InternalError
LinkageError

```
NoClassDefFoundError
NoSuchFieldError
NoSuchMethodError
OutOfMemoryError
StackOverflowError
ThreadDeath
UnknownError
UnsatisfiedLinkError
VerifyError
VirtualMachineError
```

layout manager

A layout manager is a component that has the job of positioning other components on the display window of a container. The container contains the components, but the layout manager does the work of sizing and positioning.

There are five layout managers, and each has a different method of organizing the display. A layout manager will interact with each component to determine a size appropriate for it. It uses this sizing information, along with any other constraints that may have been specified, to determine the layout of the components within the container.

Each component has a preferred size and a minimum size. These two are often the same, but they differ at times. The layout manager itself has a preferred size and a minimum size that it calculates by requesting the appropriate size information from the components that it lays out.

 Remember that the layout manager on one machine could make slightly different decisions than the layout manager on another machine. Even on very similar machines, two layout managers could make things look slightly different, so it is best not to start counting pixels when you are setting up the layout of your display windows — just use broad logical positioning for the sake of portability.

Comparisons among layout managers

This is a very brief look at how the various layout managers work:

♦ *BorderLayout*. Components are positioned against the top, bottom, left and right sides — and one is placed in the middle.

♦ *CardLayout*. Components are laid one on top of the other. Controls can be used to determine which one is visible.

- ◆ *FlowLayout.* Components are placed beside one another left to right and, if space runs out, will wrap to a new line. The layout will change as the window is resized.
- ◆ *GridBagLayout.* Components are laid out on a grid with each component given its own specifications as to how it is positioned. The squares of the grid do not all have to be the same size.
- ◆ *GridLayout.* A grid of equal-sized rectangles is defined, and one component is placed in each.

 The layout managers are **BorderLayout**, **CardLayout**, **FlowLayout**, **GridBagLayout**, and **GridLayout**.

LayoutManager

interface java.awt.LayoutManager

This is an interface for classes that lay out components in containers.

Implemented by

```
FlowLayout
GridLayout
```

Extended by

```
LayoutManager2
```

Inheritance

```
public interface java.awt.LayoutManager
```

Constructors

Returned by

An object that implements this class is returned from `Container.getLayout()`.

Methods

addLayoutComponent()

```
public abstract void addLayoutComponent(String name,
```

```
        Component component)
```

Adds the specified `component` to the layout, and assigns it the `name`.

layoutContainer()

```
    public abstract void layoutContainer(Container parent)
```

Lays out the components in the `parent` container.

minimumLayoutSize()

```
    public abstract Dimension minimumLayoutSize(Container parent)
```

Calculates the minimum size that can be used to lay out the components in the `parent` container. The layout will use the minimum size of each of the components and allow for any spacing or specific positioning that has been defined.

preferredLayoutSize()

```
    public abstract Dimension preferredLayoutSize(Container parent)
```

Calculates the preferred size for the layout of the components in the `parent` container. The layout will use the preferred size of each of the components and allow for any spacing or specific positioning that has been defined.

removeLayoutComponent()

```
    public abstract void removeLayoutComponent(Component component)
```

Removes the `component` from the layout.

 A class implements this interface to position **Components** inside a **Container**. For examples, see **FlowLayout** and **GridLayout**. Another layout manger interface is **LayoutManager2**.

LayoutManager2

interface java.awt.LayoutManager2

This is an interface for classes that lay out components in containers.

Constraints

This is an extension of the `LayoutManager` interface to add the methods needed for a layout manager to be able to base the layout on constraints. The prime example of this is the `GridBagLayout` manager that uses the `GridBagConstraints` object to size and place the components.

Implemented by

```
BorderLayout
CardLayout
GridBagLayout
```

Inheritance

```
public interface java.awt.LayoutManager2
        extends LayoutManager
            ⇑
    public interface java.awt.LayoutManager
```

Constructors

Returned by

The method `Container.getLayout()` returns a `LayoutManager` that could also be a `LayoutManager2`.

Methods

addLayoutComponent()

```
public abstract void addLayoutComponent(
            Component component,Object constraints)
```

Adds the `component` to the layout and uses the `constraints` to size and position it.

getLayoutAlignmentX()

```
public abstract float getLayoutAlignmentX(Container target)
```

Returns the preferred horizontal position of this layout manager in its parent window. The left size is 0.0, and the right is 1.0.

getLayoutAlignmentY()

```
public abstract float getLayoutAlignmentY(Container target)
```

Returns the preferred vertical position of this layout manager in its parent window. The top is 0.0, and the bottom is 1.0.

invalidateLayout()

```
public abstract void invalidateLayout(Container target)
```

Requests that the layout manager discard any information it may have gathered or calculated about the layout. This will require that everything be recalculated for the layout.

maximumLayoutSize()

```
public abstract Dimension maximumLayoutSize(Container target)
```

Returns the minimum size it would take to lay out the components in the specified target.

 A class implements this interface to position **Component**s inside a **Container**. For examples, see **BorderLayout**, **CardLayout**, and **GridBagLayout**. Another layout manger interface is **LayoutManager**.

LastOwnerException

class java.security.acl.LastOwnerException

This exception is thrown on an attempt to delete the last owner of an access control list.

Inheritance

```
public class LastOwnerException
    extends Exception
        ⇑
    public class java.lang.Exception
        extends Throwable
            ⇑
        public class java.lang.Throwable
            implements Serializable
            extends Object
                ⇑
            public class java.lang.Object
```

Constructors

```
public LastOwnerException()
```

 See deleteOwner() of **Owner**.

Lease

class java.rmi.dgc.Lease

This is a wrapper that contains a Virtual Machine identifier and a duration. This object is used to request and grant leases for remote method invocation.

Inheritance

```
public final class java.rmi.dgc.Lease
    implements Serializable
    extends Object
         ⇑
    public class java.lang.Object
```

Constructors

```
public Lease(VMID id,long duration)
```

The Lease object is constructed with a Virtual Machine id and the duration of the lease. The VMID may be null.

Returned by

An object of this class is returned from DGC.dirty().

Methods

getValue()

```
public long getValue()
```

Returns the duration of the lease.

getVMID()

```
public VMID getVMID()
```

Returns the Virtual Machine ID.

 For a description of object leasing, see **DGC**.

legacy

In software, *legacy* refers to any existing implementation or practice. This becomes important when the existing body of software is so large and/or widespread that there is no hope of changing it any time soon. Java, being a fairly young language, has very few legacy elements, but it does have some.

From 1.0 to 1.1 to 1.2 and so on

Moving from one version of Java to another creates a legacy situation because there will always be running code that uses something from a previous version—something that is now considered obsolete. Java has addressed this with the concept of *deprecation*. The old code will still run—it is still supported in the class libraries—but the compiler will complain each time it is compiled anew.

The external legacy

Some design decisions and practices in Java arose from the fact that some preexisting circumstance always existed with which Java had to be compatible. Since this is something that came to us from a prior condition—something over which the framers of Java had no control—it is known as a legacy. An example of this is the inclusion of the dollar sign as a Java letter for the purpose of creating variable names.

lexical structure

The textual source of a Java program is made up of a stream of three things:

- ◆ Tokens
- ◆ White space separating tokens
- ◆ Comments

The Java program that is to be compiled and run by the Virtual Machine is defined by the tokens. As the input character stream is being read, the ASCII characters are converted to their Unicode counterparts. Unicode escape sequences are also converted to Unicode characters. As the compiler reads the resulting Unicode input stream, it reduces it to an input stream of tokens by skipping over the white space and the comments. These tokens are the names, numbers, and punctuation that make up the Java language.

The white space characters

Tokens may be separated by any amount of white space. In most cases, the presence of white space will terminate a token—the only token capable of containing white space is the string. Apart from using it as token separators, the Java compiler will ignore white space. The white space characters are the ASCII characters shown in Table L-1.

Table L-1 ASCII White Space Characters

Octal	Decimal	Unicode	Name	Description
011	9	\u0009	HT	Ctrl-I, horizontal tab
012	10	\u000a	LF	Ctrl-J, linefeed, newline
014	12	\u000c	FF	Ctrl-L, form feed, new page
015	13	\u000d	CR	Ctrl-M, carriage return
032	26	\u001a	SUB	Ctrl-Z, SUB (substitute) (see note)
040	32	\u0020		Space

Note: The SUB character is a bit of a special case. It is treated like white space if it is found to be the last character in a source file. This is for compatibility with operating systems that use SUB as a text file terminator.

Line termination

Since Java is a free-form language, it normally doesn't care where the ends of the lines are —white space is all the same. However, the comment that begins with // continues to the end of a line, so it is necessary that the ends of the lines be detected. Java's portability requires some flexibility in the definition of a line terminator. Lines are terminated with either a single CR or LF character, the CR LF character pair, or the three-character sequence, CR CR LF.

Token separation

In most cases, the Java compiler can easily tell where one token ends and another begins even when they are placed adjacent to one another. Take this example character string:

```
average=sum/(count-10);
```

It can easily be broken into this token stream:

```
average = sum / ( count - 10 ) ;
```

There are a few cases where white space becomes important. Take this example:

```
a = b - -c;
```

It is quite easy to see that a value will first be negated and then the two values will be subtracted. Removing the spaces makes the statement ambiguous:

```
a=b--c;
```

Java, breaking the input stream into the longest tokens it can find, will get this stream of tokens:

```
a = b -- c ;
```

This results in a syntax error.

Tokens

The executable program is defined as a stream of tokens. There are five kinds of tokens:

- *Identifier.* An identifier begins with a letter and includes letters and digits.

- *Keyword.* A keyword is an identifier—such as `while` or `public` that has some special meaning in the language.

- *Literal.* A literal is a constant—that is, a number or a string. It can be an identifier that is defined to have a special value—such as `false` or `null`.

- *Separator.* A separator is used to organize or group the other tokens. Separators are punctuation characters—things like commas, periods, and parentheses.

- *Operator.* An operator is compiled into code that will perform some action on the tokens around it— + and && are examples.

 For the Java character set, see **Unicode** and **ASCII**. For escape sequences in the input stream, see **escapes**. For the format of the comments discarded during the lexical scan, see **comments**. For the specific types of tokens, see **identifiers**, **keywords**, **literals**, **strings**, **separators**, and **operators**.

LineNumberInputStream

class java.io.LineNumberInputStream

This class was designed to keep a running count of the number of input lines. This class is deprecated—use `LineNumberReader` instead.

Deprecation

The design of this class assumes that there is a one-to-one correspondence between bytes and characters. This is not true. The `LineNumberReader` class handles character streams correctly and includes the ability to count the lines.

Inheritance

```
public class java.io.LineNumberInputStream
    extends FilterInputStream
        ⇑
    public class java.io.FilterInputStream
        extends InputStream
            ⇑
        public class java.io.InputStream
```

```
extends Object
       ⇑
public class java.lang.Object
```

Constructors

```
public LineNumberInputStream(InputStream input)
```

The `LineNumberInputStream` is constructed to use `input` for reading.

Methods

available()

```
public int available()
    throws IOException
```

Returns the number of bytes immediately available—the number that can be read without blocking.

getLineNumber()

```
public int getLineNumber()
```

Returns the current line number.

mark()

```
public void mark(int readlimit)
```

This will mark the current position in the input stream; a subsequent call to `reset()` will restore the input to this position. The value of `readlimit` specifies the number of bytes that can be read before the mark is discarded. For this to work, the return value from `markSupported()` must be `true`.

read()

```
public abstract int read()
    throws IOException
```

```
public int read(byte barray[],int offset,int length)
    throws IOException
```

If no argument is supplied, this will read one `byte` of data and return it as an `int`. If `barray` is supplied, the input data is placed in the array and the number of bytes read is returned. The input data will appear beginning at `barray[offset]` for a maximum of `length` bytes. This method will block as long as there is unread data available. A return value of −1 indicates a normal end to the input stream.

reset()

```
public void reset()
    throws IOException
```

This will reposition the input stream to the location of the last call to mark(). The exception is thrown if there is no active mark. A mark will be removed (causing this method to throw an exception) if more bytes have been read than the number specified on the call to mark().

setLineNumber()

```
public void setLineNumber(int lineNumber)
```

This will set the running line counter to lineNumber.

skip()

```
public long skip(long count)
    throws IOException
```

Calling this method makes a request to have the input stream skip over count number of input bytes. The return value is the actual number of bytes skipped.

 For a nondeprecated class to do this job, see **LineNumberReader**.

LineNumberReader

class java.io.LineNumberReader

This class will perform a buffered read from an input stream and keep a running count of the line numbers.

End of the line

A line is terminated by a carriage return, a line feed, or the combination of a carriage return immediately followed by a line feed.

Inheritance

```
public class java.io.LineNumberReader
    extends BufferedReader
        ⇑
    public class java.io.BufferedReader
        extends Reader
            ⇑
        public class java.io.Reader
            extends Object
```

⇑
```
public class java.lang.Object
```

Constructors

```
public LineNumberReader(Reader input)
public LineNumberReader(Reader input,int bufferSize)
```

A new LineNumberReader is created using a Reader object to read the stream. If the bufferSize is not specified, it will default to the size used by input.

Methods

getLineNumber()

```
public int getLineNumber()
```

This method returns the current line number.

mark()

```
public void mark(int readlimit)
```

This will mark the current position in the input stream; a subsequent call to reset() will restore the input to this position. The value of readlimit specifies the number of characters that can be read before the mark is discarded. For this to work, the return value from markSupported() must be true.

read()

```
public int read()
    throws IOException
```

```
public int read(char carray[],int offset,int length)
    throws IOException
```

If no argument is supplied, this will read one character and return it as an int. If carray is supplied, the input data is placed in the array and the number of characters read is returned. The input data will appear beginning at carray[offset] for a maximum of length characters. This method will block until the read completes or there is no more data. A return value of −1 indicates a normal end to the input stream.

readLine()

```
public String readLine()
    throws IOException
```

Reads a line of text from the input stream. The returned String does not include the line termination.

reset()

```
public void reset()
     throws IOException
```

This will reposition the input stream to the location of the last call to mark(). The exception is thrown if there is no active mark. A mark will be removed (causing this method to throw an exception) if more bytes have been read than the number specified on the call to mark().

setLineNumber()

```
public void setLineNumber(int lineNumber)
```

This sets the value of the line counter to lineNumber.

skip()

```
public long skip(long count)
     throws IOException
```

Calling this method makes a request to have the input stream skip over count number of input characters. The return value is the actual number of characters skipped.

LinkageError

class java.lang.LinkageError

This error is thrown to indicate an incompatibility has arisen because one class has a dependency on a particular characteristic of another class—and the other class has changed. This can happen when the two are compiled separately.

Extended by

```
ClassCircularityError
ClassFormatError
ExceptionInInitializerError
IncompatibleClassChangeError
NoClassDefFoundError
UnsatisfiedLinkError
VerifyError
```

Inheritance

```
public class java.lang.LinkageError
```

```
        extends Error
           ⇑
    public class java.lang.Error
        extends Throwable
               ⇑
        public class java.lang.Throwable
            implements Serializable
            extends Object
               ⇑
            public class java.lang.Object
```

Constructors

```
    public LinkageError()
    public LinkageError(String message)
```

If the `message` string is supplied, it is used as a detailed message describing this particular exception.

List

class java.awt.List

This component presents a list of items and allows the user to make a selection. A scroll bar will be included if there is not enough room to display the entire list.

An item

Each item in the list is a `String` object. Inside the program, items can be addressed by either the characters in the string or the index of the item (the index being its position in the list).

An index

Item indexes are zero-based. The first item in the list is 0, the second is 1, and so on.

Inheritance

```
    public class java.awt.List
        implements ItemSelectable
        extends Component
           ⇑
        public abstract class java.awt.Component
            implements ImageObserver
            implements MenuContainer
```

```
implements Serializable
extends Object
      ⇑
public class java.lang.Object
```

Constructors

```
public List()
public List(int rows)
public List(int rows,boolean multipleMode)
```

A list can be created by specifying the number of rows to be made visible —if no row count is specified, none will be visible. If multipleMode is set to true, any number of selections can be made at one time; otherwise, only one can be made.

Methods

add()

```
public void add(String item)

public synchronized void add(String item,int index)
```

Adds the item at the specified index in the list. The item at the indexed position, and all those below it, are moved down one position to make room. If the index is not specified or is outside the range of the index values of the list, the item is added to the end of the list. This is the same as addItem().

addActionListener()

```
public synchronized void addActionListener(
       ActionListener listener)
```

Adds a listener to be notified whenever an item in the list is double-clicked.

addItem()

```
public void addItem(String item)

public synchronized void addItem(String item,int index)
```

Adds the item at the specified index in the list. The item at the indexed position, and all those below it, are moved down one position to make room. If the index is not specified or is outside the range of the index values of the list, the item is added to the end of the list. This is the same as add().

addItemListener()

```
public synchronized void addItemListener(
```

```
                              ItemListener listener)
```

Adds a listener that will receive events from the list.

addNotify()

```
public void addNotify()
```

Creates the underlying system-dependent peer for this object. This method is not normally called by the application. It is called by the container.

allowsMultipleSelections()   **deprecated**

```
public boolean allowsMultipleSelections()
```

Returns true if the list is able to accept multiple selections. This method is deprecated — use isMultipleMode().

clear()   **deprecated**

```
public synchronized void clear()
```

Removes all items from the list. This method is deprecated — use removeAll().

countItems()   **deprecated**

```
public int countItems()
```

Returns the number of items in the list. This method is deprecated — use getItemCount().

delItem()

```
public synchronized void delItem(int index)
```

Removes the item at the index.

delItems()   **deprecated**

```
public synchronized void delItems(int startIndex,int endIndex)
```

Removes all items from startIndex to endIndex. The indexing is inclusive — the items at startIndex and endIndex will both be removed. The method is deprecated — it is expected to be made accessible only inside the package in the future.

deselect()

```
public synchronized void deselect(int index)
```

Causes the item at the index not to be selected.

getItem()

```
public String getItem(int index)
```

Returns the item at the `index`. If the `index` is out of range, an `ArrayIndexOutOfBoundsException` will be thrown.

getItemCount()

```
public int getItemCount()
```

Returns a count of the number of items in the list.

getItems()

```
public synchronized String[] getItems()
```

Returns all the items in the list.

getMinimumSize()

```
public Dimension getMinimumSize()

public Dimension getMinimumSize(int rows)
```

Returns the minimum size that could be used by the `List` object to display the specified number of `rows`. If the number of rows is not specified, the current internal row count will be used.

getPreferredSize()

```
public Dimension getPreferredSize()

public Dimension getPreferredSize(int rows)
```

Returns the preferred size of the `List` object to display the specified number of `rows`. If the number of rows is not specified, the current internal row count will be used.

getRows()

```
public int getRows()
```

Returns the number of visible rows.

getSelectedIndex()

```
public synchronized int getSelectedIndex()
```

Returns the index of the selected item. If no item is selected, or if multiple items are selected, returns −1.

getSelectedIndexes()

```
public synchronized int[] getSelectedIndexes()
```

Returns an array containing the indexes of the selected items.

getSelectedItem()

```
public synchronized String getSelectedItem()
```

Returns the selected item. If no item is selected, or if multiple items are selected, returns null.

getSelectedItems()

```
public synchronized String[] getSelectedItems()
```

Returns the selected items as an array of String objects. If no items are selected, a zero-length array is returned.

getSelectedObjects()

```
public Object[] getSelectedObjects()
```

Returns the selected items as an array of Objects. If no items are selected, a zero-length array is returned.

getVisibleIndex()

```
public int getVisibleIndex()
```

Returns the index of the item most recently made visible by a call to makeVisible().

isIndexSelected()

```
public boolean isIndexSelected(int index)
```

Returns true if the item at the index has been selected.

isMultipleMode()

```
public boolean isMultipleMode()
```

Returns true if multiple selections can be made.

isSelected()   **deprecated**

```
public boolean isSelected(int index)
```

Returns true if the item at the index has been selected. This method is deprecated—use isIndexSelected().

makeVisible()

```
public synchronized void makeVisible(int index)
```

Makes the item at the index visible in the List window.

minimumSize()   **deprecated**

```
public Dimension minimumSize()
```

```
public Dimension minimumSize(int rows)
```

Returns the minimum size that could be used by the List object to display the specified number of rows. If the number of rows is not specified, the current internal row count will be used. This method is deprecated—use getMinimumSize().

paramString()

```
protected String paramString()
```

Returns debugging information. The return string describes the internal state and values of this object.

preferredSize()   deprecated

```
public Dimension preferredSize()
```

```
public Dimension preferredSize(int rows)
```

Returns the preferred size of the List object to display the specified number of rows. If the number of rows is not specified, the current internal row count will be used. This method is deprecated—use getPreferredSize(int).

processActionEvent()

```
protected void processActionEvent(ActionEvent event)
```

An ActionEvent is processed in this method by being dispatched to any registered ActionListener objects.

This method will be called only if action events have been enabled. They will be enabled whenever a listener is registered by a call to addActionListener() or there is a call to enableEvents() with the appropriate mask.

processEvent()

```
protected void processEvent(AWTEvent event)
```

This method processes events that apply to this object and passes on those that do not. If the event is an ItemEvent, the method processItemEvent() will be called. If the event is an ActionEvent, the method processItemEvent() is called. If it is neither of those, a call will be made to processEvent() of the superclass.

processItemEvent()

```
protected void processItemEvent(ItemEvent event)
```

An ItemEvent is processed in this method by being dispatched to any registered ItemListener objects.

This method will be called only if item events have been enabled. They will be enabled whenever a listener is registered by a call to addItemListener() or there is a call to enableEvents() with the appropriate mask.

remove()

```
public synchronized void remove(int index)

public synchronized void remove(String item)
```

Removes an item from the list. It can be selected by either its name or its index.

removeActionListener()

```
public synchronized void removeActionListener(
        ActionListener listener)
```

Removes the listener from the list of registered ActionListeners.

removeAll()

```
public synchronized void removeAll()
```

Removes all items from the list.

removeItemListener()

```
public synchronized void removeItemListener(
        ItemListener listener)
```

Removes the listener from the list of registered ItemListeners.

removeNotify()

```
public void removeNotify()
```

Removes the peer object of the List.

replaceItem()

```
public synchronized void replaceItem(
        String newString,int index)
```

Replaces the String of the item at the index with newString.

select()

```
public synchronized void select(int index)
```

Causes the item at the index to become selected.

setMultipleMode()

```
public synchronized void setMultipleMode(boolean setting)
```

If setting is true, the List will allow several items to be selected simultaneously. If setting is false, only one item can be selected at any one time.

setMultipleSelections()   **deprecated**

```
public synchronized void setMultipleSelections(boolean setting)
```

If setting is true, the List will allow several items to be selected simultaneously. If setting is false, only one item can be selected at any one time. This method is deprecated—use setMultipleMode().

Example

This example is a List with a collection of buttons that can be used to add and delete items, and to change the selection mode:

```
import java.awt.*;
import java.awt.event.*;
public class ModList extends Frame
            implements ActionListener {
    List list;
    TextField textField;
    public static void main(String[] arg) {
        ModList ml = new ModList();
    }
    public ModList() {
        setBackground(Color.lightGray);
        list = new List(8);
        Font font = new Font("Courier",Font.BOLD,15);
        list.setFont(font);
        list.addItem("First Item");
        list.addItem("Second Item");
        list.addItem("Third Item");
        list.addItem("Fourth Item");
        add("North",list);

        textField = new TextField(20);
        add("Center",textField);

        Panel p = new Panel();
        Button b = new Button("Add");
        b.addActionListener(this);
        p.add(b);
        b = new Button("Delete");
        b.addActionListener(this);
        p.add(b);
        b = new Button("Get");
        b.addActionListener(this);
        p.add(b);
```

```
            b = new Button("Single");
            b.addActionListener(this);
            p.add(b);
            b = new Button("Multiple");
            b.addActionListener(this);
            p.add(b);
            b = new Button("Quit");
            b.addActionListener(this);
            p.add(b);
            add("South",p);

            pack();
            show();
        }
        public void actionPerformed(ActionEvent event) {
            if(event.getActionCommand().equals("Quit"))
                System.exit(0);
            else if(event.getActionCommand().equals("Add")) {
                list.addItem(textField.getText());
            } else if(event.getActionCommand().equals(
                                    "Delete")) {
                if(list.getSelectedIndex() >= 0)
                    list.delItem(list.getSelectedIndex());
            } else if(event.getActionCommand().equals("Get"))
                {if(list.getSelectedItem() != null)

                    textField.setText(list.getSelectedItem());
            } else if(event.getActionCommand().equals(
                                    "Multiple")) {
                list.setMultipleMode(true);
            } else if(event.getActionCommand().equals(
                                    "Single")) {
                list.setMultipleMode(false);
            }
        }
    }
```

The display produced by this example is shown in Figure L-3.

Figure L-3 An example that manipulates the members of a *List*.

The List is at the top of the window. A TextField and a collection of control buttons appear at the bottom. The Add button will add the string being displayed in the text field to the List as the last member. The Delete button will delete the currently selected member from the list. The Get button will read the currently selected member from the list and write it to the TextField. The Multiple and Single buttons will change the mode of operation of the List between accepting multiple selections and accepting only a single selection.

The other noncontainer components are **Button, Label, Checkbox, Canvas, Scrollbar, Choice, TextArea,** and **TextField**.

listener

To receive an event (things such as mouse or keyboard button presses will initiate an event), a class must become a listener for the event. For the class to do this, it must implement the interface that defines the method that will be used to process the received event. This object must itself have registered as a *listener* for the event.

You can consume events

Input events are delivered to listeners before they are processed normally by the source where they originated. This allows listeners and component subclasses to "consume" the events so that the source will not process them in their default manner. For example, consuming mousePressed events on a Button component will prevent the Button from being activated.

The addXxxListener() methods

Methods of the form addXxxListener(), where Xxx is the name of the event type, are used to register objects to receive the events. Table L-2 is a list of the classes that have methods that can be used to add listeners. Table L-3 is a list of the method names and the classes in which they are implemented.

Table L-2 Classes and the Listener Methods They Implement

Method Name	Class
Adjustable	addAdjustmentListener()
Button	addActionListener()
Checkbox	addItemListener()
CheckboxMenuItem	addItemListener()
Choice	addItemListener()
Component	addComponentListener(), addFocusListener(), addKeyListener(), addMouseListener(), addMouseMotionListener()
Container	addContainerListener()
Customizer	addPropertyChangeListener()
ItemSelectable	addItemListener()
List	addActionListener(), addItemListener()
MenuItem	addActionListener()
PropertyChangeSupport	addPropertyChangeListener()
PropertyEditor	addPropertyChangeListener()
PropertyEditorSupport	addPropertyChangeListener()
Scrollbar	addAdjustmentListener()
TextComponent	addTextListener()
TextField	addActionListener()
VetoableChangeSupport	addVetoableChangeListener()
Window	addWindowListener()

Table L-3 Listener Methods and the Classes That Implement Them

Method Name	Class
addActionListener()	Button, List, MenuItem, TextField
addAdjustmentListener()	Adjustable, Scrollbar
addComponentListener()	Component
addContainerListener()	Container
addFocusListener()	Component
addItemListener()	Checkbox, CheckboxMenuItem, Choice, ItemSelectable, List
addKeyListener()	Component
addMouseListener()	Component
addMouseMotionListener()	Component

Method Name	Class
addPropertyChangeListener()	Customizer, PropertyChangeSupport, PropertyEditor, PropertyEditorSupport
addTextListener()	TextComponent
addVetoableChangeListener()	VetoableChangeSupport
addWindowListener()	Window

Most of the events, adapters, and interfaces are defined in the package java.awt.event. The PropertyChangeEvent and VetoableChangeSupport are defined in the package java.beans.

ListResourceBundle

class java.util.ListResourceBundle

This is an abstract class that contains locale resources as a list of key/object pairs.

Subclassing

A subclass is required to override getContents(), which returns an array of resources. Each item of the array is a pair of objects. One object is the String that is to be used as the resource key. The other is the object that is the resource itself—it may or may not be a String. A key string is case-sensitive.

Inheritance

```
public abstract class ListResourceBundle
    extends ResourceBundle
        ⇑
    public abstract class java.util.ResourceBundle
        extends Object
            ⇑
        public class java.lang.Object
```

Constructors

```
public ListResourceBundle()
```

Methods

getContents()

```
protected abstract Object[][] getContents()
```

Returns the entire array of resources. Each resource is a pair—a String acting as the key and the resource object itself.

getKeys()

```
public Enumeration getKeys()
```

Returns an enumeration object that contains the keys.

handleGetObject()

```
public final Object handleGetObject(String key)
```

Returns the resource object associated with the key.

Example

This is an example of how a ListResourceBundle can be used to define a set of key/resource pairs. This example is used to translate the meanings of a set of standard terms into other forms for a specific locale:

```
import java.awt.*;
import java.util.*;
public class ResourceChoice {
    static public void main(String[] arg) {
        AlabamaList aList = new AlabamaList();
        showList(aList.getContents());
        TexasList tList = new TexasList();
        showList(tList.getContents());
    }
    static private void showList(Object[][] pair) {
        for(int i=0; i<pair.length; i++) {
            System.out.println("Key " + (String)pair[i][0]

                    +"translates to " + (String)pair[i][1]);
        }
    }
}
class AlabamaList extends ListResourceBundle {
    static final Object[][] resources = {
        { "Ok", "Sure Bubba" },
        { "Cancel", "Ne'er Mine" },
        { "Quit", "Nope" },
```

```
                { "Start", "Watchout" }
        };
        public Object[][] getContents() {
            return(resources);
        }
}
class TexasList extends ListResourceBundle {
        static final Object[][] resources = {
                { "Ok", "You betcha" },
                { "Cancel", "Nah" },
                { "Quit", "Whoa" },
                { "Start", "Here it comes" }
        };
        public Object[][] getContents() {
            return(resources);
        }
}
```

The output looks like this.

```
Key Ok translates to Sure Bubba
Key Cancel translates to Ne'er Mine
Key Quit translates to Nope
Key Start translates to Watchout

Key Ok translates to You betcha
Key Cancel translates to Nah
Key Quit translates to Whoa
Key Start translates to Here it comes
```

 For more information on resources in general, see **ResourceBundle**. Also see **PropertyResourceBundle**.

literals

A literal is the declaration of a constant value formed by using a string of characters. Any Java statement that defines a constant value—a value that cannot be changed by a running program—is a literal. Literal values can be declared for any of the primitive data types. There is also the special case of the String literal, which is a string of zero or more characters surrounded by double quotes. A character literal is of type char and is one or more characters surrounded by single quotes. There is also the null keyword, which is a reference literal. Finally, there are the two boolean literals—true and false.

Unless otherwise specified, a numeric literal will default to being an `int`. If a literal contains a decimal point or an exponent indicator (e or E), it will be a `double`. A suffix (f or F) can convert it to a `float`. Another suffix (d or D) will cause it to be a `double`. Another suffix (l or L) will cause it to be a `long`.

 For types, ranges, and characteristics of literals, see **boolean**, **byte**, **char**, **short**, **int**, **long**, **float**, and **double**. For a discussion of string literals, see **string literal**.

little endian

This term describes systems that have the rightmost bit as the most significant bit. That is, the leading bit, reading from left to right, is the least significant. The "little end" comes first. All integral data in Java is big endian.

LoaderHandler

interface java.rmi.server.LoaderHandler

This is an interface defining the methods for a class loader that can operate in an RMI environment.

Inheritance

```
public interface java.rmi.server.LoaderHandler
```

Variables and constants

packagePrefix

```
public static final String packagePrefix
```

The name of the package containing the class that implements this interface.

Methods

getSecurityContext()

```
public abstract Object getSecurityContext(
        ClassLoader loader)
```

Returns the security context of the specified `loader`.

loadClass()

```
public abstract Class loadClass(String name)
    throws MalformedURLException
    throws ClassNotFoundException

public abstract Class loadClass(URL codebase,String name)
    throws MalformedURLException
    throws ClassNotFoundException
```

Loads the named class using from the location specified by the URL defined in either the `java.rmi.server.codebase` property or the URL specified as `codebase`. A `ClassNotFoundException` is thrown if the class file cannot be located. A `MalformedURLException` is thrown if there the URL is not valid.

local variable

 See **variable**.

Locale

class java.util.Locale

The `Locale` class is used to internationalize Java applets and applications. It can be used by a program to make the display adapt to a different location. This is done by making translations into different languages, and even causing it to have different sets of behavior. This class contains the information needed for collating order, dates, times, numbers, and currencies that will vary from one location to another.

Class types in the abstract

Many of the abstract base classes have a type indicator that allows them to be changed from one locale to another. For example, using `NumberFormat`, you can create a default number format, a currency format, or a percent format. The classes that derive from this base class will all inherit this new formatting information, and they can all be transformed to any new locale.

The identification of a locale

The `Locale` is just a mechanism for identifying objects, not a container for the objects themselves. The Java international architecture supplies the mechanisms for identifying the objects that will be concerned with making locale modifications. The classes that have this sort of capability will have methods that require a specific locale to be included as an argument, as well as other methods that will use the default locale.

The production of locale specific objects

A base class designed to be used as a factory of locale-specific objects provides these methods:

```
public static Locale[] getAvailableLocales()
public static String getDisplayName(Locale objectLocale,
        Locale displayLocale)
public static final String getDisplayName(
        Locale objectLocale)
```

The getDisplayName() method will throw a MissingResourceException if objectLocale is not in the list of available locales.

The names may not match

A locale characteristic can be something that exists in one place but not in another. To be accurate and complete, you will need to query each locale-modifiable class as to whether or not it knows how to handle any specific locale item. Also, when you do ask for a locale, you may not get exactly what you asked for—see **ResourceBundle.**

The language codes

Every language has a lowercase two-letter code defined by ISO-639. These codes are used to indicate the language of the locale. The two-letter codes are only used internally—the user interface should always use the name returned from a call to getDisplayLanguage(). Here are some places to find a complete list of these codes:

```
http://sizif.mf.uni-lj.si/linux/cee/std/ISO_639.html
http://www.triacom.com/a.iso639.en.htm
http://www.sil.org/sgml/iso639.html
```

The country codes

Every country has an uppercase two-letter code defined by ISO-3166. These are used to indicate the country of the locale. The two-letter codes are used internally—the user interface should always use the name returned from a call to getDisplayCountry(). These are the same two-letter codes used as the country domain names on the Internet. Here are some places to find a complete list:

```
http://www.chemie.fu-berlin.de/diverse/doc/ISO_3166.html
http://stiwww.epfl.ch/utile/iso_3166.html
http://www-s.ti.com/ti_me/docs/ctrycode.htm
```

The Variants

The variant codes are for vendor-specific or browser-specific uses. Commonly used are WIN (for Windows), MAC (for Macintosh), and POSIX.

Inheritance

```
public final class Locale
    implements Cloneable
    implements Serializable
    extends Object
            ⇑
    public class java.lang.Object
```

Variables and constants

CANADA

```
public final static Locale CANADA
```

A Locale constant for the country.

CANADA_FRENCH

```
public final static Locale CANADA_FRENCH
```

A Locale constant for the language.

CHINA

```
public final static Locale CHINA
```

A Locale constant for the country.

CHINESE

```
public final static Locale CHINESE
```

A Locale constant for the language.

ENGLISH

```
public final static Locale ENGLISH
```

A Locale constant for the language.

FRANCE

```
public final static Locale FRANCE
```

A Locale constant for the country.

FRENCH

```
public final static Locale FRENCH
```

A Locale constant for the language.

GERMAN

```
public final static Locale GERMAN
```

A `Locale` constant for the language.

GERMANY

```
public final static Locale GERMANY
```

A `Locale` constant for the country.

ITALIAN

```
public final static Locale ITALIAN
```

A `Locale` constant for the language.

ITALY

```
public final static Locale ITALY
```

A `Locale` constant for the country.

JAPAN

```
public final static Locale JAPAN
```

A `Locale` constant for the country.

JAPANESE

```
public final static Locale JAPANESE
```

A `Locale` constant for the language.

KOREA

```
public final static Locale KOREA
```

A `Locale` constant for the country.

KOREAN

```
public final static Locale KOREAN
```

A `Locale` constant for the language.

PRC

```
public final static Locale PRC
```

A `Locale` constant for the country.

SIMPLIFIED_CHINESE

```
public final static Locale SIMPLIFIED_CHINESE
```

A Locale constant for the language.

TAIWAN

```
public final static Locale TAIWAN
```

A Locale constant for the country.

TRADITIONAL_CHINESE

```
public final static Locale TRADITIONAL_CHINESE
```

A Locale constant for the language.

UK

```
public final static Locale UK
```

A Locale constant for the country.

US

```
public final static Locale US
```

A Locale constant for the country.

Constructors

```
public Locale(String language,String country)
public Locale(String language,String country,String variant)
```

The language is the two-letter code specified in ISO-639. The country is the two-letter code described in ISO-3166. The variant is the vendor- and browser-specific code.

Returned by

Objects of this class can be returned from the getLocale() methods of Applet, Component, MessageFormat, and Window. The getDefault() method of this class also returns a Locale. Arrays of Locale objects are returned from the getAvailableLocales() methods of BreakIterator, Calendar, Collator, DataFormat, and NumberFormat.

Methods

clone()

```
public Object clone()
```

Constructs a duplicate of this object.

equals()

```
public boolean equals(Object object)
```

Returns `true` if the `object` is identical to this object.

getCountry()

```
public String getCountry()
```

Returns the uppercase two-letter ISO-3166 code for the country. See Example 1.

getDefault()

```
public static synchronized Locale getDefault()
```

This method returns the default `Locale` object. See Example 1.

getDisplayCountry()

```
public final String getDisplayCountry()

public String getDisplayCountry(Locale locale)
```

This will return a displayable name of the country. If the `locale` is specified, it is used instead of this `Locale`. See Example 1.

getDisplayLanguage()

```
public final String getDisplayLanguage()

public String getDisplayLanguage(Locale locale)
```

Returns the displayable name of the language. If the displayable name is not found, the ISO code is returned. If the `locale` is specified, it is used instead of this `Locale`. See example 1.

getDisplayName()

```
public final String getDisplayName()

public String getDisplayName(Locale locale)
```

Returns a displayable name that specifies both the language and the country. If neither is not found, the ISO code is returned. If the `locale` is specified, it is used instead of this `Locale`. See Example 1.

getDisplayVariant()

```
public final String getDisplayVariant()

public String getDisplayVariant(Locale locale)
```

Returns the displayable format of the variant. If none has been defined, it returns a zero-length string. If the `locale` is specified, it is used instead of this `Locale`. See Example 1.

getISO3Country()

```
public String getISO3Country()
          throws MissingResourceException
```

This method returns a string containing the three-letter ISO abbreviation of the name of the country. If there is no three-letter definition in the locale, the `MissingResourceException` is thrown. See Example 1.

getISO3Language()

```
public String getISO3Language()
          throws MissingResourceException
```

This method returns the three-letter abbreviation of the name of the language. If there is no three-letter definition defined, the `MissingResourceException` is thrown. See Example 1.

getLanguage()

```
public String getLanguage()
```

This method returns the two-letter ISO-639 code of the language. See Example 1.

getVariant()

```
public String getVariant()
```

The method will return the name of the variant. If the variant is not found, a zero-length string will be returned.

hashCode()

```
public synchronized int hashCode()
```

On the assumption that `Locale`s are often found in hash tables, the hash value is cached for speed.

setDefault()

```
public static synchronized voidsetDefault(Locale locale)
```

Changes the default to the specified locale. It affects only the currently running program—it has no effect on the host. If this method is going to be used, it should be called when the program first starts up, because any number of classes could be programmed to use the `Locale` during their construction.

toString()

```
public final String toString()
```

Returns the name of the locale—it includes the language, the country, and the variant. The names are separated with underscore characters so that the resulting string can be used to construct names. See Example 1.

Example

This example displays the strings returned for two Locales. One is the default locale, and the other is the locale for Germany:

```
import java.util.*;
public class LocaleShow {
    public static void main(String[] arg) {
        Locale locale = Locale.getDefault();
        System.out.println("-- The default locale --");
        localeShow(locale);
        locale = Locale.GERMANY;
        System.out.println("-- The GERMANY locale --");
        localeShow(locale);
    }
    public static void localeShow(Locale locale) {
        System.out.println("toString(): \"" +
            locale + "\"");
        System.out.println("getCountry(): \"" +
            locale.getCountry() + "\"");
        System.out.println("getDisplayCountry(): \"" +
            locale.getDisplayCountry() + "\"");
        System.out.println("getISO3Country(): \"" +
            locale.getISO3Country() + "\"");
        System.out.println("getLanguage(): \"" +
            locale.getLanguage() + "\"");
        System.out.println("getDisplayLanguage(): \"" +
            locale.getDisplayLanguage() + "\"");
        System.out.println("getISO3Language(): \"" +
            locale.getISO3Language() + "\"");
        System.out.println("getDisplayName(): \"" +
            locale.getDisplayName() + "\"");
        System.out.println("getVariant(): \"" +
            locale.getVariant() + "\"");
        System.out.println("getDisplayVariant(): \"" +
            locale.getDisplayVariant() + "\"");
    }
}
```

In this execution, the default Locale was US. Here is the output.

```
-- The default locale --
```

```
toString(): "en_US"
getCountry(): "US"
getDisplayCountry(): "United States"
getISO3Country(): "USA"
getLanguage(): "en"
getDisplayLanguage(): "English"
getISO3Language(): "enu"
getDisplayName(): "English (United States)"
getVariant(): ""
getDisplayVariant(): ""
-- The GERMANY locale --
toString(): "de_DE"
getCountry(): "DE"
getDisplayCountry(): "Germany"
getISO3Country(): "DEU"
getLanguage(): "de"
getDisplayLanguage(): "German"
getISO3Language(): "deu"
getDisplayName(): "German (Germany)"
getVariant(): ""
getDisplayVariant(): ""
```

 For an example of using a `Locale` to format numbers, see **DecimalFormat**.

LocateRegistry

class java.rmi.registry.LocateRegistry

The methods of this class can be used to get a reference to the `Registry` object on this host or such an object on another host.

Inheritance

```
public final class java.rmi.registry.LocateRegistry
    extends Object
        ⇑
    public class java.lang.Object
```

Constructors

This class is a collection of static methods. There are no constructors.

Methods

createRegistry()

```
public static Registry createRegistry(int port)
    throws RemoteException
```

Creates and exports a `Registry` on the specified `port` number of the local host. A `RemoteException` is thrown on a failure to create a remote object.

getRegistry()

```
public static Registry getRegistry()
    throws RemoteException
```

```
public static Registry getRegistry(int port)
    throws RemoteException
```

```
public static Registry getRegistry(String host)
    throws RemoteException
    throws UnknownHostException
```

```
public static Registry getRegistry(String host,int port)
    throws RemoteException
    throws UnknownHostException
```

Returns the `Registry` for the specified `host` and `port`. This can be either a local or remote `Registry`. If the `host` is not specified or is `null`, the local host is assumed. If the `port` number is not specified or is not greater than zero, the well-known port number defined in the `Registry` class is assumed. An `UnknownHostException` is thrown if the host is specified but is unknown. A `RemoteException` is thrown on a failure to create a remote object.

 For more information, see **RMI**. Also see **Registry** and **RegistryHandler**.

LogStream

class java.rmi.server.LogStream

This is a mechanism used for logging error messages that could be of interest to those monitoring the RMI system.

The constants defined in the class are used to indicate the level and type of the messages being logged.

Inheritance

```
public class java.rmi.server.LogStream
    extends PrintStream
```

```
                    ⇑
        public class java.io.PrintStream
            extends FilterOutputStream
                    ⇑
            public class java.io.FilterOutputStream
                extends OutputStream
                        ⇑
                public class java.io.OutputStream
                    extends Object
                            ⇑
                    public class java.lang.Object
```

Variables and constants

BRIEF

```
    public static final int BRIEF
```

SILENT

```
    public static final int SILENT
```

VERBOSE

```
    public static final int VERBOSE
```

Constructors

Returned by

Under normal circumstances, there is only one LogStream, and a reference to it can be acquired by calling log().

Methods

getDefaultStream()

```
    public static synchronized PrintStream getDefaultStream()
```

Returns the underlying PrintStream of the LogStream.

getOutputStream()

```
    public synchronized OutputStream getOutputStream()
```

Returns the underlying OutputStream of the LogStream.

log()

```
public static LogStream log(String name)
```

Returns a LogStream identified by the specified name. If there is no current LogStream of the name, one will be created. The construction is done in this way so that various processes will be able to write their messages to the same stream by using the same name.

parseLevel()

```
public static int parseLevel(String string)
```

Converts the name of a logging level to its int value—one of the values defined as a constant in this class.

setDefaultStream()

```
public static synchronized void setDefaultStream(
        PrintStream newDefault)
```

Specifies the PrintStream to be used for all new logs.

setOutputStream()

```
public synchronized void setOutputStream(
        OutputStream out)
```

Specifies the OutputStream to be used for this LogStream.

toString()

```
public String toString()
```

Returns the name of this LogStream.

write()

```
public void write(int bvalue)
```

```
public void write(byte barray[],int offset,int length)
```

If bvalue is specified, writes a single byte of data to the output. If that byte is not a new line, it is only appended to the internal buffer. If it is a new line, the currently buffered line is output after being prefixed with the appropriate logging information.

If barray is specified, each of the bytes beginning at barray[offset] and continuing for length is treated as if it had been passed individually to the method with the int argument.

long

primitive data type

A long is a 64-bit signed integer.

The largest magnitude negative value of a long is –9,223,372,036,854,775,807. The largest positive value of a long is 9,223,372,036,854,775,808.

Just in case you would like to bring it up in a conversation, that number is nine quintillion, two hundred twenty-three quadrillion, three hundred seventy-two trillion, thirty-six billion, eight hundred fifty-four million, seven hundred seventy-five thousand, eight hundred eight.

Table L-4 lists all the ways in which the maximum and minimum values for a long can be declared.

Table L-4   Different Forms of Declaring Maximum and Minimum Values

Type	Maximum	Minimum	Minus one
Decimal	9223372036854775808L	-9223372036854775807L	-1L
Octal	0777777777777777777777L	01000000000000000000000L	01777777777777777777777L
Hexadecimal	0x7fffffffffffffffL	0x8000000000000000L	0xffffffffffffffffL
Predefined	Long.MAX_VALUE	Long.MIN_VALUE	

Literals

Literal long values can be declared in decimal, octal, or hexadecimal form. Any of these can be declared negative by being preceded with a minus sign. A long literal must always have the letter L or the letter l as a suffix—otherwise, it will default to int.

It is immaterial to the compiler whether you use an uppercase or lowercase letter to indicate a long, but the lowercase letter—depending on the font you are using—can be confusing to the eye. For example:

521   521

One of these is a 52 long, and the other is 521 int. Because the compiler doesn't care, it may be best to use the uppercase.

If you declare a literal that is valid for a long but will not fit into an int, it is necessary to append the L, or you will get a compiler error. For example,

```
long fred = 0xFFFFFFFFFFFF;     // Error
```

will generate an error message even though the value will fit nicely into a long. The compiler (which does not look across the equals sign for type information) will attempt to compile it as an int and generate an error.

Base-10 literal

A number beginning with any digit other than 0, and not containing anything other than the digits 0 through 9, is an integer. Some examples of long literals:

```
82L     63261     852L
```

Hexadecimal literal

A hexadecimal (base-16) long begins with 0x or 0X. It can contain the digits 0 through 9 and the letters A through F. The letters A through F (which represent the numeric values 10 through 15) can be either upper- or lowercase. Some examples of long hexadecimal literals are:

```
0x022L     0XA1B9L     0x99a1     0X2aL
```

The compiler will translate these as long values, since they end with the letter L or the letter l.

Octal literal

An octal (base-8) long begins with a 0 and contains only the digits 0 through 7. These are examples of octal literals:

```
05L     027L     06124531L
```

The compiler will translate these as being long values, since they end with the letter L or the letter l.

For a class to perform special int operations, see **Long**. For other integer types, see **byte**, **char**, **short**, and **int**.

Long

class java.lang.Long

This is a wrapper for the primitive data type long. It is a constant—the value contained in a Long object is set by the constructor and cannot be changed.

Inheritance

```
public final class java.lang.Integer
    extends Number
        ⇑
    public class java.lang.Number
        implements Serializable
        extends Object
            ⇑
        public class java.lang.Object
```

Variables and constants

MAX_VALUE

```
public final static long MAX_VALUE
```

This is the largest positive value that can be contained in a `long`. The value is 9223372036854775807. In hexadecimal, it is 0x7FFFFFFFFFFFFFFF.

MIN_VALUE

```
public final static long MIN_VALUE
```

This is the largest negative value that can be contained in a `long`. The value is −9223372036854775808. In hexadecimal, it is 0x8000000000000000.

TYPE

```
public final static Class TYPE
```

The `Class` object representing the primitive type `long`.

Constructors

```
public Long(long value)
public Long(String string)
        throws NumberFormatException
```

A `Long` object can be constructed directly from a `long` value, or from a string. The `string` must be a base-10 character form of an integer value; otherwise, a `NumberFormatException` is thrown.

Returned by

An object of this class is returned from `getLong()` and `valueOf()`.

Methods

byteValue()

```
public byte byteValue()
```

The value of the long is cast to a byte and returned.

doubleValue()

```
public double doubleValue()
```

The value of the long is returned as a double.

equals()

```
public boolean equals(Object object)
```

Returns true if object is a Long that contains the same value as this one.

floatValue()

```
public float floatValue()
```

Returns the value of the long as a float.

getLong()

```
public static Long getLong(String name)

public static Long getLong(String name,Long default)

public static Long getLong(String name,long default)
```

Calls System.getProperty() with name as the key. If a property is found, its value is interpreted as a character string form of a long and is translated to a long value in the instantiation of a Long object. The input string can be base-10, octal, or hexadecimal.

If the property is not found—or if the property isn't a valid integer string value—the value of the default is used. If you don't supply a default, a value of 0 is assumed.

hashCode()

```
public int hashCode()
```

Returns the hashcode for this object. Two Long wrappers that contain the same value will return the same hashcode.

intValue()

```
public int intValue()
```

Casts the value to an int and returns it.

longValue()

```
public long longValue()
```

Returns the value of the long.

parseLong()

```
public static long parseLong(String string)
        throws NumberFormatException

public static long parseLong(String string,int radix)
        throws NumberFormatException
```

The string is expected to be a long value in the specified radix (a radix of 10 is assumed if none is specified). A NumberFormatException is thrown if any character is encountered other than the ones that are valid for the base. For bases larger than 10, letters of the alphabet are used. For example, base 16 includes the letters A through F, base 17 includes G, and so on.

shortValue()

```
public short shortValue()
```

The internal value is cast to a short and returned.

toBinaryString()

```
public static String toBinaryString(long value)
```

This will convert the value into a string of 1 and 0 characters. Leading zeroes are suppressed.

toHexString()

```
public static String toHexString(long value)
```

This will convert the value into a hexadecimal number. Leading zeroes are suppressed; no leading '0x' is added, and the letters are in lowercase. Negative numbers will have the leading 'f' characters as required.

toOctalString()

```
public static String toOctalString(long value)
```

Converts the value into the character string octal form. Leading zeroes are suppressed. Negative numbers are represented with leading 1s and 7s as necessary.

toString()

```
public String toString()

public static String toString(long value)

public static String toString(long value,int radix)
```

Returns a String representation of value. If no value is supplied, the internal value of the Long is used. If no radix is specified, a radix of 10 is assumed.

valueOf()

```
public static Long valueOf(String string)
        throws NumberFormatException

public static Long valueOf(String string,int radix)
        throws NumberFormatException
```

The string is assumed to represent a long that is converted into a Long object and returned. Unless another radix is specified, a radix of 10 is assumed. If any character is encountered other that one that is valid for the radix, a NumberFormatException is thrown.

 The wrappers of the other primitive types are **Boolean, Byte, Character, Short, Integer, Float**, and **Double**.

longjmp

 For a facility that can be used to do the same thing that longjmp does in C, see **exception**.

MalformedURLException

class java.net.MalformedURLException

This exception is thrown to indicate that a URL is not syntactically correct. It could mean that no protocol was specified or that the specified protocol is unknown. It could also mean that the string simply could not be parsed.

Inheritance

```
public class java.net.MalformedURLException
    extends IOException
        ⇑
    public class java.io.IOException
        extends Exception
            ⇑
        public class java.lang.Exception
            extends Throwable
                ⇑
            public class java.lang.Throwable
                implements Serializable
                extends Object
                    ⇑
                public class java.lang.Object
```

Constructors

```
public MalformedURLException()
public MalformedURLException(String message)
```

If the message string is supplied, it is used as a detailed message describing this particular exception.

MarshalException

class java.rmi.MarshalException

This exception is thrown to indicate an error in marshaling the arguments for a remote method invocation.

Inheritance

```
public class java.rmi.MarshalException
    extends RemoteException
        ⇑
    public class java.rmi.RemoteException
        extends IOException
            ⇑
        public class java.io.IOException
            extends Exception
                ⇑
            public class java.lang.Exception
                extends Throwable
                    ⇑
                public class java.lang.Throwable
                    implements Serializable
                    extends Object
                        ⇑
                    public class java.lang.Object
```

Constructors

```
public MarshalException(String message)
public MarshalException(String message,Exception ex)
```

A MarshalException is created with a descriptive message and an optional Exception object detailing the cause of the exception being thrown at the remote location.

marshaling

 See **RMI**.

math

package java.math

This package contains a pair of classes that can be used for extended precision arithmetic.

Classes

```
BigDecimal
BigInteger
```

Math

class java.lang.Math

This is the Java standard math library. This class can be neither instantiated nor subclassed—all its methods are either constants or static methods. As much error handling as possible is handled by the methods of the class, but some out-of-range and immeasurable results are platform-dependent.

Inheritance

```
public final class Math
    extends Object
        ⇑
    public class java.lang.Object
```

Variables and constants

E

```
public final static double E
```

The mathematical constant value e. The value of E is 2.7182818284590452354.

PI

```
public final static double PI
```

The mathematical constant value pi. The value of PI is 3.14159265358979323846.

Constructors

There are no constructors—the class cannot be instantiated.

Methods

abs()

```
public static double abs(double arg)
public static float abs(float arg)
public static int abs(int arg)
public static long abs(long a)
```

Returns the absolute value of `arg`.

acos()

```
public static double acos(double cosine)
```

Returns the arc-cosine of `cosine`. The value of `cosine` must be from −1.0 through 1.0. The return value, in radians, is in the range 0.0 through PI.

asin()

```
public static double asin(double sine)
```

Returns the arc-sine of `sine`. The value of `sine` must be from −1.0 through 1.0. The return value, in radians, is in the range −PI/2.0 through PI/2.0.

atan()

```
public static double atan(double tangent)
```

Returns the arc-tangent of `tangent`. The return value, in radians, is in the range −PI/2.0 through PI/2.0.

atan2()

```
public static double atan2(double y,double x)
```

Given a pair of rectangular coordinate points `(x,y)`, this method will return, in radians, the angle that is created by a line being drawn from the origin to the point. That is, the tangent of the angle is determined by the relationship y/x, and the arc-tangent is taken. The range of the returned angle is −PI through PI.

This method can be used to convert rectangular `(x,y)` coordinates to polar `(r,theta)` coordinates. The polar angle, theta, is the value returned by this method. The radius can be calculated as

```
r = Math.sqrt((x*x) + (y*y));
```

ceil()

```
public static double ceil(double arg)
```

Returns the smallest whole number that is greater than or equal to `arg`.

cos()

```
public static double cos(double angle)
```

Returns the cosine of the angle. The angle is expressed in radians.

exp()

```
public static double exp(double exponent)
```

Raises the number e to the power of the exponent.

floor()

```
public static double floor(double arg)
```

Returns the largest whole number less than or equal to arg.

IEEEremainder()

```
public static double
          IEEEremainder(double dividend,double divisor)
```

Returns the remainder of dividend divided by divisor as defined by IEEE-754.

log()

```
public static double log(double arg)
```

Returns the natural logarithm (log to the base e) of the arg.

max()

```
public static double max(double arg1,double arg2)
public static float max(float arg1,float arg2)
public static int max(int arg1,int arg2)
public static long max(long arg1,long arg2)
```

Returns the larger of the values arg1 and arg2.

min()

```
public static double min(double arg1,double arg2)

public static float min(float arg1,float arg2)

public static int min(int arg1,int arg2)

public static long min(long arg1,long arg2)
```

Returns the smaller of the values arg1 and arg2.

pow()

```
public static double pow(double base,double exponent)
```

Returns base raised to the power of exponent.

If `base` is zero, `exponent` must be both greater than zero and a whole number. Also if `base` is negative, `exponent` must be a whole number. Failure to meet the conditions will cause an `ArithmeticException` to be thrown.

random()

```
public static synchronized double random()
```

Returns a pseudorandom number from 0.0 to 1.0.

These are called pseudorandom numbers because there is a possibility of sequences repeating themselves. The Java random number generator seeds itself by using the system clock, so the same sequences of numbers will almost never occur at the beginning.

rint()

```
public static double rint(double arg)
```

Rounds `arg` to its nearest whole number. If it is halfway between two integers, it will round up—for example, the value 4.5 will become 5.0.

round()

```
public static long round(double arg)
```

```
public static int round(float arg)
```

The value of `arg` is rounded to an integer value and returned. This is done by adding 0.5 to arg and then truncating the fractional portion. For example, 4.499 would round to 4, and 4.5 would round to 5.

sin()

```
public static double sin(double angle)
```

Returns the sine of the `angle`. The angle is expressed in radians.

sqrt()

```
public static double sqrt(double arg)
```

Returns the square root of `arg`. The value `arg` must be nonnegative.

tan()

```
public static double tan(double angle)
```

Returns the tangent of the `angle`. The angle is expressed in radians.

Example

The method `random()` returns a value in the range 0.0 to 1.0. This can be easily translated into an `int` value of a specified range:

```
public class MathRandom {
    static public void main(String arg[]) {
        for(int i=0; i<20; i++)
            System.out.print(randint(1,10) + " ");
        System.out.println();
    }

    static int randint(int low,int high) {
        int value = (int)((high-low+1)*(Math.random()));
        return(value + low);
    }
}
```

The method `randint()` will accept a pair of integer values that defines the range. The return value is some number between low and high (inclusive). Because the random number generator is seeded with the system clock, it will generate a different set of `int` values each time the program runs. Here is an example of the output from three consecutive runs:

```
10 9 10 6 6 10 5 9 5 4 4 3 3 2 7 9 9 7 5 5
2 6 9 4 6 3 6 6 5 3 3 8 9 10 9 10 6 7 4 6
1 3 8 4 3 1 9 2 9 10 1 1 10 5 1 2 8 7 8 10
```

 For more sophisticated random number generation, see **Random**.

MediaTracker

class java.awt.MediaTracker

This class will track the status of images being read from an `ImageProducer`. The `ImageProducer` could be loading the image from a file, reading it over the Internet, or generating it internally.

The only media is Image

The `MediaTracker` was originally designed to monitor different types of objects used in multimedia operations (such as audio files). As of version 1.1, only `Image` files are supported.

How to

The `MediaTracker` can be used to track the production of multiple `Image`s simultaneously. Once an instance of `MediaTracker` is created, a call is made to `addImage()` for each one to be tracked. Each `Image` added is assigned an ID number for purposes of tracking. Each `Image` can be assigned a unique number, or they can all have the same number. Status queries can be made using the ID number.

Inheritance

```
public class java.awt.MediaTracker
    implements Serializable
    extends Object
          ⇑
    public class java.lang.Object
```

Variables and constants

ABORTED

```
public static final int ABORTED
```

A status flag used to indicate that the production of the Image has been aborted.

COMPLETE

```
public static final int COMPLETE
```

A status flag used to indicate that the production of the Image was successful and has completed.

ERRORED

```
public static final int ERRORED
```

A status flag used to indicate that the production of the Image has encountered an error.

LOADING

```
public static final int LOADING
```

A status flag used to indicate that the Image is being processed.

Constructors

```
public MediaTracker(Component component)
```

A MediaTracker is constructed to track media objects for a specific component. The component is the one where the image will be drawn.

Methods

addImage()

```
public void addImage(Image image,int id)

public synchronized void addImage(Image image,int id,
        int width,int height)
```

Adds an image to the list of those being tracked. The id number will be assigned to the image inside the MediaTracker. Several images may have the same id number. If width and height are specified, the image is to be scaled and will eventually be rendered at the specified size.

checkAll()

```
public boolean checkAll()

public boolean checkAll(boolean load)
```

Returns false as long as the process of loading images is incomplete. This method will not cause the images to start loading unless load is true, and it will return false as long as the loading process has not been started. For the loading process to be considered complete, either all the images will be completely loaded, or the loading will have failed with some sort of error.

checkID()

```
public boolean checkID(int id)

public boolean checkID(int id,boolean load)
```

Returns false as long as the process of loading images with the specified id is incomplete. This method will not cause the images to start loading unless load is true, and it will return false as long as the loading process has not been started. For the loading process to be considered complete, either all the images with the specified id will be completely loaded, or the loading will have failed with some sort of error.

getErrorsAny()

```
public synchronized Object[] getErrorsAny()
```

Returns the list of errors that was encountered during loading. If there were no errors, the return is null.

getErrorsID()

```
public synchronized Object[] getErrorsID(int id)
```

Returns the list of loading errors that occurred for the specified id number. If there were no errors, the return is null.

isErrorAny()

```
public synchronized boolean isErrorAny()
```

Returns true if one or more errors have occurred during the image loading.

isErrorID()

```
public synchronized boolean isErrorID(int id)
```

Returns `true` if one or more errors have occurred during loading of images with the specified `id` number.

removeImage()

```
public synchronized void removeImage(Image image)

public synchronized void removeImage(Image image,int id)

public synchronized void removeImage(Image image,int id,
        int width,int height)
```

Removes references to the specified `image` from the list of those being tracked. If the `id` number is specified, only references to the `image` with that `id` number will be removed. If the `width` and `height` are also specified, only references to the `image` that have matching `id`, `width`, and `height` values will be removed.

statusAll()

```
public int statusAll(boolean load)
```

Returns the current set of status flags. The return value is the Boolean OR of all the flags. If `load` is true, this method will cause loading to begin.

statusID()

```
public int statusID(int id,boolean load)
```

Returns the current set of status flags of images with the specified `id` number. The return value is the Boolean OR of all the flags. If `load` is `true`, this method will cause loading to begin.

waitForAll()

```
public void waitForAll()
    throws InterruptedException

public synchronized boolean waitForAll(long milliseconds)
    throws InterruptedException
```

Starts loading all images and waits until they have finished loading — or have their loading aborted — before returning. If an error occurs during the loading of an image, that image is considered complete but the method will continue to wait for any others. If a number of milliseconds is specified, the method will return after the time has elapsed (if it expires before loading is complete) — a return value of `true` will indicate loading is complete, and a return of `false` will indicate that the timer has expired. After this method returns, it will be necessary to check the status to detect any errors. The `InterruptedException` is thrown if another thread interrupts this one.

waitForID()

```
public void waitForID(int id)
```

```
        throws InterruptedException

public synchronized boolean waitForID(int id,
            long milliseconds)
        throws InterruptedException
```

Starts loading all images of the specified id and waits until they have finished loading, or have their loading aborted, before returning. If an error occurs during the loading of an image, that image is considered complete but the method will continue to wait for any others. If a number of milliseconds is specified, the method will return after the time has elapsed (if it expires before loading is complete)—a return value of true will indicate loading is complete, and a return of false will indicate that the timer has expired. After this method returns, it will be necessary to check the status to detect any errors. The InterruptedException is thrown if another thread interrupts this one.

 For an example that uses MediaTracker to load images, see **MouseListener**.

Member

interface java.lang.reflect.Member

An object that implements this interface provides information about—and access to—a single member (field or method) of a class or an interface. That is, it *reflects* the member.

Implemented by

```
Constructor
Field
Method
```

Inheritance

```
public interface java.lang.reflect.Member
```

Variables and constants

DECLARED

```
public final static int DECLARED
```

This value is used to identify the declared members of a class or interface (as opposed to the inherited members).

PUBLIC

```
public final static int PUBLIC
```

This value is used to identify the public members of a class or interface (including inherited members).

Methods

getDeclaringClass()

```
public abstract Class getDeclaringClass()
```

Returns the Class object that represents the class or interface that declares the member or constructor reflected by this Member object.

getModifiers()

```
public abstract int getModifiers()
```

Returns the set of modifiers used to declare the member. The return value is the form that can be decoded by a Modifier object.

getName()

```
public abstract String getName()
```

Returns the simple name of the reflected member.

MemoryImageSource

class java.awt.image.MemoryImageSource

This class implements the ImageProducer interface and uses an array to produce the pixel values for an Image. This class can be used when you want to create an image by manipulating pixels and then have it converted to an Image object for display.

Inheritance

```
public class java.awt.image.MemoryImageSource
    implements ImageProducer
    extends Object
        ⇑
    public class java.lang.Object
```

Constructors

```
public MemoryImageSource(int width,int height,
```

```
        ColorModel model,byte pixel[],int offset,
        int scanSize)

public MemoryImageSource(int width,int height,
        ColorModel model,byte pixel[],int offset,
        int scanSize,Hashtable properties)

public MemoryImageSource(int width,int height,
        ColorModel model,int pixel[],int offset,
        int scanSize)

public MemoryImageSource(int width,int height,
        ColorModel model,int pixel[],int offset,
        int scanSize,Hashtable properties)

public MemoryImageSource(int width,int height,
        int pixel[],int offset,int scanSize)

public MemoryImageSource(int width,int height,
        int pixel[],int offset,
        int scanSize,Hashtable properties)
```

The `ImageProducer` can be constructed to create from an array of either byte pixel values or integer pixel values of the specified `width` and `height`. If the `ColorModel` is not specified, it will default to the RGB model. The `properties` are a set of properties to be sent to each `ImageConsumer` receiving a copy of the image. The `scanSize` is the number of pixels in each horizontal line (which is normally the same as the width of the image).

Methods

addConsumer()

```
public synchronized void addConsumer(ImageConsumer consumer)
```

Add an image consumer to the list of those that will receive output from this image producer.

isConsumer()

```
public synchronized boolean isConsumer(ImageConsumer consumer)
```

Returns `true` if the consumer is in the list of those that will receive output from this image producer.

newPixels()

```
public void newPixels()

public synchronized void newPixels(int x,int y,
        int width,int height)
```

```
public synchronized void newPixels(int x,int y,
        int width,int height,boolean framenotify)

public synchronized void newPixels(int newpixels[],
        ColorModel newmodel,int offset,int scansize)

public synchronized void newPixels(byte newpixels[],
        ColorModel newmodel,int offset,int scansize)
```

Sends a new array of image pixels to all the ImageConsumers in the list and then notifies them that the image is complete. This method only has meaning when the animation flag has been turned on with a call to setAnimation(). If a newpixels array is specified, the existing internal array of pixels is replaced with the new one—as is the color model.

If the dimensions and sizes are specified, all that will be sent is that particular rectangular region of the image. The (x,y) point is the upper-left corner of the rectangle of the specified width and height. However, if the flag was set by the setFullBufferUpdates() method, any specified rectangle will be ignored—the entire image will be sent.

If framenotify is true, the consumers will be notified by being sent a SINGLEFRAMEDONE notification that an animation frame is complete.

removeConsumer()

```
public synchronized void removeConsumer(ImageConsumer consumer)
```

Removes the consumer from the list of those that will receive image data from this object.

requestTopDownLeftRightResend()

```
public void requestTopDownLeftRightResend(
        ImageConsumer consumer)
```

This is a request that the specified consumer be delivered the image again, but in top-down left-right order.

setAnimated()

```
public synchronized void setAnimated(boolean animated)
```

If animated is true, the produced image will become a multiframe animation. If it is false, the produced image is to be a single-frame static image. This method should be called immediately after the object is constructed—after the consumers have been added but before an image is produced—to make sure the consumers receive multiframed data.

setFullBufferUpdates()

```
public synchronized void setFullBufferUpdates(boolean setting)
```

If setting is true, animation frames will be updated by being sent a complete frame, even if the request is for only a portion of the frame. This flag has no meaning if animation is not turned on. To be effective, this method should be called before any images are constructed.

startProduction()

```
public void startProduction(ImageConsumer consumer)
```

Adds a `consumer` to the list of those `ImageConsumers` that will receive image output from this object and immediately starts delivery of the image information to the entire list of `ImageConsumers`.

Example

This program paints a rectangle of pixel values and then uses a `MemoryImageSource` object to convert it to an image:

```
import java.awt.*;
import java.awt.image.*;
public class CrossFade extends Frame  {
    public static void main(String[] arg) {
        new CrossFade();
    }
    CrossFade() {
        add("Center",new CrossFadeCanvas());
        setSize(200,200);
        show();
    }
}

class CrossFadeCanvas extends Canvas {
    Image image;
    public void paint(Graphics g) {
        if(image == null) {
            int width = 200;
            int height = 200;
            int pixel[] = new int[width * height];
            int index = 0;
            for (int y = 0; y < height; y++) {
                for (int x = 0; x < width; x++) {
                    int red = (x * y) % 255;
                    int blue = (x + y) % 255;
                    int green = (x*x + y*y) % 255;
                    pixel[index++] =
                      (green << 24) | (red << 16) | blue;
                }
            }
            MemoryImageSource mis = new
MemoryImageSource(
                    width,height,pixel,0,width);
```

```
            image = createImage(mis);
        }
        g.drawImage(image,0,0,this);
    }
}
```

The pixel values—numbers in the range 0 to 255—are placed into the array and passed to the MemoryImageSource object for conversion. Figure M-1 shows the resulting display.

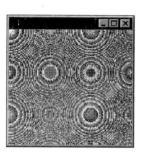

Figure M-1 The numeric pixel values are converted to an Image.

Menu

class java.awt.Menu

A Menu is a MenuItem that is used as a component of a MenuBar. It can be selected by the mouse and will display a list of MenuItems that can be selected.

Persistence

Selecting a Menu with the mouse will cause it to expand and display its list of members. The menu will remain on the display after the mouse button has been released.

Tear off

There are flags and methods of this class that deal with tear-off menus—menus that can be selected and then dragged to other locations on the screen to remain there until they are closed. Not all windowing environments support tear-off menus. Whenever they are unsupported, the settings will be silently ignored.

Extended by

PopupMenu

Inheritance

```
public class java.awt.Menu
    implements MenuContainer
    extends MenuItem
        ⇑
    public class java.awt.MenuItem
        extends MenuComponent
            ⇑
        public abstract class java.awt.MenuComponent
            implements Serializable
            extends Object
                ⇑
            public class java.lang.Object
```

Constructors

```
public Menu()
public Menu(String label)
public Menu(String label,boolean tearOff)
```

If no label is specified, the Menu will be blank. It will be a tear-off menu only if tearOff is set to true.

Returned by

Objects of this class are returned from MenuBar.add(), MenuBar.getHelpMenu(), MenuBar.getMenu(), and ResourceBundle.getMenu().

Methods

add()

```
public synchronized MenuItem add(MenuItem item)
```

```
public void add(String label)
```

Adds a new menu item to this Menu. If the item is specified as a String, a new MenuItem will be constructed using the string as its label. It will be added as the last one in the list.

addNotify()

```
public void addNotify()
```

Creates the underlying system-dependent peer for this object. This method is not normally called by the application. It is called by the container.

addSeparator()

```
public void addSeparator()
```

Adds a separator line to the bottom of the list of members.

countItems()   deprecated

```
public int countItems()
```

Returns the number of items in the list. This method is deprecated — use getItemCount().

getItem()

```
public MenuItem getItem(int index)
```

Returns the specified MenuItem from the list. The index is zero-based.

getItemCount()

```
public int getItemCount()
```

Returns a count of the number of items in the list.

insert()

```
public synchronized void insert(MenuItem menuitem,int index)
public void insert(String label,int index)
```

Inserts a new MenuItem at the specified index location. If a label is specified, a new MenuItem will be constructed. The index is zero-based. The MenuItem at the indexed position, and all those below it, are moved down to make room. An IllegalArgumentException will be thrown for an invalid index.

insertSeparator()

```
public void insertSeparator(int index)
```

Inserts a new separator at the specified index location. The index is zero-based. The MenuItem at the indexed position, and all those below it, are moved down to make room. An IllegalArgumentException will be thrown for an invalid index.

isTearOff()

```
public boolean isTearOff()
```

Returns true if this is a tear-off menu.

paramString()

```
public String paramString()
```

Returns debugging information. The return string describes the internal state and values of this object.

remove()

```
public synchronized void remove(int index)

public synchronized void remove(MenuComponent item)
```

If an item is specified, removes the item from the Menu. If an index is specified, removes the MenuItem at the specified index. The index is zero-based. The MenuItem at the indexed position, and all those below it, are moved down to make room. An IllegalArgumentException will be thrown for an invalid index.

removeAll()

```
public synchronized void removeAll()
```

Removes all items from the menu.

removeNotify()

```
public void removeNotify()
```

Removes the peer of the Menu.

 For an example. see **MenuBar**. The other classes dealing with menus are **CheckboxMenuItem**, **MenuBar**, **MenuComponent**, **MenuContainer**, **MenuItem**, **MenuShortcut**, and **PopupMenu**.

MenuBar

class java.awt.MenuBar

This is the menu bar that can be attached to a Frame. It is the menu bar across the top of the main window of an application. It is the container of all of the selectable pull-down and tear-off menus, and of the buttons and checkboxes they all contain.

Inheritance

```
public class java.awt.MenuBar
    implements MenuContainer
    extends MenuComponent
        ⇑
    public abstract class java.awt.MenuComponent
        implements Serializable
```

```
extends Object
        ⇑
public class java.lang.Object
```

Constructors

```
public MenuBar()
```

Returned by

Objects of the class are returned from `Frame.getMenuBar()` and `ResourceBundle.getMenuBar()`.

Methods

add()

```
public synchronized Menu add(Menu menu)
```

Add the `menu` to the `MenuBar`.

addNotify()

```
public void addNotify()
```

Creates the underlying system-dependent peer for this object. This method is not normally called by the application. It is called by the container.

countMenus()   **deprecated**

```
public int countMenus()
```

Returns the number of menu items in this `MenuBar`. This method is deprecated—use `getMenuCount()`.

deleteShortcut()

```
public void deleteShortcut(MenuShortcut shortcut)
```

Deletes the specified `shortcut`.

getHelpMenu()

```
public Menu getHelpMenu()
```

Returns the help menu of the `MenuBar`.

getMenu()

```
public Menu getMenu(int index)
```

Returns the `Menu` at the specified index. The index is zero-based.

getMenuCount()

```
public int getMenuCount()
```

Returns the count of the number of Menus.

getShortcutMenuItem()

```
public MenuItem getShortcutMenuItem(MenuShortcut shortcut)
```

Returns the MenuItem that is associated with the specified shortcut.

remove()

```
public synchronized void remove(int index)

public synchronized void remove(MenuComponent component)
```

Removes the item specified by component or index. The index is zero-based.

removeNotify()

```
public void removeNotify()
```

Removes the peer of the MenuBar.

setHelpMenu()

```
public synchronized void setHelpMenu(Menu menu)
```

Sets the specified menu as being the help menu.

shortcuts()

```
public synchronized Enumeration shortcuts()
```

Returns an Enumeration of the MenuShortcut objects managed by this MenuBar.

Example

This example includes the basics of menu construction and demonstrates several of the features:

```
import java.awt.*;
import java.awt.event.*;
public class MenuDemo extends Frame
            implements ActionListener {
    FileHandler fileHandler;
    MagicHandler magicHandler;
    MenuItem shazam;
    MenuItem xyzzy;
    public static void main(String[] arg) {
        new MenuDemo();
    }
```

```
MenuDemo() {
    MenuItem item;
    fileHandler = new FileHandler();
    magicHandler = new MagicHandler();
    MenuBar mb = new MenuBar();
    Menu fileMenu = new Menu("File");
    fileMenu.add(item = new MenuItem("Open"));
    item.addActionListener(fileHandler);
    fileMenu.add(item = new MenuItem("Save"));
    item.setShortcut(new MenuShortcut(KeyEvent.VK_S));
    item.addActionListener(fileHandler);
    fileMenu.add(item = new MenuItem("Save As..."));
    item.setShortcut(
            new MenuShortcut(KeyEvent.VK_S,true));
    item.setActionCommand("Saveas");
    item.addActionListener(fileHandler);
    fileMenu.addSeparator();
    fileMenu.add(item = new MenuItem("Exit"));
    item.addActionListener(this);
    fileMenu.add(item);
    mb.add(fileMenu);
    Menu magicMenu = new Menu("Magic");
    magicMenu.add(item = new MenuItem("Disable"));
    item.addActionListener(magicHandler);
    magicMenu.add(item = new MenuItem("Enable"));
    item.addActionListener(magicHandler);
    magicMenu.add(shazam = new MenuItem("Shazam"));
    shazam.addActionListener(magicHandler);
    magicMenu.add(xyzzy = new MenuItem("Xyzzy"));
    xyzzy.addActionListener(magicHandler);
    mb.add(magicMenu);
    setMenuBar(mb);
    setSize(150,300);
    show();
}
public void actionPerformed(ActionEvent event) {
    if(event.getActionCommand().equals("Exit"))
        System.exit(0);
    else
        System.out.println(event.getActionCommand());
}
class MagicHandler implements ActionListener {
    public void actionPerformed(ActionEvent event) {
        String command = event.getActionCommand();
```

```
                    if(command.equals("Enable")) {
                        xyzzy.setEnabled(true);
                        shazam.setEnabled(true);
                    } else if(command.equals("Disable")) {
                        xyzzy.setEnabled(false);
                        shazam.setEnabled(false);
                    }
                }
            }
        }

        class FileHandler implements ActionListener {
            public void actionPerformed(ActionEvent event) {
                System.out.println("FileHandler: " +
                    event.getActionCommand());
            }
        }
```

Figure M-2 shows the appearance of the menu with the accelerator keys for "Save" and "Save As." Figures M-3 and M-4 show the appearance of the menu with the magic-word buttons enabled and disabled.

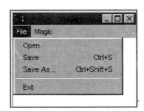

Figure M-2 A menu with accelerator keys.

Figure M-3 A menu with all its selections enabled.

Figure M-4 A menu with two of its selections disabled.

The MenuBar

A MenuBar acts as the parent component for all the other menu objects. The MenuDemo class extends Frame. The Frame class has a setMenuBar() method and will display whatever MenuBar object is passed to it. The MenuDemo constructor creates a new MenuBar object and, after adding a few menu items to it, attaches it to the Frame.

The Menu

Two Menu objects are created and attached to the MenuBar. One is the fileMenu, and the other is the magicMenu. Each one is created, has several menu objects attached to it, and then is attached to the MenuBar with a call to add().

The MenuItem

Each Menu has one or more MenuItems attached to it with the add() method of the Menu. The MenuItems are individual buttons—and each of these buttons has an ActionListener attached to it that will be notified when the button is selected.

The three ActionListeners

There are three action listeners in this example. An ActionListener is a class that implements the ActionListener interface, which requires the presence of the method actionPerformed(). An ActionListener is registered with each of the MenuItems with a call to its addActionListener() method.

The MenuDemo action listener

The method actionPerformed() in the class MenuDemo will respond to the "Exit" selection by shutting down the program. Any other selection passed to it is simply printed to System.out.

The FileHandler action listener

This is an example of using a separate class for an action listener. In the MenuDemo constructor, the class is instantiated and the object is used in the addActionListener() method of the menu selections on the "File" menu. The actionPerformed() method simply prints the name of whichever button is pressed.

The MagicHandler action listener

This is an example of using an inner class as an action listener. The MenuDemo constructor creates an instance of the class that is registered with the "Enable" and "Disable" menu items. Whenever the "Enable" button is selected, the "Shazam" and "Xyzzy" menu selections will be enabled for mouse interaction—when "Disable" is selected, the two menu selections will be disabled.

The Shortcuts

A couple of the menu items, "Save" and "Saveas," both have their setShortcut() methods called defining keystrokes for them. The "Save" selection will respond to the lowercase *s*, and the "Save As" button will respond to the uppercase *S*. Both respond to the key defined as KeyEvent.VK_S, but one is set to respond when the Shift key is being held down, and the other is not.

Also, notice that "Save As" has its command string set with a call to setActionCommand(). This is necessary when using accelerator keys to be able to read a string value in the actionPerformed() method. The "Save" menu selection does not do this, and using the accelerator key results in a null string being passed in the event.

 The other classes dealing with menus are **CheckboxMenuItem**, **Menu**, **MenuComponent**, **MenuContainer**, **MenuItem**, **MenuShortcut**, and **PopupMenu**.

MenuComponent

class java.awt.MenuComponent

This is the abstract class that is the superclass of all menu components.

Extended by

```
MenuBar
MenuItem
```

Inheritance

```
public abstract class java.awt.MenuComponent
    implements Serializable
    extends Object
        ⇑
    public class java.lang.Object
```

Constructors

```
public MenuComponent()
```

Methods

dispatchEvent()

```
public final void dispatchEvent(AWTEvent event)
```

The `event` will be distributed to all registered `ActionListeners`.

getFont()

```
public Font getFont()
```

Returns the font used for this menu component. If this component does not display text, the return is `null`.

getName()

```
public String getName()
```

Returns the name of the menu component.

getParent()

```
public MenuContainer getParent()
```

Returns the parent container of this component.

getPeer()   **deprecated**

```
public MenuComponentPeer getPeer()
```

Returns the peer. This method is deprecated because applications should not directly manipulate peers.

paramString()

```
protected String paramString()
```

Returns debugging information. The return string describes the internal state and values of this object.

postEvent()

```
public boolean postEvent(Event event)
```

Posts the specified `event`.

processEvent()

```
protected void processEvent(AWTEvent event)
```

Processes events that occur on this menu component.

removeNotify()

```
public void removeNotify()
```

Removes the peer of the menu component.

setFont()

```
public void setFont(Font font)
```

Specifies the font for a menu component that displays text.

setName()

```
public void setName(String name)
```

Specifies the name of the menu component.

toString()

```
public String toString()
```

Returns a string containing a description of the menu component.

 For an example, see **MenuBar**. For classes used to construct a menu, see **CheckboxMenuItem**, **Menu**, **MenuBar**, **MenuContainer**, **MenuItem**, **MenuShortcut**, and **PopupMenu**.

MenuContainer

interface java.awt.MenuContainer

This is the interface implemented by all menu-related containers.

Implemented by

```
Component
Frame
Menu
MenuBar
```

Inheritance

```
public interface java.awt.MenuContainer
```

Constructors

Returned by

An object implementing this interface is returned from `MenuComponent.getParent()`.

Methods

getFont()

```
public abstract Font getFont()
```

Returns the font being used for the menu items within this container.

postEvent()

```
public abstract boolean postEvent(Event event)
```

Posts an event to be propagated to a member of this menu container.

remove()

```
public abstract void remove(MenuComponent comp)
```

Removes the specified menu component.

 For classes used to construct a menu, see **CheckboxMenuItem**, **Menu**, **MenuBar**, **MenuComponent**, **MenuItem**, **MenuShortcut**, and **PopupMenu**.

MenuItem

class java.awt.MenuItem

An item on a menu that can be used to make a selection.

Extended by

```
CheckboxMenuItem
Menu
```

Inheritance

```
public class java.awt.MenuItem
    extends MenuComponent
        ⇑
    public abstract class java.awt.MenuComponent
        implements Serializable
        extends Object
            ⇑
        public class java.lang.Object
```

Constructors

```
public MenuItem()
public MenuItem(String label)
public MenuItem(String label,MenuShortcut shortcut)
```

The `label` is the text that appears on the menu item—if there is no `label`, the menu item will be blank. The optional `shortcut` defines the way in which the keyboard can be used to select the menu item.

Returned by

Objects of this class are returned from `Menu.add()`, `Menu.getItem()`, and `MenuBar.getShortcutMenuItem()`.

Methods

addActionListener()

```
public void addActionListener(ActionListener listener)
```

Adds an action listener to the menu item.

addNotify()

```
public void addNotify()
```

Creates the underlying system-dependent peer for this object. This method is not normally called by the application. It is called by the container.

deleteShortcut()

```
public void deleteShortcut()
```

Deletes the `MenuShortcut` that was assigned to this menu item.

disable()   **deprecated**

```
public synchronized void disable()
```

Disables the menu item. This method is deprecated—use `setEnabled()` instead.

disableEvents()

```
protected final void disableEvents(long eventmask)
```

Disables the events from being delivered to the menu item. The possible `eventmask` values are defined as constants in `AWTEvent`.

enable()   **deprecated**

```
public synchronized void enable()

public void enable(boolean setting)
```

Enables or disables the menu item. The method is deprecated — use `setEnabled()` instead.

enableEvents()

```
protected final void enableEvents(long eventmask)
```

Enables the events so that they will be delivered to the menu item. The possible `event-mask` values are defined as constants in `AWTEvent`. Normally, it is not necessary to call this method, because events of the appropriate types will be enabled as listeners are added to the component with `addActionListener()`.

getActionCommand()

```
public String getActionCommand()
```

Returns the string used as the command name when this menu item issues an action event.

getLabel()

```
public String getLabel()
```

Returns the label string of the menu item.

getShortcut()

```
public MenuShortcut getShortcut()
```

Returns the `MenuShortcut` object for this menu item. If there is none, `null` will be returned.

isEnabled()

```
public boolean isEnabled()
```

Returns `true` if the menu item is enabled.

paramString()

```
public String paramString()
```

Returns debugging information. The return string describes the internal state and values of this object.

processActionEvent()

```
protected void processActionEvent(ActionEvent event)
```

This method is called for the menu item to process its events. This method is called *only* with events that have been requested by a call to either `addActionListener()` or `enableEvents()`.

processEvent()

```
protected void processEvent(AWTEvent event)
```

If event is an ActionEvent, a call is made to processActionEvent(). All other event types are ignored.

removeActionListener()

```
public void removeActionListener(ActionListener listener)
```

Removes the listener from the list of ActionListeners for this menu item.

setActionCommand()

```
public void setActionCommand(String command)
```

This will define the action command—the string that is included with the ActionEvent issued by activating this menu item. If this is not set, the action command is the same as the label string.

setEnabled()

```
public synchronized void setEnabled(boolean setting)
```

If setting is true, the menu item will be enabled. If setting is false, it will be disabled.

setLabel()

```
public synchronized void setLabel(String label)
```

Specifies the label of the menu item.

setShortcut()

```
public void setShortcut(MenuShortcut shortcut)
```

Specifies the shortcut for the menu item. A MenuShortcut is a keyboard action that will select the menu item the same as a mouse click would.

For an example, see **MenuBar**. For classes used to construct a menu, see **CheckboxMenuItem**, **Menu**, **MenuBar**, **MenuContainer**, **MenuComponent**, **MenuShortcut**, and **PopupMenu**.

MenuShortcut

class java.awt.MenuShortcut

This class represents a menu keyboard shortcut—sometimes called a keyboard accelerator—that allows the user to make menu selections from the keyboard. A keyboard selection will have the same effect as if a selection had been made from the menu with the mouse.

Inheritance

```
public class java.awt.MenuShortcut
    implements Serializable
    extends Object
        ⇑
    public class java.lang.Object
```

Constructors

```
public MenuShortcut(int keycode)
public MenuShortcut(int keycode,boolean useShiftModifier)
```

A MenuShortcut is constructed to respond to a specific key. The value of keycode is one of the constants defined in KeyEvent. If useShiftModifier is specified as true, the keystroke will only be recognized when the Shift key is held down.

Returned by

A MenuShortcut object is returned from MenuItem.getShortcut().

Methods

equals()

```
public boolean equals(MenuShortcut shortcut)
```

Returns true if the shortcut object uses the same key with the same Shift-key setting as this one.

getKey()

```
public int getKey()
```

Returns the keycode of this MenuShortcut.

paramString()

```
protected String paramString()
```

Returns debugging information. The return string describes the internal state and values of this object.

toString()

```
public String toString()
```

Returns the string form of this object.

usesShiftModifier()

```
public boolean usesShiftModifier()
```

Returns true if this MenuShortcut only responds when the Shift key is being held down.

 For an example, see **MenuBar**.

MessageDigest

class java.security.MessageDigest

A message digest is a secure one-way hash function that can take an arbitrary-sized input and generate a fixed-length hash value. The algorithm used by this class can be such things as MD5 or SHA.

The API part

The API (Application Programmer Interface) of the MessageDigest is the set of methods called by applications that need message digest services. These are the public methods.

The SPI part

The SPI (Service Program Interface) is the interface implemented by providers that supply specific algorithms to be used in digesting data. These are all the methods that are prefixed by "engine." These methods are all abstract—the implementations must be supplied by a provider.

Digesting

When a MessageDigest object is created, it is already initialized and ready to receive data to be digested. The data is input with the update() methods. Once all the data has been entered through the update() methods, a digest() method is called to complete the hash computation. The digest() method will only work once for a given set of update() method calls. At any point during the life of the object, reset() can be called to reinitialize the MessageDigest.

Inheritance

```
public abstract class java.security.MessageDigest
    extends Object
        ⇑
    public class java.lang.Object
```

Constructors

```
protected MessageDigest(String algorithm)
```

A `MessageDigest` is created using the name of a specific algorithm. For a list of the standard algorithm names, see `security`.

Returned by

A `MessageDigest` object is returned from a call to `getInstance()`. They are also returned from calls to `DigestInputStream.getMessageDigest()` and `DigestOutputStream.getMessageDigest()`.

Methods

clone()

```
public Object clone()
        throws CloneNotSupportedException
```

Returns a clone of this object. This method will only work if the `Cloneable` interface has been implemented by the subclass.

digest()

```
public byte[] digest()
```

```
public byte[] digest(byte input[])
```

Completes any pending computations and returns the digest value. If an input array is specified, it will be used to update the data before the calculations begin. After this call, the `MessageDigest` will have been initialized and will be ready to receive new data for a new value.

engineDigest()

```
protected abstract byte[] engineDigest()
```

Completes the computations by performing final operations such as padding. Once the computation has been completed, the engine should be reset.

engineReset()

```
protected abstract void engineReset()
```

Resets the digest engine. Any intermediate calculations are discarded.

engineUpdate()

```
protected abstract void engineUpdate(byte input)
```

```
protected abstract void engineUpdate(byte input[],
            int offset,int length)
```

Updates the calculation by supplying it with more data. If an array is specified, `length` bytes will be used beginning at `input[offset]`.

getAlgorithm()

```
public final String getAlgorithm()
```

Returns the name of the algorithm.

getInstance()

```
public static MessageDigest getInstance(String algorithm)
    throws NoSuchAlgorithmException
```

```
public static MessageDigest getInstance(String algorithm,
        String provider)
    throws NoSuchAlgorithmException
    throws NoSuchProviderException
```

Creates a new `MessageDigest` object for the specified algorithm. A `NoSuchAlgorithmException` will be thrown if the algorithm is unknown, or if there is no subclass of `MessageDigest` available for the specified algorithm. A `NoSuchProviderException` will be thrown if the specified provider is unknown.

isEqual()

```
public static boolean isEqual(byte digesta[],byte digestb[])
```

Compares two digests and returns `true` if `digesta` is identical to `digestb`.

reset()

```
public void reset()
```

Resets the digest. It will be initialized and readied to accept input data.

toString()

```
public String toString()
```

Returns a string representation of this object.

update()

```
public void update(byte input)
```

```
public void update(byte input[])
```

```
public void update(byte input[],int offset,int length)
```

Inputs one or more bytes of data. If the `input` array is specified with `offset` and `length`, `length` bytes beginning with `input[offset]` will be used for the calculation.

 For examples of generating `MessageDigest` values, see **DigestInputStream** and **DigestOutputStream**. For a list of the standard algorithm names, see **security**.

MessageFormat

class java.text.MessageFormat

This class provides the capability to construct textual messages in a language-neutral way. Its primary purpose is to construct messages to be displayed on the screen for end users. It operates from a formatting string—a template, if you will—and converts data from objects into strings and fits them into the format of the template. The template string not only specifies the placement of each inserted string, but it can also specify the format used in converting the variable into a string.

Locale

There is no actual locale work done by an object of this class. The only job performed by this class is stringing together the output from other objects. These other objects could be using locale information to construct their strings.

The pattern string

The template that is used to create the message is a string of characters with some special formatting instructions embedded in it. Each embedded formatting instruction is set off from the body of the string by being enclosed in braces. To actually construct a message string, the `format()` method is called with an array of objects to be converted to character strings and inserted in the string. The formatting instructions in the pattern specify exactly how. For example, an occurrence of

```
{2,number}
```

means that that `object[2]` is to be formatted as a numeric string. A template string with this embedded in it would look like this:

```
"It happened {2,number} times."
```

and if `Object[2]` is, say, an `Integer` object containing the value 372, the formatted string would look like this:

```
"It happened 372 times."
```

They syntax of the embedded patterns

This is a BNF-like representation of the syntax of the embedded formatting element. As you can see, each formatting command consists of an argument (which is the index specifying which object to use) optionally followed by one or more comma-separated descriptive names. The object can be interpreted as a date, a time, a number, or a choice. For details on choice, see `ChoiceFormat`. The date and time formats can be further refined as being short, medium, long, full, or having a formatting pattern defined. Numbers can be formatted as currency, percent, integer, or having a special number format defined for them:

```
messageFormatElement := argument { "," elementFormat }
    elementFormat := "time" { "," datetimeStyle }
                   | "date" { "," datetimeStyle }
                   | "number" { "," numberStyle }
                   | "choice" { "," choiceStyle }
    datetimeStyle := "short"
                   | "medium"
                   | "long"
                   | "full"
                   | dateFormatPattern
    numberStyle := "currency"
                 | "percent"
                 | "integer"
                 | numberFormatPattern
    choiceStyle := choiceFormatPattern
```

More rules about pattern strings

◆ If the format definition consists only of the object index, as in
  { 3 }, then the object must be `String` and it is simply inserted.

◆ If `date`, `time`, or `number` has no further refinement, such as `short` or
  `medium`, a reasonable default is used.

◆ A curly brace can be included in a pattern by being surrounded by
  single quotes, as in `'{'` and `'}'`. The single quotes will be removed
  in the final string.

◆ A single quote can be included by being typed as a pair of single
  quotes, `''`. One of the single quotes will be removed in the final string.

Date format pattern and number format pattern

During formatting, a `MessageFormat` will call on other classes in the `java.text` package
to do some of the specific work. The details of date and number formatting are to be found
in the descriptions of `ChoiceFormat`, `DateFormat`, `DecimalFormat`, `NumberFormat`,
and `SimpleDateFormat`.

Inheritance

```
public class java.text.MessageFormat
    extends Format
        ⇑
    public class java.text.Format
        implements Serializable
        implements Cloneable
        extends Object
```

⇑

```
public class java.lang.Object
```

Constructors

```
public MessageFormat(String pattern)
```

A MessageFormat object is constructed by supplying it the pattern from which messages are to be constructed. The pattern is based on the syntax described above.

Methods

applyPattern()

```
public void applyPattern(String newPattern)
```

Replaces the existing pattern with a new one.

clone()

```
public Object clone()
```

Creates a duplicate of this object.

equals()

```
public boolean equals(Object object)
```

Returns true if object is a MessageFormat with the same pattern as this one.

format()

```
public final StringBuffer format(Object source,
          StringBuffer result,FieldPosition ignore)
```

```
public final StringBuffer format(Object source[],
          StringBuffer result,FieldPosition ignore)
```

```
public static String format(String pattern,Object arguments[])
```

Returns a formatted message.

If source is not an array, the single source object is used to construct a string that is appended to the result and returned.

The source is the array of objects to be inserted into the internally defined pattern. The string resulting from inserting the objects into the pattern is appended to result, and result is returned. The FieldPosition is unused.

The static form of this method is a convenience method that can be used without the necessity of creating a MessageFormat object. The pattern is used to create a String by inserting arguments into it.

If a source object is found to be missing or is of the wrong type for the format specification, a `ParseException` is thrown.

getFormats()

```
public Format[] getFormats()
```

Returns the array of formats that were set by `setFormats()`.

getLocale()

```
public Locale getLocale()
```

Gets the default `Locale`.

hashCode()

```
public int hashCode()
```

Returns the hashcode value for this object.

parse()

```
public Object[] parse(String source,ParsePosition position)
public Object[] parse(String source)
    throws ParseException
```

Reads the text of the `source`, beginning at `position`, and creates an array of objects by matching the string with the internal pattern definition.

This is not a dependable process—there are many reasons this method could fail. It will fail if something is in the source that is not in the pattern. If the process of formatting an object into the string allowed some data to be lost, it cannot be fully recovered. This method does not handle recursion. The sequence of characters could be ambiguous because of the juxtaposition with other items in the string.

parseObject()

```
public Object parseObject(String source,ParsePosition position)
```

Reads the `source` string and converts the data into an object. The `position` argument contains the index into the `source` of the first character to be read. On return, `position` is set to next character after the last one used. If an error occurs, `position` is unchanged. Leading white space is skipped, but the `position` will be set to the beginning of any trailing white space. This method does not handle recursion.

setFormat()

```
public void setFormat(int variable,Format newFormat)
```

Sets formats individually to use on parameters.

setFormats()

```
public void setFormats(Format newFormats[])
```

Sets the formats to use on parameters.

setLocale()

```
public void setLocale(Locale locale)
```

Specifies the locale to be used in converting objects to strings.

toPattern()

```
public String toPattern()
```

Returns the pattern string.

Example 1

This example uses the `format()` method to generate a string from a list of arguments and a format template:

```
import java.util.*;
import java.text.*;
public class ShootingSchedule {
    public static void main(String[] arg) {
        Object arguments[] = {
            new Date(),
            new Integer(34),
            "the greenhouse location"
        };
        String format =
            "On {0,date} at {0,time} we will be shooting"
+
            " scene {1} at {2}.";
        System.out.println(
            MessageFormat.format(format,arguments));
    }
}
```

This example shows how the indexes inside the format string are used to address the individual arguments, and how the modifiers are used to control the type of formatting. Output from this example looks like this:

```
On 28-Jul-97 at 9:01:34 AM we will be shooting
          scene 34 at the greenhouse location.
```

Example 2

This is an example of using a choice format:

```
import java.util.*;
import java.text.*;
public class HamburgerLoan {
    public static void main(String[] arg) {
        Object arguments[]  = {
            new Integer(2)
        };
        String format =
            "I will gladly pay you on " +
            "{0,choice,0#Sunday|1#Monday|2#Tuesday}" +
            " if you buy me a hamburger today.";
        System.out.println(
            MessageFormat.format(format,arguments));
    }
}
```

The entire selectable list is included in the format string. The leading zero is the index of the value into the `arguments` array (in this case, there is only one member of the array). The strings that are to be printed from the integer values are listed as number/string pairs. The output looks like this:

```
I will gladly pay you on Tuesday if you buy me a hamburger today.
```

 For the ability to format strings from specific data types, see **ChoiceFormat**, **DateFormat**, **DecimalFormat**, **NumberFormat**, and **SimpleDateFormat**.

method

Almost all executable code in a Java program is found inside methods (there is the single exception of a `static` initializer block). A *method* is defined inside a class — it has a name, a return value, and a list of arguments. Two methods with the same name and the same parameter types in the same order are said to have the same *signature*.

Simple overload

This is a simple method overload. The two methods have the same name and return type, but they have a different argument — they are different methods because they have different signatures:

```
public class Signature1 {
    double frammis(int framValue) {
```

```
            return((double)framValue);
        }
        double frammis(float framValue) {
            return((double)framValue);
        }
    }
```

Criss-cross overload

This is a valid overload. The two methods have the same names, but they have different
return values. However, because the signatures are different (one takes an int argument
and the other takes a float), there is no conflict. The compiler will always be able to tell
which is which by comparing the arguments passed to them:

```
public class Signature2 {
    double frammis(int framValue) {
        return((double)framValue);
    }
    int frammis(float framValue) {
        return((int)framValue);
    }
}
```

Erroneous overload

This class will not compile. The two methods have different signatures, but the names are
the same while the return values are different:

```
public class Signature3 {
    double frammis(int framValue) {
        return((double)framValue);
    }
    int frammis(int framValue) { // ** Error **
        return(framValue);
    }
}
```

If the compiler allowed this, it would be an ambiguous situation. There is no way for the
compiler to tell which of the two methods to call.

Simple override

If a method in a subclass has the same signature as one in the superclass, the one in the
superclass is said to be *overridden*. A call to the method will result in *only* the one in the subclass being called. This example will always print "Subclass":

```
public class Signature4 {
    public static void main(String[] arg) {
        ExtendSignature4 sig = new ExtendSignature4();
```

```
            System.out.println(sig.frammis(44));
        }
        String frammis(int framValue) {
            return("Superclass");
        }
    }
    class ExtendSignature4 extends Signature4 {
        String frammis(int framValue) {
            return("Subclass");
        }
    }
```

Failure to override

This example will not compile. The argument types are close—but they do not match. Situations arise in which a method call would be ambiguous, so an error is issued from the compiler:

```
public class Signature5 {
    public static void main(String[] arg) {
        ExtendSignature5 sig = new ExtendSignature5();
        System.out.println(sig.frammis(44));
    }
    String frammis(int framValue) {
        return("Superclass");
    }
}
class ExtendSignature5 extends Signature5 {
    String frammis(double framValue) {   // **Error**
        return("Subclass");
    }
}
```

Another failure to override

This example will not compile. The subclass attempts to override a method in the superclass with a change in the type of the return value:

```
public class Signature6 {
    public static void main(String[] arg) {
        ExtendSignature6 sig = new ExtendSignature6();
        System.out.println(sig.frammis(44));
    }
    int frammis(int framValue) {
        return(framValue);
    }
```

```
    }
class ExtendSignature6 extends Signature6 {
    double frammis(int framValue) {   // **Error**
        return((double)framValue);
    }
}
```

Return to the right

The declaration of a method requires a return value be specified. It can also have one or more modifiers (such as static, public, or protected). The return value must be adjacent to the method name. For example:

```
public int final someMethod() { ...
```

will not compile. The return type must be on the right, like either one of these:

```
public final int someMethod() { ...
final public int someMethod() { ...
```

Passing constants as arguments

All the normal conversion rules apply to variables being passed as arguments, but there is a slight variation when it comes to constants. Because of overloaded methods and possible ambiguities that could arise, constant values are not automatically narrowed. Take this example:

```
public class ConstantNarrowing {
    public static void main(String[] arg) {
        nar(44);
    }

    static void nar(short value) {
        System.out.println("The int value is " + value);
    }
}
```

This program will not compile. Even though the constant value would be perfectly valid as a short, it defaults to being an int, and there is no method that exactly matches. To make the program compile, simply cast the constant at the method call, like this:

```
nar((short)44);
```

Array arguments have moveable brackets

The brackets defining an argument as an array can be placed with the name of the argument, or with its type. Both of these are valid:

```
public static void main(String[] arg) { ...
public static void main(String arg[]) { ...
```

For information on automatic argument conversion, see **conversion**. The other place that executable statements can be written in Java is in a **static initializer**.

Method

class java.lang.reflect.Method

An object of this class provides information about—and access to—a single method within a class or an interface. That is, it *reflects* the method. The reflected method can be a class method (declared as static) or an instance method. It can even be an abstract method.

Inheritance

```
public final class java.lang.reflect.Method
    implements Member
    extends Object
        ⇑
    public class java.lang.Object
```

Constructors

Returned by

Arrays of objects of this class can be acquired by calls to Class.getMethods(), Class.getMethod(), Class.getDeclaredMethods(), and Class.getDeclaredMethod().

> Objects of this class are returned from
> Class.getDeclaredMethod
> Class.getMethod
> EventSetDescriptor.getAddListenerMethod
> EventSetDescriptor.getRemoveListenerMethod
> IndexedPropertyDescriptor.getIndexedReadMethod
> IndexedPropertyDescriptor.getIndexedWriteMethod
> MethodDescriptor.getMethod
> PropertyDescriptor.getReadMethod
> PropertyDescriptor.getWriteMethod

Methods

equals()

```
public boolean equals(Object object)
```

Returns `true` if `object` is a `Method` object reflecting the same method as this `Method` object.

getDeclaringClass()

```
public Class getDeclaringClass()
```

Returns the `Class` object that represents the class or interface that declares the method reflected by this `Method` object.

getExceptionTypes()

```
public Class[] getExceptionTypes()
```

Returns an array of `Class` objects that represent the types of checked exceptions that can be thrown by the reflected method. If there are none, a zero-length array is returned.

getModifiers()

```
public int getModifiers()
```

Returns the modifiers of the reflected method. The return value is in a format that can be decoded by a `Modifier` object.

getName()

```
public String getName()
```

Return the name of the reflected method.

getParameterTypes()

```
public Class[] getParameterTypes()
```

Returns an ordered array of `Class` objects that represents each of the argument types of the reflected method. If there are no arguments, a zero-length array is returned.

getReturnType()

```
public Class getReturnType()
```

Return a `Class` object that represents the return type of the reflected method.

hashCode()

```
public int hashCode()
```

Returns the hashcode of this object. The value of the hashcode is made up from the name of the method and the name of its declaring class.

invoke()

```
public Object invoke(Object object,Object args[])
    throws IllegalAccessException
```

```
throws IllegalArgumentException
throws InvocationTargetException
```

Calls the reflected method. The method of the `object` argument is called, and it is passed the `args` as arguments. If an argument is a primitive type, it should be supplied as a wrapper of a type that can be widened to the primitive type. The return value is that from the method—in a wrapper if the return value is a primitive type. (The one exception is that if the method's return type is `void`, `invoke()` returns `null`). If the method is `static`, the `object` argument is not used and may be `null`.

A `NullPointerException` is thrown if the method is nonstatic and `object` is null. An `IllegalArgumentException` is thrown if `object` is of the wrong class or interface, an argument supplied as a wrapper cannot be widened to the appropriate primitive type, or there is a mismatch in the number of arguments required. An `IllegalAccessException` is thrown if the method is inaccessible.

Instance methods are invoked using dynamic lookup—that is, overriding will occur based on the runtime types of the arguments.

If the reflected method throws an exception (which could be one that is not listed here since the method defines its own), the exception is wrapped in an `InvocationTargetException` and is thrown to the caller of `invoke()`.

toString()

```
public String toString()
```

Returns a string that describes the reflected method. The format is similar to the Java source-code form used to declare the method. The string contains the modifiers, followed by the return type, and the class declaring the method separated by a period from the method name. This is all followed by a list of the argument types in a comma-separated list surrounded by parentheses. This is followed by the list of check exceptions.

Example

This example creates an object and lists all of its methods:

```
import java.lang.reflect.*;
public class MethodReflection {
    public static void main(String[] arg) {
        MethodReflection mr = new MethodReflection();
        Class mrClass = mr.getClass();
        Method[] method = mrClass.getMethods();
        for(int i=0; i<method.length; i++)
            System.out.println(method[i]);
    }
    public final double sumOf(int x,double j) {
        return((double)x + j);
    }
    public final double diffOf(int x,double j) {
```

```
        return((double)x - j);
    }
}
```

The list of methods not only includes those of this class, but it also includes all the methods inherited from other classes. Here is the output:

```
public static void
MethodReflection.main(java.lang.String[])
public final native java.lang.Class
java.lang.Object.getClass()
public native int java.lang.Object.hashCode()
public boolean java.lang.Object.equals(java.lang.Object)
public java.lang.String java.lang.Object.toString()
public final native void java.lang.Object.notify()
public final native void java.lang.Object.notifyAll()
public final native void java.lang.Object.wait(long)
throws java.lang.InterruptedException
public final void java.lang.Object.wait(long,int) throws
java.lang.InterruptedException
public final void java.lang.Object.wait() throws
java.lang.InterruptedException
public final double MethodReflection.sumOf(int,double)
public final double MethodReflection.diffOf(int,double)
```

MethodDescriptor

class java.beans.MethodDescriptor

This class is used to hold the description of a method in a bean. The method described by an object of this class is available for external access.

Inheritance

```
public class java.beans.MethodDescriptor
    extends FeatureDescriptor
        ⇑
    public class java.beans.FeatureDescriptor
        extends Object
            ⇑
        public class java.lang.Object
```

Constructors

```
public MethodDescriptor(Method method)

public MethodDescriptor(Method method,
        ParameterDescriptor parameterDescriptors[])
```

The `Method` object contains the information about the method. The `ParameterDescriptor` array can be supplied to include descriptive information about each parameter.

Returned by

Arrays of `MethodDescriptor` objects are returned from `BeanInfo.getMethodDescriptors`, `EventSetDescriptor.getListenerMethodDescriptors`, and `SimpleBeanInfo.getMethodDescriptors`.

Methods

getMethod()

```
public Method getMethod()
```

Returns the `Method` object that contains all the low-level information.

getParameterDescriptors()

```
public ParameterDescriptor[] getParameterDescriptors()
```

Returns the array that contains descriptive information for each of the parameters. If there are no descriptions, `null` is returned.

methods

 See Appendix A for a complete list of methods.

microJava

 See **JavaChip**.

millisecond

A millisecond is one one-thousandth of a second. It is one thousand microseconds. Java keeps its internal time as a `long` that is the number of milliseconds since midnight, January 1, 1970.

For a wrapper class that handles date and time, see **Date.**

minus

− −=

The operators − and −= are the Java arithmetic subtraction operators. Also, the − operator can be used as the unary minus to negate a value. These operators are only valid for the Java primitive data types. Mixed-mode arithmetic is supported—the narrower of the two types is widened before the operation is performed.

The − operator performs subtraction but does not modify the operands. The −= operator performs subtraction and places the results in the left operand. These two statements are equivalent:

```
a = a - b;
a -= b;
```

Integer overflow

Integer subtraction can possibly result in a number that can't be represented in the type receiving the result. The overflow will be lost without notice. For example, these four lines of code:

```
int ivalue = 0x80000005;
System.out.println(ivalue);
ivalue -= 200;
System.out.println(ivalue);
```

will print these two values:

```
-2147483643
2147483453
```

The negative value was so large that the subtraction caused it to cycle back around to being a positive value.

For information on possible values of the data types, see **Byte, Character, Integer, Short, Long, Float,** and **Double.**

MissingResourceException

class java.util.MissingResourceException

This exception is thrown whenever an expected resource is missing.

Inheritance

```
public class java.util.MissingResourceException
    extends RuntimeException
              ⇑
    public class java.lang.RuntimeException
        extends Exception
              ⇑
        public class java.lang.Exception
            extends Throwable
              ⇑
            public class java.lang.Throwable
                implements Serializable
                extends Object
                  ⇑
                public class java.lang.Object
```

Constructors

MissingResourceException()

```
public MissingResourceException(String message,
        String classname,String key)
```

There are three pieces of information contained in a `MissingResourceException`. The `message` is the text of a detailed description of the missing resource. The `classname` is the name of the class of the missing resource. The `key` is the key value of the missing resource.

Methods

getClassName()

```
public String getClassName()
```

This will return the name of the class—the one that was supplied as part of the constructor.

getKey()

```
public String getKey()
```

This will return the key value of the resource. The key value is the one supplied to the constructor.

modifier

There are modifiers that can be used in declarations of classes, methods, and variables. Table M-1 is a list of the modifiers and a brief description of what each does.

Table M-1   The Java modifiers

Modifier	Description
abstract	An abstract class is one that cannot be instantiated. All interfaces are abstract. An abstract method is empty—it does not have a body of executable statements.
final	A final class cannot be subclassed. A final method cannot be overridden. A final variable is a constant.
native	A native method is one that is written in a language other than Java.
static	A static method is a class method—it cannot access data from the individual objects of the class. A static variable only has one instance—it is not duplicated in the individual objects.
synchronized	A synchronized method cannot be simultaneously executed by more than one thread.
transient	A transient variable is not part of the persistent information in an object and will not be serialized.
volatile	A volatile variable is one that can have its value changed by more than one thread.

 For more information on the modifiers, see the individual listings for each one.

Modifier

class java.lang.reflect.Modifier

This class can be used to decode the binary format of the access modifier definitions.

Inheritance

```
public class java.lang.reflect.Modifier
       extends Object
            ⇑
       public class java.lang.Object
```

Variables and constants

ABSTRACT

```
public final static int ABSTRACT
```

A constant representing the abstract modifier.

FINAL

```
public final static int FINAL
```

A constant representing the final modifier.

INTERFACE

```
public final static int INTERFACE
```

A constant representing the interface modifier.

NATIVE

```
public final static int NATIVE
```

A constant representing the native modifier.

PRIVATE

```
public final static int PRIVATE
```

A constant representing the private modifier.

PROTECTED

```
public final static int PROTECTED
```

A constant representing the protected modifier.

PUBLIC

```
public final static int PUBLIC
```

A constant representing the public modifier.

STATIC

```
public final static int STATIC
```

A constant representing the static modifier.

SYNCHRONIZED

```
public final static int SYNCHRONIZED
```

A constant representing the synchronized modifier.

TRANSIENT

```
public final static int TRANSIENT
```

A constant representing the transient modifier.

VOLATILE

```
public final static int VOLATILE
```

A constant representing the volatile modifier.

Constructors

```
public Modifier()
```

Methods

isAbstract()

```
public static boolean isAbstract(int mod)
```

Returns true if mod includes the abstract modifier.

isFinal()

```
public static boolean isFinal(int mod)
```

Returns true if mod includes the final modifier.

isInterface()

```
public static boolean isInterface(int mod)
```

Returns true if mod includes the interface modifier.

isNative()

```
public static boolean isNative(int mod)
```

Returns true if mod includes the native modifier.

isPrivate()

```
public static boolean isPrivate(int mod)
```

Returns true if mod includes the private modifier.

isProtected()

```
public static boolean isProtected(int mod)
```

Returns true if mod includes the protected modifier.

isPublic()

```
public static boolean isPublic(int mod)
```

Returns `true` if mod includes the `public` modifier.

isStatic()

```
public static boolean isStatic(int mod)
```

Returns `true` if mod includes the `static` modifier.

isSynchronized()

```
public static boolean isSynchronized(int mod)
```

Returns `true` if mod includes the `synchronized` modifier.

isTransient()

```
public static boolean isTransient(int mod)
```

Returns `true` if mod includes the `transient` modifier.

isVolatile()

```
public static boolean isVolatile(int mod)
```

Returns `true` if mod includes the `volatile` modifier.

toString()

```
public static String toString(int mod)
```

Returns a string describing the modifier flags in mod. The modifier names are in canonical order.

 For a description of the modifiers, see **modifier**. To find the set of modifiers, see **Class.getModifiers()** and **Member.getModifiers()**. To get the modifiers for a constructor, see **Constructor**.

monitor

If two separate threads access the same resource, they need to maintain a level of synchronization. That is, each one needs to *monitor* the other's use of the resource. In Java, there is no special class used for monitoring—synchronization is maintained by using methods available to every object.

 See the `wait()` and `notify()` methods of **Object**. Also see **synchronize**.

mouse

 For mouse cursors, see **Cursor**. For examples of handling mouse events, see **MouseListener** and **MouseMotionListener**.

MouseAdapter

class java.awt.event.MouseAdapter

This class implements the methods of the `MouseListener` interface with empty stubs. This class was designed to be used as a convenient way to construct a mouse listener by implementing only the methods of interest to the application.

Inheritance

```
public abstract class java.awt.event.MouseAdapter
    implements MouseListener
    extends Object
        ⇑
    public class java.lang.Object
```

Constructors

```
public MouseAdapter()
```

Methods

mouseClicked()

```
public void mouseClicked(MouseEvent e)
```

mouseEntered()

```
public void mouseEntered(MouseEvent e)
```

mouseExited()

```
public void mouseExited(MouseEvent e)
```

mousePressed()

```
public void mousePressed(MouseEvent e)
```

mouseReleased()

```
public void mouseReleased(MouseEvent e)
```

Example

This example displays an empty window and has an inner class that listens only for MOUSE_ENTERED events:

```java
import java.awt.*;
import java.awt.event.*;
public class EnterTheMouse extends Frame {
    public static void main(String[] arg) {
        new EnterTheMouse();
    }
    EnterTheMouse() {
        addMouseListener(new Entrance());
        setSize(100,100);
        show();
    }
    class Entrance extends MouseAdapter {
        public void mouseEntered(MouseEvent event) {
            System.out.println("IN: " + event.getPoint());
        }
    }
}
```

The class Entrance extends the MouseAdapter and overrides only the mouseEntered() method. The other methods are allowed to default to stubs. Here is some typical output:

```
IN: java.awt.Point[x=98,y=46]
IN: java.awt.Point[x=14,y=59]
IN: java.awt.Point[x=100,y=63]
IN: java.awt.Point[x=24,y=66]
IN: java.awt.Point[x=100,y=70]
IN: java.awt.Point[x=50,y=69]
IN: java.awt.Point[x=93,y=69]
IN: java.awt.Point[x=19,y=68]
```

Also see **MouseEvent, MouseListener, MouseMotionAdapter,** and **MouseMotionListener**.

MouseEvent

class java.awt.event.MouseEvent

A `MouseEvent` object contains information about mouse movement and button clicks.

Inheritance

```
public class java.awt.event.MouseEvent
    extends InputEvent
        ⇑
    public abstract class java.awt.event.InputEvent
        extends ComponentEvent
            ⇑
        public class java.awt.event.ComponentEvent
            extends AWTEvent
                ⇑
            public class java.awt.AWTEvent
                extends EventObject
                    ⇑
                public class java.util.EventObject
                    implements Serializable
                    extends Object
                        ⇑
                    public class java.lang.Object
```

Variables and constants
MOUSE_CLICKED

```
public static final int MOUSE_CLICKED
```

The ID of the event indicating that a mouse button has been pressed.

MOUSE_DRAGGED

```
public static final int MOUSE_DRAGGED
```

The ID of an event indicating that the mouse has been moved while a button was being held down.

MOUSE_ENTERED

```
public static final int MOUSE_ENTERED
```

The ID of an event indicating that the mouse pointer has entered the component window.

MOUSE_EXITED

```
public static final int MOUSE_EXITED
```

The ID of an event indicating that the mouse pointer has exited from the component window.

MOUSE_FIRST

```
public static final int MOUSE_FIRST
```

The smallest value possible of all the MouseEvent ID numbers.

MOUSE_LAST

```
public static final int MOUSE_LAST
```

The largest value possible of all the MouseEvent ID numbers.

MOUSE_MOVED

```
public static final int MOUSE_MOVED
```

The ID of an event indicating that the mouse pointer has been moved without a mouse button being held down.

MOUSE_PRESSED

```
public static final int MOUSE_PRESSED
```

The ID of an event indicating that a mouse button has been pressed.

MOUSE_RELEASED

```
public static final int MOUSE_RELEASED
```

The ID of an event indicating that a mouse button has been released.

Constructors

```
public MouseEvent(Component source,int id,long when,
        int modifiers,int x,int y,int clickCount,
        boolean popupTrigger)
```

The event is constructed to represent an occurrence on the source component. The id number is one of the event-type constants listed above. The value of when is the timestamp indicating the time the event occurred. The modifiers indicate which, if any, keyboard keys were being held down when the event occurred (see InputEvent for the modifier definitions). The values of x and y specify the mouse pointer location at the time of the event. The clickCount is used to indicate the number of times the button was pressed to generate the event. The value of popupTrigger is set to true if this event is the popup-trigger event for this platform.

Methods
getClickCount()
```
public int getClickCount()
```
Returns a count of the number of mouse clicks that caused this event.

getPoint()
```
public Point getPoint()
```
Returns the position of the mouse event within the component window.

getX()
```
public int getX()
```
Returns the x position of the mouse event—unless it has been translated, this is a count of the number of pixels from the left edge of the component.

getY()
```
public int getY()
```
Returns the y position of the mouse event—unless it has been translated, this is a count of the number of pixels from the top edge of the component.

isPopupTrigger()
```
public boolean isPopupTrigger()
```
Returns true if this mouse event was initiated by the popup-menu trigger event for this platform.

paramString()
```
public String paramString()
```
Returns debugging information. The return string describes the internal state and values of this object.

translatePoint()
```
public synchronized void translatePoint(int x,int y)
```
Translates the coordinate point of the event by the x and y amounts. These values are added to the x and y coordinate values of the event.

Also see **MouseAdapter**, **MouseListener**, **MouseMotionAdapter**, and **MouseMotionListener**.

MouseListener

interface java.awt.event.MouseListener

This is the interface implemented by classes wishing to receive mouse position and button events.

The other mouse

This interface does not handle all events from a mouse. The interface `MouseMotionListener` is capable of fielding events that track the details of mouse movement. There is an enormous amount of event traffic required for tracking every mouse movement, so it is for the sake of efficiency that the two mouse listeners were separated.

Implemented by

```
AWTEventMulticaster
MouseMotionAdapter
```

Inheritance

```
public interface java.awt.event.MouseListener
    extends EventListener
        ⇑
    public interface java.util.EventListener
```

Constructors

Returned by

Objects implementing this interface are returned from `AWTEventMulticaster.add()` and `AWTEventMulticaster.remove()`.

Methods

mouseClicked()

```
public abstract void mouseClicked(MouseEvent event)
```

This method is called whenever a mouse button is clicked. There is one of these following each pair of press and release events.

mouseEntered()

```
public abstract void mouseEntered(MouseEvent event)
```

This method is called whenever the mouse pointer enters the component.

mouseExited()

```
public abstract void mouseExited(MouseEvent event)
```

This method is called whenever the mouse pointer leaves the component.

mousePressed()

```
public abstract void mousePressed(MouseEvent event)
```

This method is called whenever a mouse button has been pressed.

mouseReleased()

```
public abstract void mouseReleased(MouseEvent event)
```

This method is called whenever a mouse button has been released.

Example

This is a simple application that displays an empty window and prints one line for each mouse event:

```
import java.awt.*;
import java.awt.event.*;
public class MouseTrap extends Frame
                implements MouseListener {
    public static void main(String[] arg) {
        new MouseTrap();
    }
    MouseTrap() {
        addMouseListener(this);
        setSize(100,100);
        show();
    }
    public void mouseClicked(MouseEvent event) {
        System.out.println("mouseClicked()");
    }
    public void mouseEntered(MouseEvent event) {
        System.out.println("mouseEntered()");
    }
    public void mouseExited(MouseEvent event) {
        System.out.println("mouseExited()");
    }
    public void mousePressed(MouseEvent event) {
```

```
            System.out.println("mousePressed()");
        }
        public void mouseReleased(MouseEvent event) {
            System.out.println("mouseReleased()");
        }
    }
```

 Also see **MouseAdapter**, **MouseEvent**, **MouseMotionAdapter**, and **MouseMotionListener**.

MouseMotionAdapter

class java.awt.event.MouseMotionAdapter

This class implements the methods of the MouseMotionListener interface with empty stubs. This class was designed to be used as a convenient way to construct a mouse motion listener by implementing only the methods of interest to the application.

Inheritance

```
public abstract class java.awt.event.MouseMotionAdapter
    implements MouseMotionListener
    extends Object
        ⇑
    public class java.lang.Object
```

Constructors

```
public MouseMotionAdapter()
```

Methods

mouseDragged()

```
public void mouseDragged(MouseEvent event)
```

mouseMoved()

```
public void mouseMoved(MouseEvent event)
```

Example

This example displays a blank window and tracks the mouse movements in it:

```
import java.awt.*;
import java.awt.event.*;
public class MoveTheMouse extends Frame {
    public static void main(String[] arg) {
        new MoveTheMouse();
    }
    MoveTheMouse() {
        addMouseMotionListener(new Motion());
        setSize(100,100);
        show();
    }
    class Motion extends MouseMotionAdapter {
        public void mouseMoved(MouseEvent event) {
            System.out.println(event.getPoint());
        }
    }
}
```

The inner class `Motion` extends the `MouseMotionAdapter` and overrides the `mouseMoved()` method to print the current position of the mouse pointer. The output looks like this.

```
java.awt.Point[x=68,y=61]
java.awt.Point[x=68,y=60]
java.awt.Point[x=115,y=48]
java.awt.Point[x=70,y=59]
```

 Also see **MouseAdapter, MouseEvent, MouseListener,** and **MouseMotionListener**.

MouseMotionListener

interface java.awt.event.MouseMotionListener

This is the interface implemented by classes wishing to receive mouse movement events.

The other mouse

This interface does not handle all the events from a mouse. The interface `MouseListener` is responsible for fielding events that track the details of a button and certain positioning.

There is an enormous amount of event traffic required for tracking every mouse movement, so it is for the sake of efficiency that these two were separated.

Implemented by

```
AWTEventMulticaster
MouseMotionAdapter
```

Inheritance

```
public interface java.awt.event.MouseMotionListener
    extends EventListener
        ⇑
    public interface java.util.EventListener
```

Constructors

Returned by

Objects implementing this interface are returned from the add() and remove() methods of AWTEventMulticaster.

Methods

mouseDragged()

```
public abstract void mouseDragged(MouseEvent event)
```

This method is called whenever the mouse pointer is moved to a new position in the component window while a mouse button is being held down. Once a dragging operation starts, the location of the mouse continues to be reported to the same component regardless of whether or not the mouse pointer remains inside the window. This continues until the mouse button is released.

mouseMoved()

```
public abstract void mouseMoved(MouseEvent event)
```

This method is called whenever the mouse pointer is moved to a new position in the component window without a mouse button being held down.

Example

This application implements both methods of the interface and prints the location of each event:

```
import java.awt.*;
```

```
import java.awt.event.*;
public class MouseMotionTrap extends Frame
            implements MouseMotionListener {
    public static void main(String[] arg) {
        new MouseMotionTrap();
    }
    MouseMotionTrap() {
        addMouseMotionListener(this);
        setSize(100,100);
        show();
    }
    public void mouseMoved(MouseEvent event) {
        System.out.println("Move: " + event.getPoint());
    }
    public void mouseDragged(MouseEvent event) {
        System.out.println("Drag: " + event.getPoint());
    }
}
```

Here is some typical output:

```
Move: java.awt.Point[x=51,y=44]
Move: java.awt.Point[x=48,y=42]
Move: java.awt.Point[x=45,y=41]
Move: java.awt.Point[x=16,y=33]
Move: java.awt.Point[x=42,y=38]
Move: java.awt.Point[x=16,y=34]
Move: java.awt.Point[x=17,y=34]
Drag: java.awt.Point[x=18,y=33]
Drag: java.awt.Point[x=19,y=32]
Drag: java.awt.Point[x=19,y=31]
Drag: java.awt.Point[x=18,y=31]
Drag: java.awt.Point[x=16,y=31]
Drag: java.awt.Point[x=11,y=30]
Drag: java.awt.Point[x=-30,y=26]
Drag: java.awt.Point[x=-55,y=23]
Drag: java.awt.Point[x=-74,y=20]
Drag: java.awt.Point[x=-76,y=20]
```

This shows the mouse being moved without the mouse pointer being held down until it reached the point (17,34), where the button was pressed and held. Mouse movement events stopped coming, and mouse drag events started. The mouse was then dragged off to the left of the window, causing the values for *x* to become negative.

Also see **MouseAdapter**, **MouseEvent**, **MouseListener**, and **MouseMotionAdapter**.

MulticastSocket

class java.net.MulticastSocket

This is a socket specially designed to operate with a multicast address.

All for one

There can be multiple recipients waiting for messages on the same multicasting address. A message sent to a specific port on a multicast address will be received by all hosts that have a process waiting at that address and port number.

A multicast address

A *multicast address,* also known as a class-D address, is any address in the range 224.0.0.1 through 239.255.255.255. A message is sent using one of these addresses and a previously agreed-upon port number.

A multicast message

A *multicast message* is a UDP message transmitted over a multicast address. A multicast message is UDP instead of TCP because TCP is designed for two-way communications. The transmitted message is assigned a time-to-live. It will be delivered to all recipients that are actively subscribed to the group in that period of time. The sender need not be subscribed as a recipient to be able to send messages—any process can send a message to a multicast group.

Time to live

Each message has a value in its header—a number called time-to-live—that determines how long attempts will be made to deliver the message to all the recipients. The time-to-live value is an 8-bit unsigned integer—the value must be in the range of 0 to 255. It actually is not a time. It is the number of hops the message will take from one host to another before the message dies.

Applets

Security precautions prevent applets from having access to multicast sockets.

Inheritance

```
public class java.net.MulticastSocket
    extends DatagramSocket
        ⇑
```

```
public class java.net.DatagramSocket
     extends Object
         ⇑
public class java.lang.Object
```

Constructors

```
public MulticastSocket()
     throws IOException
```

```
public MulticastSocket(int port)
     throws IOException
```

If the port number is specified, the multicast socket will be bound to the local port on creation.

Methods

getInterface()

```
public InetAddress getInterface()
     throws SocketException
```

Returns the multicast address.

getTTL()

```
public byte getTTL()
     throws IOException
```

Returns the default time-to-live value that will be assigned to the transmitted packets.

joinGroup()

```
public void joinGroup(InetAddress mcastaddr)
     throws IOException
```

Joins the multicast group using the address mcastaddr. An IOException is thrown if there is an error in joining, or if the address is not a multicast address.

leaveGroup()

```
public void leaveGroup(InetAddress mcastaddr)
     throws IOException
```

Leaves the multicast group with the address mcastaddr. An IOException is thrown if there is an error leaving the group, or if mcastaddr is not a multicast address.

send()

```
public synchronized void send(DatagramPacket p,byte ttl)
```

```
throws IOException
```

Sets `ttl` as the time-to-live value and sends the `DatagramPacket`. This method will assign a time-to-live for the one packet only—it does not change the default.

setInterface()

```
public void setInterface(InetAddress inf)
    throws SocketException
```

Sets the outgoing network interface for multicast packets on this socket to something other than the system default. This is useful for multihomed hosts.

setTTL()

```
public void setTTL(byte ttl)
    throws IOException
```

Sets a new default for the time-to-live value that will be attached to each outgoing message header.

Example

These code snippets show the sequence of events for joining a multicast group, sending a message, reading the responses, and leaving the group.

The group is joined by using the address "228.5.6.7" and port number 6789:

```
InetAddress group = InetAddress.getByName("228.5.6.7");
MulticastSocket s = new MulticastSocket(6789);
s.joinGroup(group);
```

A message can then be sent to the group:

```
byte[] msg = {'H', 'e', 'l', 'l', 'o'};
DatagramPacket hi = new DatagramPacket(msg, msg.length,
        group, 6789);
s.send(hi);
```

Any responses can be received:

```
byte[] buf = new byte[1000];
DatagramPacket recv = new DatagramPacket(buf,
        buf.length);
s.receive(recv);
```

On completion, the process can leave the group:

```
s.leaveGroup(group);
```

 Also see **Socket** and **InetAddress**.

multiply

* *=

The operators * and *= are the Java arithmetic multiplication operators. These operators are only valid for the Java primitive data types. Mixed-mode arithmetic is supported — the narrower type is widened before the operation is performed.

The * operator performs multiplication but does not modify the operands. The *= operator performs multiplication and places the results in the left operand. These two statements are equivalent:

```
a = a * b;
a *= b;
```

Integer multiplication

Integer multiplication will cause overflow if the resulting value is too large. No error is associated with this; the answer will simply be truncated.

Floating point multiplication

Floating-point multiplication will never throw an exception. The results, however, could be positive or negative infinity, or NaN.

For information on real numbers, see **floating point numbers**.

Naming

class java.rmi.Naming

This is the bootstrap mechanism for obtaining references to remote objects.

Addressing remote objects

The location of the remote objects is determined by using URL syntax with RMI as the protocol, like this:

```
rmi://host:port/name
```

host   Name of the registry
port   Port number of the registry
name   Name of the remote object

Inheritance

```
public final class java.rmi.Naming
    extends Object
        ⇑
    public class java.lang.Object
```

Methods

bind()

```
public static void bind(String name,Remote obj)
    throws AlreadyBoundException
    throws MalformedURLException
    throws UnknownHostException
    throws RemoteException
```

Binds the name to the specified remote object. The RemoteException is thrown if the registry could not be contacted. The AlreadyBoundException is thrown if the name is already bound.

list()

```
public static String[] list(String name)
    throws RemoteException
    throws MalformedURLException
    throws UnknownHostException
```

Returns an array of URLs in the registry. This is a snapshot of the names found in the registry. A RemoteException is thrown if the registry cannot be contacted.

lookup()

```
public static Remote lookup(String name)
    throws NotBoundException
    throws MalformedURLException
    throws UnknownHostException
    throws RemoteException
```

Returns the Remote object representing the URL specified by name. The RemoteException is thrown if the registry could not be contacted. The NotBoundException is thrown if the name cannot be found.

rebind()

```
public static void rebind(String name,Remote object)
    throws RemoteException
    throws MalformedURLException
    throws UnknownHostException
```

Rebinds the name to a new object. This will replace any binding that may already be assigned to the name. A RemoteException will be thrown if the remote registry cannot be contacted.

unbind()

```
public static void unbind(String name)
    throws RemoteException
    throws NotBoundException
    throws MalformedURLException
    throws UnknownHostException
```

Unbinds the name. A RemoteException is thrown if the registry cannot be contacted. A NotBoundException is thrown if the name is not currently bound.

Naming Convention

A naming convention has been adopted by the developers of the Java API. No naming convention is perfect, and no naming convention is perfectly followed.

There is no technical reason to follow this (or any other) naming convention—it simply acts as an aid in keeping things straight. Whenever a naming convention is followed, the code is usually easier to read once the patterns become familiar. Also, following a naming convention reduces the likelihood of inadvertently assigning two items the same name, which—in an object-oriented language with inheritance and overriding—can create some very subtle errors.

Package names

There is one reserved package name: `java`. It holds all of the API, and any class or interface not specified as belonging to a package defaults to becoming a member of the `java` package.

The naming convention for packages has been devised to include domain names of the Internet. If this naming convention is followed in the future, we will all have the advantage of being able to read the name of a package and determine its origin—and two packages from two different companies would never have identical names.

An Internet domain name, reading from left to right, moves from the narrow to the broad, as in

    elephant.animals.com

where `elephant` is one specific animal in the domain `animal` within the domain `com`. Package names run the other way—from the broad to the specific, as in

    java.awt.image

where we have the all-inclusive `java` package, which contains the subpackage `awt`, which contains the subpackage `image`. The proposed naming convention for third-party package developers is for the developer to reverse the order of the names, capitalize the domain name, and add the package name to it. For example, if the elephant of our example domain name developed a `peanut` package, its full name would be

    COM.animals.elephant.peanut

This name has a double advantage: It is easily identifiable (the name of package alone contains enough information to contact the vendor), and, since domain names are unique, there should never be a name conflict. Using an uppercase form of the domain name is intended to help reduce the possibility of confusion with other names. Whether vendors choose to follow this convention, only time will tell.

Class and interface names

The names of classes and interfaces begin with a capital letter, proceed with lowercase letters, and may or may not have other capital letters occurring in their middles. The interspersed capital letters are usually placed at the beginning of different words that were placed together to construct the name of the class or interface. Here are some examples from the API:

```
FontMetrics
Graphics
ThreadGroup
ContentHandlerFactory
```

A problem with this is that the capitalization can be inconsistent — it just depends on what the writer of the class or interface considers to be a different word. The class Checkbox could have been called CheckBox, and Hashtable could be been called HashTable.

Method names

The names of methods begin with lowercase letters but have capital letters sprinkled through them much like the names of classes and interfaces. Some examples of method names from the API are

```
appendText()
currentTimeMillis()
concat()
checkTopLevelWindow()
```

Certain types of methods occur again and again. Following specific naming conventions for these can make both code and documentation quicker and easier to read. Here is a list of names and method types:

get and set

Methods that assign and retrieve attributes or value-settings of some kind — things that can be thought of as variables — should begin with set or get. Some examples of these are

```
setDirectory()
getDirectory()
setSize();
getSize();
getApplet()
```

length

It is common to have a method return the length of the contents of a class (list, array, and so on). This method should simply be named length(), as in the File and String classes.

is

A method that tests for a condition and returns a boolean should have the prefix is. Examples of this are

```
isVisible()
isLowerCase()
isEnabled()
```

to

A method that converts a class—or the contents of a class—into another form should have the prefix to. Examples of these are

```
toString()
toLowerCase()
toByteArray()
```

Several other prefix names are used often in the API. Some of the more common ones are add, create, draw, read, remove, and write.

Variable names

The naming convention for variables is the same as that for methods. They should begin with a lowercase letter and have their internal words capitalized. It is considered bad form to have these declared as public, so there are not many of these directly accessible in the API. Here are some examples:

```
maximumValue
skipCountMinimumValue
hour
rightEndOfRedLine
```

Constant names

Any variable that has the final modifier in its declaration is a constant—it has an initial value that can never be changed. Constants should be defined in all uppercase letters with the internal words separated by underscore characters. Some examples:

```
MAX_VALUE
PI
MINIMUM_HORIZONTAL_EXTENT
```

Normally, constants should be defined with more than three characters so as not to conflict with the domain name—style package names.

Local variable and parameter names

Because these names are local to the method, they can be made up of simple lowercase acronyms and abbreviations. For example, reference to the FontMetrics class could be named fm—or the coordinates of a point could be named simply x and y. It is not uncommon to use the same naming convention that is used for variables declared outside a method—begin with a lowercase letter and sprinkle one or more capital letters through the name, like maxSize or upperLeftPixel.

For more on the names of packages, see **package**.

NaN

This is the IEEE 754 floating-point acronym for "Not a Number".

For details, see **float** or **double**.

narrowing

For the primitive types, see **conversion**. For casting an object to one of its ancestors, see **reference**.

native

keyword

Used as a modifier on the definition of a method to inform the compiler that the method body is implemented in some language other than Java.

For an example of writing a native method in C, see **JNI**.

native2ascii

utility

This program will convert native-encoded text to ASCII text. Native text is text that contains non-Unicode non-ASCII characters. The ASCII text output from native2ascii encodes Unicode characters in the form \u*XXXX*, where *XXXX* is the four-digit hexadecimal value of a Unicode character. The Java compiler, and the other Java utility programs, can only process text in Latin-1 and/or Unicode-encoded characters.

Synopsis

```
native2ascii [options] [inputfile [outputfile]]
```

options
-reverse

Perform the reverse action of converting an ASCII file with embedded Unicode into text with native-encoded characters.

-encoding <name>

Specify the name of the native encoding to be used for the conversion. If this is not specified, the value of the system property `file.encoding` will be used. Table N-1 is a list of known encoding names.

Table N-1   Native Encoding Names Known to `native2ascii`

Name	Description
8859_1	ISO Latin-1
8859_2	ISO Latin 2
8859_3	ISO Latin-3
8859_5	ISO Latin/Cyrillic
8859_6	ISO Latin/Arabic
8859_7	ISO Latin/Greek 8859_8 ISO Latin/Hebrew
8859_9	ISO Latin-5
Cp1250	Windows Eastern Europe / Latin-2
Cp1251	Windows Cyrillic
Cp1252	Windows Western Europe / Latin-1
Cp1253	Windows Greek
Cp1254	Windows Turkish
Cp1255	Windows Hebrew
Cp1256	Windows Arabic
Cp1257	Windows Baltic
Cp1258	Windows Vietnamese
Cp437	PC Original
Cp737	PC Greek
Cp775	PC Baltic
Cp850	PC Latin-1
Cp852	PC Latin-2
Cp855	PC Cyrillic
Cp857	PC Turkish
Cp860	PC Portuguese

continued

Table N-1 *continued*

Name	Description
Cp861	PC Icelandic
Cp862	PC Hebrew
Cp863	PC Canadian French
Cp864	PC Arabic
Cp865	PC Nordic
Cp866	PC Russian
Cp869	PC Modern Greek
Cp874	Windows Thai
EUCJIS	Japanese EUC
JIS	JIS
MacArabic	Macintosh Arabic
MacCentralEurope	Macintosh Central Europe
Macintosh	Latin-2
MacCroatian	Macintosh Croatian
MacCyrillic	Macintosh Cyrillic
MacDingbat	Macintosh Dingbat
MacGreek	Macintosh Greek
MacHebrew	Macintosh Hebrew
MacIceland	Macintosh Icelandic
MacRoman	Macintosh Roman
MacRomania	Macintosh Romanian
MacSymbol	Macintosh Symbol
MacThai	Macintosh Thai
MacTurkish	Macintosh Turkish
MacUkraine	Macintosh Ukrainian
SJIS	PC and Windows Japanese
UTF8	Standard UTF-8

inputfile
If the input file is omitted, the input will come from `System.in`.

outputfile
If the output file is omitted, the output will go to `System.out`.

 For more information on the Unicode character set, see **Unicode**.

NegativeArraySizeException

class java.lang.NegativeArraySizeException

This exception is thrown if an attempt is made to create an array with a negative size.

Inheritance

```
public class java.lang.NegativeArraySizeException
    extends RuntimeException
        ⇑
    public class java.lang.RuntimeException
        extends Exception
            ⇑
        public class java.lang.Exception
            extends Throwable
                ⇑
            public class java.lang.Throwable
                implements Serializable
                extends Object
                    ⇑
                public class java.lang.Object
```

Constructors

```
public NegativeArraySizeException()
public NegativeArraySizeException(String message)
```

If the `message` string is supplied, it is used as a detailed message describing this particular exception.

net

package java.net

This package contains the classes used for Internet communications.

Interfaces

```
ContentHandlerFactory
FileNameMap
SocketImplFactory
URLStreamHandlerFactory
```

Classes

```
ContentHandler
DatagramPacket
DatagramSocket
DatagramSocketImpl
HttpURLConnection
InetAddress
MulticastSocket
ServerSocket
Socket
SocketImpl
URL
URLConnection
URLEncoder
URLStreamHandler
```

Exceptions

```
BindException
ConnectException
MalformedURLException
NoRouteToHostException
ProtocolException
SocketException
UnknownHostException
UnknownServiceException
```

new

keyword

An object is created from its class definition by using the keyword new. Using new causes RAM to be dynamically allocated and a constructor called to initialize the object. The new keyword returns a reference to the object it creates.

An object from a class

Every class has at least one constructor. If there is more than one constructor, they are differentiated by their arguments. It is the name of the constructor that is specified as the argument to new, and the constructor always has the same name as the class and includes a pair of parentheses enclosing the arguments. Here are two ways to create a String object using new:

```
new String();
new String("Contents");
```

The first form uses the default constructor. The default constructor is the one with no arguments. The second form uses a string as its argument. A class may or may not have a default constructor. In fact, it is possible for a class to have no public constructor at all, thus preventing new from instantiating an object.

An object from an array

The new keyword is used to construct instances of arrays. For example:

```
int position[] = new int[30];
```

This creates an array capable of containing 30 int values. What is returned from new is the reference to an array object that holds the actual int values. This is not limited to the primitive data types—it is possible to create arrays from any class. For example:

```
String str[] = new String[10];
```

This example does not actually create String objects. It creates an array object that contains 10 references to String objects (that do not exist), and it returns a single reference to the array. The variable str holds that single reference.

 For more on the creations of arrays, see **array**.

NotActiveException

class java.io.NotActiveException

This exception is thrown to indicate that serialization or deserialization is not active.

Inheritance

```
public class java.io.NotActiveException
    extends ObjectStreamException
        ⇑
    public class java.io.ObjectStreamException
        extends IOException
            ⇑
        public class java.io.IOException
            extends Exception
                ⇑
            public class java.lang.Exception
                extends Throwable
                    ⇑
                public class java.lang.Throwable
                    implements Serializable
```

```
                                     extends Object
                                          ⇑
                            public class java.lang.Object
```

Constructors

```
            public NotActiveException()
            public NotActiveException(String message)
```

If the `message` string is supplied, it is used as a detailed message describing this particular exception.

NoClassDefFoundError

class java.lang.NoClassDefFoundError

This error will be thrown if an attempt is made (during the instantiation of an object) to load a class and the definition of it cannot be found. It existed when the class was compiled, but it can no longer be found.

Inheritance

```
            public class java.lang.NoClassDefFoundError
                extends LinkageError
                      ⇑
                public class java.lang.LinkageError
                    extends Error
                          ⇑
                    public class java.lang.Error
                        extends Throwable
                              ⇑
                        public class java.lang.Throwable
                            implements Serializable
                            extends Object
                                  ⇑
                            public class java.lang.Object
```

Constructors

```
            public NoClassDefFoundError()
            public NoClassDefFoundError(String message)
```

If the `message` string is supplied, it is used as a detailed message describing this particular exception.

NoRouteToHostException

class java.net.NoRouteToHostException

> This exception will be thrown to indicate an error in attempting to connect a socket to a remote address and port. Normally, this exception being thrown will indicate that the host is blocked by a firewall or that some intermediate router is down.

Inheritance

```
public class NoRouteToHostException
    extends SocketException
        ⇑
    public class java.net.SocketException
        extends IOException
            ⇑
        public class java.io.IOException
            extends Exception
                ⇑
            public class java.lang.Exception
                extends Throwable
                    ⇑
                public class java.lang.Throwable
                    implements Serializable
                    extends Object
                        ⇑
                    public class java.lang.Object
```

Constructors

```
public NoRouteToHostException()
public NoRouteToHostException(String message)
```

> If the message string is supplied, it is used as a detailed message describing this particular exception.

NoSuchElementException

class java.util.NoSuchElementException

> This exception is thrown when an attempt is made to read from an empty Enumeration.

Inheritance

```
public class java.util.NoSuchElementException
    extends RuntimeException
        ⇑
    public class java.lang.RuntimeException
        extends Exception
            ⇑
        public class java.lang.Exception
            extends Throwable
                ⇑
            public class java.lang.Throwable
                implements Serializable
                extends Object
                    ⇑
                public class java.lang.Object
```

Constructors

```
public NoSuchElementException()
public NoSuchElementException(String message)
```

If the `message` string is supplied, it is used as a detailed message describing this particular exception.

NoSuchFieldError

class java.lang.NoSuchFieldError

This is thrown whenever an application attempts to access or modify a field in an object, and the object has no such field. Under normal circumstances, this error is caught by the compiler, but this situation can occur when mixing classes that were not compiled together.

Inheritance

```
public class java.lang.NoSuchFieldError
    extends IncompatibleClassChangeError
        ⇑
    public class java.lang.IncompatibleClassChangeError
        extends LinkageError
            ⇑
        public class java.lang.LinkageError
            extends Error
```

```
                          ⇑
          public class java.lang.Error
              extends Throwable
                      ⇑
              public class java.lang.Throwable
                  implements Serializable
                  extends Object
                          ⇑
                  public class java.lang.Object
```

Constructors

```
      public NoSuchFieldError()
      public NoSuchFieldError(String message)
```

If the message string is supplied, it is used as a detailed message describing this particular exception.

NoSuchFieldException

class java.lang.NoSuchFieldException

This error is thrown whenever there is a reference from one class to a field in another, and the field is no longer a member of the class. This condition will normally be caught by the compiler, but it can occur at runtime when there is a mix of classes that were not compiled together.

Inheritance

```
      public class java.lang.NoSuchFieldException
          extends Exception
                  ⇑
          public class java.lang.Exception
              extends Throwable
                      ⇑
              public class java.lang.Throwable
                  implements Serializable
                  extends Object
                          ⇑
                  public class java.lang.Object
```

Constructors

```
public NoSuchFieldException()
public NoSuchFieldException(String message)
```

If the message string is supplied, it is used as a detailed message describing this particular exception.

NoSuchMethodError

class java.lang.NoSuchMethodError

This error is thrown whenever an application tries to call a method, and the method is no longer a member of the class. This condition will normally be caught by the compiler, but it can occur at runtime when there is a mix of classes that were not compiled together.

Inheritance

```
public class java.lang.NoSuchMethodError
    extends IncompatibleClassChangeError
        ⇑
    public class java.lang.IncompatibleClassChangeError
        extends LinkageError
            ⇑
        public class java.lang.LinkageError
            extends Error
                ⇑
            public class java.lang.Error
                extends Throwable
                    ⇑
                public class java.lang.Throwable
                    implements Serializable
                    extends Object
                        ⇑
                    public class java.lang.Object
```

Constructors

```
public NoSuchMethodError()
public NoSuchMethodError(String message)
```

If the message string is supplied, it is used as a detailed message describing this particular exception.

NoSuchMethodException

class java.lang.NoSuchMethodException

This exception will be thrown whenever a named method cannot be found.

Inheritance

```
public class java.lang.NoSuchMethodException
    extends Exception
        ⇑
    public class java.lang.Exception
        extends Throwable
            ⇑
        public class java.lang.Throwable
            implements Serializable
            extends Object
                ⇑
            public class java.lang.Object
```

Constructors

```
public NoSuchMethodException()
public NoSuchMethodException(String message)
```

If the message string is supplied, it is used as a detailed message describing this particular exception.

NoSuchObjectException

class java.rmi.NoSuchObjectException

This exception is thrown on an attempt to locate a remote object that does not exist.

Inheritance

```
public class NoSuchObjectException
    extends RemoteException
        ⇑
    public class java.rmi.RemoteException
        extends IOException
            ⇑
```

```
public class java.io.IOException
    extends Exception
        ⇑
    public class java.lang.Exception
        extends Throwable
            ⇑
        public class java.lang.Throwable
            implements Serializable
            extends Object
                ⇑
            public class java.lang.Object
```

Constructors

```
public NoSuchObjectException(String message)
```

The message string is used as a detailed message describing this particular exception.

NotBoundException

class java.rmi.NotBoundException

This exception is thrown to indicate that a name has not been found in the registry.

Inheritance

```
public class NotBoundException
    extends Exception
        ⇑
    public class java.lang.Exception
        extends Throwable
            ⇑
        public class java.lang.Throwable
            implements Serializable
            extends Object
                ⇑
            public class java.lang.Object
```

Constructors

```
public NotBoundException()
```

```
public NotBoundException(String message)
```

If the `message` string is supplied, it is used as a detailed message describing this particular exception.

NotOwnerException

class java.security.acl.NotOwnerException

This exception is thrown to indicate that an attempted modification of an object is not permitted. The attempted action is only permitted to an owner of the object.

Inheritance

```
public class NotOwnerException
    extends Exception
        ⇑
    public class java.lang.Fxception
        extends Throwable
            ⇑
        public class java.lang.Throwable
            implements Serializable
            extends Object
                ⇑
            public class java.lang.Object
```

Constructors

```
public NotOwnerException()
```

NotSerializableException

class java.io.NotSerializableException

This exception is thrown when an attempt is made to serialize a class that is not serializable.

Inheritance

```
public class java.io.NotSerializableException
```

```
            extends ObjectStreamException
                ⇑
    public class java.io.ObjectStreamException
            extends IOException
                ⇑
        public class java.io.IOException
            extends Exception
                ⇑
        public class java.lang.Exception
            extends Throwable
                ⇑
            public class java.lang.Throwable
                implements Serializable
                extends Object
                    ⇑
                public class java.lang.Object
```

Constructors

```
    public NotSerializableException()
    public NotSerializableException(String message)
```

If the message string is supplied, it is used as a detailed message describing this particular exception. For this exception, the message is normally the class name.

NoSuchAlgorithmException

class java.security.NoSuchAlgorithmException

This exception is thrown when an unknown cryptographic algorithm has been requested. It could be that the algorithm is known but is not available on this platform. For a list of known algorithms, see security.

Inheritance

```
    public class NoSuchAlgorithmException
        extends Exception
            ⇑
    public class java.lang.Exception
        extends Throwable
            ⇑
    public class java.lang.Throwable
```

```
        implements Serializable
      extends Object
              ⇑
      public class java.lang.Object
```

Constructors

```
      public NoSuchAlgorithmException()
      public NoSuchAlgorithmException(String message)
```

If the message string is supplied, it is used as a detailed message describing this particular exception.

NoSuchProviderException

class java.security.NoSuchProviderException

This exception is thrown to indicate that the specified security provider is unknown or is unavailable.

Inheritance

```
      public class java.security.NoSuchProviderException
        extends Exception
              ⇑
        public class java.lang.Exception
          extends Throwable
                  ⇑
          public class java.lang.Throwable
              implements Serializable
              extends Object
                    ⇑
              public class java.lang.Object
```

Constructors

```
      public NoSuchProviderException()
      public NoSuchProviderException(String message)
```

If the message string is supplied, it is used as a detailed message describing this particular exception.

not

!

This is the unary Boolean inversion operator. If a Boolean expression is `true`, this operator will convert it to `false`; and if the expression is `false`, it will convert it to `true`. For example, if the expression (a < b) results in `true`, then !(a < b) will result in `false`.

 For the not-equals operator, see **comparison**.

null

keyword

The `null` keyword is a special case in the Java language.

- ◆ It is considered to be one of the three primitive types (the others are the numeric types and the reference types).
- ◆ The word `null` is a reserved word in the Java language.
- ◆ It is not possible to declare a variable of type `null`, nor to cast an object to the `null` type.
- ◆ The `null` type can always be cast to any reference type (class, interface, or array).
- ◆ It is the default value of an uninitialized reference.
- ◆ Any reference can be compared to `null` for equality or inequality.

There are different ways you can think about `null`. Instead of thinking of it as being some sort of special language construct, you can just think of it a special literal value that will fit into any reference. If you like to think of references as containing addresses of objects (a possible implementation), then `null` is the "zero pointer"—a special address value that doesn't point anywhere. If, however, you prefer to think of references as holding some sort of object "handle" (another possible implementation), then you can think of `null` as the handle of an object that does nothing.

NullPointerException

class java.lang.NullPointerException

This is thrown to indicate an attempt was made to use `null` in a place where a nonnull value was required. This most often occurs when a reference has not been properly initialized to address an object. An attempt may have been made to access a field value of a `null` object or to call the method of a `null` object. It is common for applications to throw this exception from methods that require a nonnull method reference as an argument.

Inheritance

```
public class java.lang.NullPointerException
    extends RuntimeException
        ⇑
    public class java.lang.RuntimeException
        extends Exception
            ⇑
        public class java.lang.Exception
            extends Throwable
                ⇑
            public class java.lang.Throwable
                implements Serializable
                extends Object
                    ⇑
                public class java.lang.Object
```

Constructors

```
public NullPointerException()
public NullPointerException(String message)
```

If the `message` string is supplied, it is used as a detailed message describing this particular exception.

Number

class java.lang.Number

This is the superclass of all the numeric wrappers. Each of the subclasses provides methods to convert its own value type to or from the other types.

Extended by

```
BigDecimal
BigInteger
Byte
Double
```

```
Float
Integer
Long
Short
```

Inheritance

```
public abstract class java.lang.Number
    implements Serializable
    extends Object
        ⇑
    public class java.lang.Object
```

Constructors

```
public Number()
```

Returned by

A Number object is returned from ChoiceFormat.parse(), DecimalFormat.parse(), and NumberFormat.parse().

Methods

byteValue()

```
public byte byteValue()
```

Returns the value as a byte. It will round or truncate as necessary, and data could be lost.

doubleValue()

```
public abstract double doubleValue()
```

Returns the value as a double.

floatValue()

```
public abstract float floatValue()
```

Returns the value as a float. It will round or truncate as necessary, and data could be lost.

intValue()

```
public abstract int intValue()
```

Returns the value as an int. It will round or truncate as necessary, and data could be lost.

longValue()
```
public abstract long longValue()
```
Returns the value as a `long`. It will round as necessary, and data could be lost.

shortValue()
```
public short shortValue()
```
Returns the value as a `short`. It will round or truncate as necessary, and data could be lost.

 For a general discussion of how this works, see **wrapper**.

NumberFormat

class java.text.NumberFormat

This abstract class is the superclass for the classes that convert numbers to and from strings.

The numbers and locale

This class can be used for number formatting in a way that the resulting formatted strings will vary from one locale to another. The ideal purpose is to enable you to write code that is locale-independent—your code will adapt itself automatically. Some of the things that vary are the decimal points, the characters used for the digits, and the way that thousands are separated.

A template for number formatting

You can think of an instance of this object as a template that can be used to format numbers. Once you have the template, you can use it repeatedly to stamp out number strings in the correct format. This is the more efficient approach—creating one object and using it over and over—because determining all the locale information from the system can be expensive.

Controlling your number formats

The normal way of getting a number formatting object is to call `getNumberInstance()` to have a `NumberFormat` of the correct locale returned to you. If you want closer control, you can attempt to cast the returned `NumberFormat` to a `DecimalNumberFormat` to get closer control—in the vast majority of locales this will work.

Extended by
```
ChoiceFormat
DecimalFormat
```

Inheritance

```
public abstract class java.text.NumberFormat
    implements Cloneable
    extends Format
        ⇑
    public class java.text.Format
        implements Serializable
        implements Cloneable
        extends Object
            ⇑
        public class java.lang.Object
```

Variables and constants

FRACTION_FIELD

```
public final static int FRACTION_FIELD
```

A constant used to construct a FieldPosition object. It specifies that the position of the fractional portion of the formatted number should be returned.

INTEGER_FIELD

```
public final static int INTEGER_FIELD
```

A constant used to construct a FieldPosition object. It specifies that the position of the integer portion of the formatted number should be returned.

Constructors

```
public NumberFormat()
```

Returned by

A NumberFormat object is returned from DateFormat.getNumberInstance, NumberFormat.getCurrencyInstance, NumberFormat.getInstance, NumberFormat.getNumberInstance, and NumberFormat.getPercentInstance

Methods

clone()

```
public Object clone()
```

Makes a duplicate of this object.

equals()

```
public boolean equals(Object object)
```

Returns true if object is equal to this object.

format()

```
public final String format(double number)

public final String format(long number)

public final StringBuffer format(Object number,
        StringBuffer appendTo,FieldPosition position)

public abstract StringBuffer format(double number,
        StringBuffer appendTo,FieldPosition position)

public abstract StringBuffer format(long number,
        StringBuffer appendTo,FieldPosition position)
```

Formats number into a string. If appendTo and position are specified, the generated string will be appended to the end of the one in appendTo, which is also used as the return value. The position is updated to hold the location of the resulting string in the returned StringBuffer.

getAvailableLocales()

```
public static Locale[] getAvailableLocales()
```

Returns an array of all the locales that can be used with NumberFormat.

getCurrencyInstance()

```
public final static NumberFormat getCurrencyInstance()

public static NumberFormatgetCurrencyInstance(Locale locale)
```

Returns the NumberFormat for the currency of the specified locale. If locale is not specified, the current locale is returned.

getInstance()

```
public final static NumberFormat getInstance()

public static NumberFormat getInstance(Locale locale)
```

Returns the default NumberFormat for the locale. If no locale is specified, the default locale is assumed.

This is the same NumberFormat returned from getNumberInstance(), getCurrencyInstance(), or getPercentInstance()—exactly which one is returned depends on the locale.

getMaximumFractionDigits()

```
public int getMaximumFractionDigits()
```

Returns the maximum number of digits allowed in the fractional portion of a formatted number.

getMaximumIntegerDigits()

```
public int getMaximumIntegerDigits()
```

Returns the maximum number of digits allowed in the integer portion (the nonfractional portion) of a formatted number.

getMinimumFractionDigits()

```
public int getMinimumFractionDigits()
```

Returns the minimum number of digits allowed in the fractional portion of a formatted number.

getMinimumIntegerDigits()

```
public int getMinimumIntegerDigits()
```

Returns the minimum number of digits allowed in the integer portion (the nonfractional portion) of a formatted number.

getNumberInstance()

```
public final static NumberFormat getNumberInstance()

public static NumberFormatgetNumberInstance(Locale locale)
```

Returns a general-purpose number format object for locale. If no locale is specified, uses the default.

getPercentInstance()

```
public final static NumberFormat getPercentInstance()

public static NumberFormatgetPercentInstance(Locale locale)
```

Returns the percentage format for the locale. If no locale is specified, uses the default.

hashCode()

```
public int hashCode()
```

Returns the hashcode of this NumberFormat.

isGroupingUsed()

```
public boolean isGroupingUsed()
```

Returns `true` if grouping is used. An example of grouping is the familiar three-digit comma-separated sequences, as in 43,564,201.

isParseIntegerOnly()

```
public boolean isParseIntegerOnly()
```

Returns `true` if this `NumberFormat` will only parse integers. For example, in a number format definition that uses a decimal point to separate the integer and fractional portions of a number, the number 45.67 would become 45 because it would stop at the period—this is the *integer only* portion.

parse()

```
public abstract Number parse(String text,
         ParsePosition position)
```

```
public Number parse(String text)
     throws ParseException
```

Reads the text string and converts it to a numeric value. If the value is all integer (which is always the case if `isParseIntegerOnly()` is `true`), and if the value is within the range that can be contained in a `long`, a `Long` wrapper is returned. If the number cannot be represented as a `long`, a `Double` wrapper will be returned. If specified, the `position` will determine the starting position in `text`, and `position` will be updated to the next character after the last one read. On an error, either `null` is returned and the `position` is not updated, or a `ParseException` is thrown.

parseObject()

```
public final Object parseObject(String source,
         ParsePosition position)
```

Reads the characters of the `source` string and produces the `object`. The position will determine where reading from source begins—and it will be updated to index the first character following the last one used to produce the object. On an error, a `null` is returned and the `position` is not updated.

setGroupingUsed()

```
public void setGroupingUsed(boolean setting)
```

Specifies whether or not grouping is to be used. An example of grouping is the familiar three-digit comma-separated sequence, as in 43,564,201.

setMaximumFractionDigits()

```
public void setMaximumFractionDigits(int value)
```

Specifies the maximum number of digits allowed in the fractional portion of a formatted string. If value is less than the current setting of the minimum number of digits allowed, both minimum and maximum are set to value.

setMaximumIntegerDigits()

```
public void setMaximumIntegerDigits(int value)
```

Specifies the maximum number of digits allowed in the integer (nonfractional) portion of a formatted string. If value is less than the current setting of the minimum number of digits allowed, both minimum and maximum are set to value.

setMinimumFractionDigits()

```
public void setMinimumFractionDigits(int value)
```

Specifies the minimum number of digits allowed in the fractional portion of a formatted string. If value is greater than the current setting of the maximum number of digits allowed, both minimum and maximum are set to value.

setMinimumIntegerDigits()

```
public void setMinimumIntegerDigits(int value)
```

Specifies the maximum number of digits allowed in the integer (nonfractional) portion of a formatted string. If value is less than the current setting of the minimum number of digits allowed, both minimum and maximum are set to value.

setParseIntegerOnly()

```
public void setParseIntegerOnly(boolean setting)
```

Setting this to true will cause only the integer portion of an input string to be converted to a number. The input will halt at a period or any other nondigit character.

Example 1

This is an example of formatting the same numeric value in three locales — the default, which in this case is US, along with ITALY and GERMANY:

```
import java.text.*;
import java.util.*;
public class FormatNumber {
    public static void main(String[] arg) {
        System.out.println("..default..");
        Locale locale = Locale.getDefault();
        NumberFormat numForm =
            NumberFormat.getNumberInstance(locale);
        System.out.println(numForm.format(82.95));
        System.out.println(numForm.format(-821.873));
```

```
        System.out.println(numForm.format(84915.02));
        System.out.println("..Italy..");
        numForm =
            NumberFormat.getNumberInstance(Locale.ITALY);
        System.out.println(numForm.format(82.95));
        System.out.println(numForm.format(-821.873));
        System.out.println(numForm.format(84915.02));
        System.out.println("..Germany..");
        numForm =
    NumberFormat.getNumberInstance(Locale.GERMAN);
        System.out.println(numForm.format(82.95));
        System.out.println(numForm.format(-821.873));
        System.out.println(numForm.format(84915.02));
    }
}
```

The output looks like this:

```
..default..
82.95
-821.873
84,915.02
..Italy..
82,95
-821,873
84.915,02
..Germany..
82,95
-821,873
84.915,02
```

Example 2

This example show the results from formatting currency with three different locales—the default, which, in this case, is US, along with ITALY and GERMANY:

```
import java.text.*;
import java.util.*;
public class FormatCurrency {
    public static void main(String[] arg) {
        System.out.println("..default..");
        Locale locale = Locale.getDefault();
        NumberFormat numForm =
            NumberFormat.getCurrencyInstance(locale);
```

```
System.out.println(numForm.format(82.95));
System.out.println(numForm.format(-821.873));
System.out.println(numForm.format(84915.02));
System.out.println("..Italy..");
numForm =
    NumberFormat.getCurrencyInstance(Locale.ITALY);
System.out.println(numForm.format(82.95));
System.out.println(numForm.format(-821.873));
System.out.println(numForm.format(84915.02));
System.out.println("..Germany..");
numForm =
    NumberFormat.getCurrencyInstance(Locale.GERMAN);
System.out.println(numForm.format(82.95));
System.out.println(numForm.format(-821.873));
System.out.println(numForm.format(84915.02));
    }
}
```

A `NumberFormat` object for currency is created for each of the locales, and each is used three times for the same values. The output looks like this:

```
..default..
$82.95
($821.87)
$84,915.02
..Italy..
L. 82,95
-L. 821,87
L. 84.915,02
..Germany..
82,95 DM
-821,87 DM
84.915,02 DM
```

 For other classes that format data into strings, see **ChoiceFormat**, **DateFormat**, **DecimalFormat**, and **SimpleDateFormat**.

NumberFormatException

class java.lang.NumberFormatException

This is thrown whenever the application attempts to convert a string to one of the numeric types and the contents of the string are not valid for the conversion.

Inheritance

```
public class java.lang.NumberFormatException
    extends IllegalArgumentException
        ⇑
    public class java.lang.IllegalArgumentException
        extends RuntimeException
            ⇑
        public class java.lang.RuntimeException
            extends Exception
                ⇑
            public class java.lang.Exception
                extends Throwable
                    ⇑
                public class java.lang.Throwable
                    implements Serializable
                    extends Object
                        ⇑
                    public class java.lang.Object
```

Constructors

```
public NumberFormatException()
public NumberFormatException(String message)
```

If the `message` string is supplied, it is used as a detailed message describing this particular exception.

object

An object is either an instance of a class or an instance of an array. Objects exist only while a program is executing—they are constructed by executing specific commands.

A Java program executes by manipulating objects and the variables contained in the objects. All variables have a type, and all objects have a class.

This word has been so used and abused, it has lost its meaning in any but the strictest contexts. In Java, the word "object" refers only to a collection of data and methods that work together as a unit—that is, it is an instance of a class or array. The word `Object` (capitalized) refers the Java class that is the root superclass of all other classes.

A Java object can be created in any of several specific ways:

- ◆ Invoke the Java Virtual Machine with the name of a class file. It creates an object from the class and starts it into execution.

- ◆ Execute a `new` statement to create the instance of a class. This command allocates memory to hold an object and then calls the constructor to initialize it.

- ◆ Execute a `new` statement to create an array.

- ◆ Invoke the method `newInstance()` of the `Class` object associated with the desired object.

- ◆ Use an array initializer statement that will implicitly create an array object during class or method initialization.

- ◆ Use a quoted string that will cause the creation of a `String` object during class or method initialization.

- ◆ Use the `String` concatenation operators + and += to automatically create new `String` objects.

For access to objects, see **references**.

Object

class java.lang.Object

This class is the superclass of all classes in Java—this is the root class of the entire class hierarchy. This includes arrays, which are objects.

Since this is the universal superclass, every method of this class exists in every class in Java. In some classes, these methods are overridden and in some they are not, but they are always present.

Returning an Object

Many methods in the API return objects of this class. This fact is handy whenever a method is capable of returning—or accepting as an argument—objects of different types. The receiver of the object can simply use instanceof or cast it to whatever type it would like; if the cast doesn't take, it is of some other type. The recipient then tries another cast or discards the object as unwanted.

Inheritance

```
public class java.lang.Object
```

Constructors

```
public Object()
```

Methods

clone()

```
protected Object clone()
    throws CloneNotSupportedException
```

Creates a new object of the same class as this object. The fields of the new object are initialized with the data from the fields of this class. The constructor of the new object is not called. The newly created object is returned. See Examples 1 and 2.

For this method to succeed, the class must implement the Cloneable interface—otherwise, a CloneNotSupportedException will be thrown. This exception can also be thrown by instances of classes to limit cloning to certain specific circumstances. An OutOfMemoryError could be thrown if there is not sufficient space to create the clone.

equals()

```
public boolean equals(Object obj)
```

This method compares two objects for equality. The default method only considers an object to be equal to itself. The invocation x.equals(x) will always return true, and x.equals(y) will return true *only* if the same object is referenced — that is, if x == y is true.

The equality is *reflexive*. That is, x.equals(x) will always return true.

It is *symmetric*. That is, the return from x.equals(y) will be the same as the return from y.equals(x).

It is *consistent*. That is, invoking the method x.equals(y) repeatedly will return the same result.

For any object, x.equals(null) is false.

Two equal objects will have the same hashcode values. That is, if x.equals(y) is true, then x.hashCode() == y.hashCode() is also true.

This method is commonly overloaded, and the exact meaning of equality can have some shadings. For example, if an object contains an array of strings, are they equal if the contents of the array are equal (the string references are identical), or is it sufficient that each of the strings compare for equality by containing copies of the same characters in the same order? One can imagine circumstances in which the two objects could be considered equal if they each contained the same number of strings—that is, if the lengths of their arrays were the same.

finalize()

```
protected void finalize()
        throws Throwable
```

This method is called once by the garbage collector before the RAM being used by the object is returned to the system. A subclass can override this method to release any system resources that are being held, or to perform some other necessary cleanup. The default form of the method does nothing.

This method can throw exceptions. A thrown exception will cause the finalization of the object to be halted, but no other action takes place.

getClass()

```
public final Class getClass()
```

Every object has a Class object that represents it. This will return that Class object.

hashCode()

```
public int hashCode()
```

Returns a hashcode value for this object. This method exists for convenience in hashing objects to be stored in tables, such as java.util.Hashtable. This method will always return the same value from the same object—however, two different runs of a program could generate different hashcode values for an object. Two equal objects, such that x.equals(y) returns true, will produce the same hashcode value.

notify()

```
public final void notify()
```

This method has to do with Java synchronization. It will wake up a single thread that is sleeping on this object's monitor. A thread will sleep on a monitor by calling `wait()`.

It is expected for this method to be called by a thread that is the owner of this object's monitor. Only one thread at a time can become the owner of a monitor. A thread becomes the owner of a monitor by being the one that is executing synchronized code. It can be a synchronized method of the object, or it can be a block of synchronized code inside a method. It can also be a synchronized static method defined in the class of the object.

If the current thread is not the owner of the monitor, an `IllegalMonitorStateException` will be thrown.

notifyAll()

```
public final void notifyAll()
```

This method has to do with Java synchronization. It wakes up all threads that are sleeping on an object's monitor. The threads sleep on the monitor by calling `wait()`. This method should be called only by the thread that is the current owner of the monitor. See `notify()`. An `IllegalMonitorStateException` will be thrown if the current thread is not the owner of the monitor.

toString()

```
public String toString()
```

This method will return a string representation of the object. This is the method used by the Java system to convert an object to its string form. In most cases, the resulting string is a very concise description of the object and/or its contents. This method is not intended for automation—the string should be in a human-readable format. All subclasses should override this method to produce a descriptive string unique to itself.

The default form of this method returns a string made up of the name of the class, an at-sign, and the string form of the object's hashcode.

wait()

```
public final void wait(long timeout)
    throws InterruptedException
```

```
public final void wait(long timeout,int nanos)
    throws InterruptedException
```

```
public final void wait()
    throws InterruptedException
```

This has to do with Java synchronization. Calling this method will block the current thread until some sort of change in the object has been reported. The calling thread, which must own the object's monitor, will, by calling this method, release ownership of the monitor until either the timeout has expired or another thread issues a notification for waiting threads to wake up. The thread then waits until it can reestablish ownership of the monitor and continue execution.

If no timeout is supplied, the wait will be terminated only when this thread is awakened by another thread making a call to notify() or notifyAll(). A value for nanos can be supplied to have sub-millisecond control over the time to wait. Nanoseconds can be specified in the range 0 to 999999.

This method should be called only by a thread that is the owner of the monitor of the object. An object becomes owner of the monitor by executing synchronized code.

An IllegalArgumentException is thrown if the timeout is negative or if nanos is outside the valid range. An IllegalMonitorStateException is thrown if the current thread is not the owner of the object's monitor. An InterruptedException is thrown if another thread has interrupted this thread.

Example 1

This is an example of very simple cloning. The members (in this case, the single member string) are simply bitwise-copied to the new object:

```
public class CloneSimple implements Cloneable {
    String string;
    public static void main(String[] arg) {
        CloneSimple cs1 = new CloneSimple("original");
        try {
            CloneSimple cs2 = (CloneSimple)cs1.clone();
            System.out.println(cs2);
        } catch(Exception e) {
            System.out.println(e);
        }
    }
    public CloneSimple(String string) {
        this.string = string;
    }
    public String toString() {
        return(string);
    }
}
```

This class implements the Cloneable interface to prevent the call to clone() from throwing an exception. The method simply duplicates the object and makes a bitwise copy of the data—in this case, a String reference. Although there are no methods in the Cloneable interface, it must be implemented for the clone() method to be called correctly. This program prints the string from the duplicate, which is simply

```
original
```

Example 2

The cloning of Example 1 is known as a *shallow* copy. This can occasionally lead to undesirable results — the two clones can wind up sharing the same object internally. Here is an example of a shallow copy leading to shared objects, and an example of how it can be converted to a deep copy by overriding the `clone()` method.

First, the shallow version. Here we have a class that includes an array that is initialized in the constructor. We create an instance called `copy1` and clone it into `copy2`. We then make modifications to the array in the original:

```
public class CloneDeep implements Cloneable {
    public int[] ia;
    public static void main(String[] arg) {
        CloneDeep copy1 = new CloneDeep();
        try {
            CloneDeep copy2 = (CloneDeep)copy1.clone();
            System.out.println("Before: " + copy2);
            copy1.ia[0] = 99;
            System.out.println(" After: " + copy2);
        } catch(Exception e) {
            System.out.println(e);
        }
    }
    public CloneDeep() {
        ia = new int[3];
        for(int i=0; i<3; i++) {
            ia[i] = i + 10;
        }
    }
    public String toString() {
        String outline;
        outline = "ia:";
        for(int i=0; i<3; i++)
            outline += " " + ia[i];
        return(outline);
    }
}
```

The program prints the array values of the clone before and after modifications are made to the original. Executing the program generates this output:

```
Before: ia: 10 11 12
 After: ia: 99 11 12
```

As you can see, making a change in the copy causes the same change to occur in the original — the results of having a shallow copy.

This can be remedied by overloading the default `clone()` method with one of your own. For this example, here is a `clone()` method that will cause a deep copy:

```
protected Object clone()
        throws CloneNotSupportedException {
    CloneDeep copy = (CloneDeep)super.clone();
    copy.ia = new int[3];
    for(int i=0; i<3; i++) {
        copy.ia[i] = ia[i];
    }
    return(copy);
}
```

This method calls the `clone()` method of the superclass to get a new copy of the object—complete with any shallow or deep copying that has been coded into any of the superclasses. The method then makes copies of any objects that need to be duplicated (this could have been done with the clone methods of the copied objects, if you trust them to do deep copies). Adding this method to the `CloneDeep` class causes the output to look like this:

```
Before: ia: 10 11 12
 After: ia: 10 11 12
```

Because making a change to one did not change the other, the output shows that the two copies are independent of one another—they no longer share the array.

Example 3

This is an example of using `wait()` and `notify()` to synchronize data access from multiple threads:

```
import java.util.*;
import java.awt.*;
public class Queue {
    Vector v;
    public static void main(String[] arg) {
        Queue queue = new Queue();
        new Inserter(queue);
        new Extracter(queue);
    }
    Queue() {
        v = new Vector();
    }
    public synchronized void enQueue(Object o) {
```

```
                synchronized(v) {
                    v.addElement(o);
                    notify();
                }
            }
        public synchronized Object deQueue() {
            try {
                while(v.isEmpty())
                    wait();
                synchronized(v) {
                    Object retval = v.elementAt(0);
                    v.removeElementAt(0);
                    return(retval);
                }
            } catch(InterruptedException e) {
                return(null);
            }
        }
    }

class Inserter implements Runnable {
    Queue queue;
    Inserter(Queue queue) {
        this.queue = queue;
        new Thread(this).start();
    }
    public void run() {
        for(int i=0; ; i++) {
            Integer integer = new Integer(i);
            System.out.println("enqueue: " + integer);
            queue.enQueue(integer);
        }
    }
}

class Extracter implements Runnable {
    Queue queue;
    Extracter(Queue queue) {
        this.queue = queue;
        new Thread(this).start();
    }
    public void run() {
        while(true) {
            Integer integer = (Integer)queue.deQueue();
```

```
                            System.out.println("dequeue: " + integer);
                    }
              }
       }
```

The class `Queue` uses a `Vector` to manage a queue of objects. The method `enQueue()` adds a new member to the end of the queue, and the method `deQueue()` extracts and returns the oldest member from the front of the queue. Both of these methods are synchronized, so that only one of them can have a thread executing at a given time. Both of these threads synchronize on the `Vector` to make sure that they both don't try to do a modification at the same time. The `Inserter` object runs in a separate thread, constantly inserting objects by calling `enQueue()`. The `Extracter` object runs in another thread, constantly extracting objects by calling `deQueue()`.

Inside `enQueue()` the object is added to the `Vector` and a call is made to `notify()`. This `notify()` call will cause the `wait()` call in `deQueue()` to return. The call to `v.addElement()` is made with the `Vector` synchronized to prevent `deQueue()` from making a call to `v.removeElementAt()` until after the new element has been added.

Inside `deQueue()`, a test is made to determine whether or not the `Vector` is empty. If it is empty, a call is made to `wait()`. The call to `wait()` blocks until there is a call to `notify()`. The call to `wait()` is made inside a `try-catch` block because is it necessary to handle the exception that is thrown if `wait()` is interrupted by another thread. Once it has been determined that there is data in the `Vector`, an element is removed and returned.

The program runs until it is interrupted. Because the threads are asynchronous, the insertions and extractions can come in any order. A typical run looks like this:

```
enqueue: 0
enqueue: 1
enqueue: 2
dequeue: 0
enqueue: 3
enqueue: 4
enqueue: 5
dequeue: 1
enqueue: 6
dequeue: 2
dequeue: 3
enqueue: 7
enqueue: 8
dequeue: 4
dequeue: 5
dequeue: 6
```

```
enqueue:  9
dequeue:  7
enqueue:  10
dequeue:  8
enqueue:  11
```

ObjectInput

interface java.io.ObjectInput

The ObjectInput interface extends the DataInput interface by adding methods to include the reading of objects.

Implemented by

```
ObjectInputStream
```

Inheritance

```
public interface java.io.ObjectInput
     extends DataInput
          ⇑
public interface java.io.DataInput
```

Constructors

Returned by

An object implementing this interface is returned from RemoteCall.getInputStream().

Methods

available()

```
public abstract int available()
     throws IOException
```

Returns a count of the number of bytes that can be read without blocking.

close()

```
public abstract void close()
     throws IOException
```

Closes the stream. It should be called so that any system resources held by the stream are released.

read()

```
public abstract int read()
    throws IOException

public int read(byte barray[])
    throws IOException

public int read(byte barray[],int offset,int length)
    throws IOException
```

If no argument is supplied, this method will read one `byte` of data and return it as an `int`. If `barray` is supplied, the input data is placed in the array and the number of bytes read is returned. If `offset` and `length` are specified, the input data will appear beginning at `barray[offset]` for a maximum of `length` bytes. The default `offset` is 0, and the default `length` is the size of `barray`. This method will block as long as unread data is available. A return value of −1 indicates a normal end to the input stream.

readObject()

```
public abstract Object readObject()
    throws ClassNotFoundException
    throws IOException
```

This will read and return an object. The class that implements this interface will determine how and from where the object is read. The `ClassNotFoundException` is thrown if there is no object to be read — or if the incoming object does not have a `Class` defined for it.

skip()

```
public long skip(long count)
    throws IOException
```

Calling this method makes a request to have the input stream skip over `count` number of input bytes. The return value is the actual number of bytes skipped.

ObjectInputStream

class java.io.ObjectInputStream

An `ObjectInputStream` is capable of reading primitive data and objects that were written by an `ObjectOutputStream`.

Inheritance

```
public class java.io.ObjectInputStream
        implements ObjectInput
        implements ObjectStreamConstants
        extends InputStream
            ⇑
        public class java.io.InputStream
                extends Object
                    ⇑
                public class java.lang.Object
```

Constructors

```
public ObjectInputStream(InputStream input)
        throws IOException
        throws StreamCorruptedException
```

An object is created that uses the specified `input` for incoming data. On creation, the header information is read from the input to verify the magic number (indicating the existence of a serialized object) and the version number. If these cannot be verified, a `StreamCorruptedException` is thrown. If cannot be read from the input, an `IOException` is thrown.

Methods

available()

```
public int available()
        throws IOException
```

Returns a count of the number of bytes that can be read without blocking.

close()

```
public void close()
        throws IOException
```

Closes the input stream. This method should be called to free any system resources that are being held by the input stream.

defaultReadObject()

```
public final void defaultReadObject()
        throws IOException
        throws ClassNotFoundException
        throws NotActiveException
```

This method can only be called from the readObject() method of the class being dese-rialized. It will read the nonstatic and nontransient fields from the input stream. It will throw the NotActiveException if it is called from somewhere besides readObject().

enableResolveObject()

```
protected final booleanenableResolveObject(boolean enable)
    throws SecurityException
```

Allows objects read from the stream to replace existing objects. If the stream is a trusted class, it is allowed to enable replacement. Trusted classes are those with a null class loader. When enabled, the resolveObject() method is called for every object being deserial-ized. The SecurityException is thrown if the classloader of this stream object is nonnull.

read()

```
public abstract int read()
    throws IOException
```

```
public int read(byte barray[],int offset,int length)
    throws IOException
```

If no argument is supplied, reads one byte of data and returns it as an int. If barray is supplied, the input data is placed in the array and the number of bytes read is returned. The input data will appear beginning at barray[offset] for a maximum of length bytes. This method will block as long as there is unread data available. A return value of −1 indi-cates a normal end to the input stream.

readBoolean()

```
public boolean readBoolean()
    throws IOException
```

Reads a boolean value. An EOFException is thrown on an unexpected end-of-file.

readByte()

```
public byte readByte()
    throws IOException
```

Reads a byte value. An EOFException is thrown on an unexpected end-of-file.

readChar()

```
public char readChar()
    throws IOException
```

Reads a char value. An EOFException is thrown on an unexpected end-of-file.

readDouble()

```
public double readDouble()
    throws IOException
```

Reads a double value. An EOFException is thrown on an unexpected end-of-file.

readFloat()

```
public float readFloat()
    throws IOException
```

Reads a float value. An EOFException is thrown on an unexpected end-of-file.

readFully()

```
public void readFully(byte barray[])
    throws IOException
```

```
public void readFully(byte barray[],int offset,int length)
    throws IOException
```

This method will read an array of bytes into barray. The data will be placed into barray beginning at offset and continuing for length bytes. If offset and length are not specified, all of barray will be filled. This is a blocking read—it will not return until there is enough data to fill barray. An EOFException is thrown on an unexpected end-of-file.

readInt()

```
public int readInt()
    throws IOException
```

Reads an int value. An EOFException is thrown on an unexpected end-of-file.

readLine()

```
public String readLine()
    throws IOException
```

Reads a String. An EOFException is thrown on an unexpected end-of-file.

readLong()

```
public long readLong()
    throws IOException
```

Reads a long value. An EOFException is thrown on an unexpected end-of-file.

readObject()

```
public final Object readObject()
    throws OptionalDataException
```

```
        throws ClassNotFoundException
        throws IOException
```

Reads an object from the input stream. This method can be overridden in a subclass that wishes to use its own form of deserialization.

The `ClassNotFoundException` is thrown if there is no `Class` for the incoming object. An `InvalidClassException` is thrown if the `Class` definition is in error. A `StreamCorruptedException` is thrown to indicate an error in the incoming object definition. An `OptionalDataException` is thrown if the incoming data is primitive instead of in the form of objects.

readShort()

```
    public short readShort()
        throws IOException
```

Reads a `short` value. An `EOFException` is thrown on an unexpected end-of-file.

readStreamHeader()

```
    protected void readStreamHeader()
        throws IOException
        throws StreamCorruptedException
```

Reads and verifies the magic number and version number of the incoming data. This method is supplied so that subclasses can read and verify their own stream headers.

readUnsignedByte()

```
    public int readUnsignedByte()
        throws IOException
```

Reads an eight-bit byte as an unsigned value and returns it as an `int` in the range 0 to 255. An `EOFException` is thrown on an unexpected end-of-file.

readUnsignedShort()

```
    public int readUnsignedShort()
        throws IOException
```

Reads a 16-bit short as an unsigned value and returns it as an `int` in the range 0 to 65,535. An `EOFException` is thrown on an unexpected end-of-file.

readUTF()

```
    public String readUTF()
        throws IOException
```

Reads a string of UTF-formatted Unicode characters and converts them all to their 16-bit Unicode form. An `EOFException` is thrown on an unexpected end-of-file.

registerValidation()

```
public synchronized void registerValidation(
        ObjectInputValidation object,int priority)
    throws NotActiveException
    throws InvalidObjectException
```

Registers an object to be validated before the graph of the object is returned. The object is the object that will receive the validation callback. The priority controls the order of the defaults. The lowest priority is zero—objects with higher priority numbers are called first. While similar to those in resolveObject(), these validations are called after the entire graph has been reconstituted into an object. A typical registerValidation() method will register the object with the stream so that when all of the objects are restored, a final set of validations can be performed.

A NotActiveException will be thrown if the stream is not currently reading objects. An InvalidObjectException will be thrown if object is null.

resolveClass()

```
protected Class resolveClass(ObjectStreamClass osc)
    throws IOException
    throws ClassNotFoundException
```

This method exists to read data that was previously stored along with the object by annotateClass() of ObjectOutputStream. This method will be called once for each unique class in the stream. This method can be overridden by subclasses to read data from a different source, but it must return a Class object. The serialVersionUID values of the class and the object are compared, and if there is a mismatch, deserialization fails and an exception is thrown.

resolveObject()

```
protected Object resolveObject(Object obj)
    throws IOException
```

This method will allow trusted subclasses of ObjectInputStream to substitute one object for another during deserialization—that is, it will replace any object already in RAM with the new one being loaded. Replacing objects is disabled until enableResolveObject() is called. The enableResolveObject() method checks that the stream requesting to resolve object can be trusted. Every reference to serializable objects is passed to resolveObject(). To ensure that the private state of objects is not unintentionally exposed, only trusted streams may use resolveObject().

This method is called after an object has been read, but before it is returned from readObject(). The default resolveObject() method just returns the new object.

When a subclass is replacing objects, it must ensure that the substituted object is compatible with every field where the reference will be stored. Objects whose type is not a subclass of the type of the field or array element abort the serialization by raising an exception, and the object is not stored.

This method is called only once when each object is first encountered. All subsequent references to the object will be redirected to the new object.

skipBytes()

```
public int skipBytes(int count)
    throws IOException
```

This will cause the input stream to skip `count` number of bytes of the input stream. An `EOFException` is thrown on an unexpected end-of-file.

 For an example of object serialization, see **Serializable**. For the callback interface, see **ObjectInputValidation**.

ObjectInputValidation

interface java.io.ObjectInputValidation

This is the callback interface that allows validation of objects within a graph. `ObjectInputValidation` allows an object to be called when a complete graph of objects has been deserialized.

Inheritance

```
public interface java.io.ObjectInputValidation
```

Methods

validateObject()

```
public abstract void validateObject()
    throws InvalidObjectException
```

This will request that the object validate itself. If the object is unable to validate itself, the `InvalidObjectException` is thrown.

 For an example of serialization and for the description of the graph of an object, see **Serializable**.

ObjectOutput

interface java.io.ObjectOutput

The `ObjectOutput` interface extends the `DataOutput` interface by adding methods to include the writing of objects.

Implemented by

```
ObjectOutputStream
```

Inheritance

```
public interface java.io.ObjectOutput
    extends DataOutput
        ⇑
    public interface java.io.DataOutput
```

Constructors

Returned by

Objects implementing this interface are returned from `getOutputStream()` and `getResultStream()` of `RemoteCall`.

Methods

close()

```
public abstract void close()
    throws IOException
```

Closes the output stream. It must be called to release any resources associated with the stream.

flush()

```
public abstract void flush()
    throws IOException
```

Flushes the stream by forcing a write of any buffered output bytes.

write()

```
public abstract void write(byte barray[])
    throws IOException

public abstract void write(byte barray[],int offset,
        int length)
    throws IOException

public abstract void write(int bvalue)
    throws IOException
```

Writes one or more bytes to the output. If `bvalue` is specified, it is written as a single byte. The writing will begin at `offset` and continue for `length` bytes. The default value for `offset` is 0, and the default `length` is the entire length of the array. The method blocks until the writing is complete.

writeObject()

```
public abstract void writeObject(Object obj)
    throws IOException
```

Writes an object to the output stream. The exact form of the written object is determined by the class implementing this interface.

ObjectOutputStream

class java.io.ObjectOutputStream

An `ObjectOutputStream` is capable of writing primitive data and objects in a form that can be read by `ObjectInputStream`.

Inheritance

```
public class java.io.ObjectOutputStream
    implements ObjectOutput
    implements ObjectStreamConstants
    extends OutputStream
        ⇑
    public class java.io.OutputStream
        extends Object
            ⇑
        public class java.lang.Object
```

Constructors

```
public ObjectOutputStream(OutputStream output)
    throws IOException
```

The `ObjectOutputStream` is constructed to write to the `output` stream. The constructor writes the header.

Methods

annotateClass()

```
protected void annotateClass(Class class)
    throws IOException
```

This method exists so that subclasses can be designed to write other data in the same stream as the object. By default, this method does nothing. The corresponding method in `ObjectInputStream` is `resolveClass()`. This method will be called once for each unique class in the stream. It is called after the class name and signature have been written.

The format in which the class is written is not defined—but it must be in a form expected by `resolveClass()`. This method is not called for arrays.

close()

```
public void close()
    throws IOException
```

Closes the stream. This method must be called to make sure any resources held by the stream are released.

defaultWriteObject()

```
public final void defaultWriteObject()
    throws IOException
```

This method may only be called from the `writeObject()` method of the class being serialized; otherwise, a `NotActiveException` is thrown. It will write the nonstatic and non-transient fields to the stream.

drain()

```
protected void drain()
    throws IOException
```

Writes any locally buffered data to the output stream. It does not flush the underlying stream.

enableReplaceObject()

```
protected final booleanenableReplaceObject(boolean enable)
    throws SecurityException
```

Enables or disables the replacement of objects in the stream. If replacement is enabled, a call is made to `replaceObject()` for every object being serialized. Replacement can be enabled only if the stream is a trusted class — that is, one with a `null` class loader. If this method is called and the stream is not a trusted class, the `SecurityException` is thrown.

flush()

```
public void flush()
    throws IOException
```

Writes any buffered data to the stream and flushes the underlying stream.

replaceObject()

```
protected Object replaceObject(Object object)
    throws IOException
```

Replaces one object with another during serialization. A call must be made to `enableReplaceObject()` before this method will work. Once enabled, this method is called with every object being serialized. This method is called just as the object is about to be serialized—all subsequent method calls are made to the object returned from this method (which becomes the serialized object). It is possible to return the `null` object for serialization.

reset()

```
public void reset()
        throws IOException
```

Restores the writing state to that of a newly opened stream. That is, the fact that anything has been written to the stream will be ignored. Everything will be written to the stream again.

write()

```
public void write(byte barray[])
        throws IOException
```

```
public void write(byte barray[],int offset,int length)
        throws IOException
```

```
public void write(int bvalue)
        throws IOException
```

Writes one or more bytes to the output. If `bvalue` is specified, it is written as a single byte. The writing will begin at `offset` and continue for `length` bytes. The default value for `offset` is 0, and the default `length` is the entire length of the array. The method blocks until the writing is complete.

writeBoolean()

```
public void writeBoolean(boolean value)
        throws IOException
```

Writes a `boolean` value.

writeByte()

```
public void writeByte(int value)
        throws IOException
```

The least significant eight bits of `value` are written to the stream as a `byte` value.

writeBytes()

```
public void writeBytes(String string)
        throws IOException
```

The characters of `string` are written as a series of byte values.

writeChar()

```
public void writeChar(int value)
```

```
        throws IOException
```

The low-order 16 bits of the int are written as a char.

writeChars()

```
    public void writeChars(String string)
        throws IOException
```

The contents of the string are written as a sequence of char values.

writeDouble()

```
    public void writeDouble(double value)
        throws IOException
```

The double is written to the stream.

writeFloat()

```
    public void writeFloat(float value)
        throws IOException
```

The float is written to the stream.

writeInt()

```
    public void writeInt(int value)
        throws IOException
```

The int is written to the stream.

writeLong()

```
    public void writeLong(long value)
        throws IOException
```

The long is written to the stream.

writeObject()

```
    public final void writeObject(Object object)
        throws IOException
```

Writes object to the stream. Writes the class of the object, the signature of the class, the values of the nontransient and nonstatic fields of the class, and all the superclasses of the class. The object is written in a format that is readable by an ObjectInputStream. Default serialization can be overridden with the writeObject() and readObject() methods. If an exception is thrown, the output stream is left in an unknown state. An InvalidClassException is thrown if an error is found in the class being serialized. A NotSerializableException is thrown if the object does not implement the Serializable interface.

writeShort()

```
public void writeShort(int value)
    throws IOException
```

The least significant 16 bits of the `int` are written as a `short`.

writeStreamHeader()

```
protected void writeStreamHeader()
    throws IOException
```

Writes the magic number and version to the stream. This method is supplied so that sub-classes can write their own header information.

writeUTF()

```
public void writeUTF(String string)
    throws IOException
```

The `string` is written in UTF format.

 For an example of object streaming, see **Serializable**.

ObjectStreamClass

class java.io.ObjectStreamClass

This describes a class that can be serialized, or has been serialized, to a stream. It contains the name and the `serialVersionUID` of the class. You can look at this as being sort of a `Class` object that has special information that applies only to classes loaded from serial streams.

Inheritance

```
public class java.io.ObjectStreamClass
    implements Serializable
    extends Object
        ⇑
    public class java.lang.Object
```

Constructors

Returned by

An `ObjectStreamClass` for a specific class that has been loaded by the Virtual Machine can be found by calling `lookup()`.

Methods

forClass()

```
public Class forClass()
```

Returns the local class in the Virtual Machine that this class is mapped to. Returns `null` if there is no corresponding local class.

getName()

```
public String getName()
```

Gets the name of the class.

getSerialVersionUID()

```
public long getSerialVersionUID()
```

Returns the value of the `serialVersionUID` for this class. The value defines a set of classes—all with the same name—that have evolved from a common root class and can be serialized and deserialized using a common format.

lookup()

```
public static ObjectStreamClass lookup(Class class)
```

Uses the specified `class` to find the `ObjectStreamClass` of a class that can be serialized. Returns `null` if objects of class cannot be serialized—that is, if they do not implement the `Serializable` interface.

toString()

```
public String toString()
```

Returns a string describing this object.

ObjectStreamConstants

interface java.io.ObjectStreamConstants

A collection of constant values used for reading and writing the graphs of objects to streams. This is not a public interface—it is available only to classes in the `java.io` package.

The tags and flags

The constants that begin with `TC_` are tag values used to identify items in the stream. Most of them mark the beginning of an item, but some of them are used to indicate the end, and there is one for marking a write exception. The constants beginning with `SC_` are one-bit flag values for `ObjectStreamClasses` in the stream.

Implemented by

```
ObjectInputStream
ObjectOutputStream
```

Inheritance

```
interface java.io.ObjectStreamConstants
```

Variables and Constants

baseWireHandle

```
final static int baseWireHandle
```

The value of the first wire handle to be assigned.

SC_EXTERNALIZABLE

```
final static byte SC_EXTERNALIZABLE = 0x04;
```

The flag to indicate the object is externalizable.

SC_SERIALIZABLE

```
final static byte SC_SERIALIZABLE = 0x02;
```

The flag to indicate the object is serializable.

SC_WRITE_METHOD

```
final static byte SC_WRITE_METHOD = 0x01;
```

STREAM_MAGIC

```
final static short STREAM_MAGIC = 0xACED;
```

The magic number of a stream object. This number is included in the header as a type identifier.

STREAM_VERSION

```
final static short STREAM_VERSION = 5;
```

The version number of the stream format.

TC_ARRAY

```
final static byte TC_ARRAY = 0x75;
```

An identifier of an array.

TC_BASE

```
final static byte TC_BASE = 0x70;
```

TC_BLOCKDATA

```
final static byte TC_BLOCKDATA = 0x77;
```

An identifier of a block of optional data.

TC_BLOCKDATALONG

```
final static byte TC_BLOCKDATALONG = 0x7A;
```

An identifier of a long block data.

TC_CLASS

```
final static byte TC_CLASS = 0x76;
```

An identifier of a reference to a class.

TC_CLASSDESC

```
final static byte TC_CLASSDESC = 0x72;
```

An identifier of a class descriptor.

TC_ENDBLOCKDATA

```
final static byte TC_ENDBLOCKDATA = 0x78;
```

A tag marking the end of a block of optional data.

TC_EXCEPTION

```
final static byte TC_EXCEPTION = 0x7B;
```

A tag marking an exception during a write operation.

TC_MAX

```
final static byte TC_MAX = 0x7B;
```

TC_NULL

```
final static byte TC_NULL = 0x70;
```

An identifier of a null object reference.

TC_OBJECT

```
final static byte TC_OBJECT = 0x73;
```

An identifer of an object.

TC_REFERENCE

```
final static byte TC_REFERENCE = 0x71;
```

An identifier of a reference to the preceding object.

TC_RESET

```
final static byte TC_RESET = 0x79;
```

An identifier indicating a reset of the stream context.

TC_STRING

```
final static byte TC_STRING = 0x74;
```

An identifier of a `String`.

ObjectStreamException

class java.io.ObjectStreamException

A superclass of all exceptions specific to the object stream classes.

Extended by

```
InvalidClassException
InvalidObjectException
NotActiveException
NotSerializableException
OptionalDataException
StreamCorruptedException
WriteAbortedException
```

Inheritance

```
public abstract class java.io.ObjectStreamException
    extends IOException
        ⇑
    public class java.io.IOException
        extends Exception
            ⇑
        public class java.lang.Exception
            extends Throwable
                ⇑
            public class java.lang.Throwable
```

```
                    implements Serializable
                    extends Object
                         ⇑
                    public class java.lang.Object
```

Constructors

```
      public ObjectStreamException()
      public ObjectStreamException(String message)
```

If the `message` string is supplied, it is used as a detailed message describing this particular exception. For this exception, the message is normally the class name.

ObjID

class java.rmi.server.ObjID

This class is used to uniquely identify the objects in a remote Virtual Machine. An `ObjID` is assigned to a remote object when it is exported.

Identifying marks

To establish a unique ID, an `ObjID` contains a number and an address-space identifier with respect to a specific host.

Inheritance

```
      public final class java.rmi.server.ObjID
          implements Serializable
          extends Object
               ⇑
          public class java.lang.Object
```

Variables and constants

DGC_ID

```
      public static final int DGC_ID
```

This is the well-known ID of the distributed garbage collector.

REGISTRY_ID

```
      public static final int REGISTRY_ID
```

This is the well-known ID of the RMI registry.

Constructors

```
public ObjID()
public ObjID(int number)
```

The number is a unique well-known ID number. Supplying the number guarantees that the resulting ID will not clash with any that are generated by the default constructor.

Returned by

An object of this class is returned from the read() method.

Methods

equals()

```
public boolean equals(Object object)
```

Returns true if object is an ObjID that has identical contents to this one.

hashCode()

```
public int hashCode()
```

Returns the hashcode value for this object.

read()

```
public static ObjID read(ObjectInput in)
    throws IOException
```

Constructs an object ID using data read from the input stream.

toString()

```
public String toString()
```

Returns a string representation of this object. If the object being identified is not local, its address-space identifier is included.

write()

```
public void write(ObjectOutput out)
    throws IOException
```

Marshals the object ID to the output stream.

Observable

class java.util.Observable

An Observable class supplies an interface that enables one or more Observer classes to receive information about the internal status of the Observable class.

The Observable class has the ability to maintain a list of Observer classes. The Observable will—when a status change warrants it—cause the update() method of all the Observers to be called with the new information.

The changed flag

The Observable object maintains an internal flag indicating whether or not its state has changed. Each time the Observers are notified, the flag is set to false. The flag must be set to true before any of the Observers will be notified again.

Inheritance

```
public class java.util.Observable
      extends Object
          ⇑
    public class java.lang.Object
```

Constructors

Observable()

```
public Observable()
```

Constructs an Observable object with an empty Observer table.

Methods

addObserver()

```
public synchronized void addObserver(Observer o)
```

Adds a new observer to the list. If the Observer is already in the list, it will not be added again.

clearChanged()

```
protected synchronized void clearChanged()
```

Clears the flag indicating that the state has changed.

countObservers()

```
public synchronized int countObservers()
```

Returns a count of the number of observers.

deleteObserver()

```
public synchronized void deleteObserver(Observer obs)
```

Removes the specified observer from the list.

deleteObservers()

```
public synchronized void deleteObservers()
```

Removes all observers from the list.

hasChanged()

```
public synchronized boolean hasChanged()
```

Returns the internal state flag—`true` if it has changed, `false` if it has not.

notifyObservers()

```
public void notifyObservers()

public void notifyObservers(Object arg)
```

This method will notify the observers by calling their `update()` methods. If the internal flag indicates there has been no change, no action will be taken. If `arg` is supplied, it will be the second argument on the call to `update()`.

setChanged()

```
protected synchronized void setChanged()
```

Sets the internal flag to `true`, indicating that the state of this object has changed.

Example

This `Observable` notifies an `Observer` each time a counter reaches a multiple of 10. The `track` and `watcher` objects are created in `main()`, and, since `track` is an `Observable` and `watcher` is an `Observer`, a call can be made to `addObserver()` that adds `watcher` to the list of `Observers` maintained by `track` (in this example, it is the only member of the list):

```
import java.util.*;
public class Track extends Observable implements Runnable
{
    public static void main(String[] arg) {
        Track track = new Track();
        Thread thread = new Thread(track);
        thread.start();
        Watcher watcher = new Watcher();
```

```
                track.addObserver(watcher);
        }
        public void run() {
                int counter = 0;
                try {
                        while(true) {
                                counter++;
                                System.out.println("counter=" + counter);
                                if((counter % 10) == 0) {
                                        setChanged();
                                        notifyObservers(
                                                new Integer(counter));
                                }
                                Thread.sleep(1000);
                        }
                } catch(InterruptedException e) {
                        return;
                }
        }
}

class Watcher implements Observer {
        public void update(Observable observable,Object arg) {
                Integer i = (Integer)arg;
                System.out.println("Observer notified at " + i);
        }
}
```

Whenever the counter in track reaches an even multiple of 10, two things happen. A call is made to setChanged() to make certain the internal flag is set. (If this flag is not set, no notification will take place.) A call is then made to notifyObservers() with an object containing the value of the counter. This causes a call to be made to update() in the watcher. The argument supplied to the notifyObservers() shows up as the arg object in the call to update().

Observer

interface java.util.Observer

Any class implementing this interface can be an observer of any class that extends Observable. The Observable class will call the update() method whenever there is a change in status.

Inheritance

```
public interface java.util.Observer
```

Methods

update()

```
public abstract void update(Observable obs,Object arg)
```

This method is called by the Observable object whenever there is a change in status. The argument obs is the Observable object. The arg is a possibly null object that may be used to pass information.

 For more details and an example, see **Observable**.

octal

An octal number is a base-8 number representation using only the digits 0 through 7. Each digit represents the value of three bits.

 For declarations of octal constants for each data type, see **char**, **byte**, **short**, **int**, and **long**. For octal and other escape sequences, see **escapes**.

Operation

class java.rmi.server.Operation

This class holds the description of a Java method.

Inheritance

```
public class java.rmi.server.Operation
    extends Object
        ⇑
    public class java.lang.Object
```

Constructors

```
public Operation(String methodName)
```

An Operation object is created for a specific method.

Returned by

An array of `Operation` objects is returned from `Skeleton.getOperations()`.

Methods

getOperation()

```
public String getOperation()
```

Returns the name of the method.

toString()

```
public String toString()
```

Returns a string representation of this object.

operators and operations

 See **expressions**.

OptionalDataException

class java.io.OptionalDataException

This exception is thrown by a `readObject()` method whenever it encounters optional data. If the `eof` flag is `false`, the `length` will hold the number of bytes available to be read.

Inheritance

```
public class java.io.OptionalDataException
    extends ObjectStreamException
        ⇑
    public class java.io.ObjectStreamException
        extends IOException
            ⇑
        public class java.io.IOException
            extends Exception
                ⇑
            public class java.lang.Exception
                extends Throwable
                    ⇑
                public class java.lang.Throwable
```

```
            implements Serializable
            extends Object
                 ⇑
            public class java.lang.Object
```

Variables and constants

eof

```
    public boolean eof
```

This is `true` if there is no more data in the buffered part of the stream.

length

```
    public int length
```

This is the number of bytes available for reading from the current buffer.

OR

 See **AND**.

OutOfMemoryError

class java.lang.OutOfMemoryError

The Virtual Machine will throw this error whenever it cannot allocate the memory required to instantiate an object. This is only thrown after garbage collection has failed to free sufficient memory.

Inheritance

```
    public class java.lang.OutOfMemoryError
        extends VirtualMachineError
            ⇑
        public class java.lang.VirtualMachineError
            extends Error
                ⇑
            public class java.lang.Error
                extends Throwable
                    ⇑
                public class java.lang.Throwable
```

```
                    implements Serializable
                    extends Object
                          ⇑
                    public class java.lang.Object
```

Constructors

```
      public OutOfMemoryError()
      public OutOfMemoryError(String message)
```

If the message string is supplied, it is used as a detailed message describing this particular exception.

OutputStream

class java.io.OutputStream

This is an abstract class representing an output stream of bytes. All output stream classes are based on this class.

Extended by

```
      ByteArrayOutputStream
      FileOutputStream
      FilterOutputStream
      ObjectOutputStream
      PipedOutputStream
```

Inheritance

```
      public abstract class java.io.OutputStream
          extends Object
               ⇑
          public class java.lang.Object
```

Constructors

```
      public OutputStream()
```

Returned by

Objects of this class are returned from calls to LogStream.getOutputStream, Process.getOutputStream, Runtime.getLocalizedOutputStream, Socket.getOutputStream, SocketImpl.getOutputStream, and URLConnection.getOutputStream.

Methods

close()

```
public void close()
    throws IOException
```

Closes the output stream. It must be called to release any resources associated with the stream.

flush()

```
public void flush()
    throws IOException
```

Flushes the stream by forcing a write of any buffered output bytes.

write()

```
public void write(byte barray[])
    throws IOException

public void write(byte barray[],int offset,int length)
    throws IOException

public abstract void write(int bvalue)
    throws IOException
```

Writes one or more bytes to the output. If bvalue is specified, it is written as a single byte. The writing will begin at offset and continue for length bytes. The default value for offset is 0, and the default length is the entire length of the array. The method blocks until the writing is complete.

OutputStreamWriter

class java.io.OutputStreamWriter

Writes bytes to an output stream. If character data is written, it is converted to a byte format.

Encoding

There is an encoding scheme used to map characters to bytes. The encoding scheme used is determined by the constructor — one can be specified, or it can be allowed to default. For this class to write a character, it could be necessary to write one or more bytes to the stream — this depends on the encoding.

The encoding is done with an internal `CharToByteConverter` object.

Extended by

```
FileWriter
```

Inheritance

```
public class java.io.OutputStreamWriter
    extends Writer
        ⇑
    public class java.io.Writer
        extends Object
            ⇑
        public class java.lang.Object
```

Constructors

OutputStreamWriter()

```
public OutputStreamWriter(OutputStream output,String encoding)
    throws UnsupportedEncodingException
```

```
public OutputStreamWriter(OutputStream output)
```

An `OutputStreamWriter` can be constructed on top of an `OutputStream` with or without specifying a special encoding scheme. If encoding is not specified, the system default is used.

Methods

close()

```
public void close()
    throws IOException
```

This method will first call `flush()` and then close the output stream. Further calls to `write()` or flush() will not work. There is no error in calling `close()` more than once.

flush()

```
public void flush()
```

```
    throws IOException
```

Writes any pending output. If there are any pending output characters anywhere in the output stream, they will be sent immediately to their final destination at the end of the stream chain.

getEncoding()

```
    public String getEncoding()
```

Returns the name of the character encoding scheme. It may return `null` if the stream has been closed.

write()

```
    public void write(char carray[],int offset,int length)
        throws IOException

    public void write(int character)
        throws IOException

    public void write(String string,
            int stroffset,int strlength)throws IOException
```

Writes an array of characters, a string of characters, or a single character to the stream. For an array, the writing will begin at `carray[offset]` and continue for `length` characters. If `string` is specified, the character beginning at `stroffset` and continuing for `strlength` characters will be written.

overflow

 For the action taken whenever the result of a real-number calculation becomes too large to be represented, see **float** and **double**.

overload

This term commonly refers to the capability of an operator to perform differently depending on its context within a program. There is no facility in Java for the programmer to change or enhance the capability of any operator. While there is no programmable overloading, Java does have some built-in overloading.

Many of the arithmetic operators (+, −, *, /) will perform either floating-point or integer operations. The most overloaded operators are the plus and the plus-equals (+ and +=), which both can be used to create `String` objects from any object or primitive type. They can then be concatenated with an already-existing `String` object.

For details on just what the defined overloadings are, see **operator**. For details on string concatenation, see **String.**

override

 See **extends**.

Owner

interface java.security.acl.Owner

This is the interface for a managing owner of an Access Control List (ACL).

The first Principal

Any class that implements this interface should require that the initial principal/owner be specified on its constructor, because an owner can only be added by another owner. If there are no owners, one can never be added.

Extended by

```
Acl
```

Inheritance

```
public interface java.security.acl.Owner
```

Methods

addOwner()

```
public abstract boolean addOwner(Principal caller,
        Principal newOwner)
    throws NotOwnerException
```

The `caller` is using this method to add `newOwner` as a new owner. The method returns `true` on success and `false` on failure. A `NotOwnerException` is thrown if `caller` is not an owner.

deleteOwner()

```
public abstract boolean deleteOwner(Principal caller,
            Principal owner)
    throws NotOwnerException
    throws LastOwnerException
```

The `caller` is using this method to remove `owner` from the list of owners. A caller can use this method to remove itself. The method returns `true` if `owner` is successfully removed, and `false` if `owner` was not in the list of owners. A `NotOwnerException` is thrown if `caller` is not an owner. The `LastOwnerException` is thrown if the `caller` and the `owner` are the same, and it is the last owner—there must always be at least one owner.

isOwner()

```
public abstract boolean isOwner(Principal principal)
```

Returns `true` if `principal` is an owner of the list.

package

A package is a named group of classes, interfaces, and subpackages. A package may consist of any number of compilation units. All compilation units in the same package have access to one another. Any compilation unit that is not specified as being a part of a package is a member of the default package.

Packages are very useful for separating code into organized groups, but the primary usefulness of packages lies in creating name spaces. Identical names can be defined in several packages, and they can all be used without conflict because of their package names. If the importation of two packages reveals a name conflict in a program, the programmer simply resorts to using fully qualified names and the conflict disappears. Examples of this in the API are the classes `java.util.Date` and `java.sql.Date`. The result is that Java packages can be written and distributed without concern for possible name collisions.

The unnamed package

Whenever a compilation unit has no package declaration at its top, it becomes a member of the unnamed package. Exactly what this means will vary from one host system to another. Every system is required to have at least one unnamed package. It is possible for a system to have several. A hierarchical file system, for example, could automatically associate unnamed packages with directory names. Only one unnamed package is available at any one time—there is only one "current working directory," for example. It is common for the unnamed package to be the same as the package named `java`, which also holds the Java API.

The unnamed package exists mostly for convenience—for the development of simple or temporary programs. An application of any size should have its classes organized into packages. Or at least, if the application is small, it should have its own package.

Declaring the package name

The `package` keyword can be used at the beginning of each source file to specify the package to which the classes and interfaces will belong. If no name is specified, the classes and interfaces will be in the unnamed package, which acts much like a named package in respect to references and interrelationships.

If a package name is declared on a `package` statement, it must be the fully qualified name. That is, any public names in the file will be appended on the specified package name to become the fully qualified name. For example, this file:

```
package red.planet;
public class Mongo {
    ...
}
```

defines a class that has the fully qualified name of `red.planet.Mongo`.

Package contents and names

A package is made up of its member classes, interfaces, and other packages (known as subpackages). The name of every item in a package must be unique. This means that a subpackage and a class cannot have the same name any more than two classes could have the same name.

The names of items in a package, when addressed by their fully qualified names, are hierarchical dot-references. For example, the name `java.awt` is the name of the subpackage `awt` in the package `java`—the name `java.awt.image` is the name of the subpackage `image` in the subpackage `awt` in the package `java`.

Storing packages on disk

It is up to the host system to devise the exact method of storing packages. Packages have a hierarchical naming scheme that fits well with a hierarchical file system—just give the directories the same names as the packages and subpackages, and put things where they belong. Java can then look at the directory system and follow the name trail to the correct file. The same sort of arrangement could be made inside a database—the name of a package could be used as the key to the list of items contained in the package. Some of the items in the package could be made its subpackages to enable Java to follow the name trail to the item being sought.

This hierarchical naming structure is the reason for Java's restriction of a single public name (class or interface) per source file. This allows Java to search the hierarchy by directory and filename to find both the source and object files of the classes and interfaces it needs.

When you want a class or an interface to be in a specific package, it is necessary to put the source file into the directory named for the package *and* specify the package name at the top of the file. This may seem a bit redundant at first, but it needs to be done this way to allow the source code to be ported to nonhierarchical systems—it's the portability thing again.

Example

This is a simple example to show the relationship between package names and a hierarchical file system. Here are the file-system locations of our set of source files:

```
p/PackageNames.java
p/red/MyColor.java
p/blue/MyColor.java
p/blue/green/MyColor.java
```

The program of p/PackageNames.java is the mainline and—since it has no package name declared—is in the unnamed package. Its source code looks like this:

```
import blue.green.*;

public class PackageName {
    public static void main(String[] arg) {
        MyColor mc = new MyColor();
        System.out.println(mc);
    }
}
```

You can see that it imports everything in the blue.green package. All this program does is create a MyColor object and print out its descriptive string. We have three packages, and each of them has MyColor class in it. The one used by Java will be the one found in the imported package. The source of p/red/MyColor.java looks like this:

```
package red;

public class MyColor {
    public String toString() {
        return("Hello. I'm red.");
    }
}
```

The file p/blue/MyColor.java is in the package blue and looks like this:

```
package blue;

public class MyColor {
    public String toString() {
        return("Hello. I'm blue.");
```

```
            }
        }
```

The file `p/blue/green/MyColor`, a subpackage of `blue`, is in the package `blue.green` and looks like this:

```
package blue.green;

public class MyColor {
    public String toString() {
        return("Hello. I'm green.");
    }
}
```

The import statement specifies that the package to be searched for names is `blue.green`, so the output of the program looks like this:

```
Hello. I'm green.
```

 For more on the ability to access items from other packages, see **import** and **CLASSPATH**. For the naming of files and their contents, see **naming convention**. For the list of packages supplied as the API, see **java**. For naming restrictions on Java source code files, see **compilation unit**.

PaintEvent

class java.awt.event.PaintEvent

This event is not designed to be used in an application or applet. This is the event that causes calls to be made to the `paint()` and `update()` methods. It is in the form of an event so that it can be delivered in the event queue.

Inheritance

```
public class PaintEvent
    extends ComponentEvent
        ⇑
    public class java.awt.event.ComponentEvent
        extends AWTEvent
            ⇑
        public class java.awt.AWTEvent
            extends EventObject
                ⇑
            public class java.util.EventObject
                implements Serializable
```

```
               extends Object
                     ⇑
               public class java.lang.Object
```

Variables and constants

PAINT

```
public static final int PAINT
```

The constant defining the event that will cause a call to `paint()`.

PAINT_FIRST

```
public static final int PAINT_FIRST
```

The smallest possible value of the `PaintEvent` types.

PAINT_LAST

```
public static final int PAINT_LAST
```

The largest possible value of the `PaintEvent` types.

UPDATE

```
public static final int UPDATE
```

The constant defining the event that will cause a call to `update()`.

Constructors

```
public PaintEvent(Component component,int id,
          Rectangle updateRect)
```

The `PaintEvent` originates from a `component`. The `id` is either `PAINT` or `UPDATE`. The `updateRect` is the area of the component that needs to be painted.

Methods

getUpdateRect()

```
public Rectangle getUpdateRect()
```

Returns the rectangle defining the area of the component that needs to painted.

paramString()

```
public String paramString()
```

Returns debugging information. The return string describes the internal state and values of this object.

setUpdateRect()

```
public void setUpdateRect(Rectangle updateRect)
```

Sets the rectangle that defines the area of the component that needs to be painted.

Panel

class java.awt.Panel

This is a component that has the sole purpose of being a container of other components—it has no displayable parts. It uses a layout manager to size and position the components added to it and, in turn, is itself a component that can be added to another container. It takes a collection of components and combines them into a single component that can be dealt with as a unit.

Layout manager

The default layout manager is FlowLayout.

Extended by

```
Applet
```

Inheritance

```
public class java.awt.Panel
    extends Container
        ⇑
    public abstract class java.awt.Container
        extends Component
            ⇑
        public class java.awt.Component
            implements ImageObserver
            implements MenuContainer
            implements Serializable
            extends Object
                ⇑
            public class java.lang.Object
```

Constructors

```
public Panel()
public Panel(LayoutManager layout)
```

A `Panel` can be created with a specific layout manager, or it can use the default `FlowLayout` manager.

Methods

addNotify()

```
public void addNotify()
```

Creates the underlying system-dependent peer for this object. This method is not normally called by the application. It is called by the container.

Example 1

This example uses a couple of `Panel`s to lay out collections of buttons. The layout we want has three spaced buttons at the top, one beside the other, and a square of buttons at the bottom:

```
import java.awt.*;
public class PanelPair extends Frame{
    public static void main(String[] arg) {
        new PanelPair();
    }
    PanelPair() {
        Panel topPanel = new Panel();
        topPanel.add(new Button("left"));
        topPanel.add(new Button("middle"));
        topPanel.add(new Button("right"));
        add("North",topPanel);
        Panel bottomPanel = new Panel(new
        GridLayout(2,2));
        bottomPanel.add(new Button("one"));
        bottomPanel.add(new Button("two"));
        bottomPanel.add(new Button("three"));
        bottomPanel.add(new Button("four"));
        add("South",bottomPanel);
        pack();
        show();
    }
}
```

Two panels are used to do this. The one at the top, `topPanel`, is allowed to default to the `FlowLayout` manager, and the three buttons are added in the order they are to appear. The `bottomPanel` is created with a `GridLayout` manager—to force the buttons into a square—and the buttons are added to it. The default layout manager of the `Frame` is `BorderLayout`, so the `topPanel` is added to the frame at the "North" and `bottomPanel` is added at the "South." The result is shown in Figure P-1.

Figure P-1 A pair of *Panels* used to lay out buttons.

Example 2

A `Panel` is both a container and a component, so one `Panel` (acting as a component) can be placed inside another (acting as a container):

```
import java.awt.*;
public class PanelInPanel extends Frame{
    public static void main(String[] arg) {
        new PanelInPanel();
    }
    PanelInPanel() {
        Panel panel = new Panel(new BorderLayout());
        panel.add("North",new Checkbox("Upper check"));
        panel.add("South",new Checkbox("Lower check"));
        Panel buttonPanel = new Panel(new
        GridLayout(2,2));
        buttonPanel.add(new Button("one"));
        buttonPanel.add(new Button("two"));
        buttonPanel.add(new Button("three"));
        buttonPanel.add(new Button("four"));
        panel.add("Center",buttonPanel);
        add(panel);
        pack();
        show();
    }
}
```

The parent `Panel` is created with a `BorderLayout` manager. It has two checkboxes added to it—one at the "North" and one at the "South." Another panel, the `buttonPanel`, is created with four buttons and added to the "Center" of the original `Panel`. The result is shown in Figure P-2.

Figure P-2   One *Panel* inside another.

The other containers are **Applet, ScrollPane, Window, Dialog, FileDialog,**
and **Frame**.

ParameterDescriptor

class java.beans.ParameterDescriptor

> An object of this class can be supplied by a bean to provide additional infor-
> mation on a parameter. This is for information beyond that supplied by
> Method.
> The Java 1.1 version of this class supplies nothing that is not supplied by
> its superclass, FeatureDescriptor.

Inheritance

```
public class java.beans.ParameterDescriptor
    extends FeatureDescriptor
        ⇑
    public class java.beans.FeatureDescriptor
        extends Object
            ⇑
        public class java.lang.Object
```

Constructors

```
public ParameterDescriptor()
```

Returned by

An array of objects of this class is returned from MethodDescriptor.
getParameterDescriptors().

 For the reflection class that describes all the parameters of a method, see
Method.

paramString()

method

Many objects have a method by this name. Its primary purpose is debugging. It returns a String object that contains a description of the status and contents of the object. There is no real convention for the format of the string except that it be human-readable. It is normally a bit more detailed than the toString() method, but it is not as useful for production output because it contains internal information about the object.

parentheses

( )

Parentheses are used to group the list of comma-separated parameters on a method. They are also used for grouping terms in an arithmetic expression to force a specific operator precedence. They can also be used to cast one data type to another.

 For more information on grouping the terms of an expression, see **expression**. For information about method parameters, see **method**. For more information on casting, see **casting** and **conversion**.

ParseException

class java.text.ParseException

This exception is thrown whenever an error occurs during the scanning and reading of input text.

Inheritance

```
public class java.text.ParseException
     extends Exception
         ⇑
     public class java.lang.Exception
         extends Throwable
             ⇑
         public class java.lang.Throwable
             implements Serializable
             extends Object
```

```
                                    ⇑
              public class java.lang.Object
```

Constructors

```
    public ParseException(String message,int offset)
```

The `message` string is used as a detailed message describing this particular exception. The value of `offset` should be an index into the input string where the error was encountered.

Methods

getErrorOffset()

```
    public int getErrorOffset()
```

Returns the index into the input string where the error was encountered.

ParsePosition

class java.text.ParsePosition

Objects of this class are used as arguments to subclasses of `Format` to track and control the character positioning of input strings. It is updated by the process reading the strings.

How this class is used

When a `ParsePosition` object is created, it is given an index. This index is the character offset at which the reading of input will begin. The `ParsePosition` object is then used as an argument to the `parseObject()` method of a subclass of `Frame`. As the process proceeds—as the characters are read—this index is incremented. When the `parseObject()` has finished reading characters, the index has been moved to the next position in the input string. It can then be used again on another call to `parseObject()`.

Inheritance

```
    public class java.text.ParsePosition
        extends Object
              ⇑
        public class java.lang.Object
```

Constructors

```
    public ParsePosition(int index)
```

A new `ParsePosition` object is created by being given a specific index value—a starting location in the input string.

Methods

getIndex()

```
public int getIndex()
```

Returns the current value of the `index`.

setIndex()

```
public void setIndex(int index)
```

Sets the position to the value of `index`.

 This class is used as a utility class in **Format**.

peer

package java.awt.peer

This package contains interface definitions used by Java GUI components to communicate between the AWT and the underlying windowing system. None of these interfaces define a method that should be called from an application or an applet—these are used by objects inside the Java API. You can see by the names of the interfaces that all but a couple of them have a corresponding class implementation in the `java.awt` package. There is a one-to-one correspondence between the peer interfaces and the Java components—for example, the class `java.awt.Button` has its corresponding peer interface `java.awt.peer.ButtonPeer`.

The peer event

One member of the package that is not a component interface is the `ActiveEvent` interface. It is the interface of events that knows how to dispatch themselves. An implementation of this interface will allow an event to be placed on the queue; by calling the one method of the interface, one can have it dispatch itself. This way, objects that are not components can have things occur in threads other than the one originating the event. This must be handled with care because deadlocks are possible.

The lightweight peer

The `LightweightPeer` interface has no data or methods—it marks a component as being dependent upon a native container. Window-related events need to be routed to the underlying native container for the actual work to be done.

Interfaces

```
ActiveEvent
ButtonPeer
CanvasPeer
CheckboxMenuItemPeer
CheckboxPeer
ChoicePeer
ComponentPeer
ContainerPeer
DialogPeer
FileDialogPeer
FontPeer
FramePeer
LabelPeer
LightweightPeer
ListPeer
MenuBarPeer
MenuComponentPeer
MenuItemPeer
MenuPeer
PanelPeer
PopupMenuPeer
ScrollbarPeer
ScrollPanePeer
TextAreaPeer
TextComponentPeer
TextFieldPeer
WindowPeer
```

period

.

In Java, a period is used as a decimal point in a real number and as a dot-reference in a qualified name.

A method or field in a class or interface can be fully qualified by attaching the name of the class or interface onto the front of the item being addressed. For example, constant `MAX_VALUE` of the `Integer` class can be addressed as `Integer.MAX_VALUE`. The dot-reference name can be used to fully qualify a name—package and all—as in `java.lang.Integer.MAX_VALUE`.

 For more on using a period as a dot-reference name qualifier, see **package** and **naming convention**. For using the period as a decimal point in real numbers, see **float** and **double**.

permill

"Permill" is like "percent," except that it is based on 1,000 instead of 100. For example, 34 percent is the same as 340 permill.

Permission

interface java.security.acl.Permission

This is the interface to an object that will grant a permission. For example, it could grant access permission to some system resource.

Inheritance

```
public interface java.awt.security.Permission
```

Methods

equals()

```
public abstract boolean equals(Object object)
```

Returns true if object implements the Permission interface to grant the same permission as this one.

toString()

```
public abstract String toString()
```

Returns a string description of this Permission.

picoJava

 See **JavaChip**.

PipedInputStream

class java.io.PipedInputStream

A PipedInputStream can read data that has been written to a PipedOutputStream. This can be used for communication between two threads.

Inheritance

```
public class java.io.PipedInputStream
    extends InputStream
            ⇑
    public class java.io.InputStream
        extends Object
                ⇑
        public class java.lang.Object
```

Variables and constants

buffer

```
protected byte buffer[]
```

The internal ring buffer of the input pipe.

in

```
protected int in
```

The index into `buffer` of the next available byte. It is set to −1 if `buffer` is empty.

out

```
protected int out
```

The index into `buffer` of the next location to receive an incoming byte.

PIPE_SIZE

```
protected final static int PIPE_SIZE
```

The default size of buffer.

Constructors

```
public PipedInputStream()
```

```
public PipedInputStream(PipedOutputStream stream)
    throws IOException
```

If `stream` is specified, the `PipedInputStream` will be connected to it. If `stream` is not specified, the `PipedInputStream` is not connected (and cannot be used until it is).

Methods

available()

```
public synchronized int available()
    throws IOException
```

Returns the number of bytes that are immediately available—the number that can be read without blocking.

close()

```
public void close()
    throws IOException
```

Closes the input stream. This must be called to free any system resources that are being held by the stream.

connect()

```
public void connect(PipedOutputStream stream)
    throws IOException
```

Connects this input stream to an output stream.

read()

```
public synchronized int read()
    throws IOException
```

```
public synchronized int read(byte barray[],
        int offset,int length)
    throws IOException
```

Reads one or more bytes of data. If no argument is specified, reads and returns one byte of data. If barray is specified, reads data into the array starting at barray[offset] and continuing for length bytes and return number of bytes actually read. Blocks until data is available. Returns -1 if the end of the pipe has been reached, and thrown an IOException if the pipe is broken.

receive()

```
protected synchronized void receive(int bvalue)
    throws IOException
```

Places byte value bvalue in the input buffer as the next character received from the PipedOuputStream.

 For an example, see **PipedOutputStream**. Also see **PipedReader** and **PipedWriter**.

PipedOutputStream

class java.io.PipedOutputStream

A `PipedOutputStream` can write data to a `PipedInputStream`. This can be used for communication between two threads.

Inheritance

```
public class java.io.PipedOutputStream
    extends OutputStream
        ⇑
    public class java.io.OutputStream
        extends Object
            ⇑
        public class java.lang.Object
```

Constructors

PipedOutputStream()

```
public PipedOutputStream()
```

```
public PipedOutputStream(PipedInputStream stream)
    throws IOException
```

If `stream` is specified, the `PipedOutputStream` will be connected to it. If `stream` is not specified, the `PipedOutputStream` is not connected (and cannot be used until it is).

Methods

close()

```
public void close()
    throws IOException
```

Closes the output stream. This must be called to free any system resources that are being held by the stream.

connect()

```
public void connect(PipedInputStream stream)
    throws IOException
```

Connects this output stream to an input stream.

flush()

```
public synchronized void flush()
```

```
        throws IOException
```

Flushes the stream and notifies any readers that bytes are waiting on the pipe.

write()

```
    public void write(byte barray[],int offset,int length)
        throws IOException

    public void write(int bvalue)
        throws IOException
```

Writes one or more bytes of data to the pipe. If barray is specified, the data beginning and barray[offset] and continuing for length bytes are written. If bvalue is specified, the low-order eight bits of it are written as a single byte. Blocks until the data is actually written to the pipe.

Example

This example creates a PipedInputStream and a PipedOutputStream, connects them together, and hands each one off to its own thread so that they can communicate with one another:

```
import java.io.*;
public class PipeThread {
    public static void main(String[] arg) {
        PipedOutputStream pout = new PipedOutputStream();
        PipedInputStream pin = new PipedInputStream();
        try {
            pin.connect(pout);
        } catch(IOException e) {
            System.out.println(e);
            System.exit(1);
        }
        PipeReadBytes read = new PipeReadBytes(pin);
        PipeSendBytes send = new PipeSendBytes(pout);
        read.start();
        send.start();
    }
}
class PipeSendBytes extends Thread {
    PipedOutputStream pout;
    public PipeSendBytes(PipedOutputStream pout) {
        this.pout = pout;
    }
    public void run() {
        try {
```

```
                    for(int i=0; i<10; i++) {
                        int bvalue = (int)(255*(Math.random()));
                        pout.write(bvalue);
                    }
                    pout.close();
                } catch(IOException e) {
                    System.out.println(e);
                    return;
                }
            }
        }
        class PipeReadBytes extends Thread {
            PipedInputStream pin;
            public PipeReadBytes(PipedInputStream pin) {
                this.pin = pin;
            }
            public void run() {
                int count = 0;
                while(true) {
                    try {
                        int byteValue = pin.read();
                        if(byteValue < 0)
                            return;
                        System.out.println("Byte " + ++count +
                                ": " + byteValue);
                    } catch(IOException e) {
                        System.out.println(e);
                        return;
                    }
                }
            }
        }
```

The `PipeSendBytes` thread writes ten random byte values to the thread and then closes the pipe. The `PipeReadBytes` thread reads and counts the incoming bytes until the closing of the pipe is indicated by the −1 return value. A typical run produced this output:

```
Byte 1: 103
Byte 2: 198
Byte 3: 35
Byte 4: 70
Byte 5: 58
Byte 6: 43
Byte 7: 161
```

```
Byte 8: 247
Byte 9: 6
Byte 10: 52
```

 Also see **PipedReader** and **PipedWriter**.

PipedReader

class java.io.PipedReader

A piped character-input stream. This can be used for communication between two threads.

Inheritance

```
public class java.io.PipedReader
    extends Reader
      ⇑
    public class java.io.Reader
        extends Object
          ⇑
        public class java.lang.Object
```

Constructors

```
public PipedReader()

public PipedReader(PipedWriter pipe)
    throws IOException
```

A `PipedReader` can be created and connected to an output `pipe`, or one can be created that is not yet connected.

Methods

close()

```
public void close()
    throws IOException
```

Closes the stream.

connect()

```
public void connect(PipedWriter pipe)
    throws IOException
```

Connects the `pipe` to this reader.

read()

```
public synchronized int read(char carray[],
        int offset,int length)
    throws IOException
```

Reads one or more characters from the pipe. Reads data into the array starting at `carray[offset]` and continuing for `length` characters and returns the number of characters actually read. Blocks until data is available. Returns −1 if the end of the pipe has been reached, and throws an `IOException` if the pipe is broken.

 For an example, see **PipedWriter**. Also see **PipedInputStream** and **PipedOutputStream**.

PipedWriter

class java.io.PipedWriter

A piped character input stream. This can be used for communication between two threads.

Inheritance

```
public class java.io.PipedWriter
    extends Writer
        ⇑
    public class java.io.Writer
        extends Object
            ⇑
        public class java.lang.Object
```

Constructors

```
public PipedWriter()

public PipedWriter(PipedReader pipe)
    throws IOException
```

If `pipe` is specified, the `PipedWriter` will be connected to it. If `pipe` is not specified, a `PipedWriter` is created that is not yet connected.

Methods

close()

```
public void close()
    throws IOException
```

Closes the stream.

connect()

```
public void connect(PipedReader pipe)
    throws IOException
```

Connects pipe as the reader for this writer.

flush()

```
public void flush()
    throws IOException
```

Writes any buffered data and flushes the underlying stream.

write()

```
public void write(char carray[],int offset,int length)
    throws IOException
```

Writes one or more characters to the pipe. The data beginning at carray[offset] and continuing for length characters are written. Blocks until the data is actually written to the pipe.

Example

This example uses a PipedWriter and a PipedReader to send an array of characters from one thread to another:

```
import java.io.*;
public class PipeReadWrite {
    public static void main(String[] arg) {
        PipedWriter pout = new PipedWriter();
        PipedReader pin = new PipedReader();
        try {
            pin.connect(pout);
        } catch(IOException e) {
            System.out.println(e);
            System.exit(1);
        }
        PipeReadByteArray read =
                new PipeReadByteArray(pin);
        PipeWriteByteArray send =
                new PipeWriteByteArray(pout);
        read.start();
```

```
            send.start();
        }
    }
    class PipeWriteByteArray extends Thread {
        PipedWriter pout;
        public PipeWriteByteArray(PipedWriter pout) {
            this.pout = pout;
        }
        public void run() {
            String str = "This will be piped!";
            int length = str.length();
            char[] carray = new char[length];
            for(int i=0; i<length; i++)
                carray[i] = str.charAt(i);
            try {
                pout.write(carray,0,length);
                pout.flush();
                pout.close();
            } catch(IOException e) {
                System.out.println(e);
            }
        }
    }
    class PipeReadByteArray extends Thread {
        PipedReader pin;
        public PipeReadByteArray(PipedReader pin) {
            this.pin = pin;
        }
        public void run() {
            String str = "";
            char[] carray = new char[3];
            try {
                int count;
                do {
                    count = pin.read(carray,0,3);
                    for(int i=0; i<count; i++)
                        str += carray[i];
                } while(count > 0);
                System.out.println(str);
            } catch(IOException e) {
                System.out.println(e);
            }
        }
    }
```

The `PipedReader` and `PipedWriter` are created and passed to each of the threads via the constructor. The writer sends an array of characters extracted from a character string. Because the writer knows the exact size of the string to be sent, it sends it all at once. The reader reads up to three characters at a time —using the return count value from the `read()` method to determine how many—and concatenates them into a string as they are received. The receiver outputs the single line:

```
This will be piped!
```

 Also see **PipedInputStream** and **PipedOutputStream**.

PixelGrabber

class java.awt.image.PixelGrabber

This is an `ImageConsumer` capable of retrieving a subset of the pixels from an `Image` or an `ImageProducer`.

Incomplete information

A call to `getStatus()` should be made before information about the pixels is retrieved. Several of the methods of this class are for returning information about the retrieved pixels. These methods may return incomplete or erroneous data until the process of grabbing the pixels is complete. This is true not just for size information, but even for the `ColorModel` of the retrieved pixels.

Not only could the data be incomplete, it could be completely wrong. For example, it is possible that the `PixelGrabber` could begin using a color model other than the RGB model and, during the process of collecting the data, find that it must fall back to the default RGB model (the source could be using more than one color model). This means that the return value from `getColorModel()` could change during the pixel grabbing.

Inheritance

```
public class java.awt.image.PixelGrabber
    implements ImageConsumer
    extends Object
            ⇑
    public class java.lang.Object
```

Constructors

```
public PixelGrabber(Image image,
        int x,int y,
```

```
            int width,int height,int pixel[],
            int offset,int scansize)
    public PixelGrabber(ImageProducer imageProducer,
            int x,int y,
            int width,int height,int pixel[],
            int offset,int scansize)
    public PixelGrabber(Image image,
            int x,int y,
            int width,int height,boolean forceRGB)
```

The `PixelGrabber` will grab the rectangular area of `image` or `imageProducer` of `width` and `height` with its upper-left corner at `x` and `y`. The `x` and `y` coordinates are relative to the unscaled size of the `image`.

If the pixel array is specified, the retrieved pixels will be stored in the array in the RGB color model. The `RGB` data for pixel `(i, j)`, where `(i, j)` is inside the rectangle, is stored in the array at

```
    pixel[((j - y) * scansize) + (i - x) + offset]
```

The `offset` is the location in the `pixel` array to store the first value. The `scansize` is the distance from one row of pixels to the next.

If the pixel array is not specified, a storage location of the correct size (and the correct type for the color model) will be allocated. Also, because there is no fixed-length array to specify the size, a negative `width` or `height` value will automatically default to being the full width or height of the input image. If `forceRGB` is `true`, the results will be in the RGB color model—if `forceRGB` is `false`, the results will be determined by the input image.

Methods

abortGrabbing()

```
    public synchronized void abortGrabbing()
```

Requests that the `PixelGrabber` abort the process of grabbing pixels.

getColorModel()

```
    public synchronized ColorModel getColorModel()
```

Returns the color model of the pixels stored in the array. If the pixel array was specified on the constructor, this will always be an RGB `ColorModel`. A `null` is returned if the color model coming from the `ImageProducer` is not known.

getHeight()

```
    public synchronized int getHeight()
```

Returns the height of the grabbed rectangle. If the height is not yet known, −1 is returned.

getPixels()

```
public synchronized Object getPixels()
```

Returns the pixels. If the pixel array was not supplied to the constructor, and the pixel-grabbing is not complete, the return value will be null until the size and format of the data is known.

getStatus()

```
public synchronized int getStatus()
```

Return a bitwise OR of the current set of status flags. For a description of the possible flag bit values, see ImageObserver.

getWidth()

```
public synchronized int getWidth()
```

Returns the width of the grabbed rectangle. If the width is not yet known, −1 is returned.

grabPixels()

```
public boolean grabPixels()
        throws InterruptedException
```

```
public synchronized boolean grabPixels(long milliseconds)
        throws InterruptedException
```

Requests that the Image or ImageProducer begin delivering pixels. Blocks forever unless a timeout is specified as a number of milliseconds. This method will block until the pixels are delivered. If the pixels are all delivered, returns true. If there is an error, abort, or timeout, returns false. An InterruptedException is thrown if another thread interrupts this one.

imageComplete()

```
public synchronized void imageComplete(int status)
```

This method is implemented as a requirement of the ImageConsumer interface. It is used in the retrieval of pixels.

setColorModel()

```
public void setColorModel(ColorModel model)
```

This method is implemented as a requirement of the ImageConsumer interface. It is used in the retrieval of pixels.

setDimensions()

```
public void setDimensions(int width,int height)
```

This method is implemented as a requirement of the ImageConsumer interface. It is used in the retrieval of pixels.

setHints()

```
public void setHints(int hints)
```

This method is implemented as a requirement of the ImageConsumer interface. It is used in the retrieval of pixels.

setPixels()

```
public void setPixels(int srcX,int srcY,int srcW,
        int srcH,ColorModel model,
        byte pixels[],int srcOff,int srcScan)

public void setPixels(int srcX,int srcY,int srcW,
        int srcH,ColorModel model,
        int pixels[],int srcOff,int srcScan)
```

This method is implemented as a requirement of the ImageConsumer interface. It is used in the retrieval of pixels.

setProperties()

```
public void setProperties(Hashtable props)
```

This method is implemented as a requirement of the ImageConsumer interface. It is used in the retrieval of pixels.

startGrabbing()

```
public synchronized void startGrabbing()
```

Requests that the PixelGrabber start fetching the pixels.

status()   **deprecated**

```
public synchronized int status()
```

Returns the current status of the PixelGrabber. This method is deprecated—use getStatus().

Example

This example grabs a 4 × 4 square of pixels at location (10,10) from bluemarble.gif and prints out the RGB values for each of the 16 pixels:

```
import java.awt.*;
import java.awt.image.*;
public class Grab {
    public static void main(String[] arg) {
```

```
                    Toolkit tk = Toolkit.getDefaultToolkit();
                    Image image = tk.getImage("bluemarble.gif");

                    int x=10;
                    int y=10;
                    int width=4;
                    int height=4;
                    int[] pixel = new int[16];
                    int offset = 0;
                    int scansize = width;
                    PixelGrabber pg = new PixelGrabber(image,x,y,
                        width,height,pixel,offset,scansize);
                    try {
                        pg.grabPixels();
                    } catch(InterruptedException e) {
                        System.out.println(e);
                    }

                    for(int i=0; i<width; i++) {
                        for(int j=0; j<height; j++) {
                            int p = pixel[(j * width) + i];
                            System.out.println(
                                "pixel(" + i + "," + j + ")" +
                                " R:" + ((p >> 16) & 0xFF) +
                                " G:" + ((p >> 8) & 0xFF) +
                                " B:" + (p & 0xFF));
                        }
                    }
                }
            }
```

The output looks like this:

```
pixel(0,0) R:8 G:0 B:0
pixel(0,1) R:0 G:0 B:0
pixel(0,2) R:107 G:115 B:140
pixel(0,3) R:231 G:239 B:239
pixel(1,0) R:0 G:0 B:0
pixel(1,1) R:123 G:132 B:132
pixel(1,2) R:214 G:222 B:222
pixel(1,3) R:156 G:140 B:123
pixel(2,0) R:123 G:132 B:132
pixel(2,1) R:206 G:214 B:214
pixel(2,2) R:156 G:132 B:107
pixel(2,3) R:198 G:148 B:123
pixel(3,0) R:222 G:222 B:206
```

```
pixel(3,1) R:156 G:140 B:123
pixel(3,2) R:173 G:156 B:140
pixel(3,3) R:173 G:148 B:132
```

For the source of the pixels, see **Image** and **ImageProducer**. For a description of the methods used to retrieve pixels, see **ImageConsumer**.

plus

+ +=

The operators + and += are the Java arithmetic addition operators and the Java string concatenation operators. Also, the + operator can be used as the unary plus.

Simple addition

Arithmetic addition is valid only for the Java primitive data types. Mixed-mode arithmetic is supported — the narrower type is widened before the operation is performed. The + operator performs addition but does not modify the operands. The += operator performs addition and places the results in the left operand. These two statements are equivalent:

```
a = a + b;
a += b;
```

Integer overflow

Integer addition can possibly result in a number that can't be represented in the type receiving the result. The overflow will be lost without notice. For example, these four lines of code:

```
int ivalue = 0x7FFFFFF0;
System.out.println(ivalue);
ivalue += 100;
System.out.println(ivalue);
```

will print these two values:

```
2147483632
-2147483564
```

The original value is so large that the addition caused it to cycle back around to being a negative value.

For string concatenation, see **String** and **string literal**. For information on possible values of the data types, see **Byte**, **Character**, **Integer**, **Short**, **Long**, **Float**, and **Double**.

Point

class java.awt.Point

A simple class that contains an (x,y) point on a rectangular coordinate system. There is a redundancy among the methods: Several methods exist to set the *x* and *y* values. This is done for completeness—to parallel the same method names in the Component class.

Inheritance

```
public class java.awt.Point
        implements Serializable
        extends Object
            ⇑
        public class java.lang.Object
```

Variables and constants

x

```
public int x
```

The *x* coordinate.

y

```
public int y
```

The *y* coordinate.

Constructors

```
public Point()

public Point(Point p)

public Point(int x,int y)
```

If no arguments are supplied, a point is created with the values (0,0). Initial values can be specified with a Point object, or with the values x and y.

Returned by

A Point object is returned from

```
Component.getLocation()
Component.getLocationOnScreen()
Component.location()
```

```
ComponentPeer.getLocationOnScreen()
GridBagLayout.getLayoutOrigin()
GridBagLayout.location()
MouseEvent.getPoint()
Point.getLocation()
Rectangle.getLocation()
ScrollPane.getScrollPosition()
```

Methods

equals()

```
public boolean equals(Object obj)
```

Returns `true` only if `obj` is a `Point` object and the values of x and y match exactly. Overrides `Object.equals()`.

getLocation()

```
public Point getLocation()
```

Returns a new `Point` object that is a duplicate of this one.

hashCode()

```
public int hashCode()
```

Returns a hashcode value that is unique to these values of x and y. Overrides `Object.hashCode()`.

move()

```
public void move(int x,int y)
```

Sets the values of x and y.

setLocation()

```
public void setLocation(int x,int y)

public void setLocation(Point p)
```

Sets the values of x and y.

toString()

```
public String toString()
```

Returns a `String` for this `Point` that includes the coordinates. Overrides `Object.toString()`.

translate()

```
public void translate(int dx,int dy)
```

Translates the point. The argument values of dx and dy are added to the internal x and y coordinates. This effectively moves the point by the amounts specified by dx and dy.

 For similar wrappers, see **Dimension, Inset, Polygon, Rectangle,** and **Shape.**

pointer

 See **reference.**

Polygon

class java.awt.Polygon

A Polygon is a wrapper for an array of *x* and *y* coordinates.

The origin of a polygon

Each point in the array has one point before it and one after it. The last point in the list uses the first point as the one that follows it, and the first point uses the last point as the one to precede. This way, a polygon is always a closed figure.

The even-odd rule

The *even-odd rule,* also called the *alternating rule,* is used to determine whether or not a point is inside the polygon. The polygon in Figure P-3 has its origin (the location defined by the first point in the array) on the left. The bounded area labeled A is inside the polygon. The lines cross twice, creating the region labeled B—this region is not considered to be inside the polygon. The lines cross again creating C, which is inside, and D, which is not. This is called the even-odd rule because counting an odd or even number of crossings will tell you whether a region is inside or outside the polygon.

Figure P-3 A polygon with even and odd regions.

Inheritance

```
public class java.awt.Polygon
    implements Shape
    implements Serializable
    extends Object
        ⇑
    public class java.lang.Object
```

Variables and constants

bounds

```
protected Rectangle bounds
```

This is the smallest rectangle that will enclose the polygon. It is constructed by using the extreme points of the polygon array.

npoints

```
public int npoints
```

The total number of points in the polygon.

xpoints

```
public int xpoints[]
```

The *x* coordinates of the polygon.

ypoints

```
public int ypoints[]
```

The *y* coordinates of the polygon.

Constructors

```
public Polygon()

public Polygon(int xpoints[],int ypoints[],int npoints)
```

If no coordinates are specified, the polygon is empty. The arrays xpoints and ypoints contain *x* and *y* coordinates of each point. The arrays must be large enough to contain npoints number of points.

Methods

addPoint()

```
public void addPoint(int x,int y)
```

The values of x and y will be added onto the end of the list of the points defining the polygon.

contains()

```
public boolean contains(Point point)

public boolean contains(int x,int y)
```

Returns true if the point is inside the polygon. The even-odd rule is used to determine whether or not the point is inside.

getBoundingBox()   deprecated

```
public Rectangle getBoundingBox()
```

Returns the smallest rectangle that will enclose all the points of the polygon. This method is deprecated—use getBounds().

getBounds()

```
public Rectangle getBounds()
```

Returns the smallest rectangle that will enclose all the points of the polygon.

inside()   deprecated

```
public boolean inside(int x,int y)
```

Returns true if the point is inside the polygon. The even-odd rule is used to determine whether or not the point is inside. This method is deprecated—use contains().

translate()

```
public void translate(int deltaX,int deltaY)
```

Adds the values deltaX and deltaY to all the points of the polygon, effectively moving it to a new position.

For similar wrappers, see **Dimension, Inset, Point, Rectangle**, and **Shape**.
For an example of using a Polygon to draw a figure, see **Graphics**.

polymorphism

 See **reference**.

PopupMenu

class java.awt.PopupMenu

This is a menu that will pop up at a specified position inside a component
instead of from a pull-down menu bar.

Inheritance

```
public class java.awt.PopupMenu
     extends Menu
          ⇑
     public class java.awt.Menu
          implements MenuContainer
          extends MenuItem
                ⇑
          public class java.awt.MenuItem
               extends MenuComponent
                    ⇑
               public abstract class java.awt.MenuComponent
                    implements Serializable
                    extends Object
                         ⇑
                    public class java.lang.Object
```

Constructors

```
public PopupMenu()

public PopupMenu(String title)
```

A pop-up menu can be created with or without a title.

Returned by

An object of this class is returned from `Toolkit.createPopupMenu()`.

Methods

addNotify()

```
public synchronized void addNotify()
```

Creates the underlying system-dependent peer for this object. This method is not normally called by the application. It is called by the container.

show()

```
public void show(Component origin,int x,int y)
```

Displays the pop-up menu with its upper-left corner at the position specified by x and y relative to the `origin` component.. The `origin` component must be in the hierarchy of the parent of the menu. Both the `origin` and the `parent` must be currently displayed.

Example

This example pops up a menu in response to a mouse button inside its window:

```
import java.awt.*;
import java.awt.event.*;
public class FramePopup extends Frame
        implements MouseListener, ActionListener {
    private PopupMenu popup;
    public static void main(String[] arg) {
        new FramePopup();
    }
    FramePopup() {
        popup = new PopupMenu();
        popup.add("Move");
        popup.add("Smear");
        popup.add("Spread");
        MenuItem item = new MenuItem("Exit");
        item.addActionListener(this);
        popup.add(item);
        add(popup);
        addMouseListener(this);
        setSize(200,200);
        show();
    }
    public void mouseReleased(MouseEvent event) {
        popup.show(this,event.getX(),event.getY());
```

```
        }
    public void mouseClicked(MouseEvent event) {}
    public void mouseEntered(MouseEvent event) {}
    public void mouseExited(MouseEvent event) {}
    public void mousePressed(MouseEvent event) {}
    public void actionPerformed(ActionEvent event) {
        if(event.getActionCommand().equals("Exit"))
            System.exit(0);
    }
}
```

The PopupMenu is created and added to the Frame. Whenever the mouse button is released inside the Frame window, the show() method of the pop-up is called with the coordinates of the mouse. The resulting pop-up menu is shown in Figure P-4. The menu will display and wait for a response. The only menu item with an action attached to it is "Exit," which exits the program.

Figure P-4   A pop-up menu being displayed in front of its parent component.

 The other classes dealing with menus are **CheckboxMenuItem**, **Menu**, **MenuComponent**, **MenuContainer**, **MenuItem**, and **MenuShortcut**.

PreparedStatement

interface java.sql.PreparedStatement

This is the interface to an object that can store a precompiled SQL statement. It can then be used to efficiently execute the statement multiple times.

Know your SQL types

There are several methods for setting IN parameter values. The methods all have names in the form of "setSomething0." Care must be taken that the data types match the SQL types. For example, if the IN parameter has the SQL type INTEGER, then setInt() should be used.

The parameterIndex

The methods used to set parameter values all use a `parameterIndex` value to specify which parameter is being set. The first parameter has an index number of 1, not 0 as one might expect.

The exception

Every method of this interface is capable of throwing an `SQLException`. This means that it will be necessary to call the methods of this class inside a `try-catch` block.

Extended by

```
CallableStatement
```

Inheritance

```
public interface PreparedStatement
    extends Statement
        public interface Java.sql.Statement
```

Constructors

Returned by

An object that implements this interface can be returned from a call to `Connection.prepareStatement()`.

Methods

clearParameters()

```
public abstract void clearParameters()
    throws SQLException
```

Clears all parameter settings. Parameter values will remain unchanged for multiple uses, and they can also be replaced one at a time by setting them to new values. This method immediately clears them all.

execute()

```
public abstract boolean execute()
    throws SQLException
```

execute()

```
public abstract boolean execute(String sql)
    throws SQLException
```

Executes an SQL statement that could return multiple results.

executeQuery()

```
public abstract ResultSet executeQuery()
    throws SQLException
```

The prepared SQL query is executed, and the ResultSet resulting from the execution is returned.

executeUpdate()

```
public abstract int executeUpdate()
    throws SQLException
```

Executes an SQL statement that does not return a value, such as INSERT, UPDATE, DELETE, or a DDL statement.

setAsciiStream()

```
public abstract void setAsciiStream(int parameterIndex
        InputStream instring,int length)
    throws SQLException
```

Sets a parameter to a character string value. The string comes from the InputStream and has a maximum length. The parameterIndex determines which parameter is to receive the string. The driver will convert the string into the character set appropriate for the database.

setBigDecimal()

```
public abstract void setBigDecimal(int parameterIndex,
        BigDecimal value)
    throws SQLException
```

Sets a parameter to a BigDecimal value. The value is converted to SQL NUMERIC when it is transmitted to the database.

setBinaryStream()

```
public abstract void setBinaryStream(int parameterIndex,
        InputStream instream,int length)
    throws SQLException
```

Sets a parameter to a block of binary data. Data is read from instream, for a maximum of length bytes, and is converted to a LONGVARBINARY type before being forwarded to the database.

setBoolean()

```
public abstract void setBoolean(int parameterIndex,
        boolean value)
    throws SQLException
```

Sets a parameter to a boolean value. The driver will convert the value to an SQL BIT before sending it to the database.

setByte()

```
public abstract void setByte(int parameterIndex,byte value)
    throws SQLException
```

Sets a parameter to a `byte` value. The driver will convert the `value` to an SQL TINYINT before sending it to the database.

setBytes()

```
public abstract void setBytes(int parameterIndex,byte value[])
    throws SQLException
```

Sets a parameter to an array of `byte` values. The driver will convert the `value` to an SQL VARBINARY or LONGVARBINARY, as appropriate, before sending it to the database.

setDate()

```
public abstract void setDate(int parameterIndex,Date value)
    throws SQLException
```
Sets a parameter to a `Date` value. The driver will convert the `value` to an SQL DATE before sending it to the database.

setDouble()

```
public abstract void setDouble(int parameterIndex,double value)
    throws SQLException
```

Sets a parameter to a `double` value. The driver will convert the `value` to an SQL DOUBLE before sending it to the database.

setFloat()

```
public abstract void setFloat(int parameterIndex,float value)
    throws SQLException
```

Sets a parameter to a `float` value. The driver will convert the `value` to an SQL FLOAT before sending it to the database.

setInt()

```
public abstract void setInt(int parameterIndex,int value)
    throws SQLException
```

Sets a parameter to an `int` value. The driver will convert the `value` to an SQL INTEGER before sending it to the database.

setLong()

```
public abstract void setLong(int parameterIndex,long value)
    throws SQLException
```

Sets a parameter to a `long` value. The driver will convert the `value` to an SQL BIGINT value before sending it to the database.

setNull()

```
public abstract void setNull(int parameterIndex,int sqlType)
    throws SQLException
```

Sets a parameter to an SQL NULL. The possible values for `sqlType` are defined in `java.sql.Types`.

setObject()

```
public abstract void setObject(int parameterIndex,
        Object value,int targetSqlType)
    throws SQLException
```

```
public abstract void setObject(int parameterIndex,
        Object value)
    throws SQLException
```

```
public abstract void setObject(int parameterIndex,
        Object value,int targetSqlType,int scale)
    throws SQLException
```

Sets the value of a parameter using `value` after it has been converted to the `targetSqlType`. The possible values of `targetSqlType` are defined in `java.sql.Types`. If `targetrSqlType` is not specified, a type appropriate to the object type of the `value` will be assumed. The value is converted to its integral equivalent. The conversion may or may not require the use of `scale` — it is needed for certain Java numeric types. If the scale is not specified but turns out to be necessary, a value of 0 is assumed.

It is possible to use this method to set database-specific abstract types by using a driver that understands the Java types and specifying `targetSqlType` to be `java.sql.Types.OTHER`.

setShort()

```
public abstract void setShort(int parameterIndex,short value)
    throws SQLException
```

Sets a parameter to a `short` value. The driver will convert the `value` to an SQL SMALLINT before sending it to the database.

setString()

```
public abstract void setString(int parameterIndex,String value)
    throws SQLException
```

Sets a parameter to a `String` value. The driver will convert the `value` to an SQL VARCHAR or LONGVARCHAR (as appropriate) before sending it to the database.

setTime()

```
public abstract void setTime(int parameterIndex,Time value)
    throws SQLException
```

Sets a parameter to a Time value. The driver will convert the value to an SQL TIME before sending it to the database.

setTimestamp()

```
public abstract void setTimestamp(int parameterIndex,
        Timestamp value)
    throws SQLException
```

Sets a parameter to a Timestamp value. The driver will convert the value to an SQL TIMESTAMP before sending it to the database.

setUnicodeStream()

```
public abstract void setUnicodeStream(int parameterIndex,
        InputStream value,int length)
    throws SQLException
```

Sets a parameter to a Unicode stream. The driver will read a maximum of length Unicode characters from the input stream and convert the data into an SQL LONGVARCHAR before sending it to the database.

 For another way to execute SQL statements, see **Statement**.

primitive data types

There are two kinds of primitive types: a collection of numeric types and the one logical type. The numeric types can be further divided into integer types and floating-point types. Each of the primitive types assumes an initial value when it is created. They are all listed in Table P-1.

Table P-1   Primitive Data Types

Name	Group	Size	Kind	Initial
boolean	logical	1 bit	logical	false
byte	numeric	8 bits	signed integer	0
char	numeric	16 bits	unsigned integer	'\u0000'
short	numeric	16 bits	signed integer	0
int	numeric	32 bits	signed integer	0

Name	Group	Size	Kind	Initial
long	numeric	64 bits	signed integer	0L
float	numeric	32 bits	floating point	0.0f
double	numeric	64 bits	floating point	0.0d

 Although the specification of the Java language does not include "reference" in its list of primitive types, it could be argued that it is one. It is different from the other primitive types in that references have different types and the size of a reference is not fixed from one implementation of Java to another. References, however, are somewhat similar to pointers in other languages, and like the other Java primitives, they are atomic since they cannot be broken down any further except as bit patterns. The initial value of a reference is null.

 For performing binary operations between two different types, see **expressions**. For declaring and referencing, see **variables**. For descriptions of the primitive data types, see **boolean**, **byte**, **char**, **short**, **int**, **long**, **float**, or **double**.

Principal

interface java.security.Principal

This is the interface that represents a principal. A *principal* is an individual, a corporation, a program thread, or anything else that can be given an identity and may require permissions to take actions.

Implemented by

Identity

Extended by

Group

Inheritance

public interface java.security.Principal

Constructors

Returned by

Objects that implement this interface are returned from `AclEntry.getPrincipal()`, `Certificate.getGuarantor()`, and `Certificate.getPrincipal()`.

Methods

equals()

```
public abstract boolean equals(Object object)
```

Returns `true` if `object` is a `Principal` object representing the same entity as this one.

getName()

```
public abstract String getName()
```

Returns the name of the represented entity.

hashCode()

```
public abstract int hashCode()
```

Returns the hashcode for this `Principal`.

toString()

```
public abstract String toString()
```

Returns a string representation of this object.

 For information on maintaining lists of permissions for a `Principal`, see the **acl** package. Specifically, see **Identity**, **Certificate**, **Permission**, and **Group.**

PrintGraphics

interface java.awt.PrintGraphics

This is the interface used by an extension of the `Graphics` class designed to draw graphic objects to a printer. An object of this class is the context of a single page.

Inheritance

```
public interface java.awt.PrintGraphics
```

Constructors

Returned by

The method PrintJob.getGraphics() returns a Graphics object that implements this interface.

Methods

getPrintJob()

```
public abstract PrintJob getPrintJob()
```

Returns the PrintJob object that underlies this PrintGraphics object.

 Also see **PrintJob**.

PrintJob

class java.awt.PrintJob

This is an abstract class defining the methods to initiate and execute a print job. Its purpose is to provide access to a print-graphics object to render the output on a print device.

The print is in pixels

Printing to a printer page uses the same techniques as drawing text and graphics on a window. A Graphics object is used. The pixel resolution of the page is selected to be reasonably close to that of the display—objects printed and displayed will have similar sizes and the same ratios.

Inheritance

```
public abstract class java.awt.PrintJob
    extends Object
            ⇑
    public class java.lang.Object
```

Constructors

```
public PrintJob()
```

Returned by

A PrintJob object is returned from PrintGraphics.getPrintJob() and Toolkit.getPrintJob().

Methods

end()

```
public abstract void end()
```

Does any necessary cleanup and ends the print job.

finalize()

```
public void finalize()
```

This method is called by the garbage collector right before this object is reclaimed by the system.

getGraphics()

```
public abstract Graphics getGraphics()
```

Returns a Graphics object that will draw one page. The page will be sent to the printer whenever the dispose() method of the Graphics object is called. The returned Graphics object will implement the PrintGraphics interface.

getPageDimension()

```
public abstract Dimension getPageDimension()
```

Returns the dimensions of the page in pixels.

getPageResolution()

```
public abstract int getPageResolution()
```

Reruns the resolution of the page in pixels per inch. This may or may not correspond to the physical resolution of the printer.

lastPageFirst()

```
public abstract boolean lastPageFirst()
```

Returns true if the last page will be printed first.

Example

This example prints some lines and shapes on the default printer:

```
import java.awt.*;
import java.awt.image.*;
import java.util.*;
import java.net.*;
public class PrintDisplay extends Frame {
```

```
public static void main(String[] arg) {
    new PrintDisplay();
}
PrintDisplay() {
    Toolkit tk = Toolkit.getDefaultToolkit();
    PrintJob pj = tk.getPrintJob(this,
            "PrintDisplay",null);
    Graphics g = pj.getGraphics();
    Dimension dim = pj.getPageDimension();
    g.drawLine(0,0,dim.width,dim.height);
    g.drawLine(dim.width,0,0,dim.height);
    g.drawOval(0,0,dim.width,dim.height);
    g.drawRect(dim.width/4,dim.height/4,
        (3*(dim.width/4)),(3*(dim.height/4)));
    g.dispose();
    pj.end();
}
}
```

The default `Toolkit` is used to get a `PrintJob` object. The graphics object is then retrieved from the `PrintJob`. This example gets the pixel dimensions of the page by calling `getPageDimensions()` and uses the returned value to draw lines from corner to corner, then an oval, and then a rectangle. The printed page is shown in Figure P-5.

o
p
q

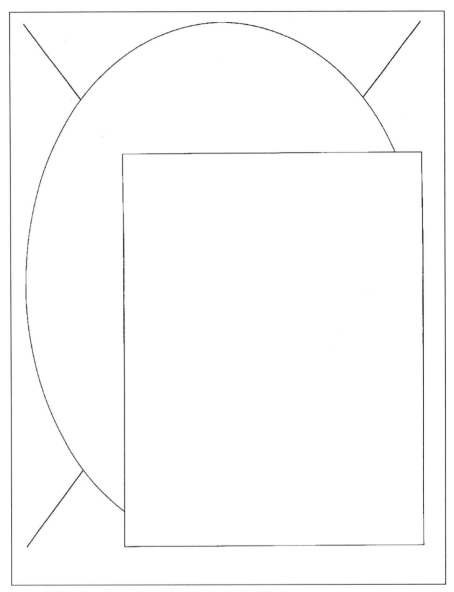

Figure P-5 The page printed by a *PrintJob* object.

 The printing capabilities in Java were new in release 1.1. Printing is a complicated process, especially when there is an attempt to do it in such a way that it
is portable across a number of platforms. The results of printing do not always
match those of the display, as is demonstrated by the fact that the line draw-

ings of this example actually performed hidden-line suppression—something not done in the on-screen display.

 Also see **Graphics** and **PrintGraphics**.

PrintStream

class java.io.PrintStream

This class will print formatted data to an output stream.

Do not use

This class is primarily for debugging. There are three of these objects in `java.lang.System` to write to `System.out` and `System.err` and to read from `System.in`. Generally speaking, objects of this class should not be used in production software. Use `PrintWriter` instead.

Exception catching

To facilitate this class being used for debugging—to make coding it quicker and easier—the methods of this class all catch the `IOException` thrown by the underlying stream. The only way to detect an error is by making a call to `checkError()`.

Difference from PrintWriter

`PrintWriter` performs automatic flushing only when one of the `println()` methods is called—not whenever a newline character is output, as in `PrintStream`. The `PrintWriter` uses the platform-dependent form of line separation. Another difference is that `PrintWriter` does not have any methods for the output of binary data—only character data.

Extended by

```
LogStream
```

Inheritance

```
public class java.io.PrintStream
    extends FilterOutputStream
        ⇑
    public class java.io.FilterOutputStream
        extends OutputStream
            ⇑
        public class java.io.OutputStream
            extends Object
                ⇑
            public class java.lang.Object
```

Constructors   deprecated

The constructors are deprecated. Use `PrintWriter` instead.

```
public PrintStream(OutputStream out)
public PrintStream(OutputStream out,boolean autoFlush)
```

A `PrintStream` is constructed on top of an `OutputStream`. If `autoFlush` is set to `true`, the output stream will be flushed each time a newline character is written.

Returned by

An object of this class is returned from `DriverManager.getLogStream()`, `LogStream.getDefaultStream()`, and `RemoteServer.getLog()`.

Methods

checkError()

```
public boolean checkError()
```

Flushes the underlying print stream and returns `true` if there has been any kind of error. The error flag is never cleared—once an error has occurred, this method will continuously return `true`.

close()

```
public void close()
```

Closes the print stream. This method will release any resources being held by the underlying stream.

flush()

```
public void flush()
```

Writes all buffered data and flushes the underlying stream.

print()

```
public void print(boolean b)

public void print(char c)

public void print(char s[])

public void print(double d)

public void print(float f)

public void print(int i)

public void print(long l)

public void print(Object obj)
```

```
public void print(String s)
```

This set of methods will format an output string appropriate for the data type passed in as the argument.

- A `boolean` will print as either "true" or "false."
- A `char` will print as the ASCII character defined by its low-order eight bits.
- A `char[]` will print as the ASCII character defined by the low-order eight bits of each member of the array.
- A `double` will print as a numeric string with a decimal—possibly an exponential form.
- A `float` will print as a numeric string with a decimal—possibly an exponential form.
- An `int` will print as a string of digits.
- A `long` will print as a string of digits.
- An `Object` is converted to a string by having its `toString()` method called.
- A `String` is printed by having the lower eight bits of each of its characters printed as ASCII. If the `String` is `null`, the word "null" is printed.

println()

```
public void println()
public void println(boolean b)
public void println(char c)
public void println(char s[])
public void println(double d)
public void println(float f)
public void println(int i)
public void println(long l)
public void println(Object obj)
public void println(String s)
```

This set of methods will format an output string appropriate for the data type—the same as `print()`—except that a newline character is added to the end of the output string. In the case where no argument is supplied, only the newline is output. Note that the newline produced as output is not the same as the '\n' character on all systems.

setError()

```
protected void setError()
```

Sets the error flag to `true`. This is the flag returned by `checkError()`.

write()

```
public void write(int bvalue)

public void write(byte barray[],int offset,int length)
```

This is a binary write. It writes the lower eight bits of the byte (or bytes) supplied as the argument. If `barray` is specified, the writing begins at `barray[offset]` and continues for `length` bytes. If `bvalue` is specified, its lower eight bits are written as a single byte. If `bvalue` is a newline character, the print stream is flushed if autoflush is turned on.

 For two examples of `PrintStream`, see **System.out** and **System.err**. For a very similar class, see **PrintWriter**.

PrintWriter

class java.io.PrintWriter

Converts objects to a text format and prints the text to an output stream.

Exception catching

The methods of this class all catch the `IOException` thrown by the underlying stream. The only way to detect an error is by making a call to `checkError()`.

Difference from PrintStream

`PrintWriter` performs automatic flushing only when one of the `println()` methods is called—not whenever a newline character is output, as in `PrintStream`. The `PrintWriter` uses the platform-dependent form of line separation. Another difference is that `PrintWriter` does not have any methods for the output of binary data—only character data.

Inheritance

```
public class PrintWriter
    extends Writer
        ⇑
    public class java.io.Writer
        extends Object
            ⇑
        public class java.lang.Object
```

Constructors

```
public PrintWriter(Writer out)

public PrintWriter(Writer out,boolean autoFlush)

public PrintWriter(OutputStream out)

public PrintWriter(OutputStream out,boolean autoFlush)
```

The PrintWriter uses out (which can be either a Writer or an OutputStream) to do the actual output. If an OutputStream is used, an OutputStreamWriter is created to do the appropriate data formatting. If autoFlush is set to true, the output will automatically be flushed on each call to a println() method.

Methods

checkError()

```
public boolean checkError()
```

Flushes the underlying print stream and returns true if there has been any kind of error. The error flag is never cleared—once an error has occurred, this method will continuously return true.

close()

```
public void close()
```

Closes the print stream. This method will release any resources being held by the underlying stream.

flush()

```
public void flush()
```

Writes all buffered data and flushes the underlying stream.

print()

```
public void print(boolean b)

public void print(char c)

public void print(char s[])

public void print(double d)

public void print(float f)

public void print(int i)

public void print(long l)

public void print(Object obj)
```

```
public void print(String s)
```

This set of methods will format an output string appropriate for the data type passed in as the argument.

- A `boolean` will print as either "true" or "false."
- A `char` will print as the ASCII character defined by its low-order eight bits.
- A `char[]` will print as the ASCII character defined by the low-order eight bits of each member of the array.
- A `double` will print as a numeric string with a decimal—possibly an exponential form.
- A `float` will print as a numeric string with a decimal—possibly an exponential form.
- An `int` will print as a string of digits.
- A `long` will print as a string of digits.
- An `Object` is converted to a string by having its `toString()` method called.
- A `String` is printed by having the lower eight bits of each of its characters printed as ASCII. If the `String` is `null`, the word "null" is printed.

println()

```
public void println()

public void println(boolean b)

public void println(char c)

public void println(char s[])

public void println(double d)

public void println(float f)

public void println(int i)

public void println(long l)

public void println(Object obj)

public void println(String s)
```

This set of methods will format an output string appropriate for the data type—the same as `print()`—except a newline character is added to the end of the output string. In the case where no argument is supplied, only the newline is output. Note that the newline produced as output is not the same as the '\n' character on all systems. If `autoFlush` was specified as `true` in the constructor, the output is flushed on each call to `println()`.

setError()

```
protected void setError()
```

Sets the error flag to `true`. This is the flag returned by `checkError()`.

write()

```
public void write(char carray[])

public void write(char carray[],int offset,int length)

public void write(int character)

public void write(String string)

public void write(String string,int offset,int length)
```

Writes one or more characters. If `carray` or `string` is specified without `offset` or `length`, the entire `string` or `carray` is written. If the argument is a `String` with `offset` and `length`, `length` characters are written beginning at `string[offset]`. If the argument is `carray` with `offset` and `length`, `length` characters are written beginning at `carray[offset]`. If `character` is specified, the low-order 16 bits are taken to be a Unicode character.

 For another class very similar to this one, see **PrintStream**.

private

keyword

 See **access**.

PrivateKey

interface java.security.PrivateKey

This is an interface for a class that is the container of a private key—a key that is closely held by an identity for use in the encryption of messages to be transmitted and the decryption of messages received.

There are no methods or constants defined for the interface. It serves as an identifying tag for any object that contains a private encryption key.

Extended by

```
DSAPrivateKey
```

Inheritance

```
public interface java.security.PrivateKey
    extends Key
        ⇑
    public interface java.security.Key
        extends Serializable
            ⇑
        public interface java.io.Serializable
```

Constructors

Returned by

Objects that implement this interface are returned from `KeyPair.getPrivate()` and `Signer.getPrivateKey()`.

 Also see **Key**, **PublicKey**, **Certificate**, and **DSAPrivateKey**.

Process

class java.lang.Process

An object of this class is used to obtain information about—and send control messages to—a separately running process.

No automatic halting

The other process is not halted by deleting any or all of its `Process` objects. To kill the other process, it is necessary to call `destroy()`.

Inheritance

```
public abstract class java.lang.Process
    extends Object
        ⇑
    public class java.lang.Object
```

Constructors

```
public Process()
```

Returned by

An object that is a subclass of this class is returned from `Runtime.exec()`.

Methods

destroy()

```
public abstract void destroy()
```

This will kill the subprocess.

exitValue()

```
public abstract int exitValue()
```

Returns the exit value issued from the other process when it halted. If the other process has not halted, an `IllegalThreadStateException` is thrown.

getErrorStream()

```
public abstract InputStream getErrorStream()
```

This method will return a readable `InputStream` that is connected to the error output stream of the process.

getInputStream()

```
public abstract InputStream getInputStream()
```

This method will return a readable `InputStream` that is connected to the standard output stream of the other process.

getOutputStream()

```
public abstract OutputStream getOutputStream()
```

This method will return a writeable `OutputStream` that is connected to the standard input stream of the other process.

waitFor()

```
public abstract int waitFor()
      throws InterruptedException
```

Blocks until the other process is no longer in execution. This will return immediately if the process is not in execution. If the wait is interrupted, an `InterruptedException` is thrown.

 For starting other processes, see **Runtime**.

properties

A property is a pair of strings—one is the key and the other the value associated with the key. A standard set of properties is defined in the System class. Table P-2 lists the set of properties that you can count on always being present.

Table P-2 Set of Standard Property Names

Key	Description
java.version	Java version number
java.vendor	Java-vendor-specific string
java.vendor.url	Java vendor URL
java.home	Java installation directory
java.class.version	Java class format version number
java.class.path	Java classpath
java.compiler.exists	This one is not always present. When it does exists, it is the name of a compiler capable of converting classes into native mode executables. See **Compiler**.
os.name	Operating system name
os.arch	Operating system architecture
os.version	Operating system version
file.separator	File separator ("/" on UNIX and Mac, "\" on Windows)
path.separator	Path separator (":" on UNIX and Mac, ";" on Windows)
line.separator	Line separator ("\n" on UNIX)
user.name	User account name
user.home	User home directory
user.dir	User's current working directory

This program lists all the standard property values of the system on which it is run.

```
import java.util.*;

public class PropertiesShow {
    static public void main(String arg[]) {
        Properties p = System.getProperties();
        Enumeration enum = p.propertyNames();
        while(enum.hasMoreElements()) {
            String property_name =
                (String)enum.nextElement();
            String property =
                p.getProperty(property_name);
```

```
                 System.out.println(property_name +
                     ": " + property);
             }
        }
    }
```

The example retrieves the `Properties` object from the `System` class and lists each one—both key and value. Of course, the exact output of this program will vary depending on the system on which it is run. Here is what it listed when I ran it on the computer being used to write this book:

```
java.home: C:\JAVA\BIN\..
awt.toolkit: sun.awt.win32.MToolkit
java.version: 1.0.2
file.separator: \
line.separator:

java.vendor: Sun Microsystems Inc.
user.name: Arthur
os.arch: x86
os.name: Windows 95
java.vendor.url: http://www.sun.com/
user.dir: C:\jr.cd\p
java.class.path: .;C:\JAVA\LIB\CLASSES;C:\JAVA\BIN\..\classes;
C:\JAVA\BIN\..\lib\classes.zip
java.class.version: 45.3
os.version: 4.0
path.separator: ;
user.home: C:\HOME
```

As you can see, all the properties are strings. The property key `line.separator` has nothing following it, but there is a blank line below it— this shows that it works.

 For manipulation of properties, see **Properties**. To access the system default properties, see **System**.

Properties

class java.util.Properties

This is a class that maintains a list of properties. The properties can persist on disk from one invocation of a program to the next. This class extends the `Hashtable` class—you can think of this class as a persistent hashtable where all the objects (both keys and values) are `Strings`.

Properties within properties

Properties objects can be nested. That is, if a sought property is not found, the Properties class will look inside an internal Properties object to find it. This is a convenient way to override a system parameter—create a Properties object that contains all the properties you wish to define and have the system properties object included as the nested Properties object.

Extended by

```
Provider
```

Inheritance

```
public class java.util.Properties
    extends Hashtable
        ⇑
    public class Hashtable
        implements Cloneable
        implements Serializable
        extends Dictionary
            ⇑
        public class Dictionary
            extends Object
                ⇑
            public class java.lang.Object
```

Variables and constants

defaults

```
protected Properties defaults
```

This is the storage location of the Properties object supplied on the constructor. It can be null. Whenever a search is made for a property and the sought property is not found in a Properties object, the search will automatically continue into the defaults Properties object. There can be several levels of these (each Properties object having its own defaults until one of them is finally null).

Constructors

```
public Properties()

public Properties(Properties defaults)
```

These will create an empty property list. The defaults may be supplied—but if not, the default is left null.

Returned by

A `Properties` object is returned from `System.getProperties()`.

Methods

getProperty()

```
public String getProperty(String key)

public String getProperty(String key,String defaultValue)
```

Returns the property that matches the specified `key`. If there is no matching key, the value from the defaults will be returned. If `defaults` is `null`, or if it returns a `null` value, `defaultValue` is returned—if the `defaultValue` is not specified, `null` is returned.

list()

```
public void list(PrintStream out)

public void list(PrintWriter out)
```

The properties can be listed to a `PrintStream` or a `PrintWriter`. This is primarily for debugging.

load()

```
public synchronized void load(InputStream inStream)
          throws IOException
```

This will load a set of properties from `inStream`. None of the existing properties are deleted before the new ones are loaded. If a new property has the same key as an existing one, the new one will replace the old one. If `inStream` has two properties with the same key, the last one loaded will prevail.

propertyNames()

```
public Enumeration propertyNames()
```

This method returns an `Enumeration` that contains all the keys contained in this property list and in the `default` property list. If you only want the properties from this list (without looking into the `defaults` list), you can use the `keys()` method inherited from `Hashtable`.

save()

```
public synchronized void save(OutputStream out,String header)
```

This method writes the properties to `out` in the same format that is expected by `load()`. Only the local properties are written—it does not write those in `defaults`. The `header` string is used as a comment at the beginning of the file.

Example

The class `MakeProps` creates a property file:

```
import java.util.*;
import java.io.*;
public class MakeProps {
    public static void main(String[] arg) {
        Properties props = new Properties();
        props.put("myprop.maximum","1080");
        props.put("myprop.minimum","820");
        props.put("user.home","/user/javapref");
        props.put("user.dir","/user/javadir");
        try {
            FileOutputStream out =
                    new
            FileOutputStream("myProperties");
            props.save(out,"My Properties");
        } catch(IOException e) {
            System.out.println(e);
        }
    }
}
```

The property file created by this program begins with the heading string and a time stamp specifying when it was created:

```
#My Properties
#Sat May 10 14:53:43 CDT 1997
myprop.maximum=1080
user.dir=/user/javadir
myprop.minimum=820
user.home=/user/javapref
```

The class `LoadProps` reads the properties from the files and combines them with the system properties in such a way that the defined local properties will override the system properties:

```
import java.util.*;
import java.io.*;
public class LoadProps {
    public static void main(String[] arg) {
        String key;
        String property;
        Properties props;
        props = System.getProperties();
        key = "user.home";
```

```
            property = props.getProperty(key);
            System.out.println(key + "=" + property);
            props = new Properties(props);
            try {
                FileInputStream in =
                            new FileInputStream("myProperties");
                props.load(in);
            } catch(IOException e) {
                System.out.println(e);
            }
            key = "user.home";
            property = props.getProperty(key);
            System.out.println(key + "=" + property);
            key = "os.version";
            property = props.getProperty(key);
            System.out.println(key + "=" + property);
        }
    }
```

A call is made to `System.getProperties()` to load the set of system properties. The "user.home" property is extracted from the system property and
printed. Next, a new `Properties` object is created using the system
`Properties` object as its nested set of properties. The "myProperties" file is
then loaded as the set of local properties. Finally, the property settings for
"user.home" and "os.version" are printed to show that the locally loaded
property has overridden the system property, but the system properties that
have not been overridden are still available. The output looks like this:

```
user.home=C:\HOME
user.home=/user/javapref
os.version=4.0
```

 For details on property composition and the property file format, see **properties**.

PropertyChangeEvent

class java.beans.PropertyChangeEvent

This event is issued to indicate that a bound or constrained property value has
been changed. This is the event that gets distributed to the
`PropertyChangeListeners` and `VetoableChangeListeners` that have registered to be notified of changes.

The old and the new

A `PropertyChangeEvent` can include both the old and new values of the property that is being changed. If the property value is a primitive type, it will be in the form of a wrapper object. Either the old value or the new value could be `null`.

A null event

The source could send a `null` property name to indicate that multiple properties have changed. In this case, the old and new values will also be `null`.

Inheritance

```
public class java.beans.PropertyChangeEvent
    extends EventObject
        ⇑
    public class java.lang.Object
```

Constructors

```
public PropertyChangeEvent(Object source,
        String propertyName,
        Object oldValue,Object newValue)
```

A property change event contains the `source` object that contains the property. The name of the property having its value changed is the `propertyName`. The value is changed from the `oldValue` to the `newValue`.

Returned by

A `PropertyChangeEvent` is returned from a call to `PropertyVetoException.getPropertyChangeEvent()`.

Methods

getNewValue()

```
public Object getNewValue()
```

Returns the new value of the property. This object could be the wrapper of a primitive Java type. The return value could be `null` if multiple properties have been changed.

getOldValue()

```
public Object getOldValue()
```

Returns the old value of the property. This object could be the wrapper of a primitive Java type. The return value could be `null` if multiple properties have been changed.

getPropagationId()

```
public Object getPropagationId()
```

Returns the propagation ID object associated with this particular update.

This method is reserved for future use. In Beans 1.0, the sole requirement is that if a listener catches a `PropertyChangeEvent` and then fires a `PropertyChangeEvent` of its own, it should then make sure that it propagates the `propagationId` field from its incoming event to its outgoing event. If listeners are written to do this, future versions will be able to use the ID number.

getPropertyName()

```
public String getPropertyName()
```

Returns the name of the property. This will be `null` if more than one property is being changed.

setPropagationId()

```
public void setPropagationId(Object propagationId)
```

Sets the propagation ID number.

 For information on the recipients of this event, see **PropertyChangeListener** and **VetoableChangeListener**. For information on the distribution of these events, see **PropertyChangeSupport** and **VetoableChangeSupport**.

PropertyChangeListener

interface java.beans.PropertyChangeListener

A `PropertyChangeListener` that has been registered with a bean will be notified whenever the value of a bound property is changed.

Inheritance

```
public interface java.beans.PropertyChangeListener
    extends EventListener
        ⇑
    public interface java.util.EventListener
```

Methods

propertyChange()

```
public abstract void propertyChange(PropertyChangeEvent event)
```

This method is called each time a bound property is changed.

 For information on bound properties, see **PropertyDescriptor**. For registration of a PropertyChangeListener, see **PropertyChangeSupport**.

PropertyChangeSupport

class java.beans.PropertyChangeSupport

An object of this class can be used as a registry for a list of PropertyChangeListeners. It also has methods that can be used to send change notifications to the registrants. This class can be used by a bean that supports bound properties—it can be used as is, or it can be subclassed.

Inheritance

```
public class java.beans.PropertyChangeSupport
    implements Serializable
    extends Object
        ⇑
    public class java.lang.Object
```

Constructors

```
public PropertyChangeSupport(Object sourceBean)
```

The sourceBean is the bean that is to be the source of any events.

Methods

addPropertyChangeListener()

```
public synchronized void
addPropertyChangeListener(PropertyChangeListener listener)
```

Adds a PropertyChangeListener to the list of those that will be notified whenever there is a change being made to a bound property.

firePropertyChange()

```
public void firePropertyChange(String propertyName,
        Object oldValue,Object newValue)
```

This method is called to report the update of a property to any registered listeners. The propertyName is the name of the property being changed. The existing value is supplied as the `oldValue`, and the modified value is the `newValue`. No notification will be made if the `oldValue` is equal to the `newValue`.

removePropertyChangeListener()

```
public synchronized void removePropertyChangeListener(
            PropertyChangeListener listener)
```

Removes the listener from the list of those that will receive notification of changes.

 Also see **PropertyDescriptor** and **PropertyChangeListener**.

PropertyDescriptor

class java.beans.PropertyDescriptor

An object of this class describes a single property of a bean. This is a property that the bean exports via a pair of accessor methods.

Accessor methods

The accessor methods follow a naming convention that enables a process to derive the names of the methods from the name of the property. For example, if the name of a property is `umpaMaximum`, the accessor methods would be `getUmpaMaximum()` and `setUmpaMaximum()`. The name of a property begins with a lowercase letter—to find the accessor methods, switch it to uppercase and prepend "set" or "get."

Constrained and vetoable

A *constrained* property, also called a *vetoable* property, is one with limits imposed on changes that can be made to it. Whenever the "set" method of a vetoable property is called, it is possible that one or more objects implementing the `VetoableChangeListener` interface will be notified via a `PropertyChangeEvent`. Any one of these is capable of throwing a `PropertyVetoException` to prevent the change from occurring.

Bound

A bound property is one that can cause a `PropertyChangeEvent` to be distributed to a list of registered `PropertyChangeListener` objects. This is very similar to a constrained property, except that there is no veto power.

Extended by

```
IndexedPropertyDescriptor
```

Inheritance

```
public class java.beans.PropertyDescriptor
    extends FeatureDescriptor
        ⇑
    public class java.beans.FeatureDescriptor
        extends Object
            ⇑
        public class java.lang.Object
```

Constructors

```
public PropertyDescriptor(String propertyName,
        Class beanClass)
    throws IntrospectionException

public PropertyDescriptor(String propertyName,
        Class beanClass,
        String getName,String setName)
    throws IntrospectionException

public PropertyDescriptor(String propertyName,
        Method getter,Method setter)
    throws IntrospectionException
```

The `propertyName` is the name of the property to be described. The `beanClass` is the `Class` object for the bean that has the property. An `IntrospectionException` is thrown if there is an exception during introspection.

The accessor method names can be specified as `getName` and `setName`. If they are not specified, they will be generated from the property name as described. If `getName` is `null`, the property is write-only. If `setName` is `null`, the property is read-only.

The accessor methods can be specified as the `Method` objects `getter` and `setter`. Either one of these being `null` will indicate that the property is either read-only or write-only.

Returned by

An array of `PropertyDescriptor` objects is returned from the `getPropertyDescriptors()` methods of `BeanInfo` and `SimpleBeanInfo`.

Methods

getPropertyEditorClass()

```
public Class getPropertyEditorClass()
```

Returns the `Class` of the `PropertyEditor` that has been registered for this property. If there is none, return `null`.

getPropertyType()

```
public Class getPropertyType()
```

Returns a Class object that describes the object, or the primitive data type, that will be returned by a call to the "get" accessor method. A null is returned if this is an indexed property that does not support nonindexed access. This could be the Class file of a primitive Java data type wrapper.

getReadMethod()

```
public Method getReadMethod()
```

Returns the Method object of the "get" accessor method. If the property is write-only, this will return null.

getWriteMethod()

```
public Method getWriteMethod()
```

Returns the Method object of the "set" accessor method. If the property is read-only, this will return null.

isBound()

```
public boolean isBound()
```

Returns true if this is a bound property. A bound property will issue a PropertyChange event to all its registered PropertyChange listeners whenever the "set" accessor method is called.

isConstrained()

```
public boolean isConstrained()
```

Returns true if this is a constrained (vetoable) property.

setBound()

```
public void setBound(boolean setting)
```

If setting is true, this will be a bound property. If setting is false, this will not be a bound property.

setConstrained()

```
public void setConstrained(boolean setting)
```

If setting is true, this will be a constrained property. If setting is false, this will not be a constrained property.

setPropertyEditorClass()

```
public void setPropertyEditorClass(Class propertyEditorClass)
```

Associates the `properyEditorClass` with this property instead of the more normal procedure of using the `PropertyEditorManager`.

For the editing of properties, see **PropertyEditor** and **PropertyEditorManager**. For more on constrained properties, see **VetoableChangeListener** and **VetoableChangeSupport**. For more on bound properties, see **PropertyChangeListener** and **PropertyChangeSupport**.

PropertyEditor

interface java.beans.PropertyEditor

This interface provides the definitions of standard access to a property of a bean. It is primarily intended for a GUI interface to have the ability to display and modify information about a bean in an interactive software development environment.

Changing property values

Internally, a bean is composed of a collection of properties (that is, attributes). Some of these properties can have their values altered to make changes in the state of the bean. The purpose of a `PropertyEditor` is to supply methods for access to the internal property values of a bean. This access can be used to automatically read and write the property values or, more commonly, to present the values to a user in such a way that they can be interactively modified.

Flexibility

An object of this class can be used to read and write the property values of a bean in a variety of ways. Most editors will only need to support a subset of the possible capabilities. For example, a very simple property text–based editor may only support `getAsText()` and `setAsText()`, and a completely graphics-based editor may ignore the text-only capabilities and support `paintValue()` and `getCustomEditor()`.

The three display styles

There are three different display styles. One or all of these may be supported by a given editor.

- The `paintValue()` method can be used to graphically draw the property on the display.
- The `getAsText()` method returns a textual description of the property value.

◆ The getTags() method can be used to return the array of all possible string values for a property.

The minimum must

A minimum set of methods must be supported by any PropertyManager. The setValue() method must be supported for argument values of the type (or types) known to this PropertyEditor. Either getCustomEditor() or setAsText() must also be supported so that the value can be modified. Each property editor should have a default constructor.

Implemented by

PropertyEditorSupport

Inheritance

public interface java.beans.PropertyEditor

Constructors

Returned by

An object implementing this interface is returned from PropertyEditorManager. findEditor().

Methods

addPropertyChangeListener()

```
public abstract void addPropertyChangeListener(
        PropertyChangeListener listener)
```

Registers a listener to be notified on a change of value of a property.

The implementer of this interface should take the responsibility of dispatching a PropertyChangeEvent to each listener whenever a property value changes. The event should specify the implementer as the source of the event and null for the property name.

getAsText()

```
public abstract String getAsText()
```

Returns the value of the property as a string that can be deciphered by a human. The string should be in a form that is readable by setAsText(). If the property cannot be represented as a string, the method returns null.

getCustomEditor()

```
public abstract Component getCustomEditor()
```

Returns a complete editor for the property. The return will be null if this feature is not supported—a call to supportsCustomEditor() can be made to test whether this method is supported. The editor is in the form of a displayable Component that has the appropriate connections and event handlers to modify the property. It will also need to dispatch the necessary PropertyChangeEvent to the registered listeners. The caller of this method can use the returned editor just as it would any other Component on the display.

getJavaInitializationString()

```
public abstract String getJavaInitializationString()
```

Returns a String containing a fragment of Java code that, when compiled, can be used to set the property to its current value.

The returned string is one that is suitable to be used in "set" accessor method of the property. For example, if the argument to the set method is an int, the string could be "34" or "–271." If the argument is a Color object, it could be "new Color(100,100,100)" or "Color.orange."

getTags()

```
public abstract String[] getTags()
```

If the value of the property is a selection from a predefined set of strings (for example, the names of the days of the week), then this method will return the entire set. If this method is supported, the PropertyEditor should also support the setAsText() method as a way of selecting one of the tags, and getAsText() as a way of determining the currently selected tag. If the value of the property cannot be represented this way, the return value is null.

getValue()

```
public abstract Object getValue()
```

Returns the value of the property. If the property value is a Java primitive type, it will be returned inside the appropriate wrapper object.

isPaintable()

```
public abstract boolean isPaintable()
```

Returns true if the paintValue() method has been implemented.

paintValue()

```
public abstract void paintValue(Graphics g,Rectangle box)
```

Paints a representation of the property value. The painting will be done using the supplied Graphics object, and it will be placed in the area specified by the box. The painting is clipped to the box. This method is functional only if isPaintable() returns true, but it is never an error to call this method.

removePropertyChangeListener()

```
public abstract void removePropertyChangeListener(
            PropertyChangeListener listener)
```

Removes the listener from the list of those that will be notified of a change in the value of a property.

setAsText()

```
public abstract void setAsText(String text)
        throws IllegalArgumentException
```

Sets the property value to that specified as the text string. An IllegalArgumentException is thrown if the text is not formatted correctly, or if the value of this property cannot be set this way. This method should be capable of parsing strings in the form of those returned from getAsText().

setValue()

```
public abstract void setValue(Object value)
```

Specifies the object to be edited by the PropertyEditor. The PropertyEditor will not modify this object—it will make a duplicate of this object to be returned as the modified value. If the value to be edited is a primitive type, it should be enclosed in an appropriate wrapper.

supportsCustomEditor()

```
public abstract boolean supportsCustomEditor()
```

Returns true if this PropertyEditor can provide a custom editor.

 For information on interfaces to properties, see **PropertyDescriptor** and **IndexedPropertyDescriptor**. To implement a property editor, see **PropertyEditorSupport**. For information on listeners to property changes, see **PropertyChangeEvent**, **PropertyChangeListener**, and **PropertyChangeSupport**.

PropertyEditorManager

class java.beans.PropertyEditorManager

The PropertyEditorManager is used to match the editable property of a bean with the appropriate PropertyEditor.

Each property of a bean is a data type—either a primitive type or a class. Each property that can be modified has a PropertyEditor designed to manage interactive editing. An application—during the process of modifying the values of the properties of a bean—will locate the appropriate editor for each property by making a call to `PropertyEditorManager.findEditor()`.

Step 1: Locate a built-in.

Some built-in editors are made available by the Java API. Editors are already defined for the Java primitive data types (`boolean`, `byte`, `short`, `int`, `long`, `float`, and `double`), as well as for the Java API classes `String`, `Color`, and `Font`.

Step 2: Locate by registry.

The next step taken by the `PropertyEditorManager` to locate an editor is to look in its own registry. The method `registerEditor()` could have been used to designate a specific editor for the requested data type. If the sought type is found in this registry, it will be the one returned to the requester. There is no naming convention required here—any name can be used for the editor.

Step 3: Locate by package.

Next, the name of the editor is assumed to be the same as the full package name of the object being edited, but with "Editor" tacked onto the name. For example, if the property class has the name "poo.bear.Widget," an attempt is made to find the editor under the name "poo.bear.WidgetEditor."

Step 4: Locate by path.

If the previous method did not turn up an editor, "Editor" is appended to the simple name of the editable class, and an attempt is made to locate the editor in all the directories on the path that was set with a call to `setEditorSearchPath()`. For example, if the search path includes "deep.dark.woods" and "main.street," and the name of the property "poo.bear.Widget," the editor will be looked for as "deep.dark.woods.WidgetEditor" and "main.street.WidgetEditor."

Inheritance

```
public class java.beans.PropertyEditorManager
     extends Object
          ⇑
     public class java.lang.Object
```

Constructors

```
public PropertyEditorManager()
```

Methods

findEditor()

```
public static PropertyEditor findEditor(Class targetType)
```

Returns a `PropertyEditor` for a property of the type represented by `targetType`. If no suitable `PropertyEditor` can be found, the method returns `null`.

getEditorSearchPath()

```
public static String[] getEditorSearchPath()
```

Returns the array of package names that will be searched for a `PropertyEditor`. This is initially set to the single package `sun.beans.editors`.

registerEditor()

```
public static void registerEditor(Class targetType,
        Class editorClass)
```

Adds a new `PropertyEditor` to the list of those available. The `targetType` is the `Class` of the data type to be edited, and the `editorClass` is the `Class` of the `PropertyEditor` being registered with the manager.

setEditorSearchPath()

```
public static void setEditorSearchPath(String path[])
```

Specifies the list of package names that will be used in the search for a `PropertyEditor` when a call made to `findEditor()`. The `path` is an array of strings — each one is a complete package name.

 For information of property editing, see **PropertyEditor**.

PropertyEditorSupport

class java.beans.PropertyEditorSupport

This class was designed to be the superclass of a Java bean `PropertyEditor`. It implements the methods defined in the `PropertyEditor` interface with reasonable default actions.

Inheritance

```
public class java.beans.PropertyEditorSupport
    implements PropertyEditor
    extends Object
        ⇑
```

```
public class java.lang.Object
```

Constructors

```
protected PropertyEditorSupport()
```

```
protected PropertyEditorSupport(Object source)
```

The protected constructor is for use by subclasses. The `source` is to be used as the source of any `PropertyChangeEvents` that are dispatched. The source should be specified unless the subclass is going to override `addPropertyChangeListener()` and distribute its own events.

Methods

addPropertyChangeListener()

```
public synchronized void addPropertyChangeListener(
        PropertyChangeListener listener)
```

Registers a listener to be notified on a change of value of a property. A `PropertyChangeEvent` will be dispatched to each listener whenever a property value changes. The event will use the object specified on the constructor as the source of the event and `null` for the property name.

firePropertyChange()

```
public void firePropertyChange()
```

Dispatches a `PropertyChangeEvent` to each listener that has been registered by a call to `addPropertyChangedListener()`.

getAsText()

```
public String getAsText()
```

Returns the value of the property as a string that can be deciphered by a human. The string will be in a form that is readable by `setAsText()`. If the property cannot be represented as a string, the method returns `null`.

getCustomEditor()

```
public Component getCustomEditor()
```

Returns a complete editor for the property. The return will be `null` if this feature is not supported—a call to `supportsCustomEditor()` can be made to test whether this feature is supported. The editor is in the form of a displayable `Component` that has the appropriate connections and event handlers to modify the property. It will also need to dispatch the necessary `PropertyChangeEvent` to the registered listeners. The caller of this method can use the returned editor just as it would any other `Component` on the display.

getJavaInitializationString()

```
public String getJavaInitializationString()
```

Returns a `String` containing a fragment of Java code that, when compiled, can be used to set the property to its current value.

The returned string is one that is suitable to be used in the "set" accessor method of the property. For example, if the argument to the set method is an `int`, the string could be "34" or "–271." If the argument is a `Color` object, it could be "new Color(100,100,100)" or "Color.orange."

getTags()

```
public String[] getTags()
```

If the value of the property is a selection from a predefined set of strings (for example, the names of the days of the week), then this method will return the entire set. If this method is supported, the `PropertyEditor` will also support the `setAsText()` method as a way of selecting one of the tags, and `getAsText()` as a way of determining the currently selected tag. If the value of the property cannot be represented this way, the return value is `null`.

getValue()

```
public Object getValue()
```

Returns the value of the property. If the property value is a Java primitive type, it will be returned inside the appropriate wrapper object.

isPaintable()

```
public boolean isPaintable()
```

Returns `true` if the `paintValue()` method has been implemented.

paintValue()

```
public void paintValue(Graphics g,Rectangle box)
```

Paints a representation of the property value. The painting will be done using the supplied `Graphics` object, and it will be placed in the area specified by the `box`. The painting is clipped to the `box`. This method is functional only if `isPaintable()` returns `true`, but it is never an error to call this method.

removePropertyChangeListener()

```
public synchronized void removePropertyChangeListener(
          PropertyChangeListener listener)
```

Removes the `listener` from the list of those that will be notified of a change in value of a property.

setAsText()

```
public void setAsText(String text)
        throws IllegalArgumentException
```

Sets   the   property   value   to   that   specified   as   the   text   string.   An
`IllegalArgumentException` is thrown if the text is not formatted correctly, or if the
value of this property cannot be set in this way. This method is capable of parsing strings in
the form of those returned from `getAsText()`.

setValue()

```
public void setValue(Object value)
```

Specifies the object to be edited by the `PropertyEditor`. The `PropertyEditor` will not
modify this object—it will make a duplicate of this object to be returned as the modified
value. If the value to be edited is a primitive type, it should be enclosed in an appropriate
wrapper.

supportsCustomEditor()

```
public boolean supportsCustomEditor()
```

Returns `true` if this `PropertyEditor` can provide a custom editor.

 For more information on a property editor, see **PropertyEditor**,
IndexedPropertyEditor, and **PropertyEditorManager**. For information
on listeners to property changes, see **PropertyChangeEvent**,
PropertyChangeListener, and **PropertyChangeSupport**.

PropertyResourceBundle

class java.util.PropertyResourceBundle

This class is an extension of the `PropertyResource` abstract class that reads
the properties and keys from an input stream—normally a disk file.

Inheritance

```
public class java.util.PropertyResourceBundle
    extends ResourceBundle
        ⇑
    public abstract class java.util.ResourceBundle
        extends Object
            ⇑
        public class java.lang.Object
```

Constructors

```
public PropertyResourceBundle(InputStream stream)
    throws IOException
```

Creates a PropertyResourceBundle from the data in stream.

Methods

getKeys()

```
public Enumeration getKeys()
```

Returns an enumeration of the property keys available in the bundle.

handleGetObject()

```
public Object handleGetObject(String key)
```

Retrieves an object from the ResourceBundle.

Example

Each line of the input file is a key/property pair. The keys are case-sensitive. In this example, we have a set of keys in the file that defines button labels:

```
import java.util.*;
import java.io.*;

public class DiskBundle {
    static public void main(String arg[]) {
        PropertyResourceBundle prb;
        FileInputStream fin;
        try {
            fin = new FileInputStream("bundle.text");
            prb = new PropertyResourceBundle(fin);
        } catch(IOException e) {
            System.err.println(e);
            return;
        }
        Enumeration enum = prb.getKeys();
        while(enum.hasMoreElements()) {
            String key = (String)enum.nextElement();
            String prop = prb.getString(key);
            System.out.println("Key=" + key + "
                    Property=" + prop);
        }
    }
}
```

The `PropertyResourceBundle` is constructed using the contents of the file bundle.text. The file contains a collection of key/property pairs, like this:

```
YesButton=Si
NoButton=No
StopButton=Alto
```

Once the file is loaded, the `getKeys()` method is called to get an `Enumeration` of all the keys. The key values are then used to retrieve the property strings. The output looks like this:

```
Key=StopButton Property=Alto
Key=YesButton Property=Si
Key=NoButton Property=No
```

 For more information and examples of resource bundles in general, see **ResourceBundle**. For another example, see **ListResourceBundle**.

PropertyVetoException

class java.beans.PropertyVetoException

This is the exception thrown by a `VetoableChangeListener` to veto a change being made to a constrained property.

Inheritance

```
public class java.beans.PropertyVetoException
    extends Exception
        ⇑
    public class java.lang.Exception
        extends Throwable
            ⇑
        public class java.lang.Throwable
            implements Serializable
            extends Object
                ⇑
            public class java.lang.Object
```

Constructors

```
public PropertyVetoException(String message,
        PropertyChangeEvent event)
```

A descriptive text message and the `PropertyChangeEvent` that caused the exception are both included.

Methods

getPropertyChangeEvent()

```
public PropertyChangeEvent getPropertyChangeEvent()
```

Returns the event that caused the exception to be thrown.

 This event is thrown from a **VetoableChangeListener** to veto a change being made to a property defined as vetoable by its **PropertyDescriptor**.

protected

 See **access**.

ProtocolException

class java.net.ProtocolException

This exception is thrown to indicate that an error has occurred in the underlying protocol. For example, there could be an error in a TCP header or the format of a MIME expression.

Inheritance

```
public class ProtocolException
    extends IOException
        ⇑
    public class java.io.IOException
        extends Exception
            ⇑
        public class java.lang.Exception
            extends Throwable
                ⇑
            public class java.lang.Throwable
                implements Serializable
                extends Object
                    ⇑
                public class java.lang.Object
```

Constructors

```
public ProtocolException()

public ProtocolException(String message)
```

If the `message` string is supplied, it is used as a detailed message describing this particular exception.

Provider

class java.security.Provider

This abstract class defines the methods used to access the facilities of a security provider. A security provider is one that implements a key generation algorithm (such as DSA, RSA, MD5, or SHA-1). A provider is identified by a name and a version number. There is a default provider — called the SUN Provider — that is supplied with the JDK.

Inheritance

```
public abstract class java.security.Provider
    extends Properties
        ⇑
    public class Properties
        extends Hashtable
            ⇑
        public class Hashtable
            implements Cloneable
            implements Serializable
            extends Dictionary
                ⇑
            public class Dictionary
                extends Object
                    ⇑
                public class java.lang.Object
```

Constructors

```
protected Provider(String name,double version,String info)
```

A `Provider` object is constructed from the `name` of the provider, the `version` number, and a string describing the provider and its services.

Returned by

A `Provider` object is returned from `Security.getProvider()`. An array of `Provider` objects is returned from `Security.getProviders()`.

Methods

getInfo()

```
public String getInfo()
```

Returns the string that is a human-readable description of the provider and its services. It is possible for the string to be an HTML document with links to more information.

getName()

```
public String getName()
```

Returns the name of the provider.

getVersion()

```
public double getVersion()
```

Returns the version number of the provider.

toString()

```
public String toString()
```

Returns a string with both the name and the version number of the provider.

 For maintaining the list of available providers, see **Security**.

ProviderException

class java.security.ProviderException

This exception is thrown as notification of a run-time problem with a provider. This can be used as-is, or it can be subclassed by providers to add specific information.

Inheritance

```
public class java.security.ProviderException
    extends RuntimeException
            ⇑
    public class java.lang.RuntimeException
        extends Exception
```

```
                                    ⇑
                        public class java.lang.Exception
                            extends Throwable
                                    ⇑
                        public class java.lang.Throwable
                            implements Serializable
                            extends Object
                                    ⇑
                            public class java.lang.Object
```

Constructors

```
public ProviderException()
```

```
public ProviderException(String message)
```

If the message string is supplied, it is used as a detailed message describing this particular exception.

public

 See **access**.

PublicKey

interface java.security.PublicKey

This is the interface of a class that is the container of a public key—the key that is published by an identity for encryption of messages that are to be sent to the entity.

No methods or constants are defined for this interface. It serves as an identifying tag for any object that contains a public encryption key.

Extended by

```
DSAPublicKey
```

Inheritance

```
public interface java.security.PublicKey
    extends Key
```

⇑
```
public interface java.security.Key
```

Constructors

Returned by

An object implementing the `PublicKey` interface is returned from `Certificate.getPublicKey()`, `Identity.getPublicKey()`, and `KeyPair.getPublic()`.

 Also see **Key**, **PrivateKey**, **Certificate**, and **DSAPrivateKey**.

PushbackInputStream

class java.io.PushbackInputStream

This is an input stream that allows characters to be pushed back after having been read. The last characters read can be put back so that the next read will fetch them again.

What is this for?

This is a convenience for applications that read and analyze the contents of character strings. Circumstances arise in which input characters are read continuously until a character does not fit the pattern. When an unwanted character is read, it can be put back so that when processing begins for the next group of characters, it will be available.

Inheritance

```
public class java.io.PushbackInputStream
    extends FilterInputStream
        ⇑
    public class java.io.FilterInputStream
        extends InputStream
            ⇑
        public class java.io.InputStream
            extends Object
                ⇑
            public class java.lang.Object
```

Variables and constants

buf

```
protected byte buf[]
```

A location to hold the pushed-back character.

pos

```
protected int pos
```

The current position in buf.

Constructors

PushbackInputStream()

```
public PushbackInputStream(InputStream in,int size)

public PushbackInputStream(InputStream in)
```

The size value determines the number of characters that can be pushed back after being read. The default size is 1.

Methods

available()

```
public int available()
    throws IOException
```

Returns the number of bytes that can be read without blocking. It includes the count of the characters that have been pushed back.

markSupported()

```
public boolean markSupported()
```

This method always returns false.

read()

```
public int read()
    throws IOException

public int read(byte barray[],int offset,int length)
    throws IOException
```

Reads one or more bytes of data from the input stream. If no argument is supplied, it reads and returns one byte. If barray is specified, it reads up to length bytes and places them in the array at barray[offset]. This method will block until at least one byte of data is available. When an array is being read, the return value is a count of the number of characters read. A return value of −1 indicates that no characters have been read and the end-of-file has been reached. The returned byte may be one that was pushed back.

unread()

```
public void unread(int character)
    throws IOException

public void unread(byte barray[])
    throws IOException

public void unread(byte barray[],int offset,int count)
    throws IOException
```

This will push back one or more bytes. If character is specified, its low-order eight bits are pushed back. If offset and count are specified, count characters beginning at barray[offset] are pushed back. If barray is specified without offset and count, all of barray is pushed back.

If there is not sufficient room in the internal push-back array, an IOException is thrown.

PushbackReader

class java.io.PushbackReader

A character-stream reader that allows characters to be pushed back into the stream.

Inheritance

```
public class PushbackReader
    extends FilterReader
        ⇑
    public class java.io.FilterReader
        extends Reader
            ⇑
        public class java.io.Reader
            extends Object
                ⇑
            public class java.lang.Object
```

Constructors

```
public PushbackReader(Reader in,int size)

public PushbackReader(Reader in)
```

The size is the number of bytes that can be pushed back at any one time. The default size is 1.

Methods

close()

```
public void close()
    throws IOException
```

Closes the stream.

markSupported()

```
public boolean markSupported()
```

This method always returns false.

read()

```
public int read()
    throws IOException

public int read(byte barray[],int offset,int length)
    throws IOException
```

Reads one or more bytes of data from the input stream. If no argument is supplied, it reads and returns one byte. If barray is specified, it reads up to length bytes and places them in the array at barray[offset]. This method will block until at least one byte of data is available. When it is reading an array, the return value is a count of the number of characters read. A return value of −1 indicates that no characters have been read and the end-of-file has been reached. The returned data could be those pushed back.

ready()

```
public boolean ready()
    throws IOException
```

Returns true if the stream is ready to be read.

unread()

```
public void unread(int character)
    throws IOException

public void unread(byte barray[])
    throws IOException

public void unread(byte barray[],int offset,int count)
    throws IOException
```

This will push back one or more bytes. If character is specified, its low-order eight bits are pushed back. If offset and count are specified, count characters beginning at barray[offset] are pushed back. If barray is specified without offset and count, all of barray is pushed back.

If there is not sufficient room in the internal push-back array, an IOException is thrown.

question mark

? :

The question mark and the colon pair form a special conditional operator used to assign one of two possible values to a variable. It is simply shorthand for a common form of an if-else block. The code shown here:

```
if(a < b)
     x = 5;
else
     x = 25;
```

can also be written this way:

```
x = a < b ? 5 : 25;
```

When this statement is executed, the `boolean` expression is evaluated. If the result is `true`, the expression following the "?" is evaluated and the result is assigned to "x"—if it is `false`, the expression following the ":" is evaluated and the result is assigned to "x."

R

radio button

For mutually exclusive buttons, sometimes called radio buttons, see **Checkbox** and **CheckboxGroup**.

radix

The numeric base of a number. If a string of digits has a radix of 10, that means it is a base-10 number. A radix of 16 is hexadecimal, and a radix of 8 is octal.

The string form of a number with a radix greater than 10 uses letters from the ASCII character set as digits. Base 16 uses the letters A through F for the values 10 through 15. This is continued for larger bases—G is used for 16, H for 17, and so on.

Random

class java.util.Random

This class can be used to generate a sequence of pseudorandom numbers.

Pseudorandom and seeding

The term *pseudorandom* refers to the fact that it is possible for sequences of numbers to be repeated. This repetition can be achieved by supplying the same seed at the beginning of each run.

Because each number in a sequence is determined by the number that came before it, any sequence of numbers—allowed to run long enough—will eventually repeat itself. However, the sequences are extremely long and this is almost never a problem.

The formula

The Random class uses a 48-bit seed modified using a linear congruential formula. This is found in Donald Knuth's *Art of Computer Programming, Volume 2*.

Extended by

SecureRandom

Inheritance

```
public class java.util.Random
    implements Serializable
    extends Object
            ⇑
    public class java.lang.Object
```

Constructors

```
public Random()
public Random(long seed)
```

A Random object can be created with or without a seed. If a seed is supplied, it will determine the sequence of generated numbers. If no seed is supplied, the Random class will use the current clock value as the seed.

Methods

next()

```
protected synchronized int next(int bits)
```

This method returns a random int value that is no larger than will fit into the specified number of bits.

nextBytes()

```
public void nextBytes(byte bytes[])
```

This method will fill the array with random values in the range 0 to 255.

nextDouble()

```
public double nextDouble()
```

This method returns a random double value in the range 0.0 through 1.0. The sequence of numbers will be uniformly distributed across the range. See Example 2.

nextFloat()

```
public float nextFloat()
```

This method returns a random float value in the range 0.0 through 1.0. The sequence of numbers will be uniformly distributed across the range.

nextGaussian()

```
public synchronized double nextGaussian()
```

This method returns a random double value. The values have a Gaussian distribution with a mean of 0.0 and a standard deviation of 1.0.

nextInt()

```
public int nextInt()
```

This will return a random integer value. The values have an even distribution across the entire range of int values — positive and negative.

nextLong()

```
public long nextLong()
```

This will return a random integer value. The values have an even distribution across the entire range of long values — positive and negative.

setSeed()

```
public synchronized void setSeed(long seed)
```

This can be used to set the seed to a specific value. Using a seed value that was the same as a previous one will cause the same sequence of pseudorandom numbers to be generated. See Example 2.

Example 1

This is an example using the next() method to produce integer values that will fit in a specified number of bits:

```
import java.util.*;
public class NextBitsRandom extends Random {
    static public void main(String arg[]) {
        NextBitsRandom nb = new NextBitsRandom();
        for(int i=0; i<25; i++)
            System.out.print(" " + nb.next(2));
        System.out.println();
        for(int i=0; i<15; i++)
            System.out.print(" " + nb.next(8));
        System.out.println();
        for(int i=0; i<5; i++)
            System.out.print(" " + nb.next(32));
    }
}
```

The number of bits of the result is determined by the number specified as the argument to next(). This example generates sequences of random numbers of 2, 8, and 32 bits. Here is the output from a typical run:

```
1 0 0 0 0 3 2 0 1 3 2 1 3 3 2 1 0 2 1 0 2 2 0 2 2
65 189 208 159 164 71 38 100 215 197 207 128 30 88 8
-1289742823 -938851026 1239415892 -1163903088 102761798
```

Example 2

This shows how calls to setSeed() can be used to cause a sequence of random numbers to be repeated:

```
import java.util.*;
public class SequenceRestart {
    public static void main(String[] arg) {
        Random r = new Random(12345);
        for(int i=0; i<5; i++)
            System.out.println(r.nextDouble());
        System.out.println();
        r.setSeed(12345);
        for(int i=0; i<5; i++)
            System.out.println(r.nextDouble());
    }
}
```

The Random object is created with a specific seed — this determines the sequence of pseudorandom numbers that will be generated. The sequence will be the same every time this program is run. A call is made to setSeed() with the same seed value, causing the entire sequence to be repeated. Here is the output:

```
0.3618031071604718
0.932993485288541
0.8330913489710237
0.32647575623792624
0.2355237906476252

0.3618031071604718
0.932993485288541
0.8330913489710237
0.32647575623792624
0.2355237906476252
```

For a simple method of generating random numbers, see `random()` in **Math**.

RandomAccessFile

class java.io.RandomAccessFile

This class is for random access reading and writing of a file.

Blocking

There are methods to read data from a file in many formats. All of these are blocking reads — that is, each will read until it has data. If there is no more data, an `EOFException` will be thrown.

UTF-8

There are methods here that read and write UTF-8-encoded strings. The disk form of these strings does not have a terminator at the end — instead they have a counter at the beginning. The counter is a 16-bit binary value that is a count of the number of encoded bytes. This count is the number of bytes in the disk file, not the number of characters in the unencoded string — the two values can be different because of the encoding.

Inheritance

```
public class java.io.RandomAccessFile
    implements DataOutput
    implements DataInput
    extends Object
        ⇑
    public class java.lang.Object
```

Constructors

RandomAccessFile()

```
public RandomAccessFile(String name,String mode)
    throws IOException

public RandomAccessFile(File file,String mode)
    throws IOException
```

A `RandomAccessFile` object can be created from the `name` of a file, or from a `File` object representing the name of the file. The `mode` string must be either "r" for read-only or "rw" for both read and write.

An IOException is thrown if some sort of input/output error occurs. A SecurityException is thrown if the requested read or write permission is denied.

Methods

close()

```
public void close()
    throws IOException
```

Closes the stream and releases any system resources allocated for it.

getFD()

```
public final FileDescriptor getFD()
    throws IOException
```

Returns the opaque file descriptor object associated with this stream.

getFilePointer()

```
public long getFilePointer()
    throws IOException
```

Returns the current file offset—the count of the number of bytes from the beginning of the file at which the next read or write operation will take place.

length()

```
public long length()
    throws IOException
```

Returns the total length of the file.

read()

```
public int read()
    throws IOException

public int read(byte barray[])
    throws IOException

public int read(byte barray[],int offset,int length)
    throws IOException
```

If no argument is supplied, this will read one byte of data and return it as an int. If barray is supplied, the input data is placed in the array and the number of bytes is returned. If offset and length are specified, the input data will appear beginning at barray[offset] for a maximum of length bytes. If offset and length are not specified, the entire array is used. This method will block until at least one byte of data is available for input. A return value of –1 indicates an end-of-file has been reached.

readBoolean()

```
public final boolean readBoolean()
    throws IOException
```

Reads a `boolean` value.

readByte()

```
public final byte readByte()
    throws IOException
```

Reads a `byte` value.

readChar()

```
public final char readChar()
    throws IOException
```

Reads a Unicode value. Two bytes are read from the file to make up the character.

readDouble()

```
public final double readDouble()
    throws IOException
```

Reads a `double` value. This method reads a `long` value as if by the `readLong()` method and then converts it to a `double` using the `Double.longBitsToDouble()` method.

readFloat()

```
public final float readFloat()
    throws IOException
```

Reads a `float` value. This method reads an `int` value as if by the `readInt()` method and then converts it to a `float` using the `Float.intBitsToFloat()` method.

readFully()

```
public final void readFully(byte barray[])
    throws IOException

public final void readFully(byte barray[],
        int offset,int length)
    throws IOException
```

This method will read an array of bytes into `barray`. The data will be placed into `barray` beginning at `offset` and continuing for `length` bytes. If `offset` and `length` are not specified, all of `barray` will be filled. This is a blocking read—it will not return until there is enough data to fill `barray`.

readInt()

```
public final int readInt()
    throws IOException
```

Reads an int value. Four bytes are read from the file and treated as the binary form of an int.

readLine()

```
public final String readLine()
    throws IOException
```

Reads a line of text and returns it as a String. A line of text is terminated by a carriage return, a newline, a carriage return immediately followed by a newline, or the end of the input stream. If line-terminating characters are found, they are returned as part of the String.

readLong()

```
public final long readLong()
    throws IOException
```

Reads a long value. Eight bytes are read from the file and treated as the binary form of a long.

readShort()

```
public final short readShort()
    throws IOException
```

Reads a short value. Two bytes are read from the file and treated as the binary form of a signed short.

readUnsignedByte()

```
public final int readUnsignedByte()
    throws IOException
```

Reads an 8-bit byte as an unsigned value and returns it as an int in the range 0 to 255.

readUnsignedShort()

```
public final int readUnsignedShort()
    throws IOException
```

Reads a 16-bit short as an unsigned value and returns it as an int in the range 0 to 65,535.

readUTF()

```
public final String readUTF()
    throws IOException
```

Reads a string of UTF-8-formatted Unicode characters and converts them to their 16-bit Unicode form. The first two bytes are read as an unsigned short and treated as a count of the number of bytes in the encoded string to follow. A `UTFDataFormatException` is thrown if a byte is found not to be a valid UTF-8 encoding.

seek()

```
public void seek(long position)
    throws IOException
```

Sets the internal file pointer so that the next read or write operation will occur at `position`. The value of positions is an index from the beginning of the file.

skipBytes()

```
public int skipBytes(int count)
    throws IOException
```

Moves the file position pointer forward by `count` bytes. The result is just as if the specified number of bytes had been read and discarded—it is possible that an `EOFException` or `IOException` could be thrown.

write()

```
public void write(byte barray[],int offset,int length)
    throws IOException

public void write(byte barray[])
    throws IOException

public void write(int bvalue)
    throws IOException
```

Writes one or more bytes to the stream. If `bvalue` is specified, the least-significant eight bits of it are written as a `byte`. If `barray` is specified, the bytes written will begin with `barray[offset]` and continue for `length` bytes. If `offset` and `length` are not specified, the entire array is written. The method will block until the data is written.

writeBoolean()

```
public final void writeBoolean(boolean value)
    throws IOException
```

Writes a `boolean` value as a single byte. Writes a 1 byte if `true` and a 0 byte if `false`.

writeByte()

```
public final void writeByte(int value)
    throws IOException
```

The least significant eight bits of `value` are written to the stream as a `byte` value.

writeBytes()

```
public final void writeBytes(String string)
    throws IOException
```

Writes the string as a sequence of bytes by discarding the high-order eight bits of each character.

writeChar()

```
public final void writeChar(int value)
    throws IOException
```

The low-order 16 bits of the int are written as a char.

writeChars()

```
public final void writeChars(String string)
    throws IOException
```

The contents of the string are written as a sequence of char values. There is no encoding—each char is written as a 16-bit value.

writeDouble()

```
public final void writeDouble(double value)
    throws IOException
```

The double is written to the stream. The eight bytes of the value are written in their binary form.

writeFloat()

```
public final void writeFloat(float value)
    throws IOException
```

The float is written to the stream. The four bytes of the value are written in their binary form.

writeInt()

```
public final void writeInt(int value)
    throws IOException
```

The int is written to the stream. The four bytes of the value are written in their binary from.

writeLong()

```
public final void writeLong(long value)
    throws IOException
```

The long is written to the stream. The eight bytes of the value are written in their binary form.

writeShort()

```
public final void writeShort(int value)
    throws IOException
```

The least-significant 16 bits of the int are written as a short. The two bytes are written in their binary form.

writeUTF()

```
public void writeUTF(String string)
    throws IOException
```

The string is written in UTF-8 format. First, two bytes are written to the file (using the writeShort() method) that are a count of the number of bytes to follow. Then, each of the encoded bytes of the string are written.

Example

This example writes some Unicode characters, a double value, and some UTF-8-encoded characters to a file and then, by repositioning, reads some of them back:

```
import java.io.*;
public class RanFile {
    public static void main(String[] arg) {
        try {
            RandomAccessFile rf =
                new
            RandomAccessFile("ranfile.data","rw");
            rf.writeChars("abcdef\u04F5");
            long position = rf.getFilePointer();
            rf.writeDouble(3.1415);
            rf.writeUTF("abcdef\u04F5");
            rf.seek(position);
            System.out.println(rf.readDouble());
            rf.seek(0L);
            for(int i=0; i<3; i++)
                System.out.println(rf.readChar());
        } catch(IOException e) {
            System.out.println(e);
        }
    }
}
```

The writeChars() method is used to write a string of Unicode characters. The getFilePointer() method is called to return the file position of the next write — the position immediately following the characters just written. A double is then written with writeDouble(), and then seven UTF-encoded characters are written. The seek() method repositions the file to the formerly marked location, and the double value is read and printed. This positions the file in front of the encoded characters, so three of them are read and printed. The output looks like this:

```
3.1415
a
b
c
```

The contents of the file, dumped in hexadecimal form, look like this:

```
      00 01 02 03 04 05 06 07 08 09 0A 0B 0C 0D 0E 0F
0000  00 61 00 62 00 63 00 64 00 65 00 66 04 F5 40 09
0010  21 CA C0 83 12 6F 00 08 61 62 63 64 65 66 D3 B5
```

The bytes 0x0000 through 0x000D hold the 16-bit Unicode characters. The bytes from 0x000E through 0x00105 are the double value. The 16-bit value at 0x0016 is the number 8, which is the count of the encoded form of the UTF-8 characters on disk. The first six characters, beginning at 0x0018, take up one byte each. The last character, which is the Unicode character '\u04F5', encodes as the 2-byte value 0xD3B5.

Reader

class java.io.Reader

This is an abstract class used as the superclass of character-reading streams. Although other methods can be overridden, its subclasses only need to implement read() and close().

Extended by

```
BufferedReader
CharArrayReader
FilterReader
InputStreamReader
PipedReader
StringReader
```

Inheritance

```
public abstract class java.io.Reader
extends Object
```

⇑
```
public class java.lang.Object
```

Variables and constants

lock

```
protected Object lock
```

Subclasses should use this object for synchronizing access to the file.

Constructors

```
protected Reader()
protected Reader(Object lock)
```

If `lock` is specified, it will be used for critical-section access of the file. If `lock` is not supplied, `this` object will be used.

Methods

close()

```
public abstract void close()
    throws IOException
```

Closes the stream. Any attempt to access the file after this method has been called will cause an `IOException` to be thrown.

mark()

```
public synchronized void mark(int readlimit)
```

This will mark the current position in the input stream; a subsequent call to `reset()` will restore the input to this position. The value of `readlimit` specifies the number of characters that can be read before the mark is discarded. For this to work, the return value from `markSupported()` must be `true`.

markSupported()

```
public boolean markSupported()
```

This method returns `true` if the `mark()` and `reset()` methods can be used to alter the flow of the input stream.

read()

```
public int read()
    throws IOException

public int read(char carray[])
```

```
        throws IOException
public int read(char carray[],int offset,int length)
        throws IOException
```

If no argument is supplied, this will read one character and return it as an `int`. If `carray` is supplied, the input data is placed in the array and the number of characters read is returned. If `offset` and `length` are specified, the input data will appear beginning at `carray[offset]` for a maximum of `length` characters. The default `offset` is zero, and the default `length` is the size of `carray`. This method will block as long as there is unread data available. A return value of −1 indicates a normal end to the input stream.

ready()

```
public boolean ready()
        throws IOException
```

This method returns `true` if there is data that can be read without blocking and `false` otherwise.

reset()

```
public synchronized void reset()
        throws IOException
```

This will reposition the input stream to the location of the last call to `mark()`. The exception is thrown if there is no active mark. A mark will be removed (causing this method to throw an exception) if more bytes have been read than the number specified in the call to `mark()`.

skip()

```
public long skip(long count)
        throws IOException
```

Calling this method makes a request to have the input stream skip over `count` number of input characters. The return value is the actual number of characters skipped.

real numbers

 See **floating point numbers**. For the Java IEEE 754 real numbers, see **float** and **double**.

Rectangle

class java.awt.Rectangle

This is a wrapper for the definition of a rectangle.

Relationship of the variables

The *x* and *y* values are the coordinates of the upper-left corner of the defined rectangle. The `height` is the distance down from *y* to the bottom of the rectangle, and the `width` is the distance from *x* to the right side of the rectangle.

Inheritance

```
public class java.awt.Rectangle
     implements Shape
     implements Serializable
     extends Object
          ⇑
     public class java.lang.Object
```

Variables and constants

height

```
public int height
```

The height of the rectangle.

width

```
public int width
```

The width of the rectangle.

x

```
public int x
```

The *x* coordinate of the rectangle.

y

```
public int y
```

The *y* coordinate of the rectangle.

Constructors

```
public Rectangle()

public Rectangle(Rectangle rectangle)

public Rectangle(int x,int y,int width,int height)

public Rectangle(int width,int height)

public Rectangle(Point point,Dimension dimension)

public Rectangle(Point p)

public Rectangle(Dimension dimension)
```

There are a number of ways to specify the initial location (the *x* and *y* coordinates) and size (the width and height values) of a Rectangle. Any values not specified on the constructor will default to zero.

Returned by

A Rectangle object is returned from

```
Component.bounds()
Component.getBounds()
Graphics.getClipBounds()
Graphics.getClipRect()
PaintEvent.getUpdateRect()
Polygon.getBoundingBox()
Polygon.getBounds()
Rectangle.getBounds()
Rectangle.intersection()
Rectangle.union()
Shape.getBounds()
```

Methods

add()

```
public void add(int x,int y)

public void add(Point point)

public void add(Rectangle rectangle)
```

Adds the specified point or rectangle to the existing rectangle. That is, the existing rectangle will be expanded in whatever directions necessary to include the specified point, or to enclose the specified rectangle.

contains()

```
public boolean contains(Point point)

public boolean contains(int x,int y)
```

Returns true if the rectangle includes the specified point. A point that is "on the line" is considered to be contained.

equals()

```
public boolean equals(Object object)
```

Returns true if object is a Rectangle with the same location and dimensions as this one.

getBounds()

```
public Rectangle getBounds()
```

Returns the bounds of the rectangle—effectively, this is a clone of Rectangle.

getLocation()

```
public Point getLocation()
```

Returns the *x* and *y* coordinates of the rectangle as a Point.

getSize()

```
public Dimension getSize()
```

Returns the size (width and height) as a Dimension.

grow()

```
public void grow(int horizontal,int vertical)
```

Expands the size of the rectangle both horizontally and vertically. The amount specified will be used for both sides of the rectangle. For example, if the value of horizontal is 10, the rectangle will expand by 10 on the left (by 10 being subtracted from *x*) and the width will be increased by 20 causing the right side to be expanded by 10. Negative values will reduce the size.

hashCode()

```
public int hashCode()
```

Returns the hashcode value of this object.

inside()   **deprecated**

```
public boolean inside(int x,int y)
```

Returns `true` if the point is inside the rectangle. This method is deprecated—use `contains()`.

intersection()

```
public Rectangle intersection(Rectangle rectangle)
```

Returns a new `Rectangle` that is the intersection of the two rectangles. The result is undefined if the two do not intersect.

intersects()

```
public boolean intersects(Rectangle rectangle)
```

Returns `true` if the two rectangles intersect.

isEmpty()

```
public boolean isEmpty()
```

Returns `true` if either the height or the width of the rectangle is not greater than zero.

move()   **deprecated**

```
public void move(int x,int y)
```

Moves the rectangle to another location. This method is deprecated—use `setLocation()`.

reshape()   **deprecated**

```
public void reshape(int x,int y,int width,int height)
```

Defines a new location and size for the rectangle. This method is deprecated—use `setBounds()`.

resize()   **deprecated**

```
public void resize(int width,int height)
```

Defines new height and width dimensions for the rectangle. This method is deprecated—use `setSize()`.

setBounds()

```
public void setBounds(Rectangle rectangle)

public void setBounds(int x,int y,int width,int height)
```

Sets the location and size to match those of the specified argument values.

setLocation()

```
public void setLocation(Point point)
```

```
public void setLocation(int x,int y)
```

Sets the *x* and *y* coordinates of the rectangle to the specified values.

setSize()

```
public void setSize(Dimension dimension)
```

```
public void setSize(int width,int height)
```

Sets the height and width of the rectangle to the specified values.

toString()

```
public String toString()
```

Returns a string containing the values of the Rectangle.

translate()

```
public void translate(int xDelta,int yDelta)
```

Moves the location of the rectangle by the amount specified as xDelta and yDelta. The values can be positive or negative.

union()

```
public Rectangle union(Rectangle rectangle)
```

Returns a new rectangle that is the union of these two—that is, it is the smallest possible Rectangle that includes the area enclosed by the two.

 For similar wrappers, see **Dimension**, **Insets**, **Point**, **Polygon**, and **Shape**.

reference

A *reference* is a special Java data type that holds the location (or handle, if you prefer) of an object. Every reference holds either the location of an object of the type for which it was defined or the special reference value null.

 This is sort of like a pointer—but only sort of. It holds what could be the address of an object or could be some sort of handle used to locate the object. The exact contents of a reference are implementation-dependent, but there are definite rules about how and where a reference can be used.

Whether or not a reference is a pointer depends on your definition of a pointer. If you consider a pointer as a holder of the necessary information to find something, then a reference is a pointer. On the other hand, if you consider a pointer to be an address in RAM—something you can index from and manipulate, then a reference is not a pointer.

A reference cannot be converted to any of the primitive types. No primitive type can be converted to a reference. Because null is a reference, even though it is a special one, it has the same conversion limitations as any other reference value. Since all objects in Java are descended from the superclass Object, all references (including arrays) can be stored in a reference of type Object.

Kinds of references

There are three kinds of references:

- References to a specific class. This type of reference can also be used for any subclass of its class.
- References to interfaces. One of these is capable of referring to any class that implements the interface it was defined for.
- References to arrays. In Java, an array is an object.

Reference declarations

All references have a type. The type of a reference is determined by its declaration, and it cannot be changed. Here are some examples of reference declarations:

```
String str;
java.util.Bitset name;
Frame frame;
int[] intArray;
```

A newly declared reference is initialized to null. For a reference to take on a value other than null, it must be assigned an object. This can be done by assigning the value from another reference, like this:

```
String str = other_str;
```

Alternatively, a new object can be created for it while it is being declared, like this:

```
String str = new String();
java.util.Bitset name = new java.util.Bitset();
Frame frame = new Frame("Title string");
int intArray[] = new int[20];
```

Modifying an object through its reference

The same object can have several references. Whenever this is the case, modifying the state or content of the object through either reference will have the same effect—the resulting change can be observed through either reference.

This is the case whether the reference is used in the same method or passed to another one. Example:

```
public class MultipleReference {
    public static void main(String[] arg) {
        ValueHolder vh1;
        ValueHolder vh2;
        vh1 = new ValueHolder();
        vh2 = vh1;
        vh1.value = 50;
        System.out.println("Start  vh1=" + vh1.value +
                " vh2=" + vh2.value);
        modify(vh1);
        System.out.println("End    vh1=" + vh1.value +
                " vh2=" + vh2.value);
    }
    public static void modify(ValueHolder vh) {
        vh.value = 99;
    }
}

class ValueHolder {
    public int value;
}
```

The output from this example shows that the two references vh1 and vh2 refer to the same object. It also shows that a reference passed to another method is still a reference to the same object. The output from the preceding example:

```
Start  vh1=50 vh2=50
End    vh1=99 vh2=99
```

This output proves that not only do vh1 and vh2 refer to the same object, but so does vh in the modify method. All of these refer to the object created by the new expression.

Operations on references

These are the contexts in which references can be used:

◆ As a qualifying name in accessing a field in an object
◆ In invoking a method
◆ With the cast operator
◆ With the concatenation operator +, which will convert a reference to a String object

◆ As the operand of the `instanceof` operator

◆ With the reference equality operators == and !=

◆ As the second and third operands of the conditional operator ?:

Polymorphism

The ability of an object to be referenced by any of the classes in its hierarchy is the Java way of implementing polymorphism. This example is designed to demonstrate the relationship between class hierarchies and references:

```
import java.awt.*;

public class PolyReference {
    public static void main(String[] arg) {
        Setter setter = new Setter();
        Dog dog = new Setter();
        Animal animal = new Setter();

        animal = setter;
        dog = setter;

        setter = (Setter)dog;
        animal = (Setter)dog;

        dog = new Dog();
        setter = (Setter)dog; //Error
    }
}

class Animal {
    private int weight;
    public void setWeight(int weight) {
        this.weight = weight;
    }
    public int getWeight() {
        return(weight);
    }
}

class Dog extends Animal {
    Color eyeColor;
    public void setEyeColor(Color eyeColor) {
        this.eyeColor = eyeColor;
    }
```

```
    public Color getEyeColor() {
        return(eyeColor);
    }
}

class Setter extends Dog {
    boolean trainedToHunt;
    public boolean isTrainedToHunt() {
        return(trainedToHunt);
    }
    public void setTrainedToHunt(boolean trainedToHunt) {
        this.trainedToHunt = trainedToHunt;
    }
}
```

Three levels of a class hierarchy are shown in this example. First is the
Animal class, which—since it has no extends statement—defaults to extending the Object class. Second, the Dog class extends the Animal class (which
means that a Dog "isa" Animal). Finally, the Setter class extends Dog (which
means that a Setter "isa" Dog). The class Polyreference declares references
to the three and creates objects to populate the references.

A reference has a class (or an interface) as its type—this type is made up of
a hierarchy of classes and/or interfaces. The reference can be used to refer to any
class or interface in the hierarchy. Building on the previous example, the following code shows that a Setter object is also a Dog object and an Animal object.

```
Setter setter = new Setter();
Dog dog = new Setter();
Animal animal = new Setter();
```

The reference value of a class can be held by a reference to any superclass
of a class. This works because of the "isa" relationships.

```
animal = setter;
dog = setter;
```

The reverse can be true, but a couple of things must be done. To assign the
value of a subclass reference to one of its superclasses, it is necessary to use a
cast like this:

```
setter = (Setter)dog;
animal = (Setter)dog;
```

The casting is accepted by the compiler since it is possible for a dog or an
animal to be a setter. Care must be taken to prevent a runtime error, as shown
here:

```
dog = new Dog();
setter = (Setter)dog; //Error at runtime
```

In this case, the object referred to by dog is not a Setter. The cast just won't take, because there are attributes of a setter beyond that of a dog and attributes cannot be added with a cast. The compiler had no way of knowing about the mismatch, but at runtime, a ClassCastException will be thrown.

References to interface types

The object of a class can be accessed through a reference to an interface that the class implements. For example, the class Stack inherits from Vector, and Vector implements a couple of interfaces. Here is the hierarchy of Stack:

```
public class java.util.Stack
    extends Vector
              ⇑
    public class java.util.Vector
        implements Cloneable
        implements Serializable
        extends Object
              ⇑
        public class java.lang.Object
```

This example includes the complete set of reference types that can contain a Stack reference:

```
import java.util.*;
import java.io.*;
public class StackDown {
    public static void main(String[] arg) {
        Stack stack = new Stack();
        Vector vector = stack;
        Cloneable cloneable = stack;
        Serializable serializable = stack;
        Object object = stack;
    }
}
```

A reference to an interface can be used as a reference to any class that implements the interface—even if the implementation is inherited.

Widening and narrowing

Reference values are widened and narrowed by being assigned from one reference type to another. If the assignment is made such that the receiving reference is guaranteed (by the reference types on each side of the assignment) to be valid, the compiler can approve it as widening and the statement will compile. On the other hand, if the compiler cannot determine whether the assignment will be valid for all possible type combinations, the compiler will require that the assignment be cast and will leave the final approval to the runtime system—in Java terminology, this is narrowing.

While it is not possible to instantiate interfaces and abstract classes, it is possible to declare a reference to an interface or abstract class and to widen or narrow a reference value into it. This is probably best explained with an example. Here is the hierarchy of java.awt.Frame:

```
public class java.awt.Frame
     implements java.awt.MenuContainer
     extends java.awt.Window
                    ⇑
     public class java.awt.Window
         extends java.awt.Container
                        ⇑
         public class java.awt.Container
             extends java.awt.Component
                            ⇑
             public class java.awt.Component
                 implements java.awt.image.ImageObserver
                 implements java.awt.MenuContainer
                 implements java.io.Serializable
                 extends java.lang.Object
                                ⇑
                 public class java.lang.Object
```

From this hierarchy, we can see that a Frame is a Window, a Container, a Component, and an Object. It also is a MenuContainer, an ImageObserver, and Serializable. Take this sequence of code:

```
Frame frame = new Frame();
Container container;
container = frame;
frame = (frame)container;
```

Assigning the frame to the container is valid. Because the frame is a container, the frame reference can be assigned to the container reference. The compiler looks at the hierarchy and allows the assignment to take place, since the result will be an object that has all the capabilities of a container.

Assigning the container reference to the frame may or may not be valid—the compiler cannot tell for sure because the container could be a reference to a Panel or a FileDialog or something that is not compatible. The compiler requires the insertion of a cast and leaves it up to the runtime system to do the checking.

There can be references to interfaces, but because an interface cannot be instantiated, the value contained in the reference must be that of the object of a class that instantiates the interface. Continuing with our example, we create the reference to an interface and assign it a value:

```
ImageObserver observer;
observer = frame;
frame = (Frame)observer;
```

The observer reference can accept the value of a frame reference because the `Frame` class implements the `ImageObserver` interface—the compiler knows this and permits the assignment. Because any number of classes could implement the interface, however, it is necessary to cast the assignment from observer to frame—this will force the runtime system to execute its conversion code and make the test for validity.

 For more about objects, see **array** and **object**. To test a reference to learn what kind of object it holds, see **instanceof**.

reflect

package java.lang.reflect

Reflection is the capability of a running Java program to discover information about fields, methods, and constructors of loaded classes. Reflection can expose all the details of the internal parts allowed by security restrictions. This is an API providing capabilities for internal inspection and manipulation of Java objects. It has classes with methods that modify elements of arrays, construct new classes, and access the fields within objects.

Interfaces

```
Member
```

Classes

```
Array
Constructor
Field
Method
Modifier
```

Exceptions

```
InvocationTargetException
```

registry

package java.rmi.registry

This package supplies access to the registry of remote method invocation. The registry contains the information describing the remote objects.

Interfaces
```
Registry
RegistryHandler
```

Classes
```
LocateRegistry
```

Registry

interface java.rmi.registry.Registry

Every network node that allows RMI connections has a `Registry`. It contains the database that maps names to remote objects.

How it works

There is only one `Registry` object on a system. At boot time, the `Registry` database is empty. Any service wishing to allow RMI stores its name in the database of the `Registry`. The stored names are included without being modified in any way (there is no parsing or analysis). The service storing the name would be wise to store its entire package name to prevent name collision — this is not required, but it is a good safety measure.

A server establishes a local service

A local service is created from a class that implements the `Remote` interface. It will have one or more method suitable for being invoked remotely. For example, it could be called `SimpleService` and be constructed this way:

```
SimpleService simserve = new SimpleService();
```

To make it available to clients, it will need to be registered. A copy of the local registry (for the default port) can be acquired like this:

```
Registry registry = LocateRegistry.getRegistry();
```

To add the new service to the registry, it is necessary to bind it by name, like this:

```
registry.bind("Simple name",simserve);
```

The service is now available to client systems — it can be accessed by the name "Simple name."

A client can access a remote service

A remote service can be accessed by the name under which it was registered by the server. To do this, it is first necessary to get a reference to the registry object on the remote system. For example:

```
Registry registry =
          LocateRegistry.getRegistry("some.system.com");
```

The client then requests the actual service from the registry by using its name, like this:

```
SimpleService simserve =
          (SimpleService)registry.lookup("Simple name");
```

The object referenced by `simserve` can have its methods called by the client just as any other object could. For example:

```
String string = simserver.toString();
```

Inheritance

```
public interface java.rmi.Registry
    extends Remote
            ⇑
    public interface java.rmi.Remote
```

Variables and constants

REGISTRY_PORT

```
public static final int REGISTRY_PORT
```

The TCP/IP well-known port number used to access a remote `Registry`.

Constructors

Returned by

References to objects that implement this interface are returned from calls to `LocateRegistry.createRegistry()`, `LocateRegistry.getRegistry()`, `RegistryHandler.registryImpl()`, and `RegistryHandler.registryStub()`.

Methods

bind()

```
public abstract void bind(String name,Remote object)
```

```
     throws RemoteException
     throws AlreadyBoundException
     throws AccessException
```

Binds the name to the specified remote object. A RemoteException is thrown if the remote operation failed. An AlreadyBoundException is thrown if the name has already been used to bind a remote object. An AccessException is thrown if the operation is not permitted.

list()

```
public abstract String[] list()
     throws RemoteException
     throws AccessException
```

Returns an array of the names in the registry. A RemoteException is thrown if the operation fails. An AccessException is thrown if the operation is not permitted.

lookup()

```
public abstract Remote lookup(String name)
     throws RemoteException
     throws NotBoundException
     throws AccessException
```

Returns the remote object associated with name. A RemoteException is thrown if the remote operation failed. A NotBoundException is found if there is no such name found in the Registry database. An AccessException is thrown if the operation is not permitted.

rebind()

```
public abstract void rebind(String name,Remote object)
     throws RemoteException
     throws AccessException
```

Replaces the binding name of the object with a new name. A RemoteException is thrown if the remote operation failed. An AccessException is thrown if the operation is not permitted.

unbind()

```
public abstract void unbind(String name)
     throws RemoteException
     throws NotBoundException
     throws AccessException
```

Removes the name from the database. A RemoteException is thrown if the remote operation failed. A NotBoundException is found if no such name was found in the Registry database. An AccessException is thrown if the operation is not permitted.

For more information, see **RMI**. Also see **RegistryHandler** and **LocateRegistry**.

RegistryHandler

interface java.rmi.registry.RegistryHandler

This is a definition of the standard methods to be used to interface with the private implementation of the Registry.

Inheritance

```
public interface java.rmi.registry.RegistryHandler
```

Methods

registryImpl()

```
public abstract Registry registryImpl(int port)
    throws RemoteException
```

This will construct and export a Registry object for the specified port. The port number must be nonzero.

registryStub()

```
public abstract Registry registryStub(String host,int port)
    throws RemoteException
    throws UnknownHostException
```

This will return a local stub that can be used to contact a remote Registry on the specified host and port.

 For more information, see **RMI**. Also see **Registry** and **LocateRegistry**.

remainder

%   %=

The operators % and %= are the Java arithmetic remainder operators—also called the modulo operators. They return the remainder from a division. These operators are only valid for the Java primitive data types. Mixed-mode arithmetic is supported—the narrower type is widened before the operation is performed.

The % operator extracts the remainder but does not modify the operands. The %= operator extracts the remainder and places the results in the left operand. These two statements are equivalent:

```
a = a % b;
a %= b;
```

You can think of the operation as a sequence of subtractions. As long as a is greater than b, the value of b is subtracted from a. As soon as a becomes some value smaller than b, the value of a is taken as the result of the operation.

 For division on both integer and real types, see **divide**. For information on real numbers, see **floating-point numbers**.

Remote

interface java.rmi.Remote

This interface is used to identify a remote object. A remote object is one that can have its methods invoked from an object in another Virtual Machine. This interface does not declare any methods—it is used as a tag to identify remotely accessible objects.

Implemented by

```
RemoteObject
```

Extended by

```
DGC
Registry
```

Inheritance

```
public interface java.rmi.Remote
```

Constructors

Returned by

Objects that implement this interface are returned from calls to `Name.lookup()` and `Registry.lookup()`.

RemoteCall

interface java.rmi.server.RemoteCall

A `RemoteCall` is an abstraction used internally by the stubs and skeletons of remote objects to carry out a remote method invocation.

Inheritance

```
public interface java.rmi.server.RemoteCall
```

Constructors

Returned by

A `RemoteCall` object is returned from `RemoteRef.newCall()`.

Methods

done()

```
public abstract void done()
    throws IOException
```

Performs cleanup after a method call has been completed.

executeCall()

```
public abstract void executeCall()
    throws Exception
```

Executes the remote method call. The `Exception` is thrown if a general exception occurs.

getInputStream()

```
public abstract ObjectInput getInputStream()
    throws IOException
```

Returns the input stream that can be used by the stub to read results or by the skeleton to read arguments.

getOutputStream()

```
public abstract ObjectOutput getOutputStream()
    throws IOException
```

Returns the output stream that the stub should use to write arguments or that the skeleton should use to write results.

getResultStream()

```
public abstract ObjectOutput getResultStream(
        boolean success)
    throws IOException
    throws StreamCorruptedException
```

Returns an output stream that could possibly be used to read header information relating to the success or failure of the remote call. This should succeed only once per remote call. The value success is set to true to indicate a normal return from the method and false to indicate an Exception was thrown. A StreamCorruptedException is thrown if this method has already been called.

releaseInputStream()

```
public abstract void releaseInputStream()
    throws IOException
```

Releases the input stream. This call could increase efficiency if the transport layer is able to release the channel early.

releaseOutputStream()

```
public abstract void releaseOutputStream()
    throws IOException
```

Releases the output stream. This call could increase efficiency if the transport layer is able to release the channel early.

 For a general description, see **RMI**. Also see **Operation**, **RemoteObject**, **RemoteRef**, **RemoteServer**, **RemoteStub**, **ServerRef**, and **Skeleton**.

RemoteException

class java.rmi.RemoteException

There has been some kind of exception at the remote location. Optionally, the exception thrown by the remote is included inside this one.

Extended by

```
AccessException
ExportException
ConnectException
ConnectIOException
MarshalException
NoSuchObjectException
```

```
ServerError
ServerException
ServerRuntimeException
SkeletonMismatchException
SkeletonNotFoundException
StubNotFoundException
UnexpectedException
UnknownHostException
UnmarshalException
```

Inheritance

```
public class java.rmi.RemoteException
    extends IOException
        ⇑
    public class java.io.IOException
        extends Exception
            ⇑
        public class java.lang.Exception
            extends Throwable
                ⇑
            public class java.lang.Throwable
                implements Serializable
                extends Object
                    ⇑
                public class java.lang.Object
```

Variables and constants

detail

```
public Throwable detail
```

Optionally, an exception received from the remote location can be held here.

Constructors

```
public RemoteException()

public RemoteException(String message)

public RemoteException(String message,Throwable except)
```

If the `message` string is supplied, it is used as a detailed message describing this particular exception. If `except` is supplied, it is placed in the variable `detail`.

Methods

getMessage()

```
public String getMessage()
```

This will produce a string describing the exception. It will use the message and `except` from the constructors, if they were supplied.

Remote Method Invocation

 See **RMI.**

RemoteObject

class java.rmi.server.RemoteObject

The `RemoteObject` class implements the `Object` class for remote objects. The methods implemented here are the ones from the `Object` class that require special treatment for remote objects.

Extended by

```
RemoteServer
RemoteStub
```

Inheritance

```
public abstract class java.rmi.server.RemoteObject
    implements Remote
    implements Serializable
    extends Object
        ⇑
    public class java.lang.Object
```

Variables and constants

ref

```
protected transient RemoteRef ref
```

The remote object represented by the `RemoteObject`.

Constructors

```
protected RemoteObject()
protected RemoteObject(RemoteRef newref)
```

A `RemoteObject` can be created and initialized to a specific remote object.

Methods

equals()

```
public boolean equals(Object object)
```

Returns `true` if `object` is a `RemoteObject` that represents the same remote object as this one.

hashCode()

```
public int hashCode()
```

Returns the hashcode value of a remote object. Two local stubs referring to the same remote object will have the same hashcode value.

toString()

```
public String toString()
```

Returns a string representation of the remote object.

 For a general description, see **RMI**. Also see **Operation**, **RemoteCall**, **RemoteRef**, **RemoteServer**, **RemoteStub**, **ServerRef**, and **Skeleton**.

RemoteRef

interface java.rmi.server.RemoteRef

A `RemoteRef` is the representation of the handle of a remote object. There are methods defined here to get a `RemoteCall` object, and to use it to call remote methods.

Extended by

```
ServerRef
```

Inheritance

```
public interface java.rmi.server.RemoteRef
```

```
     extends Externalizable
         ⇑
public interface java.io.Externalizable
     extends Serializable
             ⇑
        public interface java.io.Serializable
```

Variables and constants

packagePrefix

```
public static final String packagePrefix
```

The package containing the object at the remote location.

Methods

done()

```
public abstract void done(RemoteCall call)
    throws RemoteException
```

This method can be called after remote invocation has completed successfully to allow the remote reference to clean up the connection. This should not be called if the invocation threw an Exception. The RemoteException is thrown if the registry could not be contacted.

getRefClass()

```
public abstract String getRefClass(ObjectOutput out)
```

Returns the class name of the type that will be serialized onto the stream out.

invoke()

```
public abstract void invoke(RemoteCall call)
    throws Exception
```

Executes the RemoteCall. If an Exception is thrown by the remote method, it will be rethrown by this method so that it can be caught locally—just as if the method were being called locally. If an exception occurs because of the remote invocation itself, it is the responsibility of this method to clean up the connection before throwing the local Exception.

newCall()

```
public abstract RemoteCall newCall(RemoteObject obj,
        Operation op[],int opnum,long hash)
    throws RemoteException
```

q
r
s

Creates and returns a `RemoteCall` object that can be used to remotely call a method of the `RemoteObject`. The method to be called is the one described by `op[opnum]`. The `RemoteException` is thrown if the registry could not be contacted.

remoteEquals()

```
public abstract boolean remoteEquals(RemoteRef object)
```

Returns `true` if `object` represents a handle to the same remote object as this one.

remoteHashCode()

```
public abstract int remoteHashCode()
```

Returns the hashcode for a remote object. Two `RemoteRef` objects referring to the same remote object will return the same hashcode value.

remoteToString()

```
public abstract String remoteToString()
```

Returns a string that represents the reference to the remote object.

 For a general description, see **RMI**. Also see **Operation**, **RemoteCall**, **RemoteObject**, **RemoteServer**, **RemoteStub**, **ServerRef**, and **Skeleton**.

RemoteServer

class java.rmi.server.RemoteServer

This class provides the methods necessary for a server to export objects — that is, to make them accessible for use from remote locations. This abstract class is the superclass of all server implementations.

Extended by

```
UnicastRemoteObject
```

Inheritance

```
public abstract class java.rmi.server.RemoteServer
    extends RemoteObject
        ⇑
    public abstract class java.rmi.server.RemoteObject
        implements Remote
        implements Serializable
```

```
extends Object
       ⇑
public class java.lang.Object
```

Constructors

```
protected RemoteServer()

protected RemoteServer(RemoteRef ref)
```

Methods

getClientHost()

```
public static String getClientHost()
      throws ServerNotActiveException
```

When called from a thread actively handling a remote method invocation, the host name of the remote client is returned. The ServerNotActiveException is thrown if the thread is not handling a remote method invocation.

getLog()

```
public static PrintStream getLog()
```

Returns the stream being used to log RMI call data.

setLog()

```
public static void setLog(OutputStream out)
```

Specifies the stream to be used to log RMI call data. If out is null, logging will be turned off.

 For a general description, see **RMI**. Also see **Operation**, **RemoteCall**, **RemoteObject**, **RemoteRef**, **RemoteStub**, **ServerRef**, and **Skeleton**.

RemoteStub

class java.rmi.server.RemoteStub

This is the superclass of all client stubs. A *stub* is the representation of a remote object—it represents it by supporting the same set of methods as the remote objects, and supporting remote invocation of the methods.

Inheritance

```
public abstract class java.rmi.server.RemoteStub
    extends RemoteObject
        ⇑
    public abstract class java.rmi.server.RemoteObject
        implements Remote
        implements Serializable
        extends Object
            ⇑
        public class java.lang.Object
```

Constructors

```
protected RemoteStub()
protected RemoteStub(RemoteRef ref)
```

The construction of a `RemoteStub` may include the remote reference.

Returned by

A RemoteStub object is returned from `ServerRef.exportObject()` and `UnicastRemoteObject.exportObject()`.

Methods

setRef()

```
protected static void setRef(RemoteStub stub,
    RemoteRef ref)
```

Relates the RemoteStub to the RemoteRef.

 For a general description, see **RMI**. Also see **Operation**, **RemoteCall**, **RemoteObject**, **RemoteRef**, **RemoteServer**, **ServerRef**, and **Skeleton**.

ReplicateScaleFilter

class java.awt.image.ReplicateScaleFilter

This class will scale an image from one size to another using the simplest possible algorithm. An image is enlarged by duplicating rows and columns of pixels. An image is reduced in size by deleting rows and columns of pixels.

FilteredImageSource

This class is designed to handle an image in the form that it has as it comes from a `FilteredImageSource`.

Inheritance

```
public class java.awt.image.ReplicateScaleFilter
    extends ImageFilter
        ⇑
    public class java.awt.image.ImageFilter
        implements ImageConsumer
        implements Cloneable
        extends Object
            ⇑
        public class java.lang.Object
```

Variables and constants

destHeight

```
protected int destHeight
```

The height of the output image.

destWidth

```
protected int destWidth
```

The width of the output image.

outpixbuf

```
protected Object outpixbuf
```

A work area used in construction of the output pixel array.

srccols

```
protected int srccols[]
```

A work area used for mapping pixels during filtering.

srcHeight

```
protected int srcHeight
```

The height of the input image.

srcrows

```
protected int srcrows[]
```

A work area used for mapping pixels during filtering.

srcWidth

```
protected int srcWidth
```

The width of the input image.

Constructors

```
public ReplicateScaleFilter(int width,int height)
```

This will construct a ReplicateScaleFilter object that will output an image of the specified width and height.

Methods

setDimensions()

```
public void setDimensions(int width,int height)
```

Overrides the dimensions from the ImageProducer and sets the dimensions of the new scaled image that will be passed to the ImageConsumer.

setPixels()

```
public void setPixels(int x,int y,int w,int h,
        ColorModel model,byte pixels[],
        int off,int scansize)
```

```
public void setPixels(int x,int y,int w,int h,
        ColorModel model,int pixels[],
        int off,int scansize)
```

This does the actual filtering of the data supplied in the pixels array.

The values of x and y specify the upper-left corner of the section of the image being delivered. The width and height values specify the count of the number of pixels being delivered in each dimension. If the entire image is being delivered, the values of x and y will both be zero, and the width and height will represent the size of the entire image. The ColorModel is that of the pixels being delivered.

The pixels array contains the actual pixel values. Depending on the color model, each pixel is stored in either 32 bits or 8 bits. Because the format of the pixel data matches the ColorModel argument, it should be used for any processing of the pixel data. The implementation of this interface normally requires that the two versions of this method be identical except for the difference in the sizes of the individual pixels.

The `offset` is an index to the first pixel in the array. The `scansize` is the width of each horizontal row of pixels in the delivered rectangle. These two values are used to address the individual pixels. The address of an individual pixel is

```
pixels[px + (py * scansize) + offset]
```

where `px` and `py` are the *x* and *y* coordinates of the pixel.

setProperties()

```
public void setProperties(Hashtable props)
```

Passes along the properties from the `ImageProducer` to the `ImageConsumer` after adding (or modifying) a property indicating the scale applied.

Example

This example is an applet that loads an image file from the disk and displays it unscaled and scaled. The scaled size will change each time the mouse clicks on the applet:

```java
import java.awt.*;
import java.awt.event.*;
import java.applet.*;
import java.net.*;
import java.awt.image.*;
import java.util.*;

public class RepScaleApplet extends Applet
        implements MouseListener {
    private static final int startScale = 10;
    private static final int incrementScale = 10;
    private static final int endScale = 200;
    private int scale = startScale;
    private Image image;
    private Image scaleImage;

    public void init() {
        addMouseListener(this);
        setBackground(Color.lightGray);
        URL url = getCodeBase();
        image = getImage(url,"bluemarble.gif");
        MediaTracker mt = new MediaTracker(this);
        mt.addImage(image,1);
        try {
            mt.waitForAll();
        } catch(Exception e) {
```

```
                            e.printStackTrace();
                }
                repaint();
        }

        public void paint(Graphics g) {
                g.setColor(Color.lightGray);
                g.fillRect(0,0,getSize().width,getSize().height);
                g.drawImage(image,0,0,this);
                if(scaleImage != null) {
                        g.drawImage(scaleImage,0,
                                    image.getHeight(this),this);
                }
                g.dispose();
        }

        public void mousePressed(MouseEvent event) {
                ReplicateScaleFilter sf =
                            new ReplicateScaleFilter(scale,scale);
                ImageProducer ip = image.getSource();
                ImageProducer is = new FilteredImageSource(ip,sf);
                scaleImage = getToolkit().createImage(is);
                repaint();
                if((scale += incrementScale) > endScale)
                        scale = startScale;
        }
        public void mouseEntered(MouseEvent event) {}
        public void mouseExited(MouseEvent event) {}
        public void mouseReleased(MouseEvent event) {}
        public void mouseClicked(MouseEvent event) {}
}
```

The applet uses the value of scale to determine the size of the new image. It starts off reducing the size of the image and then changes the scaling (by increasing the value of scale) as the mouse is clicked. After just a couple of mouse clicks, it looks like Figure R-1.

Figure R-1   The image being reduced from its original size.

After a few mouse clicks, it begins to expand instead of contract as shown in Figure R-2.

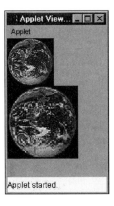

Figure R-2 The image being expanded from its original size.

 For a more sophisticated scaling algorithm, see **AverageScaleFilter**. For scaling an image within a component, see **Component.prepareImage()**.

ResourceBundle

class java.util.ResourceBundle

A *resource bundle* is a collection of locale-specific objects. It can be used to have code automatically adjust itself to a new locale.

How a ResourceBundle is used

Whenever an application needs a locale-specific object, it retrieves it from the resource bundle. This way, by using a different resource bundle for each locale, a program should move from one locale to another and operate properly without modifications. This could include more that just number formats and the order of the appearance of date values—if every prompt and display string were extracted from the resource bundle, it could include the language in which the program operates. Having the locale information isolated in a ResourceBundle makes it easier to move from one locale to another—it's just a matter of creating different ResourceBundle information for each locale.

Naming a resource

A resource bundle is a collection of objects, and related subcollections of objects. Each object can be located by name. A related subclass of objects will all have the same name except for a component added to differentiate it from the others. For example, you could start a group by creating a bundle named `GuzResource`. Then you could have a German version named `GuzResource_de`. Both these `ResourceBundles` would contain the same set of objects, but for different locales.

Locating a resource

When an application needs a resource, it uses the `getBundle()` method with the base name, or default name, for the resource. For example, if the base name of a resource is `GuzResource`, then the string "GuzResource" is used as the argument to `getBundle()`. The complete package name will need to be specified—for example, if the package name is `packet.resbun.GuzResource`, the argument will need to be "packet.resbun.GuzResource."

Information from the locale—the one supply as an argument and the default locale—will be used to modify the name to find the appropriate resource. Using information from the locale, the method will try to find the resource bundle under several names. It will first use the specified locale and then the default locale. The names are constructed from the language and country information in the locale in this order:

```
baseclass + "_" + language1 + "_" + country1 +
          "_" + variant1

baseclass + "_" + language1 + "_" + country1

baseclass + "_" + language1

baseclass

baseclass + "_" + language2 + "_" + country2 +
          "_" + variant2

baseclass + "_" + language2 + "_" + country2

baseclass + "_" + language2
```

As you can see, if the search fails to turn up an object for the specific locale, it will try the base class name without an extension. It is probably a good idea to always supply a default resource bundle without an extension as the default to operate in any locale.

Extended by

```
ListResourceBundle
LocaleData
PropertyResourceBundle
```

Inheritance

```
public abstract class java.util.ResourceBundle
    extends Object
        ⇑
    public class java.lang.Object
```

Variables and constants

parent

```
protected ResourceBundle parent
```

This is the ResourceBundle that will be searched for a resource if it is not found in this object.

Constructors

```
public ResourceBundle()
```

Returned by

A ResourceBundle is returned from getBundle().

Methods

getBundle()

```
public static final ResourceBundle getBundle(String baseName)
    throws MissingResourceException
```

```
public static final ResourceBundle getBundle(
        String baseName,Locale locale)
```

Returns the ResourceBundle object specified by baseName. The name of the ResourceBundle name will be constructed from the baseName suffixed with information from the locale.

getKeys()

```
public abstract Enumeration getKeys()
```

Returns an enumeration of the keys.

getObject()

```
public final Object getObject(String key)
    throws MissingResourceException
```

Retrieves an object from the ResourceBundle.

getString()

```
public final String getString(String key)
    throws MissingResourceException
```

Retrieves a string resource from the ResourceBundle. This is a convenience form of getObject() that can be used to get a String without casting.

getStringArray()

```
public final String[] getStringArray(String key)
    throws MissingResourceException
```

Retrieves a string resource from the ResourceBundle. This is a convenience form of getObject() that can be used to get an array of Strings without casting.

handleGetObject()

```
protected abstract Object handleGetObject(String key)
    throws MissingResourceException
```

Retrieves an object from the ResourceBundle.

setParent()

```
protected void setParent(ResourceBundle parent)
```

Sets the parent ResourceBundle. It is the one that will be searched whenever this bundle does not contain a resource.

Example 1

Inside a resource bundle, a single resource is located by its key value. Here is an example of a resource that has three keys and their associated values. A call to the getContents() method will return the table of key/value pairs. In this example, the values are also strings, but they could be any Object:

```
class GuzResource extends ListResourceBundle {
    static final Object[][] contents = {
        {"YesButton", "Yes"},
        {"NoButton", "No"},
        {"StopButton", "Stop"},
    };
    public Object[][] getContents() {
        return contents;
    }
}
```

The value of an individual key can be returned by a call to getObect(). Also, because the resources themselves are all strings, they could be returned by calling getString().

Here is the same resource bundle that has been localized for Mexico. The keys remain the same, but the values have been changed for the locale. This is identified as being the Mexico locale by having the "_mx" appended to the name of the base resource:

```
class GuzResource_mx extends ListResourceBundle {
```

```
static final Object[][] contents = {
    {"YesButton", "Si"},
    {"NoButton", "No"},
    {"StopButton", "Alto"},
};
public Object[][] getContents() {
    return contents;
}
}
```

The code to create a set of buttons with the correct labels for a locale would look something like this:

```
ResourceBundle rsrc = ResourcBundle.getBundle(
        "packet.resbun.GuzResource");
yesButton = new Button(rsrc.getString("YesButton"));
noButton = new Button(rsrc.getString("NoButton"));
stopButton = new Button(rsrc.getString("StopButton"));
```

 This example is not fully functional. The two methods getKeys() and handleGetObject() are protected in the class and are required for a functional implementation. Anyway, it is simpler to use the ListResourceBundle and PropertyResourceBundle classes for actual implementations. The following example is more complete.

Example 2

A resource bundle class can be created by overriding two methods— handleGetObject() and getKeys():

```
import java.util.*;

public class Bundle extends ResourceBundle {
    static public void main(String arg[]) {
        ResourceBundle rb =
            ResourceBundle.getBundle("Bundle");
        System.out.println("Ok-" +
            rb.getString("Ok"));
        System.out.println("Cancel-" +
            rb.getString("Cancel"));
    }
    public Object handleGetObject(String key) {
        if(key.equals("Ok"))
            return("That's just dandy");
        if(key.equals("Cancel"))
```

q
r
s

```
                    return("I don't think so");
            return(null);
    }
    public Enumeration getKeys() {
            Vector v = new Vector();
            v.addElement("Ok");
            v.addElement("Cancel");
            return((Enumeration)v);
    }
}
```

The output looks like this:

```
Ok—That's just dandy
Cancel—I don't think so
```

Because both the keys and the resources are String objects, this ResourceBundle is basically a String translator. The static method getResourceBundle() loads the object (in this case, itself) as a ResourceBundle. It then requests the values for its two keys and displays them. In this example, there are only two keys and the lookup method is crude at best, but you can easily get an idea of how it is all to work. The other method, getKeys(), is not called in this example, but it must be declared because it is an abstract method. The Vector class is an Enumeration, so it can be used to satisfy the requirement for holding an enumerated list of keys.

 For a class that simplifies implementation, see **ListResourceBundle**. For an implementation of a ResourceBundle that keeps the keys in a file on disk, see **PropertyResourceBundle**.

reserved words

 See **keywords**.

resource

In the context of Java, the term *resource* means some special sort of data file, such as an audio file or an image file. The contents of the file could be simply a configuration setting, or they could be the name of another resource. They could also refer to an input data stream.

ResultSet

interface java.sql.ResultSet

A `ResultSet` encapsulates the data resulting from the execution of a `Statement`.

Form of the data

The data is returned as rows and columns. The rows can be retrieved one at a time—in sequence. Once a row is retrieved, the columns can be accessed in random order. The internal cursor is initially positioned before the first row. The `next()` method moves the cursor to the next row. The "get" methods can be used to retrieve a column value from the current row.

The "get" methods

A "get" method is used to retrieve column data from the current row. This can be done using either the index or the name of the column. The index values are one-based—that is, the leftmost column in a row is number 1, not 0. Generally, using the index to read a column will be more efficient than using the name. Also, reading the columns sequentially, starting with 1, is more efficient than reading them randomly—and they should only be read once.

The JDBC driver will attempt to convert the data to the type specified by the "get" method. The conversion map from the database types to Java types should be included with your JDBC driver documentation.

The column names are not case-sensitive. If two columns have the same name, a retrieval by name will return the leftmost one.

The life of a ResultSet

A returned `ResultSet` is open and ready to be read. It will be closed whenever the `Statement` that read it is closed or is used to retrieve another `ResultSet`—that is, there is an internal relationship between the `Statement` and the `ResultSet`.

Inheritance

```
public interface java.sql.ResultSet
```

Constructors

Returned by

Objects implementing this interface are returned from `PreparedStatement.executeQuery()`, `Statement.executeQuery()`, `Statement.getResultSet()`, and 17 "get" methods in `DataBaseMetaData`.

Methods

clearWarnings()

```
public abstract void clearWarnings()
    throws SQLException
```

Deletes all internally held warnings. After this call, `getWarnings()` will return `null` until a new warning has been reported.

close()

```
public abstract void close()
    throws SQLException
```

Releases any resources that are held by the `ResultSet`. This is not strictly necessary since a `ResultSet` is closed automatically during garbage collection, but there may be circumstances in which it is more efficient to force the closing sooner.

findColumn()

```
public abstract int findColumn(String columnName)
    throws SQLException
```

Returns the index number of the named column.

getAsciiStream()

```
public abstract InputStream getAsciiStream(int columnIndex)
    throws SQLException
```

```
public abstract InputStream getAsciiStream(String columnName)
    throws SQLException
```

Returns the column value as a stream of ASCII characters. All data must be read from the stream before getting the value of another column — the stream is closed on the next call to a "get" method. The `available()` method of the stream may return 0 even though there is actually data available. While this is particularly suitable for LONGVARCHAR values, the JDBC driver will perform the conversion of other data types to an ASCII stream. If the value is SQL NULL, a `null` is returned.

getBigDecimal()

```
public abstract BigDecimal getBigDecimal(
        int columnIndex,int scale)
    throws SQLException
```

```
public abstract BigDecimal getBigDecimal(
        String columnName,int scale)
    throws SQLException
```

Returns the value of column as a `BigDecimal` object with `scale` digits to the right of the decimal. If the value is SQL NULL, `null` is returned.

getBinaryStream()

```
public abstract InputStream getBinaryStream(int columnIndex)
    throws SQLException

public abstract InputStream getBinaryStream(String columnName)
    throws SQLException
```

Returns the column value as a stream of binary data. All data must be read from the stream before getting the value of another column—the stream is closed on the next call to a "get" method. The `available()` method of the stream may return 0 even though there is actually data available. While this is particularly suitable for LONGVARCHAR values, the JDBC driver will perform the conversion of other data types to a binary stream. If the value is SQL NULL, a `null` is returned.

getBoolean()

```
public abstract boolean getBoolean(int columnIndex)
    throws SQLException

public abstract boolean getBoolean(String columnName)
    throws SQLException
```

Returns the value of the column as a `boolean`. If the value is SQL NULL, the result is `false`.

getByte()

```
public abstract byte getByte(int columnIndex)
    throws SQLException

getpublic abstract byte getByte(String columnName)
    throws SQLException
```

Returns the value of the column as a `byte`. If the value is SQL NULL, the result is 0.

getBytes()

```
public abstract byte[] getBytes(int columnIndex)
    throws SQLException

public abstract byte[] getBytes(String columnName)
    throws SQLException
```

Returns the value of the column as a `byte` array. The bytes will contain the raw values returned by the driver. If the value is SQL NULL, the return value is `null`.

getCursorName()

```
public abstract String getCursorName()
    throws SQLException
```

Returns the name of the SQL cursor that was used by the SQL statement that produced the data in this ResultSet. The current row of a result can be updated or deleted using a positioned update or delete statement that references the cursor name. The current row of a ResultSet is also the current row of the SQL cursor. If an update is attempted but positioned update is not supported, an SQLException will be thrown.

getDate()

```
public abstract Date getDate(int columnIndex)
    throws SQLException
```

```
public abstract Date getDate(String columnName)
    throws SQLException
```

Returns the value of the column as a java.sql.Date. If the value is SQL NULL, null is returned.

getDouble()

```
public abstract double getDouble(int columnIndex)
    throws SQLException
```

```
public abstract double getDouble(String columnName)
    throws SQLException
```

Returns the value of the column as a double. If the column is SQL NULL, 0.0 is returned.

getFloat()

```
public abstract float getFloat(int columnIndex)
    throws SQLException
```

```
public abstract float getFloat(String columnName)
    throws SQLException
```

Returns the value of the column as a float. If the column is SQL NULL, 0.0 is returned.

getInt()

```
public abstract int getInt(int columnIndex)
    throws SQLException
```

```
public abstract int getInt(String columnName)
    throws SQLException
```

Returns the value of the column as an int. If the column is SQL NULL, 0 is returned.

getLong()

```
public abstract long getLong(int columnIndex)
    throws SQLException
```

```
public abstract long getLong(String columnName)
    throws SQLException
```

Returns the value of the column as a `long`. If the column is SQL NULL, 0 is returned.

getMetaData()

```
public abstract ResultSetMetaData getMetaData()
    throws SQLException
```

Returns the `ResultSetMetaData` object for this `ResultSet`.

getObject()

```
public abstract Object getObject(int columnIndex)
    throws SQLException
```

```
public abstract Object getObject(String columnName)
    throws SQLException
```

Returns the value of the column as a Java object. The type of object will be the default mapping from the SQL type to a Java object for the JDBC driver. This method may be used to read database-specific abstract data types.

getShort()

```
public abstract short getShort(int columnIndex)
    throws SQLException
```

```
public abstract short getShort(String columnName)
    throws SQLException
```

Returns the value of the column as a `short`. If the value is SQL NULL, 0 is returned.

getString()

```
public abstract String getString(int columnIndex)
    throws SQLException
```

```
public abstract String getString(String columnName)
    throws SQLException
```

Returns the value of the column as a `String`. If the value is SQL NULL, 0 is returned.

getTime()

```
public abstract Time getTime(int columnIndex)
    throws SQLException
```

```
public abstract Time getTime(String columnName)
    throws SQLException
```

Returns the value of the column as a `java.sql.Time` object. If the value is SQL NULL, `null` is returned.

getTimestamp()

```
public abstract Timestamp getTimestamp(int columnIndex)
    throws SQLException
```

```
public abstract Timestamp getTimestamp(String columnName)
    throws SQLException
```

Returns the value of the column as a `java.sql.Timestamp` object. If the value is SQL NULL, `null` is returned.

getUnicodeStream()

```
public abstract InputStream getUnicodeStream(
        int columnIndex)
    throws SQLException
```

```
public abstract InputStream getUnicodeStream(
        String columnName)
    throws SQLException
```

Returns the column value as a stream of Unicode characters. All data must be read from the stream before getting the value of another column — the stream is closed on the next call to a "get" method. The `available()` method of the stream may return 0 even though there is actually data available. While this is particularly suitable for LONGVARCHAR values, the JDBC driver will perform the conversion of other data types to a Unicode stream. If the value is SQL NULL, a `null` is returned.

getWarnings()

```
public abstract SQLWarning getWarnings()
    throws SQLException
```

Returns the first (oldest) warning reported to this `ResultSet`. If there are other warnings, they will be chained to this one with the newest one last. The chain of warnings is cleared each time a new row is read.

These will only be the warnings caused by the `ResultSet`. Any warnings resulting from the actions of a `Statement` method will be chained to the `Statement` object.

next()

```
public abstract boolean next()
    throws SQLException
```

Moves ResultSet cursor to the next row of data, returning false if there is no next row. A ResultSet is initially positioned before the first row, and the next() method must be called to move to the first row. After that, access to each succeeding row requires another call to next().

wasNull()

```
public abstract boolean wasNull()
    throws SQLException
```

Returns true if the most recent column read with a "get" method was SQL NULL.

 The number of rows and columns and other properties of a ResultSet are available through a **ResultSetMetaData** object. For the SQL type definitions, see **Types**.

ResultSetMetaData

interface java.sql.ResultSetMetaData

An object of this class can be used to find out information about the contents of a ResultSet.

The column index

The methods that access specific columns do so by using a column number, or index. The leftmost column is number 1, not 0.

Inheritance

```
public interface java.sql.ResultSetMetaData
```

Variables and constants

columnNoNulls

```
public static final int columnNoNulls
```

The return value from isNullable() indicating that a column will not accept SQL NULL.

columnNullable

```
public static final int columnNullable
```

The return value from isNullable() indicating that a column will accept SQL NULL.

columnNullableUnknown

```
public static final int columnNullableUnknown
```

The return value from isNullable() indicating that it is not determinable whether a column will accept SQL NULL.

Constructors

Returned by

A ResultSetMetaData object is returned from ResultSet.getMetaData().

Methods

getCatalogName()

```
public abstract String getCatalogName(int column)
    throws SQLException
```

Returns the name of the column. If there is no column name, an SQLException is thrown.

getColumnCount()

```
public abstract int getColumnCount()
    throws SQLException
```

Returns the number of columns.

getColumnDisplaySize()

```
public abstract int getColumnDisplaySize(int column)
    throws SQLException
```

Returns the number of characters required to display the normal widest value of the column.

getColumnLabel()

```
public abstract String getColumnLabel(int column)
    throws SQLException
```

Returns the suggested column title to be printed and displayed.

getColumnName()

```
public abstract String getColumnName(int column)
    throws SQLException
```

Returns the name of the column.

getColumnType()

```
public abstract int getColumnType(int column)
    throws SQLException
```

Returns the SQL data type of a column. The return values are defined in `Types`.

getColumnTypeName()

```
public abstract String getColumnTypeName(int column)
    throws SQLException
```

Returns the type name for the column. Type names are data source–specific.

getPrecision()

```
public abstract int getPrecision(int column)
    throws SQLException
```

Returns the number of base-10 digits for a column that has a numeric value.

getScale()

```
public abstract int getScale(int column)
    throws SQLException
```

Returns the number of base-10 digits to the right of the decimal point for a column that has a numeric value.

getSchemaName()

```
public abstract String getSchemaName(int column)
    throws SQLException
```

Returns the schema definition name of the `column`. A zero-length `String` will return if there is no schema name.

getTableName()

```
public abstract String getTableName(int column)
    throws SQLException
```

Returns the table name of the `column`. A zero-length `String` will be returned if there is no table name.

isAutoIncrement()

```
public abstract boolean isAutoIncrement(int column)
    throws SQLException
```

Returns `true` if the column is automatically numbered (and, thus is, read-only).

isCaseSensitive()

```
public abstract boolean isCaseSensitive(int column)
    throws SQLException
```

Return `true` if the data in the `column` is case-sensitive.

isCurrency()

```
public abstract boolean isCurrency(int column)
    throws SQLException
```

Returns `true` if the `column` is a cash value.

isDefinitelyWritable()

```
public abstract boolean isDefinitelyWritable(int column)
    throws SQLException
```

Returns `true` if a write to the `column` would definitely succeed.

isNullable()

```
public abstract int isNullable(int column)
    throws SQLException
```

Returns an indicator of whether or not this `column` will accept SQL NULL. The method returns `columnNoNulls` it if will not, `columnNullable` if it will, or `columnNullableUnknown` if it is not known whether it will or not.

isReadOnly()

```
public abstract boolean isReadOnly(int column)
    throws SQLException
```

Returns `true` if the `column` is read-only.

isSearchable()

```
public abstract boolean isSearchable(int column)
    throws SQLException
```

Returns `true` if the `column` can be used in a WHERE clause.

isSigned()

```
public abstract boolean isSigned(int column)
    throws SQLException
```

Returns `true` if the `column` is a signed number.

isWritable()

```
public abstract boolean isWritable(int column)
```

```
throws SQLException
```

Returns true if it is permitted to write to the column.

 For the SQL type definitions, see **Types**.

return

keyword

This keyword will cause a method to return to its caller. This is normally done as the last statement in a method, but return can appear anywhere within the body of a method.

Returning from a void

If the method has been declared as void, there is no return value and the return statement will not accept an argument. Also, for void methods, there is an implied return at the bottom of the method—it does not have to be specified in the source code.

Returning with a value

If the method has been declared as returning any data type other than void, a return statement is required, and the return statement must be followed by an expression of the correct type.

 For more information on return values, see **method**.

RGB

 For a description of the RGB color model, see **ColorModel**.

RGBImageFilter

class java.awt.image.RGBImageFilter

This abstract class was designed to simplify the creation of an ImageFilter to modify the pixels of an image in the default RGB color model. It can be used— in conjunction with a FilteredImageSource object—to filter an existing image.

One at a time

This filter is intended to be used to modify colors one pixel at a time. Each pixel is passed to the filterRGB() method to be modified. There are other methods that accept pixels in other forms, but they all pass each pixel through filterRGB(). The pixels are converted to RGB format for filtering regardless of the color model of the ImageProducer.

Filtering by index

If the color model of the ImageProducer is an IndexColorModel, then the pixel values stored in the image are actually indexed into a palette of colors. There are two ways of handling this: In one approach, the image data can be used to extract data from the palette and the resulting RGB values can be filtered—this effectively changes the color model to RGB for output. Another way to handle it is to simply filter all the colors of the palette first, and then use the new version of the ColorModel to retrieve values for the image. The only drawback to the second method is that color filtering is done without regard to the x and y coordinates of each pixel. If the coordinates have no effect on the color filtering, then set canFilterIndexColorModel to true; otherwise, leave it set to false.

Filtering by ColorModel

If the ColorModel variables are set with a call to substituteColorModel(), another type of filtering may take place. Instead of any pixel-by-pixel filtering, if the pixel values passed into setPixels() are from the color model defined as origmodel, the pixels are passed to oldmodel with no further filtering.

An implementation

This abstract class has only one abstract method—filterRGB(). This is the only method that must be implemented to create an RGBImageFilter. The canFilterIndexColorModel value should be set to true if it doesn't matter what the coordinates are of the pixels being translated.

Inheritance

```
public abstract class java.awt.image.RGBImageFilter
    extends ImageFilter
        ⇑
    public class java.awt.image.ImageFilter
        implements ImageConsumer
        implements Cloneable
        extends Object
            ⇑
        public class java.lang.Object
```

Variables and constants

canFilterIndexColorModel

```
protected boolean canFilterIndexColorModel
```

If this is `true`, it is acceptable to apply `filterRGB()` directly to the color table entries of an `IndexColorModel` instead of performing pixel-by-pixel filtering.

newmodel

```
protected ColorModel newmodel
```

This is the `ColorModel` that has been modified for use in filtering.

origmodel

```
protected ColorModel origmodel
```

This is the unaltered color model from the `ImageProducer`.

Constructors

```
public RGBImageFilter()
```

Methods

filterIndexColorModel()

```
public IndexColorModel filterIndexColorModel(
        IndexColorModel icm)
```

Filters the contents of an `IndexColorModel` by running each of its table entries through the `filterRGB()` method. The returned object is a new `IndexColorModel` with the filtered values. It uses −1 for the *x* and *y* coordinates passed to `filterRGB()` to indicate that the pixel values do not have defined coordinates in an image.

filterRGB()

```
public abstract int filterRGB(int x,int y,int rgb)
```

This is the method that does the filtering of each pixel. The `rgb` pixel value is modified and returned. The values of x and y are the coordinates of the pixel in the image.

The values of x and y can be negative to indicate that the pixel value is not in an image (it could be from a palette). This can only happen if `canFilterIndexColorModel` is set to `true`.

filterRGBPixels()

```
public void filterRGBPixels(int x,int y,
        int width,int height,int pixels[],
```

```
               int offset,int scansize)
```

Filters the array of `pixels` by passing each one of them through the `filterRGB()` method. The values of x and y are the coordinates of the upper-left corner of the rectangle of pixels. The `width` and `height` are the dimensions of the rectangle. The `offset` is the index to the first pixel in the array, and the `scansize` is the number of pixels in each horizontal row.

setColorModel()

```
    public void setColorModel(ColorModel model)
```

This is called by the `ImageProducer` to set the color model. Normally, the `RGBImageFilter` simply overrides the color model used by the `ImageProducer` supplying the pixels and uses the RGB color model instead. However, if (1) the `model` is an `IndexColorModel` and (2) the `canFilterIndexColorModel` flag has been set to `true`, then a filtered version of the color model will be substituted.

setPixels()

```
    public void setPixels(int x,int y,
              int width,int height,ColorModel model,
              byte pixels[],int offset,int scansize)

    public void setPixels(int x,int y,
              int width,int height,ColorModel model,
              int pixels[],int offset,int scansize)
```

This is called by the `ImageProducer` to deliver pixels to the image filter. The values of x and y are the coordinates of the upper-left corner of the rectangle of pixels. The `width` and `height` are the dimensions of the rectangle. The `offset` is the index to the first pixel in the array, and the `scansize` is the number of pixels in each horizontal row.

The `model` is the color model of the `ImageProducer`. If the color model is the same as the one that has already been converted and supplied to `setColorModel`, the pixels simply pass through the new `ColorModel` object—otherwise, the pixels are converted to the RGB model and converted with calls to `filterRGB()`.

substituteColorModel()

```
    public void substituteColorModel(ColorModel origmodel,
              ColorModel newmodel)
```

Sets the color models to be used for substitution. If the pixels from the `ImageProducer` are in the `origmodel`, no filtering takes place—the pixels are simply passed directly to the `ImageConsumer` by being passed to `newmodel`.

 For an example, see **FilteredImageSource**. Also see **ImageFilter**.

rmi

package java.rmi

This package and its subpackages contain the API for remote method invocation. For a description, see **RMI**.

Packages

```
java.rmi.dgc
java.rmi.registry
package java.rmi.server
```

Interfaces

```
Remote
```

Classes

```
Naming
RMISecurityManager
```

Exceptions

```
AccessException
AlreadyBoundException
ConnectException
ConnectIOException
MarshalException
NoSuchObjectException
NotBoundException
RMISecurityException
RemoteException
ServerError
ServerException
ServerRuntimeException
StubNotFoundException
UnexpectedException
UnknownHostException
UnmarshalException
```

RMI

RMI stands for *remote method invocation*. It is the ability to make a call from an object executing in one Virtual Machine to a method of an object in another Virtual Machine. (Calling a method is also called invoking a method, thus remote method invocation.) The Virtual Machines may be on the same computer or different computers. Arguments and return values are serialized (a process known as marshaling) and passed between the two.

Figure R-3 is a diagram of the layered architecture of RMI. If you are familiar with TCP/IP, you can see how RMI is an extension of that model.

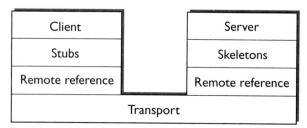

Figure R-3 The layers of RMI.

The flow of a remote invocation

Client and server

The caller of the remote method is the *client*. The remote object being called is the *server*. The client may pass objects to the server, and the server may return objects to the client.

The client calls the stub

When the client wants to call a remote method, it uses a *stub*. A stub is a local object that has the same set of methods (that is, it implements the same interface) as the remote object and acts as a proxy for the remote object. It is the job of the stub to package the information from the call and pass it to the server.

Arguments to the stub must be serializable

Objects are passed by value from the client to the server. For this to work, the passed object must be serializable. For an object to be serializable, it must implement the Serializable interface. Many classes of the Java API are serializable. Also, the Java primitive types are all serializable.

The information describing the remote method call (the method and the arguments) is serialized into a single stream of serialized data—this is called *marshaling*. This marshaling means that all arguments are passed by value, not by reference.

The skeleton is on the server side

The counterpart of the client's stub is the server's *skeleton*. It receives the marshaled stream, unmarshals it, and uses the information to call the actual method. Once it has the return value from the method, it marshals it and transmits the resulting stream back to the stub in the client. The called method could throw an exception, in which case the exception is caught and marshaled as the return value.

The stub returns to its caller

The stub receives the returned value from the skeleton on the server side. It unmarshals the data and returns to the original caller. If a serialized object was included as a return value, a new object is instantiated from the data and used as the return value. The stub could unmarshal the return value and find an exception, in which case the exception is thrown.

Distributed garbage collection

Some special considerations apply to automatic garbage collection in a distributed system. The RMI runtime system uses a reference-counting technique. Each Virtual Machine keeps track of all references to remote objects.

The count up and down on the client

Each Virtual Machine keeps a count of its references to remote objects. With the first reference (initiating a new count value of 1), a "referenced" message is sent to the remote Virtual Machine. The count is incremented and decremented locally as the number of references to the object increases and decreases. When the count reaches zero, an "unreferenced" message is sent to the server.

The count up and down on the server

Each server object keeps a list of the remote Virtual Machines that have it "referenced." When this list becomes empty (that is, there have been just as many "unreferenced" messages as "referenced" messages), the server then takes stock of its own references to the object. If there is just one, the one used for remote access, the reference is deleted and the object will be reclaimed in the normal course of events.

The dirty, the clean, and the lease

An object that has a remote reference is termed *dirty*. An object that no longer has a remote reference is termed *clean*. Whenever an object is made dirty by having another Virtual Machine added to its list, a timeout is associated with the request. This time period is known as the *lease* period.

A failure to communicate

If the lease of a client runs out (because the client system crashes or otherwise loses contact with the server), the RMI system will act as if an "unreferenced" message had arrived. If it

turns out the client has not crashed and attempts to access the object, a
RemoteException will be thrown from the server back to the client.

 For the general RMI package, see **RMI**. For the distributed garbage collection
package, see **dgc**. For the creation of stubs and skeletons, see **rmic**.

rmic

utility

This utility generates stubs and skeletons to be used in RMI. The stubs and
skeletons are generated as Java source and compiled using javac.

The input is one or more compiled Java classes that implement the Remote
interface. The input class names must be fully package-qualified. The output
class files will have the same names as the input files with "_Skel" and "_Stub"
appended to them. For example, the command

```
rmic hello.HelloImpl
```

will locate the package hello in one of the directories on the class path and,
using HelloImpl.class as input, will create the files HelloImpl_Skel.class
and HelloImpl_Stub.class as the skeleton and the stub.

Syntax

```
rmic [options] name [name ...]
```

options
-classpath <path>

This is the list of directories that rmic will use to locate the class files. This replaces the path
specified by the CLASSPATH environment variable. On UNIX and Mac, the directory
names are separated by colons; on Windows, they are separated by semicolons.

-d <directory>

Specify the name of the directory of the class hierarchy. The default is the current directory.

-depend

The compiler will recompile all classes referenced from other classes. Normally, the only
classes compiled are those that are missing, or those referred to from source code files that
are found to be out-of-date.

-g

Generate information for debugging. This includes tables containing line numbers and descriptive information of local variables. This is the information used by the Java debugging tools. By default, only line numbers are generated (and these are suppressed by the -O option).

-keepgenerated

Retain the generated Java source files for the stubs and skeletons. They will be written to the same directory as the class files.

-nowarn

Turn off all warnings.

-0

Optimize the output by inlining static, final, and private methods. Do not include line numbers, or any other debugging information. The optimization, by putting things inline, could actually make the class file larger.

-show

Operate in interactive mode by displaying the window in Figure R-4. Enter each of the package-qualified class names separated by spaces. Pressing the Compile button will create the stubs and skeletons.

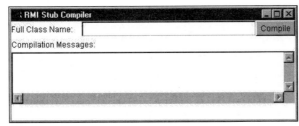

Figure R-4 The GUI interface to `rmic`.

-verbose

Print out messages about which messages are being compiled and what class files are being loaded.

Environment

CLASSPATH

This environment variable is used to supply rmic with a list of directories that hold the class files that will be used to resolve references. It is a list of directory names separated by colons on UNIX and Apple, and by semicolons on Windows.

 For information on how the stubs and skeletons are used, see **RMI**. For the Java compiler, see **javac**.

RMIClassLoader

class java.rmi.server.RMIClassLoader

This class provides static methods to load classes over the network. The loading can be from a specified URL or from a URL specified by the property java.rmi.server.codebase.

Inheritance

```
public class java.rmi.server.RMIClassLoader
    extends Object
        ⇑
    public class java.lang.Object
```

Constructors

There are no constructors. This class is a collection of static methods.

Methods

getSecurityContext()

```
public static Object getSecurityContext(
        ClassLoader loader)
```

Returns the security context of loader. The security context is a URL.

loadClass()

```
public static Class loadClass(String name)
    throws MalformedURLException
    throws ClassNotFoundException

public static Class loadClass(URL codebase,String name)
```

```
throws MalformedURLException
      ClassNotFoundException
```

Loads the named class. If codebase is specified, it will be loaded from there—if not, it will be loaded from the URL specified by the system property java.rmi.server.codebase. A MalformedURLException will be thrown if the specified URL is not valid (or is missing from java.rmi.server.codebase). A ClassNotFoundException will be thrown if class cannot be found.

 Also see **ClassLoader**.

RMIFailureHandler

interface java.rmi.server.RMIFailureHandler

This interface defines the method that is invoked when the RMI runtime is unable to create a Socket or ServerSocket. An RMIFailureHandler is registered with a call to RMISocketFactory.setFailureHandler().

Inheritance

```
public interface java.rmi.server.RMIFailureHandler
```

Constructors

Returned by

A class implementing this interface is returned from RMISocketFactory.getFailureHandler().

Methods

failure()

```
public abstract boolean failure(Exception exception)
```

This method is called whenever the RMI runtime is not able to create Socket or ServerSocket using the RMISocketFactory. The exception is the one that occurred during the attempt to create the Socket or ServerSocket. A return value of true indicates that there should be a retry.

q
r
s

rmiregistry

utility

The `rmiregistry` will start a local RMI object registry that listens to the specified port.

A remote-object registry is the bootstrap naming service of RMI that binds names to objects. Clients can use the names to locate remote objects made available for remote method invocation. Once the client locates the object, it can be directed—by invoking methods of the object—to other objects on the same host.

Synopsis

```
rmiregistry [port]
```

There are no options other than the port number. If no port number is specified, the default value 1099 is used.

The `rmiregistry` is generally run in the background. On UNIX, the command would be

```
rmiregistry &
```

and on Windows, it would be

```
start rmiregistry
```

 For the Java methods used to start a registry, see **LocateRegistry**. For the methods used to locate a name within a registry, see **Naming**. Also see **RMI**.

RMISecurityException

class java.rmi.RMISecurityException

This exception is thrown to indicate that a security exception has occurred.

Inheritance

```
public class java.rmi.RMISecurityException
    extends SecurityException
        ⇑
    public class SecurityException
        extends RuntimeException
            ⇑
```

```
public class java.lang.RuntimeException
    extends Exception
        ⇑
public class java.lang.Exception
    extends Throwable
        ⇑
    public class java.lang.Throwable
        implements Serializable
        extends Object
            ⇑
        public class java.lang.Object
```

Constructors

```
public RMISecurityException(String name)
public RMISecurityException(String name,String message)
```

If the message string is supplied, it is used as a detailed message describing this particular exception.

RMISecurityManager

class java.rmi.RMISecurityManager

This is the security manager for RMI stubs. It is used to define the security policy for applications (but not for applets). Whenever code is loaded as a stub, the RMISecurityManager disables all functions except for class definition and access.

Without an RMISecurityManager being set, RMI will load stub classes only from the local file system in the directories specified in CLASSPATH. To set an RMISecurityManager, call setSecurityManager() like this:

```
System.setSecurityManager(new RMISecurityManager());
```

If a program is executed without a security manager having been set, RMI will load stub classes only from the local files as defined by CLASSPATH.

Inheritance

```
public class RMISecurityManager
    extends SecurityManager
        ⇑
    public class java.lang.SecurityManager
        extends Object
```

⇑
```
public class java.lang.Object
```

Constructors
```
public RMISecurityManager()
```

Methods

checkAccept()
```
public synchronized void checkAccept(String host,int port)
```
This method always throws an RMISecurityException for stubs. Stubs cannot accept connections to a port.

checkAccess()
```
public synchronized void checkAccess(Thread t)

public synchronized void checkAccess(ThreadGroup g)
```
This method always throws an RMISecurityException for stubs. Stubs cannot manipulate threads or thread groups.

checkAwtEventQueueAccess()
```
public void checkAwtEventQueueAccess()
```
This method always throws an RMISecurityException for stubs. Stubs cannot access the event queue.

checkConnect()
```
public synchronized void checkConnect(String host,int port)

public void checkConnect(String host,
        int port,Object context)
```
Stubs can make network connections if called through the RMI transport. A port number of −1 indicates that this will be a query of the IP address of the host. Optionally, a system-dependent context can be supplied to specify a security context. An RMISecurityException is thrown to deny permission.

checkCreateClassLoader()
```
public synchronized void checkCreateClassLoader()
```
This method always throws an RMISecurityException for stubs. Stubs cannot create class loaders (or even execute the method of a ClassLoader).

checkDelete()

```
public void checkDelete(String file)
```

This method always throws an RMISecurityException for stubs. Stubs cannot delete files.

checkExec()

```
public synchronized void checkExec(String command)
```

This method always throws an RMISecurityException for stubs. Stubs are not allowed to spawn processes.

checkExit()

```
public synchronized void checkExit(int status)
```

This method always throws an RMISecurityException for stubs. Stubs are not allowed to exit the Virtual Machine.

checkLink()

```
public synchronized void checkLink(String lib)
```

This method always throws an RMISecurityException for stubs. Stubs are not allowed to link to dynamic libraries.

checkListen()

```
public synchronized void checkListen(int port)
```

This method always throws an RMISecurityException for stubs. Stubs are not allowed to link to listen to any port.

checkMemberAccess()

```
public void checkMemberAccess(Class cls,int which)
```

All nonstubs have access to default, package, and private declarations. All stubs are allowed access to public information. An RMISecurityException will be thrown if permissions is denied.

checkMulticast()

```
public void checkMulticast(InetAddress maddr)
```

```
public void checkMulticast(InetAddress maddr,byte ttl)
```

This method always throws an RMISecurityException for stubs. Stubs are not allowed to join, leave, send, or receive IP multicasts.

checkPackageAccess()

```
public synchronized void checkPackageAccess(
        String package)
```

This method will throw an RMISecurityException if the stub is denied access to the package.

checkPackageDefinition()

```
public synchronized void checkPackageDefinition(
        String package)
```

This method will throw an RMISecurityException if the stub is denied the ability to define classes in the named package.

checkPrintJobAccess()

```
public void checkPrintJobAccess()
```

This method always throws an RMISecurityException for stubs. Stubs are not allowed access to a printer.

checkPropertiesAccess()

```
public synchronized void checkPropertiesAccess()
```

Stubs are not allowed to access the entire system properties list, only properties explicitly labeled as accessible to stubs. This method is called from System. An RMISecurityException is thrown to deny permission.

checkPropertyAccess()

```
public synchronized void checkPropertyAccess(String key)
```

Stubs can access certain system properties—the ones for which the special ".rmi" version is "true." For example, the system property "user.name" can be accessed by a stub only if the property "user.name.rmi" is "true." The method constructs the RMI form of the key from the one passed to it and throws an RMISecurityException if it is not defined.

checkRead()

```
public synchronized void checkRead(String file)

public void checkRead(String file,Object context)

public synchronized void checkRead(FileDescriptor fd)
```

This method always throws an RMISecurityException for stubs. Stubs are not allowed to read files. Optionally, a system-dependent context can be supplied to specify a security context.

checkSecurityAccess()

```
public void checkSecurityAccess(String provider)
```

This method always throws an RMISecurityException for stubs. Stubs are not allowed to perform security provider operations.

checkSetFactory()

```
public synchronized void checkSetFactory()
```

This method always throws a SecurityException to deny the ability to set a networking-related object factory.

checkSystemClipboardAccess()

```
public void checkSystemClipboardAccess()
```

This method always throws an RMISecurityException for stubs. Stubs are not allowed access to the system clipboard.

checkTopLevelWindow()

```
public synchronized boolean checkTopLevelWindow(
        Object window)
```

This method always returns false for stubs and true otherwise. Stubs may be allowed to create top-level windows, but they can carry warnings.

checkWrite()

```
public synchronized void checkWrite(String file)
```

```
public synchronized void checkWrite(FileDescriptor fd)
```

This method always throws an RMISecurityException for stubs. Stubs are not allowed to write to files.

getSecurityContext()

```
public Object getSecurityContext()
```

Gets the URL of the security context—an object that summarizes the current execution environment. This is the context argument passed to some other methods of this class.

 For more information on how security managers work, see **SecurityManager**.

RMISocketFactory

class java.rmi.server.RMISocketFactory

The RMISocketFactory is used by the RMI runtime to obtain client and server sockets for RMI calls.

Three attempts to connect

Three attempts are made to complete the connection.

First, the RMISocketFactory attempts to make a direct connection to the remote Virtual Machine. This could fail because of the presence of a firewall.

Second, the runtime uses HTTP with the explicit port number of the server. This could also be prohibited by the firewall.

Third, an HTTP to a cgi-bin script on the server is used to POST the RMI call. An application may set the source of sockets for RMI. In this case, the application is responsible for offering sockets that will penetrate a firewall.

The failure handler

The RMISocketFactory has an RMIFailureHandler that is notified whenever there is a failure to make a connection. The single method defined in the RMIFailureHandler interface is failure(). As long as this method returns true, the RMI will try again to make the connection. If it returns false, there will be no retry. The default RMIFailureHandler simply returns false, so if you want retries to occur, you will need to implement your own.

Inheritance

```
public abstract class java.rmi.server.RMISocketFactory
    extends Object
        ⇑
    public class java.lang.Object
```

Constructors

```
public RMISocketFactory()
```

Returned by

An object of this class is returned from getSocketFactory().

Methods

createServerSocket()

```
public abstract ServerSocket createServerSocket(int port)
    throws IOException
```

Creates a server socket on the specified port. Port number 0 represents the anonymous port.

createSocket()

```
public abstract Socket createSocket(String host,int port)
    throws IOException
```

Creates a client socket connected to the specified host and port.

getFailureHandler()

```
public static RMIFailureHandler getFailureHandler()
```

Returns the failure handler.

getSocketFactory()

```
public static RMISocketFactory getSocketFactory()
```

Returns the socket factory object that is used by RMI.

setFailureHandler()

```
public static void setFailureHandler(
        RMIFailureHandler handler)
```

Sets the failure handler.

setSocketFactory()

```
public static void setSocketFactory(RMISocketFactory fac)
    throws IOException
```

Sets the RMISocketFactory from which the RMI runtime will get its sockets. This method can only be called once. A SecurityException will be thrown if the SecurityManager does not allow setting the socket factory.

 For more on security, see **SecurityManager** and **RMISecurityManager**. Also see **RMIFailureHandler**.

rounding

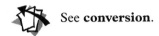 See **conversion**.

RuleBasedCollator

class java.text.RuleBasedCollator

This is a table-driven collator. The `RuleBasedCollator` maps characters to sort keys.

Caveats

This is a simple collator. Complex or elaborate languages may require more complex processing than can be done here.

Secondary ordering is always applied. See `collation`.

Any Unicode character not covered by values in the table will simply drop to the end of the collation order.

The Unicode private-use characters, \uE800 through \uF8FF, are all treated as identical.

The character relational operators

There are four possible relationships between characters, and there are two special operators.

Table R-1   Collation Table Operators

Operator	Meaning
<	As a primary difference, the character on the left comes before the one on the right.
;	As a secondary difference, the character on the left comes before the one on the right.
,	As a tertiary difference, the character on the left comes before the one on the right.
=	There is no collation difference in these characters.
@	All the accent differences (the secondary comparisons) are to be done in reverse order, as in French.
&	The reset operator. The character that follows this operator determines the position in the table at which the relations that follow it will be inserted.

The comparison operators

The table controlling the collation is a `String` containing a list that defines the character sorting order, and the type of comparison to be made between each. For example,

```
"< a < b < c"
```

means a is less than b, and b is less than c. To create a table for an entire set of characters, you must include all of them in the string. More than one character can be included in a single position. For example, we can get a caseless compare like this:

```
"< a,A < b,B < c,C"
```

The comma operator specifies that the difference is only by case—the tertiary relationship. To consider upper- and lowercase identical so that they will not even be considered in the sort, write this:

```
"< a = A < b = B < c = C"
```

The reset operator

The reset operator can be used to specify things out of order. What happens is that when the reset operator (&) is encountered, the character following it (which must be one that has already been encountered in the table) specifies the location at which the table information following it is to be inserted. For example, writing

```
"< a < b < d & b < c"
```

is exactly the same as if

```
"< a < b < c < d"
```

had been written because the reset operator folds the information following back into the earlier location in the string.

The characters that can be ignored

All characters that come before the first '<' character in the string are ignored. For example, to ignore hyphens in words, simply put that character at the very beginning of the table string, like this:

```
"- < a < b < c"
```

Operators as characters

The operators can be entered as characters in the table by being enclosed in quotes, as in

```
"< '<' < '>' < ','"
```

Combination characters

Multiple characters can be collated as single entities simply by entering them in the table, like this:

```
"< f <fl < Fl < fi < Fi"
```

Inheritance

```
public class java.text.RuleBasedCollator
    extends Collator
        ⇑
    public class java.text.Collator
        implements Cloneable
        implements Serializable
        extends Object
            ⇑
        public class java.lang.Object
```

Constructors

```
public RuleBasedCollator(String rules)
    throws ParseException
```

Constructs a `RuleBasedCollator` using the `rules` as the table. Throws a `ParseException` if the `rules` string is not valid.

Methods

clone()

```
public Object clone()
```

Returns a duplicate of this object.

compare()

```
public int compare(String source,String target)
```

Return the result of a comparison of `source` and `target` using the collation rules. If `source` is less than `target`, a negative number is returned; if it is greater, a positive number is returned; and if they are equal, zero is returned.

equals()

```
public boolean equals(Object object)
```

Returns `true` if object is a `RuleBasedCollator` with the same rules as this one.

getCollationElementIterator()

```
public CollationElementIterator
        getCollationElementIterator(String source)
```

Returns a `CollationElementIterator` object for `source`.

getCollationKey()

```
public CollationKey getCollationKey(String source)
```

Returns a `CollationKey` for the `source` string based on the rules. The `CollationKey` can be used for quick string comparisons.

getRules()

```
public String getRules()
```

Returns the collation rules table that was supplied to the constructor.

hashCode()

```
public int hashCode()
```

Returns a hashcode for this object.

 Also see **CollationElementIterator**, **CollationKey**, and **Collator**.

Runnable

interface java.lang.Runnable

The implementation of this interface enables an instance of the class to be run as an independent thread.

A thread is alive while `run()` **is alive**

When a thread is started, the method `run()` is called. As long as the `run()` method is in execution, the thread is active. When `run()` returns, the thread becomes inactive—it is no longer running.

More than one way to make a thread

An object that subclasses the class `Thread` can be run as a thread. However, there are circumstances—because of the single inheritance—in which this is not convenient. A class can simply implement `Runnable` and become threadable. This is done by having a class instantiate a `Thread` instance while passing itself in as the argument. See Example 1.

Overriding the `run()` **method**

This interface only has the one method—`run()`. There are other methods that can be used for threading (see `Thread`), and if you plan on doing more than simple threading, you may be better off inheriting your class from `Thread`.

Implemented by

```
Thread
```

Inheritance

```
public interface java.lang.Runnable
```

Methods

run()

```
public abstract void run()
```

This method is called to activate a thread. When this method returns, the thread becomes deactivated.

Example

This program runs two threads that each print lines after random delays:

```
public class Runner implements Runnable {
    static char tag = 'A';
    public static void main(String[] arg) {
        Runner runner = new Runner();
        Thread thread = new Thread(runner);
        thread.start();
        thread = new Thread(runner);
        thread.start();
    }
    public void run() {
        char myTag;
        synchronized(this) {
            myTag = tag++;
        }
        System.out.println(myTag + " Start");
        for(int i=0; i<3; i++) {
            try {
                Thread.sleep(randint(500,3000));
                System.out.println(myTag + " Loop");
            } catch(InterruptedException e) {
                System.out.println(e);
            }
        }
        System.out.println(myTag + " End");
    }
```

```
final private int randint(int low,int high) {
    return(((int)((high-low+1)*(Math.random()))) +
low);      }
}
```

The `main()` method creates a pair of threads using the `Runner` object. Each thread is kicked off by a call to `start()`, which causes a new thread of execution to be started and the method `run()` to be called.

The `run()` method gets a tag for itself and increments the tag value for use by the next thread. (Because we are dealing with threads, it is always advisable to put statements that modify common data items inside synchronized blocks.) Each thread displays a "Start" message and a "Stop" message and in between—at intervals varying from half a second to three seconds—a "Loop" message. Output from the program looks like this:

```
A Start
B Start
A Loop
A Loop
B Loop
A Loop
A End
B Loop
B Loop
B End
```

The fact that the messages of A and B are intertwined demonstrates that the two threads are running simultaneously.

 For a more robust way of creating threads, see **Thread**.

Runtime

class java.lang.Runtime

This class supplies access to the facilities of the Virtual Machine and to certain facilities of the underlying operating system.

Inheritance

```
public class java.lang.Runtime
    extends Object
        ⇑
    public class java.lang.Object
```

Constructors

Returned by

There is never more than one instance of this class. A reference to it is returned from `getRuntime()`.

Methods

exec()

```
public Process exec(String command)
    throws IOException

public Process exec(String command,String envp[])
    throws IOException

public Process exec(String cmdarray[])
    throws IOException

public Process exec(String cmdarray[],String envp[])
    throws IOException
```

Executes the `command` string as a separate process. An object of the `Process` class is returned—it can be used to control and communicate with the other process. A `SecurityException` is thrown if the current process is prohibited from creating the sub-process.

The `command` is a single-line command in the same form in which it would be entered from a screen prompt.

The array `envp` contains the settings of environment variables. Each member of the array is a `String` in the format `name=value`.

The `cmdarray` is the command line broken up into component parts. It has the same end result as if they were all separated by spaces as one `command`.

exit()

```
public void exit(int status)
```

Terminates the currently running Virtual Machine and sends the status value to the system. By convention, any nonzero status indicates an abnormal termination. This method does not return—although a `SecurityException` may be thrown by the security manager.

freeMemory()

```
public long freeMemory()
```

Returns the amount of free memory available. A call to `gc()` to perform garbage collection may increase the value returned from this method. Because of the dynamic nature of the system, the value returned should be treated as only an approximation. The value returned is always less than the value returned by `totalMemory()`.

gc()

```
public void gc()
```

Runs the garbage collector. This method suggests that the Virtual Machine attempt to recover some memory by recovering the space allocated to objects that are no longer in use. When this method has returned, the Virtual Machine will have made an effort at some quick memory recovery.

 Strictly speaking, there is no need to call this method. The garbage will be collected automatically by the system. However, there could be some circumstances in which it is more efficient to have your application reclaim memory sooner rather than later.

getLocalizedInputStream()   **deprecated**

```
public InputStream
       getLocalizedInputStream(InputStream input)
```

This method is deprecated. Use an `InputStreamReader` with a `BufferedReader` instead.

Creates a localized version of an input stream that will convert input characters of the local system into Unicode. If the `input` stream is already localized, it may be returned directly without modification.

getLocalizedOutputStream()   **deprecated**

```
public OutputStream
       getLocalizedOutputStream(OutputStream output)
```

This method is deprecated. It is better to use an `OuputStreamWriter`, `BufferedWriter`, and the `PrintWriter` classes.

Creates a localized version of an output stream. This method takes an `OutputStream` and converts it to an equivalent `OutputStream` in which Unicode characters have been converted to the local character set. If the stream is already localized, it will be returned unaltered.

getRuntime()

```
public static Runtime getRuntime()
```

Returns the runtime object associated with this currently running application.

load()

```
public synchronized void load(String filename)
```

Loads a dynamic library. The `filename` must be the complete path name of the library. If the library is not found, an `UnsatisfiedLinkError` is thrown. If there is a security manager, it is possible to have a `SecurityException` thrown if access to the library is denied.

If you are running java_g (the debugging version of the Virtual Machine), the library name will have the characters "_g" inserted before the ".so" file extension of the shared library. For example, if the library name is fred.so, it will be changed to fred_g.so. The same is true of Win32 — the library name fred.dll will be changed to fred_g.dll.

loadLibrary()

```
public synchronized void loadLibrary(String libname)
```

Loads the named dynamic library. The mapping from libname to the actual library name is done in a system-dependent way. If this method is called more than once with the same name, all but the first calls are ignored. If there is a security manager, its checkLink() method is called with the libname — this may result in a SecurityException. An UnsatisfiedLinkError is thrown if libname does not exist.

runFinalization()

```
public void runFinalization()
```

Runs the finalization methods of any objects that are pending finalization.

The garbage collection process includes calling the finalize() method of all the objects right before their memory is put back into circulation. It is possible for the garbage collector to have several objects ready for processing that have not had the finalize() method called yet. A call to runFinalization() is a request that these finalize() methods be called.

runFinalizersOnExit()

```
public static void runFinalizersOnExit(boolean setting)
```

Either sets or clears the flag that determines whether or not the finalize() methods of all objects should be called as the program exits. By default this is disabled, which means that there will be finalizers that are not executed as the Virtual Machine shuts down.

This method can be called only if the security manager will allow this program to exit.

totalMemory()

```
public long totalMemory()
```

Returns the total amount of memory in the Virtual Machine.

traceInstructions()

```
public void traceInstructions(boolean setting)
```

Enables or disables the tracing of instructions. If tracing is enabled, the Virtual Machine is being requested to print a detailed trace of each instruction as it is executed. Where the output is directed is system-dependent. It can be turned on and off any number of times, which will start and stop the tracing. If tracing is not supported, this request will be ignored.

traceMethodCalls()

```
public void traceMethodCalls(boolean setting)
```

Enables or disables the tracing of method calls. If tracing is enabled, the Virtual Machine is being requested to print a detailed trace of each method call as it is executed. Where the output is directed is system-dependent. It can be turned on and off any number of times, which will start and stop the tracing. If tracing is not supported, this request will be ignored.

RuntimeException

class java.lang.RuntimeException

This is the superclass of the family of exceptions thrown during normal operation of the Virtual Machine. A method is not required to declare any of these exceptions in its `throws` clause.

Extended by

```
ArithmeticException
ArrayStoreException
ClassCastException
EmptyStackException
IllegalArgumentException
IllegalMonitorStateException
IllegalStateException
IndexOutOfBoundsException
MissingResourceException
NegativeArraySizeException
NoSuchElementException
NullPointerException
ProviderException
SecurityException
```

Inheritance

```
public class java.lang.RuntimeException
    extends Exception
        ⇑
        public class java.lang.Exception
            extends Throwable
```

```
                              ⇑
                   public class java.lang.Throwable
                        implements Serializable
                        extends Object
                              ⇑
                   public class java.lang.Object
```

Constructors

```
public RuntimeException()
public RuntimeException(String message)
```

If the message string is supplied, it is used as a detailed message describing this particular exception.

scope

The scope of a name is the region in which it has effect. Scope is the natural result of the location in which a name is declared—but this can be modified, to some degree, with the access keywords `public`, `private`, and `protected`.

From Outer to Inner

Here is a list and a description of the scopes from the largest (outermost) to the smallest (innermost).

Top-level scope

This is the largest scope—Java puts no limitations on the outermost scope. The broadness of this scope is really determined by the host system. This is the scope of the top-level packages, and a package name never hides any of its internal names.

Package scope

Class and interface declarations, by default, have the scope level of the entire package in which they are declared. If no package is specified (by using the `package` keyword), a class or interface defaults to being a member of the unnamed package—this is a package the same as any other, except it has no name.

Compilation-unit scope

This scoping level can be thought of as the classes and interfaces in a single source file, and the items referenced externally through the `import` statement. Several classes and interfaces can be defined in one source file, but only one of them (the one with the same name as the file) can have more than compilation-unit scope. The `import` statement can limit the items being imported by being very specific with the single-type import (such as `import java.awt.Graphics`), or it can provide a more inclusive type-on-demand import (such as `import java.awt.*`). The latter form includes more names into the scope.

Class scope

Variables and constants declared within a class, but outside a method, are available from the point of their declaration to the end of the compilation unit. For example, this code will not compile:

```
public class ScopeTest {
    int a = b;   // Error. Forward reference.
    int b = 10;
}
```

Methods and classes declared inside a class also have class scope, but with no such forward reference limitation as exists with variables. This code will compile cleanly:

```
void showHands() {
    System.out.println(hands());
}
String hands() {
    return("Hands");
}
```

Parameter scope

The scope of a method or constructor parameter is the entire body of the method or constructor.

Block scope

Declaration of variables inside a block within a method have the same forward reference limitation as those at the class level. A block can be an entire method or subset of it as defined by opening and closing braces. This code will cause an error:

```
public class ScopeTest {
    void poo() {
        int m = n;   // Error. Forward reference.
        int n = 10;
    }
}
```

for scope

This is a special case of the block scope. Any variable declared as part of the for statement is included in the scope of the body of the loop. For example:

```
public class ForScopeTest {
    public static void main(String[] arg) {
        // The variable i is undefined here
        for(int i=0; i<10; i++) {
            System.out.println("i=" + i);
        }
        // The variable i is undefined here
    }
}
```

The variable i is declared inside the parentheses of the for statement, which defines its scope as being from the point of its declaration to the end of the code block, but no further. The variable cannot be accessed after the loop has exited.

Exception-handler scope

There is a special case of scoping that occurs with the catch statement in a try-catch block. The parameter—the instance of the Exception class that is the argument of the catch statement—has the scope of the block associated with catch. Syntactically, this is similar to parameter scope. For example, the exception variable is available inside this catch block:

```
try {
    ...
} catch(Exception exception) {
    System.out.println(exception);
}
```

Hidden Names

It is possible for a variable to be hidden from a region of the code that would normally be within its scope. Take this example:

```
public class HiddenScope {
    static int bob = 333;
    public static void main(String[] arg) {
        bigBob();
        littleBob();
    }
    public static void bigBob() {
        int bob = 999;
        System.out.println("bigBob=" + bob);
    }
    public static void littleBob() {
        System.out.println("littleBob=" + bob);
    }
}
```

There are two bobs in this program—one is defined classwide and has the value 333, and the other is defined in the method bigBob() and has the value 999. This is the output from the program:

```
bigBob=999
littleBob=333
```

As you can see, the local declaration of bob completely masks the classwide definition.

This particular kind of hiding only works for variables that are outside the scope of a method. A variable name inside a method cannot be declared in such a way that it hides another variable name inside the same method. You cannot, for example, have nested `for` loops that use the same variable name for counters.

Inadvertent data hiding can be the source of bugs that are difficult to find. It is, for example, possible to hide the names of classes with local variables and methods. Visual code inspection makes the code appear to be doing one thing while is actually doing something else. The best defense against having this happen is to establish a reasonable naming convention. The Java language specification defines one (see **naming convention**) that has been used to write all the distributed libraries and API.

For information on accessibility of names in other scopes, see **access**. For more details on variable scoping within a class, see **variable**.

Scrollbar

class java.awt.Scrollbar

The graphical scroll bar component.

The name of the bubble

That little movable graphic piece in the middle of a scroll bar is variously called a slider, a thumb, and a bubble. Java documentation uses "bubble." You will sometime find the term "slider" used to refer to the whole scroll bar.

The orientation

A scroll bar can be in one of two orientations. When the bubble runs from side to side, the orientation is horizontal. When the bubble runs up and down, the orientation is vertical.

The maximum and minimum

The purpose of a scroll bar is to allow the user to move easily between minimum and maximum values. This is done by using the mouse to move the bubble from one end of the scroll bar to the other. The minimum and maximum values are programatically adjustable. In horizontal orientation, the minimum is on the left. In vertical orientation, the minimum is at the top. When you are setting these values, note that the minimum must always be smaller than the maximum, so if you wish to reverse the values you will have to do so programmatically.

Changing the value by dragging

The bubble itself can be mouse-dragged from one position to another to change the value of the scroll bar. Multiple `AdjustmentEvents` are sent to the `AdjustmentListeners` while a mouse is being dragged—the program is constantly updated with new bubble positions. The scaled adjustment settings of block and unit are ignored—the bubble moves by adding or subtracting 1.

There is a pixel limitation to the granularity of the move. If, for example, the minimum value is 100 and the maximum value is 10,000, then you have more range than you have pixels. Dragging the bubble by even a single pixel will cause the value to be changed by more than 1.

The visible amount and the value

The value of the *visible amount* determines the size of the bubble, and how far it can travel. For example, if the minimum value is 0 and the maximum value is 200, a visible amount setting of 20 will cause the bubble to cover 10 percent of the available distance between the ends of the `Scrollbar`. The value of the bubble at the left or bottom will be 0, and that at the right or top will be 180—the largest possible value is the maximum less the visible amount. You can think of the value of the scroll bar as being determined by the position of the bubble closest to the minimum end of the scroll bar.

Changing the value by a unit

There is a button at each end of a scroll bar. Each time one of these buttons is selected, the value is adjusted by the *unit* value. If the button at the top or left is selected, the value of unit is subtracted—at the maximum end it is added. The unit value defaults to 1, but it can be set to anything. This value is also called the *line* value because it is commonly used to scroll a window by the height of one line of text.

Changing the value by a block

Selecting the background space of the scroll bar—that space between the bubble and either of the end buttons—will cause the value to be adjusted by the *block* amount. If the mouse selection is made on the minimum side of the button, the block value will be subtracted— on the maximum side it will be added. The block value defaults to 10, but it can be set to anything. This value is also called the *page* value because it is commonly used to scroll a window the height of one full page of text.

The numbers will always fit

A few simple rules must be followed for the settings of a scroll bar to make sense. For example, the size of the bubble must fit in the minimum/maximum range. The rules are simple enough that any value set by calling one of the methods can be automatically adjusted to fit. If you are going to make changes, you will need to make sure that you make them in the correct order—if you set the minimum and maximum values first, the others will fit no matter what the previous values happen to be.

Inheritance

```
public class Scrollbar
      implements Adjustable
```

```
        extends Component
             ⇑
    public abstract class java.awt.Component
            implements ImageObserver
            implements MenuContainer
            implements Serializable
            extends Object
                 ⇑
            public class java.lang.Object
```

Variables and constants

HORIZONTAL

```
    public static final int HORIZONTAL
```

Designates horizontal orientation.

VERTICAL

```
    public static final int VERTICAL
```

Designates vertical orientation.

Constructors

```
    public Scrollbar()

    public Scrollbar(int orientation)

    public Scrollbar(int orientation,int value,
            int visible,int minimum,int maximum)
```

Constructs a Scrollbar with the orientation being either VERTICAL or HORIZONTAL. The default is VERTICAL. The value is the current position of the bubble—it defaults to 0. The value of visible is the number of visible units —the default is 10. The minimum is the smallest possible value for the scroll bar—the default is 0. The maximum is the largest possible value for the scroll bar—the default is 100. An IllegalArgumentException will the thrown for an unknown value for orientation.

Methods

addAdjustmentListener()

```
    public synchronized void addAdjustmentListener(
            AdjustmentListener listener)
```

Adds the listener to the list of those that will receive an AdjustmentEvent whenever the value changes.

addNotify()

```
public void addNotify()
```

Creates the underlying system-dependent peer for this object. This method is not normally called by the application. It is called by the container.

getBlockIncrement()

```
public int getBlockIncrement()
```

Returns the block increment amount. This is the amount the bubble will move when the arrow at either end of the scroll bar is selected.

getLineIncrement()   **deprecated**

```
public int getLineIncrement()
```

Returns the unit increment. This is the distance the bubble will move each time one of the arrows at the end of the scroll bar is selected. This method is deprecated—use getUnitIncrement().

getMaximum()

```
public int getMaximum()
```

Returns the maximum value.

getMinimum()

```
public int getMinimum()
```

Returns the maximum value.

getOrientation()

```
public int getOrientation()
```

Returns the orientation—either VERTICAL or HORIZONTAL.

getPageIncrement()   **deprecated**

```
public int getPageIncrement()
```

Returns the page increment. This is the amount the bubble will move when the arrow at either end of the scroll bar is selected. This method is deprecated—use getBlockIncrement().

getUnitIncrement()

```
public int getUnitIncrement()
```

Returns the unit increment. This is the distance the bubble will move each time one of the arrows at the end of the scroll bar is selected.

getValue()

```
public int getValue()
```

Returns the current bubble position.

getVisible()   **deprecated**

```
public int getVisible()
```

Returns the visible amount of the scroll bar. This method is deprecated — use getVisibleAmount().

getVisibleAmount()

```
public int getVisibleAmount()
```

Returns the visible amount of the scroll bar.

paramString()

```
protected String paramString()
```

Returns debugging information. The return string describes the internal state and values of this object.

processAdjustmentEvent()

```
protected void processAdjustmentEvent(AdjustmentEvent e)
```

The event is dispatched to each member of the list of registered listeners. This method will not be called unless there has been a registration of a listener with a call to addAdjustmentListener(), or AdjustmentEvents have been enabled by a call to enableEvents().

processEvent()

```
protected void processEvent(AWTEvent e)
```

If the event is an AdjustmentEvent, a call is made to processAdjustmentEvent(). If it is not an AdjustmentEvent, the processEvent() method of the superclass is called.

removeAdjustmentListener()

```
public synchronized void removeAdjustmentListener(
          AdjustmentListener listener)
```

Removes the listener from the list of those that will receive an AdjustmentEvent whenever the value changes.

setBlockIncrement()

```
public synchronized void setBlockIncrement(int value)
```

Sets the value of the block increment.

setLineIncrement()

```
public void setLineIncrement(int v)
```

Sets the value of the unit increment. This method is deprecated—use `setUnitIncrement()`.

setMaximum()

```
public synchronized void setMaximum(int value)
```

Sets the maximum value.

setMinimum()

```
public synchronized void setMinimum(int value)
```

Sets the minimum value.

setOrientation()

```
public synchronized void setOrientation(int orientation)
```

Sets the orientation to either `HORIZONTAL` or `VERTICAL`.

setPageIncrement()

```
public void setPageIncrement(int value)
```

Sets the block increment. This method is deprecated—use `setBlockIncrement()`.

setUnitIncrement()

```
public synchronized void setUnitIncrement(int value)
```

Sets the unit increment.

setValue()

```
public synchronized void setValue(int value)
```

Sets the current value. This will set the bubble position. If the requested value is below the minimum, or above the maximum, it will be automatically adjusted.

setValues()

```
public synchronized void setValues(int value,
        int visible,int minimum,int maximum)
```

This method sets the current `value`, the `visible` amount, the `minimum`, and the `maximum`. The values must fit within their normal constraints. The minimum must be less than the maximum, and the visible amount must be positive and fit inside the bounds of minimum and maximum. No exception is thrown—the values will be automatically adjusted to fit.

setVisibleAmount()

```
public synchronized void setVisibleAmount(int value)
```

Sets the visible amount. This is, in effect, the size of the bubble.

Example

This example uses a `Canvas` to interactively display the current value settings of a `Scrollbar`:

```
import java.awt.*;
import java.awt.event.*;
public class ShowBar extends Frame
        implements AdjustmentListener {
    Scrollbar scrollbar;
    OneLine oneLine;
    int value;
    public static void main(String[] arg) {
        new ShowBar();
    }
    public ShowBar() {
        addWindowListener((WindowListener)new WinMon());
        oneLine = new OneLine();
        add("Center",oneLine);
        scrollbar = new Scrollbar(Scrollbar.HORIZONTAL);
        scrollbar.setVisibleAmount(15);
        scrollbar.setBlockIncrement(5);
        scrollbar.setUnitIncrement(3);
        scrollbar.addAdjustmentListener(this);
        add("South",scrollbar);
        pack();
        show();
    }
    public void adjustmentValueChanged(AdjustmentEvent e) {
        value = e.getValue();
        oneLine.repaint();
    }
    class OneLine extends Canvas {
        OneLine() {
            setSize(400,40);
        }
        public void paint(Graphics g) {
            g.drawString("min=" + scrollbar.getMinimum()
            + " max=" + scrollbar.getMaximum() +
            " visible=" +
            scrollbar.getVisibleAmount() + " block=" +
```

```
                scrollbar.getBlockIncrement() +
                " unit=" + scrollbar.getUnitIncrement()
                +" value=" + value,
                20,20);
        }
    }
    class WinMon extends WindowAdapter {
        public void windowClosing(WindowEvent event) {
            System.exit(0);
        }
    }
}
```

The `Scrollbar` is allowed to default to a range of 0 to 100. The visible amount, the block value, and the increment value are all set differently so that you can see the different effect each one has on the value. Figure S-1 shows the window with the `Canvas` and the `Scrollbar`.

min=0 max=100 visible=15 block=5 unit=3 value=32

Figure S-1   A `Scrollbar` with its settings and current value displayed.

The other components are **Button, Canvas, Checkbox, Choice, Label, List, TextArea,** and **TextField**. The menu components are **Menu, MenuBar, MenuItem,** and **CheckboxMenuItem**.

ScrollPane

class java.awt.ScrollPane

This is a container implementing both horizontal and vertical scrolling of a single child component. It uses scroll bars to allow the user to view a component that is too large to all be displayed at once. This container is a bit of a special case—it can contain only one component, and it has its own built-in layout manager.

Scroll bar policy

There are three settings of the scroll bar policy.

The scroll bars can be set to appear only if they are needed. That is, if the component fits entirely within the ScrollPane window, there will be no scroll bars. If any portion of the component extends beyond the sides of the ScrollPane, however, a horizontal scroll bar will appear, and similarly, if any portion of the component extends beyond the top or bottom of the ScrollPane, a vertical scroll bar will appear.

The policy can be set to always display the scroll bars. In this case, there will always be scroll bars present even when the entire component is being displayed inside the ScrollPane window.

The policy can be set to never display scroll bars. In this case, the position of the ScrollPane cannot be adjusted by the user, but it can still be adjusted inside the program.

Scroll bar placement

The scroll bar placement (left or right, top or bottom) is controlled by the host windowing system, not by the ScrollPane.

The Insets and the Scrollbars

Inset objects are used to defined the amount of border space around the edges, and any space used by the scroll bars. The Inset values are automatically adjusted to allow for the scroll bars.

The Adjustables

Two Adjustable objects (one for vertical positioning and one for horizontal positioning) are used to track and adjust the current position of the component. Care should be taken when setting values of the Adjustable objects because certain values (such as minimum and maximum values, and the amount that is visible) are set in the ScrollPane and should not be adjusted by the application.

Inheritance

```
public class ScrollPane
    extends Container
        ⇑
    public abstract class java.awt.Container
        extends Component
            ⇑
        public class java.awt.Component
            implements ImageObserver
            implements MenuContainer
            implements Serializable
            extends Object
                ⇑
            public class java.lang.Object
```

Variables and constants

SCROLLBARS_ALWAYS

```
public static final int SCROLLBARS_ALWAYS
```

The value used for setting the scroll bar policy to always have the scroll bars displayed.

SCROLLBARS_AS_NEEDED

```
public static final int SCROLLBARS_AS_NEEDED
```

The value used for setting the scroll bar policy to have the scroll bars appear only if they are needed.

SCROLLBARS_NEVER

```
public static final int SCROLLBARS_NEVER
```

The value used for setting the scroll bar policy to never have the scroll bars appear.

Constructors

```
public ScrollPane()
public ScrollPane(int scrollbarPolicy)
```

The value of `scrollbarPolicy` is one of the constants just defined—the default is `SCROLLBARS_AS_NEEDED`. The initial size of the `ScrollPane` is 100×100.

Methods

addImpl()

```
protected final void addImpl(Component component,
        Object constraints,int index)
```

Sets the `component` as the one being displayed by the `ScrollPane`. If another component has already been assigned, it will be replaced by this one.

The `constraints` and `index` are not applicable, because a `ScrollPane` contains only one component—use `null` for the `constraints` and 0 (first) or –1 (last) for the `index`.

addNotify()

```
public void addNotify()
```

Creates the underlying system-dependent peer for this object. This method is not normally called by the application. It is called by the container.

doLayout()

```
public void doLayout()
```

Lays out the component. This will resize the child component to its preferred size and determine whether, and where, the scroll bars are to be displayed. The scroll bars are set to represent the current position of the component.

getHAdjustable()
```
public Adjustable getHAdjustable()
```
Returns the Adjustable object representing the horizontal position.

getHScrollbarHeight()
```
public int getHScrollbarHeight()
```
Returns the pixel height occupied by a horizontal scroll bar. This value will be the same whether or not the scroll bar is being displayed.

getScrollbarDisplayPolicy()
```
public int getScrollbarDisplayPolicy()
```
Returns the current policy for displaying scroll bars.

getScrollPosition()
```
public Point getScrollPosition()
```
Returns the x and y coordinate points of the upper-left-hand corner of the rectangular area of the child component that is now being displayed in the ScrollPane window. This is a convenience method that determines the coordinates by querying the two Adjustable objects.

getVAdjustable()
```
public Adjustable getVAdjustable()
```
Returns the Adjustable object representing the vertical position.

getViewportSize()
```
public Dimension getViewportSize()
```
Returns the pixel height and width of area of the ScrollPane used to display the child component.

getVScrollbarWidth()
```
public int getVScrollbarWidth()
```
Returns the pixel width occupied by a vertical scroll bar. This value will be the same whether or not the scroll bar is being displayed.

layout()   **deprecated**
```
public void layout()
```

Lays out the component. This will resize the child component to its preferred size and determine whether, and where, the scroll bars are to be displayed. The scroll bars are set to represent the current position of the component. This method is deprecated—use `doLayout()`.

paramString()

```
public String paramString()
```

Returns debugging information. The return string describes the internal state and values of this object.

printComponents()

```
public void printComponents(Graphics g)
```

Prints the child component of the `ScrollPane` onto the specified `Graphics` object.

setLayout()

```
public final void setLayout(LayoutManager mgr)
```

This method does nothing. It is here to prevent the layout manager from being set.

setScrollPosition()

```
public void setScrollPosition(int x,int y)

public void setScrollPosition(Point p)
```

Scrolls the windows—both horizontally and vertically—so that the specified x and y coordinates of the child component are at the upper-left corner of the `ScrollPane`. If the values x and y are outside the displayable range of the component, they will be automatically adjusted to the nearest valid values. This is a convenience method that interfaces with the `Adjustable` objects.

The values of x and y will be adjusted to assure that no space will be left over if the component is large enough to fill the `ScrollPane` window. For example, if the component is 200 pixels wide and the `ScrollPane` is 150 pixels wide, the maximum possible value of x will be 50. This way, there is no way to position the component that leaves space to its right. The minimum values for x and y are 0.

Example

This example draws an image onto a `Canvas` and makes portions of it available through a `ScrollPane`:

```
import java.awt.*;
import java.awt.event.*;
public class ImageScroller extends Frame {
    public static void main(String[] arg) {
        new ImageScroller("hubble.jpeg");
```

```
            }
        public ImageScroller(String imageFileName) {
            addWindowListener(
                        (WindowListener)new WindowMonitor());
            Toolkit tk = Toolkit.getDefaultToolkit();
            Image image = tk.getImage(imageFileName);
            MediaTracker mt = new MediaTracker(this);
            mt.addImage(image,1);
            try {
                mt.waitForAll();
            } catch(Exception e) {
                e.printStackTrace();
            }
            ImageCanvas ic = new ImageCanvas(image);
            ScrollPane sc = new ScrollPane();
            sc.add(ic);
            add(sc);
            pack();
            show();
        }
    class ImageCanvas extends Canvas {
        Image image;
        public ImageCanvas(Image image) {
            this.image = image;
            setSize(image.getWidth(this),
                        image.getHeight(this));
        }
        public void paint(Graphics g) {
            g.drawImage(image,0,0,this);
        }
    }
    class WindowMonitor extends WindowAdapter {
        public void windowClosing(WindowEvent event) {
            System.exit(0);
        }
    }
}
```

The inner class ImageCanvas sizes itself to fit an image. Whenever the paint() method is called, the entire area of the Canvas is covered with the Image. The ImageCanvas object is not added directly to the Frame—a ScrollPane is added to the Frame and the ImageCanvas is added to the ScrollPane as its child component. The ScrollPane is allowed to default to its initial size of 100×100, and the window first appears as shown in Figure S-2. After the scroll bars have been moved and the window has been resized a bit, it can look like Figure S-3. If the `ScrollPane` is expanded, along either axis, to a size that exposes the entire component, and if the policy is `SCROLLBARS_AS_NEEDED` (which is the default), the unnecessary scroll bar will not be displayed, as shown in Figure S-4.

Figure S-2 The default size and configuration of a *ScrollPane*.

Figure S-3 A `ScrollPane` displaying a small area of an image.

Figure S-4 A `ScrollPane` can be set to show only the necessary scroll bars.

For other `Container` classes see **Applet, Dialog, FileDialog, Frame, Window,** and **Panel**. Also see **ContainerEvent** and **ContainerListener**.

SecureRandom

class java.security.SecureRandom

This is a pseudorandom number generator designed to create numbers that are cryptographically strong. The numbers are generated using the SHA-1 hash algorithm.

Seeding

A `SecureRandom` object requires a 20-byte seed. The default constructor will automatically seed the random number generator with a 20-byte seed. While the seeding algorithm in JDK 1.1 seems robust, it has not been thoroughly studied or widely deployed.

The seeding is based on the number of times one thread yields while waiting for another to sleep for a specified interval. This can cause a delay of several seconds in generating the seed — exactly how long depends on the underlying hardware. The delay only occurs for the first call to the constructor, because subsequent calls will use the same pseudorandom number generator to create the seed bits.

Even though the same generator is used over and over, no information about the bits produced in one seed should be carried over to the next seed. If you want to produce completely unrelated seeds, however, the following code will cause the seeds to be generated from scratch (along with a delay for each one):

```
new SecureRandom(SecureRandom.getSeed(20));
```

Inheritance

```
public class java.security.SecureRandom
     extends Random
          ⇑
     public class java.util.Random
          implements Serializable
          extends Object
               ⇑
          public class java.lang.Object
```

Constructors

```
public SecureRandom()
public SecureRandom(byte seed[])
```

If the 20-byte seed is not provided, one will be automatically generated. It could be preferable to use the `seed` argument if the user has some source of highly random values.

Methods

getSeed()

```
public static byte[] getSeed(int numBytes)
```

Returns an array of random bytes suitable for use as the seed to a random number generator. This seed generator is somewhat costly in terms of the amount of time it takes to generate the bytes.

next()

```
protected final int next(int numBits)
```

Returns a random number that will fit in the specified number of bits. For example, if the value of numBits is 4, the returned number will be from 0 to 16 (that is, from 0x00000000 to 0x0000000F). The value of numBits can be from 1 to 32.

nextBytes()

```
public synchronized void nextBytes(byte bytes[])
```

Fills the array of bytes with random values. This is the basic random number generator used by the other methods of this class (except for seeds). Overriding this method will change the behavior of the class.

setSeed()

```
public synchronized void setSeed(byte seed[])

public void setSeed(long seed)
```

Reseeds the random number generator. The seed argument value is combined with the existing seed—it does not replace it—which means this call cannot be made to set up a repetition of a sequence of random numbers.

 Other random number generators are **Random** and **Math.random()**.

security

package java.security

Packages

```
java.security.acl
java.security.interfaces
```

Interfaces

```
Certificate
Key
```

```
Principal
PrivateKey
PublicKey
```

Classes

```
DigestInputStream
DigestOutputStream
Identity
IdentityScope
KeyPair
KeyPairGenerator
MessageDigest
Provider
SecureRandom
Security
Signature
Signer
```

Exceptions

```
DigestException
InvalidKeyException
InvalidParameterException
KeyException
KeyManagementException
NoSuchAlgorithmException
NoSuchProviderException
ProviderException
SignatureException
```

security

standard names

The Java Security API requires and utilizes a set of standard names for various algorithms, padding schemes, providers, and such. These names are used as String arguments to (and return values from) many of the methods in the java.security package.

DES

The Data Encryption Standard, as defined by NIST in FIPS 46-1 and 46-2.

DSA

The Digital Signature Algorithm, as defined in Digital Signature Standard, NIST FIPS 186. This standard defines a digital signature algorithm that uses the RawDSA asymmetric transformation along with the SHA-1 message digest algorithm.

IDEA

The International Data Encryption Algorithm (IDEA) from ASCOM Systec, Switzerland.

MD2

The Message Digest Algorithm RSA-MD2, as defined by RSA DSI in RFC 1423.

MD2/RSA

The Signature Algorithm obtained by combining the RSA AsymmetricCipher Algorithm with the MD2 MessageDigest Algorithm.

MD5

The Message Digest Algorithm RSA-MD5, as defined by RSA DSI in RFC 1321.

MD5/RSA

The Signature Algorithm obtained by combining the RSA AsymmetricCipher Algorithm with the MD5 MessageDigest Algorithm.

RawDSA

The asymmetric transformation described in NIST FIPS 186, described as the "DSA Sign Operation" and the "DSA Verify Operation," applied prior to creating a digest. The input to RawDSA is always 20 bytes long.

RC2

The SymmetricCipher Algorithm proprietary to RSA DSI.

RC4

The SymmetricCipher Algorithm proprietary to RSA DSI.

RSA

The Rivest, Shamir, and Adleman AsymmetricCipher Algorithm. RSA encryption is defined in the RSA Laboratory Technical Note PKCS#1.

SHA-1 (also SHA)

The Secure Hash Algorithm, as defined in the Secure Hash Standard, NIST FIPS 180-1.

SHA-1/RSA

The Signature Algorithm obtained by combining the RSA AsymmetricCipher Algorithm with the SHA-1 MessageDigest Algorithm.

Security

class java.security.Security

This class is a collection of static methods that can be used to access and manage the list of security Providers.

The provider list

The providers are kept in a prioritized list. The highest priority is number 1, the next priority is number 2, and so on. They are added to the list in priority order with no two providers at the same level, and no gaps in the numbers.

Inheritance

```
public final class java.security.Security
        extends Object
            ⇑
        public class java.lang.Object
```

Constructors

There are no constructors. This class is a collection of static methods.

Methods

addProvider()

```
public static int addProvider(Provider provider)
```

Adds a security provider to the end of the list—the lowest priority. The return value is the position in which it was added. A return of −1 indicates it was not added because it was already in the list.

getAlgorithmProperty()

```
public static String getAlgorithmProperty(
        String algorithm,String property)
```

Returns the value of the property of the named security algorithm.

getProperty()

```
public static String getProperty(String key)
```

Returns the value of the security property specified by the `key`.

getProvider()

```
public static Provider getProvider(String name)
```

Returns the named `Provider`. If no provider by the specified name has been installed, a `null` is returned.

getProviders()

```
public static Provider[] getProviders()
```

Returns an array containing all the installed providers.

insertProviderAt()

```
public static int insertProviderAt(Provider provider,
        int position)
```

Inserts a security `provider` into the list at the priority position specified. The one already at that position, and all those below it, are moved down by one to make room. The return value is the position in which it was inserted. It is possible that the specified position will be ignored and the new provider will be added at the end. A return of −1 indicates the `provider` was not added because it was already in the list.

removeProvider()

```
public static void removeProvider(String name)
```

Removes the named provider from the list. If the provider is not in the list, no action is taken.

setProperty()

```
public static void setProperty(String key,String property)
```

Sets the `property` value for the `key`.

 For a list of security algorithm names, see **security**.

SecurityException

class java.lang.SecurityException

Thrown by the security manager to indicate a security violation.

Extended by

```
RMISecurityException
```

Inheritance

```
public class java.lang.SecurityException
    extends RuntimeException
        ⇑
    public class java.lang.RuntimeException
        extends Exception
            ⇑
        public class java.lang.Exception
            extends Throwable
                ⇑
            public class java.lang.Throwable
                implements Serializable
                extends Object
                    ⇑
                public class java.lang.Object
```

Constructors

```
public SecurityException()

public SecurityException(String message)
```

If the message string is supplied, it is used as a detailed message describing this particular exception.

SecurityManager

class java.lang.SecurityManager

This is an abstract class that aids applications in implementing a security policy by creating a security manager that will put limits on accessibility.

There is only one

There is only one security manager object, and it cannot be replaced. The most well-known example of this is the security manager of a Java-enabled Web browser that prevents applets from accessing any local information—it can't even determine the name of the user and the current working directory. Once a security manager is installed, it cannot be replaced, and because the security manager is loaded before any applets are loaded, an applet cannot have any effect on the security.

The security manager is not required. If no security manager is present, everything is allowed.

A list of permissions

As a Java application executes, the presence of a security manager will cause the Java runtime to call the security manager for things that could possibly be forbidden. If the security manager disallows an action, it cannot be done. The things that are permitted and forbidden can vary according to the user, the group the user is in, the particular Java class making the request, the source from which an object was loaded, and any number of other factors. The interface to the security manager — defined by this abstract class — is standard, but the implementation is very system-dependent.

The check methods

This class consists mainly of methods that begin with the word "check." These are the methods called to request permission to take some action or other. The calls to these methods are inside the Java library and are made every time a potentially sensitive action is about to be taken. These methods prohibit actions by throwing a `SecurityException`. If an action is permitted, the method simply returns. The default implementation of all the check methods is to prohibit the action.

There is one exception — the method `checkTopLevelWindow()` returns `true` or `false`.

Setting and getting

The security manager is installed by calling `System.setSecurityManager()`. To get a reference to the security manager, call `System.getSecurityManager()`.

Extended by

RMISecurityManager

Inheritance

```
public class java.lang.SecurityManager
    extends Object
        ⇑
    public class java.lang.Object
```

Variables and constants

inCheck

```
protected boolean inCheck
```

Whenever this value is `true`, it indicates that a security check is in progress.

Constructors

```
protected SecurityManager()
```

If a security manager has already been installed, another one cannot be created—the constructor will throw `SecurityException` if one already exists.

Returned by

A `SecurityManager` is returned from a call to `System.getSecurityManager()`.

Methods

checkAccept()

```
public void checkAccept(String host,int port)
```

Checks permission to accept a socket connection from the specified `host` and `port`. This method is called from the `ServerSocket` class. A `SecurityException` is thrown to deny permission.

checkAccess()

```
public void checkAccess(Thread g)
```

Checks permission for the calling thread to modify the thread argument. This method is called from methods in the `Thread` class. A `SecurityException` is thrown to deny permission.

checkAccess()

```
public void checkAccess(ThreadGroup g)
```

Checks permission for the calling thread to modify the thread group argument. This method is called by the `ThreadGroup` class. A `SecurityException` is thrown to deny permission.

checkAwtEventQueueAccess()

```
public void checkAwtEventQueueAccess()
```

Checks permission for a client to access the AWT event queue. A `SecurityException` is thrown to deny permission.

checkConnect()

```
public void checkConnect(String host,int port)
public void checkConnect(String host,int port,
    Object context)
```

Checks permission for the calling thread to open a socket connection to the specified host and port. A port number of –1 indicates that this will be a query of the IP address of the host. Optionally, a system-dependent `context` can be supplied to specify a security context. A `SecurityException` is thrown to deny permission.

checkCreateClassLoader()

```
public void checkCreateClassLoader()
```

Checks permission for the calling thread to create a class loader. A `SecurityException` is thrown to deny permission.

checkDelete()

```
public void checkDelete(String file)
```

Checks permission for the calling thread to delete the `file`. A `SecurityException` is thrown to deny permission.

checkExec()

```
public void checkExec(String cmd)
```

Checks permission for the current thread to create a subprocess. This method is invoked from the class `Runtime`. A `SecurityException` is thrown to deny permission.

checkExit()

```
public void checkExit(int status)
```

Checks permission for the current thread to cause the Virtual Machine to halt with the specified `status`. This method is invoked from the `Runtime` class. A `SecurityException` is thrown to deny permission.

checkLink()

```
public void checkLink(String library)
```

Checks permission for the current thread to dynamically link code from the name `library`. This method is invoked by the `LoadLibrary` class. A `SecurityException` is thrown to deny permission.

checkListen()

```
public void checkListen(int port)
```

Checks permission for the current thread to wait for a connection request on the specified port. A `SecurityException` is thrown to deny permission.

checkMemberAccess()

```
public void checkMemberAccess(Class class,int which)
```

Checks permission for a client to access members. A `SecurityException` is thrown to deny permission.

checkMulticast()

```
public void checkMulticast(InetAddress maddr)
```

```
public void checkMulticast(InetAddress maddr,byte ttl)
```

Checks permission for the current context to use IP multicast. The argument `maddr` is the multicast address to use, and `ttl` is the value to send if permitted. A `SecurityException` is thrown to deny permission.

checkPackageAccess()

```
public void checkPackageAccess(String pkg)
```

Checks permission for the current thread to access the specified package. This method is called by the class loader. A `SecurityException` is thrown to deny permission.

checkPackageDefinition()

```
public void checkPackageDefinition(String pkg)
```

Check permission for the calling thread to define classes in the named package. This method is called by the class loader. A `SecurityException` is thrown to deny permission.

checkPrintJobAccess()

```
public void checkPrintJobAccess()
```

Check permission for a client to initiate a print job. A `SecurityException` is thrown to deny permission.

checkPropertiesAccess()

```
public void checkPropertiesAccess()
```

Cheek permission for the calling thread to access and modify the system properties. This method is called from `System`. A `SecurityException` is thrown to deny permission.

checkPropertyAccess()

```
public void checkPropertyAccess(String key)
```

Check permission for the thread to access the property with the specified `key` name. This is called by `System.getProperty()`. A `SecurityException` is thrown to deny permission.

checkRead()

```
public void checkRead(FileDescriptor fd)

public void checkRead(String file)

public void checkRead(String file,Object context)
```

Checks permission for the calling thread or the `context` to read from the `fd` or the `file`. A `SecurityException` is thrown to deny permission. The context object is acquired with a call to `getSecurityContext()`. A `SecurityException` is thrown to deny permission.

checkSecurityAccess()

```
public void checkSecurityAccess(String action)
```

Checks whether this thread can perform the described action. A SecurityException is thrown to deny permission.

checkSetFactory()

```
public void checkSetFactory()
```

Checks permission for the current thread to set the socket factory used by ServerSocket and Socket, or the stream-handler factory used by URL. A SecurityException is thrown to deny permission.

checkSystemClipboardAccess()

```
public void checkSystemClipboardAccess()
```

Checks permission for the current thread to access the system clipboard. A SecurityException is thrown to deny permission.

checkTopLevelWindow()

```
public boolean checkTopLevelWindow(Object window)
```

Checks permission for the current thread to be able to show a top-level window—the one supplied as window. A SecurityException is thrown to deny permission.

If permission is not completely denied, this method returns a boolean value. A return of true grants permission. While a return of false does not prohibit the action, if the thread chooses to ignore the advice, the window should have some sort of visual warning.

checkWrite()

```
public void checkWrite(FileDescriptor fd)
```

```
public void checkWrite(String file)
```

Checks permission for the current thread to write the file or fd. A SecurityException is thrown to deny permission.

classDepth()

```
protected int classDepth(String name)
```

Returns the stack depth of the named class.

classLoaderDepth()

```
protected int classLoaderDepth()
```

Returns the stack depth of the most recently executing method of any class that was defined using a class loader. A return of −1 indicates that no such method is in execution.

currentClassLoader()

```
protected ClassLoader currentClassLoader()
```

Returns an object describing the most recent class loader executing on the stack.

currentLoadedClass()

```
protected Class currentLoadedClass()
```

Returns the current `Class` with a `ClassLoader` on the execution stack.

getClassContext()

```
protected Class[] getClassContext()
```

Returns the current execution stack as an array of classes. The element `Class[0]` is the currently executing method, and `Class[1]` is the one that called it.

getInCheck()

```
public boolean getInCheck()
```

Returns `true` if there is a security check in progress.

getSecurityContext()

```
public Object getSecurityContext()
```

Creates and returns an object that summarizes the current execution environment. This is the `context` argument passed to some other methods of this class. This can be used by a trusted method to determine whether its operations on behalf of another — possibly untrusted — method should be permitted. See `checkConnect()` and `checkRead()`.

getThreadGroup()

```
public ThreadGroup getThreadGroup()
```

Returns this thread's thread group. Any new threads spawned by this thread will, by default, be members of this group. This method can be overridden by a security manager to specify a group for each thread.

inClass()

```
protected boolean inClass(String name)
```

Returns `true` if the named class is on the execution stack.

inClassLoader()

```
protected boolean inClassLoader()
```

Returns `true` if the `ClassLoader` is not equal to `null`.

For accessing and installing a security manager, see **System**.

semicolon

;

In Java, the semicolon is used as the terminator of a statement. It is required at the end of every declaration, whether or not there is an initial value, like this:

```
int a;
int b = 42;
int[] c = {1,2,3};
```

It is also required at the end of every imperative statement, like this:

```
a += b;
b /= 39.0 / Math.sqrt(max);
```

The closing brace of a block is sufficient—no semicolon is required:

```
if(a < b) {
    j = 15;
} // No semicolon required here
```

There is a special use of the semicolon in the `for` loop. The first two expressions (but not the third) require a semicolon. For example:

```
for(iter = 0; iter < 10; iter++) ...
```

Extra semicolons are ignored

Extra semicolons are ignored. Any place you can put one semicolon, you can put several. Also, semicolons where they are not necessary (providing they don't come in the middle of a statement of some sort) are also ignored. For example, there is no need for a semicolon at the end of a class declaration, but it is perfectly acceptable:

```
class fred { int height };
```

 Also see **comma**. For a special use of the semicolon, see **for**.

SequenceInputStream

class java.io.SequenceInputStream

This class can be used to attach input streams together end-to-end. The reading of input will switch from one stream to another, reading to the end of each one, until all the streams have been read. To the application, it appears that the input is all coming in from one stream. Each stream is closed as it reaches end-of-file.

Inheritance

```
public class java.io.SequenceInputStream
    extends InputStream
      ⇑
    public class InputStream
        extends Object
          ⇑
        public class java.lang.Object
```

Constructors

SequenceInputStream()

```
public SequenceInputStream(Enumeration enumeration)

public SequenceInputStream(InputStream s1,InputStream s2)
```

The enumeration contains the list of InputStream objects to be used as input. A SequenceInputStream can also be constructed by using just two streams, s1 and s2.

Methods

available()

```
public abstract int available()
    throws IOException
```

Returns the number of bytes immediately available—the number that can be read without blocking.

close()

```
public void close()
    throws IOException
```

Closes the input stream. This will call the close() methods of the current input stream and of any input streams from which reading has not yet begun.

read()

```
public abstract int read()
    throws IOException

public int read(byte barray[],int offset,int length)
    throws IOException
```

If no argument is supplied, this will read one byte of data and return it as an int. If barray is supplied, the input data is placed in the array and the number of bytes read is returned. The input data will appear beginning at barray[offset] for a maximum of length bytes. If barray is null, length bytes are read and discarded. This method will block until at least one byte of data is available. A return value of −1 indicates a normal end to the input stream.

Example

This example uses a SequenceInputStream to read two files as if they were a single file:

```
import java.io.*;
public class Sequencer {
    public static void main(String[] arg) {
        try {
            FileInputStream file1 =
                new FileInputStream("file1.txt");
            FileInputStream file2 =
                new FileInputStream("file2.txt");
            SequenceInputStream sis =
                new SequenceInputStream(file1,file2);
            int character = sis.read();
            while(character != -1) {
                System.out.print((char)character);
                character = sis.read();
            }
        } catch(IOException e) {
            System.out.println(e);
        }
    }
}
```

Once the input files are open, a SequenceInputStream object is created using both of them. Each character is read and displayed. With two one-line files as input, the output looked like this:

```
This is the text of file1.
This is the text of file2.
```

Serializable

interface java.io.Serializable

For a class to have the capability of being serialized, it must implement this interface.

No methods or fields

This interface has no methods and no fields. It is only used to identify the class as being serializable.

Graph

An object, when serialized, exists as a sequence of bytes. A serialized object, along with all its contained serialized objects and primitive types, is called the *graph* form of an object. Whenever the data from an object is being deserialized from its graph, a new object is instantiated to hold it.

Subclassing

A subclass of a class implementing this interface is also serializable. If a subclass implements this interface, and its superclass does not, it is the responsibility of the subclass to implement the code necessary to serialize and deserialize the data of the superclass. The subclass can only do this if the superclass has a default (no argument) constructor that is accessible to the subclass—if there is no such constructor, it is an error to declare the subclass serializable (it is a runtime error, not a compiler error). During deserialization, the default constructor of a nonserializable superclass will be used to initialize the superclass. Any other initialization is the responsibility of the serializable subclass.

Field and stream

During deserialization, the fields of the serializable class (and its subclasses) will have their values initialized from the incoming stream. It could happen that there is an object (used as a field in a serialized class) that does not support serialization—this causes a NotSerializableException to be thrown to identify the class of the offending object.

Transient and static

Normal fields inside an object are written to the stream and then restored to their original values when the object is restored. Fields that are declared as transient are neither written to the stream nor restored—they are considered to hold only temporary values that have nothing to do with the actual state of the object. The values of static fields are not included in the streaming process because they are a part of the class as a whole, not any individual object.

Special handling

It is possible that classes will require special handling. These classes should implement methods with these signatures. Once you have implemented these methods, you have assumed the responsibility for serialization or deserialization of the state of the entire object:

```
private void writeObject(java.io.ObjectOutputStream out)
    throws IOException

private void readObject(java.io.ObjectInputStream in)
    throws IOException
    throws ClassNotFoundException
```

The `writeObject()` method is called during serialization to handle any special output to the output stream. The `readObject()` method is called during deserialization to restore the data written by `writeObject()`.

The `ObjectOutputStream` and `ObjectInputStream` classes have methods to convert objects and primitive types for input and output. These classes have special methods that can only be used for this purpose.

Changing classes

A class definition may have changed between the time its state was written to a stream and the time that it was read back. In this circumstance, any fields found in the incoming stream that are not members of the class are ignored. Any new fields—ones that are in the class but have no values in the stream—are allowed to assume their normal default values.

Preventing serialization

The serialization of an object can be prevented by implementing `writeObject()` and throwing the `NotSerializableException`. In the same way, the deserialization of an object can be prevented by throwing the `NotSerializableException` from `readObject()`.

Implemented by

```
BitSet
Boolean
BorderLayout
BreakIterator
Calendar
CardLayout
Character
CheckboxGroup
Collator
Color
Component
Cursor
Date
```

```
DateFormatSymbols
DecimalFormatSymbols
Dimension
Event
EventObject
File
FlowLayout
Font
FontMetrics
Format
GridBagConstraints
GridLayout
Hashtable
Identity
InetAddress
Insets
Lease
Locale
MenuComponent
MenuShortcut
Number
ObjectStreamClass
ObjID
Point
Polygon
PropertyChangeSupport
Random
Rectangle
RemoteObject
String
StringBuffer
SystemColor
Throwable
TimeZone
UID
URL
Vector
VetoableChangeSupport
VMID
```

Extended by

```
Externalizable
Key
```

Inheritance

```
public interface java.io.Serializable
```

Example

This example shows the implementation of a persistent object by using `ObjectOutputStream` and `ObjectInputStream` to write an object to a file and read it back in again. The `Streamer` class is defined as `Serializable`, like this:

```
import java.io.*;
public class Streamer implements Serializable {
    private int ivalue;
    private double dvalue;
    Streamer() {
        ivalue = 11;
        dvalue = 34.1;
    }
    public void setIvalue(int setting) {
        ivalue = setting;
    }
    public void setDvalue(double setting) {
        dvalue = setting;
    }
    public String toString() {
        return("Streamer: i=" + ivalue + " d=" + dvalue);
    }
}
```

The example implements the `Serializable` interface and has the two fields, `ivalue` and `dvalue`, that will need to be included in the stream to save the entire state of a `Streamer` object. This `StreamOutIn` program creates a `Streamer` object, streams it to a disk file, and then reads it back in as a new object:

```
import java.io.*;
public class StreamOutIn {
    public static void main(String[] arg) {
        Streamer s1 = new Streamer();
        Streamer s2;
        s1.setIvalue(999);
        s1.setDvalue(999.999);
        System.out.println(s1);
        try {
            FileOutputStream fos =
                new FileOutputStream("Streamer.data");
            ObjectOutputStream oos =
```

```
                          new ObjectOutputStream(fos);
                oos.writeObject(s1);
        } catch(IOException e) {
            System.out.println(e);
        }
        try {
            FileInputStream fis =
                    new FileInputStream("Streamer.data");
            ObjectInputStream ois =
                    new ObjectInputStream(fis);
            s2 = (Streamer)ois.readObject();
            System.out.println(s2);
        } catch(IOException e) {
            System.out.println(e);
        } catch(ClassNotFoundException e) {
            System.out.println(e);
        }
    }
}
```

The state of s1 is printed before it is written to disk, and the state of s2 is
printed after it has been loaded back in from disk. The output of the program
looks like this:

```
Streamer: i=999 d=999.999
Streamer: i=999 d=999.999
```

A hexadecimal dump of the resulting file shows that the streamed object
includes the name of the class, and the names of the individual streamed fields:

```
00 01 02 03 04 05 06 07 08 09 0A 0B 0C 0D 0E 0F
AC ED 00 05 73 72 00 08 53 74 72 65 61 6D 65 72    ....sr..Streamer
AA 8A FB C5 63 8D A2 BD 02 00 02 44 00 06 64 76    ....c......D..dv
61 6C 75 65 49 00 06 69 76 61 6C 75 65 78 70 40    alueI..ivaluexp@
8F 3F FD F3 B6 45 A2 00 00 03 E7                   .?...E.....
```

 For other members of the API dealing with serialization, see
**ObjectOutputStream, ObjectInputStream, ObjectOutput,
ObjectInput,** and **Externalizable.**

serialver

utility

This is a utility program to return the version number of a serializable class. This number is a 64-bit `serialVersionUID` that will change each time any part of the class changes.

Syntax

```
serialver [-show] [classname ...]
```

options

-show

This option will display a window like the one in Figure S-5 that will accept the name of a class and display the `serialVersionUID` number.

Figure S-5   The GUI window of the serialver utility.

 For more information, see **ObjectStreamClass**

serialVersionUID

This is a unique 64-bit number generated from a `Serializable` class. The number will change whenever any modification is made to the class.

 For a utility that will display the `serialVersionUID` of a class, see **serialver**. Also see **ObjectStreamClass**.

server

package java.rmi.server

Interfaces

```
LoaderHandler
```

RemoteCall
RemoteRef
RMIFailureHandler
ServerRef
Skeleton
Unreferenced

Classes

LogStream
ObjID
Operation
RemoteObject
RemoteServer
RemoteStub
RMIClassLoader
RMISocketFactory
UID
UnicastRemoteObject

Exceptions

ExportException
ServerCloneException
ServerNotActiveException
SkeletonMismatchException
SkeletonNotFoundException
SocketSecurityException

ServerCloneException

class java.rmi.server.ServerCloneException

This exception is thrown to indicate a failed attempt to clone a remote object.

Inheritance

```
public class java.rmi.server.ServerCloneException
    extends CloneNotSupportedException
        ⇑
    public class java.lang.CloneNotSupportedException
        extends Exception
            ⇑
        public class java.lang.Exception
```

```
extends Throwable
        ⇑
public class java.lang.Throwable
        implements Serializable
        extends Object
                ⇑
        public class java.lang.Object
```

Variables and constants

detail

```
public Exception detail
```

The original exception that caused this one to be thrown.

Constructors

```
public ServerCloneException(String message)

public ServerCloneException(String message,Exception detail)
```

The `message` string is supplied as a message describing this particular exception. If the `detail` is included, it is the one that was originally thrown, causing this exception to be thrown.

Methods

getMessage()

```
public String getMessage()
```

Returns the message string that was included on the constructor. If the message string is `null`, the method returns the one from the inner `detail` exception (which could also be `null`).

ServerError

class java.rmi.ServerError

This error is thrown to report an error on the server.

Inheritance

```
public class java.rmi.ServerError
    extends RemoteException
```

```
                          ⇑
            public class java.rmi.RemoteException
                 extends IOException
                          ⇑
              public class java.io.IOException
                  extends Exception
                          ⇑
                public class java.lang.Exception
                    extends Throwable
                          ⇑
                  public class java.lang.Throwable
                      implements Serializable
                      extends Object
                          ⇑
                    public class java.lang.Object
```

Constructors

```
public ServerError(String message,Error error)
```

A `ServerError` is created with a descriptive `message` and the original `error` that caused this one to be thrown.

ServerException

class java.rmi.ServerException

This exception is thrown to report an exception on the remote server.

Inheritance

```
public class java.rmi.ServerException
     extends RemoteException
         ⇑
    public class java.rmi.RemoteException
         extends IOException
             ⇑
        public class java.io.IOException
            extends Exception
                ⇑
          public class java.lang.Exception
              extends Throwable
                  ⇑
```

```
public class java.lang.Throwable
      implements Serializable
      extends Object
            ⇑
      public class java.lang.Object
```

Constructors

```
public ServerException(String message)

public ServerException(String message,Exception exception)
```

The ServerException is created with a descriptive message and, optionally, the original exception that caused this one to be thrown.

ServerNotActiveException

class java.rmi.server.ServerNotActiveException

This exception is thrown to indicate that some action was requested that can only be performed when the server is active, and that it is not currently active.

Inheritance

```
public class java.rmi.server.ServerNotActiveException
    extends Exception
        ⇑
    public class java.lang.Exception
        extends Throwable
            ⇑
        public class java.lang.Throwable
              implements Serializable
              extends Object
                  ⇑
          public class java.lang.Object
```

Constructors

```
public ServerNotActiveException()

public ServerNotActiveException(String message)
```

If the message string is supplied, it is used as a detailed message describing this particular exception.

ServerRef

interface java.rmi.server.ServerRef

A ServerRef represents the server-side handle of a remote object.

Inheritance

```
public interface java.rmi.server.ServerRef
      extends RemoteRef
          ⇑
      public interface java.rmi.server.RemoteRef
            extends Externalizable
                ⇑
            public interface java.io.Externalizable
                  extends Serializable
                      ⇑
                  public interface java.io.Serializable
```

Methods

exportObject()

```
public abstract RemoteStub exportObject(Remote obj,
        Object data)
    throws RemoteException
```

Locates, or creates, a client RemoteStub for the specified remote object. The data is information necessary to export the object, such as the port number.

getClientHost()

```
public abstract String getClientHost()
    throws ServerNotActiveException
```

When called from a thread currently handling a remote method invocation, the method returns the host name of the client. A ServerNotActiveException is thrown if the thread is not currently handling a remote method invocation.

 For a general description, see **RMI**. Also see **Operation**, **RemoteCall**, **RemoteObject**, **RemoteRef**, **RemoteServer**, **RemoteStub**, and **Skeleton**.

ServerRuntimeException

class java.rmi.ServerRuntimeException

This exception is thrown to report a runtime error on the server.

Inheritance

```
public class java.rmi.ServerRuntimeException
    extends RemoteException
        ⇑
    public class java.rmi.RemoteException
        extends IOException
            ⇑
        public class java.io.IOException
            extends Exception
                ⇑
            public class java.lang.Exception
                extends Throwable
                    ⇑
                public class java.lang.Throwable
                    implements Serializable
                    extends Object
                        ⇑
                    public class java.lang.Object
```

Constructors

```
public ServerRuntimeException(String message,
        Exception exception)
```

A `ServerRuntimeException` is created with a descriptive message and the original exception that caused this one to be thrown.

ServerSocket

class java.net.ServerSocket

This class implements server sockets. A *server socket* binds itself to a port on the local host and waits for a network message to arrive. Whenever a message arrives, the application using the server socket will act on the message and, possibly, use the socket to respond.

The factory and the firewall

The actual work of the server socket is performed by a `SocketImpl` object. A `SocketImpl` object is created by a `SocketImplFactory`. The `SocketImplFactory` can be set by the application to create sockets that know how to deal with the local firewall. If no socket factory is specified, the default factory will be used to create plain sockets.

The backlog

As requests for connections arrive, they are queued. This is known as the backlog. If the queue is full, any newly arriving connection requests will be denied.

Inheritance

```
public class java.net.ServerSocket
    extends Object
        ⇑
    public class java.lang.Object
```

Constructors

```
public ServerSocket(int port)
    throws IOException

public ServerSocket(int port,int backlog)
    throws IOException

public ServerSocket(int port,int backlog,InetAddress bindAddr)
    throws IOException
```

A `ServerSocket` is created for a specific local `port` number. Specifying a port number of 0 will cause the constructor to select a free port number. If the size of the `backlog` is not specified, it will default to 50. The `bindAddr` can be used in the case of a multihomed host (one that has more than one IP address) to specify which address is to be used—if `bindAddr` is `null` or is not specified, the socket will accept connections on all of its addresses. An `IOException` is thrown if the socket cannot be opened.

Returned by

A `ServerSocket` is returned from `RMISocketFactory.createServerSocket()`.

Methods

accept()

```
public Socket accept()
```

```
        throws IOException
```

Using the connection request at the head of the backlog queue makes a connection. If no connection request is in the queue, this method will block until one appears. An `InterruptedIOException` is thrown if the `accept()` times out (see SO_TIMEOUT earlier under this heading), but the socket is still valid.

close()

```
    public void close()
        throws IOException
```

Closes the socket.

getInetAddress()

```
    public InetAddress getInetAddress()
```

Returns the local address of this socket.

getLocalPort()

```
    public int getLocalPort()
```

Returns the local port number of this socket.

getSoTimeout()

```
    public synchronized int getSoTimeout()
        throws IOException
```

Returns the setting for SO_TIMEOUT. A return of zero indicates that the timeout is set to infinity.

implAccept()

```
    protected final void implAccept(Socket s)
        throws IOException
```

This method does the actual connection work for `accept()` (the `accept()` method simply creates a `Socket` and calls this method). This method exists to be overridden to implement any special actions required to make a connection to a client.

setSocketFactory()

```
    public static synchronized void setSocketFactory(
            SocketImplFactory factory)
        throws IOException
```

Specifies the socket factory for this application. This method can only be called once. A `SocketException` will be thrown if the factory has already been defined.

setSoTimeout()

```
public synchronized void setSoTimeout(int timeout)
       throws SocketException
```

Sets the SO_TIMEOUT value to a specified number of milliseconds — a value of zero disables the timer and effectively sets it to infinity.

toString()

```
public String toString()
```

Returns a string including the address and port number of this socket.

 For a client socket, see **Socket**. For an abstract class that can be extended to implement special sockets, see **SocketImpl**. For a UDP socket, see **DatagramSocket** and **DatagramSocketImpl**.

Shape

interface java.awt.Shape

This is an interface for objects designed to represent a geometric shape.

Changes are coming

This documents the Java 1.1 version. This interface is expected to be revised in the upcoming Java2D project. It is meant to provide a common interface for various existing geometric AWT classes and methods that operate on them. Since it may be superseded or expanded in the future, developers should avoid implementing this interface in their own classes until it is completed in a later release.

Implemented by

```
Polygon
Rectangle
```

Inheritance

```
public interface java.awt.Shape
```

Constructors

Returned by

An object returning this interface is returned from Graphics.getClip().

Methods

getBounds()

```
public abstract Rectangle getBounds()
```

Returns a bounding box of the shape. This is the smallest rectangle possible that will include all points that define the shape.

shift left

This operator can be used to shift the bits of any of the integer primitives (byte, short, char, int, and long) a specified number of bits to the left. The abandoned bit positions on the right will be zero-filled.

The arguments

The operand on the left is the one to be shifted, and the operand on the right is the number of bits of the shift. The only difference between the operators is that <<= places the result in the operand on the left, and << does not.

Changing signs

Shifting bits to the left will cause the sign of the value to reverse if the value of the leftmost bit (the sign bit) changes. This is true for all types except char, which is an unsigned value.

 Also see **shift right**.

shift right

This operator can be used to shift the bits of any of the integer primitives (byte, short, char, int, and long) a specified number of bits to the right.

The arguments

The operand on the left is the one to be shifted, and the operand on the right is the number of bits of the shift. The operators >>= and >>>= place the result in the operand on the left—the operators >> and >>> do not.

Sign extension

The operators >> and >>= will sign-extend by duplicating the leftmost bit into all the bits that were abandoned by the shift operation. The operators >>> and >>>= will always zero-fill any bits abandoned on the left.

Also see **shift left.**

short

primitive data type

A short is a 16-bit signed integer.

The largest magnitude negative value of a short is –32,768. The largest positive value of a short is 32,767.

Table S-1 lists all the ways in which the maximum and minimum values for a short can be declared.

Table S-1   The Different Forms for Declaring Maximum and Minimum Values

Type	Maximum	Minimum	Minus One
Decimal	32767	-32768	-1
Octal	077777	0100000	0177777
Hexadecimal	0x7fff	0x8000	0xffff
Pre-defined	Short.MAX_VALUE	Short.MIN_VALUE	

Literals

Short constants can be declared in decimal, octal, or hexadecimal form. Any of these can be declared negative by being preceded with a minus sign.

Base-10 literal

A number beginning with any digit other than 0, and containing only the digits 0 through 9, is a base-10 literal. Some examples of short literals:

```
82    -5632    852
```

Hexadecimal literal

A hexadecimal (base-16) integer begins with 0x or 0X. It can contain the digits 0 through 9 and the letters A through F. The letters A through F (which represent the decimal values 10 through 15) can be either upper- or lowercase. Some examples of hexadecimal literals are these:

```
0x022    0X71B9    -0x99a    0X2a
```

 Hexadecimal values greater than 0x7FFF are positive values that have no representation as a short—the values from 0x8000 through 0xFFFF will fit into a short but represent negative numbers. The Java compiler will generate an error for this statement:

```
short s = 0xFFFF;    // Error
```

The insertion of the value can be forced by using a cast, like this:

```
short s = (short)0xFFFF;
```

Octal literal

An octal (base-8) literal begins with a 0 and contains only the digits 0 through 7. One octal digit represents, at most, three bits. These are examples of octal literals:

```
05    052    017777
```

 Octal values greater than 077777 are positive values that will not fit into a short—the values from 0100000 through 0177777 will fit into a short but represent negative values. The Java compiler will generate an error for this statement:

```
short s = 0100000;    // Error
```

The insertion of the value can be forced by using a cast, like this:

```
short s = (short)0100000;
```

Possible values for a short range from –32768 to +32767. Byte octal literals range from –077777 to +077777—which does not include –32768 (internally represented as 0177777). To write this value in octal, it is necessary to cast it this way:

```
short s = (short)0177777;
```

 For other integer types, see **byte, char, int,** and **long**.

Short

class java.lang.Short

This is a wrapper for the primitive data type `short`. It is a constant—the value contained in a `Short` object is set by the constructor and cannot be changed.

Inheritance

```
public final class java.lang.Short
    extends Number
        ⇑
    public class java.lang.Number
        implements Serializable
        extends Object
            ⇑
        public class java.lang.Object
```

Variables and constants

MAX_VALUE

```
public final static short MAX_VALUE
```

The maximum possible value of a `short`. It is 32767.

MIN_VALUE

```
public final static short MIN_VALUE
```

The most negative possible value of a `short`. It is –32768.

TYPE

```
public final static Class TYPE
```

The class object that represents the `short` primitive type.

Constructors

```
public Short(short value)

public Short(String string)
    throws NumberFormatException
```

A `Short` is constructed from a `value`, or from a `string` that holds the base-10 digits of a value. The `NumberFormatException` is thrown if the string is not a string of base-10 digits within the range of a `short`.

Returned by

A Short object is returned from the decode() and valueOf() methods.

Methods

byteValue()

```
public byte byteValue()
```

Casts the short to a byte and returns the value.

decode()

```
public static Short decode(String string)
        throws NumberFormatException
```

Converts the string characters into a short value and returns it as a Short object. The string can be in the Java standard forms for decimal, hexadecimal, or octal values. A NumberFormatException is thrown if the string cannot be decoded.

doubleValue()

```
public double doubleValue()
```

Widens the short to a double and returns the value.

equals()

```
public boolean equals(Object object)
```

Returns true if object is a Short object and it contains the same value as this one.

floatValue()

```
public float floatValue()
```

Widens the short value to a float and returns it.

hashCode()

```
public int hashCode()
```

Returns the hashcode for this Short.

intValue()

```
public int intValue()
```

Widens the short value to an int and returns it.

longValue()

```
public long longValue()
```

Widens the short value to a long and returns it.

parseShort()

```
public static short parseShort(String string)
    throws NumberFormatException
```

```
public static short parseShort(String string,int radix)
    throws NumberFormatException
```

A short value is built from a string that holds the digit characters. The default radix is 10. The NumberFormatException is thrown if the string is not a string of digits of the proper radix that produces an integer value within the range of a short.

shortValue()

```
public short shortValue()
```

Returns the short value.

toString()

```
public static String toString(short svalue)
```

```
public String toString()
```

Converts svalue to a string of base-10 digits and returns it. If svalue is not specified, the short value of this object is used.

valueOf()

```
public static Short valueOf(String string,int radix)
    throws NumberFormatException
```

```
public static Short valueOf(String string)
    throws NumberFormatException
```

Converts the digits of the string into a short value and creates a Short object for the value. The default radix is 10. The digits must be of the specified radix, and the value must be within the range that can be contained in a short or a NumberFormatException will be thrown.

 The wrappers of the other primitive types are **Boolean, Byte, Character, Long, Integer, Float,** and **Double.**

signature

 The signature of a method includes its name and argument list. See **method.**

Signature

class java.security.Signature

This is the wrapper of a digital signature.

A digital signature

A digital signature uses an algorithm (such as DSA or RSA with MD5) to provide a method of digital authentication of the signer of a document, or of any other digital data.

A dual-purpose class

This class can be used for one of two purposes. It can be initialized with a private key for the generation of encoded signatures—or it can be initialized with a public key for the verification of encoded signature.

The SPI

Several of the methods of this class are SPI (Service Provider Interface) methods. These are the abstract methods that define the interface to be implemented by providers when supplying specific algorithms. There is a corresponding API method for each SPI method. The SPI methods all begin with `engine`. For example, the API method `sign()` calls the SPI method `engineSign()`.

Three steps to create a signature

1. Initialize. When the `Signature` object is first created, it is in an uninitialized state. It must be initialized for creating a signature with a call to `initSign()`.
2. Update. The act of supplying the data to the `Signature` to be signed is known as *updating*. The `update()` method can be called repeatedly to do this one byte at a time, or else it can be called with an array of bytes each time.
3. Sign. Once the `Signature` has been updated with all the data, the final step is to generate an X.509-encoded signature by making a call to `sign()`.

Three steps to verify a signature

1. Initialize. When the `Signature` object is first created, it is in an uninitialized state. It must be initialized for verification by making a call to `initVerify()`.
2. Update. The act of supplying the data to the `Signature` to be verified is known as *updating*. The `update()` method can be called

repeatedly to do this one byte at a time, or else it can be called with an array of bytes each time.

3. Verify. Once the Signature has been updated with all the data, the final step is to call verify(). A return value of true indicates the signature is valid, and a return of false indicates that it is not.

Inheritance

```
public abstract class java.security.Signature
    extends Object
        ⇑
    public class java.lang.Object
```

Variables and constants

SIGN

```
protected static final int SIGN
```

One of the possible values of state. It indicates that the object has been initialized and is ready to be signed.

state

```
protected int state
```

The current state of the Signature.

UNINITIALIZED

```
protected static final int UNINITIALIZED
```

One of the possible values of state. It indicates that the object has not yet been initialized.

VERIFY

```
protected static final int VERIFY
```

One of the possible values of state. It indicates that the object has been initialized and is ready for verification.

Constructors

```
protected Signature(String algorithm)
```

Uses the named security algorithm to create a Signature object.

Returned by

A Signature object is returned from getInstance().

Methods

clone()

```
public Object clone()
     throws CloneNotSupportedException
```

Returns a duplicate of this object. If the implementation does not support cloning, a CloneNotSupportedException is thrown.

engineGetParameter()

```
protected abstract Object engineGetParameter(String parameter)
     throws InvalidParameterException
```

SPI. Returns the value associated with the parameter.

This method supplies a general-purpose mechanism to get the various parameters of this object. A parameter can be any settable parameter for the algorithm, such as a size, a source of random bits, or an indication of whether or not to perform a specific computation. There is no uniform naming scheme. An InvalidParmeterException is thrown if the parameter is unknown.

engineInitSign()

```
protected abstract void engineInitSign(PrivateKey privateKey)
     throws InvalidKeyException
```

SPI. Initializes this object for signing by using the PrivateKey. The InvalidKeyException is thrown if the PrivateKey is not initialized properly.

engineInitVerify()

```
protected abstract void engineInitVerify(PublicKey publicKey)
     throws InvalidKeyException
```

SPI. Initializes this object for verification by using the PublicKey of the identity that is going to be verified. The InvalidKeyException is thrown if the PublicKey is not initialized properly.

engineSetParameter()

```
protected abstract void engineSetParameter(
          String parameter,Object value)
     throws InvalidParameterException
```

SPI. Sets the value associated with parameter.

This method supplies a general-purpose mechanism to set the various parameters of this object. A `parameter` can be any settable parameter for the algorithm, such as a size, a source of random bits, or an indication of whether or not to perform a specific computation. There is no uniform naming scheme. An `InvalidParmeterException` is thrown if the `parameter` is unknown.

engineSign()

```
protected abstract byte[] engineSign()
    throws SignatureException
```

SPI. Returns the X.509-encoded signature for all the data that has been updated so far. A `SignatureException` will be thrown if the `Signature` has not been properly initialized.

engineUpdate()

```
protected abstract void engineUpdate(byte b)
    throws SignatureException

protected abstract void engineUpdate(byte data[],
        int offset,int length)
    throws SignatureException
```

SPI. Updates the data being signed or verified. The data can be a single byte, or an array of bytes. If an array is specified, the update will be `length` bytes beginning at `data[offset]`. A `SignatureException` is thrown if the `Signature` object has not been properly initialized.

engineVerify()

```
protected abstract boolean engineVerify(byte sigBytes[])
    throws SignatureException
```

SPI. Returns `true` if the X.509-encoded signature passed in as `sigBytes` is verified as being correct. A `SignatureException` is thrown if the `Signature` object has not been properly initialized.

getAlgorithm()

```
public final String getAlgorithm()
```

Returns the name of the algorithm being used.

getInstance()

```
public static Signature getInstance(String algorithm)
    throws NoSuchAlgorithmException

public static Signature getInstance(String algorithm,
        String provider)
```

```
      throws NoSuchAlgorithmException
      throws NoSuchProviderException
```

Instantiates and returns a Signature object implementing the specified algorithm. If the default provider package contains a Signature, an implementation of it will be returned. Specifying a Provider will override the default. If the named algorithm is not available, other packages will be searched. A NoSuchAlgorithmException is thrown if the algorithm is not found. A NoSuchProviderException will be thrown if the specified provider is not known.

getParameter()

```
   public final Object getParameter(String parameter)
      throws InvalidParameterException
```

Returns the value of the specified parameter.

This method supplies a general-purpose mechanism to get the various parameters of this object. A parameter can be any settable parameter for the algorithm, such as a size, a source of random bits, or an indication of whether or not to perform a specific computation. There is no uniform naming scheme. An InvalidParmeterException is thrown if the parameter is unknown.

initSign()

```
   public final void initSign(PrivateKey privateKey)
      throws InvalidKeyException
```

Initializes this object for signing by using the PrivateKey. The InvalidKeyException is thrown if the PrivateKey is not initialized properly.

initVerify()

```
   public final void initVerify(PublicKey publicKey)
      throws InvalidKeyException
```

Initializes this object for verification by using the PublicKey of the identity that is going to be verified. The InvalidKeyException is thrown if the PublicKey is not initialized properly.

setParameter()

```
   public final void setParameter(String param,Object value)
      throws InvalidParameterException
```

Sets the value associated with the parameter.

This method supplies a general-purpose mechanism to set the various parameters of this object. A parameter can be any settable parameter for the algorithm, such as a size, a source of random bits, or an indication of whether or not to perform a specific computation. There is no uniform naming scheme. An InvalidParmeterException is thrown if the parameter is unknown.

sign()

```
public final byte[] sign()
    throws SignatureException
```

Returns the X.509-encoded signature for all the data that has been updated so far. A SignatureException will be thrown if the Signature has not been properly initialized.

toString()

```
public String toString()
```

Returns a string that includes the state and the name of the algorithm.

update()

```
public final void update(byte b)
    throws SignatureException
```

```
public final void update(byte data[])
    throws SignatureException
```

```
public final void update(byte data[],
        int offset,int length)
    throws SignatureException
```

Updates the data being signed or verified. The data can be a single byte, or an array of bytes. The update will be length bytes beginning at data[offset]—if length and offset are not specified, the entire array is used. A SignatureException is thrown if the Signature object has not been properly initialized.

verify()

```
public final boolean verify(byte signature[])
    throws SignatureException
```

Returns true if the supplied signature verifies the contents supplied to the update() method. The signature bytes are expected to be X.509-encoded.

A call to this method resets the Signature object to the state it was in right after it was initialized for verification by the call to initVerify()—this call resets the object in such a way that it can be used to verify multiple signatures that require the same public key.

 For a list of security algorithm names, see **security**. Also see **Certificate, Signer,** and **Identity**.

SignatureException

class java.security.SignatureException

This exception is thrown to indicate an error with creating or validating a Signature.

Inheritance

```
public class SignatureException
    extends Exception
        ⇑
    public class java.lang.Exception
        extends Throwable
            ⇑
        public class java.lang.Throwable
            implements Serializable
            extends Object
                ⇑
            public class java.lang.Object
```

Constructors

```
public SignatureException()
public SignatureException(String message)
```

If the message string is supplied, it is used as a detailed message describing this particular exception.

Signer

class java.security.Signer

An object of this class represents an Identity — it can also be used to digitally sign data. This object can be used to contain both the private and public keys, so it should be closely held by the owner of the private key.

Inheritance

```
public abstract class java.security.Signer
    extends Identity
        ⇑
    public abstract class java.security.Identity
```

```
                    implements Principal
                    implements Serializable
                    extends Object
                        ⇑
                    public class java.lang.Object
```

Constructors

```
      protected Signer()

      public Signer(String name)

      public Signer(String name,IdentityScope scope)
          throws KeyManagementException
```

A Signer is created using the name of an identity. The scope of the identity is optional. A KeyManagementException is thrown if there is already an identity with the same name and scope.

The default constructor is protected and should only be used by subclasses for serialization.

Methods

getPrivateKey()

```
      public PrivateKey getPrivateKey()
```

Returns the private key of this Signer. Returns null if the key has not been set.

setKeyPair()

```
      public final void setKeyPair(KeyPair pair)
          throws InvalidParameterException
          throws KeyException
```

Sets the public and private key pair for this signer. An InvalidParameterException will be thrown if either key is not properly initialized. A KeyException is thrown if the key cannot be set.

toString()

```
      public String toString()
```

Returns a string describing the Signer.

 For more on signature and verification, see **Signature** and **Certificate**.

SimpleBeanInfo

class java.beans.SimpleBeanInfo

This is a support class designed to simplify the process of writing a `BeanInfo` class. All the methods of the `BeanInfo` interface are implemented to return `null` (or some other appropriate value) to indicate that the information is not available. In subclassing this class, it is only necessary to implement the methods that will return useful information.

Inheritance

```
public class java.beans.SimpleBeanInfo
    implements BeanInfo
    extends Object
        ⇑
    public class java.lang.Object
```

Constructors

```
public SimpleBeanInfo()
```

Methods

getAdditionalBeanInfo()

```
public BeanInfo[] getAdditionalBeanInfo()
```

Returns `null`.

getBeanDescriptor()

```
public BeanDescriptor getBeanDescriptor()
```

Returns `null`.

getDefaultEventIndex()

```
public int getDefaultEventIndex()
```

Returns −1.

getDefaultPropertyIndex()

```
public int getDefaultPropertyIndex()
```

Returns −1.

getEventSetDescriptors()

```
public EventSetDescriptor[] getEventSetDescriptors()
```

Returns null.

getIcon()

```
public Image getIcon(int iconKind)
```

Returns null.

getMethodDescriptors()

```
public MethodDescriptor[] getMethodDescriptors()
```

Returns null.

getPropertyDescriptors()

```
public PropertyDescriptor[] getPropertyDescriptors()
```

Returns null.

loadImage()

```
public Image loadImage(String resourceName)
```

This method can be used to load icon images. It uses the resourceName as the path name of the file, relative to the current directory, and loads it as an Image object. If the load fails, the return is null.

 For information on defined constants, and for a description of the values returned from the methods, see **BeanInfo.** For more general information, see **Introspector**.

SimpleDateFormat

class java.text.SimpleDateFormat

This class will convert dates between their Java internal form and a localized string form.

Other ways to do this

Some alternative date and time formatting facilities are a bit more sophisticated than this one. See **DateFormat** for the methods getTimeInstance(), getDateInstance(), and getDateTimeInstance().

The format string

A string of characters is used to control the formatting of output strings and the expected format of the input string. Table S-2 lists the characters of this string along with their meanings. Each of these characters can be repeated a number of times to indicate the desired size of the particular data field. For example, "yyyy" will print "1997" and "yy" will print "97."

Any characters not in this table (such as ':' or '/') will be inserted into the output. Characters from the table can be included in the output by being enclosed in single quotes. A single-quote character is written as two single quotes.

Table S-2   The Formatting Control Characters

Character	Meaning in the Format
a	The A.M. and P.M. marker, for example, AM and PM.
D	The day of the year. The number will be zero-filled to fit the requested size.
d	The day of the month. The number will be zero-filled to fit the requested size.
E	The day of the week. If there are less than four of these, the short form of the text is used.
F	The day of the week in the month, for example, the second Sunday of the month. The number will be zero-filled to fit the requested size.
G	The era, such as A.D. and B.C.
h	The hour of a 12-hour clock. The values range from 1 through 12. If there are two or more, the number will be zero-filled to fit.
H	The hour of a 24-hour clock. The values range from 0 through 23. If there are two or more, the number will be zero-filled to fit.
k	The hour in the day, a number in the range 1 through 24. If there are two or more, it will be zero-filled to fit.
m	The minute of the hour. If there are two or more, it will be zero-filled to fit.
M	The month. If there are three or more, the name of the month is used—two or less, the number of the month.
s	The second of the minute. If there are two or more, it will be zero-filled to fit.
S	The millisecond of the second. If there are two or more, it will be zero-filled to fit.
w	The week in the year. If there is more than one of these, the number will be zero-filled to fit the requested size.
W	The week in the month. This is always a single digit, but the number will be zero-filled to fit the requested size.
y	The year. If there are one or two of these, the year is two digits. If there are more, the year is four digits.
z	The time zone. If there are four or more of these, the long form will be used, for example, "Central Standard Time." If there are three or less, the short form will be used, for example, "CST."

Inheritance

```
public class java.text.SimpleDateFormat
    extends DateFormat
        ⇑
    public class java.text.DateFormat
        implements Cloneable
        extends Format
            ⇑
        public class java.text.Format
            implements Serializable
            implements Cloneable
            extends Object
                ⇑
            public class java.lang.Object
```

Constructors

```
public SimpleDateFormat()

public SimpleDateFormat(String pattern)

public SimpleDateFormat(String pattern,Locale locale)

public SimpleDateFormat(String pattern,
        DateFormatSymbols formatData)
```

The pattern is a string containing characters that determine the format of the date string. If the pattern is not specified, a default will be used. If the locale is not specified, the default will be used. The formatData argument will determine the set of symbols used for such things as A.M. and P.M. notations. If formatData is not specified, one will be generated automatically using the appropriate locale.

Methods

applyLocalizedPattern()

```
public void applyLocalizedPattern(String pattern)
```

Replaces the string that controls the formatting with this localized pattern.

applyPattern()

```
public void applyPattern(String pattern)
```

Replaces the sting that controls the formatting with this one. This can be a nonlocalized string.

clone()

```
public Object clone()
```

Returns a duplicate of this object.

equals()

```
public boolean equals(Object object)
```

Returns `true` if `object` is a `SimpleDateFormat` that contains the same pattern string as this one.

format()

```
public StringBuffer format(Date date,
          StringBuffer appendTo,FieldPosition position)
```

Uses the `date` for the data to format a string. The new string is appended onto the end of `appendTo`, and the result is returned. The position is the specification of an alignment of a field, and on output, it specifies the location of the field in the output string.

getDateFormatSymbols()

```
public DateFormatSymbols getDateFormatSymbols()
```

Returns the `DateFormatSymbols` object being used to format the strings.

hashCode()

```
public int hashCode()
```

Returns a hashcode value for this object.

parse()

```
public Date parse(String text,ParsePosition position)
```

Reads the `text` string, translates the characters found there into an internal date, and return it as a `Date` object. The `position` specifies the starting location of the date in the `text` string; it is updated to index one character beyond the last one used to construct the date.

setDateFormatSymbols()

```
public void setDateFormatSymbols(DateFormatSymbols symbols)
```

Specifies a new `DateFormatSymbols` object to be used in the formatting of date strings.

toLocalizedPattern()

```
public String toLocalizedPattern()
```

Returns a localized version of the pattern string used to format dates.

toPattern()

```
public String toPattern()
```

Returns the nonlocalized pattern string used to format dates.

Example

This examples demonstrates output of a few different formats on the same input data:

```
import java.text.*;
import java.util.*;
public class DateStringer {
    static String[] form = {
        "EEE, MMM d, ''yy",
        "h:mm a",
        "hh 'o''''clock' a, zzzz",
        "K:mm a, z",
        "yyyyy.MMMMM.dd GGG hh:mm aaa"
    };
    public static void main(String[] arg) {
        FieldPosition fp = new FieldPosition(0);
        Date date = new Date();
        SimpleDateFormat sdf;
        for(int i=0; i<form.length; i++) {
            StringBuffer sb = new StringBuffer();
            sdf = new SimpleDateFormat(form[i]);
            System.out.println("\""+form[i]+"\"");
            System.out.println("  "+sdf.format(date,sb,
                fp));
        }
    }
}
```

This example instantiates a Date object and formats it with several different formatting strings. The output looks like this:

```
"EEE, MMM d, ''yy"
  Mon, May 26, '97
"h:mm a"
  1:35 PM
"hh 'o''''clock' a, zzzz"
  01 o'clock PM, Pacific Daylight Time
"K:mm a, z"
  1:35 PM, PDT
```

```
"yyyyy.MMMMM.dd GGG hh:mm aaa"
 1997.May.26 AD 01:35 PM
```

 For other date and time classes, see **Calendar**, **GregorianCalendar**, **TimeZone**, **DateFormat**, and **DateFormatSymbols**.

SimpleTimeZone

class java.util.SimpleTimeZone

This is a representation of the time zone for use with a modern Gregorian calendar.

Simplicity

This class does not handle historical changes. It is a set of simple operations intended to be used for practical modern-day operations.

Inheritance

```
public class java.util.SimpleTimeZone
    extends TimeZone
        ⇑
    public abstract class java.util.TimeZone
        implements Serializable
        implements Cloneable
        extends Object
            ⇑
        public class java.lang.Object
```

Constructors

```
public SimpleTimeZone(int rawOffset,String ID)

public SimpleTimeZone(int rawOffset,String ID,
        int startMonth,int startDayOfWeekInMonth,
        int startDayOfWeek,int startTime,
        int endMonth,int endDayOfWeekInMonth,
        int endDayOfWeek,int endTime)
```

The rawOffset is the hour-count from the base UT (GMT). The ID is a time zone name as returned from TimeZone.getAvailableID(). To create a SimpleTimeZone for your default time zone, use TimeZone.getDefault() for the ID.

The simpler form of the constructor should be used for a SimpleTimeZone that does not use daylight savings time. All of the other arguments have to do with daylight savings time. The startMonth is a number from 0 through 11 (with 0 representing January) indicating the starting month of daylight savings time.

The startDayOfWeek is a value from 0 through 6, with 0 representing Sunday, that specifies which day of the week daylight savings time starts. The startDayOfWeekInMonth is a number specifying the count from the beginning (or ending) of the month of the start of daylight savings time—a negative value indicates that the count should be from the end of the month. For example, if the startDayOfWeek is 0 indicating Sunday, a startDayOfWeekInMonth of −1 would indicate the last Sunday of the month—a startDayOfWeekInMonth of 2 would indicate the second Sunday of the month. The startTime is the starting time—it is a count of the number of milliseconds since midnight.

The arguments that begin with end contain the same sort of values as the ones that begin with start—collectively, they mark the end of daylight savings time.

Methods

clone()

```
public Object clone()
```

Returns a duplicate of this object.

equals()

```
public boolean equals(Object object)
```

Returns true if object is a SimpleTimeZone that represents the same time zone as this one.

getOffset()

```
public int getOffset(int era,int year,int month,
          int day,int dayOfWeek,int millis)
```

Returns the offset from UT for the specified date. The offset will be adjusted for daylight savings time. The returned value is a positive or negative number that should be added to the UT value to get the local time, or subtracted from the local time to get the UT value.

The era is either GegorianCalendar.AD or GregorianCalendar.BC. The year is the full four-digit year number. The month is a number from 0 to 11. The day is the day of the month. The dayOfWeek is a number from 0 through 6, with 0 being Sunday. The milliseconds argument is the number of milliseconds since midnight.

getRawOffset()

```
public int getRawOffset()
```

Returns the offset of this `TimeZone` from UT without consideration for daylight savings time. The returned value is a positive or negative number that should be added to the UT value to get the local time, or subtracted from the local time to get UT value.

hashCode()

```
public synchronized int hashCode()
```

Returns the hashcode value for this object.

inDaylightTime()

```
public boolean inDaylightTime(Date date)
```

Returns `true` if the `date` is in daylight savings time in this `TimeZone`.

setEndRule()

```
public void setEndRule(int month,int dayOfWeekInMonth,
        int dayOfWeek,int time)
```

Sets the rule for ending daylight savings time. See the description of the constructor arguments.

setRawOffset()

```
public void setRawOffset(int offsetMillis)
```

Changes the time zone offset from UT to the value specified as `offsetMillis`. The value is a positive or negative number that should be added to the UT value to get the local time, or subtracted from the local time to get the UT value.

setStartRule()

```
public void setStartRule(int month,int dayOfWeekInMonth,
        int dayOfWeek,int time)
```

Sets the rule for starting daylight savings time. See the description of the constructor arguments.

setStartYear()

```
public void setStartYear(int year)
```

Sets the year that daylight savings time was started in this time zone.

useDaylightTime()

```
public boolean useDaylightTime()
```

Returns `true` if this `SimpleTimeZone` is set up to use daylight savings time.

 Also see **Calendar**, **GregorianCalendar**, and **TimeZone**.

single quote

/

The single quote is used to declare character literals (character constants).

For declaration of character constants, see **char** and **Unicode**.

Skeleton

interface java.rmi.server.Skeleton

Every skeleton class generated by the `rmic` stub compiler implements this interface. A skeleton class is a server-side entity that receives method-call information from a remote invocation and invokes the actual method—it then returns the result of the invocation.

Inheritance

```
public interface java.rmi.server.Skeleton
```

Methods

dispatch()

```
public abstract void dispatch(Remote obj,
        RemoteCall theCall,int opnum,long hash)
    throws Exception
```

This method will unmarshal the arguments in the RemoteCall and call the actual method of the Remote object. It then will marshal the return value (or Exception) and return it to the remote caller. The Exception is thrown if a general exception occurs—not if an exception occurs in the call to the method.

getOperations()

```
public abstract Operation[] getOperations()
```

Returns an array of Operation objects representing the methods of the object represented by this Skeleton.

For a general description, see **RMI**. Also see **Operation, RemoteCall, RemoteObject, RemoteRef, RemoteServer, RemoteStub,** and **ServerRef**.

SkeletonMismatchException

class java.rmi.server.SkeletonMismatchException

This exception is thrown when a call is received that does not match the skeleton. This can happen when a method name/signature has been changed in either the stub or the skeleton, but not in both. That is, it happens when the stub and the skeleton were generated by `rmic` from different versions of the classes.

Inheritance

```
public class java.rmi.server.SkeletonMismatchException
    extends RemoteException
        ⇑
    public class java.rmi.RemoteException
    extends IOException
        ⇑
    public class java.io.IOException
        extends Exception
            ⇑
        public class java.lang.Exception
            extends Throwable
                ⇑
            public class java.lang.Throwable
                implements Serializable
                extends Object
                    ⇑
                public class java.lang.Object
```

Constructors

```
public SkeletonMismatchException(String message)
```

The `message` string is supplied as a detailed message describing this particular exception.

SkeletonNotFoundException

class java.rmi.server.SkeletonNotFoundException

This exception is thrown to indicate that there is no skeleton on the server to match the stub on the client that is making a remote method invocation.

Inheritance

```
public class java.rmi.server.SkeletonNotFoundException
    extends RemoteException
        ⇑
    public class java.rmi.RemoteException
        extends IOException
            ⇑
        public class java.io.IOException
            extends Exception
                ⇑
            public class java.lang.Exception
                extends Throwable
                    ⇑
                public class java.lang.Throwable
                    implements Serializable
                    extends Object
                        ⇑
                    public class java.lang.Object
```

Constructors

```
public SkeletonNotFoundException(String message)
```

```
public SkeletonNotFoundException(String message,
        Exception exception)
```

The message string is supplied as a detailed message describing this particular exception. Optionally, an exception can be included as a further description.

Socket

class java.net.Socket

This class implements client sockets. *A client socket* binds itself to a local port and uses it to connect and communicate with a server socket on a remote host. The client socket and the server socket then act as the two end points of a communications link.

The factory and the firewall

The actual work of the socket is performed by a SocketImpl object. A SocketImpl object is created by a SocketImplFactory. The SocketImplFactory can be set by the application to create sockets that know how to deal with the local firewall.

SO_TIMEOUT

The SO_TIMEOUT value is the number of milliseconds a call to read() on the socket input stream will block while waiting for data. A value of zero disables the timer and will cause read() to block forever. If the timeout expires, an InterruptedIOException is thrown. The value of SO_TIMEOUT must be set before a call is made to read().

Inheritance

```
public class java.net.Socket
    extends Object
        ⇑
    public class java.lang.Object
```

Constructors

```
protected Socket()

protected Socket(SocketImpl impl)
    throws SocketException

public Socket(String host,int port)
    throws UnknownHostException
    throws IOException

public Socket(InetAddress address,int port)
    throws IOException

public Socket(String host,int port,
        InetAddress localAddr,int localPort)
    throws IOException

public Socket(InetAddress address,int port,
        InetAddress localAddr,int localPort)
    throws IOException

public Socket(String host,int port,boolean stream)
    throws IOException  *** deprecated ****

public Socket(InetAddress host,int port,boolean stream)
    throws IOException  *** deprecated ****
```

If the SocketImpl is not specified, a Socket is created with the default SocketImpl. The new Socket will be connected to a remote server if it is specified (either by host and port or by address and port). The localAddr and localPort can be used to specify which IP address and port number will be used locally to bind the socket (the localAddr address may be needed for hosts that have more than one IP address).

The forms that use the `stream` argument to create a UDP connection are deprecated—use `DatagramSocket` instead.

If the application has specified a `SocketImplFactory` to create sockets to operate with a firewall or proxy server, the factory will be used to create the actual socket. If not, the default will be used to create a plain socket.

Returned by

A Socket object is returned from `RMISocketFactory.createSocket()` and `ServerSocket.accept()`.

Methods

close()

```
public synchronized void close()
    throws IOException
```

Closes the socket.

getInetAddress()

```
public InetAddress getInetAddress()
```

Returns the address of the connection on the remote host.

getInputStream()

```
public InputStream getInputStream()
    throws IOException
```

Returns an input stream that can be used to read from this socket.

getLocalAddress()

```
public InetAddress getLocalAddress()
```

Returns the local address to which this socket is bound.

getLocalPort()

```
public int getLocalPort()
```

Returns the local port number to which this socket is bound.

getOutputStream()

```
public OutputStream getOutputStream()
    throws IOException
```

Returns an output stream that can be used to write to this socket.

getPort()

```
public int getPort()
```

Returns the port number of the remote host.

getSoLinger()

```
public int getSoLinger()
    throws SocketException
```

Returns the setting of the value SO_LINGER. A return of −1 indicates that the option is disabled.

getSoTimeout()

```
public synchronized int getSoTimeout()
    throws SocketException
```

Returns the setting for SO_TIMEOUT. A return of 0 indicates that there is no timeout—that is, the timeout is infinite.

getTcpNoDelay()

```
public boolean getTcpNoDelay()
    throws SocketException
```

Returns true if TCP_NDELAY is enabled.

setSocketImplFactory()

```
public static synchronized void setSocketImplFactory(
        SocketImplFactory factory)
    throws IOException
```

Specifies the socket factory for this application. This method can only be called once. A SocketException will be thrown if the factory has already been defined.

setSoLinger()

```
public void setSoLinger(boolean setting,int value)
    throws SocketException
```

If setting is true, SO_LINGER is enabled and set to the time specified by value. If setting is false, SO_LINGER is disabled.

setSoTimeout()

```
public synchronized void setSoTimeout(int timeout)
    throws SocketException
```

Sets the SO_TIMEOUT value to a specified number of milliseconds—a value of zero disables the timer and effectively sets it to infinity.

setTcpNoDelay()

```
public void setTcpNoDelay(boolean setting)
    throws SocketException
```

If the setting is true, TCP_NODELAY will be set (that is, Nagles's algorithm will be enabled). If setting is false, it will be disabled.

toString()

```
public String toString()
```

Returns a string that contains a description of this socket.

 For a server socket, see **ServerSocket**. For an abstract class that can be extended to implement special sockets, see **SocketImpl**. For a UDP socket, see **DatagramSocket** and **DatagramSocketImpl**.

SocketException

class java.net.SocketException

This exception is thrown to indicate a protocol error, such as a TCP error.

Extended by

```
BindException
ConnectException
NoRouteToHostException
```

Inheritance

```
public class java.net.SocketException
    extends IOException
        ⇑
    public class java.io.IOException
        extends Exception
            ⇑
        public class java.lang.Exception
            extends Throwable
                ⇑
            public class java.lang.Throwable
                implements Serializable
                extends Object
                    ⇑
                public class java.lang.Object
```

Constructors

```
public SocketException()
public SocketException(String message)
```

If the `message` string is supplied, it is used as a detailed message describing this particular exception.

SocketImpl

class java.net.SocketImpl

This is the superclass of all classes that implement a socket. This is used to implement both client and server sockets. A client socket is one that requests connections over the Internet—a server socket is one that waits for connection requests. The methods defined here are for simple sockets that do not go through a firewall or proxy server.

Inheritance

```
public abstract class java.net.SocketImpl
    implements SocketOptions
    extends Object
            ⇑
    public class java.lang.Object
```

Variables and constants

address

```
protected InetAddress address
```

The IP address of the remote end of this socket.

fd

```
protected FileDescriptor fd
```

The file descriptor object for this socket.

localport

```
protected int localport
```

The local port number to which this socket is connected.

port

```
protected int port
```

The port number on the remote host to which this socket is connected.

Constructors

```
public SocketImpl()
```

Returned by

An object of this class is returned from SocketImplFactory.createSocketImpl().

Methods

accept()

```
protected abstract void accept(SocketImpl socket)
        throws IOException
```

Accepts a connection to socket.

available()

```
protected abstract int available()
        throws IOException
```

Returns the number of bytes that can be read from the socket without blocking.

bind()

```
protected abstract void bind(InetAddress host,int port)
        throws IOException
```

Binds this socket to the specified host and port.

close()

```
protected abstract void close()
        throws IOException
```

Closes the socket.

connect()

```
protected abstract void connect(String host,int port)
        throws IOException
```

```
protected abstract void connect(InetAddress address,
            int port)
        throws IOException
```

Connects this socket to the specified remote host and port.

create()

```
protected abstract void create(boolean stream)
    throws IOException
```

Creates either a stream socket (if stream is true) or a datagram socket (if stream is false).

getFileDescriptor()

```
protected FileDescriptor getFileDescriptor()
```

Returns the file descriptor (the fd field) of this socket.

getInetAddress()

```
protected InetAddress getInetAddress()
```

Returns the address of the remote host.

getInputStream()

```
protected abstract InputStream getInputStream()
    throws IOException
```

Returns an input stream that can be used to read from this socket.

getLocalPort()

```
protected int getLocalPort()
```

Returns the local port number of this socket.

getOutputStream()

```
protected abstract OutputStream getOutputStream()
    throws IOException
```

Returns an output stream that can be used to write to this socket.

getPort()

```
protected int getPort()
```

Returns the port number of the remote host.

listen()

```
protected abstract void listen(int queueSize)
    throws IOException
```

Sets the maximum queue size for incoming connection requests to queueSize. If a remote host makes a connection request while the queue is full, the connection request will be refused.

toString()

```
public String toString()
```

Returns a string that includes the local and remote host and port numbers.

 Also see **SocketImplFactory**. For a client socket, see **Socket**. For a server socket, see **ServerSocket**. For a UDP socket, see **DatagramSocket** and **DatagramSocketImpl**.

SocketImplFactory

interface java.net.SocketImplFactory

This interface is the definition of a factory that produces socket objects.

Inheritance

```
public interface java.net.SocketImplFactory
```

Methods

createSocketImpl()

```
public abstract SocketImpl createSocketImpl()
```

Creates and returns a new SocketImpl object.

 This interface is used by **Socket** and **ServerSocket**. For a UDP socket, see **DatagramSocket** and **DatagramSocketImpl**.

SocketSecurityException

class java.rmi.server.SocketSecurityException

Inheritance

```
public class java.rmi.server.SocketSecurityException
    extends ExportException
        ⇑
    public class java.rmi.server.ExportException
        extends RemoteException
            ⇑
        public class java.rmi.RemoteException
```

```
extends IOException
        ⇑
public class java.io.IOException
    extends Exception
            ⇑
    public class java.lang.Exception
        extends Throwable
                ⇑
        public class java.lang.Throwable
            implements Serializable
            extends Object
                    ⇑
            public class java.lang.Object
```

Constructors

```
public SocketSecurityException(String message)

public SocketSecurityException(String message,
        Exception ex)
```

The message string is supplied as a detailed message describing this particular exception. An optional Exception can be included as a further explanation of why this one was thrown.

source

See **compilation unit**.

sql

package java.sql

Interfaces

```
CallableStatement
Connection
DatabaseMetaData
Driver
PreparedStatement
ResultSet
ResultSetMetaData
Statement
```

Classes

```
Date
DriverManager
DriverPropertyInfo
Time
Timestamp
Types
```

Exceptions

```
DataTruncation
SQLException
SQLWarning
```

SQLException

class java.sql.SQLException

An exception of this class is thrown on a database access error. Several pieces of information are supplied with the exception.

Description

The string describing the error is used as the Java exception error message. It is available with a call to getMessage().

The SQL state

There is a string format defined by the XOPEN SQL state conventions to describe the reason for an exception in terms of the SQL status. The meanings of strings of this format are defined in the XOPEN SQL specification.

An error code

Unless an exceptional situation arises, this will be the error code value from the underlying database.

The next exception

This may not be the only exception pending. If not, all other SQL exceptions are in a chain linked below this one. Depending on the circumstances, one exception may be more informative of the situation than another.

Extended by

```
SQLWarning
```

Inheritance

```
public class java.sql.SQLException
    extends Exception
        ⇑
    public class java.lang.Exception
        extends Throwable
            ⇑
        public class java.lang.Throwable
            implements Serializable
            extends Object
                    ⇑
            public class java.lang.Object
```

Constructors

```
public SQLException()

public SQLException(String message)

public SQLException(String message,String SQLState)

public SQLException(String message,String SQLState,
        int vendorCode)
```

The `message` is a description of the reason for the exception. The default `message` is `null`. The `SQLState` is the XOPEN-style string specifying the SQL error. The default `SQLState` is `null`. The `vendorCode` is the error code number from the underlying database. The default `vendorCode` is zero.

Returned by

An `SQLException` object is returned from `getNextException()`.

Methods

getErrorCode()

```
public int getErrorCode()
```

Returns the error code from the underlying database.

getNextException()

```
public SQLException getNextException()
```

Returns the next `SQLException`—returns `null` if there are none.

getSQLState()

```
public String getSQLState()
```

Returns the XOPEN-style description of the error.

setNextException()

```
public synchronized void
          setNextException(SQLException exception)
```

Chains exception as the last one in the list.

 Also see **SQLWarning**.

SQLWarning

class java.sql.SQLWarning

Objects of this class are used to report database access warnings. Warnings are silently chained to the object whose method caused the warning to be generated.

Extended by

```
DataTruncation
```

Inheritance

```
public class java.sql.SQLWarning
    extends SQLException
        ⇑
    public class java.sql.SQLException
        extends Exception
            ⇑
        public class java.lang.Exception
            extends Throwable
                ⇑
            public class java.lang.Throwable
                implements Serializable
                extends Object
                    ⇑
                public class java.lang.Object
```

Constructors

```
public SQLWarning()

public SQLWarning(String message)

public SQLWarning(String message,String SQLState)

public SQLWarning(String message,String SQLState,
            int vendorCode)
```

The message is a description of the reason for the exception. The default message is null. The SQLState is the XOPEN-style string specifying the SQL error. The default SQLState is null. The vendorCode is the error code number from the underlying database. The default vendorCode is zero.

Returned by

An SQLWarning object is returned from Connection.getWarnings(), ResultSet.getWarnings(), SQLWarning.getNextWarning(), and Statement.getWarnings().

Methods

getNextWarning()

```
public SQLWarning getNextWarning()
```

Returns the next SQLWarning chained to this one. If there is none, the return is null.

setNextWarning()

```
public void setNextWarning(SQLWarning warning)
```

Chains warning as the last one in the list.

 For more details on the contents, see **SQLException**.

Stack

class java.util.Stack

An object of this class will maintain a stack of objects. It is a LIFO object container—last in, first out. Any object can be pushed onto the stack, including the null object.

Inheritance

```
public class java.util.Stack
```

```
extends Vector
       ⇑
public class java.util.Vector
      implements Cloneable
      implements Serializable
      extends Object
                ⇑
      public class java.lang.Object
```

Constructors

```
public Stack()
```

Methods

empty()

```
public boolean empty()
```

Returns `true` if the stack is empty.

peek()

```
public synchronized Object peek()
```

Returns a reference to the object on top of the stack but leaves the contents of the stack undisturbed. If the stack is empty, an `EmptyStackException` is thrown.

pop()

```
public synchronized Object pop()
```

Removes the top element from the stack and returns it. If the stack is empty, an `EmptyStackException` is thrown.

push()

```
public Object push(Object element)
```

Pushes the `element` on the stack.

search()

```
public synchronized int search(Object element)
```

If the specified element is on the stack, its distance from the stop of the stack is returned (the top being zero). If the element is not on the stack, −1 is returned.

For other classes that can contain references, see **Hashtable** and **Vector.**

StackOverflowError

class java.lang.StackOverflowError

This error is thrown by the Virtual Machine when the stack space has been exhausted. This can happen if an application has a recursive method that runs away.

Inheritance

```
public class java.lang.StackOverflowError
    extends VirtualMachineError
    ⇑
    public class java.lang.VirtualMachineError
        extends Error
        ⇑
        public class java.lang.Error
            extends Throwable
            ⇑
            public class java.lang.Throwable
                implements Serializable
                extends Object
                ⇑
                public class java.lang.Object
```

Constructors

```
public StackOverflowError()

public StackOverflowError(String message)
```

If the message string is supplied, it is used as a detailed message describing this particular exception.

Statement

interface java.sql.Statement

A Statement object is used to execute an SQL statement and retrieve the results it produces from a database.

The result set

At any one time, there can only be one ResultSet open for a Statement. This means that if the retrieval of one ResultSet is interleaved with the retrieval of another, the two must be produced from different Statements. Calling one of the methods to execute a Statement will cause an open ResultSet to be closed.

The exception

Every method of this interface is defined as being capable of throwing an SQLException. This means it will be necessary to call the methods of this class inside a try-catch block.

Extended by

PreparedStatement

Inheritance

public interface java.sql.Statement

Constructors

Returned by

An object that implements this interface is returned from Connection.createStatement().

Methods

cancel()

```
public abstract void cancel()
    throws SQLException
```

Cancels the execution of the current statement. The execution methods themselves block until completed, so it would be necessary to call this method from another thread.

clearWarnings()

```
public abstract void clearWarnings()
    throws SQLException
```

Deletes the entire chain of warnings that are being held. Once this call is made, a call to getWarnings() will return null until another warning is reported for this Statement.

close()

```
public abstract void close()
    throws SQLException
```

Closes the Statement and releases its resources. It is not strictly necessary to call this method because the close will happen automatically during garbage collection, but it may be advisable to release system resources as soon as possible.

execute()

```
public abstract boolean execute(String sql)
    throws SQLException
```

Executes an SQL statement that could return multiple results. This would be the method of choice for executing an unknown SQL string. This method, used in conjunction with `getMoreResults()`, `getResultSet()`, and `getUpdateCount()`, enables the retrieval of multiple results. This method returns `true` if the result from the execution is a `ResultSet`, and `false` if it is either an updated count or no result was returned.

executeQuery()

```
public abstract ResultSet executeQuery(String sql)
    throws SQLException
```

Executes an SQL statement that returns a single `ResultSet`. The `ResultSet` returns the data produced by the query.

executeUpdate()

```
public abstract int executeUpdate(String sql)
    throws SQLException
```

Executes SQL statements that do not return data. For example, this could be used to execute an INSERT, UPDATE, or DELETE statement.

getMaxFieldSize()

```
public abstract int getMaxFieldSize()
    throws SQLException
```

Returns the maximum number of bytes that can be consumed by any column that has the data type BINARY, VARBINARY, LOGVARBINARY, CHAR, VARCHAR, or LOGVARCHAR. If data of one of these types exceeds this limit, it will be quietly truncated. A return value of zero means there is no limit.

getMaxRows()

```
public abstract int getMaxRows()
    throws SQLException
```

Returns a count of the maximum number of rows that can be contained in a `ResultSet`. If the limit is exceeded, the excess rows are quietly dropped. A return value of zero means there is no limit.

getMoreResults()

```
public abstract boolean getMoreResults()
    throws SQLException
```

Moves the internal result-cursor to the next result from the execution of an SQL statement. A return value of `true` indicates that the result is a `ResultSet`. A return of `false` means either that there are no more results or that the result is an update count (a call can be made to `getUpateCount()` to determine which). A call to this method will close a `ResultSet` from this statement that may be open.

getQueryTimeout()

```
public abstract int getQueryTimeout()
    throws SQLException
```

Returns the number of seconds the driver will wait for a `Statement` to execute. A return value of zero means there is no timeout. If this timeout limit is exceeded by one of the execute methods, an `SQLException` will be thrown.

getResultSet()

```
public abstract ResultSet getResultSet()
    throws SQLException
```

Returns the current result as a `ResultSet`. It can be called only once for each result. The return value will be `null` if there is no result, or if the result is an update count that can be returned by `getUpdateCount()`.

getUpdateCount()

```
public abstract int getUpdateCount()
    throws SQLException
```

Returns the current result in the form of an update count. If there is no result, or if the result is a `ResultSet`, −1 is returned. This method can only be called once for each result.

getWarnings()

```
public abstract SQLWarning getWarnings()
    throws SQLException
```

Returns the head of a link-list of warnings that were reported to this `Statement`. All subsequent warnings will be linked to this one—the oldest one remains at the head of the chain. The warnings posted because of processing a `ResultSet` will appear here. The entire chain is deleted each time a statement is executed.

setCursorName()

```
public abstract void setCursorName(String name)
    throws SQLException
```

Defines the name of the SQL cursor that will be used in the execution of this `Statement`. Once defined, the name can subsequently be used by another `Statement` to position the cursor for update and delete, and to identify the result-row in the `ResultSet`. If the database does not support updates or deletes, this method does nothing. Cursor names must be unique within a `Connection`.

There must be two `Statement` objects used in update and delete operations. One is used to position the cursor, and the other, to perform the action. This is necessary because of the one-to-one relationship between a `Statement` and a `ResultSet`.

setEscapeProcessing()

```
public abstract void setEscapeProcessing(boolean setting)
    throws SQLException
```

Turns escape processing on or off—by default, it is on. If it is on, the driver will perform escape substitution before sending SQL commands to the database.

setMaxFieldSize()

```
public abstract void setMaxFieldSize(int max)
    throws SQLException
```

Specifies the maximum number of bytes that can be included in any column that has the data type BINARY, VARBINARY, LOGVARBINARY, CHAR, VARCHAR, or LOGVARCHAR. If of one of these types exceeds this limit it will be quietly truncated. A value of zero means there is no limit.

setMaxRows()

```
public abstract void setMaxRows(int max)
    throws SQLException
```

Specifies the maximum number of rows that can be contained in a `ResultSet`. If the limit is exceeded, the excess rows are quietly dropped. A setting of zero means there is no limit.

setQueryTimeout()

```
public abstract void setQueryTimeout(int seconds)
    throws SQLException
```

Specifies the number of seconds that the driver is to wait for a `Statement` to execute. A setting of zero means there is no timeout. If this timeout limit is exceeded by one of the execute methods, an `SQLException` will be thrown.

For a method of executing precompiled SQL statements, see **PreparedStatement**.

static

Two things can be declared static in Java — methods and fields.

A static field

This is also called a *static variable* or a *class variable*. There will never be more than one copy of a static field. A nonstatic field is duplicated once for every object, but a static field remains the property of the class, and every object referring to the field refers to the same value. It is not possible to include a static declaration of a variable inside a method — even if the method itself is static.

A static method

A static method is like a static field — it is a part of the class, not an object. A static method can only refer to other static entities of the class (static fields or other static methods). A nonstatic method can use `this` to refer to the current object — a static method does not have a `this` reference. A static method can be called even if there are no instances of the object, because it never refers to an object (unless one is explicitly passed to it).

Example 1

This example demonstrates that there is only one copy of a static variable. The static variable `colorName` is defined in the class `ColorName`. Two classes, `BlueName` and `RedName`, inherit the field because they both extend the class `ColorName`. What they really inherit is the ability to address the same field:

```
public class StaticColorName extends ColorName {
    public static void main(String[] arg) {
        System.out.println(colorName);
        BlueName bn = new BlueName();
        bn.doBlue();
        System.out.println(colorName);
        RedName rn = new RedName();
        rn.doRed();
        System.out.println(colorName);
    }
}

class ColorName {
    public static String colorName = "SCN: ";
}

class BlueName extends ColorName {
    public void doBlue() {
        ColorName cn = new ColorName();
```

```
                colorName += "Blue ";
          }
    }

    class RedName extends ColorName {
          public void doRed() {
                ColorName cn = new ColorName();
                colorName += "Red ";
          }
    }
```

The class StaticColorName also extends ColorName, so it has access to the same field. Here is the output from the program:

```
SCN:
SCN: Blue
SCN: Blue Red
```

Each of these lines is output from StaticColorName, and as you can see, each object modifies the same field value.

Example 2

This example demonstrates that static variables can be accessed from static and nonstatic methods:

```
public class StaticShare {
    static int counter;
    String name;
    int myCounter;
    public static void main(String[] arg) {
        System.out.println("Starting counter: " +
                StaticShare.getCounter());
        StaticShare s1 = new StaticShare("red");
        StaticShare s2 = new StaticShare("white");
        StaticShare s3 = new StaticShare("blue");
        System.out.println(s1);
        System.out.println(s2);
        System.out.println(s3);
        System.out.println("Ending counter: " +
                StaticShare.getCounter());
    }
    public StaticShare(String name) {
        this.name = name;
        myCounter = ++counter;
    }
```

```
public String toString() {
    return("The name " + name +
            " has the value " + myCounter);
}
public static int getCounter() {
    return(counter);
}
}
```

The counter is incremented whenever a new object is created, and the value is copied into the local variable myCounter as a sort of unique ID number for each one. The static method getCounter() can be called by using the name of the class (being static, it is not associated with any object), and because the counter is also static, it is able to return the value that will be used by the next instantiation of an object. This is done before any objects are created and again after several objects have been created. The output looks like this:

```
Starting counter: 0
The name red has the value 1
The name white has the value 2
The name blue has the value 3
Ending counter: 3
```

 Also see **static initializers**.

static initializers

There is one place for executable code in Java other than inside a method—inside a *static initializer*. This is a block of code used to set the initial value of a static field.

No exceptions

A static initializer block cannot throw checked exceptions. This cannot be done directly or indirectly (by calling a method that throws an exception). Although a static initializer cannot throw an exception, it can catch one—it is valid to include a try-catch block inside the static initializer.

An unreliable combination

Because static initializer code can instantiate objects and call methods, it is possible to write a program such that the initialization of class A could require that class B be initialized, and class B could, in turn, depend on class A. This cannot be reliably detected by the compiler (because A and B could be compiled separately), so when this happens, some of the variables may simply not be initialized.

Example

This example initializes an array such that each member of the array is the sum of the previous two (this is known as the Fibonacci sequence):

```
public class StaticInit {
    private static int[] fibo = new int[10];
    private static int fiboTotal;
    static {
        fibo[0] = 0;
        fibo[1] = 1;
        for(int i=2; i<10; i++)
            fibo[i] = fibo[i-1] + fibo[i-2];
        fiboTotal = fiboSum();
    }
    public static void main(String[] arg) {
        for(int i=0; i<10; i++)
            System.out.print(fibo[i] + " ");
        System.out.println();
        System.out.println("Total: " + fiboTotal);
    }
    private static int fiboSum() {
        int sum = 0;
        for(int j=0; j<10; j++)
            sum += fibo[j];
        return(sum);
    }
}
```

The static variables fibo and fiboTotal are both initialized in the same static initializer block. First, the array is initialized in a loop, and then the static method fiboSum() is called to return the sum of the values. The output looks like this:

```
0 1 1 2 3 5 8 13 21 34
Total: 88
```

 Also see **static**.

StreamCorruptedException

class java.io.StreamCorruptedException

Thrown when control information read from an object stream violates internal consistency checks.

Inheritance

```
public class java.io.StreamCorruptedException
    extends ObjectStreamException
        ⇑
    public class java.io.ObjectStreamException
        extends IOException
            ⇑
        public class java.io.IOException
            extends Exception
                ⇑
            public class java.lang.Exception
                extends Throwable
                    ⇑
                public class java.lang.Throwable
                    implements Serializable
                    extends Object
                        ⇑
                    public class java.lang.Object
```

Constructors

```
public StreamCorruptedException()
public StreamCorruptedException(String message)
```

If the message string is supplied, it is used as a detailed message describing this particular exception.

StreamTokenizer

class java.io.StreamTokenizer

This will read an input stream and perform a lexical scan—that is, it will break it up into a stream of input tokens that are returned one at a time. The tokenization is controlled by a table and a group of control flags. It has the ability to recognize identifiers, numbers, quoted strings, and various forms of comments.

Input characters

The input characters are limited to the extended ASCII character set—that is, the Unicode values '\u0000' through '\u00FF'. Any incoming character can have more than one of the following attributes: white space, alphabetic, numeric, string quote, and comment character.

Flag controls

Flag settings control whether or not line separators are to be returned as tokens, whether C-style comments should be recognized and skipped, whether C++-style comments should be skipped, and whether there is automatic conversion of identifiers to lowercase.

Default character categories

These are the default settings for placing characters into categories:

- The char values 'A' through 'Z', 'a' through 'z', and '\u00A0 through '\u00FF' are alphabetic.
- The char values '\u0000' through '\u0020' are white space.
- The '/' character is a comment.
- Both the single-quote and double-quote characters are string-quote characters.
- Numeric strings are parsed and have their values placed in nval.
- The ends of lines are ignored—they are treated as white space.
- There is no recognition of C- or C++- style comments.

Inheritance

```
public class java.io.StreamTokenizer
    extends Object
        ⇑
    public class java.lang.Object
```

Variables and constants

nval

```
public double nval
```

If the current token is numeric—indicated by ttype being set to TT_NUMBER—its value will be found in nval.

sval

```
public String sval
```

If the current token is a word—indicated by ttype being set to TT_WORD—the character string of the word will be found in sval. Also, if the input token is a quoted string—indicated by ttype containing a quote character—the body of the string will be found in sval.

TT_EOF

```
public final static int TT_EOF
```

Indicates that the end of the input stream has been reached.

TT_EOL

```
public final static int TT_EOL
```

Indicates that the end of the line has been reached.

TT_NUMBER

```
public final static int TT_NUMBER
```

Indicates that the current token is some kind of numeric value.

TT_WORD()

```
public final static int TT_WORD
```

Indicates that the current token is a word.

ttype

```
public int ttype
```

Following a call to nextToken(), ttype is set to the token type.

If the token is a single character, the character itself is the value of ttype. For a quoted string, ttype holds a quote character and the string itself is placed in sval. If the token is a word, the value TT_WORD is in ttype and the word is in sval. If the token is a number, its numeric value is in nval and ttype is set to TT_NUMBER. The value TT_EOL is in ttype if eolIsSignificant(true) has been called and the end of a line has been reached. Finally, ttype is set to TT_EOF when the end of the input stream has been reached.

Constructors

```
public StreamTokenizer(Reader reader)
public StreamTokenizer(InputStream is)                    deprecated
```

A tokenizer is constructed to use the specified input stream.

 StreamTokenizer(InputStream is) is a deprecated constructor because creating a tokenizer this way does not properly convert bytes into characters. The preferred way to set up an input token stream is to use a Reader, as shown in Example 1.

Methods

commentChar()

```
public void commentChar(int character)
```

Defines the comment character to be character. The tokenizer will ignore all characters from this one to the end of the line it is on.

eolIsSignificant()

```
public void eolIsSignificant(boolean setting)
```

Sets the flag that determines whether or not the end of line should be returned as a token. If this flag is set to `true`, `nextToken()` will, when encountering the end of a line, set `ttype` to `TT_EOL` and return without reading any more characters from the input stream. If the flag is set to `false`, line endings are ignored and treated as white space.

The end of a line is a carriage return, a newline, or the combination of a carriage return followed by a newline.

lineno()

```
public int lineno()
```

Returns the current line number.

lowerCaseMode()

```
public void lowerCaseMode(boolean setting)
```

Sets the flag that determines whether the letters in all the word tokens should be converted to lowercase.

nextToken()

```
public int nextToken()
    throws IOException
```

Gets the next token from the input stream. Information about the token may be put into `nval` and `sval`. The token type is set in `ttype` and returned.

ordinaryChar()

```
public void ordinaryChar(int character)
```

Removes any special significance that has been assigned to a `character`. If a character has been specified—specifically or by default—as being a comment character, a word component, a string delimiter, white space, or a number character, a call to this method will remove that special characteristic. Hereafter, the tokenizer will treat the character as a single character token and set `ttype` to the character itself.

ordinaryChars()

```
public void ordinaryChars(int low,int high)
```

Removes any special significance from all characters in the inclusive range `low` through `high`. It is just as if `ordinaryChar()` had been called for each one of them.

parseNumbers()

```
public void parseNumbers()
```

Specifies that incoming number tokens should be parsed and have their value placed in nval. The digit characters '0' through '9' along with the decimal point and minus sign are the twelve characters that can be used to make up numbers that are parsed this way — they all have the numeric attribute.

pushBack()

```
public void pushBack()
```

A call to this method will cause the next call to nextToken() to return the current value of ttype and make no modifications to the other fields. It is just as if the same token were fetched from the input stream again.

quoteChar()

```
public void quoteChar(int character)
```

Specifies that matching pairs of characters are to be used as the quote characters that delimit strings. When this character is encountered, the ttype is set to the character value and sval is set to the string of characters between it and the next character. Inside this string, the standard escapes (such as '\n' and '\t') are recognized and converted to the correct Unicode character.

resetSyntax()

```
public void resetSyntax()
```

Completely clears the syntax table so that characters have no special meaning — this is like calling ordinaryChars() on the entire character set.

slashSlashComments()

```
public void slashSlashComments(boolean setting)
```

Specifies whether the C++ style of double-slash comments is recognized. If the method is called with setting as true, all characters from a pair of slash characters to the end of a line will be skipped.

slashStarComments()

```
public void slashStarComments(boolean setting)
```

Specifies whether C-style slash-asterisk comments are to be recognized. If this method is called with setting as true, all characters from a slash-asterisk pair through a matching asterisk-slash pair are discarded.

toString()

```
public String toString()
```

Returns the string form of the current token.

whitespaceChars()

```
public void whitespaceChars(int low,int high)
```

Specifies that all characters in the inclusive range `low` through `high` are white-space characters and will be used only to separate tokens in the input stream.

wordChars()

```
public void wordChars(int low,int high)
```

Specifies that all characters in the inclusive range `low` through `high` are to be considered valid to be part of a word. A *word* is a combination of a word character followed by one or more word or number characters.

 To break a `String` object into tokens, see **StringTokenizer**.

String

class java.lang.String

This class is the Java standard form of a character string.

A part of the language

This class is very much a part of the Java language. The compiler automatically converts all quoted literal strings into objects of the `String` class. It is the only class that will work with operators—the '+' and '+=' operators will both concatenate strings. Any class or primitive type will be automatically converted directly into a string form when it is an operand of one of the concatenation operators. All objects have a `toString()` method that will do the string conversion (some objects override the `toString()` method; others just use the default inherited from the `Object` class).

This object contains a constant

The value of a `String` object cannot be modified. The instantiation of an object of this class always assigns the character string values, and these cannot be changed. This is known as being *immutable*. There is another class, the `StringBuffer` class, that can be used to modify the contents of a character string. The `StringBuffer` class is, thus, a *mutable* class.

The `toString()` method

Every object in Java can be converted to a `String` object. The `Object` class has the `toString()` method that does the conversion, and every class has the ability of overriding this method to form the string in its own way. Whenever a Java object is implicitly converted to a `String`, the method `toString()` is called to do the job.

Inheritance

```
public final class java.lang.String
    implements Serializable
    extends Object
        ⇑
    public class java.lang.Object
```

Constructors

```
public String()

public String(String otherString)

public String(char charArray[])

public String(char charArray[],int offset,int count)

public String(byte asciiArray[],
        int hibyte,int offset,int count)                    deprecated

public String(byte asciiArray[],
        int hibyte)                                         deprecated

public String(byte byteArray[],int offset,int count,
        String encoding)
    throws UnsupportedEncodingException

public String(byte byteArray[],String encoding)
    throws UnsupportedEncodingException

public String(byte byteArray[],int offset,int length)

public String(byte byteArray[])

public String(StringBuffer stringBuffer)
```

If no argument is specified, a zero-length string is constructed.

If otherString is specified, a new string is constructed that contains exactly the same characters as otherString.

If charArray is specified, a String object is constructed that holds count characters beginning at charArray[offset]. If offset and count are not specified, the entire charArray is used. If the offset and count are such that the final index would be past the end of charArray, a StringIndexOutOfBoundsException is thrown.

The constructors with the asciiArray argument are deprecated because they do not use a proper method of converting eight-bit ASCII characters to Unicode. They operate by using the characters from the asciiArray as the least significant eight bits of the Unicode character and inserting eight bits of the hibyte value as the most significant. If offset and count are specified, a

`String` with `count` characters is constructed starting with `asciiArray [offset]`. A `StringIndexOutOfBoundsException` is thrown if `asciiArray` is not large enough to hold all the specified characters.

If `byteArray` is specified, a `String` is constructed from the `count` byte values beginning at byte `Array[offset]`. If `offset` and `count` are not specified, the entire `byteArray` is used. The 8-bit bytes are converted to 16-bit Unicode characters using the named `encoding` scheme. If no `encoding` scheme is named, the default encoding is used. If the named `encoding` scheme cannot be found, an `UnsupportedEncodingException` is thrown.

If `stringBuffer` is specified, a `String` object is constructed that has the same content as the `stringBuffer`.

The implied constructors

There are constructors that are built into Java. These statements are equivalent—they will all produce a string that contains the same four characters:

```
String str = "fred";

String str = new String("fred");

String str = "fr" + "ed";

String str = "fr";
str += "ed;
```

Methods

charAt()

```
public char charAt(int index)
```

Returns the character at the `index`. The first character is at index 0. A `StringIndexOutOfBoundsException` is thrown if the `index` is invalid.

compareTo()

```
public int compareTo(String anotherString)
```

The return value is positive if `anotherString` is greater than this one, negative if it is less than this one, and zero if they are identical. The comparison is done character by character on the values of the Unicode until a mismatch is found or the ends of both `Strings` are reached. If two `Strings` of different lengths, but otherwise the same, are compared, the longer `String` is considered greater.

concat()

```
public String concat(String otherString)
```

Creates a new `String` by concatenating the `otherString` characters onto the end of those of this string. If `otherString` has a length of zero, this object is returned.

copyValueOf()

```
public static String copyValueOf(char data[],
    int offset,int count)
```

```
public static String copyValueOf(char data[])
```

This method creates a new String object using count characters beginning with data[offset]. If offset and count are not specified, the entire array is used.

endsWith()

```
public boolean endsWith(String suffix)
```

Returns true if the rightmost characters of this string exactly match the entire string suffix.

equals()

```
public boolean equals(Object anObject)
```

Returns true if anObject is a String object that holds exactly the same characters as this one.

equalsIgnoreCase()

```
public boolean equalsIgnoreCase(String anotherString)
```

Returns true if anotherString has the same set of characters as this one without regard to upper- or lowercase.

getBytes()

```
public byte[] getBytes(String encoding)
    throws UnsupportedEncodingException
```

```
public byte[] getBytes()
```

```
public void getBytes(int srcBegin,int srcEnd,
    byte dst[],int dstBegin)                          deprecated
```

Converts this String into an array of bytes using the named encoding scheme. If no encoding scheme is named, the default is used. An UnsupportedEncodingException is thrown if the named encoding scheme is unknown.

The forms of this method that do not use encoding are deprecated because they do not properly convert the Unicode to byte values.

getChars()

```
public void getChars(int srcBegin,int srcEnd,
    char dst[],int dstBegin)
```

Copies characters from the string to the dst character array. The characters from index srcBegin through srcEnd-1 are copied—the total number of characters copied is srcEnd − srcBegin. The characters are copied into dst beginning at dst[dstBegin]. A StringIndexOutOfBoundsException is thrown if the indexing is invalid.

hashCode()

```
public int hashCode()
```

Returns the hashcode value for this object.

indexOf()

```
public int indexOf(int character)

public int indexOf(int character,int fromIndex)

public int indexOf(String string)

public int indexOf(String str,int fromIndex)
```

Returns the index of the first occurrence of character or string. The search starts with fromIndex—the default value of fromIndex is 0. A zero-length string is always found at the beginning of the search. The method returns −1 if the character or string is not found.

intern()

```
public String intern()
```

Returns a String object that, internally, keeps its characters in a common pool. Every call to intern() for the same String values will return the same string reference value. That is, if two strings holding the same set of characters have been interned, they will be exactly the same string. See Example 1.

lastIndexOf()

```
public int lastIndexOf(int character)

public int lastIndexOf(int character,int fromIndex)

public int lastIndexOf(String string)

public int lastIndexOf(String string,int fromIndex)
```

Returns the index of the last occurrence of the character or the string in this String. This String is searched backward beginning at fromIndex. If fromIndex is not specified, the search starts at the end of this String. A zero-length string is always found at the beginning of the search. If it is not found, the method returns −1.

length()

```
public int length()
```

Returns a count of the number of characters in this String.

regionMatches()

```
public boolean regionMatches(int thisOffset,
    String otherString,int otherOffset,int count)

public boolean regionMatches(boolean ignoreCase,
    int thisOffset,String otherString,int otherOffset,
    int length)
```

Returns `true` if the regions of this `String` beginning at `thisOffset` and the `otherString` beginning at `otherOffset` are identical for `count` characters. If `ignoreCase` is `true`, a caseless comparison is made. If there is a mismatch anywhere in the range, or if the combination of indexes and lengths is invalid for either string, `false` is returned.

replace()

```
public String replace(char oldChar,char newChar)
```

Returns a `String` that results from replacing all occurrences of `oldChar` with `newChar`. If `oldChar` does not appear in the string, this `String` is returned.

startsWith()

```
public boolean startsWith(String prefix,int offset)

public boolean startsWith(String prefix)
```

Returns `true` if an exact match of `prefix` is found in this string at the `offset`. The default value for `offset` is zero.

substring()

```
public String substring(int beginIndex)

public String substring(int beginIndex,int endIndex)
```

Returns a new `String` that is a substring of this one. The new substring starts at `beginIndex` and continues through the character at `endIndex` −1. If `endIndex` is not specified, the substring will include all characters to the end of the string. A `StringIndexOutOfBoundsException` is thrown if `beginIndex` or `endIndex` is invalid.

toCharArray()

```
public char[] toCharArray()
```

Returns the contents of this `String` as a `char` array.

toLowerCase()

```
public String toLowerCase(Locale locale)

public String toLowerCase()
```

Returns a new String with all the characters converted to lowercase. If they are specified, the method uses the rules of the locale. If the case shift causes no changes to be made, this String is returned.

toString()

```
public String toString()
```

This method returns this object.

toUpperCase()

```
public String toUpperCase(Locale locale)

public String toUpperCase()
```

Returns a new String with all the characters converted to uppercase. If they are specified, the method uses the rules of the locale. If the case shift causes no changes to be made, this String is returned.

trim()

```
public String trim()
```

Removes all white-space characters from both the beginning and the end of the String.

valueOf()

```
public static String valueOf(Object object)

public static String valueOf(char data[])

public static String valueOf(char data[],
    int offset,int count)

public static String valueOf(boolean bvalue)

public static String valueOf(char character)

public static String valueOf(int intValue)

public static String valueOf(long longValue)

public static String valueOf(float floatValue)

public static String valueOf(double doubleValue)
```

Returns a String representation of the argument.

For an object, the Object.toString method is called to construct the String. If object is null, the String "null" is returned. For the character array, a new String object is created that holds the char values. If offset and count are specified, count characters beginning with data[offset] are used. The bvalue argument will produce the String "true" or "false." If character is specified, the returned String has a length of one and contains the character. The numeric types (intValue, longValue, `floatValue`, and `doubleValue`) all have the `toString()` method of their wrappers called to make the conversion.

Example 1

Two strings that come from different places, but that have the same contents, can be interned to become the same string:

```java
public class StringIntern {
    public static void main(String[] arg) {
        String a = "bub";
        a += "ba";
        String b = "bubba";
        if(a != b)
            System.out.println("BEFORE: mismatch.");
        else
            System.out.println("BEFORE: match.");
        a = a.intern();
        b = b.intern();
        if(a != b)
            System.out.println("AFTER: mismatch.");
        else
            System.out.println("AFTER: match.");
    }
}
```

In this example, the strings a and b are identical, but they came about in different ways. A comparison of their reference values shows that they are different String objects. They are then both "interned"; that is, they both are used to instantiate new versions of themselves using the characters from the common pool. This conversion leaves only one String object with two references to it. The output looks like this:

```
BEFORE: mismatch.
AFTER: match.
```

Example 2

The string concatenation operator '+' combined with the ability to have anything (object or primitive type) converted to a string brings out a slight ambiguity. The left-to-right associativity of the operator '+' can cause it to act very differently depending on the order of evaluation. Take this example:

```java
public class StringConcat {
    public static void main(String[] arg) {
        show("\"abc\" + 1","abc" + 1);
```

```
            show("1 + \"abc\"",1 + "abc");
            show("1 + \"abc\" + 2",1 + "abc" + 2);
            show("1 + 2 + \"abc\"",1 + 2 + "abc");
            show("\"abc\" + 1 + 2","abc" + 1 + 2);
        }
        public static void show(String s1,String s2) {
            System.out.println(s1 + " = " + s2);
        }
    }
```

The `StringConcat` class shows the results of concatenating strings and integer values in different orders. The output looks like this:

```
"abc" + 1 = abc1
1 + "abc" = 1abc
1 + "abc" + 2 = 1abc2
1 + 2 + "abc" = 3abc
"abc" + 1 + 2 = abc12
```

Whenever the value on either side of a plus sign is a `String`, the value on the other side is automatically converted to a `String` and the two are concatenated together. If both sides are numeric, however, they will be arithmetically added. This causes some of the results to be order-dependent, as you can see from the varied results of the last two lines. To overcome the ambiguity, simply use parentheses to tell Java which operation should be performed first.

 Also see **StringBuffer** and **string literal**.

StringBuffer

class java.lang.StringBuffer

A `StringBuffer` contains a sequence of characters that can be altered by calling methods of the class. The internal allocation of space is adjusted automatically as string operations are performed. The principal methods of the class are the `append()` and `insert()` methods, which are overloaded to accept any Java data type.

Synchronized

This class is safe for simultaneous access from more than one thread. The methods are all synchronized to prohibit collisions.

A part of the language

Like the `String` class, this class is known to the compiler. Whenever operations, such as concatenation, are performed on literal strings or on the `String` class, the compiler will use a `StringBuffer` class to perform the actual operations for the sake of efficiency. The result of the operation, however, will always be a `String` object.

The capacity and the length

There are two sizes associated with `StringBuffer`. Its length is a count of the number of characters it contains. Its capacity is the number of characters that can be held without the `StringBuffer` having to allocate more memory.

Inheritance

```
public final class java.lang.StringBuffer
       implements Serializable
       extends Object
          ⇑
       public class java.lang.Object
```

Constructors

```
public StringBuffer()

public StringBuffer(int capacity)

public StringBuffer(String string)
```

A `StringBuffer` can be created empty, or with an initial `string`. The default capacity is 16, plus the length of the initial string, if one is specified. An initial `capacity` can be specified for the sake of efficiency. For example, if you know in advance that the longest string you will have is 80 characters, then you may want to set the initial capacity to 90 or so to avoid the necessity of requiring another allocation as the string expands. A `NegativeArraySizeException` is thrown if capacity is less than zero.

Methods

append()

```
public synchronized StringBuffer append(Object object)

public synchronized StringBuffer append(String string)

public synchronized StringBuffer append(char charArray[])

public synchronized StringBuffer append(char charArray[],
       int offset,int length)
```

```
public StringBuffer append(boolean bvalue)

public synchronized StringBuffer append(char character)

public StringBuffer append(int ivalue)

public StringBuffer append(long lvalue)

public StringBuffer append(float fvalue)

public StringBuffer append(double dvalue)
```

The argument, or arguments, here are used in a call to `String.valueOf()` to convert the argument to a character string. The resulting string is appended onto the end of character array already in the `StringBuffer`.

capacity()

```
public int capacity()
```

Returns the current capacity—the number of characters that can be contained without further memory allocation.

charAt()

```
public synchronized char charAt(int index)
```

Returns the character at the index. The first character is at index 0. The last character is at `length()` −1. If an invalid index value is specified, a `StringIndexOutOfBoundsException` is thrown.

ensureCapacity()

```
public synchronized voidensureCapacity(int minimumCapacity)
```

Ensures that the `StringBuffer` has already allocated enough capacity to hold `minimumCapacity` number of characters. A new memory allocation is made if necessary. If a new allocation is necessary, the new size will be either the `minimumCapacity` or double the old capacity plus two—whichever is greater. If `minimumCapacity` is negative, the method call is ignored.

getChars()

```
public synchronized void getChars(int srcBegin,
    int srcEnd,char dst[],int dstBegin)
```

Copies characters from the internal array to the `dst` character array beginning at `dst[dstBegin]`. The internal characters indexed form `srcBegin` through `srcEnd` −1 are copied. This means that `srcEnd` − `srcBegin` is the character count. If any index values are invalid, a `StringIndexOutOfBoundsException` is thrown.

insert()

```
public synchronized StringBuffer insert(int offset,Object obj)
public synchronized StringBuffer insert(int offset,String str)
public synchronized StringBuffer insert(int offset,char str[])
public StringBuffer insert(int offset,boolean bvalue)
public synchronized StringBuffer insert(int offset,
    char character)
public StringBuffer insert(int offset,int ivalue)
public StringBuffer insert(int offset,long lvalue)
public StringBuffer insert(int offset,float fvalue)
public StringBuffer insert(int offset,double dvalue)
```

The argument following the offset argument is used in a call to String.valueOf() to create a character string. The resulting string is inserted into the character array already in the StringBuffer. The character at offset, and any characters to its right, are shifted to the right to make room. A StringIndexOutOfBoundsException is thrown if offset is invalid.

length()

```
public int length()
```

Returns the count of the number of characters in the StringBuffer.

reverse()

```
public synchronized StringBuffer reverse()
```

Reverses the order of the characters in the internal array.

setCharAt()

```
public synchronized void setCharAt(int index,char character)
```

The character at index is replaced with character. If the index is not valid, a StringIndexOutOfBoundsException is thrown. For this to work, a character must already have been placed at this position. For example, if you have StringBuffer with a capacity of 16, but only two or three characters have actually been put into the array, an attempt to use setCharAt() with an index of 10 will result in a StringIndexOutOfBoundsException.

setLength()

```
public synchronized void setLength(int newLength)
```

If there are more than newLength characters in the array, they are removed. If there are fewer, null characters, '\u0000', are used to fill out the string to newLength.

toString()

```
public String toString()
```

Creates a `String` object that contains the characters from this `StringBuffer` and returns it.

 For the ability to separate a string into tokens, see **StringTokenizer**. For an immutable string, see **String**.

StringBufferInputStream

class java.io.StringBufferInputStream

Deprecated. This class is deprecated because it does not properly handle the conversion of characters to bytes. Use `StringReader` instead.

This class will read the bytes of an input stream of 16-bit characters and use only the least significant eight bits of each.

Inheritance

```
public class java.io.StringBufferInputStream
    extends InputStream
        ⇑
    public abstract class java.io.InputStream
        extends Object
            ⇑
        public class java.lang.Object
```

Variables and constants

buffer

```
protected String buffer
```

The `String` from which the byte values are read.

count

```
protected int count
```

The number of characters in `buffer`.

pos

```
protected int pos
```

The index of the next character in `buffer`.

Constructors

```
public StringBufferInputStream(String string)
```

The input stream will read from the string characters.

Methods

available()

```
public synchronized int available()
```

This will return the number of bytes left to be read from the input string.

read()

```
public synchronized int read()

public synchronized int read(byte barray[],
        int offset,int count)
```

If barray is specified, the byte values from barray[offset] for count bytes are placed into the array and the actual number of bytes read is returned. If no argument is specified, the next byte from the input stream is returned. Each byte value is lower eight bits of the next character — a value in the range from 0 to 255. The end of the input string is indicated by −1 being returned.

reset()

```
public synchronized void reset()
```

This returns the input pointer back to the first character of the input string.

skip()

```
public synchronized long skip(long count)
```

This will skip over count characters in the input string just as if they had been read and discarded. The return value is the number of characters skipped, which could be fewer than requested if the end of the input string is reached.

StringCharacterIterator

class java.text.StringCharacterIterator

This class can be used to read the characters from a String in forward or reverse order.

Beyond the string

When iteration has returned the last character in the requested direction, the value `DONE` is returned for the next character. This value is defined in the interface `CharacterIterator` as being '\uFFFF'.

Inheritance

```
public final class java.text.StringCharacterIterator
    implements CharacterIterator
    extends Object
        ⇑
    public class java.lang.Object
```

Constructors

```
public StringCharacterIterator(String text)

public StringCharacterIterator(String text,int index)

public StringCharacterIterator(String text,
        int begin,int end,int index)
```

A `StringCharacterIterator` is constructed for a specific string. The `index` specifies the starting position in the string. It is a zero-based index with a default value of zero. If `begin` and `end` are specified, they define the subset of the string to be used—the character at `begin` is at index zero.

Methods

clone()

```
public Object clone()
```

Creates a duplicate of this object.

current()

```
public char current()
```

Returns the character at the current index. Returns `DONE` if the current position is past the end of the text.

equals()

```
public boolean equals(Object object)
```

Returns `true` if `object` is a `StringCharacterIterator` containing the same string as this one.

first()

```
public char first()
```

Sets the index to the first character in the string and returns the character.

getBeginIndex()

```
public int getBeginIndex()
```

Returns the starting index of the text. If begin and end were not specified on the constructor, this will always be zero—otherwise, it will be the value of begin.

getEndIndex()

```
public int getEndIndex()
```

Returns the ending index of the text. If begin and end were not specified on the constructor, this will always be one less than the length of the string.

getIndex()

```
public int getIndex()
```

Returns the value of the current index.

hashCode()

```
public int hashCode()
```

Returns the hashcode value of this object.

last()

```
public char last()
```

Sets the index on the last character in the string and returns the character.

next()

```
public char next()
```

Increments the index by one and returns the character from the new location. If the results of incrementing the index would go beyond the end of the string, the increment does not take place and DONE is returned.

previous()

```
public char previous()
```

Decrements the index by one and returns the character from the new location. If the results of decrementing the index would go beyond the beginning of the string, the decrement does not take place and DONE is returned.

setIndex()

```
public char setIndex(int index)
```

Sets the internal index to `index` and returns the character at that location. An `IllegalArgumentException` is thrown if the index is out of bounds.

StringIndexOutOfBoundsException

class java.lang.StringIndexOutOfBoundsException

This is thrown by `StringBuffer` and `String` methods to indicate that an index is less than zero or beyond the last character in the string.

Inheritance

```
public class java.lang.StringIndexOutOfBoundsException
    extends IndexOutOfBoundsException
        ⇑
    public class java.lang.IndexOutOfBoundsException
        extends RuntimeException
            ⇑
        public class java.lang.RuntimeException
            extends Exception
                ⇑
            public class java.lang.Exception
                extends Throwable
                    ⇑
                public class java.lang.Throwable
                    implements Serializable
                    extends Object
                        ⇑
                    public class java.lang.Object
```

Constructors

```
public StringIndexOutOfBoundsException()

public StringIndexOutOfBoundsException(String string)

public StringIndexOutOfBoundsException(int index)
```

If the `message` string is supplied, it is used as a detailed message describing this particular exception. If the index is specified, it is the value of the invalid index being reported.

string literal

A string literal is a collection of characters surrounded with double quotes. This is a typical string literal:

```
"Hello, world"
```

You can include any character in the string except a double quote (which defines the end of the string) or a backslash (which marks the beginning of an escape sequence). To insert either of these characters into a string, use the escape sequence of a single backslash in front of it. For example, this is how to insert a double quote into a string:

```
"This quote \" is inside the string"
```

In the same way, a backslash can be inserted into a string like this:

```
"This backslash \\ is inside the string"
```

In both of these examples, the leading (leftmost) backslash will be discarded and the character following it will be included as a character in the string. There are other escape sequences, including special ASCII characters and Unicode—see **escapes**.

 The Unicode escapes '\u000a' (line feed) and '\u000d' (carriage return) should never be used inside a string literal. Use '\n' for line feed and '\r' for carriage return. The Java compiler scans the source for Unicode escape sequences and converts them to their Unicode equivalents before it breaks the input source into tokens. If either of the Unicode escapes appears in a string literal, it is the same as if the string has been split across lines—a compiler error will result.

The empty string

A string can be empty—that is, it can contain zero characters, like this:

```
""
```

There's not much information there, but this form can sometimes be handy for a placeholder. There are circumstances where a reference to a String object will require some value other than a null, so you can use the empty string.

All literals become String objects

Whenever the compiler finds a string literal in the code, it creates an object of the class String. The following code demonstrates two ways of creating a String object from a string literal:

```
String str
str = "A brand new string";
str = new String("A brand new string");
```

As far as Java is concerned, there is no fundamental difference in these two methods of creating a `String` object. Different compilers may implement the details of the code a bit differently, but in both cases, the semantics are the same.

The string literals are in a common pool

There is one extra step that is performed by the compiler on string literals—they are all "interned." In effect, this line of code is executed after the `String` object is created from a literal:

```
str = str.intern()
```

This adds the text of the string to a global pool of strings. This means there is only one copy of duplicate string literals because identical strings are shared. This is true for `String` objects constructed from literals, but not true for those constructed from other `String` objects. Take this example:

```
public class StringLiteralPool {
    public static void main(String[] arg) {
        String cat = "cat";
        String walk = "walk";
        String cw = "catwalk";
        System.out.println(cw == "catwalk");
        System.out.println(cw == "cat" + "walk");
        System.out.println(cw == "ca" + "twa" + "lk");
        System.out.println(cw == AnotherClass.cw);
        System.out.println(cw == (cat + walk));
        System.out.println(cw == ("cat" + walk).intern());
    }
}

class AnotherClass {
    static String cw = "catwalk";
}
```

The class `StringLiteralPool` produces the string "catwalk" in a number of ways. It does it by concatenating it from parts and even reading it from another class. Because the classes are both running in the same Java machine, they are subject to sharing the same pool. The output reports on the reference values being equal—not just the characters in the string. The output of a test run looked like this:

```
true
```

```
true
true
true
false
true
```

They all refer to the same pool entry except the next-to-last entry—the one that is a concatenation of two previously defined `String` objects. This is not crucial because—as you can see from the last entry in the list—it is always possible to force any string to be in the global pool by calling the method `intern()`.

Concatenation of strings

Each string literal must be completed in one line. There is no continuation character that can be used to break a string into more than one line. However, there is the concatenation operator (the plus sign) that can be used to do the same thing. Java will combine these two strings:

```
"These two parts" + " will become one."
```

into this single string:

```
"These two parts will become one."
```

Because we are dealing with a free-form language, the two halves of the original string could have been put on two separate lines like this:

```
"These two parts" +
    " will become one."
```

Of course, there is no limit to the number of string literals that can be combined this way. This would also work:

```
"These " + "parts " + "will " + "become " + "one."
```

 The strict definition of the Java language states that each of these literals will be compiled into `String` objects and then they will be concatenated together. However, a `String` object is immutable. This means once it has been created, it cannot be modified. Following this strict rule would mean that a minimum of nine `String` objects would be created—and eight of them destroyed—just to construct the results of that last example. What really happens is that the compiler does the concatenation (probably using a `StringBuffer` object as a work area) and then generates code to build a single `String` object.

 For information on escape sequences in strings, see **escapes**. For information on string concatenation, see **plus**. For information on the `String` class, see **String**.

StringReader

class java.io.StringReader

This class will read characters from a RAM-resident string.

Inheritance

```
public class java.io.StringReader
    extends Reader
        ⇑
    public class java.io.Reader
        extends Object
            ⇑
        public class java.lang.Object
```

Constructors

```
public StringReader(String string)
```

Constructs a StringReader that uses string for input.

Methods

close()

```
public void close()
```

Closes the stream.

mark()

```
public void mark(int readAheadLimit)
    throws IOException
```

Marks the current position in the stream. A call to reset() will restore the input pointer to this location. The readAheadLimit is ignored.

markSupported()

```
public boolean markSupported()
```

This method always returns true.

read()

```
public int read()
    throws IOException
```

```
public int read(char carray[],int offset,int count)
    throws IOException
```

If no argument is specified, a single character is read and returned. If `carray` is specified, up to `count` characters are placed in the array beginning at `carray[offset]`.

ready()

```
public boolean ready()
```

This method always returns `true`.

reset()

```
public void reset()
    throws IOException
```

This will restore input to the location set by a call to `mark()`. An `IOException` is thrown if there has never been a call to `mark()`.

skip()

```
public long skip(long count)
    throws IOException
```

The input location pointer will move forward by `count` characters. It is just as if `count` characters were read and discarded.

 Also see **StringWriter**.

StringSelection

class java.awt.datatransfer.StringSelection

This class encapsulates a block of text in a form that is capable of being transferred from one object to another through the clipboard.

 The methods imply an ability to retrieve the data in different flavors, and in the future, that may be true. In the initial release, version 1.1, the only flavor supported is plain text—the "java.lang.String" flavor.

Inheritance

```
public class java.awt.datatransfer.StringSelection
    implements Transferable
    implements ClipboardOwner
    extends Object
```

⇑
```
public class java.lang.Object
```

Constructors

```
public StringSelection(String text)
```

The constructor accepts the text to be transferred as a `String` object.

Methods

getTransferData()

```
public synchronized ObjectgetTransferData(DataFlavor flavor)
        throws UnsupportedFlavorException
        throws IOException
```

Returns the data (the plain text) in the requested flavor. An `UnsupportedFlavorException` is thrown if the specified flavor is not supported. An `IOException` could be thrown if the data cannot be read from where it was supposed to have been stored.

getTransferDataFlavors()

```
public synchronized DataFlavor[] getTransferDataFlavors()
```

Returns an array of all the flavors in which the data can be returned.

isDataFlavorSupported()

```
public boolean isDataFlavorSupported(DataFlavor flavor)
```

Returns `true` if the data can be returned in the specified `flavor`.

lostOwnership()

```
public void lostOwnership(
        Clipboard clipboard,Transferable contents)
```

This method is required by the `ClipboardOwner` interface, but it does nothing.

 For an example of transferring plain text using the clipboard, see **Clipboard**.

StringTokenizer

class java.util.StringTokenizer

This class can be used to break a `String` into its component tokens. The delimiters default to the set of white-space characters but can be further refined. The delimiters can even be changed from one token to the next.

Inheritance

```
public class java.util.StringTokenizer
    implements Enumeration
    extends Object
        ⇑
    public class java.lang.Object
```

Constructors

```
public StringTokenizer(String string)

public StringTokenizer(String string,
        String delimiters)

public StringTokenizer(String string,
        String delimiters,boolean returnTokens)
```

This will construct a StringTokenizer based on the specified string. The delimiters are the group of characters that will be used to separate the tokens. If no delimiters are specified, the default is the set of white-space characters— space, tab, carriage return, and newline ("\t\r\n"). If returnTokens is set to true, the delimiters will each be returned as tokens—otherwise, they are discarded.

Methods

countTokens()

```
public int countTokens()
```

This will return the number of tokens left to be retrieved by making calls to nextToken().

hasMoreElements()

```
public boolean hasMoreElements()
```

Returns true if there are more tokens. This method is here so that the class can be used as an Enumeration.

hasMoreTokens()

```
public boolean hasMoreTokens()
```

Returns true if there are more tokens.

nextElement()

```
public Object nextElement()
```

Returns the next token. If there are no tokens, a NoSuchElementException is thrown. The method exists so that the class can be used as an enumeration.

nextToken()

```
public String nextToken()

public String nextToken(String delimiters)
```

Returns the next token. If delimiters is specified, the StringTokenizer will switch to the new set of delimiters before extracting the token, and the new delimiters will remain in effect until they are changed again. If there are no tokens, a NoSuchElementException is thrown.

Example

This simple example uses the default white space as the delimiters:

```
import java.util.*;
public class Tokens {
    public static void main(String[] arg) {
        StringTokenizer st =
            new StringTokenizer("Is this your hat?");
        System.out.println("There are " +
            st.countTokens() + " tokens.");
        while(st.hasMoreTokens())
            System.out.println(st.nextToken());
    }
}
```

The output looks like this:

```
There are 4 tokens.
Is
this
your
hat?
```

 For general string manipulation, see **String**. To extract tokens from an input stream, see **StreamTokenizer**.

StringWriter

class java.io.StringWriter

This is an output character stream that collects the written characters internally. The stored characters can be used to create a String. The internal storage buffer size is increased automatically as characters are written to it.

Inheritance

```
public class java.io.StringWriter
    extends Writer
        ⇑
    public class java.io.Writer
        extends Object
            ⇑
        public class java.lang.Object
```

Constructors

```
public StringWriter()
protected StringWriter(int initialSize)
```

The initialSize is the number of bytes initially allocated to hold characters—if it is not specified, a reasonable default is assumed. Specifying an initial size can be a matter of efficiency—if you have a maximum count of the number of characters that will be written, the allocation of storage space can be done just once.

Methods

close()

```
public void close()
```

Closes the stream but does not release the internal buffer—the characters will still be available.

flush()

```
public void flush()
```

Flushes the stream.

getBuffer()

```
public StringBuffer getBuffer()
```

Returns the StringBuffer that is used as internal character storage.

toString()

```
public String toString()
```

Converts the internal StringBuffer to a String and returns it.

write()

```
public void write(int character)

public void write(char carray[],int offset,int count)
```

```
public void write(String string)

public void write(String string,int offset,int count)
```

Writes one or more characters. Writes a single character, or writes a portion of an array of characters. One character is written if `character` is specified. If `string` is specified without `offset` and `count`, the entire `string` is written. If `offset` and `count` are specified, `count` characters are written beginning at the index specified by `offset`.

 Also see **StringReader**.

stub

 See **RMI**.

StubNotFoundException

class java.rmi.StubNotFoundException

This exception is thrown to report a missing stub.

Inheritance

```
public class java.rmi.StubNotFoundException
    extends RemoteException
        ⇑
    public class java.rmi.RemoteException
        extends IOException
            ⇑
        public class java.io.IOException
            extends Exception
                ⇑
            public class java.lang.Exception
                extends Throwable
                    ⇑
                public class java.lang.Throwable
                    implements Serializable
                    extends Object
                        ⇑
                    public class java.lang.Object
```

r
s
t

Constructors

```
public StubNotFoundException(String message)

public StubNotFoundException(String message,
          Exception exception)
```

A StubNotFoundException is created with a descriptive string and, optionally, the original exception that caused this one to be thrown.

subclass

A subclass is a class that is derived from another class through inheritance. That is, a subclass is one that extends another class. In Java, every class except the Object class is a subclass.

 See **class**.

super

keyword

This keyword can be used to directly address the superclass or a member of the superclass. You can think of it as the this reference of the superclass. For example, to call a constructor of the superclass, use the form super(). If the subclass has overloaded a method, the one in the superclass can be called explicitly by using the form super.methodName().

 Also see **this** and **constructor**.

superclass

 See **Class**.

switch

The switch keyword is used, in conjunction with the case and default keywords, to execute one way of a possible multiway branch. It has an integer as its argument and will execute the single case statement that matches the value. For example:

```
switch(expression) {
case 1:
    System.out.println("Case 1");
    break;
case 2:
    System.out.println("Case 2");
case 3:
    System.out.println("Case 3");
    break;
default:
    System.out.println("The default case");
    break;
}
```

In this example, if the expression evaluates to 1, the string "Case 1" will print and the break statement will then break out of the block. If the expression evaluates to 2, the string "Case 2" will print, then the string "Case 3" will print, and then the break statement will break out of the block (notice that without the break statement, the flow of execution will drop right through to the next case). If the expression isn't 1, 2, or 3, the string "The default case" will execute and then the break statement will break out of the block.

Variable declarations

It is valid to declare local variables inside switch statements as long as they are declared before they are used and initialized within the case where they are going to be used. Here is an example of a valid program doing this:

```
public class SwitchVariable {
    public static void main(String[] arg) {
        int sw = 2;
        switch(sw) {
        case 1:
            int ivar;
            break;
        case 2:
            ivar = 33;
            System.out.println("ivar= " + ivar);
            break;
        }
    }
}
```

Even though the flow of execution skipped case 1—the location of the declaration statement—the variable ivar is found to exist in case 2. However, any initial value settings that may have been present in case 1 would not have occurred. If the inner part of the example had been this:

```
case 1:
      int ivar = 33;
      break;
case 2:
      System.out.println("ivar= " + ivar);
      break;
```

then the compiler would have assumed that ivar had not been initialized and would have generated an error message according to the rules of *definite assignment,* which will not allow access to an uninitialized variable. Here is another variation of the inner part that won't work:

```
case 2:
      ivar = 33;
      System.out.println("ivar= " + ivar);
      break;
case 1:
      int ivar;
      break;
```

This is the same as the original working form except for a change of order. This will cause a compile error because the flow of execution will have not come to the declaration yet and ivar does not exist.

 For other control flow keywords, see **do, for,** and **while**.

SyncFailedException

class java.io.SyncFailedException

Inheritance

```
public class java.io.SyncFailedException
      extends IOException
          (
      public class java.lang.Object
```

Constructors

```
public SyncFailedException(String message)
```

The message string is used as a detailed message describing this particular exception.

synchronized

keyword

Multiple threads can access the same data without conflict by use of the synchronized keyword to limit the access to one thread at a time. If it is possible that one thread could be reading data while another is updating it, the action should be synchronized—this is true even for reading primitive data types.

A synchronized method

A method can be declared as synchronized. For example:

```
public synchronized setValue(int newSetting) {
    value = newSetting;
}
```

Whenever the setValue() method has been called by one thread, the object is locked. No other thread will be able to call this method—or any other synchronized method—of the same object. If another thread attempts to call a synchronized method of an object that is locked by another thread, it is blocked and will wait until the lock is released.

A synchronized static method

It is possible to synchronize static methods. For example:

```
public static synchronized setValue(int newSetting) {
    value = newSetting;
}
```

Whenever a thread calls this method, all static synchronized methods for the class are locked. This has no effect on synchronized methods of the object—they will not be locked by this call.

Constructors don't need synchronization

There is no need to synchronize a constructor, because it can only be executed when an object is being instantiated. This can only occur in one thread—no other thread can have access to the object until after the constructor has returned.

Overriding synchronized methods

A subclass can override a synchronized method, causing it to be either synchronized or not. That is, the method in the child class does not inherit the synchronized characteristic of the method in the parent class. However, the method in the parent class does not change—if a synchronized method in the parent class is called explicitly, it will be a synchronized call.

A synchronized object

It is possible to execute synchronized code by locking the data instead of the method. Say, for example, that it is necessary to update an array, and the update should be synchronized. This is one way that it could be done:

```
private int[] iarray = new int[30];
...
public void updateArray(int delta) {
    synchronized(iarray) {
        for(int i=0; i<30; i++)
            iarray[i] += delta;
    }
}
```

In this example, the `iarray` becomes a synchronized object. The class can include any number of methods that use the statement `synchronized(iarray)`, and only one of them can possibly be in execution at any one time.

It is not required that the updated data itself be the locking object. It is sometimes more convenient to create an object for the sole purpose of locking. Here is an alternative approach to the example that updates the array:

```
private Object lockObject = new Object();
private int[] iarray = new int[30];
...
public void updateArray(int delta) {
    synchronized(lockObject) {
        for(int i=0; i<30; i++)
            iarray[i] += delta;
    }
}
```

 For communication between synchronized threads, see **Object.wait()** and **Object.notify()**.

System

class java.lang.System

This class supplies some system-level information and services to an application. Among these are standard input, standard output, and standard error streams. There is also access to external property information so that an application can find out something about the environment it is running in. An application can use this information to determine locations of files and directories.

Inheritance

```
public final class java.lang.System
    extends Object
        ⇑
    public class java.lang.Object
```

Variables and constants

err

```
public final static PrintStream err
```

The standard error output stream—already open and ready to accept data. Normally, this output will go directly to the user's terminal, although its actual destination can be redirected to another location. By convention, errors that require immediate attention are written to this stream. This is not dependable, though, because some windowing environments simply discard the data. See Example 1.

in

```
public final static InputStream in
```

The standard input stream—already open and ready to be read. Normally, this input stream is from the keyboard, but there are other possible sources of data. For instance, if this process was spawned as a child process, the parent process may have assumed the responsibility of supplying data for this stream.

out

```
public final static PrintStream out
```

The standard output stream—already open and ready to accept data. Normally, this output will go directly to the user's terminal, although its actual destination can be redirected to another location. Sending data to this stream is undependable because some windowing environments simply discard the data. See Example 1.

Constructors

There are no constructors—this class is a collection of static methods.

Methods

arraycopy()

```
public static void arraycopy(Object source,
    int sourceIndex,Object destination,
    int destinationIndex,int count)
```

Copies data from one array to another. The copying begins at source[sourceIndex] and copies count array members into the target beginning at destination[destinationIndex].

If there is only one array—that is, the source and destination arrays are the same—the copying is done as if a temporary array were made and the items copied back. This means that an overlapping copy within a single array is a valid operation. The arraycopy() method can be used to insert or close gaps in a single array.

If an ArrayStoreException is thrown, the destination array will not have been modified. The exception will be thrown if either the source or the destination is not an array, the two arrays have components of different primitive types, or one array contains objects and the other, primitive types.

An ArrayIndexOutOfBoundsException is thrown if the count and index arguments would cause an access outside the bounds of either array.

An ArrayStoreException is thrown if any member of one array cannot be converted by assignment to the other array. In this case, any copying done before the exception was encountered will be left intact—that is, the copying could have been partially completed.

currentTimeMillis()

```
public static long currentTimeMillis()
```

Returns the current time in milliseconds. This is a count of the number of milliseconds since midnight, January 1, 1970. See **Date**.

exit()

```
public static void exit(int status)
```

Terminates the running of the Virtual Machine. The argument is the status code returned to the system—by convention, a nonzero value indicates abnormal termination. This method calls Runtime.exit(), which never returns normally. If this thread is prohibited from halting the Virtual Machine, a SecurityException is thrown.

gc()

```
public static void gc()
```

Suggests to the Virtual Machine that the garbage collector should be run. If there is any memory that the garbage collector can retrieve quickly, it will make its best effort to do so. This does not mean that all free memory has been recovered. There is a sequence of steps to be followed, and some of these take time—this method does not block while that time is spent. What this method does is cause the garbage collector to get the "easy ones."

getenv()   deprecated

```
public static String getenv(String name)
```

Returns the `String` value assigned to an environment variable. If the environment variable is not defined, `null` is returned. This method is deprecated because environment variables are not universal to all operating systems.

getProperties()

```
public static Properties getProperties()
```

Returns an object that contains a list of the current system properties. If there is a security manager, a call is made to its `checkPropertiesAccess()` method with no arguments—this could result in a `SecurityException` being thrown. For a description of the standard set of system properties, see **properties**.

getProperty()

```
public static String getProperty(String key)
```

```
public static String getProperty(String key,String default)
```

Retrieves the system property specified by `key`. If access to the property is prohibited by the security manager, a `SystemException` will be thrown. If there is no property that matches the `key`, the `default` is returned—if no `default` is specified, `null` is returned.

getSecurityManager()

```
public static SecurityManager getSecurityManager()
```

Returns a reference to the `SecurityManager`. If there is no security manager, the method returns `null`.

identityHashCode()

```
public static int identityHashCode(Object object)
```

Returns the hashcode value for `object` by ignoring methods that have overridden `Object.hashCode()`. If `object` is `null`, the hashcode is zero.

load()

```
public static void load(String filename)
```

Loads the file as a dynamic library. The filename must be its complete path name. This method calls `Runtime.load()`. A `SecurityException` will be thrown if permission is not granted to load the library. If the file does not exist, an `UnsatisfiedLinkError` is thrown.

loadLibrary()

```
public static void loadLibrary(String libname)
```

Loads the system library specified by `libname`. The manner in which `libname` is mapped to an actual library is system–dependent. If this thread cannot load the library, a `SecurityException` is thrown. If the library is not found, an `UnsatisfiedLinkError` is thrown.

runFinalization()

```
public static void runFinalization()
```

Runs the `finalize()` methods of any objects pending finalization. This finalization is a normal part of garbage collection. A call to this method requests that the Virtual Machine call the finalize methods of the discarded objects.

runFinalizersOnExit()

```
public static void runFinalizersOnExit(boolean setting)
```

Enables or disables running of the `finalize()` methods as the Virtual Machine exits. By default, the Java runtime will shut down without bothering to run the finalizers, but calling this method with a `setting` of `true` will guarantee that they will be executed.

setErr()

```
public static void setErr(PrintStream stream)
```

This will replace `err`—the standard error output stream.

setIn()

```
public static void setIn(InputStream stream)
```

This will replace `in`—the standard input stream.

setOut()

```
public static void setOut(PrintStream stream)
```

This will replace `out`—the standard output stream.

setProperties()

```
public static void setProperties(Properties props)
```

This will replace the standard system `Properties` object with `props`. It will become the `Properties` object returned by the `getProperty()` method. If this thread is prohibited from this action, a `SecurityException` is thrown. If `props` is `null`, the current set of system properties is discarded.

setSecurityManager()

```
public static void setSecurityManager(SecurityManager s)
```

This method is used to specify the system security manager. A `SecurityException` will be thrown if there is already a security manager — this can only happen once. If the argument is `null`, no action is taken.

 For more information on system-level methods, see **Runtime**. For system-level property information, see **properties**. For information on the security manager, see **SecurityManager** and **RMISecurityManager**.

SystemColor

class java.awt.SystemColor

This class contains the standard set of colors used to display the GUI objects on the screen.

Changing colors

The actual RGB values of these colors could be changed from one system to another. Also, the meanings of the system colors could change dynamically if there is an index into a palette or some other local color scheme. To make a comparison between a nonsymbolic `Color` object and one of the system colors defined here, use the `getRGB()` method instead of the `equals()` method.

Inheritance

```
public final class java.awt.SystemColor
    implements Serializable
    extends Color
        ⇑
    public class java.awt.Color
        implements Serializable
        extends Object
            ⇑
        public class java.lang.Object
```

Variables and constants

ACTIVE_CAPTION

```
public static final int ACTIVE_CAPTION
```

Index to the background color of a caption.

ACTIVE_CAPTION_BORDER

```
public static final int ACTIVE_CAPTION_BORDER
```

Index to the color of a caption border.

ACTIVE_CAPTION_TEXT

```
public static final int ACTIVE_CAPTION_TEXT
```

Index to the color of active caption text.

activeCaption

```
public static final SystemColor activeCaption
```

The background color for captions in window borders.

activeCaptionBorder

```
public static final SystemColor activeCaptionBorder
```

The border color for captions in window borders.

activeCaptionText

```
public static final SystemColor activeCaptionText
```

The text color for captions in window borders.

CONTROL

```
public static final int CONTROL
```

The index to the control background color.

control

```
public static final SystemColor control
```

The background color for control objects.

CONTROL_DK_SHADOW

```
public static final int CONTROL_DK_SHADOW
```

The index to the control dark shadow color.

CONTROL_HIGHLIGHT

```
public static final int CONTROL_HIGHLIGHT
```

The index to the control highlight color.

CONTROL_LT_HIGHLIGHT

```
public static final int CONTROL_LT_HIGHLIGHT
```

The index to the control light highlight color.

CONTROL_SHADOW

```
public static final int CONTROL_SHADOW
```

The index to the control shadow color.

CONTROL_TEXT

```
public static final int CONTROL_TEXT
```

The index to the control text color.

controlDkShadow

```
public static final SystemColor controlDkShadow
```

The dark shadow color for control objects.

controlHighlight

```
public static final SystemColor controlHighlight
```

The regular highlight color for control objects.

controlLtHighlight

```
public static final SystemColor controlLtHighlight
```

The light highlight color for control objects.

controlShadow

```
public static final SystemColor controlShadow
```

The regular shadow color for control objects.

controlText

```
public static final SystemColor controlText
```

The text color for control objects.

r
s
t

desktop

```
public static final SystemColor desktop
```

The color of the desktop background.

DESKTOP

```
public static final int DESKTOP
```

The index to the desktop background color.

INACTIVE_CAPTION

```
public static final int INACTIVE_CAPTION
```

The index to the inactive caption background color.

INACTIVE_CAPTION_BORDER

```
public static final int INACTIVE_CAPTION_BORDER
```

The index to the inactive caption border color.

INACTIVE_CAPTION_TEXT

```
public static final int INACTIVE_CAPTION_TEXT
```

The index to the inactive caption text color.

inactiveCaption

```
public static final SystemColor inactiveCaption
```

The background color for inactive captions in window borders.

inactiveCaptionBorder

```
public static final SystemColor inactiveCaptionBorder
```

The border color for inactive captions in window borders.

inactiveCaptionText

```
public static final SystemColor inactiveCaptionText
```

The text color for inactive captions in window borders.

INFO

```
public static final int INFO
```

The index to the info background color.

info

```
public static final SystemColor info
```

The background color for info/help text.

INFO_TEXT

```
public static final int INFO_TEXT
```

The index to the info text color.

infoText

```
public static final SystemColor infoText
```

The text color for info/help text.

menu

```
public static final SystemColor menu
```

The background color for menus.

MENU

```
public static final int MENU
```

The index to the menu background color.

MENU_TEXT

```
public static final int MENU_TEXT
```

The index to the menu text color.

menuText

```
public static final SystemColor menuText
```

The text color for menus.

NUM_COLORS

```
public static final int NUM_COLORS
```

The total number of system colors in the array.

scrollbar

```
public static final SystemColor scrollbar
```

The background color for scroll bars.

SCROLLBAR

```
public static final int SCROLLBAR
```

The index to the scrollbar background color.

TEXT

```
public static final int TEXT
```

The index to the text background color.

text

```
public static final SystemColor text
```

The background color for text components.

TEXT_HIGHLIGHT

```
public static final int TEXT_HIGHLIGHT
```

The index to the text highlight color.

TEXT_HIGHLIGHT_TEXT

```
public static final int TEXT_HIGHLIGHT_TEXT
```

The index to the text highlight text color.

TEXT_INACTIVE_TEXT

```
public static final int TEXT_INACTIVE_TEXT
```

The index to the text inactive text color.

TEXT_TEXT

```
public static final int TEXT_TEXT
```

The index to the text color.

textHighlight

```
public static final SystemColor textHighlight
```

The background color for highlighted text.

textHighlightText

```
public static final SystemColor textHighlightText
```

The text color for highlighted text.

textInactiveText

```
public static final SystemColor textInactiveText
```

The text color for inactive text.

textText

```
public static final SystemColor textText
```

The text color for text components.

WINDOW

```
public static final int WINDOW
```

The index to the window background color.

window

```
public static final SystemColor window
```

The background color for windows.

WINDOW_BORDER

```
public static final int WINDOW_BORDER
```

The index to the window border color.

WINDOW_TEXT

```
public static final int WINDOW_TEXT
```

The index to the window text color.

windowBorder

```
public static final SystemColor windowBorder
```

The border color for windows.

windowText

```
public static final SystemColor windowText
```

The text color for windows.

Methods

getRGB()

```
public int getRGB()
```

Returns the RGB value for the color.

toString()

```
public String toString()
```

Returns a string representation of this color.

 For more information on colors, see **Color** and **RGB**.

text

package java.text

Interfaces

CharacterIterator

Classes

ChoiceFormat
CollatedString
Collation
CollationElementIterator
DateFormat
DateFormatData
DecimalFormat
Format
FormatStatus
MessageFormat
NumberFormat
NumberFormatData
ParseStatus
SimpleDateFormat
SortKey
StringCharacterIterator
TableCollation
TextBoundary

Exceptions

FormatException

TextArea

class java.awt.TextArea

A TextArea object is a component that displays multiple lines of text. It can be set for interactive editing, or it can be set to a display-only mode.

Inheritance

```
public class java.awt.TextArea
    extends TextComponent
        ⇑
    public class java.awt.TextComponent
        extends Component
            ⇑
        public abstract class java.awt.Component
            implements ImageObserver
            implements MenuContainer
            implements Serializable
            extends Object
                ⇑
            public class java.lang.Object
```

Variables and constants

SCROLLBARS_BOTH

```
public static final int SCROLLBARS_BOTH
```

Creates and displays both vertical and horizontal scroll bars.

SCROLLBARS_HORIZONTAL_ONLY

```
public static final int SCROLLBARS_HORIZONTAL_ONLY
```

Creates and displays only the horizontal scroll bar.

SCROLLBARS_NONE

```
public static final int SCROLLBARS_NONE
```

Suppresses the creation of the scroll bars.

SCROLLBARS_VERTICAL_ONLY

```
public static final int SCROLLBARS_VERTICAL_ONLY
```

Creates and displays only the vertical scroll bar.

Constructors

```
public TextArea()

public TextArea(String text)

public TextArea(int rows,int columns)

public TextArea(String text,int rows,int columns)

public TextArea(String text,int rows,int columns,
        int scrollbars)
```

The text is the initial text that will be displayed in the window. The rows and columns values can be used to specify the dimension of the display area in terms of character counts. The scrollbars can be specified by using one of the four constants defined in this class — the default is SCROLLBARS_BOTH.

Methods

addNotify()

```
public void addNotify()
```

Creates the underlying system-dependent peer for this object. This method is not normally called by the application. It is called by the container.

append()

```
public synchronized void append(String string)
```

Appends string onto the end of the text.

appendText()   **deprecated**

```
public void appendText(String string)
```

Appends string onto the end of the text. The method is deprecated — use append().

getColumns()

```
public int getColumns()
```

Returns the number of character columns in the text area.

getMinimumSize()

```
public Dimension getMinimumSize()

public Dimension getMinimumSize(int rows,int columns)
```

Returns the minimum size of the TextArea in terms of pixels. If the rows and columns are specified, the method sets the minimum TextArea to the size necessary to hold that number of rows and columns and then returns the resulting pixel dimensions.

getPreferredSize()

```
public Dimension getPreferredSize()

public Dimension getPreferredSize(int rows,int columns)
```

Returns the preferred size of the TextArea in terms of pixels. If the rows and columns are specified, the method sets the preferred TextArea to the size necessary to hold that number of rows and columns and then returns the resulting pixel dimensions.

getRows()

```
public int getRows()
```

Returns the number of rows of characters in the display area.

getScrollbarVisibility()

```
public int getScrollbarVisibility()
```

Returns the value designating which scroll bars this TextArea has. The return value is one of the constant values defined in this class.

insert()

```
public synchronized void insert(String string,
            int position)
```

Inserts the string into the text at the specified position.

insertText()   **deprecated**

```
public void insertText(String string,int position)
```

Inserts the string into the text at the specified position. This method is deprecated—use insert().

minimumSize()   **deprecated**

```
public Dimension minimumSize()

public Dimension minimumSize(int rows,int columns)
```

Returns the minimum size of the TextArea in terms of pixels. If the rows and columns are specified, the method sets the minimum TextArea to the size necessary to hold that number of rows and columns and then returns the resulting pixel dimensions. This method is deprecated—use getMinimumSize().

paramString()

```
protected String paramString()
```

Returns debugging information. The return string describes the internal state and values of this object.

preferredSize()

```
public Dimension preferredSize()

public Dimension preferredSize(int rows,int columns)
```

Returns the preferred size of the TextArea in terms of pixels. If the rows and columns are specified, the method sets the preferred TextArea to the size necessary to hold that number of rows and columns and then returns the resulting pixel dimensions. This method is deprecated—use getPreferredSize().

replaceRange()

```
public synchronized void replaceRange(String string,
             int start,int end)
```

Deletes the text in the range specified by start and end, and replaces it with the text in string.

replaceText()

```
public void replaceText(String string,int start,int end)
```

Deletes the text in the range specified by start and end, and replaces it with the text in string. This method is deprecated—use replaceRange().

setColumns()

```
public void setColumns(int columns)
```

Specifies the number of columns of characters in the display area. An IllegalArgumentException is thrown if columns is less than 0.

setRows()

```
public void setRows(int rows)
```

Specifies the number of rows of characters in the display area. An IllegalArgumentException is thrown if rows is less than 0.

Example

This example displays a TextArea that can be used to print text to System.out:

```
import java.awt.*;
import java.awt.event.*;
public class TextAreaDemo extends Frame
            implements ActionListener {
    TextArea textArea;
```

```
        public static void main(String[] arg) {
            new TextAreaDemo();
        }
        public TextAreaDemo() {
            textArea = new TextArea();
            add("Center",textArea);
            Panel p = new Panel();
            Button b = new Button("Get All");
            b.addActionListener(this);
            p.add(b);
            b = new Button("Get Selection");
            b.addActionListener(this);
            p.add(b);
            b = new Button("Select All");
            b.addActionListener(this);
            p.add(b);
            b = new Button("Clear");
            b.addActionListener(this);
            p.add(b);
            b = new Button("Quit");
            b.addActionListener(this);
            p.add(b);
            add("South",p);
            pack();
            show();
        }
        public void actionPerformed(ActionEvent event) {
            String command = event.getActionCommand();
            if(command.equals("Get All")) {
                System.out.println(textArea.getText());
            } else if(command.equals("Get Selection")) {

                System.out.println(textArea.getSelectedText());
            } else if(command.equals("Select All")) {
                textArea.selectAll();
            } else if(command.equals("Clear")) {
                textArea.setText("");
            } else if(command.equals("Quit")) {
                System.exit(0);
            }
        }
    }
```

Figure T-1 shows the window as it first appears, with a couple of lines of text typed into it.

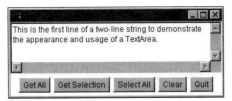

Figure T-1   A *TextArea* displaying two
                 lines of text.

Even though two scroll bars are displayed, they are disabled because there is no hidden text. Figure T-2 shows the same TextArea after it has been reduced in size to hide some text—the horizontal scroll bar has become activated because of the hidden text.

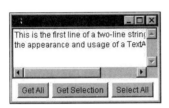

Figure T-2   A *TextArea* with text extending
                 beyond the window.

Figure T-3 shows the TextArea with selected text.

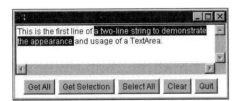

Figure T-3   A *TextArea* with selected text.

Pressing the "Get All" button causes all of the text to be read by calling getText(). This is the output from the program:

```
This is the first line of a two-line string to demonstrate
the appearance and usage of a TextArea.
```

Pressing the "Get Selected" button causes only the selected text to be read by calling getSelectedText(). This is the output from the program:

```
a two-line string to demonstrate
the appearance
```

For a single-line edit window, see **TextField**. For more methods dealing with editing (such as text selection and cursor control), see **TextComponent**. Also see **TextEvent** and **TextListener**.

TextComponent

class java.awt.TextComponent

This is a component that manages editable text. It can be set for interactive editing, or it can be set to a display-only mode. This is the superclass that supplies editing capabilities to `TextArea` (a multiline text editor) and `TextField` (a single-line text editor).

Position in the text

Several methods in this class deal with the positions of characters in the text. A position is a zero-based index value. The selected text is defined as a pair of indexes—one that designates the first character selected and one that designates the character just past (to the right of) the selected area. There is also the *caret*—the cursor that specifies the insertion point of the editable text—that is also positioned by a zero-based index.

Extended by

```
TextArea
TextField
```

Inheritance

```
public class java.awt.TextComponent
    extends Component
        ⇑
    public abstract class java.awt.Component
        implements ImageObserver
        implements MenuContainer
        implements Serializable
        extends Object
            ⇑
        public class java.lang.Object
```

Variables and constants

textListener

```
protected transient TextListener textListener
```

The text listeners registered for events from this object.

Constructors

This class has no public constructors.

Methods

addTextListener()

```
public void addTextListener(TextListener listener)
```

Adds the listener to the list of those that will receive TextEvents issued by this component.

getCaretPosition()

```
public int getCaretPosition()
```

Returns the current position of the text-insertion caret.

getSelectedText()

```
public synchronized String getSelectedText()
```

Returns the selected text. If no text is selected, the return value will be a zero-length string.

getSelectionEnd()

```
public synchronized int getSelectionEnd()
```

Returns the position of the character following the selected text. If no text is selected, this is 0.

getSelectionStart()

```
public synchronized int getSelectionStart()
```

Returns the position of the first character of the selected text. This will be 0 if the selected text starts with the first character, or if there is no selected text.

getText()

```
public synchronized String getText()
```

Returns the entire text.

isEditable()

```
public boolean isEditable()
```

Returns true if the text is editable.

paramString()

```
protected String paramString()
```

Returns debugging information. The return string describes the internal state and values of this object.

processEvent()

```
protected void processEvent(AWTEvent e)
```

If the event is a TextEvent, the processTextEvent() method will be called. If it is not a TextEvent, a call is made to the processEvent() method of the superclass.

processTextEvent()

```
protected void processTextEvent(TextEvent e)
```

Processes the TextEvent by dispatching a copy of it to each member of the textListener list. This method will not be called unless a listener has been registered by calling addTextListener() or events have been enabled with a call to enableEvents().

removeNotify()

```
public void removeNotify()
```

Removes the peer of the TextComponent.

removeTextListener()

```
public void removeTextListener(TextListener listener)
```

Removes the specified listener from the list of registered TextListeners.

select()

```
public synchronized void select(int selectionStart,
        int selectionEnd)
```

Sets the text from selectionStart to selectionEnd as the selected text.

selectAll()

```
public synchronized void selectAll()
```

Sets all the text as the selected text.

setCaretPosition()

```
public void setCaretPosition(int position)
```

Sets the insertion caret to a new position. An IllegalArgumentException is thrown if position is outside the range of the existing characters.

setEditable()

```
public synchronized void setEditable(boolean setting)
```

If setting is true, the TextComponent will become editable. If it is false, the component will become display-only.

setSelectionEnd()

```
public synchronized void setSelectionEnd(int position)
```

Sets the end of the selected text to the position. The value will be adjusted to follow the selection start position and to fit within the length of the text.

setSelectionStart()

```
public synchronized void setSelectionStart(int position)
```

Sets the start of the selected text to position. The value will be adjusted to precede the selection end position and to be nonnegative.

setText()

```
public synchronized void setText(String text)
```

Replaces the text of the component with text.

 The subclass for multiline editing is **TextArea**. The subclass for single-line editing is **TextField**. Also see **TextEvent** and **TextListener**.

TextEvent

class java.awt.event.TextEvent

This is the event delivered to TextListeners when a text event occurs, such as a keystroke in a text window.

Inheritance

```
public class TextEvent
    extends AWTEvent
        ⇑
    public class AWTEvent
        extends EventObject
            ⇑
        public class java.util.EventObject
            implements Serializable
            extends Object
```

⇑
```
public class java.lang.Object
```

Variables and constants

TEXT_FIRST

```
public static final int TEXT_FIRST
```

The lowest possible value of any `TextEvent` ID number.

TEXT_LAST

```
public static final int TEXT_LAST
```

The highest possible value of any `TextEvent` ID number.

TEXT_VALUE_CHANGED

```
public static final int TEXT_VALUE_CHANGED
```

The event indicating a change to the text.

Constructors

```
public TextEvent(Object source,int id)
```

A `TextEvent` is constructed by specifying the text component `source` and the `id` number indicating the event type.

Methods

paramString()

```
public String paramString()
```

Returns debugging information. The return string describes the internal state and values of this object.

 Also see **TextEventListener**. The text components derived from **TextComponent** are **TextArea** and **TextField**.

TextField

class java.awt.TextField

A `TextArea` object is a component that displays a single line of text. It can be set for interactive editing, or it can be set for a display-only mode.

The echo character

By setting a special echo character, the `TextField` can be made to disguise the input by displaying the one special character for all characters entered. The real input characters are maintained internally; only the display is disguised. This is commonly used for password entry.

Inheritance

```
public class java.awt.TextField
    extends TextComponent
        ⇑
    public class java.awt.TextComponent
        extends Component
            ⇑
        public abstract class java.awt.Component
            implements ImageObserver
            implements MenuContainer
            implements Serializable
            extends Object
                ⇑
            public class java.lang.Object
```

Constructors

```
public TextField()

public TextField(String text)

public TextField(int columns)

public TextField(String text,int columns)
```

The construction of a `TextField` has two options. It can be constructed with `text` that is initially displayed in the window. It can also be constructed with a specific number of characters displayed.

Methods

addActionListener()

```
public synchronized void addActionListener(
        ActionListener listener)
```

Adds the listener to the list of those that will receive `ActionEvents` from the `TextField`.

addNotify()

```
public void addNotify()
```

Creates the underlying system-dependent peer for this object. This method is not normally called by the application. It is called by the container.

echoCharIsSet()

```
public boolean echoCharIsSet()
```

Returns `true` if an echo character has been specified.

getColumns()

```
public int getColumns()
```

Returns the number of columns in the `TextField`.

getEchoChar()

```
public char getEchoChar()
```

Returns the character that is to be used for echoing. The return value is 0 if the echo character has not been set.

getMinimumSize()

```
public Dimension getMinimumSize()

public Dimension getMinimumSize(int columns)
```

Returns the minimum size of the `TextField` in terms of pixels. If the `columns` are specified, the method sets the minimum `TextArea` to the size necessary to hold that number of character columns and then returns the resulting pixel dimensions.

getPreferredSize()

```
public Dimension getPreferredSize()

public Dimension getPreferredSize(int columns)
```

Returns the preferred size of the `TextField` in terms of pixels. If the `columns` are specified, the method sets the preferred `TextArea` to the size necessary to hold that number of character columns and then returns the resulting pixel dimensions.

minimumSize()   deprecated

```
public Dimension minimumSize()

public Dimension minimumSize(int columns)
```

Returns the minimum size of the `TextField` in terms of pixels. If the `columns` are specified, the method sets the minimum `TextArea` to the size necessary to hold that number of character columns and then returns the resulting pixel dimensions. This method is deprecated—use `getMinimumSize()`.

paramString()

```
protected String paramString()
```

Returns debugging information. The return string describes the internal state and values of this object.

preferredSize()   **deprecated**

```
public Dimension preferredSize()
```

```
public Dimension preferredSize(int columns)
```

Returns the preferred size of the TextField in terms of pixels. If the columns are specified, the method sets the preferred TextArea to the size necessary to hold that number of character columns and then returns the resulting pixel dimensions. This method is deprecated—use getPreferredSize().

processActionEvent()

```
protected void processActionEvent(ActionEvent event)
```

The event is dispatched to each member of the list of registered listeners. This method will not be called unless a listener has been registered with a call to addActionListener() or ActionEvents have been enabled by a call to enableEvents().

processEvent()

```
protected void processEvent(AWTEvent event)
```

If the event is an ActionEvent, a call is made to processActionEvent(). If it is not an ActionEvent, the processEvent() method of the superclass is called.

removeActionListener()

```
public synchronized void removeActionListener(
        ActionListener listener)
```

Removes the specified listener from the list of registered ActionListeners.

setColumns()

```
public void setColumns(int columns)
```

Sets the number of columns for this TextField. An IllegalArgumentException is thrown if columns is less than 0.

setEchoChar()

```
public void setEchoChar(char character)
```

Sets the echo character. If this is set, it will be the only character displayed. Specifying a character of 0 will clear any previous setting.

setEchoCharacter()   **deprecated**

```
public void setEchoCharacter(char character)
```

Sets the echo character. If this is set, it will be the only character displayed. Specifying a character of 0 will clear any previous setting. This method is deprecated — use setEchoCharacter().

Example

This is an example of a TextField that can be set to receive characters with or without echoing them to the display:

```java
import java.awt.*;
import java.awt.event.*;
public class TextFieldDemo extends Frame
                implements ActionListener {
    TextField textField;
    public static void main(String[] arg) {
        new TextFieldDemo();
    }
    public TextFieldDemo() {
        textField = new TextField();
        add("Center",textField);
        Panel p = new Panel();
        Button b = new Button("Set Echo");
        b.addActionListener(this);
        p.add(b);
        b = new Button("Clear Echo");
        b.addActionListener(this);
        p.add(b);
        b = new Button("Clear");
        b.addActionListener(this);
        p.add(b);
        b = new Button("Quit");
        b.addActionListener(this);
        p.add(b);
        add("South",p);
        pack();
        show();
    }
    public void actionPerformed(ActionEvent event) {
        String command = event.getActionCommand();
        if(command.equals("Clear")) {
            textField.setText("");
        } else if(command.equals("Set Echo")) {
```

```
                    textField.setEchoChar('*');
            } else if(command.equals("Clear Echo")) {
                    textField.setEchoChar((char)0);
            } else if(command.equals("Quit")) {
                    System.exit(0);
            }
        }
    }
}
```

The buttons "Set Echo" and "Clear Echo" toggle it between the two modes. Figure T-4 shows the display with the characters visible, and Figure T-5 shows the display with the same text, but with the echo character set to an asterisk.

Figure T-4 A *TextField* in the default mode of visible characters.

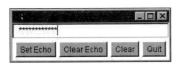

Figure T-5 A *TextField* with the echo character set to *"*"*.

For a multiline edit window, see **TextArea**. For more methods dealing with editing (such as text selection and cursor control), see **TextComponent**. To display a single line of text, see **Label**. Also see **TextEvent** and **TextListener**.

TextListener

interface java.awt.event.TextListener

The listener interface used to receive TextEvents.

Implemented by

```
AWTEventMulticaster
```

Inheritance

```
public interface java.awt.event.TextListener
```

```
            extends EventListener
                   ⇑
      public interface java.util.EventListener
```

Constructors

Returned by

Objects implementing this interface are returned from AWTEventMulticaster.add() and AWTEventMulticaster.remove().

Methods

textValueChanged()

```
   public abstract void textValueChanged(TextEvent event)
```

This method is called whenever the text changes.

 This **TextEvent** is dispatched from **TextField** and **TextArea**.

this

keyword

The keyword this is the reference that exists inside a method of an object and can be used whenever the method needs to explicitly refer to its own object. The this variable—present in every nonstatic method—is a reference variable that refers to the enclosing object.

Static methods don't have this

For the this keyword to have any meaning, it must refer to an object. Static methods—also called class methods—are a part of the class, not part of an object, and can be executed whether or not there are any objects in existence. Therefore, this has no meaning inside a static method.

Example

The two most common uses of this are to allow one constructor to call another and to qualify references to variable names. This example shows how each of these work:

```
public class ConstructorCall {
    private String string;
    private int count;
```

```
public static void main(String[] arg) {
    ConstructorCall cc = new ConstructorCall();
    System.out.println(cc);
}
ConstructorCall() {
    this("Default string");
}
ConstructorCall(String string) {
    this(string,3);
}
ConstructorCall(String string,int count) {
    this.string = string;
    this.count = count;
}
public String toString() {
    String outstring = string + " count=" + count;
    return(outstring);
}
}
```

This class has three constructors. There is the default, the one that requires a String, and the one that requires both a String and an int. The default constructor uses this, with a default String, to make a call to the one requiring a String—this way there is no need for the default constructor to do anything else. In turn, the constructor that requires only a String uses a default int value and calls the constructor that requires both a String and an int.

The constructor that requires both a String and an int puts the values passed to it into object-level variables. The names of the arguments and the object-level variables are the same, so the keyword this is used to specify that the references are to the object-level variables—otherwise, the local variables would hide them.

 Also see **constructor** and **super**.

thread

A *thread* is the line of execution followed by an application or an applet. Every Java program in execution is executed in a thread. It is possible for the one program to be executing simultaneously in more than one thread.

A thread has states

A thread can be created and not started—it is said to be *inactive*. Once a thread has started running (the run() method of the Runnable interface has been called), the thread is then *active*. An active thread can be temporarily *suspended* and later *resumed* where it left off. A thread will *stop* when it returns from the `run()` method, or it can be forcibly halted by a call to the `stop()` method.

Priority

Every thread is assigned a *priority*. Those with higher priorities have execution preference over those with lower priorities. When one thread starts another, the new thread initially has the same priority as the one that started it.

There are daemons

A thread may be marked as being a *daemon*. A newly started thread is a daemon if (and only if) the thread that started it is also a daemon. The only difference between a daemon thread and a user thread is that the Virtual Machine will continue to run as long as there is at least one nondaemon thread in execution—once there are nothing but daemon threads left running, the Virtual Machine ceases execution. An entire thread group can be designated as a daemon group.

There are groups

For security reasons, threads can be placed into thread groups. These groups nest—one thread group can contain another. Threads within a group have permission to modify one another and to modify threads lower in the thread group hierarchy, but they cannot modify threads outside of their group or above them in the hierarchy. Every thread belongs to a group—the default is for a thread to be in the same group as the thread that created it.

Single-thread operation

When the Virtual Machine first starts a program, it does so by creating a single thread calling the `main()` method of the class named on the command line. If this method calls `Runtime.exit()`, the thread dies and the Virtual Machine halts.

 Also see **Runnable**, **Thread**, and **ThreadGroup**.

Thread

class java.lang.Thread

A thread is one instance of the execution of a program by the Virtual Machine. Different threads can be completely different programs—or they can simply be different incarnations of the same program. The `Thread` class allows an application to create a new thread in the Virtual Machine and have itself, or another object, run in the new thread.

Inheritance

```
public class Thread
    implements Runnable
    extends Object
        ⇑
    public class java.lang.Object
```

Variables and constants

MAX_PRIORITY

```
public final static int MAX_PRIORITY
```

The maximum priority that can be assigned to any thread.

MIN_PRIORITY

```
public final static int MIN_PRIORITY
```

The minimum priority that can be assigned to any thread.

NORM_PRIORITY

```
public final static int NORM_PRIORITY
```

The normal priority assigned to a thread.

Constructors

```
public Thread()

public Thread(Runnable target)

public Thread(String name)

public Thread(ThreadGroup group,String name)

public Thread(ThreadGroup group,Runnable target)

public Thread(Runnable target,String name)

public Thread(ThreadGroup group,Runnable target,String name)
```

The creation of a new thread involves three possible arguments—all of which are optional.

The new thread will assume the priority setting of the thread creating it. This can be altered by a subsequent call to setPriority(). If the creating thread is tagged as being a daemon, the new thread will also be tagged as a daemon. A subsequent call to setDaemon() can be made to alter the setting.

A SecurityExcecption is thrown if the current thread cannot create a new thread.

target

The target is the object that will be executed as a thread. It must implement the Runnable interface (which only requires that the method run() be implemented). If a nonnull target is specified, its run() method will be called when the thread is started. If target is null, or is not supplied, the class creating the thread is used for the new thread —which means it must implement Runnable.

name

The name specifies the name of the new thread. If name is not supplied or is null, a name will be generated. Generated names are in the form Thread-n, where *n* is some number.

group

The group specifies which group the new thread will belong to. If a nonnull group is specified, the checkAccess() method of group will be called with no arguments—this could result in a SecurityException being thrown. If group is null or is not included in the argument list, the new thread will belong to the same group as the thread that creates the new thread.

Returned by

A Thread object is returned from the method currentThread().

Methods

activeCount()

```
public static int activeCount()
```

Returns the count of the number of active threads in this thread group.

checkAccess()

```
public void checkAccess()
```

Checks with the security manager and throws a SecurityException if permission is denied to make modifications to this thread.

countStackFrames()

```
public int countStackFrames()
```

Returns a count of the number of stack frames in this thread. If the thread is not currently suspended, an IllegalThreadStateException is thrown.

currentThread()

```
public static Thread currentThread()
```

Returns the currently executing thread object.

destroy()

```
public void destroy()
```

Destroys this thread. There is no cleanup—any blocked monitors remain locked.

dumpStack()

```
public static void dumpStack()
```

Prints the stack trace. This method is intended for debugging.

enumerate()

```
public static int enumerate(Thread tarray[])
```

Places a copy of the Thread object of every active thread into tarray and returns a count of the number in the array. This method gets an enumeration from the ThreadGroup object and uses the results to populate the array.

getName()

```
public final String getName()
```

Returns the name of the thread.

getPriority()

```
public final int getPriority()
```

Returns the priority of the thread.

getThreadGroup()

```
public final ThreadGroup getThreadGroup()
```

Returns this thread's ThreadGroup object.

interrupt()

```
public void interrupt()
```

Interrupts the thread. A call to this method sets a flag that can be checked by calls to interrupted() or isInterrupted().

interrupted()

```
public static boolean interrupted()
```

Returns true if the current thread has been interrupted. This method returns true if interrupt() has been called on the currently executing thread, and false if not.

isAlive()

```
public final boolean isAlive()
```

Returns true if the current thread is alive. A thread is alive if its start() method has been called and it has not yet died.

isDaemon()

```
public final boolean isDaemon()
```

Returns true if this thread is a daemon.

isInterrupted()

```
public boolean isInterrupted()
```

Returns true if the current thread has been interrupted. This method returns true if interrupt() has been called on this thread, and false if not.

join()

```
public final void join()
      throws InterruptedException

public final synchronized void join(long millis)
      throws InterruptedException

public final synchronized void join(long millis,
         int nanos)
      throws InterruptedException
```

This thread will wait, at most, the specified number of milliseconds and then die. If millis is zero (or is not specified), it will wait forever. A finer granularity can be specified for time by using nanos to add a nanosecond increment to millis. The value of nanos can be in the range of 0 through 999999. An InterruptedException is thrown if another thread has interrupted this one. An IllegalArgumentException is thrown if millis is negative or nanos is outside its valid range.

resume()

```
public final void resume()
```

This method resumes execution of a suspended thread. If the thread is alive but suspended, it will resume. A SecurityException is thrown if the calling thread does not have permission for this action. See suspend().

run()

```
public void run()
```

This method is called by the system to execute the thread. This method is required for all Runnable objects, and subclasses of this class should override this method to do the work of the thread. The default method in the Thread object does nothing — it simply returns, which terminates the thread.

setDaemon()

```
public final void setDaemon(boolean setting)
```

If setting is `true`, converts this thread to a daemon thread. If setting is `false`, converts this thread to a nondaemon thread. This method cannot be called once the thread has started—an `IllegalThreadStateException` is thrown if the thread is active.

setName()

```
public final void setName(String name)
```

Changes the name that was assigned to the thread when it was constructed. This will throw a `SecurityException` if this level of access is denied.

setPriority()

```
public final void setPriority(int newPriority)
```

Changes the priority of the thread to `newPriority`. An `IllegalArgumentException` is thrown if `newPriority` is outside the range from `MIN_PRIORITY` to `MAX_PRIORITY`. This will cause a `SecurityException` if this level of access is denied.

sleep()

```
public static void sleep(long millis)
    throws InterruptedException
```

```
public static void sleep(long millis,int nanos)
    throws InterruptedException
```

This thread will cease execution for `millis` milliseconds. The granularity of the sleep time can be made smaller by specifying `nanos` as the number of nanoseconds to be added to `millis`. While sleeping, the thread does not lose ownership of any monitors. An `InterrupedException` is thrown if another thread interrupts this thread while it is sleeping. An `IllegalArgumentException` is thrown if `millis` is negative or if `nanos` is outside the range of 0 through 999999.

start()

```
public synchronized void start()
```

This method is called by the Virtual Machine to spawn execution of a new thread. The current thread—the one calling this method—will simply return from the method. Inside this method, a new thread is created that does not return—the method calls the `run()` method, which holds the executable code of the new thread. This method will throw an `IllegalThreadStateException` to indicate that the thread has already been started.

stop()

```
public final void stop()
```

```
public final synchronized void stop(Throwable throwable)
```

Ceases execution of the thread. The thread is expected to halt immediately and throw a ThreadDeath object as an exception. If throwable is specified, it will be thrown instead of ThreadDeath. This method can be called for a thread that has not yet started—starting after that will cause it to terminate immediately. If throwable is null, a NullPointerException is thrown to the caller of the method. A SecurityException will be thrown if permission is denied.

 Under normal circumstances, the application should not specify the throwable. It is important that the system receive the thrown ThreadDeath so that the thread will actually die.

suspend()

```
public final void suspend()
```

Suspends the thread. If the thread is alive, it will suspend execution until it is resumed. A SecurityException will be thrown if the current thread does not have permission for this kind of access. See resume().

toString()

```
public String toString()
```

Returns the string representation of this thread. The string will include the name, the priority, and the thread group.

yield()

```
public static void yield()
```

This will cause the thread to pause briefly and then resume automatically. The purpose is to allow other threads more execution time.

Example

This example demonstrates one of the two ways of starting a separate thread. (The other uses the Runnable interface.) This example creates three instances of the SimpleThread class and starts each one in its own thread:

```
public class SimpleThread extends Thread {
    String tag;
    long sleepTime;
    public static void main(String[] arg) {
        SimpleThread st;
        st = new SimpleThread("A",3000);
        System.out.println(".....starting A");
        st.start();
        st = new SimpleThread("B",1000);
        System.out.println(".....starting B");
```

```
        st.start();
        st = new SimpleThread("C",2000);
        System.out.println(".....starting C");
        st.start();
    }
    SimpleThread(String tag,long sleepTime) {
        this.tag = tag;
        this.sleepTime = sleepTime;
    }
    public void run() {
        try {
            System.out.println(tag + " started");
            Thread.sleep(sleepTime);
            System.out.println(tag + " ended");
        } catch(InterruptedException e) {
            System.out.println(e);
        }
    }
}
```

Each thread is given a different number of milliseconds to sleep. The threads don't synchronize themselves in any way (other than the length of time of the sleep), so there is a race condition that occurs as the three are starting up. Here is the output from a typical run:

```
.....starting A
.....starting B
A started
.....starting C
B started
C started
B ended
C ended
A ended
```

You can see by the fact that the output is intertwined that the three are running concurrently. The main() method creates and starts all three threads. As it turns out, after A and B were started, but before C was started, the A thread began by printing the "starting" message from the run() method. Then C got its start. All three slept—each using its own setting for the amount of time to sleep—and then printed their ending statements. The one that slept the longest was the last to stop.

 For another way to create threads, and more examples, see **Runnable** and **Applet**. For a general discussion of Java threads, see **thread**.

ThreadDeath

class java.lang.ThreadDeath

A ThreadDeath object is thrown from a thread whenever its stop() method is called with no arguments.

Don't catch ThreadDeath

An application should not catch this exception unless there is some overpowering reason that some cleanup be done immediately. Even if it is caught, it should be rethrown as soon as possible to make sure that the thread actually dies.

How ThreadDeath **is handled**

This error is handled a bit differently that most. Normally, the default error handler will print a diagnostic and, sometimes, cease execution of the Virtual Machine. A ThreadDeath exception is processed silently—the thread is quietly deleted from the system and the exception object is discarded.

Why is ThreadDeath **an** Error**?**

ThreadDeath inherits from Error instead of Exception because it must be passed up to the system and it is common for application code to simply catch all the Exceptions and sort it all out later. Even though it is not an abnormal occurrence, it is thrown as an Error so that it won't inadvertently be trapped.

Inheritance

```
public class java.lang.ThreadDeath
    extends Error
        ⇑
    public class java.lang.Error
        extends Throwable
            ⇑
        public class java.lang.Throwable
            implements Serializable
            extends Object
                ⇑
            public class java.lang.Object
```

Constructors

```
public ThreadDeath()
```

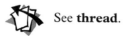 See **thread**.

ThreadGroup

class java.lang.ThreadGroup

A *thread group* includes a set of one or more threads. In addition, a thread group can include other thread groups. The result is that a thread group forms a hierarchical tree of threads with one `ThreadGroup` object as its root.

Security manager

Several methods in this class require that access permission be granted by the `SecurityManager`. If no `SecurityManager` has been installed, all permissions are granted. To get permission, the `checkAccess()` method is called with no argument, and if permission is not granted, the method will throw a `SecurityException`.

Inheritance

```
public class ThreadGroup
    extends Object
        ⇑
    public class java.lang.Object
```

Constructors

```
public ThreadGroup(String name)
public ThreadGroup(ThreadGroup parent,String name)
```

A `ThreadGroup` is constructed by being given a name. If the `parent` is not specified, the `parent` will be the `ThreadGroup` of the currently running thread. The `checkAccess()` method of the parent group is called with no arguments, resulting in a `SecurityException` being thrown if permission is not granted. A `NullPointerException` is thrown if `parent` is `null`.

Returned by

An object of this class is returned from `SecurityManager.getThreadGroup()`, `Thread.getThreadGroup()`, and `ThreadGroup.getParent()`.

Methods

activeCount()

```
public int activeCount()
```

Returns a count of the number of active threads in this group, and in all groups that have this one as an ancestor.

activeGroupCount()

```
public int activeGroupCount()
```

Returns a count of the number of active groups that have this one as an ancestor.

allowThreadSuspension()

```
public boolean allowThreadSuspension(boolean setting)
```

The Virtual Machine uses this method to control low memory implicit suspension.

checkAccess()

```
public final void checkAccess()
```

Determines whether the currently running thread has permission to modify this thread group. If permission is granted, the method will return normally—if it is denied by the security manager, a SecurityException will be thrown.

destroy()

```
public final void destroy()
```

Destroys this thread group and all the thread groups that have this one as an ancestor. An IllegalThreadStateException is thrown if this group or any subgroup is not empty. A SecurityException is thrown if this thread cannot modify the thread group.

enumerate()

```
public int enumerate(Thread list[])

public int enumerate(Thread list[],boolean recurse)

public int enumerate(ThreadGroup list[])

public int enumerate(ThreadGroup list[],boolean recurse)
```

Places a reference of every active Thread or ThreadGroup in the array and returns a count of the number included. If the recurse flag is true, references to the active threads or active thread groups in all the subgroups are included. The return value is a count of the number of references placed in the array. If the array is not large enough to hold all the threads, the ones that will not fit are ignored. The methods activeCount() and activeGroupCount() could be used to get an estimate of the size of the array.

getMaxPriority()

```
public final int getMaxPriority()
```

Returns the maximum priority value allowed for members of this group.

getName()

```
public final String getName()
```

Returns the name assigned to this ThreadGroup when it was constructed.

getParent()

```
public final ThreadGroup getParent()
```

Returns the parent of this `ThreadGroup`. If `null` is returned, this is the top-level thread group.

isDaemon()

```
public final boolean isDaemon()
```

Returns `true` if this group is a daemon `ThreadGroup`. A daemon `ThreadGroup` will be destroyed automatically when its last member thread or thread group is destroyed.

isDestroyed()

```
public synchronized boolean isDestroyed()
```

Returns `true` if this thread group has been destroyed.

list()

```
public void list()
```

Prints information about this thread group to System.out. This method is intended for debugging.

parentOf()

```
public final boolean parentOf(ThreadGroup group)
```

Returns `true` if `group` is either this `ThreadGroup` or one of its ancestors.

resume()

```
public final void resume()
```

This will call the `resume()` method on all threads and thread groups in this thread group. A `SecurityException` is thrown if this level of access is refused by the security manager.

setDaemon()

```
public final void setDaemon(boolean setting)
```

If `setting` is `true`, this `ThreadGroup` will be tagged as being a daemon group. If setting is `false`, the group will be marked as a user `ThreadGroup`. If the security manager disallows this level of access, a `SecurityException` will be thrown.

setMaxPriority()

```
public final void setMaxPriority(int priority)
```

This will set the maximum priority allowed for any thread in the group. Threads in the group that are already running at a higher priority are not affected. The security manager can disallow this operation by throwing a `SecurityException`.

stop()

```
public final void stop()
```

Halts all processes in the group by calling the `stop()` methods of all the threads and thread groups. If this level of access is forbidden, a `SecurityException` will be thrown.

suspend()

```
public final void suspend()
```

Suspends all processes in this group by calling the `suspend()` method of all the threads and thread groups. If this level of access is forbidden, a `SecurityException` will be thrown.

toString()

```
public String toString()
```

Returns a string representation of this `ThreadGroup`.

uncaughtException()

```
public void uncaughtException(Thread thread,
        Throwable throwable)
```

This method is called by the Virtual Machine to report that an uncaught exception has been thrown by `thread`. If this is not the root of the `ThreadGroup` tree, the `uncaughtException()` method of the parent group is called with the same arguments. If this is the root (if there is no parent group), the situation is handled locally. If `throwable` is a `ThreadDeath` object, no action is taken. If throwable is not `ThreadDeath`, the `throwable.printStackTrace()` method is called to print the stack to `System.err`. This method can be overridden to provide alternative ways of handling uncaught exceptions.

 For a description of threads and thread groups, see **thread**.

throw

keyword

The `throw` statement has as its one argument a throwable object. When the `throw` statement is executed, execution flow of the method is immediately terminated. The execution flow moves to the method that called this one, and there the throwable object will either be caught or passed on up to the next higher-calling method. This continues until there is a `catch` statement with an argument that matches the type of the throwable object.

Objects are commonly thrown to report errors and exceptions, but throw statements can be executed at any time with any throwable object.

For examples of throwing and catching objects, see **exception**.

throws

keyword

This is used as part of the declaration of a method to declare that the method `throws` a certain error or exception. The thrown object may originate in the method, or it can originate in a lower-level method that uses the `throws` keyword for the same purpose as this one. Using `throws` in the declaration, an exception can be thrown past any number of method calls.

Java only requires that checked exceptions be declared as being thrown. Unchecked exceptions can be thrown with or without appearing in a `throws` statement.

 For a description of checked exceptions, and for examples of throwing and catching objects, see **exception**.

Throwable

class java.lang.Throwable

This is the superclass of all errors and exceptions. Only objects that inherit `Throwable` can be the arguments of the `throw`, `throws`, and `catch` keywords. A `Throwable` object contains a copy of the execution stack at the moment of its creation. It can optionally include a text message that gives information about why it was thrown. Several of its subclasses include other information that can be used to help determine the reason for its having been thrown.

Extended by

```
Error
Exception
```

Inheritance

```
public class java.lang.Throwable
    implements Serializable
    extends Object
        ⇑
    public class java.lang.Object
```

Constructors

```
public Throwable()
public Throwable(String message)
```

If the `message` string is supplied, it is used as a detailed message describing this particular exception or error. The stack trace is automatically filled in by the constructor.

Returned by

A `Throwable` object is returned from `ExceptionInInitializerError.getException()`, `InvocationTargetException.getTargetException()`, and `Throwable.fillInStackTrace()`.

Methods

fillInStackTrace()

```
public Throwable fillInStackTrace()
```

This method can be used to insert a stack trace. This can be useful for an application that wishes to rethrow an exception or an error. This method simply replaces the stack trace already in the object with the stack trace of the location where this method is called.

getLocalizedMessage()

```
public String getLocalizedMessage()
```

The default implementation of this method is the same as `getMessage()`. This method can be overridden to produce a localized description of the `Throwable`.

getMessage()

```
public String getMessage()
```

Returns the detail message that was supplied on the constructor. If no message was supplied, the method returns `null`.

printStackTrace()

```
public void printStackTrace()

public void printStackTrace(PrintStream stream)

public void printStackTrace(PrintWriter stream)
```

This will format the stack trace into a readable form and write it to `stream`. If `stream` is not specified, it is written to `System.err`.

toString()

```
public String toString()
```

Returns a short description of the object.

 For examples of throwing and catching `Throwable` objects, see **exception**.

tilde

~

This is the one's complement operator. It takes an integer argument and converts the one-bits to zero and the zero-bits to one.

Example

This example initializes the integer value `before` and stores its one's complement into `after`:

```
public class OnesComplement {
    public static void main(String[] arg) {
        int before;
        int after;
        before = 0xA5F6F981;

        after = ~before;
        System.out.println(Integer.toBinaryString(before));
        System.out.println("0" +
                Integer.toBinaryString(after));
    }
}
```

The before and after values are printed as series of ones and zeroes. Notice that each one has been toggled:

```
10100101111101101111100110000001
01011010000010010000011001111110
```

It was necessary to put an extra zero on the front of the printed `after` value to make the line up—this is because the method `toBinaryString()` suppresses leading zeros.

 For the other bitwise operators, see **ampersand** and **bar**.

time

 See **date**.

Time

class java.sql.Time

This is an extension of `java.util.Date` to add the ability of JDBC to identify it as an SQL TIME value. There is formatting and parsing specially designed to support the JDBC escape syntax for time values.

Inheritance

```
public class java.sql.Time
    extends Date
        ⇑
    public class java.util.Date
            implements Serializable
            implements Cloneable
            extends Object
                ⇑
            public class java.lang.Object
```

Constructors

```
public Time(long time)
public Time(int hour,int minute,int second)
```

The value of `time` is the number of milliseconds since midnight, January 1, 1970, GMT. The `hour` value is from 0 to 23. The `minute` value is from 0 to 59. The `second` value is from 0 to 59.

Returned by

A Time object is returned from `CallableStatement.getTime()`, `ResultSet.getTime()`, and `Time.valueOf()`.

Methods

getDate()

```
public int getDate()
```

Returns the day of the month. This is a number from 1 to 31.

getDay()

```
public int getDay()
```

Returns the day of the week. This is a number from 0 to 6, with 0 as Sunday.

getMonth()

```
public int getMonth()
```

Returns the month. This is a number from 0 to 11, with 0 as January.

getYear()

```
public int getYear()
```

Returns the year. To get the actual year, add 1900.

setDate()

```
public void setDate(int day)
```

Sets the day of the month. The day is a number from 1 to 31.

setMonth()

```
public void setMonth(int month)
```

Sets the month. The month is a number from 0 to 11, with 0 as January.

setTime()

```
public void setTime(long time)
```

Sets the time. The time value is a count of the number of milliseconds since midnight, January 1, 1970, GMT.

setYear()

```
public void setYear(int year)
```

Sets the year. The year value is the actual year minus 1900.

toString()

```
public String toString()
```

Returns a string representation of the time and date in JDBC escape format.

valueOf()

```
public static Time valueOf(String string)
```

Converts the string from the JDBC escape format to a Time object.

For access to individual data columns, see **ResultSet**.

Timestamp

class java.sql.Timestamp

This is an extension of `java.util.Date` to add the ability of JDBC to identify it as an SQL TIMESTAMP value. It adds the capability of holding an SQL TIMESTAMP nanosecond value, and formatting and parsing is specially designed to support the JDBC escape syntax for timestamp values.

Nanoseconds on the side

This class adds the `nanos` value as a new piece of data separate from the millisecond value stored in `Date`. The inherited `Date` is capable of storing data accurate only to one second. Fractional portions of the second — all subsecond durations — are stored separately. The result is that calling any of the time-returning methods that are inherited from `Date` — `getTime()`, for example — will result in a time value accurate to only one second. The method `getNanos()` can be called to retrieve the fractional portion of the timestamp. Also, the calculated hashcode value does not consider the fractional portion — the same value will be returned for any timestamps that represent the same second.

Inheritance

```
public class java.sql.Timestamp
    extends Date
        ⇑
    public class java.util.Date
        implements Serializable
        implements Cloneable
        extends Object
            ⇑
        public class java.lang.Object
```

Constructors

```
public Timestamp(long time)

public Timestamp(int year,int month,int date,
        int hour,int minute,int second,int nano)
```

If a `time` value is supplied, it is the number of milliseconds since midnight, January 1, 1970, GMT. The `year` is the actual year minus 1900. The `month` is a value from 0 to 11. The day is a value from 1 to 31. The hour is a value from 0 to 23. The minute is a value from 0 to 59. The second is a value from 0 to 59. The value of nano ranges from 0 to 999,999,999.

Returned by

A Timestamp object is returned from CallableStatement.getTime(), ResultSet.getTime(), and Timestamp.valueOf().

Methods

after()

```
public boolean after(Timestamp timestamp)
```

Returns true if this Timestamp is later than timestamp.

before()

```
public boolean before(Timestamp timestamp)
```

Returns true if this Timestamp is earlier than timestamp.

equals()

```
public boolean equals(Timestamp timestamp)
```

Returns true if this Timestamp and timestamp represent exactly the same time.

getNanos()

```
public int getNanos()
```

Returns the fractional value of the Timestamp. The returned value is a count of nanoseconds — to get the millisecond value, divide the returned value by 1,000,000.

setNanos()

```
public void setNanos(int nanos)
```

Sets the fractional portion of the Timestamp to the specified number of nanoseconds.

toString()

```
public String toString()
```

Returns the value in the JDBC timestamp escape format. The returned string is in the form
```
yyyy-mm-dd hh:mm:ss.fffffffff
```

valueOf()

```
public static Timestamp valueOf(String string)
```

Converts a string in the JDBC timestamp escape format to a `Timestamp` object. The format of the string is

```
yyyy-mm-dd hh:mm:ss.fffffffff
```

 Also see **Time**.

TimeZone

class java.util.TimeZone

This class represents a time zone. It is capable of determining daylight savings time.

The default time zone

Normally, all that is needed is a call to `getDefault()` to retrieve the local time zone—the one where the program is executing.

The time zone ID

The creation of a `TimeZone` can be controlled by using a time zone ID. For example, use "CDT" for central daylight time, or "MST" for mountain standard time.

```
TimeZone tz = TimeZone.getTimeZone("PST");
```

The method `getAvailableIDs()` can be used to get a complete list of the known IDs.

Extended by

```
SimpleTimeZone
```

Inheritance

```
public abstract class java.util.TimeZone
    implements Serializable
    implements Cloneable
    extends Object
        ⇑
    public class java.lang.Object
```

Constructors

```
public TimeZone()
```

Returned by

Two static methods in this class that return `TimeZone` objects are `getDefault()` and `getTimeZone()`. Objects of this class are also returned from `getTimeZone()` methods in `Calendar` and `DateFormat`.

Methods

clone()

```
public Object clone()
```

Creates a duplicate of this object.

getAvailableIDs()

```
public static synchronized String[] getAvailableIDs()
```

```
public static synchronized String[] getAvailableIDs(int offset)
```

Returns an array of all the ID strings known to exist at the specified `offset` from GMT. If the `offset` is not specified, all ID strings are returned.

getDefault()

```
public static synchronized TimeZone getDefault()
```

Returns the default `TimeZone`.

getID()

```
public String getID()
```

Returns the ID string of this `TimeZone`.

getOffset()

```
public abstract int getOffset(int era,int year,int month,
            int day,int dayOfWeek,int milliseconds)
```

Returns the offset from UT for the specified date. The offset will be adjusted for daylight savings time. The returned value is a positive or negative number that should be added to the UT value to get the local time or subtracted from the local time to get the UT value.

The `era` is either `GregorianCalendar.AD` or `GregorianCalendar.BC`. The `year` is the full four-digit year number. The `month` is a number from 0 to 11. The `day` is the day of the month. The `dayOfWeek` is a number from 0 through 6, with 0 being Sunday. The `milliseconds` argument is the number of milliseconds since midnight.

getRawOffset()

```
public abstract int getRawOffset()
```

s
t
u

Returns the offset of this TimeZone from UT without consideration for daylight savings time. The returned value is a positive or negative number that should be added to the UT value to get the local time or subtracted from the local time to get the UT value.

getTimeZone()

```
public static synchronized TimeZone getTimeZone(String id)
```

Returns the TimeZone for the given id.

inDaylightTime()

```
public abstract boolean inDaylightTime(Date date)
```

Returns true of the date is in daylight savings time in this TimeZone.

setDefault()

```
public static synchronized void setDefault(TimeZone zone)
```

Changes zone to the default time zone.

setID()

```
public void setID(String id)
```

Changes the TimeZone ID string to id. It does not change any other data.

setRawOffset()

```
public abstract void setRawOffset(int offsetMillis)
```

Changes the time zone offset from UT to the value specified as offsetMillis. The value is a positive or negative number that should be added to the UT value to get the local time or subtracted from the local time to get the UT value.

useDaylightTime()

```
public abstract boolean useDaylightTime()
```

Returns true if this time zone uses daylight savings time.

 For an example of using a TimeZone to format date output, see **DateFormat**. For classes that make use of the TimeZone, see **Calendar**, **GregorianCalendar**, and **DateFormat**. Also see **SimpleTimeZone**.

token

 For information about breaking an input stream into a set of tokens, see **lexical structure.** For the specific types of tokens, see **identifiers, keywords, integer literals, floating-point literals, character literals, strings, separators,** and **operators**.

Toolkit

class java.awt.Toolkit

This is an AWT toolkit. It supplies the lowest level of Java access to the local GUI. For the most part, the methods of this class are not used directly in an applet or application, but there are some notable exceptions. There are methods here to convert raw graphical data into displayable images, return information about fonts, find out the size and resolution of the display, and get system property information.

The peers are here

Each component of the AWT has a peer object that does the work for the component for each operating system. The methods of the `Toolkit` class are used as the source of the peer objects. For example, whenever a button is created, the method `Toolkit.createButton()` is called to deliver the peer. The actual implementation of the peer will be different on, say, Windows from that on Solaris. Windows has a button built into the operating system, and Solaris normally uses a Motif button widget. The AWT is ported from one system to another by porting the peers of the Toolkit from one system to another.

Inheritance

```
public abstract class java.awt.Toolkit
     extends Object
             ⇑
     public class java.lang.Object
```

Constructors

```
public Toolkit()
```

Returned by

A `Toolkit` is returned from `Componenet.getToolkit()`, `ComponentPeer.getToolkit()`, `Toolkit.getDefaultToolkit()`, and `Window.getToolkit()`.

Methods

beep()

```
public abstract void beep()
```

Emits an audio beep.

checkImage()

```
public abstract int checkImage(Image image,
        int width,int height,ImageObserver observer)
```

Returns the status of the construction of an `image`. The `image` is constructed to the specified width and height for the default screen.

createButton()

```
protected abstract ButtonPeer createButton(Button target)
```

Returns a peer for the `Button`.

createCanvas()

```
protected abstract CanvasPeer createCanvas(Canvas target)
```

Returns a peer for the `Canvas`.

createCheckbox()

```
protected abstract CheckboxPeer createCheckbox(
        Checkbox target)
```

Returns a peer for the `Checkbox`.

createCheckboxMenuItem()

```
protected abstract CheckboxMenuItemPeer
        createCheckboxMenuItem(CheckboxMenuItem target)
```

Returns a peer for the `CheckBoxMenuItem`.

createChoice()

```
protected abstract ChoicePeer createChoice(Choice target)
```

Returns a peer for the `Choice`.

createComponent()

```
protected LightweightPeer createComponent(Component target)
```

Returns a peer for the Component. The returned peer has no window. This allows the Component and the Container classes to be extended directly to create windowless components that are defined entirely in Java.

createDialog()

```
protected abstract DialogPeer createDialog(Dialog target)
```

Returns a peer for the Dialog.

createFileDialog()

```
protected abstract FileDialogPeer createFileDialog(
        FileDialog target)
```

Returns a peer for the FileDialog.

createFrame()

```
protected abstract FramePeer createFrame(Frame target)
```

Returns a peer for the Frame.

createImage()

```
public abstract Image createImage(ImageProducer producer)
```

Returns a peer for the ImageProducer.

createImage()

```
public Image createImage(byte imagedata[])

public abstract Image createImage(byte imagedata[],
        int imageoffset,int imagelength)
```

Creates an image that is stored in imagedata as an array of bytes. The imagedata must be a raw-data form that is known to the Toolkit, such as GIF or JPEG. Either the entire array will be used, or the image data will be found at imagedata[imageoffset] and have a length of imagelength.

createLabel()

```
protected abstract LabelPeer createLabel(Label target)
```

Returns a peer for the Label.

createList()

```
protected abstract ListPeer createList(List target)
```

Returns a peer for the List.

createMenu()

```
protected abstract MenuPeer createMenu(Menu target)
```

Returns a peer for the Menu.

createMenuBar()

```
protected abstract MenuBarPeer createMenuBar(
        MenuBar target)
```

Returns a peer for the MenuBar.

createMenuItem()

```
protected abstract MenuItemPeer createMenuItem(
        MenuItem target)
```

Returns a peer for the MenuItem.

createPanel()

```
protected abstract PanelPeer createPanel(Panel target)
```

Returns a peer for the Panel.

createPopupMenu()

```
protected abstract PopupMenuPeer createPopupMenu(
        PopupMenu target)
```

Returns a peer for the PopupMenu.

createScrollbar()

```
protected abstract ScrollbarPeer createScrollbar(
        Scrollbar target)
```

Returns a peer for the Scrollbar.

createScrollPane()

```
protected abstract ScrollPanePeer createScrollPane(
        ScrollPane target)
```

Returns a peer for the ScrollPane.

createTextArea()

```
protected abstract TextAreaPeer createTextArea(
        TextArea target)
```

Returns a peer for the `TextArea`.

createTextField()

```
protected abstract TextFieldPeer createTextField(
        TextField target)
```

Returns a peer for the `TextField`.

createWindow()

```
protected abstract WindowPeer createWindow(Window target)
```

Returns a peer for the `Window`.

getColorModel()

```
public abstract ColorModel getColorModel()
```

Returns the color model used by the screen.

getDefaultToolkit()

```
public static synchronized Toolkit getDefaultToolkit()
```

Returns the default `Toolkit` object. This will be the `Toolkit` specified by the system property `awt.toolkit`. An `AWTError` is thrown if the `Toolkit` cannot be found or cannot be instantiated.

getFontList()

```
public abstract String[] getFontList()
```

Returns an array of the names of the fonts that are available on this system. Table T-1 lists the names of the fonts that are deprecated as of version 1.1 of Java, and the names that should be used in their place.

Table T-1   The Deprecated Font Names and Their Replacements

Deprecated	Use
TimesRoman	Serif
Helvetica	SansSerif
Courier	Monospaced
ZapfDingbats	(none)

While ZapfDingbats is deprecated as being a separate font name, Unicode defines Dingbat characters from '\u2700' through '\u27BF'.

getFontMetrics()

```
public abstract FontMetrics getFontMetrics(Font font)
```

Returns the `FontMetrics` object for the specified font. The returned metrics information includes information such as height and width for the default display.

getFontPeer()

```
protected abstract FontPeer getFontPeer(String name,
            int style)
```

Returns a peer for the named font in the specified style. The possible values of `style` are defined in the `Font` class.

getImage()

```
public abstract Image getImage(String filename)
```

```
public abstract Image getImage(URL url)
```

Creates and returns an `Image` by reading the pixel information from the named file. The file can be in a remote location specified by a URL. The data must be in one of the recognized formats (GIF or JPEG).

getMenuShortcutKeyMask()

```
public int getMenuShortcutKeyMask()
```

Returns an event modifier mask appropriate for keyboard menu accelerators (also called shortcuts). This method should be overridden if the control key is not the correct key to use for accelerators.

getNativeContainer()

```
protected static Container getNativeContainer(
            Component component)
```

This method provides native peers with the ability to query the native container of a native component..

getPrintJob()

```
public abstract PrintJob getPrintJob(Frame frame,
            String jobtitle,Properties props)
```

Initiates a printing operation on the native platform and returns a `PrintJob` object for it. A `null` is returned if the print job was canceled by the user.

getProperty()

```
public static String getProperty(String key,
          String defaultValue)
```

Returns the value string of a system property. The property is named as the key. If the key is not found, the defaultValue is returned in its place.

getScreenResolution()

```
public abstract int getScreenResolution()
```

Returns the screen resolution in pixels per inch.

getScreenSize()

```
public abstract Dimension getScreenSize()
```

Returns the size of the screen in inches.

getSystemClipboard()

```
public abstract Clipboard getSystemClipboard()
```

Returns an instance of the local system clipboard. There can be several Clipboard objects at any one time, but this is the one that interfaces with the clipboard capabilities of the native platform.

getSystemEventQueue()

```
public final EventQueue getSystemEventQueue()
```

Returns the EventQueue being used by the applet or application. The returned EventQueue could be the same one being used by other applets; but it may not, so no assumptions should be made as to whether or not this is a shared queue.

getSystemEventQueueImpl()

```
protected abstract EventQueue getSystemEventQueueImpl()
```

loadSystemColors()

```
protected void loadSystemColors(int systemColors[])
```

Copies the system colors into the array.

prepareImage()

```
public abstract boolean prepareImage(Image image,
          int width,int height,ImageObserver observer)
```

Prepares an image, at the specified width and height, for rendering on the default screen.

sync()

```
public abstract void sync()
```

Synchronizes the graphics state. This will flush any previously written graphic information—which could be buffered waiting for more—to the screen. This can be useful when doing animation.

Example 1

This example uses the default toolkit to list the names of the locally available fonts:

```
import java.awt.*;
public class FontList {
    public static void main(String[] arg) {
        Toolkit tk = Toolkit.getDefaultToolkit();
        String[] fontlist = tk.getFontList();
        for(int i=0; i<fontlist.length; i++)
            System.out.println(fontlist[i]);
        System.exit(0);
    }
}
```

The output looks like this:

```
Dialog
SansSerif
Serif
Monospaced
Helvetica
TimesRoman
Courier
DialogInput
ZapfDingbats
```

Example 2

This example lists some of the system-dependent information available from the Toolkit:

```
import java.awt.*;
public class ScreenData {
    public static void main(String[] arg) {
        Toolkit tk = Toolkit.getDefaultToolkit();
        tk.beep();
        System.out.println("Color model: " +
```

```
            tk.getColorModel());
        System.out.println("Screen resolution: " +
            tk.getScreenResolution());
        System.out.println("Screen size: " +
            tk.getScreenSize());
        System.exit(0);
    }
}
```

The output looked like this on a machine that uses the index color model:

```
Color model: java.awt.image.IndexColorModel@1cc91d
Screen resolution: 96
Screen size: java.awt.Dimension[width=800,height=600]
```

 Also see **properties**.

TooManyListenersException

class java.util.TooManyListenersException

Certain special cases arise in which there can be only one listener (these are known as *unicast*) as opposed to the normal situation in which there can be several (known as *multicast*). This exception is thrown when there is more than one listener in a unicast situation.

On the throws clause

This is a checked exception, so whenever you encounter a method declared as

```
throws TooManyListenersException
```

you can take it as an indicator that you have encountered the special case in which there can only be one listener, and you can write your code accordingly.

Inheritance

```
public class java.util.TooManyListenersException
    extends Exception
        ⇑
    public class java.lang.Exception
        extends Throwable
            ⇑
        public class java.lang.Throwable
            implements Serializable
```

```
             extends Object
                    ⇑
        public class java.lang.Object
```

Constructors

```
        public TooManyListenersException()
        public TooManyListenersException(String string)
```

If the `message` string is supplied, it is used as a detailed message describing this particular exception.

 For more on events and event listeners, see **EventObject** and **EventListener**.

Transferable

interface java.awt.datatransfer.Transferable

The interface used to implement classes that can be placed onto a `Clipboard` and retrieved.

Implemented by

```
        StringSelection
```

Inheritance

```
        public interface java.awt.datatransfer.Transferable
```

Constructors

Returned by

The object implementing this interface can be retrieved from a clipboard by making a call to `Clipboard.getContents()`.

Methods

getTransferData()

```
        public abstract Object getTransferData(DataFlavor flavor)
            throws UnsupportedFlavorException
            throws IOException
```

Returns a data object in the form specified by `flavor`. An `UnsupportedFlavorException` is thrown if the data cannot be represented in the form specified by the `flavor`. An `IOException` will be thrown if the data is no longer available.

getTransferDataFlavors()

```
public abstract DataFlavor[] getTransferDataFlavors()
```

Returns an array of all the flavors into which this data can be converted and returned. The array should be ordered with the most preferred flavors first.

isDataFlavorSupported()

```
public abstract boolean isDataFlavorSupported(
        DataFlavor flavor)
```

Returns `true` if this flavor is supported.

 For an example of using this interface to transfer data, see **Clipboard**.

transient

Class member variables can be declared as transient. This has no meaning in the current version of Java, but there are plans for future expansion into the area of persistent objects. All the variables in a class could become persistent, with the exception of those marked transient. For example, the class

```
public class Balloon {
        int maximumVolume;
        Color color;
        transient int currentVolume;
}
```

contains three variables. Two of these are parts of the basic definition of a `Balloon` object—the third, `currentVolume`, is a changeable value and there is no need to save it when saving the definition of the `Balloon`.

 For information on how `transient` affects serialization, see **Serializable**.

true

keyword

This is the constant `boolean` value. It is part of the Java language.

try

keyword

This keyword is used to declare a block containing code that could possibly throw one or more execeptions.

For examples of using `try` to `throw` and `catch` objects, see **exception**.

types

Java is a strongly typed language. This means that Java knows the type of everything at compile time. That the Java compiler knows the types of things also means that it knows their capabilities — the types and ranges of data that each can hold, and what operations can be performed on them.

The types are divided into three categories: the *primitive* types, the *reference* types, and the *null* type.

Primitive

The primitive types include the numeric types (both integer and floating-point), and the `boolean` type. The integer types are `char`, `byte`, `short`, `int`, and `long`. The floating-point types are `float` and `double`.

Reference

There are three kinds of references: class references, interface references, and array references.

null

The `null` type is a special case. Its value can be assigned to any reference. It is, in fact, the value assumed by an unitialized reference.

Any of the types can be stored in variables, passed as arguments, and returned from methods. All but the `null` type can have operations performed on them.

For more on the special `null` type, see **null**.

Types

class java.sql.Types

This is a collection of constant values used to identify the SQL column types. The numeric values of these type definitions match those in XOPEN.

Inheritance

```
public class java.sql.Types
    extends Object
        ⇑
    public class java.lang.Object
```

Variables and constants

BIGINT

```
public static final int BIGINT
```

The Java equivalent is `long`.

BINARY

```
public static final int BINARY
```

The Java equivalent is a `byte` array.

BIT

```
public static final int BIT
```

The Java equivalent is `boolean`.

CHAR

```
public static final int CHAR
```

The Java equivalent is `String`.

DATE

```
public static final int DATE
```

The Java equivalent is `java.sql.Date`.

DECIMAL

```
public static final int DECIMAL
```

The Java equivalent is `java.sql.Numeric`.

DOUBLE

```
public static final int DOUBLE
```

The Java equivalent is `double`.

FLOAT

```
public static final int FLOAT
```

The Java equivalent is `double`.

INTEGER

```
public static final int INTEGER
```

The Java equivalent is `int`.

LONGVARBINARY

```
public static final int LONGVARBINARY
```

The Java equivalent is `String`.

LONGVARCHAR

```
public static final int LONGVARCHAR
```

The Java equivalent is `String`.

NULL

```
public static final int NULL
```

There is no direct Java equivalent—this is the SQL specification for "no value."

NUMERIC

```
public static final int NUMERIC
```

The Java equivalent is `java.sql.Numeric`.

OTHER

```
public static final int OTHER
```

This is the indicator of an SQL type that is database-specific. The JDBC driver will map it to a type that can be accessed via `getObect()` and `setObject()` of ResultSet.

REAL

```
public static final int REAL
```

The Java equivalent is `float`.

SMALLINT

```
public static final int SMALLINT
```

The Java equivalent is short.

TIME

```
public static final int TIME
```

The Java equivalent is java.sql.Time.

TIMESTAMP

```
public static final int TIMESTAMP
```

The Java equivalent is java.sql.Timestamp.

TINYINT

```
public static final int TINYINT
```

The Java equivalent is byte.

VARBINARY

```
public static final int VARBINARY
```

The Java equivalent is a byte array.

VARCHAR

```
public static final int VARCHAR
```

The Java equivalent is a byte array.

 For access to SQL data columns, see **ResultSet** and **Statement**. To determine the type of a column, see **ResultSetMetaData**.

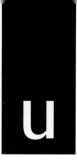

UID

class java.rmi.server.UID

This class is used to create a unique identifier for the host on which it originates.

A pure ID

A *pure* identifier can be created by using the constructor with no arguments. The result will be a unique identifier for the host machine if (1) the machine takes more than one second to reboot and (2) the machine's clock is never set backward. An ID that is universally unique can be created by pairing a UID with an InetAddress.

A well-known ID

A *well-known* ID can be created by using the constructor that takes a short argument. Any value can be used, so there are 65,535 unique well-known UIDs possible. It is guaranteed that any well-known ID will be different from a *pure* ID.

Inheritance

```
public final class UID
      implements Serializable
      extends Object
          ⇑
      public class java.lang.Object
```

Constructors

```
public UID()
public UID(short num)
```

Generates a pure UID with no argument or a well-known ID from a short value.

Returned by

A UID object is returned from the read() method.

Methods

equals()

```
public boolean equals(Object obj)
```

Returns `true` if the `Object` is `UID` with the same ID value as this one.

hashCode()

```
public int hashCode()
```

Returns the hashcode value of this object.

read()

```
public static UID read(DataInput in)
    throws IOException
```

Returns the `UID` from the input stream. An `IOException` is thrown if there is an error with the stream, or if the `UID` is malformed.

toString()

```
public String toString()
```

Returns a string representation of the UID value.

write()

```
public void write(DataOutput out)
    throws IOException
```

Writes the UID to the output stream.

UltraJava

 See **JavaChip**.

underflow

 For the action taken whenever the result of a real-number calculation becomes too small to be represented, see **byte, short, int, long, float,** and **double.**

UnexpectedException

class java.rmi.UnexpectedException

This exception is thrown to indicate that something unexpected happened at the remote site.

Inheritance

```
public class UnexpectedException
    extends RemoteException
        ⇑
    public class java.rmi.RemoteException
        extends IOException
            ⇑
        public class java.io.IOException
            extends Exception
                ⇑
            public class java.lang.Exception
                extends Throwable
                    ⇑
                public class java.lang.Throwable
                    implements Serializable
                    extends Object
                        ⇑
                    public class java.lang.Object
```

Constructors

```
public UnexpectedException(String message)

public UnexpectedException(String message,
        Exception exception)
```

The message string is supplied as a detailed message describing this particular exception. The optional exception can be included as the original exception causing this one to be thrown.

UnicastRemoteObject

class java.rmi.server.UnicastRemoteObject

This class represents a remote object that can only be referenced while the process on the server is alive.

Implementing the remote object

This class is provided as support for point-to-point active object references (method calls with arguments, and the returned result) using TCP/IP. A remote object should extend `UnicastRemoteObject`. If it does not, it will need to implement the `RemoteObject` interface and assume the responsibility of the correct semantics of `hashCode()`, `equals()`, and `toString()`—these must behave properly for remote objects.

Inheritance

```
public class java.rmi.server.UnicastRemoteObject
    extends RemoteServer
       ⇑
    public abstract class java.rmi.server.RemoteServer
        extends RemoteObject
           ⇑
        public abstract class java.rmi.server.RemoteObject
            implements Remote
            implements Serializable
            extends Object
               ⇑
            public class java.lang.Object
```

Constructors

```
protected UnicastRemoteObject()
    throws RemoteException
```

Creates and exports a `UnicastRemoteObject` on an anonymous port.

Methods

clone()

```
public Object clone()
    throws CloneNotSupportedException
```

Returns a clone of the remote object. The `CloneNotSupportedException` is thrown if the cloning has not been implemented for the object.

exportObject()

```
public static RemoteStub exportObject(Remote obj)
    throws RemoteException
```

Exports the `Remote` object so that it will be able to be called remotely. The `RemoteException` is thrown if the export fails.

For a general discussion, see **RMI**.

Unicode

Unicode is a standard character set in which each character is represented by 16 bits. This means there can be as many as 65,535 distinct characters. Java programs can be written using Unicode version 1.1. For information about Unicode, contact `http://unicode.org` or `ftp://unicode.org`.

Categories

The Unicode characters are placed into categories. Each category — designated by a two-letter code — is either a normative category (having to do with the basic origin or nature of the character) or an informative category (having to do with information about the character other than its origin). Tables U-1 and U-2 list all the categories.

Table U-1 The Unicode Normative Categories

Category	Description
Mn	Mark, Non-Spacing
Mc	Mark, Combining
Nd	Number, Decimal Digit
No	Number, Other
Zs	Separator, Space
Zl	Separator, Line
Zp	Separator, Paragraph
Cc	Other, Control or Format
Co	Other, Private Use
Cn	Other, Not Assigned

Table U-2 The Unicode Informative Categories

Category	Description
Lu	Letter, Uppercase
Ll	Letter, Lowercase
Lt	Letter, Titlecase

continued

Table U-2 *continued*

Category	Description
Lm	Letter, Modifier
Lo	Letter, Other
Pd	Punctuation, Dash
Ps	Punctuation, Open
Pe	Punctuation, Close
Po	Punctuation, Other
Sm	Symbol, Math
Sc	Symbol, Currency
So	Symbol, Other

Physical appearance

Two Unicode characters from entirely different alphabets can have the same physical appearance, but inside Java, they are very different. For example, the Latin capital letter *A* has a Unicode hex value of 0x0041. The Greek capital letter alpha looks identical but is represented internally by the hex value 0x0391.

The three cases

For the most part, there are only two cases—uppercase and lowercase—but some characters have a third case. This third case is known as the *titlecase*. These characters have the physical appearance of two letters combined into one. For example, there is the character that has the uppercase form "NJ" and the lowercase form "nj"—it also has the titlecase form "Nj." The titlecase form is appropriate for use when rendering a word in lowercase with initial capitals, as for a book title—thus, the name "titlecase."

Character blocks

The Unicode numeric values are grouped into blocks of characters and alphabets, as shown in Table U-3. The values in the first two columns specify the range of the block in hexadecimal. The first entry in the table, the one listed as Basic Latin, is the ASCII character set.

Table U-3 Unicode Character Set Blocks

Start Code	End Code	Block Name
0000	007F	Basic Latin
0080	00FF	Latin-1 Supplement
0100	017F	Latin Extended-A
0180	024F	Latin Extended-B
0250	02AF	IPA Extensions
02B0	02FF	Spacing Modifier Letters
0300	036F	Combining Diacritical Marks
0370	03FF	Greek
0400	04FF	Cyrillic
0530	058F	Armenian
0590	05FF	Hebrew
0600	06FF	Arabic
0900	097F	Devanagari
0980	09FF	Bengali
0A00	0A7F	Gurmukhi
0A80	0AFF	Gujarati
0B00	0B7F	Oriya
0B80	0BFF	Tamil
0C00	0C7F	Telugu
0C80	0CFF	Kannada
0D00	0D7F	Malayalam
0E00	0E7F	Thai
0E80	0EFF	Lao
0F00	0FBF	Tibetan
10A0	10FF	Georgian
1100	11FF	Hangul Jamo
1E00	1EFF	Latin Extended Additional
1F00	1FFF	Greek Extended
2000	206F	General Punctuation
2070	209F	Superscripts and Subscripts
20A0	20CF	Currency Symbols
20D0	20FF	Combining Marks for Symbols
2100	214F	Letterlike Symbols
2150	218F	Number Forms
2190	21FF	Arrows
2200	22FF	Mathematical Operators
2300	23FF	Miscellaneous Technical
2400	243F	Control Pictures

continued

Table U-3 *continued*

Start Code	End Code	Block Name
2440	245F	Optical Character Recognition
2460	24FF	Enclosed Alphanumerics
2500	257F	Box Drawing
2580	259F	Block Elements
25A0	25FF	Geometric Shapes
2600	26FF	Miscellaneous Symbols
2700	27BF	Dingbats
3000	303F	CJK Symbols and Punctuation
3040	309F	Hiragana
30A0	30FF	Katakana
3100	312F	Bopomofo
3130	318F	Hangul Compatibility Jamo
3190	319F	Kanbun
3200	32FF	Enclosed CJK Letters and Months
3300	33FF	CJK Compatibility
4E00	9FFF	CJK Unified Ideographs
AC00	D7A3	Hangul Syllables
D800	DB7F	High Surrogates
DB80	DBFF	High Private Use Surrogates
DC00	DFFF	Low Surrogates
E000	F8FF	Private Use
F900	FAFF	CJK Compatibility Ideographs
FB00	FB4F	Alphabetic Presentation Forms
FB50	FDFF	Arabic Presentation Forms-A
FE20	FE2F	Combining Half Marks
FE30	FE4F	CJK Compatibility Forms
FE50	FE6F	Small Form Variants
FE70	FEFF	Arabic Presentation Forms-B
FF00	FFEF	Halfwidth and Fullwidth Forms
FEFF	FEFF	Specials
FFF0	FFFF	Specials

Digit blocks

There are several sets of digits other than the familiar ASCII (or ISO-LATIN) digits 0 through 9 (which are the Unicode digits \u0030 through \u0039). The sets of digits are listed in Table U-4. (In the Unicode specification, these are all tagged as being in the "Nd" category.)

Table U-4 Unicode Digit Blocks

Start Code	End Code	Block Name
0030	0039	Basic Latin digits ('0' through '9')
0660	0669	Arabic-Indic digits
06F0	06F9	Extended Arabic-Indic digits
0966	096F	Devanagari digits
09E6	09EF	Bengali digits
0A66	0A6F	Gurmukhi digits
0AE6	0AEF	Gujarati digits
0B66	0B6F	Oriya digits
0BE7	0BEF	Tamil digits
0C66	0C6F	Telugu digits
0CE6	0CEF	Kannada digits
0D66	0D6F	Malayalam digits
0E50	0E59	Thai digits
0ED0	0ED9	Lao digits
0F20	0F29	Tibetan digits
FF10	FF19	Fullwidth digits

For details on inserting Unicode characters into ASCII text, see **escapes**. The primitive Unicode data type in Java is **char**. For information about the Unicode wrapper class, see **Character**. For a list of the first 127 Unicode characters, see **ASCII**. For the Java ways to sort Unicode, see **collation**. For the conversion of Unicode to and from native characters, see **native2ascii**.

union

There is nothing in Java that is like a C union. However, it is possible to construct one using a `ByteArrayOutputStream` and a `ByteArrayInputStream`.

universal time

The standard basis of time in Java is UT (Universal Time). This also known as UTC (Coordinated Universal Time) and GMT (Greenwich Mean Time).

UnknownError

class java.lang.UnknownError

This is thrown by the Virtual Machine whenever a serious—but unknown—error has occurred.

Inheritance

```
public class java.lang.UnknownError
    extends VirtualMachineError
        ⇑
    public class java.lang.VirtualMachineError
        extends Error
            ⇑
        public class java.lang.Error
            extends Throwable
                ⇑
            public class java.lang.Throwable
                implements Serializable
                extends Object
                    ⇑
                public class java.lang.Object
```

Constructors

```
public UnknownError()
public UnknownError(String message)
```

If the `message` string is supplied, it is used as a detailed message describing this particular exception.

UnknownHostException

class java.net.UnknownHostException

This exception is thrown to indicate a failure in determining the IP address of a named host.

Inheritance

```
public class java.net.UnknownHostException
    extends IOException
```

```
            ⇑
public class java.io.IOException
    extends Exception
            ⇑
    public class java.lang.Exception
        extends Throwable
                ⇑
        public class java.lang.Throwable
            implements Serializable
            extends Object
                    ⇑
            public class java.lang.Object
```

Constructors

```
public UnknownHostException()
public UnknownHostException(String host)
```

An `UnknownHostException` can optionally be created containing the name of the `host`.

 Also see **java.rmi.UnknownHostException**.

UnknownHostException

class java.rmi.UnknownHostException

This exception is thrown to indicate that the specified host is not known.

Inheritance

```
public class java.rmi.UnknownHostException
    extends RemoteException
            ⇑
    public class java.rmi.RemoteException
        extends IOException
                ⇑
        public class java.io.IOException
            extends Exception
                    ⇑
            public class java.lang.Exception
                extends Throwable
                        ⇑
```

```
public class java.lang.Throwable
    implements Serializable
    extends Object
            ⇑
    public class java.lang.Object
```

Constructors

```
public UnknownHostException(String message)

public UnknownHostException(String message,Exception exception)
```

An `UnknownHostException` can optionally be created containing the name of the `host`. The `message` string is supplied as a detailed message describing this particular exception.

 Also see **java.net.UnknownHostException**.

UnknownServiceException

class java.net.UnknownServiceException

This exception is thrown to indicate either that the MIME type returned by a URL connection is unknown or that the application is attempting to write to a read-only URL connection.

Inheritance

```
public class java.net.UnknownServiceException
    extends IOException
            ⇑
    public class java.io.IOException
        extends Exception
                ⇑
        public class java.lang.Exception
            extends Throwable
                    ⇑
            public class java.lang.Throwable
                implements Serializable
                extends Object
                        ⇑
                public class java.lang.Object
```

Constructors

```
public UnknownServiceException()
public UnknownServiceException(String message)
```

If the message string is supplied, it is used as a detailed message describing this particular exception.

UnmarshalException

class java.rmi.UnmarshalException

This exception is thrown to indicate an error during the unmarshaling of the stream arriving from the remote system.

Inheritance

```
public class java.rmi.UnmarshalException
    extends RemoteException
        ⇑
    public class java.rmi.RemoteException
        extends IOException
            ⇑
        public class java.io.IOException
            extends Exception
                ⇑
            public class java.lang.Exception
                extends Throwable
                    ⇑
                public class java.lang.Throwable
                    implements Serializable
                    extends Object
                        ⇑
                    public class java.lang.Object
```

Constructors

```
public UnmarshalException(String message)

public UnmarshalException(String message,Exception exception)
```

An UnmarshalException can optionally be created containing the original exception that caused this one to be thrown. The message string is supplied as a detailed message describing this particular exception.

Unreferenced

interface java.rmi.server.Unreferenced

This interface is implemented by a remote object wishing to be notified when no other objects are referring to it.

Inheritance

```
public interface java.rmi.server.Unreferenced
```

Methods

unreferenced()

```
public abstract void unreferenced()
```

This method will be called when the last reference to this remote object is withdrawn.

 For more information, see **RMI**.

UnsatisfiedLinkError

class java.lang.UnsatisfiedLinkError

This will be thrown when the Virtual Machine cannot resolve a Java reference to a native-code method.

Inheritance

```
public class java.lang.UnsatisfiedLinkError
    extends LinkageError
        ⇑
    public class java.lang.LinkageError
        extends Error
            ⇑
        public class java.lang.Error
            extends Throwable
                ⇑
            public class java.lang.Throwable
                implements Serializable
                extends Object
                    ⇑
                public class java.lang.Object
```

Constructors

```
public UnsatisfiedLinkError()
public UnsatisfiedLinkError(String message)
```

If the message string is supplied, it is used as a detailed message describing this particular exception.

unsigned

There is no way to declare an unsigned value in Java as there is in C++. The only unsigned data type is char, which is designed to contain a Unicode character.

 For the only unsigned data type, see **char**.

UnsupportedEncodingException

class java.io.UnsupportedEncodingException

This will be thrown when a specified character encoding method is not supported.

Inheritance

```
public class java.io.UnsupportedEncodingException
    extends IOException
        ⇑
    public class java.io.IOException
        extends Exception
            ⇑
        public class java.lang.Exception
            extends Throwable
                ⇑
            public class java.lang.Throwable
                implements Serializable
                extends Object
                    ⇑
                public class java.lang.Object
```

Constructors

```
public UnsupportedEncodingException()
public UnsupportedEncodingException(String message)
```

If the message string is supplied, it is used as a detailed message describing this particular exception.

UnsupportedFlavorException

class java.awt.datatransfer.UnsupportedFlavorException

This exception is thrown indicating that the requested data does not support the requested flavor.

Inheritance

```
public class java.awt.datatransfer.UnsupportedFlavorException
    extends Exception
        ⇑
public class java.lang.Exception
    extends Throwable
        ⇑
    public class java.lang.Throwable
        implements Serializable
        extends Object
            ⇑
        public class java.lang.Object
```

Constructors

```
public UnsupportedFlavorException(DataFlavor flavor)
```

The exception is constructed to include the flavor that was not supported.

URL

class java.net.URL

This is the wrapper for a Uniform Resource Locator—the address of a resource on the World Wide Web. For all practical purposes, an object of this class can be considered immutable.

Finding the stream handler

Whenever a URL object is instantiated, a protocol-specific URLStreamFactory is created (unless one already exists). That is, if a new instance is the first instance of URL with this protocol, a protocol-specific URLStreamHandler is created to handle it.

If there has been a URLStreamHandlerFactory set up by the application, then it will be used to create the stream protocol handler.

If no URLStreamHandlerFactory has been set up—or if the one that has been set up returns null—the constructor will look for the system property java.handler. protocol.pkgs. The value of the property is a list of packages separated by the vertical bar character (|). Using each of the package names, an attempt is made to load

    <package>.<protocol>.Handler

For example, if a package name is mypackage.hndlr and the protocol is http, there will be an attempt to load

    mypackage.hndlr.http.Handler

If there is still no handler, the constructor will attempt to load the class named

    sun.net.www.protocol.<protocol>.Handler

For example, if the protocol is HTTP, it will attempt to load

    sun.net.www.protocol.http.Handler

If this fails, then the MalformedURLException is thrown.

A Web resource

The resource addressed by the URL can simply be a file, or it can be a more complicated object. The URL can be a database query (such as is the case with a search engine), or it can include information to cause the returned data to configure itself (such as is the case of a tag to locate a particular spot within a Web page), or it can be the name of a program that will produce a customized Web page for the particular user (the sort of thing that is done by certain news services).

A URL begins with the protocol

A URL always includes a protocol. The most common protocol is HTTP, but there are other protocols, such as FTP, Gopher, and file. The HTTP protocol (HyperText Transfer Protocol) is used to transmit Web pages. The FTP protocol (File Transfer Protocol) is used to copy files from one location to another. The file "protocol" can be used to address files on the local host—no transmission protocol is necessary.

Absolute and relative

Every URL can be put into one of two categories—either it is absolute or it is relative. An absolute URL is the completely qualified name of a resource. An absolute URL can unambiguously locate the resource from anywhere on the Web. For example, the URL

    http://www.idgbooks.com/index.html

can be used from anywhere in the world to locate the file index.html on the host www.idgbooks.com and use http to transfer the file.

A relative URL can be used if no network is involved. For example:

```
http:pub/index.html
```

addresses the file `index.html` in the subdirectory `pub` on the local host. Another form of a relative URL specifies the host but not the file. For example:

```
http://www.idgbooks.com/
```

addresses a host, but not a specific file. In this case, the server will automatically fill in the file-name `index.html` or perform some other default action.

There can be a port number

The transmission protocol involved is TCP/IP, so a port number must be sent to the server. In the case of the URL, a default port number is generated according to the protocol. For example, the port number for HTTP is 80. This number can be specified in the URL this way:

```
http://www.idgbooks.com:80/index.html
```

This is needed only in special cases when the default must be overridden. The default port number for a protocol is called the *well-known* port number.

The anchor or the reference

Information can be appended to the end of a URL string for use as an anchor or a reference. An *anchor* is a special label in HTML; if a URL has an anchor, the local browser will immediately scroll to that section of the document. This idea was broadened for use in a query for sites (such as search engines and databases) that use the information as a key to locate data and generate an HTML document to be delivered to the client. These references can be quite elaborate—there is no size limitation on the transmitted URL string.

The anchor or the reference is separated from the body of the URL string with a question mark (?) character or an octothorpe (#). The octothorpe is used for HTML tags. These can be used in any combination that makes sense to the server.

Inheritance

```
public final class java.net.URL
    implements Serializable
    extends Object
         ⇑
    public class java.lang.Object
```

Constructors

```
public URL(String protocol,String host,int port,String file)
    throws MalformedURLException
```

```
public URL(String protocol,String host,String file)
    throws MalformedURLException
```

```
public URL(URL context,String spec)
    throws MalformedURLException
```

```
public URL(String spec)
    throws MalformedURLException
```

The URL is created for a specific protocol, host computer, port number, and file name. If the port number is not specified or is specified as –1, the default well-known port number for the protocol will be used.

The spec is the text string of a URL beginning with the protocol and containing the host and/or file information. If a nonnull context is specified, the URL is constructed from the spec within the context. The spec can then be incomplete and have its missing parts filled in from the context. For example, if the spec contains only a filename, the protocol, host, and port will be taken from the context and combined with the filename to create the resulting URL.

The spec can be an incomplete form, so some rules about its syntax are needed. If the string contains a colon (:) that comes before the first slash (/), the text preceding the colon is assumed to be the protocol.

A MalFormedURLException is thrown if a URLStreamHandler cannot be located. Because the URLStreamHandler is protocol specific, this will happen if the protocol name is invalid.

Returned by

An object of this class is returned from Applet.getCodeBase(), Applet.getDocumentBase(), AppletStub.getCodeBase(), AppletStub.getDocumentBase(), Class.getResource(), ClassLoader.getResource(), ClassLoader.getSystemResource(), and URLConnection.getURL().

Methods

equals()

```
public boolean equals(Object object)
```

Returns true if object is a URL representing the same resource in the same way as this one.

getContent()

```
public final Object getContent()
    throws IOException
```

Opens a connection and reads the contents of the URL. This is the same as calling openConnection() and then calling getConnect().

getFile()

```
public String getFile()
```

Returns the filename portion of the URL.

getHost()

```
public String getHost()
```

Returns the host name portion of the URL. If the URL is relative to the local host, this could be a zero-length string.

getPort()

```
public int getPort()
```

Returns the port number of the URL. If there is no port number, as could be the case with a relative URL, the return value is −1.

getProtocol()

```
public String getProtocol()
```

Returns the name of the protocol for this URL.

getRef()

```
public String getRef()
```

Returns the anchor, or reference, portion of this URL.

hashCode()

```
public int hashCode()
```

Returns the hashcode value for this object.

openConnection()

```
public URLConnection openConnection()
    throws IOException
```

Returns a URLConnection object that represents a connection to the remote object referred to by the URL. This could return a connection that is already open, or it could open a new one with a call to openConnection() of the protocol handler.

openStream()

```
public final InputStream openStream()
    throws IOException
```

Opens the connection to the URL and returns an input stream for reading from the connection. This is the same as calling openConnection() and then getStream().

sameFile()

```
public boolean sameFile(URL other)
```

Returns true if the other URL and this one are the same, exclusive of any anchor or reference specifications.

set()

```
protected void set(String protocol,String host,
        int port,String file,String ref)
```

Sets the internal values of the URL. This is not a public method and the class is final, so this method can called only by a URLStreamHandler.

setURLStreamHandlerFactory()

```
public static synchronized voidsetURLStreamHandlerFactory(
        URLStreamHandlerFactory factory)
```

This method is used to set the URLStreamHandlerFactory to be used by the application. This method can only be called once—the factory cannot be changed after it has been set. An error is thrown if the URLStreamHandlerFactory has already been set.

toExternalForm()

```
public String toExternalForm()
```

Uses the internal values to create the string form of a URL.

toString()

```
public String toString()
```

Returns a string representation of the object. This is the same as calling toExternalForm().

Example 1

This example takes the string form of a URL from the command line and uses it to create a URL object. It then prints each of its various parts:

```
import java.net.*;
public class UrlParts {
    public static void main(String[] arg) {
        try {
            URL url = new URL(arg[0]);
            System.out.println("File name: " +
                    url.getFile());
            System.out.println("Host name: " +
                    url.getHost());
            System.out.println("Port number: " +
```

```
                                        url.getPort());
                    System.out.println("Protocol: " +
                                url.getProtocol());
                    System.out.println("Reference: " +
                                url.getRef());
                } catch(MalformedURLException e) {
                    System.out.println(e);
                }
            }
        }
    }
```

Entering this URL string on the command line:

```
http://www.x.com:80/index.html#survey?max
```

will generate this output:

```
File name: /index.html
Host name: www.x.com
Port number: 80
Protocol: http
Reference: survey?max
```

Example 2

This is a minimal example of the code required for reading the HTML of a Web page from a remote site:

```
import java.net.*;
import java.io.*;
public class GimmeWebPage {
    public static void main(String[] arg) {
        try {
            int character;
            URL url = new URL(arg[0]);
            BufferedInputStream bin =
                (BufferedInputStream)url.getContent();
            while((character = bin.read()) > 0)
                System.out.print((char)character);
            System.out.println();
        } catch(Exception e) {
            System.out.println(e);
            System.exit(0);
        }
    }
```

```
            }
    }
```

The name of a Web page is specified on the command line, like this:

```
java GimmeWebPage http://www.idgbooks.com
```

A URL is created from the command line argument, and the `getContent()` method is called. The input stream returned from `getContent()` is used to copy the HTML text, character by character, to `System.out`.

 Also see **URLStreamHandler** and **URLConnection**. For the encoding of strings that are valid to be used as the reference portion of a URL, see **URLEncoder**.

URLConnection

class java.net.URLConnection

This abstract class is the superclass of all classes that represent a communications link between an application and a URL.

The one-step connection

If a `URLConnection` object is created for a URL that already has a connection established, then no further action is necessary — the connection will have been made. If there is no active connection, there will need to be a second step.

The two-step connection

If a `URLConnection` object is created for a URL that does not have a connection established, at least one other step will be needed to make the connection. A connection is made by calling the `connect()` method, but it may be necessary to use some of the "set" methods to configure the `URLConnection` object — this must be done before a connection can be made.

The defaults are reasonable

The default settings were designed to handle the most common situations and can generally be left as they are.

Extended by

```
HttpURLConnection
```

Inheritance

```
public abstract class java.net.URLConnection
    extends Object
        ⇑
    public class java.lang.Object
```

Variables and constants

allowUserInteraction

```
protected boolean allowUserInteraction
```

If this is true, the human-interaction items of the URL will be used (things such as popping up a dialog and waiting for a response). If it is set to false, no human interaction will occur. This will initially default to false, but the default can be changed by calling setDefaultAllowUserInteraction() before instantiating the URLConnection object.

connected

```
protected boolean connected
```

This defaults to false and is set to true once a connection has been established.

doInput

```
protected boolean doInput
```

This is set to true to indicate that the URL connection will be for input. A single connection can be used for both input and output. The default is true.

doOutput

```
protected boolean doOutput
```

This is set to true to indicate that the URL connection will be used for output. A single connection can be used for both input and output. The default is false.

fileNameMap

```
public static FileNameMap fileNameMap
```

An object for converting the name of a file to MIME format.

ifModifiedSince

```
protected long ifModifiedSince
```

This is a date stamp that is tested against the URL and will retrieve a new copy only if it has been modified since the time of the date stamp. The value is the number of milliseconds since January 1, 1970, GMT. The default is zero to indicate that it should always be retrieved.

url

```
protected URL url
```

The URL of the remote resource. This is initially set to the URL value supplied on the constructor.

useCaches

```
protected boolean useCaches
```

This is set to true to request that the protocol read from a cache if the object is available. If it is false, the URLConnection must always try to get a new copy of the object.

Constructors

```
protected URLConnection(URL url)
```

A URLConnection() object is created from a specific url.

Returned by

Objects of this class are returned from the openConnection() methods of URL and URLStreamHandler.

Methods

connect()

```
public abstract void connect()
    throws IOException
```

Opens a communications link to the resource specified by the URL. If the communications link has already been established, this method will do nothing.

getAllowUserInteraction()

```
public boolean getAllowUserInteraction()
```

Returns the value of the allowUserInteraction flag.

getContent()

```
public Object getContent()
    throws IOException
```

Retrieves the object addressed by the URL. A call is first made to getContentType() to determine the type of object. An instanceof operation should be performed to verify the type of object received.

The type of object being retrieved will need to be determined so that this method will be able to create an appropriate object. This is done by the ContentHandlerFactory specified in a call to setContentHandlerFactor(). If there is no ContentHandlerFactory, or if it returns null, an attempt will be made to load the class named

        sun.net.www.content.<type>

where <type> is formed by taking the content-type string, replacing all slash characters with a period ('.'), and replacing all other nonalphanumeric characters with the underscore character (_). The alphanumeric characters are specifically the 26 uppercase ASCII letters *A* through *Z,* the 26 lowercase ASCII letters *a* through *z,* and the 10 ASCII digits *0* through *9.* If no class can be found for the object, or if it is not a subclass of ContentHandler, then an UnknownServiceException is thrown to indicate that the protocol is not accepted.

getContentEncoding()

    public String getContentEncoding()

Returns the content-encoding header field. If it is not known, the method returns null.

getContentLength()

    public int getContentLength()

Returns the content-length header field value. If it is not known, the method returns −1.

getContentType()

    public String getContentType()

Returns the content-type header field. If it is not known, the method returns null.

getDate()

    public long getDate()

Returns the value of the data header field. Returns zero if it is not known. The value is the number of milliseconds since January 1, 1970, GMT.

getDefaultAllowUserInteraction()

    public static boolean getDefaultAllowUserInteraction()

Returns the default value of the allowUserInteraction field. This is the setting that will be assigned to the allowUserInteraction field whenever a new URLConnection is created.

getDefaultRequestProperty()

    public static String getDefaultRequestProperty(
            String key)

Returns the default value of the request property. This is the request property that will be set whenever a new URLConnection is created.

getDefaultUseCaches()

```
public boolean getDefaultUseCaches()
```

Returns the default value of the useCaches flag. This is the default that will be assigned whenever a new URLConnection is created.

getDoInput()

```
public boolean getDoInput()
```

Returns the value of the doInput flag.

getDoOutput()

```
public boolean getDoOutput()
```

Returns the value of the doOutput flag.

getExpiration()

```
public long getExpiration()
```

Returns the expiration date of the data for this URL. Returns zero if it is not known. The value is the number of milliseconds since January 1, 1970, GMT.

getHeaderField()

```
public String getHeaderField(String name)

public String getHeaderField(int number)
```

Returns the value of the specified header field specified by name. The number can be used to specify which header field. The method returns null if there is no such header field.

getHeaderFieldDate()

```
public long getHeaderFieldDate(String name,long default)
```

Assumes that the named header field is a date and parses it—returns the result as the number of milliseconds since January 1, 1970, GMT. If the named field is not found, the default is returned.

getHeaderFieldInt()

```
public int getHeaderFieldInt(String name,int default)
```

Assumes that the named header field is an integer value—parses it and returns the results. If there is no such header field, the method reruns the default.

getHeaderFieldKey()

```
public String getHeaderFieldKey(int number)
```

Returns the key value of the header field specified by the number. Returns `null` if there is no such header field.

getIfModifiedSince()

```
public long getIfModifiedSince()
```

Returns the value of `ifModifiedSince`.

getInputStream()

```
public InputStream getInputStream()
    throws IOException
```

Returns an input stream that can be used to read from the connection. An `UnknownServiceException` is thrown if the protocol of the URL is not supported.

getLastModified()

```
public long getLastModified()
```

Returns the value of the last-modified header field. It is a count of the number of milliseconds since January 1, 1970, GMT. If the value is not known, zero is returned.

getOutputStream()

```
public OutputStream getOutputStream()
    throws IOException
```

Returns an output stream that can be used to write to the connection. An `UnknownServiceException` is thrown if the protocol of the URL is not supported.

getRequestProperty()

```
public String getRequestProperty(String key)
```

Returns the value of the general request property of this connection.

getURL()

```
public URL getURL()
```

Returns the URL.

getUseCaches()

```
public boolean getUseCaches()
```

Returns the value of the `useCaches` flag.

guessContentTypeFromName()

```
protected static String guessContentTypeFromName(
        String urlName)
```

Makes an attempt to determine the content type of an object based on the rightmost portion of urlName. For example, if urlName ends with ".html," it is assumed to be a Web page.

guessContentTypeFromStream()

```
public static StringguessContentTypeFromStream(InputStream is)
    throws IOException
```

Makes an attempt to determine the type of input stream based on the characters that first arrive as the stream is read. This can be used to overcome an erroneous or misleading content-type specification.

setAllowUserInteraction()

```
public void setAllowUserInteraction(boolean setting)
```

Sets the value of allowUserInteraction.

setContentHandlerFactory()

```
public static synchronized void setContentHandlerFactory(
        ContentHandlerFactory factory)
```

Sets the ContentHandlerFactory that will be used by all URLConnection objects. This method can only be called once. An attempt to set the factory again will result in an Error being thrown.

setDefaultAllowUserInteraction()

```
public static void setDefaultAllowUserInteraction(
        boolean setting)
```

Sets the value of the allowUserInteraction field for all future URLConnection objects.

setDefaultRequestProperty()

```
public static void setDefaultRequestProperty(
        String key,String value)
```

Sets the value of the general-request property. Whenever a URLConnection is created, it is initialized with these properties. The key is the keyword for the property, and the value is its associated value.

setDefaultUseCaches()

```
public void setDefaultUseCaches(boolean setting)
```

Sets the value of defaultUseCaches.

setDoInput()

```
public void setDoInput(boolean setting)
```

Sets the value of doInput.

setDoOutput()

```
public void setDoOutput(boolean setting)
```

Sets the value of doOutput.

setIfModifiedSince()

```
public void setIfModifiedSince(long ifmodifiedsince)
```

Sets the value of ifModifiedSince.

setRequestProperty()

```
public void setRequestProperty(String key,String value)
```

Sets the general request property for this URLConnection. The key is the keyword for the property, and the value is its associated value.

setUseCaches()

```
public void setUseCaches(boolean setting)
```

Sets the value of useCaches.

toString()

```
public String toString()
```

Returns a string representation of this URLConnection.

 Also see **URL**.

URLEncoder

class java.net.URLEncoder

This is a utility class for converting a String into a MIME format called "x-www-form-urlencoded." The resulting string is suitable for use as the reference portion—the parameter values to the right of the filename—of a URL.

The conversion process

Each individual character is examined. The ASCII characters A–Z, a–z, and 0–9 are left unchanged. The ASCII space character ( ) is converted to a plus sign (+). All other characters are converted to three-character sequences in the form "%00," where "00" is the two-digit hexadecimal value of the lower eight bits of the character value.

Inheritance

```
public class java.net.URLEncoder
    extends Object
        ⇑
    public class java.lang.Object
```

Constructors

This class cannot be instatiated—it just has the one static method.

Methods

encode()

```
public static String encode(String string)
```

The string is converted to the MIME "x-www-form-urlencoded" format and returned.

Example

Using this simple program:

```
import java.net.*;
public class DoEncode {
    public static void main(String[] arg) {
        System.out.println(URLEncoder.encode(arg[0]));
    }
}
```

converted this string:

```
Hold varlet, what're ye 'bout?
```

into this string:

```
Hold+varlet%2c+what%27re+ye+%27bout%3f
```

 For a description of how this encoding can be used for HTML references, see **URL**.

URLStreamHandler

class java.net.URLStreamHandler

This is the superclass of all protocol stream handlers. A stream handler knows how to make and operate a connection for a specific protocol, such as HTTP, FTP, or Gopher.

It comes from the factory

For the most part, an instance of a URLStreamHandler is not created directly in an application—it is normally selected by the protocol name of a URL and established as the result of creating a URLConnection object.

Inheritance

```
public abstract class java.net.URLStreamHandler
    extends Object
        ⇑
    public class java.lang.Object
```

Constructors

```
public URLStreamHandler()
```

Returned by

A URLStreamHandler object is returned from
URLStreamHandlerFactory.createURLStreamHandler().

Methods

openConnection()

```
protected abstract URLConnection openConnection(URL url)
    throws IOException
```

Opens a connection to the resource referenced by the url. This method is overridden by a subclass so that the particulars of protocol-specific connections can be implemented. The IOException is thrown to report any error that occurs during the connection.

parseURL()

```
protected void parseURL(URL url,String spec,
        int start,int limit)
```

Parses spec—the string form of a URL—and inserts the results into the supplied url object. Any inherent context already in the url (filename, host, protocol, or such) that is not included in the spec will not be overwritten in the url. The string is parsed as if it were an HTTP specification—this will usually be correct for other protocols, but there are some minor exceptions.

The value of start is the index to the first character of spec to be included in the parse—it should be pointed to the first character following the colon (:) following the protocol name (if there is one). The limit is the index of the character just past the end of the parse—it should be the index of the octothorpe (#) (if there is one).

setURL()

```
protected void setURL(URL url,String protocol,
         String host,int port,String file,String ref)
```

Sets the fields of the URL to the values specified in the other arguments. The protocol is the protocol of the URL, the host is the name of the host computer, the port is the TCP/IP port number, the file is the name of the resource file, and the ref is the string that follows the octothorpe (#) to act as an anchor.

toExternalForm()

```
protected String toExternalForm(URL url)
```

Returns the standard string form of the url.

For more information on the URLStreamHandler, see **URL, URLConnection,** and **URLStreamHandlerFactory.**

URLStreamHandlerFactory

interface java.net.URLStreamHandlerFactory

This is the interface implemented by the factory that produces URLStreamHandler objects.

Inheritance

```
public interface java.net.URLStreamHandlerFactory
```

Methods

createURLStreamHandler()

```
public abstract URLStreamHandler createURLStreamHandler(
         String protocol)
```

Creates and returns a `URLStreamHandler` instance for the specified protocol. The `protocol` argument is the name of a protocol, such as HTTP or FTP.

 Also see **URL**, **URLConnection**, and **URLStreamHandler**.

UT or UTC

The standard basis of time in Java is UT (Universal Time). This is also known as UTC (Coordinated Universal Time) and GMT (Greenwich Mean Time).

UTF or UTF8

 See **Unicode**.

UTFDataFormatException

class java.io.UTFDataFormatException

This exception is thrown whenever a malformed UTF-8 string is encountered when reading data.

Inheritance

```
public class java.io.UTFDataFormatException
    extends IOException
        ⇑
    public class java.io.IOException
        extends Exception
            ⇑
        public class java.lang.Exception
            extends Throwable
                ⇑
            public class java.lang.Throwable
                implements Serializable
                extends Object
                    ⇑
                public class java.lang.Object
```

Constructors

```
public UTFDataFormatException()
public UTFDataFormatException(String message)
```

If the `message` string is supplied, it is used as a detailed message describing this particular exception.

util

package java.util

This is the package of utility classes with such items as calendar arithmetic, lists, and stacks.

Packages

```
zip
```

Interfaces

```
Enumeration
EventListener
Observer
```

Classes

```
BitSet
Calendar
Date
Dictionary
EventObject
GregorianCalendar
Hashtable
ListResourceBundle
Locale
Observable
Properties
PropertyResourceBundle
Random
ResourceBundle
SimpleTimeZone
Stack
StringTokenizer
TimeZone
Vector
```

t
u
v

Exceptions

EmptyStackException
MissingResourceException
NoSuchElementException
TooManyListenersException

variable

A variable is a location in memory that is assigned a name and a data type. It holds a value of that type and can be used for storage and retrieval of values. The contents of a variable can be changed in two ways. A value can be placed into it with an assignment operator (such as =, +=, or –=), or it can be altered with the increment and decrement operators (++ and ––).

The value contained in a variable is guaranteed by Java to be of the correct type. These checks are mostly made at compile time, but some checks are also made at run time.

The seven kinds of variables

Class variables

A *class variable* is one that is not replicated during instantiation. There is never more than one occurrence of it—the one that is created when the class is loaded. It is declared in a class with the keyword `static`. All variables declared in an interface are class variables by default.

Instance variables

An *instance variable* is one for which a new copy is created with each instantiation. A unique copy of an instance variable will exist in every object created from a class and all of its subclasses. It goes out of existence when the object goes out of existence. All variables defined in a class without the keyword `static` are instance variables.

Array components

Array components are the unnamed variables that make up the individual members of an array. They come into existence when an array is created and disappear when the array is no longer referenced.

Method parameters

Every argument passed to a method causes the creation of a new parameter variable containing the value of the argument. Such a *method parameter* ceases to exist when the method returns.

Constructor parameters

Every argument passed to a constructor causes the creation of a new parameter variable containing the value of the argument. Such a *constructor parameter* ceases to exist when the constructor returns.

Exception-handler parameters

A variable is constructed by the `catch` statement whenever it handles an exception. This variable, the *exception-handler parameter,* is a reference to the thrown exception. Its existence ends when the `catch` block completes.

Local variables

Whenever the flow of execution enters a block (or a `for` statement), a new *local variable* is created for every variable declaration anywhere in that block (or within the `for` statement). A local variable ceases to exist whenever the flow of execution leaves its block (or the block of its `for` statement).

Initial values

The compiler will not allow code to be generated that references an uninitialized variable. Method and constructor parameters are initialized to their corresponding argument values. Local variables must be assigned a value before they can be used, but other variables do not — they are all automatically assigned default values by the compiler. The numeric primitive types all default to zero, a `boolean` type defaults to `false`, and a reference defaults to `null`.

Local variables

A local variable is one that is declared inside a block of executable code. This means that local variables always reside inside methods. A local variable cannot be declared `static`.

Normally, you can consider a local variable to be created where the flow of execution reaches its declaration — but you will need to think of the `switch` statement as a special case. Even though the flow of execution may skip over unselected case statements, it acknowledges the presence of local variable declarations by bringing them into existence.

 For array variable existence, see **array** and **garbage collection**. For a local variable in a `for` loop, see **for**. A local variable must have had a value assigned before it can be used — see **definite assignment**. For information on local variable declaration inside a `switch` statement, see **switch**. For information on sharing data through variables, see **static**.

Vector

class java.util.Vector

A `Vector` object has the ability to manage an array of objects. The array will automatically grow in size as new objects are added. The class is really just a thin wrapper around an array of objects.

Capacity management

A `Vector` will automatically allocate space as needed. The amount of space it has allocated at any one time is normally more than it needs. It is done this way for efficiency. Because of the overhead involved with each RAM allocation, it is done in chunks. There are methods that allow you to tune the size of these chunks to optimize the `Vector` for the way that you are going to be using it.

Duplicate entries

The `Vector` class will store any kind of object—it pays no attention to the value of its contents. In fact, the same object can be inserted into the array any number of times. There are methods that can be used to search for an object from the beginning (to find its first occurrence), from the end (to find its last occurrence), and even from somewhere in the middle.

The null object

It is valid to have the `null` object as an element of the array.

Extended by

```
Stack
```

Inheritance

```
public class java.util.Vector
    implements Cloneable
    implements Serializable
    extends Object
            ⇑
    public class java.lang.Object
```

Variables and constants

capacityIncrement

```
protected int capacityIncrement
```

The size of the increment. This controls the amount of RAM that is to be allocated each time the Vector needs to expand the capacity of its array of references. For example, if this value is 5, with each allocation space will be added to hold five more objects. The default setting of zero causes the current size of the array to be doubled on each allocation.

elementCount

```
protected int elementCount
```

A count of the number of objects.

elementData

```
protected Object elementData[]
```

The array of objects.

Constructors

```
public Vector()

public Vector(int initial)

public Vector(int initial,int increment)
```

The constructors create an empty Vector object. If initial is supplied, it will specify the number of objects that can be held in the initial array allocation. The initial default is 10. If increment is specified, it will determine the number of new spaces that are allocated each time the vector needs to grow in size. The increment will default to zero and simply double its size with each allocation.

Methods

addElement()

```
public final synchronized void addElement(Object obj)
```

Adds a new object as the last element of the vector.

capacity()

```
public final int capacity()
```

Returns the current capacity of the vector. This value changes only when new space is allocated—it is always greater than or equal to the value returned by size().

clone()

```
public synchronized Object clone()
```

This method returns a copy of this vector. It is a shallow copy in the sense that the array and the counts are duplicated, but the individual objects held in the vector are not duplicated.

contains()

```
public final boolean contains(Object element)
```

Returns `true` if the specified `element` is in the vector.

copyInto()

```
public final synchronized void copyInto(Object anArray[])
```

The elements in the vector are copied into the array. If the array is too small to hold them all, an `ArrayIndexOutOfBoundsException` is thrown.

elementAt()

```
public final synchronized Object elementAt(int index)
```

This returns the element at the `index`. If there is no element at the specified `index`, an `ArrayIndexOutOfBoundsException` is thrown.

elements()

```
public final synchronized Enumeration elements()
```

This method returns an `Enumeration` object that can be used to access all the elements in the vector.

ensureCapacity()

```
public final synchronized voidensureCapacity(int capacity)
```

This will, if necessary, adjust the `capacity` of the vector up to the specified amount. The `capacity` is the number of objects the `Vector` can hold.

firstElement()

```
public final synchronized Object firstElement()
```

This returns the first element of the `Vector`. If it is empty, a `NoSuchElementException` is thrown.

indexOf()

```
public final int indexOf(Object element)
```

```
public final synchronized intindexOf(Object element,int index)
```

This method will search for the specified `element` and return its index. If an `index` is specified, the search will begin there—if not, the search will begin at the first element of the array. The search is made from its starting point and continues to the end of the array, ignoring all the elements that come before the starting point. If element is not found, −1 is returned.

insertElementAt()

```
public final synchronized void
          insertElementAt(Object element,int index)
```

This method will insert element at the specified index. To make room, the elements already in the array —at index and above —will be moved up by one to make room. If the index is invalid, an ArrayIndexOutOfBoundsException is thrown.

isEmpty()

```
public final boolean isEmpty()
```

This will return true if there are no elements in the array.

lastElement()

```
public final synchronized Object lastElement()
```

This returns the last element of the Vector. If the array is empty, a NoSuchElementException is thrown.

lastIndexOf()

```
public final int lastIndexOf(Object element)
```

```
public final synchronized int
          lastIndexOf(Object element,int index)
```

This is a reverse search. It will start at the end of the array (or at the specified index) and search toward the front of the array for element. The method will return the index at which element is found or, if it is not found, the method will return −1.

removeAllElements()

```
public final synchronized void removeAllElements()
```

Empties the vector.

removeElement()

```
public final synchronized booleanremoveElement(Object element)
```

Searches for the element and, if found, removes it. The search proceeds from the beginning of the array, and if there is more than one occurrence of the element, only the first one will be removed. If the element was found and removed, the return value is true; otherwise, it is false.

removeElementAt()

```
public final synchronized void removeElementAt(int index)
```

The element at the `index` is removed. The elements in the array that have indexes greater than this one are all shifted down by one to fill the gap. If the specified `index` is not valid, an `ArrayIndexOutOfBoundsException` is thrown.

setElementAt()

```
public final synchronized void
        setElementAt(Object element,int index)
```

This method will replace the element at `index` with a new one. If `index` is not valid, an `ArrayIndexOutOfBoundsException` is thrown.

setSize()

```
public final synchronized void setSize(int newSize)
```

This method sets the number of elements in the array. Any elements beyond the end of the new size are discarded. If the size expands the array, the new elements are all `null`.

size()

```
public final int size()
```

This method returns the number of elements in the array. This is always less than or equal to the value returned by `capacity()`.

toString()

```
public final synchronized String toString()
```

This method will convert the `Vector` object to a `String`. It does this by converting each member of the array to a `String` and then concatenating them all together. This means the `String` will be very long for large arrays. This mostly has use in debugging.

trimToSize()

```
public final synchronized void trimToSize()
```

This will reduce the capacity of the internally allocated array to fit exactly the number of elements in the array. This can be used if there is a need to reduce the amount of storage taken up by a `Vector` object. After this is done, the `Vector` will still operate normally—the next insertion of an element will cause a new allocation to be made.

 For other classes that can contain references, see **Hashtable** and **Stack**.

u

v

w

VerifyError

class java.lang.VerifyError

This is thrown whenever the verifier detects a class file that contains some internal inconsistency or a security problem.

Inheritance

```
public class java.lang.VerifyError
    extends LinkageError
        ⇑
    public class java.lang.LinkageError
        extends Error
            ⇑
        public class java.lang.Error
            extends Throwable
                ⇑
            public class java.lang.Throwable
                implements Serializable
                extends Object
                    ⇑
                public class java.lang.Object
```

Constructors

```
public VerifyError()
public VerifyError(String message)
```

If the message string is supplied, it is used as a detailed message describing this particular exception.

VetoableChangeListener

interface java.beans.VetoableChangeListener

This is the interface of a class that will be notified whenever a vetoable change is being made to a bean. A vetoable property, also known as a constrained property, can have change attempts reversed by a VetoableChangeListener. The VetoableChangeListener will need to be registered with a bean to be notified of any attempts to change a constrained property.

Inheritance

```
public interface java.beans.VetoableChangeListener
    extends EventListener
        ⇑
    public interface java.util.EventListener
```

Methods

vetoableChange()

```
public abstract void vetoableChange(PropertyChangeEvent event)
    throws PropertyVetoException
```

This method is called whenever a constrained property has been changed. The event contains information describing the property and both the old and new values of the change. The PropertyVetoException is thrown if the property change should be rolled back to the old value.

 See **PropertyChangeEvent**, **PropertyDescriptor**, **PropertyVetoException**, and **VetoableChangeSupport**.

VetoableChangeSupport

class java.beans.VetoableChangeSupport

An object of this class can be used as a registry to hold a list of VetoableChangeListeners. It also has methods that can be used to send change notifications to the registrants. This class can be used by a bean that supports constrained properties—it can be used as is, or it can be subclassed.

Inheritance

```
public class java.beans.VetoableChangeSupport
    implements Serializable
    extends Object
        ⇑
    public class java.lang.Object
```

Constructors

```
public VetoableChangeSupport(Object sourceBean)
```

The sourceBean is the bean that is to be the source of any events.

Methods

addVetoableChangeListener()

```
public synchronized void addVetoableChangeListener(
        VetoableChangeListener listener)
```

Adds a `VetoableListener` to the list of those that will be notified whenever a vetoable change is being made.

fireVetoableChange()

```
public void fireVetoableChange(String propertyName,
        Object oldValue,Object newValue)
    throws PropertyVetoException
```

This method is called to report the update of a property to any registered listeners. The `propertyName` is the name of the property being changed. The existing value is supplied as the `oldValue`, and the modified value is the `newValue`. No notification will be made if the `oldValue` is equal to the `newValue`.

The `PropertyVetoException` is thrown in the event of a veto—the property will then be rolled back to the `oldValue`.

removeVetoableChangeListener()

```
public synchronized void removeVetoableChangeListener(
        VetoableChangeListener listener)
```

Removes the listener from the list of those that will receive notification of changes.

 Also see **PropertyDescriptor** and **VetoableChangeListener**.

view

A Java bean has the ability to expose its interfacing controls and internal capabilities. Objects can be instantiated that contain the information. One object will describe certain aspects; another object will describe other aspects. These groupings of the capabilities of a bean are called *views*—each is a slightly different way of looking at a bean.

Virtual Machine

Java Virtual Machine (JVM)

The Java Virtual Machine is a program that loads and executes class files. It contains the lowest-level run-time facilities of Java. It is an interpreter in the sense that it reads a sequence of opcodes (the bytecodes) and executes one or more native instructions for each one of them. It is a virtual machine in the sense that, while it is executing a program, it maintains a program counter, registers, and stacks.

Data types

The JVM offers direct support for all the Java primitive types: `byte`, `short`, `char`, `int`, `long`, `float`, and `double`. It also uses two other data types internally —the `object` type (which holds the address of an object) and the `returnAddress` type (which holds a return address used to exit a method).

Registers

The JVM has a set of 32-bit special-purpose registers. The registers are machine addresses of locations in memory. Each register has a name.

frame

This register points to the execution environment structure.

optop

This register points to the top of the operand stack.

pc

This register points to the next bytecode to be executed.

vars

This register references the memory space of the local variables.

Local variables

Each Java method has its own fixed-size block of local variables allocated when the method is called. Local variables are all 32 bits and are addressed as offsets from the `vars` register. The 64-bit data types consume two local variable positions but are addressed only by the offset of the first 32-bit location.

The operand stack

The JVM instructions pop their operands from a stack, perform the operations, and push the results back onto the stack. The stack is also used to pass arguments and return results. It is 32 bits wide. Each primitive data type has specialized instructions that know how to work with its values from the stack. Instructions must match the type on the stack—it is not possible to push one data type and then manipulate it using the opcode for another type. This rule is enforced by the bytecode verifier.

The stack is not contiguous—each method invocation is allocated its own stack frame. Each individual stack can be expanded as required. Because all dynamic memory in Java comes from stack allocation, an `OutOfMemoryError` can be thrown only when there is insufficient RAM to create or expand a stack.

Exception and error propagation

An exception or an error will cause a `Throwable` object to be created and thrown. This results in an immediate departure from the current point of execution.

Things that can cause an exception

- A dynamic linkage failure occurs. A class file may not be found, or the one that is found may not be valid.
- A run-time error, such as a null pointer reference, occurs.
- The program executes a `throw` statement.
- An asynchronous event, such as `Thread.stop()`, is received from another thread.

The throwing of an exception

When an exception occurs, the `catch` clauses defined for the method are inspected. Each `catch` clause specifies the range of instructions for which it is responsible and describes the type of exception it can handle—it also has the address of the code to handle the exception.

If a matching `catch` clause is found, control branches to the handler code, and normal execution will continue from wherever the `catch` clause leaves off (after executing the `finally` clause). If no `catch` code is found inside a method, the method returns to its caller and the search continues there. The search will continue until all the nested `catch` clauses have been examined, and if none were found to match, the default exception handler is executed.

Garbage collection

Objects in Java are recycled—garbage collected—automatically by the JVM. There is no way that an application can specifically delete an object. The algorithm for garbage collection is unspecified and will vary from one implementation of the JVM to another. Although the data areas are garbage-collected in every version of the JVM, recycling of the area used to hold class definitions began with Java 1.1.

 To execute the JVM, see **java**. For loading classes for execution, see **ClassLoader**.

VirtualMachineError

class java.lang.VirtualMachineError

This is thrown when an error is detected in the Virtual Machine. Either it has run out of resources, or something is wrong in the machine itself.

Extended by

```
InternalError
StackOverflowError
OutOfMemoryError
UnknownError
```

Inheritance

```
public class java.lang.VirtualMachineError
    extends Error
        ⇑
    public class java.lang.Error
        extends Throwable
            ⇑
        public class java.lang.Throwable
            implements Serializable
            extends Object
                ⇑
            public class java.lang.Object
```

Constructors

```
public VirtualMachineError()
public VirtualMachineError(String message)
```

If the message string is supplied, it is used as a detailed message describing this particular exception.

Visibility

interface java.beans.Visibility

This interface defines methods that can be used to query a bean as to whether or not it is capable of operating in a non-GUI situation—some can and some can't. If the bean can be used in a non-GUI environment, this interface also defines the methods to request that it do so.

A modified interface

The use of this interface is considered to be an advanced technique for expert bean developers. To avoid confusion with the simpler interfaces, this one does not use the standard "get" and "set" method-naming convention.

Inheritance

```
public interface java.beans.Visibility
```

Methods

avoidingGui()

```
public abstract boolean avoidingGui()
```

Returns true if this bean is currently avoiding the use of any GUI capabilities because of an earlier call to dontUseGui().

dontUseGui()

```
public abstract void dontUseGui()
```

Specifies that this bean should not use the GUI.

needsGui()

```
public abstract boolean needsGui()
```

Returns true if this bean needs the GUI and cannot operate without it.

okToUseGui()

```
public abstract void okToUseGui()
```

Notifies the bean that the GUI is available for use.

VMID

class java.rmi.dgc.VMID

This class holds the identifier of a Virtual Machine. An identifier value is unique among all Virtual Machines. This identification is necessary for garbage collection of resources held by remote Virtual Machines, and it also has other uses.

Conditions of uniqueness

A unique ID for every possible installation of the Virtual Machine can be achieved if certain conditions are met. First, the condition for uniqueness of `java.rmi.server.UID` must be satisfied. Second, an address can be obtained for the host—one that is unique and remains constant for the lifetime of the object. A dial-up account is an example of a situation in which the address will change, causing a change in the ID.

Inheritance

```
public final class java.rmi.dgc.VMID
    implements Serializable
    extends Object
           ⇑
    public class java.lang.Object
```

Constructors

```
public VMID()
```

Returned by

A `VMID` object is returned from `Lease.getVMID()`.

Methods

equals()

```
public boolean equals(Object object)
```

Returns `true` if `object` is a `VMID` with the same identifier as this one.

hashCode()

```
public int hashCode()
```

Returns the hashcode value for this object.

isUnique()

```
public static boolean isUnique()
```

Returns `true` only if the criteria to create a unique `VMID` have been met.

toString()

```
public String toString()
```

Returns a string representation of this object.

void

The Java language requires that every method have a declared return type. This is the type to use in declaring a method that returns nothing.

Void

class java.lang.Void

This is a wrapper class for the primitive type void. There is one global instance of the Void class, and no others can be instantiated. It exists for the sole purpose of being a placeholder.

What is this for?

The wrappers of the primitive data types (Integer, Double, and so on) all contain a TYPE field that holds the reference to their defining Class object. In this way, objects of these wrappers can be mixed together in a container of some sort, and they can be identified by looking at the TYPE field of each one. The Void wrapper works the same way—it can be intermixed with the other wrappers as a placeholder.

Inheritance

```
public final class java.lang.Void
    extends Object
        ⇑
    public class java.lang.Object
```

Variables and constants

TYPE

```
public final static Class TYPE
```

The Class that represents the primitive type void.

volatile

keyword

If a variable is declared in such a way that its contents could be changed by more than one thread, and if the threads execute in such a way that it is not necessary to use synchronized to make sure that there are no collisions, the variable should be declared as `volatile`. This is information used by the compiler to make sure that the variable is freshly loaded each time it is referenced, instead of using a previously loaded value.

u
v
w

while

keyword

This language keyword takes, as its one argument, a Boolean expression; it will repeatedly execute a block of code as long as the expression is `true`. If the expression is `false` at the beginning, the block will never execute (unlike the do/while pair, which will always execute the block at least once).

The `while` block

A loop is written with `while` at its top like this:

```
while(boolean expression) {
    body of the loop
}
```

The body of the loop will execute after the Boolean expression has been tested. If the Boolean expression evaluates to `true`, the body will be executed. This continues until the Boolean expression is `false`.

The `break` statement

A `break` statement will cause the `while` block to exit immediately. For example, this loop will print the values 0 and 1 and then exit the loop:

```
int i = 0;
while(i++ < 5) {
    if(i == 2)
        break;
    System.out.println(i);
}
```

It is also possible to use a label on the `break` statement by labeling the loop itself, in this way:

```
int i = 0;
whileLabel: while(i++ < 5) {
    if(i == 2)
```

```
            break whileLabel;
        System.out.println(i);
    }
```

The advantage of using a label is the ability to break from nested loops of
do, for, and while. This break statement will break both loops because it
breaks out to the label:

```
int i = 0;
whileLabel: while(i++ < 5) {
    int j = 0;
    while(j++ < 5) {
        if(j == 2)
            break whileLabel;
        System.out.println(j);
    }
}
```

The continue statement

A continue statement will cause the while block to jump to the top and test
for the next iteration. This loop will print the values 0, 1, 3, 4, and 5. The value
2 is skipped by the continue statement:

```
int i = 0;
while(i++ < 5) {
    if(i == 2)
        continue;
    System.out.println(i);
}
```

It is also possible to use a label on the continue statement by labeling the
loop itself, in this way:

```
int i = 0;
whileLabel: while(i++ < 5) {
    if(i == 2)
        continue whileLabel;
    System.out.println(i);
}
```

One advantage of using a label is the ability to continue the iteration of an
outer loop in the case of nested do, for, and while loops. This continue statement will go to the test at the bottom of the outer do loop:

```
int i = 0;
whileLabel: while(i++ < 5) {
```

```
        int j = 0;
        while(j++ < 5) {
            if(j == 2)
                continue whileLabel;
            System.out.println(j);
        }
    }
```

 The other iteration keywords are **for** and **do**. There is conditional execution with **if** and **switch**.

white space

 For the white-space characters accepted by the compiler, see **lexical structure**.

widening

 For widening of the primitive types, see **conversion**. Also see **reference**.

Window

class java.awt.Window

A `Window` object is a top-level display area with no borders and no menu bar. It is suitable for a pop-up display or dialog. It is modal—that is, it will grab the mouse and keyboard focus and hold them as long as it is being displayed.

Layout manager

The default layout manager is `BorderLayout`.

Events

The events generated by a `Window` are `WindowOpened` and `WindowClosed`.

Extended by
```
Dialog
Frame
```

Inheritance

```
public class java.awt.Window
    extends Container
        ⇑
    public abstract class java.awt.Container
        extends Component
            ⇑
        public class java.awt.Component
            implements ImageObserver
            implements MenuContainer
            implements Serializable
            extends Object
                ⇑
            public class java.lang.Object
```

Constructors

```
public Window(Frame parent)
```

A Window is initially constructed as being invisible. The parent is the owner of the Window.

Returned by

An object of this class is returned from WindowEvent.getWindow().

Methods

addNotify()

```
public void addNotify()
```

Creates the underlying system-dependent peer for this object. This method is not normally called by the application. It is called by the container.

addWindowListener()

```
public synchronized void
        addWindowListener(WindowListener listener)
```

Adds a listener that will be sent the events issuing from the Window.

dispose()

```
public void dispose()
```

This method must be called to release any resources that are being held by the Window.

getFocusOwner()

```
public Component getFocusOwner()
```

Returns the child component of the `Window` that currently has the focus. If the `Window` is not active, no component has the focus, so the return value can be `null`.

getLocale()

```
public Locale getLocale()
```

Returns the locale of the `Window`. If none has been set, the default is returned.

getToolkit()

```
public Toolkit getToolkit()
```

Returns the `Toolkit` for the `Window`.

getWarningString()

```
public final String getWarningString()
```

Returns the text that will be displayed for windows that are not secure. The string is defined by the system property "awt.appletWarning." If no such property has been defined, the returned string is "Warning: Applet Window."

isShowing()

```
public boolean isShowing()
```

Returns `true` if the `Window` is currently being displayed.

pack()

```
public void pack()
```

Causes the layout manager to calculate the sizes and positions of all the components and lay them out for display.

postEvent() deprecated

```
public boolean postEvent(Event event)
```

Posts an event to this `Window`. This method is deprecated — use `dispatchEvent()` instead.

processEvent()

```
protected void processEvent(AWTEvent event)
```

If `event` is a `WindowEvent`, the process `WindowEvent()` method is called. If not, the event is propagated up with a call to `processEvent()` of the superclass.

processWindowEvent()

```
protected void processWindowEvent(WindowEvent event)
```

This method will dispatch the event to all `WindowListeners`. This method will not be called with events unless at least one listener has been registered, or unless a call has been made to `enableEvents()`.

removeWindowListener()

```
public synchronized void
          removeWindowListener(WindowListener listener)
```

Removes a `listener` that has been previously registered by a call to `addWindowListener()`.

show()

```
public void show()
```

Displays the window. This will make it visible, if necessary, and bring it to the front of the stacking order.

toBack()

```
public void toBack()
```

Moves the `Window` to the back of the stacking order.

toFront()

```
public void toFront()
```

Moves the `Window` to the front of the stacking order.

WindowAdapter

class java.awt.event.WindowAdapter

This is an adapter class that can be extended by classes wishing to receive window events. All the required methods of the `WindowListener` interface have been implemented as empty—it is only necessary for a subclass to override the methods it wants to use.

Inheritance

```
public abstract class java.awt.event.WindowAdapter
     implements WindowListener
     extends Object
```

⇑
```
public class java.lang.Object
```

Constructors

```
public WindowAdapter()
```

Methods

windowActivated()

```
public void windowActivated(WindowEvent e)
```

This method is called whenever a window is activated.

windowClosed()

```
public void windowClosed(WindowEvent e)
```

This method is called whenever a window has been closed. This happens after the window has been closed as the result of a call to `hide()` or `destroy()`.

windowClosing()

```
public void windowClosing(WindowEvent e)
```

This method is called when a window is closing—the closing operation can be overridden at this point. This happens when the user selects "Quit" from the window's system menu. No action is taken by the system before or after this call—it is up to the application to hide or destroy the window.

windowDeactivated()

```
public void windowDeactivated(WindowEvent e)
```

This method is called whenever a window is deactivated.

windowDeiconified()

```
public void windowDeiconified(WindowEvent e)
```

This method is called whenever a window is deiconified.

windowIconified()

```
public void windowIconified(WindowEvent e)
```

This method is called whenever a window is being iconified.

windowOpened()

```
public void windowOpened(WindowEvent e)
```

This method is called whenever a window has been opened. This will only happen the first time a window is made visible.

 Also see **WindowListener** and **WindowEvent**. For an example, see **Frame**.

WindowEvent

class java.awt.event.WindowEvent

This is used to report window events to a WindowListener.

Inheritance

```
public class java.awt.event.WindowEvent
    extends ComponentEvent
        ⇑
    public class java.awt.event.ComponentEvent
        extends AWTEvent
            ⇑
        public class java.awt.AWTEvent
            extends EventObject
                ⇑
            public class java.util.EventObject
                implements Serializable
                extends Object
                    ⇑
                public class java.lang.Object
```

Variables and constants

WINDOW_ACTIVATED

```
public static final int WINDOW_ACTIVATED
```

The ID of the window activated event type.

WINDOW_CLOSED

```
public static final int WINDOW_CLOSED
```

The ID of the window closed event type.

WINDOW_CLOSING

```
public static final int WINDOW_CLOSING
```

The ID of the window closing event type.

WINDOW_DEACTIVATED

```
public static final int WINDOW_DEACTIVATED
```

The ID of the window deactivated event type.

WINDOW_DEICONIFIED

```
public static final int WINDOW_DEICONIFIED
```

The ID of the window deiconified event type.

WINDOW_FIRST

```
public static final int WINDOW_FIRST
```

This is the lowest possible value of the ID of any WindowEvent.

WINDOW_ICONIFIED

```
public static final int WINDOW_ICONIFIED
```

The ID of the window iconified event type.

WINDOW_LAST

```
public static final int WINDOW_LAST
```

The highest possible value of the ID of any WindowEvent.

WINDOW_OPENED

```
public static final int WINDOW_OPENED
```

The ID of the window opened event type.

Constructors

```
public WindowEvent(Window source,int id)
```

A WindowEvent is constructed containing the source window of the event and the id number of the event.

Methods

getWindow()

```
public Window getWindow()
```

Returns the Window that was the source of the event.

paramString()

```
public String paramString()
```

Returns debugging information. The return string describes the internal state and values of this object.

 See **WindowListener** and **WindowAdapter**.

WindowListener

interface java.awt.event.WindowListener

This is the interface for event listeners that wish to receive window events.

Implemented by

```
AWTEventMulticaster
WindowAdapter
```

Inheritance

```
public interface java.awt.event.WindowListener
    extends EventListener
        ⇑
public interface java.util.EventListener
```

Constructors

Returned by

An object implementing this interface is returned from AWTEventMulticaster.add() and AWTEventMulticaster.remove().

Methods

windowActivated()

```
public abstract void windowActivated(WindowEvent e)
```

This method is called whenever a window is activated.

windowClosed()

```
public abstract void windowClosed(WindowEvent e)
```

This method is called whenever a window has been closed. This happens after the window has been closed as the result of a call to `hide()` or `destroy()`.

windowClosing()

```
public abstract void windowClosing(WindowEvent e)
```

This method is called when a window is closing—the closing operation can be overridden at this point. This happens when the user selects "Quit" from the window's system menu. There is no action taken by the system before or after this call—it is up to the application to hide or destroy the window.

windowDeactivated()

```
public abstract void windowDeactivated(WindowEvent e)
```

This method is called whenever a window is deactivated.

windowDeiconified()

```
public abstract void windowDeiconified(WindowEvent e)
```

This method is called whenever a window is deiconified.

windowIconified()

```
public abstract void windowIconified(WindowEvent e)
```

This method is called whenever a window is being iconified.

windowOpened()

```
public abstract void windowOpened(WindowEvent e)
```

This method is called whenever a window has been opened. This will only happen the first time a window is made visible.

 Also see **WindowAdapter** and **WindowEvent**. For an example of a `WindowListener`, using the `WindowAdapter`, see **Frame**.

wrapper

A *wrapper* is a class that contains data or an object of a specific type and has the ability of performing special operations on the data or object. It is a convenient encapsulation of data in such a way that it can be acted upon as a single entity. An example of this is an Internet socket—which consists of the identity of a host and a port number—that is contained in a Java `Socket` object and has a set of methods that can be used to manipulate it and pass commands to it.

The most common wrappers are the Java API wrapper classes for the primitive data types. One reason for enclosing a primitive type in a wrapper class is so that it can be stored in a hash table just like any other object. Another reason is that the wrapper has methods that can be performed on the primitive type, such as converting to and from various character string representations.

 The wrappers of the primitive types are **Boolean, Byte, Character, Short, Integer, Long, Float, Double,** and **Void.**

WriteAbortedException

class java.io.WriteAbortedException

A `WriteAbortedException` is thrown during a read when one of the `ObjectStreamExceptions` was thrown during writing. The stream is reset to its initial state, and all references to objects already processed are discarded.

Inheritance

```
public class java.io.WriteAbortedException
    extends ObjectStreamException
        ⇑
    public class java.io.ObjectStreamException
        extends IOException
            ⇑
        public class java.io.IOException
            extends Exception
                ⇑
            public class java.lang.Exception
                extends Throwable
                    ⇑
                public class java.lang.Throwable
                    implements Serializable
                    extends Object
                        ⇑
                    public class java.lang.Object
```

Variables and constants

detail

```
public Exception detail
```

The exception that caused this one to be thrown.

Constructors

```
public WriteAbortedException(String message,Exception detail)
```

The constructor requires both a descriptive message and the original exception that caused this one to be thrown.

Methods

getMessage()

```
public String getMessage()
```

If the detail exception is not null, and if it has a detailed message string, this method will return it.

Writer

class java.io.Writer

This is an abstract class for writing to character streams.

Subclassing

At a minimum, to create a nonabstract subclass, it is necessary only to implement write(), flush(), and close(). Other methods may need to be overwritten in view of special considerations.

Writing one character

There is a write() method to write a single character to the stream. It is not very efficient. If much writing is to be done, it would probably be best to override the method to use some sort of buffering.

Extended by

```
BufferedWriter
CharArrayWriter
FilterWriter
OutputStreamWriter
PipedWriter
PrintWriter
StringWriter
```

Inheritance

```
public abstract class java.io.Writer
    extends Object
        ⇑
    public class java.lang.Object
```

Variables and constants

lock

```
protected Object lock
```

This object used to synchronize operations on the stream. A subclass should use `lock`, instead of `this` or some local variable, to allow for the circumstance of several synchronized stream objects.

Constructors

Writer()

```
protected Writer()
```

```
protected Writer(Object lock)
```

If the `lock` is specified, it will be used as the synchronizing object for critical-section stream access. If it is not supplied, `this` will be used as the lock object.

Methods

close()

```
public abstract void close()
    throws IOException
```

This method will first call `flush()` and then close the output stream. Further calls to `write()` or `flush()` will not work. There is no error in calling `close()` more than once.

flush()

```
public abstract void flush()
    throws IOException
```

Any pending output is written. If there are any pending output characters anywhere in the output stream, they will be sent immediately to their final destination at the end of the stream chain.

write()

```
public void write(char carray[])
    throws IOException
```

```
public abstract void write(char carray[],int offset,int length)
     throws IOException
```

```
public void write(int character)
     throws IOException
```

```
public void write(String string)
     throws IOException
```

```
public void write(String string,int stroffset,int strlength)
     throws IOException
```

Writes an array of characters, a string of characters, or a single character to the stream. The lowest-order 16 bits of `character` are written to the stream as a single Unicode character (the high-order 16 bits are ignored). For an array, the writing will begin at `carray[offset]` and continue for `length` characters. If `offset` and `length` are not specified, the entire array is written. If `string` is specified, the character beginning at `stroffset` and continuing for `strlength` characters will be written. If `stroffset` and `strlength` are not specified, the entire string is written.

zip

package java.util.zip

This package is an API that can be used to compress Java class files and other Java resources into a single file. A Java class can be executed directly from a compressed file, and, thus, a Java applet or application can be distributed and installed as a single file. An API is also included to read and write general-purpose zip files.

Interfaces

Checksum

Classes

Adler32
CRC32
CheckedInputStream
CheckedOutputStream
Deflater
DeflaterOutputStream
GZIPInputStream
GZIPOutputStream
Inflater
InflaterInputStream
ZipEntry
ZipFile
ZipInputStream
ZipOutputStream

Exceptions

DataFormatException
ZipException

ZipConstants

interface java.util.zip.ZipConstants

This interface contains a set of constants that are necessary to the internal operation of `ZipEntry`, `ZipFile`, `ZipInputStream`, and `ZipOutputStream`. The values are for internal use only, as the interface is accessible only to classes inside the package.

ZipEntry

class java.util.zip.ZipEntry

This class is used to represent a single entry in a ZIP file. A `ZipEntry` object is used by `ZipOutputFile` and `ZipInputFile` to read and write the individual entries in a ZIP file.

Inheritance

```
public class java.util.zip.ZipEntry
      implements ZipConstants
      extends Object
          ⇑
      public class java.lang.Object
```

Variables and constants

DEFLATED

```
public static final int DEFLATED
```

An indicator that the data has been compressed (deflated).

STORED

```
public static final int STORED
```

An indicator that the data has not been compressed.

Constructors

```
public ZipEntry(String name)
```

A `ZipEntry` is constructed with the specified name. The name is considered to be that of a directory if it ends with a slash (/). A `NullPointerException` is thrown if name is null.

Returned by

An object of this class is returned from `ZipFile.getEntry()` and `ZipInputStream.getNextEntry()`.

Methods

getComment()

```
public String getComment()
```

Returns the comment string. If there is none, return `null`.

getCompressedSize()

```
public long getCompressedSize()
```

Returns the compressed size of the data. If it is not known, returns −1. If the data is stored uncompressed, there will be no change in its size.

getCrc()

```
public long getCrc()
```

Returns the CRC-32 checksum of the uncompressed data. Returns −1 if it is not known.

getExtra()

```
public byte[] getExtra()
```

Returns the extra field data. Returns `null` if there is none.

getMethod()

```
public int getMethod()
```

Returns the specifier of the compression method. The return value is either `STORED` or `DEFLATED`—or else −1 if no method is specified.

getName()

```
public String getName()
```

Returns the name of this entry.

getSize()

```
public long getSize()
```

Returns the uncompressed size of the data. Returns −1 if it is not known.

x
y
z

getTime()

```
public long getTime()
```

Returns the modification time of the entry. It is a number of milliseconds since January 1, 1970. The method returns −1 if that time is not known.

isDirectory()

```
public boolean isDirectory()
```

Returns `true` if this is a directory entry. A directory is defined as a name that ends with a slash (/) character.

setComment()

```
public void setComment(String comment)
```

Sets the comment string.

setCrc()

```
public void setCrc(long crc)
```

Sets the value of the CRC-32 checksum for the uncompressed data. An `IllegalArgumentException` is thrown if the value is less than 0 or greater than 0xFFFFFFFF.

setExtra()

```
public void setExtra(byte extra[])
```

Sets the optional `extra` data field. An `IllegalArgumentException` is thrown if `extra` is larger that 0xFFFFF bytes.

setMethod()

```
public void setMethod(int method)
```

Specifies the compression method for the entry. An `IllegalArgumentException` is thrown unless this is either `STORED` or `DEFLATED`.

setSize()

```
public void setSize(long size)
```

Sets the size of the uncompressed data. An `IllegalArgumentException` is thrown if the size is less than 0 or greater than 0xFFFFFFFF.

setTime()

```
public void setTime(long time)
```

Specifies the modification time of the data. It is the number of milliseconds since January 1, 1970.

toString()

```
public String toString()
```

Returns a string representation of the ZIP entry.

Example

This example uses ZipOutputStream to create a ZIP file and then uses ZipInputStream to read the contents of the file. A zip file will normally hold the contents of several other files—each one represented by a ZipEntry object —but this example simply uses a String as the data for each of three entries in the ZIP file. The file produced from this example can be used with an unzip utility to recreate the files (and their directories):

```
import java.io.*;
import java.util.zip.*;
public class Zipper {
    ZipOutputStream zipOut;
    ZipInputStream zipIn;
    public static void main(String[] arg) {
        Zipper zipper = new Zipper();
        zipper.write("mystuff.zip");
        zipper.read("mystuff.zip");
    }
    public void write(String filename) {
        try {
            FileOutputStream fo =
                    new FileOutputStream(filename);
            zipOut = new ZipOutputStream(fo);
            putEntry("toons",
              "This is the contents for toons.");
            putEntry("alley/oop",
              "This is the contents for Alley Oop.");
            putEntry("pogo/possum",
              "This is the contents of Pogo Possum.");
            zipOut.close();
        } catch (IOException e) {
            System.out.println(e);
        }
    }
    public void putEntry(String name,String data)
                throws IOException {
        ZipEntry entry = new ZipEntry(name);
        zipOut.putNextEntry(entry);
        byte[] arr = data.getBytes();
```

```
            zipOut.write(arr,0,arr.length);
            zipOut.closeEntry();
    }
    public void read(String filename) {
        byte[] arr = new byte[10];
        try {
            FileInputStream fi =
                    new FileInputStream(filename);
            zipIn = new ZipInputStream(fi);
            ZipEntry entry = zipIn.getNextEntry();
            while(entry != null) {
                System.out.println("Name:" +
                        entry.getName());
                int count = zipIn.read(arr,0,arr.length);
                while(count > 0) {
                    for(int i=0; i<count; i++)
                        System.out.print((char)arr[i]);
                    count =zipIn.read(arr,0,arr.length);
                }
                System.out.println();
                entry = zipIn.getNextEntry();
            }
            zipIn.close();
        } catch (IOException e) {
            System.out.println(e);
        }
    }
}
```

A FileOutputStream is created by opening the file myfile.zip for output.
This stream is then used to create a ZipOutputStream object. The method
putEntry() is called three times with the name and content of a file. The first
file, toon, has no path, but the files oop and possum both are defined as being
in a subdirectory. The putEntry() method creates a ZipEntry using the name
of the file and, allowing all the settings of the ZipEntry to default, writes the
header of the entry with a call to putNextEntry(). Following this, all the data
from the file is written (in this example, it is the string passed in as the second
argument to putEntry()). After all the data are written, a call is made to
closeEntry() to mark the end of that entry and get the file ready for another
one. After the ZIP file has been written, a call is made to close() to flush any
pending output to disk.

Reading the file is very much like writing it—the ZipEntry objects that
were created and written are now read from the file and used to recover the
data that was stored for writing. Once the ZipInputStream is created from the
FileInputStream that was opened to read the file, the ZipEntry objects are

read by calling `getNextEntry()` and the data for each one is read and displayed. The output looks like this:

```
Name:toons
This is the contents for toons.
Name:alley/oop
This is the contents for Alley Oop.
Name:pogo/possum
This is the contents of Pogo Possum.
```

 A `ZipEntry` is used to read and write zip files by **ZipInputStream** and **ZipOutputStream**.

ZipException

class java.util.zip.ZipException

This exception is thrown to indicate a problem in the format of the contents of a ZIP file.

Inheritance

```
public class java.util.zip.ZipException
    extends IOException
        ⇑
    public class java.io.IOException
        extends Exception
            ⇑
        public class java.lang.Exception
            extends Throwable
                ⇑
            public class java.lang.Throwable
                implements Serializable
                extends Object
                    ⇑
                public class java.lang.Object
```

Constructors

```
public ZipException()
public ZipException(String message)
```

If the `message` string is supplied, it is used as a detailed message describing this particular exception.

ZipFile

class java.util.zip.ZipFile

This class uses `RandomAccessFile` to read the contents of a ZIP file. It will read both compressed and uncompressed entries.

Inheritance

```
public class ZipFile
    implements ZipConstants
    extends Object
        ⇑
    public class java.lang.Object
```

Constructors

```
public ZipFile(String fileName)
    throws ZipException
    throws IOException
```

```
public ZipFile(File file)
    throws ZipException
    throws IOException
```

Opens the specified ZIP file for reading. A `ZipException` is thrown if there is a format error in the ZIP file. The `IOException` is thrown if there is an error opening or reading the file.

Methods

close()

```
public void close()
    throws IOException
```

Closes the file.

entries()

```
public Enumeration entries()
```

Returns an enumeration of the ZIP file entries.

getEntry()

```
public ZipEntry getEntry(String name)
```

Returns the named ZIP file entry. The `name` should be the complete path name as used inside the ZIP file. A `null` is returned if there is no such `name`.

getInputStream()

```
public InputStream getInputStream(ZipEntry zipEntry)
    throws IOException
```

Returns an input stream that can be used to read the file specified by `zipEntry`. A `ZipException` will be thrown if a ZIP format error occurs.

getName()

```
public String getName()
```

Returns the path name of the ZIP file.

 For reading and writing ZIP files, see **ZipInputStream** and **ZipOutputStream**. For the class representing a single ZIP file entry, see **ZipEntry**.

ZipInputStream

class java.util.zip.ZipInputStream

This is an input stream that can be used to read ZIP files. It will read both compressed and uncompressed entries from the file.

Inheritance

```
public class java.util.zip.ZipInputStream
    implements ZipConstants
    extends InflaterInputStream
        ⇑
    public class java.util.zip.InflaterInputStream
        extends FilterInputStream
            ⇑
        public class java.io.FilterInputStream
            extends InputStream
                ⇑
            public class java.io.InputStream
                extends Object
                    ⇑
                public class java.lang.Object
```

Constructors

```
public ZipInputStream(InputStream in)
```

A ZipInputStream is constructed using an existing InputStream.

Methods

close()

```
public void close()
    throws IOException
```

Closes the input stream.

closeEntry()

```
public void closeEntry()
    throws IOException
```

Closes the current incoming ZipEntry and positions the file pointer at the beginning of the next entry. A ZipException is thrown if a ZIP file error occurs.

getNextEntry()

```
public ZipEntry getNextEntry()
    throws IOException
```

Reads the next ZIP file entry and positions the stream at the beginning of its data. A ZipException is thrown if there is a ZIP file error.

read()

```
public int read(byte barray[],int offset,int length)
    throws IOException
```

Reads up to length bytes from the ZIP file and stores the data beginning at barray[offset] for a maximum of length bytes. This method will block until some data is available. The return value is the actual number of bytes read, or −1 if there is no more data for the ZipEntry. A ZipException will be thrown if there is a ZIP file error.

skip()

```
public long skip(long count)
    throws IOException
```

Skips over count bytes of the current ZipEntry. A ZipException will be thrown if there is a ZIP file format error.

 For an example using a ZipInputStream to read a zip file, see **ZipEntry**. Also see **ZipOutputStream** in **Inflater**.

ZipOutputStream

class java.util.zip.ZipOutputStream

This is an output stream for writing files in the ZIP format. Files can be written either compressed or uncompressed.

Inheritance

```
public class java.util.zip.ZipOutputStream
    implements ZipConstants
    extends DeflaterOutputStream
        ⇑
    public class java.lang.Object
```

Variables and constants

DEFLATED

```
public static final int DEFLATED
```

An indicator that the data has been compressed (deflated).

STORED

```
public static final int STORED
```

An indicator that the data has not been compressed.

Constructors

```
public ZipOutputStream(OutputStream out)
```

A `ZipOutputStream` is constructed using an existing `OutputStream`.

Methods

close()

```
public void close()
    throws IOException
```

Closes the output stream. A `ZipException` is thrown if a ZIP file error occurs.

closeEntry()

```
public void closeEntry()
    throws IOException
```

x
y
z

Closes the current `ZipEntry` and positions the stream to write the next one. A `ZipException` is thrown if a ZIP format error has occurred.

finish()

```
public void finish()
    throws IOException
```

Finishes writing the contents to the ZIP output stream without closing the underlying stream. This method is for use when multiple filters are being used in the same output stream. A `ZipException` is thrown if a ZIP file error occurs.

putNextEntry()

```
public void putNextEntry(ZipEntry entry)
    throws IOException
```

Begins writing a new `ZipEntry` and positions the file to the beginning of the new data. This will close the currently `ZipEntry` if it is still active. If no compression method has been specified for the entry, the default will be used. The current time will be assumed if no modification time was specified. A `ZipException` is thrown if a ZIP file error occurs.

setComment()

```
public void setComment(String comment)
```

This will set the `comment` string for the ZIP file. An `IllegalArgumentException` is thrown if the length is greater than 0xFFFF bytes.

setLevel()

```
public void setLevel(int level)
```

Sets the compression level for entries that are to be DEFLATED. The default setting is `DEFAULT_COMPRESSION`. The compression levels are defined in `Deflater`. An `IllegalArgumentException` is thrown if the level is not valid.

setMethod()

```
public void setMethod(int method)
```

Sets the default compression method. The default will be used whenever the compression method is not specified in the `ZipEntry`. This is initially set to DEFLATED. An `IllegalArgumentException` is thrown if the `method` is invalid.

write()

```
public synchronized void write(byte barray[],
        int offset,int length)
    throws IOException
```

Writes `length` bytes beginning at `barray[offset]` to the current `ZipEntry` data. This will block until all the bytes are written. A `ZipException` will be thrown if there is a ZIP file error.

 For an example of using a `ZipOutputStream` to create a zip file, see **ZipEntry**. Also see **ZipInputStream** and **Deflater**.

ZLIB

The ZLIB compression library is not protected by any patents. The full specification is available in the RFCs 1950 (the ZLIB format), 1951 (deflate format), and 1952 (the GZIP format). These plain-text documents can be found at `ftp://ds.internic.net/rfc`.

 For classes to perform `ZLIB` compression, see **Deflater** and **Inflater**. For classes that implement `ZLIB` directly to and from a file, see **DeflaterOutputStream** and **InflaterInputStream**.

appendix

a

Table of Methods

This appendix lists all method names in alphabetical order. Each method is followed by a list of all the classes or interfaces in which it is defined. Once a class or interface is determined, it can be looked up directly by its name in the book. Use this table to jog your memory when you remember the name of a method but can't recall the class in which it is defined. You can also compare the listing here against the hierarchy of a class to determine which superclass defines it—even if it is overridden. Finally, you can use this list to make certain you are not inadvertently overriding an existing method.

Method Name	Class or Interface Name
abortGrabbing()	PixelGrabber
abs()	BigDecimal, BigInteger, Math
accept()	FilenameFilter, ServerSocket, SocketImpl
acceptsURL()	Driver
acos()	Math
action()	Component
actionPerformed()	AWTEventMulticaster, ActionListener
activeCount()	Thread, ThreadGroup
activeGroupCount()	ThreadGroup
add()	AWTEventMulticaster, BigDecimal, BigInteger, Calendar, Choice, ChoicePeer, Component, Container, GregorianCalendar, List, ListPeer, Menu, MenuBar, Rectangle
addActionListener()	Button, List, MenuItem, TextField
addAdjustmentListener()	Adjustable, Scrollbar
addCertificate()	Identity
addComponentListener()	Component
addConsumer()	FilteredImageSource, ImageProducer, MemoryImageSource
addContainerListener()	Container
addElement()	Vector

continued

Method Name	Class or Interface Name
addEntry()	Acl
addFocusListener()	Component
addHelpMenu()	MenuBarPeer
addIdentity()	IdentityScope
addImage()	MediaTracker
addImpl()	Container, ScrollPane
addInternal()	AWTEventMulticaster
addItem()	Choice, ChoicePeer, List, ListPeer, MenuPeer
addItemListener()	Checkbox, CheckboxMenuItem, Choice, ItemSelectable, List
addKeyListener()	Component
addLayoutComponent()	BorderLayout, CardLayout, FlowLayout, GridBagLayout, GridLayout, LayoutManager, LayoutManager2
addMember()	Group
addMenu()	MenuBarPeer
addMouseListener()	Component
addMouseMotionListener()	Component
addNotify()	Button, Canvas, Checkbox, CheckboxMenuItem, Choice, Component, Container, Dialog, FileDialog, Frame, Label, List, Menu, MenuBar, MenuItem, Panel, PopupMenu, ScrollPane, Scrollbar, TextArea, TextField, Window
addObserver()	Observable
addOwner()	Owner
addPermission()	AclEntry
addPoint()	Polygon
addPropertyChangeListener()	Customizer, PropertyChangeSupport, PropertyEditor, PropertyEditorSupport
addProvider()	Security
addSeparator()	Menu, MenuPeer
addTextListener()	TextComponent
addVetoableChangeListener()	VetoableChangeSupport
addWindowListener()	Window
AdjustForGravity()	GridBagLayout
adjustmentValueChanged()	AWTEventMulticaster, AdjustmentListener
after()	Calendar, Date, GregorianCalendar, Timestamp
allProceduresAreCallable()	DatabaseMetaData
allTablesAreSelectable()	DatabaseMetaData
allowThreadSuspension()	ThreadGroup
allowsMultipleSelections()	List
and()	BigInteger, BitSet
andNot()	BigInteger
annotateClass()	ObjectOutputStream

Method Name	Class or Interface Name
append()	StringBuffer, TextArea
appendText()	TextArea
appletResize()	AppletStub
applyLocalizedPattern()	DecimalFormat, SimpleDateFormat
applyPattern()	ChoiceFormat, DecimalFormat, MessageFormat, SimpleDateFormat
ArrangeGrid()	GridBagLayout
arraycopy()	System
asin()	Math
atan()	Math
atan2()	Math
attributeNames()	FeatureDescriptor
available()	BufferedInputStream, ByteArrayInputStream, FileInputStream, FilterInputStream, InputStream, LineNumberInputStream, ObjectInput, ObjectInputStream, PipedInputStream, PushbackInputStream, SequenceInputStream, SocketImpl, StringBufferInputStream
avoidingGui()	Visibility
beep()	Toolkit
before()	Calendar, Date, GregorianCalendar, Timestamp
beginValidate()	ContainerPeer
bind()	DatagramSocketImpl, Naming, Registry, SocketImpl
bitCount()	BigInteger
bitLength()	BigInteger
booleanValue()	Boolean
bounds()	Component
brighter()	Color
byteValue()	Byte, Double, Float, Integer, Long, Number, Short
bytesWidth()	FontMetrics
canRead()	File
canWrite()	File
cancel()	Statement
capacity()	StringBuffer, Vector
ceil()	Math
certificates()	Identity
charAt()	String, StringBuffer
charValue()	Character
charWidth()	FontMetrics
charsWidth()	FontMetrics
checkAccept()	RMISecurityManager, SecurityManager
checkAccess()	RMISecurityManager, SecurityManager, Thread, ThreadGroup
checkAll()	MediaTracker

continued

Method Name	Class or Interface Name
checkAwtEventQueueAccess()	RMISecurityManager, SecurityManager
checkConnect()	RMISecurityManager, SecurityManager
checkCreateClassLoader()	RMISecurityManager, SecurityManager
checkDelete()	RMISecurityManager, SecurityManager
checkError()	PrintStream, PrintWriter
checkExec()	RMISecurityManager, SecurityManager
checkExit()	RMISecurityManager, SecurityManager
checkID()	MediaTracker
checkImage()	Component, ComponentPeer, Toolkit
checkLink()	RMISecurityManager, SecurityManager
checkListen()	RMISecurityManager, SecurityManager
checkMemberAccess()	RMISecurityManager, SecurityManager
checkMulticast()	RMISecurityManager, SecurityManager
checkPackageAccess()	RMISecurityManager, SecurityManager
checkPackageDefinition()	RMISecurityManager, SecurityManager
checkPermission()	Acl, AclEntry
checkPrintJobAccess()	RMISecurityManager, SecurityManager
checkPropertiesAccess()	RMISecurityManager, SecurityManager
checkPropertyAccess()	RMISecurityManager, SecurityManager
checkRead()	RMISecurityManager, SecurityManager
checkSecurityAccess()	RMISecurityManager, SecurityManager
checkSetFactory()	RMISecurityManager, SecurityManager
checkSystemClipboardAccess()	RMISecurityManager, SecurityManager
checkTopLevelWindow()	RMISecurityManager, SecurityManager
checkWrite()	RMISecurityManager, SecurityManager
childResized()	ScrollPanePeer
classDepth()	SecurityManager
classLoaderDepth()	SecurityManager
clean()	DGC
clear()	BitSet, Calendar, Hashtable, List, ListPeer
clearBit()	BigInteger
clearChanged()	Observable
clearParameters()	PreparedStatement
clearRect()	Graphics
clearWarnings()	Connection, ResultSet, Statement
clipRect()	Graphics
clone()	AclEntry, BitSet, BreakIterator, Calendar, CharacterIterator, ChoiceFormat, Collator, DateFormat, DateFormatSymbols, DecimalFormat, DecimalFormatSymbols, Format, GregorianCalendar, GridBagConstraints, Hashtable, ImageFilter, Insets, Locale, MessageDigest, MessageFormat, NumberFormat,

Method Name	Class or Interface Name
	Object, RuleBasedCollator, Signature, SimpleDateFormat, SimpleTimeZone, StringCharacterIterator, TimeZone, UnicastRemoteObject, Vector
close()	BufferedReader, BufferedWriter, CharArrayReader, CharArrayWriter, Connection, DatagramSocket, DatagramSocketImpl, DeflaterOutputStream, FileInputStream, FileOutputStream, FilterInputStream, FilterOutputStream, FilterReader, FilterWriter, GZIPInputStream, GZIPOutputStream, InputStream, InputStreamReader, ObjectInput, ObjectInputStream, ObjectOutput, ObjectOutputStream, OutputStream, OutputStreamWriter, PipedInputStream, PipedOutputStream, PipedReader, PipedWriter, PrintStream, PrintWriter, PushbackReader, RandomAccessFile, Reader, ResultSet, SequenceInputStream, ServerSocket, Socket, SocketImpl, Statement, StringReader, StringWriter, Writer, ZipFile, ZipInputStream, ZipOutputStream
closeEntry()	ZipInputStream, ZipOutputStream
command()	Compiler
commentChar()	StreamTokenizer
commit()	Connection
compare()	Collator, RuleBasedCollator
compareTo()	BigDecimal, BigInteger, CollationKey, String
compileClass()	Compiler
compileClasses()	Compiler
complete()	Calendar
componentAdded()	AWTEventMulticaster, ContainerAdapter, ContainerListener
componentHidden()	AWTEventMulticaster, ComponentAdapter, ComponentListener
componentMoved()	AWTEventMulticaster, ComponentAdapter, ComponentListener
componentRemoved()	AWTEventMulticaster, ContainerAdapter, ContainerListener
componentResized()	AWTEventMulticaster, ComponentAdapter, ComponentListener
componentShown()	AWTEventMulticaster, ComponentAdapter, ComponentListener
computeFields()	Calendar, GregorianCalendar
computeTime()	Calendar, GregorianCalendar
concat()	String
connect()	Driver, PipedInputStream, PipedOutputStream, PipedReader, PipedWriter, SocketImpl, URLConnection
consume()	AWTEvent, InputEvent
contains()	Component, Hashtable, Polygon, Rectangle, Vector
containsKey()	Hashtable
controlDown()	Event
copyArea()	Graphics
copyInto()	Vector
copyValueOf()	String
cos()	Math
countComponents()	Container

continued

Method Name	Class or Interface Name
countItems()	Choice, List, Menu
countMenus()	MenuBar
countObservers()	Observable
countStackFrames()	Thread
countTokens()	StringTokenizer
create()	DatagramSocketImpl, Graphics, SocketImpl
createButton()	Toolkit
createCanvas()	Toolkit
createCheckbox()	Toolkit
createCheckboxMenuItem()	Toolkit
createChoice()	Toolkit
createComponent()	Toolkit
createContentHandler()	ContentHandlerFactory
createDialog()	Toolkit
createFileDialog()	Toolkit
createFrame()	Toolkit
createImage()	Component, ComponentPeer, Toolkit
createLabel()	Toolkit
createList()	Toolkit
createMenu()	Toolkit
createMenuBar()	Toolkit
createMenuItem()	Toolkit
createPanel()	Toolkit
createPopupMenu()	Toolkit
createRegistry()	LocateRegistry
createScrollPane()	Toolkit
createScrollbar()	Toolkit
createServerSocket()	RMISocketFactory
createSocket()	RMISocketFactory
createSocketImpl()	SocketImplFactory
createStatement()	Connection
createTextArea()	Toolkit
createTextField()	Toolkit
createURLStreamHandler()	URLStreamHandlerFactory
createWindow()	Toolkit
current()	BreakIterator, CharacterIterator, StringCharacterIterator
currentClassLoader()	SecurityManager
currentLoadedClass()	SecurityManager
currentThread()	Thread
currentTimeMillis()	System

Method Name	Class or Interface Name
darker()	Color
dataDefinitionCausesTransactionCommit()	DatabaseMetaData
dataDefinitionIgnoredInTransactions()	DatabaseMetaData
decapitalize()	Introspector
decode()	Byte, Certificate, Color, Font, Integer, Short
defaultReadObject()	ObjectInputStream
defaultWriteObject()	ObjectOutputStream
defineClass()	ClassLoader
deflate()	Deflater, DeflaterOutputStream
delItem()	List, MenuPeer
delItems()	List, ListPeer
delMenu()	MenuBarPeer
delete()	File
deleteObserver()	Observable
deleteObservers()	Observable
deleteOwner()	Owner
deleteShortcut()	MenuBar, MenuItem
deliverEvent()	Component, Container
deregisterDriver()	DriverManager
deselect()	List, ListPeer
destroy()	Applet, Process, Thread, ThreadGroup
digest()	MessageDigest
digit()	Character
dirty()	DGC
disable()	Compiler, Component, ComponentPeer, MenuItem, MenuItemPeer
disableEvents()	Component, MenuItem
disconnect()	HttpURLConnection
dispatch()	Skeleton
dispatchEvent()	Component, MenuComponent
dispose()	ComponentPeer, Frame, Graphics, MenuComponentPeer, Window
divide()	BigDecimal, BigInteger
divideAndRemainder()	BigInteger
doLayout()	Component, Container, ScrollPane
doesMaxRowSizeIncludeBlobs()	DatabaseMetaData
done()	RemoteCall, RemoteRef
dontUseGui()	Visibility
doubleToLongBits()	Double

continued

Method Name	Class or Interface Name
doubleValue()	BigDecimal, BigInteger, Byte, Double, Float, Integer, Long, Number, Short
drain()	ObjectOutputStream
draw3DRect()	Graphics
drawArc()	Graphics
drawBytes()	Graphics
drawChars()	Graphics
drawImage()	Graphics
drawLine()	Graphics
drawOval()	Graphics
drawPolygon()	Graphics
drawPolyline()	Graphics
drawRect()	Graphics
drawRoundRect()	Graphics
drawString()	Graphics
dumpStack()	Thread
echoCharIsSet()	TextField
elementAt()	Vector
elements()	Dictionary, Hashtable, Vector
empty()	Stack
enable()	Compiler, Component, ComponentPeer, MenuItem, MenuItemPeer
enableEvents()	Component, MenuItem
enableReplaceObject()	ObjectOutputStream
enableResolveObject()	ObjectInputStream
encode()	Certificate, URLEncoder
end()	Deflater, Inflater, PrintJob
endValidate()	ContainerPeer
endsWith()	String
engineDigest()	MessageDigest
engineGetParameter()	Signature
engineInitSign()	Signature
engineInitVerify()	Signature
engineReset()	MessageDigest
engineSetParameter()	Signature
engineSign()	Signature
engineUpdate()	MessageDigest, Signature
engineVerify()	Signature
ensureCapacity()	StringBuffer, Vector
entries()	Acl, ZipFile
enumerate()	Thread, ThreadGroup
eolIsSignificant()	StreamTokenizer

Method Name	Class or Interface Name
equals()	BigDecimal, BigInteger, BitSet, Boolean, Byte, Calendar, Character, ChoiceFormat, CollationKey, Collator, Color, Constructor, DataFlavor, Date, DateFormat, DateFormatSymbols, DecimalFormat, DecimalFormatSymbols, Dimension, Double, Field, File, Float, Font, GregorianCalendar, Identity, InetAddress, Insets, Integer, Locale, Long, MenuShortcut, MessageFormat, Method, NumberFormat, ObjID, Object, Permission, Point, Principal, Rectangle, RemoteObject, RuleBasedCollator, Short, SimpleDateFormat, SimpleTimeZone, String, StringCharacterIterator, Timestamp, UID, URL, VMID
equalsIgnoreCase()	String
exec()	Runtime
execute()	PreparedStatement, Statement
executeCall()	RemoteCall
executeQuery()	PreparedStatement, Statement
executeUpdate()	PreparedStatement, Statement
exists()	File
exit()	Runtime, System
exitValue()	Process
exp()	Math
exportObject()	ServerRef, UnicastRemoteObject
failure()	RMIFailureHandler
fill()	InflaterInputStream
fill3DRect()	Graphics
fillArc()	Graphics
fillInStackTrace()	Throwable
fillOval()	Graphics
fillPolygon()	Graphics
fillRect()	Graphics
fillRoundRect()	Graphics
filterIndexColorModel()	RGBImageFilter
filterRGB()	RGBImageFilter
filterRGBPixels()	RGBImageFilter
finalize()	ColorModel, Deflater, FileInputStream, FileOutputStream, Graphics, Inflater, Object, PrintJob
findColumn()	ResultSet
findEditor()	PropertyEditorManager
findLoadedClass()	ClassLoader
findSystemClass()	ClassLoader
finish()	Deflater, DeflaterOutputStream, GZIPOutputStream, ZipOutputStream
finished()	Deflater, Inflater
firePropertyChange()	PropertyChangeSupport, PropertyEditorSupport

continued

Method Name	Class or Interface Name
fireVetoableChange()	VetoableChangeSupport
first()	BreakIterator, CardLayout, CharacterIterator, StringCharacterIterator
firstElement()	Vector
flipBit()	BigInteger
floatToIntBits()	Float
floatValue()	BigDecimal, BigInteger, Byte, Double, Float, Integer, Long, Number, Short
floor()	Math
flush()	BufferedOutputStream, BufferedWriter, CharArrayWriter, DataOutputStream, FilterOutputStream, FilterWriter, Image, ObjectOutput, ObjectOutputStream, OutputStream, OutputStreamWriter, PipedOutputStream, PipedWriter, PrintStream, PrintWriter, StringWriter, Writer
focusGained()	AWTEventMulticaster, FocusAdapter, FocusListener
focusLost()	AWTEventMulticaster, FocusAdapter, FocusListener
following()	BreakIterator
forClass()	ObjectStreamClass
forDigit()	Character
forName()	Class
format()	ChoiceFormat, DateFormat, DecimalFormat, Format, MessageFormat, NumberFormat, SimpleDateFormat
freeMemory()	Runtime
gc()	Runtime, System
gcd()	BigInteger
generateKeyPair()	KeyPairGenerator
get()	Array, BitSet, Calendar, Dictionary, Field, Hashtable
getAbsolutePath()	File
getActionCommand()	ActionEvent, Button, MenuItem
getAddListenerMethod()	EventSetDescriptor
getAdditionalBeanInfo()	BeanInfo, SimpleBeanInfo
getAddress()	DatagramPacket, InetAddress
getAdjustable()	AdjustmentEvent
getAdjustmentType()	AdjustmentEvent
getAdler()	Deflater, Inflater
getAlgorithm()	Key, KeyPairGenerator, MessageDigest, Signature
getAlgorithmProperty()	Security
getAlignment()	FlowLayout, Label
getAlignmentX()	Component, Container
getAlignmentY()	Component, Container
getAllByName()	InetAddress
getAllowUserInteraction()	URLConnection
getAlpha()	ColorModel, DirectColorModel, IndexColorModel

Method Name	Class or Interface Name
getAlphaMask()	DirectColorModel
getAlphas()	IndexColorModel
getAmPmStrings()	DateFormatSymbols
getApplet()	AppletContext
getAppletContext()	Applet, AppletStub
getAppletInfo()	Applet
getApplets()	AppletContext
getAsText()	PropertyEditor, PropertyEditorSupport
getAscent()	FontMetrics
getAsciiStream()	ResultSet
getAudioClip()	Applet, AppletContext
getAutoCommit()	Connection
getAvailableIDs()	TimeZone
getAvailableLocales()	BreakIterator, Calendar, Collator, DateFormat, NumberFormat
getBackground()	Component
getBeanClass()	BeanDescriptor
getBeanDescriptor()	BeanInfo, SimpleBeanInfo
getBeanInfo()	Introspector
getBeanInfoSearchPath()	Introspector
getBeginIndex()	CharacterIterator, FieldPosition, StringCharacterIterator
getBestRowIdentifier()	DatabaseMetaData
getBigDecimal()	CallableStatement, ResultSet
getBinaryStream()	ResultSet
getBlockIncrement()	Adjustable, Scrollbar
getBlue()	Color, ColorModel, DirectColorModel, IndexColorModel
getBlueMask()	DirectColorModel
getBlues()	IndexColorModel
getBoolean()	Array, Boolean, CallableStatement, Field, ResultSet
getBoundingBox()	Polygon
getBounds()	Component, Polygon, Rectangle, Shape
getBuffer()	StringWriter
getBundle()	ResourceBundle
getByName()	InetAddress
getByte()	Array, CallableStatement, Field, ResultSet
getBytes()	CallableStatement, ResultSet, String
getCalendar()	DateFormat
getCanonicalPath()	File
getCaretPosition()	TextComponent, TextComponentPeer
getCatalog()	Connection

continued

Method Name	Class or Interface Name
getCatalogName()	ResultSetMetaData
getCatalogSeparator()	DatabaseMetaData
getCatalogTerm()	DatabaseMetaData
getCatalogs()	DatabaseMetaData
getChar()	Array, Field
getCharacterInstance()	BreakIterator
getChars()	String, StringBuffer
getCheckboxGroup()	Checkbox
getChecksum()	CheckedInputStream, CheckedOutputStream
getChild()	ContainerEvent
getClass()	Object
getClassContext()	SecurityManager
getClassLoader()	Class
getClassName()	MissingResourceException
getClasses()	Class
getClickCount()	MouseEvent
getClientHost()	RemoteServer, ServerRef
getClip()	Graphics
getClipBounds()	Graphics
getClipRect()	Graphics
getCodeBase()	Applet, AppletStub
getCollationElementIterator()	RuleBasedCollator
getCollationKey()	Collator, RuleBasedCollator
getColor()	Color, Graphics
getColorModel()	Component, ComponentPeer, PixelGrabber, Toolkit
getColumnCount()	ResultSetMetaData
getColumnDisplaySize()	ResultSetMetaData
getColumnLabel()	ResultSetMetaData
getColumnName()	ResultSetMetaData
getColumnPrivileges()	DatabaseMetaData
getColumnType()	ResultSetMetaData
getColumnTypeName()	ResultSetMetaData
getColumns()	DatabaseMetaData, GridLayout, TextArea, TextField
getComment()	ZipEntry
getComponent()	ComponentEvent, Container
getComponentAt()	Component, Container
getComponentCount()	Container
getComponentType()	Class
getComponents()	Container
getCompressedSize()	ZipEntry

Method Name	Class or Interface Name
getConnection()	DriverManager
getConstraints()	GridBagLayout
getConstructor()	Class
getConstructors()	Class
getContainer()	ContainerEvent
getContent()	ContentHandler, URL, URLConnection
getContentEncoding()	URLConnection
getContentLength()	URLConnection
getContentType()	URLConnection
getContentTypeFor()	FileNameMap
getContents()	Clipboard, ListResourceBundle
getCountry()	Locale
getCrc()	ZipEntry
getCrossReference()	DatabaseMetaData
getCurrencyInstance()	NumberFormat
getCurrent()	CheckboxGroup
getCursor()	Component
getCursorName()	ResultSet
getCursorType()	Frame
getCustomEditor()	PropertyEditor, PropertyEditorSupport
getCustomizerClass()	BeanDescriptor
getData()	DatagramPacket
getDataSize()	DataTruncation
getDatabaseProductName()	DatabaseMetaData
getDatabaseProductVersion()	DatabaseMetaData
getDate()	CallableStatement, Date, ResultSet, Time, URLConnection
getDateFormatSymbols()	SimpleDateFormat
getDateInstance()	DateFormat
getDateTimeInstance()	DateFormat
getDay()	Date, Time
getDecimalFormatSymbols()	DecimalFormat
getDecimalSeparator()	DecimalFormatSymbols
getDeclaredClasses()	Class
getDeclaredConstructor()	Class
getDeclaredConstructors()	Class
getDeclaredField()	Class
getDeclaredFields()	Class
getDeclaredMethod()	Class
getDeclaredMethods()	Class

continued

Method Name	Class or Interface Name
getDeclaringClass()	Class, Constructor, Field, Member, Method
getDecomposition()	Collator
getDefault()	Locale, TimeZone
getDefaultAllowUserInteraction()	URLConnection
getDefaultCursor()	Cursor
getDefaultEventIndex()	BeanInfo, SimpleBeanInfo
getDefaultPropertyIndex()	BeanInfo, SimpleBeanInfo
getDefaultRequestProperty()	URLConnection
getDefaultStream()	LogStream
getDefaultToolkit()	Toolkit
getDefaultTransactionIsolation()	DatabaseMetaData
getDefaultUseCaches()	URLConnection
getDescent()	FontMetrics
getDigit()	DecimalFormatSymbols
getDirectory()	FileDialog
getDisplayCountry()	Locale
getDisplayLanguage()	Locale
getDisplayName()	FeatureDescriptor, Locale
getDisplayVariant()	Locale
getDoInput()	URLConnection
getDoOutput()	URLConnection
getDocumentBase()	Applet, AppletStub
getDouble()	Array, CallableStatement, Field, ResultSet
getDriver()	DriverManager
getDriverMajorVersion()	DatabaseMetaData
getDriverMinorVersion()	DatabaseMetaData
getDriverName()	DatabaseMetaData
getDriverVersion()	DatabaseMetaData
getDrivers()	DriverManager
getEchoChar()	TextField
getEditorSearchPath()	PropertyEditorManager
getEncoded()	Key
getEncoding()	InputStreamReader, OutputStreamWriter
getEndIndex()	CharacterIterator, FieldPosition, StringCharacterIterator
getEntry()	ZipFile
getEras()	DateFormatSymbols
getErrorCode()	SQLException
getErrorOffset()	FormatException, ParseException
getErrorStream()	Process
getErrorsAny()	MediaTracker

Method Name	Class or Interface Name
getErrorsID()	MediaTracker
getEventSetDescriptors()	BeanInfo, SimpleBeanInfo
getException()	ExceptionInInitializerError
getExceptionTypes()	Constructor, Method
getExpiration()	URLConnection
getExportedKeys()	DatabaseMetaData
getExtra()	ZipEntry
getExtraNameCharacters()	DatabaseMetaData
getFD()	FileInputStream, FileOutputStream, RandomAccessFile
getFailureHandler()	RMISocketFactory
getFamily()	Font
getField()	Class, FieldPosition
getFields()	Class
getFile()	FileDialog, URL
getFileDescriptor()	DatagramSocketImpl, SocketImpl
getFilePointer()	RandomAccessFile
getFilenameFilter()	FileDialog
getFilterInstance()	ImageFilter
getFirstDayOfWeek()	Calendar
getFloat()	Array, CallableStatement, Field, ResultSet
getFocusOwner()	Window
getFollowRedirects()	HttpURLConnection
getFont()	Component, Font, FontMetrics, Graphics, MenuComponent, MenuContainer
getFontList()	Toolkit
getFontMetrics()	Component, ComponentPeer, Graphics, Toolkit
getFontPeer()	Toolkit
getForeground()	Component
getFormat()	Certificate, Key
getFormats()	ChoiceFormat, MessageFormat
getG()	DSAParams
getGraphics()	Component, ComponentPeer, Image, PrintJob
getGreatestMinimum()	Calendar, GregorianCalendar
getGreen()	Color, ColorModel, DirectColorModel, IndexColorModel
getGreenMask()	DirectColorModel
getGreens()	IndexColorModel
getGregorianChange()	GregorianCalendar
getGroupingSeparator()	DecimalFormatSymbols
getGroupingSize()	DecimalFormat

continued

Method Name	Class or Interface Name
getGuarantor()	Certificate
getHAdjustable()	ScrollPane
getHSBColor()	Color
getHScrollbarHeight()	ScrollPane, ScrollPanePeer
getHeaderField()	URLConnection
getHeaderFieldDate()	URLConnection
getHeaderFieldInt()	URLConnection
getHeaderFieldKey()	URLConnection
getHeight()	FontMetrics, Image, PixelGrabber
getHelpMenu()	MenuBar
getHgap()	BorderLayout, CardLayout, FlowLayout, GridLayout
getHost()	URL
getHostAddress()	InetAddress
getHostName()	InetAddress
getHours()	Date
getHumanPresentableName()	DataFlavor
getID()	AWTEvent, TimeZone
getISO3Country()	Locale
getISO3Language()	Locale
getIcon()	BeanInfo, SimpleBeanInfo
getIconImage()	Frame
getIdentifierQuoteString()	DatabaseMetaData
getIdentity()	IdentityScope
getIfModifiedSince()	URLConnection
getImage()	Applet, AppletContext, Toolkit
getImportedKeys()	DatabaseMetaData
getInCheck()	SecurityManager
getIndex()	CharacterIterator, DataTruncation, ParsePosition, StringCharacterIterator
getIndexInfo()	DatabaseMetaData
getIndexedPropertyType()	IndexedPropertyDescriptor
getIndexedReadMethod()	IndexedPropertyDescriptor
getIndexedWriteMethod()	IndexedPropertyDescriptor
getInetAddress()	ServerSocket, Socket, SocketImpl
getInfinity()	DecimalFormatSymbols
getInfo()	Identity, Provider
getInputStream()	Process, RemoteCall, Socket, SocketImpl, URLConnection, ZipFile
getInsets()	Container, ContainerPeer
getInstance()	Calendar, Collator, DateFormat, KeyPairGenerator, MessageDigest, NumberFormat, Signature

Method Name	Class or Interface Name
getInstanceOf()	Beans
getInt()	Array, CallableStatement, Field, ResultSet
getInteger()	Integer
getInterface()	MulticastSocket
getInterfaces()	Class
getItem()	Choice, ItemEvent, List, Menu
getItemCount()	Choice, List, Menu
getItemSelectable()	ItemEvent
getItems()	List
getJavaInitializationString()	PropertyEditor, PropertyEditorSupport
getKey()	MenuShortcut, MissingResourceException
getKeyChar()	KeyEvent
getKeyCode()	KeyEvent
getKeyModifiersText()	KeyEvent
getKeyText()	KeyEvent
getKeys()	ListResourceBundle, PropertyResourceBundle, ResourceBundle
getLabel()	Button, Checkbox, MenuItem
getLanguage()	Locale
getLastModified()	URLConnection
getLayout()	Container
getLayoutAlignmentX()	BorderLayout, CardLayout, GridBagLayout, LayoutManager2
getLayoutAlignmentY()	BorderLayout, CardLayout, GridBagLayout, LayoutManager2
getLayoutDimensions()	GridBagLayout
GetLayoutInfo()	GridBagLayout
getLayoutOrigin()	GridBagLayout
getLayoutWeights()	GridBagLayout
getLeading()	FontMetrics
getLeastMaximum()	Calendar, GregorianCalendar
getLength()	Array, DatagramPacket
getLimits()	ChoiceFormat
getLineIncrement()	Scrollbar
getLineInstance()	BreakIterator
getLineNumber()	LineNumberInputStream, LineNumberReader
getListenerMethodDescriptors()	EventSetDescriptor
getListenerMethods()	EventSetDescriptor
getListenerType()	EventSetDescriptor
getLocalAddress()	DatagramSocket, Socket
getLocalHost()	InetAddress
getLocalPatternChars()	DateFormatSymbols

continued

Method Name	Class or Interface Name
getLocalPort()	DatagramSocket, DatagramSocketImpl, ServerSocket, Socket, SocketImpl
getLocale()	Applet, Component, MessageFormat, Window
getLocalizedInputStream()	Runtime
getLocalizedMessage()	Throwable
getLocalizedOutputStream()	Runtime
getLocation()	Component, Point, Rectangle
getLocationOnScreen()	Component, ComponentPeer
getLog()	RemoteServer
getLogStream()	DriverManager
getLoginTimeout()	DriverManager
getLong()	Array, CallableStatement, Field, Long, ResultSet
getLowestSetBit()	BigInteger
getMajorVersion()	Driver
getMapSize()	IndexColorModel
getMaxAdvance()	FontMetrics
getMaxAscent()	FontMetrics
getMaxBinaryLiteralLength()	DatabaseMetaData
getMaxCatalogNameLength()	DatabaseMetaData
getMaxCharLiteralLength()	DatabaseMetaData
getMaxColumnNameLength()	DatabaseMetaData
getMaxColumnsInGroupBy()	DatabaseMetaData
getMaxColumnsInIndex()	DatabaseMetaData
getMaxColumnsInOrderBy()	DatabaseMetaData
getMaxColumnsInSelect()	DatabaseMetaData
getMaxColumnsInTable()	DatabaseMetaData
getMaxConnections()	DatabaseMetaData
getMaxCursorNameLength()	DatabaseMetaData
getMaxDecent()	FontMetrics
getMaxDescent()	FontMetrics
getMaxFieldSize()	Statement
getMaxIndexLength()	DatabaseMetaData
getMaxPriority()	ThreadGroup
getMaxProcedureNameLength()	DatabaseMetaData
getMaxRowSize()	DatabaseMetaData
getMaxRows()	Statement
getMaxSchemaNameLength()	DatabaseMetaData
getMaxStatementLength()	DatabaseMetaData
getMaxStatements()	DatabaseMetaData
getMaxTableNameLength()	DatabaseMetaData

Method Name	Class or Interface Name
getMaxTablesInSelect()	DatabaseMetaData
getMaxUserNameLength()	DatabaseMetaData
getMaximum()	Adjustable, Calendar, GregorianCalendar, Scrollbar
getMaximumFractionDigits()	NumberFormat
getMaximumIntegerDigits()	NumberFormat
getMaximumSize()	Component, Container
getMenu()	MenuBar, ResourceBundle
getMenuBar()	Frame, ResourceBundle
getMenuCount()	MenuBar
getMenuShortcutKeyMask()	Toolkit
getMessage()	InvalidClassException, RemoteException, ServerCloneException, Throwable, WriteAbortedException
getMessageDigest()	DigestInputStream, DigestOutputStream
getMetaData()	Connection, ResultSet
getMethod()	Class, MethodDescriptor, ZipEntry
getMethodDescriptors()	BeanInfo, SimpleBeanInfo
getMethods()	Class
getMimeType()	DataFlavor
getMinimalDaysInFirstWeek()	Calendar
getMinimum()	Adjustable, Calendar, GregorianCalendar, Scrollbar
getMinimumFractionDigits()	NumberFormat
getMinimumIntegerDigits()	NumberFormat
getMinimumSize()	Component, ComponentPeer, Container, List, ListPeer, TextArea, TextAreaPeer, TextField, TextFieldPeer
getMinorVersion()	Driver
GetMinSize()	GridBagLayout
getMinusSign()	DecimalFormatSymbols
getMinutes()	Date
getMode()	FileDialog
getModifiers()	ActionEvent, Class, Constructor, Field, InputEvent, Member, Method
getMonth()	Date, Time
getMonths()	DateFormatSymbols
getMoreResults()	Statement
getMultiplier()	DecimalFormat
getNaN()	DecimalFormatSymbols
getName()	Acl, Class, Clipboard, Component, Constructor, FeatureDescriptor, Field, File, Font, Identity, Member, MenuComponent, Method, ObjectStreamClass, Principal, Provider, Thread, ThreadGroup, ZipEntry, ZipFile
getNanos()	Timestamp

continued

Method Name	Class or Interface Name
getNativeContainer()	Toolkit
getNegativePrefix()	DecimalFormat
getNegativeSuffix()	DecimalFormat
getNewValue()	PropertyChangeEvent
getNextEntry()	ZipInputStream
getNextEvent()	EventQueue
getNextException()	SQLException
getNextWarning()	SQLWarning
getNumberInstance()	DateFormat, NumberFormat
getNumericFunctions()	DatabaseMetaData
getNumericValue()	Character
getObject()	CallableStatement, ResourceBundle, ResultSet
getOffset()	SimpleTimeZone, TimeZone
getOldValue()	PropertyChangeEvent
getOperation()	Operation
getOperations()	Skeleton
getOrientation()	Adjustable, Scrollbar
getOutputStream()	LogStream, Process, RemoteCall, Socket, SocketImpl, URLConnection
getP()	DSAParams
getPageDimension()	PrintJob
getPageIncrement()	Scrollbar
getPageResolution()	PrintJob
getParameter()	Applet, AppletStub, DataTruncation, Signature
getParameterDescriptors()	MethodDescriptor
getParameterInfo()	Applet
getParameterTypes()	Constructor, Method
getParams()	DSAKey
getParent()	Component, File, MenuComponent, ThreadGroup
getPath()	File
getPatternSeparator()	DecimalFormatSymbols
getPeer()	Component, Font, MenuComponent
getPerMill()	DecimalFormatSymbols
getPercent()	DecimalFormatSymbols
getPercentInstance()	NumberFormat
getPermissions()	Acl
getPixelSize()	ColorModel
getPixels()	PixelGrabber
getPoint()	MouseEvent
getPort()	DatagramPacket, Socket, SocketImpl, URL
getPositivePrefix()	DecimalFormat

Method Name	Class or Interface Name
getPositiveSuffix()	DecimalFormat
getPrecision()	ResultSetMetaData
getPredefinedCursor()	Cursor
getPreferredSize()	Component, ComponentPeer, Container, List, ListPeer, TextArea, TextAreaPeer, TextField, TextFieldPeer
getPrimaryKeys()	DatabaseMetaData
getPrincipal()	AclEntry, Certificate
getPrintJob()	PrintGraphics, Toolkit
getPriority()	Thread
getPrivate()	KeyPair
getPrivateKey()	Signer
getProcedureColumns()	DatabaseMetaData
getProcedureTerm()	DatabaseMetaData
getProcedures()	DatabaseMetaData
getPropagationId()	PropertyChangeEvent
getProperties()	System
getProperty()	Image, Properties, Security, System, Toolkit
getPropertyChangeEvent()	PropertyVetoException
getPropertyDescriptors()	BeanInfo, SimpleBeanInfo
getPropertyEditorClass()	PropertyDescriptor
getPropertyInfo()	Driver
getPropertyName()	PropertyChangeEvent
getPropertyType()	PropertyDescriptor
getProtocol()	URL
getProvider()	Security
getProviders()	Security
getPublic()	KeyPair
getPublicKey()	Certificate, Identity
getQ()	DSAParams
getQueryTimeout()	Statement
getRGB()	Color, ColorModel, DirectColorModel, IndexColorModel, SystemColor
getRGBdefault()	ColorModel
getRawOffset()	SimpleTimeZone, TimeZone
getRead()	DataTruncation
getReadMethod()	PropertyDescriptor
getRed()	Color, ColorModel, DirectColorModel, IndexColorModel
getRedMask()	DirectColorModel
getReds()	IndexColorModel
getRef()	URL

continued

Method Name	Class or Interface Name
getRefClass()	RemoteRef
getRegistry()	LocateRegistry
getRemaining()	Inflater
getRemoveListenerMethod()	EventSetDescriptor
getRepresentationClass()	DataFlavor
getRequestMethod()	HttpURLConnection
getRequestProperty()	URLConnection
getResource()	Class, ClassLoader
getResourceAsStream()	Class, ClassLoader
getResponseCode()	HttpURLConnection
getResponseMessage()	HttpURLConnection
getResultSet()	Statement
getResultStream()	RemoteCall
getReturnType()	Method
getRows()	GridLayout, List, TextArea
getRules()	RuleBasedCollator
getRuntime()	Runtime
getSQLKeywords()	DatabaseMetaData
getSQLState()	SQLException
getScale()	ResultSetMetaData
getScaledInstance()	Image
getSchemaName()	ResultSetMetaData
getSchemaTerm()	DatabaseMetaData
getSchemas()	DatabaseMetaData
getScope()	Identity
getScreenResolution()	Toolkit
getScreenSize()	Toolkit
getScrollPosition()	ScrollPane
getScrollbarDisplayPolicy()	ScrollPane
getScrollbarVisibility()	TextArea
getSearchStringEscape()	DatabaseMetaData
getSeconds()	Date
getSecurityContext()	LoaderHandler, RMIClassLoader, RMISecurityManager, SecurityManager
getSecurityManager()	System
getSeed()	SecureRandom
getSelectedCheckbox()	CheckboxGroup
getSelectedIndex()	Choice, List
getSelectedIndexes()	List, ListPeer
getSelectedItem()	Choice, List

Method Name	Class or Interface Name
getSelectedItems()	List
getSelectedObjects()	Checkbox, CheckboxMenuItem, Choice, ItemSelectable, List
getSelectedText()	TextComponent
getSelectionEnd()	TextComponent, TextComponentPeer
getSelectionStart()	TextComponent, TextComponentPeer
getSentenceInstance()	BreakIterator
getSerialVersionUID()	ObjectStreamClass
getShort()	Array, CallableStatement, Field, ResultSet
getShortDescription()	FeatureDescriptor
getShortMonths()	DateFormatSymbols
getShortWeekdays()	DateFormatSymbols
getShortcut()	MenuItem
getShortcutMenuItem()	MenuBar
getSigners()	Class
getSize()	Component, Dimension, Font, Rectangle, ZipEntry
getSoLinger()	Socket
getSoTimeout()	DatagramSocket, ServerSocket, Socket
getSocketFactory()	RMISocketFactory
getSource()	EventObject, Image
getSourceString()	CollationKey
getState()	Checkbox, CheckboxMenuItem
getStateChange()	ItemEvent
getStatus()	PixelGrabber
getStrength()	Collator
getString()	CallableStatement, ResourceBundle, ResultSet
getStringArray()	ResourceBundle
getStringFunctions()	DatabaseMetaData
getStyle()	Font
getSuperclass()	Class
getSystemClipboard()	Toolkit
getSystemEventQueue()	Toolkit
getSystemEventQueueImpl()	Toolkit
getSystemFunctions()	DatabaseMetaData
getSystemResource()	ClassLoader
getSystemResourceAsStream()	ClassLoader
getSystemScope()	IdentityScope
getTTL()	DatagramSocketImpl, MulticastSocket
getTableName()	ResultSetMetaData
getTablePrivileges()	DatabaseMetaData

continued

Method Name	Class or Interface Name
getTableTypes()	DatabaseMetaData
getTables()	DatabaseMetaData
getTags()	PropertyEditor, PropertyEditorSupport
getTargetException()	InvocationTargetException
getTcpNoDelay()	Socket
getText()	BreakIterator, Label, TextComponent, TextComponentPeer
getThreadGroup()	SecurityManager, Thread
getTime()	Calendar, CallableStatement, Date, ResultSet, ZipEntry
getTimeDateFunctions()	DatabaseMetaData
getTimeInMillis()	Calendar
getTimeInstance()	DateFormat
getTimeZone()	Calendar, DateFormat, TimeZone
getTimestamp()	CallableStatement, ResultSet
getTimezoneOffset()	Date
getTitle()	Dialog, Frame
getToolkit()	Component, ComponentPeer, Window
getTotalIn()	Deflater, Inflater
getTotalOut()	Deflater, Inflater
getTransactionIsolation()	Connection
getTransferData()	StringSelection, Transferable
getTransferDataFlavors()	StringSelection, Transferable
getTransferSize()	DataTruncation
getTransparentPixel()	IndexColorModel
getTreeLock()	Component
getType()	Character, Cursor, Field
getTypeInfo()	DatabaseMetaData
getURL()	DatabaseMetaData, URLConnection
getUnicodeStream()	ResultSet
getUnitIncrement()	Adjustable, Scrollbar
getUpdateCount()	Statement
getUpdateRect()	PaintEvent
getUseCaches()	URLConnection
getUserName()	DatabaseMetaData
getVAdjustable()	ScrollPane
getVMID()	Lease
getVScrollbarWidth()	ScrollPane, ScrollPanePeer
getValue()	Adjustable, AdjustmentEvent, Adler32, CRC32, Checksum, FeatureDescriptor, Lease, PropertyEditor, PropertyEditorSupport, Scrollbar
getVariant()	Locale
getVersion()	Provider

Method Name	**Class or Interface Name**
getVersionColumns()	DatabaseMetaData
getVgap()	BorderLayout, CardLayout, FlowLayout, GridLayout
getViewportSize()	ScrollPane
getVisible()	Scrollbar
getVisibleAmount()	Adjustable, Scrollbar
getVisibleIndex()	List
getWarningString()	Window
getWarnings()	Connection, ResultSet, Statement
getWeekdays()	DateFormatSymbols
getWhen()	InputEvent
getWidth()	Image, PixelGrabber
getWidths()	FontMetrics
getWindow()	WindowEvent
getWordInstance()	BreakIterator
getWriteMethod()	PropertyDescriptor
getX()	DSAPrivateKey, MouseEvent
getY()	DSAPublicKey, MouseEvent
getYear()	Date, Time
getZeroDigit()	DecimalFormatSymbols
getZoneStrings()	DateFormatSymbols
getenv()	System
gotFocus()	Component
grabPixels()	PixelGrabber
grow()	Rectangle
guessContentTypeFromName()	URLConnection
guessContentTypeFromStream()	URLConnection
handleEvent()	Component, ComponentPeer
handleGetObject()	ListResourceBundle, PropertyResourceBundle, ResourceBundle
hasChanged()	Observable
Hashtable()	Constructor
hasMoreElements()	Enumeration, StringTokenizer
hasMoreTokens()	StringTokenizer
hashCode()	BigDecimal, BigInteger, BitSet, Boolean, Byte, Character, ChoiceFormat, CollationKey, Collator, Color, Constructor, Date, DateFormat, DateFormatSymbols, DecimalFormat, DecimalFormatSymbols, Double, Field, File, Float, Font, GregorianCalendar, Identity, InetAddress, Integer, Locale, Long, MessageFormat, Method, NumberFormat, ObjID, Object, Point, Principal, Rectangle, RemoteObject, RuleBasedCollator, Short, SimpleDateFormat, SimpleTimeZone, String, StringCharacterIterator, UID, URL, VMID

continued

Method Name	Class or Interface Name
hide()	Component, ComponentPeer
HSBtoRGB()	Color
identities()	IdentityScope
identityEquals()	Identity
identityHashCode()	System
IEEEremainder()	Math
imageComplete()	ImageConsumer, ImageFilter, PixelGrabber
imageUpdate()	Component, ImageObserver
implAccept()	ServerSocket
inClass()	SecurityManager
inClassLoader()	SecurityManager
inDaylightTime()	SimpleTimeZone, TimeZone
indexOf()	String, Vector
inflate()	Inflater
init()	Applet
initSign()	Signature
initVerify()	Signature
initialize()	DSAKeyPairGenerator, KeyPairGenerator
insert()	Choice, Menu, StringBuffer, TextArea, TextAreaPeer
insertElementAt()	Vector
insertProviderAt()	Security
insertSeparator()	Menu
insertText()	TextArea, TextAreaPeer
insets()	Container, ContainerPeer
inside()	Component, Polygon, Rectangle
instantiate()	Beans
intBitsToFloat()	Float
intValue()	BigDecimal, BigInteger, Byte, Double, Float, Integer, Long, Number, Short
intern()	String
internalGet()	Calendar
interrupt()	Thread
interrupted()	Thread
intersection()	Rectangle
intersects()	Rectangle
invalidate()	Component, Container
invalidateLayout()	BorderLayout, CardLayout, GridBagLayout, LayoutManager2
invoke()	Method, RemoteRef
isAbsolute()	File
isAbstract()	Modifier
isActionKey()	KeyEvent

Method Name	Class or Interface Name
isActive()	Applet, AppletStub
isAlive()	Thread
isAltDown()	InputEvent
isAncestorOf()	Container
isArray()	Class
isAssignableFrom()	Class
isAutoIncrement()	ResultSetMetaData
isBold()	Font
isBound()	PropertyDescriptor
isCaseSensitive()	ResultSetMetaData
isCatalogAtStart()	DatabaseMetaData
isClosed()	Connection
isConstrained()	PropertyDescriptor
isConsumed()	AWTEvent, InputEvent
isConsumer()	FilteredImageSource, ImageProducer, MemoryImageSource
isControlDown()	InputEvent
isCurrency()	ResultSetMetaData
isDaemon()	Thread, ThreadGroup
isDataFlavorSupported()	StringSelection, Transferable
isDecimalSeparatorAlwaysShown()	DecimalFormat
isDefined()	Character
isDefinitelyWritable()	ResultSetMetaData
isDesignTime()	Beans
isDestroyed()	ThreadGroup
isDigit()	Character
isDirectory()	File, ZipEntry
isEditable()	TextComponent
isEmpty()	Dictionary, Hashtable, Rectangle, Vector
isEnabled()	Component, MenuItem
isEqual()	MessageDigest
isErrorAny()	MediaTracker
isErrorID()	MediaTracker
isExpert()	FeatureDescriptor
isFile()	File
isFinal()	Modifier
isFocusTraversable()	Component, ComponentPeer
isGroupingUsed()	NumberFormat
isGuiAvailable()	Beans
isHidden()	FeatureDescriptor

continued

Method Name	Class or Interface Name
isISOControl()	Character
isIdentifierIgnorable()	Character
isInDefaultEventSet()	EventSetDescriptor
isIndexSelected()	List
isInfinite()	Double, Float
isInstance()	Class
isInstanceOf()	Beans
isInterface()	Class, Modifier
isInterrupted()	Thread
isItalic()	Font
isJavaIdentifierPart()	Character
isJavaIdentifierStart()	Character
isJavaLetter()	Character
isJavaLetterOrDigit()	Character
isLeapYear()	GregorianCalendar
isLenient()	Calendar, DateFormat
isLetter()	Character
isLetterOrDigit()	Character
isLowerCase()	Character
isMember()	Group
isMetaDown()	InputEvent
isMimeTypeEqual()	DataFlavor
isModal()	Dialog
isMulticastAddress()	InetAddress
isMultipleMode()	List
isNaN()	Double, Float
isNative()	Modifier
isNegative()	AclEntry
isNullable()	ResultSetMetaData
isOwner()	Owner
isPaintable()	PropertyEditor, PropertyEditorSupport
isParseIntegerOnly()	NumberFormat
isPlain()	Font
isPopupTrigger()	MouseEvent
isPrimitive()	Class
isPrivate()	Modifier
isProbablePrime()	BigInteger
isProtected()	Modifier
isPublic()	Modifier
isReadOnly()	Connection, DatabaseMetaData, ResultSetMetaData

Method Name	Class or Interface Name
isResizable()	Dialog, Frame
isSearchable()	ResultSetMetaData
isSelected()	List
isSet()	Calendar
isShiftDown()	InputEvent
isShowing()	Component, Window
isSigned()	ResultSetMetaData
isSpace()	Character
isSpaceChar()	Character
isStatic()	Modifier
isSynchronized()	Modifier
isTearOff()	Menu
isTemporary()	FocusEvent
isTitleCase()	Character
isTransient()	Modifier
isUnicast()	EventSetDescriptor
isUnicodeIdentifierPart()	Character
isUnicodeIdentifierStart()	Character
isUnique()	VMID
isUpperCase()	Character
isValid()	Component
isVisible()	Component
isVolatile()	Modifier
isWhitespace()	Character
isWritable()	ResultSetMetaData
itemStateChanged()	AWTEventMulticaster, ItemListener
jdbcCompliant()	Driver
join()	DatagramSocketImpl, Thread
joinGroup()	MulticastSocket
keyDown()	Component
keyPressed()	AWTEventMulticaster, KeyAdapter, KeyListener
keyReleased()	AWTEventMulticaster, KeyAdapter, KeyListener
keyTyped()	AWTEventMulticaster, KeyAdapter, KeyListener
keyUp()	Component
keys()	Dictionary, Hashtable
last()	BreakIterator, CardLayout, CharacterIterator, StringCharacterIterator
lastElement()	Vector
lastIndexOf()	String, Vector
lastModified()	File

continued

Method Name	Class or Interface Name
lastPageFirst()	PrintJob
layout()	Component, Container, ScrollPane
layoutContainer()	BorderLayout, CardLayout, FlowLayout, GridBagLayout, GridLayout, LayoutManager
leave()	DatagramSocketImpl
leaveGroup()	MulticastSocket
length()	File, RandomAccessFile, String, StringBuffer
lineno()	StreamTokenizer
list()	Component, Container, File, Naming, Properties, Registry, ThreadGroup
listen()	SocketImpl
load()	Properties, Runtime, System
loadClass()	ClassLoader, LoaderHandler, RMIClassLoader
loadImage()	SimpleBeanInfo
loadLibrary()	Runtime, System
loadSystemColors()	Toolkit
locate()	Component, Container
location()	Component, GridBagLayout
log()	LogStream, Math
longBitsToDouble()	Double
longValue()	BigDecimal, BigInteger, Byte, Double, Float, Integer, Long, Number, Short
lookup()	Naming, ObjectStreamClass, Registry
lookupConstraints()	GridBagLayout
loop()	AudioClip
lostFocus()	Component
lostOwnership()	ClipboardOwner, StringSelection
lowerCaseMode()	StreamTokenizer
makeVisible()	List, ListPeer
mark()	BufferedInputStream, BufferedReader, ByteArrayInputStream, CharArrayReader, FilterInputStream, FilterReader, InputStream, LineNumberInputStream, LineNumberReader, Reader, StringReader
markSupported()	BufferedInputStream, BufferedReader, ByteArrayInputStream, CharArrayReader, FilterInputStream, FilterReader, InputStream, PushbackInputStream, PushbackReader, Reader, StringReader
max()	BigDecimal, BigInteger, Math
maximumLayoutSize()	BorderLayout, CardLayout, GridBagLayout, LayoutManager2
members()	Group
metaDown()	Event
min()	BigDecimal, BigInteger, Math
minimumLayoutSize()	BorderLayout, CardLayout, FlowLayout, GridBagLayout, GridLayout, LayoutManager

Method Name	Class or Interface Name
minimumSize()	Component, ComponentPeer, Container, List, ListPeer, TextArea, TextAreaPeer, TextField, TextFieldPeer
mkdir()	File
mkdirs()	File
mod()	BigInteger
modInverse()	BigInteger
modPow()	BigInteger
mouseClicked()	AWTEventMulticaster, MouseAdapter, MouseListener
mouseDown()	Component
mouseDrag()	Component
mouseDragged()	AWTEventMulticaster, MouseMotionAdapter, MouseMotionListener
mouseEnter()	Component
mouseEntered()	AWTEventMulticaster, MouseAdapter, MouseListener
mouseExit()	Component
mouseExited()	AWTEventMulticaster, MouseAdapter, MouseListener
mouseMove()	Component
mouseMoved()	AWTEventMulticaster, MouseMotionAdapter, MouseMotionListener
mousePressed()	AWTEventMulticaster, MouseAdapter, MouseListener
mouseReleased()	AWTEventMulticaster, MouseAdapter, MouseListener
mouseUp()	Component
move()	Component, Point, Rectangle
movePointLeft()	BigDecimal
movePointRight()	BigDecimal
multiply()	BigDecimal, BigInteger
nativeSQL()	Connection
needsDictionary()	Inflater
needsGui()	Visibility
needsInput()	Deflater, Inflater
negate()	BigDecimal, BigInteger
newCall()	RemoteRef
newInstance()	Array, Class, Constructor
newLine()	BufferedWriter
newPixels()	MemoryImageSource
next()	BreakIterator, CardLayout, CharacterIterator, CollationElementIterator, Random, ResultSet, SecureRandom, StringCharacterIterator
nextBytes()	Random, SecureRandom
nextDouble()	ChoiceFormat, Random
nextElement()	Enumeration, StringTokenizer
nextFloat()	Random

continued

Method Name	Class or Interface Name
nextFocus()	Component
nextGaussian()	Random
nextInt()	Random
nextLong()	Random
nextToken()	StreamTokenizer, StringTokenizer
normalizeMimeType()	DataFlavor
normalizeMimeTypeParameter()	DataFlavor
not()	BigInteger
notify()	Object
notifyAll()	Object
notifyObservers()	Observable
nullPlusNonNullIsNull()	DatabaseMetaData
nullsAreSortedAtEnd()	DatabaseMetaData
nullsAreSortedAtStart()	DatabaseMetaData
nullsAreSortedHigh()	DatabaseMetaData
nullsAreSortedLow()	DatabaseMetaData
okToUseGui()	Visibility
on()	DigestInputStream, DigestOutputStream
openConnection()	URL, URLStreamHandler
openStream()	URL
or()	BigInteger, BitSet
ordinaryChar()	StreamTokenizer
ordinaryChars()	StreamTokenizer
pack()	Window
paint()	Canvas, Component, ComponentPeer, Container
paintAll()	Component
paintComponents()	Container
paintValue()	PropertyEditor, PropertyEditorSupport
paramString()	AWTEvent, ActionEvent, AdjustmentEvent, Button, Checkbox, CheckboxMenuItem, Choice, Component, ComponentEvent, Container, ContainerEvent, Dialog, Event, FileDialog, FocusEvent, Frame, ItemEvent, KeyEvent, Label, List, Menu, MenuComponent, MenuItem, MenuShortcut, MouseEvent, PaintEvent, ScrollPane, Scrollbar, TextArea, TextComponent, TextEvent, TextField, WindowEvent
parentOf()	ThreadGroup
parse()	ChoiceFormat, Date, DateFormat, DecimalFormat, MessageFormat, NumberFormat, SimpleDateFormat
parseByte()	Byte
parseInt()	Integer
parseLevel()	LogStream

Method Name	Class or Interface Name
parseLong()	Long
parseNumbers()	StreamTokenizer
parseObject()	DateFormat, Format, MessageFormat, NumberFormat
parseShort()	Short
parseURL()	URLStreamHandler
peek()	DatagramSocketImpl, Stack
peekEvent()	EventQueue
permissions()	AclEntry
play()	Applet, AudioClip
pop()	Stack
postEvent()	Component, EventQueue, MenuComponent, MenuContainer, Window
pow()	BigInteger, Math
preferredLayoutSize()	BorderLayout, CardLayout, FlowLayout, GridBagLayout, GridLayout, LayoutManager
preferredSize()	Component, ComponentPeer, Container, List, ListPeer, TextArea, TextAreaPeer, TextField, TextFieldPeer
prepareCall()	Connection
prepareImage()	Component, ComponentPeer, Toolkit
prepareStatement()	Connection
previous()	BreakIterator, CardLayout, CharacterIterator, StringCharacterIterator
previousDouble()	ChoiceFormat
primaryOrder()	CollationElementIterator
print()	Component, ComponentPeer, Container, PrintStream, PrintWriter
printAll()	Component
printComponents()	Container, ScrollPane
printStackTrace()	Throwable
println()	DriverManager, PrintStream, PrintWriter
PrintWriter()	PrintWriter
processActionEvent()	Button, List, MenuItem, TextField
processAdjustmentEvent()	Scrollbar
processComponentEvent()	Component
processContainerEvent()	Container
processEvent()	Button, Checkbox, CheckboxMenuItem, Choice, Component, Container, List, MenuComponent, MenuItem, Scrollbar, TextComponent, TextField, Window
processFocusEvent()	Component
processItemEvent()	Checkbox, CheckboxMenuItem, Choice, List
processKeyEvent()	Component
processMouseEvent()	Component

continued

Method Name	Class or Interface Name
processMouseMotionEvent()	Component
processTextEvent()	TextComponent
processWindowEvent()	Window
propertyChange()	PropertyChangeListener
propertyNames()	Properties
push()	Stack
pushBack()	StreamTokenizer
put()	Dictionary, Hashtable
putNextEntry()	ZipOutputStream
quoteChar()	StreamTokenizer
random()	Math
read()	BufferedInputStream, BufferedReader, ByteArrayInputStream, CharArrayReader, CheckedInputStream, DataInputStream, DigestInputStream, FileInputStream, FilterInputStream, FilterReader, GZIPInputStream, InflaterInputStream, InputStream, InputStreamReader, LineNumberInputStream, LineNumberReader, ObjID, ObjectInput, ObjectInputStream, PipedInputStream, PipedReader, PushbackInputStream, PushbackReader, RandomAccessFile, Reader, SequenceInputStream, StringBufferInputStream, StringReader, UID, ZipInputStream
readBoolean()	DataInput, DataInputStream, ObjectInputStream, RandomAccessFile
readByte()	DataInput, DataInputStream, ObjectInputStream, RandomAccessFile
readChar()	DataInput, DataInputStream, ObjectInputStream, RandomAccessFile
readDouble()	DataInput, DataInputStream, ObjectInputStream, RandomAccessFile
readExternal()	Externalizable
readFloat()	DataInput, DataInputStream, ObjectInputStream, RandomAccessFile
readFully()	DataInput, DataInputStream, ObjectInputStream, RandomAccessFile
readInt()	DataInput, DataInputStream, ObjectInputStream, RandomAccessFile
readLine()	BufferedReader, DataInput, DataInputStream, LineNumberReader, ObjectInputStream, RandomAccessFile
readLong()	DataInput, DataInputStream, ObjectInputStream, RandomAccessFile
readObject()	ObjectInput, ObjectInputStream
readShort()	DataInput, DataInputStream, ObjectInputStream, RandomAccessFile
readStreamHeader()	ObjectInputStream
readUTF()	DataInput, DataInputStream, ObjectInputStream, RandomAccessFile
readUnsignedByte()	DataInput, DataInputStream, ObjectInputStream, RandomAccessFile
readUnsignedShort()	DataInput, DataInputStream, ObjectInputStream, RandomAccessFile
ready()	BufferedReader, CharArrayReader, FilterReader, InputStreamReader, PushbackReader, Reader, StringReader
rebind()	Naming, Registry
receive()	DatagramSocket, DatagramSocketImpl, PipedInputStream
regionMatches()	String

Method Name	Class or Interface Name
registerDriver()	DriverManager
registerEditor()	PropertyEditorManager
registerOutParameter()	CallableStatement
registerValidation()	ObjectInputStream
registryImpl()	RegistryHandler
registryStub()	RegistryHandler
rehash()	Hashtable
releaseInputStream()	RemoteCall
releaseOutputStream()	RemoteCall
remainder()	BigInteger
remoteEquals()	RemoteRef
remoteHashCode()	RemoteRef
remoteToString()	RemoteRef
remove()	AWTEventMulticaster, Choice, ChoicePeer, Component, Container, Dictionary, Frame, Hashtable, List, Menu, MenuBar, MenuContainer
removeActionListener()	Button, List, MenuItem, TextField
removeAdjustmentListener()	Adjustable, Scrollbar
removeAll()	Choice, Container, List, ListPeer, Menu
removeAllElements()	Vector
removeCertificate()	Identity
removeComponentListener()	Component
removeConsumer()	FilteredImageSource, ImageProducer, MemoryImageSource
removeContainerListener()	Container
removeElement()	Vector
removeElementAt()	Vector
removeEntry()	Acl
removeFocusListener()	Component
removeIdentity()	IdentityScope
removeImage()	MediaTracker
removeInternal()	AWTEventMulticaster
removeItemListener()	Checkbox, CheckboxMenuItem, Choice, ItemSelectable, List
removeKeyListener()	Component
removeLayoutComponent()	BorderLayout, CardLayout, FlowLayout, GridBagLayout, GridLayout, LayoutManager
removeMember()	Group
removeMouseListener()	Component
removeMouseMotionListener()	Component
removeNotify()	Component, Container, List, Menu, MenuBar, MenuComponent, TextComponent

continued

Method Name	Class or Interface Name
removePermission()	AclEntry
removePropertyChangeListener()	Customizer, PropertyChangeSupport, PropertyEditor, PropertyEditorSupport
removeProvider()	Security
removeTextListener()	TextComponent
removeVetoableChangeListener()	VetoableChangeSupport
removeWindowListener()	Window
renameTo()	File
repaint()	Component, ComponentPeer
replace()	String
replaceItem()	List
replaceObject()	ObjectOutputStream
replaceRange()	TextArea, TextAreaPeer
replaceText()	TextArea, TextAreaPeer
requestFocus()	Component, ComponentPeer
requestTopDownLeftRightResend()	FilteredImageSource, ImageProducer, MemoryImageSource
resendTopDownLeftRight()	ImageFilter
reset()	Adler32, BufferedInputStream, BufferedReader, ByteArrayInputStream, ByteArrayOutputStream, CRC32, CharArrayReader, CharArrayWriter, Checksum, CollationElementIterator, Deflater, FilterInputStream, FilterReader, Inflater, InputStream, LineNumberInputStream, LineNumberReader, MessageDigest, ObjectOutputStream, Reader, StringBufferInputStream, StringReader
resetSyntax()	StreamTokenizer
reshape()	Component, ComponentPeer, Rectangle
resize()	Applet, Component, Rectangle
resolveClass()	ClassLoader, ObjectInputStream
resolveObject()	ObjectInputStream
resume()	Thread, ThreadGroup
reverse()	StringBuffer
RGBtoHSB()	Color
rint()	Math
roll()	Calendar, GregorianCalendar
rollback()	Connection
round()	Math
run()	Runnable, Thread
runFinalization()	Runtime, System
runFinalizersOnExit()	Runtime, System
sameFile()	URL
save()	Properties

Method Name	Class or Interface Name
saveInternal()	AWTEventMulticaster
scale()	BigDecimal
search()	Stack
secondaryOrder()	CollationElementIterator
seek()	RandomAccessFile
select()	Choice, ChoicePeer, List, ListPeer, TextComponent, TextComponentPeer
selectAll()	TextComponent
send()	DatagramSocket, DatagramSocketImpl, MulticastSocket
set()	Array, BitSet, Calendar, Field, URL
setActionCommand()	Button, MenuItem
setAddress()	DatagramPacket
setAlignment()	FlowLayout, Label, LabelPeer
setAllowUserInteraction()	URLConnection
setAmPmStrings()	DateFormatSymbols
setAnimated()	MemoryImageSource
setAsText()	PropertyEditor, PropertyEditorSupport
setAsciiStream()	PreparedStatement
setAutoCommit()	Connection
setBackground()	Component, ComponentPeer
setBeanInfoSearchPath()	Introspector
setBigDecimal()	PreparedStatement
setBinaryStream()	PreparedStatement
setBit()	BigInteger
setBlockIncrement()	Adjustable, Scrollbar
setBoolean()	Array, Field, PreparedStatement
setBound()	PropertyDescriptor
setBounds()	Component, ComponentPeer, Rectangle
setByte()	Array, Field, PreparedStatement
setBytes()	PreparedStatement
setCalendar()	DateFormat
setCaretPosition()	TextComponent, TextComponentPeer
setCatalog()	Connection
setChanged()	Observable
setChar()	Array, Field
setCharAt()	StringBuffer
setCheckboxGroup()	Checkbox, CheckboxPeer
setChoices()	ChoiceFormat
setClip()	Graphics
setColor()	Graphics

continued

Method Name	Class or Interface Name
setColorModel()	ImageConsumer, ImageFilter, PixelGrabber, RGBImageFilter
setColumns()	GridLayout, TextArea, TextField
setComment()	ZipEntry, ZipOutputStream
setConstrained()	PropertyDescriptor
setConstraints()	GridBagLayout
setContentHandlerFactory()	URLConnection
setContents()	Clipboard
setCrc()	ZipEntry
setCurrent()	CheckboxGroup
setCursor()	Component, ComponentPeer, Frame
setCursorName()	Statement
setDaemon()	Thread, ThreadGroup
setData()	DatagramPacket
setDate()	Date, PreparedStatement, Time
setDateFormatSymbols()	SimpleDateFormat
setDecimalFormatSymbols()	DecimalFormat
setDecimalSeparator()	DecimalFormatSymbols
setDecimalSeparatorAlwaysShown()	DecimalFormat
setDecomposition()	Collator
setDefault()	Locale, TimeZone
setDefaultAllowUserInteraction()	URLConnection
setDefaultRequestProperty()	URLConnection
setDefaultStream()	LogStream
setDefaultUseCaches()	URLConnection
setDesignTime()	Beans
setDictionary()	Deflater, Inflater
setDigit()	DecimalFormatSymbols
setDimensions()	CropImageFilter, ImageConsumer, ImageFilter, PixelGrabber, ReplicateScaleFilter
setDirectory()	FileDialog, FileDialogPeer
setDisplayName()	FeatureDescriptor
setDoInput()	URLConnection
setDoOutput()	URLConnection
setDouble()	Array, Field, PreparedStatement
setEchoChar()	TextField, TextFieldPeer
setEchoCharacter()	TextField, TextFieldPeer
setEditable()	TextComponent, TextComponentPeer
setEditorSearchPath()	PropertyEditorManager
setElementAt()	Vector
setEnabled()	Component, ComponentPeer, MenuItem, MenuItemPeer

Method Name	Class or Interface Name
setEndRule()	SimpleTimeZone
setEras()	DateFormatSymbols
setErr()	System
setError()	PrintStream, PrintWriter
setEscapeProcessing()	Statement
setExpert()	FeatureDescriptor
setExtra()	ZipEntry
setFailureHandler()	RMISocketFactory
setFile()	FileDialog, FileDialogPeer
setFilenameFilter()	FileDialog, FileDialogPeer
setFirstDayOfWeek()	Calendar
setFloat()	Array, Field, PreparedStatement
setFollowRedirects()	HttpURLConnection
setFont()	Component, ComponentPeer, Graphics, MenuComponent
setForeground()	Component, ComponentPeer
setFormat()	MessageFormat
setFormats()	MessageFormat
setFullBufferUpdates()	MemoryImageSource
setGregorianChange()	GregorianCalendar
setGroupingSeparator()	DecimalFormatSymbols
setGroupingSize()	DecimalFormat
setGroupingUsed()	NumberFormat
setGuiAvailable()	Beans
setHelpMenu()	MenuBar
setHgap()	BorderLayout, CardLayout, FlowLayout, GridLayout
setHidden()	FeatureDescriptor
setHints()	AreaAveragingScaleFilter, ImageConsumer, ImageFilter, PixelGrabber
setHours()	Date
setHumanPresentableName()	DataFlavor
setID()	TimeZone
setIconImage()	Frame, FramePeer
setIfModifiedSince()	URLConnection
setIn()	System
setInDefaultEventSet()	EventSetDescriptor
setIndex()	CharacterIterator, ParsePosition, StringCharacterIterator
setInfinity()	DecimalFormatSymbols
setInfo()	Identity
setInput()	Deflater, Inflater
setInt()	Array, Field, PreparedStatement

continued

Method Name	Class or Interface Name
setInterface()	MulticastSocket
setKeyChar()	KeyEvent
setKeyCode()	KeyEvent
setKeyPair()	Signer
setLabel()	Button, ButtonPeer, Checkbox, CheckboxPeer, MenuItem, MenuItemPeer
setLayout()	Container, ScrollPane
setLength()	DatagramPacket, StringBuffer
setLenient()	Calendar, DateFormat
setLevel()	Deflater, ZipOutputStream
setLineIncrement()	Scrollbar, ScrollbarPeer
setLineNumber()	LineNumberInputStream, LineNumberReader
setLocalPatternChars()	DateFormatSymbols
setLocale()	Component, MessageFormat
setLocation()	Component, Point, Rectangle
setLog()	RemoteServer
setLogStream()	DriverManager
setLoginTimeout()	DriverManager
setLong()	Array, Field, PreparedStatement
setMaxFieldSize()	Statement
setMaxPriority()	ThreadGroup
setMaxRows()	Statement
setMaximum()	Adjustable, Scrollbar
setMaximumFractionDigits()	NumberFormat
setMaximumIntegerDigits()	NumberFormat
setMenuBar()	Frame, FramePeer
setMessageDigest()	DigestInputStream, DigestOutputStream
setMethod()	ZipEntry, ZipOutputStream
setMinimalDaysInFirstWeek()	Calendar
setMinimum()	Adjustable, Scrollbar
setMinimumFractionDigits()	NumberFormat
setMinimumIntegerDigits()	NumberFormat
setMinusSign()	DecimalFormatSymbols
setMinutes()	Date
setModal()	Dialog
setMode()	FileDialog
setModifiers()	KeyEvent
setMonth()	Date, Time
setMonths()	DateFormatSymbols
setMultipleMode()	List, ListPeer

Method Name	Class or Interface Name
setMultipleSelections()	List, ListPeer
setMultiplier()	DecimalFormat
setNaN()	DecimalFormatSymbols
setName()	Acl, Component, FeatureDescriptor, MenuComponent, Thread
setNanos()	Timestamp
setNegativePermissions()	AclEntry
setNegativePrefix()	DecimalFormat
setNegativeSuffix()	DecimalFormat
setNextException()	SQLException
setNextWarning()	SQLWarning
setNull()	PreparedStatement
setNumberFormat()	DateFormat
setObject()	Customizer, PreparedStatement
setOrientation()	Scrollbar
setOut()	System
setOutputStream()	LogStream
setPageIncrement()	Scrollbar, ScrollbarPeer
setPaintMode()	Graphics
setParameter()	Signature
setParent()	ResourceBundle
setParseIntegerOnly()	NumberFormat
setPatternSeparator()	DecimalFormatSymbols
setPerMill()	DecimalFormatSymbols
setPercent()	DecimalFormatSymbols
setPixels()	AreaAveragingScaleFilter, CropImageFilter, ImageConsumer, ImageFilter, PixelGrabber, RGBImageFilter, ReplicateScaleFilter
setPort()	DatagramPacket
setPositivePrefix()	DecimalFormat
setPositiveSuffix()	DecimalFormat
setPrincipal()	AclEntry
setPriority()	Thread
setPropagationId()	PropertyChangeEvent
setProperties()	CropImageFilter, ImageConsumer, ImageFilter, PixelGrabber, ReplicateScaleFilter, System
setProperty()	Security
setPropertyEditorClass()	PropertyDescriptor
setPublicKey()	Identity
setQueryTimeout()	Statement
setRawOffset()	SimpleTimeZone, TimeZone

continued

Method Name	Class or Interface Name
setReadOnly()	Connection
setRef()	RemoteStub
setRequestMethod()	HttpURLConnection
setRequestProperty()	URLConnection
setResizable()	Dialog, DialogPeer, Frame, FramePeer
setRows()	GridLayout, TextArea
setScale()	BigDecimal
setScrollPosition()	ScrollPane, ScrollPanePeer
setSeconds()	Date
setSecurityManager()	System
setSeed()	Random, SecureRandom
setSelectedCheckbox()	CheckboxGroup
setSelectionEnd()	TextComponent
setSelectionStart()	TextComponent
setShort()	Array, Field, PreparedStatement
setShortDescription()	FeatureDescriptor
setShortMonths()	DateFormatSymbols
setShortWeekdays()	DateFormatSymbols
setShortcut()	MenuItem
setSigners()	ClassLoader
setSize()	Component, Dimension, Rectangle, Vector, ZipEntry
setSoLinger()	Socket
setSoTimeout()	DatagramSocket, ServerSocket, Socket
setSocketFactory()	RMISocketFactory, ServerSocket
setSocketImplFactory()	Socket
setStartRule()	SimpleTimeZone
setStartYear()	SimpleTimeZone
setState()	Checkbox, CheckboxMenuItem, CheckboxMenuItemPeer, CheckboxPeer
setStrategy()	Deflater
setStrength()	Collator
setString()	PreparedStatement
setStub()	Applet
setSystemScope()	IdentityScope
setTTL()	DatagramSocketImpl, MulticastSocket
setTcpNoDelay()	Socket
setText()	BreakIterator, Label, LabelPeer, TextComponent, TextComponentPeer
setTime()	Calendar, Date, PreparedStatement, Time, ZipEntry
setTimeInMillis()	Calendar
setTimeZone()	Calendar, DateFormat
setTimestamp()	PreparedStatement

Method Name	Class or Interface Name
setTitle()	Dialog, DialogPeer, Frame, FramePeer
setTransactionIsolation()	Connection
setURL()	URLStreamHandler
setURLStreamHandlerFactory()	URL
setUnicast()	EventSetDescriptor
setUnicodeStream()	PreparedStatement
setUnitIncrement()	Adjustable, ScrollPanePeer, Scrollbar
setUpdateRect()	PaintEvent
setUseCaches()	URLConnection
setValue()	Adjustable, FeatureDescriptor, PropertyEditor, PropertyEditorSupport, ScrollPanePeer, Scrollbar
setValues()	Scrollbar, ScrollbarPeer
setVgap()	BorderLayout, CardLayout, FlowLayout, GridLayout
setVisible()	Component, ComponentPeer
setVisibleAmount()	Adjustable, Scrollbar
setWeekdays()	DateFormatSymbols
setXORMode()	Graphics
setYear()	Date, Time
setZeroDigit()	DecimalFormatSymbols
setZoneStrings()	DateFormatSymbols
shiftDown()	Event
shiftLeft()	BigInteger
shiftRight()	BigInteger
shortValue()	Byte, Double, Float, Integer, Long, Number, Short
shortcuts()	MenuBar
show()	CardLayout, Component, ComponentPeer, Dialog, PopupMenu, PopupMenuPeer, Window
showDocument()	AppletContext
showStatus()	Applet, AppletContext
sign()	Signature
signum()	BigDecimal, BigInteger
sin()	Math
size()	BitSet, ByteArrayOutputStream, CharArrayWriter, Component, DataOutputStream, Dictionary, Hashtable, IdentityScope, Vector
skip()	BufferedInputStream, BufferedReader, ByteArrayInputStream, CharArrayReader, CheckedInputStream, FileInputStream, FilterInputStream, FilterReader, InflaterInputStream, InputStream, LineNumberInputStream, LineNumberReader, ObjectInput, Reader, StringBufferInputStream, StringReader, ZipInputStream
skipBytes()	DataInput, DataInputStream, ObjectInputStream, RandomAccessFile

continued

Method Name	Class or Interface Name
slashSlashComments()	StreamTokenizer
slashStarComments()	StreamTokenizer
sleep()	Thread
sqrt()	Math
start()	Applet, Thread
startGrabbing()	PixelGrabber
startProduction()	FilteredImageSource, ImageProducer, MemoryImageSource
startsWith()	String
status()	PixelGrabber
statusAll()	MediaTracker
statusID()	MediaTracker
stop()	Applet, AudioClip, Thread, ThreadGroup
storesLowerCaseIdentifiers()	DatabaseMetaData
storesLowerCaseQuotedIdentifiers()	DatabaseMetaData
storesMixedCaseIdentifiers()	DatabaseMetaData
storesMixedCaseQuotedIdentifiers()	DatabaseMetaData
storesUpperCaseIdentifiers()	DatabaseMetaData
storesUpperCaseQuotedIdentifiers()	DatabaseMetaData
stringWidth()	FontMetrics
substituteColorModel()	RGBImageFilter
substring()	String
subtract()	BigDecimal, BigInteger
supportsANSI92EntryLevelSQL()	DatabaseMetaData
supportsANSI92FullSQL()	DatabaseMetaData
supportsANSI92IntermediateSQL()	DatabaseMetaData
supportsAlterTableWithAddColumn()	DatabaseMetaData
supportsAlterTableWithDropColumn()	DatabaseMetaData
supportsCatalogsInDataManipulation()	DatabaseMetaData
supportsCatalogsInIndexDefinitions()	DatabaseMetaData
supportsCatalogsInPrivilegeDefinitions()	DatabaseMetaData
supportsCatalogsInProcedureCalls()	DatabaseMetaData
supportsCatalogsInTableDefinitions()	DatabaseMetaData
supportsColumnAliasing()	DatabaseMetaData
supportsConvert()	DatabaseMetaData
supportsCoreSQLGrammar()	DatabaseMetaData
supportsCorrelatedSubqueries()	DatabaseMetaData
supportsCustomEditor()	PropertyEditor, PropertyEditorSupport
supportsDataDefinitionAndDataManipulationTransactions()	DatabaseMetaData

Method Name	Class or Interface Name
supportsDataManipulationTransactionsOnly()	DatabaseMetaData
supportsDifferentTableCorrelationNames()	DatabaseMetaData
supportsExpressionsInOrderBy()	DatabaseMetaData
supportsExtendedSQLGrammar()	DatabaseMetaData
supportsFullOuterJoins()	DatabaseMetaData
supportsGroupBy()	DatabaseMetaData
supportsGroupByBeyondSelect()	DatabaseMetaData
supportsGroupByUnrelated()	DatabaseMetaData
supportsIntegrityEnhancementFacility()	DatabaseMetaData
supportsLikeEscapeClause()	DatabaseMetaData
supportsLimitedOuterJoins()	DatabaseMetaData
supportsMinimumSQLGrammar()	DatabaseMetaData
supportsMixedCaseIdentifiers()	DatabaseMetaData
supportsMixedCaseQuotedIdentifiers()	DatabaseMetaData
supportsMultipleResultSets()	DatabaseMetaData
supportsMultipleTransactions()	DatabaseMetaData
supportsNonNullableColumns()	DatabaseMetaData
supportsOpenCursorsAcrossCommit()	DatabaseMetaData
supportsOpenCursorsAcrossRollback()	DatabaseMetaData
supportsOpenStatementsAcrossCommit()	DatabaseMetaData
supportsOpenStatementsAcrossRollback()	DatabaseMetaData
supportsOrderByUnrelated()	DatabaseMetaData
supportsOuterJoins()	DatabaseMetaData
supportsPositionedDelete()	DatabaseMetaData
supportsPositionedUpdate()	DatabaseMetaData
supportsSchemasInDataManipulation()	DatabaseMetaData
supportsSchemasInIndexDefinitions()	DatabaseMetaData
supportsSchemasInPrivilegeDefinitions()	DatabaseMetaData
supportsSchemasInProcedureCalls()	DatabaseMetaData
supportsSchemasInTableDefinitions()	DatabaseMetaData
supportsSelectForUpdate()	DatabaseMetaData
supportsStoredProcedures()	DatabaseMetaData
supportsSubqueriesInComparisons()	DatabaseMetaData
supportsSubqueriesInExists()	DatabaseMetaData
supportsSubqueriesInIns()	DatabaseMetaData
supportsSubqueriesInQuantifieds()	DatabaseMetaData
supportsTableCorrelationNames()	DatabaseMetaData
supportsTransactionIsolationLevel()	DatabaseMetaData
supportsTransactions()	DatabaseMetaData

continued

Method Name	Class or Interface Name
supportsUnion()	DatabaseMetaData
supportsUnionAll()	DatabaseMetaData
suspend()	Thread, ThreadGroup
sync()	FileDescriptor, Toolkit
tan()	Math
tertiaryOrder()	CollationElementIterator
testBit()	BigInteger
textValueChanged()	AWTEventMulticaster, TextListener
toBack()	Window, WindowPeer
toBigInteger()	BigDecimal
toBinaryString()	Integer, Long
toByteArray()	BigInteger, ByteArrayOutputStream, CollationKey
toCharArray()	CharArrayWriter, String
toExternalForm()	URL, URLStreamHandler
toFront()	Window, WindowPeer
toGMTString()	Date
toHexString()	Integer, Long
toLocaleString()	Date
toLocalizedPattern()	DecimalFormat, SimpleDateFormat
toLowerCase()	Character, String
toOctalString()	Integer, Long
toPattern()	ChoiceFormat, DecimalFormat, MessageFormat, SimpleDateFormat
toString()	AWTEvent, Acl, AclEntry, BigDecimal, BigInteger, BitSet, Boolean, BorderLayout, Byte, ByteArrayOutputStream, CardLayout, Certificate, CharArrayWriter, Character, CheckboxGroup, Class, Color, Component, Constructor, Date, DigestInputStream, DigestOutputStream, Dimension, Double, Event, EventObject, Field, File, Float, FlowLayout, Font, FontMetrics, Graphics, GridBagLayout, GridLayout, Hashtable, Identity, IdentityScope, InetAddress, Insets, Integer, Locale, LogStream, Long, MenuComponent, MenuShortcut, MessageDigest, Method, Modifier, ObjID, Object, ObjectStreamClass, Operation, Permission, Point, Principal, Provider, Rectangle, RemoteObject, ServerSocket, Short, Signature, Signer, Socket, SocketImpl, StreamTokenizer, String, StringBuffer, StringWriter, SystemColor, Thread, ThreadGroup, Throwable, Time, Timestamp, UID, URL, URLConnection, VMID, Vector, ZipEntry
toTitleCase()	Character
toUpperCase()	Character, String
totalMemory()	Runtime
traceInstructions()	Runtime
traceMethodCalls()	Runtime
transferFocus()	Component
translate()	Event, Graphics, Point, Polygon, Rectangle
translatePoint()	MouseEvent

Method Name	Class or Interface Name
trim()	String
trimToSize()	Vector
unbind()	Naming, Registry
uncaughtException()	ThreadGroup
union()	Rectangle
unread()	PushbackInputStream, PushbackReader
unreferenced()	Unreferenced
update()	Adler32, CRC32, Checksum, Component, MessageDigest, Observer, Signature
useDaylightTime()	SimpleTimeZone, TimeZone
usesLocalFilePerTable()	DatabaseMetaData
usesLocalFiles()	DatabaseMetaData
usesShiftModifier()	MenuShortcut
usingProxy()	HttpURLConnection
UTC()	Date
valid()	FileDescriptor
validate()	Component, Container
validateObject()	ObjectInputValidation
validateTree()	Container
valueOf()	BigDecimal, BigInteger, Boolean, Byte, Date, Double, Float, Integer, Long, Short, String, Time, Timestamp
verify()	Signature
vetoableChange()	VetoableChangeListener
wait()	Object
waitFor()	Process
waitForAll()	MediaTracker
waitForID()	MediaTracker
wasNull()	CallableStatement, ResultSet
whitespaceChars()	StreamTokenizer
windowActivated()	AWTEventMulticaster, WindowAdapter, WindowListener
windowClosed()	AWTEventMulticaster, WindowAdapter, WindowListener
windowClosing()	AWTEventMulticaster, WindowAdapter, WindowListener
windowDeactivated()	AWTEventMulticaster, WindowAdapter, WindowListener
windowDeiconified()	AWTEventMulticaster, WindowAdapter, WindowListener
windowIconified()	AWTEventMulticaster, WindowAdapter, WindowListener
windowOpened()	AWTEventMulticaster, WindowAdapter, WindowListener
wordChars()	StreamTokenizer

continued

Method Name	Class or Interface Name
write()	BufferedOutputStream, BufferedWriter, ByteArrayOutputStream, CharArrayWriter, CheckedOutputStream, DataOutput, DataOutputStream, DeflaterOutputStream, DigestOutputStream, FileOutputStream, FilterOutputStream, FilterWriter, GZIPOutputStream, LogStream, ObjID, ObjectOutput, ObjectOutputStream, OutputStream, OutputStreamWriter, PipedOutputStream, PipedWriter, PrintStream, PrintWriter, RandomAccessFile, StringWriter, UID, Writer, ZipOutputStream
writeBoolean()	DataOutput, DataOutputStream, ObjectOutputStream, RandomAccessFile
writeByte()	DataOutput, DataOutputStream, ObjectOutputStream, RandomAccessFile
writeBytes()	DataOutput, DataOutputStream, ObjectOutputStream, RandomAccessFile
writeChar()	DataOutput, DataOutputStream, ObjectOutputStream, RandomAccessFile
writeChars()	DataOutput, DataOutputStream, ObjectOutputStream, RandomAccessFile
writeDouble()	DataOutput, DataOutputStream, ObjectOutputStream, RandomAccessFile
writeExternal()	Externalizable
writeFloat()	DataOutput, DataOutputStream, ObjectOutputStream, RandomAccessFile
writeInt()	DataOutput, DataOutputStream, ObjectOutputStream, RandomAccessFile
writeLong()	DataOutput, DataOutputStream, ObjectOutputStream, RandomAccessFile
writeObject()	ObjectOutput, ObjectOutputStream
writeShort()	DataOutput, DataOutputStream, ObjectOutputStream, RandomAccessFile
writeStreamHeader()	ObjectOutputStream
writeTo()	ByteArrayOutputStream, CharArrayWriter
writeUTF()	DataOutput, DataOutputStream, ObjectOutputStream, RandomAccessFile
xor()	BigInteger, BitSet
yield()	Thread

appendix

b

What's on the CD-ROM?

The CD-ROM contains every example used in the book. It also contains the Sun Java Development Kit for versions 1.0.2 and 1.1.4. To access all the documentation and links, load the file index.html from the root directory of the CD-ROM.

Using the Examples from the Book

The book is arranged alphabetically, and so is the sample code on the CD-ROM. Inside the Examples directory is the code for each letter. That is, any code listed under the letter *A* in the book will be in the A directory, the examples for *B* are in the B directory, and so on.

Every example is a complete standalone program, which means every sample source file contains a public class. The name of each example is the same as its name in the book. Its filename on disk is always the same as the name of the public class defined in the example.

For example, under the letter *C* there is a listing for CardLayout, which is a description of java.awt.CardLayout. There is a Java application program that is named CardCanvases that is an example of using CardLayout. On the CD-ROM, this program can be found inside the C directory, and the name of the file is CardCanvases.java. It has a class file named CardCanvases.class that can be executed by a Virtual Machine — the one supplied with the JDK is named java — so it can be executed using this command:

```
java CardCanvases
```

If an example is in the form of an applet, you will find both a class file and an HTML file that can be used by the applet viewer to run it. The HTML file always has the same name as the applet. For example, under *B* in the book there is an entry for Button (a description of java.awt.Button) that has a sample applet named SimpleButton. The source for the applet is in the B directory and is named SimpleButton.java. It has been compiled into SimpleButton.class, and, because an applet can only be run as part of a Web

1587

page, there is a small HTML file for it named `SimpleButton.html`. It can be executed by using `appletviewer` — a simple Web browser that only displays applets — with this command:

```
appletviewer SimpleButton.html
```

Some examples require data. If there is an input file required, it is on the CD-ROM in the same directory as the sample code. If output is required, it will be necessary for you to execute the program from some place other than the CD-ROM so that you will have write capabilities. Normally, there is no need to be able to write to a disk — this is mostly reserved for examples demonstrating how Java writes to files.

Installing the Sun Java Development Kit

Included on the CD-ROM are the Sun JDK versions 1.0.2 and 1.1.4 for Windows and Solaris. (For the Macintosh, only the JDK 1.0.2 is available.) This includes the compiled API classes in the form of the `classes.zip` file, the complete set of utility programs, and the HTML documentation that was automatically generated from the source code of the API. For more information on these utilities and how to use them, see the Java Development Kit.

Also included on disc is the Java Runtime Environment (also known as the "Java Runtime" or "JRE"), which consists of the Java Virtual Machine, the Java Core Classes, and supporting files. It is the runtime part of the JDK — no compiler, no debugger, and no tools. The JRE is the smallest set of executables and files that constitute the standard Java platform.

Table B-1 lists the Windows and Solaris contents of the Sun JDK filenames on the CD-ROM. Because many browsers have not implemented JDK 1.1 as yet, you may wish to create applets using JDK 1.0. Be aware that some new capabilities have been added to version 1.1 that are incompatible with a version 1.0-based browser.

Table B-1   Contents of Windows and Solaris JDK Files on the CD-ROM

File	Contains
`JDK-1_0_2-solaris2-sparc.tar`	JDK 1.0.2 for Solaris SPARC
`JDK-1_0_2-solaris2-x86.tar`	JDK 1.0.2 for Solaris x86
`JDK-1_0_2-win32-x86.exe`	JDK 1.0.2 for Windows NT/95
`JDK_1_0_2_apidocs.zip`	JDK 1.0.2 Documentation in HTML format
`jdk1.1.4-solaris2-sparc.bin`	JDK 1.1.4 for Solaris SPARC
`jdk114.exe`	JDK 1.1.4 for Windows NT/95

File	Contains
`jdk114doc.zip`	JDK 1.1.4 Documentation in HTML format
`jdk114doc.tar`	JDK 1.1.4 Documentation in HTML format
`jdk1.1.4-beta-solaris2-x86.bin`	JDK 1.1.4 for Solaris *x*86
`jre114.exe`	JRE 1.1.4 for Windows NT/95
`jre114i.exe`	JRE 1.1.4 international for Windows NT/95
`jre1_1_4-beta-solaris2-x86.bin`	JRE 1.1.4 beta for Solaris x86
`jre1_1_4-solaris2-sparc.bin`	JRE 1.1.4 for Solaris SPARC

There is complete installation documentation for each JDK — and for the documentation — included on the CD-ROM. Load `index.html` from the CD-ROM and select the version you wish to install on your system.

Java API Hierarchy Map

The API of Java consists of a collection of class and interface definitions. Every class is derived, at its root, from `java.lang.Object`. This appendix contains a diagram of the complete API, showing the relative position of every class. The diagram contains every class, along with the interfaces implemented by each. Here's how you should interpret the entries:

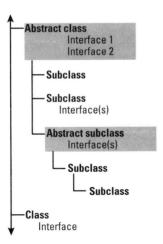

The diagram can be used to trace every class back to its root (through its superclasses) as well as to find all the classes derived from it (its subclasses). Because the diagram also lists the interfaces implemented by each class, you can determine from the hierarchy which interfaces, if any, a class inherits from its superclasses.

java.lang.Object

java.awt.AWTEvent

—**java.awt.event.ActionEvent**

—**java.awt.event.AdjustmentEvent**

—**java.awt.event.ComponentEvent**

—**java.awt.event.ContainerEvent**

—**java.awt.event.FocusEvent**

java.awt.event.InputEvent

—**java.awt.event.KeyEvent**

—**java.awt.event.MouseEvent**

—**java.awt.event.PaintEvent**

—**java.awt.event.WindowEvent**

—**java.awt.event.ItemEvent**

—**java.awt.event.TextEvent**

—**java.awt.AWTEventMulticaster**
java.awt.event.ComponentListener
java.awt.event.ContainerListener
java.awt.event.FocusListener
java.awt.event.KeyListener
java.awt.event.MouseListener
java.awt.event.MouseMotionListener
java.awt.event.WindowListener
java.awt.event.ActionListener
java.awt.event.ItemListener
java.awt.event.AdjustmentListener
java.awt.event.TextListener

—**java.awt.BorderLayout**
java.awt.LayoutManager2
java.io.Serializable

—**java.awt.CardLayout**
java.awt.LayoutManager2
java.io.Serializable

—**java.awt.CheckboxGroup**
java.io.Serializable

—**java.awt.Color**
java.io.Serializable

—**java.awt.SystemColor**
java.io.Serializable

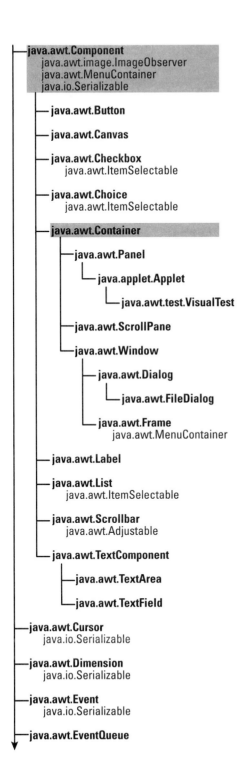

java.awt.Component
java.awt.image.ImageObserver
java.awt.MenuContainer
java.io.Serializable

— **java.awt.Button**

— **java.awt.Canvas**

— **java.awt.Checkbox**
java.awt.ItemSelectable

— **java.awt.Choice**
java.awt.ItemSelectable

— **java.awt.Container**

 — **java.awt.Panel**

  └ **java.applet.Applet**

   └ **java.awt.test.VisualTest**

 — **java.awt.ScrollPane**

 └ **java.awt.Window**

  — **java.awt.Dialog**

   └ **java.awt.FileDialog**

  └ **java.awt.Frame**
   java.awt.MenuContainer

— **java.awt.Label**

— **java.awt.List**
java.awt.ItemSelectable

— **java.awt.Scrollbar**
java.awt.Adjustable

└ **java.awt.TextComponent**

 — **java.awt.TextArea**

 └ **java.awt.TextField**

— **java.awt.Cursor**
java.io.Serializable

— **java.awt.Dimension**
java.io.Serializable

— **java.awt.Event**
java.io.Serializable

— **java.awt.EventQueue**

—**java.awt.FlowLayout**
    java.awt.LayoutManager
    java.io.Serializable

—**java.awt.Font**
    java.io.Serializable

—**java.awt.FontMetrics**
    java.io.Serializable

—**java.awt.Graphics**

—**java.awt.GridBagConstraints**
    java.lang.Cloneable
    java.io.Serializable

—**java.awt.GridBagLayout**
    java.awt.LayoutManager2
    java.io.Serializable

—**java.awt.GridLayout**
    java.awt.LayoutManager
    java.io.Serializable

—**java.awt.Image**

—**java.awt.Insets**
    java.lang.Cloneable
    java.io.Serializable

—**java.awt.MediaTracker**
    java.io.Serializable

—**java.awt.MenuComponent**
    java.io.Serializable

    — **java.awt.MenuBar**
        java.awt.MenuContainer

    └ **java.awt.MenuItem**

        — **java.awt.CheckboxMenuItem**
            java.awt.ItemSelectable

        └ **java.awt.Menu**
            java.awt.MenuContainer

           └**java.awt.PopupMenu**

—**java.awt.MenuShortcut**
    java.io.Serializable

—**java.awt.Point**
    java.io.Serializable

—**java.awt.Polygon**
    java.awt.Shape
    java.io.Serializable

—java.awt.**PrintJob**

—java.awt.**Rectangle**
    java.awt.Shape
    java.io.Serializable

—java.awt.**Toolkit**

—java.awt.datatransfer.**Clipboard**

—java.awt.datatransfer.**DataFlavor**

—java.awt.datatransfer.**StringSelection**
    java.awt.datatransfer.Transferable
    java.awt.datatransfer.ClipboardOwner

—java.awt.event.**ComponentAdapter**
    java.awt.event.ComponentListener

—java.awt.event.**ContainerAdapter**
    java.awt.event.ContainerListener

—java.awt.event.**FocusAdapter**
    java.awt.event.FocusListener

—java.awt.event.**KeyAdapter**
    java.awt.event.KeyListener

—java.awt.event.**MouseAdapter**
    java.awt.event.MouseListener

—java.awt.event.**MouseMotionAdapter**
    java.awt.event.MouseMotionListener

—java.awt.event.**WindowAdapter**
    java.awt.event.WindowListener

—java.awt.image.**ColorModel**

    — java.awt.image.**DirectColorModel**

    └— java.awt.image.**IndexColorModel**

—java.awt.image.**FilteredImageSource**
    java.awt.image.ImageProducer

—java.awt.image.**ImageFilter**
    java.awt.image.ImageConsumer
    java.lang.Cloneable

    — java.awt.image.**CropImageFilter**

    — java.awt.image.**RGBImageFilter**

    └— java.awt.image.**ReplicateScaleFilter**

        └—java.awt.image.**AreaAveragingScaleFilter**

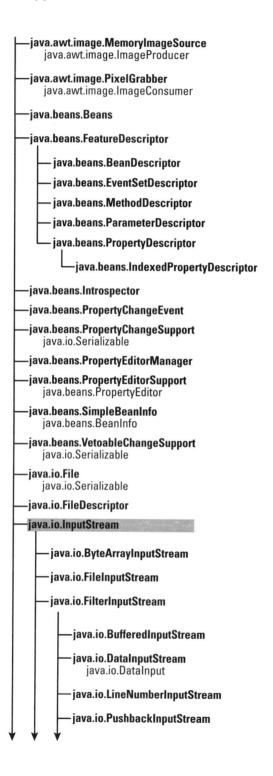

—**java.awt.image.MemoryImageSource**
 java.awt.image.ImageProducer

—**java.awt.image.PixelGrabber**
 java.awt.image.ImageConsumer

—**java.beans.Beans**

—**java.beans.FeatureDescriptor**

— **java.beans.BeanDescriptor**

— **java.beans.EventSetDescriptor**

— **java.beans.MethodDescriptor**

— **java.beans.ParameterDescriptor**

— **java.beans.PropertyDescriptor**

—**java.beans.IndexedPropertyDescriptor**

—**java.beans.Introspector**

—**java.beans.PropertyChangeEvent**

—**java.beans.PropertyChangeSupport**
 java.io.Serializable

—**java.beans.PropertyEditorManager**

—**java.beans.PropertyEditorSupport**
 java.beans.PropertyEditor

—**java.beans.SimpleBeanInfo**
 java.beans.BeanInfo

—**java.beans.VetoableChangeSupport**
 java.io.Serializable

—**java.io.File**
 java.io.Serializable

—**java.io.FileDescriptor**

—**java.io.InputStream**

— **java.io.ByteArrayInputStream**

— **java.io.FileInputStream**

— **java.io.FilterInputStream**

— **java.io.BufferedInputStream**

— **java.io.DataInputStream**
 java.io.DataInput

— **java.io.LineNumberInputStream**

— **java.io.PushbackInputStream**

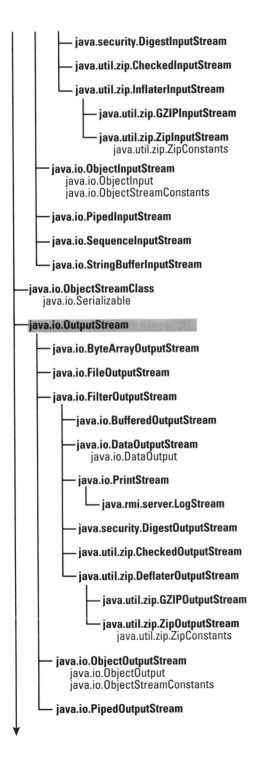

java.security.**DigestInputStream**

java.util.zip.**CheckedInputStream**

java.util.zip.**InflaterInputStream**

java.util.zip.**GZIPInputStream**

java.util.zip.**ZipInputStream**
java.util.zip.ZipConstants

java.io.**ObjectInputStream**
java.io.ObjectInput
java.io.ObjectStreamConstants

java.io.**PipedInputStream**

java.io.**SequenceInputStream**

java.io.**StringBufferInputStream**

java.io.**ObjectStreamClass**
java.io.Serializable

java.io.**OutputStream**

java.io.**ByteArrayOutputStream**

java.io.**FileOutputStream**

java.io.**FilterOutputStream**

java.io.**BufferedOutputStream**

java.io.**DataOutputStream**
java.io.DataOutput

java.io.**PrintStream**

java.rmi.server.**LogStream**

java.security.**DigestOutputStream**

java.util.zip.**CheckedOutputStream**

java.util.zip.**DeflaterOutputStream**

java.util.zip.**GZIPOutputStream**

java.util.zip.**ZipOutputStream**
java.util.zip.ZipConstants

java.io.**ObjectOutputStream**
java.io.ObjectOutput
java.io.ObjectStreamConstants

java.io.**PipedOutputStream**

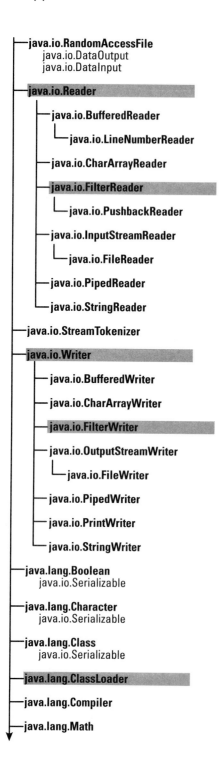

—**java.io.RandomAccessFile**
    java.io.DataOutput
    java.io.DataInput

—**java.io.Reader**

    —**java.io.BufferedReader**

        └—**java.io.LineNumberReader**

    —**java.io.CharArrayReader**

    —**java.io.FilterReader**

        └—**java.io.PushbackReader**

    —**java.io.InputStreamReader**

        └—**java.io.FileReader**

    —**java.io.PipedReader**

    └—**java.io.StringReader**

—**java.io.StreamTokenizer**

—**java.io.Writer**

    —**java.io.BufferedWriter**

    —**java.io.CharArrayWriter**

    —**java.io.FilterWriter**

    —**java.io.OutputStreamWriter**

        └—**java.io.FileWriter**

    —**java.io.PipedWriter**

    —**java.io.PrintWriter**

    └—**java.io.StringWriter**

—**java.lang.Boolean**
    java.io.Serializable

—**java.lang.Character**
    java.io.Serializable

—**java.lang.Class**
    java.io.Serializable

—**java.lang.ClassLoader**

—**java.lang.Compiler**

—**java.lang.Math**

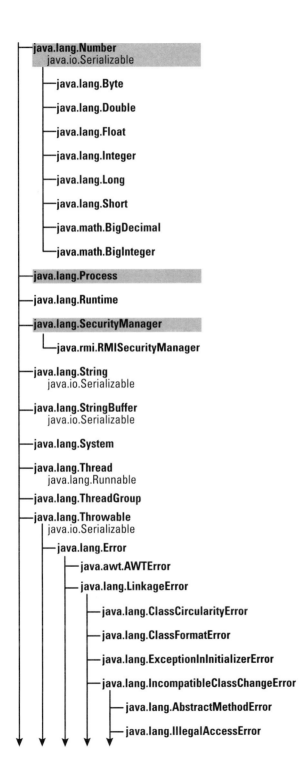

java.lang.**Number**
java.io.Serializable

—java.lang.**Byte**

—java.lang.**Double**

—java.lang.**Float**

—java.lang.**Integer**

—java.lang.**Long**

—java.lang.**Short**

—java.math.**BigDecimal**

—java.math.**BigInteger**

—java.lang.**Process**

—java.lang.**Runtime**

—java.lang.**SecurityManager**

——java.rmi.**RMISecurityManager**

—java.lang.**String**
java.io.Serializable

—java.lang.**StringBuffer**
java.io.Serializable

—java.lang.**System**

—java.lang.**Thread**
java.lang.Runnable

—java.lang.**ThreadGroup**

—java.lang.**Throwable**
java.io.Serializable

—java.lang.**Error**

——java.awt.**AWTError**

——java.lang.**LinkageError**

———java.lang.**ClassCircularityError**

———java.lang.**ClassFormatError**

———java.lang.**ExceptionInInitializerError**

———java.lang.**IncompatibleClassChangeError**

————java.lang.**AbstractMethodError**

————java.lang.**IllegalAccessError**

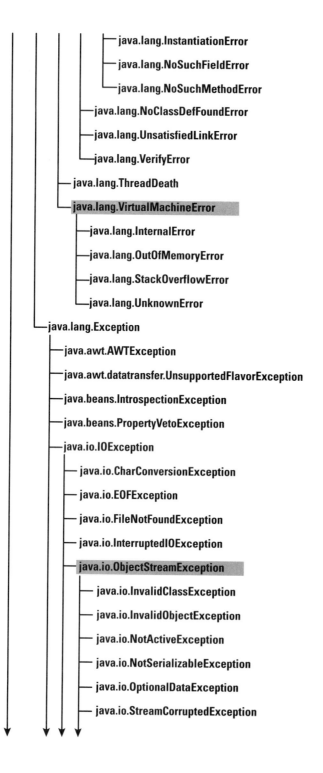

- java.lang.InstantiationError
- java.lang.NoSuchFieldError
- java.lang.NoSuchMethodError
- java.lang.NoClassDefFoundError
- java.lang.UnsatisfiedLinkError
- java.lang.VerifyError
- java.lang.ThreadDeath
- java.lang.VirtualMachineError
  - java.lang.InternalError
  - java.lang.OutOfMemoryError
  - java.lang.StackOverflowError
  - java.lang.UnknownError
- java.lang.Exception
  - java.awt.AWTException
  - java.awt.datatransfer.UnsupportedFlavorException
  - java.beans.IntrospectionException
  - java.beans.PropertyVetoException
  - java.io.IOException
    - java.io.CharConversionException
    - java.io.EOFException
    - java.io.FileNotFoundException
    - java.io.InterruptedIOException
    - java.io.ObjectStreamException
      - java.io.InvalidClassException
      - java.io.InvalidObjectException
      - java.io.NotActiveException
      - java.io.NotSerializableException
      - java.io.OptionalDataException
      - java.io.StreamCorruptedException

```
          └──java.io.WriteAbortedException
    ─── java.io.SyncFailedException
    ─── java.io.UTFDataFormatException
    ─── java.io.UnsupportedEncodingException
    ─── java.net.MalformedURLException
    ─── java.net.ProtocolException
    ─── java.net.SocketException
        ┌── java.net.BindException
        ├── java.net.ConnectException
        └──java.net.NoRouteToHostException
    ─── java.net.UnknownHostException
    ─── java.net.UnknownServiceException
    ─── java.rmi.RemoteException
        ┌── java.rmi.AccessException
        ├── java.rmi.ConnectException
        ├── java.rmi.ConnectIOException
        ├── java.rmi.MarshalException
        ├── java.rmi.NoSuchObjectException
        ├── java.rmi.ServerError
        ├── java.rmi.ServerException
        ├── java.rmi.ServerRuntimeException
        ├── java.rmi.StubNotFoundException
        ├── java.rmi.UnexpectedException
        ├── java.rmi.UnknownHostException
        ├── java.rmi.UnmarshalException
        ├── java.rmi.server.ExportException
        │   └──java.rmi.server.SocketSecurityException
        ├── java.rmi.server.SkeletonMismatchException
        └──java.rmi.server.SkeletonNotFoundException
```

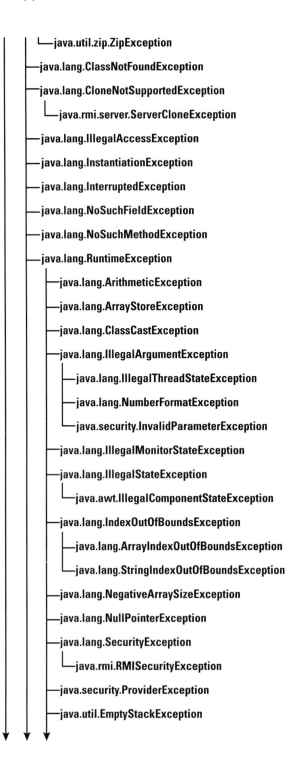

└─ java.util.zip.ZipException

├─ java.lang.ClassNotFoundException

├─ java.lang.CloneNotSupportedException

    └─ java.rmi.server.ServerCloneException

├─ java.lang.IllegalAccessException

├─ java.lang.InstantiationException

├─ java.lang.InterruptedException

├─ java.lang.NoSuchFieldException

├─ java.lang.NoSuchMethodException

├─ java.lang.RuntimeException

   ├─ java.lang.ArithmeticException

   ├─ java.lang.ArrayStoreException

   ├─ java.lang.ClassCastException

   ├─ java.lang.IllegalArgumentException

      ├─ java.lang.IllegalThreadStateException

      ├─ java.lang.NumberFormatException

      └─ java.security.InvalidParameterException

   ├─ java.lang.IllegalMonitorStateException

   ├─ java.lang.IllegalStateException

      └─ java.awt.IllegalComponentStateException

   ├─ java.lang.IndexOutOfBoundsException

      ├─ java.lang.ArrayIndexOutOfBoundsException

      └─ java.lang.StringIndexOutOfBoundsException

   ├─ java.lang.NegativeArraySizeException

   ├─ java.lang.NullPointerException

   ├─ java.lang.SecurityException

      └─ java.rmi.RMISecurityException

   ├─ java.security.ProviderException

   ├─ java.util.EmptyStackException

— java.util.**MissingResourceException**

— java.util.**NoSuchElementException**

— java.lang.reflect.**InvocationTargetException**

— java.rmi.**AlreadyBoundException**

— java.rmi.**NotBoundException**

— java.rmi.server.**ServerNotActiveException**

— java.security.**DigestException**

— java.security.**KeyException**

  — java.security.**InvalidKeyException**

  — java.security.**KeyManagementException**

— java.security.**NoSuchAlgorithmException**

— java.security.**NoSuchProviderException**

— java.security.**SignatureException**

— java.security.acl.**AclNotFoundException**

— java.security.acl.**LastOwnerException**

— java.security.acl.**NotOwnerException**

— java.sql.**SQLException**

  — java.sql.**SQLWarning**

    — java.sql.**DataTruncation**

— java.text.**ParseException**

— java.util.**TooManyListenersException**

— java.util.zip.**DataFormatException**

— java.lang.**Void**

— java.lang.reflect.**Array**

— java.lang.reflect.**Constructor**
  java.lang.reflect.Member

— java.lang.reflect.**Field**
  java.lang.reflect.Member

— java.lang.reflect.**Method**
  java.lang.reflect.Member

— java.lang.reflect.**Modifier**

```
├─java.net.ContentHandler

├─java.net.DatagramPacket

├─java.net.DatagramSocket
│   └─java.net.MulticastSocket

├─java.net.DatagramSocketImpl
│   java.net.SocketOptions

├─java.net.InetAddress
│   java.io.Serializable

├─java.net.ServerSocket

├─java.net.Socket

├─java.net.SocketImpl
│   java.net.SocketOptions

├─java.net.URL
│   java.io.Serializable

├─java.net.URLConnection
│   └─java.net.HttpURLConnection

├─java.net.URLEncoder

├─java.net.URLStreamHandler

├─java.rmi.Naming

├─java.rmi.dgc.Lease
│   java.io.Serializable

├─java.rmi.dgc.VMID
│   java.io.Serializable

├─java.rmi.registry.LocateRegistry

├─java.rmi.server.ObjID
│   java.io.Serializable

├─java.rmi.server.Operation

├─java.rmi.server.RMIClassLoader

├─java.rmi.server.RMISocketFactory

├─java.rmi.server.RemoteObject
│   java.rmi.Remote
│   java.io.Serializable

├─java.rmi.server.RemoteServer
│   └─java.rmi.server.UnicastRemoteObject
```

java.rmi.server.RemoteStub

java.rmi.server.UID
java.io.Serializable

java.security.Identity
java.security.Principal
java.io.Serializable

— **java.security.IdentityScope**

— **java.security.Signer**

java.security.KeyPair

java.security.KeyPairGenerator

java.security.MessageDigest

java.security.Security

java.security.Signature

java.sql.DriverManager

java.sql.DriverPropertyInfo

java.sql.Types

java.text.BreakIterator
java.lang.Cloneable
java.io.Serializable

java.text.CollationElementIterator

java.text.CollationKey

java.text.Collator
java.lang.Cloneable
java.io.Serializable

— **java.text.RuleBasedCollator**

java.text.DateFormatSymbols
java.io.Serializable
java.lang.Cloneable

java.text.DecimalFormatSymbols
java.lang.Cloneable
java.io.Serializable

java.text.FieldPosition

java.text.Format
java.io.Serializable
java.lang.Cloneable

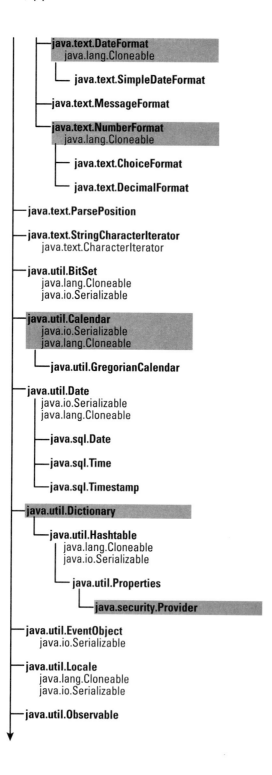

java.text.**DateFormat**
java.lang.Cloneable

└── java.text.**SimpleDateFormat**

java.text.**MessageFormat**

java.text.**NumberFormat**
java.lang.Cloneable

├── java.text.**ChoiceFormat**

└── java.text.**DecimalFormat**

java.text.**ParsePosition**

java.text.**StringCharacterIterator**
java.text.CharacterIterator

java.util.**BitSet**
java.lang.Cloneable
java.io.Serializable

java.util.**Calendar**
java.io.Serializable
java.lang.Cloneable

└── java.util.**GregorianCalendar**

java.util.**Date**
java.io.Serializable
java.lang.Cloneable

├── java.sql.**Date**

├── java.sql.**Time**

└── java.sql.**Timestamp**

java.util.**Dictionary**

└── java.util.**Hashtable**
java.lang.Cloneable
java.io.Serializable

└── java.util.**Properties**

└── java.security.**Provider**

java.util.**EventObject**
java.io.Serializable

java.util.**Locale**
java.lang.Cloneable
java.io.Serializable

java.util.**Observable**

—**java.util.Random**
| java.io.Serializable

   └—**java.security.SecureRandom**

—**java.util.ResourceBundle**

   ├—**java.text.resources.LocaleData**

       ├— **java.text.resources.LocaleElements**

       ├— **java.text.resources.LocaleElements_ar**

       ├— **java.text.resources.LocaleElements_be**

       ├— **java.text.resources.LocaleElements_bg**

       ├— **java.text.resources.LocaleElements_ca**

       ├— **java.text.resources.LocaleElements_cs**

       ├— **java.text.resources.LocaleElements_da**

       ├— **java.text.resources.LocaleElements_de**

       ├— **java.text.resources.LocaleElements_de_AT**

       ├— **java.text.resources.LocaleElements_de_CH**

       ├— **java.text.resources.LocaleElements_el**

       ├— **java.text.resources.LocaleElements_en**

       ├— **java.text.resources.LocaleElements_en_CA**

       ├— **java.text.resources.LocaleElements_en_GB**

       ├— **java.text.resources.LocaleElements_en_IE**

       ├— **java.text.resources.LocaleElements_es**

       ├— **java.text.resources.LocaleElements_et**

       ├— **java.text.resources.LocaleElements_fi**

       ├— **java.text.resources.LocaleElements_fr**

       ├— **java.text.resources.LocaleElements_fr_BE**

       ├— **java.text.resources.LocaleElements_fr_CA**

       ├— **java.text.resources.LocaleElements_fr_CH**

       ├— **java.text.resources.LocaleElements_hr**

       ├— **java.text.resources.LocaleElements_hu**

       ├— **java.text.resources.LocaleElements_is**

       ├— **java.text.resources.LocaleElements_it**

       ├— **java.text.resources.LocaleElements_it_CH**

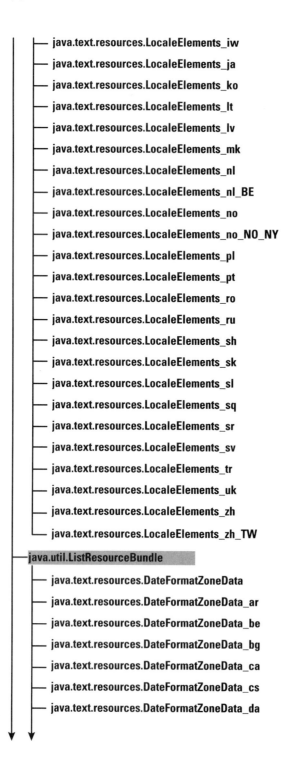

- java.text.resources.LocaleElements_iw
- java.text.resources.LocaleElements_ja
- java.text.resources.LocaleElements_ko
- java.text.resources.LocaleElements_lt
- java.text.resources.LocaleElements_lv
- java.text.resources.LocaleElements_mk
- java.text.resources.LocaleElements_nl
- java.text.resources.LocaleElements_nl_BE
- java.text.resources.LocaleElements_no
- java.text.resources.LocaleElements_no_NO_NY
- java.text.resources.LocaleElements_pl
- java.text.resources.LocaleElements_pt
- java.text.resources.LocaleElements_ro
- java.text.resources.LocaleElements_ru
- java.text.resources.LocaleElements_sh
- java.text.resources.LocaleElements_sk
- java.text.resources.LocaleElements_sl
- java.text.resources.LocaleElements_sq
- java.text.resources.LocaleElements_sr
- java.text.resources.LocaleElements_sv
- java.text.resources.LocaleElements_tr
- java.text.resources.LocaleElements_uk
- java.text.resources.LocaleElements_zh
- java.text.resources.LocaleElements_zh_TW

java.util.ListResourceBundle

- java.text.resources.DateFormatZoneData
- java.text.resources.DateFormatZoneData_ar
- java.text.resources.DateFormatZoneData_be
- java.text.resources.DateFormatZoneData_bg
- java.text.resources.DateFormatZoneData_ca
- java.text.resources.DateFormatZoneData_cs
- java.text.resources.DateFormatZoneData_da

— java.text.resources.**DateFormatZoneData_de**

— java.text.resources.**DateFormatZoneData_de_AT**

— java.text.resources.**DateFormatZoneData_de_CH**

— java.text.resources.**DateFormatZoneData_el**

— java.text.resources.**DateFormatZoneData_en**

— java.text.resources.**DateFormatZoneData_en_CA**

— java.text.resources.**DateFormatZoneData_en_GB**

— java.text.resources.**DateFormatZoneData_en_IE**

— java.text.resources.**DateFormatZoneData_es**

— java.text.resources.**DateFormatZoneData_et**

— java.text.resources.**DateFormatZoneData_fi**

— java.text.resources.**DateFormatZoneData_fr**

— java.text.resources.**DateFormatZoneData_fr_BE**

— java.text.resources.**DateFormatZoneData_fr_CA**

— java.text.resources.**DateFormatZoneData_fr_CH**

— java.text.resources.**DateFormatZoneData_hr**

— java.text.resources.**DateFormatZoneData_hu**

— java.text.resources.**DateFormatZoneData_is**

— java.text.resources.**DateFormatZoneData_it**

— java.text.resources.**DateFormatZoneData_it_CH**

— java.text.resources.**DateFormatZoneData_iw**

— java.text.resources.**DateFormatZoneData_ja**

— java.text.resources.**DateFormatZoneData_ko**

— java.text.resources.**DateFormatZoneData_lt**

— java.text.resources.**DateFormatZoneData_lv**

— java.text.resources.**DateFormatZoneData_mk**

— java.text.resources.**DateFormatZoneData_nl**

— java.text.resources.**DateFormatZoneData_nl_BE**

— java.text.resources.**DateFormatZoneData_no**

— java.text.resources.**DateFormatZoneData_no_NO_NY**

— java.text.resources.**DateFormatZoneData_pl**

— java.text.resources.**DateFormatZoneData_pt**

— java.text.resources.**DateFormatZoneData_ro**

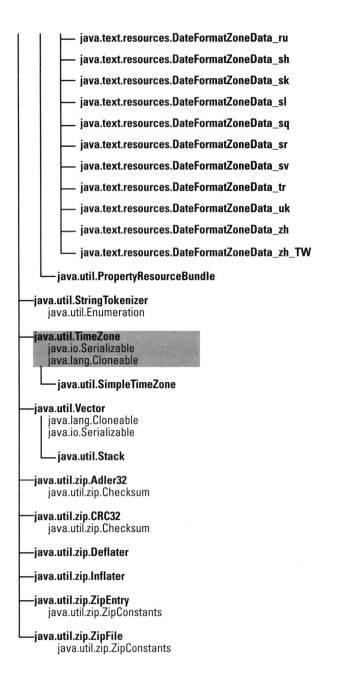

— java.text.resources.DateFormatZoneData_ru

— java.text.resources.DateFormatZoneData_sh

— java.text.resources.DateFormatZoneData_sk

— java.text.resources.DateFormatZoneData_sl

— java.text.resources.DateFormatZoneData_sq

— java.text.resources.DateFormatZoneData_sr

— java.text.resources.DateFormatZoneData_sv

— java.text.resources.DateFormatZoneData_tr

— java.text.resources.DateFormatZoneData_uk

— java.text.resources.DateFormatZoneData_zh

— java.text.resources.DateFormatZoneData_zh_TW

— java.util.PropertyResourceBundle

— java.util.StringTokenizer
  java.util.Enumeration

— java.util.TimeZone
  java.io.Serializable
  java.lang.Cloneable

  — java.util.SimpleTimeZone

— java.util.Vector
  java.lang.Cloneable
  java.io.Serializable

  — java.util.Stack

— java.util.zip.Adler32
  java.util.zip.Checksum

— java.util.zip.CRC32
  java.util.zip.Checksum

— java.util.zip.Deflater

— java.util.zip.Inflater

— java.util.zip.ZipEntry
  java.util.zip.ZipConstants

— java.util.zip.ZipFile
  java.util.zip.ZipConstants

IDG Books Worldwide, Inc. End-User License Agreement

READ THIS. You should carefully read these terms and conditions before opening the software packet(s) included with this book ("Book"). This is a license agreement ("Agreement") between you and IDG Books Worldwide, Inc. ("IDGB"). By opening the accompanying software packet(s), you acknowledge that you have read and accept the following terms and conditions. If you do not agree and do not want to be bound by such terms and conditions, promptly return the Book and the unopened software packet(s) to the place you obtained them for a full refund.

1. **License Grant.** IDGB grants to you (either an individual or entity) a nonexclusive license to use one copy of the enclosed software program(s) (collectively, the "Software") solely for your own personal or business purposes on a single computer (whether a standard computer or a workstation component of a multiuser network). The Software is in use on a computer when it is loaded into temporary memory (RAM) or installed into permanent memory (hard disk, CD-ROM, or other storage device). IDGB reserves all rights not expressly granted herein.

2. **Ownership.** IDGB is the owner of all right, title, and interest, including copyright, in and to the compilation of the Software recorded on the disk(s) or CD-ROM ("Software Media"). Copyright to the individual programs recorded on the Software Media is owned by the author or other authorized copyright owner of each program. Ownership of the Software and all proprietary rights relating thereto remain with IDGB and its licensers.

3. **Restrictions On Use and Transfer.**

   (a) You may only (i) make one copy of the Software for backup or archival purposes, or (ii) transfer the Software to a single hard disk, provided that you keep the original for backup or archival purposes. You may not (i) rent or lease the Software, (ii) copy or reproduce the Software through a LAN or other network system or through any computer subscriber system or bulletin-board system, or (iii) modify, adapt, or create derivative works based on the Software.

   (b) You may not reverse engineer, decompile, or disassemble the Software. You may transfer the Software and user documentation on a permanent basis, provided that the transferee agrees to accept the terms and conditions of this Agreement and you retain no copies. If the Software is an update or has been updated, any transfer must include the most recent update and all prior versions.

4. **Restrictions On Use of Individual Programs.** You must follow the individual requirements and restrictions detailed for each individual program in Appendix B of this Book. These limitations are also contained in the individual license agreements recorded on the Software Media. These limitations may include a requirement that after using the program for a specified period of time, the user must pay a registration fee or discontinue use. By opening the Software packet(s), you will be agreeing to abide by the licenses and restrictions for these individual programs that are detailed in Appendix B and on the Software Media. None of the

material on this Software Media or listed in this Book may ever be redistributed, in original or modified form, for commercial purposes.

5. Limited Warranty.

(a) IDGB warrants that the Software and Software Media are free from defects in materials and workmanship under normal use for a period of sixty (60) days from the date of purchase of this Book. If IDGB receives notification within the warranty period of defects in materials or workmanship, IDGB will replace the defective Software Media.

(b) IDGB AND THE AUTHOR OF THE BOOK DISCLAIM ALL OTHER WARRANTIES, EXPRESS OR IMPLIED, INCLUDING WITHOUT LIMITATION IMPLIED WARRANTIES OF MERCHANTABILITY AND FITNESS FOR A PARTICULAR PURPOSE, WITH RESPECT TO THE SOFTWARE, THE PROGRAMS, THE SOURCE CODE CONTAINED THEREIN, AND/OR THE TECHNIQUES DESCRIBED IN THIS BOOK. IDGB DOES NOT WARRANT THAT THE FUNCTIONS CONTAINED IN THE SOFTWARE WILL MEET YOUR REQUIREMENTS OR THAT THE OPERATION OF THE SOFTWARE WILL BE ERROR FREE.

(c) This limited warranty gives you specific legal rights, and you may have other rights that vary from jurisdiction to jurisdiction.

6. Remedies.

(a) IDGB's entire liability and your exclusive remedy for defects in materials and workmanship shall be limited to replacement of the Software Media, which may be returned to IDGB with a copy of your receipt at the following address: Software Media Fulfillment Department, Attn.: *Java Master Reference*, IDG Books Worldwide, Inc., 7260 Shadeland Station, Ste. 100, Indianapolis, IN 46256, or call 1-800-762-2974. Please allow three to four weeks for delivery. This Limited Warranty is void if failure of the Software Media has resulted from accident, abuse, or misapplication. Any replacement Software Media will be warranted for the remainder of the original warranty period or thirty (30) days, whichever is longer.

(b) In no event shall IDGB or the author be liable for any damages whatsoever (including without limitation damages for loss of business profits, business interruption, loss of business information, or any other pecuniary loss) arising from the use of or inability to use the Book or the Software, even if IDGB has been advised of the possibility of such damages.

(c) Because some jurisdictions do not allow the exclusion or limitation of liability for consequential or incidental damages, the above limitation or exclusion may not apply to you.

7. U.S. Government Restricted Rights. Use, duplication, or disclosure of the Software by the U.S. Government is subject to restrictions stated in paragraph (c)(1)(ii) of the Rights in Technical Data and Computer Software clause of DFARS 252.227-7013, and in subparagraphs (a) through (d) of the Commercial Computer—Restricted Rights clause at FAR 52.227-19, and in similar clauses in the NASA FAR supplement, when applicable.

8. **General.** This Agreement constitutes the entire understanding of the parties and revokes and supersedes all prior agreements, oral or written, between them and may not be modified or amended except in a writing signed by both parties hereto that specifically refers to this Agreement. This Agreement shall take precedence over any other documents that may be in conflict herewith. If any one or more provisions contained in this Agreement are held by any court or tribunal to be invalid, illegal, or otherwise unenforceable, each and every other provision shall remain in full force and effect.

Java™ Developers Kit Version 1.0.2 Copyright and License Information

JAVA™ Web development products are owned and licensed exclusively by Sun Microsystems, Inc. Copyright © 1992–96 Sun Microsystems, Inc. All rights reserved. Java and all Java-based names and logos, including the Coffee Cup and Duke, are trademarks of Sun Microsystems, Inc., and refer to Sun's Java Technologies. Products bearing authorized "JAVA-Compatible" Logo are based upon Sun's JAVA and technology, and are compatible with the API's for such technology.

Sun grants to you ("Licensee") a non-exclusive, non-transferable license to use the Java binary code version (hereafter, "Binary Software") without fee. Licensee may distribute the Binary Software to third parties provided that the copyright notice and this statement appear on all copies. Licensee agrees that the copyright notice and this statement will appear on all copies of the software, packaging, and documentation or portions thereof.

In the event Licensee creates additional classes or otherwise extends the Applet Application Programming Interface (AAPI), licensee will publish the specifications for such extensions to the AAPI for use by third-party developers of Java-based software, in connection with licensee's commercial distribution of the Binary Software.

RESTRICTED RIGHTS: Use, duplication, or disclosure by the government is subject to the restrictions as set forth in subparagraph (c) (1) (ii) of the Rights in Technical Data and Computer Software Clause as DFARS 252.227-7013 and FAR 52.227-19.

SUN MAKES NO REPRESENTATIONS OR WARRANTIES ABOUT THE SUITABILITY OF THE BINARY SOFTWARE, EITHER EXPRESS OR IMPLIED, INCLUDING BUT NOT LIMITED TO THE IMPLIED WARRANTIES OF MERCHANTABILITY, FITNESS FOR A PARTICULAR PURPOSE, OR NON-INFRINGEMENT. SUN SHALL NOT BE LIABLE FOR ANY DAMAGES SUFFERED BY LICENSEE AS A RESULT OF USING, MODIFYING OR DISTRIBUTING THE BINARY SOFTWARE OR ITS DERIVATIVES.

By downloading, using, or copying this Binary Software, Licensee agrees to abide by the intellectual property laws, and all other applicable laws of the U.S., and the terms of this License. Ownership of the software shall remain solely in Sun Microsystems, Inc.

Sun shall have the right to terminate this license immediately by written notice upon Licensee's breach of, or non-compliance with, any of its terms. Licensee shall be liable for any infringement or damages resulting from Licensee's failure to abide by the terms of this License.

The JDK 1.0.2 binary release is based in part on the work of the Independent
JPEG Group.
Developed by Sun Microsystems, Inc.
2550 Garcia Avenue
Mountain View, CA 94043
Copyright © 1994, 1995, Sun Microsystems, Inc.

Java™ Development Kit Version 1.1.4
Binary Code License

This binary code license ("License") contains rights and restrictions associated with
use of the accompanying software and documentation ("Software"). Read the
License carefully before installing the Software. By installing the Software, you agree
to the terms and conditions of this License.

1. **Limited License Grant.** Sun grants to you ("Licensee") a non-
   exclusive, non-transferable limited license to use the Software without fee
   for evaluation of the Software and for development of Java™ compatible
   applets and applications. Licensee may make one archival copy of the
   Software and may re-distribute complete, unmodified copies of the
   Software to software developers within Licensee's organization to avoid
   unnecessary download time, provided that this License conspicuously
   appear with all copies of the Software. Except for the foregoing, Licensee
   may not re-distribute the Software in whole or in part, either separately or
   included with a product. Refer to the Java Runtime Environment Version
   1.1.4 binary code license (http://java.sun.com/products
   /jdk/1.1/index.html) for the availability of runtime code which may
   be distributed with Java compatible applets and applications.

2. **Java Platform Interface.** Licensee may not modify the Java Platform
   Interface ("JPI", identified as classes contained within the "java" package
   or any subpackages of the "java" package), by creating additional classes
   within the JPI or otherwise causing the addition to or modification of the
   classes in the JPI. In the event that Licensee creates any Java-related API
   and distributes such API to others for applet or application development,
   Licensee must promptly publish an accurate specification for such API
   for free use by all developers of Java-based software.

3. **Restrictions.** Software is confidential copyrighted information of Sun and
   title to all copies is retained by Sun and/or its licensors. Licensee shall not
   modify, decompile, disassemble, decrypt, extract, or otherwise reverse
   engineer Software. Software may not be leased, assigned, or sublicensed, in
   whole or in part. Software is not designed or intended for use in on-line
   control of aircraft, air traffic, aircraft navigation or aircraft communications;
   or in the design, construction, operation or maintenance of any nuclear
   facility. Licensee warrants that it will not use or redistribute the Software
   for such purposes.

4. **Trademarks and Logos.** This License does not authorize Licensee to use
   any Sun name, trademark, or logo. Licensee acknowledges that Sun owns
   the Java trademark and all Java-related trademarks, logos, and icons
   including the Coffee Cup and Duke ("Java Marks") and agrees to: (i)
   comply with the Java Trademark Guidelines at http://java.sun.com/
   trademarks.html; (ii) not do anything harmful to or inconsistent with

Sun's rights in the Java Marks; and (iii) assist Sun in protecting those rights, including assigning to Sun any rights acquired by Licensee in any Java Mark.

5. **Disclaimer of Warranty.** Software is provided "AS IS," without a warranty of any kind. ALL EXPRESS OR IMPLIED REPRESENTATIONS AND WARRANTIES, INCLUDING ANY IMPLIED WARRANTY OF MERCHANTABILITY, FITNESS FOR A PARTICULAR PURPOSE OR NON-INFRINGEMENT, ARE HEREBY EXCLUDED.

6. **Limitation of Liability.** SUN AND ITS LICENSORS SHALL NOT BE LIABLE FOR ANY DAMAGES SUFFERED BY LICENSEE OR ANY THIRD PARTY AS A RESULT OF USING OR DISTRIBUTING SOFTWARE. IN NO EVENT WILL SUN OR ITS LICENSORS BE LIABLE FOR ANY LOST REVENUE, PROFIT, OR DATA, OR FOR DIRECT, INDIRECT, SPECIAL, CONSEQUENTIAL, INCIDENTAL, OR PUNITIVE DAMAGES, HOWEVER CAUSED AND REGARDLESS OF THE THEORY OF LIABILITY, ARISING OUT OF THE USE OF OR INABILITY TO USE SOFTWARE, EVEN IF SUN HAS BEEN ADVISED OF THE POSSIBILITY OF SUCH DAMAGES.

7. **Termination.** Licensee may terminate this License at any time by destroying all copies of Software. This License will terminate immediately without notice from Sun if Licensee fails to comply with any provision of this License. Upon such termination, Licensee must destroy all copies of Software.

8. **Export Regulations.** Software, including technical data, is subject to U.S. export control laws, including the U.S. Export Administration Act and its associated regulations, and may be subject to export or import regulations in other countries. Licensee agrees to comply strictly with all such regulations and acknowledges that it has the responsibility to obtain licenses to export, re-export, or import Software. Software may not be downloaded, or otherwise exported or re-exported (i) into, or to a national or resident of, Cuba, Iraq, Iran, North Korea, Libya, Sudan, Syria, or any country to which the U.S. has embargoed goods; or (ii) to anyone on the U.S. Treasury Department's list of Specially Designated Nations or the U.S. Commerce Department's Table of Denial Orders.

9. **Restricted Rights.** Use, duplication, or disclosure by the United States government is subject to the restrictions as set forth in the Rights in Technical Data and Computer Software Clauses in DFARS 252.227-7013(c) (1) (ii) and FAR 52.227-19(c) (2) as applicable.

10. **Governing Law.** Any action related to this License will be governed by California law and controlling U.S. federal law. No choice of law rules of any jurisdiction will apply.

11. **Severability.** If any of the above provisions are held to be in violation of applicable law, void, or unenforceable in any jurisdiction, then such provisions are herewith waived to the extent necessary for the License to be otherwise enforceable in such jurisdiction. However, if in Sun's opinion deletion of any provisions of the License by operation of this paragraph unreasonably compromises the rights or increases, the liabilities of Sun or its licensors, Sun reserves the right to terminate the License and refund the fee paid by Licensee, if any, as Licensee's sole and exclusive remedy.

my2cents.idgbooks.com

Register This Book — And Win!

Visit **http://my2cents.idgbooks.com** to register this book and we'll automatically enter you in our monthly prize giveaway. It's also your opportunity to give us feedback: let us know what you thought of this book and how you would like to see other topics covered.

Discover IDG Books Online!

The IDG Books Online Web site is your online resource for tackling technology — at home and at the office.

Ten Productive and Career-Enhancing Things You Can Do at www.idgbooks.com

1. Nab source code for your own programming projects.

2. Download software.

3. Read Web exclusives: special articles and book excerpts by IDG Books Worldwide authors.

4. Take advantage of resources to help you advance your career as a Novell or Microsoft professional.

5. Buy IDG Books Worldwide titles or find a convenient bookstore that carries them.

6. Register your book and win a prize.

7. Chat live online with authors.

8. Sign up for regular e-mail updates about our latest books.

9. Suggest a book you'd like to read or write.

10. Give us your 2¢ about our books and about our Web site.

Not on the Web yet? It's easy to get started with *Discover the Internet*, at local retailers everywhere.